THE WORLD CUP WHO'S WHO

50 YEARS OF ENGLAND WORLD CUP FOOTBALL

1950-2002

FOREWORD BY NOBBY STILES MBE

A BRITESPOT PUBLICATION

FOREWORD

NOBBY STILES M.B.E.

It's a great honour to be asked to contribute to a book about the true greats of English football. Any player will tell you that being involved in a World Cup is the pinnacle of their career, whatever the outcome, because you know you have pitted yourself against the best in the world.

Of course, winning the World Cup is even better. 1966 not only changed the lives of me and my team mates for ever but it has also become a defining moment in the history of the nation - the afternoon when England became champions of the world, at Wembley, in front of 100,000 screaming fans after beating Germany 4-2 in extra time!

Dreams don't come any sweeter than this and I never tire of people telling me their favourite memories of that incredible day. My own are somewhat different - I was so shattered at the end of it all that I don't even remember doing the famous jig I'm constantly reminded of.

What I'll never forget though is the pure joy of the final whistle and the startled look on George Cohen's face as I jumped on top of him. I also remember feeling on top of the world as I went up to collect my medal from the Queen… and the hell my wife Kay gave me afterwards for not putting my teeth in for the occasion.

The World Cup is undoubtedly the most important sporting occasion on earth. Some people may argue for the Olympics but, for me, football is the people's game and nothing brings a nation together or generates as much passion as their national team going for the ultimate prize.

As a player you know that even if you are lucky enough to ever reach that level of ability there will still only be two or three World Cups during your career so getting there becomes a hugely important target.

I was only 24 in 1966 and I suddenly found myself playing in the same team as such truly world class players as Bobby Charlton, Gordon Banks and Bobby Moore against the very best the world could offer. It's nice to have that calibre of player round you when you're told your job is to go and mark Eusebio out of the game!

But it's not just about the handful of truly great players that appear only a few times in any generation. They might provide the spark of inspiration that can change a game but it's the entire squad that can win or lose a tournament.

We had an incredible team spirit in 1966 and although Geoff Hurst may have scored a hat-trick in the final his contribution was no more important in a way than that of Ron Springett who never got a game but made us laugh throughout.

In the same way every player mentioned in this book has played a part in England's World Cup history and they can all be truly proud of the contributions they have made.

THE WORLD CUP WHO'S WHO

50 YEARS OF ENGLAND WORLD CUP FOOTBALL
1950-2002

Since England first entered the World Cup in 1950 the game of football has changed dramatically. Today it is all about style and technique with the coaches, accompanied by the respective managers, continuously planning and working out tactics to overcome the opposition.

There are more competitions to enter, the players' wages have risen to new proportions, attendances (especially in the Premiership) are exceptionally good and the stadiums are now looking high-class with several added accessories.

As in years gone by and indeed as in every sport, footballers want to represent their country and when selected they wear the national colours with pride.

The record books show that over the years, since international soccer was first introduced way back in 1872, well over 1,200 players have represented England at home and abroad but only a selected few of course have played in the World Cup.

Owing to circumstances, England missed out in the 1930, 1934 and 1938 tournaments before making a rather moderate first appearance in the Finals in 1950. Thereafter, in 1954, 1958 and 1962, they did a shade better and then in 1966, under the guidance of manager Alf Ramsey, the Jules Rimet Trophy was proudly held aloft by Bobby Moore after West Germany had been beaten 4-2 in an epic Final at Wembley.

England were confident of retaining the World Cup four years later, but the Germans gained sweet revenge in Leon.

After missing out in 1974 and 1978, Ron Greenwood guided England to the Finals in Spain. Their followed a trip to Mexico under Bobby Robson in 1986, but unfortunately in the sweltering heat the Hand of God, delivered by Diego Maradona, ended all hopes of success!

Four years later in Italy, it was failure from the penalty spot (once more versus the Germans) that proved to be England's downfall, and in 1994, with the Finals being staged in the USA; England surprisingly failed to qualify.

Then came 1998 in France, with Glenn Hoddle in charge, yet again it was vital misses from the 12-yard spot (against Argentina in the quarter-final) that ended any chance of further World Cup glory for England.

Now in 2002 England have a chance to triumph again, this time under Swedish-born manager Sven Goran-Eriksson.

With the Finals taking place in the Far East (Japan and South Korea) for the very first time, all England supporters will be hoping that the goal-touch of Michael Owen and Emile Heskey, the defensive qualities of Gareth Southgate and Sol Campbell, the midfield efficiency of Steven Gerrard, Paul Scholes and skipper David Beckham and the form of 'keeper David Seaman will prove decisive under the sun….. just like it was in 1966.

What better way to celebrate the Queen's Golden Jubilee with a World Cup victory?

All the England players (and managers) named for each of the World Cup Finals in 1954, 1958, 1962, 1966, 1970, 1982, 1986, 1990 and 1998 are listed in this book with the inclusion of Sven Goran Eriksson's potential list of players for 2002; their respective career records evident for all to note.

I feel this publication is what all the votaries of English soccer have been waiting for. Authentic and profusely illustrated, it is a true guide, a complete statistical who's who of England in the World Cup as well as a detailed history of every single World Cup that has taken place since its conception in 1930.

TONY MATTHEWS
May 2002

THE WORLD CUP WHO'S WHO - 1950-2002, 50 YEARS OF ENGLAND WORLD CUP FOOTBALL
A Britespot Publication

First Published in Great Britain by
Britespot Publishing Solutions Limited
Chester Road, Cradley Heath, West Midlands B64 6AB

May 2002

ISBN 1 904103 10 3

Cover design and layout © Britespot Publishing Solutions Limited

Printed and bound in Great Britain by
Cradley Print Limited, Chester Road, Cradley Heath, West Midlands B64 6AB

Acknowledgments
As the author, I would like to give a special thank you to Ian Nannestad for assisting me with the clarification of the facts and figures contained in this book; also sincere gratitude to David Barber from the Football Association for his assistance and likewise to John Russell, along with Jim Cadman, Neville Evans, Dan Davies, Tom Roe and Tony Williamson who have loaned several items of memorabilia. Also, a special thank you to Bob Bond who allowed the use of his fantastic caricatures to help make this publication very special indeed.
I would also like to thank Empics and Allsports for supplying a number of photographs and of course, there is a special thank you to Roger Marshall, Paul Burns, and Chris Sweet at Britespot Publishing, not forgetting my wife Margaret who once again has given me great encouragement all down the line.

Dedicated to all the players, past and present, who have represented England in the World Cup Finals.

THE WORLD CUP WHO'S WHO

50 YEARS OF ENGLAND WORLD CUP FOOTBALL

1950-2002

CONTENTS

1ST WORLD CUP

Group Matches

Group 1

Team	P	W	D	L	Pts
Argentina	3	3	0	0	6
Chile	3	2	0	1	4
France	3	1	0	2	2
Mexico	3	0	0	3	0

13-Jul	France : Mexico	4:1
15-Jul	Argentina : France	1:0
16-Jul	Chile : Mexico	3:0
19-Jul	Chile : France	1:0
19-Jul	Argentina : Mexico	6:3
22-Jul	Argentina : Chile	3:1

Group 2

Team	P	W	D	L	Pts
Yugoslavia	2	2	0	0	4
Brazil	2	1	0	1	2
Bolivia	2	0	0	2	0

14-Jul	Yugoslavia : Brazil	2:1
17-Jul	Yugoslavia : Bolivia	4:0
20-Jul	Brazil : Bolivia	4:0

Group 3

Team	P	W	D	L	Pts
Uruguay	2	2	0	0	4
Romania	2	1	0	1	2
Peru	2	0	0	2	0

14-Jul	Romania : Peru	3:1
18-Jul	Uruguay : Peru	1:0
21-Jul	Uruguay : Romania	4:0

Group 4

Team	P	W	D	L	Pts
USA	2	2	0	0	4
Paraguay	2	1	0	1	2
Belgium	2	0	0	2	0

13-Jul	USA : Belgium	3:0
17-Jul	USA : Paraguay	3:0
20-Jul	Paraguay : Belgium	1:0

The first World Cup tournament was planned by FIFA at its 1928 congress. Five countries applied to host the inaugural competition – Holland, Italy, Spain, Sweden and Uruguay. Uruguay was chosen for three reasons: in recognition of its status as Olympic champions in 1924 and 1928; the fact that 1930 marked the 100th anniversary of the country's independence; the Uruguayan FA offered to pay all the entrants travel and hotel expenses in full.

A total of 13 countries entered, although European involvement was minimal with just four participants – Belgium, France, Romania and Yugoslavia. The teams were divided into three groups of three and one of four, with group winners advancing to the semi-finals.

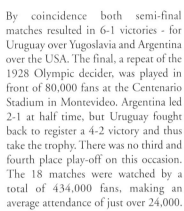

The opening matches took place on 13 July when France defeated Mexico 4-1 and USA beat Belgium 3-0. The first ever World Cup goal was scored by Lucien Laurent of France. Two players claim the first hat-trick – Bertran Patenaude of USA against Paraguay (some sources suggest he scored two with the third being an own goal) and Guillermo Stabile of Argentina against Mexico.

By coincidence both semi-final matches resulted in 6-1 victories - for Uruguay over Yugoslavia and Argentina over the USA. The final, a repeat of the 1928 Olympic decider, was played in front of 80,000 fans at the Centenario Stadium in Montevideo. Argentina led 2-1 at half time, but Uruguay fought back to register a 4-2 victory and thus take the trophy. There was no third and fourth place play-off on this occasion. The 18 matches were watched by a total of 434,000 fans, making an average attendance of just over 24,000.

Final Competition

Semi-finals

26-Jul	Argentina : USA	6:1
27-Jul	Uruguay : Yugoslavia	6:1

Final

30-Jul	Uruguay : Argentina	4:2

Did You Know?

For the first ever World Cup there are no qualifying rounds - participation is by invitation only. Because of recession and the long voyage to Uruguay by ship, lots of European teams declined to take part. In Romania, a decree from King Carol gave the players three months off from their jobs and a guarantee that they will be re-employed on their return. The king himself is also active as coach, but after a great performance from the host country, the king's men have to pack their bags for an early trip home.

There still seems to be a difference of opinion on a statistical point of footballing interest: while FIFA and a number of other sources give America's Bertram Patenaude the honour of having scored the first World Cup hat trick (17 July 1930, against Paraguay), others say it was Guillermo Stabile of Argentina who was first, with three goals two days later against Mexico.

The whole of this World Cup takes place in a single city, Montevideo, with its three stadiums (Centenario, Pocitos and Parque Central).

The tournament in Spain in 1982, with 24 teams participating for the first time, was held in no less than 14 cities and used 17 stadia (two each in Barcelona, Madrid and Seville) to stage the 52 matches.

ITALY 1934

2ND WORLD CUP

Final Competition

Preliminary Round

27-May	Spain : Brazil	3:1
27-May	Austria : France	3:2
27-May	Germany : Belgium	5:2
27-May	Switzerland : Netherlands	3:2
27-May	Czechoslovakia : Romania	2:1
27-May	Italy : USA	7:1
27-May	Hungary : Egypt	4:2
27-May	Sweden : Argentina	3:2

Quarter Finals

31-May	Czech : Switzerland	3:2
31-May	Germany : Sweden	2:1
31-May	Austria : Hungary	2:1
31-May	Italy : Spain	1:1
01-Jun	Italy : Spain	1:0

Semi-finals

03-Jun	Czechoslovakia : Germany	3:1
03-Jun	Italy : Austria	1:0

3rd/4th Place

07-Jun	Germany : Austria	3:2

Final

10-Jun	Italy : Czechoslovakia	2:1

Did You Know?

The final between the host country Italy and Czechoslovakia is also a meeting between two of the best goalkeepers of all time, Gianpiero Combi and Frantisek Planicka. Both concede a goal in regular playing time, and in extra time Italy get another to win 2-1.

Upon the final whistle, Combi sticks to the plan he made the day before the final and carries out his intention to retire immediately from football.

The second World Cup competition attracted 32 entries and for the first time a qualifying competition took place. All countries, including hosts Italy, were required to qualify, although three – Chile, Peru and Turkey withdrew without playing a match.

The Irish Free State (now Republic of Ireland) entered the competition but were eliminated in the qualifiers. Twelve of the 16 finalists were from Europe, the others being Argentina, Brazil, Egypt and USA. Argentina and Brazil both walked over in their preliminary games, while the USA emerged from the four entrants in North and Central America, defeating Mexico in Rome shortly before the start of the finals.

Uruguay declined to enter so did not defend their title. A straight knock-out format was used to decide the competition. The finalists were Italy, who defeated USA, Spain and Austria to reach the last two, and Czechoslovakia, conquerors of Romania, Switzerland and Germany. Germany took third place after a 3-2 win over Austria.

A crowd of 50,000 attended the final in Rome's Stadio Nazionale and although the Czechs opened the scoring through Antonin Puc, the hosts equalised through Raimondo Orsi and snatched a winner in extra time from Angelo Schiavio.

The Italians included three Argentinian oriundi (foreign-born players who qualified through Italian parents or grandparents) – Enrico Guaita, Orsi and Luis Monti. Monti had also played for Argentina in the final in 1930 and is thus the only man to have appeared in two World Cup final matches for different countries. Three players finished joint-leading scorers in the competition with four goals – Edmund Conen (Germany), Oldrich Nejedly (Czechoslovakia) and Schiavio (Italy).

Imre Markos of Hungary became the first player to be sent off in the finals when he was dismissed by Italian referee Francesco Mattea in a second-round tie against Austria. 17 matches were played altogether attracting 395,000 spectators at an average of 23,000 per match.

SWITZERLAND 1954

5TH WORLD CUP

Group Matches

Group 1

Team	P	W	D	L	Pts
Brazil	2	1	1	0	3
Yugoslavia	2	1	1	0	3
France	2	1	0	1	2
Mexico	2	0	0	2	0

16-Jun	Brazil : Mexico	5 : 0
16-Jun	Yugoslavia : France	1 : 0
19-Jun	France : Mexico	3 : 2
19-Jun	Brazil : Yugoslavia	1 : 1

Group 2

Team	P	W	D	L	Pts
Hungary	2	2	0	0	4
Turkey	3	1	0	2	2
West Germany	3	2	0	1	2
Korea Rep	2	0	0	2	0

17-Jun	W. Germany : Turkey	4 : 1
17-Jun	Hungary : Korea Rep	9 : 0
20-Jun	Hungary : W. Germany	8 : 3
20-Jun	Turkey : Korea Rep	7 : 0
23-Jun	W. Germany : Turkey	7 : 2

Group 3

Team	P	W	D	L	Pts
Uruguay	2	2	0	0	4
Austria	2	2	0	0	4
Czechoslovakia	2	0	0	2	0
Scotland	2	0	0	2	0

16-Jun	Uruguay : Czechoslovakia	2 : 0
16-Jun	Austria : Scotland	1 : 0
19-Jun	Uruguay : Scotland	7 : 0
19-Jun	Austria : Czechoslovakia	5 : 0

A record number of 45 countries entered for the 1954 World Cup, although six entries were refused and Poland, Peru and Taiwan withdrew from the competition. The Home International Championships again served as a qualifying round, with England and Scotland earning the right to travel to the finals.

The 16 finalists included 12 from Europe, plus Brazil and Uruguay from South America, Mexico from Central America and South Korea from Asia. Neither Argentina nor USSR entered the competition.

The arrangements for the finals were changed yet again, with the countries divided into four pools, each containing four teams. Two from each group were seeded and did not meet at this stage, thus each team played just twice with the top two going through to the second phase from when the competition reverted to a straight knock-out format.

England led Belgium 3-1 in their opening match thanks to two goals from Ivor Broadis and a brave diving header from Nat Lofthouse. But they were pegged back to 3-3 at the end of 90 minutes and the match eventually finished as a 4-4 draw after extra-time, Lofthouse notching his second of the game.

England then defeated Switzerland 2-0, thanks to fine goals by the Wolverhampton Wanderers duo of Jimmy Mullen and Dennis Wilshaw and a terrific display of defensive work by their club colleague Billy Wright, and so passed into the quarter finals.

Scotland had a more troubled time. They were unable to select any players from Glasgow Rangers, the club being unwilling to release them as they themselves were on tour, and they then rather unluckily lost 1-0 to Austria in their opening match. Manager Andy Beattie then resigned and they were eliminated following a 7-0 thrashing by Uruguay.

This set up a quarter-final clash between England and the holders, but poor goalkeeping by Gil Merrick contributed to a 4-2 defeat despite goals from Lofthouse and Tom Finney.

The other games at this stage saw a remarkable encounter between Switzerland and Austria, the hosts having led 3-0 at one stage before going out 7-5, the total of 12 goals in one match remaining as a record for the finals.

Elsewhere the favourites Hungary beat Brazil 4-2 in a vicious match that has become known as the 'Battle of Berne' in which three players were sent off and fighting continued after the match in the dressing rooms.

In the semi-finals, West Germany thrashed Austria 6-1 while Hungary beat Uruguay 4-2. The Hungarians were firm favourites going into the final being unbeaten since May 1950 and having won the 1952 Olympic Games title.

Their success seemed assured after Ferenc Puskas and Zoltan Czibor gave them a 2-0 lead early on, but West Germany fought back to gain a surprise 3-2 victory with goals from Max Morlock and Helmut Rahn (2). The match attracted an attendance of 60,000 to the Wankdorf Stadium in Berne.

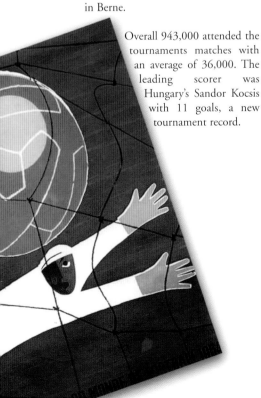

Overall 943,000 attended the tournaments matches with an average of 36,000. The leading scorer was Hungary's Sandor Kocsis with 11 goals, a new tournament record.

Group 4

Team	P	W	D	L	Pts
England	2	1	1	0	3
Italy	3	1	0	2	2
Switzerland	3	2	0	1	2
Belgium	2	0	1	1	1

17-Jun	England : Belgium	4:4
17-Jun	Switzerland : Italy	2:1
20-Jun	Italy : Belgium	4:1
20-Jun	England : Switzerland	2:0
23-Jun	Switzerland : Italy	4:1

Final Competition

Quarter Finals

26-Jun	Uruguay : England	4:2
26-Jun	Austria : Switzerland	7:5
27-Jun	Hungary : Brazil	4:2
27-Jun	W. Germany : Yugoslavia	2:0

Semi-finals

30-Jun	W. Germany : Austria	6:1
30-Jun	Hungary : Uruguay	4:2

3rd/4th Place

03-Jun	Austria : Uruguay	3:1

Final

04-Jun	W. Germany : Hungary	3:2

England's squad in 1954
Manager: Walter Winterbottom

Goalkeepers
Ted Burgin
(Sheffield United)
Gil Merrick
(Birmingham City)

Full-backs
Ken Green
(Birmingham City)
Ron Staniforth
(Huddersfield Town)
Roger Byrne
(Manchester United)

Half-backs
Jimmy Dickinson
(Portsmouth)
Bill McGarry
(Huddersfield Town)
Syd Owen
(Luton Town)
Billy Wright
(Wolverhampton Wanderers)

Forwards
Ivor Broadis
(Manchester City)
Tom Finney
(Preston North End)
Nat Lofthouse
(Bolton Wanderers)
Stanley Matthews
(Blackpool)
Jimmy Mullen
(Wolverhampton Wanderers)
Albert Quixall
(Sheffield Wednesday)
Tommy Taylor
(Manchester United)
Dennis Wilshaw
(Wolverhampton Wanderers)

Reserves *did not travel*
Ken Armstrong
(Chelsea)
Johnny Haynes
(Fulham)
Bedford Jezzard
(Fulham)
Allenby Chilton
(Manchester United)
Harry Hooper
(West Ham United)

Sir Walter Winterbottom Manager
(1950-54-58-62)
See 1950 World Cup (Brazil) for personal profile.

Ted Burgin Goalkeeper

27 TED BURGIN
Sheffield United

Born: Bradfield, Yorks, 29 April 1927.
Career: Alford Town, Sheffield United (professional, March 1949), Doncaster Rovers (December 1957), Leeds United (March 1958), Rochdale (January 1961-66), Glossop. Ted Burgin was a wholehearted goalkeeper, yet one of the most injury-prone players in the Football League during the 1950s! He broke his leg twice, suffered nine arm fractures, several cracked ribs and a broken collarbone. Nevertheless he still made nearly 600 first-class appearances Teken to Switzerland for the 1954 World Cup finals as cover for Gil Merrick, he had earlier toured Australia with the FA in 1951 and won two England 'B' caps in 1954.
World Cup Finals Record: 1954: 0A

Gil Merrick Goalkeeper

Born: Sparkhill, Birmingham, 26 January 1922.
Career: Solihull Town (July 1937), Birmingham City (amateur August 1938, professional August 1939, retired as a player in May 1960, then appointed manager, June 1960-April 1964), Bromsgrove Rovers (manager, August 1967), Atherstone Town (manager, 1970-71). Guested for Northampton Town, Nottingham Forest and West Bromwich Albion during WW2. Probably the best goalkeeper in Great Britain during the mid-1950s, Gil Merrick with his huge hands, heavy body and dapper moustache had the misfortune to be between the posts when England conceded 13 goals in two internationals against Hungary in 1953 and 1954. However, he bounced back and continued to perform exceedingly well, helping Blues win the Second Division championship in 1955, reach the FA Cup final a year later, having earlier helped his club win the Football League (South) title in 1946 and the Second Division crown in 1948.

As a manager he guided Blues to the 1961 Inter Cities Fairs Cup final and to victory over rivals Aston Villa in the 1963 League Cup final. He appeared in 551 first-class matches for Blues as well as starring in 172 wartime games. He won 23 full caps for England (1951-54) and played for the Football League representative side on 11 occasions.
World Cup Finals Record: 1954: 3A 0G

Ken Green Full-back

Born: London, 27 April 1924.
Died: Sutton Coldfield, West Midlands, June 2001.
Career: Millwall (amateur, 1940), Birmingham City (professional, November 1943). Retired April 1959. Later ran a sub-post office in Handsworth, Birmingham. Durable full back Ken Green scored two goals in 443 League and Cup appearances for Birmingham City. He played in their 1948 and 1955 Second Division championship winning sides and collected a runners-up medal after their 1956 FA Cup final defeat by Manchester City. He gained two England 'B' caps, twice represented the Football League and was a reserve in Switzerland for the 1954 World Cup finals.
World Cup Finals Record: 1954 0A

Ron Staniforth Full-back
Born: Newton Heath, Manchester, 13 April 1924.
Died: 1988.
Career: Newton Albion, Stockport County (professional, October 1946), Huddersfield Town (May 1952), Sheffield Wednesday (July 1955), Barrow (player-manager October 1959, retiring as a player in 1961, continuing as manager until July 1964), Sheffield Wednesday (assistant-coach, July 1960, chief coach, March 1971).

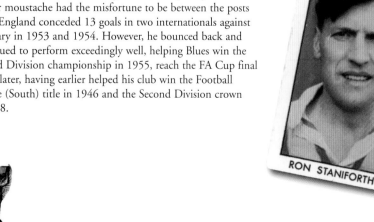

RON STANIFORTH

Ron Staniforth was a traditional right back, cool and composed under pressure, a good clean kicker with fine positional sense and useful turn of speed. He won two Second Division championship medals with Sheffield Wednesday (1956 and 1959) and made a total of 473 League appearances with his four clubs. He was capped eight times by England (1954-58) and partnered Roger Byrne in the 1954 World Cup finals. He was in the side beaten 7-1 by Hungary in Budapest a month before going to Switzerland.
World Cup Finals Record: 1954: 3A 0G

Roger Byrne Full-back

Born: Gorton, Manchester, 8 February 1929.
Died: Munich, 6 February 1958.
Career: Ryder Brow YC, Manchester United (professional March 1949 until his death).

Roger Byrne was a classy footballer and a terrific captain who was once an outside left, before developing into one of the finest left backs in the world. He went on to appear in 280 games and score 20 goals for Manchester United. After National Service in the RAF he made his Football League debut against Liverpool in 1951, establishing himself in the first XI that very same season and ending it as a goal-scoring left-winger as United clinched the First Division championship. He soon settled down in the number three position and from there went on to skipper both club and country. He won two more League Championship medals (1956 and 1957) and appeared in an FA Cup final as well. He played in 33 consecutive internationals for England, in three 'B' team matches and six times for the Football League. It was a body blow to United and England when he lost his life in the Munich air crash.

As a teenager Roger played in the same forward-line for Ryder Brow Youth Club as the future Lancashire and England fast bowler Brian Statham.
World Cup Finals Record: 1954: 3A 0G

Jimmy Dickinson, MBE Half-back

See 1950 World Cup (Brazil) for personal profile.

Bill McGarry Half-back

Born: Stoke-on-Trent, 10 June 1927.
Career: Northwood Mission, Port Vale (amateur, April 1945, professional, June 1945), Huddersfield Town (£10,000, March 1951), Bournemouth (£2,000, player-manager, March 1961), Watford (manager, July 1963-October 1964), Ipswich Town (manager, October 1964-November 1968), Wolverhampton Wanderers (manager, November 1968-May 1976), Saudi Arabia (coach, June 1976-October 1977), Newcastle United (manager, November 1977-August 1980),

Brighton & Hove Albion (scout, briefly, 1980), Power Dynamo, Zambia (coach, 1981), Zambian national team (coach, 1982), Wolverhampton Wanderers (manager September-November 1985), later as a coach in Bophuthatswana (1993-94).

Capped by England on four occasions (1954-56) and once at 'B' team level, right-half Bill McGarry also toured South Africa with the FA in 1956 and played once for the Football League side. He was originally an inside right, but found his true vocation as a wing half, and although far from being spectacular, he was a stern tackler and smart passer who amassed over 600 appearances in League and Cup football for his three clubs. As manager of Ipswich, he guided them to the Second Division title in 1968, and he won the League Cup with Wolves in 1974, having guided them to the UEFA Cup final two years earlier.
World Cup Finals Record: 1954: 2A 0G

Syd Owen Half-back

Born: Birmingham, 29 February 1922.
Died January 1999.
Career: Yardley YMCA (Birmingham), Birmingham City (professional, October 1945), Luton Town (June 1947, appointed manager on retiring, May 1959-May 1960), Leeds United (coach, May 1960), Birmingham City (assistant-manager, October 1975-September 1977), Hull City (coach, December 1977-February 1978), Manchester United (Youth team coach, May 1978-April 1981, then scout until August 1982).

Having started his career as a wing half, Syd Owen became a commanding centre half who made 388 League appearances for Luton Town, skippering the Hatters in the 1959 FA Cup final - his last game for the club. He won three England caps, playing in the 7-1 defeat in Hungary prior to the World Cup finals in Switzerland in 1954, represented the Football League twice and toured Australia, South Africa and the West Indies with the FA party. He was voted 'Footballer of the Year' in 1959.
World Cup Finals Record: 1954: 1A 0G

Billy Wright, CBE Half-back

See 1950 World Cup (Brazil) for personal profile.

Bobby Robson, CBE Forward

Born: Sacriston, Co Durham, 18 February 1933.
Career: Langley Park FC, Fulham (professional, May 1950), West Bromwich Albion (£25,000, March 1956), Fulham (£20,000, August 1962- May 1967, also Oxford University, trainer/coach, season 1965-66), Fulham (manager, January-November 1968), Ipswich Town (manager, January 1969-July 1982), England ('B' team manager, January 1978-July 1982, national team manager, July 1982-July 1990), PSV Eindhoven (manager, August 1990-May 1992), Sporting Lisbon (coach, May 1992-May 1993), Porto (coach, July 1994-June 1996), Barcelona (coach, season 1996-97), PSV Eindhoven, again (coach, 1997-99), Newcastle United (manager, September 1999 to date).

Bobby Robson was a goal-scoring inside right before he was converted into an attacking wing half at West Brom. A highly effective player, always full of running and a fine marksman in his time, he played in a total of 583 League games during his career and netted 133 goals. He struck four goals in his 20 full internationals for England (1957-62), appeared in one U-23 game, represented the Football League on five occasions and toured South Africa with the FA in 1956. As a manager, he guided Ipswich to a Texaco Cup final win in 1973, FA Cup glory in 1978, UEFA Cup success in 1981 and also led Porto to victory in the Portuguese Cup in 1994 and to the domestic championship two years later.
World Cup Finals Record (as a player): 1958: 3A 0G; 1962: 0A

Bobby Smith Forward

Born: Lingdale, Yorks, 22 February 1933.
Career: Chelsea (amateur, July 1948, professional May 1950), Tottenham Hotspur (£16,000, December 1955), Brighton & Hove Albion (£5,000, May 1964), Hastings United (October 1965-March 1967), Banbury United (1967, retiring in 1970). Later became a part-time driver and labourer.

Stockily built, as strong as an ox, Bobby Smith was a brave, hard-working, shoulder-charging centre forward of the old brigade who certainly grabbed his fair share of goals with his bustling style that gave defenders nightmares! He packed a ferocious right-foot shot, could head the ball hard and accurate and was never short of stamina. A great competitor, he was part of that wonderful Spurs side of the late fifties, early '60s, under the control of manager Bill Nicholson. Bobby scored 208 goals in 317 games for Spurs. A League championship winner in 1961, he netted in both the 1961 and 1962 FA Cup final victories and was a key figure when the European Cup Winners' Cup was won in 1963. He was Spurs' top marksman in their double-winning season (1960-61) with 33 goals, having earlier equalled Ted Harper's 1930-31 seasonal record of 36 League goals. He was appeared for the London representative team in the 1958 Inter Cities Fairs Cup final and helped Brighton win the Fourth Division title in 1965. Bobby also hit 13 goals in 15 full international appearances for England (1960-63) with eight coming in his first five outings. He was a member of England's 1958 World Cup squad but was not called up for the 1962 Finals despite playing in two qualifying games against Luxembourg and Portugal.
World Cup Finals Record: 1958: 0A

Reserve Did not travel

* West Bromwich Albion's **Maurice Setters** (born 1936) He was named as a reserve for the 1958 World Cup Finals in Sweden, but unfortunately he failed to gain a senior cap for England, although he did represent his country in several youth and 16 Under-23 internationals, while also playing for the FA XI and Young England. Setters now lives in Bawtry, near Doncaster.

CHILE 1962

7TH WORLD CUP

Group Matches

Group 1

Team	P	W	D	L	Pts
Soviet Union	3	2	1	0	5
Yugoslavia	3	2	0	1	4
Uruguay	3	1	0	2	2
Colombia	3	0	1	2	1

30-May	Uruguay : Colombia	2:1
31-May	Soviet Union : Yugoslavia	2:0
02-Jun	Yugoslavia : Uruguay	3:1
03-Jun	Soviet Union : Colombia	4:4
06-Jun	Soviet Union : Uruguay	2:1
07-Jun	Yugoslavia : Colombia	5:0

Group 2

Team	P	W	D	L	Pts
West Germany	3	2	1	0	5
Chile	3	2	0	1	4
Italy	3	1	1	1	3
Switzerland	3	0	0	3	0

30-May	Chile : Switzerland	3:1
31-May	W. Germany : Italy	0:0
02-Jun	Chile : Italy	2:0
03-Jun	W. Germany : Switzerland	2:1
06-Jun	W. Germany : Chile	2:0
07-Jun	Italy : Switzerland	3:0

Group 3

Team	P	W	D	L	Pts
Brazil	3	2	1	0	5
Czechoslovakia	3	1	1	1	3
Mexico	3	1	0	2	2
Spain	3	1	0	2	2

30-May	Brazil : Mexico	2:0
31-May	Czechoslovakia : Spain	1:0
02-Jun	Brazil : Czechoslovakia	0:0
03-Jun	Spain : Mexico	1:0
06-Jun	Brazil : Spain	2:1
07-Jun	Mexico : Czechoslovakia	3:1

Chile was awarded the 1962 World Cup finals, thus Argentina once again missed out on hosting the competition. The country had suffered a severe earthquake in August 1960, but recovered sufficiently to construct several new stadiums and host the competition efficiently. Sadly the man who had done so much to bring the tournament to Santiago, Chilean FA president Carlos Dittborn died shortly before the finals began.

A total of 56 countries entered the competition, with England being the sole British representatives amongst the 16 finalists. This was achieved after they successfully negotiated a qualifying group containing Luxembourg and Portugal. For the second finals in succession there was no representative from either Asia or Africa.

Once again the finalists were divided into groups of four, with the format the same as in 1958 in Sweden.

The opening rounds were perhaps most memorable for the loss of Pele (with a pulled hamstring that kept him out of the remainder of the tournament) and a series of violent encounters.

The most notorious of these was the tie between Chile and Italy which earned the title 'The Battle of Santiago'. English referee Ken Aston had his hands full and his whistle in his mouth from the word go. Italian defender Giorgio Ferrini was sent off after just seven minutes, although it was some time before he actually left the field, escorted by armed police. Then shortly before the interval Italy's, Mario David was also dismissed. There were several incidents involving Chile's Leonel Sanchez (the son of a former professional boxer!) during which another Italian suffered a broken nose. Italy defended resolutely with nine men but their resistance was broken 16 minutes from time when Jaime Ramirez headed home. Jorge Toro then made it 2-0 in the closing stages. After studying a film of the game, FIFA banned Ferrini for one game and severely admonished both David and Sanchez. West Germany went on to win the group, with Chile finishing second.

The winners of group one were USSR, ahead of Yugoslavia. Brazil, the favourites, were unbeaten as they topped group three, two points clear of Czechoslovakia while Hungary won group four with England second.

England lost their opening game 2-1 against Hungary in front of a very sparse crowd, Ron Flowers netting the goal from the penalty spot. Manager Walter Winterbottom needed a victory over Argentina in their second fixture and with debutant Alan Peacock in fine form the team romped to a 3-1 win, the scorers being Flowers (with another penalty), Bobby Charlton and Jimmy Greaves. They then went on to claim second spot in the group by goal difference over Argentina with a disappointing 0-0 draw against Bulgaria. England met the holders Brazil in the quarter final, Gerry Hitchens equalising Garrincha's first half goal. However the Brazilians turned on the style after the break and with Garrincha in superb form they went on to win 3-1.

In the semi finals Brazil beat the hosts 4-2 in front of the tournament's largest crowd, 76,594, and Czechoslovakia accounted for Yugoslavia 3-1. Chile then joyfully claimed third place before Brazil went on to retain their trophy with another 3-1 win in front of an attendance of 69,000 at the Nacional Stadium in santiago. Amarildo, Zito and Vava scored for the winners, with Josef Masopust netting for the Czechs.

Six players shared the honour of being joint top-scorers with 4 goals each – Garrincha and Vava (Brazil), Florian Albert (Hungary), Valentin Ivanov (USSR), Dragan Jerkovic (Yugoslavia) and Leonel Sanchez (Chile). There were six dismissals, three of them involving teams playing against Chile. Vaclav Masek's goal for Czechoslovakia against Mexico in a Group 3 game was timed at just 15 seconds after the kick-off, the fastest-ever in the World Cup finals.

A growing problem was the number of players who were switching countries – Italy included Enrique Sivori (Argentina) and Jose Altafini (Brazil) while Spain had Jose Santamaria (Uruguay) and Ferenc Puskas (Hungary) in their squad. FIFA responded by tightening all of the rules in this area.

However, attendances were at their lowest level since 1934, 776,000 watching the 32 games at an average of 24,250.

Group 4

Team	P	W	D	L	Pts
Hungary	3	2	1	0	5
England	3	1	1	1	3
Argentina	3	1	1	1	3
Bulgaria	3	0	1	2	1

30-May	Argentina : Bulgaria	1:0
31-May	Hungary : England	2:1
02-Jun	England : Argentina	3:1
03-Jun	Hungary : Bulgaria	6:1
06-Jun	Hungary : Argentina	0:0
07-Jun	England : Bulgaria	0:0

Final Competition

Quarter Finals

10-Jun	Chile : Soviet Union	2:1
10-Jun	Brazil : England	3:1
10-Jun	Czechoslovakia : Hungary	1:0
10-Jun	Yugoslavia : W. Germany	1:0

Semi-finals

13-Jun	Brazil : Chile	4:2
13-Jun	Czech : Yugoslavia	3:1

3rd/4th Place

16-Jun	Chile : Yugoslavia	1:0

Final

17-Jun	Brazil : Czechoslovakia	3:1

CHILE 1962

Did You Know?

Arica, 3 June: the Soviet Union are leading the less-fancied Colombian team 4:1 after an hour's play and look like cruising to victory. Then Colombia draw level in a nine-minute interval, during which Lev Yashin - the "Black Spider" - in the Soviet goal had a nightmare spell. However, this is another exception that proves the rule: Lev Yashin is rated as the best goalkeeper in World Cup history. The FIFA trophy for the best keeper in a World Cup competition, introduced in 1994, is named after him in honour of his fine performances.

There are some famous names to be found in the list of the fastest goals: Bryan Robson took 27 seconds to beat France's keeper Ettori in 1982; four years earlier Bernard Lacombe needed 37 to put the ball past Italy's Dino Zoff. The absolute record is held by Vaclav Masek, who scored for Czechoslovakia against Mexico in 1962 after just 15 seconds. (This did not stop the Mexicans, with their legendary keeper Carbajal, from winning the match 3:1). A very surprising honour is held by San Marino, in particular by their then 22-year old player Davide Gualtieri, who scored just 9 seconds after the kick-off whistle in his team's final qualifying match in November 1993 - against England, no less.

England's squad in 1962
Manager: Walter Winterbottom

Goalkeepers
Alan Hodgkinson
(Sheffield United)
Ron Springett
(Sheffield Wednesday)

Full-backs
Jimmy Armfield
(Blackpool)
Don Howe
(West Bromwich Albion)
Ramon Wilson
(Huddersfield Town)

Half-backs
Stan Anderson
(Sunderland)
Ron Flowers
(Wolverhampton Wanderers)
Bobby Moore
(West Ham United)
Maurice Norman
(Tottenham Hotspur)
Peter Swan
(Sheffield Wednesday)
Jimmy Adamson
(Burnley)

Forwards
Bobby Charlton
(Manchester United)
John Connelly
(Burnley)
Bryan Douglas
(Blackburn Rovers)
George Eastham
(Arsenal)
Jimmy Greaves
(Tottenham Hotspur)
Johnny Haynes
(Fulham)
Gerry Hitchens
(Inter Milan)
Roger Hunt
(Liverpool)
Alan Peacock
(Middlesbrough)
Bobby Robson
(West Bromwich Albion)

ENGLAND 1966

WORLD CHAMPIONSHIP
JULES RIMET CUP
ENGLAND 1966

WORLD CUP WILLIE
ENGLAND 1966

1966 WORLD
CUP FINAL
ENGLAND
JULY 11 to 30

WEMBLEY
EVERTON
SHEFFIELD
SUNDERLAND
ASTON VILLA
MANCHESTER
MIDDLESBROUGH
WHITE CITY

EMPIRE STADIUM
WEMBLEY

WORLD CHAMPIONSHIP
1966
Jules Rimet Cup
FINAL TIE

S. Follows. SECRETARY,
THE FOOTBALL ASSOCIATION

SATURDAY JULY 30
KICK-OFF 3 p.m.

SOUTH STAND £5

(SEE PLAN & CONDITIONS ON BACK)
TO BE RETAINED

ENTER AT
K
TURNSTILES

ENTRANCE
36
ROW
12
SEAT
16

WORLD · CHAMPIONSHIP · JULES RIMET CUP
· ENGLAND · 1966 ·

CUP
FOOTBALL
CHAMPIONSHIP
1966

'EVENING STANDARD'
WORLD CUP SPECIAL
by
Bernard Joy
Former Arsenal & England Centre half

Authoritative guide
to the 8th World Cup
including details of
teams and matches
to be played from
July 11th to July 30th

BEAVERBROOK NEWSPAPERS PUBLICATION
PRICE THREE SHILLINGS

Sir Alf Ramsey Manager
(1966-70)
See 1950 World Cup (Brazil) for personal profile.

Gordon Banks, OBE Goalkeeper

Born: Sheffield, 30 December 1937.
Career: Millspaugh Steelworks, Rawmarsh Welfare, Chesterfield (professional, October 1955), Leicester City (May 1959), Stoke City (£52,000, April 1967-May 1973), Fort Lauderdale Strikers (March 1977).

Gordon Banks was a tremendous goalkeeper, one of the greatest the game has ever produced and for years he was regarded as the best the world over - admired by Pele, Eusebio and many more. He made over 300 senior appearances in seven seasons at Filbert Street and in 1966 conceded only three goals when England won the World Cup. He inspired Stoke City to League Cup glory in 1972, the year he was elected both 'Footballer of the Year' and 'Sportsman of the Year'. However, Gordon quit English soccer in 1973 after being involved a car crash that resulted in him losing the sight of one eye, but later returned to make an impact playing in the NASL. During his career he appeared in more than 650 senior games (510 in the Football League). He won 73 international caps - a record at the time for a goalkeeper - and he also represented the Football League and played in two U-23 matches. His brilliant one handed save from Pele's header in the World Cup finals group game against Brazil in 1970 is regarded as one of the greatest ever made by a goalkeeper.
World Cup Finals Record: 1966: 6A 0G; 1970: 3A 0G

Peter Bonetti Goalkeeper

Born: Putney, London, 27 September 1941.
Career: Chelsea (amateur, July 1958, professional April 1959; released May 1975, re-engaged October 1975), Dundee United (July 1979-May 1980), later served Chelsea and England as a goalkeeping coach, and also Birmingham City (part-time) and a handful of other clubs. Capped seven times by England at senior level (1966-70) and on 12 occasions by the U-23s, as well as playing in four matches for the Football League side, goalkeeper Peter Bonetti, 'The Cat', was brilliant at times when playing for Chelsea for whom he made 729 senior appearances. He gained winners' medals for victories in the FA Youth Cup (1960), League Cup (1965), FA Cup (1970) and European Cup Winners' Cup (1971), while also collecting runners-up medals in the FA Cup in 1967 and League Cup five years later. His last England outing was in that ill-fated quarter-final tie with West Germany in Leon, Mexico in 1970 when he deputised for Gordon Banks. Prior to that 3-2 defeat he had conceded only one goal in six matches for his country.
World Cup Finals Record: 1966: 0A; 1970: 1A 0G

Ron Springett Goalkeeper
See 1962 World Cup (Chile) for personal profile.

Jimmy Armfield Full-back
See 1962 World Cup (Chile) for personal profile.

Gerry Byrne Full-back

Born: Liverpool, 29 August 1938.
Career: Liverpool (amateur, August 1953, professional August 1955, retired through injury, December 1969).
A reserve for the 1966 World Cup finals, Gerry Byrne was an efficient right or left full back. Never found wanting and always seeking to use the ball rather than giving it the heave-ho, he played through practically the whole of the 1965 FA Cup final victory over Leeds United with a broken shoulder. He also won a Second Division championship medal with the Reds (1962), followed by two League title medals (1964 and 1966) and a runners-up prize in the European Cup Winners' Cup, also in 1966. He made 330 first-class appearances for Liverpool and won two full England caps (against Scotland in 1963 and Norway in 1966).
World Cup Finals Record: 1966: 0A

George Cohen, MBE Full-back

Born: Kensington, London, 22 October 1939.
Career: Fulham (amateur, July 1955, professional October 1956, retired through injury, March 1969), Fulham (Youth team manager, January 1970-June 1971).

Sure-footed right-back George Cohen was quick, a clean tackler with an unobtrusive style, making him a natural choice in Alf Ramsey's wingless England side of the 1960s when he formed a fine partnership with Ray Wilson in front of Gordon Banks. He established himself in the Cottagers' first XI halfway through the 1957-58 season and went on to amass a fine record of 459 senior appearances for the London club (six goals scored).

He missed only 22 League games out of a possible 422 played by Fulham between November 1957 and December 1967, eventually retiring in 1969 as a result of a knee injury.

George won 37 full England caps and six at U-23 level. He successfully battled against cancer with the same determination and willpower that he displayed against the dashing wingers who opposed him in the late fifties and 1960s.

World Cup Finals Record: 1966: 6A 0G

Ray Wilson Full-back

See 1962 World Cup (Chile) for personal profile.

Jack Charlton, MBE Full-back

Born: Ashington, Northumberland, 8 May 1935.
Career: Leeds United (amateur, July 1950, professional May 1952-May 1973), Middlesbrough (manager, May 1973-April 1977), Sheffield Wednesday (manager, October 1977-May 1983) Middlesbrough (caretaker-manager, March-May 1984), Newcastle United (manager, June 1984-May 1985), Republic of Ireland (caretaker-boss February 1986, manager to 1996)

Jack Charlton developed into one of the finest defenders in European soccer. He made his Football League debut for Leeds against Doncaster Rovers in April 1953, but owing to National Service he had to wait fifteen months for his next senior game!

He finally established himself in Leeds' first XI in 1955-56, taking over from the great John Charles who moved into the attack. Jack represented the Football League in 1957 and was the back bone of the Leeds defence when the Second Division championship was won in 1964. A year later, having gained the first of 35 full England caps, he played in the beaten FA Cup final side.

A vital member of Alf Ramsey's World Cup squad in 1966. He played his heart out at Wembley against the Germans, and four years later was again in the England party for the 1970 Finals in Mexico, playing against Czechoslovakia. Voted 'Footballer of the Year' in 1967, he helped Leeds win the Football League Cup and the Fairs Cup in 1968. The following year he was in their First Division championship-winning side and in 1972 proudly grasped the FA Cup, having been a loser again in 1970.

Jack amassed 770 senior appearances for Leeds (95 goals scored, a remarkable total of a central defender). Nicknamed 'The Giraffe', he was powerful in the air and tackled like a tiger, often averting danger when no one thought he could even reach the ball! As manager, he saw Middlesbrough win the Second Division championship by a mile in 1974 and gain victory in the Anglo-Scottish Cup twelve months later. He lifted the Owls out of Division Three in 1980 and then guided the Irish to the 1988 European Championship finals and to successive World Cup finals, in 1990 and 1994. He's the older brother of Bobby.

World Cup Finals Record: 1966: 6A 0G; 1970: 1A 0G

Allan Clarke Forward

Born: Willenhall, Staffs, 31 July 1946.
Career: Walsall (apprentice, July 1961, professional August 1963), Fulham (£35,000, March 1966), Leicester City (£150,000, June 1968), Leeds United (£165,000, July 1969), Barnsley (player-manager, May 1978-October 1980), Leeds United (manager, October 1980-June 1982), Scunthorpe United (manager, February 1983-August 1984), Barnsley (manager, July 1985-November 1989), Lincoln City (manager, June-November 1990).

From a footballing family, Allan 'Sniffer' Clarke had an instinctive nose for goals and scored 223 in a total of 513 League appearances - paradoxically the sides he managed gained a reputation for their lack of goals! Twice involved in record transfers, he played in four FA Cup finals and was a winner once, with Leeds in 1972, when he scored the deciding goal against Arsenal. He helped the Elland Road club win the Fairs Cup in 1971 and the First Division championship in 1974. As a manager he guided Leeds and Scunthorpe to promotion from Divisions Two and Three respectively in 1979 and 1983. Capped six times at U-23 level, Allan won 19 full caps (1970-75) scoring 10 goals, including a penalty on his debut against Czechoslovakia in the World Cup finals of 1970.
World Cup Finals Record: 1970: 1A 1G

Sir Geoff Hurst, MBE Forward

See 1966 World Cup (England) for personal profile.

Francis Lee Forward

Born: Westhoughton, Lancs, 29 April 1944
Career: Bolton Wanderers (professional, May 1961), Manchester City (£60,000, October 1967), Derby County (£110,000, August 1974, retired in May 1976). Now a successful businessman, based in Bolton, he also owns and trains racehorses. Francis Lee was an aggressive, short, stocky footballer who made his reputation as an outside right before switching to the centre forward berth. His bustling style brought him a rich harvest of goals (many of them penalties). Indeed, in 1971-72 he was regarded as the penalty expert when netting 15 times from the spot for Manchester City, a record.

He served City for seven years during which time he claimed a total of 143 goals in 321 League and Cup games, helping the Maine Road club win the First Division title, the FA Cup, the League Cup and European Cup Winners' Cup in the space of three years (1968-70). He won his second First Division championship medal with Derby (1975) before retiring in 1976 with a career record of 279 goals in 514 League and Cup games for his three English clubs. An England Youth international, he was capped 27 times at senior level (1969-72) scoring 10 goals. He also played for the Football League representative side and a United Kingdom XI.
World Cup Finals Record: 1970: 3A 0G

Peter Osgood Forward

Born: Windsor, Berks, 20 February 1947.
Career: Chelsea (amateur March 1964, professional, September 1964), Southampton (£275,000, March 1974), Norwich City (on loan, November 1976), Philadelphia Fury (December 1977), Chelsea (£25,000, December 1978). Retired, September 1979 and later assisted on the corporate side at Stamford Bridge on match days.

An immensely talented footballer, able to play as an out-and-out striker or in midfield, Peter Osgood had flair and ability, and his opportunism made him one of the most exciting players of his generation, certainly at Chelsea. Highly spirited and often unpredictable, he was not the easiest of players to handle off the field, but on it he was a great asset to the team he represented. He scored 150 goals in 380 first-class appearances in his two spells at Stamford Bridge. An England Youth international, Peter gained six U-23 and four senior caps (three won in 1970, one in 1973) as well as representing the Football League on three occasions. He gained two FA Cup winners' medals, with Chelsea in 1970 (scoring in the replay against Leeds) and in 1976 with Southampton. He was a European Cup Winners' Cup final winner in 1971 and a year later a loser in the League Cup final. He broke his leg in 1966 and was out of action for seven months.
World Cup Finals Record: 1970: 0+2A 0G

Martin Peters, MBE Forward

See 1966 World Cup (England) for personal profile.

GERMANY 1974

10TH WORLD CUP

Group Matches

Group 1

Team	P	W	D	L	Pts
East Germany	3	2	1	0	5
West Germany	3	2	0	1	4
Chile	3	0	2	1	2
Australia	3	0	1	2	1

14-Jun	W.Germany : Chile	1:0
14-Jun	E. Germany : Australia	2:0
18-Jun	Chile : E. Germany	1:1
18-Jun	Australia : W. Germany	0:3
22-Jun	Australia : Chile	0:0
22-Jun	E. Germany : W. Germany	1:0

Group 2

Team	P	W	D	L	Pts
Yugoslavia	3	1	2	0	4
Brazil	3	1	2	0	4
Scotland	3	1	2	0	4
Zaire	3	0	0	3	0

13-Jun	Brazil : Yugoslavia	0:0
14-Jun	Zaire : Scotland	0:2
18-Jun	Scotland : Brazil	0:0
18-Jun	Yugoslavia : Zaire	9:0
22-Jun	Scotland : Yugoslavia	1:1
22-Jun	Zaire : Brazil	0:3

Group 3

Team	P	W	D	L	Pts
Netherlands	3	2	1	0	5
Sweden	3	1	2	0	4
Bulgaria	3	0	2	1	2
Uruguay	3	0	1	2	1

15-Jun	Uruguay : Netherlands	0:2
15-Jun	Sweden : Bulgaria	0:0
19-Jun	Bulgaria : Uruguay	1:1
19-Jun	Netherlands : Sweden	0:0
23-Jun	Sweden : Uruguay	3:0
23-Jun	Bulgaria : Netherlands	1:4

The World Cup continued to grow and for 1974 there were 99 entries, although 11 countries later withdrew including USSR who refused to travel to Chile for a play-off game due to political reasons. England were drawn against Poland and Wales in the qualifying rounds, but although they won their opening match in Cardiff 1-0, they could only draw against Wales at Wembley and in Poland.

They therefore needed to beat Poland in the decider, but despite having home advantage they only managed a disappointing draw and this was enough to earn the Poles a place in the finals. Scotland, however, qualified for the first time since 1958.

The finals had a new format, although they began in the traditional way with four groups of four. The top two in each group then entered a second phase of two groups of four. The countries finishing top of their respective groups then met in the final.

The Scots had a disappointing campaign, defeating Zaire 2-0 and then managing a goalless draw with Brazil. They really needed to win the final group game against Yugoslavia but a 1-1 draw meant they were eliminated.

Group runners-up Poland and Brazil met in the third-place play-off, with the Poles surprisingly victorious 1-0. The final was played out in Munich's Olympia Stadion and had a sensational start when the Dutch scored in the first minute through a Neeskens penalty, and this before a single German had touched the ball. However despite their technical ability, they failed to press home their advantage and it was the Germans with goals from Brietner and Müller who took the trophy in front of an attendance of 77,833.

Grzegorz Lato of Poland finished up as the tournament's leading scorer with seven goals. The increase in matches led to a new record aggregate attendance of 1,774,022, but the average was slightly down at 46,685.

Group 4

Team	P	W	D	L	Pts
Poland	3	3	0	0	6
Argentina	3	1	1	1	3
Italy	3	1	1	1	3
Haiti	3	0	0	3	0

15-Jun	Poland : Argentina	3:2
15-Jun	Italy : Haiti	3:1
19-Jun	Haiti : Poland	0:7
19-Jun	Argentina : Italy	1:1
23-Jun	Argentina : Haiti	4:1
23-Jun	Poland : Italy	2:1

Second Round

Group A

Team	P	W	D	L	Pts
Netherlands	3	3	0	0	6
Brazil	3	2	0	1	4
East Germany	3	0	1	2	1
Argentina	3	0	1	2	1

26-Jun	Netherlands : Argentina	4:0
26-Jun	Brazil : E. Germany	1:0
30-Jun	E. Germany : Netherlands	0:2
30-Jun	Argentina : Brazil	1:2
03-Jul	Netherlands : Brazil	2:0
03-Jul	Argentina : E. Germany	1:1

Group B

Team	P	W	D	L	Pts
West Germany	3	3	0	0	6
Poland	3	2	0	1	4
Sweden	3	1	0	2	2
Yugoslavia	3	0	0	3	0

26-Jun	Yugoslavia : W. Germany	0:2
26-Jun	Sweden : Poland	0:1
30-Jun	W. Germany : Sweden	4:2
30-Jun	Poland : Yugoslavia	2:1
03-Jul	Sweden : Yugoslavia	2:1
03-Jul	Poland : W. Germany	0:1

Final Competition

3rd/4th Place

06-Jul	Brazil : Poland	0:1

Final

07-Jul	Netherlands : W. Germany	1:2

Did You Know?

East Germany's 1-0 win over their political enemies from the west, on opposition territory too, may not have had much meaning in the sporting sense since both teams had already qualified for the next round. It certainly had an emotional effect, however: the West Germans were shaken and their captain Franz Beckenbauer reacted in a manner unusual for this part of the world - he held a crisis meeting with the team and later appeared on television to explain the situation to an unsettled public. With evident success - 20 years after the "Wonder of Bern" the West Germans went on to win their second World Cup.

Scotland, as has since become their wont, failed to qualify for the second round of the World Cup final tournament, but they came very close. One win and two draws in their group matches were still not enough and they were eliminated early. To add to their disappointment they finally proved to be the only undefeated team of the competition.

11TH WORLD CUP

Group Matches

Group 1

Team	P	W	D	L	Pts
Italy	3	3	0	0	6
Argentina	3	2	0	1	4
France	3	1	0	2	2
Hungary	3	0	0	3	0

02-Jun	Argentina : Hungary	2:1
02-Jun	Italy : France	2:1
06-Jun	Argentina : France	2:1
06-Jun	Italy : Hungary	3:1
10-Jun	France : Hungary	3:1
10-Jun	Italy : Argentina	1:0

Group 2

Team	P	W	D	L	Pts
Poland	3	2	1	0	5
West Germany	3	1	2	0	4
Tunisia	3	1	1	1	3
Mexico	3	0	0	3	0

01-Jun	W. Germany : Poland	0:0
02-Jun	Tunisia : Mexico	3:1
06-Jun	Poland : Tunisia	1:0
06-Jun	W. Germany : Mexico	6:0
10-Jun	Poland : Mexico	3:1
10-Jun	W. Germany : Tunisia	0:0

Group 3

Team	P	W	D	L	Pts
Austria	3	2	0	1	4
Brazil	3	1	2	0	4
Spain	3	1	1	1	3
Sweden	3	0	1	2	1

03-Jun	Sweden : Brazil	1:1
03-Jun	Austria : Spain	2:1
07-Jun	Brazil : Spain	0:0
07-Jun	Austria : Sweden	1:0
11-Jun	Brazil : Austria	1:0
11-Jun	Spain : Sweden	1:0

The competition attracted more than 100 entries for the first time ever, but as 11 withdrew only 96 nations actually took part.

England were drawn in a tough qualifying group with Finland, Luxembourg and Italy, but although they won five of their six games they failed to progress to the finals on goal difference. They were not the only high profile country who failed to qualify – both USSR and Uruguay were also eliminated at the same stage.

Scotland carried the British flag in Argentina but had another disappointing campaign, losing 3-1 to Peru and then stumbling to a 1-1 draw against Iran. A substantial victory was needed in the final group game against Holland but although they performed well a 3-2 victory meant they were out of the tournament on goal difference.

Holland qualified comfortably for the final, but Group B was much closer and Argentina needed to beat Peru by at least four goals in their final game to go through. They won 6-0, condemning the Brazilians to the consolation of a third-place play-off victory against Italy.

So Holland once again faced the task of defeating the hosts to win the trophy, and once again fell at the final hurdle. In front of 76,985 spectators, the match went to extra-time before Argentina ran out worthy 3-1 winners. Scorers were Kempes (2) and Bertoni for Argentina with Nanninga replying for the Dutch.

Mario Kempes (Argentina) was the tournament's top marksman with six goals. Attendances were a little disappointing – a total of 1,610, 215 averaging out at 42,374.

Group 4

Team	P	W	D	L	Pts
Peru	3	2	1	0	5
Netherlands	3	1	1	1	3
Scotland	3	1	1	1	3
Iran	3	0	1	2	1

03-Jun	Peru : Scotland	3:1
03-Jun	Netherlands : Iran	3:0
07-Jun	Scotland : Iran	1:1
07-Jun	Netherlands : Peru	0:0
11-Jun	Scotland : Netherlands	3:2
11-Jun	Peru : Iran	4:1

Second Round

Group A

14-Jun	W. Germany : Italy	0:0
14-Jun	Netherlands : Austria	5:1
18-Jun	Italy : Austria	1:0
18-Jun	W. Germany : Netherlands	2:2
21-Jun	Netherlands : Italy	2:1
21-Jun	Austria : W. Germany	3:2

Group B

14-Jun	Argentina : Poland	2:0
14-Jun	Brazil : Peru	3:0
18-Jun	Argentina : Brazil	0:0
18-Jun	Poland : Peru	1:0
21-Jun	Brazil : Poland	3:1
21-Jun	Argentina : Peru	6:0

Final Competition

3rd/4th Place

24-Jun	Brazil : Italy	2:1

Final

25-Jun	Argentina : Netherlands	3:1

Bryan mostly operated in midfield throughout his superb career. He was an aggressive competitor with endless stamina. He had awareness, was creative, possessed excellent passing skills and powerful shot, was a superb header of the ball and had an appetite for hard work. He made almost 250 first-class appearances for Albion before adding 465 to his tally with United (100 goals scored). Beside his quota of full international caps, he also played twice for the England 'B' team and starred in seven U-21 games, having earned Youth honours as a teenager. Bryan retired with an overall total of 832 competitive appearances under his belt (for club and country). He scored 172 goals.

World Cup Finals Record: 1982: 4A 2G; 1986: 2A 0G; 1990: 2A 0G

Ray Wilkins, MBE Midfielder

Born: Hillingdon, Middlesex, 14 September 1956.
Career: Chelsea (apprentice 1971, professional October 1973), Manchester United (£825,000, August 1979), AC Milan (£1.5 million, June 1984), Paris St Germain (July 1987), Glasgow Rangers (November 1987), Queen's Park Rangers (November 1989), Crystal Palace (May 1994), Queen's Park Rangers (non-contract player, November 1994 then player-manager, briefly), Wycombe Wanderers (free, September 1996), Hibernian (free, September 1996), Millwall (free, January 1997), Leyton Orient (non-contract, February 1997 - retired as a player May 1997), Chelsea (assistant-manager, 1998-2001), Watford (assistant-manager, summer 2001).

Ray Wilkins made more than 900 club and international appearances - 608 in the Football League alone. He scored over 60 goals. Winner of 84 full England caps, he also represented his country at Schools, Youth, U-21 and U-23 levels and was an FA Cup winner with Manchester United in 1983 and a Scottish Premiership and Skol League Cup winner with Rangers in 1988-89. A midfield play-maker, with superb passing ability he was nicknamed 'The Crab' by his Old Trafford boss Ron Atkinson - because he seemed to move sideways more often than he went forward! He was Chelsea's youngest-ever captain at the age of 18, leading the Blues to promotion from Division Two in 1976. He was awarded the CBE in the Queen's Birthday Honours' List in June 1993 for services to football.

World Cup Finals Record: 1982: 5A 0G; 1986: 2A 0G

Steve Coppell Forward

Born: Croxteth, Liverpool, 9 July 1955.
Career: Tranmere Rovers (amateur June 1973, professional January 1974), Manchester United (£60,000, February 1975-October 1983 when he retired). Crystal Palace (manager, then Technical Director at Selhurst Park, 1984-93), Manchester City (manager, 1996), Crystal Palace (two further spells as manager, 1997-98 & 1999-2000), Brentford (manager, 2001-02).

Right-winger Steve Coppell made 396 first-class appearances (206 in successive Football League games) for Manchester United and scored 70 goals. Fast, clever and direct, with a powerful right-foot shot, he won one England U-21 cap and followed up with 42 senior international appearances, scoring seven times. He was an FA Cup winner with United in 1977 and a loser in both the 1976 and 1979 Finals as well as collecting a League Cup runners-up medal in 1983. Chief Executive of the Football League Managers' Association and a former PFA chairman, Steve was the Football League's youngest manager when he first took charge of Crystal Palace in 1984. He guided the Eagles to promotion from Division Two, albeit via the play-offs in 1989, and then took them to Wembley for the FA Cup final against his old club, United, in 1990.

World Cup Finals Record: 1982: 4A 0G

Trevor Francis Forward

Born: Plymouth, 19 April 1954

Career: Birmingham City, (junior, June 1969, professional May 1971), Detroit Express, NASL (May-August 1978), Nottingham Forest (£1.18 million, February 1979), Detroit Express (on loan, June-August 1979), Manchester City (£1.2 million, September 1981), Sampdoria (£800,000, July 1982), Atalanta of Bergamo (£900,000, July 1983), Glasgow Rangers (free transfer, September 1987), Queen's Park Rangers (£75,000, March 1988, then player-manager from December 1988), Sheffield Wednesday (player, February 1991, then player-manager June 1991, retiring as a player in May 1993), Birmingham City (manager, May 1996-October 2001), Crystal Palace (manager, November 2001).

Trevor Francis made a massive impact as a 16-year-old by scoring four goals for Birmingham City against Bolton Wanderers. He never looked back and developed into one of England's finest post-war marksmen. With pace, flair and ability, he was lethal anywhere within shooting distance of goal. He was brave, confident and above all, had the desire to win. He enjoyed running with the ball but most of all he loved to see it fly into the net - and during an excellent career he scored over 220 goals in more than 750 appearances at club and international level. Britain's first £1 million footballer when he moved from Birmingham City to Nottingham Forest, Trevor headed home the winning goal for Forest in the 1979 European Cup Final and a year was a Football League Cup runner-up when Wolves won 1-0 at Wembley. An Italian Cup winner with Sampdoria (1985) he helped Rangers win the Scottish League Cup (1988) and then assisted Sheffield Wednesday to gain promotion from the Second Division (1991), the same year that the Owls won the League Cup, beating Manchester United 1-0. He was twice a runner-up in 1993 as manager at Hillsborough, Wednesday losing in both the finals of the League Cup and FA Cup to Arsenal. Later he guided Birmingham into the First Division play-offs two seasons running and to the 2001 League Cup final, which was won by Liverpool at Cardiff's Millennium Stadium.

Capped by England six times at Youth team level, he played five games for the U-23s and went on to win a total of 52 full caps, scoring 12 goals.

World Cup Finals Record: 1982: 5A 2G

Kevin Keegan, OBE Forward

Born: Armthorpe, near Doncaster, 14 February 1951.

Career: Scunthorpe United (apprentice December 1967, professional December 1968), Liverpool (£33,000, May 1971), SV Hamburg (£500,000, June 1977), Southampton (£400,000, July 1980), Newcastle United (£100,000, August 1982, retired May 1984), Newcastle United (manager, February 1992-97), Fulham (manager/chief operating officer, season 1998-May 1999), also England (caretaker-manager, February 1999 - for four games - then senior coach/manager from May 1999-October 2000), Manchester City (manager, May 2001).

He lived in Spain from 1984-92.

Regarded as one of Liverpool's greatest-ever footballers, Kevin Keegan was described by Ivan Ponting (author of Liverpool: Player by Player, 1998) as follows ... "He was a darting, irrepressible imp of a player, scampering to all corners of his opponents, territory and not loath to forage for the ball in his own half. Quick, brave and apparently inexhaustible, he possessed a sureness of touch with both feet which enabled him to trick defenders in tight spaces and, even at only 5ft 8ins, carried a potent aerial threat."

He scored 100 goals in 321 appearances for Liverpool, helping them win three League championships (1973, 1976 and 1977), the FA Cup in 1974 (when he scored twice against his future club Newcastle), lift the UEFA Cup in 1973 and 1976, and claim the coveted European Cup in 1977. He was also voted as 'Footballer of the Year' in 1976. After leaving Anfield he was twice acclaimed 'European Footballer of the Year' (1978 & 1979) and received the accolade of being the West German 'Footballer of the Year' also in 1978. He helped Hamburg win the Bundesliga title in 1979 and reach the European Cup final in 1980. After netting 40 goals in 76 outings for Saints, he grabbed 49 in only 85 first-team games for Newcastle, helping the Magpies, amidst great excitement, gain promotion from Division Two in 1984. As a manager he took Fulham into the Premiership in 2001 before leading Manchester City to the verge of promotion by the middle of the following season. He resigned as England boss, saying he couldn't stand the pressure! Kevin scored 21 goals in 63 full internationals (1972-82). He also played in one unofficial international, collected five U-21 caps, and was awarded the OBE for services to football in 1982.

World Cup Finals Record: 1982: 0+1A 0G

Paul Mariner Forward

Born: Bolton, 22 May 1953.
Career: Chorley, Plymouth Argyle (£22,500, July 1973), Ipswich Town (£200,000 plus John Peddelty, September 1976), Arsenal (£150,000, February 1984), Portsmouth (free transfer, July 1986, retired May 1988).

An FA Cup and UEFA Cup winner with Ipswich Town (1978 and 1981 respectively) centre forward Paul Mariner won 35 caps for England at senior level between March 1977 and May 1985, scoring 13 goals. He also collected seven 'B' caps. He replaced the injured Cyrille Regis in Ron Greenwood's 1982 World Cup squad. A positive striker, very useful in the air, Paul had power and pace and was a constant threat to defenders throughout his career. He scored 223 goals in 630 League and Cup matches, including 136 in 335 games for Ipswich where his manager was Bobby Robson.
World Cup Finals Record: 1982: 5A 2G

Peter Withe Forward

Born: Liverpool, 30 August 1951.
Career: Smith Coggins, Southport (amateur July 1970, professional, August 1971), Barrow (December 1971), Port Elizabeth & Arcadia Shepherds in South Africa (during 1972-73), Wolverhampton Wanderers (£13,500, November 1973), Portland Timbers, NASL (May 1975), Birmingham City (£50,000, August 1975), Nottingham Forest (£42,000, September 1976), Newcastle United (£200,000, August 1978), Aston Villa (£500,000, May 1980), Sheffield United (free transfer, July 1985), Birmingham City (again, on loan September-November 1987), Huddersfield Town (player/coach, July 1988), Aston Villa (assistant-manager/coach, January-October 1991), Wimbledon (manager, October 1991-January 1992), Port Vale (Football in the Community officer, 1992-95), Aston Villa (youth development officer, 1995, then chief scout), Thailand (national team coach/soccer advisor, seasons 2000-03).

Peter Withe was a powerful centre forward, strong in the air, clever at holding up play and then slotting in vital goals either with his head or feet. He was a goal-scoring nomad whose playing career spanned almost 20 years during which time he netted over 200 goals in more than 600 appearances while serving with 15 different clubs at various levels in different countries. He gained a League Championship medal with Forest in 1978, and won another with Villa in 1981. He also scored the deciding goal when the latter club won the 1982 European Cup final. Peter scored once in his eleven international outings with England (1981-85). He was taken as a reserve striker to the 1982 World Cup finals but was not used by manager Ron Greenwood.
World Cup Finals Record: 1982: 0A

Tony Woodcock Forward

Born: Eastwood, Nottingham, 6 December 1955.
Career: Nottingham Forest (apprentice, professional January 1974), Lincoln City (on loan, February 1976), Doncaster Rovers (on loan, September 1976), 1FC Köln (November 1979), Arsenal (£500,000, June 1982), 1FC Köln (July 1986), Fortuna Dusseldorf. On retirement (1991) he continued to live and coach in Germany.

Tony Woodcock loved to run at defenders. A pacy striker, with skill and determination, he often appeared unnoticed inside the penalty area and scored some stunning goals as well as claiming his fair share of tap-ins! Positive in style, he could use both feet and was not the easiest of players to mark, defenders often having trouble to contain his forceful, direct approach to the game. He netted 16 times in his 42 senior internationals for England (1978-86) as well as appearing in two 'B' and two U-21 matches for his country. At club level he scored 68 goals in 169 games for Arsenal and 62 in 180 outings for Forest, with whom he won a League championship medal (1978), two League Cup winners' medals (1978 and 1979), and a European Cup winners' medal (also in 1979).
World Cup Finals Record: 1982: 1+1A 0G

MEXICO 1986

13TH WORLD CUP

Group Matches

Group A

Team	P	W	D	L	Pts
Argentina	3	2	1	0	5
Italy	3	1	2	0	4
Bulgaria	3	0	2	1	2
Korea Republic	3	0	1	2	1

31-May	Bulgaria : Italy	1:1
02-Jun	Argentina : Korea Rep.	3:1
05-Jun	Italy : Argentina	1:1
05-Jun	Korea Rep : Bulgaria	1:1
10-Jun	Korea Rep : Italy	2:3
10-Jun	Argentina : Bulgaria	2:0

Group B

Team	P	W	D	L	Pts
Mexico	3	2	1	0	5
Paraguay	3	1	2	0	4
Belgium	3	1	1	1	3
Iraq	3	0	0	3	0

03-Jun	Belgium : Mexico	1:2
04-Jun	Paraguay : Iraq	1:0
07-Jun	Mexico : Paraguay	1:1
08-Jun	Iraq : Belgium	1:2
11-Jun	Iraq : Mexico	0:1
11-Jun	Paraguay : Belgium	2:2

Group C

Team	P	W	D	L	Pts
Soviet Union	3	2	1	0	5
France	3	2	1	0	5
Hungary	3	1	0	2	2
Canada	3	0	0	3	0

01-Jun	Canada : France	0:1
02-Jun	Soviet Union : Hungary	6:0
05-Jun	France : Soviet Union	1:1
06-Jun	Hungary : Canada	2:0
09-Jun	Soviet Union : Canada	2:0
09-Jun	Hungary : France	0:3

There were 121 entries and only nine withdrawals for the 1986 World Cup tournament, thus once again establishing a new record of participants.

England were drawn in a group with Finland, Northern Ireland, Romania and Turkey and qualified comfortably with a record of four wins and four draws, including an 8-0 thrashing of the Turks in Istanbul. Scotland also reached the finals although they required a play-off victory over Australia to do so.

The tournament was originally planned to take place in Colombia but they were forced to drop out and Mexico was chosen as an alternative, thus becoming the first nation to stage the finals for a second time.

The 24 finalists were again divided into six groups of four for the opening round. A total of 16 teams (first and second in each group and the four third-placed teams with the best records) went through to the second phase, which was now run as a straight knock-out tournament.

England opened with a disappointing 1-0 defeat to Portugal, going down to a late goal resulting from a defensive error. However, perhaps of greater significance was the fact that key midfield man Bryan Robson was taken off with a shoulder injury.

Next up was Morocco and England again struggled to take control. For a second time in succession Robson was helped off injured, and Ray Wilkins' dismissal meant the team did well to secure a 0-0 draw.

Everything depended on the final group match against Poland and for once the team played to form, a superb hat-trick by Gary Lineker clinching a 3-0 win and a place in the second round.

Argentina (on five points) won Group A, with Italy finishing second and Bulgaria third. Mexico, Paraguay and Belgium qualified in that order from Group B (after a crowd of 110,000 had seen Mexico's star man Hugo Sanchez miss a last-minute penalty in the 1-1 draw with Paraguay).

USSR and France topped the table and duly progressed from Group C. In Group D Northern Ireland struggled, drawing 1-1 with Algeria in their opening match and then losing to Spain and Brazil who were the two teams to qualify for the next phase.

Finally, Scotland too had a disappointing time in Group E, gaining just a single point from a goalless draw against Uruguay and finishing bottom of the table. The South Americans passed into the knock-out stages along with Denmark and West Germany.

England then met Paraguay in the second round and although they took some time to establish control of the match, they eventually achieved a comfortable victory with two goals from Lineker and another from Peter Beardsley. Other ties saw Spain thrash Denmark 5-1 with Butragueno netting four times and Belgium defeating USSR 4-3 in extra-time, Igor Belanov hitting a hat-trick for the losers.

France showed their growing re-emergence as a footballing power with a 2-0 win over Italy and the other ties saw Argentina, Brazil, Mexico and West Germany progress.

Group D

Team	P	W	D	L	Pts
Brazil	3	3	0	0	6
Spain	3	2	0	1	4
Northern Ireland	3	0	1	2	1
Algeria	3	0	1	2	1

01-Jun	Spain : Brazil	0:1
03-Jun	Algeria : Northern Ireland	1:1
06-Jun	Brazil : Algeria	1:0
07-Jun	Northern Ireland : Spain	1:2
12-Jun	Northern Ireland : Brazil	0:3
12-Jun	Algeria : Spain	0:3

Group E

Team	P	W	D	L	Pts
Denmark	3	3	0	0	6
West Germany	3	1	1	1	3
Uruguay	3	0	2	1	2
Scotland	3	0	1	2	1

04-Jun	Uruguay : W. Germany	1:1
04-Jun	Scotland : Denmark	0:1
08-Jun	Denmark : Uruguay	6:1
08-Jun	W. Germany : Scotland	2:1
13-Jun	Scotland : Uruguay	0:0
13-Jun	Denmark : W. Germany	2:0

Group F

Team	P	W	D	L	Pts
Morocco	3	1	2	0	4
England	3	1	1	1	3
Poland	3	1	1	1	3
Portugal	3	1	0	2	2

02-Jun	Morocco : Poland	0:0
03-Jun	Portugal : England	1:0
06-Jun	England : Morocco	0:0
07-Jun	Poland : Portugal	1:0
11-Jun	England : Poland	3:0
11-Jun	Portugal : Morocco	1:3

Mark retired in 1999.

Like his father Tony, Mark Hateley was a very useful and effective centre forward. A strong header of the ball, he had pace (when required), could fire in a shot with both feet and was generally a very mobile and aggressive attacker who gave defenders plenty to think about.

He failed to win any club honours south of the border but whilst at Ibrox Park he helped Rangers capture five successive Premier Division championships (1991-95 inclusive), lift two Scottish Cups (1992 and 93) and three Scottish League Cups (1990-92-93). Tony scored 177 goals in 428 appearances for his six British clubs, including 113 in 220 outings for Rangers. Capped 32 times by England at senior level (1984-92), scoring nine goals, he won recognition as a youth team player and starred in 10 U-21 internationals.

World Cup Finals Record: 1986: 2+1A 1G

Gary lineker, OBE Striker

Born: Leicester, 30 November 1960
Career: Leicester City (apprentice, July 1977, professional November 1978), Everton (£800,00, plus a further £250,000 later on, July 1985), Barcelona (£2.75 million, July 1986), Tottenham Hotspur (£1.2 million, July 1989), Nagoya Grampus Eight, Japan (£900,000, November 1991). Gary is now a popular sports presenter for television (Match of The Day & They Think It's All Over Now among his programmes). He was awarded the OBE for services to football in the 1992 New Year's Honours List.

Gary Lineker developed into one of the finest marksmen in world football. Sharp and incisive, with a quick turn of foot, he was a real poacher, being in the right place at the right time to plant the ball into the net. He was also brave inside the box and although not particularly strong looking he could deliver a pretty powerful shot, and he wasn't a bad header of the ball either! He scored 103 goals in 216 games for Leicester, did exceedingly well in Spain, helping Barcelona to win their domestic Cup in 1988 and the European Cup Winners' Cup the following year, notched 38 goals in only 52 outings with Everton (all in one season) and then netted 80 times in 138 appearances for Spurs before rounding off his career in Japan. A Second Division championship winner with Leicester (1980) and a vital member of the Foxes' promotion-winning side in 1983, he was then an FA Cup finalist with Everton (1986) before missing a penalty in the 1991 FA Cup final which Spurs still managed to win. He was voted both the FWA 'Footballer of the Year' and the PFA 'Footballer of the Year' in 1986. An England 'B' international, Gary went on to gain 80 full caps (1984-92), scoring 48 goals, one less than the all-time record held by Bobby Charlton. He won the 'Golden Boot' for being top scorer in the 1986 World Cup finals (his tally of six including a hat-trick against Poland). He is also a fine cricketer who once scored a century for Leicestershire CCC and a member of the MCCC.

World Cup Finals Record: 1986: 5A 6G; 1990: 7A 4G

ITALY 1990

14TH WORLD CUP

Group Matches

Group A

Team	P	W	D	L	Pts
Italy	3	3	0	0	6
Czechoslovakia	3	2	0	1	4
Austria	3	1	0	2	2
USA	3	0	0	3	0

09-Jun	Italy : Austria	1:0
10-Jun	USA : Czechoslovakia	1:5
14-Jun	Italy : USA	1:0
15-Jun	Austria : Czechoslovakia	0:1
19-Jun	Italy : Czechoslovakia	2:0
19-Jun	Austria : USA	2:1

Group B

Team	P	W	D	L	Pts
Cameroon	3	2	0	1	4
Romania	3	1	1	1	3
Argentina	3	1	1	1	3
Soviet Union	3	1	0	2	2

08-Jun	Argentina : Cameroon	0:1
09-Jun	Soviet Union : Romania	0:2
13-Jun	Argentina : Soviet Union	2:0
14-Jun	Cameroon : Romania	2:1
18-Jun	Argentina : Romania	1:1
18-Jun	Cameroon : Soviet Union	0:4

Group C

Team	P	W	D	L	Pts
Brazil	3	3	0	0	6
Costa Rica	3	2	0	1	4
Scotland	3	1	0	2	2
Sweden	3	0	0	3	0

10-Jun	Brazil : Sweden	2:1
11-Jun	Costa Rica : Scotland	1:0
16-Jun	Brazil : Costa Rica	1:0
16-Jun	Sweden : Scotland	1:2
20-Jun	Sweden : Costa Rica	1:2
20-Jun	Brazil : Scotland	1:0

For the first time in the history of the competition the number of countries fell, with 116 nations entering of which 12 withdrew for various reasons. England qualified as a result of finishing second to Sweden in a group that also contained Poland and Albania. Their record was impressive – three wins and three draws, with ten goals scored and not a single one conceded. Republic of Ireland made it to the finals for the first time and Scotland surprised many observers by qualifying ahead of France who had finished in third place in 1986.

The format for the finals was exactly the same as it had been four years previously, the 24 finalists splitting into six groups of four from which the top two in each section and the four third-placed teams with the best records going forward to a knock-out stage.

England met Republic of Ireland in their opening fixture and carved out a hard-earned 1-1 draw, Gary Lineker scoring on eight minutes before Kevin Sheedy levelled on 72.

They then played out a goalless encounter with Holland, a match in which they were on top for long periods but unable to score. That left them having to beat Egypt to qualify for the next stage - and they did, but only just, Mark Wright grabbing the all-important goal on 58 minutes to earn a 1-0 victory. Republic of Ireland finished runners-up with Holland third, all three qualifying for the second phase.

Italy powered through from their Group A with a 100 per-cent record, with the well-equipped Czechs a fighting second. Cameroon, who caused a major upset when they beat Argentina 1-0 in their opening game, won Group B, ahead of Romania with Argentina going through in third spot.

In Group C Scotland began with an embarrassing 1-0 defeat at the hands of Costa Rica, then beat Sweden before falling to Brazil. It was not enough to earn a place in the next round, however, and only Brazil and Costa Rica progressed.

West Germany beat second-placed Yugoslavia 4-1 and the UAE 5-1 in winning group D (with Colombia also going through) while inconsistent Spain, Belgium and Uruguay all edged forward from Group E.

England were drawn against Belgium in the second round and the teams were matched closely throughout. With no goals after 90 minutes extra time was required, but it was not until the final minutes that the deadlock was broken. Paul Gascoigne's free kick was skilfully volleyed home by David Platt and England were in the last eight.

The biggest surprise came in Naples where the veteran striker Roger Milla netted twice as Cameroon beat Colombia 2-1 in extra time. Argentina eliminated Brazil 1-0 with a goal from Claudio Caniggia while Republic of Ireland scraped through on penalties against Romania. The other teams progressing to the quarter finals were Czechoslovakia, West Germany, Italy and Yugoslavia.

England's next opponents were Cameroon and although they took the lead with a David Platt goal they soon found themselves 2-1 down after the impressive Africans struck twice in three minutes mid-way through the second half. Gary Lineker equalised with a penalty with 15 minutes left and added a second in extra time to send his team into the semi finals for the first time since 1966.

Elsewhere Italy beat Republic of Ireland 1-0, West Germany beat Czechoslovakia by the same score and Argentina triumphed over Yugoslavia in a penalty shoot-out.

So the semi-finals saw Argentina play Italy in Naples on 3 July and West Germany take on England in Turin the following day. A crowd of almost 60,000 witnessed a 1-1 draw in Naples, Caniggia equalising for the South Americans. This remained the scoreline after extra-time and then in a tense, nervous penalty shoot-out Argentina held their nerve to go through.

Group D

Team	P	W	D	L	Pts
West Germany	3	2	1	0	5
Yugoslavia	3	2	0	1	4
Colombia	3	1	1	1	3
U. Arab Emirates	3	0	0	3	0

09-Jun	A.Emirates : Colombia	0:2
10-Jun	W .Germany : Yugoslavia	4:1
14-Jun	Yugoslavia : Colombia	1:0
15-Jun	W .Germany : A.Emirates	5:1
19-Jun	W .Germany : Colombia	1:1
19-Jun	Yugoslavia : A.Emirates	4:1

Group E

Team	P	W	D	L	Pts
Spain	3	2	1	0	5
Belgium	3	2	0	1	4
Uruguay	3	1	1	1	3
Korea Republic	3	0	0	3	0

12-Jun	Belgium : Korea Republic	2:0
13-Jun	Uruguay : Spain	0:0
17-Jun	Korea Republic : Spain	1:3
17-Jun	Belgium : Uruguay	3:1
21-Jun	Belgium : Spain	1:2
21-Jun	Korea Republic : Uruguay	0:1

Group F

Team	P	W	D	L	Pts
England	3	1	2	0	4
Netherlands	3	0	3	0	3
Republic of Ireland	3	0	3	0	3
Egypt	3	0	2	1	2

11-Jun	England : Rep of Ire	1:1
12-Jun	Netherlands : Egypt	1:1
16-Jun	England : Netherlands	0:0
17-Jun	Rep of Ire : Egypt	0:0
21-Jun	England : Egypt	1:0
21-Jun	Rep of Ire : Netherlands	1:1

ITALY 1990

14TH WORLD CUP

Final Competition

Round of 16

23-Jun	Czech : Costa Rica	4:1
23-Jun	Cameroon : Colombia	2:1
24-Jun	W.Germany : Netherlands	2:1
24-Jun	Brazil : Argentina	0:1
25-Jun	Italy : Uruguay	2:0
25-Jun	Rep of Ire : Romania	0:0
26-Jun	Spain : Yugoslavia	1:2
26-Jun	England : Belgium	1:0

Quarter Finals

30-Jun	Yugoslavia : Argentina	0:0
30-Jun	Italy : Rep of Ireland	1:0
01-Jul	W .Germany : Czech	1:0
01-Jul	England : Cameroon	3:2

Semifinals

03-Jul	Italy : Argentina	1:1
04-Jul	W .Germany : England	1:1

Final

08-Jul	W .Germany : Argentina	1:0

Did You Know?

Like Julius Caesar before him, Salvatore "Toto" Schillaci came, saw and conquered. For three weeks he was Italy's hero. Originally from Palermo but on the books of Juventus, he had played only one international match before the World Cup Italy 90 started. In the first Italian game he came on as a substitute and scored the 1:0 winner against Austria four minutes later. He was back on the bench again for the USA match, but was then used in every game and scored in every one too.

A crowd of 62,628 witnessed a much better encounter between England and the Germans. The two teams were evenly matched until Andreas Brehme put his side ahead just before the hour with a shot that took a wicked deflection and looped over Peter Shilton. England fought back to equalise ten minutes from time when Paul Parker's cross was guided home by Gary Lineker and the scores remained at 1-1 through to the end of extra time.

In another nail-biting penalty shoot-out, it was the Germans who looked the more composed and to the bitter disappointment of everyone associated with England, went through 4-3 after both Stuart Pearce and Chris Waddle had failed to score!

Italy then defeated England 2-1 to win the third-place play-off. Nevertheless it was still the country's best performance in the competition for 24 years.
The final, played in front of 73,603 spectators in Rome's Olympic Stadium, was one of the poorest in the history of the World Cup. Argentina had two men sent off and West Germany eventual clinched the trophy with a controversially-awarded penalty four minutes from time, that was converted by Brehme.

Overall however this was a most disappointing tournament, dominated by defensive play and ill discipline, a record total of 16 players being sent off. England gained some consolation when they received the World Cup's Fair Play Award.

Salvatore Schillaci (Italy) headed the scoring charts with six goals. Attendances were just short of those in 1986, with the 52 fixtures watched by 2,515,168 fans averaging at 48,368 per match.

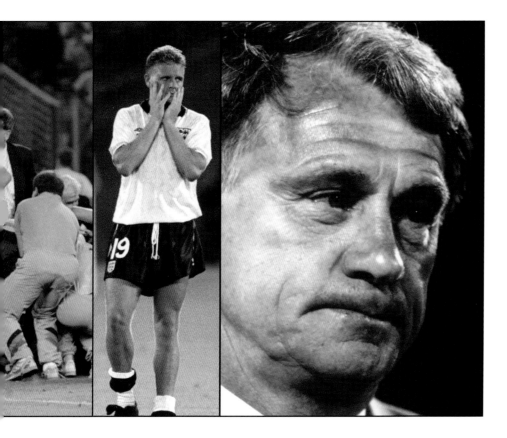

England's squad in 1990
Manager: Bobby Robson

Goalkeepers
Dave Beasant
(Chelsea)
Peter Shilton
(Derby County)
Chris Woods
(Glasgow Rangers)

Full-backs
Tony Dorigo
(Chelsea)
Paul Parker
(Queen's Park Rangers)
Stuart Pearce
(Nottingham Forest)
Gary Stevens
(Everton)

Defenders
Terry Butcher
(Ipswich Town)
Des Walker
(Nottingham Forest)
Mark Wright
(Derby County)

Midfielders
Paul Gascoigne
(Tottenham Hotspur)
Steve Hodge
(Nottingham Forest)
David Platt
(Aston Villa)
Steve McMahon
(Liverpool)
Bryan Robson
(Manchester United)
Trevor Steven
(Glasgow Rangers)
Chris Waddle
(Tottenham Hotspur)
Neil Webb
(Manchester United)

Strikers
John Barnes
(Liverpool)
Peter Beardsley
(Liverpool)
Steve Bull
(Wolverhampton Wanderers)
Gary Lineker
(Tottenham Hotspur)

Bobby Robson, CBE
Manager
(1986-90)
See 1958 World Cup
(Sweden) for personal profile.

Dave Beasant Goalkeeper

Born: Willesden, London,
20 March 1959.
Career: Edgware Town,
Wimbledon (£1,000, August
1979), Newcastle United
(£800,000, June 1988), Chelsea
(£725,000, January 1989),
Grimsby Town (on loan, October
1992), Wolverhampton Wanderers
(on loan, January 1993),
Southampton (£300,000,
November 1993), Nottingham
Forest (August 1997), Portsmouth
(non-contract, July 2001).
An FA Cup winner with Wimbledon in 1988 (thanks to his
penalty save from Liverpool's John Aldridge) goalkeeper Dave
Beasant was added to the 1990 World Cup squad by manager
Bobby Robson as cover for Peter Shilton and Chris Woods. He
won two full and seven 'B' caps for England. Showing superb
reflexes for a big man (6ft 4ins and 14st 3lbs) Dave passed the
milestone of 850 League and Cup appearances early in the
2001-02 season. He helped the Dons rise from the Fourth to
the First Division in rapid time during the early 1980s
before winning a First Division championship medal
with Forest (1998).
World Cup Finals Record: 1990: 0A

Peter Shilton, MBE, OBE Goalkeeper
See 1982 World Cup (Spain) for personal profile.

Chris Woods Goalkeeper
See 1986 World Cup (Mexico) for personal profile.

Tony Dorigo Full-back

Born: Melbourne, Australia,
31 December 1965
Career: Aston Villa
(apprentice, July 1981,
professional July 1983),
Chelsea (£475,000, May
1987), Leeds United
(£300,000, May 1991),
Torino (free, June 1997),
Derby County (free, October
1998), Stoke City (free, July
2000, retired, May 2001).
Tony now works for ITV
Sports as a football pundit.
Tony Dorigo was a very
efficient left back who enjoyed
his forays into enemy
territory! Capped by England
15 times at senior level, he
also appeared in seven 'B' and
11 U-21 internationals, acting as captain several times in the
latter category. A Second Division championship winner with
Chelsea in 1989, he also helped the London club win the Full
Members Cup in 1990 before assisting Leeds to lift the FA
Charity Shield and First Division title in 1992. He appeared in
well over 600 competitive games during his playing career.
World Cup Finals Record: 1990: 1A 0G

Paul Parker Full-back

Born: West Ham, London,
4 April 1964.
Career: Fulham (apprentice,
June 1980, professional, April
1982), Queen's Park Rangers
(£300,000, June 1987),
Manchester United (£2
million, August 1991), Derby
County (free transfer, August
1996), Sheffield United
(November 1996), Fulham
(non-contract, January 1997),
Chelsea (March 1997), Heybridge Swifts (1998-99),
Farnborough Town (1999-2000), Ashford Town (director of
football), Chelmsford City (coach, January 2000,
appointed manager in 2001 season).
Right back Paul Parker made over 180 appearances for Fulham,
160 for QPR and 146 for Manchester United before his career
started to wind down. An adaptable, compact defender, with
exceptional positional sense, he enjoyed bringing the ball out of
defence and setting up an attack rather than giving it a huge
kick downfield, hoping it found a colleague.

He represented England at four different levels during a fine career, winning eight U-21, three 'B' and 19 senior caps following his appearances for the Youth team. He was a League Cup winner in 1992, a Premiership winner in 1993 and 1994, also an FA Cup winner in the latter year as well as helping Manchester United win the Charity Shield in 1993.
World Cup Finals Record: 1990: 6A 0G

Stuart Pearce Full-back

Born: Hammersmith, London, 24 April 1962.
Career: Wealdstone, Coventry City (£25,000, October 1983), Nottingham Forest (£200,000, June 1985), Newcastle United (free transfer, July 1997), West Ham United (free, August 1999), Manchester City (free, July 2001-May 2002).

Resolute left back, totally competitive, with great determination and will-power, Stuart 'Psycho' Pearce gave opposing wingers no room whatsoever, neither did he give them too much time on the ball before he was in with a crunching tackle! A player who had a 'they shall not pass' attitude, was combative, robust when required, a real tough guy who packed a thunderous left foot shot, especially from dead-ball situations. Twice a League Cup winner with Forest (1989 and 1990), he was also a winner in the Simod Cup (1989) and Zenith Data Systems Cup (1992). He was capped 78 times by England at senior level (1987-2000), scoring five goals. He also played in one U-21 match. Stuart (with Chris Waddle) had the ill luck to miss from the spot in the penalty shoot-out with West Germany in the World Cup semi-final in Turin in 1990. But like a true professional, he bounced back and in similar situations later on he didn't miss! When the 2001-02 season came to and end Stuart had amassed close on 800 appearances at club and international level and had netted over 100 goals.
World Cup Finals Record: 1990: 6A 0G

Gary Stevens Full-back
See 1986 World Cup (Mexico) for personal profile.

Terry Butcher Defender
See 1982 World Cup (Spain) for personal profile.

Des Walker Defender
Born: Hackney, London, 26 November 1965.
Career: Nottingham Forest (apprentice, January 1982, professional November 1983), Sampdoria (£1.5 million, August 1992), Sheffield Wednesday (£2.7 million, July 1993-2001). Des Walker scored the winning goal in the 1991 FA Cup final - for Spurs against his own club Nottingham Forest when he inadvertently guided the ball past his own keeper! A defender with pace, Des was also an exceptionally fine positional player who could head a ball strongly with direction, tackle tigerishly and deliver a telling long pass, very rarely hammering the ball hopefully downfield. A League Cup winner in 1989 and 1990 and also a recipient of both a Simod Cup and Zenith Data Systems Cup winners' medal in 1989 and 1992, Des made almost 350 senior appearances for Forest before spending a season in Italy's Serie 'A'. He returned to the English scene and went on to play in a further 362 games for the Owls before his contract ran out at the end of the 2000-01 season, but he was still retained by the club. He won seven U-21 and 59 senior caps for England, the latter being between 1989-94.
World Cup Finals Record: 1990: 7A 0G

Mark Wright Defender

Born: Dorchester-on-Thames, Oxfordshire, 1 August 1963.
Career: Oxford United (juniors, August 1979, professional August 1980), Southampton (£80,000, March 1982), Derby County (£760,000, August 1987), Liverpool (£2.2 million, July 1991-September 1998 when he retired), Southport (manager, December 1999), Oxford United (manager May to November 2001).

Mark Wright was a solid central defender, as hard as iron, aggressive, tenacious in the tackle and a player who never gave up a lost cause. He made over 220 appearances for Saints, more than 170 for Derby and 210 for Liverpool as well as winning 45 full caps for England (1984-96), one goal scored, the winner in the World Cup game against Egypt in Palermo in 1990. He also played in four U-21 internationals. Surprisingly, his only club honour was an FA Cup winners' medal with Liverpool in 1992.

World Cup Finals Record: 1990: 6A 1G

Paul Gascoigne
Midfielder

Born: Gateshead, 27 May 1967
Career: Newcastle United (schoolboy forms 1980, apprentice, June 1983, professional May 1985), Tottenham Hotspur (£2.3 million, July 1988, plus an additional £350,000 later), Lazio (£3.5 million, May 1992), Glasgow Rangers (£4.3 million, July 1995), Middlesbrough (£3.45 million, March 1998), Everton (free, July 2000), Burnley (March 2002).

'Gazza' is a brilliant footballer despite having a somewhat high profile and controversial career. A class performer, he is a world-beater on his day. When the ball is at his feet, seemingly tied their by the proverbial piece of string, there is no better sight in football than a fully fit Paul Gascoigne running menacingly at defenders, weaving, jinking, swerving this way and that, trying to create space for a shot or to deliver a pass to a colleague. In his prime (in the mid-1990s) he was a joy to watch and the supporters loved him - not so opponents! During the 2001-02 season he reached the personal milestone of 450 senior appearances at club and international level, and was fast approaching the 120-goal mark. An FA Youth Cup winner in 1985 (with Newcastle) and although carried off injured he collected an FA Cup winners' medal in 1991 (with Spurs) and then added two Scottish League championships, plus Scottish League Cup and Scottish Cup winners' medals to his collection north of the border. Capped 57 times by England at senior level (1989-98), 10 goals scored, Paul appeared for the Youth team, also winning four 'B' and 13 U-21 caps.

World Cup Finals Record: 1990: 6A 0G

Steve Hodge Midfielder

See 1986 World Cup (Mexico) for personal profile.

David Platt Midfielder

Born: Oldham, 10 June 1966.
Career: Chadderton, Manchester United (professional, July 1984), Crewe Alexandra (free, January 1985), Aston Villa (£200,000, February 1988), Bari (£5.5 million, July 1991), Juventus (£6.5 million, June 1992), Sampdoria (£5.25 million, August 1993), Arsenal (£4.75 million, July 1995), Sampdoria (free, as player-coach/manager, August-November 1998), Nottingham Forest (player-manager, August 1999), England Under-21 coach (July 2001).

Attacking midfielder David Platt became Britain's most expensive footballer (in terms of total transfer fees of £22.2 million) when he joined Arsenal in 1995. He netted 60 goals in 152 games for Crewe, struck 68 in almost 150 outings for Villa, secured another 30 in just over 100 matches in Italy and added 15 more to his tally in 108 outings for Arsenal and one in seven games for Forest. With 27 goals in 62 international appearances for England, Platt is now in the top ten of his country's leading marksmen of all-time. He also represented England 'B' on three occasions, starred in three U-21 matches and gained both a Premiership and FA Cup winners' medal with Arsenal in 1997-98.

World Cup Finals Record: 1990: 3+3A 3G

Steve McMahon Midfielder

Born: Liverpool, 20 August 1961.
Career: Everton (apprentice, June 1977, professional August 1979), Aston Villa (£300,000, May 1983), Liverpool (£350,000, September 1985), Manchester City (December 1991), Swindon Town (player-manager, November 1994, retired as a player in 1996, but retained manager's job until October 1999), Blackpool (manager, January 2000).

An aggressive, hard-tackling, totally committed central midfielder, Steve McMahon gained medals galore at Anfield - three League championships (1986, 1988 and 1990), two for winning the FA Cup (1988 and 1989), the European Super Cup (1989) and three FA Charity Shields (1986, 1988 and 1989).

He earned 17 full caps for England (1988-91) and he also represented his country in six U-21 and two 'B' internationals. Steve made 120 first team appearances for Everton (14 goals scored), he had 91 outings for Aston Villa (7 goals), starred in 277 matches for Liverpool (50 goals), played 90 times for Manchester City (one goal) and had 51 games for Swindon, whom he guided to the Second Division championship in 1996. Steve was once a ball boy at Goodison Park for a Merseyside derby.

World Cup Finals Record: 1990: 3+1A 0G

Bryan Robson, OBE
Midfielder
See 1982 World Cup (Spain) for personal profile.

Trevor Steven Midfielder
See 1986 World Cup (Mexico) for personal profile.

Chris Waddle Midfielder
See 1986 World Cup (Mexico) for personal profile.

Neil Webb Midfielder
Born: Reading, Berks, 30 July 1963.
Career: Reading (associated schoolboy, September 1978, apprentice, June 1979, professional, November 1980), Portsmouth (£87,500, June 1982), Nottingham Forest (£250,000, June 1985), Manchester United (£1.5 million, July 1989), Nottingham Forest (£800,000, November 1992), Swindon Town (on loan, October 1994), Grimsby Town (non-contract, August 1996), Aldershot Town, Reading Town, Combined Counties League (manager, 2000-01).
Neil Webb was a competitive midfielder who made well over 700 appearances at club and international level, scoring more than 140 goals. He won a League Cup winners' medal with Forest in 1989 and an FA Cup winners' medal with Manchester United in 1990, but was substituted in the 1991 League Cup final when United lost. On his return to Forest he helped them reach the Premiership in 1994. Capped by England at Youth level, he represented his country in 26 senior internationals (4 goals scored) and appeared in three U-21 games, starred four times for the 'B' team and also played for the Football League. He was a member of Bobby Robson's 1990 World Cup final squad.
**World Cup Finals Record:
1990: 0+1A 0G**

John Barnes, MBE Striker
See 1986 World Cup (Mexico) for personal profile.

Peter Beardsley Striker
See 1986 World Cup (Mexico) for personal profile.

Steve Bull, MBE Striker
Born: Tipton, Staffs, 28 March 1965.
Career: Tipton Town, West Bromwich Albion (July 1984, professional August 1985), Wolverhampton Wanderers (£65,000 combined with Andy Thompson, November 1986; retired May 1999 to join the Molineux coaching staff); later Hereford United (player-coach, season 2000-01), then PRO with Wolves.
Given away by WBA, all-action, robust striker Steve Bull - affectionately known as 'Bully' - became Wolves' greatest-ever marksman, scoring 306 goals in 559 first-class appearances. He helped the Molineux club win the Fourth and Third Division championships in 1987 and 1988 and also the Sherpa Van Trophy at Wembley in the latter year. Capped initially by England at 'B' and U-21 levels, he went on to appear in 13 full internationals, scoring on his debut against Scotland in 1989 and later adding three more goals to his tally. Steve was taken to the 1990 World Cup finals by manager Bobby Robson ahead of Tony Cottee and Alan Smith.
World Cup Finals Record: 1990: 1+3A 0G

Gary lineker, OBE Striker
See 1986 World Cup (Mexico) for personal profile.

USA 1994

15TH WORLD CUP

Group Matches

Group A

Team	P	W	D	L	Pts
Romania	3	2	0	1	6
Switzerland	3	1	1	1	4
USA	3	1	1	1	4
Colombia	3	1	0	2	3

18-Jun	USA : Switzerland	1:1
18-Jun	Colombia : Romania	1:3
22-Jun	Romania : Switzerland	1:4
22-Jun	USA : Colombia	2:1
26-Jun	USA : Romania	0:1
26-Jun	Switzerland : Colombia	0:2

Group B

Team	P	W	D	L	Pts
Brazil	3	2	1	0	7
Sweden	3	1	2	0	5
Russia	3	1	0	2	3
Cameroon	3	0	1	2	1

19-Jun	Cameroon : Sweden	2:2
20-Jun	Brazil : Russia	2:0
24-Jun	Brazil : Cameroon	3:0
24-Jun	Sweden : Russia	3:1
28-Jun	Russia : Cameroon	6:1
28-Jun	Brazil : Sweden	1:1

Group C

Team	P	W	D	L	Pts
Germany	3	2	1	0	7
Spain	3	1	2	0	5
Korea Republic	3	0	2	1	2
Bolivia	3	0	1	2	1

17-Jun	Germany : Bolivia	1:0
17-Jun	Spain : Korea Republic	2:2
21-Jun	Germany : Spain	1:1
23-Jun	Korea Republic : Bolivia	0:0
27-Jun	Bolivia : Spain	1:3
27-Jun	Germany : Korea Republic	3:2

The 15th World Cup attracted a new record of 147 entries and although 17 nations subsequently withdrew there were still 130 participants. South Africa entered for the first time following their readmission to FIFA.

England failed to qualify for the first time since 1978. Grouped together with Holland, Norway, Poland, San Marino and Turkey they failed to win a single game against either Holland or Norway who both progressed to the finals. Even their performances against San Marino were not particularly convincing and although they won the away tie 7-1 they suffered the humiliation of conceding the quickest goal in World Cup history. Davide Gualtieri scored after just seven seconds, before an English player had even touched the ball.

Northern Ireland, Scotland and Wales all failed to make it to the finals, but Republic of Ireland qualified for the second time in succession, just pipping Denmark for second place in their group. Other notable absentees included France (for the second time in succession), Poland and Portugal.

The format for the finals was the same as in 1986 and 1990.

Romania won Group A, with Switzerland and USA also going through to the next stage.

The hosts opening 1-1 draw with Switzerland at Detroit's Pontiac Silverdome created history as the first-ever World Cup match played completely indoors.

In Group B Brazil and Sweden made it to the knock-out stages, both remaining unbeaten. Although Russia beat Cameroon 6-1 in their final match they still failed to make it through, but Oleg Salenko created a new record by scoring five times in a single match. Group C saw Germany and Spain progress while Nigeria surprised many by topping Group D, Bulgaria and Argentina finishing second and third.

Republic of Ireland caused a major upset by beating Italy in their opener with a Ray Houghton goal and this enabled them to scrape through along with Mexico and Italy in what was the tightest of the groups. Finally, Holland, Saudi Arabia and Belgium finished 1-2-3 in Group F.

The second round saw Republic of Ireland eliminated by Holland, while Brazil defeated the hosts 1-0. The surprises came from Romania, who put out Argentina 3-2, and Nigeria who took Italy to extra time before succumbing to Roberto Baggio's penalty. Also making it through to the quarter finals were Germany, Spain, Sweden and Bulgaria.

Italy, Brazil, Bulgaria (who knocked out the Germans) and Sweden made it through to the last four. The semi-finals saw Italy beat Bulgaria 2-1 in New York while Brazil edged out Sweden by the same score in Los Angeles. Sweden then hammered Bulgaria 4-0 to take third place.

The Final took place in Los Angeles at the Rose Bowl in front of 94,194 spectators, but it proved to be a dismal affair. Brazil and Italy playing out a 0-0 draw before the South Americans clinched their fourth title in a penalty shoot-out after Roberto Baggio fired Italy's fifth spot-kick high over the bar.

Hristo Stoichkov (Bulgaria) and Oleg Salenko (Russia) were joint-top scorers with six goals apiece.

This time there were 227 yellow cards handed out with 15 players being shown red. The attendances were at record levels, the 52 matches attracting a staggering total of 3,567,415 spectators – a million higher than the previous best – while the average of 68,604 was also a new all-time high. Overall the tournament was a huge success despite the disappointing final.

Group D

Team	P	W	D	L	Pts
Nigeria	3	2	0	1	6
Argentina	3	2	0	1	6
Bulgaria	3	2	0	1	6
Greece	3	0	0	3	0

21-Jun	Argentina : Greece	4:0
21-Jun	Nigeria : Bulgaria	3:0
25-Jun	Argentina : Nigeria	2:1
26-Jun	Bulgaria : Greece	4:0
30-Jun	Greece : Nigeria	0:2
30-Jun	Argentina : Bulgaria	0:2

Group E

Team	P	W	D	L	Pts
Mexico	3	1	1	1	4
Republic of Ireland	3	1	1	1	4
Italy	3	1	1	1	4
Norway	3	1	1	1	4

18-Jun	Italy : Rep of Ireland	0:1
19-Jun	Norway : Mexico	1:0
23-Jun	Italy : Norway	1:0
24-Jun	Mexico : Rep of Ireland	2:1
28-Jun	Italy : Mexico	1:1
28-Jun	Rep of Ireland : Norway	0:0

Group F

Team	P	W	D	L	Pts
Netherlands	3	2	0	1	6
Saudi Arabia	3	2	0	1	6
Belgium	3	2	0	1	6
Morocco	3	0	0	3	0

19-Jun	Belgium : Morocco	1:0
20-Jun	Netherlands : S. Arabia	2:1
25-Jun	S. Arabia : Morocco	2:1
25-Jun	Belgium : Netherlands	1:0
29-Jun	Morocco : Netherlands	1:2
29-Jun	Belgium : S. Arabia	0:1

Final Competition

First Round

02-Jul	Spain : Switzerland	3:0
02-Jul	Germany : Belgium	3:2
03-Jul	Saudi Arabia : Sweden	1:3
03-Jul	Romania : Argentina	3:2
04-Jul	Brazil : USA	1:0
04-Jul	Netherlands : Rep of Ire	2:0
05-Jul	Nigeria : Italy	1:2
05-Jul	Mexico : Bulgaria	1:1

Quarter Finals

09-Jul	Italy : Spain	2:1
09-Jul	Netherlands : Brazil	2:3
10-Jul	Romania : Sweden	2:2
10-Jul	Bulgaria : Germany	2:1

Semi-finals

13-Jul	Bulgaria : Italy	1:2
13-Jul	Sweden : Brazil	0:1

3rd/4th Place

16-Jul	Sweden : Bulgaria	4:0

Final

17-Jul	Brazil : Italy	0:0
		(3:2 penalty kicks)

FRANCE 1998

16TH WORLD CUP

Group Matches

Group A

Team	P	W	D	L	Pts
Brazil	3	2	0	1	6
Norway	3	1	2	0	5
Morocco	3	1	1	1	4
Scotland	3	0	1	2	1

10-Jun	Morocco : Norway	2:2
10-Jun	Brazil : Scotland	2:1
16-Jun	Scotland : Norway	1:1
16-Jun	Brazil : Morocco	3:0
23-Jun	Scotland : Morocco	0:3
23-Jun	Brazil : Norway	1:2

Group B

Team	P	W	D	L	Pts
Italy	3	2	1	0	7
Chile	3	0	3	0	3
Austria	3	0	2	1	2
Cameroon	3	0	2	1	2

11-Jun	Italy : Chile	2:2
11-Jun	Cameroon : Austria	1:1
17-Jun	Chile : Austria	1:1
17-Jun	Italy : Cameroon	3:0
23-Jun	Italy : Austria	2:1
23-Jun	Chile : Cameroon	1:1

Group C

Team	P	W	D	L	Pts
France	3	3	0	0	9
Denmark	3	1	1	1	4
South Africa	3	0	2	1	2
Saudi Arabia	3	0	1	2	1

12-Jun	S. Arabia : Denmark	0:1
12-Jun	France : South Africa	3:0
18-Jun	France : S. Arabia	4:0
18-Jun	South Africa : Denmark	1:1
24-Jun	France : Denmark	2:1
24-Jun	South Africa : S. Arabia	2:2

There were again new records for the number of entries to the 16th World Cup, with 174 applications and only four withdrawals. England qualified by heading a group that also included Georgia, Italy, Moldova and Poland. Scotland also made it to the finals as the best runner-up in the European groups, but Republic of Ireland lost out in a play-off with Belgium.

The tournament adopted the 'Golden Goal' rule for the first time, from now onwards matches entering extra time would be decided by the first team to score.

The finals were now expanded to include 32 nations, starting off in eight groups of four from which the top two entered a second-phase knock-out stage.

England needed to get off to a winning start and they achieved their aim, beating Tunisia 2-0 in Marseille with goals by Alan Shearer (42 minutes) and Paul Scholes (90). However their second fixture against Romania presented them with problems and they went a goal down shortly after half time.

Michael Owen equalised seven minutes from time but the Romanians grabbed a late winner to tie up a 2-1 victory.

The team responded positively to the set back and registered a 2-0 victory over Colombia in their final game (Darren Anderton and David Beckham with a cracking free-kick the scorers) to qualify for the next stage, along with Romania who actually won the group.

Scotland again failed to shine. An opening day defeat by holders Brazil was still a respectable result, but they could then only draw with Norway and were beaten 3-0 by Morocco.

Brazil and Norway went through from the group.

Beaten finalists from 1994, Italy topped Group B with three wins out of three. Chile also came through.

France won all three matches to claim top spot in Group C with Denmark finishing second.

Group D

Team	P	W	D	L	Pts
Nigeria	3	2	0	1	6
Paraguay	3	1	2	0	5
Spain	3	1	1	1	4
Bulgaria	3	0	1	2	1

12-Jun	Paraguay : Bulgaria	0:0
13-Jun	Spain : Nigeria	2:3
19-Jun	Nigeria : Bulgaria	1:0
19-Jun	Spain : Paraguay	0:0
24-Jun	Spain : Bulgaria	6:1
24-Jun	Nigeria : Paraguay	1:3

Group E

Team	P	W	D	L	Pts
Netherlands	3	1	2	0	5
Mexico	3	1	2	0	5
Belgium	3	0	3	0	3
Korea Republic	3	0	1	2	1

13-Jun	Korea Rep : Mexico	1:3
13-Jun	Netherlands : Belgium	0:0
20-Jun	Netherlands : Korea Rep	5:0
20-Jun	Belgium : Mexico	2:2
25-Jun	Belgium : Korea Rep	1:1
25-Jun	Netherlands : Mexico	2:2

Group F

Team	P	W	D	L	Pts
Germany	3	2	1	0	7
Yugoslavia	3	2	1	0	7
Iran	3	1	0	2	3
USA	3	0	0	3	0

14-Jun	Yugoslavia : Iran	1:0
15-Jun	Germany : USA	2:0
21-Jun	Germany : Yugoslavia	2:2
21-Jun	USA : Iran	1:2
25-Jun	Germany : Iran	2:0
25-Jun	USA : Yugoslavia	0:1

Nigeria and Paraguay were one and two in Group D, thus eliminating Spain and the previous tournaments semi-finalists Bulgaria. Edgy Holland (easily the best-supported team apart from France) and Mexico survived the challenge of Belgium to qualify from Group E. Germany and Yugoslavia bagged seven points apiece to ease through group F and Argentina won their three matches (including a 5-0 romp over Jamaica) to top group H and qualify with Croatia.

The second round matches were staged at eight different venues.

Brazil, not in good form, still beat Chile 4-1 in Paris, with Ronaldo scoring twice. Vieri scored for Italy as they defeated Norway 1-0 in front of 60,000 fans in Marseille.

France, hesitant at times, just got the better of a plucky Paraguayan side by a goal to nil in Lens, Laurent Blanc grabbing the all-important winner six minutes from the end of extra-time to claim the first-ever World Cup 'Golden Goal'.

Denmark whipped Nigeria 4-1 in Saint-Denis where the crowd was 79,500. Germany scored twice in the last quarter-of-an-hour to end Mexico's hopes at 2-1 in Montpellier, Oliver Bierhoff notching the winner on 86 minutes. Holland squeezed past Yugoslavia by 2-1 in Toulouse thanks to a last-minute goal by midfielder Edgar Davids. Davor Suker's penalty on the stroke of half time was enough to see Croatia get past a stubborn Romanian side in Bordeaux.

Then England, after failing once more to convert from the spot in the penalty shoot-out, were ousted by Argentina in St Etienne, a result that stunned the nation and, indeed, the players and manager Glenn Hoddle who certainly deserved better!

Alan Shearer's 10th minute penalty cancelled out an identical effort by Gabriel Batistuta for the South Americans as early as the 6th minute. Michael Owen then scored one of the goals of the tournament to give England a 16th minute 2-1 lead.

FRANCE 1998

16TH WORLD CUP

Group G

Team	P	W	D	L	Pts
Romania	3	2	1	0	7
England	3	2	0	1	6
Colombia	3	1	0	2	3
Tunisia	3	0	1	2	1

15-Jun	Romania : Colombia	1:0
15-Jun	England : Tunisia	2:0
22-Jun	Colombia : Tunisia	1:0
22-Jun	Romania : England	2:1
26-Jun	Romania : Tunisia	1:1
26-Jun	Colombia : England	0:2

Group H

Team	P	W	D	L	Pts
Argentina	3	3	0	0	9
Croatia	3	2	0	1	6
Jamaica	3	1	0	2	3
Japan	3	0	0	3	0

14-Jun	Argentina : Japan	1:0
14-Jun	Jamaica : Croatia	1:3
20-Jun	Japan : Croatia	0:1
21-Jun	Argentina : Jamaica	5:0
26-Jun	Japan : Jamaica	1:2
26-Jun	Argentina : Croatia	1:0

Final Competition
First Round

27-Jun	Brazil : Chile	4:1
27-Jun	Italy : Norway	1:0
28-Jun	Niger : Denmark	1:4
28-Jun	France : Paraguay	1:0
29-Jun	Germany : Mexico	2:1
29-Jun	Netherlands : Yugoslavia	2:1
30-Jun	Argentina : England	2:2
	(4:3 penalty kicks)	
30-Jun	Romania : Croatia	0:1

Zanetti equalised right on half time and having been reduced to ten men following the dismissal of Beckham for a petulant kick at fellow midfielder Simone, England thought they had won it when Sol Campbell headed what looked to be a perfectly legitimate goal. But this was ruled out and the tie went to penalties.

Shearer, Paul Merson and Owen scored for England, but Paul Ince (first) and then David Batty (with the vital last kick) had their efforts saved by goalkeeper Roa and Argentina somehow stole through 4-3 on spot-kicks.

In the quarter finals, Brazil, playing better, beat Denmark 3-2 in Nantes with Rivaldo netting twice on this occasion.

France were held to 0-0 draw by Italy in Saint Denis where the turnout was 77,000. They proceeded to win the penalty shoot-out 4-3 when Di Biagio missed Italy's fifth spot kick.

Croatia accounted for a disappointing German side by 3-0 in Lyon and Holland, courtesy of Bergkamp's brilliant last-minute strike, and Holland defeated Argentina 2-1 in Marseille.

The first semi final, in Marseille saw Brazil beat Holland 4-2 on penalties after a 1-1 draw. The Dutch, who missed from the spot in open play, again fluffed two 12-yard kicks with Cocu and Ronald de Boer the culprits.

A day later France, with 76,000 fans packed inside the Saint Denis Stadium, just got the better of Croatia by 2-1, right wing back Thuram scoring in the 47th and 70th minutes to cancel out Suker's opener just after half-time.

Croatia beat Holland 2-1 to grab third place before France, confidence sky high, took on Brazil in the final in front of 75,000 fans at Saint-Denis. Brazil, including an out-of-sorts Ronaldo were defeated 3-0 by a rampant French side whose goals came from Zinedine Zidane (27 and 45 minutes) and Emmanuel Petit (90).

France certainly had the strongest defence, and perhaps more flair in midfield while their attack at times looked sharp and incisive. They deserved to win.

For the record 22 players were shown red cards in France '98. Cup Final hero Zinedine Zidane being one of the early dismissals for a first class stamp on Fouad Amin in the second game 4-0 win over Saudi Arabia.

Croatia's Davor Suker was the leading scorer with six goals ...out of the overall total of 167 that were netted in the 64 games played.

Attendances were back to their pre-1994 levels, 2,775,400 watching the 64 matches, averaging out at 43,366.

France shared the World Cup's Fair Play Award with England.

Quarter Finals

03-Jul	Italy : France	0:0
	(3:4 penalty kicks)	
03-Jul	Brazil : Denmark	3:2
04-Jul	Germany : Croatia	0:3
04-Jul	Netherlands : Argentina	2:1

Semi-finals

07-Jul	Brazil : Netherlands	1:1
	(4:2 penalty kicks)	
08-Jul	France : Croatia	2:1

3rd/4th Place

| 11-Jul | Netherlands : Croatia | 1:2 |

Final

| 12-Jul | Brazil : France | 0:3 |

Did You Know?

In sporting terms, France '98 will go down in history as a successful World Cup. Increasing the number of competitors to 32 removed the safety net previously available to a table of 24 teams to qualify through the back door into the last 16 as one of the best third-placed teams. This time around, it was do or die in the group round matches. Teams therefore went all out for goals rather than relying on defence.

Most countries went about this with creative design and not brute force, enabling the world to discover such fresh young talents as Ariel Ortega (Argentina), Thierry Henry (France) and Michael Owen (England). Owen earned the distinction of scoring one of the most breathtaking goals of the whole World Cup, where 171 hit the target in a total of 64 matches. Davor Suker (Croatia) was the top scorer with six goals.

FRANCE 1998

England's squad in 1998
Manager: Glenn Hoddle

Goalkeepers
Tim Flowers
(Blackburn Rovers)
Nigel Martyn
(Leeds United)
David Seaman
(Arsenal)

Full-backs
Graeme Le Saux
(Chelsea)
Gary Neville
(Manchester United)

Defenders
Tony Adams
(Arsenal)
Sol Campbell
(Tottenham Hotspur)
Rio Ferdinand
(West Ham United)
Martin Keown
(Arsenal)
Gareth Southgate
(Aston Villa)

Midfielders
Darren Anderton
(Tottenham Hotspur)
David Batty
(Newcastle United)
David Beckham
(Manchester United)
Paul Ince
(Liverpool)
Robert Lee
(Newcastle United)
Steve McManaman
(Liverpool)
Paul Scholes
(Manchester United)

Strikers
Les Ferdinand
(Tottenham Hotspur)
Paul Merson
(Middlesbrough)
Michael Owen
(Liverpool)
Alan Shearer
(Newcastle United)
Teddy Sheringham
(Manchester United)

Glenn Hoddle Manager

(1998)
See 1982 World Cup (Spain) for personal profile.

Tim Flowers Goalkeeper
Born: Kenilworth, Warwickshire, 3 February 1967
Career: Wolverhampton Wanderers (apprentice, June 1983, professional August 1984), Southampton (£70,000, June 1986), Swindon Town (on loan, March 1987 & November 1987), Blackburn Rovers (£2.4 million, November 1993), Leicester City (£1.1 million, July 1999).
A goalkeeper with fine reflexes and courageous technique, Tim

Flowers had already made well over 500 first-class appearances by the time he joined Leicester City. Unfortunately, after a fine start, he struggled with back and hip injuries at Filbert Street. He helped Blackburn win the Premiership in 1995 and Leicester the League Cup in 2000. Capped 11 times by England at senior level, he also served his country in seven U-21 internationals having earlier played for the Youth team. Tim was in Glenn Hoddle's World Cup squad in 1998 but wasn't called into action.
World Cup Finals Record: 1998: 0A

Nigel Martyn Goalkeeper
Born: St Austell, Cornwall, 11 August 1966
Career: St Blazey, Bristol Rovers (August 1987), Crystal Palace (£1 million, November 1989), Leeds United (£2.25 million, July 1996).
Britain's first million pound goalkeeper when he joined Crystal Palace in 1989 after making 124 appearances for Bristol Rovers, Nigel Martyn played a further 349 games for the Selhurst Park club before transferring to Elland Road. He has served Leeds brilliantly over the past five years, amassing in excess of 250 senior appearances and taking his total of full England caps to almost 20, having earlier represented his country in 11 U-21 and six 'B' internationals. Unfortunately he has had Arsenal's David Seaman to contest the number one position with since 1990, acting as his understudy in the 1998 World Cup finals in France. Standing 6ft 2ins tall and weighing well over 14 stone, a great frame for the player billed as the last line of defence, Nigel has been one of the most consistent 'keepers in the Premiership.

A fine shot-stopper, he is brave, confident when going for high crosses and above all he commands his penalty area with great authority. In 1990 he gained a Third Division championship medal with Palace and added a Zenith Data Systems Cup winners' medal to his collection a year later before collecting a First Division championship medal in 1994.
World Cup Finals Record: 1998: 0A

David Seaman Goalkeeper
Born: Rotherham, 19 September 1963.
Career: Leeds United (apprentice, June 1979, professional September 1981), Peterborough United (£4,000, August 1982), Birmingham City (£100,000, October 1984), Queen's Park Rangers (£225,000, August 1986), Arsenal (£1.3 million, May 1990).

A terrific shot-stopper, agile and commanding in the air, David Seaman was regarded as one of the finest goalkeepers in world football during the mid-1990s. Unspectacular but utterly reliable, he made a difficult job look easy at times. He struggled with injury during 2001-02 and as a result will miss the World Cup finals in Japan and South Korea. A Division One winner with Arsenal in 1991 and a member of the Gunners' Premiership title-winning side of 1998, he was also an FA Cup winner in 1993 and 1998, triumphed in the European Cup Winners' Cup final in 1994 and won an FA Charity Shield prize in 1998, while also collecting a handful of runners-up medals. He made over 100 appearances for Peterborough more than 80 for Blues 175 for QPR and has now played in excess of 500 games for the Gunners and helped them reach the 2002 FA Cup Final. Capped ten times by England at U-21 level, David has also played in six 'B' internationals and now has 65 senior caps under his belt. Ironically he was virtually given away by Leeds as an 18 year-old in 1982. Fourteen years later the Elland Road club paid £2.25 million for Nigel Martyn, who, for the last few years has understudied him in the England set-up!
World Cup Finals Record: 1998: 4A 0G

Graeme Le Saux Full-back

Born: Jersey, 17 October 1968
Career: St Paul's FC (Jersey), Chelsea (free transfer, December 1987), Blackburn Rovers (£750,000, March 1993), Chelsea (£5 million, August 1997).

A fine attacking left back or an occasional midfielder, Graeme Le Saux suffered his fair share of injuries between 1999 and 2001 which clearly upset his rhythm and indeed his chances of establishing himself in the England side.

When fit his overall play was impressive, his sweet left foot allied to a strong presence made him one of the game's finest attacking left-sided defenders. Also able to play effectively in midfield, he has now passed the milestone of 400 appearances at club level and is well on his way to topping the 300 mark for Chelsea (two spells) whilst helping them reach the 2002 FA Cup Final. A Premiership winner in 1995 with Blackburn, Graeme also helped Chelsea win the League Cup and European Super Cup in 1998 and the FA Charity Shield in 2000. He has four U-21, two 'B' and 36 full caps in his locker (one goal scored at senior level) and was a member of England's 1998 World Cup final squad in France.
World Cup Finals Record: 1998: 4A 0G

Gary Neville Full-back

Born: Bury, 18 February 1975.
Career: Manchester United (YTS, June 1991, professional January 1993).
Able to play consistently well at right back or in a central defensive role, Gary Neville - steady, unflurried with sound positional sense - has been a vital ingredient in the Manchester United defence for seven years, since establishing himself in the first XI towards the end of the 1994-95 season. Honoured by England at Youth team level, he has now gained more than 40 senior caps. He was an FA Youth Cup winner with United in 1992 and since then has added five Premiership titles to his collection (1996-97-99-2000-01), plus two FA Cup final victories (1996 and 1999), a European Cup triumph (1999) and one FA Charity Shield success (1996). He is now well on his way to reaching the milestone of 350 first-class appearances for United.
World Cup Finals Record: 1998: 3A 0G

Tony Adams Defender

Born: Romford, Essex 10 October 1966.
Career: Arsenal (schoolboy forms, November 1980, apprentice, April 1983, professional January 1984).
An exceptional defender, totally committed, resilient, teak-tough and the most successful Arsenal captain ever, Tony Adams suffered his fair share of injuries during the late 1990s and announced his retirement from international football in 2001, having gained a total of 66 full caps (one goal scored). He also played for his country at youth level and in four 'B' and five U-21 games. He helped the Gunners win two First Division championships (1989 & 1991), the Premiership title (in 1998), two League Cups (in 1987 and 1993), two FA Cups (1993, 1998), the European Cup Winners' Cup (1984) and the FA Charity Shield (1998). Tony has now made well over 660 senior appearances for the Gunners, scoring almost 50 goals.
World Cup Finals Record: 1998: 4A

Sol Campbell Defender

Born: Newham, London, 18 September 1974
Career: Newham Schools, Tottenham Hotspur (apprentice, summer 1990, professional, September 1992), Arsenal (June 2001).

Physically strong in defence with a timely tackle and good heading ability, Sol Campbell appeared in 315 games for Spurs before controversially moving to arch rivals Arsenal at the end of the 2000-01 season. A League Cup winner in 1999, he represented England nine times as a youth team player, appeared once for the 'B' team and starred in eleven Under-21 internationals while also making 40 appearances at senior level during his time at White Hart Lane. Partnered his future team-mate Tony Adams at the heart of Glenn Hoddle's World Cup.

World Cup Finals Record: 1998: 4A 0G

Rio Ferdinand Defender

Born: Peckham, London, 8 November 1978
Career: West Ham United (apprentice, June 1994, professional November 1995), AFC Bournemouth (on loan, November 1996), Leeds United (£18 million, November 2000).

A reserve defender in Glenn Hoddle's World Cup squad in France, 1998, Rio Ferdinand made 158 appearances for the Hammers before his record-breaking transfer to Elland Road. An immensely talented footballer, thoughtful and stylish, with good control and perfect positioning, he looks set for a long and successful career in the game at club and international level, having already won almost 20 full caps to go with those he gained as a Youth and U-21 player.

World Cup Finals Record: 1998: 0A

Martin Keown Defender

Born: Oxford, 24 July 1966
Career: Arsenal (apprentice, June 1982, professional February 1984), Brighton & Hove Albion (on loan, February 1985), Aston Villa (£200,000, June 1986), Everton (£750,000, August 1989), Arsenal (£2 million, February 1993).

After being sold by Arsenal before he was 20, Martin Keown returned to Highbury seven years later a fully matured professional with well over 250 League appearances safely under his belt and he was an England international! A solid, reliable defender, he formed a superb partnership at the back for the Gunners with Tony Adams who also accompanied him on international duty. A wholehearted player, strong in the air and on the floor, Martin has now amassed a fine record with the London club of almost 400 senior games, helping the Gunners achieve the Premiership and FA Cup double in 1998 as well as collecting two Charity Shield winners medals (1998 and 1999). Most recently helping them reach the 2002 FA Cup Final. Capped almost 40 times by England at senior level (his first in 1992 against France), two goals scored, he had earlier represented his country as a youth team player and has also gained one 'B' and eight U-21 caps. He was in Glenn Hoddle's 1998 World Cup final squad in France but was not called off the bench.

World Cup Finals Record: 1998: 0A

Gareth Southgate Defender

Born: Watford, 3 September 1970
Career: Crystal Palace (trainee, January 1987, professional January 1989), Aston Villa (£2.5 million, July 1995), Middlesbrough (£6.5 million, July 2001).
Gareth Southgate controls things at the back with assurance and determination. He is rarely flustered and is certainly never given the run around by an opposing striker. He can perform equally as well as a sweeper or centre back, possesses fine positional sense and his strong in the air and precise on the ground. He made 191 senior appearances for Palace and 242 for Aston Villa before joining his former team-mate Ugo Ehiogu at Middlesbrough. Gareth helped Palace win the First Division title in 1994 and skippered Villa to victory in the 1996 League Cup final. Capped over 40 times by England at senior level (his first came as a substitute against Portugal in 1996) Gareth has so far netted one goal, and he had the misfortune to miss a vital penalty against West Germany at Wembley in Euro '96. But, like the true professional he is, he bounced back and played in the 1998 World Cup finals and Euro 2000.
World Cup Finals Record: 1998: 1+1A 0G

Darren Anderton Midfielder

Born: Southampton, 3 March 1972.
Career: Portsmouth (trainee, June 1988, professional February 1990), Tottenham Hotspur (£1.75 million, June 1992).
Darren is a very fine international-class wide midfielder with great vision and accuracy both when crossing the ball and shooting at goal. He was troubled with injuries during the late

1990s but recovered to help Spurs win the League Cup in 1999. Capped once by England at 'B' level, he appeared in 12 U-21 matches and has now won over 30 senior caps for his country (seven goals). Darren has also made close on 300 first-class appearances for Spurs, scoring more than 40 goals.
World Cup Finals Record: 1998: 4A 1G

David Batty Midfielder

Born: Leeds, 2 December 1968.
Career: Leeds United (associated schoolboy, 1983, apprentice, June 1985, professional August 1987), Blackburn Rovers (£2.75 million, October 1993), Newcastle United (£3.75 million, March 1996), Leeds United (£4.4 million, December 1998).
Widely acknowledged for his combative approach, hard-working central midfielder David Batty made 257 appearances for Leeds during his first spell at Elland Road. He followed up with 71 outings for Blackburn and 114 for Newcastle before returning to the Yorkshire club. A Second Division title winner in 1990, he gained a First Division championship medal two years later when he was also a winner in the FA Charity Shield.
Capped five times by England at 'B' level and on seven occasions by the U-21s, he has now collected more than 40 senior caps. David had the misfortune to miss the vital penalty in the World Cup second round shoot-out with Argentina in St Etienne in June 1998.
World Cup Finals Record: 1998: 2+2A 0G

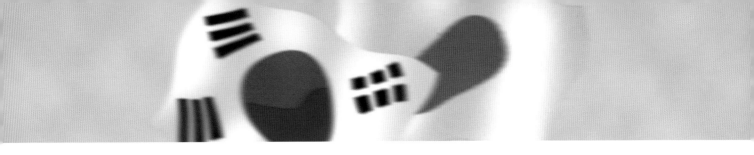

Sol Campbell Defender
(See 1998 World Cup (France) for personal profile

Ashley Cole Defender
Born: Stepney, London,
20 December 1980
Career: Arsenal (trainee, June 1997,
professional November 1998),
Crystal Palace (on loan,
February-May 2000).
Already capped by England at
Youth, Under-21 and senior levels,
attacking left-back Ashley Cole has
showed a maturity beyond his years
in the Premiership over the last two
seasons, while also catching the eye
at international level. His surging
runs and tigerish tackling, along
with his competitiveness, has
certainly been a great asset to
Arsenal whom he helped reach the
2002 FA Cup Final, despite tedious
injury problems.

Rio Ferdinand Defender
Born: Peckham, London,
8 November 1978
Career: West Ham United
(apprentice, June 1994,
professional November 1995),
AFC Bournemouth (on loan,
November 1996), Leeds
United (£18 million,
November 2000).
A reserve
defender in
Glenn Hoddle's
World Cup
squad in France,
1998, Rio Ferdinand
made 158 appearances for
the Hammers before his
record-breaking transfer to
Elland Road. An immensely
talented footballer, thoughtful
and stylish, with good control
and perfect positioning, he
looks set for a long and
successful career in the game
at club and international
level, having already won
almost 20 full caps to go
with those he gained as a
Youth and U-21 player.
**World Cup Finals
Record: 1998: 0A**

Martin Keown Defender
See 1998 World Cup (France) for personal profile

Danny Mills Defender
Born: Norwich, 18 May 1977
Career: Norwich City (trainee, June 1993, professional
November 1994), Charlton Athletic (£350,000, March 11998),
Leeds United (£4.37 million, July 1999).

Honoured by England as a Youth team player, Danny Mills
added 14 Under-21 caps to his international collection before
making his senior debut against Mexico in June 2001. He
recovered from an injury-ravaged 1999-2000 season to become
one of the finest attacking right-backs in the Premiership, while
also being able to fill in as an emergency centre-half. He has a
positive approach, is particularly sure-footed and gets in some
timely interceptions. He is now marching on towards the
milestone of 250 appearances at club level.

Gary Neville Defender
See 1998 World Cup (France) for personal profile

Gareth Southgate Defender
See 1998 World Cup (France) for personal profile

David Beckham Midfielder

See 1998 World Cup (France) for personal profile

Nicky Butt Midfielder

Born: Manchester, 21 January 1975
Career: Boundary Park Juniors, Manchester United (apprentice,

June 1991, professional January 1993) An all-action, non-stop midfielder with an aggressive presence on the pitch, Nicky Butt developed through the junior ranks at Old Trafford to become an important member of Sir Alex Ferguson's senior squad. Recognised by England at Schoolboy, Youth and Under-21 levels (seven appearances for the latter) he is now well on his way to gaining 20 senior caps for his country. He helped United win the Premiership trophy in 1996, 1997, 1999, 2000 and 2001, the FA Cup in 1996 (having been a finalist a year earlier), the European Cup in 1999, the FA Charity Shield in 1996 and 1997 and the FA Youth Cup in 1992. Butt, who has made well over 300 appearances for United, is contracted to stay at Old Trafford until 2005

Joe Cole Midfielder

Born: Islington, London, 8 November 1981
Career: West Ham United (trainee, June 1997, professional 1998).

After recovering from a broken leg that brought the 1999-2000 season to an abrupt end, West Ham's talented midfielder Joe Cole quickly made up for lost time with some fine performances over the next two campaigns, during which time he made his full England debut against Mexico in June 2001, having already won caps at Schoolboy, Youth and U-21 levels.

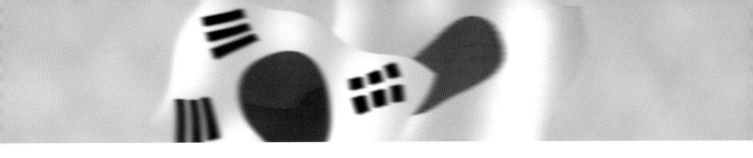

Kieron Dyer Midfielder

Born: Ipswich,
29 December 1978
Career: Ipswich Town (trainee,
June 1995, professional
January 1997), Newcastle
United (£6 million, July 1999).
Sidelined for long spells during
seasons 2000-01 and 2001-02,
when fit and on top of his
game, exciting wide-midfielder
Kieron Dyer will cause
defenders all sorts of problems.
Quick and lively, with good
control, he loves to run with
the ball and although not a
prolific scorer, he always looks
dangerous when in range of the
goal. He has been capped by
England at four different levels:
senior, 'B', Under-21
and Youth.

Steven Gerrard Midfielder

Born: Huyton, 30 May 1980
Career: Liverpool (trainee, June 1996,
professional February 1998).
A key member of Liverpool's triple Cup winning side of 2001,
Steven Gerrard developed into the complete midfielder under
the shrewd guidance of Anfield boss Gerard Houllier.
Despite a persistent back problem, he can run, chase, tackle,
shoot, create and defend - a real workhorse. Voted the PFA's
'Young Player of the Year' in 2001, he has now passed the
milestone of 100 appearances for Liverpool.

Owen Hargreaves Midfielder

Born: Canada, January 1981
Career: Bayern Munich (trainee, 1997,
professional summer 1999).
Strong-running, hard-working right-
sided midfielder Owen Hargreaves has
done exceedingly well over the last two
seasons in the German Bundesliga,
helping Bayern Munich win the
European Champions Cup in 2001.
With speculation mounting as to
whether he would play for Canada,
Wales, England or Germany, he finally
chose England and after impressing at
Under-21 level, he made his senior
debut as a late substitute in that 5-1
drubbing of Germany in a World Cup
qualifier in Munich last year.

Frank Lampard Midfielder

Born: Romford, 20 June 1978
Career: West Ham United (trainee, June 1994, professional
July 1995), Swansea City on loan, October-November 1995),
Chelsea (£11 million).
Son of the former West Ham full-back of the same name, Frank
Lampard, like his father, is a forceful, hard-working footballer,
with an eye for goal. He has represented England at Youth,
Under-21 (19 caps gained), 'B' and senior levels, and was
instrumental in helping Chelsea reaching the 2002
FA Cup Final.

Danny Murphy Midfielder

Born: Chester, 18 March 1977

Career: Crewe Alexandra (trainee, June 1993, professional March 1994), Liverpool (£1.5 million, July 1997), Crewe Alexandra (on loan, March-May 1999).

After well over 160 appearances for Crewe, Danny Murphy took almost three years before establishing himself in the Liverpool first XI, with half of his first 100 outings for the Merseysiders coming as a substitute. Mainly a midfield 'destroyer', he can also play as a support striker and at times turns up defending his own penalty area. Capped by England at Schoolboy, Youth, Under-21 and senior levels, he is a real honest-to-goodness competitor with a big heart and a terrific engine. Along with fellow midfielder Gerrard and strikers Fowler, Heskey and Owen, he was part of Liverpool's triple Cup winning side of 2001.

Trevor Sinclair Midfielder

Born: Dulwich, 2 March 1973

Career: Blackpool (trainee, June 1989, professional August 1990), Queen's Park Rangers (£750,000, August 1993), West Ham United (£2.3 million, January 1998).

Having made 140 appearances for Blackpool and 190 for QPR, right-sided midfielder (or an occasional right wing-back) Trevor Sinclair has now amassed in excess of 150 for the Hammers. A tricky, purposeful player, with good speed and tremendous shot, he has been capped by England at Youth, U-21 (14 times), 'B' and senior levels.

Robbie Fowler Striker

Born: Liverpool, 9 April 1975

Career: Liverpool (trainee, June 1991, professional April 1992), Leeds United (£11 million, December 2001).

Robbie Fowler scored more than 170 goals in well over 300 competitive games for Liverpool before joining Leeds. One of the best finishers in the game, he was twice a League Cup winner with the Merseysiders and figured in their triple Cup success of 2001. Capped over 20 times by England at senior level, he has also represented his country at Under-18, Under-21 and 'B' team levels.

Paul Scholes Midfielder

See 1998 World Cup (France) for personal profile

Emile Heskey Striker

Born: Leicester, 11 January 1978
Career: Leicester City (trainee, June 1994, professional October 1995), Liverpool (£11 million, March 2000).

As strong as an ox, Emile Heskey was regarded as one of the best strikers in the country, even in Europe, after scoring 12 goals in 12 games for Liverpool early in the 2000-01 season. He has tremendous pace, can head a ball as powerful as some players can kick one, and his right foot shots sometimes fly towards the goal like shells. He scored 46 goals in 197 games for Leicester, also gaining two league Cup winners' medals. He then joined up with Michael Owen and Robbie Fowler at Anfield and helped Liverpool win three major Cup finals in 2001. Heskey has been capped by England at Youth, Under-21, 'B' and senior levels, with 20 appearances to his name in the latter category.

Teddy Sheringham Striker

See 1998 World Cup (France) for personal profile.

Darius Vassell Striker

Born: Birmingham, 13 June 1980.
Career: Aston Villa (trainee, June 1996, professional April 1998).

A powerful young striker, quick and decisive, Darius Vassell was used as a substitute over 50 times by Aston Villa during his first three seasons of senior football (from 1998) before finally establishing himself in the side, alongside the Colombian Juan Pablo Angel in 2001-02. He scored a spectacular equalizing goal on his full international debut, in the 1-1 draw with Holland in Amsterdam in February 2002. Vassell has also played in almost a dozen Under-21 games for his country.

Michael Owen Striker

See 1998 World Cup (France) for personal profile.

ENGLAND'S BEST EVER WORLD CUP TEAM?

We have selected what we think is our best ever England World Cup team. What is your best ever team?

Back Row (Left to Right): Jimmy Armfield, Nobby Stiles, Gordon Banks, Tony Adams, Ray Wilson, Billy Wright, Alf Ramsey (Manager)

Front Row (Left to Right): David Beckham, Bobby Charlton, Bobby Moore, Michael Owen, Tom Finney

The Liverpool-Born Black Community An Issue of Identification *by Dr. R. H. Costello*

This article featured in Diverse Magazine, 2008.

The history of the Liverpool Black Community seems to have been strangely ignored in the dialogue on asylum seekers and immigration by government pundits. The Liverpool Black Community is distinguished from others by its continuity, some Black Liverpudlians being able to trace their roots in Liverpool for as many as ten generations. This community dates back to even before the American War of Independence, which caused numbers of free Black Loyalists to settle in London and the growing township. Early settlers ranged from freed slaves and Black servants to the student sons and daughters of African rulers, who had visited the port from at least the 1730s.

*Ray takes some time out from signing his book, **Black Liverpool 1730–1918**, at St. George's Hall, 2003.*

Liverpool's Black community is some three centuries old, but incredibly, still faces the difficulties of identification. Although not all the Liverpool Black Community is of dual heritage, the majority of those born in Liverpool are. Much of the difficulty of identification of the Liverpool Black Community lies in the fact that, from its beginnings, the Liverpool Black population has indeed been a mixed race community, the result of more male settlers than female; freed Black American soldiers arriving in 1782 after the American War of Independence, to be followed throughout the 19th and 20th centuries by African and West Indian sailors, soldiers and workers.

The very definition of a 'mixed-race' society is fraught with difficulty, and this is one of the problems of acknowledgement, even in Liverpool. All the current terms are inadequate: the term 'halfcaste' has long been discredited, but even newer terms – 'mixed race' and 'dual heritage' have their own problems. 'Dual Heritage' suggests a child living with the supposed 'dilemma' of each parent having a different culture or background. This may not be the case in many Liverpool children with both European and African genes, as any intermarriage may have taken place generations ago. Thus, a child who appears to have 50-50 genes may not have one Black parent and one White parent, but could be the product of a community which became a distinct multi-racial community literally centuries ago, just as Mexicans and many Central and South Americans have now evolved from being considered half Native American (or 'Indian', as they were wrongly called) and half Spanish to distinct ethnic identities.

The Liverpool Black Community remains invisible because of a lack of knowledge of the history of how this unique community, the oldest Black community in Europe, came about and the many people who have contributed to it. Those who do know of the existence of this invisible people might suppose that their presence, though vaguely 'old', is not more than a generation or so, in common with other Black settlements in Britain, following two world wars.

The presence of an almost homogeneous people derived from many nations.

Eking out their existence as a secret under-culture in a state of suppression for over two and a half centuries comes as a surprise to many.

The Liverpool Black Community would appear to have been continually added to since its beginning, an additional problem in identification, as newer Black settlers and visitors, each with their own language, culture and religion, has been thrown into the melting pot that is the present-day Black Community.

School approaches to dealing with issues of race have not helped the identification of the needs of the Liverpool Black child, often with no ill intention. Very often, the route to understanding people of different races has been through studying what are essentially purified national identities – a Nigerian family, life in a Chinese town, an Indian village, the Bedouin tent.

The problem is that some children in Liverpool do not fit neatly into these categories, being not only of dual racial ancestry, but triple – African, Chinese and English (or often Irish). To those teachers and others, the question might arise: surely, children of this sort of, for want of a better term, 'dual heritage' must occur in many parts of Britain as individuals and can hardly be considered to be people in their own right requiring appropriate attention in the school curriculum? Or are they, as a large distinct group in Liverpool, precisely that – a distinct people?

Liverpool, or indeed Britain, cannot afford to have any particular section of a community within a community ignored forever – a situation which has pertained for at least two and a half centuries, the first Black children being born in Liverpool in the 1750s. More children were born to Black American Loyalists in Liverpool after 1782. One such Black Loyalist to establish a Liverpool-born family was originally known as Cato or James Cato, a slave name. After running away to sea as a child and actually serving on ships involved in the slave trade, he joined the Royal Navy and changed his name to James Brown, serving upon no less than Lord Nelson's flagship *Victory* at the time of the battle of Trafalgar in 1804.

The Vauxhall/Scotland Road area held a special Commemorative Mass for James Clarke. The Tribute to Mr. Clarke was attended by members of his family (above) and residents. Members of the Merseyside Guyana Association also attended the Mass. A plaque was unveiled, and the Acting High Commissioner for Guyana, Marion Herbert, gave a reading during the service.
[Courtesy: Scottie Press]

James Clarke was a 'Black Liverpudlian' distinguished by being a Black man in Liverpool with a street named after him. Born around 1886, Jim's great gift was swimming, and he often saved people from drowning.

After saving around nine or ten children from the local canal, he decided to do something about it. He started going along to the local swimming baths to teach them how to swim. Negative attitudes towards racial intermarriage has a history dating back many centuries in Britain. The following extract from **Black Liverpool** demonstrates prevalent thinking on mixed marriage nearly a century ago:

"Addressing the first meeting of the Liverpool Board of Eugenics Society, under its JEW title 'The Liverpool Hereditary Society' in 1920, the Rev. James Hamilton expressed his belief in the eminence of the British nation over others by virtue of inherited powers and 'its own great common blood-stream, always differing more or less from all others.'"

The Liverpool-born Black community is here to stay. It is about time that its image as an underprivileged community is properly addressed. The first step needs to be recognition of the community's long history and work towards meeting its specific needs.

The African Presence in Liverpool

Dr. Costello provided an historic insight into both the past and present development of the Liverpool-born Black community. Here, I identify some landmarks, families and the more 'visible' and recorded links with Liverpool and Africa.

It is difficult to know where to start, there are so many ties. Maybe an 'appropriate' starting point would be the city centre of Liverpool during the month of September 1766:

Williamson's Liverpool Advertiser 12th September 1766

"At the Exchange Coffee House, in Water Street, this day, the 12th instant, September at 10 o'clock precisely, eleven negroes (for sale) imported by the Angola."

Slaves on the Dock – 18th century Liverpool watercolour drawing by B. Reading – part of the Mayer collection in Liverpool Public Library.

Liverpool Chronicle 15th December 1768

"For sale a fine negroe boy of about 4 feet 5 inches high. Of a sober, tractable, humane disposition. Eleven or twelve years – talks English very well and can dress hair in a tolerable way."

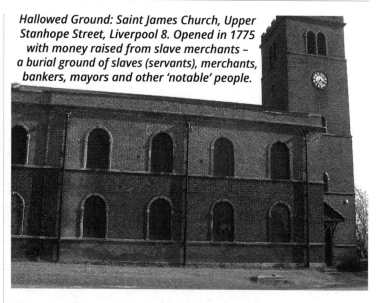

Hallowed Ground: Saint James Church, Upper Stanhope Street, Liverpool 8. Opened in 1775 with money raised from slave merchants – a burial ground of slaves (servants), merchants, bankers, mayors and other 'notable' people.

The practice of auctioning slaves on the streets of Liverpool during the mid 18th century was fairly widespread. One observer commented:

"One street in town was nicknamed Negro Row, and negro slaves were occasionally sold by auction in the shops, warehouses and coffee houses, and also on the steps of custom house."

– G. Williams 1887

Most were sold as Black servants, who were in constant demand. Liverpool excelled in the trade, and by the end of the 18th century, they controlled 70% of Britain's slave trade. The legacy can be seen in a number of Liverpool street names originating from slave ship merchants or those involved in the trade – the names of slave traders like Earle, Tarleton and Cunliffe.

The results of such involvement would see a significant growth of the population in the city. For a more comprehensive insight, see *Liverpool and Slavery* (Facebook). At this stage, most Black settlement was concentrated in the south docks area of the city, Upper Pitt Street being a melting pot of nationalities and boarding homes. Or as described by an Irish Liverpudlian:

"The negroes, many of whom are firemen and trimmers on the Elder Dempster 'monkey' boats, had their headquarters on Gore Street and Stanhope Street at the foot of which, into the Coburg dock, the monkey boats used to come from sea."

Gore Street derives from the Goree (a slave island) ruled by the Dutch, as well as Jamaica Street.

The Slavery Abolition Act 1830 came into operation by 1834, although slavery across the British Empire was not abolished until 1838. Despite this 'loss', maritime trade continued to grow. The trade was now in a variety of goods, other than human bondage. They left the trade with a healthy record, transporting 1,360,000 African people in over 5,000 voyages made by Liverpool vessels. More than half of all slaves sold by English traders were the property of Liverpool merchants. The city became prosperous with grand buildings, rich families and a succession of slave-owning lord mayors, all from the toil and inhumane treatment of African peoples.

Right: George Wayland and his wife Sara Ann Wayland; left: Emma Lawrence and John Isaac Quarless.
[Courtesy: Colin Wayland]

The experience of the slave trade had both socially and economically created a structure of White superiority towards the African. Black people were seen as an inferior class. This would be reflected throughout the 19th century. Racist ideas and practices prevailed. The myths of sex and 'half-castes' had become part of the scientific debate on race. One theory, for example, concluded that 'half-caste' children were inferior in length of life and fertility (president of the Anthropological Society of London), culminating in similar racist reports such as Muriel Fletcher's (1930) 'Report on an Investigation into the Colour Problem in Liverpool and other ports'.

The continued growth of the Liverpool Black community is also linked with the settlement of African seamen, who were employed to perform work deemed unsuitable for White seamen in the tropics, and African labour was cheaper! The majority of unemployed West Africans had arrived as firemen and trimmers on the Elder Dempster Line ships and were predominately Kru men from Liberia via Freetown, Sierra Leone. They were seafaring people with a tradition in ship and sea work and established contact with European merchants along the Liberian coast. All efforts were made, via legislation and violence, to exclude Black labour and was to expose the racial politics of the National Union of Seamen.

The number of Liverpool Black families who could trace their ancestry back to slavery must be high. I would like to mention the Quarless family, as **one** example of the slave connection in our city.

The name Quarless derives from slavery, and all people with the name Quarless are related directly to slavery. Quarless originates from the name *Quarles's* – one of the slaves belonging to Quarles or a slave from the Quarles plantation. The family were from South Carolina with plantations all over the West Indies, owning hundreds of slaves.

The history of the Quarless family alone spans many generations. I only identify some aspects of their experience to demonstrate the Liverpool Black presence; a more in-depth look can be found on *Liverpool & Merseyside Remembered* website.

Ernest A Quarless
1906–1988

The Quarless family are renowned and respected in the city of Liverpool, and afar. They have so much talent, in so many different fields and accordingly are featured in other areas of this historical document.

The life of the late Ernest Arthur Quarless is just one chapter in the family's ongoing contribution to the Liverpool Black experience.

When John Isaiah Quarless came to Liverpool in 1895, he was at lodgings in 18, Pitt Street, where Abraham and Alice Lawrence were the lodging masters (landlords).

It was here that he would meet his future wife, Elizabeth, the daughter of Abraham and Alice. John and Elizabeth were married at St. Michael's Church, Pitt Street, on 11th August 1898. The couple would have twelve children, Ernest Quarless being one. It was rumoured, as a result of research conducted in 2013 on the role of volunteers during the First World War, Ernest had joined the British West Indian Regiment as a 'boy soldier'. If this was true, he would have participated in two world wars! Further research would eventually prove the rumours to be incorrect. It was discovered there was another Ernest Quarless, born in Barbados 1890, who was a member of the first Barbados contingent of the West Indian Regiment. He was killed in action and buried in a World War One cemetery in Marseille, France. After many years as a merchant seaman, Ernest continued to make his contribution to the war effort by sailing on dangerous convoys moving cargos of goods and troops across the Atlantic and around the globe from 1941 until August 1944.

His commitment went even further. In March 1944, Ernest signed up with Langibby Castle, a passenger ship converted for the D-Day landings. They trained at Bracklesham Bay, West Sussex. His Disembarkation Book, registers him as 'Special Operations for the Liberation of Europe'. He was involved in the Normandy landings, transporting troops to the beaches of Juno, Omaha and Utah, and later Le Harve. By August 1944, he had signed off from the navy forever. His career at sea was over, two months after the D-Day landings. What did he experience on those beaches?

Pitt Street during the 1930s. The area was to be bombed during the 1942 blitz resulting in the eventual demolition of the impressive St. Michaels Church in 1946.

John and Elizabeth Quarless

For his work and contributions to the war effort, he was commemorated with the 1939–44 War Medal the Atlantic Star – African Star – Italy Star and the Pacific Star. Although he was heavily involved in the France/Germany campaign, by virtue of his involvement in the D-Day landings, he never qualified for this award, as the criteria covered a period of eleven months' engagement in his campaign from 6th June 1944 to 8th May 1945.

THE AFRICAN STAR

Thanks to Ray Quarless for his help and guidance on the war exploits of Ernest.

St James Church, Toxteth Park

St. James (Anglican) Church, in Upper Parliament Street, Toxteth, has played a role in the social life of Liverpool's Black community – a 10-acre site that once had up to 58,000 graves, the last burial in July 1936. More recently, the church, reopened as St. James in the City in 2010, has continued its revival, acknowledging that the cemetery had many slaves (servants) and local family graves, the vast majority of which were removed. The article below demonstrates Liverpool's 'ongoing' relationship with the slave trade; note references to the undoubted tourist benefits.

A major transformation worth £47m including the UK's first monument to victims of the slave trade is to begin in Toxteth. The massive project will see St James Church on the corner of Upper Parliament Street and Park Road, a LCHF member, refurbished, and an 'African Garden of Remembrance' placed in the graveyard in recognition on the many slaves who were buried there. The council hopes the monument will be a 'major pilgrimage attraction bringing tourists and particularly religious sightseers from America, the Caribbean and West Africa'. There are also around 400 jobs likely to be created by the 'St James Quarter', with around 200 in the construction phase and the same amount working in the health centre, nursery, sports hall and visitor centre which will also form part of the scheme.

The regeneration project will also provide new housing. It will be undertaken jointly by the council and LivServ, a charity linked to the Anglican diocese and specifically created for the project. The church, built in 1775, is Grade II listed but has fallen into disrepair in recent years. It will be brought back to life to provide community projects including projects as varied as pre-marriage preparation to drug addiction support, an arts academy and debt counselling. Congratulations to Rev. Neil Short for driving through the church's restoration and earning himself a well-earned pat on the back from the Liverpool Cultural Heritage Forum Committee.

The 'vision' would ultimately fail.

– Source: *Liverpool Cultural Heritage Forum*

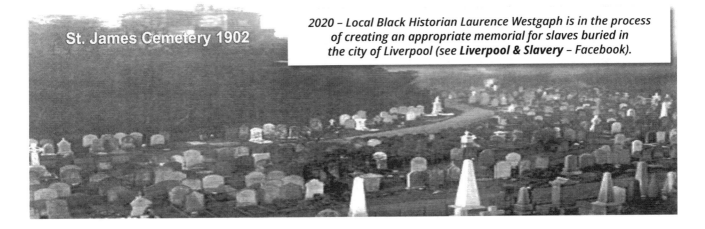

St. James Cemetery 1902

*2020 – Local Black Historian Laurence Westgaph is in the process of creating an appropriate memorial for slaves buried in the city of Liverpool (see **Liverpool & Slavery** – Facebook).*

The Real John Archer 1863–1932

John Richard Archer was born in 3, Blake Street, Liverpool, UK in 1863, living with his father, Richard, from Barbados and his Irish mother, Mary. You could say that his rise from the streets of Liverpool to become the Lord Mayor of Battersea, London remained part of the 'hidden' history of the city for many years. Local Black-White historians etc. have since, rightly, recognised the remarkable achievements of John Archer, and there is now no shortage of literature on his life. The Liverpool City Council's decision to display an appropriate portrait of the ex-Mayor on the walls of Liverpool Town Hall was the culmination of 'community' pressure for Black achievement to be recognised in the city. The oil canvas portrait (below) is the work of Liverpool-born Black artist Paul Clarkson (b.1964).

John Archer: Liverpool Town Hall Presence

Former Deputy Lord Mayor Liverpool UK Petrona Lashley (1994)

It was fitting that John Archer would have a successful political career outside of Liverpool, especially in regard to his appointment as the Lord Mayor of Battersea in 1913. He was from a city with a legacy of elected lord mayors involved in the slave trade 'industry'. He also came from a city that was once on the verge of appointing their first Black Lord Mayor in Liverpool.

Petrona Lashley RIP was born in Barbados and came to the UK when she was just 17. She trained as a nurse in Hampshire, where she met the man who became the father of her four children. Petrona moved to Liverpool because the ships he worked on docked in the city. She worked as a nurse at the homeopathic hospital, brought up her children, and became an equal opportunities officer in the National Health Service and subsequently with the Obstetrics and Gynaecology Trust.

By 1991, Petrona was elected councillor for the Granby Ward. She replaced the outgoing Liverpool Black Labour councillor, elected in 1987, Liz Drysdale (see *99 Reasons For Change*). Petrona, locally called Pet, was well-known and respected in the constituency. She was a big character with a kind heart, reflected in her work in the NHS. Here she was, the only Black councillor at the time, out of 99, thrust into the world of a city growing rapidly from the fruits of regeneration. It would be true to say that her term as Granby councillor was fairly uneventful, as Petrona worked her way through the maze of committees, agendas, surgeries, complaints, social services and school governing bodies.

All this would change in May 1994. The Labour-led Liverpool Council unanimously elected Petrona as Deputy Lord Mayor of Liverpool. Pet would be the next Mayor of Liverpool in 1995. What an achievement! Pet was one of us. The Black community had to rub their eyes when they saw Liverpool could not only have a Black female mayor but also someone locals knew. Just too good to be true. Little did we know that the vote of confidence displayed by the Labour Group in May would crumble in August, ending the political dream of a Black lady mayoress in waiting and become the talk of the town for all the wrong reasons! Criminal convictions from 20 years previously became front-page news, epitomising the powers of both criminalisation and the well-known 'crime' news publication, the *Liverpool Echo*.

The road for John Archer was not paved with gold. We will see how he was able to respond to his critics. For Petrona Lashley, the path was littered with obstacles.

Since the Royal Charter of King John designated Liverpool as a Borough in 1207, there has never been a Black mayor in over 700 years. For the Liverpool Black community, her achievements, rising from adversity to such political heights, are an integral part of our history and a lesson on the 'tactics' used to stifle such development. This document fully recognises the achievements of Petrona Lashley. As a former Deputy Mayoress of Liverpool, she should be displayed alongside John Archer and Anna Rothery (see p. 120) in the City of Liverpool Town Hall.

John Archer left Liverpool as a young man. He was a seaman and travelled around the world; he met his future wife, Bertha, in Canada. By his early twenties, he was a photographer and married to Bertha. They moved to London where they set up a photographer's shop, based in Battersea Park Road. His political career began in 1906, when he stood as the Liberal candidate for Battersea Borough Council and was elected. By 1913, he was the Lord Mayor of Battersea – the first Black lord mayor in Britain. The **Daily Mail** informed the UK public:

ELECTION OF THE FIRST BLACK MAYOR – 10th November 1913

For the first time in the history of this country a man of colour has been elected mayor of a borough. The honour has fallen to Mr John Richard Archer, a photographer, of Battersea Park Road, who by thirty votes to twenty-nine was last night elected Mayor of Battersea, by the Progressive Party. His opponent was Mr W.G. Moore, a West End tailor. Mr Archer has hitherto kept secret the place of his birth. Last night, on donning his chain of office, he revealed the secret in a dramatic speech. He said:

"I am a man of colour. Many things have been said about me which are absolutely untrue. I think you ought to show the same respect for me as you would a white man. I am the son of a man who was born in the West Indies. I was born in a little, obscure village in England that you may never have heard of – Liverpool. I am a Lancastrian born and bred."

"MY MOTHER WAS IRISH."

"My mother [here Mr Archer spoke with great emotion] was just my mother. She was not born in Burma, as some newspapers stated. She was not born at Rangoon. My mother was Irish."

Quoting "East is East and West is West and never the twain shall meet," Mr Archer added: "There is a still an older phrase than this: 'God hath made of one blood all nations of the earth to dwell.'

"Surely it is just that if a man is born under the British flag he should have the same rights as a white man. The colour of my skin can never affect the heart. My election means a new era in history. The news will go forth to all the coloured nations of the world."

The initial reaction to his appointment was fairly predictable:

"Do you know that I have had letters since I have been Mayor calling my mother some of the foulest names that it is possible for a mother to be called ('Shame'). Before I was Mayor I received no opposition on the Council. I have been made to feel my position more than any man who has ever occupied this chair, not because I am a member of the Council, but because I am a man of colour. My dead mother has been called in question because she married a coloured man ('Shame'). Am I not a man, the same as any other man? Have I not got feelings the same as any other? I may be wrong when I come here and meet this opposition, but would not any other man in my position think the opposition was because of his colour? If it's not then I say, as a man, I apologize to you."

– Archer speaking at Battersea Town Hall, December 1913.

The results of World War One were devastating in terms of loss of life and tragic injuries. The pain of war was glossed over by promises of 'A Land Fit For Heroes'.

On 24th November 1918, Prime Minister David Lloyd George (below) gave a speech in Wolverhampton. The Armistice, two weeks earlier, saw him as 'the man who won the war'.

"What is our task? To make Britain a fit country for heroes to live in. I am not using the word 'heroes' in any spirit of boastfulness, but in the spirit of humble recognition of fact. I cannot think what these men have gone through. I have been there at the door of the furnace and witnessed it, but that is not being in it, and I saw them march into the furnace. There are millions of men who will come back. Let us make this a land fit for such men to live in. There is no time to lose. I want us to take advantage of this new spirit. Don't let us waste this victory merely in ringing joybells."

The first government act aimed at the restriction of 'immigration' to Britain, was the 1905 Aliens Act: in this case, the Aliens were Jewish. The act was designed to restrict Eastern European Jewish immigration into Britain. The term 'alien' was used to describe anyone not considered to be a British citizen/subject. Then followed the 1914 Aliens Restriction Act, or more precisely the British Nationality and Status of Aliens Act, which depicted all Germans as aliens/potential enemies. We got the all-clear:

"The following persons shall be deemed to be natural-born British subjects. Any person born within His Majesty's dominions and allegiance."

At this stage, 'we' were British subjects.

By 1915, more than 30,000 German people had been interned, which was basically held in prison camps. The 1914 act also required all Foreign Nationals (aliens) to register with the police, with the threat of internment or deportation. Many Liverpool Blacks were stopped under this act. Anti-German riots took place across the country. On 7th May 1915, *RMS Lusitania* was hit by a German torpedo and sank off the coast of Ireland, with many of the crew being from Liverpool. Riots broke out from 8th May to 11th May 1915, starting in the north end of the city. The trouble moved to the south end of Liverpool, where a crowd estimated as over 2,000 made their way to Pork shops, associated with Germans, along Mill Street, Northumberland Street, Windsor Street, North Hill Street, Upper Hill Street, Warwick Street, St James, Lodge Lane and Crown Street. Police had been posted on guard outside many shops, but they had little chance of stopping the huge crowds, who smashed windows and looted the contents of stores. Many Chinese establishments were also damaged. In all, 200 properties were destroyed across the city.

Anti-German Riots in Liverpool following the Loss of the RMS Lusitania.

Before 1914, Britain was an unequal society. This was despite the country being one of the world's/Europe's leading superpowers.

When Britain entered the war in August 1914, the British public saw it as a celebration. Street parties were held. The government only wanted 100,000 volunteers in the call to arms; they got 750,000. It soon became clear that this was going to be a long and brutal war. The reality would see 700,000 military deaths and over a million wounded (Home Front).By 1916, the voluntary call to arms was replaced by conscription. By the time the war officially ended in November 1918, the country was in turmoil with chronic unemployment, poverty, strikes and riots (both military and public). By January 1918, rationing was introduced, and everyone had to register with a butcher and grocer. Sugar was the first to be rationed.

By the end of April 1918, meat, butter, margarine and cheese were added to the list of rationed foods, and the government issued ration cards. The 1919 Versailles Peace Conference saw European powers divide up the Germany's African colonies (see p. 21) – no one from Africa was invited to the conference!

(see p. 21)

FOOD OFFICE.

NATIONAL RATION BOOK (B).

INSTRUCTIONS.

Read carefully these instructions and the leaflet which will be sent you with this Book

1. The person named on the reference leaf as the holder of this ration book must write his name and address in the space below, and must write his name and address, and the serial number (printed upside down on the back cover), in the space provided to the left of each page of coupons.

"There is ample evidence that the treatment of soldiers was a reflection of the system they had left in the homeland. Most officers were drawn from the upper classes and the level of punishment for minor infractions could only be described as unacceptable. A court martial of a few officers could quickly pass a death sentence. The provisions for troops was also sub standard in regard to rations, clothes and boots etc. There were numerous mutinies. One particular incident was to depict the plight of black troops. It must be remembered that more than four million men and women from Britain's colonies volunteered for service during the first and second world wars. Thousands died, thousands went missing in action, and many more were wounded or spent years as Prisoners of War. But until now their sacrifice has been largely ignored by the mother country they fought to protect."

– Simon Webb, *Guardian*, November 2002

At the end of the war, the British West Indian Regiment (BWIR) was chiefly stationed in and around the Southern Italian coastal town of Taranto. While White soldiers were being readied for demobilisation and were awarded a pay rise, the men of the BWIR were still put to service, including constructing toilets for White soldiers. On 6th December, the 9th Battalion of the BWIR refused orders and put forward a petition of complaint, signed by 180 sergeants. Three days later, the 10th Battalion also refused orders. Sixty of the men were then tried for mutiny and sentenced to between three and five years in prison. One man was imprisoned for twenty years, and another was executed. The British West Indies Regiment received more than eighty medals for bravery between 1914 and 1918.

There was little doubt that the promises of a home fit for heroes was little more than rhetoric. The returning soldiers/merchant seaman etc., both Black and White, found themselves virtually destitute. There was a shortage of employment, food – a land in strife. It wasn't long before Black people/communities would be held responsible and targeted throughout the United Kingdom, culminating in the 1919 race riots in Liverpool and afar.

CHARLES WOOTTON

By Louis Julienne

1919 RACE RIOTS LIVERPOOL

There is ample information on the 1919 Liverpool Race Riots. Despite the coverage, there is little in regard to photographic evidence of the violence and destruction!

*One hundred years later*_ There are now higher educational courses pertaining to riots and their causes. There exists numerous books, research and dissertations that unearth the events of 1919. In order to understand what happened 100 years ago, I read countless media reports, documents and most information available. It soon became clear that the press, directly and indirectly, blamed the 'disturbances' on the presence of Black people/communities, as clearly demonstrated by our own Liverpool Lord Mayor John Ritchie (p. 19) and consequently the Assistant Head of the Liverpool Police Force (p. 28). There is no doubt that the war contribution of 'Black people' was not recognised and rarely acknowledged. This was epitomised by the decision to exclude Black troops from the infamous 1919 'Peace March' (p. 20) What a message!

During the course of the research, there were conflicting accounts of events during the 1919 Liverpool riots. There were, however, sources that provided the sequence of events. For those who want to delve further into the 'disturbances', I would suggest the following publications:

Black 1919 sets out the economic and social causes of the riots. The book also looks at Britain's relationship with its empire and colonial subjects. Furthermore, it examines, not only the role of the Liverpool police in the riots, but also provides 'enlightening' testimony/evidence from some of the court cases that followed.

Ernest Marke (***Old Man Trouble***) was born in Sierra Leone, but at age 14, in 1915, he decided to stow away to England. Lying about his age (telling the recruiting officer he was 18), he enlisted in the British Army, along with his pal Tommy McCauley, a young African who was also from Sierra Leone. On his return to the city in 1918, as we know there were no jobs for Black people in Liverpool (pp. 18–19). He was involved in the riots and tells of his many 'near death' escapes from White mobs, and recalls one such incident:

"On another occasion myself and this boy from St Lucia we got off the bus at Lime Street, walking towards the Adelphi Hotel, when suddenly this crowd saw us, like a pack of wolves they started chasing us. They was shouting 'black bastard, nigger.' We really were frightened. Again it was a woman who saved me."

His most telling observation was directed towards the Liverpool Police Force:

"The police refused to help black victims because some of them were very prejudiced."

The 8-page booklet was produced by the Charles Wootton Centre, with text by local writer Louis Julienne. It was published as part of events for the 60th Anniversary of Charles Wootton's death, the objective being to raise funds for a commemorative plaque on Charles Wootton's grave. The booklet provided a local Black perspective on the riots and causes. It is able to identify local people linked to Wootton and exactly where he resided and fought for his life. There is also a fairly extensive chronology of local and national press coverage of the disturbances.

Other sources include: '1919 – The Murder of Charles Wootton', Jeremy Hawthorn, *Nerve Magazine*; Henfrey and Law, *A History of Race and Racism in Liverpool* (please see p. 61 for name update).

Having been part of the war effort, Black people had the minimum expectation of equal treatment. This would be nothing more than an illusion.

In many ways, the aspirations of Black people differed little from the aspirations of White people. They both wanted to return to a city fit for heroes. We know all the ingredients for unrest were present in 1919. This was compounded by the long-standing dispute(s) on the docks of Liverpool. There is ample information on this in the aforementioned publications (p. 26). It can be summed up: White British seamen considered Black seamen or 'foreign labour' as cheap labour. In 1919, their belief that the government/companies were conspiring to take advantage of the postwar decline in shipping tonnage, introduce wage cuts and usurp their position, was strong. It was in part from this feeling that rioting broke out (Henfrey and Law, 1981). In reality, their view was supported by the Seamen's Union. If we add the existing sexual jealousy, with Black and White relationships 'more' visible to returning servicemen in Liverpool, we can see the inevitability. Despite all the factors leading to the riots, the major motivation, in all cities and countries, was further fuelled by racial hatred.

It was no surprise that most, if not all, rioting would occur in Britain's major seaports. The Glasgow Harbour Riot January 1919, was the first – only months after the war had ended:

"Glasgow Harbour riot of January 1919 – black British colonial sailors were branded as unfair economic competitors by the National Seamen's Union and their local delegates, chased out of the merchant marine hiring yard by white sailors when they sought jobs, beaten in the street, attacked in their boarding homes and targeted for mass arrest by police, called in to halt the disorder. This was soon followed by others in South Shields, Salford, London, Hull, Liverpool, Newport, Cardiff and Barry. Five people were killed in the wave of port rioting, dozens more were seriously injured and there were over 250 arrests as the police, and often troops, struggled to control the rioters."

– Jacqueline Jenkinson, University of Stirling

In America, the 1919 race riots were known as the Red Summer Riots. The Red Summer refers to the summer and early autumn of 1919, which was marked by hundreds of deaths and higher casualties across the United States, as a result of racial riots that occurred in more than three dozen cities and one rural county. In most instances, Whites attacked African Americans. In some cases, many Black people fought back, notably in Chicago and Washington D.C. The highest number of fatalities occurred in the rural area around Elaine, Arkansas, where five Whites and an estimated 140 Black people were killed; Chicago and Washington D.C. had 38 and 15 deaths, respectively, and many more injured, with extensive property damage in Chicago.

Rioting first broke out in Liverpool on Thursday, 5th June 1919. It began in a pub in Great George Square, involving an altercation between Blacks and Scandinavians. The police arrived and decided to arrest the Black men. They made there way to Upper Pitt Street, the area of hostels and houses occupied by Black people/families. The police were followed by an angry White crowd. Charles Wootton lived as a lodger at 18, Upper Pitt Street. The house was owned by a Liverpool Black woman, Mrs. Gibson, who had been widowed by the war. In order to make ends meet, she let the top part of her house to lodgers. Number 18 was the second house on the street to be wrecked. The windows were all smashed, and Mrs. Gibson's children screamed.

Although the door being barricaded, the mob eventually smashed it down. Charles Wootton faced the mob with an axe, injuring two of the attackers. The police arrived and arrested Charles Wootton: he was one of 12 arrested that night. Despite pleas of self-defence by Mrs. Gibson and her lodgers, Charles was arrested. The mob were now outside thirsting for revenge. They 'managed' to drag Charles Wootton away from the police, who in turn escaped the clutches of the mob and ran towards the docks, with the police and lynch mob in deadly pursuit.

The circumstances of Charles Wootton's death leave more questions than answers. It is said that he was apprehended by two policemen on the Queen's Dock.

The lynch mob grabbed him, again, and he ended up in the River Mersey being pelted with bricks. His body was recovered several hours later. Charles Wootton was 24 and had served in the Royal Navy but was unable to find work. No murder investigation ever proceeded. The inquest opened and closed in a single day. It was said that *"the dead man was reasonably believed to have fired at the police and he was escaping lawful arrest."* The stone that hit him was thrown from the 'middle' of the crowd, while a police officer was trying to rescue him, they said. The jury recorded the events without calling it an unlawful killing. It is ironic that 'a policeman' had tried to rescue him, when on two occasions they had surrendered custody to the lynch mob. A young man who fought for his country was 'murdered' in Liverpool, for being Black. The attacks continued with hundreds of Black residents being held in police stations for their own protection, while gangs attacked Black occupied homes, hostels and individuals. (Charles Wootton Centre/Jeremy Hawthorn).

The responses to the atrocities were predictable, as the media gave their full support to getting rid of the 'problem', namely the Black population. The question of job competition was settled under the 1920 Aliens Order and Special Restriction (Coloured Alien Seamen) Order. For the time being, in 1919, we were still not considered aliens. The Government was concerned about the uprisings (BWIR) in their respective colonies. Following inter-departmental discussions in June 1919, the Government reached the decision that a repatriation policy was the best solution to the issues raised by the seaport rioting. On 23rd June 1919, four days after the initial inter-departmental meeting, the Colonial Secretary, Lord Milner (left) issued a 'Memorandum on the Repatriation of Coloured Men' and introduced the term 'paid repatriation'. He made the following statement:

"I am seriously concerned at the continued disturbances due to racial ill feeling against coloured men in our large sea ports. These riots are serious enough from the point of view of the maintenance of order in this country, but they are even more serious in regard to their possible effect in the colonies. I have every reason to fear that when these men get back to their own colonies they might be tempted to revenge themselves on the white minorities there, unless we can do something to show that His Majesty's Government is not insensible to their complaints.

"I am convinced that if we wish to get rid of the coloured population whose presence here is causing so much trouble, we must pay the expense of doing so ourselves. It will not be great."

The Home Office sent letters to police forces of several of the riot locations requesting the particulars of the *"unemployed coloured population"* with a view to inducing Black colonial residents *"to return to their own countries as quickly as possible,"* even though it was conceded that it was *"not possible to compulsorily deport any coloured men who were British subjects."*

Liverpool Assistant Head Constable Lionel Everett (left) responded to the Home Office request within ten days. The Liverpool Police had identified 285 males with an interest in repatriation. Almost 50% were Sierra Leonians, with a mix from Ghana, Nigeria and the West Indies. I do not know how many took up the invitation! All 285 were interviewed and no doubt would have shed some light on the untold stories of the 1919 riots. Only one thing was for sure – there were a lot of future bridges for Black people/families to cross in the city of Liverpool, after being victims of such violent racial attacks. Could you really believe the same hostility would manifest itself after WWII?

The Rialto 1928–1981

was virtually born in the shadow of the Rialto, residing in a Kru House in 93, Upper Parliament Street, but don't remember too much.

As a child, I vaguely recall going to Saturday matinees. We would all sing, before the show, a song that went... *We come along on Saturday morning greeting everybody with a smile...* which was a little better than the 'Hairy Sausages' shout in the Granby (The Princes) Picture House. We cheered the native Indians and booed the cowboys, and I wondered why they used bow and arrows against guns. *The Three Musketeers*, *Zorro Rides Again* – all good adventure and excitement. Although not allowed, we would navigate our way around the building and were aware of its splendour.

As a teenager, I attended a dance or two and spent some time practising the twist, I think! They did not like people (us) hanging around on the marble front, and sometimes a police jeep would park nearby, in the taxi rank, to assist the elegantly dressed 'doorman'. To me, the building was a major icon. It was a meeting place, similar to meeting a date under Dickie Lewis (Lewis's). It was 'ours' – the Rio, as we called it – an integral part of Liverpool's Black community, a landmark in the city. In reality, it was never really ours; it was just located in our neighbourhood from 1927.

Ballroom dancing originated in England in the late 18th and early 19th centuries, in which these dances, such as the waltz, were performed by the upper and elite classes of society in ballrooms and parties. It was, in effect, social dancing for the privileged, leaving folk dancing for the lower classes. Traditional ballroom dances included the waltz, foxtrot, tango, quickstep, Viennese waltz, rumba, cha-cha, swing, jive, samba, mambo and the bolero.

The Rialto opened in October 1927, with William Boyd in *The Last Frontier*. The resident orchestra was Billy Cotton's London 12-piece Savannah Band.

There was an 18-feet deep stage and a dance hall that could accommodate 500 dancers. The ballroom was decorated with large, painted murals, giving Venetian views. There was the Rialto Garden Café, which had 60 tables, and was decorated with painted murals of the Wye Valley. Also included was a fully equipped billiard hall. There was a fairly strict dress code as males wore lounge suits and the ladies in their evening gowns. It was a popular venue. If you wanted to dance on Sunday, you had to join the Sunday club. Monday was dancers' night, and all the dance teachers and competition dancers would use the evening for practice. There is little doubt that a colour bar existed. Local Black artists, such as the late, great Derry Wilkie, complained. This is confirmed in people's recollections, one 'gentleman' summed it all up:

"I used to love going to the Rialto between 1959 and 1963 when I was a student Civil Engineer. I lived in one of the scruffy terrace houses off Princes Avenue. Hall Graham was the band leader. He was dedicated to dance band music and there were about 10 or 12 band members. Faith Brown won a talent contest and became resident singer. The room was enormous. At first, they limited the numbers to 800. We were all white working class or middle class. The men wore their best suits and the women wore beautiful tailored dresses. Towards the end there was a change of management and there was a change in the ethnicity of the patrons. The newcomers couldn't dance and they despised those who could. Numbers were not limited. The dancers were driven out and the place became a dump."

The Rank Organisation closed the Rialto on 29th February 1964, with Doris Day in *The Thrill of It All* and Ab Abspoel in *Silent Raid (De Overal)*. The building was converted into a furniture store by Swainbanks Ltd. John Swainbanks was a distinguished Conservative councillor, representing the Granby Ward in 1968. Swainbanks Antique Furniture Stores were well known in Liverpool, maybe more so in the Liverpool Black community. We were now welcome in the 'new' Rialto. It was unfortunate that such an icon was a target of the 1981 disturbances and no coincidence that some buildings were set on fire while others were left alone. This in many ways reflected the feelings of many involved in the mayhem. Nevertheless, the Rialto Ballroom was a beacon on Upper Parliament Street and an integral part of Liverpool Black history. The Rialto banned all 'non-Whites' during the war period.

Marching Off to War

Black American Soldiers in England during World War Two.

The British Empire and Dominions raised a total of 8,586,000 men for military service. This did not include the Liverpool/Black British or the arrival of Americans.

There is no question about the contribution of Black people to both world wars; this was despite the hostility and treatment by armed forces and government(s). Once again, we would become the scapegoats for the postwar economic problems of Britain. Government legislation throughout the 1920s ensured that racist laws were now enshrined in British policy. The view was clear as Black seamen were a threat to White labour. Following WWI, the emphasis turned on the sons and daughters of mixed-race relationships, epitomised in Liverpool with an organisation set up in 1929, the Association for the Welfare of Half-Caste Children (p. 17).

When the British engaged Hitler, 1939, soldiers of all races from the Commonwealth fought alongside each other. Liverpool was a German target.

Liverpool was the largest port on the west coast and of vital importance to the British war effort. The Nazi bombing of Liverpool in May 1941, known as the 'May Blitz', took 4,000 lives, according to Wikipedia. The list, however, can never be complete, due to unidentified and unrecorded deaths, only surpassed by London (30,000 fatalities). Life had changed little for the Liverpool Black community, still located in the slum areas of the city and still bottom of the economic ladder. It was nevertheless ironic that the war would prove to be a 'short-lived' economic boost for Black employment in the city. The final bombing of Liverpool came in January 1942 and demolished parts of Upper Stanhope Street (*A Crucial Port – Liverpool in WWII, Caroline Lewis*, 2004).

In 1942, 1.5 million American servicemen arrived in Britain, both Black and White. Thousands were dispersed to bases across the city, Aintree racecourse housing 17,000. Yet the largest US base was in Burtonwood, Warrington. It housed tens of thousands of troops during the war and into the 1960/70s. There was nevertheless a serious problem, since the US military had a segregationist policy, based on race lines. This military apartheid had been in operation since the War of Independence in 1775. Would the British Government allow America to carry out their 'racist' practices on our shores, in our city? The answer to the question, as we now know, is YES THEY WOULD.

Lewis's Department Store, Ranelagh Street, Liverpool.

Firstly, US Congress passed the Visiting Forces Act in August 1942, which stated that Black soldiers abroad were to be subjected to the same restrictions and racial segregation as they were back home. Although the British Government ignored segregation within the barracks, they refused US Army requests that the men should be segregated from the British/Liverpool White population. The Home Office issued a statement to shed some light on the situation:

"It is not the policy of His Majesty's Government that any discrimination as regards the treatment of coloured troops should be made by British authorities. The Secretary of State, therefore, would be glad if you would be good enough to ensure that the police do not make any approach to the proprietors of public houses, restaurants, cinemas or other places of entertainment with a view of discriminating against coloured troops."

As we will see, there were varied responses to this 'directive', and it transpired that White GIs were prominent in encouraging the public and proprietors to discriminate against Black servicemen. There were many commentators on the experience of Black GIs in Liverpool and afar. Two comments stood out to me:

- GIs were *"overpaid, oversexed and over here."*

- *"The general consensus of opinion seems to be that the only American soldiers with decent manners are the negroes."* (George Orwell – Author)

We can use the above to measure the impact of the US Visiting Forces Act 1942.

It was a fact the Yanks, including Black troops, earned four or five times more than their British Counterparts – definitely overpaid in comparison to British salaries.

Around 70,000 women married US soldiers during WWII, with 6,500 marrying GIs who were stationed at Burtonwood. With their pay five times that of a British soldier and all the glamour of Hollywood around them, the servicemen proved irresistible to the many young ladies who became 'GI brides' (*GI Brides: The Wartime Girls Who Crossed the Atlantic for Love*, Barrett and Calvi, 2013). However, not all GI babies were able to stay with their fathers, among the 9,000 babies born out of wedlock. It should also be considered that US laws prevented many Black servicemen from marrying. *GI Brides* describes the experience of Dr. Deborah Prior, born to a White mother and a Black American serviceman. She found herself (age 5) residing in a special home for 'mixed race' children, known as Holnicote House. It would be appropriate to say the GIs were oversexed. Pastor Ekarte founded the African Churches Mission in Liverpool which, from 1945–1949, looked after 'brown babies' (media description) – the unwanted offspring of Black American GIs and the city's White women. Hundreds of residents lined the streets for the pastor's funeral – a Nigerian man who dedicated his life to the people of our city, a true Liverpool 8 legend.

Pastor G Daniel Ekarte, minister, social activist, 1896-1964, at his Hill Street base.
[Courtesy: Liverpool Images]

Over Here was a fact. Servicemen were part of the Allied Forces fighting a dictator/fascism. The arrival of American servicemen, with their segregationist policies, was to have a dramatic impact across the country and in particular the city of Liverpool. On the one hand, we had the determination of White GIs to ensure that Black troops were treated in the same discriminatory manner as back home and on the barracks. On the other hand, we had the 'ordinary' Brit who saw them as part of the war effort. There were numerous incidents where White members of the public sided with Black Americans against discrimination and the American Military Police (MPs). One such incident was coined the 'Battle' of Bamber Bridge (1943).

There was a US military base in Bamber Bridge during WWII. The town hosted the 1511th Quartermaster Truck regiment, part of the 8th Air Force – a Black battalion.

American commanders had been demanding a colour bar in the town's social outlets. The 'demands' backfired, as many pubs posted *Black Troops Only* signs on their doors and windows. This was not an uncommon sight across the country: many establishments had displayed signs welcoming Black GIs, some stating White servicemen were not welcome. The people in the town had generally accepted the men. It was 24th June 1943, around 10pm, when a small number of Black troops were drinking with locals in the Ye Old Hob Inn. Two White Military Policemen (MPs) entered and targeted one of the soldiers, namely Private Eugene Nunn. He had no pass. It was widely known, by Black soldiers at least, that American MPs could be as deadly as the KKK. The standard racial slurs were deployed. An argument ensued between the Black soldiers and the White MPs, with local people and British servicewomen siding with Nunn and his comrades. A confrontation was avoided despite a bottle been brandished by Private Adams and a gun drawn by a military policeman.

"By 4.00am June 25th – Private Nunn was dead and four people wounded (two soldiers and two MPs), black soldiers were arrested. At a subsequent court martial, 32 black soldiers were found guilty of various crimes including mutiny, seizing arms, rioting, and firing upon officers and MPs. The sentences were all reduced on appeal, with the poor leadership and use of racial slurs, by MPs, considered mitigating factors."

– The Battle of Bamber Bridge – Updated

This would be the most violent confrontation of many. A high percentage of the conflict was down to White and Black Americans and no doubt sexual jealousy. Add racism, Black and White relationships, friendships, association, alcohol, media, (un)employment, housing and policy – a lethal mix.

Looking For Work – The Black Seaman's Mission Pool Canteen, 1940s Liverpool.
[Courtesy: Diane Frost]

At this stage in Liverpool Black history, the so-called 'coloured quarter' was located in the South docklands – a community experiencing the same race issues, which had been victims of racial violence and knew the realities of being Black in Liverpool. Black GIs came to a city with R&B, blues and jazz and no (legal) segregation policies – an education for all.

Let's be honest: the Black GIs have fond memories of their Liverpool experience. They may have experienced racism, but it could never compare to their treatment back home.

The Black GIs held regular dances on the American bases. They brought their music, dances and culture. They provided excitement in those dreary days. They spread the popularity of R&B, blues and jazz. Their experience was mostly positive in the city, although it would be wrong to say it was all good. Over time, with the encouragement of White American servicemen or US administrated 'segregation orders', establishments began to practise colour bars: The Grafton, Aintree Institute, Rialto Ballroom and Reece's Dance Hall.

One way to measure the Black GI experience is by examining how White America was reacting. Most White Americans believed that the British were too hospitable towards Black servicemen and soon turned their anger towards England. An American corporal, writing home from Cheltenham, was bitter about the British and the 'niggers' and wrote:

"Believe it or not the English seem to actually prefer them over white boys. Especially the girls, not that I give a hang for them anyhow, but it is disgusting to say the least. Maybe the South is right, keep them in line one way or another. That is enough to make me inclined to look down on the English in general to start with."

– When Jim Crow Met John Bull

The White Americans literally began taking things into their own hands in a determined effort to enforce the US Visiting Forces Act 1942. There were numerous incidents of White troops taking Black men who were with White women from their partner and making him walk on the other side of the road. Most were physically attacked or racially abused. We must remember that, back home, countless Black people were murdered for any contact with a White women or just for being Black. This conduct was becoming an embarrassment. The situation was spiralling out of control.

In Liverpool, Black people were employed in many sectors of the war industry across the city. A group of 300 technicians were recruited from the West Indies to live and work in Liverpool. They not only faced discrimination in finding homes or work, but were targets of the White American servicemen 'crusade'. The affront on British subjects was unacceptable. Trinidadian Cricketer (Sir) Learie Costantine was appointed (left) as a Welfare Officer. His task was to represent those recruited on war work in Liverpool. Despite his work, it was impossible for him to stem the tide of violence and colour bars. Nevertheless, he highlighted the experience of the Technicians to the Ministry of Labour:

"The bitterness being created amongst the Technicians by these attacks on coloured British subjects by white Americans. I am loath to believe that coloured subjects of the Empire who are here on vital work would be attacked at random and at the will and pleasure of these American soldiers without means of redress."

– Black American Soldiers in WWII Britain

The statement had little to no impact on the increasing use of segregationist-style behaviour in cities like Liverpool. The fact that Churchill's government allowed such policy in cities and towns, and the fact he NEVER wanted any American Black soldiers to set foot on our soil told its own story. This was verified at a Cabinet War Debate in October 1943. A minister pointed out that one of his Black colonial staff was excluded from a restaurant. The prime minister's response:

"That's all right if he takes his banjo with him they'll think he is one of the band.

– When Jim Crow Met John Bull)

1948 was another violent year all over the world – Accra, Tripoli, Cairo, Barcelona, France, Calcutta, Paris, Gold Coast, Bombay Riots – following Gandhi's death.

Despite all the strife, there were some significant developments. The 1948 National Assistance Act planting the seeds for the Welfare State and the belief that 'they' were only coming over here to exploit 'our' welfare system. The 1948 Nationality Act created the status of *Citizen of the United Kingdom and Colonies* as the national citizenship of the United Kingdom. It would be correct to say that this was to be the last immigration act that welcomed their 'subjects'. All future acts would be based on restriction. The year also saw the arrival of the Empire Windrush at the Tilbury Docks in Essex (June 1948).

John Hazel, Harold Wilmot and John Richards arrive at Tilbury Docks in 1948.
[Courtesy: British Library]

Once again, Black people were seen as the problem for unemployment. The circumstances were no different than 1919 in Liverpool. All the same ingredients and responses existed.

August 1948 saw White mobs on the streets of Liverpool's Southend district. Over a period of three days, Black individuals, clubs, cafés and houses were attacked. As in 1919, Black people in the city defended themselves as best as possible against thousands of marauding White mobs. In reality, it was not just the lynch mobs that were a danger, but also the behaviour of the Liverpool police force, who clearly failed to protect the 'coloured quarter'.

Despite rampaging White mobs, police decided to raid 'negro' establishments. The similarities to the Cardiff race attacks were apparent. Black people in Cardiff believed police used such tactics under the pretence that undesirable activities, such as drug use and prostitution, were practised in Black cafés and 'negro' clubs. One such raid of a Black club in Liverpool saw 30 arrests and numerous injuries (*Manchester Guardian* 3/8/1948). The recently formed Stanley House (p. 37) was attacked, as Whites seemed determined to destroy any property associated with Black people. Hundreds attacked a Black seamen's hostel. Barricading the building to prevent the mobs from entering would be in vain, as the police responded by forcing their way in and arresting those defending the hostel and their lives (150 arrests in city docks – *Post* 3/8/1948). As always when the police were involved, those arrested were predominantly Black.

NO IRISH

NO BLACKS

NO DOGS.

Sign of the Times: Open Racism prior to Race Relations Act 1965.
[Courtesy: Maurice Mcleod]

At the final count, 50 Black people were charged for defending themselves. The media coverage, as in 1919, put the blame firmly on the Black presence, with provocative headlines such as 'Police Enter Negro Club' and 'Arrests in City Docks'. After generations of residence in Liverpool, we were still seen as aliens or foreigners. Across the country, racism was rampant. Ironically, it was Black America that suffered more during this postwar period, where lynching and murder of Black people were regular events, celebrated by White men, women and children alike, just like a Klan hanging was cause for a party.

Fortunately, no deaths were recorded in the 1948 Liverpool riots. There was, however, a clear need for Black communities to organise for their own safety and well-being. It was also clear that the 1948 Nationality Act had done little to elevate the status of Black people as British subjects, in Liverpool or the UK.

Stanley House

Left to rot – a deteriorating Stanley House in 1986.
[Courtesy: Mike Robinson]

There were no organisations or anti-racist groups of note, consequently little political action. The Communist Party was a lone voice against this racial oppression.

Such was the case that Pastor Ekarte (p. 33) was the equivalent to Marcus Garvey. The appointment of Learie Constantine by the Colonial Office failed. The Liverpool Advisory Committee, set up to monitor the position of the Black community and recommended repatriation, failed. The 'revamped' Liverpool Association for the Welfare of Coloured Children (p.17) produced a report showing the inequalities of the subject group, no surprise there, failed.

Dr. Moody encouraged Black resistance. His organisation had many prominent members, such as Jomo Kenyatta, ex-president of Kenya. They fought for racial equality and civil rights for Black people. The organisation created a platform for local political action. Many years before Black American Servicemen arrived in Liverpool, he wrote in the League's Journal, *Keys*, in 1934:

"The colour bar as it operates in Great Britain, especially in Cardiff, Liverpool, Hull and London, is getting worse."

The West Indian Technicians formed a branch of the League of Coloured Peoples in Liverpool. Dr. Moody set up a British Committee to advise them. He made his way to Liverpool, from Cardiff, to challenge the racist American/Liverpool actions, and would play a major role in bringing about the formation of Stanley House Community Centre (Sir Joseph Cleary Centre).

Born Harold Arundel Moody in Kingston, Jamaica, the doctor was refused a post at King's College because of his colour. In 1913, he opened his own GP in Peckham.

He formed the League of Coloured Peoples in 1931, which fought for racial equality and civil rights in Britain. The behaviour of the White American servicemen and their segregationist practices led to Dr. Moody (right) holding several meetings with the Bishop of Liverpool, Archbishop Richard Downey (left).

The bishop had made strong statements condemning the Colour Bar in Liverpool. He fully supported the call for a community centre, for both Black and White people in Liverpool 8. The League of Coloured Peoples held its Annual General Meeting in 1943 in 130, Upper Parliament Street. The building had opened in 1872 as St Margaret's Home for Girls, and finished up as Stanley House Community Centre. The achievement had created a centre that would be pivotal to the development of the Black community.

In 1944, the Pan-African Federation was formed and became the British section of the Pan-African Congress Movement. The first meeting was attended by Eddie Du Plan, the first appointed community officer at Stanley House.

Stanley, as we called it, was to become a major resource for many generations of Black and White kids. I personally loved playing football there, especially under the lights. There are so many stories to tell and so many memories. It seems that I watched Stanley House deteriorate for more years than I care to remember. The following recollection will give readers some idea of the good times and activities that Stanley provided:

"Stanley House, which sat at the junction of Park Way and Upper Parliament Street, was more of a 'Social Centre' than a 'Club' club. Originally, it opened in 1944 with the help of the Colonial Office. It consisted of a large hall (it was here that I saw the Chants' first public appearance at a Christmas Party for children) that could be used to hold 'dances', along with a gymnasium in the basement (used by world champion boxers Hogan Kid Bassey and Dick Tiger), a library and many small meeting rooms and a bar on the second floor. It also housed a nursery and youth club (where I once performed gymnastics for MP Bessie Braddock). There was an interesting headline in the Evening Express on 11th January 1955 declaring 'Lord Derby visits the Jungle'. The article went on to say that Lord Derby went into Liverpool's 'Jungle' last night to listen to negro spirituals and calypsos, and he gave his full blessing to the work of Stanley House in Upper Parliament Street."

– Liverpool 8 – Toxteth.com

There is no doubt that Stanley was more than a 'youth' club. The fact that it was targeted by White mobs during the 1948 attacks on the Black community was a vivid demonstration of how people viewed the resource. In truth, the centre was utilised by both Black and White people, which reflected the make-up of the community. It produced great football teams, boxers and artists in every field. It is now a row of houses and a loss to the cultural aspects of the city.

At the time of writing, we have been watching the same deterioration of the Caribbean Centre (p. 68) and have witnessed the destruction of most 'Black' social outlets in the Liverpool 8 area.

Birth of the Blues

COSMIC AMBASSADOR HI·FI

FRIDAY TO MONDAY

25 PRINCESS ROAD

Poster courtesy Leroy Cooper

Liverpool 8 was renowned for its nightlife: pubs/clubs flourished in the area. In a city that practised colour bars, everyone was welcome in L8, Black and White.

In 1861, the famous author Charles Dickens, accompanied by a Police Superintendent, took a stroll down the dockland slums of Liverpool. The area had a vibrant life of its own. While walking down Pitt Street, they came across a public house with a mainly Black clientele, who came together to enjoy the music of a 'fiddle and tambourine band'. The superintendent noted:

"They generally kept together these poor fellows, because they were at a disadvantage singly, and liable to slights in the neighboring streets." – Black Slaves in Britain

Charles Dickens was more vivid and recalls the 'Dark Jacks' (Black seamen and shore workers) at the public house:

"The jovial black landlord presided over a scene of merriment and dancing, kept up with childish, good humored enjoyment. The white women there looked the least depraved I had seen anywhere that night." – A History of Race and Racism in Liverpool

The truth is that music is an integral part of 'Liverpool Black' culture. For me, and I'm sure most would agree, without music, it would be a hard(er) road to travel. Music has told our story throughout generations of pain, love, anger, enjoyment, excitement, tears and pride. It touches all our emotions through blues, jazz, R&B, soul, Motown, reggae and rap. I have passed through many of the venues below. I would highly recommend *Liverpool 8 Toxteth. com* and Donna Palmer (*The Changing Club Scene of Liverpool 8 – Nerve 14*), for a more in-depth view of club life in L8. Both articles, from L8 people, provide insight into the origins and characters, of local clubs in the area.

GRANBY TOXTETH REVIEW
1950-A-Z OF LOCAL PUBS & CLUBS-2002

African Johnny's Club	Grapes, the	Pun Club, the
Alhambra, the	Greek Club, the	Red Duster, the
All Nations, the	High life, the	Rialto, the
Alex, the	Ibo, the	Sadies
Arab Club, the	International, the	Sink, the
Aaron, the	Jamaica House	Silver Sands, the
Beacon, the	Johnson's	Snake pit, the
Bedford Club, the	Kirkland's	Sixty Eight, the
Babalou, the	Kismayo, the	Somali Club, the
Cotton Club, the	Kitty's	Silver Swallow, the
Calabar	Kit Kat Club, the	St. James Pub
Carousel, the	Kru Club, the	Stanley House
Clock, the	Lamphills	Sierra Leone, the
Charmers	Lola's	Timepiece, the
Dressler, the	Lucky Club, the	Tudor, the
Dutch Eddies	Masonic, the	Thompson's Club
Embassy, the	Mediterranean, the	West Indian Club, the
Federation, the	Merseyside, Caribbean	Wilkies Club
Fat Johnny's	Nigerian Club, the	Willow, the
Freetown, the	One o One, the	Yoruba, the
Ghana Club, the	One Hundred Club, the	
Gladray, the	Palm Cove, the	

Let us look at the position of Liverpool's Black population at this Stage. Since the end of WWII and the bombing of the South Docks, Black families were being 'relocated'.

The Black residents of the South Dock Streets, such as Pitt Street, Cornwallis Street, Frederick Street and the Sparling Street areas were moved to the Liverpool 8 area, which evolved to the Granby Toxteth Neighbourhood (please see p. 93 – *From Slums to Turner Prize* – for a more detailed account). The next generation had arrived: the Liverpool-born Black population, the sons and daughters of inter-racial liaisons.

My mate once said there were more White men in the Gladray than Black men in the Northend. He was referring to the Gladray Social Club on Upper Parliament Street, Liverpool 8. The club was run by two Liverpool Black women, namely Gladys and Rachel RIP (left), hence the *Glad-Ray*. The club could claim to be the most cosmopolitan out of an abundance of clubs located in the Liverpool 8 area. Both Black and White people frequented all the clubs. Yet the Gladray offered a more 'exotic' form of entertainment and became the first strip club in the city, with local stripper Gloria being a star turn. The venue attracted men from all over Liverpool and afar. Their reputation was legendary, attracting all nationalities. The club was utilised by local people in the evenings. It was vibrant with regular live music.

It is said that a clampdown on drinking dens in the city centre in 1957, in order to spruce up the city for an anniversary celebration, saw an increase of shebeens in the neighbourhood. The Black community had always held 'houseparties' where people could get together to dance and listen to music, or clubs would stay open until the early hours. The Shebeen, an unlicensed venue selling alcohol and liqueur, was accelerated by West Indians. Yet it was the local Liverpool Blacks holding regular unlicensed events, which we now called Blues.

The Beacon Social Club was just a few doors away from the Gladray, in 114, Upper Parliament, and Stanley House. The club was run by former boxer (below right) Joe Bygraves. It is no better described than through the eyes of local woman, Annette Reid Excel, who was a teenager at the time. Her aunty was a barmaid at the club, and Annette summed up the impact of the Beacon (edited version):

"My recollection of the Beacon Social Club coming into being was the initial buzz in our house as the negotiation, renovation and refurbishment of the  *Beacon was in progress. It opened in 1956/7. I was a teenager at the time but still in school. My Aunty Gertrude (known as Auntie G) recalls bars closed at 10pm in those days, dancing went on till midnight. Upstairs was the restaurant in which my mother, Lilian Reid, worked for a while. Live Jazz bands were replaced by sound systems. Colour bars were operated in many clubs, therefore we provided our own. These clubs were very popular, not only with the community but also with American GIs and seamen. The Beacon was an appropriate name as it did provide a huge beam of light in the local community, as did the other locally owned clubs."*

Influence of Youth Clubs

Welcome: The Methodist Youth and Community Manager Spencer Joel –
"We are an integral part of Liverpool's Black community – it's from children to adults."

As we entered the 1960s, I was a schoolboy. I knew nothing about race riots, nothing about J Archer or Liverpool's role in slavery. It was not part of the school syllabus.

I did know about 10 Little Niggers, Little Black Sambo, the golly(wog) on the jar and Sparky – the adventures of a Black boy who wore a grass skirt. I did know that 'our' African elders, fathers and uncles were gentlemen. They dressed 'sharp'; they were polite and urged their children to pursue education. Most maintained the 'Mother Country' ideology, while others talked about returning to Africa, which is maybe why the majority of Liverpool-born Black kids spoke Liverpudlian (Scouse) and what we called (African) pidgin English, although we also adopted the colloquial street backslang.

There was an abundance of youth clubs in Liverpool 8 during the late 60s/70s, in and around the Black community. Each had their own specialities – great football facilities, gyms, boxing, outings or positive activities. This was a period when youth workers would be out on the streets encouraging kids to become a member of their local youth club. As you would imagine, there were nevertheless, some territorial issues. In general, it would be fair to say that the majority of Black youth frequented the following: Stanley House; Robert Jones; Methodist; Unity Boys Club; The Blackie; The Rodney Methodist.

Manager, Spencer Joel, was quite right: the Meth is an institution in L8. Spencer was one of the first Liverpool-born Black people to gain a YMCA Diploma in Youth Work. He is from a family who have made major contributions to Liverpool Black history. For a more detailed account of the Methodist Youth Centre, please see *Granby Toxteth Review*, Issue 8.

Bobby Nyahoe

Peter Eyo

Black youth in the sixties faced the same racism as their forefathers. Their response would change the face of race relations in Liverpool and the country.

I asked Bill Harpe (above), director and co-founder of the Blackie: *"How do you think Black youth saw the Blackie?"* He said, *"I shouldn't (and can't really anyway) try to sum up all the different ways Black youth saw the Blackie. I hope that I can sum up something of the history with facts and memories."* May I (editor) just add that a trip downhill (Duke Street) to the Blackie was a trip outside L8 to the former 'colour quarter'. Numerous confrontations occurred with White gangs, the skins(heads), or John Bulls (JBs) as we called them. I won't mention what they called us! So why would young Black lads and girls 'risk' the walk? (see *Young Gifted and on Track* – Black-e). Back to Bill:

"Let me start at the beginning. A great deal of background planning went into the creation of the Blackie. The proposals – basically for a regional arts centre incorporating the elements of both a community centre and contemporary arts centre – were written by Wendy (Harpe) (below left), and myself in March 1966. Then came the search for the right sort of location. The Great George Street Congregational Church was up for sale. Wendy persuaded Peter Moores (below right) to buy it through his Foundation in mid 1967. A small team moved in and opened the doors in autumn 1967 – myself, Bobby Nyahoe (who lived in the building) and Charles Stokes (volunteer). We were then known officially, as the Great Georges Community Arts Project (Great Georges Project). Wendy was running the Bluecoat at that time, although in a relatively short time, she moved to join the Blackie.

The name Blackie – originally the 'Black Church' grew on us. It seemed natural, given that these early years were also the days of Black Power, Black is Beautiful and Young Gifted and Black. A history of the name can be found on the Black-e Website."

The Blackie had arrived.

The youth of Toxteth and L1 (predominantly though not exclusively Black) who first visited in 1967 and then made the Blackie their home, was initially drawn in by two attractions.

The inflatables were an entirely new invention, originally appearing at the Blackie as part of a contemporary art event, the Movie Show in 1969 (the commercial bouncy castle had not been invented). Recognising their potential for play, the Blackie staff designed and created their first inflatable (The Hamburger, grey and circular) in autumn 1971, which proved to be immensely popular. A succession of DIY inflatables were created, with youth joining the staff in design, cutting and gluing, and were given names (The Killer, The Blob, The Wedge (with covering cargo net).

The other great attractions were the Soul Discos, with senior discos on Sunday evenings and junior discos on Saturday evenings. Powerful soulful sounds were provided by Radio Doom (Dave Kay, Nodder Knowler, Jeff Hartley, Kevin McBride), and the lightshow (swirling colours, geometric patterns, cartoons, photos of superstars etc.) by Nova Express (Jim Macritchie, Paul Brown). The latest soulful records came courtesy of the US Air Force base at Burtonwood, with revolutionary wisdom of the Last Poets featuring alongside the dance and the confidence-raising rhythms of James Brown, Sly and the Family Stone, Jackson Five, Stevie Wonder, Edwin Starr, Earth Wind & Fire, Parliament, Johnny Nash and many more. Radio Doom did not hold on to their skills and expertise. They shared this with the youth (all male) who became DJs themselves, with Ramone Serrano (as Dr. Disco) taking over the junior disco. Later on, participants in the youth programme – including Stevie Smith, Jay Williams and Eddie Tago – joined the Blackie Team as full-time apprentices.

Waiting for the Sunday Disco (L–R): Josh Amo, Roy Forrester, Mick Snowball, Daryl Husband, Tom Branch, Kevin Benson, Ambrose Rice, Steve Smith, Mick Amo. [Courtesy: Black-E Archive]

In effect, these two attractions define what became, and might be described as, the rainbow culture of the Blackie – with the soul disco having its roots in Black Caribbean culture – and the inflatable in the predominantly White European culture of the contemporary arts. In fact, the Blackie became a partnership between the predominantly Black youth who made it their home and the predominantly White artists who had started things off. It may not have been an official partnership, but it was a real partnership, and the rest followed naturally, as the following examples taken mainly from the first 10, 20 and 30 years go to show.

Once video equipment had been acquired in the 1970s (at that time a rare and almost unknown piece of up-to-the-minute equipment), a rule was put in place. The video equipment could only be used by a team made up of both youth and the staff. The team recorded performances by the Temptations and The Chilites. They interviewed Michael Jackson and Paul and Linda McCartney. The performances were played back by the youth to learn the dance routines, as were Soul Train.

Contributing significantly to the youth programme was Peter Eyo. He took the lead in the video recording programme and bringing the Persuasions to the Black-E.

A history of the Blackie would suggest that the boys benefited more than the girls. In some ways, this was true, though the girls were always the leaders when it came to disco dancing, including performing at the Royal College of Art in London. The girls also played a leading part in the themed play schemes exploring fashion, cooking, writing etc., with Wendy (Harpe) and Sally (Morris) leading the way for women and girls in the cultural programme. The girls benefited from participation in projects exploring women's issues as 'Sisterhood is Powerful', 'Every Witch Way', 'Sister to Shakespeare', and in such dedicated projects as 'Ipi Tombi' and 'Not Just Sitting Pretty', set up to benefit girls.

Well-attended film shows organised by youth and staff included Black Panther films with information on the Party's 10-point programme, together with films of liberation struggles around the world.

Having first been influenced by the Last Poets at the soul discos, we then met the Poets in person when they came for a one-week residency, **Blessed Are Those Who Struggle**, performing at the Blackie, and touring L8 with workshops and talks, and returning again to celebrate the Blackie's 20th Birthday in 1988.

It was a friendship that continued. The Blackie also featured in the documentary **The Hustler's Convention** which celebrated the 70th birthday of the Grandfather of Rap.

Editor's note: *Since Bill wrote this article, Jalal Ruriddin (left) sadly passed away in June 2018. RIP.*

These are only a few examples chosen from the first 30 years, and we are now close to our 50th year. It sometimes takes many years to understand – or at least to describe – what we were doing. We can now say (with the words of The Last Poets) that what we were offering the youth of Toxteth and Liverpool 1 from 1967 onwards was *"affection protection and direction"* and we are still doing that for youth today. We can also now say that we were (and still are) offering youth *"what, they want, what they need and what they never dreamt of."* We learnt (and still learn) a great deal from each other. The soul discos, the films of the Black Panthers, the encounters with Jon Hendricks, the Persuasions and the Last Poets were an education to me and others on the Black-E team. No doubt the encounters with artists such as Edith Stephens, Annea Lockwood, Meredith Monk, John Latham and Judy Chicago were an education to the Blackie youth. Given that the Blackie embraced (and still does) all of the arts – cookery, fashion, painting, singing, dancing, drama...the list goes on – no doubt we got (and are still getting) a good, all-round education.

We are still on an adventure. As I write this piece, I am remembering the Halloween adventure by Blackie youngsters early yesterday evening at the Blackie, showing off their costumes and their circus skills, and then later in the evening at the Blackie, we were honoured to be chosen for the launch of Howard Gayle's autobiography **61 Minutes in Munich**, and found ourselves discussing a revival of soul discos (for over-30s), meeting with KRS-ONE for the first time and discussing a prospective 'Hip Hop School'. There are more adventures ahead. There are also more struggles ahead.

The Green Jackets

THE YOUNG PANTHERS

FREE ANGELA

The 60s was a pivotal decade for Black history. Motown, MLK, Civil Rights, Vietnam, Hippies, Ali, Powell, Black Panthers, the assassinations of Malcolm X, Kennedy...

The Liverpool Black experience had all the same ingredients as Black America. One minute, we had 'skiffle' haircuts and the next, we had afro combs and long black leather coats. We had been through the 'ghettoisation' process. Toxteth was officially the 'Black quarter'. We more or less emulated Black America in fashion, music, dance, language, police relations, poverty, prison and resistance. At this time in Liverpool Black history, demarcation lines still existed. There were many areas where you were not welcome and events you did not attend alone. In fact, the Black community was surrounded by such areas. Colour Bars, 'unofficially' were still in practice in city centre venues: racism was alive and kicking. The fact that there was such a close-knit community, most people knew of these locations. The community was also surrounded by a cluster of police stations: Hope Street, Essex Street, Kingsley Road, Lawrence Road, Cheapside, Lark Lane and Orphan Street to name a few! All the above were factors contributing to the evolution of the Green Jackets.

This insight into the Green Jackets does not necessarily identify any particular structure or founders of the group, although local campaigners like Joe Joel (left), Mr. Joel snr (Stanley House) and Bobby Nyahoe worked tirelessly, via educational programmes, with local Black youth. This article looks at the activities of the Green Jackets, their motivations, their role models, their hangouts and their recollections. Mainly, but not exclusively, they were Black/White/Chinese youth from the streets of L8 who challenged the prevailing racism in the city and consequently became the 'local resistance' to the community and a 'gang' to the local police.

As we know, Black people had been 'victims' of numerous racial attacks, including two race riots. The youth knew that organisation was essential.

It became clear that these kids were educated when it came to the issue of race and our status in the city of Liverpool. Many, but not all, passed through the same routes as teenagers. They also had their own social experience of racism in common. Some had been through the care/ judicial system and others in minor institutions. In reality, they all had their own skills and aspirations. Yeah, these were kids, male and female, like others, from the 'inner city' Liverpool slum areas. They were 'L8' youth reflecting the diverse nature of the neighbourhood. It did appear that, mainly, three venues proved to be influential to the youth along the way.

Stanley House had excellent facilities: one of the finest snooker halls in the North West, where Snooker World Champion Joe Davies once gave an exhibition; football, basketball, boxing, karate and chess. Workshops included pottery, reading and printing. Some recall seeing their first Black Father Christmas (Daddy White) at the centre. Local people worked in the building and knew the families of the youth. At this stage, there was a tight-knit community, specifically within Liverpool-born Black families. On the one hand, the centre had many activities that attracted the youth; on the other hand, it practised a fairly strict disciplinary policy, responding to bad behaviour. There was little doubt that a section of the youth began to 'extend' their knowledge. Being in Stanley House was a different experience to being on the streets.

Bobby Nyahoe – a respected Liverpool-born Black activist – would forge a close relationship with the youth. Usually, after Stanley, they would make their way to Bobby's basement flat in Upper Parliament Street. Here they would regularly read, and digest, such books as *Soledad Letters* (George Jackson) and *Soul on Ice* (Eldridge Cleaver). They knew the plight of Angela Jackson and the brutal murder of 17-year-old Black Panther, Bobby Hutton (April 1968). So here they were – sharing the experience through Stanley House and the Berkley/Stanhope/Granby Street connection. Bobby acted as another step in the forging solidarity of the more or less teenage group.

The situation in regard to racism was dire across the country. It was in the next venue that the Black kids would take another vital step – The Blackie.

Please see pp. 42-45 for a comprehensive insight into the activities pertaining to Black history. There are differing views as to how the 'partnership' with local Black youth and the Blackie came about. Green Jackets recall a day in 1967 when, walking past the building, they were invited inside by Blackie staff and volunteers, adding that, *"Black kids did not get invited into buildings."* They initially saw the staff as hippies, with whom they had good relations, but soon realised these people were also artists and creative. They heard that local gangs were 'harassing' staff and users, and proceeded to defend the venue as their own. The relationship blossomed. Now the group would 'see' the reality of civil rights. They would 'see' the struggles of Black people across the world as just as meaningful and would enhance their own skills and motivations.

The introduction of the 1965 Race Relations Act it failed to gloss over the overt racism displayed in the 60s. Enoch Powell's 'Rivers of Blood' speech in 1968 was seen as the highlight of the racist decade; however, what happened in Smethwick, Birmingham told its own story. The 1964 General Election saw Conservative MP Peter Griffiths win a seat on the slogan 'If you want a nigger for a neighbour, vote Labour'. A year later in 1965, political activist Malcolm x (below) made a visit to the UK, just 9 days before his assassination. He stood in the infamous Marshall Street, in Birmingham, where no Black residents were allowed to live.

The civil rights campaigner visited on 12th February 1965 because at the time, Smethwick was considered a hotbed of racial tension. He did not hold back:

"I have come," he told reporters, *"because I am disturbed by reports that coloured people in Smethwick are being treated badly I have heard they are being treated as the Jews were under Hitler.*

"I would not wait for the fascist elements in Smethwick to erect gas ovens."

The youths gave no definitive answer as to when it was decided to wear green jackets. It 'just evolved', they said. The full uniform comprised of Como Shoes, black trousers (strides) and a green jacket (Balfur) while some added black gloves and an Afro comb. The youth had always moved together across the city. Signing on was a problem in Renshaw Street and Northend locations. They went as a group for their own protection. In fact, they had contributed to 'no go' areas in the Berkley/Stanhope Street district; they had been barred from certain venues and had become a target for the Merseyside Police. The latter is summed up by a very illuminating incident. One day, they made a trip to the Army & Navy Store in Liverpool's city centre. It was here where they purchased their green jackets. On arrival, there was a police jeep parked outside the store. They entered the store and were informed that the shop no longer stocked the jackets in question. It turned out that the city of Manchester also had a Green Jackets group. They went to an Army & Navy store in Denton, Manchester. Not only did they get their jackets, but they could not believe the number of Black people who were employed in the store. This was a shock to Liverpool Black kids, born in a city where if a Black person wanted to work in a shop, they would have to get their own shop!

The youth hung around certain venues in the city centre. They have fond memories of Probe Virgin and Silly Billies in Whitechapel. They frequented News from Nowhere, Lewis's and Reeces Cafés, St. John's Market, Top Rank and, as we will see, ventured into hostile areas.

Who were their role models? They don't identify movies stars or sport personalities, with the exception of Mohammed Ali, Cassius Marcellus Clay, at the time.

Their role models derived from Black America and Black struggles across the world. They spoke highly of the 'older Black lads who had held their own against all the odds'. The saying 'you've got a chip on your shoulder' demonstrates Liverpool Black and White youth questioning/correcting racist attitudes/beliefs. They kept themselves fit, the Liverpool Anglican Cathedral (The Kitty) being a regular venue for a training and meeting place. Their numbers had grown. For example, a lot of L8 White kids were part of the Green Jackets – hence the 'Black and Whites' – and the Young Panther Party along the way. They were now known across the city and respected around city centre venues. In reality, the Green Jackets had their last 'official' get-together at the Falkner Estate (1972 – *Toxteth Riots, 1981*).

This article does not tell the full story of the Green Jackets. It does, however, attempt to show that the 1960s was a decade when 'revolution was in the air'. Vietnam protests, Black Panthers and Black music. It was also a period of mods, rockers, skinheads, hippies etc. and Black struggle. The Green Jackets were rebellious, aware and stuck together. They found themselves involved in numerous 'racial' clashes across the city and afar (below – no chronological order).

- *Wavertree Park – The Mystery*
- *Church Street – Skinheads*
- *Sheil Road – Ice Rink*
- *Green Lane – Old Swan*
- *West Derby Road*
- *Sheil Road Fair – Newsham Park*
- *Sefton Park – Skinheads*
- *St. Georges School – Mill Street*
- *Dingle Lane School*
- *St. Johns Market*
- *Lime Street – Football Fans*
- *New Brighton Fair*
- *Dale Street/Fontenoy – Signing On*
- *Renshaw Hall – Signing On*
- *Berkley Street/Stanhope – Police*

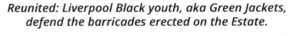
Reunited: Liverpool Black youth, aka Green Jackets, defend the barricades erected on the Estate.

The Green Jackets: major contribution to Liverpool Black history and resistance.

THE LIVERPOOL 8 ACTION GROUP

L8 Action Group Members Picket at LCRC, 1976.
[Courtesy: Black-E Archive]

Merseyside Community Relations Council Admin Staff Members, 1980s.

Community Relations

The 1965 Race Relations Act outlawed racial discrimination in public places and the promotion of hatred on the grounds of colour, race, ethnicity or origins, an offence.

I can say from the outset that I was employed by the Merseyside Community Relations Council (MCRC) for many years. During the 1970/80/90s, I was appointed as the first Liverpool 8 fieldworker, followed by other local people. I was later employed as a Public Education Officer. It is from this experience that I comment on Community Relations in Liverpool. The establishment of the Liverpool Community Relations Council (LCRC) was approved at a meeting in Liverpool Town Hall on 16th February 1970, and officially opened in October. It was initially located in Upper Parliament Street, L8 (2, Rialto Buildings). Liverpool Black legend Dorothy Kuya was appointed as the first senior community relations officer in the city. They were immediately inundated with 97 Black complaints of police harassment as a 'specially' trained police task force (OSD) patrolled the streets of Liverpool 8.

The first Annual Report reflected the high level of diversity in the city. There were 108 individual members, 7 associate members and 111 member organisations. The Council's Executive Committee had 10 different nationalities. There were also major religions – Catholic, Protestant, Muslim, Hindu, Greek – as well as Nigerian, Chinese, Jamaican and Somali minorities. (*LCRC Annual Report* – July 1971). Dorothy, in her first year with the Council, put the vision of 'Community Relations' into a fairly 'prophetic' perspective:

Dorothy Kuya 1933-2013 RIP

"The concept of community relations is a bold one, the idea of bringing a crosssection of the community together to support the objects laid down in our Constitution – which is to help the citizens of Liverpool of all races, beliefs and cultures to live together in harmony. It is challenging in these days when race is a political issue and the relationship between the groups living in our inner urban areas are under strain."

– Report of the Community Relations Officer, 1971

The swinging 60s was no doubt a decade when a new generation of Liverpool-born Blacks began to challenge a system that had maintained its discriminatory practices and stereotypical views of Black people with little to no opposition. This was no better demonstrated by the BBC who would screen the **Black and White Minstrel Show** until 1978. We had endured the presence of **10 Little Niggers**, Alf Garnet's **Till Death Do Us Part**, **Love Thy Neighbour**, **Steptoe and Son** and **Mind Your Language** etc. The 1970s would see rising levels of unrest – civil war in Northern Ireland, strikes, inflation, unemployment, changing fashion trends, Edward Heath, Harold Wilson, Margaret Thatcher and racist immigration legislation. In 1974, the geographical boundaries of the Liverpool Community Relations Council (LCRC) were expanded and the name changed to the Merseyside Community Relations Council (MCRC). In reality, complaints of racial discrimination came from all over Merseyside. Crucially, it was not known how many 'coloured people' there were in Liverpool. The population census 1971-1991 had failed to answer this question. Despite this, they described Toxteth as an area *"roughly defined as being that which lies within half a mile of Upper Parliament Street on the south ward side"* and the space in which *"the greatest concentration of the city's ethnic minority population lived."*

Race relations and immigration continued as issues in the UK. The 1976 Race Relations Act created what the British media would describe as the 'Race Industry'.

Despite the vast number of nationalities being 'represented' by the Council, there had been little development for us, Liverpool Black people. In 1976, the emerging Liverpool 8 Action Group, a group of local people, began a picket outside the Community Relations Council (CRC). We see throughout this historic document that this form of protest would epitomise the direct action tactics of Liverpool Black groups. The issue in question was a post that was specifically designated to the Liverpool Black community, namely the Liverpool 8 (L8) fieldworker. The Council had made an appointment. The successful candidate was Black and born in Liverpool. The Group demanded that the L8 post should be occupied by someone from Liverpool 8. At the time, the late Very Rev Edward Henry Patey, priest, was not only the Dean of Liverpool, but also the chairperson of the MCRC Executive Committee. Protesters informed the dean that they also intended to protest outside the cathedral. The issue would be amicably resolved, and the L8 Group demands were met. The L8 post was to become a permanent position for local Blacks.

Community race councils were situated in most cities across the UK. Each had their own diverse populations to link with. We should not forget that this was a decade of racial violence and rhetoric. This was the era when race councils were more than needed. The National Front was formed in 1967, followed by the British Movement. The Monday Club was a regular right wing venue for Tory MPs. There would be a succession of racist groups formed during this period. The response would bring about a clear demarcation between anti-fascist and fascist.

The Very Rev. Edward Henry Patey 1915–2005. With the Bee Gees at the Liverpool Anglican Cathedral, 1967. [Photo: Getty Images]

The Campaign Against Racism and Fascism (CARF) originated in the 70s and the Anti Nazi League (ANL) in 1977. The Notting Hill Riots in 1976, The Battle of Lewisham 1977, the death of Blair Peach, the death of Kevin Gately, to name a few. Meanwhile in the city of Liverpool, racism continued to be present in most areas; lack of Black teachers, high unemployment, no equal opportunities in Liverpool City Council, police racism, no Black councillor...the list was endless. The most notable developments of the era included: Falkner Estate Riots, *Listener* Article, Liverpool Black Sisters, Charles Wootton Centre, Liverpool Black Organisation, Merseyside Anti-Racist Alliance, LARCAA, L8 Anti Apartheid Group and the Elimu Study School.

The role of the Council and its relationship with the community and government was summed up by the MCRC Chairperson (left):

"Given the range and scope of our work, as wide and multi-faceted as racism itself MCRC inevitably attracts controversy and criticism, for being too radical and vociferous for some, and too conciliatory and moderate for others; for being to responsive to grass-roots concerns or being involved in trying to change the policies and practices of mainstream institutions."

– Gideon Ben-Tovim, MCRC, Annual Report 1983–4

I t was 1976 when I joined the MCRC. I was initially appointed as a caseworker before being employed as the Liverpool 8 Fieldworker (1976–81).

I would return to the MCRC as the Public Education Officer (1987–91). At this stage, the 1976 Race Relations Act was in effect, and for the first time it identified direct and indirect discrimination and established the Commission for Racial Equality (CRE). The latter enabled complaints of racial discrimination to be investigated, replacing the ineffective Race Relations Board in courts and tribunals. The 'race industry' was firmly established. Despite this development, it was basically undermined by the 1971 Immigration Act. The Act targeted Commonwealth citizens; many lost their automatic right to remain in the UK, which had been enshrined in the 1948 Nationality Act.

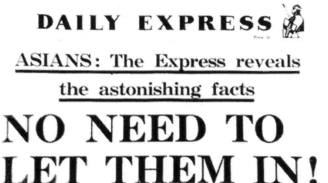

The 'race industry' was a high-profile subject for the UK media. Most coverage was negative and critical. The arrival of 'thousands' of Asians fleeing from Uganda in the early 70s was a hot anti-immigrant topic. Nevertheless, 'race training' was ridiculed, and the blackboard would become the whiteboard. Such 'initiatives' as the latter were not on the MCRC agenda. In reality, the race industry would be short-lived, as race legislation evolved. The 1976 Race Relations Act would effectively be the last 'Race Act' in the UK.

Under Margaret Thatcher, the Conservative Party began moving sharply to the right over most economic and social issues well before the 1979 election victory. In January 1981, they passed a new Nationality Act, which effectively removed the rights of British citizenship to significant numbers of New Commonwealth citizens, who had been previously classed as British subjects. By 2010, the Equality Act had replaced the Equal Pay Act 1970, Race Relations Act 1976, Sex Discrimination Act 1995, Employment Equality (Religion or Belief) Regulations 2003, Disability Discrimination Act 1995, Employment Equality (Sexual Orientation) Regulations 2003 and the Employment Equality (Age) Regulations 2006. The Act ensured that racism was basically marginalised and made part of, integrated, those groups who experienced discrimination because of their age, gender, sexual orientation or religious beliefs.

This was put in perspective by a 'racist' Conservative councillor (Barnet), Tom Davey, in 2008. Mr. Davey (left) was known as the 'social cleansing' conservative, and he made a number of racist and inappropriate comments, such as *"more excited than Harold Shipman in a nursing home."*

All his comments were discovered on Facebook. He believed that his job-hunting might be made easier if he were *"a black female wheelchair bound amputee who is sexually attracted to other women"* (Political Scapegoats).

It would not be to difficult to write an essay on the differences (albeit some similarities) between RACISM and DISCRIMINATION. Suffice it to say, there is a big difference. Black American writer Julius Lester (left) shed some light on the contrast; in the 1960s, Black radical explained it this way:

"Having achieved the 'possible' dream of ending American apartheid – of enshrining racial equality in the law – we are now pursuing the 'impossible' dream of ending racism."

The level of 'public' racism had continued unabated – Powell's 'Rivers of Blood' speech at the Conservative Association meeting in Birmingham, on 20th April 1968.

In January 1976, Margaret Thatcher, then leader of the opposition, gave what would be known as the 'Swamped Speech'. She told *World in Action* (ITV), *"People are really rather afraid that this country might be swamped by people with a different culture."* Such a statement was fully in line with right wing groups like the National Front and the anti-immigrant sentiments of the UK public. In many ways, the Tory Government had taken the mantle away from the NF. I would like to highlight one particular 'racist rant' from an unexpected source. Eric Clapton was an international superstar, known as the father of 'modern blues based rock' – a guitarist compared to the great Jimi Hendrix. He left the Yardbirds in 1965 to join John Mayall & the Bluesbreakers, then formed Cream in 1966. Clapton's blues' influences were legends like Muddy Waters, Sonny Boy Williamson and Robert Johnson. Clapton would take what he had learned from these blues greats and turn basic blues into a powerhouse of rock that would captivate younger audiences and influence young guitarists for generations to come. It is ironic that his 'racist' rant at the Birmingham Odeon on 5th August 1976 (below) would inspire the creation of the 'Rock Against Racism' event:

"I don't want you here, in the room or in my country," Clapton declared. *"Listen to me, man! I think we should vote for Enoch Powell. Enoch's our man. I think Enoch's right, I think we should send them all back. Stop Britain from becoming a black colony. Get the foreigners out. Get the wags out. Get the coons out. Keep Britain white. I used to be into dope, now I'm into racism. It's much heavier, man. Fucking wags, man. Fucking Saudis taking over London. Bastard wags. Britain is becoming overcrowded and Enoch will stop it and send them all back. The black wags and coons and Arabs and fucking Jamaicans don't belong here, we don't want them here. This is England, this is a white country, we don't want any black wags and coons living here. We need to make clear to them they are not welcome. England is for white people, man. We are a white country. I don't want fucking wags living next to me with their standards. This is Great Britain, a white country. What is happening to us, for fuck's sake?"*

– Clapton, Birmingham Odeon, 1976

The comments were more disgusting because his first British hit, in 1974, was a cover of 'Black' reggae star Bob Marley's 'I Shot the Sheriff'. Just two years later, Clapton was cursing Jamaicans (*"they don't belong here"*). Personally, from what I remember, he was a good guitarist, but there is more to the blues than hitting the right notes at the right time. Speaking at a Q&A session in London, following the screening of his *Life in12 Bars* documentary, January 2018, he apologised:

"I was so ashamed of who I was, a kind of semi-racist, which didn't make sense. Half of my friends were black, I dated a black woman and I championed black music."

Here we go!! It had became common practice to make vulgar and racist comments one day and apologise the next (or 42 years later). In this incident, Clapton blamed drugs for his outburst. I'm disgusted. Since then, he has collaborated with numerous Black musicians, like BB King; in an ironic way, he had 'championed Black music' and no doubt 'genuinely' regretted the 1976 outburst!

In my opinion, the demise of 'Community Relations' was a vital loss to communities across the UK. There were so many dedicated people amongst staff, management and members. Many are depicted in this historic document. The MCRC played a vital role in combatting racism across Merseyside, despite being under the shackles of Governmental Race Policy and funding.

Falkner Estate 1972

As we shall see in the Slums to Turner Prize (p. 93), slum clearance in Liverpool was accelerated following the destruction caused during the Second World War.

In 1933, all authorities were required to concentrate efforts on slum clearance; each had to submit a programme of building and demolition, aimed at eliminating slums from their districts. Urban decline was also closely associated with multiple deprivation, a category which combined material poverty with other indicators, including the condition of housing and the reputation of the neighbourhood. In 1955, the Liverpool Medical Officer of Health estimated that there were 88,000 unfit dwellings in the city (45% of the total housing stock). Ten years later, little had been done to tackle the problem, and the number was still 78,000; 33,000 of these homes were in Toxteth, Abercromby and Everton, and a massive programme of slum clearance was initiated. Rows and rows of uniform terraces were demolished and replaced with high- and low-rise flats, new houses and maisonettes. Many people moved or were forced away from the area. 42 square miles of Liverpool were affected by the clearances, and 88 action areas were identified across Toxteth, Abercromby, Everton and Kirkdale (University of Leicester). Throughout the early 60s, my mum was always saying: "We are on the Housing List." Little did I know, at the time, that 18,000 other households in Liverpool were also on that City Council waiting list (Shelter). Urban decline was a feature of the 70s. It was a major issue in the city.

The studies/research of urban areas was at its peak. In fact, I would say that Liverpool had to be one the most researched cities in the UK. Numerous Government Select Committees, sociologists, academics etc. would comment on social conditions in Liverpool. Labour Prime

Minister Harold Wilson (left) would initiate the Urban Programme in 1968 following an extensive study of urban areas facing acute social problems in the fields of education, housing, health and welfare. On 22nd July 1968, the government had completed the first stage of their study on urban areas in the country. The House of Lords met to discuss the implications of the Bill. The programme had put a specific emphasis on 'Areas of Special Need': the Toxteth area of inner Liverpool met all the criteria. These problems were further compounded by race discrimination and disadvantage.

The Home Secretary, James Callaghan, was to make the intentions of the Act quite clear and identified measures aimed at addressing 'areas of special need':

"The Government have now completed the first stage of their study of urban areas facing acute social problems in the fields of education, housing, health and welfare. Many of these areas include concentrations of immigrants.

"The study shows that large and expanding programmes are already having an impact in each of the main social services concerned and that in education and housing in particular, and in areas of immigrant settlement, priorities have been established within existing policies to increase the flow of aid to particular areas of special need. Nevertheless there remain areas of severe social deprivation in a number of our cities and towns—often scattered in relatively small pockets. They require special help to meet their social needs and to bring their physical services to an adequate level.

"The Government propose to initiate an urban programme to help tackle the social problems of the communities concerned. Action be required on a number of fronts and the programme must necessarily, be a continuing one. I propose to open discussions with the local authority associations and seek their co-operation in working out the basis on which help can most effectively be provided. Corresponding discussions in Scotland would he carried out by my right honourable friend the Secretary of State for Scotland. But I can inform the House that the Government are Toggle showing location of Column 687 prepared to introduce legislation at the earliest opportunity to provide a new specific grant, in addition to the existing Rate Support Grant, to assist this programme. Under Section 11 of the Local Government Act 1966 grants are already payable in respect of expenditure on staff in areas of immigrant settlement. The new grant will be payable to other areas, including any in Scotland, that meet the necessary conditions, and in respect of any item of expenditure falling within the programme. Its percentage rate will be a matter for discussion with the local authority associations. Subject to Parliament passing the necessary legislation, the new grant will be payable retrospectively on expenditure incurred under the programme in the present financial year. The extra cost of this new and additional aid has been set against general economies made in the course of the normal processes of managing the public expenditure programme."

– Hansard, vol. 295, cc. 686-93

So here we are, four years later, in August 1972. None of the above had necessarily, at this stage, had any major impact on the housing or environmental situation. Without a doubt, the Liverpool Black population had gained little. Section 11 funding, for example, was for the provision of 'ethnic minority' communities. The reality is that it was only available to immigrant groups. It was ironic that the Merseyside Community Relations Council administrated the fund for the Home Office on the one hand, but protested at the exclusion of the Liverpool Black population on the other. During the late 60s, the surrounding streets of what would become known as the Falkner Estate were demolished, although St. Nathaniel Church (Oliver Street) remained (below).

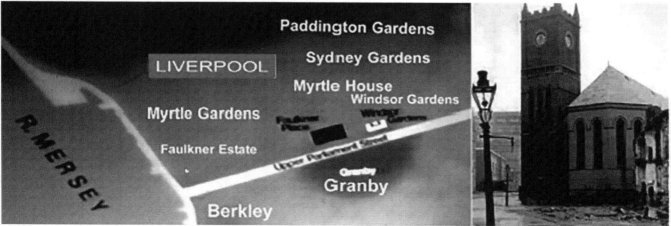

St. Nathaniel's was an Anglican church which stood between Upper Parliament Street and Crown Street in an area known as Windsor. It opened in 1869 initially as a mission church from St. Clement's on nearby Beaumont Street. The main body of the church was destroyed by fire in 1900 but re-opened in 1904. St. Nathaniel's stood for many years in a wasteland until it was demolished in 1993. Falkner Estate was also referred to as St. Nathaniel's.

Falkner Estate under early construction, overlooked by Myrtle Gardens and Myrtle House.

I need to clarify a few matters. The deteriorating state of housing in Liverpool had been happening over a long period; it affected both Black and White families. This was definitely the situation in Liverpool 8. At this point in 1972, there were 42,000 households on the City Council Housing List (Shelter 72). The estate was surrounded by a number of dilapidated tenement blocks including Myrtle Gardens, Myrtle House, Windsor Gardens and Sydney Gardens. Although in the minority, Black families lived in all of these Gardens over the years, experiencing the same hardship. Throughout the years, there were many racial clashes with Liverpool Black and White youth. Now we had a situation where a 'new' estate was being built smack in the middle of a crumbling infrastructure. It was also a period when the media was full of horror 'stories' of immigrants having preferential treatment in the housing market! What also contributed to the 'clashes' was the fact that Myrtle Gardens residents watched the development from the first brick to the first furniture van. Finally, in regard to clarification, I need to let readers know that I was present during the 'disturbances'.

A Falkner Estate resident behind her smashed windows.

I recall that it was all around the Black community that the estate had been attacked by 'skinheads' the night before. We was aware that the estate had only recently began housing residents, although not fully completed. We made our way to the estate and were immediately met by the Merseyside Police. We expressed our concerns about events of the previous evening and the fact that most of the residents were families with children or were elderly. They assured us that they were patrolling the area and making sure the residents would be safe from any further attacks. We, reluctantly, naively, accepted the explanation and left the scene.

This was disgusting. Local Black and White families, also on the housing waiting list for many years, found themselves under attack. The police patrols failed to protect the residents, consequently breaking their 'promise' to ensure no repeat of the violence. This was not 1919. This was a generation of Liverpool Black people who were resisting such racism, at great risk.

Thames TV screened a documentary (*Racial Tension*), in which they spoke with residents from Falkner Estate and Windsor Gardens AFTER the attack on their homes.

For those who may want a more in-depth view, I would recommend the excellent *Racial Tension* documentary. It explores the views of residents from all sides, both Black and White perspectives. Suffice it to say, the attacks were repeated. We will see the response to these racially motivated actions. Gangs of White youths invaded the estate, smashing cars, windows, attacking and racially abusing people.

Photo one is a family – mother and daughter on Falkner Estate. They were abused and stones thrown at their home. *"I'm made up to be able to get a decent bath,"* said the young daughter. She believed the attacks were based on jealousy of local Black families moving to decent homes. Her mother was angry at the racial abuse and stated:

"We sent for the coloured boys for our protection. There was no coloured boys on the Estate when this happened, there was none at all. We sent for them to come and beat those skinheads."

Photo two is also a Falkner Estate resident (Josie) who found herself under attack. She pointed out how local White people had watched furniture vans arriving and targeted any Black people. Josie phoned the police during the attacks. She told them about youths with bottles and stones shouting 'niggers all out, get back to your tents'. They said they only had a few officers and she retorted, *"Get more."* He said, *"You would have to get on to the Home Secretary about that."*

Photo three is of a rare Black Windsor Gardens resident (Martha). She pointed out that this trouble had been going on for five months. During the attacks, she would witness an incident where police arrested a White youth in the Gardens. Some of the neighbours began shouting 'nigger lovers' to the police. Martha was angry at what she described as this 'nigger business'. She pointed out quite clearly that she, and her children, were born and bred in Liverpool. They did not mess with her family in the Gardens, Martha acknowledged that there were many nice neighbours, however, she recalls events:

"Some of the neighbours around here, supposed to be your neighbours, shouting 'nigger lovers, nigger lovers' to the police and 'get the niggers out'. I saw the hatred in them."

Those conducting the interviews must have been impressed at the strength and determination shown by these Liverpool Black and White women. They did not know the history of the Liverpool-born Black population. They did not know how these families arrived on the Estate-Gardens.

Events demonstrated quite clearly that this was not a White neighbourhood fighting to ensure 'immigrants' were not given preferential treatment in the housing market.

We returned to the estate. This time, there was no turning back and no negotiation with the Merseyside Police. We had decided to protect the residents ourselves. We set up a barricade! Well, you could call it a barricade – a selection of bins and debris blocking the main entrance to the estate. It should be remembered there had been many racial clashes over the years, before the estate was built. This was despite Black families residing in these gardens. What was never reported were the numerous clashes that occurred outside the barricades, the police arresting one of our lads and dropping him off to the skinheads, the police jeep turned over on Grove Street and the stabbing of a Black youth on the same street. The police would eventually rush the barricade with bin lids, rather than shields, and seize some form of temporary control.

The control was soon ended as youths erected a more solid barricade, now supported by steel mesh fencing. The residents fully supported the action. There was also a problem when some had to go home in the evenings, some still in school. The journey from the estate to the Granby area was fraught with danger. Many were stopped and searched, others arrested after leaving the estate. After four or five days, a clandestine operation by the police would end the conflict. A wagon, which looked like a removal van, was full of police. If we add police dogs and undercover police, the estate found itself surrounded – the Home Secretary must have helped. Up to 10 Black youth were arrested, ending up in juvenile/magistrates' courts. Many were held on remand for so long, they were old enough to be sentenced to detention centres. The conflict effectively stopped. Once again, we came under attack in the city of Liverpool. This time, we stood firm.

Local kids at play in Windsor Gardens.   *Local kids at play in Falkner Estate.*

CHARLES WOOTTON

1974-2000

WHAT WENT WRONG?

PHOTO BY YOUTH BASE

The origins of the Charles Wootton Centre can be traced back to the Liverpool Black activism of the 1970s and a succession of high-level governmental subcommittees.

Once again, clarification is required. At the time of writing, research has unearthed a document that puts a shadow over the spelling of Charles Wootton, not his history or fate. A document was located that states his REAL name is Charles Wotten. I have included the document in question and the subsequent plaque erected on the Queen's Dock in 2016. The plaque was the idea of historian and broadcaster David Olusoga. As a community who had only known the name Wootton for at least forty-two years, it was a surprise!

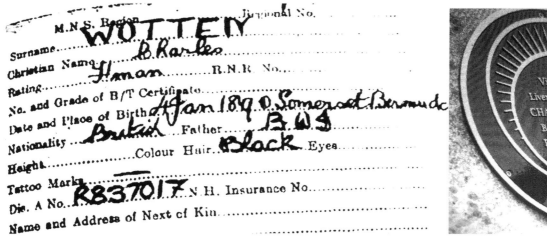

The CWC was always in a 'funding crisis'. As a former Chair, I recall such a 'crisis' regarding Employment Training, and the council removed some core funding, under sensational headlines (below). The Labour-run council 'turned' the screw on agencies who joined the ET scheme.

City refuses cash for hi-tech centre

"Charles Wootton chairman David Clay said last night:

'While we admire the Council's principled stand, we have no choice but to put ourselves in the Scheme. We have to face financial reality This smacks of discrimination.'"

– Liverpool Echo and Daily Post (2nd September 1988)

LIVERPOOL EDUCATION COMMITTEE

Liverpool

Meeting Their Needs

Working Party Examining the Educational Needs and Provision for the Children & Liverpool born Descendents of Immigrants

1974

ADULT EDUCATION
(an experimental Project)

5, Rialto Buildings, Upper Parliament Street, Liverpool L8 ITB Tel 0151 708 9698
Sponsored by Inner City Area

A 1973 report by a Government Select Committee on Race Relations Immigration/Education criticised Liverpool's education system as it found that the Black community was disadvantaged both inside and outside school. Liverpool was criticised for its inability to provide a lead to other LEAs with substantial ethnic minority populations. In the words of the Committee report: *"Liverpool left us with a profound sense of uneasiness."* Ironically, a Liverpool Education Committee Report (1973: **Meeting Their Needs** – left) was to provide further validation of their lack of progress in education. What began as an Inner City Study (below) would be a stepping stone for the arrival of the Adult Education Centre in 1974, which would transform into a major educational resource for the local community.

By 1978, they relocated from their Rialto base to 148, Upper Parliament Street, directly facing the Falkner Estate. The decision to change the name to the Charles Wootton Centre, honouring Charles, was a reflection of a Management Committee, composed of local people, in a hurry to build a strong educational structure. The funding position was as difficult as the ideological fight to have Black Studies as an integral part of mainstream education. For now, such studies were confined to the Centre.

The 1980s was a 'conflictual' era. Despite threats to funding, the CWC also managed to survive the 1981 Riots, a militant city council and turned around a funding crisis.

It is relevant to sum up how far the CWC had developed as they approached the 1990s. As we know, the Centre originated from the fact, supported by numerous reports and research that clearly exposed how Black school leavers and local adults were not represented in the fields of further and higher education. There was no doubt that the CWC was to become a platform for young people to prepare for the world of higher education. Along with the Access to Higher Education Project, the 'Charlie' as we knew it, was becoming a major educational resource in the community and the city. They nurtured the talents and skills of both young and adults with courses and activities, and increased the representation of Black people within our universities and colleges on Merseyside. It became clear that there was a thin line between education and (local) politics. This was no more apparent when the CWC allowed the 'controversial' Liverpool 8 Defence Committee to utilise their premises in 1981. This did not go down too well with their funding 'masters'.

If the 1980s was turbulent then the 1990s promised to be a decade of educational excellence. The 1991 Annual General Meeting agreed to replace the word 'Centre' with 'College'.

The CWC began to establish a firmer financial base with monies from both the Liverpool City Council and the European Social Fund. This enabled the CWC to deliver access courses and to innovate and corroborate within the field of further education. They were maintaining their proud record of increasing the number of Black students. By 1992, the Centre was celebrating (left) 'official' college status.

There was little stopping the rapid developments. Major strides were being made in the field of Black Studies, **Mark Christian** (below 1) being a major influence. The excellent *Charles Wootton News*, innovative partnerships, a diversity of courses, links to further education for students, purchase of the building, an Honorary Fellow of John Moores University award for the director **Ben Aguna** known as Chief Ben (below 2), as well as a former CWC Director, **Clare Dove** (below 4). MP **Bernie Grant** (below 3) became a CWC Patron, and by 1994, relations with Liverpool City Council appeared to have been on a positive road, with City Council Chief Executive **Peter Bounds** (below 5) stating:

"The College stands as a living symbol of the developing partnership between Liverpool's black community and Liverpool City Council."

The college Black Studies Tutor, (Dr.) Mark Christian, who would become a master scholar in the field of Black Studies, commented in 1994:

"We have played a key role in the battle against institutionalised racism. Arguably, Black Studies provides the basis and the future for the Charles Wootton College."

Despite the success story, all was not well. There were calls from Liverpool City Council for an inspection of the college, with concerns regarding administration.

By 1996, the Education Subcommittee of Liverpool Council was considering report DE/292/96 on provisions for students at the college and a culmination of previous negative reports on the governance of the college. The report was concerned that the conditions of grant aid were not being met. The meeting decided to assign the Head of the Education Services to work with the college. By 1997, the Head was reporting *"a deteriorating of relations between officers and the college."* The council reiterated their call for an inspection. The relationship was going downhill. By 1998, report DE211 was being considered. The main feature of the document was the continued non-cooperation from the director of the college. Meanwhile, the director had lodged a complaint of racism, demanding an apology.

Kensington Councillor Marbrow (above) in his role as Chair of the Lifelong Select Committee, would describe the college administration process as being 'poor'. Eventually, the Government Office for Merseyside intervened. They agreed to provide consultants who would look at the college's financial systems. By April 1999, the Education Department, utilising a firm of Black Manchester consultants, inspected the CWC. The inspection was completed in June 1999. The report was critical of the management and support systems, but had nothing but praise for the high level of teaching at the college. They made a number of recommendations and concluded:

"The challenge for the college is to develop and modernise its management of staff and resources, and thereby secure a long-term funding base. If that can be done, without losing its character or community spirit, the Charles Wootton College will be able to not only survive but flourish and grow."

In the same month (June), Councillor Marbrow stated that the college director's refusal to retire was in breach of grant aid. By August 2000, the college was closed. This was a shock to many people. This was despite press warnings, the street-level rumours of low staff moral and the damming statements of Councillor Marbrow and consecutive Council Education Committee Reports. There was no immediate statement from the Granby councillors or the college director, that I can recall. We only had the street view and an apparent lack of local protest, with the exception of the concerned Consortium of Black Organisations (CBO).

Let us put this into a clearer perspective. I do not profess to know all the details that led to the closure of this iconic 'community' institution. I do know that we had a city council that was more concerned about the terms and conditions of Grant Aid than the preservation of the college. I also know that months previously, the same council had issued the Slave Apology (p. 105). As we know, the Apology included a lot of rhetoric, which is still proving to be such. They said they would *"recognise and respond to the city's multiracial inheritance."* They failed to do so in the case of the college. Since the Apology (1999), we have witnessed the continued destruction of our multiracial institutions. The reality was that a major part of our 'multiracial inheritance' was converted to luxury apartments called Parliament Square (below). We can see quite clearly how the history of the college was given little respect or recognition!

Parliament Square   From £120,000

Cliff Marshall | Howard Gayle

1973  **1976** **1977**  **1981**

On the one hand, Cliff Marshall: a boyhood Evertonian. On the other, Howard Gayle: a boyhood Liverpudlian. Both Liverpool lads. Both talented footballers. Both Black!

To understand the implications of the above statement, we have to remember we are talking about the 1960/70s. There was racism everywhere. Football was no exception. There was a 'sprinkling' of emerging Black players in the football league. Racism on the terraces was alive and kicking; open hostility was the order of the day. Clyde Best (1968–76) at West Ham was one of the emerging Black pioneers to play First Division football in England. In fact, West Ham and West Bromwich Albion, at one stage, must have had more Black players in their squads than the rest of the First Division. This was not the case on Merseyside.

There were two specific incidents which I 'mostly' remember to this day – you know those occasions when you can't do anything about it.

The first was at Goodison Park, 1965/66 season. As a teenager, I followed the Reds everywhere. I was in the Park End with the Reds fans when Mike Trebilcock came by the barrier to collect the ball for a corner – he was met with a hail of spit and racist abuse.

The other occasion was at Anfield in an evening game against Leeds United, in the same season. Leeds were a team to be reckoned with at the time. It was a big game under the lights, just before they would meet again in the 1965 FA Cup Final. Albert Johanneson, known as the 'Black Flash' played in his all-white Real Madrid type kit. He dazzled under the lights as 20,000-plus Kopites repeatedly sang 'Go back to Africa' and 'Cocoa Pops'. They did not realise that the Leeds right back, Paul Reaney, was also Black. Nor did the country recognise that Reaney was the first Black player to appear for the England National team in 1968, nine years before the debut of Viv Anderson, who is widely credited as the first Black player to appear for England.

There were virtually no Black professionals in English football when, in January 1961, Albert arrived in the city of Leeds from South Africa. He made history by becoming the first Black player to appear in an FA Cup final. He would make 200 appearances and score 68 goals. He passed away in Leeds in 1995, an alcoholic, penniless and in recluse. He was buried in a pauper's grave. He was recognised by Leeds Utd in 2000 when a plaque was unveiled at Elland Road.

This was the toxic arena that **Cliff Marshall** and **Howard Gayle** would have to face.

Mike Trebilcock 1965–68

Albert Johanneson 1961–70

Clyde Best 1969–76

Paul Reaney 1961–78

Cliff Marshall was born in Toxteth, Stanhope Street, on 4th November 1955. During his teenage years, he played for Liverpool, Everton, Lancashire and England Schoolboys.

Initially, Cliff played at centre half. While still at school, he was invited for a trial, ironically, by Liverpool FC. A teacher believed his speed would benefit him if he played on the wing. He took the advice, was signed on by the Reds and would spend his 'short' career in this position. This was just the beginning. After a successful teenage career, he found himself with many options. His father wanted him to go to Manchester United FC. He would not only meet with United's Will McGuinness, but also received an invitation from Liverpool FC. His love for the Toffees was strong, and he turned down both opportunities, later recalling, *"I could have gone to Liverpool or Man United, but I was always going to choose Everton."* He was signed by Everton's Billy Bingham (below) in 1973. He was part of the first-team squad by the 1974/5 season, following a pre-season tour in Athens. He became the first Liverpool Black player to sign for Everton FC, following the departure of Cornish-born Black player Mike Trebilcock in January 1968.

He would make his Everton debut on 11th January 1975, coming on as a substitute in a 3-0 win over Leicester City in the First Division. He made his first full start for the club the following week on 8th January in another 3-0 win, away to Birmingham City. He would make one further league start and one FA Cup appearance for the remainder of the 1974/5 season. He would only make three further starts in the 1975/6 season. Despite Bingham urging him to stay at the club, he decided to leave. He went to America, joining the Miami Torres, mingling with players such as the brilliant Pele and George Best, two childhood heroes. He would stay for a season and effectively end his career at Southport FC still only in his early twenties. He would, years later, explain his decision.

Cliff had his own opinion on football tactics. This was reflected in his admiration of George Best. He saw himself as an 'old school' winger, running at defences and getting around the outside. He revealed that this was an issue at Everton during his period at the club. He was told by a coach that his first priority was to defend. He would later comment, *"I got a bit disillusioned."*

"I love playing football; football was my first love. But what disillusioned me was some of the coaches had said your first priority is to defend and I didn't like that. I'm an attacker, defending should be my second priority. I moved on." He was practical about his position as the only Black player at the club and would later state, *"I didn't see it as any different. If you are good enough then you will play. There were chants and sometimes bananas thrown onto the pitch in the early days. It didn't affect me. I just got on with it and played the game."* Cliff was still Everton through and through and would eventually join the former Everton Players Foundation (below) a charitable organisation set up for ex-Blues. He made a major contribution to Liverpool Black history. Respect – from a Red to a Blue (see toffeeweb.com).

Cliff Marshall – Joe Royal – Roberto Martinez – Graham Stuart

Howard Gayle was born in Toxteth in May 1958. He played for Bedford FC, Liverpool FC, Birmingham City, Blackburn Rovers, Fulham, Newcastle, Sunderland, Stoke...

I could write a book about Howard, but he already wrote one, in October 2016. The book is appropriately titled *61 Minutes In Munich*. I would recommend that everyone read it if they want some insight into Liverpool Black life and the obstacles that Howard had to navigate. Howard, or Gayley as we know him, was well respected in amateur circles across the

dodgy football pitches in the city. He played for Bedford FC, a well-established team based in the Black community of Liverpool. They were known as a 'Black' team, despite the fact that they fielded both Black and White players. If racism was rampant in the professional ranks then you can imagine what it was like playing for a 'Black' team at the amateur level in Liverpool. Insight into the latter can be found on p. 111 (Amateur Football L8). Suffice it to say, Liverpool 8 teams were a force to be reckoned with. Most kids in Liverpool dream of playing professionally for the local teams. Howard had the same dream, and against all the odds, he would open the door for local Black kids to dream. In fact, he summed it up:

"For lads who'd been brought up here and watched the Liverpool sides throughout the years, to sign with them is a dream. When you come from Liverpool, you don't want to be just a footballer, but a footballer who plays for Liverpool or Everton."

It was no easy road for Howard. He was part of a family including two older brothers, with professional potential. They realised their younger brother was special and would play a major role in his football development. They were part of a generation of Liverpool Black families who stood up against racism, on and off the pitch. Howard would maintain those 'basic' principles throughout his 19-year (1974–93) career. By 1974, Howard was on the road to a professional career. He joined the youth ranks of Liverpool FC, progressing through the youth team and the A and B teams. He made Liverpool Reserves (156 appearances) under Roy Evans and was offered a professional contract in 1977 by Bob Paisley (above). The first Liverpool FC Black player, his career has been well documented since that historical moment in Liverpool Black history. Since retiring, Howard has worked tirelessly with kids/youth teams, passing on his experience, one of the few who remain dedicated to young footballers in the area. He has always stood by his principles. This was demonstrated in his refusal of an MBE (Member of the Most Excellent Order of the British Empire) in August 2016 – the award for his work with 'Show Racism the Red Card'. He was clear, stating that acceptance would be a betrayal:

"To all of the Africans who have lost their lives, who have suffered as a result of Empire."

Liverpool FC Team April 1981 v Bayern Munich (see bottom 1st left)   *Blackburn Rovers 1987–92*

Caribbean Centre 1976–2020

The Caribbean Centre was completed in 1976 and officially opened on 7th October 1977 by the Bishop of Liverpool, the Right Reverend David Sheppard.

The Caribbean Centre was officially closed in March 2013 and left to deteriorate. Despite ongoing negotiations, since 2013, the Centre has been left to rot. At the time of writing (2019), the Centre has been 'occupied' by local people, who in turn have been restoring the building and grounds, with amazing success. I will return to this development with an update on the circumstances (p. 71); I would first like to shed some light on the origins of the Caribbean Centre.

There were many people who contributed to the origins and the development of the Centre. It would become a major community venue. It had cricket teams, domino teams, football teams, basketball teams, annual carnivals and provided space for most community events, from birthday celebrations to weddings. Known as the Carib, it would soon become the only venue in the city that could be described as providing a facility for the Afro-Caribbean/Black community in the city of Liverpool. In truth, it was a venue enjoyed by all nationalities, Black and White.

Two Jamaicans in UK appointed JPs

The Kingston Gleaner – Thursday, 22nd December 1966

The headline, proudly, announced the appointment of two Jamaicans, in Bristol (Mr. Alman Buntin) and Liverpool (Mr. James Wynter). Both had been made a Justice of Peace, in their respective cities. Mr. Wynter would serve on the Licensing Committee. He commented: "I would consider the appointment a great honour both to myself and for Jamaica." Jimmy, as he was known, had arrived in England, from Jamaica, in 1941. He was part of the first West Indian volunteers to work in factories during the war effort. He worked for many years as an Engineer turner at Imperial Metals Ltd. He would play a vital role in Liverpool's Black community. He was the first West Indian JP in Liverpool and possibly the first Black individual to join the Liverpool judiciary. He was a member of the Stanley House Community Centre from 1947 and was appointed as the Warden of the Centre between 1953–55. His role in the unification of the West Indian community in Liverpool cannot be overstated.

James Wynter, with the ubiquitous and respected Councillor Bessie Braddock.

In 1970, the late Jimmy Wynter JP managed to get an entire West Indian community to form the Merseyside Caribbean Council, with a membership of 24 representatives from each Association: Guyana, Jamaica,Trinidad and Tobago, Barbados and St. Lucia. He selflessly put his energy to the service of an entire community, producing ideas and programmes of action for the betterment of West Indians in Liverpool. He believed that the task of creating a community centre for West Indians and their friends was not an easy one. He believed it would provide a bridge between the host community and West Indians, particularly for those young people who feel they are not wholly British, although he did express his belief in a more eloquent manner:

"I am a West Indian who believes the Merseyside Caribbean Council, is essential to a civilized community and to the development and attainment that will be realized."

– Community Perspectives MCRC

By 1972, with the Community Relations Council, the Caribbean made an application for a grant under the leadership of Jimmy Wynter, to build a Community Centre.

The application through the Urban Aid Programme was rejected. In 1973, a second application was submitted. It was supported by the local authority, and a local petition campaign was also launched, against the first refusal. The Petition read:

"Residents of the Liverpool 8 and surrounding areas, do hereby protest most strongly at the refusal of the Home Office to approve the application for Urban Aid for a Community Centre made by the Merseyside Caribbean Council. We honestly believe in and strongly back the views of the Merseyside Caribbean Council that there is an urgent and necessary need for the project for which the aid is required and hereby call upon the Minister to reconsider, and therefore reverse his decision."

Over 10,000 signatures were collected. The application was approved in 1974, and £108,000 was granted to the Merseyside Caribbean Council to erect its new centre, funded by the Urban Aid Programme. 75% of the cost came from the Home Office and 25% from Liverpool City Council. The Centre was completed in 1976.

Steve Biko Housing Association Staff. Providing affordable homes. A successful and innovative community housing initiative.

On 7th October 1977, a plaque to mark the official opening of the new Caribbean was unveiled by the Bishop of Liverpool, the Right Reverend David Sheppard, ironically a former professional cricketer. Mr. Wynter, as President of the Caribbean Council, said at the opening of the Centre:

"I cannot yet say that great events awaits us as West Indians in this country. But in social affairs and in all the fields of our effort we must continue in the way we have already firmly established, as one united Organisation. May this foundation continue to witness the works of dedicated men to the service of the people of the community."

There is no way you can discuss the Caribbean Centre without identifying the role and influence of the late Herbie Higgins – a beacon in the community and in many ways the face of the Caribbean Centre. He was involved in the creation of the Centre from day one, along with Mr. Wynter and the Caribbean Council. It would take many pages to catalogue the work and contributions of Herbie. Nevertheless we can identify a 'few' significant milestones:

Herbie Higgins MBE 1929-2011

- Initiated the Merseyside Caribbean Carnival in 1978;
- Worked with Paul McCartney at Liverpool Performing Arts;
- Awarded an MBE in 1996;
- Merit Award from the Federation of Black Housing 2003;
- Lay visitor to prisons;
- Instrumental in setting up Steve Biko Housing (see above);
- Herbie Higgins Court named in his honour – Steve Biko;
- Active Trade Unionist;
- Sat on Employment Tribunal Panel.

His contribution to the City of Liverpool was immeasurable.

So here we are: 2019 – six years since closure. Six years of abandonment, neglect and negotiations. Six years of watching and reminiscing – six years too long!

A few of the flags displayed outside the Caribbean Centre as locals take over the building in 2019, six years after its closure.

If every picture tells a story then the above flags provide an accurate overview of the Black experience in Liverpool (8). They have witnessed the destruction of 'our' social outlets and community/educational based organisations. Most are quickly, in private hands, converted to luxury apartments at 'unaffordable' prices for local people. Investing in Liverpool 8 property is a very profitable 'business'. For a more in-depth insight into this development, there are various sources via Facebook/Google, including the **African Caribbean Heritage Centre Board** (the Board) and the **Save The L8 Caribbean Centre** websites.

This message was provocative and demonstrated the 'gulf' between the Board and the local 'occupation'. It failed to acknowledge that since the closure of the Centre in 2013, the Board have ensured that the Centre still stands, six years later. I would say they defended our culture through-out that period. They have faced years of procedures, legalities and impact on family life. As local people, their objective has always been to save the Caribbean. Without the Board, it would already have been demolished and no doubt become part of a gated 'housing' complex.

The Board is the 'Accountable Body' with the City Council and 'interested parties' in regard to the location of the 'new' Centre. The occupation has threatened to derail the 'ongoing' talks and specifications. On the other hand, we now have local people taking the situation into their own hands. They have made tremendous strides, in regard to the renovation of the 'original' building and its grounds. We know throughout 'our' history, when action is taken, it is direct action. Both sides want the Centre, and they should 'meet' and discuss a way forward. Jimmy Wynter (p. 70) said:

"We must continue in the way we have already firmly established, as one united Organisation."

November 2 1978   Spring Books   25p

The Listener

ON THE MERSEY BEAT by Reporter Martin Young

It is a poignant scene, though that is not how the police of Merseyside would describe it! Less poignant, by far, is the other major social problem they face: the half-caste problem.

Policemen in general and detectives in particular, are not racialist, despite what many Black groups believe. Yet they are the first to define the problem of half-castes in Liverpool. Many are the products of liaisons between black seamen and white prostitutes in Liverpool 8, the red-light district. Naturally, they do not grow up with any kind of recognisable home life. Worse still, after they have done the round of homes and institutions, they gradually realise they are nothing. The Negroes will not accept them as Blacks, and whites just assume they are coloureds. As a result, the half-caste community of Merseyside, or more particularly Liverpool, is well outside recognised society.

BLACKLASH

BBC article sparks protest and threat of legal action

ANGRY Liverpool blacks are ready to take the BBC to court. They say a story in the BBC publication The Listener is untrue and will cause more trouble in the city.

And they warn people living in Liverpool 8 are condemned in The Listener as prostitutes and outcasts, say members of Merseyside Anti-racialist Alliance and Merseyside Community Relations Council.

Wow. Who would hold such deep-rooted contempt for the sons and daughters of Black and White parents?

I apologise for the poor quality of this *Liverpool Daily Post* article from 24th November 1978, but it reflects the level of anger that had spread across the city and throughout the indigenous Liverpool Black population. At the time of the comments, the Merseyside Anti-Racialism Alliance (MARA) had just been formed, while the Liverpool Black Organisation (LBO) was still finalising 'our' constitution. It was at a MARA meeting where the *Listener* comments were raised. The first MARA Chairperson, the late, inspirational, activist Rashid Mufti (below) agreed that a public meeting should be called.

The meeting was held at the Stanley House Community Centre. The meeting was well attended, with over 250 people from all sections of the Liverpool 8 community. During the course of an angry meeting, more details were to be revealed about the BBC's controversial documentary.

BBC TV screened a documentary about the work of the Merseyside Police Force, called *Merseybeat*. It transpired that one of its programmes was found to have deeply insulting material about the Liverpool Black community. The BBC *Listener* magazine would reproduce the material (p. 72), and reporter Martin Young would claim that the information came from the Merseyside Police.

Anger at the article erupted at a noisy protest meeting on Tuesday night when over 250 people decided to take legal advice on the report.

"This shows the disgust people have over the article," said David Clay, a community fieldworker in Toxteth who helped set up the meeting.

"The article seems to say that people here are prostitutes or outcasts.

"I am a product of a white mother and a black father. My mother was not a prostitute and my father was not even a sailor. The article is offensive," he said.

"It will cause more trouble. A lot of things have happened in the past in Liverpool 8 but it could get worse. Race relations in the city, if they ever existed, are deteriorating," he warned.

Mr. Clay also warned of a backlash against the police because of the article:

"Who gave the reporter the information? A lot of people believe it was the police and they will go even more against the police.

"They believe the police are like that anyway but now they have got it in writing," said Mr. Clay.

A demonstration is planned for tomorrow and hundreds of Toxteth people are expected to take to the streets in protest.

It was decided to organise a Protest March. A petition would be presented to the Chief Constable (Hope Street) and BBC Radio Merseyside Offices (Sir Thomas Street).

Further demands included a call for a police investigation and the BBC to apologise. The demonstration took place on 25th November 1978 (below) and was successful, with no trouble of any note. The BBC refused to repudiate the article. However, the Merseyside Chief Constable, Ken Oxford, did carry out an investigation, declaring that he *"deplored the utterance of the remarks"* and *"regretted there was nothing more that could be done."*

Investigation concluded!

Part of the Listener Protest on 25th November 1978.

It was clear that the 1970s were ending in conflict. The relationship between the Liverpool Black community and Merseyside Police was at an all time low. Following the *Listener* revelations, the Merseyside Community Relations Council (MCRC) suspended their role in the Police Liaison Committee. By 1980, both the MCRC and the Liverpool Black Organisation (pp. 75–79) would send numerous letters, a petition and organise a protest march, and describe the Police Liaison Committee as a 'window dressing' exercise for the police. Despite the abundance of evidence of increasing hostility and friction between the police and the community, the chief constable would appear on television and speak of the *"Excellent relationship between the police and the Liverpool 8 community"* (*Granada Reports*, 28th/29th May 1980).

Eva Ohajuru
1st Feb 1928 to 23rd May 2016
Wife, mother, grandmother, great-grandmother
and mother to many more.

The Liverpool Black Organisation

As a founding member, one of many, of the LBO, I have to be honest and say that it was a most positive experience in regard to community activism.

It is with the greatest respect this historic document highlights the late Eva Ohajuru (p. 75), a positive role model in the Liverpool Black community. When the LBO was formed, it was Eva who made and designed the Organisation flag (below). The flag was draped on Eva's coffin.

The gesture was acknowledged by all LBO members and across the Black community. It demonstrated the impact of an organisation that was formed almost 40 years ago. The flag continues to be present at most anti-racist events, including Black Lives Matter. It still acts as a symbol that there is a Liverpool Black population in the city. This insight will take a general look at LBO's activities and present my view as to why the organisation basically folded in 1981.

The organisation was officially launched in June 1979. Nevertheless, most of 1978 was spent determining the organisation's constitution. The latter was vital. Everybody had a view. The organisation was formed for Liverpool-born Black people. Our history and culture dictated that the LBO would have White members, and it did. Positions such as Chair, Secretary etc. were to be held by local Blacks. It had already been determined that the organisation did not want any statutory funding. Everyone knew the consequences of funding dependence. All meetings were held in Stanley House. The organisation was determined to build a strong community structure, break down local apathy and directly challenge racism. In order to achieve the latter, with the help of the British Council of Churches (BCC), some members of the LBO participated in the Alinsky Training Project on behalf of the organisation, and I was fortunate to be one of them.

Saul David Alinsky (30th January 1909 – 12th June 1972) was an American community organiser and writer. He is generally considered to be the founder of modern community organising. He is often noted for his book *Rules for Radicals* (left; 1971). For a more in-depth understanding of Alinsky tactics, this book is recommended. At this stage, we worked with an Alinsky trainer from Ireland, Hank O'Mahony. His work was building strong community-led organisations. Our work was to use the project in regard to tactics, within a legal framework. Alinsky made it clear tactics meant 'doing what you can with what you have'. What we had was a Black organisation, not only with a lot of talent and ideas, but also a lifetime experience of racism in the city/country. This was an attempt to represent the interests of a very large ethnic group in an organised way. Areas of concern for the LBO included police relations, Stop and Search procedures and employment.

The first rule of change is controversy. You can't get away from it for the simple reason that all issues are controversial. Change means movement, and movement means friction, and friction means heat, and heat means controversy (Alinsky). The LBO was good at controversy. Another rule that encouraged community participation *"is one your people enjoy"* (Alinsky), and the organisation achieved this. In truth, the very name Liverpool Black Organisation would bring a sense of pride within the community, regardless of whether people were LBO members. This is why the LBO flag is still a symbol of resistance/identity (thanks to former member Alan Gayle).

Despite the short duration of the LBO (1978–81), the direct approach to racism continued to be a trademark in the future of local Black protest and organisation.

The training would prove effective. Within a month of formation, the organisation noted a planned demonstration by the Liverpool Trades Council, March Against Racism (July 1979). It was decided that the LBO would lead the march, from the Black community, with our flag. Suffice it to say, we achieved all the latter as well as concessions from the Trade Council in relation to Equal Opportunity within the City Council. Ongoing problems in the relationship between the police and the Liverpool Black community would continue. The first year of the MCRC (June 71) saw 50% of their casework consisting of police complaints. The Police Community Liaison Scheme was failing. The Community Relations Council described it as 'window dressing'. The Liverpool Black Organisation marched to Admiral Police Station (September 1980) and placed the coffin outside, in protest, stating: *Police Liaison – RIP*. The coffin was also used at the Oxford Out Demonstration (below) in 1981. *[Photo by Manny Uchegbu; Courtesy of Desery Normah]*

Stop and Search was at its peak. Liverpool had its own unique powers. The power to stop and search individuals was given to the Liverpool police under the Corporation Act 1922 and further enshrined in Section 50(b) of the Merseyside County Act.

The Act enabled police to *"search any person who may be reasonably suspected of having or conveying in any manner anything stolen or unlawfully obtained."* Such encounters involved a degree of physical and verbal confrontation. A 'specially' trained Merseyside Police Task Force was let loose on the Black community in 1969. Patrolling the streets of the area would usually incur many Section 50b's. They were intimidating and an overtly racist Task Force. In two separate cases, they planted drugs on two Liverpool Black men of good character. Both were found not guilty (*Police Power & Black People*). The Task Force would last for 8 years, until it was disbanded by the new Chief Constable Kenneth Oxford in 1977. Basically, he replaced the Task Force para-military style jeeps for transit vans and renamed it the Operational Support Division (OSD), to be deployed in districts with *"longstanding crime problems."* The LBO submitted evidence to the Home Affairs Committee 1980/1 and the report concluded:

"Racial disadvantage in Liverpool is in a sense the most disturbing case of racial disadvantage in the United Kingdom, because there can be no question of cultural problems of newness of language, and it offers a grim warning to all of Britain's cities that racial disadvantage cannot be expected to disappear by natural causes. The Liverpool Black Organisation warned the Subcommittee, 'what you see in Liverpool is a sign of things to come'. We echo that warning."

– October 1980

The above tells us that there was no issue with language or cultural differences. The LBO knew that the issue was based on colour. This was reflected during an incident that occurred in a former city centre Army & Navy Store, in Ranelagh Street (p. 78).

When a 15-year-old youth informed the LBO that he had been accused of stealing a coat, it was an opportunity to deploy the Alinsky tactics again: The Half Penny Protest.

Security staff had demanded to see the inside of his coat, claiming it had been stolen from the store. The youth was adamant that it was his own coat. He was eventually wrestled to the ground and 'his' coat ripped off. It transpired that he was telling the truth. He complained to the store, via a solicitor. He was informed that, *"Following a full investigation into your complaints we fully support the actions of our security staff."*

At this particular time, halfpennies were legal tender in Britain. In fact, you could legally spend up to 40p in halfpennies, so you can imagine the difficulties that would arise if, for example, you paid your bus fare with 80 halfpennies. One of the fundamental principles of Alinsky tactics was that every action brings about a reaction. It was how you plan for the reaction that is crucial. It was decided to visit the store at the peak shopping time, Saturday morning. The planning had been meticulous as well as fun. Some would pretend to faint, others untangle laces. There would be a halfpenny group who would purchase goods across the eight tills we had identified, basically just causing inconvenience to shoppers and staff alike. Small items would be purchased with halfpennies. A solicitor and a vicar were at the door to deal with any reaction. This was a legal protest that would happen every Saturday. Within two hours, the management asked us what we wanted. We presented the store with a list of demands, including reimbursement for the youth and a pledge to become an equal opportunity employer. All demands were met. Community action had achieved a victory. We later visited the store to apologise to staff for the inconvenience.

You could say that it was circumstances, namely, the 1981 Toxteth riots, that saw the demise of the Liverpool Black Organisation. Following derogatory remarks about 'half-caste' in the *Caribbean Times* made by the Director of the Caribbean Centre, the Liverpool Black Organisation occupied the building during May 1981, until a number of demands were met, including:

- Issue an apology for inappropriate remarks;
- Representation of locals on the Caribbean Community Council;
- More facilities and activities for youth.

The centre was occupied 24/7. During the day, inflatables were provided for local kids, and the centre remained vibrant. Negotiations dragged on. The full-time occupation attracted a lot of media attention. It was surprising to see the presence of both European and national press.

The realities of supporting and containing an occupation on a 24-hour basis is a pressure situation. It did lead to a major spilt in the organisation. Ironically, it was the media presence that would bring about this issue, or the ideological direction of the LBO. The press wanted to know who had taken the action and why. I, and other members, were not happy with press statements from LBO members. They all started with "A community spokesperson said…" We were of the opinion that the occupation was a Liverpool Black Organisation initiative, voted for unanimously and financed by the LBO. Any statement should start with "An LBO spokesperson said…" Nevertheless, it was argued that this was a 'community occupation', hence community spokesperson. This subtle difference of opinion was never resolved within the organisation, as the start of the Toxteth riots would override the issue.

On 6th July 1981, the Liverpool Black Organisation would 'officially' cease to operate under that name. It was in Stanley House (p. 85) that hundreds of residents met for a public meeting, called by the LBO. It was decided to set up a Defence Committee to act on behalf of those involved in the disturbances. Future press statements would read: "The (L8) Defence Committee said…" Despite this, the LBO loomed large in most Black social actions. I have no regrets for being part of the LBO – a vital contribution to Liverpool Black history.

Toxteth Riots 1981–85

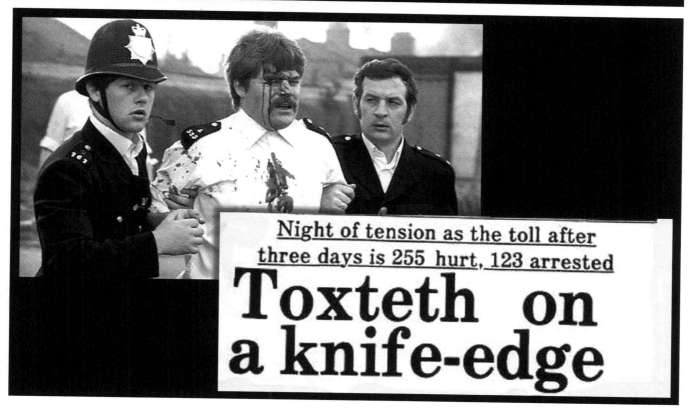

Night of tension as the toll after three days is 255 hurt, 123 arrested

Toxteth on a knife-edge

Well, here we are – the 1980s; the position of Liverpool's Black community unchanged. It would be a turbulent decade for the city, and race would remain a factor.

The city had its share of tragedy including the murder of Liverpool (Black) legend Willie Osu (below), John Lennon, riots, Heysel and Hillsborough. Police relations continued to deteriorate: *"The police give special surveillance of the Liverpool 8 area which leads to antagonism between the community and the police." – Sick City: Community Relations in Liverpool, 1974*

"We consider that it is youth who are stopped and harassed most. We believe that special attention should be focused on the Liverpool 8 area where Black youth suffer an additional attack of racial insult." – Merseyside Trade Union Inquiry: Allegations of Police Violence, 1980

"The cycle of frequent encounters with the law, together with the assumptions, mythology and even procedures constitute in some ways the 'criminalisation' of a group of Liverpool-born people, the majority of whom come from stable and supportive homes in which there is no history of involvement in the courts on the part of the parents, but some on the part of most of the children, especially males." – Patterns of Discriminatory Behaviour by Police and in the Courts facing the locally born Black Population in Liverpool, McNabb, Melish and Ben-Tovim, 1972

"Allegations of police discrimination have been sufficiently well documented for it to be accepted that police misbehaviour does exist." – Community Relations in Liverpool, 1974

It was of little surprise that on Friday, 3rd July 1981, an altercation between Black youth and police resulted in an arrest and the escape of the intended suspect. It was the fuse that would lead to the use of CS Gas, one death, many injuries, many burning buildings, many arrests and the most violent of disturbances in the country. For a more in-depth view, there is an abundance of information on the 1981 'uprising'. You may have guessed – I was there!

It is from this latter perspective that I comment on the 1981 Toxteth Riots.

It was terrifying. *"We had no protective equipment: just these round shields and an ordinary copper's helmet with a flimsy plastic visor. We had no tactical awareness or skills in riot control."*

– Det. Superintendent Tim Keelan, who was a PC during the 1981 Toxteth Riots

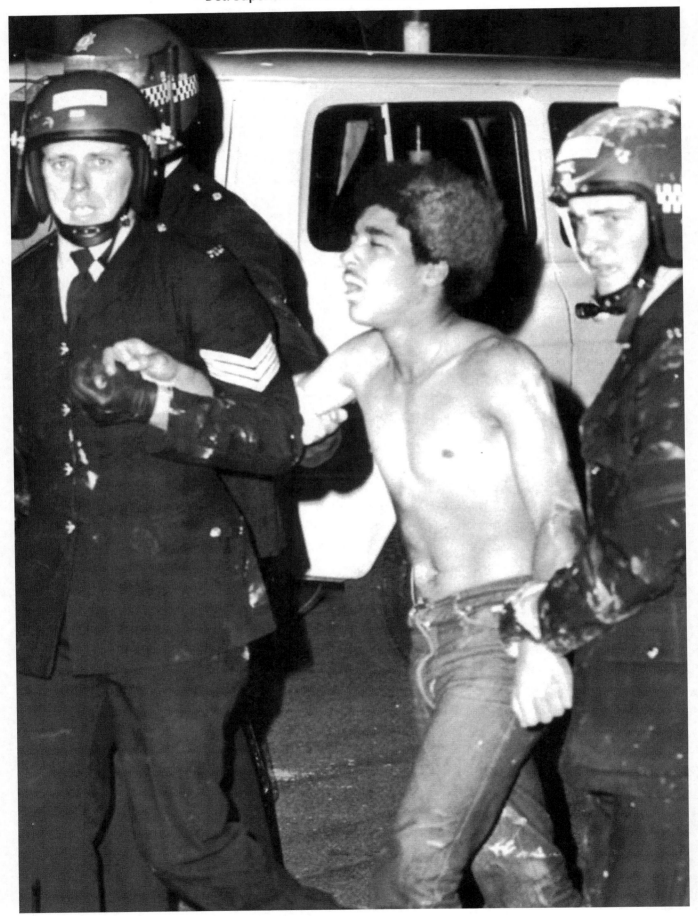

As in any riot situation, there are many controversies, interpretations and opinions, usually made from the 'outside looking in'. I wish to comment from the 'inside'!

The view of former PC Keelen (p. 80), that the Force lacked any 'tactical awareness or skills in riot control' was a fairly accurate assessment. This document has already demonstrated how Liverpool Police conducted themselves when the Black community was under attack in 1919, 1948, 1972 and 1979. They took the opportunity to arrest anyone Black who took up arms in an effort to defend themselves – who else would protect them? They allowed Charles Wootton to die at the hands of a lynch mob. There are not many people in the Liverpool Black community who do not believe/know that both the police and the judiciary are riddled with racism. I would like to comment on a few significant incidents during the disturbances.

The Use of CS Gas on the Mainland

At around 2am on the morning of 6th July 1981, Merseyside Police Chief Constable Kenneth Oxford ordered a change in tactics and authorised the use of CS gas, or 'tear gas', on the rioters. In order to comprehend this decision, we have to briefly outline the circumstances. There was a clear demarcation line between 'rioters' and 'looters'. Although the conflict began in Liverpool 8, with Black youth and police, it attracted communities from all over Merseyside, some to vent their own anger on Merseyside Police and others to take the 'open' opportunity to pillage.

There is little doubt that the 5th–6th July 1981 was the most violent and destructive period of the riots. There were times when the use of CS Gas would have been fully justified. I, for one, always maintain that it was not necessary at the time it was deployed. The majority of 'rioters' had left the scene, and those remaining were people sitting on steps, milling around as some youths providing an exhibition of car 'wheelies'. In short, there was no threat to the city centre, despite the police still not having complete control. Any police advance would have been 100% successful. Despite inappropriate projectiles being used in the pretence that the city centre was under threat, the Home Secretary, retrospectively, approved the decision.

The Evacuation of Princes Park Geriatric Hospital

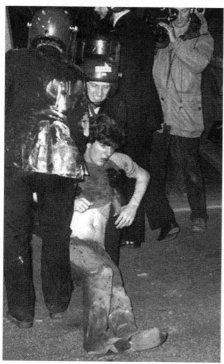

The hospital was situated next door to the then burning century-old Racquet Club at 146, Upper Parliament Street. There were 100 elderly patients at the hospital who were endangered. The rioters, like the police, did not want any harm to come to the patients. Not only was it agreed to allow ambulances and taxis to escort the 'residents' to safety, but it was facilitated by the 'rioters', who directly assisted in the evacuation. The riot was with the police, not elderly residents. It was ironic that the first taxi was attacked by a rioter. The latter action was based on the racism of many Liverpool taxis not stopping for Black folk when for hire. Nevertheless, the rioters turned against him. Little did they know that 25–30 CS gas grenades awaited. I could not believe that Oxford would be the recipient of a CBE and knighthood!

Although the troubles continued with sporadic clashes with police and youth, no one imagined that the police 'tactics' would bring about the death of a disabled youth.

Mobile Pursuit Tactics

A second wave of rioting began on 27th July 1981 and continued into the early hours of 28th July, with police being attacked with missiles and a number of cars being set alight. However, on this occasion, the Merseyside Police Force responded by driving vans and Land Rovers at high speed into the crowds, quickly dispersing them. This 'mobile pursuit tactic' had been developed as a riot control technique in Northern Ireland by the Royal Ulster Constabulary and had been employed with success in quelling the Moss Side riots by the Greater Manchester Police.

Local disabled man David Moore (p. 81) died after being struck by a police van on a mobile pursuit mission, while another, Paul Conroy (p. 81), had his back broken after being run over by a Land Rover. Chief Constable Oxford responded to critics of his 'mobile pursuit' tactics in his normal arrogant and insensitive manner, by telling journalists, *"They can see the vehicles coming and they know what will happen if they get in the way."*

Mr. Oxford was a very opinionated Chief Constable in every situation. For now, the 80s would continue with conflict, as officers tried to come to terms with the 'events' of July 1981, no doubt many with 'revenge' in mind. 1st October 1985 would present an opportunity for 'riot control'.

Rampage in Toxteth after court uproar

From Peter Davenport, Liverpool

The investigations into the death of a London man in Toxteth Sports Centre led to the arrest of four local Black youth. They were charged with 'causing an affray' at Toxteth Sports Centre on 10th August 1985. It would be the catalyst to further confrontations.

There is ample information on the events of October 1985. I will briefly explore the lead-up to the 'clashes'. On 1st October 1985, Liverpool Magistrates' Court was the venue for the youth charged with affray. It was a hot day, 80 degrees, when a group of Liverpool Black youth arrived at the court. They asked the usher(s) where the case was to be held. As we know, a large group of Black people wishing to be part of the public gallery is no straightforward matter. After almost two hours of battling to get a seat, the Stipendiary Magistrate, Norman Wootton, remanded the youths to Risley Remand Centre. This is how the youth saw an affray case dealt with – an excessive police presence, mendacity (lies) of ushers and the knowledge that the Black presence was resented. The youth did not react kindly to what was considered to be:

"Deliberate delays. Why did we have to wait for almost two hours at the Court? They said they did not have the papers. It was all too much and they have only got themselves to blame."

– Dave Smith RIP (below left), L8 Fieldworker, *Liverpool Echo*, 2nd October 1985

The mood home was angry, and Hope Street Police Station was a target of stones and a reminder of Toxteth 1981 events. This was only to be the start – by the time the youths had reached Princes Avenue, cars had been overturned and set alight. The Merseyside Police decided to cordon off the area. By the early evening, an uneasy stand-off existed as youths positioned themselves behind burnt-out cars on Granby Street, with police situated in nearby Selborne/Mulgrave Street.

There was little doubt the events that followed would show quite clearly, to me, that the police were on a revenge mission, eager to demonstrate their newfound expertise in 'riot control'.

The stand-off continued as the 'older' element of the community were trying to figure out ways to prevent the youth and police clashing.

The Liverpool 8 Law Centre, of which I was Chair at the time, held a meeting that evening, which included the Bishop of Liverpool (below left). It was decided to approach both the youth and the police. We made our way to Granby Street led by the bishop. Who could have devised a better plan? We approached the youths – we all knew each other – it's a difficult situation. We tell them that there is real danger. The police are determined and prepared, and intent on revenge, while the youth are angry but no match for the armoured Transit vans and Land Rovers. They listen. If the police leave the area, we will go home, they say. There is trust here.

We make our way to the police ranks. There is fear. Lights flash in our eyes. Can we talk, we are here with the bishop? We have spoken to the group on Granby – they will leave if you pull out. OK, they said, but we are not all moving out at once and will withdraw slowly. OK, we said.

As we entered Granby Street, Land Rovers began moving slowly behind us on their way from the area. Suddenly they are screeching into Granby Street, down the road and along the sidewalks. I hear someone shout "I told you not to trust them!" – but wait...there are also hordes of police in riot gear rushing into Granby swinging big sticks and attacking anyone in sight. We and the bishop had to scramble in the dirt as one of the lads saved him from fatal injury. There was little time to contemplate how the officer in charge could tell such bare-faced lies to the bishop. I'm OK, a few near misses from baton and wheel. Shouts of niggers and Black B's.

Catholic Bishop Derek Worlock (left) and Anglican Archbishop David Sheppard (right)
caught up in the middle of the action on Granby Street (centre), Tuesday, 1st October 1985.

The result would see injuries to 18 people and 13 arrests. It was said that the police had ignored orders to retreat and decided to attack. I don't know if the latter is true, but I certainly believed it. Nevertheless, I do know that they had agreed to move out. The 'mobile pursuit' tactics were deployed successfully, with no distinction between rioter and onlooker.

The Merseyside Police Committee met a week later (15th October 1985). The Committee, in particular the Chair Mrs. Simey, continued their war of words with the chief constable. The meeting was presented with a 1,000-signature petition, demanding an inquiry into the police tactics and behaviour. The petition complained that police vehicles were aggressively deployed and officers from the infamous Operation Support Division had used 'racist and intimidatory tactics', concluding that:

"We as mothers, fathers, ratepayers and members of the community demand to know why the police waged a war of attrition on our community."

In a city that did not carry out an Inquiry following the 1981 riots, the demand was ignored.

Liverpool 8 Defence Committee

M. Uchegbu

Part of the Oxford Out Demonstration organised by the L8 Defence Committee, 15th August 1981.
Credit: M. Uchegbu

As readers are aware, the L8 Defence Committee was formed following a public meeting, held at Stanley House Community Centre on 6th July 1981 (p. 78).

When the public meeting commenced, the atmosphere was one of confusion and anxiety. At this stage, there had been over 100 arrests. Many of those present had no idea where their family or friends were located or being held. It was decided to set up a committee, which would become the Liverpool 8 (L8) Defence Committee. The group was open to all members of the local community. It was agreed that the committee would be based in the Charles Wootton Centre and open to the community. The general objectives of the L8DC were identified, as shown below:

LIVERPOOL 8 DEFENCE COMMITTEE

c/o Charles Wootton Centre, 248 Upper Parliament Street, Liverpool 8.   Tel: 051-708 9698/8188

The Liverpool 8 Defence Committee was set up to:

- ARRANGE legal help – bail – solicitors;
- ARRANGE transport to and from Risley Remand Centre;
- COORDINATE information about what is happening to people in custody;
- COLLECT statements from witnesses of police brutality, of which there are many;
- GIVE advice about compensation or damaged property.

The formation of such committees has been widespread in Liverpool. One in particular was the emergence of the Jimmy Kelly Action Committee in 1979. The death of local Huyton man Jimmy Kelly while in police custody galvanised family members, friends and local people to oppose the Merseyside Police. The similarities of the Borough of Knowsley and Toxteth, in regard to policing, were evident. Toxteth was in its fifth year of living with a Merseyside Police Task Force (p. 77). In 1974, Knowsley got the notorious K-Division Task Force, covering Huyton, Kirkby, Speke and Halewood. Their trail of destruction included the deaths of Kenneth Williams (1974), John Lannon (1978) and Michael Kavanagh. The violence towards the Yates and Guy families and the death of Jimmy Kelly (1979) all culminated in the Gerty Report in September 1990, while the Chief Constable (above) refused to share the contents. Another similarity was the reaction of the police/media. The chair of the Police Federation, James Jardine, called the Jimmy Kelly Committee *"Ragbags – communist – criminal elements and police bashers"* (Tommy Banks, Chair of Action Group).

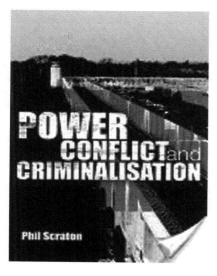

The experience of the Jimmy Kelly Action Committee and the role of the infamous K-Division is fully documented by Phil Scraton. His 'grassroots' investigation is an enlightening journey tracing the historical development of the Merseyside Police and their relationship and priorities with working-class communities on Merseyside (left). Recommended.

Like the Jimmy Kelly Action Committee, the L8 Defence Committee was a target of both the police and media. The chief constable described us as 'Black hooligans' and 'criminals'. I do not know many from the area who did not believe that Kenneth Oxford was the author of the *Listener* Article in 1979 (p. 72), and there was no love lost in his relationship with Toxteth or Knowsley.

There is no doubt that the L8DC carried out the main objectives that were determined at the meeting. The war against Oxford and the press was never-ending.

Defence Committee members protest outside Risley Remand Centre, Warrington, August 1981.

Defence Committee protest police – community meeting at the university, August 1981 (RIP).

Chief Constable Kenneth Oxford continued to utter 'ongoing arrogant statements' while refusing to acknowledge that racism was at the heart of police and Black community conflict. He made his feelings quite clear in the *Liverpool Echo* (6th July 1981): *"This was not a racial issue. It was exclusively a crowd of Black hooligans intent on making life unbearable and indulging in criminal activity."*

To state that no 'racial issues were involved' was to ignore a history of conflict between Merseyside Police and Black Liverpool residents. This was reinforced when police made racist chants and used racist language during the 1981 and 1985 disturbances. Suffice it to say that the police and the media did all in their power to try and turn the people of Liverpool against the L8DC. The *Daily Mail* unearthed the fact that some members of the L8DC had criminal convictions. Like the Kelly Committee, we did not conduct a criminal check of members. In reality, the community becomes the committee; they march, demonstrate and protest under an L8 banner. The *Liverpool Echo* published a scathing 'personal' attack on the very foundations of the L8DC:

ECHOCOMMENT

Liverpool Echo. Tuesday, March 2. 1982

JUST what authority have Liverpool 8 Defence Committee to represent the people of Toxteth? None whatsoever.

Not democratically elected, they have no mandate to speak for the people. No right to order their lives

Yet this group, which includes self-admitted ex-criminals, has become a mouthpiece, vigilante force and political pressure group claiming to represent thousands who live in Toxteth.

How they work was demonstrated to journalists twice yesterday

At an official Press conference at the troubled St. Saviour's School a photographer's camera was snatched, the film torn from it. A radio reporter was jostled until he handed over his tape

At the end of the conference Liverpool's chief publicity officer said Pressmen

"I have spoken to members of the Liverpool 8 Defence Committee and they have said there will be no trouble if you all just get into your cars and drive off. If you don't, I cannot give you any guarantees."

In a second incident at another afternoon Press conference, defence committee members even entered the room to threaten and insult a radio reporter and demand his tape.

At one point the tape was thrown back at the reporter, after committee members had listened to it.

Assault, threats, censorship . . pressmen are better equipped than many to protect themselves from such things, but we are glad that city council leader Sir Trevor Jones is calling for reports on the incidents, and has promised to refer them to the Chief Constable.

The *Echo* comment also compared Toxteth to *"parts of bomb-torn Belfast, where the rule of law no longer stretches."*

What the article 'forgot' to mention is why they were actually at the so-called 'troubled' St. Saviour's (Infant) School. Was it violence? No. Was it insolence? No. Was it troubled children? No. Was it bullying? No. It was basically confusing approaches to the racial identity of our kids. It was a curriculum issue, a teacher/parent issue.

Let us put the *Liverpool Echo* into some perspective. I do so as a former member of the L8DC, a Black Liverpudlian and a reader of the paper for a lifetime. As far as we were concerned, the paper, as usual, was seeking a 'sensational' headline about a 'troubled' school in Toxteth. The L8DC intervened with their direct action approach. In fact, the school was just over the road from the Defence Committee headquarters.

The *Liverpool Echo/Daily Post* had a history of negative reports about the Black community, and Liverpool 8 in general. Many people I know do not buy the *Echo* and say it is racist. Such a view was not solely based on their negative reporting throughout the 60/70/80s. With the exception of football/sports, Black people were mostly depicted in crime-related articles. Usually, they would be looking for a 'Toxteth Man' – 'Half-Caste' – 'Coloured'.

The article ignores the fact that the L8DC was established at a public meeting. How are Black people made democratically acceptable by the *Liverpool Echo*? There were no democratically elected Black councillors in the city, there were no Black journalists in the *Liverpool Echo* pool, and there were no Black radio reporters – within a community that had withstood a history of criminalisation. Who was democratically electing Black people to anything unless it was a race-related job? Maybe the next time Black people want to help themselves – mothers, sons and daughters – ring the *Liverpool Echo*!

L8 Defence Committee Protesters at the Oxford Out March.

The Sam Bond Affair 1984–87

The turbulence of the 80s continued – Marvin Gaye's death, Garden Festival – Miners – Marley – Liverpool Militant Council...a decade ending with the Hillsborough Tragedy.

Liverpool City Council appointed London man Sam Bond as a Principle Race Relations Advisor on 9th October 1984. It would bring about 28 months of conflict with the Liverpool Black community and the newly elected, Militant influenced, Labour-run council. It would be a dramatic period. There is an abundance of information on the events. In fact, both sides published books stating their own perspectives and view of the conflict.

The appointment cannot be seen in isolation from events that led to the October decision. Throughout the saga, it was described as a 'struggle' between the Liverpool Black Caucus and the Militant Liverpool Council. Media outlets showed little interest in the history of the Caucus or how the idea of a Race Unit originated. I would like to highlight some of this history.

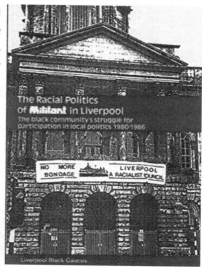

After many years of 'ongoing' meetings, discussions, setbacks, pressure and protests, the city council adopted an equal opportunity policy in 1981. Part of the agreement included the setting up of a Race Relations Liaison Committee. The committee would comprise 12 city councillors (from across the political spectrum) and 12 representatives from Black organisations. It was ironic that it was the city council who came up with the idea of such a positive structure. The committee was established in 1981, an its objectives were to develop policies, programmes and initiatives in the field of race relations. The idea of a 'Race Unit' was one of many strategic plans to come out of such a relationship. After the retirement of the first Caucus 12 (1981–83), a solid foundation for the ongoing partnership had been established.

A meeting of community groups in the Merseyside Community Relations Council (July 1983) was held in order to elect the composition of the next Caucus 12. The July meeting voted in 12 people who would form the liaison with the 12 Liverpool councillors, and the serious work of reaching their objectives was continued. It transpired that the Race Relations Unit was made top of the 'militant' agenda. The MCRC would comment:

"Possibly the most significant decision taken by the Committee (/City Council/Caucus) this year and agreed upon by the City's Policy and Finance Committee has been the plan for setting up a Race Relations Unit in the Chief Executive's Department, consisting of new posts: Principle Race Relations Advisor, Researcher, Training Officer, Complaints Officer and Administrative Assistant"

– Merseyside Community Relations Council Annual Report, 1983–84

I had no direct involvement in the caucus but was in the 'No Bond' camp. To complicate matters, I had applied for one of the 'other' posts and been shortlisted. I went for my interview on 10th October, unaware that the appointment of Sam Bond, the day before, was in dispute. An official trade union picket (NALGO) was outside the council building protesting against the appointment of Sam Bond as the Principle Race Relations Advisor. At that time, I guess I was in agreement with the No Bond position, although my reason being that he wasn't from Liverpool, let alone Toxteth. Little did I know that this battle would become a 'war', and you know what – no job Interview!

The Caucus was transformed from elected and respected subcommittee members, to participating in a no-holds-barred political and public battle (October 84 – March 87).

Sam Bond

Following the Bond appointment on 9th October 1984, events were to spiral out of control:

10th October	A group of pickets occupied the council leader's (Derek Hatton) office. Mr. Hatton declares that the post would be re-advertised.
11th October	The District Labour Party reversed the decision to re-advertise, claiming that Mr Hatton had been intimidated by 'mobs and gangsters'.
17th October	Public meeting in Liverpool 8 condemns the council turnaround.
20th October	Joint Shop Stewards Committee support the re-advertising of the post.
24th October	Race Relations Liaison Committee suspended by the city council.
14th November	March by Black Caucus (above) to Town Hall and disruption of city council meeting.

These tit-for-tat tactics would continue throughout the conflict. It was ironic that the relationship with the Black community and the militant fraction would deteriorate to such a level. No doubt L8 Defence Committee members will recall the support of the militant group during the preparations of the Oxford Out demonstration. There appeared to be some affinity with the Black community. Similar to us, they were also targets of negative media (*Gangsters Run the Town Hall* – **Echo**, 28th November); In terms of any policy on race, the militants had always accepted that discrimination existed. Nevertheless, they considered it to be part of the overall class struggle and had to be solved within that wide framework, otherwise it would alienate many working-class White people from identifying with the struggle. In Marxist terms, when the people own the means of production and a classless society exists, then there would be no racism.

We had a lot of respect for the militant faction, as they were prepared to take on the Thatcher Government to protect the resources of Liverpool people. We would argue that racism is so ingrained and institutionalised, that just to depend on Marxism to eradicate inequality and racism is unrealistic to Black struggle. Such beliefs were scorned as coming from the so-called experts of the race industry. This issue was deeper than the race industry. It had become a community rebellion. The militant attempts to divide the community with a few opportunistic local Blacks (Merseyside Action Group) would backfire. They would desert the militants and publicly expose their future plans for Black folk. Militant was wrong about Sam Bond, just as they were, a year later, with their redundancy blunders!

99 Reasons for Change

Liz Drysdale

Liz Drysdale outside the Adelphi

1988 (Image: Mirrorpix)

At the time of writing (August 2019), the City of Liverpool Labour Party has elected local Councillor Anna Rothery as the first Black Lord Mayor in Liverpool history (p. 120).

The honour of being the first Liverpool-born Black city councillor belongs to the late Glynn George Pratt (below), when elected by the Liverpool and Merseyside County Council in 1981. He remained the only Liverpool Black male to have achieved such a feat until 2019 (p. 118).

Glynn Pratt 1931-2003 RIP

Vote

| Delroy Burris | X |

1987 was another year of racial strife across Liverpool and the UK. The Community Relations Council declared 87 as the year to 'Combat Racial Terrorism'; Sam Bond left the city (19th March); John Barnes signed for Liverpool FC (June); Winston Silcott was sentenced to life imprisonment; the Federation of Black Organisations field two Independent candidates in the Granby local elections; an arson attack on a Sikh Temple; the formation of the Falkner Estate Action Group; the success of the Black Social Workers Group; Black Conservative MP John Taylor urges Black people to vote Tory; the election of four Black MPs in the House of Commons (Diane Abbott, Paul Boateng, Bernie Grant, Keith Vaz). On 7th May 1987, Liz Drysdale (p. 91) would become the first Liverpool-born Black female councillor for the Granby Ward and the city. This historic achievement was in a city with 99 ward councillors at the time!

Elizabeth Drysdale was always one to speak her mind, especially if the subject concerned the Liverpool Black community. This article provides a brief insight into local events pertaining to the 1987 Granby Ward local elections. Liz had spent many years working in the voluntary sector, including The Charles Wootton Centre, South Liverpool Personnel, Black Sisters, Women's Technology Centre and the Heseltine-inspired ITEC. At the time when she made the decision to accept the Labour District Party selection, Liz had been working with the Independent election plans of the Federation of Black Organisations, who had selected Delroy Burris (RIP) and Shaun Deckon as the Granby candidates. She would have been aware that the Labour Group in Liverpool was entering a new era as the militant faction struggled for their survival. Such rationale would fall on deaf ears in a community just recovering from the Sam Bond fiasco.

The fact that Liz perused her decision to its final conclusion would cause some conflict in the Black community. Street walls displayed the opinions of the Federation of Black Organisations – 'Liz Drysdale is a traitor' was the general message. Such opinion did not deter Liz from opening the political doors for those who questioned why we lived in a city with an 8% Black population and no Liverpool Black councillor from a total of 99.

Vote

| Shaun G. Deckon | X |

Granby (10,387), 3 seats

M Ali (L/SDP)	1,087
Mary Armstrong (C)	179
G S Ben-Tovim (Lab)	2,836
June Brandwood (C)	160
D Burris (Fed. Black Orgs)	360
E F Caddick (Comm)	138
S G Deckon (Fed. Black Orgs)	290
Elizabeth Drysdale (Lab)	2,874
Henrietta Edwards (C)	189
B E Grocott (L/SDP)	1,128
P Hughes (Lab)	2,770
Carol Laidlaw (L/SDP)	1,226

No change

The May 1987 election result was not only to confirm the end of the Bond saga, but also saw the formation of a new Labour Council leadership, led by Harry Rimmer and his deputy Alan Dean. There was a renewed optimism that the city had 'better' times ahead. Liz was the only representative Liverpool Black voice in the city council chambers at the time.

From Slums to Turner Prize

To understand how a vibrant Granby was reduced to 'Four Streets', we have to trace the demographic movement of Black families/people across the city of Liverpool.

There is now research depicting the timeline of how a 'Black community' was more or less 'relocated' from the South Dock area to the Granby/Toxteth area. I would highly recommend the following publications for a more comprehensive insight (I will indicate by number when sources are used).

1. *From Pitt Street To Granby* – Writing On The Wall

2. *Social Infrastructure in Granby/Toxteth* – Uduka and Ben-Tovim

3. *Racial Discrimination in Liverpool City Council* – CRE Investigation, 1989

4. *Why Were The Four Streets Emptied Out Anyway* – Jonathan Brown

5. *The Regeneration Game – Who Wins and Who Loses?* – Dennis Mason

In this particular era in Liverpool Black history, there still remained an identifiable 'coloured quarter' or Liverpool Black community on Merseyside. More eloquently described as the *"inner city population resident in certain postcode areas of South Liverpool"* (2).

The area has been daubed with many different descriptions – The Jungle (p. 38), The Ghetto, Southend, Parley, Toxteth, Berkley, L8, The 8... I will briefly describe the area before relocation accelerated.

Princes Road Synagogue   *Greek Orthodox Church*   *Welsh Presbyterian Church*

The Granby/Toxteth area had originally been part of Toxteth Park, owned by the Molyneaux family until 1785. The land was purchased by private developers after the Earl of Sefton was allowed, by an Act of Parliament, to grant building leases.

The location quickly developed from the 18th century, and by the end of the 19th century was one of the most elegant in the city. The area was mostly populated by merchants, diplomats and high-level civil servants (2). The Avenue (Princes Boulevard) was built in the 1860s for the well-to-do classes, known as the Princes Mansions.

Cairns Street

The streets around the Boulevard were built between 1846 and 1914, mainly terraced housing (left) predominantly built by Welsh contractors. It was known as a middle-class, multi-national neighbourhood, many coming from Eastern Europe, including Litvak Jews, Polish and others (2), reflected in the large concentration of religious institutions (above). The composition of the area changed at a rapid pace.

The composition of the Granby area began to change at the end of WWII. The bombing of the South Docks (pp. 34–36) resulted in a large-scale clearance programme.

The movement of middle-class residents away from the Granby-Toxteth area had been an ongoing reality prior to WWII, many moving to suburban areas such as Allerton and Childwall. The postwar government proceeded with their plans to deal with 'slum' housing and bomb damage in most urban areas across the country. Most local councils saw the provision of council housing as the most effective tool. In the case of Liverpool, the majority of 'immigrants' did not meet the criteria for council housing, while local Black families found the council reluctant to provide 'local' housing options and would be offered housing in predominantly White areas (2). Consequently, most of the Black population found ourselves living in rented rooms in multiple occupancy houses with minimal amenities, with Stanhope Street and Parliament Street a core area for Black residents. Landlords owned flats in various states of decay, renting out for as long as it took the council to serve a demolition or compulsory order.

MIDDLE-CLASS MOVEMENT AWAY FROM TOXTETH

(Social Infrastructure in Granby/Toxteth –p. 8)

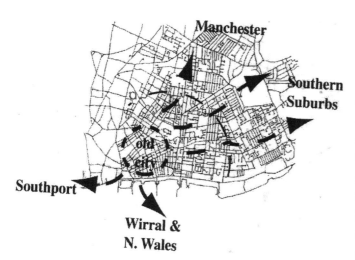

Slum clearance in the 1940s would become the forerunner to never-ending urban programmes, including European funding and housing association development. Liverpool docks was booming during the 1950s, as both cargo and passenger ships reached their peak. This saw more African seamen settle in Granby along with the older established Black community in the area. It is relevant to ask why the area had deteriorated to such an extent since the elegant beginnings of the 18th century. Middle-class migration saw many of the properties in the area falling into disrepair as landlords converted houses into multiple flats, including 'Princes Mansions' (p. 94) and renting them to mostly Black residents. Slum clearance would reach its peak in the 1960s and Granby would rapidly decline.

The 60s would see the construction of a number of 'walk up' and 'tower block' flats in Toxteth and the Dingle neighbourhoods. Granby became the focus of mass demolition. Liverpool City Council condemned most of the terraced housing in Granby as slums and issued compulsory orders. This led to the large-scale demolition of terraced housing. Large parts of the area were left with cleared sites and derelict streets (5). The mention of Granby Street or Toxteth conjured up images of a run-down, dangerous, no-go area. Despite the loss of many services in the area, Granby Street remained a thriving shopping location. The mass demolition would continue into the 70s as we witnessed the realities of so-called slum clearance:

"Whole streets on either side of Granby Street were demolished, clubs closed and the shops on Granby Street were severed from their main source of passing trade when a housing estate was built (Falkner Estate), severing Granby from Upper Parliament Street. Consequently within a few years Granby Street, once thriving, filled with customers of different nationalities and ethnicities, would visibly decline." (5)

As the 60s fizzled out, demolition/slum clearance would become regeneration. Liverpool City Council adopted a policy of improving substandard older houses. This was good news for areas like Granby Street: *"Despite the mass destruction, there still remained around 700 homes that were well constructed, with a solid and practical infrastructure."* (5)

The move towards regeneration would see the setting up of Shelter's Neighbourhood Action Project (SNAP 1969–72). The office was located on the front line: Granby Street.

The introduction of the SNAP Project between 1969 and 1972 was an attempt to stop the demolition of the remaining terraced housing in the Granby area and bring the empty properties back into use. It would be correct to say that the project was 'successful'. It managed to refurbish *"over half of the remaining 740 homes"* (5). For the project, it was not just about the refurbishment; they also believed it was essential to fully involve the local community in the renovation process. They worked hand in hand with the community and set up one of the country's first housing cooperatives, which would be responsible for the renovation process. The housing co-ops were supported by the Cooperative Development Services (CDS), a locally based organisation committed to working with the community on the renovations. They were *"grassroots providers"* (5) who would, years later, become Plus Dane Housing. SNAP would utilise the services of Merseyside Improved Housing (MIH), which became Riverside Housing and Liverpool Housing Trust (LHT).

It transpired that the renovations carried out by the Associations were considered 'substandard', or *"no more than a sticking plaster, rather than a cure for Granby"* (5). The 1974 Housing Act would prove to be a turning point for Liverpool City Council Housing Department. The Act continued the push of regeneration, giving local authorities the power to declare an area a Housing Action Area (HAA). Council housing in the city was in a state of decay. It wasn't long before the wholesale transfer of council housing to Housing Associations. By the 1980s, the Government introduced the 'Estate Action Programmes', which would soon lead to housing associations becoming the main providers of social housing. You could say that Granby was punished following the 1981 disturbances. Houses were boarded up and others left to rot. Worse still, Liverpool Housing Trust abandoned the properties they owned in Granby claiming it was because of *"persistent vandalism and break-ins. Housing Associations also claimed they could not rent out the empty homes, failing to mention that the houses were in a poor state of disrepair."* (5)

Granby Residents Association

The decline of Granby had been a long and painful process. The once thriving street lost its services, post office, chip shop, launderette, bookies, barbers, butchers...

The Commission for Race Equality (CRE) issued a non-discrimination notice against Liverpool City Council Housing Department. In 1989, the CRE conducted a formal investigation into Liverpool's Housing Department. It clearly showed the discriminatory practices towards minority families, summed up in the preface of the Investigation Report:

"The report is concerned with racial discrimination in Liverpool City Council. It showed that the Council discriminated both directly and indirectly in the way in which it nominated members of ethnic minorities to poorer properties. This discrimination existed even in those parts of the South City area of Liverpool where the local ethnic minority population tends to be concentrated."

– Michael Day, Chair Commission For Racial Equality, May 1989 (3)

Following the 1981 riots, the demolition plans resulted in more tenants being forced out of their homes by the council, via compulsory purchase orders. The demolition plans were opposed by remaining residents. It was in February 1993 that the Granby Residents Association (GRA) was formed by Anna Tullulah and Paul Agoro (RIP) in their living room at 59, Cawdor Street. Residents in and around Granby Street received letters from the three main housing associations (LHT, Riverside and CDS), proposing the demolition of their homes. The GRA fought for many years to save what they could of Granby Street. During those years, numerous governmental housing projects emerged, promising the renaissance of Granby, all flattering to deceive – HMR Pathfinder, Renewal Area, Estate Action Programme, Urban Regeneration Strategy, Housing Market Renewal... One of the most 'misleading' was the Granby Toxteth Partnership and their so-called Granby Master Plan, approved by the city council in 2004. It did not get off to a positive start. During the same year, the municipal elections took the whole of the Granby ward with part of the former Abercromby ward, containing the Canning area and parts of Dingle and Toxteth areas, as well as Princes Park itself – the Liverpool Women's Hospital is also within its boundaries – and changed the Granby ward to the Princes ward. Regeneration had officially moved to the gentrification stage.

Gentrification is defined as the process of repairing and rebuilding homes, roads and businesses in a deteriorating area (such as an urban neighbourhood) accompanied by an influx of middle-class or affluent people and often results in the displacement of earlier, usually poorer residents, in a neighbourhood under-going gentrification. However, there remained a number of obstacles, not withstanding resident resistance. The question still remained: how do you attract these professional/affluent people to live in Toxteth?

Let us put this development into perspective. Toxteth was not the only Black neighbourhood in the UK going through this gentrification process. Tiger Bay (Cardiff) – Wales' oldest Black community – saw the removal of planning constraints, creating numerous homes for middle-class executives, while local people were displaced into less desirable estates. Tiger Bay, with a similar history to Black Liverpool, was renamed Cardiff Bay. In Manchester's Moss Side, development was not coupled with employment. In Birmingham, developmental monies were spent on the city centre Bull Ring. At the time of writing, the 'gentrification' Princes Avenue Step Scheme (2020) has commenced the refurbishment plans on the Avenue – not a Black worker on site – although they will display public artwork to celebrate the history and people of Toxteth and Liverpool.

"*The former Transatlantic Slavery Gallery (TSG) was so successful that we have expanded it to create the new International Slavery Museum*" (Int. Slave Museum).

The new International Slavery Museum was opened in the city of Liverpool in 2007. Before we look at the impact of the museum, on the Liverpool economy, we have to recall the Slave Apology by Liverpool City Council in December 1999.

The Liverpool Slave Apology is well documented across the country. I think you know my opinion (p. 64). A protest was held by Black groups (left), who described consultations as 'farcical'. The city council expressed its shame and apologised:

"The Council also commits itself to programmes of action with full participation of Liverpool's Black communities which will seek to combat all forms of racism and discrimination and will recognise and respond to the city's multiracial inheritance and celebrate the skills and talent of all its people."

The main protesters included the Consortium of Black Organisations (CBO), which was formed as a platform for Black enterprise to be part of the Liverpool economic/regeneration surge and the Liverpool Anti-Racist and Community Arts Association (LARCAA) which was established to provide a platform for Black artists and trace the history of Black Liverpool. Maria O'Reilly, Chair of the CBO, described the Apology as *"a publicity stunt"*, *"window dressing and a public relations exercise."* Mark Brown (CBO), with acute foresight, accused the council of *"using the Black community as a Millennium Trophy in the shop window to promote an unreal multi-racial corporate image of Liverpool."* Finally, Jimmy Hernandez (LARCAA) believed there was a *"lack of clarification – we were a bit like there's been no consultation about this – what does this mean, what does an apology for the city's role in slavery actually mean?"*

The local media told us the £10m Slave Trade Museum would be biggest in the country and attract at least 500,000 visitors a year – they were right! At the opening of the International Slavery Museum Gala Dinner (August 2007), museum director David Fleming would comment: *"We are determined that people will remember the strength and the bravery of the enslaved Africans."*

The ISM was/is so successful they decided to completely take control of Black History, both locally and Internationally. In no chronological order, they displayed Black Sambo, Minstrels, Black Jacks, gollywogs... Jessie Jackson, MLK Family, etc. The most 'insulting' to me was the introduction of the KKK (wizard) uniform (p. 100). All the aforementioned should not be in an International Slave Museum.

Their is little doubt that a city in denial of its racist past, and present was now calling the shots. They had now realised the economical tourist benefits to the city. All our (Black) major institutions had diminished since the Slave Apology in 1999, starting with the Charles Wootton Centre in 2000. Regeneration had turned its full cycle, and no Black groups or organisations reaped any of the benefits. The cultural industries excluded any equal participation, and *"Cultural funding was in the hands of White-led and almost exclusive flagships including The Tate, Philharmonic, Liverpool Institute of Performing Arts, NMGM Conservation Centre, St. George's Hall, Playhouse, Everyman"* (see LARCAA). The Mersey visitor economy breaks the £4.5bn barrier, as they continue to tell/sell our story!

The Entertainers

Little Tony   George   Tony   Wally

Marsha Ambrosius

Junior Spencer

Malik Al Nasir

Esco Williams

Tommy Browne

The Chants at the Cavern

It would not be possible for me to do justice to the wide range of Liverpool Black entertainers. There are a number of sources providing a more in-depth insight.

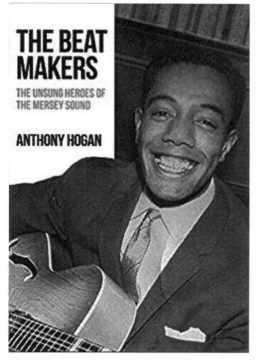

The Beat Makers describes the often-overlooked Black music scene in Liverpool. Although not solely concentrating on the Black contribution to the Merseybeat, it without doubt highlights some magic moments, including the career of Liverpool's own Derry Wilkie, who was *"the first Merseybeat artist to play in Hamburg and to release a record along with the Seniors"* (Anthony Hogan), and the influence of Lord Woodbine (left – with Paul McCartney/Alan Williams), who was basically their manager, along with Alan Williams. It was the multi-talented Woodbine (Harold Phillips) who introduced the Beatles to Hamburg and Liverpool's Black community, as well as forming the city's first all-Caribbean steel band in 1955. For more insight into this relationship, please see *The Man Who Put The Beat Into the Beatles*; *Mersey Beat: A Black Perspective*; 'Lord Woodbine: The forgotten sixth Beatle'; and 'Black Liverpudlian angles on the Beatles' history' (James McGrath).

In 1992, Phillips was offended to discover that he (and Williams) had been air brushed out of a version of the Arnhem photograph, then on display at the Liverpool Playhouse. The omission later prompted Phillips to speculate whether *"the great Beatle publicity machine didn't want any Black man associated with their boys"* (*The Observer*, 2nd August 1998).

I have included the 'original' photo in question (below) with the Beatles, Allan and Beryl Williams and Lord Woodbine: Arnhem War Memorial (16th August 1960).

I also recommend *The Music of Liverpool 8* on Facebook, from Liverpool Black soul legend Ramon 'Sugar' Deen.

Bill Harry (below), the creator of the *Mersey Beat* newspaper in the early 1960s, was one of a few who acknowledged the Black musical influences in Liverpool.

Almost 50 years later, the magic of those years is the subject of books, documentaries and exhibitions – a tribute to the efforts of many local individuals and groups. For my part, I would like to conclude this section with my recollections of the 'soul' days of the 1960/70s. As a teenager, I recall that live music venues were plentiful, from Liverpool to Chester. Geno Washington and The Ram Jam Band, Ike and Tina Turner and the Ikettes, Jimmy James and the Vagabonds, Ben E King, James Brown, Smokey, Tempts, Drifters, Tops, Stax, Motown, jazz and reggae. The *Blues & Soul* magazine was my bible.

Many of the local Black groups would appear on the Masonic, a public house in the city centre. Absolute class. The In Crowd's (p. 106) version of 'The In Crowd', released by Dobie Gray (1964), would move any crowd. The Chants single 'A Lover's Story' (1967) should have made the top 10. Bernie Wenton also formed the Buzz Brothers with Willie and Bobby. Despite winning *Stars in Their Eyes* (1991), he was never given the recognition he deserved. Nevertheless, the Buzz Brothers group is named on Mathew Street's Wall of Fame. The deep emotion of Ebony Gray (2) singing Labre Siffre's 'Something Inside So Strong', the stirring rendition of 'Old Man River' by the Gems and the Real Thing 'classic' 'Children of the Ghetto'... Gerald and Colin Ayreety (1) Sugar Deen (3) The Harlems, The Valentines, Distinction, Rudy, Delado, Simply Soul, the Russian, L8 Connection and Soul 8... For me, the late legend Tommy Browne (p. 106) was inspirational. So many exciting artists. I apologise to those not included.

★★★ TOWN GATE SOCIAL CLUB - GREAT HARWOOD ★★★
CABARET - FRIDAY - SATURDAY - SUNDAY at 10 p.m.

THE GEMS

Fantastic Coloured Show Group
Liverpool's Latest Recording Stars
★ Radio 1 ★
ON STAGE 10-30 p.m.

The Gems:

Denny Christian
Tommy Brown
Roger Christian
Lawrence Griffin
Robbie Ellis
(replaced Dave Clay)

The Sports Personalities

ONE FORMED
FROM MANY
E pluribus unum

A. Lewis

ALFIE LEWIS
ROLL OF HONOUR

1977 Junior British Champion
1983 World Champion
1987 World Champion
1990 World Champion
1981 Third in World
        Championships
1985 Second in World
        Championships

1980 European Champion
1981 European Champion
1982 European Champion
1986 European Champion
1988 European Champion
1990 European Champion
1989 European Cup
14 British Championships
Captain of the Great Britain
Team since 1980

British Team coach 1990

Voted Fighter of the Decade
1990
Voted Combat Magazine's
Fighter of the Year 1985
HALL OF FAME 1989

Gloria Hyatt – Liverpool and Northern 100 Metres Champion

The success of the L8 community in the world of sport is phenomenal in every genre. I could not do the subject justice, only provide a taste of the existing talent.

The Heritage Development Company originated in 2016 and continued in the tradition of highlighting the history of Black Liverpool. 'Old school' local Black activists (left) Louis Julienne, Albert Fontenot and Ray Quarless are joined by newly elected Mayor (Anna Rothery), for the opening of their latest exhibition *Black Punch/Black to the Future*: historical coverage of Liverpool Black and L8 boxers. This followed the excellent *Legacy of Liverpool Black Music Exhibition*.

Below: *1. Rodney Mac; 2. Trent Alexander-Arnold; 3. Donna Alleyne; 4. Nakita Parris; 5. Fidel O'Rourke; 6. Abdi Sharif; 7. Remi Savage; 8. Katarina Johnson-Thompson; 9. Anyika Onuora; 10. Marcel Braithwaite; 11. Michael Ihiekwe; 12. Layton Julienne Nichols signing for LFC 2017 at 8 years of age; 12a. Marcus Lewis.*

Amateur Football in L8

Old School Liverpool Black Squad

Coach: Howard Gayle (Gayley)
Manager: Stephen Skeete (Bull)
Assistant: Dave Clay (Clayman)

Substitutes

John Stevens
Ste Estridge
Ian Prendergast (Spongy)
Alan Martins (Bert)
Arthur Miriah
Jay Sampson
Tony Morris (Mogsy)

On Standby

Ray Quintel
Ian Stephens
Ian Braithwaite
Eddie Clarke

Ray Warren   Eddie Johnson (Johno)   Neil Clarke (Smiler)   Chris Hoy

Chris Browne   Steve Davies (Davo)   Michael Owalabi (The Gaffer –Capt.)   Eugene Lamb (Lama)

Charles Kadri (Kads)   Rodney McDonald (Maca)

There is no dispute that the FA Sunday Cup, aka National Cup, is the most prestigious trophy in Sunday Amateur Football across the country.

F.A.
SUNDAY CUP
FINAL
SEASON 1988/89

SOVEREIGN RUBBER   SOVEREIGN RUBBER

Almethak F.C.
versus
East Levenshulme F.C.
at
Edgeley Park
on
Sunday 14th May, 1989

OFFICIAL PROGRAMME
PRICE 50p

The FA Sunday Cup trophy was presented to the Football Association (FA) by the football-loving Shah of Iran, Mohammed Reza Shah Pahlavia, as a gift to mark the centenary of the FA in 1963. It was made by an Iranian silversmith (above). Since its introduction in the 1964-65 season, Liverpool teams have won the coveted trophy on 13 occasions and been runners-up 6 times, Croxteth-based Lobster FC being the first Scouse winners in the 1978-9 season. Liverpool 8 local teams have a share in the glory. Nicosia led the way with two wins (1990–1/2003–4). Dingle Rail won it first in 1981–2, while Almethak (above) swept up all before them in their debut 1988–9 season, winning the FA Sunday Cup – Liverpool Sunday League Premier Title and the Ken Gillies Memorial Cup.

Renowned journalist and author, **Hyder Jaward (inset), is in the process of researching Black footballers/teams in Liverpool – an eagerly awaited publication with the full support of local footballers past and present.**

After 40+ years involvement in amateur football as a player and manager, I have to give 100% praise to those dedicated league committee members and team managers, who have ensured that grassroot football survives. The centre photo (below) epitomises this: where the old school committee members of the Liverpool Business Houses (LBH) League dealt with 7 cup finals in one day. Left to Right: Billy Flanagan, Jack Mercer, Bill Roberts, Jack Lavender **[Pic by Billy Flanagan Picturebook]**. During most of my 'stint', amateur football was thriving across the city. Liverpool 8 (L8) had an abundance of teams. Sefton Park was the home ground for most. So-called 'Black' teams emerged because the teams were formed in the Black community and associated with local establishments/pubs, e.g. Stanley House, Bedford FC, Methodist, Caribbean, Coach and Horses, The Windsor, Toxteth SC, Kavanaghs, Sana/Yeman FC (top), Tiber Puma Almethak (bottom) – mostly local Black managers.

In reality, the so-called 'Black' teams also had White players while most of the teams across the area, and the city, had a 'sprinkling' of Black players. Most, not all, of the L8 teams played in the Liverpool and District Sunday League/Liverpool Business Houses League; most Saturday teams were in the Liverpool League or the Liverpool and District CMS League. As you may imagine, any competitive game (for points or friendly) against our Dingle (L8) neighbours, who had some great sides – e.g. Dingle Rail, St. Pat's, Mt. Carmel, Farmers Arms, Etnaward Ward, Pineapple, to name a few – would be a full head-on 'derby'. They were just the local clashes. I would like to believe that all 'Black' teams dealt with racism and won the respect of most Liverpool teams and respective leagues via their skill and determination, not to mention being 'Scousers'.

There was a period when amateur football was in decline. Countless teams were folding, local playing fields being closed, including Sefton Park. The rising ground hire fees, the closure of many pubs, criticism of the strict 'financial control' of league committees and the 'apathy' of young players all played a part. The most worrying development was the fall of leagues, established for countless years, such as the Wirral League (46 years), where League Secretary, Dave Lea, must be commended for his dedication to amateur football on the Wirral. We have seen a revival as the District Sunday League and the Liverpool Business Houses flourish (see *Amateur football is dying on Merseyside* – Corinthian).

Black to the Future

Curtis Jones (left) started playing for Liverpool FC at under-9s level. By the age of 17, he had signed a professional contract.

He made his first team debut (Jan 2019) v Wolves in the FA Cup, followed by v MK Dons (EFL Sept 2019) and v Arsenal (EFL Oct 2019), making his Premier debut v Bournemouth (Dec 2019) and scoring the winner v Everton (Jan FA Cup 3rd Round).

Meshech (Shack) Speares (right) aka 'Mr Notorious' began his boxing career in 2017 in the lightweight division.

He has recently turned professional and has been successful in all of his six outings to date.

Speares is an exciting local prospect, hard-working and determined to make a major impact in his respective division.

Sisterhood

Meeting Place
Liverpool Black Sisters

photo By LBS

is Powerful

Ifully acknowledge that this historic document has been from a Liverpool Black male perspective. In reality, the contributions of both Black and White women has been crucial.

It would only be right for me to show recognition to the pivotal role of White mothers with Black children or in a relationship with a Black male. They became the topic of racial abuse, and some found themselves disowned by immediate family.

Most showed an inner strength aimed at protecting their children from this direct racism. Many of these mothers were single parents raising Black families in a 'challenging' environment.

It was not long before local Black women started to form groups/organisations of their own.

For the purposes of 'equality', *Sisterhood is Powerful* has been compiled by two respected Liverpool Black women.

We are honoured to be asked by Dave (Clay) to contribute our thoughts to this historic documentation of Liverpool Black History.

We cannot name every woman who campaigned, made personal sacrifices or volunteered to challenge racism and fought for justice and equality, whilst themselves facing racism, sexism and discrimination. We ask you, the reader, to remember who stood beside you when on protest campaigns whilst working for racial justice, including yourself. This way, no one is forgotten: you could scribble their name in the margins of the book or email the author (daveyclay@hotmail.com) so they are recorded and no longer hidden from our history.

Looking back, we reflected on the negative image of Black women stereotypes – aggressive, sexual and ugly. The 'Fletcher Report' demonstrated how academics influenced and perpetuated the stereotypes from the 1930s onwards, evidenced in the 70s by the *Listener* article. In the late 50s and 60s, we had been influenced by American civil rights: the Black Panther movement was relevant to us Black women. The media demonised Angela Davies as a terrorist. We, as Black teenagers, started the embryonic Black women's movement looking for guidance and a solution to racism as Black youth formed the Green Jackets (p. 42) and us women joining this movement.

In developing our sense of self-worth as a Black women's movement, our struggles came as a challenge to the White feminist movement; influenced by Germaine Greer and others, it did not extend to our community. For example, we attended an L8 Women's group meeting in the 80s, held at the Mona pub in Liverpool town centre. There were no Black women present, with around 50 White women. We attended to protest about a Black woman who had contacted the then Rape Crisis group, with an all-White staff. After she disclosed that she had been raped, she was asked if the attacker was Black or White – she said Black. The racist response from the call handler was "what do you expect from a Black man?"

Much of our struggles intertwined with defence against racism, directed at both men and women. We were, and still are, the descendants of over five hundred years of indigenous Black Liverpudlians, against a background of Enoch Powell's Rivers of Blood speech and the 1940s Windrush racism. As Black women, we organised to provide the social infrastructure, that, despite paying council tax, Liverpool 8 was denied. Our fathers found themselves unable to access social clubs in White communities and formed their own social and welfare clubs to meet the challenge of unequal allocation of resources by Liverpool City Council and others to Liverpool 8 and for Black families settled across Merseyside. We as women looked to campaign for equal access to welfare and social infrastructure, hence our Black women's movement developed into an organisation called Liverpool Black Sisters, at first a loose alliance of all Black women interested in women's equality and racial justice across every aspect of our rights, including our family mental health services, sheltered accommodation for Black elders, childcare, campaigns against police brutality and domestic violence.

These were campaigns which took us to challenge mainstream politics and saw the formation of many organisations, including the Liverpool Black Organisation, Federation of Liverpool Black Organisations, Consortium of Black Organisations, Black Caucus and the Liverpool 8 Defence Committee. The FLBO (p. 92) stood two independent candidates as a direct challenge to the discrimination perpetuated by the Labour administration. Lack of access to employment and discrimination of the few Black workers they employed, and we had two Black women councillors, one vilified by local and national press (p. 13) for her personal life when she was very young, which had no bearing on her political ability or skills, the other (p. 91) retired, exhausted and worn down by the constant battle against racism. In conclusion, much of the social welfare voluntary structure developed in the Black community has either closed down or been absorbed into mainstream provision, moving away from the Black service users' approach.

Funding streams are not meeting grassroots need. Most of the Black service provision has been taken over by large White voluntary organisations.

The constraints of the Legal Services Commission has closed law centres across the country, not least Liverpool 8, and that expertise is lost to large law firms who themselves have had to amalgamate to meet contract demands. Women were at the forefront of these developments, providing the stability, tenacity and working as equals alongside men in the struggles for racial justice. On the political front, we now have five black councillors, three of whom are women, a Black woman mayoress and a newly appointed Liverpudlian Black Member of Parliament. Whilst this is a cause for pride, we still have little access to employment in the city centre, despite our youngsters achieving in higher education. Millions of pounds of investment in the city over the past ten years, new schools built and unaffordable housing has not yet translated into access of apprenticeships for our youth. We as women have watched husbands and partners racially abused, our children beaten and criminalised in the 70s and 80s by racist police and the criminal justice system. We have campaigned against every attempt to dehumanise us as women and as a community. We have changed things by our opposition to injustice. We are encouraged to see young women going forward doing the same for us in education, health, legal services, housing, domestic violence, drugs service, mental health, film, arts, anti-racism, politics and childcare. For further insight, check Suzanne Morris (Suzy Mo) – a member of the Liverpool Black Sisters for over 25 years – who sums up the work of the group (see Museum of Liverpool: *Liverpool Black Sisters Doing It for Themselves*).

Thanks Linda and Maria for your ongoing contribution to Liverpool Black History

As the sisters rightly state, they *"have changed things by our opposition to injustice."* So many Liverpool Blacks have made significant contributions in most areas; I identify a few of many:

Education: Wally Brown, Claire Dove, Debbie Mende, Gloria Hyatt, Dave Clay, Lenford White, John Cole, Irene Loh Lynn, Linda Loy, Albert Fontenot, Alex Bennett, Pam Brown, Ruby Dixon, Annette Tagoe.

Academia: Ray Costello, Stephen Small, Mark Christian, Mike Boyle, David Thompson, Maurice Bessman.

Housing: Louis Julienne, Ray Quarless, Tracey Gore, Dennis Mason, Sonia Bassey, Paul Peng, David Wilkie.

Probation/Care/Health/Employment: John Joel, Manneh Brown, Michelle Cox, Judith Cummings, Karl Smith, Yvonne Griffin, Sunsha, Geraldine and Paul Ambrosius, Nze, Joe Joel, Ray Smith, Martha Igbinovia.

Law/Legal: George White, Maria O'Reilly, Alan Gayle, Solly Bassey, Felicia Oshodi, Dave Smith, Donna Maria.

Liverpool Black Sisters march against police brutality, 1991.

BALL OF CONFUSION

Photo: Alan Thompson

Kim Johnson (inset) is Liverpool's first Black MP (12th December 2019), while Joanne Marie Anderson (Princes Park) and Calvin Smeda (Picton) were also elected as councillors in their respective constituencies.

The decade was ending on a positive note with historical achievements, including the first Liverpool Black Lord Mayor and MP for 700 years. The election of Kim Johnson (Riverside) as a Member of Parliament clearly demonstrated how the Liverpool Black community/Individuals have progressed, politically, since the appointment of Glynn Pratt, almost 30 years previously (p. 92).

I have endeavoured throughout this historical document to be honest and give my perspective on events that have impacted the Liverpool Black community, and where possible provide supporting evidence. Despite the latter, this final section has to be articulated from a more personal point of view. There are many aspects of the Liverpool Black experience that, I believe, have contributed towards our 'position' today, including:

1. The loss of our local clubs and social outlets (p. 40);
2. The 'destruction' of Granby Street (p. 94);
3. The effects of Regeneration/Gentrification (p. 96);
4. The demise of local Black voluntary/educational organisations and groups (p.102);
5. The increase of mental health issues in the area;
6. The realities of Black-on-Black violence/drug abuse;
7. The redirection of funding to other minority groups;
8. Institutionalised racism.

Mary Seacole House

Before commenting on the above factors, I am proud to note that many of our present generation of young people are excelling in education and competing for professional vocations. Respect to those parents and families. There is little doubt that the gradual loss of local 'social venues' (1) had a devastating effect in regard to social interaction. Clubs and pubs, frequented mostly by local Black and White families throughout the generations, soon became part of the Liverpool 8 'housing boom'. The demise of Granby Street (2), as both a legendary shopping and meeting location, had a similar impact. It is clear to see why the Caribbean Centre 'occupation' (p. 69) was conducted with such determination. The effects of compulsory purchase orders, housing policies and gentrification (p. 98) split up large sections of the established community, put into a realistic perspective by the late Dorothy Kuya (p. 98).

There are many reasons why organisations disband. The voluntary sector is dependent on funding, usually from government sources, local councils or charitable organisations. In all such situations, there are terms and conditions that have to be adhered to. The lifespan of such organisations is always precarious. Despite this, many Liverpool Black organisations were approaching a quarter of century in existence. Most were formed to address issues of racism and exclusion in public sectors, including education, employment, law, police relations, Black history, arts, community relations, social services, anti-apartheid and youth. All provided a service to the Black/White community. They are gone, and what remains was predicted by Mark Brown in his comments following the Slave Apology: *"Using the Black community as a Millennium Trophy in the shop window to promote an unreal multi-racial corporate image of Liverpool"* (p. 105). You could say we now have a 'Black Elite'!

The growth of mental health services in Liverpool 8 is a clear signal that all may not be well in regard to the mental state of our area. Mary Seacole House (MSH) was established during the early 1990s to cater for 'minorities' with mental health issues, fulfilling the original vision/ work of the Granby Community Mental Health Group. The fact that the MSH need more resources confirms the demand for their service. Increasing mental health issues are having a direct impact within the Liverpool Black community (see 'Mental Health in L8: The Debate' – *Granby Toxteth Review*, Issue 5).

The early years of the new millennium would bring a 'new' dimension to the Liverpool Black community. Between 2000 and 2003, there had been five murders involving firearms.

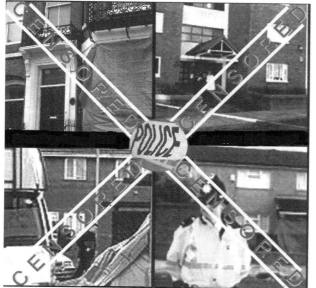

The experiences of the Liverpool multiracial population had entrenched what I would describe as a 'sense of community', namely a Black community. These murders were a blow to that belief.

As editor of the **Granby Toxteth Review**, I wrote to Merseyside Chief Constable Norman Bettison (27th November 2003) and asked a specific question: *"How many Black people have been murdered, via the use of firearms, since 2000?"* The chief passed the request on to the Major Incidents Team, who responded (15th December 2003): *"Between 2000 and 2003, there have been five murders involving firearms, whereby the victims have been Afro Caribbean."*

In fact, the victims were mostly Liverpool-born Black people. It was a period when Black-on-Black violence was at its peak, with countless families affected.

In 2020, we must ask the questions: how many Black youth have been murdered via the use of a knife or gun? Is Black-on-Black violence a reality in Liverpool? The answers do not equal 'a sense of community'. One thing for sure is that the Liverpool Black population is now dispersed and low down in the pecking order of 'minorities'. I would add that this is reflected both economically and socially. I have endeavoured to provide an historic overview of the Liverpool Black experience since 1919. I have made it clear that it is based on my own perspective and involvement in some of the issues identified. It was never possible to include ALL our history, characters, organisations, experiences or those magic and tragic moments. To compensate for this, I have included, where possible, sources that provide further information on the subject. None of this would have been 'real' grassroots without the help of those who contributed to the GoFundMe campaign – so humbled and proud. So many people helped me, in particular my friends. I needed their feedback, opinions and advice. We are all part of the same experience of being Black and born in Liverpool. We all have a Liverpool Black History.

A small contribution to Liverpool Black History.

Acknowledgements:

Gideon Ben Tovim
Ray Quarless
Jay Sampson
Ivan Freeman
Graham Lee
Dennis Mason
Steve Smith
Bill Harpe
Mark Sweeney
Joe Joel
Howard Gayle
Grant Jackson
Mark Christian
Gloria Hyatt

km
10 km = 6.2 miles

🕐 h

	Bordeaux	Clermont-Ferrand	Dijon	Dunkerque	Grenoble	Le Havre	Lyon	Marseille	Nancy	Nantes	Paris	Reims	Strasbourg	Toulouse	Tours
Bordeaux		375 / 3:45	650 / 6:25	883 / 8:00	664 / 6:10	658 / 6:10	540 / 5:10	641 / 5:50	860 / 8:10	353 / 3:15	586 / 5:20	722 / 6:30	945 / 8:55	242 / 2:20	348 / 3:10
Clermont-Ferrand	375 / 3:45		338 / 3:10	716 / 6:30	275 / 2:45	580 / 5:35	166 / 1:45	470 / 4:25	544 / 5:00	536 / 4:45	427 / 3:55	563 / 5:00	635 / 5:45	378 / 3:45	335 / 3:00
Dijon	650 / 6:25	338 / 3:10		577 / 5:05	301 / 2:50	508 / 4:50	196 / 1:55	502 / 4:35	216 / 2:10	640 / 5:45	315 / 3:05	296 / 2:40	331 / 3:10	675 / 6:30	416 / 3:40
Dunkerque	883 / 8:00	716 / 6:30	577 / 5:05		878 / 7:35	311 / 3:00	763 / 6:40	1069 / 9:25	473 / 4:50	640 / 5:55	295 / 3:00	283 / 2:40	630 / 6:15	971 / 8:55	543 / 5:00
Grenoble	664 / 6:10	275 / 2:45	301 / 2:50	878 / 7:35		765 / 6:55	110 / 1:15	306 / 2:50	515 / 4:35	792 / 7:10	572 / 5:10	598 / 5:05	573 / 5:10	530 / 4:45	607 / 5:25
Le Havre	658 / 6:10	580 / 5:35	508 / 4:50	311 / 3:00	765 / 6:55		660 / 6:00	966 / 8:45	543 / 5:30	384 / 3:50	207 / 2:15	359 / 3:20	703 / 6:15	848 / 7:50	308 / 3:05
Lyon	540 / 5:10	166 / 1:45	196 / 1:55	763 / 6:40	110 / 1:15	660 / 6:00		312 / 2:55	403 / 3:40	685 / 6:05	466 / 4:15	492 / 4:10	492 / 4:25	537 / 4:50	490 / 4:25
Marseille	641 / 5:50	470 / 4:25	502 / 4:35	1069 / 9:25	306 / 2:50	966 / 8:45	312 / 2:55		709 / 6:25	985 / 8:40	773 / 7:00	798 / 6:55	802 / 7:10	403 / 3:50	797 / 7:05
Nancy	860 / 8:10	544 / 5:00	216 / 2:10	473 / 4:50	515 / 4:35	543 / 5:30	403 / 3:40	709 / 6:25		753 / 6:45	385 / 3:40	196 / 2:25	161 / 1:45	885 / 8:20	553 / 4:50
Nantes	353 / 3:15	536 / 4:45	640 / 5:45	640 / 5:55	792 / 7:10	384 / 3:50	685 / 6:05	985 / 8:40	753 / 6:45		389 / 3:40	525 / 4:45	869 / 7:40	585 / 5:10	215 / 2:10
Paris	586 / 5:20	427 / 3:55	315 / 3:05	295 / 3:00	572 / 5:10	207 / 2:15	466 / 4:15	773 / 7:00	385 / 3:40	389 / 3:40		146 / 1:30	490 / 4:25	679 / 6:15	245 / 2:20
Reims	722 / 6:30	563 / 5:00	296 / 2:40	283 / 2:40	598 / 5:05	359 / 3:20	492 / 4:10	798 / 6:55	196 / 2:25	525 / 4:45	146 / 1:30		353 / 3:10	815 / 7:20	373 / 3:25
Strasbourg	945 / 8:55	635 / 5:45	331 / 3:10	630 / 6:15	573 / 5:10	703 / 6:15	492 / 4:25	802 / 7:10	161 / 1:45	869 / 7:40	490 / 4:25	353 / 3:10		972 / 9:05	695 / 6:05
Toulouse	242 / 2:20	378 / 3:45	675 / 6:30	971 / 8:55	530 / 4:45	848 / 7:50	537 / 4:50	403 / 3:50	885 / 8:20	585 / 5:10	679 / 6:15	815 / 7:20	972 / 9:05		528 / 5:15
Tours	348 / 3:10	335 / 3:00	416 / 3:40	543 / 5:00	607 / 5:25	308 / 3:05	490 / 4:25	797 / 7:05	553 / 4:50	215 / 2:10	245 / 2:20	373 / 3:25	695 / 6:05	528 / 5:15	

1 : 4 500 000

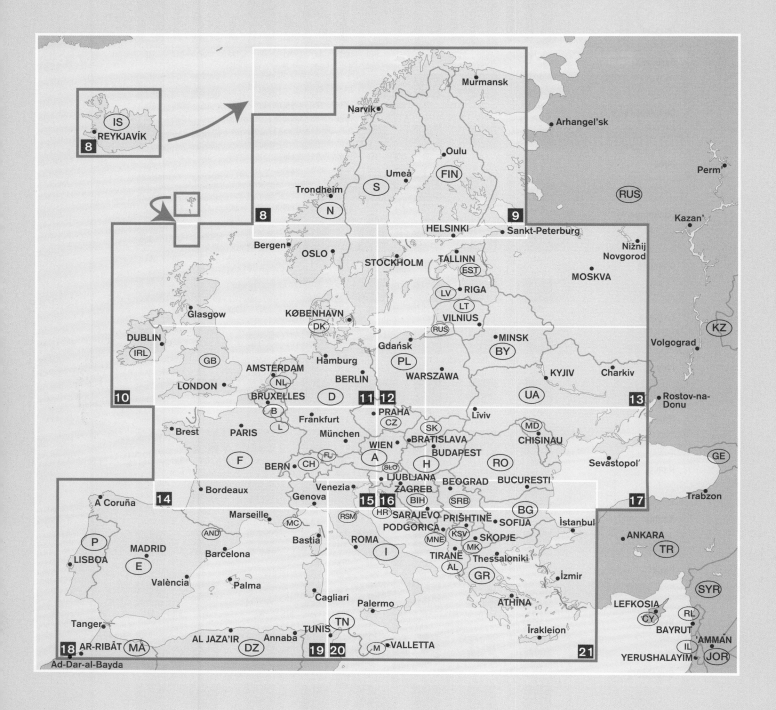

1 : 4 500 000

Légende / Legenda — Zeichenerklärung / Objaśnienia znaków — Legend / Vysvětlivky — Segni convenzionali / Legenda — Sinais convencionais / Legenda — Signos convencionales / Tumač znakova

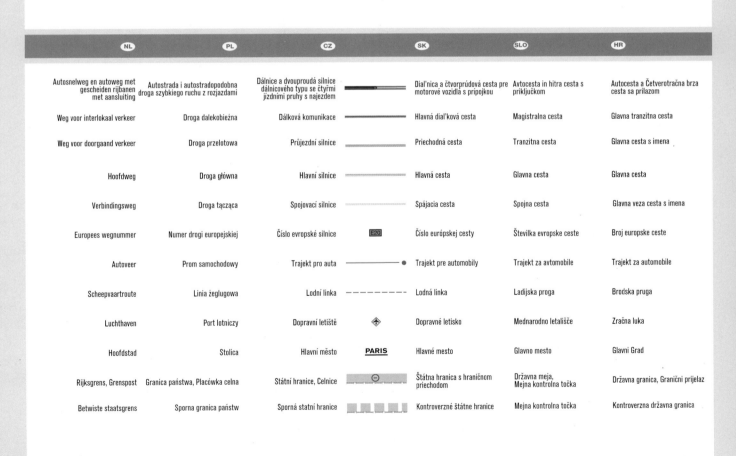

(F)	(D)	(UK)	(I)	(P)	(E)
Autoroute et chaussée double de type autoroutier avec point de jonction	Autobahn und autobahnähnliche Schnellstraße mit Anschlussstelle	Motorway and dual carriageway with motorway characteristics	Autostrada e doppio carreggiata di tipo autostradale con stazione	Auto-estrada e via rápida de faixas separadas com ramal de acesso	Autopista y autovía con enlace
Route à grande circulation	Fernverkehrsstraße	Trunk road	Strada di grande comunicazione	Estrada nacional principal	Ruta de larga distancia
Route de transit	Durchgangsstraße	Thoroughfare	Strada di attraversamento	Estrada de trânsito	Carretera de tránsito
Route principale	Hauptstraße	Main road	Strada principale	Estrada principal	Carretera principal
Route de communication	Verbindungsstraße	Connecting road	Strada di collegamento	Estrada de ligação	Carretera de enlace
Numéro de route européenne	Europastraßennummer	European road number [E20]	Numero di strada europea	Número de estrada europeia	Número de carretera europea
Bac pour automobiles	Autofähre	Car ferry	Traghetto per automobili	Balsa para viaturas	Ferry
Ligne de navigation	Schifffahrtslinie	Shipping route	Linea maríttima	Linha de navegação	Ruta marítima
Aéroport	Verkehrsflughafen	Airport	Aeroporto	Aeroporto	Aeroporto
Capitale	Hauptstadt	Capital PARIS	Capitale di Stato	Capital	Capital
Frontière d'État, Point de contrôle	Staatsgrenze, Grenzkontrollstelle	National boundary, Check-point	Confine di Stato, Punto di controllo	Fronteira nacional, Posto de controlo	Frontera de Estado, Control
Frontière d'État contestée	Umstrittene Staatsgrenze	Disputed international boundary	Confine di stato contestato	Fronteira nacional disputável	Frontera estatal discutida

(NL)	(PL)	(CZ)	(SK)	(SLO)	(HR)
Autosnelweg en autoweg met gescheiden rijbanen met aansluiting	Autostrada i autostradopodobna droga szybkiego ruchu z rozjazdami	Dálnice a dvouproudá silnice dálnicového typu se čtyřmi jízdními pruhy s najezdem	Dial'nica a čtvorprúdová cesta pre motorové vozidlá s prípojkou	Avtocesta in hitra cesta s priključkom	Autocesta a Četverotračna brza cesta sa prilazom
Weg voor interlokaal verkeer	Droga dalekobieżna	Dálková komunikace	Hlavná dial'ková cesta	Magistralna cesta	Glavna tranzitna cesta
Weg voor doorgaand verkeer	Droga przelotowa	Průjezdní silnice	Priechodná cesta	Tranzitna cesta	Glavna cesta s imena
Hoofdweg	Droga główna	Hlavní silnice	Hlavná cesta	Glavna cesta	Glavna cesta
Verbindingsweg	Droga tącząca	Spojovací silnice	Spájacia cesta	Spojna cesta	Glavna veza cesta s imena
Europees wegnummer	Numer drogi europejskiej	Číslo evropské silnice [E20]	Číslo európskej cesty	Številka evropske ceste	Broj europske ceste
Autoveer	Prom samochodowy	Trajekt pro auta	Trajekt pre automobily	Trajekt za avtomobile	Trajekt za automobile
Scheepvaartroute	Linia żeglugowa	Lodní linka	Lodná linka	Ladijska proga	Brodska pruga
Luchthaven	Port lotniczy	Dopravní letiště	Dopravné letisko	Mednarodno letališče	Zračna luka
Hoofdstad	Stolica	Hlavní město PARIS	Hlavné mesto	Glavno mesto	Glavni Grad
Rijksgrens, Grenspost	Granica państwa, Placówka celna	Státní hranice, Celnice	Štátna hranica s hraničnom priechodom	Državna meja, Mejna kontrolna točka	Državna granica, Granični prijelaz
Betwiste staatsgrens	Sporna granica państw	Sporná statní hranice	Kontroverzné štátne hranice	Mejna kontrolna točka	Kontroverzna državna granica

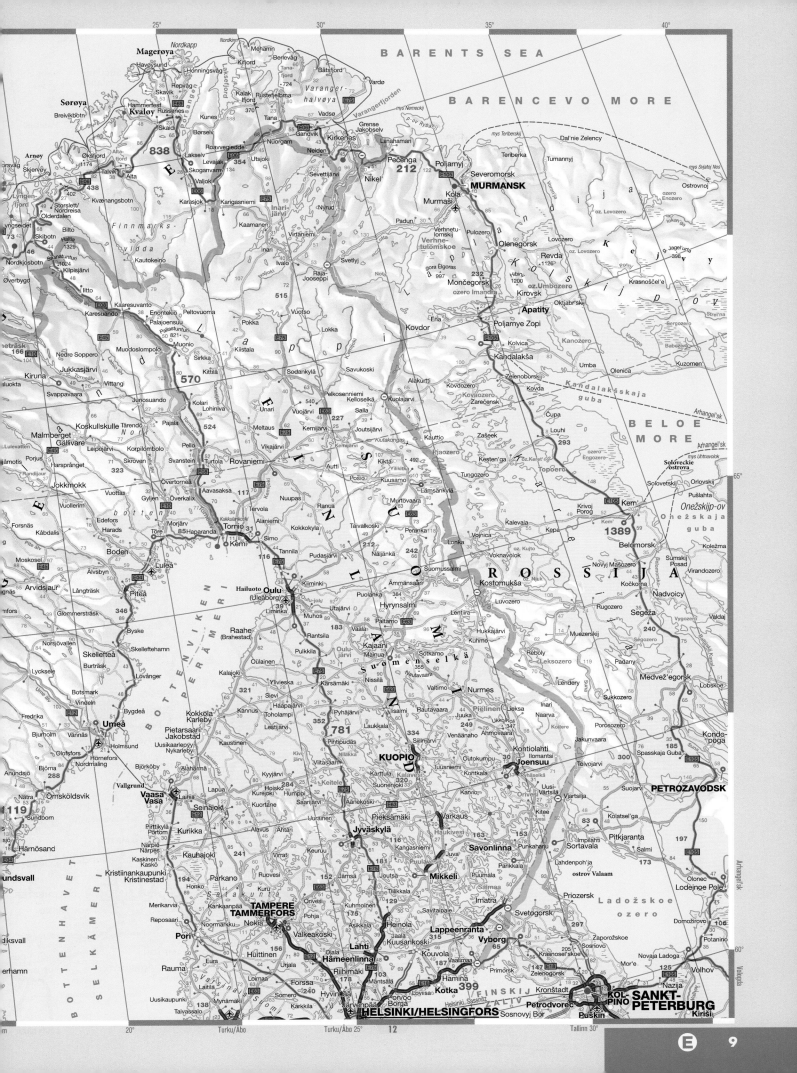

1 : 300 000

Légende
Zeichenerklärung

Legend
Segni convenzionali

CIRCULATION (F) / VERKEHR (D)
(UK) TRAFFIC / (I) COMUNICAZIONI

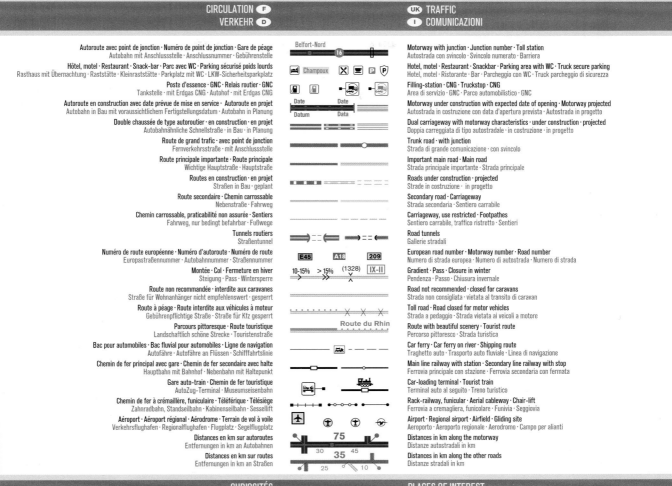

Autoroute avec point de jonction · Numéro de point de jonction · Gare de péage Autobahn mit Anschlussstelle · Anschlussnummer · Gebührenstelle	Motorway with junction · Junction number · Toll station Autostrada con svincolo · Svincolo numerato · Barriera
Hôtel, motel · Restaurant · Snack-bar · Parc avec WC · Parking sécurisé poids lourds Rasthaus mit Übernachtung · Raststätte · Kleinraststätte · Parkplatz mit WC · LKW-Sicherheitsparkplatz	Hotel, motel · Restaurant · Snackbar · Parking area with WC · Truck secure parking Hotel, motel · Ristorante · Bar · Parcheggio con WC · Truck parcheggio di sicurezza
Poste d'essence · GNC · Relais routier · GNC Tankstelle · mit Erdgas CNG · Autohof · mit Erdgas CNG	Filling-station · CNG · Truckstop · CNG Area di servizio · GNC · Parco automobilistico · GNC
Autoroute en construction avec date prévue de mise en service · Autoroute en projet Autobahn in Bau mit voraussichtlichem Fertigstellungsdatum · Autobahn in Planung	Motorway under construction with expected date of opening · Motorway projected Autostrada in costruzione con data d'apertura prevista · Autostrada in progetto
Double chaussée de type autoroutier · en construction · en projet Autobahnähnliche Schnellstraße · in Bau · in Planung	Dual carriageway with motorway characteristics · under construction · projected Doppia carreggiata di tipo autostradale · in costruzione · in progetto
Route de grand trafic · avec point de jonction Fernverkehrsstraße · mit Anschlussstelle	Trunk road · with junction Strada di grande comunicazione · con svincolo
Route principale importante · Route principale Wichtige Hauptstraße · Hauptstraße	Important main road · Main road Strada principale importante · Strada principale
Routes en construction · en projet Straßen in Bau · geplant	Roads under construction · projected Strade in costruzione · in progetto
Route secondaire · Chemin carrossable Nebenstraße · Fahrweg	Secondary road · Carriageway Strada secondaria · Sentiero carrabile
Chemin carrossable, praticabilité non assurée · Sentiers Fahrweg, nur bedingt befahrbar · Fußwege	Carriageway, use restricted · Footpaths Sentiero carrabile, traffico ristretto · Sentieri
Tunnels routiers Straßentunnel	Road tunnels Gallerie stradali
Numéro de route européenne · Numéro d'autoroute · Numéro de route Europastraßennummer · Autobahnnummer · Straßennummer	European road number · Motorway number · Road number Numero di strada europea · Numero di autostrada · Numero di strada
Montée · Col · Fermeture en hiver Steigung · Pass · Wintersperre	Gradient · Pass · Closure in winter Pendenza · Passo · Chiusura invernale
Route non recommandée · interdite aux caravanes Straße für Wohnanhänger nicht empfehlenswert · gesperrt	Road not recommended · closed for caravans Strada non consigliata · vietata al transito di caravan
Route à péage · Route interdite aux véhicules à moteur Gebührenpflichtige Straße · Straße für Kfz gesperrt	Toll road · Road closed for motor vehicles Strada a pedaggio · Strada vietata ai veicoli a motore
Parcours pittoresque · Route touristique Landschaftlich schöne Strecke · Touristenstraße	Route with beautiful scenery · Tourist route Percorso pittoresco · Strada turistica
Bac pour automobiles · Bac fluvial pour automobiles · Ligne de navigation Autofähre · Autofähre an Flüssen · Schifffahrtslinie	Car ferry · Car ferry on river · Shipping route Traghetto auto · Trasporto auto fluviale · Linea di navigazione
Chemin de fer principal avec gare · Chemin de fer secondaire avec halte Hauptbahn mit Bahnhof · Nebenbahn mit Haltepunkt	Main line railway with station · Secondary line railway with stop Ferrovia principale con stazione · Ferrovia secondaria con fermata
Gare auto-train · Chemin de fer touristique AutoZug-Terminal · Museumseisenbahn	Car-loading terminal · Tourist train Terminal auto al seguito · Treno turistico
Chemin de fer à crémaillère, funiculaire · Téléférique · Télésiège Zahnradbahn, Standseilbahn · Kabinenseilbahn · Sessellift	Rack-railway, funicular · Aerial cableway · Chair-lift Ferrovia a cremagliera, funicolare · Funivia · Seggiovia
Aéroport · Aéroport régional · Aérodrome · Terrain de vol à voile Verkehrsflughafen · Regionalflughafen · Flugplatz · Segelflugplatz	Airport · Regional airport · Airfield · Gliding site Aeroporto · Aeroporto regionale · Aerodromo · Campo per alianti
Distances en km sur autoroutes Entfernungen in km an Autobahnen	Distances in km along the motorway Distanze autostradali in km
Distances en km sur routes Entfernungen in km an Straßen	Distances in km along the other roads Distanze stradali in km

---

CURIOSITÉS / SEHENSWÜRDIGKEITEN
PLACES OF INTEREST / INTERESSE TURISTICO

Localité particulièrement intéressante Besonders sehenswerter Ort	Place of particular interest Località di particolare interesse
Ville très recommandée Sehr sehenswerter Ort	Very interesting city Località molto interessante
Monument culturel particulièrement intéressant · Monument culturel très recommandé Besonders sehenswertes kulturelles Objekt · Sehr sehenswertes kulturelles Objekt	Cultural monument of particular interest · Very interesting cultural monument Monumento di particolare interesse · Monumento molto interessante
Monument naturel particulièrement intéressant · Monument naturel très recommandé Besondere Natursehenswürdigkeit · Natursehenswürdigkeit	Natural object of particular interest · Very interesting natural monument Monumento naturale di particolare interesse · Monumento naturale molto interessante
Autres curiosités: culture - nature Sonstige Sehenswürdigkeiten: Kultur - Natur	Other objects of interest: culture - nature Altre curiosità: cultura - natura
Jardin botanique, parc intéressant · Jardin zoologique Botanischer Garten, sehenswerter Park · Zoologischer Garten	Botanical gardens, interesting park · Zoological gardens Giardino botanico, parco interessante · Giardino zoologico
Parc national, parc naturel · Point de vue Nationalpark, Naturpark · Aussichtspunkt	National park, nature park · Scenic view Parco nazionale, parco naturale · Punto panoramico
Église · Chapelle · Église en ruines · Monastère · Monastère en ruines Kirche · Kapelle · Kirchenruine · Kloster · Klosterruine	Church · Chapel · Church ruin · Monastery · Monastery ruin Chiesa · Cappella · Rovine di chiesa · Monastero · Rovine di monastero
Château, château fort · Château fort en ruines · Monument · Moulin à vent · Grotte Schloss, Burg · Burgruine · Denkmal · Windmühle · Höhle	Palace, castle · Castle ruin · Monument · Windmill · Cave Castello, fortezza · Rovine di fortezza · Monumento · Mulino a vento · Grotta

Place names shown in example: BORDEAUX · BIARRITZ · St. Pierre · Chateau · Grotte · Cascade · ★ Dolmen · ★ Gorge

---

AUTRES INDICATIONS / SONSTIGES
OTHER INFORMATION / ALTRI SEGNI

Terrain de camping permanent · saisonniers · Auberge de jeunesse · Hôtel, motel, auberge, refuge, village touristique Campingplatz ganzjährig · saisonal · Jugendherberge · Hotel, Motel, Gasthaus, Berghütte, Feriendorf	Camping site permanent · seasonal · Youth hostel · Hotel, motel, inn, refuge, tourist colony Campeggio tutto l'anno · stagionale · Ostello della gioventù · Hotel, motel, albergo, rifugio, villaggio turistico
Terrain de golf · Marina · Cascade Golfplatz · Jachthafen · Wasserfall	Golf-course · Marina · Waterfall Campo da golf · Porto turistico · Cascata
Piscine · Station balnéaire · Plage recommandée Schwimmbad · Heilbad · Empfehlenswerter Badestrand	Swimming pool · Spa · Recommended beach Piscina · Terme · Spiaggia raccomandabile
Tour · Tour radio, tour de télévision · Phare · Bâtiment isolé Turm · Funk-, Fernsehturm · Leuchtturm · Einzelgebäude	Tower · Radio or TV tower · Lighthouse · Isolated building Torre · Torre radio o televisiva · Faro · Edificio isolato
Mosquée · Ancienne mosquée · Église russe orthodoxe · Cimetière militaire Moschee · Ehemalige Moschee · Russisch-orthodoxe Kirche · Soldatenfriedhof	Mosque · Former mosque · Russian orthodox church · Military cemetery Moschea · Antica moschea · Chiesa ortodossa russa · Cimitero militare
Frontière d'État · Point de contrôle international · Point de contrôle avec restrictions Staatsgrenze · Internationale Grenzkontrollstelle · Grenzkontrollstelle mit Beschränkung	National boundary · International check-point · Check-point with restrictions Confine di Stato · Punto di controllo internazionale · Punto di controllo con restrizioni
Limite administrative · Zone interdite Verwaltungsgrenze · Sperrgebiet	Administrative boundary · Prohibited area Confine amministrativo · Zona vietata
Forêt · Lande Wald · Heide	Forest · Heath Foresta · Landa
Sable et dunes · Mer recouvrant les hauts-fonds Sand und Dünen · Wattenmeer	Sand and dunes · Tidal flat Sabbia e dune · Barena

Sinais convencionais
Signos convencionales

Legenda
Objaśnienia znaków

TRÁFICO (E)
TRÂNSITO (P)

(CZ) DOPRAVA
(NL) VERKEER

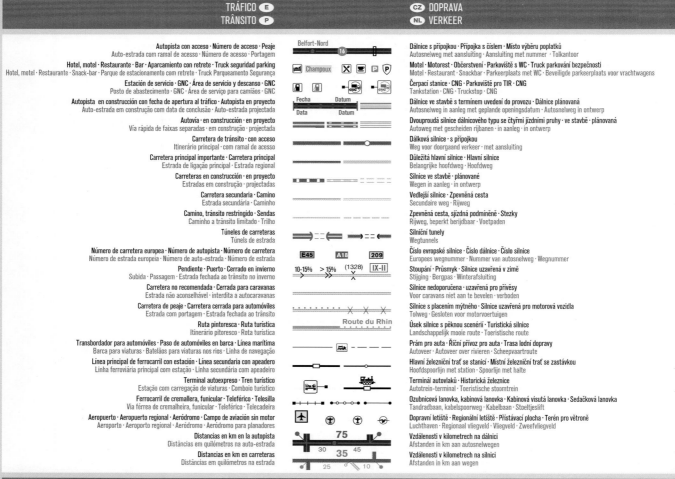

Español / Português	Čeština / Nederlands
Autopista con acceso · Número de acceso · Peaje Auto-estrada com ramal de acesso · Número de acesso · Portagem	Dálnice s připojkou · Připojka s číslem · Místo výběru poplatků Autosnelweg met aansluiting · Aansluiting met nummer · Tolkantoor
Hotel, motel · Restaurante · Bar · Aparcamiento con retrete · Truck seguridad parking Hotel, motel · Restaurante · Snack-bar · Parque de estacionamento com retrete · Truck Parqueamento Segurança	Motel · Motorest · Občerstvení · Parkoviště s WC · Truck parkování bezpečnosti Motel · Restaurant · Snackbar · Parkeerplaats met WC · Beveiligde parkeerplaats voor vrachtwagens
Estación de servicio · GNC · Área de servicio y descanso · GNC Posto de abastecimento · GNC · Área de serviço para camiãos · GNC	Čerpací stanice · CNG · Parkoviště pro TIR · CNG Tankstation · CNG · Truckstop · CNG
Autopista en construcción con fecha de apertura al tráfico · Autopista en proyecto Auto-estrada em construção com data de conclusão · Auto-estrada projectada	Dálnice ve stavbě s termínem uvedení do provozu · Dálnice plánovaná Autosnelweg in aanleg met geplande openingsdatum · Autosnelweg in ontwerp
Autovía · en construcción · en proyecto Vía rápida de faixas separadas · em construção · projectada	Dvouproudá silnice dálnicového typu se čtyřmi jízdními pruhy · ve stavbě · plánovaná Autoweg met gescheiden rijbanen · in aanleg · in ontwerp
Carretera de tránsito · con acceso Itinerário principal · com ramal de acesso	Dálková silnice · s připojkou Weg voor doorgaand verkeer · met aansluiting
Carretera principal importante · Carretera principal Estrada de ligação principal · Estrada regional	Důležitá hlavní silnice · Hlavní silnice Belangrijke hoofdweg · Hoofdweg
Carreteras en construcción · en proyecto Estradas em construção · projectadas	Silnice ve stavbě · plánované Wegen in aanleg · in ontwerp
Carretera secundaria · Camino Estrada secundária · Caminho	Vedlejší silnice · Zpevněná cesta Secundaire weg · Rijweg
Camino, tránsito restringido · Sendas Caminho a trânsito limitado · Trilho	Zpevněná cesta, sjízdná podmíněně · Stezky Rijweg, beperkt berijdbaar · Voetpaden
Túneles de carreteras Túnels de estrada	Silniční tunely Wegtunnels
Número de carretera europea · Número de autopista · Número de carretera Número de estrada europeia · Número de auto-estrada · Número de estrada	Číslo evropské silnice · Číslo dálnice · Číslo silnice Europees wegnummer · Nummer van autosnelweg · Wegnummer
Pendiente · Puerto · Cerrado en invierno Subida · Passagem · Estrada fechada ao trânsito no inverno	Stoupání · Průsmyk · Silnice uzavřená v zimě Stijging · Bergpas · Winterafsluiting
Carretera no recomendada · Cerrada para caravanas Estrada não aconselhável · interdita a autocaravanas	Silnice nedoporučena · uzavřená pro přívěsy Voor caravans niet aan te bevelen · verboden
Carretera de peaje · Carretera cerrada para automóviles Estrada com portagem · Estrada fechada ao trânsito	Silnice s placením mýtného · Silnice uzavřená pro motorová vozidla Tolweg · Gesloten voor motorvoertuigen
Ruta pintoresca · Ruta turística Itinerário pitoresco · Rota turística	Úsek silnice s pěknou scenérií · Turistická silnice Landschappelijk mooie route · Toeristische route
Transbordador para automóviles · Paso de automóviles en barca · Línea marítima Barca para viaturas · Batelãos para viaturas nos rios · Linha de navegação	Prám pro auta · Říční přívoz pro auta · Trasa lodní dopravy Autoveer · Autoveer over rivieren · Scheepvaartroute
Línea principal de ferrocarril con estación · Línea secundaria con apeadero Linha ferroviária principal com estação · Linha secundária com apeadeiro	Hlavní železniční trať se stanicí · Místní železniční trať se zastávkou Hoofdspoorlijn met station · Spoorlijn met halte
Terminal autoexpreso · Tren turístico Estação com carregação de viaturas · Comboio turístico	Terminál autovlaků · Historická železnice Autotrein-terminal · Toeristische stoomtrein
Ferrocarril de cremallera, funicular · Teleférico · Telesilla Via férrea de cremalheira, funicular · Teleférico · Telecadeira	Ozubnicová lanovka, kabinová lanovka · Kabinová visutá lanovka · Sedačková lanovka Tandradbaan, kabelspoorweg · Kabelbaan · Stoeltjeslift
Aeropuerto · Aeropuerto regional · Aeródromo · Campo de aviación sin motor Aeroporto · Aeroporto regional · Aeródromo · Aeródromo para planadores	Dopravní letiště · Regionální letiště · Přistávací plocha · Terén pro větroně Luchthaven · Regionaal vliegveld · Vliegveld · Zweefvliegveld
Distancias en km en la autopista Distâncias em quilómetros na auto-estrada	Vzdálenosti v kilometrech na dálnici Afstanden in km aan autosnelwegen
Distancias en km en carreteras Distâncias em quilómetros na estrada	Vzdálenosti v kilometrech na silnici Afstanden in km aan wegen

---

PUNTOS DE INTERÉS
PONTOS DE INTERESSE

ZAJÍMAVOSTI
BEZIENSWAARDIGHEDEN

Español / Português	Čeština / Nederlands
Población de interés especial Povoação de interesse especial	Turisticky pozoruhodná lokalita Bijzonder bezienswaardige plaats
Localidad de mucho interés Povoação muito interessante	Velmi zajímavé místo Zeer bezienswaardige plaats
Monumento cultural de interés especial · Monumento cultural de mucho interés Monumento cultural de interesse especial · Monumento cultural de muito interesse	Turistická pozoruhodná kulturní památka · Velmi zajímavý kulturní památka Bijzonder bezienswaardig cultuurmonument · Zeer bezienswaardig cultuurmonument
Curiosidad natural de interés · Curiosidad natural Monumento natural de interesse especial · Monumento natural de muito interesse	Turistická pozoruhodná přírodní památka · Velmi zajímavý přírodní památka Bijzonder bezienswaardig natuurmonument · Zeer bezienswaardig natuurmonument
Otras curiosidades: cultura - naturaleza Outros pontos de interesse: cultura - natureza	Jiné zajímavosti: kultura - příroda Overige bezienswaardigheden: cultuur - natuur
Jardín botánico, parque de interés · Jardín zoológico Jardim botânico, parque interessante · Jardim zoológico	Botanická zahrada, pozoruhodný park · Zoologická zahrada Botanische tuin, bezienswaardig park · Dierentuin
Parque nacional, parque natural · Vista pintoresca Parque nacional, parque natural · Vista panorâmica	Národní park, přírodní park · Krásný výhled Nationaal park, natuurpark · Mooi uitzicht
Iglesia · Ermita · Iglesia en ruinas · Monasterio · Ruina de monasterio Igreja · Capela · Ruína de igreja · Mosteiro · Ruína de mosteiro	Kostel · Kaple · Zřícenina kostela · Klášter · Zřícenina kláštera Kerk · Kapel · Kerkruïne · Klooster · Kloosterruïne
Palacio, castillo · Ruina de castillo · Monumento · Molino de viento · Cueva Palácio, castelo · Ruínas castelo · Monumento · Moinho de vento · Gruta	Zámek, hrad · Zřícenina hradu · Pomník · Větrný mlýn · Jeskyně Kasteel, burcht · Burchtruïne · Monument · Windmolen · Grot

---

OTROS DATOS
DIVERSOS

JINÉ ZNAČKY
OVERIGE INFORMATIE

Español / Português	Čeština / Nederlands
Camping todo el año · estacionales · Albergue juvenil · Hotel, motel, restaurante, refugio, aldea de vacaciones Parque de campismo durante todo o ano · sazonal · Pousada da juventude · Hotel, motel, restaurante, abrigo de montanha, aldeia turística	Kempink s celoročním provozem · sezóní · Ubytovna mládeže · Hotel, motel, hostinec, horská bouda, rekreační středisko Kampeerterrein het gehele jaar · seizoensgebonden · Jeugdherberg · Hotel, motel, restaurant, berghut, vakantiekolonie
Campo de golf · Puerto deportivo · Cascada Área de golfe · Porto de abrigo · Cascata	Golfové hřiště · Jachtařský přístav · Vodopád Golfterrein · Jachthaven · Waterval
Piscina · Baño medicinal · Playa recomendable Piscina · Termas · Praia recomendável	Plovárna · Lázně · Doporučená pláž Zwembad · Badplaats · Mooi badstrand
Torre · Torre de radio o televisión · Faro · Edificio aislado Torre · Torre de telecomunicação · Farol · Edifício isolado	Věž · Rozhlasová, televizní věž · Maják · Jednotlivá budova Toren · Radio of T.V. mast · Vuurtoren · Geïsoleerd gebouw
Mezquita · Antigua mezquita · Iglesia rusa-ortodoxa · Cementerio militar Mesquita · Mesquita antiga · Igreja russa ortodoxa · Cemitério militar	Mešita · Dřevější mešita · Ruský ortodoxní kostel · Vojenský hřbitov Moskee · Voormalig moskee · Russisch orthodox kerk · Militaire begraafplaats
Frontera nacional · Control internacional · Control con restricciones Fronteira nacional · Posto de controlo internacional · Posto de controlo com restrição	Státní hranice · Hraniční přechod · Hraniční přechod se zvláštními předpisy Rijksgrens · Internationaal grenspost · Grenspost met restrictie
Frontera administrativa · Zona prohibida Limite administrativo · Área proibida	Správní hranice · Zakázaný prostor Administratieve grens · Afgesloten gebied
Bosque · Landa Floresta · Charneca	Les · Vřesoviště Bos · Heide
Arena y dunas · Aguas bajas Areia e dunas · Baixio	Písek a duny · Mělké moře Zand en duinen · Bij eb droogvallende gronden

1 : 300 000

Vysvětlivky
Legenda

Legenda
Tumač znakova

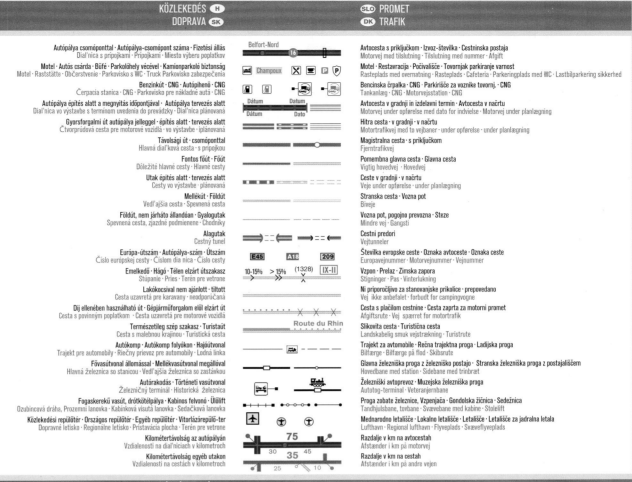

KÖZLEKEDÉS (H) / DOPRAVA (SK)
(SLO) PROMET / (DK) TRAFIK

Autópálya csomóponttal · Autópálya-csomópont száma · Fizetési állás
Dial'nica s pripojkami · Pripojkami · Miesto výberu poplatkov

Avtocesta s priključkom · Izvoz-številka · Cestninska postaja
Motorvej med tilslutning · Tilslutning med nummer · Afgift

Motel · Autós csárda · Büfé · Parkolóhely vécével · Kamionparkoló biztonság
Motel · Raststätte · Občerstvenie · Parkovisko s WC · Truck Parkovisko zabezpečenia

Motel · Restauracija · Počivališče · Tovornjak parkiranje varnost
Rasteplads med overnatning · Rasteplads · Cafeteria · Parkeringsplads med WC · Lastbilparkering sikkerhed

Benzinkút · CNG · Autópihenő · CNG
Čerpacia stanica · CNG · Parkovisko pre nákladné autá · CNG

Bencinska črpalka · CNG · Parkirišče za voznike tovornj. · CNG
Tankanlæg · CNG · Motorvejsstation · CNG

Autópálya építés alatt a megnyitás időpontjával · Autópálya tervezés alatt
Dial'nica vo výstavbe s terminom uvedenia do prevádzky · Dial'nica plánovaná

Avtocesta v gradnji in izdelavni termin · Avtocesta v načrtu
Motorvej under opførelse med dato for indvielse · Motorvej under planlægning

Gyorsforgalmi út autópálya jelleggel · építés alatt · tervezés alatt
Čtvorprúdová cesta pre motorové vozidlá · vo výstavbe · iplánovaná

Hitra cesta · v gradnji · v načrtu
Motortrafikvej med to vejbaner · under opførelse · under planlægning

Távolsági út · csomóponttal
Hlavná dial'ková cesta · s pripojkou

Magistralna cesta · s priključkom
Fjerntrafikvej

Fontos főút · Főút
Dôležité hlavné cesty · Hlavné cesty

Pomembna glavna cesta · Glavna cesta
Vigtig hovedvej · Hovedvej

Utak építés alatt · tervezés alatt
Cesty vo výstavbe · plánovaná

Ceste v gradnji · v načrtu
Veje under opførelse · under planlægning

Mellékút · Földút
Vedl'ajšia cesta · Spevnená cesta

Stranska cesta · Vozna pot
Biveje

Földút, nem járháto állandóan · Gyalogutak
Spevnená cesta, zjazdné podmienené · Chodníky

Vozna pot, pogojno prevozna · Steze
Mindre vej · Gangsti

Alagutak
Cestný tunel

Cestni predori
Vejtunneler

Európa-útszám · Autópálya-szám · Útszám
Číslo európskej cesty · Číslom dia nica · Číslo cesty

Številka evropske ceste · Oznaka avtoceste · Oznaka ceste
Europavejnummer · Motorvejnummer · Vejnummer

Emelkedő · Hágó · Télen elzárt útszakasz
Stúpanie · Pries · Terén pre vetrone

Vzpon · Prelaz · Zimska zapora
Stigninger · Pas · Vinterlukning

Lakókocsival nem ajánlott · tiltott
Cesta uzavretá pre karavany · neodporúčaná

Ni priporočljivo za stanovanjske prikolice · prepovedano
Vej ikke anbefalet · forbudt for campingvogne

Díj ellenében használható út · Gépjárműforgalom elől elzárt út
Cesta s povinným poplatkom · Cesta uzavretá pre motorové vozidlá

Cesta s plačilom cestnine · Cesta zaprta za motorni promet
Afgiftsrute · Vej spærret for motortrafik

Természetileg szép szakasz · Turistaút
Cesta s malebnou krajinou · Turistická cesta

Slikovita cesta · Turistična cesta
Landskabelig smuk vejstrækning · Turistrute

Autókomp · Autókomp folyókon · Hajóútvonal
Trajekt pre automobily · Riečny prievoz pre automobily · Lodná linka

Trajekt za avtomobile · Rečna trajektna proga · Ladijska proga
Bilfærge · Bilfærge på flod · Skibsrute

Fővasútvonal állomással · Mellékvasútvonal megállóval
Hlavná železnica so stanicou · Vedl'ajšia železnica so zastávkou

Glavna železniška proga z železniško postajo · Stranska železniška proga z postajališčem
Hovedbane med station · Sidebane med trinbræt

Autórakodás · Történeti vasútvonal
Železničný terminál · Historická železnica

Železniški avtoprevoz · Muzejska železniška proga
Autotog-terminal · Veteranjernbane

Fogaskerekű vasút, drótkötélpálya · Kabinos felvonó · Ülőlift
Ozubincová dráha, Prozemni lanovka · Kabínková visutá lanovka · Sedačková lanovka

Proga zobate železnice, Vzpenjača · Gondolska žičnica · Sedežnica
Tandhjulsbane, tovbane · Svævebane med kabine · Stolelift

Közlekedési repülőtér · Országos repülőtér · Egyéb repülőtér · Vitorlázórepülő-ter
Dopravné letisko · Regionálne letisko · Pristavácia plocha · Terén pre vetrone

Mednarodno letališče · Lokalno letališče · Letališče za jadralna letala
Lufthavn · Regional lufthavn · Flyveplads · Svæveflyveplads

Kilométertávolság az autópályán
Vzdialenosti na dial'niciach v kilometroch

Razdalje v km na avtocestah
Afstænder i km på motorvej

Kilométertávolság egyéb utakon
Vzdialenosti na cestách v kilometroch

Razdalje v km na cestah
Afstænder i km på andre vejen

Belfort-Nord
16
Champoux
Dátum Datum
Dátum Dato
E45 A18 209
10-15% > 15% (1328) IX-II
Route du Rhin
75
30 35 45
25 10

LÁTVÁNYOSSÁGOK / ZAUJÍMAVOST
ZAMINIVOSTI / SEVÆRDIGHEDER

Különösen látványos település
Mimoriadne pozoruhodné miesto

Posebej zanimivo naselje
Særlig seværdig by

Nagyon látványos hely
Vel'mi pozoruhodnév miesto

Zelo zanimivo naselje
Meget seværdig by

Különösen nevezetes műemlék · Nagyon látványos műemlék
Mimoriadne pozoruhodné kultúra objekt · Vel'mi pozoruhodnév kultúra objekt

Posebej zanimiva kulturna znamenitost · Zanimiva kulturna znamenitost
Særlig seværdig kulturmindesmærke · Meget Seværdig kulturmindesmærke

Különösen nevezetes természeti érték · Nagyon látványos természeti érték
Mimoriadna prírodná zaujímavost' · Zaujímavost'

Posebej zanimiva naravna znamenitost · Zanimiva naravna znamenitost
Særlig seværdig naturmindesmærke · Meget seværdig naturmindesmærke

Egyéb látnivaló: kultúra - természet
Iná pozoruhodnosťi: kultúra - prírroda

Druge znamenitosti: kultura - priroda
Andre seværdigheder: kultur - natur

Botanikus kert, látványos park · Állatkert
Botanická záhrada, Pozoruhodný park · Zoologická záhrada

Botanični vrt, zanimiv park · Živalski vrt
Botanisk have, seværdig park · Zoologisk have

Nemzeti park, természeti park · Kilátópont
Národný park, Prírodný park · Vyhliadka

Narodni park, naravni park · Razgledišče
Nationalpark, naturpark · Udsigtspunkt

Templom · Kápolna · Templomrom · Kolostor · Kolostorrom
Kostol · Kaplnka ·Zrúcanina kostola · Kláštor · Zrúcanina kláštora

Cerkev · Kapela · Razvalina cerkve · Samostan · Samostanska razvalina
Kirke · Kapel · Kirkeruin · Kloster · Klosterruin

Kastély, vár · Várrom · Emlékmű · Szélmalom · Barlang
Zámok, Hrad · Zrúcanina hradu · Pomník · Veterný mlyn · Jaskyňa

Graščina, grad · Razvalina grada · Spomenik · Mlin na veter · Jama
Slot, borg · Borgruin · Mindesmærke · Vejrmølle · Hule

BORDEAUX
BIARRITZ
St. Pierre · Chateau
Grotte · Cascade
Dolmen · Gorge

EGYÉB / INÉ ZNAČKY
DRUGI ZNAKI / ANDET

Kemping hely egész évben nyitva · szezonális · Ifjúsági szállás · Szálloda, motel, vendéglő, menedékház, nyaralótelep
Kemping celoročný · sezónne · Mládežnícka ubytovňa · Hotel, motel, hostinec, horská chata, rekreačné stredisko

Kamp celo leto · sezonske · Mladinski hotel · Hotel, motel, gostišče, planinska koča, počitniško naselje
Campingplads hele året · sæsonbestemte · Vandrerhjem · Hotel, motel, restaurant, bjerghytte, ferieby

Golfpálya · Jachtkikötő · Vízesés
Golfové ihrisko · Pristav pre plachetnice · Vodopád

Igrišče za golf · Marina · Slap
Golfbane · Lystbådehavn · Vandfald

Uszoda · Gyógyfürdő · Ajánlatos strand
Kúpalisko · Kúpele · Pláž vhodná na kúpanie

Bazen · Toplice · Obala primerna za kopanje
Svømmebad · Kurbad · God badestrand

Torony · Rádió- vagy tévétorony · Világítótorony · Magában álló épület
Veža · Rozhlasový, televízny stožiar · Maják · Osamote stojacá budova

Stolp · Radijski ali televizijski stolp · Svetilnik · Posamezno poslopje
Tårn · Telemast · Fyrtårn · Isoleret bygning

Mecset · Egykori mecset · Oroszkeleti templom · Katonatemető
Mešita · Ehemalige Moschee · Ruský ortodoxný kostol · Vojenský cintorín

Džamija · Nekdanja džamija · Rusko-pravoslavna cerkev · Vojaško pokopališče
Moské · Fordums moské · Russisk ortodoks kirke · Militærisk kirkegård

Államhatár · Nemzetközi határátlépő · Korlátozott átjárhatóságú határátkelőhely
Štátna hranica · Medzinárodný hraničný priechod · Hraničný priechod s obmedzením

Državna meja · Mednarodni mejni prehod · Mejna kontrolna točka z omejitvijo
Rigsgrænse · International grænsekontrol · Grænsekontrol med indskrænkning

Közigazgatási határ · Zárt terület
Administratívna hranica · Zakázaná oblasť

Upravna meja · Zaprto območje
Regionsgrænse · Spærret område

Erdő · Puszta
Les · Pustatina

Gozd · Goljava
Skov · Hede

Homok, föveny · Watt-tenger
Piesok a duny · Plytčina

Pesek in sipine · Bibavični pas
Sand og klitter · Vadehav

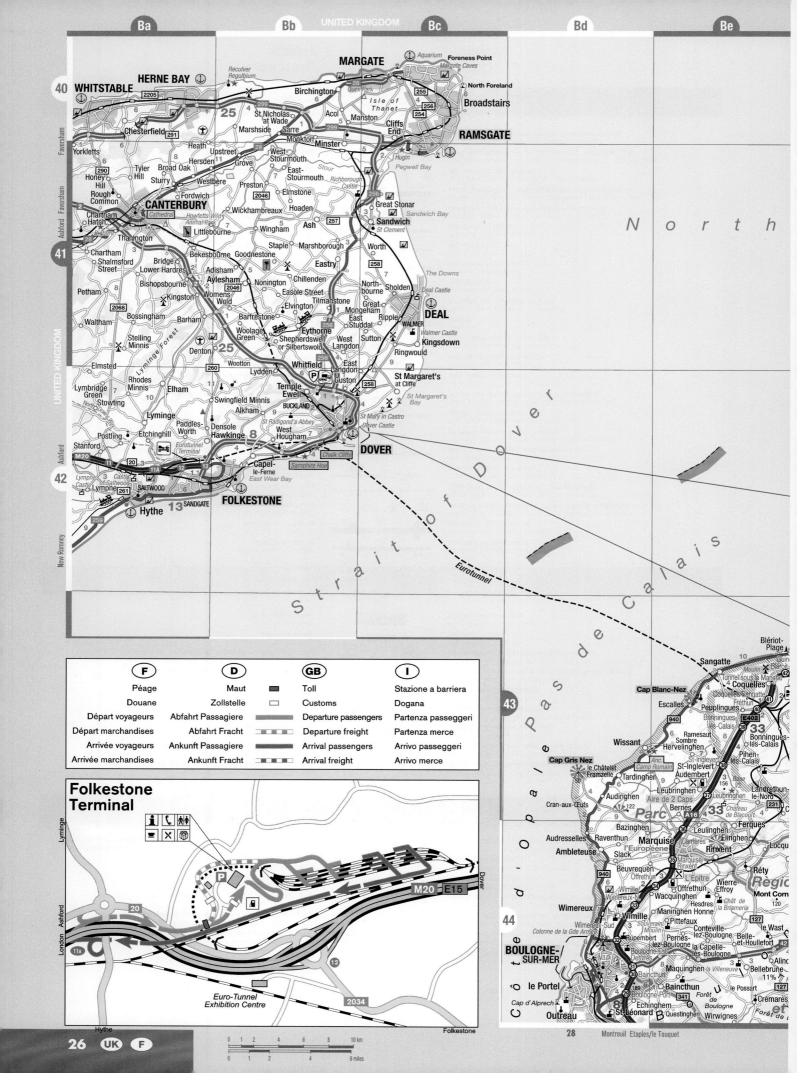

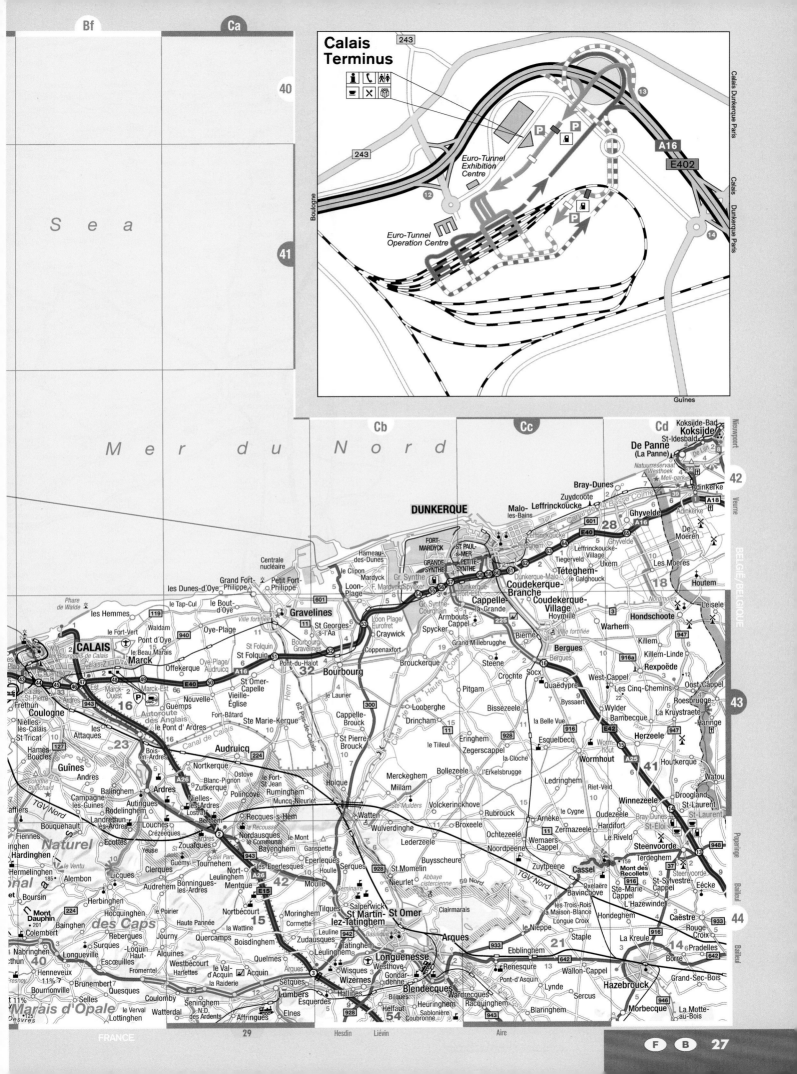

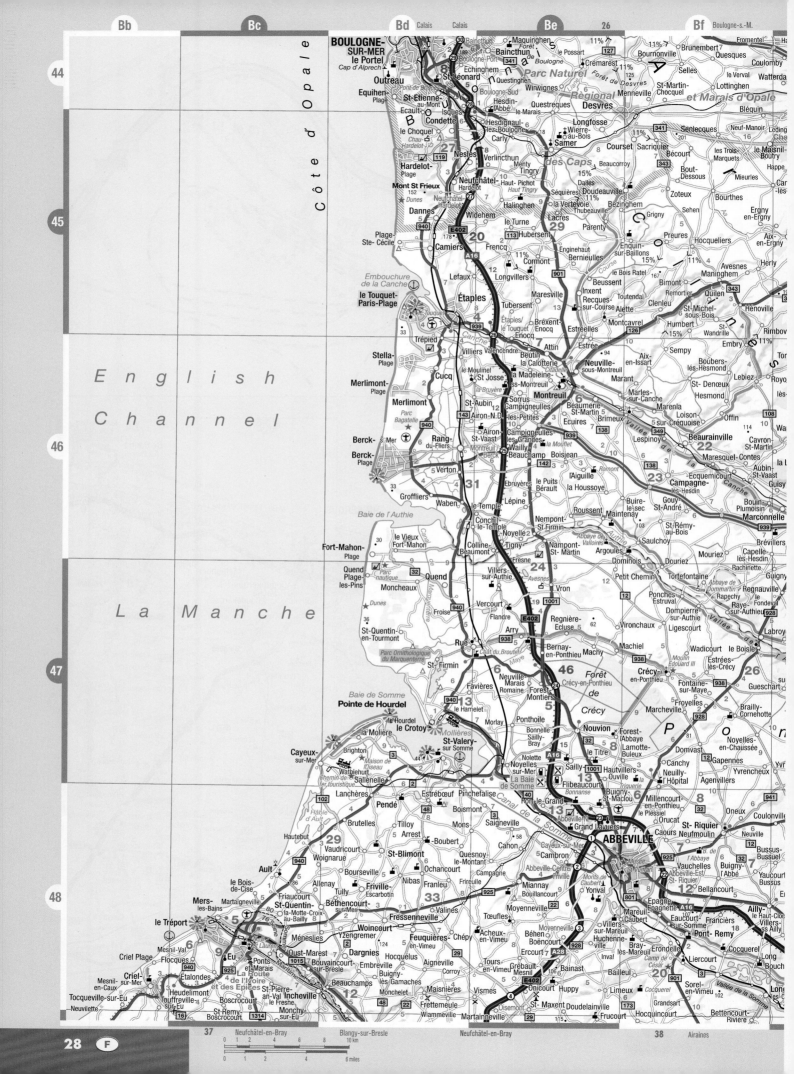

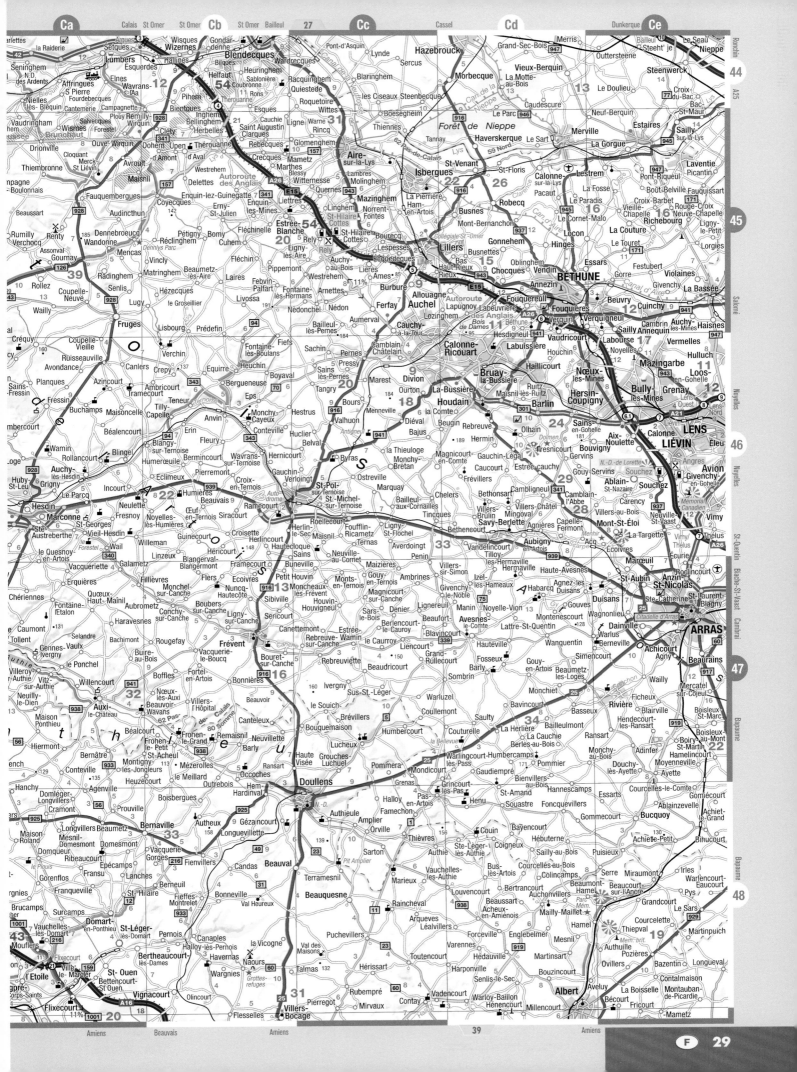

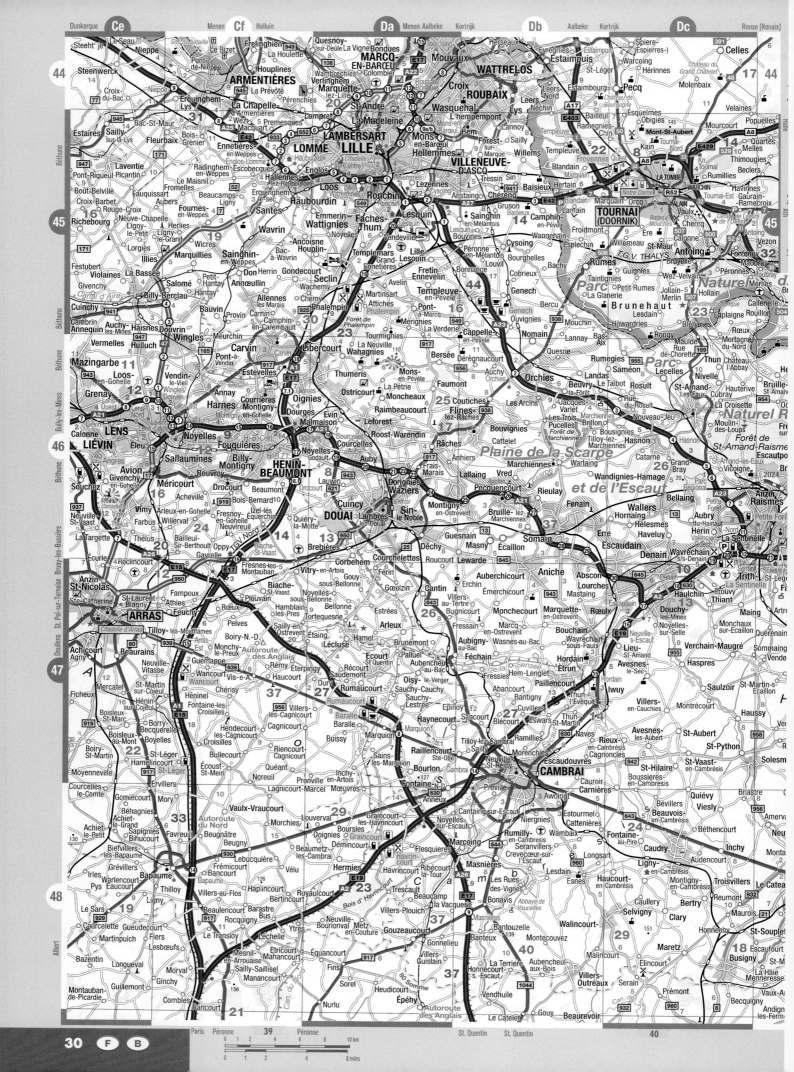

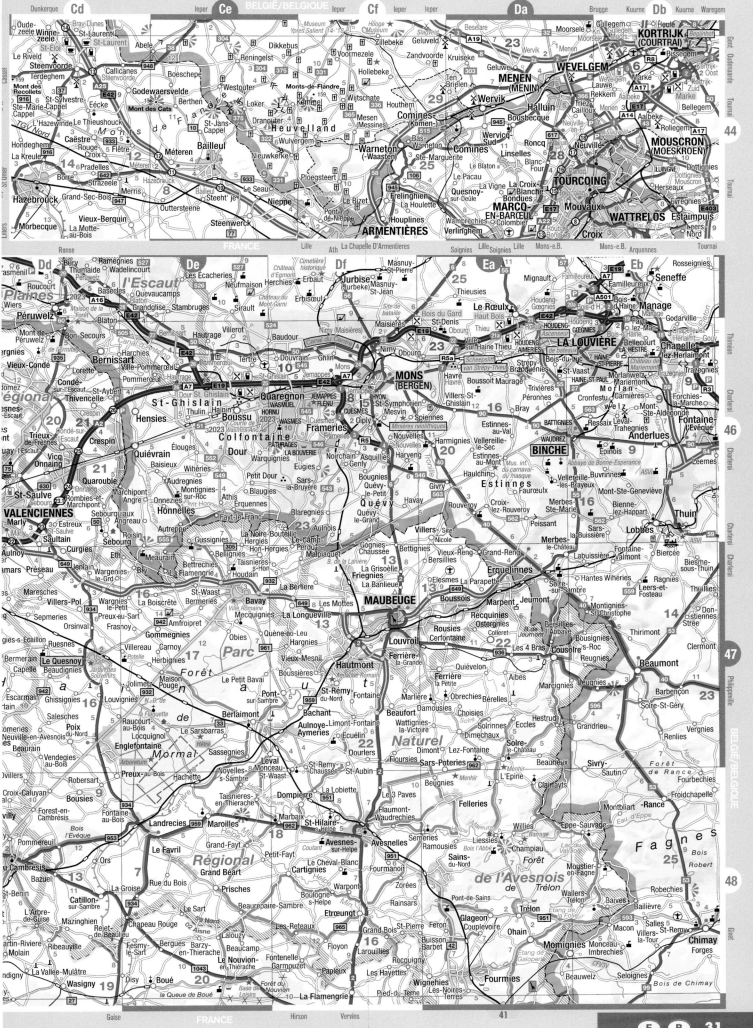

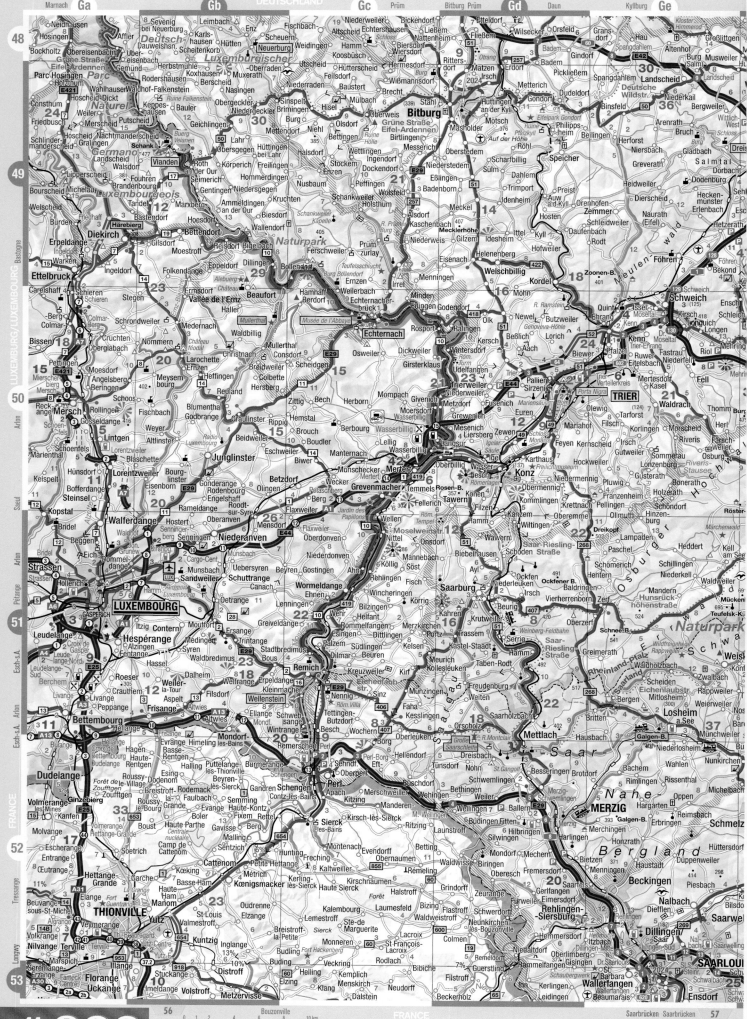

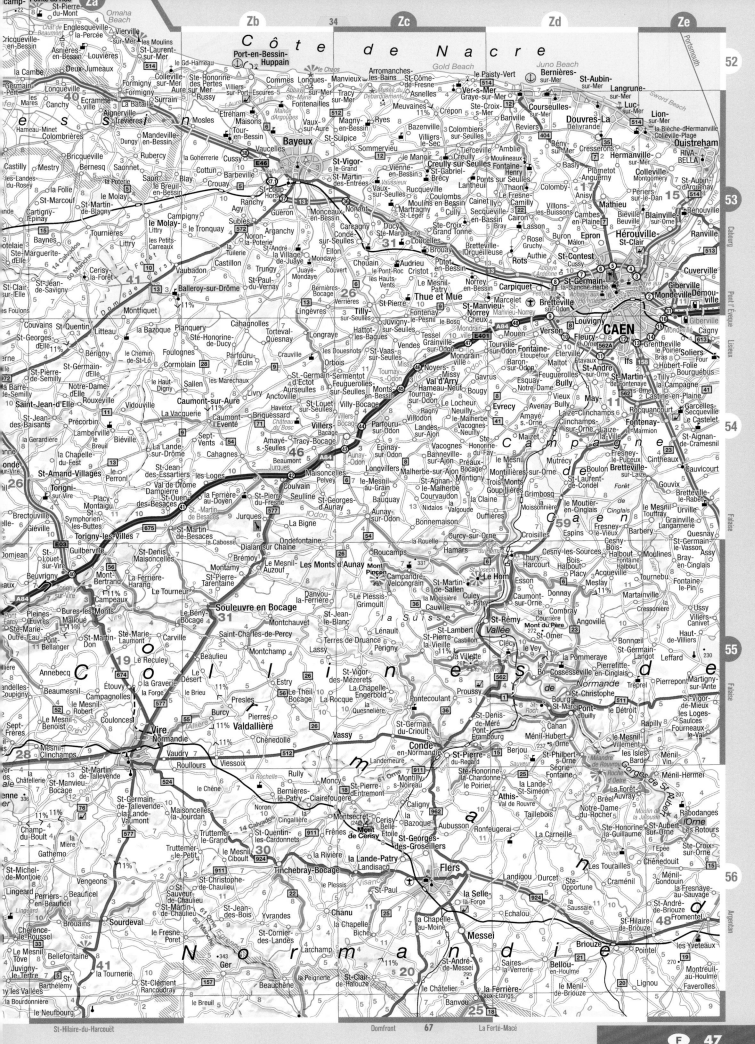

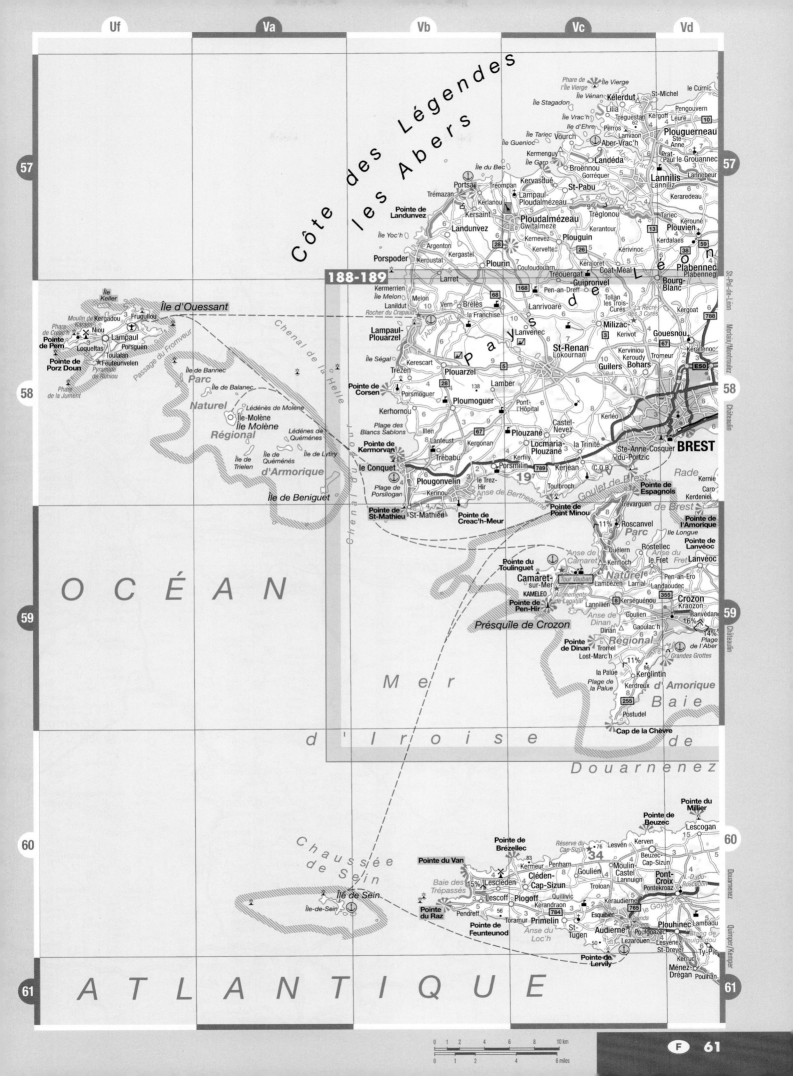

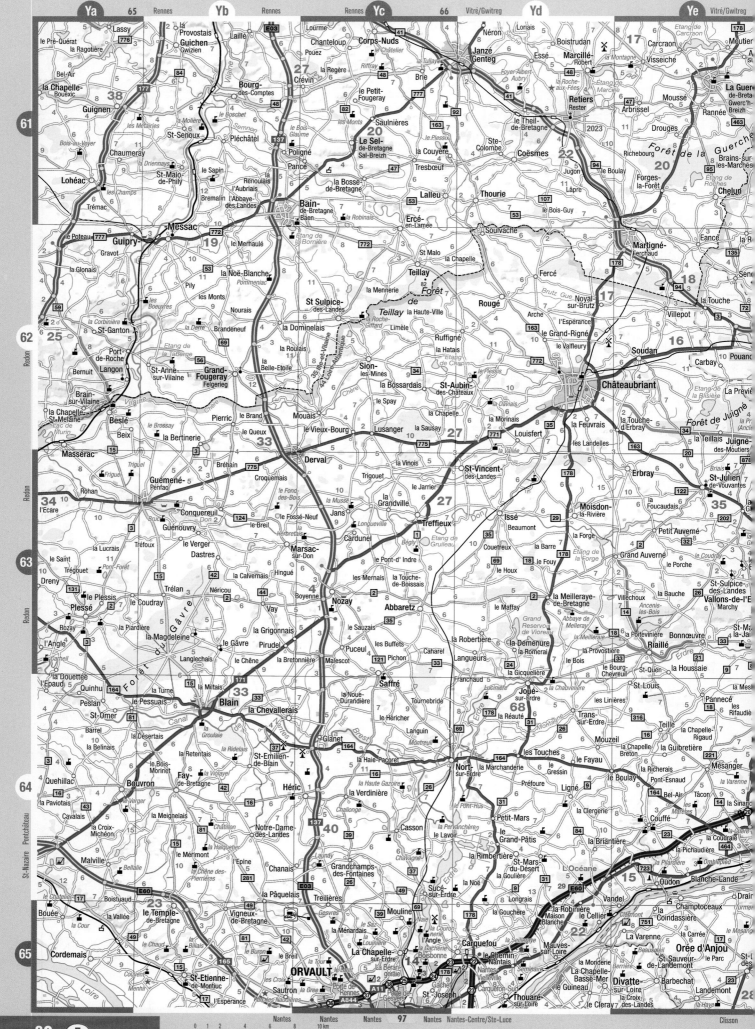

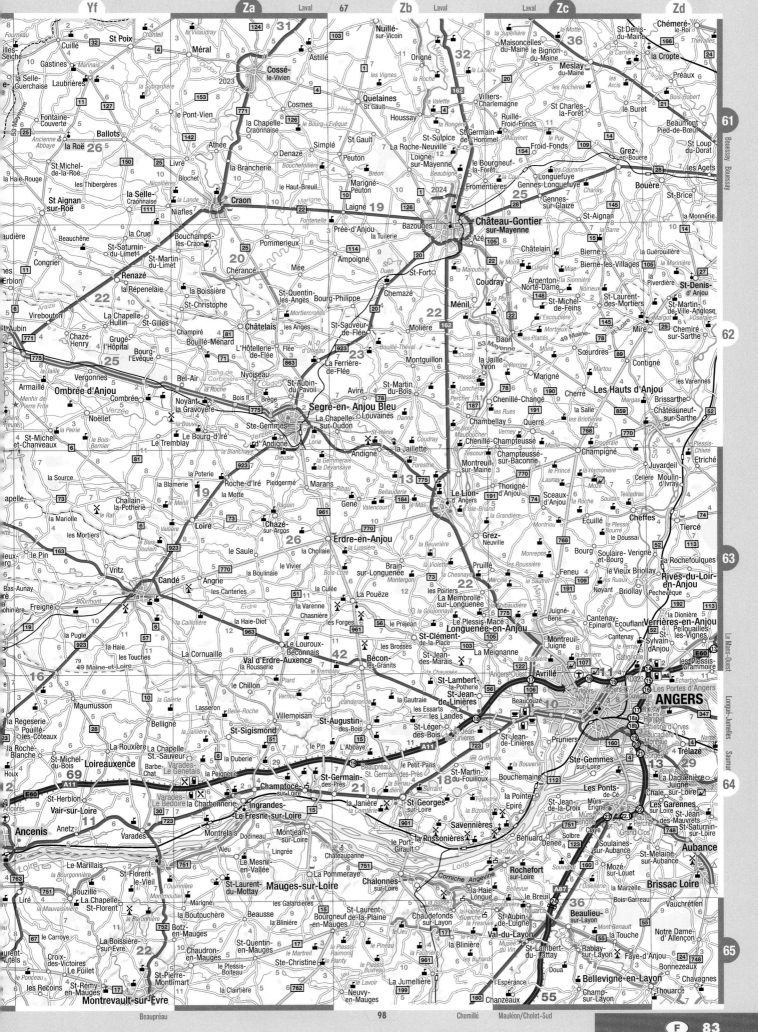

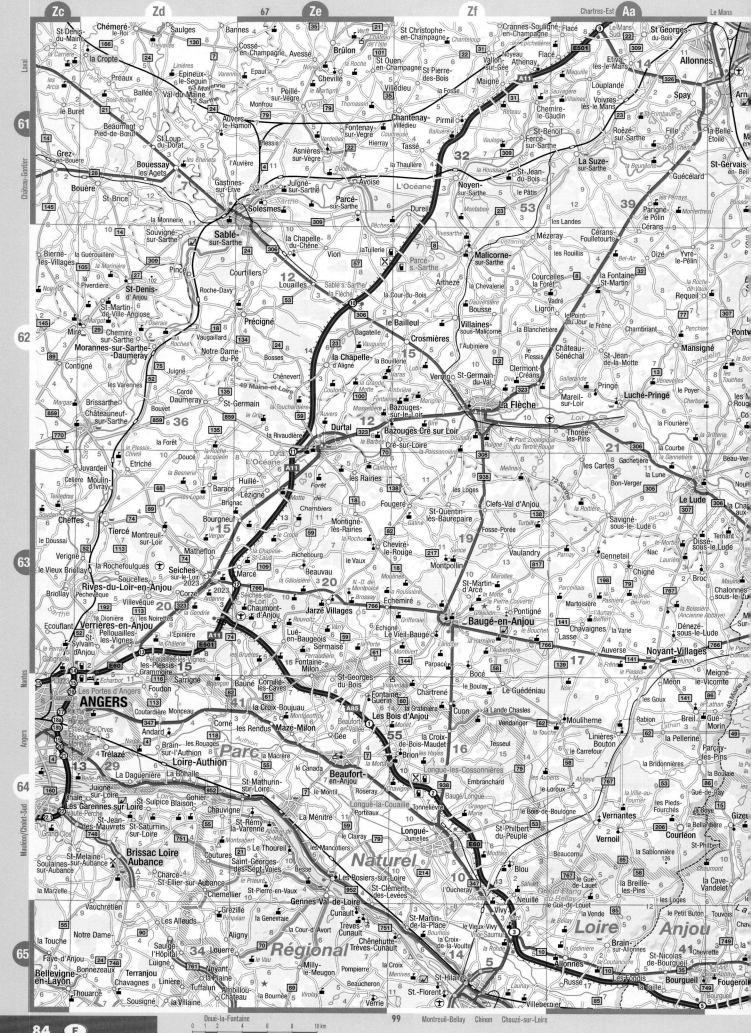

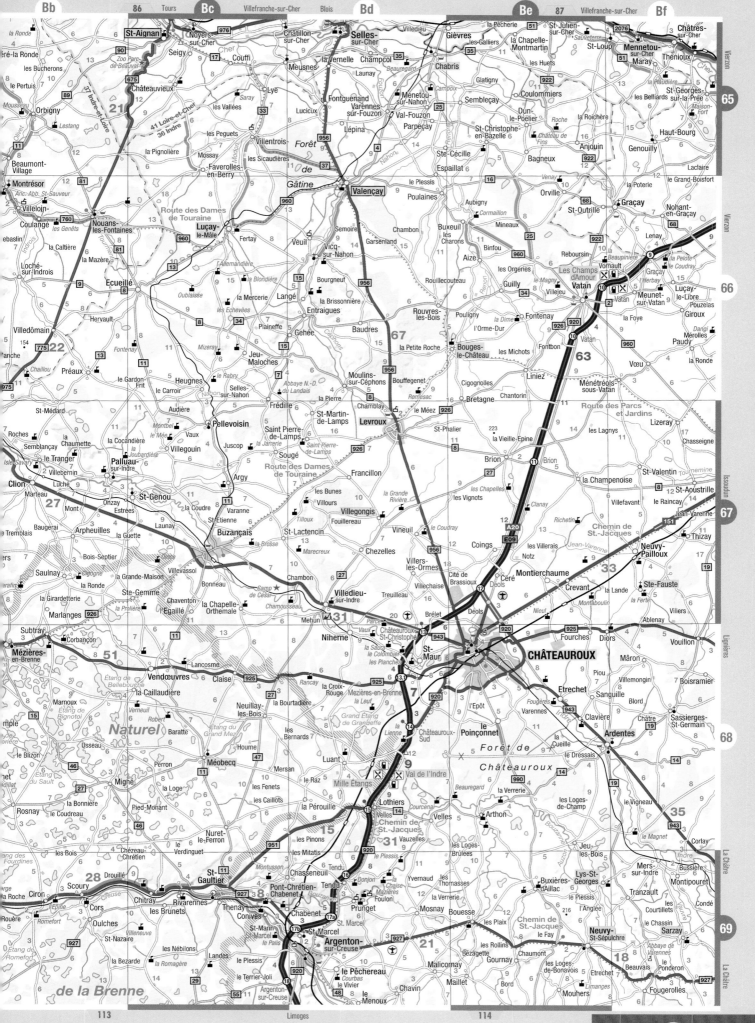

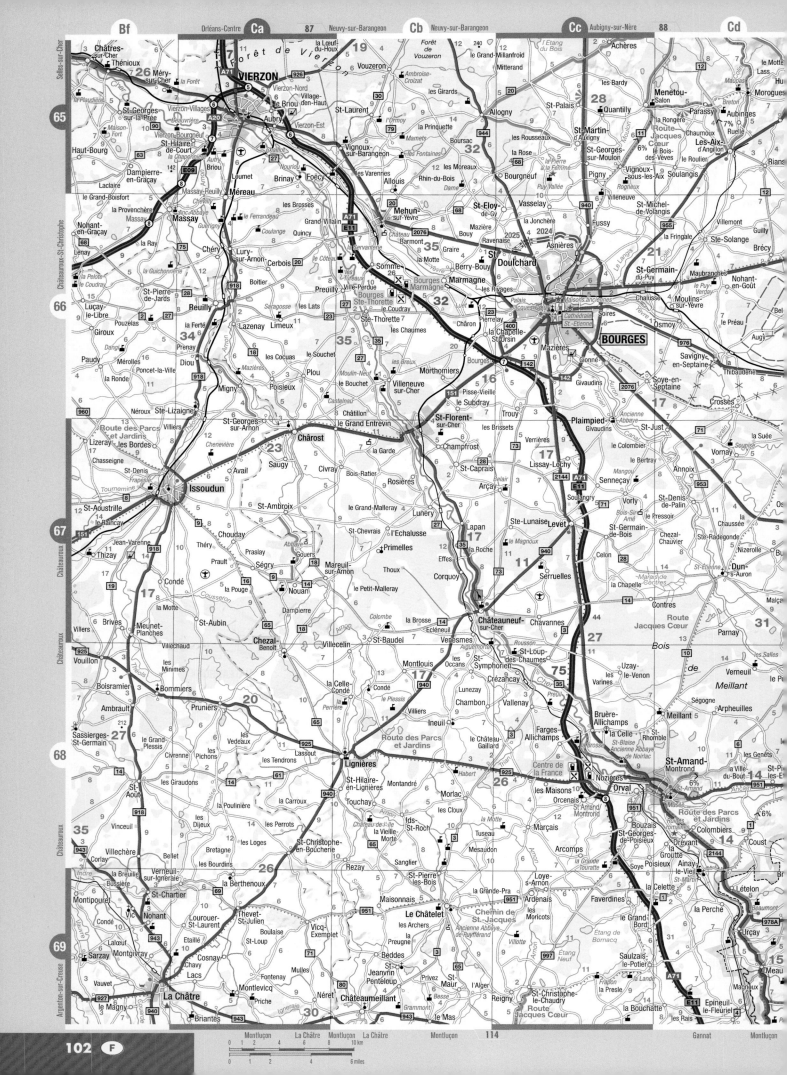

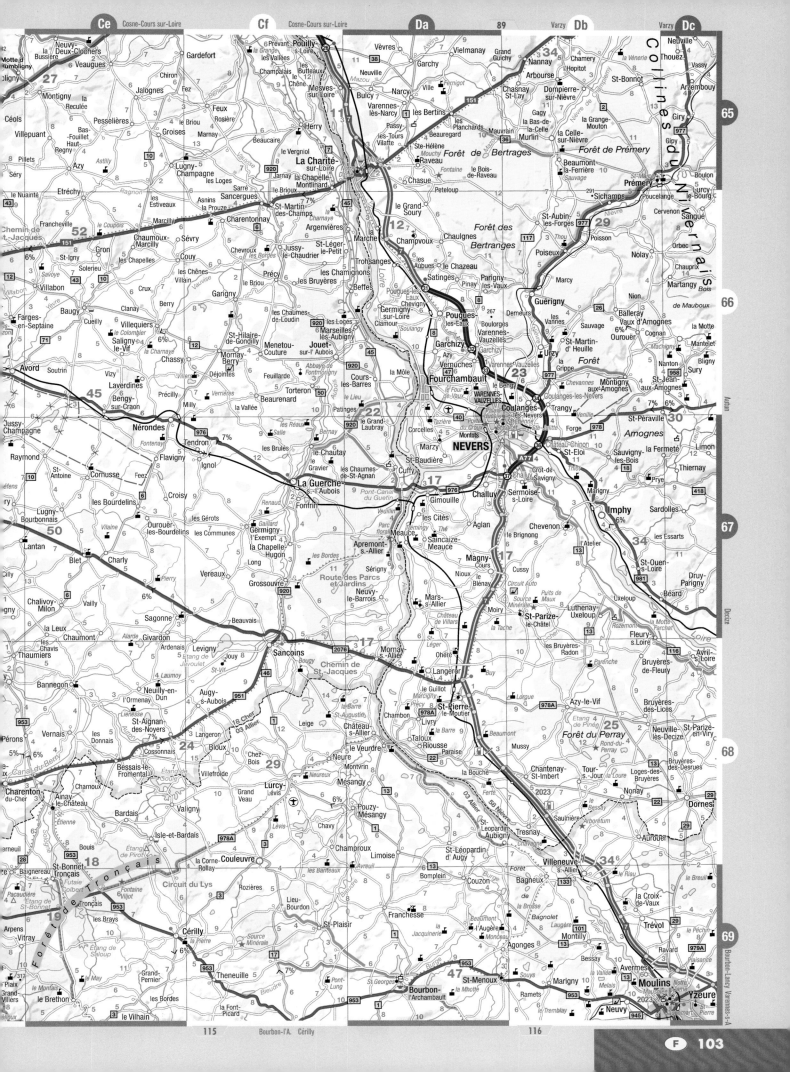

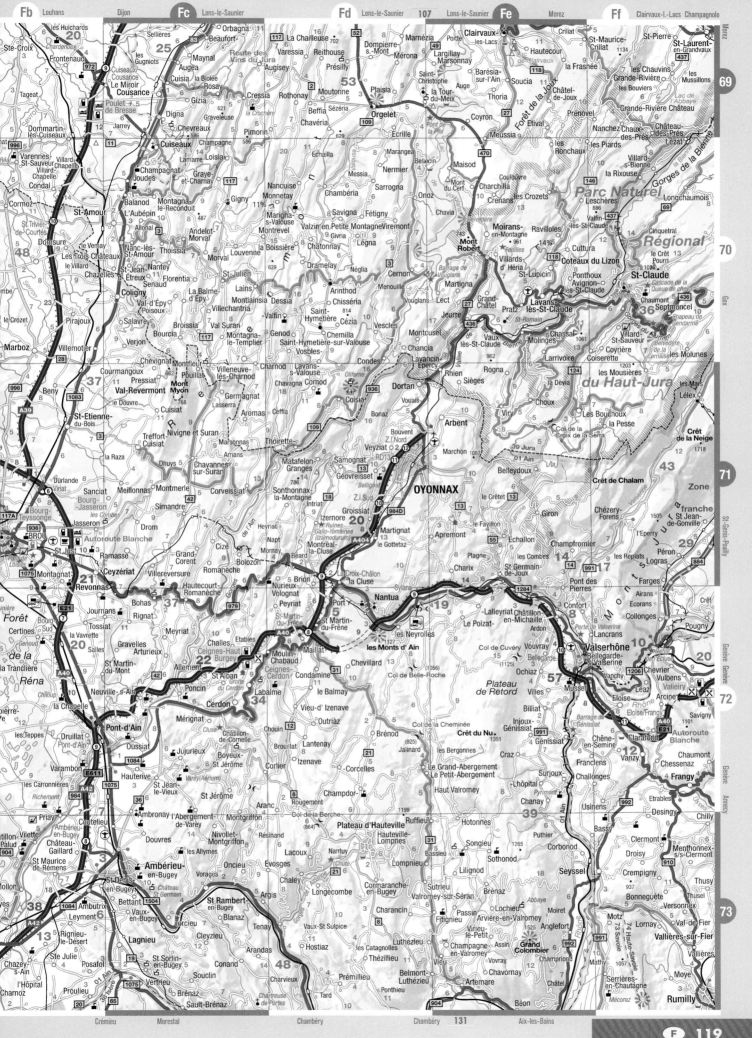

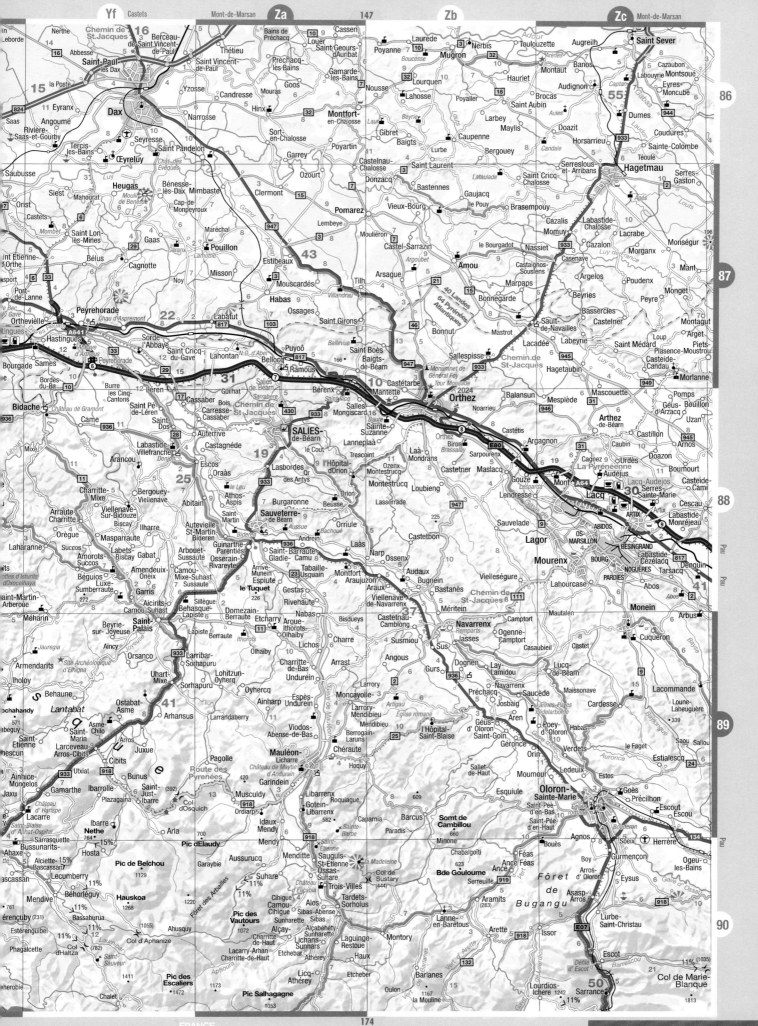

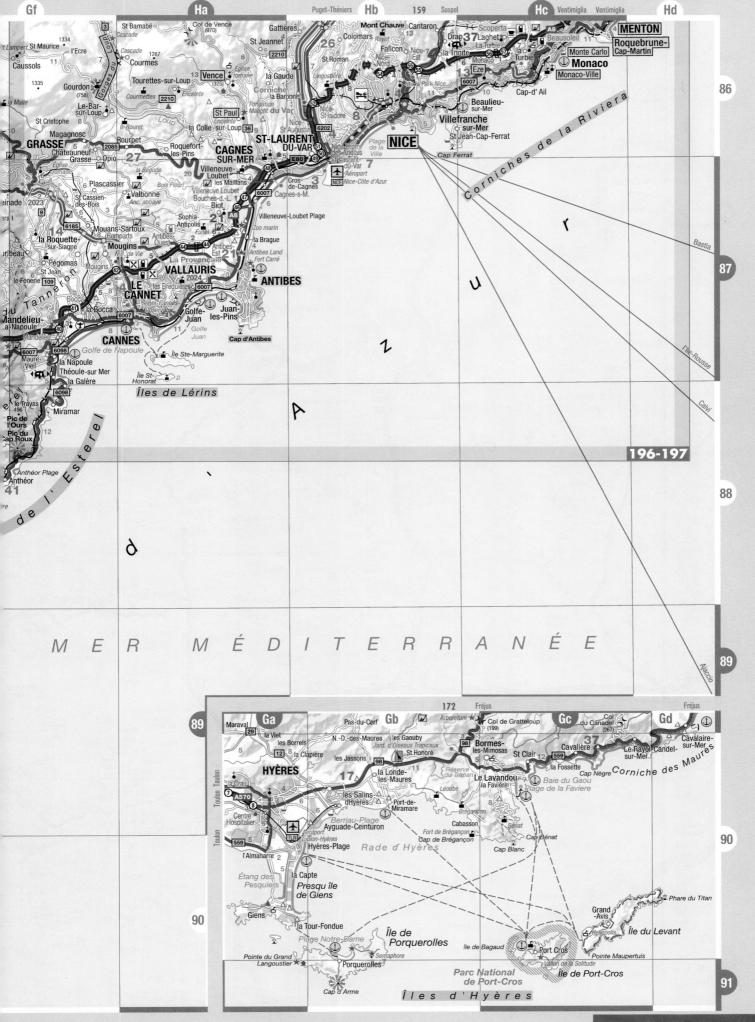

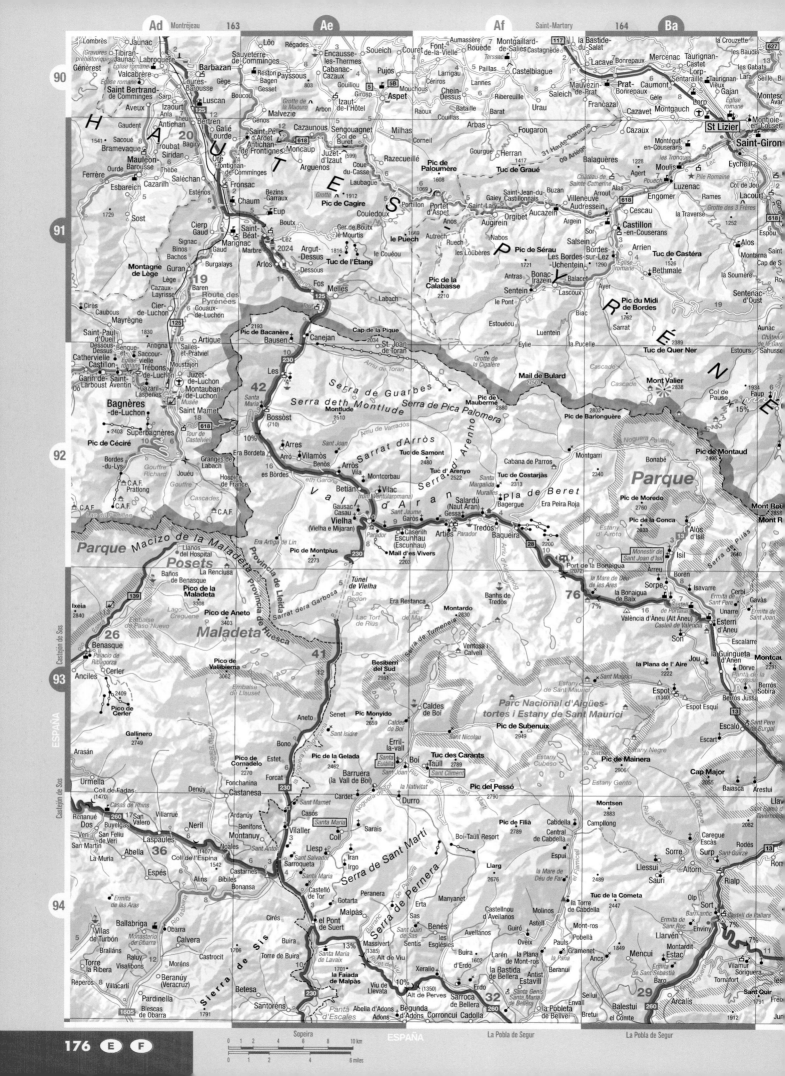

Bourg-Blanc
Plabennec
23
Kergonc Kervillerm
Kernoas 77
Scaven 2,5
Lanorven Kergrenn
Leslevret
Coatanéa
I'Ile Gouesnou
Kersaint-
-Plabennec 3,5
Kléongar de Kéralias
Kerarmérien
Cozglouet
Quillien 91
D788
Gouesnou
Aéroport régional de
Brest-Guipavas
Keralénoc 95
17
Fuzoret 76
Trémeur Braz
Pentraon 84
l'Ile Lesquélen
Lesquélen
Château Saint-Thonan
Pen ar
Quinquis
Saint-Elven
Pen ar Forêt
Keraiber Kerudalar 12
Keramézec D770
Quilifigan le Penfrat
Lestréonc
le Mézou
Saint-Eloi
Kerargac
Botiguéry
Bel-Air
Trémaria
France
Trémaouézan Penguilly
Keriel Kervéléoc Lanneuffret
Begavel Guernévez
Monastère
de Kerbénéat
le Lez Elom
Run Poulzic
N12 35 Kerellé
Morlaix
Moulin
de Brezel
D712
Mescoat
Cosquer Cleuzéver

BREST
(34)   62
Rade de Brest
Pointe du Corbeau
gnols
de l'Armorique 12
Ile Ronde
te de
ngue
Pointe de
Kerdéniel
Ile Longue
Pointe de Lanvéoc

Baie de Douarnenez

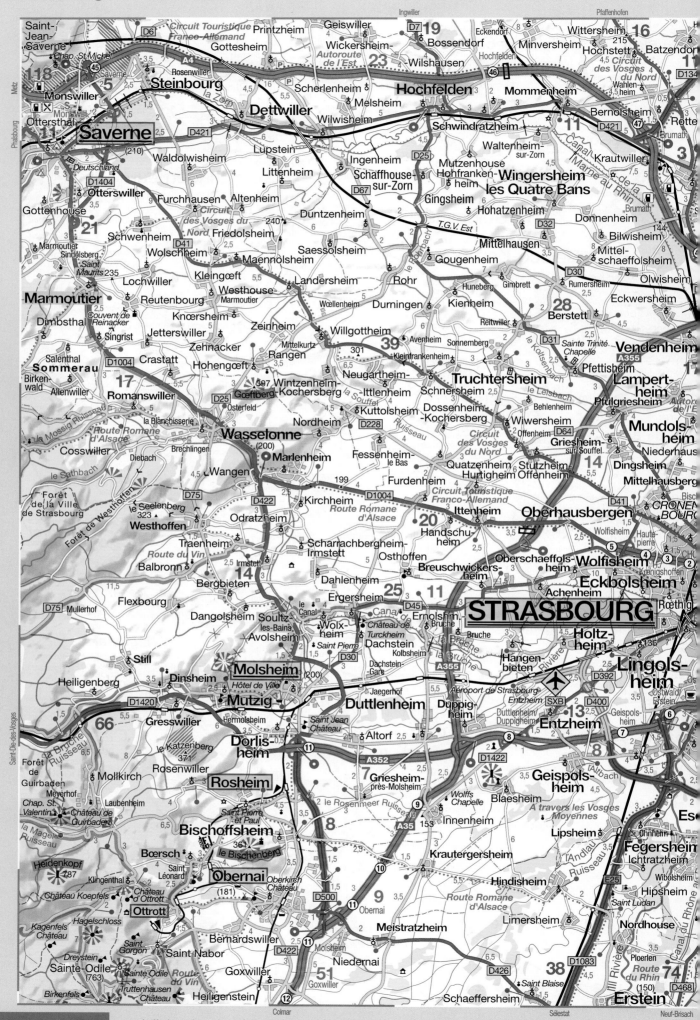

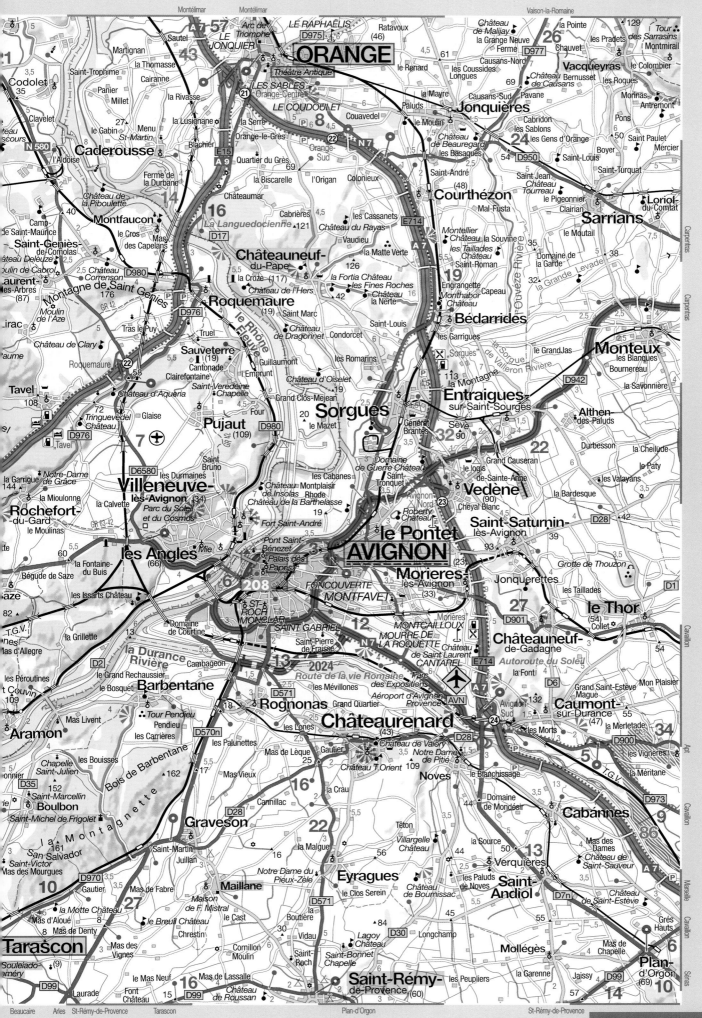

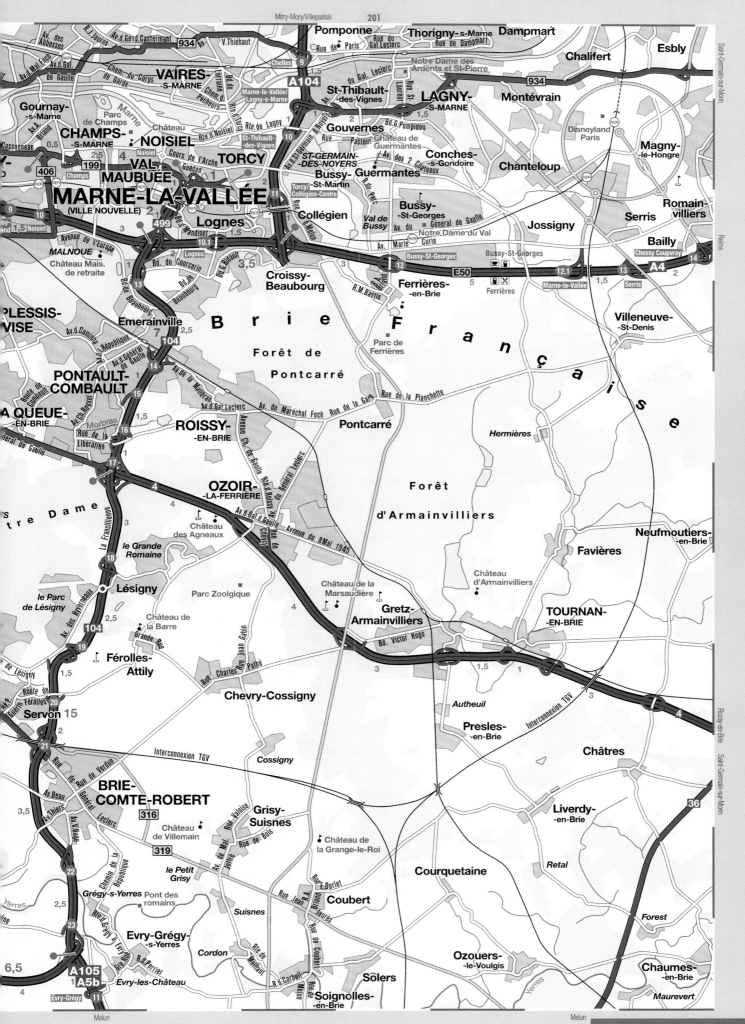

Av. des
Abbesses
R.J.Jaurès
Av.d.Gend.Casterman
934
V.Thiébaut
Pomponne
Rue du Gal.Leclerc
Thorigny-s-Marne
Rue de Dampmart
Dampmart
Chalifert
Esbly

Av.d.Mal.Foch
Av.d.Gal.
de Gaulle
Chem.-du-Corps
de Garde
Chelles
9
Rue de Paris
Notre Dame des
Ardents et St-Pierre
934

Gournay-
s-Marne
Av.A.
Briant
Parc
de Champs
VAIRES-
S-MARNE
A104
Lorraine
Rue.d.Pêcheurs
Bd.de
St-Thibault-
des-Vignes
Av. du Gal.Leclerc
Rue St.
LAGNY-
S-MARNE
Montévrain

0,5
Cossonneau
CHAMPS-
S-MARNE
Château
NOISIEL
Marne-la-Vallée/
Lagny-s-Marne
1
Rte. de Lagny
1,5
Laurent
Disneyland
Paris
Magny-
le-Hongre

406
Champs
199
2,5
4
Noisiel
Cours de l'Arche
Guédon
TORCY
St-Thibault-
des-Vignes
10
Gouvernes
Rue
Bd.G.Pompidou
Pasteur
Château de
Guermantes
Conches-
s-Gondoire
Chanteloup
Romain-
villiers

VAL
MAUBUÉE
499
MARNE-LA-VALLÉE
(VILLE NOUVELLE)
2
1
Guédon
ST-GERMAIN-
DES-NOYERS
Bussy-
St-Martin
Guermantes
Av. des 2 Châteaux
Serris

9
10
Lognes
11
Avenue de l'Europe
Lognes
1,5
Collégien
Val de
Bussy
Bussy-
St-Georges
Av. du
Général de Gaulle
Jossigny
Bailly
Chessy Coupvray

1,5
Noisiel
Bd.Mandinet
10.1
3,5
Rue d.Melun
Av. Marie
Notre Dame du Val
Curie
14
A4

Bd. du Courcerin
Bd.G.Breault
Croissy-
Beaubourg
3
Bussy-St-Georges
Bussy-St-Georges
12
E50
12.1
A4
Serris

13
Bd de
Beaubourg
R.M.Bastié
Ferrières-
en-Brie
5
Ferrières
Marne-la-Vallée
2

PLESSIS-
VISE
Emerainville
2,5
Brie
Parc de
Ferrières
Villeneuve-
St-Denis

Av.d.Camille
Av.du Général de Gaulle
Av.d. République
7
104
Forêt de
Pontcarré
Fran
çais
e

PONTAULT-
COMBAULT
14
Av. de la Malnoue
15
Rue de la Gare
Rue de la Planchette

LA QUEUE-
EN-BRIE
Route de
Combault
Av.d.Gal.Leclerc
Av. du Maréchal Foch
Pontcarré
Hermières

Av.Ch.Rouvel
Morbras
Rue de la
Libération
16
1,5
ROISSY-
EN-BRIE

1
17
4
OZOIR-
LA-FERRIÈRE
Forêt
d'Armainvilliers
Neufmoutiers-
en-Brie

tre Dame
La Francilienne
4
Av.d.Gal.de Gaulle
Avenue du 8 Mai 1945
Favières
Château
d'Armainvilliers

3
Château
des Agneaux
Rue du Général Leclerc
Rue de Chevry

18
le Grande
Romaine
Château de la
Marsaudière
Gretz-
Armainvilliers
TOURNAN-
EN-BRIE

Lésigny
Parc Zoologique
4

le Parc
de Lésigny
Av. des Buyerneaux
2,5
Château de
la Barre
Bd. Victor Hugo

104
Grande Rue
Rue Charles
Rue Jean Gabin
Pathé
3
1,5
1

19
Férolles-
Attily
Autheuil

de Lésigny
1,5
Chevry-Cossigny
Presles-
en-Brie
Châtres

Route de
Férolles
20
Servon
15
Cossigny
Interconnexion TGV
3
4

2
21
Interconnexion TGV

Rue de Verdun
Liverdy-
en-Brie
36

3,5
Av.Beau
Av.Thiers
Av. Général Leclerc
BRIE-
COMTE-ROBERT
316
Grisy-
Suisnes
Rue Valoise
Retal

Château de
Villemain
319
Rue de Bois
Château de
la Grange-le-Roi
Courquetaine
Forest

22
Chemin de la
République
le Petit
Grisy
Av. du Mal. Joffre
Rue
Rue Dorlet

Grégy-s-Yerres
Pont des
romains
Suisnes
Rue Jean
R.A.
Briard
Coubert
Ozouers-
le-Voulgis
Chaumes-
en-Brie

2,5
Evry-Grégy-
s-Yerres
Cordon
Rte de
Meilland
Rue Jaurès
Solers

23
6,5
A105
1A5b
Evry-les-Château
R.d.Perrier
R.d.Corbeil
Soignolles-
en-Brie
Maurevert

4
Evry-Grégy
11
Yerres

1:20.000

CARTE D'ASSEMBLAGE   BLATTÜBERSICHT   KEY MAP   QUADRO D'UNIONE
ÍNDICE DE MAPA   MAPA ÍNDICE   OVERZICHTSKAART   SKOROWIDZ ARKUSZY
KLAD MAPOVÝCH LISTŮ   KLAD MAPOVÝCH LISTOV   PREGLED LISTOV   PREGLED LIST

1 : 20 000

Légende / Legenda (F)	Zeichenerklärung / Objaśnienia znaków (D)	Legend / Vysvětlivky (UK)			Segni convenzionali / Legenda (I)	Sinais convencionais / Legenda (P)	Signos convencionales / Tumač znakova (E)
Autoroute	Autobahn	Motorway			Autostrada	Auto-estrada	Autopista
Route à quatre voies	Vierspurige Straße	Road with four lanes			Strada a quattro corsie	Estrada com quatro faixas	Carretera de cuatro carriles
Route de transit	Durchgangsstraße	Thoroughfare			Strada di attraversamento	Estrada de trânsito	Carretera de tránsito
Route principale	Hauptstraße	Main road			Strada principale	Estrada principal	Carretera principal
Autres routes	Sonstige Straßen	Other roads			Altre strade	Outras estradas	Otras carreteras
Rue à sens unique - Zone piétonne	Einbahnstraße - Fußgängerzone	One-way street - Pedestrian zone			Via a senso unico - Zona pedonale	Rua de sentido único - Zona de peões	Calle de dirección única - Zona peatonal
Information - Parking	Information - Parkplatz	Information - Parking place			Informazioni - Parcheggio	Informação - Parque de estacionamento	Información - Aparcamiento
Chemin de fer principal avec gare	Hauptbahn mit Bahnhof	Main railway with station			Ferrovia principale con stazione	Linha principal ferroviária com estação	Ferrocarril principal con estación
Autre ligne	Sonstige Bahn	Other railway			Altra ferrovia	Linha ramal ferroviária	Otro ferrocarril
Métro	U-Bahn	Underground			Metropolitana	Metro	Metro
Tramway	Straßenbahn	Tramway			Tram	Eléctrico	Tranvía
Bus d'aéroport	Flughafenbus	Airport bus			Autobus per l'aeroporto	Autocarro c. serviço aeroporto	Autobús al aeropuerto
Poste de police - Bureau de poste	Polizeistation - Postamt	Police station - Post office			Posto di polizia - Ufficio postale	Esquadra da polícia - Correios	Comisaria de policia - Correos
Hôpital - Auberge de jeunesse	Krankenhaus - Jugendherberge	Hospital - Youth hostel			Ospedale - Ostello della gioventù	Hospital - Pousada da juventude	Hospital - Albergue juvenil
Église - Église remarquable	Kirche - Sehenswerte Kirche	Church - Church of interest			Chiesa - Chiesa interessante	Igreja - Igreja interessante	Iglesia - Iglesia de interés
Synagogue - Mosquée	Synagoge - Moschee	Synagogue - Mosque			Sinagoga - Moschea	Sinagoga - Mesquita	Sinagoga - Mezquita
Monument - Tour	Denkmal - Turm	Monument - Tower			Monumento - Torre	Monumento - Torre	Monumento - Torre
Zone bâtie, bâtiment public	Bebaute Fläche, öffentliches Gebäude	Built-up area, public building			Caseggiato, edificio pubblico	Área urbana, edifício público	Zona edificada, edificio público
Zone industrielle	Industriegelände	Industrial area			Zona industriale	Zona industrial	Zona industrial
Parc, bois	Park, Wald	Park, forest			Parco, bosco	Parque, floresta	Parque, bosque

(NL)	(PL)	(CZ)			(SK)	(SLO)	(HR)
Autosnelweg	Autostrada	Dálnice			Diaľnica	Avtocesta	Autocesta
Weg met vier rijstroken	Droga o czterech pasach ruchu	Čtyřstopá silnice			Stvorprúdová cesta	Stiripasovna cesta	Cesta sa četiri traka
Weg voor doorgaand verkeer	Droga przelotowa	Průjezdní silnice			Prejazdná cesta	Tranzitna cesta	Tranzitna cesta
Hoofdweg	Droga główna	Hlavní silnice			Hlavná cesta	Glavna cesta	Glavna cesta
Overige wegen	Drogi inne	Ostatní silnice			Ostatné cesty	Druge ceste	Ostale ceste
Straat met eenrichtingsverkeer - Voetgangerszone	Ulica jednokierunkowa - Strefa ruchu pieszego	Jednosměrná ulice - Pěší zóna			Jednosmerná cesta - Pešia zóna	Enosmerna cesta - Površine za pešce	Jednosmjerna ulica - Pješačka zona
Informatie - Parkeerplaats	Informacja - Parking	Informace - Parkoviště			Informácie - Parkovisko	Informacije - Parkirišče	Informacije - Parkiralište
Belangrijke spoorweg met station	Kolej główna z dworcami	Hlavní železnice s stanice			Hlavná železnica so stanicou	Glavna železniška proga z železniško postajo	Glavna željeznička pruga sa kolodvorom
Overige spoorweg	Kolej drugorzędna	Ostatní železnice			Ostatné železnice	Druga železniška proga	Ostala željeznička traka
Ondergrondse spoorweg	Metro	Metro			Podzemná dráha	Podzemska železnica	Podzemna željeznica
Tram	Linia tramwajowa	Tramvaj			Električka	Tramvaj	Tramvaj
Vliegveldbus	Autobus dojazdowy na lotnisko	Letištní autobus			Letiskový autobus	Letališki avtobus	Autobus zračnog pristaništa
Politiebureau - Postkantoor	Komisariat - Poczta	Policie - Poštovní úřad			Polícia Poštový úrad	Policijska postaja - Pošta	Policijska postaja - Pošta
Ziekenhuis - Jeugdherberg	Szpital - Schronisko młodzieżowe	Nemocnice - Ubytovna mládeže			Nemocnica - Mládežnícka ubytovňa	Bolnišnica - Mladinski hotel	Bolnica - Omladinski hotel
Kerk - Bezienswaardige kerk	Kościół - Kościół zabytkowy	Kostel - Zajímavý kostel			Kostol - Pozoruhodný kostol	Cerkev - Zanimiva cerkev	Crkva - Znamenita crkva
Synagoge - Moskee	Synagoga - Meczet	Synagoga - Mešita			Synagóga - Mešita	Sinagoga - Džamija	Sinagoga - Džamija
Monument - Toren	Pomnik - Wieża	Pomník - Věž			Pomník - Veža	Spomenik - Stolp	Spomenik - Toranj
Bebouwing, openbaar gebouw	Obszar zabudowany, budynek użyteczności publicznej	Zastavěná plocha, veřejná budova			Zastavaná plocha, verejná budova	Stanovanjske zgradbe, javna zgradba	Izgradnja, javna zgradna
Industrieterrein	Obszar przemysłowy	Průmyslová plocha			Priemyselná plocha	Industrijske zgradbe	Industrijska zona
Park, bos	Park, las	Park, les			Park, les	Park, gozd	Park, šuma

Avignon

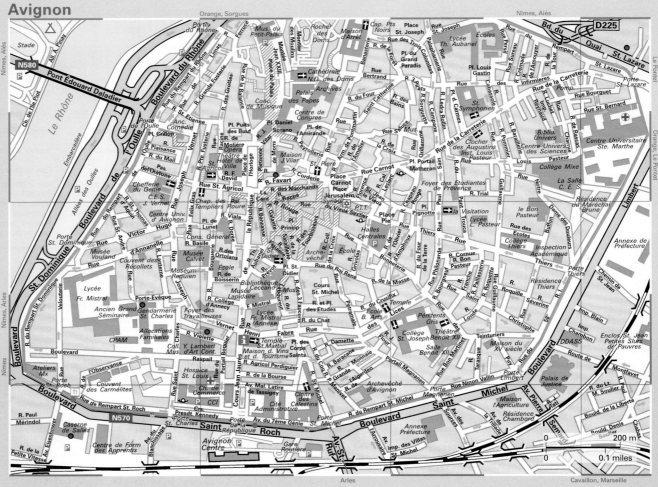

Bordeaux

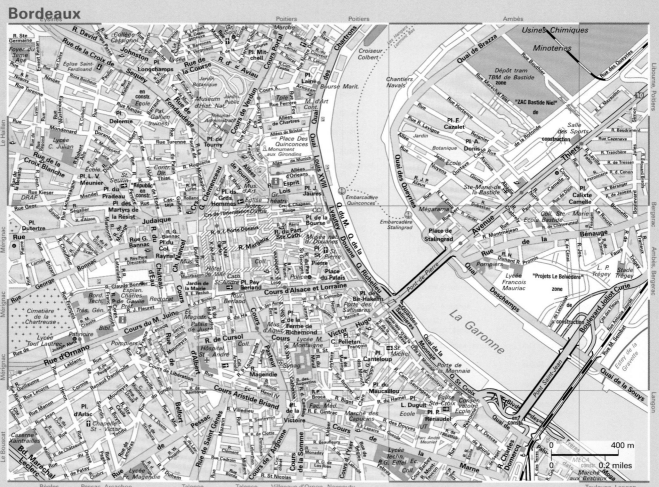

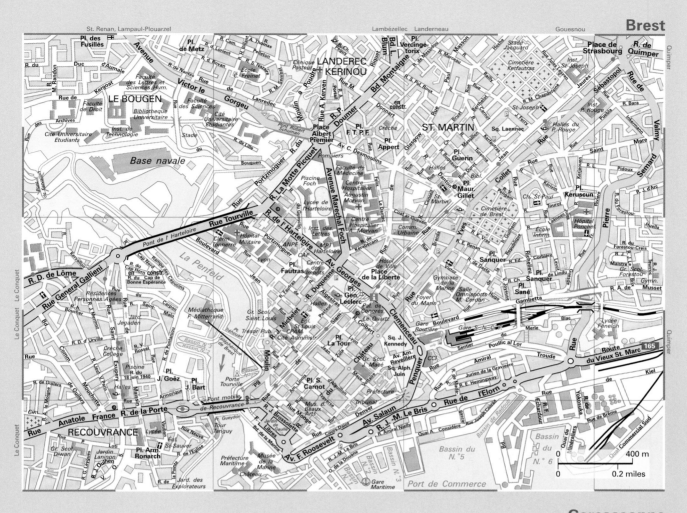

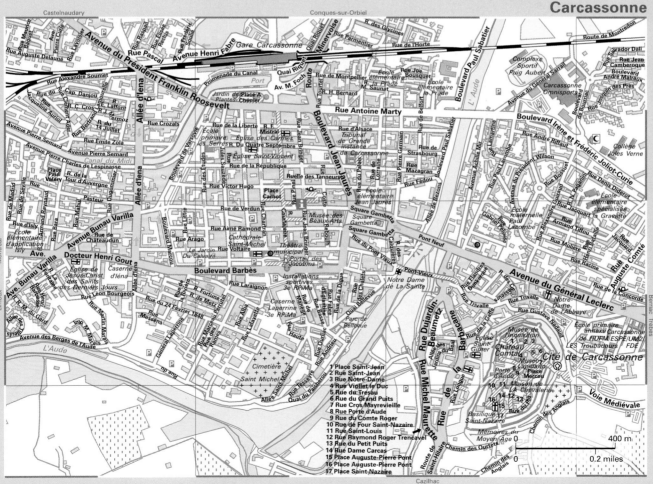

1 Place Saint-Jean
2 Rue Saint-Jean
3 Rue Notre-Dame
4 Rue Viollet le Duc
5 Rue du Trésau
6 Rue du Grand Puits
7 Rue Cros Mayrevieille
8 Rue Porte d'Aude
9 Rue du Comte Roger
10 Rue de Four Saint-Nazaire
11 Rue Saint-Louis
12 Rue Raymond Roger Trencavel
13 Rue du Petit Puits
14 Rue Dame Carcas
15 Place Auguste-Pierre Pont
16 Place Auguste-Pierre Pont
17 Place Saint-Nazaire

SAINT-OUEN D111   **MARCHE AUX PUCES** D14   A1   N301

MONTMARTRE

18

9

MARAIS

3

10

12150 Auberoques 12 152 Da 82
59249 Aubers 59 30 Ce 45
70190 Aubertans 70 93 Ga 64
17220 Aubertière, l' 17 110 Za 72
64290 Aubertin 64 162 Zd 89
05260 Auberts, les 05 144 Gb 80
26340 Auberts, les 26 143 Fb 81
14640 Auberville 14 48 Zf 53
76170 Auberville-la-Campagne 76 36 Ad 51
76450 Auberville-la-Manuel 76 36 Ad 50
76110 Auberville-la-Renault 76 36 Ac 50
93300 Aubervillers 93 51 Cc 55
32420 Aubes, les 32 163 Ae 88
15120 Aubespeyre 15 139 Cc 80
48600 Aubespeyre 48 141 Dd 80
10150 Aubeteire 10 73 Ea 58
03110 Aubeterre 03 116 Db 71
16210 Aubeterre-sur-Dronne 16 124 Ab 77
16250 Aubeville 16 123 Zf 76
27940 Aubevoye 27 50 Bb 53
33430 Aubiac 33 135 Ze 82
46110 Aubiac 46 138 Bd 78
47310 Aubiac 47 149 Ad 84
19380 Aubiat 19 138 Be 78
63260 Aubiat 63 116 Db 73
33240 Aubie-et-Espessas 33 135 Zd 78
63170 Aubière 63 128 Da 74
86320 Aubière 86 112 Ae 70
32270 Aubiet 32 163 Ae 87
48130 Aubigeyres 48 140 Db 80
30140 Aubignac 30 154 Df 84
43350 Aubignac 43 129 De 77
84810 Aubignan 84 155 Fa 84
07400 Aubignas 07 142 Ed 81
63420 Aubignat 63 128 Da 76
35250 Aubigné 35 65 Yc 59
49540 Aubigné 49 98 Zd 65
79110 Aubigné 79 111 Zf 72
72800 Aubigné-Racan 72 85 Ab 62
42940 Aubigneux 42 129 Df 74
70140 Aubigney 70 92 Fd 65
04200 Aubignosc 04 157 Ff 84
03460 Aubigny 03 103 Da 68
14700 Aubigny 14 48 Ze 55
36210 Aubigny 36 101 Be 66
77950 Aubigny 77 71 Ce 57
79390 Aubigny 79 99 Zf 68
80400 Aubigny 80 40 Da 50
80800 Aubigny 80 39 Cc 49
85430 Aubigny 85 97 Yd 69
89560 Aubigny 89 89 Dc 63
59265 Aubigny-au-Bac 59 30 Da 47
02590 Aubigny-aux-Kaisnes 02 40 Da 50
62690 Aubigny-en-Artois 62 29 Cd 46
02820 Aubigny-en-Laonnois 02 40 De 52
21170 Aubigny-en-Plaine 21 106 Fb 66
21340 Aubigny-la-Ronce 21 105 Ed 67
85430 Aubigny-les-Clouzeaux 85 97 Yd 69
08150 Aubigny-les-Pothées 08 41 Ec 50
21540 Aubigny-lès-Sombernon 21 91 Ed 65
52190 Aubigny-sur-Badin 52 92 Fb 62
18700 Aubigny-sur-Nère 18 88 Cc 64
16110 Aubilly 51 53 Df 53
12110 Aubin 12 139 Cb 81
64230 Aubin 64 162 Zd 88
18220 Aubinges 18 102 Cd 65
72270 Aubinière, l' 72 84 Zf 62
62140 Aubin-Saint-Vaast 62 28 Bf 46
66490 Aubiry 66 179 Ce 93
08270 Auboncourt-Vauzelles 08 41 Ec 51
25520 Aubonne 25 108 Gb 66
30620 Aubord 30 169 Eb 86
54580 Auboué 54 56 Ff 53
79100 Auboué 79 99 Zf 67
64330 Aubous 64 162 Zf 87
12470 Aubrac 12 140 Cf 81
26110 Aubres 26 155 Fb 82
85140 Aubretière, l 85 97 Ye 68
55120 Aubréville 55 55 Fa 54
35470 Aubriais, l' 35 82 Yb 61
36370 Aubris, les 36 113 Bb 69
08320 Aubrives 08 42 Ee 48
62390 Aubrometz 62 29 Cb 47
18100 Aubry 18 102 Ca 65
59135 Aubry-du-Hainaut 59 30 Dc 46
61160 Aubry-en-Exmes 61 48 Aa 56
61120 Aubry-le-Pantheau 61 48 Ab 55
58400 Aubues, les 58 103 Da 66
68150 Aubure 68 60 Hb 59
30190 Aubussargues 30 154 Eb 84
23200 Aubusson 23 114 Cb 73
61100 Aubusson 61 47 Zc 56
63120 Aubusson-d'Auvergne 63 128 Dd 74
80110 Aubvillers 80 39 Cc 50
59950 Auby 59 30 Da 46
22100 Aucaleuc 22 65 Xf 58
31140 Aucamville 31 164 Bc 87
82600 Aucamville 82 150 Bb 86
09800 Aucazein 09 176 Af 91
20133 Auccià = Ucciani CTC 182 If 96
26340 Aucelon 26 143 Fc 81
70500 Aucey-la-Plaine 50 66 Yd 57
32000 Auch 32 163 Ad 87
23460 Auchaise 23 126 Bf 74
33480 au Chalet 33 134 Za 79
85200 Auchay-sur-Vendée 85 110 Za 70
62260 Auchel 62 29 Cc 45
80560 Auchonvillers 80 29 Cd 48
59310 Auchy 59 30 Db 46
62190 Auchy-au-Bois 62 29 Cc 45
60360 Auchy-la-Montagne 60 38 Ca 51
62770 Auchy-lès-Hesdin 62 29 Ca 46
62138 Auchy-les-Mines 62 30 Ce 45
55400 Aucourt 55 55 Fe 53
65400 Aucun 65 174 Ze 91
30580 Audabiac 30 154 Ec 84
64400 Audaux 64 161 Zb 88
20116 Auddè = Aullène CTC 183 Ka 98
17770 Audebert 17 123 Zd 73
79170 Audebert, La Brousse- 79 98 Zd 66
64170 Audéjus 64 161 Zc 88
39700 Audelange 39 107 Fd 66
52240 Audeloncourt 52 75 Fd 60
62250 Audembert 62 26 Be 43
59540 Audencourt 59 30 Dc 48
33980 Audenge 33 134 Yf 80
50440 Auderville 50 33 Ya 50
03190 Audes 03 115 Cd 70
25170 Audeux 25 93 Ff 65
45300 Audeville 45 71 Cb 59
06750 Audibergue, l' 06 158 Ge 86
36180 Audière 36 101 Bc 67
29770 Audierne 29 61 Vc 60
02300 Audignicourt 02 40 Da 52
40500 Audignon 40 161 Zc 86
02120 Audigny 02 40 Dd 49
25400 Audincourt 25 94 Gf 64
62560 Audincthun 62 29 Ca 45
62179 Audinghen 62 26 Bd 43
40400 Audon 40 146 Zb 86
50480 Audouville-la-Hubert 50 33 Ye 52
62890 Audrehem 62 27 Bf 44
09800 Audressein 09 176 Af 91
62164 Audresselles 62 26 Bd 44
14250 Audrieu 14 47 Zc 53
24260 Audrix 24 137 Af 79
62370 Audruiq 62 27 Ca 43
54560 Audun-le-Roman 54 43 Ff 52
57390 Audun-le-Tiche 57 43 Ff 52
31360 Audureaux 31 164 Ae 90
67480 Auenheim 67 59 Ia 56
31580 Auèrets 31 163 Ac 90
28150 Auffains 28 70 Bd 59
78610 Auffargis 78 50 Bf 56
76720 Auffay 76 37 Ba 50
28360 Aufferville 28 69 Bc 59
77570 Aufferville 77 71 Cd 59
78930 Auffreville-Brasseuil 78 50 Be 55
08370 Auflance 08 42 Fb 51
64450 Auga 64 162 Zd 88
56800 Augan 56 81 Xe 61
08380 Auge 08 41 Eb 49
13990 Auge 13 155 Ee 86
16170 Augé 16 123 Zf 73
23170 Auge 23 114 Cb 71
39130 Auge 39 119 Fe 69
79400 Augé 79 111 Ze 70
39190 Augea 39 119 Fc 69
43370 Augeac 43 141 De 79
39380 Augerans 39 107 Fd 66
63740 Augère 63 127 Ce 74
03210 Augère, l' 03 103 Da 69
23210 Augères 23 114 Be 72
23400 Augères 23 114 Be 73
63680 Augères-Haute 63 127 Ce 76
63930 Augerolles 63 128 Dd 74
17800 Augers, les 17 123 Zc 75
60800 Auger-Saint-Vincent 60 52 Ce 53
77560 Augers-en-Brie 77 52 Dc 56
45330 Augerville-la-Rivière 45 71 Cc 59
04230 Augès 04 157 Ff 84
42460 Auges, les 42 117 Ea 72
86160 Auget 86 112 Ac 70
36160 Augette, l' 36 114 Ca 70
76850 Augeville 76 37 Bb 51
70500 Augicourt 70 93 Ff 62
24300 Augignac 24 124 Ae 75
09800 Augirein 09 176 Af 91
33820 Augirons, les 33 122 Zc 77
39270 Augisey 39 119 Fc 69
63340 Augnat 63 128 Db 76
32120 Augnax 32 163 Ae 86
87120 Augne 87 126 Be 74
57685 Augny 57 56 Ga 54
28800 Augonville 28 70 Bc 59
72600 Augotterie, l' 72 68 Ab 59
40200 Augreilh 40 161 Zc 86
61270 Auguaise 61 49 Ad 56
13500 Auguette 13 170 Ef 88
02220 Augy 02 53 Dd 52
18800 Augy 18 102 Cd 66
89290 Augy 89 89 Dd 62
18600 Augy-sur-Aubois 18 103 Cf 68
17770 Aujac 17 123 Zd 73
30200 Aujac 30 155 Ed 83
30450 Aujac 30 154 Ea 82
32300 Aujan-Mournède 32 163 Ad 88
05310 Aujards, les 05 145 Gd 80
30250 Aujargues 30 154 Ea 86
52190 Aujeurres 52 92 Fb 62
12630 Aujols 12 152 Ce 82
46090 Aujols 46 150 Bd 82
07600 Aulagnet, l' 07 142 Eb 80
05500 Aulagnier, l' 05 144 Ga 80
47120 Aulaines 72 68 Ac 59
30120 Aulas 30 153 Dd 84
63500 Aulhat-Flat 63 128 Db 75
31190 Auliat 19 126 Bf 76
20116 Aullène CTC 183 Ka 98
63510 Aulnat 63 127 Cd 75
10240 Aulnay 10 74 Ec 58
17470 Aulnay 17 111 Zd 72
86330 Aulnay 86 99 Aa 67
51130 Aulnay-aux-Planches 51 53 Df 56
51240 Aulnay-l'Aître 51 54 Ed 56
45390 Aulnay-la-Rivière 45 71 Cc 59
93600 Aulnay-sous-Bois 93 51 Cc 55
27180 Aulnay-sur-Iton 27 49 Ba 55
51150 Aulnay-sur-Marne 51 53 Eb 54
78126 Aulnay-sur-Mauldre 78 50 Bf 55
72600 Aulneaux, les 72 68 Ac 58
51130 Aulnizeux 51 53 Df 56
88300 Aulnois 88 76 Fe 59
55170 Aulnois-en-Perthois 55 55 Fa 57
02000 Aulnois-sous-Laon 02 40 Dd 51
55200 Aulnois-sous-Vertuzey 55 55 Fe 56
57590 Aulnois-sur-Seille 57 56 Gb 55
77120 Aulnoy 77 52 Da 55
59620 Aulnoye-Aymeries 59 31 Df 47
59300 Aulnoy-lez-Valenciennes 59 30 Dd 47
52160 Aulnoy-sur-Aube 52 91 Fa 62
23210 Aulon 23 113 Be 72
31420 Aulon 31 164 Ae 89
65240 Aulon 65 175 Ab 91
80460 Ault 80 28 Bc 48
09140 Aulus-les-Bains 09 177 Bc 92
70190 Aulx-lès-Cromary 70 93 Ga 64
17770 Aumagne 17 123 Zd 73
26560 Aumagne 26 156 Fd 83
76390 Aumale 76 38 Be 50
31160 Aumassère 31 163 Af 90
80140 Aumâtre 80 38 Be 49
51110 Auménancourt 51 41 Ea 52
51110 Auménancourt-le-Petit 51 41 Ea 52
83390 Aumérade 83 171 Ga 89
62550 Aumerval 62 29 Cc 45
34530 Aumes 34 167 Dc 88
30770 Aumessas 30 153 Dd 85
57710 Aumetz 57 43 Ff 52
50630 Aumeville-Lestre 50 34 Ye 51
23300 Aumône, l' 23 113 Bd 71
12300 Aumont 12 139 Cb 81
19160 Aumont 19 126 Cb 76
19400 Aumont 19 138 Bf 78
39800 Aumont 39 107 Fd 67
80640 Aumont 80 38 Bf 49
48130 Aumont-Aubrac 48 140 Db 80
60300 Aumont-en-Halatte 60 51 Cd 53
88640 Aumontzey, Granges- 88 77 Ge 59
28250 Aumoy 28 69 Ba 57
31360 Aumur 39 106 Fc 66
09140 Aunac 09 176 Ba 91
12470 Aunac 12 139 Ce 81
43370 Aunac 43 141 Df 79
16460 Aunac-sur-Charente 16 111 Ab 73
28700 Aunainville 28 70 Be 58
11140 Aunat 11 178 Ca 92
45130 Aunay 45 87 Be 61
76220 Aunay 76 38 Be 52
53260 Aunay, l' 53 67 Zb 61
85140 Aunay, l' 85 97 Yf 68
58110 Aunay-en-Bazois 58 104 De 66
61500 Aunay-les-Bois 61 68 Ab 57
53100 Aunay-Play, l' 53 67 Zb 59
28700 Aunay-sous-Auneau 28 70 Be 58
28500 Aunay-sous-Crécy 28 50 Bb 56
14260 Aunay-sur-Odon 14 47 Zc 54
28700 Auneau 28 70 Be 58
60390 Auneuil 60 38 Bf 52
46300 Auniac 46 137 Bc 80
61200 Aunou-le-Faucon 61 48 Aa 56
61500 Aunou-sur-Orne 61 68 Ab 57
77710 Aunoy, l' 77 72 Da 59
87470 Auphelle 87 126 Be 74
81530 Aupilières 81 152 Cc 86
43260 Aupinhac 43 141 Ea 78
76730 Auppegard 76 37 Ba 50
83630 Aups 83 171 Gb 87
63660 au Puy 63 129 Df 76
14140 Auquainville 14 48 Ab 54
76630 Auquemesnil 76 37 Bb 49
84120 Auquiers, les 84 171 Fd 86
32600 Auradé 32 164 Ba 87
47140 Auradou 47 149 Ae 82
31190 Auragne 31 164 Bd 88
79350 Auraire, l' 79 98 Zd 67
56400 Auray 56 79 Xa 63
08400 Aure 08 54 Ed 53
43110 Aurec-sur-Loire 43 129 Eb 76
87220 Aureil 87 125 Bc 74
40200 Aureilhan 40 146 Ye 83
13930 Aureille 13 170 Ef 86
88320 Aureil-Maison 88 76 Fe 60
26340 Aurel 26 143 Fb 80
84390 Aurel 84 156 Fc 84
12130 Aurelle-Verlac 12 140 Da 81
17260 Aurenne 17 122 Zb 75
32500 Aurenque 32 149 Ad 85
32100 Aurens 32 148 Ac 85
32400 Aurensan 32 162 Ze 87
65390 Aurensan 65 162 Aa 89
04320 Aurent 04 158 Ge 84
48150 Aures 48 153 Dc 83
14520* Aure sur Mer 14 47 Za 52
31320 Aureville 31 164 Bc 88
50390 Aureville 50 33 Yc 52
11330 Auriac 11 178 Cc 91
12210 Auriac 12 139 Ce 80
19220 Auriac 19 126 Ca 77
64450 Auriac 64 162 Ze 88
24320 Auriac-de-Bourzac 24 124 Ab 76
24290 Auriac-du-Périgord 24 137 Ba 78
12120 Auriac-Lagast 12 152 Cd 84
15500 Auriac-L'Église 15 128 Da 77
47120 Auriac-sur-Dropt 47 136 Ab 81
31460 Auriac-sur-Vendinelle 31 165 Be 87
23400 Auriat 23 126 Bd 73
31190 Auribail 31 164 Bc 88
06810 Auribeau 06 173 Gf 87
84400 Auribeau 84 156 Fc 85
40500 Aurice 40 147 Zc 86
65700 Auriébat 65 162 Aa 88
63210 Aurières 63 127 Cf 74
31260 Auriet 31 164 Ba 90
31420 Aurignac 31 164 Af 89
15000 Aurillac 15 139 Cc 79
32450 Aurimont 32 164 Ae 87
31570 Aurin 31 165 Be 87
13390 Auriol 13 171 Fd 88
34210 Auriol, l' 34 166 Cd 88
07120 Auriolles 07 154 Eb 82
33790 Auriolles 33 135 Aa 80
64350 Aurions-Idernes 64 162 Zf 87
38142 Auris 38 144 Ga 78
06660 Auron 06 158 Gf 83
13121 Aurons 13 170 Fa 87
33124 Auros 33 135 Zf 82
33730 au Ros 33 147 Zd 82
03460 Aurouer 03 103 Db 68
48600 Auroux 48 141 De 80
15500 Aurouze 15 128 Da 77
48300 Aurouzet 48 141 De 80
14240* Aurseulles 14 34 Zb 54
85670 Auspierre, l' 85 97 Yc 68
16560 Aussac 16 124 Ab 74
81600 Aussac 81 151 Ca 85
32170 Aussat 32 163 Ab 88
31260 Ausseing 31 164 Ba 90
64230 Aussevielle 64 162 Zd 88
12390 Aussibal 12 139 Cb 82
81200 Aussillon 81 166 Cb 88
81200 Aussillon-Village 81 166 Cb 88
73500 Aussois 73 133 Ge 77
08310 Aussonce 08 41 Eb 52
31840 Aussonne 31 164 Bb 86
32140 Aussos 32 163 Ad 88
64130 Aussurucq 64 161 Za 90
41240 Autainville 41 86 Bc 61
26110 Autanne 26 156 Fb 83
25110 Autechaux 25 93 Gc 64
25150 Autechaux-Roide 25 94 Ge 64
28330 Autels-Villevillon, les 28 69 Af 59
31190 Auterive 31 164 Bc 88
32550 Auterive 32 163 Ad 87
82500 Auterive 82 149 Af 85
64270 Auterrive 64 161 Yf 88
02360 Autes, les 02 41 Eb 50
70180 Autet 70 92 Fe 63
60390 Auteuil 60 51 Ca 52
78770 Auteuil 78 50 Be 55
64390 Autevielle-Saint-Martin-Bideren 64 161 Za 88
08240 Authe 08 42 Ef 52
28220 Autheuil 28 69 Bb 60
61190 Autheuil 61 69 Ae 57
27490 Autheuil-Authouillet 27 50 Bb 54
60890 Autheuil-en-Valois 60 52 Da 53
80600 Autheux 80 29 Cb 48
27420 Authevernes 27 50 Bd 53
63114 Authezat 63 128 Db 75
14280 Authie 14 35 Zd 53
80560 Authie 80 29 Cc 48
80600 Authieule 80 29 Cc 48
27170 Authieux, les 27 49 Af 54
27220 Authieux, les 27 50 Bb 55
76520 Authieux, les 76 49 Ba 52
76750 Authieux, les 76 37 Bb 51
61240 Authieux-du-Puits, les 61 48 Ab 56
14140 Authieux-Papion, les 14 48 Aa 54
76690 Authieux-Ratiéville 76 37 Ba 51
14130 Authieux-sur-Calonne, les 14 48 Ab 53
58700 Authiou 58 89 Dc 65
70190 Authoison 70 93 Ga 64
04200 Authon 04 157 Ga 83
41310 Authon 41 85 Af 63
28330 Authon-du-Perche 28 69 Af 59
17770 Authon-Ebéon 17 123 Zd 73
91410 Authon-la-Plaine 91 70 Bf 58
27290 Authou 27 49 Ae 53
80300 Authuille 80 29 Cd 48
39100 Authume 39 106 Fd 66
71270 Authumes 71 106 Fb 67
26400 Autichamp 26 143 Ef 80
34480 Autignac 34 167 Db 88
76740 Autigny 76 37 Af 50
88300 Autigny-la-Tour 88 76 Fe 58
52300 Autigny-le-Grand 52 75 Fa 58
52300 Autigny-le-Petit 52 75 Fa 58
62610 Autingues 62 27 Bf 43
46400 Autoire 46 138 Bf 79
70700 Autoreille 70 93 Fe 64
78770 Autouillet 78 50 Be 55
43450 Autrac 43 128 Da 77
38880 Autrans 38 143 Fd 77
38112* Autrans-Méaudre en Vercors 38 143 Fc 78
09800 Autrech 09 176 Af 91
37110 Autrèche 37 86 Af 63
90140 Autrechêne 90 94 Gf 63
60350 Autrêches 60 40 Da 52
55120 Autrécourt-sur-Aire 55 55 Fa 54
02250 Autremencourt 02 40 De 50
54450 Autrepierre 54 77 Ge 57
02580 Autreppes 02 41 Df 49
76190 Autretot 76 36 Ae 51
02300 Autreville 02 40 Db 51
88300 Autreville 88 76 Ff 58
55700 Autréville-Saint-Lambert 55 42 Fa 51
52120 Autreville-sur-la-Renne 52 74 Ef 60
54380 Autreville-sur-Moselle 54 56 Ga 56
54160 Autrey 54 76 Ga 57
88700 Autrey 88 77 Ge 59
70110 Autrey-lès-Cerre 70 93 Gc 63
70100 Autrey-lès-Gray 70 92 Fc 64
21570 Autricourt 21 74 Ed 61
08240 Autruche 08 42 Ef 52
45480 Autruy-sur-Juine 45 71 Ca 59
08250 Autry 08 54 Ef 53
03210 Autry-Issards 03 116 Da 69
45500 Autry-le-Châtel 45 88 Cd 63
71400 Autun 71 105 Eb 67
82220 Auty 82 150 Bc 83
06260 Auvare 06 158 Gf 85
51800 Auve 51 54 Ee 54
33910 Auvergnats, les 33 135 Ze 78
27250 Auvergny 27 49 Ae 55
91830 Auvernaux 91 71 Cc 57
43300 Auvers 43 140 Dc 79
50500 Auvers 50 33 Ye 53
49490 Auverse 49 84 Aa 63
72300 Auvers-le-Hamon 72 84 Zd 61
91580 Auvers-Saint-Georges 91 71 Cb 58
72540 Auvers-sous-Montfaucon 72 68 Zf 60
95430 Auvers-sur-Oise 95 51 Cb 54
70100 Auvet-et-la-Chapelotte 70 92 Fd 63
81470 Auvezines 81 165 Bf 87
44210 Auvière, l' 44 96 Xf 66
72300 Auvière, l' 72 84 Zd 61
17800 Auvignac 17 123 Zc 75
87600 Auvignac 87 125 Af 73
82340 Auvillar 82 149 Af 84
14340 Auvillars 14 48 Aa 53
21250 Auvillars-sur-Saône 21 106 Fa 66
60290 Auvillers 60 39 Cc 52
08260 Auvillers-les-Forges 08 41 Ec 49
28360 Auvilliers 28 70 Bc 59
76270 Auvilliers 76 38 Bd 50
45270 Auvilliers-en-Gâtinais 45 71 Cd 61
AD600 Auvinyà ◘ AND 177 Bd 94
50500 Auxais 50 33 Ye 53
33680 aux Andraux 33 134 Yf 79
39700 Auxange 39 107 Fd 65
47150 Aux Anjeaux 47 137 Af 81
21360 Auxant 21 105 Ed 66
32170 Aux-Aussat 32 163 Ab 88
87130 Aux-Barres 87 126 Bd 75
90200 Auxelles-Bas 90 94 Ge 62
90200 Auxelles-Haut 90 94 Ge 62
89000 Auxerre 89 89 Dd 62
21190 Auxey-Duresses 21 105 Ee 67
42990 aux Gouttes 42 129 Df 74
62390 Auxi-le-Château 62 29 Ca 47
15300 Auxillac 15 139 Cf 78
48500 Auxillac 48 140 Db 82
60000 Aux Marais 60 38 Ca 52
58800 Auxois 58 89 De 65
10130 Auxon 10 73 Df 60
70000 Auxon 70 93 Gb 62
89630 Auxon 89 90 Df 64
25870 Auxon-Dessous 25 93 Ff 65
25870 Auxon-Dessus 25 93 Ff 65
21130 Auxonne 21 106 Fc 65
25870 Auxons, les 25 93 Ff 65
71520 Aux Truges 71 117 Ec 70
45340 Auxy 45 71 Cc 60
71400 Auxy 71 105 Ec 67
33690 Auzac 33 148 Zf 82
46300 Auzac 46 138 Bd 80
88140 Auzainvilliers 88 76 Ff 59
30140 Auzas 30 154 Ea 84
31360 Auzas 31 164 Af 89
09220 Auzat 09 177 Bc 92
63570 Auzat-sur-Allier 63 128 Db 76
85200 Auzay 85 110 Za 70
76190 Auzebosc 76 36 Ae 51
55800 Auzécourt 55 55 Ef 55
63590 Auzelles 63 128 Dd 75
81800 Auzérals, les 81 150 Be 85
15240 Auzers 15 127 Cc 77
04140 Auzet 04 157 Gb 83
55120 Auzéville-en-Argonne 55 55 Fa 54
31320 Auzeville-Tolosane 31 164 Bc 87
34390 Auziale 34 167 Cf 87
31650 Auzielle 31 165 Bd 87
87290 Auzillac 87 113 Bb 72
12390 Auzits 12 139 Cb 81
63320 Auzolette 63 128 Da 75
15110 Auzolles 15 140 Cf 79
63420 Auzolles 63 128 Cf 76
43390 Auzon 43 128 Dc 76
37110 Auzouer-en-Touraine 37 86 Af 63
76640 Auzouville-Auberbosc 76 36 Ad 51
76760 Auzouville-L'Esneval 76 37 Af 51
76116 Auzouville-sur-Ry 76 37 Bb 52
76730 Auzouville-sur-Saâne 76 37 Af 50
20146 A Vacca CTC 185 Ka 99
36100 Avail 36 102 Ca 67
86270 Availlé 86 100 Ae 68
86530 Availles-en-Châtellerault 86 100 Ad 68
86460 Availles-Limouzine 86 112 Ad 72
79170 Availles-sur-Chizé 79 111 Zd 72
35130 Availles-sur-Seiche 35 66 Ye 61
79600 Availles-Thouarsais 79 99 Zf 67
42840 Avaize 42 117 Ea 72
65240 Avajan 65 175 Ac 91
81160 Avalats, les 81 151 Cb 85
10110 Avaleur 10 74 Ec 60
17530 Avallon 17 122 Yf 74
89200 Avallon 89 90 Df 64
73260 Avanchers, les 73 132 Gc 76
05230 Avançon 05 144 Gb 81
08300 Avançon 08 41 Eb 52
57640 Avancy 57 56 Gb 53
25720 Avanne-Aveney 25 107 Ff 65
10400 Avant-lès-Marcilly 10 73 Dd 58
10240 Avant-lès-Ramerupt 10 74 Eb 58
86170 Avanton 86 99 Ab 69
20225 Avapessa CTC 180 If 93
41500 Avaray 41 86 Bd 62
08190 Avaux 08 41 Ea 52
69610 Aveize 69M 130 Ec 74
42330 Aveizieux 42 129 Ec 75
30430 Avejan 30 154 Eb 83
83310 Avelan, l' 83 172 Gd 89
21120 Avelanges 21 91 Fa 63
80270 Avelesges 80 38 Bf 49
59710 Avelin 59 30 Da 45
60650 Avelon 60 38 Bf 52
80300 Aveluy 80 39 Cd 48
69430 Avenas 69D 118 Ed 71
14210 Avenay 14 35 Zd 54
51160 Avenay-Val-d'Or 51 53 Ea 54
34260 Avène 34 152 Da 86
61160 Avenelles 61 48 Aa 56
25720 Aveney 25 107 Ff 65
67370 Avenheim 67 58 Hd 56
38630 Avenières Veyrins-Thuellin, les 38 131 Fd 75
06260 Avenos 06 158 Gf 85
32120 Avensac 32 149 Af 86
33480 Avensan 33 134 Zb 78
87370 Avent 87 113 Bc 72
65660 Aventignan 65 163 Ad 90
27630 Aveny 27 50 Bd 54
65380 Averan 65 162 Aa 90
62127 Averdoingt 62 29 Cc 46
41330 Averdon 41 86 Bb 62
03000 Avermes 03 103 Db 69
95450 Avernes 95 50 Bf 54
61470 Avernes-Saint-Gourgon 61 48 Ab 55
61310 Avernes-sous-Exmes 61 48 Ab 56
73480 Avérole 73 133 Ha 77
32310 Avéron 32 148 Ac 85
32290 Avéron-Bergelle 32 162 Aa 86

240 | Auberoques

38930 Avers 38 144 Fe 80
53700 Averton 53 67 Ze 59
59440 Avesnelles 59 31 Df 48
62650 Avesnes 62 28 Bf 45
80140 Avesnes-Chaussoy 80 38 Bf 49
76220 Avesnes-en-Bray 76 38 Be 52
72260 Avesnes-en-Saosnois 72 68 Ac 59
76630 Avesnes-en-Val 76 37 Bc 49
62810 Avesnes-le-Comte 62 29 Cd 47
59129 Avesnes-lès-Aubert 59 30 Dc 47
59296 Avesnes-le-Sec 59 30 Dc 47
59440 Avesnes-sur-Helpe 59 31 Df 48
44460 Avessac 44 81 Ya 63
72350 Avessé 72 67 Ze 61
65370 Aveux 65 176 Ad 90
31350 Avezac 31 163 Ad 89
65130 Avezac-Prat-Lahitte 65 163 Ac 90
32380 Avezan 32 149 Ae 85
30120 Avèze 30 153 Dd 85
63690 Avèze 63 127 Cd 75
72400 Avezé 72 69 Ae 59
74570 Aviernoz 74 120 Gb 73
89240 Avigneau 89 89 Dc 62
84000 Avignon 84 155 Ee 85
38650 Avignonet 38 144 Fd 79
31290 Avignonet-Lauragais 31 165 Be 88
39200 Avignon-lès-Saint-Claude 39 119 Ff 70
89270 Avigny 89 89 De 63
54490 Avillers 54 43 Fe 53
88500 Avillers 88 76 Gb 59
55210 Avillers-Sainte-Croix 55 55 Fe 54
25680 Avilley 25 93 Gb 64
60300 Avilly 60 51 Cd 53
60300 Avilly-Saint-Léonard 60 51 Cd 53
20215 A Vinzulasca = Venzolasca CTC 181 Kc 94
62210 Avion 62 30 Ce 46
55600 Avioth 55 43 Fc 51
49500 Aviré 49 83 Zb 62
10340 Avirey-Lingey 10 74 Eb 60
27930 Aviron 27 49 Ba 54
51190 Avize 51 53 Ea 55
55270 Avocourt 55 55 Fa 53
37420 Avoine 37 99 Ab 65
61150 Avoine 61 48 Zf 56
72430 Avoise 72 84 Ze 61
77300 Avon 77 71 Ce 58
79800 Avon 79 111 Zf 70
62310 Avondance 62 29 Ca 46
26410 Avondons, les 26 143 Fd 81
10290 Avon-la-Pèze 10 73 Dd 58
37220 Avon-les-Roches 37 100 Ac 66
18520 Avord 18 103 Cd 66
74110 Avoriaz 74 121 Ge 71
21350 Avosnes 21 91 Ed 64
21580 Avot 21 91 Fa 63
25690 Avoudrey 25 108 Gc 66
01170 Avouzon 01 120 Ga 71
52130 Avrainville 52 75 Fa 57
54385 Avrainville 54 56 Ff 56
88130 Avrainville 88 76 Gb 58
91630 Avrainville 91 71 Cb 57
50300 Avranches 50 46 Yd 56
81190 Avraniers, les 81 151 Ca 84
88630 Avranville 88 75 Fd 58
80500 Avre 80 39 Cd 50
60130 Avrechy 60 39 Cc 52
52140 Avrecourt 52 75 Fd 61
58170 Avrée 58 104 Df 68
74350 Avregny 74 120 Ga 72
76730 Avremesnil 76 37 Af 49
73240 Avressieux 73 131 Fe 75
10130 Avreuil 10 73 Ea 60
60310 Avricourt 60 39 Cf 51
54450 Avricourt (Meurthe et Moselle) 54 57 Ge 57
57810 Avricourt (Moselle) 57 57 Ge 57
73500 Avrieux 73 133 Ge 77
70150 Avrigney-Virey 70 93 Fe 64
89660 Avrigny 89 90 Dd 64
54150 Avril 54 56 Ff 53
49240 Avrillé 49 83 Zc 63
85440 Avrillé 85 109 Yd 70
37340 Avrillé-les-Ponceaux 37 85 Ab 64
03130 Avrilly 03 117 Df 70
27240 Avrilly 27 49 Ba 55
61700 Avrilly 61 67 Zc 57
77760 Avrilmont 77 71 Cd 59
58300 Avril-sur-Loire 58 103 Dc 68
89600 Avrolles 89 73 De 60
62560 Avroult 62 29 Ca 45
74330 Avully 74 120 Ga 73
20290 A Vulpaiola = Volpajola CTC 181 Kc 93
20167 A Vulpaja CTC 182 Ie 97
17800 Avy 17 123 Zc 75
59400 Awoingt 59 30 Db 48
11140 Axat 11 178 Cb 92
09250 Axiat 09 177 Be 92
09110 Ax-les-Thermes 09 177 Bf 92
51160 Ay 51 53 Ea 54
63390 Ayat-sur-Sioule 63 115 Cf 72
51150* Aÿ-Champagne 51 53 Ea 54
63970 Aydat 63 128 Cf 75
64330 Aydie 64 162 Zf 87
64490 Aydius 64 174 Zc 90
88600 Aydoilles 88 77 Gd 59
19310 Ayen 19 125 Bb 77
80500 Ayencourt 80 39 Cd 51
09800 Ayer 09 176 Ba 91
63560 Ayes, les 63 115 Ce 72
47400 Ayet 47 148 Ab 82
62116 Ayette 62 29 Ce 47
13015 Aygalades, les 13 170 Fc 88
83400 Ayguade-Ceinturon 83 171 Gb 90
66360 Ayguatébia 66 178 Cb 93
33640 Ayguemorte-les-Graves 33 135 Zd 80
32120 Aygues-Mortes 32 149 Ae 86
31450 Ayguesvives 31 165 Bd 88
32410 Ayguetinte 32 148 Ac 86
64240 Ayherre 64 160 Ye 88
63470 Aymards, les 63 127 Cd 74
15200 Aymons 15 127 Cb 77
73470 Ayn 73 131 Fe 75
46120 Aynac 46 138 Bf 80
70200 Aynans, les 70 94 Gc 63
09400 Aynat 09 177 Bd 91
15250 Ayrens 15 139 Cb 79
12240 Ayres 12 151 Ca 83
48240 Ayres, les 48 153 Df 83
12310 Ayrinhac 12 152 Ce 82
11430 Ayrolle, l' 11 167 Da 90
35470 Baen = Bain-de-Bretagne 35 82 Yb 61
86190 Ayron 86 99 Aa 69
65400 Ayros-Arbouix 65 175 Zf 90
65120 Ayrues 65 175 Zf 92
74130 Ayse 74 120 Gc 72
12430 Ayssènes 12 152 Ce 84
12510 Ayssiols 12 152 Cc 82
57300 Ay-sur-Moselle 57 56 Gb 53
17440 Aytré 17 110 Yf 72
08000 Ayvelles, les 08 42 Ee 50
65400 Ayzac-Ost 65 175 Zf 90
32800 Ayzieu 32 148 Zf 85
33820 Azac 33 122 Zc 77
55150 Azannes-et-Soumazannes 55 55 Fc 53
39100 Azans 39 106 Fd 66
31380 Azas 31 165 Be 86
23800 Azat 23 113 Bd 71
23210 Azat-Châtenet 23 114 Be 72
87360 Azat-le-Ris 87 113 Ba 71
79400 Azay-le-Brulé 79 111 Ze 70
36290 Azay-le-Ferron 36 100 Ba 67
37190 Azay-le-Rideau 37 100 Ac 65
37270 Azay-sur-Cher 37 85 Af 64
37310 Azay-sur-Indre 37 100 Af 65
79130 Azay-sur-Thouet 79 98 Zd 69
41100 Azé 41 86 Af 61
71260 Azé 71 118 Ee 70
54210 Azelot 54 76 Gb 57
12130 Azémars, les 12 140 Cf 82
23160 Azerables 23 113 Bc 70
54122 Azerailles 54 77 Ge 58
24210 Azerat 24 137 Ba 78
43390 Azérat 43 128 Dc 76
65380 Azereix 65 162 Zf 89
65170 Azet 65 175 Ac 92
50310 Azeville 50 34 Ye 52
34210 Azillanet 34 166 Ce 89
11700 Azille 11 166 Cd 89
20190 Azilone-Apaza CTC 184 Ka 97
20190 Azilonu = Azilone CTC 184 Ka 97
62310 Azincourt 62 29 Ca 46
12620 Azinières 12 152 Cf 84
85490 Aziré 85 110 Zc 70
69790 Azolette 69D 117 Ec 71
57810 Azoudange 57 57 Ge 56
71230 Azu 71 105 Ec 69
40140 Azur 40 146 Ye 86
18220 Azy 18 103 Ce 65
58600 Azy 58 103 Da 66
58240 Azy-le-Vif 58 103 Db 68
02400 Azy-sur-Marne 02 52 Dc 54
20121 Azzana CTC 182 If 96

B

55700 Baâlon 55 42 Fb 52
08430 Baâlons 08 42 Ee 51
34360 Babeau-Bouldoux 34 167 Cf 88
86300 Babijère, la 86 112 Ae 69
24170 Babiot 24 137 Ba 80
60400 Babœuf 60 40 Da 51
43170 Babonnès 43 141 Dd 79
03470 Babus, les 03 116 De 70
19140 Baby 19 125 Bd 76
77480 Baby 77 72 Dc 58
15190 Bac, le 15 127 Ce 76
24630 Bac, le 24 125 Ba 75
82230 Bacan 82 150 Bd 85
59147 Bac-à-Wavrin 59 30 Cf 45
54120 Baccarat 54 77 Ge 58
31550 Baccarets, les 31 165 Bd 89
20246 Baccialu CTC 181 Ka 93
45130 Baccon 45 87 Bd 61
02300 Bac-d'Arblincourt, le 02 40 Db 51
46230 Bach 46 150 Be 82
59138 Bachant 59 31 Df 47
31420 Bachas 31 164 Af 89
05700 Bachas, le 05 156 Fe 83
19290 Bachelerie, la 19 126 Cb 75
24210 Bachellerie, la 24 137 Ba 78
62390 Bachimont 62 29 Ca 47
60240 Bachivillers 60 50 Bf 53
31440 Bachos 31 176 Ad 91
59830 Bachy 59 30 Db 45
50530 Bacilly 50 46 Yd 56
51400 Baconnes 51 54 Ec 54
44210 Baconnière 44 96 Xf 65
44210 Baconnière 44 96 Xf 66
53240 Baconnière, la 53 66 Za 59
43230 Bacou 43 128 Dd 77
60120 Bacouel 60 39 Cc 51
80480 Bacouel-sur-Selle 80 38 Cb 50
57590 Bacourt 57 56 Gc 55
27930 Bacquepuis 27 49 Ba 54
27440 Bacqueville 27 37 Bc 53
76730 Bacqueville-en-Caux 76 37 Ba 50
62840 Bac-Saint-Maur 62 30 Ce 45
15800 Badailhac 15 139 Cd 79
24120 Badaillac 24 137 Bb 78
48000 Badaroux 48 140 Dd 81
13410 Badasset 13 170 Fb 87
12370 Badassou 12 166 Ce 86
36200 Badecon-le-Pin 36 113 Bd 69
24390 Badefols-d'Ans 24 125 Bb 77
24150 Badefols-sur-Dordogne 24 137 Ae 79
56870 Baden 56 80 Xa 63
11800 Badens 11 166 Cd 89
86460 Badeuil 86 112 Ad 71
58330 Badières, les 58 104 Dc 66
38300 Badinières, Eclose- 38 131 Fb 75
43150 Badioux, les 43 141 Df 79
54122 Badménil 54 77 Ge 58
88330 Badménil-aux-Bois 88 77 Gd 59
13129 Badon 13 169 Ee 88
54540 Badonviller 54 77 Gf 58
24130 Badoux 24 136 Ab 79
48340 Badroux 48 140 Db 82
67320 Baerendorf 67 57 Ha 55
57230 Baerenthal 57 58 Hd 55
03390 Bæut 03 115 Cf 71
33620 Bafave 33 135 Ze 78
88460 Baffe, la 88 77 Gd 60
63600 Baffie 63 129 De 76
44680 Baffrie, la 44 96 Yb 66
30140 Bagard 30 154 Ea 84
33190 Bagas 33 135 Zf 81
40110 Bagatelle 40 147 Zb 84
72200 Bagatelle 72 84 Ze 62
46800 Bagat-en-Quercy 46 150 Bb 82
01380 Bâgé-Dommartin 01 118 Ef 71
01380 Bâgé-le-Châtel 01 118 Ef 71
31510 Bagen 31 176 Ae 90
09230 Bagert 09 164 Ba 90
11100 Bages 11 167 Cf 90
12400 Bages 12 152 Cf 85
66670 Bages 66 179 Cf 93
15190 Bagil 15 127 Ce 77
31510 Bagiry 31 176 Ad 91
46270 Bagnac-sur-Célé 46 138 Ca 81
15190 Bagnard 15 127 Ce 76
24750 Bagnas 24 136 Ae 78
79800 Bagnault 79 111 Zf 70
86350 Bagné 86 112 Ad 71
77720 Bagneaux 77 72 Cf 57
89190 Bagneaux 89 73 Dd 59
77167 Bagneaux-sur-Loing 77 71 Ce 59
40140 Bagnère, la 40 160 Ye 86
31230 Bagnères, les 31 163 Ae 88
65200 Bagnères-de-Bigorre 65 162 Aa 90
31110 Bagnères-de-Luchon 31 176 Ad 92
02290 Bagneux 02 40 Db 52
03460 Bagneux 03 103 Db 69
36210 Bagneux 36 101 Be 65
54170 Bagneux 54 76 Ff 57
79290 Bagneux 79 99 Ze 66
92320 Bagneux 92 51 Cb 56
10340 Bagneux-la-Fosse 10 74 Eb 61
20270 Bagni di Puzzichellu = Bains de Puzzichellu CTC 183 Kc 96
17160 Bagnizeau 17 111 Ze 73
87370 Bagnol 87 113 Bd 72
11600 Bagnoles 11 166 Cc 89
61140 Bagnoles-de-l'Orne Normandie 61 67 Zd 57
03240 Bagnolets, les 03 116 Da 71
63810 Bagnols 63 127 Cd 76
69620 Bagnols 69D 118 Ed 73
83600 Bagnols-en-Forêt 83 172 Ge 87
48190 Bagnols-les-Bains 48 141 Dd 81
30200 Bagnols-sur-Cèze 30 155 Ed 84
21700 Bagnot 21 106 Fa 66
51260 Bagrieux 51 73 De 57
27700 Baguelande, la 27 50 Bc 53
35120 Baguer-Morvan 35 65 Yb 57
35120 Baguer-Pican 35 65 Yb 57
83440 Baguier, le 83 172 Gd 87
66540 Baho 66 179 Ce 92
40500 Bahus 40 162 Zd 86
40320 Bahus-Soubiran 40 162 Zd 86
28140 Baigneaux 28 70 Be 60
28360 Baigneaux 28 70 Bd 58
33760 Baigneaux 33 135 Ze 80
41290 Baigneaux 41 86 Bb 62
03360 Baignereau 03 103 Cd 69
70000 Baignes 70 93 Ga 63
16360 Baignes-Sainte-Radegonde 16 123 Ze 76
21450 Baigneux-les-Juifs 21 91 Ed 63
28150 Baignolet 28 70 Bd 59
40380 Baigts 40 161 Zb 86
64300 Baigts-de-Béarn 64 161 Za 87
87380 Baile 87 125 Bc 75
34670 Baillargues 34 168 Ea 87
32420 Baillasbat 32 163 Ae 88
35460 Baillé 35 66 Yd 58
37260 Baillé 37 85 Ad 65
28320 Bailleau-Armenonville 28 70 Bd 57
28120 Bailleau-le-Pin 28 70 Bb 58
28300 Bailleau-l'Evêque 28 70 Bc 58
66320 Baillestavy 66 178 Cd 93
33114 Baillet 33 134 Zb 81
95560 Baillet-en-France 95 51 Cb 54
61160 Bailleuil 61 48 Zf 56
27220 Bailleul 27 49 Bb 55
59270 Bailleul 59 30 Ce 44
80490 Bailleul 80 38 Bf 48
72200 Bailleul, le 72 84 Zf 62
62127 Bailleul-aux-Cornailles 62 29 Cc 46
27260 Bailleul-la-Cormeilles 27 48 Ac 53
60190 Bailleul-le-Soc 60 39 Cd 52
62550 Bailleul-lès-Pernes 62 29 Cc 45
62123 Bailleulmont 62 29 Cd 47
76660 Bailleul-Neuville 76 37 Bc 50
62580 Bailleul-Sir-Berthoult 62 30 Cf 46
60930 Bailleul-sur-Thérain 60 38 Cb 52
60140 Bailleval 60 39 Cc 52
22380 Baillie, la 22 64 Xe 57
76660 Baillolet 76 37 Bc 50
95270 Baillon 95 51 Cc 54
41170 Baillou 41 69 Af 61
41320 Bailly 41 87 Bf 65
58800 Bailly 58 90 De 65
60170 Bailly 60 39 Cf 52
78870 Bailly 78 51 Ca 55
89530 Bailly 89 90 Dd 62
52130 Bailly-aux-Forges 52 74 Ef 58
77720 Bailly-Carrois 77 72 Cf 57
76660 Bailly-en-Campagne 76 37 Bc 49
76630 Bailly-en-Rivière 76 37 Bc 49
10330 Bailly-le-Franc 10 74 Ed 57
77700 Bailly-Romainvilliers 77 52 Ce 55
80870 Bainast 80 28 Be 48
62360 Baincthun 62 28 Be 44
35470 Bain-de-Bretagne 35 82 Yb 61
62850 Bainghen 62 27 Bf 44
43370 Bains 43 141 De 78
23240 Bains, les 23 114 Bd 72
20113 Bains de Baraci CTC 184 If 98
20153 Bains de Guitera CTC 183 Ka 97
66500 Bains-de-Molitg, les 66 178 Cc 93
20270 Bains de Puzzichellu CTC 183 Kc 96
88240 Bains-les-Bains 88 76 Gb 60
35600 Bains-sur-Oust 35 81 Xf 62
54290 Bainville-aux-Miroirs 54 76 Gb 58
88270 Bainville-aux-Saules 88 76 Ga 59
54550 Bainville-sur-Madon 54 76 Ga 57
45390 Bainvilliers 45 71 Cc 59
10410 Baires 10 73 Ea 59
06420 Bairols 06 158 Ha 85
08390 Bairon et ses environs 08 42 Ee 51
35680 Bais 35 66 Ye 60
53160 Bais 53 67 Zd 59
61210 Baise 61 48 Ze 56
59780 Baisieux 59 30 Db 45
13680 Baisses, les 13 170 Fa 87
34330 Baïssescure 34 166 Ce 87
59132 Baives 59 31 Eb 48
07210 Baix 07 142 Ee 80
38118 Baix 38 131 Fc 74
66390 Baixas 66 179 Ce 92
80300 Baizieux 80 39 Cd 49
51270 Baizil, le 51 53 De 55
32140 Bajon 32 163 Ad 88
32120 Bajonnette 32 149 Ae 86
81470 Bajos 81 165 Bf 87
09130 Bajou 09 164 Bc 89
62150 Bajus 62 29 Cc 46
20137 Bala CTC 185 Kb 99
09800 Balacet 09 176 Af 91
46230 Balach 46 150 Bd 83
46600 Baladou 46 138 Bd 79
15170 Baladour, le 15 128 Cf 77
60250 Balagny-sur-Thérain 60 51 Cc 53
09800 Balaguères 09 176 Ba 91
09700 Balaguier 09 165 Be 90
12260 Balaguier-d'Olt 12 138 Bf 81
12380 Balaguier-sur-Rance 12 152 Cd 85
47250 Balahade 47 148 Aa 82
39120 Balaiseaux 39 106 Fc 67
65400 Balaïtous 65 174 Ze 91
08160 Balaives-et-Butz 08 42 Ee 50
01360 Balan 01 131 Fa 73
39160 Balanod 39 119 Fc 70
33470 Balanos 33 134 Za 81
64300 Balansun 64 161 Zb 88
17600 Balanzac 17 122 Za 74
32250 Balarin 32 148 Ab 85
34540 Balaruc-les-Bains 34 168 De 88
34540 Balaruc-le-Vieux 34 168 De 88
44160 Balasson 44 81 Xf 64
80700 Balâtre 80 39 Cf 50
35500 Balazé 35 66 Ye 59
07120 Balazuc 07 142 Ec 81
15150 Balbarie, la 15 138 Ca 79
42510 Balbigny 42 129 Eb 74
38260 Balbins 38 131 Fb 76
67310 Balbronn 67 60 Hc 57
67600 Baldenheim 67 60 Hd 59
68270 Baldersheim 68 95 Hc 62
77320 Baleine 77 52 Dc 56
50450 Baleine, la 50 46 Ye 55
64460 Baleix 64 162 Zf 88
40240 Balen 40 148 Zf 84
87470 Balendeix 87 126 Be 74
20167 Baleone CTC 182 Ie 97
82120 Baléry 82 149 Af 85
09420 Balès 09 177 Bc 91
37160 Balesmes 37 100 Ae 67
52200 Balesmes-sur-Marne 52 92 Fc 62
31580 Balesta 31 163 Ad 89
32390 Baleyron 32 149 Ad 86
47120 Baleyssagues 47 136 Aa 80
68740 Balgau 68 95 Hd 61
20226 Balgudè = Belgodere CTC 180 Ka 93
82120 Balignac 82 149 Af 85
10330 Balignicourt 10 74 Ec 57
27130 Balines 27 49 Af 56
62610 Balinghem 62 27 Bf 43
64330 Baliracq-Maumusson 64 162 Ze 87
64510 Baliros 64 162 Ze 89
33730 Balizac 33 135 Zd 82
33112 Balizac 33 134 Zb 77
91160 Ballainvilliers 91 51 Cb 56
74140 Ballaison 74 120 Gb 71
91610 Ballancourt-sur-Essonne 91 71 Cc 57
37510 Ballan-Miré 37 85 Ad 64
17160 Ballans 17 123 Ze 74
03130 Ballans, les 03 116 De 70
50170 Ballant 50 66 Yd 57
08400 Ballay 08 42 Ee 52
87290 Balledent 87 113 Bb 72
53340 Ballée 53 84 Zd 61
58130 Balleray 58 103 Db 66
14490 Balleroy-sur-Drôme 14 34 Za 53
68210 Ballersdorf 68 95 Ha 63
88170 Balléville 88 76 Ff 59
49260 Balloire 49 99 Zf 66
17290 Ballon 17 110 Za 72
37600 Ballon 37 100 Ba 66
72290 Ballon 72 68 Ab 59
26560 Ballons 26 156 Fd 83
72290 Ballon-Saint Mars 72 68 Ab 59
71220 Ballore 71 117 Ec 69
63230 Ballot 63 127 Ce 73
53350 Ballots 53 83 Yf 61
77118 Balloy 77 72 Da 58
31130 Balma 31 164 Bc 87
01430 Balmay, le 01 119 Fd 72
38142 Balme, la 38 144 Ga 78
73170 Balme, la 73 131 Fe 74
39320 Balme-d'Epy, la 39 119 Fc 70
74330 Balme-de-Sillingy, la 74 120 Ga 73
74230 Balme-de-Thuy, la 74 120 Gb 73
38390 Balme-les-Grottes, la 38 131 Fc 73
26100 Balmes, les 26 143 Fa 78
48500 Balmes, les 48 153 Db 82
74600 Balmont 74 132 Ga 74
10210 Balnot-la-Grange 10 73 Eb 61
10110 Balnot-sur-Laignes 10 74 Ec 60
20160 Balogna CTC 182 Ie 95
21330 Balot 21 91 Ec 62
24580 Balou 24 137 Af 78
12510 Balsac 12 151 Cc 82
23320 Balsac 23 114 Be 71
68210 Balschwiller 68 95 Hb 62
68320 Baltzenheim 68 60 Hd 60
01340 Balvay 01 118 Fb 71
16430 Balzac 16 124 Aa 74
59470 Bambecque 59 27 Cd 43
57690 Bambiderstroff 57 57 Gd 54
88260 Bambois, le 88 76 Ff 60
29380 Banaleg = Bannalec 29 79 Wb 61
48500 Banassac-Canilhac 48 153 Db 82
09400 Banat 09 177 Bd 91
12310 Banc 12 152 Ce 82
64430 Banca 64 160 Yd 90
05130 Banchet, le 05 157 Ga 82
02140 Bancigny 02 41 Ea 50
62450 Bancourt 62 30 Cf 48
70290 Ban-de-Champagney, le 70 94 Ge 62
67130 Ban-de-la-Roche, le 67 60 Hb 58
88520 Ban-de-Laveline 88 77 Ha 59
88210 Ban-de-Sapt 88 77 Ha 58
83150 Bandol 83 171 Fe 90
01990 Baneins 01 118 Ef 72
63330 Baneize 63 115 Cd 72
24150 Baneuil 24 136 Ae 79
56360 Bangor 56 80 We 65
12140 Banhars 12 139 Cd 80
63230 Banière 63 127 Cf 74
65200 Banios 65 175 Ab 90
23120 Banize 23 114 Ca 73
86550 Banlègre 86 112 Ac 69
30450 Banlève, la 30 154 Df 82
59600 Banlieue, la 59 31 Df 47
29380 Bannalec 29 79 Wb 61
25560 Bannans 25 107 Gb 67
89400 Bannard 89 89 Dd 61
18300 Bannay 18 88 Cf 64
51270 Bannay 51 53 De 55
57220 Bannay 57 57 Gc 54
07460 Banne 07 154 Ea 82
07510 Banne 07 141 Ea 80
18210 Bannegon 18 103 Ce 68
50440 Bannery 50 33 Ya 50
46400 Bannes 46 138 Bf 80
51230 Bannes 51 53 Df 56
52360 Bannes 52 92 Fc 61
53340 Bannes 53 67 Zd 61
13790 Bannettes, les 13 171 Fd 88
14940 Banneville-la-Campagne 14 48 Ze 53
14260 Banneville-sur-Ajon 14 47 Zc 54
81500 Bannières 81 165 Be 87
18300 Bannon 18 88 Ce 65
55300 Bannoncourt 55 55 Fd 55
77970 Bannost-Villagnon 77 52 Db 56
04150 Banon 04 156 Fd 84
40500 Banos 40 161 Zc 86
81240 Banquet, le 81 166 Cc 87
39380 Bans 39 107 Fd 67
05290 Bans, les 05 144 Gb 79
57220 Ban Saint-Jean, le 57 57 Gd 53
57050 Ban-Saint Martin, le 57 56 Ga 54
63570 Bansat 63 128 Dc 76
63740 Banson 63 127 Ce 74
71500 Bantanges 71 106 Fa 69
23140 Bantardeix 23 114 Ca 72
59266 Banteux 59 30 Db 48
95420 Banthelu 95 50 Be 54
55110 Bantheville 55 42 Fa 52
59554 Bantigny 59 30 Db 47
59266 Bantouzelle 59 30 Db 48
68490 Bantzenheim 68 95 Hd 62
15270 Banut, la 15 127 Cd 76
90800 Banvillars 90 94 Ge 63
14480 Banville 14 35 Zd 53
61450 Banvou 61 47 Zc 57
66300 Banyuls-dels-Aspres 66 179 Cf 93
66650 Banyuls-sur-Mer 66 179 Da 94
56150 Baod = Baud 56 80 Wf 61
89430 Baon 89 90 Ea 61
76190 Baons-le-Comte 76 36 Ae 51
28200 Bapaume 28 69 Bb 60
62450 Bapaume 62 30 Cf 48
74170 Baptieu, le 74 133 Ge 74
12270 Bar 12 151 Ca 83
19800 Bar 19 126 Be 76
49430 Baracé 49 84 Zd 63
63660 Baracucher 63 129 Df 75
47420 Baradé 47 148 Aa 83
63480 Baraduc 63 129 De 74
30140 Barafort 30 154 Df 84
11410 Baraigne 11 165 Be 89
09350 Baraillas 09 164 Bb 90
21350 Barain 21 91 Ed 64
36270 Baraize 36 113 Bd 70
62860 Baralle 62 30 Da 47
24220 Baran 24 137 Ba 79
88230 Barançon 88 77 Ha 60
88310 Baranges, les 88 77 Ge 61
32430 Baraque, la 32 164 Af 86
87310 Baraque, la 87 125 Ba 74
48700 Baraque-de-Boislong 48 140 Dd 80
48300 Baraque-de-L'Air 48 141 De 80
48170 Baraque-de-la-Motte 48 141 Dd 80
48100 Baraque-du-Plo 48 140 Db 81
07240 Baraques, les 07 142 Ed 79

Baraques, les | 241

43210 Baraques, les 43 129 Ea 77
54890 Baraques, les 54 56 Ff 54
88240 Baraques, les 88 76 Gb 60
88250 Baraques, les 88 77 Gf 60
12800 Baraque-Saint-Jean 12 151 Cb 84
70800 Baraques-Chardin, les 70 93 Gb 61
70000 Baraques-de-Borey, les 70 93 Gb 63
26420 Baraques-en-Vercors, les 26 143 Fc 78
12160 Baraqueville 12 151 Cc 83
13011 Barasse, la 13 170 Fc 89
62124 Barastre 62 30 Cf 48
31160 Barat 31 176 Af 90
81310 Barat 81 150 Be 85
05200 Baratier 05 145 Gc 81
36500 Baratte 36 101 Bc 68
65140 Barbachen 65 162 Aa 88
20253 Barbaggio CTC 181 Kc 92
20253 Barbaghju = Barbaggio CTC 181 Kc 92
50170 Barbaie, la 50 66 Yd 58
11800 Barbaira 11 166 Cd 89
08430 Barbaise 08 42 Ed 50
86300 Barbalières, les 86 100 Ad 69
54450 Barbas 54 77 Gf 57
47230 Barbaste 47 148 Ab 83
12200 Barbat 12 151 Bf 82
85630 Barbâtre 85 96 Xe 67
31510 Barbazan 31 176 Ad 90
65690 Barbazan-Debat 65 162 Aa 89
65360 Barbazan-Dessus 65 162 Aa 89
19390 Barbazange 19 126 Bf 76
44370 Barbe-Chat 44 83 Yf 64
44450 Barbechat 44 82 Ye 65
13330 Barben, la 13 170 Fb 87
13570 Barbentane 13 155 Ee 85
10180 Barberey-aux-Moines 10 73 Df 58
10600 Barberey-Saint-Sulpice 10 73 Ea 58
03140 Barberier 03 116 Db 71
74660 Barberine 74 121 Gf 72
14220 Barbery 14 47 Zd 54
60810 Barbery 60 51 Cd 53
33840 Barbes, les 33 148 Zf 83
40110 Barbet 40 147 Zb 84
14400 Barbeville 14 47 Zb 53
33125 Barbey 33 134 Zc 81
77130 Barbey 77 72 Da 58
24590 Barbeyroux 24 137 Bc 79
88640 Barbey-Seroux 88 77 Gf 60
16140 Barbezières 16 111 Zf 73
16300 Barbezieux-Saint-Hilaire 16 123 Zf 76
26300 Barbières 26 143 Fa 79
58300 Barbiers, les 58 104 Dd 67
69440 Barbieux 69M 130 Ed 75
03140 Barbignat 03 116 Da 71
21410 Barbirey-sur-Ouche 21 105 Ee 65
77630 Barbizon 77 71 Cd 58
88390 Barbonfaing 88 76 Gb 60
51120 Barbonne-Fayel 51 53 De 57
54360 Barbonville 54 76 Gc 57
32150 Barbotan-les-Thermes 32 148 Zf 85
25210 Barboux, le 25 108 Ge 66
10400 Barbuise 10 73 Dd 57
08300 Barby 08 41 Eb 51
27170 Barc 27 49 Ae 54
20275 Barcaggio CTC 181 Kc 90
66420 Barcarès, le 66 179 Da 92
26120 Barcelonne 26 143 Fa 79
32720 Barcelonne-du-Gers 32 162 Ze 86
04400 Barcelonnette 04 158 Gd 82
57830 Barchain 57 57 Gf 56
03380 Barchaux, les 03 115 Cc 70
03360 Barchères 03 116 Db 70
20290 Barchetta CTC 181 Kc 93
05110 Barcillonnette 05 157 Ff 82
32170 Barcugnan 32 163 Ac 88
64130 Barcus 64 161 Zb 89
77910 Barcy 77 52 Cf 54
42600 Bard 42 129 Ea 75
43360 Bard 43 128 Dc 76
09100 Bardaille, la 09 165 Be 90
03360 Bardais 03 103 Ce 68
16500 Barde, la 16 112 Ad 72
17360 Barde, la 17 135 Zf 78
23300 Barde, la 23 113 Bd 71
40200 Barde, la 40 146 Yf 83
17120 Bardécille 17 122 Za 75
42310 Bardet 42 117 Df 72
09200 Bardies 09 176 Bb 90
82340 Bardigues 82 149 Af 84
31580 Bardins, les 31 89 Db 64
21430 Bard-le-Régulier 21 105 Eb 66
21460 Bard-lès-Epoisses 21 90 Eb 63
70140 Bard-lès-Pesmes 70 92 Fd 65
45130 Bardon, le 45 87 Bd 61
03250 Bardonnet, le 03 116 De 72
85150 Bardonnière, la 85 97 Yc 69
64520 Bardos 64 160 Ye 88
24560 Bardou 24 136 Ae 80
76480 Bardouville 76 37 Af 52
18110 Bardy, les 18 102 Cc 65
87480 Bardys, les 87 113 Bc 73
39700 Baree, la 39 107 Fe 66
65120 Barèges 65 175 Aa 91
65120 Bareilles 65 175 Zf 92
65240 Bareilles 65 175 Ac 91
06470 Barels 06 158 Gf 84
67130 Barembach 67 60 Hb 58
31440 Baren 31 176 Ad 91
76360 Barentin 76 37 Af 51
50720 Barenton 50 66 Zb 57
02000 Barenton-Bugny 02 40 Dd 51
02000 Barenton-Cel 02 40 Dd 51
02270 Barenton-sur-Serre 02 40 De 50
31580 Barères 31 163 Ad 89
39130 Barésia-sur-L'Ain 39 119 Fe 69
50760 Barfleur 50 33 Ye 50
42600 Barge 42 129 Ea 75
04530 Barge, la 04 145 Ge 81
63600 Barge, la 63 129 De 75
83840 Bargème 83 172 Gd 86
03250 Bargeon 03 116 Dd 72
21910 Barges 21 106 Fa 65
43340 Barges 43 141 Df 79
70500 Barges 70 93 Ff 61
43340 Bargettes 43 141 Df 79
20245 Barghiana CTC 182 Ie 94
63380 Bargignat 63 127 Cd 73
60620 Bargny 60 52 Cf 53
45740 Bargoudière, la 45 87 Be 62
63940 Bargues 63 129 De 76
07450 Baricaude, la 07 141 Eb 80
33190 Barie 33 135 Zf 81
85500 Barillère, la 85 97 Yf 67
27130 Barils, les 27 49 Ae 56
64160 Barinque 64 162 Ze 88
19410 Bariolet, le 19 126 Bd 76
02700 Barisis 02 40 Db 51
71640 Barizey 71 105 Ee 68
09230 Barjac 09 164 Ba 90
30430 Barjac 30 154 Ec 83
48000 Barjac 48 140 Dc 81
83670 Barjols 83 171 Ga 87
21580 Barjon 21 91 Ef 63
24440 Barjou 24 137 Ae 80
40090 Barlac 40 147 Zb 85
64570 Barlanes 64 161 Zb 90
55000 Bar-le-Duc 55 55 Fb 56
04140 Barles 04 157 Gb 83
08240 Bar-lès-Buzancy 08 42 Ef 52
65100 Barlest 65 162 Zf 90
80200 Barleux 80 39 Cf 49
79400 Barlière, la 79 111 Ze 70
18260 Barlieu 18 88 Cd 64
62620 Barlin 62 29 Cd 46
62810 Barly 62 29 Cd 47
80600 Barly 80 29 Cb 47
18500 Barmont 18 102 Cb 66
87130 Barnagaud 87 126 Bd 75
07330 Barnas 07 141 Eb 81
04240 Barnaud 04 158 Ge 85
71340 Barnaudière, la 71 117 Ea 71
26310 Barnave 26 143 Fc 81
71540 Barnay-Dessous 71 105 Ec 66
63310 Barnazat 63 116 Dc 73
77111 Barneau 77 51 Ce 57
50270 Barneville-Carteret 50 33 Yb 52
14600 Barneville-la-Bertran 14 35 Ab 52
50270 Barneville-Plage 50 46 Yb 52
27310 Barneville-sur-Seine 27 37 Af 52
53110 Baroche-Gondouin, la 53 67 Zd 58
54150 Baroches, les 54 56 Ff 53
61330 Baroche-sous-Lucé, la 61 67 Zc 57
76260 Baromesnil 76 37 Bc 49
30700 Baron 30 154 Eb 84
33750 Baron 33 135 Ze 80
60300 Baron 60 51 Ce 53
71120 Baron 71 117 Eb 70
06700 Baronne, la 06 173 Ha 86
27220 Baronnie, la 27 50 Bb 55
14210 Baron-sur-Odon 14 35 Zd 54
57340 Baronville 57 57 Gd 55
14620 Barou-en-Auge 14 48 Zf 55
47290 Barouille 47 136 Ad 81
10200 Baroville 10 74 Ee 59
38790 Baroz, le 38 131 Fa 75
33114 Barp, le 33 134 Zb 81
13710 Barque, la 13 170 Fc 88
76390 Barques 76 38 Be 50
27170 Barquet 27 49 Af 54
26130 Barquets, les 26 155 Ee 82
67140 Barr 67 60 Hc 58
12440 Barraban 12 151 Cb 83
33450 Barrade, la 33 135 Zd 79
42370 Barrage du Rouchain 42 117 Df 72
03120 Barrais-Bussolles 03 116 De 71
30770 Barral, le 30 153 Dd 85
32350 Barran 32 163 Ac 87
65240 Barrancoueu 65 175 Ac 91
48500 Barraque-de-Trémolet 48 153 Db 82
63440 Barraques 63 115 Cf 72
05500 Barraques, les 05 144 Ga 80
04380 Barras 04 157 Ga 84
24130 Barrat 24 136 Ab 79
89260 Barrault 89 72 Db 59
64390 Barraute-Camu 64 161 Za 88
38530 Barraux 38 132 Ff 76
81320 Barre 81 166 Ce 86
17450 Barre, la 17 110 Yf 72
41360 Barre, la 41 85 Af 62
44330 Barre, la 44 97 Ye 66
44520 Barre, la 44 82 Yd 63
58110 Barre, la 58 104 Dd 66
64600 Barre, la 64 160 Yc 87
70190 Barre, la 70 93 Gb 64
85250 Barre, la 85 97 Ye 67
86300 Barre, la 86 100 Ad 69
86500 Barre, la 86 112 Ae 71
87520 Barre, la 87 113 Ba 73
85550 Barre-de-Monts, la 85 96 Xf 67
48400 Barre-des-Cévennes 48 153 Dd 83
50810 Barre-de-Semilly, la 50 34 Yf 54
27330 Barre-en-Ouche, la 27 49 Ad 55
44130 Barrel 44 82 Ya 64
04330 Barrême 04 157 Gc 85
86160 Barrerie, la 86 112 Ac 70
45140 Barres, les 45 70 Be 61
45760 Barres, les 45 87 Ca 61
53300 Barres, les 53 67 Zc 58
70400 Barres, les 70 94 Ge 63
85700 Barres, les 85 98 Zb 68
89520 Barres, les 89 89 Db 63
16300 Barret 16 123 Ze 76
39800 Barretaine 39 107 Fe 68
26570 Barret-de-Lioure 26 156 Fc 83
05300 Barret-le-Bas 05 156 Fe 83
05300 Barret-le-Haut 05 156 Fe 83
20228 Barrettali CTC 181 Kc 91
24410 Barreyrie 24 123 Aa 77
12290 Barri 12 152 Ce 82
15800 Barriac 15 139 Ce 79
15700 Barriac-les-Bosquets 15 139 Cb 78
43270 Barribas 43 129 De 77
08240 Barricourt 08 42 Fa 52
24190 Barrière, la 24 136 Ab 78
19330 Barrières, les 19 126 Bd 77
40270 Barrières, les 40 147 Zd 85
81140 Barrières, les 81 150 Be 85
44530 Barrisset 44 81 Xf 63
16700 Barro 16 111 Ab 73
63330 Barrot 63 115 Ce 72
69440 Barrot 69M 130 Ed 75
32230 Barrottes 32 163 Ab 87
37350 Barrou 37 100 Ae 67
47500 Barrou 47 137 Af 82
24800 Barroutie, la 24 125 Ba 76
84330 Barroux, le 84 155 Fa 84
82160 Barry 82 150 Be 83
82150 Barry, le 82 149 Ba 82
82290 Barry-d'Islemade 82 150 Bb 84
12600 Bars 12 139 Cd 80
24210 Bars 24 137 Ba 78
32300 Bars 32 163 Ab 87
04210 Bars, le 04 157 Ff 85
26150 Barsac 26 143 Fb 80
33720 Barsac 33 135 Ze 81
19170 Barsanges 19 126 Ca 75
57450 Barst 57 57 Ge 54
10200 Bar-sur-Aube 10 74 Ee 59
06620 Bar-sur-Loup, le 06 173 Gf 86
10110 Bar-sur-Seine 10 74 Ec 60
25420 Bart 25 94 Ge 64
87200 Bart 87 125 Af 73
68870 Bartenheim 68 95 Hc 63
68870 Bartenheim-la-Chaussée 68 95 Hd 63
40430 Barthe 40 147 Zc 83
65230 Barthe 65 163 Ac 89
12600 Barthe, la 12 139 Ce 80
46230 Barthe, la 46 150 Bd 83
81700 Barthe, la 81 165 Ca 87
65250 Barthe-de-Neste, la 65 163 Ac 90
25440 Bartherans 25 107 Ff 66
09500 Barthes 09 165 Be 90
82100 Barthes, les 82 149 Bb 84
09700 Barthète, la 09 165 Bd 89
12120 Barthie, la 12 152 Cc 84
03380 Bartillat 03 115 Cc 71
20246 Bartollaciu CTC 181 Kb 92
82270 Bartou 82 150 Bd 83
65100 Bartrès 65 162 Zf 90
27230 Barville 27 49 Ac 54
61170 Barville 61 68 Ac 58
88300 Barville 88 76 Fe 58
76450 Barville, Cany- 76 36 Ad 50
45340 Barville-en-Gâtinais 45 71 Cc 60
17120 Barzan 17 122 Za 75
64530 Barzum 64 162 Zf 89
02170 Barzy-en-Thiérache 02 31 De 48
02850 Barzy-sur-Marne 02 53 Dd 54
70270 Bas, le 70 94 Gd 62
59310 Bas-Aix 59 30 Db 45
63210 Bas-Angle 63 127 Ce 74
49440 Bas-Aunay 49 83 Ye 63
86260 Bas-Bourg 86 100 Ae 68
44430 Bas-Briacé 44 97 Yd 65
64220 Bascassan 64 161 Ye 90
04330 Bas-Chaudol, le 04 157 Gb 85
40090 Bascons 40 147 Zd 86
82110 Bascoulesse 82 149 Bb 83
50220 Bas-Courtils 50 66 Yd 57
32190 Bascous 32 148 Aa 86
18700 Bascule, la 18 87 Cb 64
14860 Bas-de-Bréville 14 48 Ze 53
58700 Bas-de-la-Celle, le 58 103 Db 65
71110 Bas-des-Augères, le 71 117 Ea 71
43210 Bas-en-Basset 43 129 Ea 77
85190 Baserière, la 85 97 Yc 68
18220 Bas-Fouillet 18 103 Ce 65
72130 Bas-Frété 72 68 Aa 59
54620 Baslieux 54 43 Fe 52
51170 Baslieux-lès-Fismes 51 40 De 53
51700 Baslieux-sous-Châtillon 51 53 De 54
14610 Basly 14 47 Zd 53
56620 Bas-Pont-Scorff, le 56 79 Wd 61
62190 Bas-Rieux 62 29 Cd 45
88400 Bas-Rupts 88 77 Gf 60
73410 Bassa 73 132 Ff 74
64220 Bassaburua 64 161 Yf 90
16120 Bassac 16 123 Zf 75
87130 Bassade, la 87 126 Bd 74
34290 Bassan 34 167 Db 88
33190 Bassanne 33 135 Zf 81
16570 Basse 16 123 Aa 74
34800 Basse 34 167 Db 87
23500 Basse, la 23 126 Cb 73
50500 Basse-Addeville, la 50 46 Ye 52
86150 Basse-Barbade, la 86 112 Ad 71
79270 Bassée 79 110 Zc 71
59480 Bassée, la 59 30 Ce 45
12200* Bas Ségala, le 12 151 Ca 83
44115 Basse-Goulaine 44 97 Yd 65
61360 Basse-Gravelle 61 68 Ac 58
57970 Basse Ham 57 44 Gb 52
67220 Bassemberg 67 60 Hb 58
23300 Basseneuille 23 113 Bc 71
14670 Basseneville 14 35 Zf 53
71130 Bassenier 71 104 Df 69
33530 Bassens 33 135 Zc 79
73000 Bassens 73 132 Ff 75
40700 Bassercles 40 161 Zc 87
57570 Basse-Rentgen 57 44 Gb 52
86200 Basses 86 99 Aa 66
89260 Basses-Bergeries, les 89 72 Dc 59
20132 Bassetta CTC 183 Ka 97
62123 Basseux 62 29 Cd 47
70210 Basse-Vaivre, la 70 76 Ga 61
77750 Bassevelle 77 52 Db 55
83340 Basse-Verrerie, la 83 172 Gc 88
57690 Basse-Vigneulles 57 57 Gd 54
01260 Bassieu 01 119 Fd 73
15240 Bassignac 15 127 Cc 77
19430 Bassignac-le-Bas 19 138 Bf 78
19220 Bassignac-le-Haut 19 126 Ca 77
70800 Bassigney 70 93 Gb 62
24330 Bassilac et Auberoche 24 124 Ae 77
18260 Bassinerie, la 18 88 Cd 64
57260 Bassing 57 57 Ge 55
02380 Bassoles-Aulers 02 40 Dc 51
52240 Bassoncourt 52 75 Fd 60
89400 Bassou 89 89 Dd 61
32320 Bassoues 32 163 Ab 87
51300 Bassu 51 54 Ee 56
51300 Bassuet 51 54 Ee 56
64200 Bassussarry 64 160 Yc 88
74910 Bassy 74 119 Fe 73
64190 Bastanès 64 161 Zb 88
32170 Bastanous 32 163 Ac 88
20119 Bastelica CTC 182 Ka 96
20129 Bastelicaccia CTC 182 If 97
40360 Bastennes 40 161 Zb 87
20200 Bastia CTC 181 Kc 92
20200 Bastìa = Bastia CTC 181 Kc 92
12120 Bastide, la 12 152 Cd 83
12470 Bastide, la 12 140 Cf 81
15400 Bastide, la 15 127 Ce 77
15500 Bastide, la 15 140 Db 78
24240 Bastide, la 24 136 Ac 80
30630 Bastide, la 30 154 Ec 83
33460 Bastide, la 33 134 Zc 78
33730 Bastide, la 33 147 Zd 82
40110 Bastide, la 40 147 Zb 85
43580 Bastide, la 43 141 Dd 79
48700 Bastide, la 48 140 Dd 80
64430 Bastide, la 64 160 Yd 89
66110 Bastide, la 66 179 Cd 93
83840 Bastide, la 83 172 Gd 86
13220 Bastide-Blanche 13 170 Fa 88
83560 Bastide-Blanche 83 171 Fe 87
83420 Bastide-Blanche, la 83 172 Gd 89
83470 Bastide-Blanche, la 83 171 Fe 88
12200 Bastide-Capdenac, la 12 151 Bf 82
12470 Bastide-d'Aubrac, la 12 139 Ce 81
09350 Bastide-de-Besplas, la 09 164 Bb 89
09500 Bastide-de-Bousignac, la 09 177 Bf 90
11420 Bastide-de-Couloumat, la 11 165 Be 89
09700 Bastide-de-Lordat, la 09 165 Be 90
30330 Bastide-d'Engras, la 30 154 Ec 84
09240 Bastide-de-Sérou, la 09 177 Bc 90
84240 Bastide-des-Jourdans, la 84 156 Fd 86
09160 Bastide-du-Salat, la 09 176 Af 90
12200 Bastide-l'Evêque, la 12 151 Ca 82
12490 Bastide-Pradines, la 12 152 Da 84
48250 Bastide-Puylaurent, la 48 141 Df 81
48150 Bastides, les 48 153 Db 83
84570 Bastides, les 84 156 Fb 84
12550 Bastide-Solages, la 12 151 Cd 85
09600 Bastide-sur-l'Hers, la 09 178 Bf 91
84580 Bastidon-du-Pradon 84 156 Fa 86
84120 Bastidonne, la 84 171 Fd 86
12290 Bastié, la 12 152 Cd 83
17120 Bastille, la 17 122 Zb 75
46350 Bastit, le 46 138 Bd 79
46500 Bastit, le 46 138 Bd 80
21121 Bas-Val-Suzon 21 91 Ef 64
23260 Basville 23 127 Cc 73
31160 Bataille 31 176 Af 90
48600 Bataille, la 48 141 Dd 80
79110 Bataille, la 79 111 Zf 72
88260 Bataille, la 88 76 Ga 60
36700 Bataillerie, la 36 100 Ba 67
38270 Bataillouse 38 130 Ef 76
57810 Bataville 57 57 Ge 56
32130 Batcrabère, la 32 164 Af 87
78730 Bâte, la 78 70 Ca 57
40430 Bathariére 40 147 Zc 83
54370 Bathelémont-lès-Bauzemont 54 57 Gd 56
26260 Bathernay 26 143 Ef 77
73540 Bâthie, la 73 132 Gc 75
04170 Bâtie 04 158 Gc 84
04120 Bâtie, la 04 158 Gd 86
05120 Bâtie, la 05 145 Gd 80
38650 Bâtie, la 38 143 Fd 79
26310 Bâtie-des-Fonds, la 26 143 Fd 81
38490 Bâtie-Divisins, la 38 131 Fd 75
38110 Bâtie-Montgascon, la 38 131 Fd 75
05700 Bâtie-Montsaléon, la 05 144 Fe 82
05230 Bâtie-Neuve, la 05 144 Gb 81
26160 Bâtie-Rolland, la 26 142 Ef 81
70130 Bâties, les 70 93 Fd 63
05000 Bâtie-Vieille, la 05 144 Ga 81
27220 Bâtigny 27 50 Bb 55
37310 Batilly 37 100 Af 65
54980 Batilly 54 56 Ff 53
61150 Batilly 61 48 Ze 56
45340 Batilly-en-Gâtinais 45 71 Cc 60
45420 Batilly-en-Puisaye 45 88 Cf 63
56500 Bâtiment, le 56 80 Xa 61
32410 Bâtisse, la 32 148 Ac 85
40320 Bats 40 162 Zd 87
65130 Batsère 65 163 Ab 90
33720 Batsères 33 135 Zd 81
25640 Battenans-les-Mines 25 93 Gb 64
25380 Battenans-Varin 25 108 Ge 65
68390 Battenheim 68 95 Hc 62
88130 Battexey 88 76 Gb 58
54115 Battigny 54 76 Ff 58
70100 Battrans 70 92 Fd 64
19600 Battut 19 137 Bc 78
32600 Battut 32 164 Bb 87
15230 Battut, le 15 139 Ce 79
19550 Battut, le 19 126 Ca 76
12800 Batut, le 12 151 Cb 83
46600 Batut, le 46 138 Bc 78
67500 Batzendorf 67 58 He 56
44740 Batz-sur-Mer 44 81 Xd 65
63950 Bauberty 63 127 Cd 75
21340 Baubigny 21 105 Ee 67
44860 Bauche 44 97 Yc 66
44520 Bauche, la 44 82 Ye 63
73360 Bauche, la 73 132 Fe 76
73210 Bauches, les 73 133 Ge 75
37600 Bauchetière, la 37 100 Ba 67
56150 Baud = Badd 56 80 Wf 61
51260 Baudement 51 73 De 57
71800 Baudemont 71 117 Eb 71
95710 Baudemont 95 50 Bd 54
33650 Baudes 33 135 Zc 81
78120 Baudicourt 78 70 Bf 57
50480 Baudienville 50 33 Ye 52
38840 Baudiere, la 38 143 Fb 78
89550 Baudières, les 89 90 Dd 61
40310 Baudignan 40 148 Aa 84
55130 Baudignécourt 55 75 Fc 57
04250 Baudinard 04 157 Ga 83
83630 Baudinard-sur-Verdon 83 171 Ga 86
09200 Baudis, les 09 176 Ba 90
70300 Baudoncourt 70 93 Gc 62
55170 Baudonvilliers 55 55 Fa 56
50000 Baudre 50 34 Yf 54
52110 Baudrecourt 52 74 Ef 58
57580 Baudrecourt 57 56 Gc 55
64800 Baudreix 64 162 Ze 89
55260 Baudrémont 55 55 Fc 55
36110 Baudres 36 101 Bd 66
28310 Baudreville 28 70 Bf 59
50250 Baudreville 50 33 Yc 53
76560 Baudribosc 76 37 Af 50
88500 Baudricourt 88 76 Ga 59
71370 Baudrières 71 106 Fa 68
36220 Baudrussais 36 100 Ba 68
83630 Bauduen 83 171 Gb 86
85340 Bauduère, la 85 109 Ya 69
49150 Baugé-en-Anjou 49 84 Zf 63
36700 Baugerai 36 101 Bb 67
87370 Baugiraud 87 113 Bc 72
18800 Baugy 18 103 Ce 66
71110 Baugy 71 117 Ea 71
32160 Baulat 32 162 Aa 87
70160 Baulay 70 93 Ga 62
45130 Baule 45 87 Bd 62
47600 Baulens 47 148 Ac 84
31550 Baulias 31 165 Bd 89
21410 Baulme-la-Roche 21 91 Ee 64
02330 Baulne-en-Brie 02 53 Dd 55
55270 Baulny-Charpentry 55 55 Fa 53
35580 Baulon 35 65 Ya 61
09000 Baulou 09 177 Bd 90
04120 Baume, la 04 158 Gc 85
04260 Baume, la 04 158 Gd 83
05150 Baume, la 05 156 Fd 82
30480 Baume, la 30 154 Ea 84
74430 Baume, la 74 120 Gd 71
26120 Baume-Cornillane, la 26 143 Fa 80
26790 Baume-de-Transit, la 26 155 Ef 82
26730 Baume d'Hostun, la 26 143 Fb 78
25110 Baume-les-Dames 25 93 Gc 64
39210 Baume-les-Messieurs 39 107 Fd 68
04260 Baumelle, la 04 158 Gd 83
30770 Baumes 30 153 Dc 85
84360 Baumes 84 156 Fb 86
05260 Baumes, les 05 144 Gb 80
06470 Baumette, la 06 158 Gf 84
13890 Baumettes, les 13 170 Ef 86
05140 Baumugne 05 144 Fe 81
16140 Baunac 16 111 Aa 73
49140 Bauné 49 84 Ze 64
50500 Baupte 50 33 Yd 53
14260 Bauquay 14 47 Zc 54
89500 Bauquins, les 89 72 Dc 60
33880 Baurech 33 135 Zd 80
35190 Baussaine, la 35 65 Ya 59
86200 Baussay 86 99 Aa 66
59221 Bauvin 59 30 Cf 45
84410 Baux, les 84 156 Fb 84
27160 Baux-de-Breteuil, les 27 49 Ae 55
27180 Baux-Sainte-Croix, les 27 49 Ba 55
54370 Bauzemont 54 57 Gd 56
56300 Bauzo, le 56 64 Wf 60
41250 Bauzy 41 86 Bd 63
25550 Bavans 25 94 Ge 64
59570 Bavay 59 31 De 47
80260 Bavelincourt 80 39 Cc 49
14860 Bavent 14 48 Ze 53
39100 Baverans 39 107 Fd 66
90800 Bavilliers 90 94 Ge 63
59670 Bavinchove 59 27 Cc 44
62158 Bavincourt 62 29 Cd 47
31310 Bax 31 164 Bb 89
40210 Baxente 40 146 Yf 83
08290 Bay 08 41 Eb 50
70150 Bay 70 92 Fe 65
74190 Bay 74 121 Ge 73
24150 Bayac 24 136 Ae 80
63570 Bayard 63 128 Db 76
52170 Bayard-sur-Marne 52 75 Fa 57
33230 Bayas 33 135 Ze 78
04400 Bayasse 04 158 Ge 83
29300 Baye 29 79 Wc 61
51270 Baye 51 53 De 55
58110 Baye 58 104 Dd 66
88150 Bayecourt 88 77 Gc 59
10310 Bayel 10 74 Ee 59
80560 Bayencourt 80 29 Cd 48
62910 Bayenghem-les-Eperlesques 62 27 Ca 44
16460 Bayers 16 111 Ab 73
03500 Bayet 03 116 Db 71
16700 Bayette, la 16 112 Ab 72
14400 Bayeux 14 47 Zb 53
47120 Bayle 47 136 Ab 80
07220 Bayne 07 142 Ed 82
14330 Baynes 14 34 Za 53
54290 Bayon 54 76 Gb 58
26230 Bayonne 26 155 Ef 82
64100 Bayonne 64 160 Yd 88
04250 Bayons 04 157 Ga 82
63700 Bayons, les 63 115 Cf 71
71340 Bayons, les 71 117 Df 71
33710 Bayon-sur-Gironde 33 135 Zc 78
08240 Bayonville 08 42 Fa 52

242 | Baraques, les

34380 Bertrand 34 153 Dd 86
11310 Bertrande 11 166 Cb 88
81440 Bertrandié 81 165 Ca 86
83340 Bertrands, le 83 172 Gb 88
57310 Bertrange 57 56 Gb 53
33290 Bertranot 33 134 Zb 79
18340 Bertray, le 18 102 Cc 67
81700 Bertre 81 165 Bf 87
65370 Bertren 65 176 Ad 91
48160 Bertresque, la 48 154 Df 83
76450 Bertreville 76 36 Ad 50
76590 Bertreville-Saint-Ouen 76 37 Ba 50
24320 Bertric-Burée 24 124 Ac 77
54120 Bertrichamps 54 77 Ge 58
02190 Bertricourt 02 41 Ea 52
76890 Bertrimont 76 37 Ba 50
88520 Bertrimoutier 88 77 Ha 59
59980 Bertry 59 30 Dc 48
89700 Béru 89 90 Df 62
10160 Bérulle 10 73 Dd 59
72610 Bérus 72 68 Aa 58
29440 Berven 29 62 Vf 57
76560 Berville 76 37 Ae 50
95810 Berville 95 51 Ca 53
27520 Berville-en-Roumois 27 49 Ae 53
27170 Berville-la-Campagne 27 49 Af 54
57550 Berviller-en-Moselle 57 57 Gd 53
14170 Bervilles 14 48 Zf 54
27210 Berville-sur-Mer 27 36 Ac 52
76480 Berville-sur-Seine 76 37 Af 52
71960 Berzé-la-Ville 71 118 Ee 70
71960 Berzé-le-Châtel 71 118 Ee 70
07580 Berzème 07 142 Ed 81
51800 Berzieux 51 54 Ee 54
02200 Berzy-le-Sec 02 52 Db 52
04420 Bès 04 157 Gb 83
48310 Bès, le 48 140 Da 80
08450 Besace, la 08 42 Ef 51
08460 Besace, la 08 41 Ec 50
39800 Besain 39 107 Fe 68
25000 Besançon 25 107 Ga 65
26300 Bésayes 26 143 Fa 79
64260 Bescat 64 162 Zd 90
26110 Bésignan 26 156 Fb 83
44650 Bésillère, la 44 97 Yc 67
64150 Besingrand 64 161 Zc 88
44290 Beslé 44 82 Ya 62
50800 Beslon 50 46 Yf 55
02300 Besmé 02 40 Da 51
02500 Besmont 02 41 Ea 49
70230 Besnans 70 93 Gb 64
50640 Besnardière, la 50 66 Yf 57
44160 Besné 44 81 Xf 64
50390 Besneville 50 46 Yc 52
28190 Besnez 28 69 Bb 57
53500 Besnières 53 66 Za 58
02870 Besny-et-Loizy 02 40 Dd 51
16250 Bessac 16 123 Zf 76
44750 Bessac 44 81 Ya 64
15320 Bessaire-de-Lair 15 140 Db 79
18210 Bessais-le-Fromental 18 103 Ce 68
43200 Bessamorel 43 141 Ea 78
34550 Bessan 34 167 Dc 88
95550 Bessancourt 95 51 Cb 54
73480 Bessans 73 133 Gf 77
43370 Bessarioux 43 141 Df 79
07150 Bessas 07 154 Eb 82
23460 Bessat 23 126 Bf 73
63210 Bessat 63 127 Cf 74
42660 Bessat, le 42 130 Ed 76
03000 Bessay 03 103 Db 69
28150 Bessay 28 70 Bd 59
85320 Bessay 85 109 Yf 69
03340 Bessay-sur-Allier 03 116 Dc 70
19140 Bessde, la 19 126 Bd 75
15140 Besse 15 139 Cc 78
16140 Bessé 16 111 Aa 73
24550 Besse 24 137 Ba 80
38142 Besse 38 144 Gb 78
43130 Besse 43 129 Df 77
49350 Besse 49 84 Ze 64
12430 Besse, la 12 152 Ce 84
19150 Besse, la 19 126 Bf 77
63660 Besse, la 63 129 Df 75
81310 Bessède 81 150 Be 85
11140 Bessède-de-Sault 11 178 Ca 92
63610 Besse-et-Saint-Anastaise 63 128 Cf 75
30160 Bességes 30 154 Ea 83
23170 Besse-Mathieu 23 114 Cc 71
69690 Bessenay 69M 130 Ed 74
82170 Bessens 82 150 Bb 85
15220 Besserols 15 139 Cc 80
30450 Besses 30 154 Ea 82
46100 Besses 46 138 Ca 80
34190 Besses, les 34 153 Dc 85
72310 Bessé-sur-Braye 72 85 Ae 61
83890 Besse-sur-Issole 83 171 Gb 88
09500 Besset 09 165 Bf 90
43150 Besset 43 141 Ea 79
48340 Besset, le 48 140 Da 82
19170 Bessette, la 19 126 Bf 74
48300 Bessettes 48 141 De 80
42520 Bessey 42 130 Ee 76
21360 Bessey-en-Chaume 21 105 Ee 66
21360 Bessey-la-Cour 21 105 Ed 66
21110 Bessey-lès-Cîteaux 21 106 Fa 66
43170 Besseyre-Saint-Mary, la 43 140 Dc 79
81320 Bessière 81 167 Cf 86
12130 Bessière, la 12 140 Da 82
48340 Bessière, la 48 140 Da 81
31660 Bessières 31 150 Bd 86
48130 Bessils 48 140 Db 80
79000 Bessines 79 110 Zc 71
87250 Bessines-sur-Gartempe 87 113 Bc 72
38160 Bessins 38 131 Fb 77
19200 Bessole 19 127 Cc 76
63790 Bessolles 63 127 Cf 75
15100 Bessols 15 140 Da 79
03210 Besson 03 116 Db 70
90160 Bessoncourt 90 94 Gf 63
46210 Bessonies 46 138 Ca 80
48200 Bessons, les 48 140 Db 80
77760 Bessonville 77 71 Cd 59
46310 Bessous 46 137 Bc 80
09500 Bessous, les 09 165 Be 90
10170 Bessy 10 73 Ea 57
89270 Bessy-sur-Cure 89 90 De 63
40200 Bestaven 40 146 Yf 83
23100 Besth, le 23 127 Cc 74
09250 Bestiac 09 177 Be 92
57670 Besville 57 57 Ge 55
19380 Bétaille 19 138 Bf 77
46110 Bétaille 46 138 Be 79
70500 Betaucourt 70 93 Ff 61
65230 Betbèze 65 163 Ad 89
40240 Betbezer-d'Armagnac 40 148 Ze 85
32420 Betcave-Aguin 32 163 Ae 88
09160 Betchat 09 164 Ba 90
12270 Bételle 12 151 Bf 83
23270 Bétête 23 114 Ca 70
08190 Bethancourt 08 41 Ea 51
60129 Béthancourt-en-Valois 60 52 Cf 53
02300 Béthancourt-en-Vaux 02 40 Da 51
87120 Bethe 87 126 Be 74
55100 Béthelainville 55 55 Fb 53
78300 Béthemont 78 51 Bf 55
95840 Béthemont-la-Forêt 95 51 Cb 54
59540 Béthencourt 59 30 Dc 48
60140 Béthencourt 60 39 Cc 52
62127 Bethencourt 62 29 Cd 46
76340 Béthencourt 76 37 Bd 49
80130 Béthencourt-sur-Mer 80 28 Bd 48
80190 Béthencourt-sur-Somme 80 39 Cf 50
36190 Bethenet 36 114 Bd 70
51490 Bétheniville 51 54 Ec 53
51450 Bétheny 51 53 Ea 53
55270 Béthincourt 55 55 Fb 53
86310 Béthines 86 113 Af 69
60320 Béthisy-Saint-Martin 60 52 Ce 53
60320 Béthisy-Saint-Pierre 60 52 Ce 53
09800 Bethmale 09 176 Ba 91
51260 Béthon 51 73 Dd 57
72610 Béthon 72 68 Aa 58
70400 Béthoncourt 70 94 Ge 63
62690 Bethonsart 62 29 Cd 46
28330 Béthonvilliers 28 69 Af 59
90150 Bethonvilliers 90 94 Gf 62
63260 Bethueix, le 63 116 Db 72
62400 Béthune 62 29 Cd 45
10500 Bétignicourt 10 74 Ec 58
65220 Betmont 65 163 Ab 89
77320 Béton-Bazoches 77 52 Dd 56
70120 Betoncourt-les-Ménétriers 70 93 Fe 62
70210 Betoncourt-Saint-Pancras 70 93 Gb 61
70500 Betoncourt-sur-Mance 70 92 Fe 62
23160 Bétoulle, la 23 113 Bd 70
87620 Betoulles, les 87 125 Ba 74
32110 Bétous 32 162 Aa 86
40550 Betoy 40 146 Ye 85
32730 Betplan 32 163 Ab 88
65120 Betpouey 65 175 Aa 91
65230 Betpouy 65 163 Ac 89
64350 Bétracq 64 162 Zf 87
67660 Betschdorf 67 58 Hf 55
54640 Bettainvillers 54 56 Ff 53
51330 Bettancourt-la-Longue 51 54 Ef 56
57220 Bettange 57 57 Gc 53
01500 Bettant 01 119 Fc 73
57930 Bettborn 57 57 Ha 56
88450 Bettegney-Saint-Brice 88 76 Gb 59
57640 Bettelainville 57 56 Gb 53
80290 Bettembos 80 38 Bf 50
80270 Bettencourt-Rivière 80 28 Bf 49
80610 Bettencourt-Saint-Ouen 80 38 Ca 48
68560 Bettendorf 68 95 Hb 63
65130 Bettes 65 163 Ab 90
76190 Betteville 76 36 Ae 51
74170 Bettex, le 74 121 Gd 73
59600 Bettignies 59 31 Df 47
57480 Betting 57 44 Gd 52
57800 Betting 57 57 Ge 54
68480 Bettlach 68 95 Hc 63
35830 Betton 35 65 Yc 59
73390 Betton-Bettonet 73 132 Gb 75
88500 Bettoncourt 88 76 Ga 58
52230 Bettoncourt-le-Haut 52 75 Fb 58
59570 Bettrechies 59 31 De 47
57510 Bettring 57 57 Gf 54
57410 Bettviller 57 58 Hb 54
67320 Bettwiller 67 57 Hb 55
60620 Betz 60 52 Cf 54
43260 Betz, le 43 141 Ea 78
37600 Betz-le-Château 37 100 Af 67
62150 Beugin 62 29 Cd 46
35350 Beuglais, la 35 65 Ya 57
62450 Beugnâtre 62 30 Cf 48
85400 Beugné-L'Abbé 85 110 Ye 70
02210 Beugneux 02 52 Dc 53
59216 Beugnies 59 31 Ea 48
89570 Beugnon 89 73 De 60
79130 Beugnon, le 79 98 Zc 69
79310 Beugnon, le 79 111 Ze 69
85390 Beugnon, le 85 98 Zb 69
62124 Beugny 62 30 Cf 48
06470 Beuil 06 158 Gf 84
88490 Beulay, le 88 77 Ha 59
70310 Beulotte-la-Guillaume 70 94 Gd 61
70310 Beulotte-Saint-Laurent 70 94 Ge 61
25720 Beure 25 107 Ga 65
10140 Beurey 10 74 Ec 59
21320 Beurey-Bauguay 21 105 Ec 65
55000 Beurey-sur-Saulx 55 55 Fa 56
63220 Beurières 63 129 De 76
21350 Beurizot 21 91 Ec 64
17250 Beurlay 17 122 Zb 73
56130 Beurnais 56 81 Xe 64
52110 Beurville 52 74 Ee 59
64390 Beüsse 64 161 Za 88
62170 Beussent 62 28 Be 45
64800 Beuste 64 162 Ze 89
62170 Beutin 62 28 Be 46
33700 Beutre 33 134 Zb 80
57100 Beuvange-sous-Saint-Michel 57 43 Ga 52
02130 Beuvardes 02 53 Dc 54
54620 Beuveille 54 43 Fe 52
54115 Beuvezin 54 76 Ff 58
76890 Beuville 76 37 Ba 50
14100 Beuvillers 14 48 Ab 54
54560 Beuvillers 54 43 Ff 52
80700 Beuvraignes 80 39 Ce 51
62250 Beuvrequen 62 26 Be 44
76220 Beuvreuil 76 38 Bd 51
50420 Beuvrigny 50 47 Yf 55
58210 Beuvron 58 89 Dc 64
14430 Beuvron-en-Auge 14 35 Zf 53
62660 Beuvry 62 29 Ce 45
59310 Beuvry-la-Forêt 59 30 Db 46
57580 Beux 57 56 Gb 55
86120 Beuxes 86 99 Ab 66
29120 Beuzec 29 78 Ve 61
29790 Beuzec-Cap-Sizun 29 61 Vc 60
29900 Beuzec-Conq 29 78 Wa 61
27210 Beuzeville 27 48 Ac 52
50480 Beuzeville-au-Plain 50 33 Ye 52
50360 Beuzeville-la-Bastille 50 46 Yd 52
76850 Beuzeville-la-Giffarde 76 37 Bb 51
76210 Beuzeville-la-Grenier 76 36 Ac 51
76450 Beuzeville-la-Guérard 76 36 Ad 50
76210 Beuzevillette 76 36 Ad 51
57175 Bevange 57 56 Ga 53
38690 Bévenais 38 131 Fc 76
70110 Beveuge 70 94 Gc 63
57645 Béville 57 56 Gb 54
28700 Béville-le-Comte 28 70 Be 58
59217 Bévillers 59 30 Dc 48
04200 Bevons 04 157 Ff 83
21220 Bévy 21 106 Ef 65
15130 Bex, le 15 139 Cc 79
01290 Bey 01 118 Ef 71
71620 Bey 71 106 Ef 68
33450 Beychac-et-Caillau 33 135 Zd 79
33250 Beychevelle 33 134 Zb 78
19330 Beylie, la 19 126 Bd 77
40370 Beylongue 40 147 Zb 85
15170 Beynac 15 140 Cf 78
87700 Beynac 87 125 Bb 74
24220 Beynac-et-Cazenac 24 137 Ba 79
19190 Beynat 19 138 Be 78
19250 Beynat 19 126 Ca 75
04270 Beynes 04 157 Gb 85
13104 Beynes 13 169 Ee 87
78650 Beynes 78 50 Bf 55
19250 Beynette 19 126 Ca 75
01700 Beynost 01 130 Fa 73
65410 Beyrède-Jumet 65 175 Ac 91
57570 Beyren-lès-Sierck 57 44 Gb 52
40440 Beyres 40 160 Yd 87
64230 Beyrie-en-Béarn 64 162 Zd 88
40700 Beyries 40 161 Zc 87
64120 Beyrie-sur-Joyeuse 64 161 Yf 89
19230 Beyssac 19 125 Bc 76
19390 Beyssac 19 126 Bf 76
43320 Beyssac 43 141 De 78
47200 Beyssac 47 136 Aa 81
19230 Beyssenac 19 125 Bb 76
54760 Bey-sur-Seille 54 56 Gb 56
33230 Beytoure 33 135 Zf 78
12700 Bez 12 138 Ca 81
12300 Bez, le 12 139 Cb 81
81260 Bez, le 81 166 Cc 87
09100 Bézac 09 165 Bd 90
24240 Bézage 24 136 Ac 80
36340 Bézagette 36 101 Be 69
77970 Bezalles 77 52 Db 56
12190 Bézamat 12 139 Ce 81
76220 Bézancourt 76 38 Bd 52
54370 Bezange-la-Grande 54 57 Gc 56
57630 Bezange-la-Petite 57 57 Gd 56
51430 Bezannes 51 53 Df 53
36800 Bezarde, la 36 101 Bb 69
45290 Bézards, les 45 88 Ce 62
06510 Bézaudun 06 158 Ha 86
26460 Bézaudun-sur-Bine 26 143 Fb 81
54380 Bezaumont 54 56 Ga 55
21310 Bèze 21 92 Fb 64
19170 Bezeau 19 126 Bf 75
24220 Bézenac 24 137 Ba 79
80640 Bézencourt 80 38 Bf 49
03170 Bézenet 03 115 Cf 71
32130 Bézéril 32 164 Af 87
24550 Bezet 24 137 Ba 81
30120 Bez-et-Esparon 30 153 Dd 85
34500 Béziers 34 167 Db 88
40110 Bezin 40 147 Zb 84
62650 Bezinghem 62 28 Be 45
31440 Bezins-Garraux 31 176 Ae 91
56500 Bézo, le 56 80 Xb 61
11300 Bezole, la 11 178 Ca 90
32310 Bezolles 32 148 Ab 86
12340 Bezonnes 12 152 Cd 82
95100 Bezons 95 51 Cb 55
30320 Bezouce 30 154 Ec 85
21310 Bézouotte 21 92 Fc 64
30450 Bézout 30 154 Df 82
11500 Bézu, le 11 178 Cb 91
83136 Bezud 83 171 Ff 88
32140 Bézues-Bajon 32 163 Ad 88
27480 Bézu-la-Forêt 27 38 Bd 52
02310 Bézu-le-Guéry 02 52 Db 54
27660 Bézu-Saint-Eloi 27 50 Be 53
02400 Bézu-Saint-Germain 02 52 Dc 54
09800 Biac 09 176 Af 91
80200 Biaches 80 39 Cf 49
62118 Biache-Saint-Vaast 62 30 Cf 47
63750 Bialon 63 127 Cd 75
39290 Biarne 39 106 Fc 66
25520 Bians-les-Usiers 25 108 Gb 67
86580 Biard 86 112 Ab 69
50540 Biards, les 50 66 Ye 57
46230 Biargues 46 150 Bd 82
80190 Biarre 80 39 Cf 50
64200 Biarritz 64 160 Yc 88
40390 Biarrotte 40 160 Ye 87
46130 Biars 46 138 Bf 79
46130 Biars-sur-Cère 46 138 Bf 79
88470 Biarville 88 77 Gf 58
40170 Bias 40 146 Ye 84
47300 Bias 47 149 Ae 82
42380 Biaud 42 129 Ea 76
40390 Biaudos 40 160 Ye 87
87500 Biaugeas 87 125 Bb 75
81190 Bibel 81 151 Cb 84
57870 Biberkirch 57 57 Ha 57
57320 Bibiche 57 44 Gc 53
67360 Biblisheim 67 58 He 55
69690 Bibost 69M 130 Ed 74
20140 Bicchisano, Petreto- CTC 182 If 98
20140 Bicchisgià, Pitretu- CTC 182 If 98
94800 Bicêtre 94 51 Cc 56
43800 Bichaix 43 141 Df 78
02300 Bichancourt 02 40 Db 51
01480 Bicheron 01 118 Ee 72
58110 Biches 58 104 Dd 66
87290 Bicheuil 87 113 Bb 72
31530 Bichou 31 164 Bb 87
57635 Bickenholtz 57 57 Hb 56
63460 Bicom 63 116 Db 72
54200 Bicqueley 54 56 Ff 57
64520 Bidache 64 161 Yf 88
09230 Bidaousse, la 09 164 Ba 90
64780 Bidarray 64 160 Yd 89
64210 Bidart 64 160 Yc 88
41270 Bidaudières, les 41 69 Af 60
57260 Bidestroff 57 57 Ge 55
57660 Biding 57 57 Ge 54
18370 Bidoire, la 18 114 Cb 69
07700 Bidon 07 155 Ed 82
88170 Biécourt 88 76 Ff 59
68480 Biederthal 68 95 Hc 64
39150 Bief-des-Maisons 39 107 Ga 68
39250 Bief-du-Fourg 39 107 Ga 68
39800 Biefmorin 39 107 Fd 67
42310 Biefs, les 42 116 De 72
62450 Biefvillers-lès-Bapaume 62 30 Ce 48
09140 Bielle 09 177 Bb 92
64260 Bielle 64 174 Zd 90
76210 Bielleville 76 36 Ac 51
17600 Bien-Assis 17 122 Yf 74
80140 Biencourt 80 38 Be 49
55290 Biencourt-sur-Orge 55 75 Fc 57
28120 Bienfol 28 69 Bb 58
87600 Biennac 87 125 Af 74
76850 Biennais 76 37 Ba 51
62570 Bientques 62 29 Cb 44
60280 Bienville 60 39 Ce 52
62111 Bienvillers-au-Bois 62 29 Cd 47
77750 Biercy 77 52 Da 55
32160 Bières-d'Armagnac 32 162 Aa 87
08300 Biermes 08 41 Ec 52
60490 Biermont 60 39 Ce 51
10800 Bierne 10 73 Ea 59
53290 Bierné 53 84 Zc 62
59380 Bierne 59 27 Cc 43
61160 Bierre 61 48 Zf 55
21390 Bierre-lès-Semur 21 90 Eb 64
89200 Bierry 89 90 Df 63
89420 Bierry-les-Belles-Fontaines 89 90 Eb 63
09320 Biert 09 177 Bb 91
76750 Bierville 76 37 Bb 51
68600 Biesheim 68 60 Hd 60
52340 Biesles 52 75 Fb 60
67720 Bietlenheim 67 58 He 56
33210 Bieujac 33 135 Zf 81
02290 Bieuxy 02 40 Db 52
56310 Bieuzy 56 79 Wf 61
56330 Bieuzy-Lanvaux 56 80 Xa 62
50160 Biéville 50 47 Za 54
14112 Biéville-Beuville 14 47 Ze 53
14270 Biéville-en-Auge 14 35 Zf 54
14270 Biéville-Quétiéville 14 35 Zf 54
02860 Bièvres 02 40 De 52
08370 Bièvres 08 42 Fb 51
91570 Bièvres 91 51 Cb 56
88430 Biffontaine 88 77 Ge 59
40410 Biganon 40 147 Zb 82
33380 Biganos 33 134 Za 81
24260 Bigaroque 24 137 Af 79
16170 Bignac 16 123 Aa 74
33230 Bignac 33 135 Zf 78
56500 Bignan 56 80 Xb 61
17400 Bignay 17 110 Zc 73
14260 Bigne, la 14 47 Zb 54
08310 Bignicourt 08 41 Ec 52
51300 Bignicourt-sur-Marne 51 54 Ed 56
51340 Bignicourt-sur-Saulx 51 54 Ee 56
35000 Bignon 35 65 Yb 60
44140 Bignon, le 44 97 Yd 66
53170 Bignon-du-Maine, le 53 67 Zc 61
45210 Bignon-Mirabeau, le 45 72 Cf 60
35137 Bignonnet, le 35 65 Ya 59
86800 Bignoux 86 100 Ac 69
20252 Bigorno CTC 181 Kb 93
20252 Bigornu = Bigorno CTC 181 Kb 93
53240 Bigottière, la 53 67 Zb 59
53440 Bigottière, la 53 67 Zd 59
24130 Bigounin, le 24 136 Ab 79
20620 Biguglia CTC 181 Kc 93
02490 Bihécourt 02 40 Da 49
76420 Bihorel 76 37 Ba 52
62121 Bihucourt 62 30 Ce 48
44117 Bilac 44 81 Xe 65
79100 Bilazais 79 99 Zf 67
43000 Bilhac 43 141 Df 78
64260 Bilhères 64 174 Zd 90
28170 Bilheux 28 69 Bc 57
20100 Bilia CTC 184 If 99
19120 Billac 19 138 Be 79
24320 Billac 24 124 Ac 76
28190 Billancelles 28 69 Bb 58
80190 Billancourt 80 39 Cf 50
92100 Billancourt 92 51 Cb 56
87340 Billanges, les 87 113 Bd 73
85230 Billarderies, les 85 96 Xf 67
71540 Billaudot, les 71 105 Ec 66
33500 Billaux, les 33 135 Ze 79
35133 Billé 35 66 Ye 59
17920 Billeau, le 17 122 Yf 74
39250 Billecul 39 107 Ga 68
55100 Billemont 55 55 Fc 54
60890 Billemont 60 52 Da 53
64140 Billère 64 162 Zd 89
21130 Billey 21 106 Fc 66
03120 Billezois 03 116 Dd 71
22230 Billiaie 22 64 Xe 59
01200 Billiat 01 119 Fe 72
73170 Billième 73 132 Fe 74
56190 Billiers 56 81 Xd 63
01300 Billieu 01 131 Fe 74
56420 Billio 56 80 Xc 61
56190 Billion 56 80 Xc 63
63160 Billom 63 128 Dc 74
52220 Billory 52 74 Ee 58
46270 Billoux 46 138 Ca 81
03260 Billy 03 116 Dc 71
14370 Billy 14 48 Ze 54
41130 Billy 41 86 Bd 65
79600 Billy 79 98 Ze 68
62138 Billy-Berclau 62 30 Cf 45
58270 Billy-Chevannes 58 104 Dc 66
51400 Billy-le-Grand 51 53 Eb 54
21450 Billy-lès-Chanceaux 21 91 Ee 63
62420 Billy-Montigny 62 30 Cf 46
55210 Billy-sous-les-Côtes 55 55 Fe 54
55230 Billy-sous-Mangiennes 55 43 Fd 53
02200 Billy-sur-Aisne 02 40 Dc 52
58500 Billy-sur-Oisy 58 89 Dc 64
02210 Billy-sur-Ourcq 02 52 Db 53
33770 Bilos 33 134 Za 81
62570 Bilques 62 29 Cb 44
68340 Bilsteinthal 68 60 Hb 59
68127 Biltzheim 68 60 Hc 61
67170 Bilwisheim 67 58 Hd 56
20100 Bilzese CTC 184 Ka 99
62650 Bimont 62 28 Be 45
39570 Binans 39 107 Fd 69
51800 Binarville 51 54 Ef 53
41240 Binas 41 86 Bc 61
60850 Binaux, les 60 38 Be 52
67600 Bindernheim 67 60 Hd 59
36150 Binfou 36 101 Be 66
50490 Bingard, le 50 33 Yc 54
21270 Binges 21 92 Fb 65
22520 Binic-Étables-sur-Mer 22 64 Xb 57
57410 Bining 57 58 Hb 54
50390 Biniville 50 33 Yd 52
31440 Binos 31 176 Ad 91
51700 Binson-et-Orquigny 51 53 De 54
46500 Bio 46 138 Be 80
82000 Bio 82 150 Bc 85
74500 Bioge 74 120 Gd 71
38690 Biol 38 131 Fc 76
39190 Biolée, la 39 119 Fc 69
73410 Biolle, la 73 132 Ff 74
63640 Biollet 63 115 Ce 73
50140 Bion 50 66 Za 57
57170 Bioncourt 57 56 Gc 56
74170 Bionnay 74 133 Ge 73
57220 Bionville-sur-Nied 57 57 Gc 54
73540 Biorges 73 132 Gc 75
06410 Biot 06 173 Ha 87
81260 Biot 81 166 Cd 87
74430 Biot, le 74 120 Gd 71
82800 Bioule 82 150 Bd 84
12500 Biounac 12 139 Ce 82
16700 Bioussac 16 112 Ab 72
07130 Biousse 07 142 Ee 79
26110 Biove, la 26 156 Fb 83
03800 Biozat 03 116 Db 72
16120 Birac 16 123 Zf 75
33430 Birac 33 147 Zf 82
82000 Birac 82 150 Bc 84
47200 Birac-sur-Trec 47 136 Ab 82
32350 Biran 32 163 Ac 86
24310 Biras 24 124 Ad 77
24220 Birat 24 137 Ba 79
33840 Biret 33 148 Zf 83
64700 Biriatou 64 160 Yb 88
01330 Birieux 01 118 Fa 73
67440 Birkenwald 67 58 Hb 57
67160 Birlenbach, Drachenbronn- 67 58 Hf 55
44210 Birochère, la 44 96 Xf 66
17310 Biroire, la 17 109 Yd 73
17800 Biron 17 123 Zd 75
24540 Biron 24 137 Af 81
40600 Biscarrosse 40 146 Yf 82
40600 Biscarrosse-Plage 40 146 Ye 82
64120 Biscay 64 161 Yf 88
57660 Bischdorf = Bistroff 57 57 Ge 55
67800 Bischheim 67 60 He 57
67340 Bischholtz 67 58 Hd 55
67870 Bischoffsheim 67 60 Hc 58
67260 Bischtroff-sur-Sarre 67 57 Ha 55
68320 Bischwihr 68 60 Hc 60
67240 Bischwiller 67 58 He 56
64190 Bisdueys 64 161 Za 89
07530 Bise 07 142 Ec 80
74360 Bise 74 121 Ge 70
68580 Bisel 68 95 Hb 63
20112 Bisene CTC 185 Ka 99
16360 Bises, les 16 123 Ze 77
20128 Bisinao CTC 184 If 97
20128 Bisinau = Bisinao CTC 184 If 97
20235 Bisinchi CTC 181 Kb 94
55300 Bislée 55 55 Fc 55
28150 Bisseau 28 70 Bd 59
67260 Bissert 67 57 Ha 55
51150 Bisseuil 51 53 Ea 54

Bisseuil | 245

21520 Bissey-la-Côte 21 91 Ee 61
21330 Bissey-la-Pierre 21 91 Ec 61
71390 Bissey-sous-Cruchaud 71 105 Ee 68
59380 Bissezeele 59 27 Cc 43
19430 Bissiere, la 19 138 Bf 79
14370 Bissières 14 35 Zf 54
14380 Bisson, le 14 46 Yf 55
02830 Bissy 02 41 Ea 49
71260 Bissy-la-Mâconnaise 71 118 Ee 70
71460 Bissy-sous-Uxelles 71 118 Ee 69
71460 Bissy-sur-Fley 71 105 Ed 69
17490 Bistandille, la 17 123 Ze 73
47400 Bistauzac 47 136 Ab 82
57220 Bisten-en-Lorraine 57 57 Gd 54
57660 Bistroff = Bischdorf 57 57 Ge 55
19320 Bitarelle, la 19 126 Ca 77
19800 Bitarelle, la 19 126 Be 77
57230 Bitche = Bitsch 57 58 Hc 54
33730 Biton 33 135 Zd 82
45300 Bitry 45 71 Cb 59
58310 Bitry 58 89 Da 64
60350 Bitry 60 40 Da 52
57230 Bitsch = Bitche 57 58 Hc 54
67350 Bitschhoffen 67 58 Hd 55
68620 Bitschwiller-lès-Thann 68 94 Ha 62
32380 Bivès 32 149 Ae 85
38330 Biviers 38 132 Fe 77
50440 Biville 50 33 Yb 51
76890 Biville-la-Baignarde 76 37 Ba 50
76730 Biville-la-Rivière 76 37 Af 50
76630 Biville-sur-Mer 76 37 Bb 49
61190 Bivilliers 61 68 Ad 57
AD600 Bixessarri ◘ AND 177 Bc 94
30420 Bizac 30 154 Eb 86
43370 Bizac 43 141 De 79
60130 Bizancourt 60 39 Cc 52
11200 Bizanet 11 167 Cf 90
64320 Bizanos 64 162 Zd 89
52500 Bize 52 92 Fd 61
65150 Bize 65 175 Ac 90
11120 Bize-Minervois 11 167 Cf 89
03170 Bizeneuille 03 115 Ce 70
01290 Biziat 01 118 Ef 71
57480 Bizing 57 44 Gd 52
56250 Bizole 56 80 Xc 62
79120 Bizon 79 111 Zf 71
38690 Bizonnes 38 131 Fc 76
25210 Bizot, le 25 108 Ge 66
71710 Bizots, les 71 105 Ec 68
61290 Bizou 61 69 Ae 58
65150 Bizous 65 163 Ac 90
41290 Bizy 41 86 Bd 61
69460 Blacé 69D 118 Ed 72
84750 Blace 84 156 Fc 85
69460 Blaceret 69D 118 Ee 72
05230 Blache 05 144 Gb 81
04230 Blache, la 04 157 Fe 84
26400 Blache, la 26 143 Fa 80
26700 Blaches, les 26 155 Ee 82
04530 Blachière, la 04 145 Ge 81
60650 Blacourt 60 38 Bf 52
76190 Blacqueville 76 37 Af 51
51300 Blacy 51 54 Ed 56
89440 Blacy 89 90 Ea 63
63640 Bladeix, le 63 115 Ce 73
67113 Blaesheim 67 60 Hd 57
31700 Blagnac 31 164 Bc 87
08110 Blagny 08 42 Fb 51
21310 Blagny-sur-Vingeanne 21 92 Fc 64
33138 Blagon 33 134 Za 80
33190 Blaignac 33 135 Zf 81
33340 Blaignan 33 122 Za 77
44130 Blain 44 82 Yb 64
60460 Blaincourt 60 51 Cc 53
10500 Blaincourt-sur-Aube 10 74 Ec 58
76116 Blainville-Crevon 76 37 Bb 51
54360 Blainville-sur-L'Eau 54 76 Gc 57
50560 Blainville-sur-Mer 50 46 Yc 54
14550 Blainville-sur-Orne 14 47 Ze 53
62173 Blairville 62 29 Ce 47
08400 Blaise 08 42 Ed 52
52330 Blaise 52 74 Ef 59
51300 Blaise-sous-Arzillières 51 54 Ed 56
51290 Blaise-sous-Hauteville 51 74 Ee 57
49320 Blaison-Saint-Sulpice 49 84 Zd 64
52330 Blaisy 52 75 Ef 59
21540 Blaisy-Bas 21 91 Ee 64
21540 Blaisy-Haut 21 91 Ee 64
07000 Blaizac 07 142 Ec 80
31350 Blajan 31 163 Ad 89
48500 Blajoux 48 153 Dc 82
17700 Blameré 17 110 Za 72
49440 Blamerie, la 49 83 Yf 63
25310 Blamont 25 94 Gf 64
54450 Blâmont 54 77 Gf 57
81700 Blan 81 165 Ca 87
46500 Blanat 46 138 Be 80
01230 Blanaz 01 119 Fc 73
12360 Blanc 12 167 Cf 86
24440 Blanc 24 136 Ae 80
33340 Blanc 33 122 Yf 77
18410 Blancafort 18 88 Cd 63
36300 Blanc Coubernard, le 36 100 Ba 69
50220 Blancdinière, la 50 46 Ye 57
21320 Blancey 21 91 Ec 65
60120 Blancfossé 60 38 Cb 51
59223 Blanc-Four 59 30 Da 44
72600 Blanchardière, la 72 68 Ac 59
85110 Blanchardière, la 85 96 Yb 67
86100 Blanchards, les 86 100 Ac 67
57260 Blanche Église 57 57 Ge 56
91530 Blancheface 91 71 Ca 57
08290 Blanchefosse-et-Bay 08 41 Eb 50
44521 Blanche-Lande 44 82 Ye 64
24660 Blancherie, la 24 136 Ae 78
67130 Blancherupt 67 77 Hb 58
72270 Blanchetière, la 72 84 Zf 62
52700 Blancheville 52 75 Fb 59
93150 Blanc-Mesnil, le 93 51 Cc 55
31220 Blancotte 31 164 Ba 89
62370 Blanc-Pignon 62 27 Ca 43
38930 Blancs, les 38 143 Fd 80
51130* Blancs-Coteaux 51 53 Df 55
28120 Blandainville 28 69 Bb 59
30770 Blandas 30 153 Dd 85
38730 Blandin 38 131 Fc 76
53270 Blandouet-Saint Jean 53 67 Ze 60
31310 Blandy 31 164 Bb 90
77115 Blandy 77 72 Ce 57
91150 Blandy 91 71 Cb 59
62270 Blangerval-Blangermont 62 29 Cb 47
80430 Blangiel 80 38 Be 50
14130 Blangy-le-Château 14 48 Ab 53
80290 Blangy-sous-Poix 80 38 Ca 50
76340 Blangy-sur-Bresle 76 38 Bd 49
62770 Blangy-sur-Ternoise 62 29 Cb 46
80440 Blangy-Tronville 80 39 Cc 49
43800 Blanlhac 43 129 Df 78
22600 Blanlin 22 64 Xb 60
89200 Blannay 89 90 De 63
21430 Blanot 21 105 Eb 65
71250 Blanot 71 118 Ee 70
32270 Blanquefort 32 164 Ae 86
32600 Blanquefort 32 164 Ba 87
33290 Blanquefort 33 134 Zc 79
47500 Blanquefort-sur-Briolance 47 137 Af 81
28500 Blanville 28 50 Bc 56
71870 Blany 71 118 Ee 70
24640 Blanzac 24 125 Af 77
43350 Blanzac 43 141 Df 78
87300 Blanzac 87 113 Ba 72
17160 Blanzac-lès-Matha 17 123 Zd 73
16250 Blanzac-Porcheresse 16 123 Aa 76
46200 Blanzaguet 46 138 Bd 79
16320 Blanzaguet-Saint-Cybard 16 124 Ab 76
63112 Blanzat 63 128 Da 74
86400 Blanzay 86 112 Ab 71
17470 Blanzay-sur-Boutonne 17 111 Zd 72
55400 Blanzée 55 55 Fd 54
71450 Blanzy 71 105 Ec 68
08190 Blanzy-la-Salonnaise 08 41 Eb 52
02160 Blanzy-lès-Fismes 02 53 De 52
12230 Blaquererie, la 12 153 Db 85
12100 Blaquière, la 12 152 Da 84
60220 Blargies 60 38 Be 50
25640 Blarians 25 93 Gb 64
59173 Blaringhem 59 29 Cc 44
04120 Blaron 04 158 Gd 85
46330 Blars 46 138 Be 81
78270 Blaru 78 50 Bc 54
48000 Blasièges 48 140 Dc 82
33540 Blasimon 33 135 Zf 80
86170 Blaslay 86 99 Ab 68
43380 Blassac 43 140 Dc 77
07110 Blat, le 07 141 Eb 81
59126 Blaton, le 59 30 Da 44
48100 Blatte, la 48 140 Da 81
81360 Blaucau 81 166 Cc 86
23140 Blaudeix 23 114 Ca 71
50390 Blauderie, la 50 33 Yc 52
38690 Blaune 38 131 Fc 76
06440 Blausasc 06 159 Hc 86
84570 Blauvac 84 155 Fb 84
12440 Blauzac 12 151 Cb 83
30700 Blauzac 30 154 Ec 85
23700 Blavepeyre 23 115 Cc 72
19190 Blavignac 19 138 Be 78
48200 Blavignac 48 140 Db 79
62810 Blavincourt, Beaufort- 62 29 Cc 47
43700 Blavozy 43 141 Df 78
14400 Blay 14 47 Za 53
33600 Blayais, les 33 134 Zb 80
12170 Blaye 12 151 Cc 84
33113 Blaye 33 135 Zc 81
33390 Blaye 33 134 Zc 78
81400 Blaye-les-Mines 81 151 Ca 84
47470 Blaymont 47 149 Af 83
32100 Blaziert 32 148 Ac 85
52300 Blécourt 52 75 Fa 58
59268 Blécourt 59 30 Db 47
04420 Blégiers 04 157 Gc 83
39110 Blegny 39 107 Ff 67
50500 Bléhou 50 46 Yd 53
89230 Bleigny-le-Carreau 89 89 De 61
54450 Blémerey 54 77 Ge 57
88500 Blémerey 88 76 Ga 58
58470 Blénay, le 58 103 Da 67
62575 Blendecques 62 29 Cb 44
89220 Bléneau 89 88 Cf 62
77940 Blennes 77 72 Da 59
54700 Blénod-lès-Pont-à-Mousson 54 56 Ga 55
54113 Blénod-lès-Toul 54 76 Fe 57
60240 Bléquencourt 60 51 Ca 53
62380 Bléquin 62 28 Bf 45
02300 Blérancourdelle 02 40 Da 51
02300 Blérancourt 02 40 Da 51
55120 Blercourt 55 55 Fb 54
37150 Bléré 37 86 Af 65
62231 Blériot-Plage 62 27 Be 43
35750 Bléruais 35 65 Xf 60
33670 Blésignac 33 135 Ze 80
43450 Blesle 43 128 Db 77
02400 Blesmes 02 52 Dc 54
51340 Blesms 51 54 Ee 56
23200 Blessac 23 114 Ca 73
21690 Blessey 21 91 Ee 64
52120 Blessonville 52 75 Fa 60
62120 Blessy 62 29 Cb 45
18350 Blet 18 103 Ce 67
05100 Blétonnet, le 05 145 Ge 79
39140 Bletterans 39 106 Fc 68
43000 Bleu 43 141 De 78
88410 Bleurville 88 76 Ff 60
89110 Bleury 89 89 Dc 61
28700 Bleury-Saint-Symphorien 28 70 Be 57
88320 Blévaincourt 88 75 Fe 60
72600 Blèves 72 68 Ac 58
45300 Bléville 45 71 Cb 59
28170 Blévy 28 49 Bb 57
48190 Bleymard, le 48 141 De 82
12240 Bleys 12 151 Cb 83
81170 Bleys 81 151 Bf 84
60860 Blicourt 60 38 Ca 51
67650 Blienschwiller 67 60 Hc 58
57200 Bliesbruck 57 57 Hb 54
57200 Blies-Ebersing 57 57 Ha 54
57200 Blies-Guersviller 57 57 Ha 54
57200 Blies-Schweyen 57 57 Ha 54
04330 Blieux 04 157 Gc 85
10500 Blignicourt 10 74 Ed 58
10200 Bligny 10 74 Ed 59
51170 Bligny 51 53 Df 53
58270 Bligny 58 103 Dc 66
89210 Bligny-en-Othe 89 73 Dd 60
21200 Bligny-lès-Beaune 21 106 Ee 67
21440 Bligny-le-Sec 21 91 Ee 64
21360 Bligny-sur-Ouche 21 105 Ee 66
60190 Blincourt 60 39 Cd 52
62770 Blingel 62 29 Ca 46
49120 Blinière, la 49 83 Zb 65
49620 Blinière, la 49 83 Za 65
53320 Blinière-Rogat, la 53 66 Za 60
24330 Blis-et-Born 24 137 Af 77
58120 Blismes 58 104 De 66
36300 Blizon, le 36 101 Bb 68
53400 Blochet 53 83 Za 61
68740 Blodelsheim 68 95 Hd 61
41000 Blois 41 86 Bb 63
39210 Blois-sur-Seille 39 107 Fe 68
11700 Blomac 11 166 Cd 89
03390 Blomard 03 115 Cf 71
08260 Blombay-Morency 08 41 Ec 50
56800 Blond 56 81 Xd 61
87300 Blond 87 113 Ba 72
70500 Blondefontaine 70 93 Ff 61
41210 Blondellerie, la 41 87 Bf 63
74230 Blonniere, la 74 120 Gb 73
14910 Blonville 14 36 Aa 53
14910 Blonville-sur-Mer 14 48 Aa 52
36120 Blord 36 101 Bf 68
76460 Blosseville 76 36 Ae 49
50480 Blosville 50 46 Ye 52
79360 Blotière, la 79 111 Zd 71
63440 Blot-L'Église 63 115 Cf 72
68730 Blotzheim 68 95 Hc 63
49160 Blou 49 84 Zf 64
32230 Blousson-Sérian 32 163 Ab 88
50800 Bloutière, la 50 46 Ye 55
03320 Bloux 03 103 Cf 68
74150 Bloye 74 132 Ff 74
82300 Bloyne, la 82 150 Bd 84
74290 Bluffy 74 132 Gb 73
52110 Blumeray 52 74 Ef 58
77171 Blunay 77 72 Dc 57
25250 Blussans 25 94 Gd 64
39130 Blye 39 107 Fe 69
01150 Blyes 01 131 Fb 73
14690 Bô, le 14 47 Zd 55
64160 Boast 64 162 Ze 88
12360 Bobes 12 167 Da 86
93000 Bobigny 93 51 Cc 55
22100 Bobital 22 65 Xf 58
27330 Bocage, le 27 49 Ae 55
76690 Bocasse, le 76 37 Ba 51
06150 Bocca, la 06 173 Gf 87
20137 Bocca di l'Oru CTC 185 Kb 99
49150 Bocé 49 84 Zf 63
57220 Bockange 57 56 Gc 53
20136 Bocognano CTC 182 Ka 96
88270 Bocquegney 88 76 Gb 59
61550 Bocquence 61 48 Ac 55
56350 Bocquéreux 56 81 Xe 63
22980 Boculé, le 22 65 Xe 58
56390 Bodéan 56 80 Xa 62
22210 Bodéléno 22 64 Xc 60
22320 Bodéo, la 22 64 Xa 59
56370 Bodérin 56 80 Xb 63
29460 Bodévintin 29 62 Ve 58
29400 Bodilis 29 62 Vf 57
03270 Bodiment 03 116 Dd 72
53420 Bodinière, la 53 66 Za 59
56930 Bodion 56 64 Xa 61
29540 Bodizel 29 63 Wb 59
56480 Boduic 56 79 Wf 60
47550 Boé 47 149 Ad 84
61560 Boëcé 61 68 Ac 57
74420 Boëge 74 120 Gc 71
64510 Boeil-Bezing 64 162 Ze 89
42130 Boën 42 129 Ea 74
03450 Boënat 03 115 Cf 71
80870 Boëncourt 80 28 Be 48
67530 Bœrsch 67 60 Hc 58
59299 Boeschepe 59 30 Ce 44
59189 Bœseghem 59 29 Cc 45
67390 Bœsenbiesen 67 60 Hd 59
45390 Boësse 45 71 Cc 60
79150 Boësse 79 98 Zd 67
72400 Boëssé-le-Sec 72 68 Ad 60
89770 Bœurs-en-Othe 89 73 De 60
62390 Boffles 62 29 Cb 47
07440 Boffres 07 142 Ee 79
74250 Bogève 74 120 Gc 71
08120 Bogny-sur-Meuse 08 42 Ee 49
63750 Bogros 63 127 Cd 75
07340 Bogy 07 130 Ee 77
02110 Bohain-en-Vermandois 02 40 Dc 49
56140 Bohal 56 81 Xd 62
49800 Bohalle, la 49 84 Zd 64
29820 Bohars 29 61 Vc 58
01250 Bohas 01 119 Fc 72
44540 Bohinière, la 44 83 Ye 63
28130 Boigneville 28 70 Bd 57
91720 Boigneville 91 71 Cc 58
45760 Boigny-sur-Bionne 45 87 Ca 61
65150 Boila 65 163 Ac 90
28310 Boinville 28 70 Be 59
28700 Boinville-au-Chemin 28 70 Bd 58
78930 Boinville-en-Mantois 78 50 Be 55
55400 Boinville-en-Woëvre 55 55 Fe 53
78660 Boinville-le-Gaillard 78 70 Bf 58
78200 Boinvilliers 78 50 Bd 55
07690 Boiray 07 130 Ed 77
58110 Boire 58 104 Dd 67
44450 Boire-Courant 44 97 Yd 65
48600 Boirelac 48 140 Dd 80
45720 Boires-d'en-Haut, les 45 88 Cd 63
18370 Boiron, le 18 114 Cb 70
28200 Boirreville 28 69 Bc 60
56460 Boiry 56 81 Xd 62
62156 Boiry-Notre-Dame 62 30 Cf 47
62175 Boiry-Saint-Martin 62 29 Ce 47
17240 Bois 17 122 Zc 76
64270 Bois 64 161 Za 88
44440 Bois, le 44 82 Yd 63
73260 Bois, le 73 133 Gc 76
73350 Bois, le 73 133 Ge 76
22630 Bois, les 22 65 Xf 58
36300 Bois, les 36 101 Bb 69
71130 Bois, les 71 117 Df 69
27330 Bois-Anzeray 27 49 Ae 55
27250 Bois-Arnault 27 49 Ae 56
60650 Bois-Aubert 60 38 Bf 51
85310 Bois-aux-Moines 85 97 Ye 68
23290 Bois-Auzareix 23 113 Bd 72
77510 Bois-Baudry 77 52 Db 55
86170 Bois-Baudry 86 99 Zf 68
18250 Boisbelle 18 88 Cd 65
80600 Boisbergues 80 29 Cb 48
62320 Bois-Bernard 62 30 Cf 46
37270 Bois-Bidault 37 85 Af 65
03250 Bois-Blanc 03 116 Dd 72
85480 Bois-Bonnaud, le 85 97 Ye 69
16480 Boisbreteau 16 123 Ze 77
71210 Bois-Bretoux 71 105 Ec 68
61570 Boischampré 61 48 Zf 56
41320 Bois-Chavant 41 87 Bf 65
45340 Boiscommun 45 71 Cc 60
59144 Boiscrête, la 59 31 De 47
39220 Bois-d'Amont 39 120 Ga 69
29370 Bois-Daniel 29 78 Wa 60
49250 Bois d'Anjou, les 49 84 Ze 64
78390 Bois-d'Arcy 78 51 Ca 56
89660 Bois-d'Arcy 89 89 De 63
49390 Bois-de-Boulogne, le 49 84 Zf 64
19410 Bois-de-Bourzat 19 125 Bc 76
85710 Bois-de-Céné 85 96 Ya 67
88600 Bois-de-Champ 88 77 Ge 59
80460 Bois-de-Cise, le 80 28 Bc 48
28800 Bois-de-Feugères 28 70 Bc 59
88390 Bois-de-Girancourt, le 88 76 Gc 60
39230 Bois-de-Grand 39 106 Fd 68
85330 Bois-de-la-Chaise 85 96 Xe 66
16480 Bois-Delage 16 123 Zf 76
89450 Bois-de-la-Madeleine, les 89 90 Dd 64
31390 Bois-de-la-Pierre 31 164 Ba 88
29610 Bois-de-la-Roche 29 62 Wb 57
33240 Bois-de-Lion, le 33 135 Zd 78
28630 Bois-de-Mivoie 28 70 Bc 58
76160 Bois-d'Ennebourg 76 37 Bb 52
71600 Bois-de-Paray, le 71 117 Ea 70
58400 Bois-de-Raveau, le 58 103 Da 65
10160 Bois-de-Rigny, le 10 73 Dd 59
38090 Bois-de-Roche, le 38 131 Fa 75
45260 Bois-de-Romaison, les 45 88 Cd 61
70200 Bois-Derrière 70 94 Gc 62
37350 Bois-des-Cours, le 37 100 Ae 67
63460 Bois-des-Lapins 63 115 Da 72
76390 Bois-des-Puits 76 38 Be 50
18220 Bois-des-Vèves, le 18 102 Cc 65
03120 Bois-Dieu 03 116 Dd 72
62500 Boisdinghem 62 27 Ca 44
69620 Bois-d'Oingt, le 69D 118 Ed 73
77970 Boisdon 77 52 Db 56
12780 Bois-du-Four 12 152 Cf 83
51340 Bois-du-Roi, le 51 54 Ef 56
27150 Boisemont 27 50 Bc 53
95000 Boisemont 95 51 Bf 54
62610 Bois-en-Ardres 62 27 Bf 43
28270 Bois-Fautray 28 49 Ba 56
44680 Bois-Flamberge 44 96 Yb 66
71230 Bois-Francs, les 71 105 Ec 69
49610 Bois-Garreau 49 83 Zc 65
28220 Boisgasson 28 69 Ba 60
76780 Bois-Gaultier 76 37 Bc 51
35360 Boisgervilly 35 65 Xf 60
58150 Bois-Gibault 58 88 Cf 65
37370 Bois-Girault 37 85 Ad 63
59280 Bois-Grenier 59 30 Cf 45
50500 Bois-Grimot 50 34 Ye 53
76750 Bois-Guilbert 76 37 Bc 51
76420 Bois-Guillaume 76 37 Ba 52
60240 Bois-Guillaume, le 60 50 Bf 53
35134 Bois-Guy, le 35 82 Yd 61
14220 Bois-Halbout 14 47 Zd 54
27260 Bois-Hellain, le 27 48 Ac 53
76750 Bois-Héroult 76 37 Bc 51
91150 Bois-Herpin 91 71 Cb 58
76190 Bois-Himont 76 36 Ae 51
27180 Bois-Hubert 27 49 Af 54
76590 Bois-Hulin 76 37 Ba 50
49500 Bois II 49 83 Za 62
62170 Boisjean 62 28 Be 46
27620 Bois-Jérôme-Saint-Ouen 27 50 Bd 54
87190 Bois-Jeune 87 113 Bb 71
16490 Bois-Jura 16 112 Ac 72
41100 Bois-la-Barbe 41 86 Ba 62
07310 Bois-Lantal 07 142 Eb 79
80150 Boisle, le 80 28 Bf 47
27220 Bois-le-Roi 27 50 Bc 55
77590 Bois-le-Roi 77 71 Ce 58
02270 Bois-lès-Pargny 02 40 Dd 50
62175 Boisleux-au-Mont 62 30 Ce 47
62175 Boisleux-Saint-Marc 62 30 Ce 47
76160 Bois-l'Evêque 76 37 Bb 52
87160 Bois-Mandé 87 113 Bc 71
72560 Bois-Martin 72 68 Ab 61
79300 Boismé 79 98 Zd 68
27910 Bois Meigle 27 37 Bb 52
54620 Boismont 54 43 Fe 52
80230 Boismont 80 28 Be 48
45290 Boismorand 45 88 Ce 62
44130 Bois-Morinet, le 44 82 Yb 64
79110 Bois-Naudouin 79 111 Zf 72
16320 Boisné-La Tude 16 124 Ab 76
27800 Boisney 27 49 Ad 54
04250 Bois-Noir 04 157 Gb 82
27330 Bois-Normand-près-Lyre 27 49 Ae 55
14380 Bois-Olivier, le 14 46 Yf 55
17580 Bois-Plage-en-Ré, le 17 109 Yd 71
79260 Boisragon 79 111 Ze 70
36120 Boisramier 36 102 Bf 68
03700 Bois-Randenay, le 03 116 Dc 72
62650 Bois Ratel, le 62 28 Be 45
18290 Bois-Ratier 18 102 Cb 67
80640 Boisrault 80 38 Bf 49
17150 Boisredon 17 123 Zc 77
18410 Bois-Renard 18 87 Cb 63
28350 Bois-Renault, le 28 49 Ba 56
76590 Bois-Robert, les 76 37 Ba 49
50200 Boisroger 50 46 Yc 54
77710 Boisroux 77 72 Cf 59
24170 Boissac 24 137 Ba 80
87110 Boissac 87 125 Bb 74
71800 Bois-Sainte-Marie 71 117 Ec 71
48170 Boissanfeuilles 48 141 De 81
28800 Boissay 28 70 Bd 59
45410 Boissay 45 70 Be 60
76660 Boissay 76 37 Bc 49
76750 Boissay 76 37 Bc 51
27490 Boissaye, la 27 50 Bb 54
17700 Boisse 17 110 Zc 72
24560 Boisse 24 136 Ad 80
01120 Boisse, la 01 130 Fa 73
28120 Boisseau 28 69 Bb 58
41290 Boisseau 41 86 Bb 62
45480 Boisseaux 45 70 Bf 59
31230 Boissède 31 164 Ae 88
61570 Boissei-la-Lande 61 48 Aa 56
63122 Boisséjour 63 128 Da 74
42990 Boissel 42 129 Df 74
49230 Boisselière, la 49 97 Yf 66
80300 Boisselle, la 80 39 Ce 48
12300 Boisse-Penchot 12 139 Cb 81
36700 Bois-Septier 36 101 Bb 67
43300 Boisserette 43 140 Dc 78
79360 Boisserolles 79 110 Zd 72
34160 Boisseron 34 154 Ea 86
77120 Boisserotte, la 77 52 Da 56
73320 Boisses, les 73 133 Gf 75
15600 Boisset 15 139 Cb 80
30210 Boisset 30 154 Ec 85
34220 Boisset 34 166 Ce 88
43500 Boisset 43 129 Df 77
84750 Boisset, le 84 156 Fd 85
42210 Boisset-lès-Montrond 42 129 Eb 75
27120 Boisset-les-Prévanches 27 50 Bb 55
78910 Boissets 78 50 Bd 55
42560 Boisset-Saint-Priest 42 129 Ea 75
77350 Boissettes 77 71 Cd 57
63420 Boisseuge 63 128 Da 76
43450 Boisseuges 43 128 Db 77
17700 Boisseuil 17 110 Zb 72
24390 Boisseuilh 24 125 Bb 77
01190 Boissey 01 118 Ef 70
14170 Boissey 14 48 Aa 54
34390 Boissezon 34 167 Cf 87
81490 Boissezon 81 166 Cc 87
81320 Boissezon-de-Masviel 81 167 Cf 86
47110 Boissie 47 149 Ad 82
27220 Boissière 27 50 Bc 55
34150 Boissière 34 168 Dd 87
39240 Boissière 39 119 Fd 70
46330 Boissière 46 138 Be 81
53160 Boissière 53 67 Ze 59
14340 Boissière, la 14 35 Aa 54
29710 Boissière, la 29 78 Ve 60
53800 Boissière, la 53 83 Za 62
24640 Boissière-d'Ans, la 24 125 Af 77
85600 Boissière-de-Montaigu, la 85 97 Ye 67
85430 Boissière-des-Landes, la 85 109 Yd 69
44430 Boissière-du-Doré, la 44 97 Ye 65
78125 Boissière-École, la 78 50 Bd 56
79310 Boissière-en-Gâtine, la 79 111 Zd 69
30114 Boissières 30 154 Eb 86
43130 Boissières 43 129 Ea 77
46150 Boissières 46 137 Bc 81
49110 Boissière-sur-Evre, la 49 83 Yf 65
79200 Boissière-Thouarsaise, la 79 98 Ze 68
77350 Boissise-la-Bertrand 77 71 Cd 57
77310 Boissise-le-Roi 77 71 Cd 57
30500 Boisson 30 154 Eb 83
15300 Boissonière, la 15 127 Cf 78
12350 Boissonnade, la 12 151 Cb 82
87150 Boissonnie, la 87 125 Af 74
28210 Boissy 28 50 Bd 56
56430 Boissy 56 64 Xd 61
77760 Boissy-aux-Cailles 77 71 Cd 59
60440 Boissy-Fresnoy 60 52 Cf 54
95650 Boissy-L'Aillerie 95 51 Ca 54
27300 Boissy-Lamberville 27 49 Ad 53
91690 Boissy-la-Rivière 91 71 Ca 58
60240 Boissy-le-Bois 60 50 Bf 53
27520 Boissy-le-Châtel 27 49 Ae 53
77169 Boissy-le-Châtel 77 52 Da 56
91590 Boissy-le-Cutte 91 71 Cb 58
51210 Boissy-le-Repos 51 53 Dd 55
91870 Boissy-le-Sec 91 70 Ca 58
28340 Boissy-lès-Perche 28 49 Af 56
61110 Boissy-Maugis 61 69 Ae 58
78200 Boissy-Mauvoisin 78 50 Bd 55
94470 Boissy-Saint-Léger 94 51 Cd 56
78490 Boissy-sans-Avoir 78 50 Be 56
91790 Boissy-sous-Saint-Yon 91 71 Cb 57
27240 Boissy-sur-Damville 27 49 Ba 55
35150 Boistrudan 35 66 Yd 61
44260 Boistuaud 44 82 Ya 64

246 | Bissey-la-Côte

13200 Boisverdun 13 169 Ee 88
16360 Bois-Vert 16 123 Ze 76
28150 Boisville-la-Saint-Père 28 70 Be 59
74570 Boisy 74 120 Ga 72
50800 Boisyvon 50 46 Yf 56
18120 Boitier 18 102 Ca 66
61500 Boitron 61 68 Ab 57
77750 Boitron 77 52 Db 55
56130 Boizeul, le 56 81 Xe 63
25330 Bolandoz 25 107 Ga 66
29640 Bolazec 29 63 Wc 58
76210 Bolbec 76 36 Ac 51
57570 Boler 57 44 Gb 52
88100 Bollé, la 88 77 Gf 59
84500 Bollène 84 155 Ee 83
06450 Bollène-Vesubie, la 06 159 Hc 85
50250 Bolleville 50 33 Yc 53
76210 Bolleville 76 36 Ad 51
59470 Bollezeele 59 27 Cb 43
06420 Bolline, la 06 159 Hb 84
68540 Bollwiller 68 95 Hb 61
52310 Bologne 52 75 Fa 59
22740 Boloï 22 63 Wf 56
01450 Bolozon 01 119 Fc 71
66210 Bolquère 66 178 Ca 93
67150 Bolsenheim 67 60 Hd 58
15170 Bolzat 15 140 Da 78
76110 Bomambusc 76 36 Ac 51
33121 Bombannes 33 134 Yf 78
48500 Bombes 48 152 Da 83
77160 Bombon 77 71 Cf 57
33210 Bommes 33 135 Zd 81
36120 Bommiers 36 102 Bf 68
37800 Bommiers 37 100 Ad 66
13510 Bompard 13 170 Fc 87
09400 Bompas 09 177 Bd 91
66430 Bompas 66 179 Cf 92
03160 Bomplein 03 103 Da 69
62960 Bomy 62 29 Cb 45
58330 Bona 58 104 Dc 66
35350 Bonaban 35 65 Ya 57
09800 Bonac-Irazein 09 176 Af 91
82230 Bonanech 82 150 Bd 85
32410 Bonas 32 148 Ac 86
12500 Bonauberg 12 139 Cf 81
59258 Bonavis 59 30 Db 48
01100 Bonaz 01 119 Fd 71
70150 Bonboillon 70 92 Fe 64
28150 Boncé 28 70 Bd 59
38290 Bonce 38 131 Fa 74
53960 Bonchamp-lès-Laval 53 67 Zb 60
02350 Boncour 02 41 Df 51
27120 Boncourt 27 50 Bb 54
28260 Boncourt 28 50 Bc 55
54800 Boncourt 54 56 Fe 53
21700 Boncourt-le-Bois 21 106 Ef 66
55200 Boncourt-sur-Meuse 55 55 Fd 56
45300 Bondaroy 45 71 Cb 59
25230 Bondeval 25 94 Gf 64
76400 Bondeville 76 36 Ac 50
58220 Bondieuse 58 89 Db 65
31340 Bondigoux 31 150 Bd 85
86130 Bondilly 86 100 Ac 68
37320 Bondis, les 37 100 Ae 65
48400 Bondons, les 48 153 Dd 82
17150 Bondou 17 123 Zc 77
91070 Bondoufle 91 71 Cc 57
59910 Bondues 59 30 Da 44
87510 Bondy 87 125 Ba 73
93140 Bondy 93 51 Cc 55
22110 Bonen 22 63 We 59
47240 Bon-Encontre 47 149 Ae 83
30450 Bonevaux 30 154 Ea 82
77720 Bonfruit 77 52 Cf 57
60000 Bongenoult 60 38 Ca 52
63160 Bongheat 63 128 Dc 74
63290 Bonhomme 63 116 Dd 73
68650 Bonhomme, le 68 77 Ha 59
48600 Boniac 48 141 Dd 80
20169 Bonifacio CTC 185 Ka 100
20100 Bonifazinca CTC 184 If 99
58140 Bonin 58 104 Df 65
60510 Bonlier 60 38 Ca 52
39130 Bonlieu 39 107 Ff 69
26160 Bonlieu-sur-Roubion 26 142 Ef 81
64240 Bonloc 64 160 Ye 88
23340 Bon-Martin 23 126 Bf 74
09100 Bonnac 09 165 Bd 89
15500 Bonnac 15 128 Da 77
87270 Bonnac-la-Côte 87 113 Bb 73
63620 Bonnafond 63 127 Cd 74
81330 Bonnaigue, la 81 151 Cc 86
25680 Bonnal 25 93 Gc 63
48100 Bonnalbert 48 140 Da 81
59242 Bonnance 59 30 Db 45
86400 Bonnardelière, la 86 111 Ab 71
19370 Bonnat 19 126 Be 75
23220 Bonnat 23 114 Bf 71
63310 Bonnat 63 116 Dc 73
74140 Bonnatrait 74 120 Gc 70
39190 Bonnaud 39 106 Fc 69
25870 Bonnay 25 93 Ga 64
71460 Bonnay 71 118 Ed 69
80800 Bonnay 80 39 Cd 49
74380 Bonne 74 120 Gb 71
36500 Bonneau 36 101 Bc 67
27500 Bonnebos 27 36 Ad 52
14340 Bonnebosq 14 48 Aa 53
58190 Bonneçon 58 89 De 64
52360 Bonnecourt 52 75 Fc 61
45460 Bonnée 45 88 Cc 62
56130 Bonne-Façon, la 56 81 Xe 63
38090 Bonnefamille 38 131 Fa 75
61270 Bonnefoi 61 49 Ad 56
12470 Bonnefon 12 140 Cf 81
03440 Bonnefond 03 115 Cf 70
19170 Bonnefond 19 126 Bf 75
48200 Bonnefons 48 140 Db 80
23250 Bonnefont 23 114 Be 72
32350 Bonnefont 32 163 Ac 87
43510 Bonnefont 43 141 De 79
65220 Bonnefont 65 163 Ac 89
87130 Bonnefont 87 125 Bd 74
39800 Bonnefontaine 39 107 Fe 68
57370 Bonne-Fontaine 57 58 Hb 56
40330 Bonnegarde 40 161 Zb 87
74150 Bonneguète 74 119 Ff 73
02400 Bonneil 02 52 Dc 54
23500 Bonneix, le 23 126 Ca 74
78830 Bonnelles 78 70 Ca 57
80860 Bonnelle Sailly-Bray 80 28 Be 47
35270 Bonnemain 35 65 Yb 58
14260 Bonnemaison 14 47 Zc 54
27380 Bonnemare 27 37 Bc 53
15600 Bonnemayoux 15 139 Cb 80
65130 Bonnemazon 65 163 Ab 90
21250 Bonnencontre 21 106 Fa 66
47150 Bonnenouvelle 47 137 Af 81
73450 Bonnenuit 73 145 Gc 78
37290 Bonnerie, la 37 100 Af 68
81260 Bonnéry 81 166 Cc 87
11270 Bonnérys 11 165 Bf 89
16390 Bonnes 16 124 Aa 77
86300 Bonnes 86 100 Ad 69
19250 Bonnesaigne 19 126 Cb 76
44380 Bonne-Source 44 96 Xd 65
02400 Bonnesvalyn 02 52 Db 54
55130 Bonnet 55 75 Fc 57
72110 Bonnétable 72 68 Ac 59
25210 Bonnétage 25 108 Ge 65
33370 Bonnetan 33 135 Zd 80
12560 Bonneterre 12 152 Da 82
24320 Bonnetie, la 24 124 Ac 76
16120 Bonneuil 16 123 Zf 75
36310 Bonneuil 36 113 Bb 70
79120 Bonneuil 79 111 Aa 71
79370 Bonneuil 79 111 Ze 71
86300 Bonneuil 86 112 Ad 69
60123 Bonneuil-en-Valois 60 52 Cf 53
60120 Bonneuil-les-Eaux 60 38 Cb 50
86210 Bonneuil-Matours 86 100 Ad 68
94380 Bonneuil-sur-Marne 94 51 Cc 56
28800 Bonneval 28 69 Bc 59
43160 Bonneval 43 129 De 77
73260 Bonneval 73 132 Gc 75
73480 Bonneval 73 133 Ha 76
73700 Bonneval 73 133 Ge 75
26410 Bonneval-en-Diois 26 143 Fd 81
25560 Bonnevaux 25 107 Gb 68
74360 Bonnevaux 74 121 Ge 71
25620 Bonnevaux-le-Prieuré 25 107 Gb 66
41800 Bonneveau 41 85 Ae 62
70700 Bonnevent-Velloreille 70 93 Ff 64
12120 Bonneviale 12 152 Ce 83
16170 Bonneville 16 123 Zf 73
23250 Bonneville 23 114 Be 72
74130 Bonneville 74 120 Gc 72
80670 Bonneville 80 29 Cb 48
50360 Bonneville, la 50 33 Yd 52
27290 Bonneville-Aptot 27 49 Ae 53
14130 Bonneville-la-Louvet 14 48 Ac 53
27190 Bonneville-sur-Iton, la 27 49 Ba 55
14800 Bonneville-sur-Touques 14 48 Aa 52
49380 Bonnezeaux 49 83 Zd 65
36800 Bonnière, la 36 101 Bb 68
60112 Bonnières 60 38 Bf 51
78270 Bonnières-sur-Seine 78 50 Bd 54
16230 Bonnieure 16 124 Ab 73
84480 Bonnieux 84 156 Fb 86
62890 Bonningues-les-Ardres 62 27 Ca 44
62340 Bonningues-lès-Calais 62 26 Be 43
14700 Bonnœil 14 47 Zd 55
44540 Bonnœuvre 44 82 Ye 63
36190 Bonnu 36 113 Bd 70
64300 Bonnut 64 161 Zb 87
45420 Bonny-sur-Loire 45 88 Cf 63
56400 Bono 56 80 Xa 63
09160 Bonrepaux 09 176 Ba 90
65330 Bonrepos 65 163 Ac 89
31590 Bonrepos-Riquet 31 165 Bd 86
31470 Bonrepos-sur-Aussonnelle 31 164 Ba 87
22570 Bon Repos sur Blavet 22 63 Wf 59
89630 Bon-Ru, le 89 90 Ea 64
26170 Bons 26 156 Fd 83
AD200 Bons, les ◘ AND 177 Bd 93
12150 Bonsecours 12 152 Da 82
76240 Bonsecours 76 37 Ba 52
74890 Bons-en-Chablais 74 120 Gc 71
04200 Bons-Enfants, les 04 157 Ff 84
61380 Bonsmoulins 61 49 Ad 57
42160 Bonson 42 129 Eb 75
06830 Bonsons 06 159 Hb 85
14420 Bons-Tassilly 14 48 Ze 55
15310 Bontat, la 15 139 Cb 78
26110 Bonté, la 26 156 Fa 82
79390 Bontellerie, la 79 99 Zf 68
04240 Bontes 04 158 Gd 85
89140 Bonval 89 72 Da 59
72800 Bon-Verger, le 72 84 Aa 63
73130 Bonvillard 73 132 Gc 76
73140 Bonvillard 73 133 Gd 77
73460 Bonvillard 73 132 Gb 75
73220 Bonvillaret 73 132 Gb 75
28630 Bonville 28 70 Bd 58
54300 Bonviller 54 57 Gc 57
54300 Bonviller-la-Petite 54 57 Gd 57
60120 Bonvillers 60 39 Cc 51
60730 Bonvillers 60 51 Cb 53
88260 Bonvillet 88 76 Ga 60
02420 Bony 02 40 Db 49
33910 Bonzac 33 135 Ze 78
55160 Bonzée-en-Woëvre 55 55 Fd 54
40160 Bôo, le 40 146 Yf 82
67860 Boofzheim 67 60 He 59
40370 Boos 40 146 Za 85
76520 Boos 76 37 Bb 52
65400 Boô-Silhent 65 175 Zf 90
67390 Bootzheim 67 60 Hd 59
22170 Boqueho 22 63 Xa 58
60820 Boran-sur-Oise 60 51 Cc 53
64490 Borce 64 174 Zc 91
79600 Borcq-sur-Airvault 79 99 Zf 68
23210 Bord 23 113 Bd 72
36340 Bord 36 114 Be 69
87290 Bord 87 113 Bb 72
87500 Bord 87 125 Ba 75
56360 Bordardué 56 80 Wf 65
24380 Bordas 24 136 Ad 78
23220 Bordat 23 114 Bf 71
10110 Borde, la 10 74 Ec 60
19140 Borde, la 19 125 Bd 76
19140 Borde, la 19 126 Bd 76
71140 Borde, la 71 104 De 69
77820 Borde, la 77 71 Cf 57
33000* Bordeaux 33 135 Zc 79
27420 Bordeaux-Saint-Clair 27 50 Bd 53
76790 Bordeaux-Saint-Clair 76 36 Ab 50
56360 Bordelanne 56 80 We 64
33580 Bordepaille 33 135 Aa 81
64800 Bordères 64 162 Ze 89
40270 Bordères-et-Lamensans 40 147 Zd 86
65590 Bordères-Louron 65 175 Ac 91
65320 Bordères-sur-L'Echez 65 162 Aa 89
56360 Borderhouat 56 80 Wf 65
19120 Borderie, la 19 138 Be 79
24600 Borderie, la 24 124 Ab 77
19600 Borderies, les 19 137 Bc 78
12310 Bordes 12 152 Cf 82
32330 Bordes 32 148 Ab 86
64350 Bordes 64 162 Zf 88
64510 Bordes 64 162 Ze 89
65190 Bordes 65 163 Ab 89
03350 Bordes, les 03 115 Ce 69
11230 Bordes, les 11 178 Bf 91
19160 Bordes, les 19 126 Cb 76
23460 Bordes, les 23 126 Bf 73
28360 Bordes, les 28 70 Bc 59
36100 Bordes, les 36 102 Bf 67
37600 Bordes, les 37 100 Ba 66
45460 Bordes, les 45 88 Cc 62
58420 Bordes, les 58 104 Dd 65
58800 Bordes, les 58 89 De 65
71350 Bordes, les 71 106 Fa 67
77120 Bordes, les 77 52 Da 56
77120 Bordes, les 77 52 Da 56
78720 Bordes, les 78 50 Bf 57
86320 Bordes, les 86 112 Ae 70
89500 Bordes, les 89 72 Dc 60
89520 Bordes, les 89 89 Db 63
10800 Bordes-Aumont, les 10 73 Ea 59
31210 Bordes-de-Rivière 31 163 Ad 90
40300 Bordes-du-Ba 40 161 Yf 87
31110 Bordes-du-Lys 31 176 Ad 92
21440 Bordes Pillot 21 91 Ee 64
23300 Bordessoule 23 113 Bc 71
09350 Bordes-sur-Arize, les 09 164 Bc 90
09800 Bordes-sur-Lez, les 09 176 Ba 91
09800 Bordes-Uchentein 09 176 Ba 91
31830 Bordettes, les 31 164 Bb 87
30160 Bordezac 30 154 Ea 83
47340 Bordiels, les 47 149 Ae 83
17430 Bords 17 110 Zb 73
23230 Bord-Saint-Georges 23 114 Cb 71
07310 Borée 07 141 Eb 79
85480 Borelière, la 85 97 Yf 69
04200 Borelly 04 157 Ff 83
05230 Borels, les 05 144 Gb 81
06450 Boréon, le 06 159 Hb 84
17270 Boresse-et-Marton 17 123 Zf 77
60300 Borest 60 51 Ce 53
70110 Borey 70 93 Gc 63
74230 Borgeal, le 74 120 Gc 73
06440 Borghéas 06 159 Hb 86
20290 Borgo CTC 181 Kc 93
20290 Borgo CTC 181 Kd 93
20290 Borgo = U Borgu CTC 181 Kd 93
12120 Borie, la 12 152 Cd 83
12390 Borie, la 12 151 Cb 82
19210 Borie, la 19 125 Bc 76
46310 Borie, la 46 137 Bc 81
48000 Borie, la 48 153 Dd 82
81600 Borie, la 81 151 Bf 85
34480 Borie-Nouvelle, la 34 167 Da 87
46260 Bories 46 150 Be 82
74930 Boringes 74 120 Gb 72
20146 Borivoli CTC 185 Ka 99
83230 Bormes-les-Mimosas 83 172 Gc 90
12470 Born 12 140 Cf 81
47210 Born 47 136 Ae 81
31340 Born, le 31 150 Bd 85
48000 Born, le 48 141 Dd 81
39570 Bornay 39 107 Fd 69
24440 Born-de-Champs 24 136 Ae 80
26410 Borne 26 143 Fd 80
43350 Borne 43 141 De 78
18250 Borne, la 18 88 Cd 65
23200 Borne, la 23 114 Ca 73
41300 Borne, la 41 87 Ca 65
74130 Borne, le 74 120 Gc 73
60540 Bornel 60 51 Cb 53
90100 Boron 90 94 Ha 63
59190 Borre 59 30 Cd 44
82270 Borredon 82 150 Bd 83
83400 Borrels, les 83 171 Ga 90
24590 Borrèze 24 137 Bc 79
62128 Borry-Becquerelle 62 30 Ce 47
84360 Borrys, les 84 156 Fb 86
16360 Bors de-Baigne 16 123 Ze 77
16190 Bors-de-Montmoreau 16 124 Ab 76
19700 Bort 19 126 Be 76
56360 Borticado 56 80 We 64
19110 Bort-les-Orgues 19 127 Cd 76
63190 Bort-L'Étang 63 128 Dc 74
54290 Borville 54 76 Gc 58
56360 Borvran 56 80 Wf 65
19290 Bos, le 19 126 Ca 74
34700 Bosc 34 167 Dc 86
09000 Bosc, le 09 177 Bc 91
17360 Boscamnant 17 123 Zf 77
76780 Bosc-Asselin 76 37 Bc 51
27520 Bosc-Bénard-Commin 27 37 Af 53
76680 Bosc-Bérenger 76 37 Bb 51
76750 Bosc-Bordel 76 37 Bc 51
76720 Bosc-de-Sévis, le 76 37 Ba 50
27370 Bosc du Theil, le 27 49 Ae 53
76750 Bosc-Edeline 76 37 Bc 51
76710 Bosc-Guérard-Saint-Adrien 76 37 Ba 51
22250 Boschais, le 22 64 Xd 59
27520 Boscherville 27 49 Af 53
76220 Bosc-Hyons 76 38 Bd 52
76850 Bosc-le-Hard 76 37 Bb 51
76680 Bosc-Mesnil 76 37 Bc 51
61470 Bosc-Renoult, le 61 48 Ab 55
27330 Bosc-Renoult-en-Ouche 27 49 Ae 55
27520 Bosc-Renoult-en-Rumois 27 49 Ae 53
76260 Boscrocourt 76 37 Bc 48
27670 Bosc-Roger-en-Roumois, le 27 49 Af 53
76750 Bosc-Roger-sur-Buchy 76 37 Bc 51
64290 Bosdarros 64 162 Zd 89
27310 Bosgouet 27 37 Af 52
27520 Bosguérard-de-Marcouville 27 49 Ae 53
27190 Boshion, le 27 49 Ba 55
71330 Bosjean 71 106 Fc 68
02250 Bosmont-sur-Serre 02 41 Df 50
23400 Bosmoreau-les-Mines 23 114 Be 72
27670 Bosnormand 27 49 Af 53
13390 Bosq, le 13 171 Fd 88
14210 Bosq, le 14 35 Zc 54
40600 Bosque 40 146 Yf 82
13130 Bosque, la 13 170 Fa 87
34360 Bosque, le 34 167 Cf 88
80160 Bosquel 80 38 Cb 50
27480 Bosquentin 27 38 Bd 52
50270 Bosquet, le 50 33 Yb 52
50580 Bosqueville 50 46 Yb 52
27800 Bosrobert 27 49 Ae 53
23200 Bosroger 23 114 Cb 73
27670 Bosroumois 27 49 Af 53
10140 Bossancourt 10 74 Ed 59
37240 Bossard, le 37 100 Ae 66
44590 Bossardais, la 44 82 Yc 62
37290 Bossay-sur-Claise 37 100 Af 68
25210 Bosse 25 108 Gd 66
41290 Bosse 41 86 Bb 61
12350 Bosse, la 12 151 Ca 82
72400 Bosse, la 72 68 Ad 59
35320 Bosse-de-Bretagne, la 35 82 Yc 61
37240 Bossée 37 100 Ae 66
67330 Bosselshausen 67 58 Hd 56
67270 Bossendorf 67 58 Hd 56
72300 Bosses 72 84 Ze 62
24130 Bosset 24 136 Ac 79
08350 Bosseval-et-Briancourt 08 42 Ef 50
74160 Bossey 74 120 Ga 72
38260 Bossieu 38 131 Fa 76
74400 Bossons, les 74 121 Ge 73
33350 Bossugan 33 135 Zf 80
29930 Bossulan 29 78 Wb 61
08290 Bossus-lès-Rumigny 08 41 Eb 49
03300 Bost 03 116 Dd 71
03390 Bost 03 115 Cf 70
63300 Bost 63 128 Dd 74
71320 Bost 71 104 Ea 68
24560 Bost, le 24 136 Ad 80
24700 Bost, le 24 135 Aa 78
56490 Bos-Tarju, le 56 64 Xd 60
40090 Bostens 40 147 Zd 85
87230 Bosvieux 87 125 Ba 74
76450 Bosville 76 36 Ae 50
50430 Bot, le 50 46 Yc 53
61340 Botagne, la 61 69 Ae 58
90400 Botans 90 94 Gf 63
29370 Botbodern 29 78 Wa 61
29540 Bot-Carrec 29 63 Wb 59
22320 Bothan, le 22 63 Wf 59
19120 Bothies, les 19 138 Be 79
22480 Bothoa 22 63 Wf 58
22140 Botlézan 22 63 We 57
22160 Botmel 22 63 Wd 58
29690 Botmeur 29 62 Wa 58
29910 Botquélen 29 78 Wb 61
56630 Botquelvez 56 79 Wd 60
56320 Botquenven 56 79 Wd 60
29650 Botsorhel 29 63 Wc 57
20129 Bottacina CTC 182 If 97
40410 Botte 40 147 Zb 82
47120 Botte 47 136 Ab 80
27250 Bottereaux, les 27 49 Ae 55
56500 Bottine, la 56 80 Xb 61
49110 Botz-en-Mauges 49 83 Yf 65
45430 Bou 45 87 Ca 61
78410 Bouafle 78 50 Bf 55
27700 Bouafles 27 50 Bc 53
76390 Bouafles 76 38 Be 49
09310 Bouan 09 177 Bd 92
37110 Bouardière, la 37 85 Ae 62
40310 Bouau 40 148 Aa 85
44830 Bouaye 44 96 Yb 66
62990 Boubers-lès-Hesmond 62 28 Bf 46
62270 Boubers-sur-Canche 62 29 Cb 47
80210 Boubert, Mons- 80 28 Bd 48
60240 Boubiers 60 50 Bf 53
77470 Boubigny 77 52 Cf 55
87150 Boubon 87 124 Ae 74
19200 Boubouleix, le 19 127 Cc 75
32550 Boucagnères 32 163 Ad 87
30240 Boucanet, le 30 168 Ea 87
71300 Boucansaud 71 105 Ec 68
40260 Boucaou 40 146 Yf 85
18260 Boucard 18 88 Ce 64
64340 Boucau 64 160 Yd 87
50250 Boucaux, les 50 33 Yd 53
13320 Bouc-Bel-Air 13 170 Fc 88
03150 Boucé 03 116 Dc 71
61570 Boucé 61 48 Zf 57
50240 Bouceel 50 66 Yd 57
16350 Bouchage, le 16 112 Ac 72
38510 Bouchage, le 38 131 Fd 74
87320 Bouchage, le 87 112 Af 71
59111 Bouchain 59 30 Db 47
42110 Bouchala 42 130 Ec 74
53800 Bouchamps-lès-Craon 53 83 Za 62
06470 Bouchanières 06 158 Gf 84
43520 Bouchat, le 43 141 Eb 78
71480 Bouchat, le 71 118 Fb 70
87700 Bouchats, les 87 125 Ba 74
18360 Bouchatte, la 18 115 Cd 69
13200 Bouchaud 13 169 Ed 87
03130 Bouchaud, le 03 117 Df 71
16170 Bouchauds, les 16 123 Zf 74
36230 Bouchauds, les 36 114 Be 69
63390 Bouchauds, les 63 115 Ce 72
86210 Bouchaux, les 86 100 Ae 68
80200 Bouchavesnes-Bergen 80 39 Cf 49
58240 Bouché, la 58 103 Da 68
28220 Bouche-d'Aigre 28 69 Bb 61
87120 Bouchefarol 87 126 Be 74
63770 Boucheix, le 63 115 Ce 73
63850 Boucheix, le 63 127 Ce 76
49080 Bouchemaine 49 83 Zc 64
57220 Boucheporn 57 57 Gd 54
77710 Bouchereau 77 72 Ce 59
23500 Boucheresse 23 126 Cb 74
74110 Boucherie, la 74 121 Ge 72
24270 Boucheron, le 24 125 Ba 76
26790 Bouchet 26 155 Ef 83
15100 Bouchet, le 15 140 Da 78
16140 Bouchet, le 16 111 Zf 73
18290 Bouchet, le 18 102 Cb 66
36300 Bouchet, le 36 100 Bb 68
43200 Bouchet, le 43 129 Ea 77
58370 Bouchet, le 58 104 Df 67
63580 Bouchet, le 63 128 Dc 75
74230 Bouchet, le 74 132 Gc 74
86140 Bouchet, le 86 99 Ab 68
86200 Bouchet, le 86 99 Aa 67
43510 Bouchet-Saint-Nicolas, le 43 141 De 79
27150 Bouchevilliers 27 38 Be 52
04260 Bouchier 04 158 Gd 83
05120 Bouchier 05 145 Gd 79
80910 Bouchoir 80 39 Ce 50
17340 Boucholeurs, les 17 110 Yf 72
33840 Bouchon 33 147 Zd 83
80830 Bouchon 80 38 Ca 48
55500 Bouchon-sur-Saulx, le 55 75 Fb 57
58150 Bouchot 58 88 Cf 65
39370 Bouchoux, les 39 119 Fe 71
51310 Bouchy-Saint-Genest 51 53 Dd 57
07270 Boucieux-le-Roi 07 142 Ee 78
25360 Bouclans 25 107 Gb 65
30190 Boucoiran 30 154 Eb 85
08250 Bouconville 08 54 Ee 53
60240 Bouconvillers 60 50 Bf 53
55300 Bouconville-sur-Madt 55 55 Fe 55
02860 Bouconville-Vauclair 02 40 De 52
46350 Boucot 46 137 Bc 80
31510 Boucou 31 176 Ad 90
76560 Boucourt 76 36 Ae 50
54200 Boucq 54 56 Fe 56
24800 Boudeau 24 124 Ae 76
24580 Bouderie, la 24 137 Af 78
35270 Bouderie, la 35 65 Yb 58
63340 Boudes 63 128 Db 76
76560 Boudeville 76 37 Af 50
12110 Boudie, la 12 139 Cb 81
73270 Boudin 73 133 Gd 74
36300 Boudinière, la 36 100 Ba 68
82200 Boudou 82 149 Ba 84
31580 Boudrac 31 163 Ad 89
36800 Boudre, la 36 113 Bc 69
21520 Boudreville 21 91 Ee 61
54560 Boudrezy 54 43 Fe 52
47290 Boudy-de-Beauregard 47 136 Ae 81
02450 Boué 02 40 De 48
31360 Boué, le 31 164 Af 90
44260 Bouée 44 81 Ya 65
36170 Bouëe, la 36 113 Bc 70
64330 Boueilh-Boueilho-Lasque 64 162 Ze 87
64330 Boueilho 64 162 Zd 87
19160 Boueix 19 126 Cb 76
63330 Boueix, le 63 127 Cd 73
76270 Bouelles 76 37 Bc 50
72390 Bouër 72 68 Ad 60
53290 Bouère 53 83 Zd 61
53290 Bouessay 53 84 Zd 61
36200 Bouesse 36 101 Be 69
31190 Bouet 31 164 Bc 89
03380 Bouets, les 03 114 Cc 70
16410 Bouëx 16 124 Ab 75
35340 Bouëxière, la 35 66 Yd 59
35133 Bouëxière, le 35 66 Ye 58
36110 Bouffegenet 36 101 Bd 66
95570 Bouffémont 95 51 Cb 54
85600 Boufféré 85 97 Yd 67
82440 Bouffière, la 82 150 Bd 84
02160 Bouffignereux 02 41 Df 52
41270 Bouffry 41 69 Ba 60
80540 Bougainville 80 38 Ca 49
64230 Bougarber 64 162 Zd 88
09320 Bougarelt 09 177 Bc 91
46200 Bougayrou, le 46 138 Bd 79
23160 Bougazeau, le 23 113 Bd 70
28160 Bougeâtre 28 69 Bb 59
38150 Bougé-Chambalud 38 130 Ef 77
71590 Bougerot 71 106 Ef 67
40460 Bougès, le 40 134 Yf 82
36110 Bouges-le-Château 36 101 Be 66
70500 Bougey 70 93 Ff 62
28130 Bouglainval 28 70 Bd 57
77570 Bougligny 77 71 Cd 59
47250 Bouglon 47 148 Aa 82
17800 Bougneau 17 123 Zc 75
31470 Bougnol 31 164 Ba 88
70170 Bougnon 70 93 Ga 62
79800 Bougon 79 111 Zf 70
79260 Bougouin 79 111 Ze 71
29233 Bougourouan 29 62 Vf 56

Bougourouan | 247

81800 Bouyayo 81 150 Be 86
09220 Bouychet 09 177 Bd 92
17100 Bouyers, les 17 122 Zb 74
10220 Bouy-Luxembourg 10 73 Eb 58
06510 Bouyon 06 158 Ha 86
46130 Bouyrissac 46 138 Be 79
81360 Bouyrol 81 166 Cb 86
82440 Bouyrolle 82 150 Bc 84
81630 Bouysse, la 81 150 Bd 85
46120 Bouyssou, le 46 138 Bf 80
10400 Bouy-sur-Orvin 10 72 Dc 58
39130 Bouzailles 39 107 Fe 69
18200 Bouzais 18 102 Cc 68
52110 Bouzancourt 52 74 Ef 59
54930 Bouzanville 54 76 Ga 58
63910 Bouzel 63 128 Db 74
21200 Bouze-lès-Beaume 21 105 Ee 66
88270 Bouzemont 88 76 Gb 59
44350 Bouzeray 44 81 Xd 64
71150 Bouzeron 71 105 Ee 67
88390 Bouzey 88 76 Gc 60
24250 Bouzic 24 137 Bb 80
46330 Bouziès 46 138 Bd 82
46330 Bouziès-Bas 46 138 Bd 82
32500 Bouzigue, la 32 149 Ae 86
34140 Bouzigues 34 168 Dd 88
49530 Bouzillé 49 83 Yf 64
31420 Bouzin 31 164 Af 89
80300 Bouzincourt 80 39 Cd 48
43700 Bouzols 43 141 Df 78
32290 Bouzon-Gellenave 32 162 Aa 86
46600 Bouzonie, la 46 138 Bd 78
54800 Bouzonville 54 56 Fe 54
57320 Bouzonville 57 57 Gd 53
45300 Bouzonville-aux-Bois 45 71 Cb 60
45300 Bouzonville-en-Beauce 45 71 Cb 59
04400 Bouzoulières 04 158 Gd 82
51150 Bouzy 51 53 Ea 54
45460 Bouzy-la-Forêt 45 88 Cc 61
55190 Bovée-sur-Barboure 55 55 Fd 57
35330 Bovel 35 81 Ya 61
80540 Bovelles 80 38 Ca 49
74250 Bovère 74 120 Gc 72
80440 Boves 80 39 Cc 49
02870 Bovette, la 02 40 Dc 51
46800 Bovila 46 149 Bb 82
01300 Bovinel 01 131 Fe 74
55500 Bovioles 55 55 Fc 57
64400 Boy 64 161 Zd 90
81190 Boyals 81 151 Cb 84
17190 Boyardville 17 109 Ye 73
62134 Boyaval 62 29 Cb 46
49390 Boye, la 49 84 Aa 64
62128 Boyelles 62 30 Ce 47
44170 Boyenne 44 82 Yb 63
42460 Boyer 42 117 Eb 72
71700 Boyer 71 106 Ef 69
71740 Boyer 71 117 Eb 71
37340 Boyères 37 85 Ac 64
01640 Boyeux-Saint-Jérôme 01 119 Fc 72
12640 Boyne 12 152 Da 83
45300 Boynes 45 71 Cc 60
01190 Boz 01 118 Ef 70
07410 Bozas 07 142 Ed 78
73350 Bozel 73 133 Gd 76
12340 Bozouls 12 139 Ce 82
55120 Brabant-en-Argonne 55 55 Fa 54
55800 Brabant-le-Roi 55 55 Ef 55
55100 Brabant sur-Meuse 55 55 Fb 53
19800 Brach 19 126 Bf 77
33480 Brach 33 134 Za 78
52110 Brachay 52 75 Fa 58
38790 Brachet, le 38 131 Fa 75
76730 Brachy 76 37 Af 50
41250 Bracieux 41 86 Bd 63
39110 Bracon 39 107 Ff 67
15290 Braconat 15 139 Cb 79
16110 Braconne, la 16 124 Ac 74
76370 Bracquemont 76 37 Ba 49
76850 Bracquetuit 76 37 Ba 51
76680 Bradiancourt 76 37 Bc 51
50870 Braffais 50 46 Ye 56
81630 Bragards, les 81 150 Bd 85
30260 Bragassargues 30 154 Ea 85
31470 Bragayrac 31 164 Ba 88
15700 Brageac 15 127 Cb 77
10340 Bragelogne 10 74 Eb 61
71350 Bragny-sur-Saône 71 106 Fa 67
48150 Bragouse, la 48 153 Dc 83
06600 Brague, la 06 173 Ha 87
07140 Brahic 07 154 Ea 82
25640 Braillans 25 93 Ga 65
80150 Brailly-Cornehotte 80 28 Bf 47
21350 Brain 21 91 Ed 64
39800 Brainans 39 107 Fd 67
02220 Braine 02 53 Dd 52
44830 Brains 44 96 Yb 65
72550 Brains-sur-Gée 72 68 Zf 60
53350 Brains-sur-les-Marches 53 83 Ye 61
49650 Brain-sur-Allonnes 49 84 Aa 65
49800 Brain-sur-L'Authion 49 84 Zd 64
49220 Brain-sur-Longuenée 49 83 Zb 63
35660 Brain-sur-Vilaine 35 82 Ya 62
50200 Brainville 50 46 Yd 54
54800 Brainville 54 56 Fe 54
52150 Brainville-sur-Meuse 52 75 Fd 59
35490 Brais 35 66 Yc 58
44600 Brais 44 81 Xe 65
54170 Braisey-au-Plain 54 76 Ff 57
54170 Braisey-la-Côte 54 76 Ff 57
03360 Braize 03 103 Cd 69
54740 Bralleville 54 76 Gb 58
11150 Bram 11 165 Ca 89
68550 Bramaly 68 94 Ha 61
73500 Bramans 73 133 Ge 77
46240 Bramarie 46 138 Bd 81
63210 Bramauds, les 63 127 Cf 74
13370 Brame-Jean 13 170 Fb 86
81310 Brames-Aigues 81 151 Bf 85
76740 Brametot 76 37 Af 50
65370 Bramevaque 65 176 Ad 91
48000 Bramonas 48 140 Dc 82
05600 Bramousse 05 145 Ge 80
17210 Bran 17 123 Ze 76
33830 Bran, le 33 134 Za 81
64290 Brana 64 162 Zd 89
19500 Branceilles 19 138 Be 78
53400 Brancherie, la 53 83 Za 61
89113 Branches 89 89 Dc 61
88630 Brancourt 88 75 Fe 58
02320 Brancourt-en-Laonnois 02 40 Dc 51
02110 Brancourt-le-Grand 02 40 Dc 49
44590 Brand, le 44 82 Yb 62
44320 Brandais, le 44 96 Ya 66
86200 Brandallière, la 86 99 Ab 67
44680 Branday, le 44 96 Yb 66
24380 Brande, la 24 136 Ad 79
28140 Brandelon 28 70 Be 60
35390 Brandeneuf 35 82 Yb 62
56700 Brandérion 56 80 We 62
17110 Brandes, les 17 122 Za 75
17139 Brandes, les 17 110 Yf 71
86400 Brandes, les 86 112 Ab 72
83470 Brandine 83 171 Fe 88
56390 Brandivy 56 80 Xa 62
71520 Brandon 71 118 Ed 70
12350 Brandonnet 12 151 Ca 82
51290 Brandonvillers 51 74 Ed 57
02130 Branges 02 53 Dc 53
71500 Branges 71 106 Fb 69
38510 Brangues 38 131 Fd 74
44530 Branleix 44 81 Xf 63
70320 Branleure, la 70 93 Gc 61
89150 Brannay 89 72 Da 59
25340 Branne 25 94 Gc 64
33420 Branne 33 135 Ze 80
33124 Brannens 33 135 Zf 82
30110 Branoux-les-Taillades 30 154 Df 83
04120 Brans 04 158 Gc 86
39290 Brans 39 107 Fd 65
03500 Bransat 03 116 Db 71
51140 Branscourt 51 53 De 53
77620 Bransles 77 71 Cf 60
86480 Brantelay 86 111 Aa 70
84390 Brantes 84 156 Fc 83
10220 Brantigny 10 74 Ec 58
88130 Brantigny 88 76 Gb 58
33910 Brantirat 33 135 Zf 78
24310 Brantôme 24 124 Ad 76
24310 Brantôme en Périgord 24 124 Ad 76
14430 Branville 14 35 Aa 53
50440 Branville-Hague 50 33 Yb 51
55400 Braquis 55 55 Fd 54
14123 Bras 14 35 Ze 54
83149 Bras 83 171 Ff 88
12550 Brasc 12 152 Cd 85
04270 Bras-d'Asse 04 157 Ga 85
40330 Brasempouy 40 161 Zb 87
02400 Brasles 02 52 Dc 54
37120 Braslou 37 99 Ac 66
29190 Brasparts 29 62 Wa 59
09000 Brassac 09 177 Bd 91
24440 Brassac 24 137 Ae 80
34220 Brassac 34 166 Ce 87
81260 Brassac 81 166 Cd 87
82190 Brassac 82 149 Af 83
63570 Brassac-les-Mines 63 128 Db 76
72360 Brassardière 72 85 Ab 62
17460 Brasseau 17 122 Zb 74
55300 Brasseitte 55 55 Fd 55
33590 Brasserie, la 33 122 Za 76
12470 Brasses, les 12 140 Cf 81
60810 Brasseuse 60 51 Ce 53
43100 Brassey 43 140 Db 77
55100 Bras-sur-Meuse 55 55 Fc 53
58140 Brassy 58 90 Df 65
80160 Brassy 80 38 Ca 50
54610 Bratte 54 56 Gb 56
52290 Braucourt 52 74 Ee 57
85200 Braud, la 85 110 Zb 69
19160 Braud, le 19 127 Cb 77
33820 Braud-et-Saint-Louis 33 122 Zc 77
54260 Braumont 54 43 Fd 52
33125 Braut 33 134 Zb 81
55170 Brauvilliers 55 75 Fa 57
04240 Braux 04 158 Ge 85
08120 Braux 08 42 Ee 49
10500 Braux 10 74 Ec 58
21390 Braux 21 91 Ec 64
52120 Braux-le-Châtel 52 74 Ef 60
51800 Braux-Sainte-Cohière 51 54 Ee 54
51800 Braux-Saint-Rémy 51 54 Ef 54
69610 Bravarel, la 69M 130 Ec 74
20230 Bravone CTC 183 Kd 95
31490 Brax 31 164 Bb 87
47310 Brax 47 149 Ad 83
10800 Bray 10 73 Ea 59
14740 Bray 14 35 Zd 53
27170 Bray 27 49 Af 54
60810 Bray 60 51 Ce 53
63560 Bray 63 115 Cf 72
71250 Bray 71 118 Ee 69
72240 Bray, le 72 67 Zf 60
59123 Bray-Dunes 59 27 Cd 42
02880 Braye 02 40 Dc 52
02000 Braye-en-Laonnais 02 40 Dd 52
02140 Braye-en-Thiérache 02 41 Df 50
14190 Bray-en-Cinglais 14 47 Ze 55
45460 Bray-en-Val 45 87 Cc 62
37120 Braye-sous-Faye 37 99 Ac 67
37330 Braye-sur-Maulne 37 85 Ab 63
95710 Bray-et-Lû 95 50 Be 54
14190 Bray-la-Campagne 14 48 Ze 54
80580 Bray-lès-Mareuil 80 28 Bf 48
03350 Brays, les 03 103 Ce 69
45460 Bray-Saint-Aignan 45 87 Cc 62
02480 Bray-Saint-Christophe 02 40 Da 50
77480 Bray-sur-Seine 77 72 Db 58
80340 Bray-sur-Somme 80 39 Ce 49
21430 Brazey-en-Morvan 21 105 Eb 65
21470 Brazey-en-Plaine 21 106 Fb 66
33990 Bré 33 122 Yf 77
35310 Bréal-sous-Montfort 35 65 Ya 60
35370 Bréal-sous-Vitré 35 66 Yf 60
95640 Bréançon 95 51 Ca 54
77720 Bréau 77 72 Cf 57
30120 Bréau-et-Salagosse 30 153 Dd 85
76110 Bréauté 76 36 Ac 51
51320 Bréban 51 74 Ec 57
62117 Brebières 62 30 Da 46
90140 Brebotte 90 94 Gf 63
44410 Bréca 44 81 Xe 64
35530 Brécé 35 66 Yd 60
53120 Brecé 53 67 Zb 58
50370 Brécey 50 46 Yf 56
47260 Brech 47 136 Ac 82
56400 Brech 56 79 Xa 62
88300 Bréchaincourt 88 75 Fe 59
88350 Bréchainville 88 75 Fc 58
28210 Bréchamps 28 50 Bd 56
32240 Brechan 32 148 Ze 85
47600 Bréchan 47 148 Ab 83
68210 Bréchaumont 68 94 Ha 62
71400 Brèche 71 105 Ec 67
37330 Brèches 37 85 Ac 63
58420 Brèches 58 104 Dd 65
43270 Bréchiniac 43 129 De 77
57220 Brecklange 57 57 Gc 53
74550 Brécorens 74 120 Gc 71
50160 Brectouville 50 47 Yf 54
02210 Brécy 02 52 Dc 54
18220 Brécy 18 102 Cd 66
89113 Brécy 89 89 Dc 62
08400 Brécy-Brières 08 42 Ee 53
74410 Brédannaz 74 132 Ga 74
33650 Brède, la 33 135 Zc 80
19200 Brédèche, la 19 127 Cb 75
50390 Brédonchel 50 33 Yc 52
50170 Brée 50 66 Yd 57
53150 Brée 53 67 Zc 60
61100 Bréel 61 47 Zd 56
17840 Brée-les-Bains, la 17 109 Yd 72
49500 Brège 49 83 Za 62
87380 Bregeat 87 126 Bd 75
24290 Bregegère 24 137 Bb 78
44210 Bregeonnière, la 44 96 Xf 66
03310 Brégère, la 03 115 Ce 71
24340 Bregnac 24 124 Ac 76
09000 Bregne 09 177 Bc 91
01300 Brégnier-Cordon 01 131 Fd 75
74250 Brégny 74 120 Gc 72
83670 Bréguière, la 83 171 Ga 87
60440 Brégy 60 52 Cf 54
44290 Bréhain 44 82 Yb 63
57340 Bréhain 57 57 Gd 55
54190 Bréhain-la-Ville 54 43 Ff 52
50290 Bréhal 50 46 Yc 55
56580 Bréhan 56 64 Xb 60
22510 Bréhand 22 64 Xc 58
22580 Brehec-en-Plouha 22 63 Xa 56
37130 Bréhémont 37 85 Ac 65
55150 Bréhéville 55 42 Fb 52
29170 Bréhoulou 29 78 Vf 61
57720 Breidenbach 57 58 Hc 54
49490 Breil 49 84 Aa 64
44310 Breil, le 44 97 Yc 66
44590 Breil, le 44 82 Yb 63
44680 Breil, le 44 96 Ya 66
44880 Breil, le 44 82 Yb 65
35140 Breil-Bernier, le 35 66 Yd 59
79220 Breilbon 79 111 Zd 70
49390 Breil-les-Pins, la 49 84 Aa 64
22230 Breil-Pignard 22 64 Xd 59
72370 Breil-sur-Mérize, le 72 68 Ac 60
06540 Breil-sur-Roya 06 159 Hd 85
15250 Breisse 15 139 Cc 78
57570 Breistroff-la-Grande 57 44 Gb 52
57970 Breistroff-la-Petite 57 44 Gb 52
67220 Breitenau 67 60 Hb 59
67220 Breitenbach 67 60 Hb 58
68380 Breitenbach-Haut-Rhin 68 77 Ha 60
87460 Breix 87 126 Bd 74
15230 Bréjal, le 15 139 Ce 79
23140 Brejassoux 23 114 Bf 71
29810 Brélès 29 61 Vb 58
36130 Brelet 36 101 Bd 67
22140 Brélidy 22 63 We 57
80470 Brely 80 38 Cb 49
35470 Brémalin 35 82 Yb 61
57230 Bremendehlerhof 57 58 Hd 54
54540 Bréménil 54 77 Gf 57
27770 Brémien, le 27 50 Bb 56
67160 Bremmelbach 67 58 Hf 55
25190 Brémoncourt 25 94 Ha 64
54290 Brémoncourt 54 76 Gc 58
25530 Bremondans 25 108 Gc 65
76220 Brémontier-Merval 76 38 Bd 51
14260 Brémoy 14 47 Zb 55
85470 Brem-sur-Mer 85 96 Yb 69
21400 Brémur-et-Vaurois 21 91 Ed 62
26260 Bren 26 143 Ef 78
56120 Bréna 56 81 Xc 61
11500 Brenac 11 178 Ca 91
12420 Brenac 12 139 Ce 80
48600 Brenac 48 140 Dd 80
34650 Brenas 34 167 Db 87
16290 Brénat 16 123 Aa 74
63500 Brenat 63 128 Db 75
01150 Brénaz 01 131 Fc 73
01260 Brénaz 01 119 Fe 73
29880 Brendaouez 29 62 Vd 57
02220 Brenelle 02 40 Dd 52
29250 Brenesquen 29 62 Vf 56
12430 Brengues 12 152 Ce 84
46320 Brengues 46 138 Be 81
52200 Brennes 52 92 Fb 62
76720 Brennetuit 76 37 Ba 50
29690 Brennilis 29 62 Wa 58
01110 Brénod 01 119 Fd 72
83840 Brenon 83 158 Gd 86
60870 Brenouille 60 51 Cd 53
48000 Brenoux 48 140 Dd 82
01300 Brens 01 131 Fe 74
74890 Brens 74 120 Gc 71
74890 Brenthonne 74 120 Gc 71
04340 Bréole, la 04 157 Gb 82
43230 Brequeille, la 43 141 Dd 77
83560 Brérac, la 83 171 Ff 87
56920 Brérec 56 64 Xb 60
25440 Brères 25 107 Ff 66
39230 Bréry 39 107 Fd 68
07230 Brès 07 141 Ea 82
12120 Brès 12 152 Cd 83
17490 Bresdon 17 123 Zf 73
25120 Bréseux, les 25 94 Ge 65
70140 Bresilley 70 107 Fd 65
30450 Brésis 30 154 Df 82
80300 Bresle 80 39 Cd 49
60510 Bresles 60 38 Cb 52
03210 Bresnay 03 116 Db 70
61190 Bresolettes 61 49 Ad 57
46320 Bresquéjouls 46 138 Bf 81
33990 Bresquette, la 33 122 Yf 77
88250 Bresse, la 88 77 Gf 60
71460 Bresse-sur-Grosne 71 105 Ee 69
21560 Bressey-sur-Tille 21 92 Fb 65
03000 Bressollees 03 116 Db 69
01360 Bressolles 01 131 Fa 73
43450 Bressolles 43 128 Da 76
81320 Bressolles 81 166 Cf 86
82710 Bressols 82 150 Bc 85
38320 Bresson 38 144 Fe 78
52230 Bressoncourt 52 75 Fc 58
79300 Bressuire 79 98 Zd 67
13840 Brest 13 170 Fc 87
29200 Brest 29 61 Vd 58
70300 Brest 70 93 Gc 62
27350 Brestot 27 36 Ae 52
74500 Bret 74 121 Ge 70
79110 Bret 79 111 Zf 72
36110 Bretagne 36 101 Be 66
36400 Bretagne 36 102 Ca 68
87200 Bretagne 87 112 Af 73
90130 Bretagne 90 94 Ha 63
27300 Bretagne, la 27 49 Ad 54
32800 Bretagne-d'Armagnac 32 148 Aa 85
40280 Bretagne-de-Marsan 40 147 Zd 85
27220 Bretagnolles 27 50 Bc 55
45250 Breteau 45 88 Cf 62
35160 Bréteil 35 65 Ya 60
21110 Bretenière 21 106 Fa 65
25640 Bretenière, la 25 93 Gb 64
39700 Bretenière, la 39 107 Fd 66
39120 Bretenières 39 107 Fd 67
46130 Bretenoux 46 138 Bf 79
41320 Bretets, les 41 87 Bf 65
60120 Breteuil 27 49 Af 55
60120 Breteuil 60 38 Cb 51
61270 Bréthel 61 49 Ad 56
52000 Brethenay 52 75 Fa 60
78660 Bréthencourt 78 70 Bf 57
03350 Brethon, le 03 115 Ce 69
58200 Bretignelle 58 89 Da 64
25110 Bretigney-Notre-Dame 25 93 Gb 65
79140 Bretignolles 79 98 Zc 67
53110 Brétignolles-le-Moulin 53 67 Zc 58
85470 Brétignolles-sur-Mer 85 96 Ya 69
01210 Brétigny 01 120 Ga 71
21490 Brétigny 21 92 Fa 64
27800 Brétigny 27 49 Ae 53
28630 Brétigny 28 70 Bd 58
60400 Brétigny 60 40 Da 51
86380 Brétigny 86 99 Ac 68
91220 Brétigny-sur-Orge 91 71 Cb 57
61110 Bretoncelles 61 69 Af 58
10200 Bretonnière, la 10 74 Ee 59
27190 Bretonnière, la 27 49 Ba 54
28500 Bretonnière, la 28 50 Bb 56
44390 Bretonnière, la 44 82 Yb 63
50290 Bretonnière, la 50 46 Yc 55
58330 Bretonnière, la 58 104 Dc 66
77120 Bretonnière, la 77 52 Da 56
85320 Bretonnière, la 85 109 Ye 70
25380 Bretonvillers 25 108 Gd 65
17700 Brette 17 110 Za 72
72250 Brette-les-Pins 72 85 Ac 61
68780 Bretten 68 94 Ha 62
80290 Brettencourt 80 38 Bf 50
16240 Brettes 16 111 Aa 72
50110 Bretteville 50 33 Yc 51
76890 Bretteville 76 37 Ba 51
76110 Bretteville-du-Grand-Caux 76 36 Ac 51
14190 Bretteville-le-Rabet 14 48 Ze 54
14740 Bretteville-L'Orgueilleuse 14 35 Zc 53
76560 Bretteville-Saint-Laurent 76 37 Af 50
50430 Bretteville-sur-Ay 50 33 Yc 53
14170 Bretteville-sur-Dives 14 48 Zf 54
14680 Bretteville-sur-Laize 14 47 Ze 54
14760 Bretteville-sur-Odon 14 35 Zd 54
57320 Brettnach 57 57 Gd 53
31530 Bretx 31 164 Bb 86
70300 Breuches 70 93 Gb 62
58460 Breugnon 58 89 Dc 64
58140 Breugny 58 90 Df 64
17330 Breuil 17 111 Zd 72
22350 Breuil 22 65 Xf 59
23220 Breuil 23 114 Bf 71
29590 Breuil 29 62 Vf 59
51140 Breuil 51 40 De 53
60350 Breuil 60 39 Cf 52
80400 Breuil 80 39 Cf 50
88340 Breuil 88 77 Gd 61
95770 Breuil 95 50 Be 53
23400 Breuil, la 23 114 Be 73
03120 Breuil, le 03 116 Dd 71
03420 Breuil, le 03 115 Cd 71
10130 Breuil, le 10 73 Df 60
14170 Breuil, le 14 48 Zf 55
16140 Breuil, le 16 123 Zf 73
16170 Breuil, le 16 123 Zf 74
16330 Breuil, le 16 123 Aa 74
17470 Breuil, le 17 111 Ze 73
17570 Breuil, le 17 122 Yf 74
17600 Breuil, le 17 122 Za 74
19510 Breuil, le 19 126 Bd 75
22980 Breuil, le 22 64 Xe 58
23190 Breuil, le 23 115 Cc 73
24210 Breuil, le 24 137 Af 78
24270 Breuil, le 24 125 Bb 76
24310 Breuil, le 24 124 Ac 76
28120 Breuil, le 28 69 Bb 58
36300 Breuil, le 36 100 Af 69
36310 Breuil, le 36 113 Bb 70
41330 Breuil, le 41 86 Bb 62
44140 Breuil, le 44 97 Yd 66
44270 Breuil, le 44 96 Yb 66
49750 Breuil, le 49 83 Zc 65
50160 Breuil, le 50 47 Za 54
50850 Breuil, le 50 47 Zb 57
51210 Breuil, le 51 53 Dd 55
69620 Breuil, le 69D 118 Ed 73
71300 Breuil, le 71 105 Eb 68
71670 Breuil, le 71 105 Ec 68
79130 Breuil, le 79 98 Zd 69
79220 Breuil, le 79 111 Zd 70
79260 Breuil, le 79 111 Zd 70
87300 Breuilaufa 87 113 Ba 72
85120 Breuil-Barret 85 98 Zb 69
17490 Breuil-Bâtard, le 17 123 Zf 73
79320 Breuil-Bernard, le 79 98 Zc 68
78930 Breuil-Bois-Robert 78 50 Be 55
35720 Breuil-Caulnette, le 35 65 Ya 58
79300 Breuil-Chaussée 79 98 Zc 67
79110 Breuil-Coiffaud, le 79 111 Aa 72
16560 Breuil-d'Anais, le 16 124 Ab 74
86400 Breuil-d'Haleine, le 86 112 Ab 72
14130 Breuil-en-Auge, le 14 48 Ab 53
14330 Breuil-en-Bessin, le 14 47 Za 53
24380 Breuilh 24 136 Ae 78
24230 Breuilh, le 24 136 Aa 79
17700 Breuil-la-Réorte 17 110 Zb 72
16140 Breuillaud 16 111 Zf 73
23100 Breuille, la 23 127 Cc 74
36400 Breuille, la 36 102 Bf 69
89520 Breuille, la 89 89 Db 63
17330 Breuilles 17 110 Zc 72
60840 Breuil-le-Sec 60 39 Cc 52
17920 Breuillet 17 122 Yf 74
91650 Breuillet 91 71 Cb 57
60600 Breuil-le-Vert 60 39 Cc 52
03500 Breuilly 03 116 Db 71
17870 Breuil-Magné 17 110 Za 73
27640 Breuilpont 27 50 Bc 55
79150 Breuil-sous-Argenton, le 79 98 Zd 67
63340 Breuil-sur-Couze, le 63 128 Db 76
52300 Breuil-sur-Marne 52 75 Fa 57
70190 Breurey 70 93 Ga 64
70160 Breurey-lès-Faverney 70 93 Ga 62
67112 Breuschwickersheim 67 60 Hd 57
16400 Breuty 16 124 Aa 75
52240 Breuvannes-en-Bassigny 52 75 Fd 60
71500 Breuve 71 106 Fb 68
51240 Breuvery-sur-Coole 51 54 Eb 55
50260 Breuville 50 33 Yb 51
55600 Breux 55 43 Fc 51
91650 Breux-Jouy 91 71 Cb 57
27570 Breux-sur-Avre 27 49 Ba 56
41160 Brévainville 41 69 Bb 61
78980 Bréval 78 50 Bd 55
50500 Brévands 50 46 Ye 53
39100 Brevans 39 106 Fd 66
38380 Brévardière 38 132 Fe 77
14130 Brévedent, le 14 48 Ab 53
29260 Breventoc 29 62 Vd 57
58530 Brèves 58 89 Dd 64
78610 Bréviaires, les 78 50 Be 56
10450 Bréviandes 10 73 Ea 59
14140 Bréviaire, la 14 48 Aa 55
14860 Bréville 14 48 Ze 53
16370 Bréville 16 123 Ze 74
62140 Brévillers 62 29 Ca 46
80600 Brévillers 80 29 Cc 47
50290 Bréville-sur-Mer 50 46 Yc 55
70400 Brevilliers 70 94 Ge 63
08140 Brévilly 08 42 Fa 51
52200 Brévoines 52 92 Fb 61
50630 Brévole 50 33 Yd 51
10220 Brévonnes 10 74 Ec 58
62170 Bréxent-Enocq 62 28 Be 45
25240 Brey-et-Maison-du-Bois 25 107 Gb 68
33650 Breyra 33 135 Zc 80
26120 Breyrons, les 26 143 Fa 79
49260 Brézé 49 99 Zf 65
29450 Brézéhant 29 62 Wa 58
05190 Bréziers 05 157 Gb 82
11270 Brézilhac 11 165 Ca 89
17120 Brézillas 17 122 Za 75
38590 Brézins 38 131 Fb 76
28270 Brézolles 28 49 Ba 56
28270 Brezolles 28 50 Bf 55
15230 Brezons 15 139 Ce 79
12600 Brézou, le 12 139 Ce 80
17600 Briagne 17 122 Za 75
03500 Briailles 03 116 Db 71
82710 Brial 82 150 Bb 85
34220 Brian 34 166 Ce 88
04200 Briançon 04 157 Ga 83
05100 Briançon 05 145 Gd 79
37500 Briançon 37 99 Ab 66
06850 Briançonnet 06 158 Ge 85
50620 Brianderie, la 50 46 Ye 53
34650 Briandes 34 167 Db 86
21390 Brianny 21 90 Ec 64
71110 Briant 71 117 Ea 71
36400 Briantes 36 114 Ca 69
44850 Briantière, la 44 82 Yd 64
45250 Briare 45 88 Ce 63
45390 Briarres-sur-Essonne 45 71 Cc 59
04200 Briasc 04 157 Ff 83
59730 Briastre 59 30 Dc 48
81390 Briatexte 81 165 Bf 86
52700 Briaucourt 52 75 Fb 59

Briaucourt | 249

70800 Briaucourt 70 93 Gb 62
37340 Briche, la 37 85 Ab 64
52120 Bricon 52 74 Ef 60
28300 Briconville 28 69 Bc 57
51310 Bricot-la-Ville 51 53 Dd 56
50260 Bricquebec-en-Cotentin 50 33 Yc 52
50340 Bricquebosq 50 33 Yb 51
14710 Bricqueville 14 47 Za 53
50290 Bricqueville-sur-Mer 50 46 Yc 55
45310 Bricy 45 70 Be 60
73570 Brides-les-Bains 73 133 Gd 76
73520 Bridoire, la 73 131 Fe 75
49390 Bridonnières, la 49 84 Aa 64
37600 Bridoré 37 100 Ba 66
02870 Brie 02 40 Dc 51
09700 Brie 09 165 Bd 89
16590 Brie 16 124 Ab 74
35150 Brie 35 66 Yc 61
79100 Brie 79 99 Zf 67
80200 Brie 80 39 Cf 49
16210 Brie-Bardenac 16 123 Zf 77
29510 Briec 29 78 Wa 60
77170 Brie-Comte-Robert 77 51 Cd 56
38320 Brie-et-Angonnes 38 144 Fe 78
50450 Brief, le 50 46 Yd 55
33840 Briel 33 147 Ze 82
35370 Brielles 35 66 Yf 60
10140 Briel-sur-Barse 10 74 Ec 59
71290 Brienne 71 118 Fa 69
10500 Brienne-la-Vieille 10 74 Ed 58
10500 Brienne-le-Château 10 74 Ed 58
08190 Brienne-sur-Aisne 08 41 Ea 52
42720 Briennon 42 117 Ea 72
89210 Brienon-sur-Armançon 89 73 Dd 61
08400 Brières 08 54 Ee 52
91150 Brières-les-Scellés 91 71 Ca 58
42620 Brierette 42 117 Df 71
89380 Bries, les 89 89 Dd 61
17520 Brie-sous-Archiac 17 123 Ze 76
16300 Brie-sous-Barbezieux 16 123 Zf 76
16300 Brie-sous-Chalais 16 123 Aa 77
17160 Brie-sous-Matha 17 123 Ze 74
17120 Brie-sous-Mortagne 17 122 Zb 76
17810 Brieu, le 14 47 Zb 55
79800 Brieuil 79 111 Zf 71
08240 Brieulles-sur-Bar 08 42 Ef 52
55110 Brieulles-sur-Meuse 55 55 Fb 52
61160 Brieux 61 48 Zf 55
43700 Brieves-Charensac 43 141 Df 78
54150 Briey 54 56 Ff 53
63820 Briffons 63 127 Cd 74
48600 Briges 48 141 De 80
80410 Brighton 80 28 Bd 47
33860 Brignac 33 123 Zd 77
34800 Brignac 34 167 Dc 87
49430 Brignac 49 84 Zd 63
56430 Brignac 56 64 Xd 60
19310 Brignac-la-Plaine 19 125 Bc 77
69530 Brignais 69M 130 Ee 74
95640 Brignancourt 95 50 Bf 54
49700 Brigné 49 98 Zd 65
29350 Brigneau 29 79 Wb 62
31480 Brignemont 31 149 Af 86
29560 Brigneun 29 62 Ve 59
29890 Brignogan-Plage 29 62 Ve 57
83170 Brignoles 83 171 Ga 88
47140 Brignols 47 149 Ae 82
30190 Brignon 30 154 Eb 85
43370 Brignon, le 43 141 Df 79
58470 Brignon, le 58 103 Db 67
38190 Brignoud 38 132 Ff 77
23250 Brigoux 23 114 Bf 73
06430 Brigue, la 06 159 Hd 84
86290 Brigueil-le-Chantre 86 113 Ba 70
16420 Brigueuil 16 112 Af 73
91640 Briis-sous-Forges 91 51 Ca 57
16500 Brillac 16 112 Ae 72
56370 Brillac 56 80 Xb 63
85200 Brillac 85 110 Za 70
04700 Brillanne, la 04 157 Ff 85
10240 Brillecourt 10 74 Ec 58
50330 Brillevast 50 33 Yd 51
59178 Brillon 59 30 Db 46
55000 Brillon-en-Barrois 55 55 Fa 56
33920 Brillouet 33 135 Zc 78
85210 Brillouet 85 110 Yf 69
45310 Brilly 45 70 Be 60
62170 Brimeux 62 28 Bf 46
51220 Brimont 51 53 Ea 52
18120 Brinay 18 102 Ca 65
58110 Brinay 58 104 De 67
68870 Brinckheim 68 95 Hc 63
69126 Brindas 69M 130 Ee 74
22170 Bringolo 22 63 Xa 57
58420 Brinon-sur-Beuvron 58 89 Dc 65
18410 Brinon-sur-Sauldre 18 87 Cb 63
54280 Brin-sur-Seille 54 56 Gc 56
77930 Brinvillé 77 71 Cd 57
39570 Briod 39 107 Fd 69
49125 Briollay 49 84 Zc 63
12400 Briols 12 152 Cf 85
01460 Brion 01 119 Fd 71
36110 Brion 36 101 Be 67
38590 Brion 38 131 Fc 77
48310 Brion 48 140 Da 80
49250 Brion 49 84 Zf 64
63610 Brion 63 128 Cf 76
71190 Brion 71 105 Eb 67
86160 Brion 86 112 Ac 70
89400 Brion 89 72 Dc 61
27800 Brionne 27 49 Ae 53
23000 Brionne, la 23 114 Be 71
79290 Brion-près-Thouet 79 99 Ze 66
21570 Brion-sur-Ource 21 91 Ed 61
48310 Brion-Vieux 48 140 Da 80
01470 Briord 01 131 Fc 74
72110 Briosne-lès-Sables 72 68 Ac 59
60210 Briot 60 38 Bf 51
18120 Briou 18 102 Ca 65
41370 Briou 41 86 Bc 62
18100 Briou, le 18 102 Ca 65
18140 Briou, le 18 103 Ce 65
18140 Briou, le 18 103 Cf 66
18300 Briou, le 18 88 Ce 65
45460 Briou, le 45 88 Cc 61
43100 Brioude 43 128 Dc 77
63190 Brioux 63 128 Dc 73
18140 Brioux, le 18 103 Cf 65
79170 Brioux-sur-Boutonne 79 111 Ze 72
61220 Briouze 61 47 Zd 56
80540 Briquemesnil-Floxicourt 80 38 Ca 49
08240 Briquenay 08 42 Ef 52
14240 Briquessard 14 34 Zb 54
50200 Briqueville-la-Blouette 50 46 Yd 54
64240 Briscous 64 160 Ye 88
64240 Briscous-les Salines 64 160 Yd 88
73100 Brison 73 132 Ff 74
74130 Brison 74 120 Gc 72
73100 Brison-Saint-Innocent 73 132 Ff 74
17390 Brisquettes 17 122 Ye 74
34190 Brissac 34 153 De 85
49320* Brissac Loire Aubance 49 83 Zd 64
37600 Brissandière, la 37 100 Af 67
28410 Brissard 28 50 Bc 56
49330 Brissarthe 49 83 Zd 62
02240 Brissay-Choigny 02 40 Dc 50
18340 Brissets, les 18 102 Cc 67
36110 Brissonnière, la 36 101 Bd 66
02240 Brissy-Hamégicourt 02 40 Dc 50
26420 Britière, la 26 143 Fc 79
44530 Brivé 44 81 Xf 64
82600 Brivecastel 82 149 Ba 85
19100 Brive-la-Gaillarde 19 125 Bd 78
36100 Brives 36 102 Bf 67
72150 Brives 72 85 Ad 62
17800 Brives-sur-Charente 17 123 Zd 74
19120 Brivezac 19 138 Bf 78
50700 Brix 50 33 Yc 51
55140 Brixey-aux-Chanoines 55 75 Fe 58
17770 Brizambourg 17 123 Zd 74
37220 Brizay 37 99 Ac 66
86110 Brizay 86 99 Ab 67
55250 Brizeaux 55 55 Fa 54
58140 Brizon 58 90 Df 65
49490 Broc 49 84 Aa 63
63500 Broc 63 128 Db 76
06510 Broc, le 06 159 Hb 86
40420 Brocas 40 147 Zc 84
40500 Brocas 40 161 Zb 86
61290 Brochard 61 69 Ae 57
27150 Broche, la 27 38 Bd 53
33920 Brochet 33 123 Zd 77
85230 Brochets, les 85 96 Xf 67
04120 Brochiers, les 04 157 Gb 85
21220 Brochon 21 106 Ef 65
14430 Brocottes 14 35 Zf 53
80430 Brocourt 80 38 Be 49
55120 Brocourt-en-Argonne 55 55 Fb 54
19380 Brocs-Haut, les 19 126 Be 78
29870 Broënnou 29 61 Vc 57
27270 Broglie 27 49 Ad 54
25600 Brognard 25 94 Gf 63
08380 Brognon 08 41 Eb 49
21490 Brognon 21 92 Fb 64
21250 Broin 21 106 Fa 66
21220 Broindon 21 106 Fa 65
39320 Broissia 39 119 Fc 70
73340 Broissieux 73 132 Ga 74
60210 Brombos 60 38 Bf 51
15320 Bromesterie, la 15 140 Db 79
45390 Bromilles 45 71 Cc 59
12600 Brommat 12 139 Ce 79
12600 Brommes 12 139 Ce 79
63230 Bromont-Lamothe 63 127 Ce 73
69500 Bron 69M 130 Ef 74
52500 Broncourt 52 92 Fd 62
22250 Bronn = Broons 22 65 Xe 59
51330 Bronne 51 54 Ed 55
57535 Bronvaux 57 56 Ga 53
28800 Bronville 28 70 Bc 59
22250 Broons = Bronn 22 65 Xe 59
35220 Broons-sur-Vilaine 35 66 Yd 60
19400 Broquerie, la 19 138 Bf 78
60220 Broquiers 60 38 Be 51
12480 Broquiès 12 152 Ce 84
16480 Brossac 16 123 Zf 77
07340 Brossainc 07 130 Ee 77
03120 Brossards, les 03 116 Dd 71
49700 Brossay 49 99 Ze 66
36310 Brosse 36 113 Bb 70
03120 Brosse, la 03 116 Dd 71
10130 Brosse, la 10 73 Df 60
18190 Brosse, la 18 102 Cb 67
28160 Brosse, la 28 69 Bb 59
44320 Brosse, la 44 96 Xf 65
49360 Brosse, la 49 98 Zc 66
71140 Brosse, la 71 116 De 69
77460 Brosse, la 77 72 Ce 59
27160 Brosse, les 27 49 Af 56
77940 Brosse-Montceaux, la 77 72 Da 58
03500 Brosses 03 116 Db 71
89660 Brosses 89 89 De 63
18120 Brosses, les 18 102 Ca 66
41300 Brosses, les 41 87 Ca 65
49370 Brosses, les 49 83 Zb 63
79350 Brosses, les 79 98 Zd 67
85250 Brossière, la 85 97 Yf 68
58440 Brossiers, les 58 88 Cf 64
27930 Brosville 27 49 Ba 54
30210 Brot 30 155 Ed 84
33720 Brot 33 135 Zd 81
70300 Brotte-lès-Luxeuil 70 93 Gc 62
70180 Brotte-lès-Ray 70 92 Fe 63
52000 Brottes 52 75 Fa 60
28160 Brou 28 69 Bb 59
17320 Brouage 17 122 Yf 73
50150 Brouains 50 47 Za 56
35120 Broualan 35 65 Yc 58
89500 Brouarde, les 89 72 Da 60
14250 Brouay 14 35 Zc 53
05800 Brouce, la 05 144 Ff 80
24210 Brouchaud 24 125 Ba 77
80400 Brouchy 80 40 Da 50
57220 Brouck 57 57 Gd 54
59630 Brouckerque 59 27 Cb 43
57565 Brouderdorff 57 57 Ha 56
33840 Broudon, le 33 148 Zf 83
17620 Broue 17 122 Za 74
28410 Broué 28 50 Bd 56
46090 Brouelles 46 137 Bc 81
56780 Brouel Mones 56 80 Xb 63
55700 Brouennes 55 42 Fb 51
32350 Brouilh-Monbert, le 32 163 Ac 87
66560 Brouilla 66 179 Cf 93
43500 Brouillac 43 129 Df 77
01430 Brouillat 01 119 Fd 72
51170 Brouillet 51 53 De 53
87800 Brouillet 87 125 Bb 74
33210 Brouquet 33 135 Ze 81
33720 Brouquet 33 135 Zd 81
33124 Brouqueyran 33 135 Ze 82
83330 Broussan 83 171 Ff 89
23340 Broussas 23 126 Bf 74
15250 Brousse 15 139 Cc 79
23360 Brousse 23 114 Be 70
23700 Brousse 23 115 Cc 73
63490 Brousse 63 128 Dc 75
81440 Brousse 81 165 Ca 86
15150 Brousse, la 15 138 Ca 78
16390 Brousse, la 16 124 Ab 77
17160 Brousse, la 17 111 Zd 73
19450 Brousse, la 19 126 Bd 76
24450 Brousse, la 24 125 Af 75
48220 Brousse, la 48 153 De 82
63410 Brousse, la 63 115 Cf 73
79150 Brousse, la 79 98 Zd 66
12480 Brousse-le-Château 12 152 Cd 85
79190 Brousses, les 79 111 Aa 72
11390 Brousses-et-Villaret 11 166 Cb 88
52130 Brousseval 52 74 Ef 58
33410 Broussey 33 135 Ze 80
55190 Broussey-en-Blois 55 55 Fd 57
55200 Broussey-en-Woëvre 55 55 Fe 56
15240 Broussoles 15 127 Cc 77
63850 Broussoux-le-Lac 63 127 Ce 76
51230 Broussy-le-Grand 51 53 Df 56
51230 Broussy-le-Petit 51 53 De 56
77177 Brou-sur-Chantereine 77 51 Cd 55
52230 Brouthières 52 75 Fb 58
88600 Brouvelieures 88 77 Ge 59
54120 Brouville 54 77 Ge 58
84390 Brouville 84 156 Fc 84
57635 Brouviller 57 57 Ha 56
91150 Brouy 91 71 Cb 59
09240 Brouzenac 09 177 Bc 90
30580 Brouzet-lès-Alès 30 154 Eb 84
30260 Brouzet-lès-Quissac 30 154 Df 85
85260 Brouzils, les 85 97 Ye 67
59470 Broxeele 59 27 Cb 44
71190 Broye 71 105 Eb 67
70140 Broye-Aubigney-Montseugny 70 92 Fd 65
70100 Broye-les-Loups-et-Verfontaine 70 92 Fc 64
51120 Broyes 51 53 De 56
60120 Broyes 60 39 Cc 51
88700 Brû 88 77 Ge 58
15500 Bru, le 15 128 Da 77
43210 Bruaille 43 129 Ea 76
71500 Bruailles 71 106 Fb 69
07270 Bruas, le 07 142 Ee 78
62700 Bruay-la-Buissière 62 29 Cd 46
59860 Bruay-l'Escaut 59 31 Dd 46
24110 Bruc 24 136 Ad 78
80690 Brucamps 80 29 Ca 48
47130 Bruch 47 148 Ac 83
57350 Bruch 57 57 Gf 53
42130 Bruchet 42 129 Df 74
50480 Brucheville 50 46 Ye 52
50500 Brucholerie, la 50 33 Ye 53
14160 Brucourt 14 35 Zf 53
35550 Bruc-sur-Aff 35 81 Xf 62
83119 Brue-Auriac 83 171 Ff 87
68440 Bruebach 68 95 Hc 62
78440 Brueil-en-Vexin 78 50 Be 54
12330 Bruéjouls 12 151 Cc 82
15220 Bruel 15 139 Cc 80
15310 Bruel 15 139 Cd 78
48100 Bruel 48 140 Db 81
48230 Bruel 48 140 Db 82
12220 Bruel, le 12 151 Cb 82
45130 Bruère, la 45 87 Bd 62
18200 Bruère-Allichamps 18 102 Cc 68
37120 Bruères, les 37 99 Ac 66
72500 Bruère-sur-Loir, la 72 85 Ac 63
85530 Bruffière, la 85 97 Ye 66
11300 Brugairolles 11 165 Ca 90
43170 Brugeire, la 43 140 Dd 79
24160 Brugère, la 24 125 Bb 77
48260 Brugère, la 48 140 Da 80
63880 Brugeron, le 63 129 De 74
64800 Bruges-Capbis-Mifaget 64 162 Ze 90
03700 Brugheas 03 116 Dc 72
63340 Brugière 63 128 Da 76
47260 Brugnac 47 148 Ac 82
81140 Brugnac 81 150 Be 85
23000 Brugnat 23 114 Bf 71
32500 Brugnens 32 149 Ae 85
51530 Brugny-Vaudancourt 51 53 Df 55
30580 Bruguière, la 30 154 Ec 84
30770 Bruguière, la 30 153 Dc 85
31150 Bruguières 31 164 Bc 86
59490 Bruille-lez-Marchiennes 59 30 Db 46
59199 Bruille-Saint-Amand 59 30 Dd 46
05150 Bruis 05 143 Fd 82
07150 Brujas 07 154 Eb 82
79230 Brûlain 79 111 Ze 71
35330 Brulais, les 35 81 Xf 61
57340 Brulange 57 57 Gd 55
83330 Brulat, le 83 171 Fe 89
53410 Brûlatte-Saint-Isle, la 53 66 Za 60
02120 Brûlé, le 02 40 De 49
18150 Brulès, les 18 103 Cf 67
27570 Brulés, les 27 49 Ba 56
88600 Bruleux, le 88 77 Gd 60
54200 Bruley 54 56 Fe 56
61390 Brullemail 61 48 Ab 57
69690 Brullioles 69M 130 Ec 74
72350 Brûlon 72 67 Ze 61
87230 Brumas 87 125 Ba 75
67170 Brumath 67 58 He 56
02810 Brumetz 02 52 Da 54
29710 Brumphuez 29 78 Vd 61
81600 Brunarié, la 81 151 Bf 86
12100 Brunas 12 152 Da 84
07210 Brune 07 142 Ee 80
02360 Brunehamel 02 41 Eb 50
28400 Brunelles 28 69 Af 59
11400 Brunels, les 11 165 Ca 88
62240 Brunembert 62 28 Bf 44
59151 Brunémont 59 30 Da 47
04210 Brunet 04 157 Ga 85
04250 Brunet 04 157 Ff 83
33113 Brunet 33 147 Zd 82
06850 Brunet, le 06 158 Ge 85
86350 Brunetière, la 86 112 Ad 71
36800 Brunets, les 36 101 Bc 69
15220 Brunie, la 15 139 Cb 80
46500 Brunie, la 46 138 Be 80
82800 Bruniquel 82 150 Bd 84
05350 Brunissard 05 145 Ge 80
91800 Brunoy 91 51 Cd 56
13460 Bruns, les 13 169 Ec 87
16300 Bruns, les 16 123 Ze 76
84410 Bruns, les 84 156 Fb 84
68350 Brunstatt 68 95 Hb 62
76630 Brunville 76 37 Bb 49
60130 Brunvillers-la-Motte 60 39 Cc 51
76780 Bruquedalle 76 37 Bc 51
04270 Brusc 04 157 Ga 85
83140 Brusc, le 83 171 Fe 90
80200 Brusle 80 39 Da 49
12360 Brusque 12 152 Cf 86
04420 Brusquet, le 04 157 Gb 84
12340 Brussac 12 139 Ce 81
70150 Brussey 70 93 Fe 65
69690 Brussieu 69M 130 Ed 74
51300 Brusson 51 54 Ee 56
22100 Brusvily 22 65 Xf 58
56360 Bruté 56 79 We 64
80230 Brutelles 80 28 Bd 48
54800 Bruville 54 56 Ff 54
86510 Brux 86 111 Ab 71
55300 Bruxières-sous-les-Côtes 55 55 Fe 55
03120 Bruyère, la 03 116 Dd 72
42130 Bruyère, la 42 129 Df 74
42600 Bruyère, la 42 129 Df 75
69850 Bruyère, la 69M 130 Ed 75
71600 Bruyère, la 71 117 Ea 70
71110 Bruyère-Bresson, la 71 117 Df 71
61120 Bruyère-Fresnay, la 61 48 Ab 55
88600 Bruyères 88 77 Ge 59
03120 Bruyères, les 03 116 De 71
03150 Bruyères, les 03 116 Dc 70
18140 Bruyères, les 18 103 Cf 66
71220 Bruyères, les 71 117 Ec 70
58240 Bruyères-de-Fleury 58 103 Db 68
58390 Bruyères-des-Desrues 58 103 Dc 68
58300 Bruyères-des-Lices 58 103 Db 68
02860 Bruyères-et-Montbérault 02 40 Dd 51
91680 Bruyères-le-Châtel 91 71 Cb 57
58240 Bruyères-Radon, les 58 103 Db 68
02000 Bruyères-sur-Fère 02 40 Dd 52
02130 Bruyères-sur-Fère 02 52 Dc 53
95820 Bruyères-sur-Oise 95 51 Cb 54
02220 Bruys 02 53 Dd 53
35170 Bruz 35 65 Yb 60
31190 Bruzes, les 31 164 Bc 88
59144 Bry 59 31 De 47
28410 Bû 28 50 Bc 56
50640 Buais-Les-Monts 50 66 Za 57
40320 Buanes 40 162 Zd 86
50540 Buat, le 50 66 Ye 57
61300 Buat, le 61 49 Ad 56
61190 Bubertré 61 68 Ad 57
56310 Bubry 56 79 We 61
78530 Buc 78 51 Ca 56
90800 Buc 90 94 Ge 63
50500 Bucaille 50 46 Ye 52
27700 Bucaille, la 27 50 Bc 53
60480 Bucamps 60 39 Cb 51
78200 Bucehlay 78 50 Be 55
10190 Bucey-en-Othe 10 73 Df 59
70700 Bucey-lès-Gy 70 93 Ff 64
70360 Bucey-lès-Traves 70 93 Ff 63
62310 Buchamps 62 29 Ca 46
03440 Buchatière 03 115 Cf 70
10800 Buchères 10 73 Ea 59
37460 Bucherons, les 37 101 Bb 65
52330 Buchey 52 74 Ef 59
60640 Buchoire 60 39 Da 51
67330 Buchsweiler = Bouxwiller 67 58 Hc 56
57420 Buchy 57 56 Gb 55
76750 Buchy 76 37 Bc 51
02500 Bucilly 02 41 Ea 49
62116 Bucquoy 62 29 Ce 48
20136 Bucugnà = Bocognano CTC 182 Ka 96
02880 Bucy-le long 02 40 Dc 52
45410 Bucy-le-Roy 45 70 Bf 60
02870 Bucy-lès-Cerny 02 40 Dd 51
02350 Bucy-lès-Pierrepont 02 41 Df 51
45140 Bucy-Saint-Liphard 45 87 Be 61
57920 Budange 57 56 Gb 53
57270 Budange-sous-Justemont 57 56 Ga 53
23170 Budelière 23 115 Cc 71
57970 Buding 57 44 Gb 53
57970 Budling 57 56 Gb 52
33720 Budos 33 135 Zd 81
18300 Bué 18 88 Ce 65
65120 Bué 65 175 Zf 92
57370 Buechelberg 57 58 Hb 56
27730 Bueil 27 50 Bc 55
37370 Bueil-en-Touraine 37 85 Ad 63
01310 Buellas 01 118 Fa 71
74660 Buet, le 74 121 Gf 72
68210 Buethwiller 68 95 Ha 63
87130 Buffangeas 87 126 Bd 74
25440 Buffard 25 107 Fe 66
73140 Buffaz, la 73 133 Gc 77
86270 Bufferières, les 86 100 Ae 68
44390 Buffets, les 44 82 Yc 63
12210 Buffières 12 140 Cf 80
12370 Buffières 12 152 Ce 85
71250 Buffières 71 117 Ed 70
70500 Buffignécourt 70 93 Ga 62
21500 Buffon 21 90 Eb 63
48150 Buffre, le 48 153 Dc 83
11190 Bugarach 11 178 Cc 91
65220 Bugard 65 163 Ab 89
82190 Bugat, le 82 149 Af 83
43170 Bugeac 43 140 Dc 79
19170 Bugeat 19 126 Bf 75
19410 Bugénie, la 19 125 Bd 76
45120 Buges 45 71 Ce 60
16200 Buges, les 16 123 Ze 74
63210 Buges, les 63 127 Ce 74
76930 Buglise 76 36 Aa 51
40990 Buglose 40 146 Za 86
64190 Bugnein 64 161 Zb 88
59151 Bugnicourt 59 30 Da 47
52210 Bugnières 52 75 Fa 61
25520 Bugny 25 108 Gc 67
24260 Bugue, le 24 137 Af 79
22710 Buguélès 22 63 We 55
67470 Buhl 67 59 Ia 55
68530 Buhl 68 95 Hb 61
57400 Buhl-Lorraine 57 57 Ha 56
14170 Buhot, le 14 48 Zf 54
22300 Buhulien 22 63 Wd 56
95770 Buhy 95 50 Be 53
60380 Buicourt 60 38 Be 51
80132 Buigny-L'Abbé 80 28 Bf 48
80220 Buigny-lès-Gamaches 80 37 Bd 48
80132 Buigny-Saint-Maclou 80 28 Be 48
11140 Buillac 11 178 Cb 92
61500 Buillon, le 61 68 Aa 57
02500 Buire 02 41 Ea 49
62390 Buire-au-Bois 62 29 Ca 47
80200 Buire-Courcelles 80 39 Da 49
62870 Buire-le-Sec 62 28 Be 46
80300 Buire-sur-L'Ancre 80 39 Cd 49
02620 Buironfosse 02 41 Df 49
38122 Buis 38 130 Fa 76
87140 Buis 87 113 Bb 72
34380 Buis, le 34 153 Dd 86
26170 Buis-les-Baronnies 26 156 Fb 83
05500 Buissard 05 144 Ga 81
38500 Buisse, la 38 131 Fd 76
38530 Buissière, la 38 132 Ff 76
87500 Buisson 87 125 Ba 75
89440 Buisson 89 90 Df 63
19320 Buisson, la 19 126 Ca 77
48100 Buisson, le 48 140 Db 81
51300 Buisson, le 51 54 Ee 56
84110 Buisson, le 84 155 Fa 83
59610 Buisson-Barbet 59 31 Df 48
54110 Buissoncourt 54 56 Gc 56
27220 Buisson-Crosson 27 50 Bb 55
24480 Buisson-de-Cadouin, le 24 137 Af 79
04700 Buissonnades, les 04 157 Ff 85
28100 Buissons, les 28 50 Bc 56
88220 Buissons, les 88 76 Gc 60
15350 Buissou 15 127 Cc 76
27240 Buis-sur-Damville 27 49 Ba 56
62860 Buissy 62 30 Da 47
24420 Bujadelle 24 125 Af 77
87460 Bujaleuf 87 126 Bd 74
50530 Bulaine, la 50 46 Yd 56
55250 Bulainville 55 55 Fb 55
65130 Bulan 65 175 Ab 90
22160 Bulat-Pestivien 22 63 We 58
58400 Bulcy 58 103 Da 65
56420 Buléon 56 80 Xb 61
88140 Bulgnéville 88 76 Ff 59
63350 Bulhon 63 116 Dc 73
28800 Bullainville 28 70 Bd 59
25560 Bulle 25 107 Gb 67
62128 Bullecourt 62 30 Cf 47
60130 Bulles 60 39 Cb 52
73400 Bulles 73 132 Gc 74
54113 Bulligny 54 76 Ff 57
78830 Bullion 78 51 Bf 57
28160 Bullou 28 69 Bb 59
14320 Bully 14 35 Zd 54
42260 Bully 42 117 Ea 73
69210 Bully 69M 130 Ed 73
76270 Bully 76 37 Bc 50
62160 Bully-les-Mines 62 29 Ce 46
08450 Bulson 08 42 Ef 51
88700 Bult 88 77 Gd 59
65400 Bun 65 174 Zf 91
33125 Bun, le 33 135 Zc 82
11340 Bunague, la 11 178 Bf 91
63600 Bunanges 63 129 De 75
21400 Buncey 21 91 Ed 62
36500 Bunes, les 36 101 Bd 67
62130 Buneville 62 29 Cc 47
20169 Bunifaziu = Bonifacio CTC 185 Ka 100
23500 Bunleix 23 126 Ca 74
91720 Buno-Bonnevaux 91 71 Cc 58
64120 Bunus 64 161 Yf 89
80400 Buny 80 39 Cf 50
16110 Bunzac 16 124 Ac 74
84480 Buoux 84 156 Fc 85
20240 Bura CTC 183 Kb 97
27320 Buray 27 49 Bb 56
67260 Burbach 67 57 Ha 55
01510 Burbanche, la 01 131 Fd 73
62151 Burbure 62 29 Cc 45
38690 Burcin 38 131 Fc 76

250 | Briaucourt

14410 Burcy 14 47 Zb 55
77760 Burcy 77 71 Cd 59
42220 Burdignes 42 130 Ed 77
74420 Burdignin 74 120 Gc 71
38580 Burdin, le 38 132 Ga 77
55290 Bure 55 75 Fc 57
57710 Bure 57 43 Ff 52
61170 Buré 61 68 Ac 57
54730 Buré-la-Ville 54 43 Fd 51
21290 Bure-les-Templiers 21 91 Ef 62
85340 Burelière, la 85 109 Yb 69
02140 Burelles 02 41 Df 50
50420 Burellière, la 50 46 Yf 55
54370 Bures 54 57 Gd 56
61170 Bures 61 68 Ac 57
72130 Bures 72 68 Zf 59
78630 Bures 78 50 Bf 55
76660 Bures-en-Bray 76 37 Bc 50
14350 Bures-les-Monts 14 47 Za 55
14670 Bures-sur-Dives 14 48 Ze 53
91190 Bures-sur-Yvette 91 51 Ca 56
53170 Buret, le 53 84 Zc 61
27190 Burey 27 49 Af 55
55140 Burey-en-Vaux 55 75 Fe 57
55140 Burey-la-Côte 55 75 Fe 57
65190 Burg 65 163 Ab 89
31440 Burgalays 31 176 Ad 91
64390 Burgaronne 64 161 Za 88
16260 Burgaud 16 124 Ac 73
31330 Burgaud, le 31 150 Ba 86
25170 Burgille 25 93 Fe 65
87800 Burgnec 87 125 Ba 74
20143 Burgo CTC 184 If 98
20143 Burgu = Burgo CTC 184 If 98
31190 Burguerolles 31 164 Bc 88
12290 Burguière, la 12 152 Cf 83
71260 Burgy 71 118 Ee 70
17770 Burie 17 123 Zd 74
38122 Burin, le 38 130 Fa 76
54450 Buriville 54 77 Ge 57
81100 Burlats 81 166 Cb 87
57170 Burlioncourt 57 57 Gd 55
71460 Burnand 71 105 Ed 69
25470 Burnevillers 25 94 Ha 65
68520 Burnhaupt-le-Bas 68 95 Ha 62
68520 Burnhaupt-le-Haut 68 95 Ha 62
14610 Buron 14 35 Zd 53
63270 Buron 63 128 Db 75
72400 Buron, le 72 68 Ad 60
64160 Buros 64 162 Ze 88
64330 Burosse-Mendousse 64 162 Ze 87
64520 Burre 64 161 Yf 87
09000 Burret 09 177 Bc 91
61500 Bursard 61 68 Ab 57
33730 Burthe, la 33 147 Zd 82
54210 Burthecourt-aux-Chênes 54 76 Gb 57
22160 Burthulet 22 63 Wd 58
57220 Burtoncourt 57 56 Gc 53
41190 Bury 41 86 Bb 63
57420 Bury 57 56 Ga 54
60250 Bury 60 39 Cc 53
83560 Bury 83 171 Ga 87
07450 Burzet 07 141 Eb 80
71460 Burzy 71 105 Ed 69
62124 Bus 62 30 Cf 48
68220 Buschwiller 68 95 Hd 63
59137 Busigny 59 40 Dc 48
80700 Bus-la-Mesiere 80 39 Ce 51
80560 Bus-lès-Artois 80 29 Cd 48
41160 Busloup 41 86 Ba 61
80140 Busménard 80 38 Bd 49
62350 Busnes 62 29 Cd 45
62920 Busnettes 62 29 Cd 45
81300 Busque 81 151 Bf 86
15500 Bussac 15 128 Da 77
24350 Bussac 24 124 Ad 77
43300 Bussac 43 141 Dd 78
87600 Bussac 87 124 Ae 74
17210 Bussac-Forêt 17 123 Zd 77
17100 Bussac-sur-Charente 17 122 Zc 74
20147 Bussaglia CTC 182 Id 95
27630 Bus-Saint-Rémy 27 50 Bd 54
88540 Bussang 88 94 Gf 61
23150 Busseau 23 114 Ca 72
79240 Busseau, le 79 98 Zc 69
21510 Busseaut 21 91 Ed 62
19200 Bussejoux 19 127 Cc 75
63270 Busséol 63 128 Db 74
23320 Busserolles 23 114 Be 72
24360 Busserolles 24 124 Ad 74
21580 Busserotte-et-Montenaille 21 91 Ef 63
86350 Busseroux 86 112 Ac 71
48500 Busses 48 140 Db 82
03270 Busset 03 116 Dd 72
02810 Bussiares 02 52 Db 54
03380 Bussière 03 115 Cc 71
12600 Bussière 12 139 Ce 80
23700 Bussière 23 115 Cd 72
36230 Bussière 36 101 Bf 69
58170 Bussière 58 104 Df 68
63380 Bussière 63 127 Cd 73
63440 Bussière 63 115 Cf 72
18250 Bussière, la 18 88 Ce 65
45230 Bussière, la 45 88 Ce 62
86310 Bussière, la 86 100 Ae 69
89520 Bussière, la 89 89 Db 63
24360 Bussière-Badil 24 124 Ad 75
87330 Bussière-Boffy 87 112 Af 72
23320 Bussière-Dunoise 23 114 Be 71
87230 Bussière-Galant 87 125 Ba 75
23300 Bussière-Madeleine, la 23 113 Bc 71
23260 Bussière-Maraud 23 114 Cb 73
87320 Bussière-Poitevine 87 112 Af 71
21580 Bussières 21 91 Ef 63
42510 Bussières 42 129 Eb 73
58340 Bussières 58 104 Dd 67
63330 Bussières 63 115 Cd 72
70190 Bussières 70 93 Ff 64
71960 Bussières 71 118 Ee 70
77750 Bussières 77 52 Db 55
89630 Bussières 89 90 Ea 64
23130 Bussières, les 23 114 Cb 72
23600 Bussière-Saint-Georges 23 114 Ca 70
52500 Bussières-Champesvaine 52 92 Fd 62
63260 Bussières-et-Pruns 63 116 Db 72
21360 Bussière-sur-Ouche, la 21 105 Ee 65
52700 Busson 52 75 Fc 59
56380 Busson, le 56 81 Xf 61
20136 Bussu CTC 182 Ka 96
80200 Bussu 80 39 Cf 49
64220 Bussunarits-Sarrasquette 64 161 Ye 90
80135 Bussus-Bussuel 80 28 Ca 48
18130 Bussy 18 102 Cd 67
58120 Bussy 58 104 Df 66
60400 Bussy 60 39 Cf 51
71550 Bussy 71 104 Ea 66
87120 Bussy 87 126 Be 74
42260 Bussy-Albieux 42 129 Ea 74
51290 Bussy-aux-Bois 51 74 Ed 57
89400 Bussy-en-Othe 89 72 Dd 60
55000 Bussy-la-Côte 55 55 Fa 56
21540 Bussy-la-Pesle 21 91 Ee 64
58420 Bussy-la-Pesle 58 89 Dc 65
51600 Bussy-le-Château 51 54 Ed 54
21150 Bussy-le-Grand 21 91 Ed 63
51330 Bussy-le-Repos 51 54 Ee 55
89500 Bussy-le-Repos 89 72 Db 60
80800 Bussy-lès-Daours 80 39 Cc 49
80290 Bussy-lès-Poix 80 38 Ca 50
51320 Bussy-Lettrée 51 54 Eb 56
77600 Bussy-Saint-Georges 77 51 Ce 55
67320 Bust 67 58 Hb 56
20212 Bustanico CTC 183 Kb 95
20212 Bustanicu = Bustanico CTC 183 Kb 95
64220 Bustince-Iriberry 64 161 Ye 89
14190 Bû-sur-Rouvres, le 14 48 Ze 54
67350 Buswiller 67 58 Hd 56
25320 Busy 25 107 Ff 65
24190 But, le 24 136 Ac 78
61570 But, le 61 48 Zf 56
58430 Buteaux, les 58 104 Df 67
55160 Butgnéville 55 55 Fe 54
70190 Buthiers 70 93 Ga 64
77760 Buthiers 77 71 Cc 59
76890 Butot 76 37 Ba 51
76450 Butot-Vénesville 76 36 Ad 50
95430 Butry-sur-Oise 95 51 Cb 54
19170 Butte, la 19 126 Bf 75
50250 Butte, la 50 46 Yd 53
89360 Butteaux 89 73 De 61
18140 Butteaux, les 18 88 Cf 65
55270 Butte de Montfaucon 55 55 Fa 53
72240 Butte-de-Saint-Calais, la 72 67 Ze 60
67430 Butten 67 57 Hb 55
56120 Buttes-de-Couessou, les 56 64 Xc 61
80400 Buverchy 80 39 Cf 50
39800 Buvilly 39 107 Fe 67
38630 Buvin 38 131 Fd 75
36140 Buxerette, la 36 114 Be 70
21290 Buxerolles 21 91 Ef 62
63720 Buxerolles 63 116 Db 73
86180 Buxerolles 86 99 Ac 69
55300 Buxerulles 55 55 Fd 55
10110 Buxeuil 10 74 Ec 60
36150 Buxeuil 36 101 Be 66
37160 Buxeuil 37 100 Ae 67
36230 Buxières-d'Aillac 36 101 Be 69
52240 Buxières-lès-Clefmont 52 75 Fc 60
52320 Buxières-lès-Froncles 52 75 Fa 59
03440 Buxières-les-Mines 03 115 Cf 70
52000 Buxières-lès-Villiers 52 75 Fa 60
63700 Buxières-sous-Montaigut 63 115 Cf 71
10110 Buxières-sur-Arce 10 74 Ec 60
71390 Buxy 71 105 Ee 68
42260 Buy 42 129 Ea 73
59285 Buysscheure 59 27 Cc 44
09800 Buzan 09 176 Af 91
36500 Buzançais 36 101 Bc 67
02200 Buzancy 02 40 Dc 53
08240 Buzancy 08 42 Ef 52
12150 Buzareingues 12 152 Cf 82
63210 Buzaudon 63 127 Ce 74
88220 Buzegney 88 76 Gc 60
12150 Buzeins 12 152 Cf 82
47160 Buzet-sur-Baïse 47 148 Ab 83
31660 Buzet-sur-Tarn 31 150 Bd 86
64680 Buziet 64 162 Zd 90
34160 Buzignargues 34 154 Ea 86
44140 Buzinières, les 44 97 Yc 66
65140 Buzon 65 162 Aa 88
55400 Buzy 55 55 Fe 53
58210 Buzy 58 89 Dc 64
64260 Buzy 64 162 Zd 90
25440 By 25 107 Ff 66
33340 By 33 122 Za 76
25320 Byans-sur-Doubs 25 107 Ff 66
62130 Byras 62 29 Cc 46
59380 Byssaert 59 27 Cc 43

C

29270 Caarhaix-Plouguer 29 63 Wc 59
65710 Cabadur 65 175 Ab 91
12500 Cabanac 12 140 Cf 82
65350 Cabanac 65 163 Ab 89
31160 Cabanac-Cazaux 31 176 Ae 90
33650 Cabanac-et-Villagrains 33 135 Zc 81
31480 Cabanac-Séguenville 31 149 Ba 86
13310 Cabanasse, la 13 169 Ef 87
24130 Cabane, la 24 136 Ab 79
63420 Cabane, la 63 128 Cf 76
65170 Cabane, la 65 175 Ab 92
81190 Cabane, la 81 151 Cb 84
04320 Cabane-des-Bas-Pasqueires 04 158 Ge 84
12240 Cabanelles 12 151 Cb 82
85580 Cabane-Neuve 85 109 Ye 70
12290 Cabanes 12 152 Cf 83
12800 Cabanès 12 151 Cb 83
81500 Cabanès 81 165 Bf 86
34130 Cabanes, les 34 168 Ea 87
13460 Cabanes-de-Cambon 13 169 Ec 87
65440 Cabanes-de-Camoudiet 65 175 Ab 91
11560 Cabanes-de-Fleury, les 11 167 Db 89
31460 Cabanial, le 31 165 Bf 87
81140 Cabanne 81 150 Be 84
13440 Cabannes 13 155 Ef 85
15150 Cabannes 15 138 Ca 79
81320 Cabannes 81 166 Ce 86
09310 Cabannes, les 09 177 Be 92
81170 Cabannes, les 81 151 Bf 84
83670 Cabanons, les 83 171 Ga 87
12100 Cabanous 12 152 Cf 84
33420 Cabara 33 135 Zf 80
17430 Cabariot 17 110 Za 73
83340 Cabasse 83 171 Gb 88
83230 Cabasson 83 172 Gb 90
40310 Cabeil 40 148 Aa 85
12210 Cabels 12 139 Ce 80
81330 Cabès 81 151 Cc 86
66330 Cabestany 66 179 Cf 92
58220 Cabets, les 58 89 Da 64
30430 Cabiac 30 154 Eb 83
64410 Cabidos 64 162 Zd 87
41150 Cabinette 41 86 Ba 63
47380 Cabirol 47 136 Ad 81
14260 Cabosse, la 14 47 Zb 54
14390 Cabourg 14 48 Zf 53
49510 Cabournes, les 49 98 Zb 65
46330 Cabrerets 46 138 Bd 81
34480 Cabrerolles 34 167 Da 87
11160 Cabrespine 11 166 Cc 88
46170 Cabrette, la 46 150 Bc 83
12220 Cabriac 12 139 Cb 81
30210 Cabrières 30 154 Ec 85
34800 Cabrières 34 167 Dc 87
84240 Cabrières-d'Aigues 84 156 Fc 86
84220 Cabrières-d'Avignon 84 156 Fa 85
13480 Cabriès 13 170 Fc 88
48400 Cabrillac 48 153 Dd 84
06530 Cabris 06 172 Gf 87
09400 Cabus 09 177 Bd 91
32190 Cacarens 32 148 Ab 85
20100 Cacciabello CTC 184 If 99
94230 Cachan 94 51 Cc 56
40120 Cachen 40 147 Zd 84
63580 Cacherat 63 128 Dc 76
80800 Cachy 80 39 Cc 49
81600 Cadalen 81 151 Bf 85
09240 Cadarcet 09 177 Bd 90
33750 Cadarsac 33 135 Ze 79
31550 Cadau 31 165 Bd 88
33140 Cadaujac 33 135 Zc 80
12330 Cadayrac 12 139 Cd 82
65240 Cadéac 65 175 Ac 91
32380 Cadeilhan 32 149 Ae 86
32220 Cadeilhan 32 163 Af 88
22600 Cadélac 22 64 Xb 59
56220 Caden 56 81 Xe 63
31540 Cadenac 31 165 Bf 88
57990 Cadenbronn 57 57 Gf 54
13170 Cadeneaux, les 13 170 Fc 88
12490 Cadenède 12 152 Cf 84
84160 Cadenet 84 170 Fc 86
84860 Caderousse 84 155 Ee 84
17600 Cadeuil 17 122 Za 74
83740 Cadière-d'Azur, la 83 171 Fe 89
30200 Cadignac 30 155 Ed 84
32330 Cadignan 32 148 Ab 85
24130 Cadillac 24 136 Ab 79
33410 Cadillac 33 135 Ze 81
33240 Cadillac-en-Fronsadais 33 135 Zd 79
64330 Cadillon 64 162 Zf 87
32300 Cadiran-de-Bas 32 163 Ac 87
81340 Cadix 81 152 Cc 85
81470 Cadix 81 165 Bf 87
29140 Cadol 29 78 Wa 61
13950 Cadolive 13 171 Fd 88
56860 Cadouarn 56 80 Xb 63
56420 Cadoudal 56 80 Xb 62
24480 Cadouin 24 137 Af 80
48500 Cadoule 48 153 Db 82
12440 Cadoulette 12 151 Cb 83
33180 Cadoume 33 122 Zb 77
12200 Cadours 12 151 Ca 82
31480 Cadours 31 164 Ba 86
86500 Cadrie, la 86 112 Af 70
46160 Cadrieu 46 138 Bf 82
14123 Caen 14 35 Ze 54
27930 Caër 27 49 Bb 54
29390 Caéro 29 78 Wb 60
59190 Caëstre 59 30 Cd 44
37310 Café-Brûlé, le 37 100 Af 65
62132 Caffiers 62 26 Be 43
33350 Cafol 33 135 Zf 79
82110 Cagnac 82 150 Bb 83
81130 Cagnac-les-Mines 81 151 Ca 85
20228 Cagnano CTC 181 Kc 91
06800 Cagnes-sur-Mer 06 173 Ha 87
64370 Cagnez 64 161 Zc 88
62182 Cagnicourt 62 30 Cf 47
59161 Cagnoncles 59 30 Db 47
40300 Cagnotte 40 161 Yf 87
14630 Cagny 14 35 Ze 54
80330 Cagny 80 39 Cc 49
14240 Cahagnes 14 47 Zb 54
14490 Cahagnolles 14 34 Zb 54
27420 Cahaignes 27 50 Bd 53
61430 Cahan 61 47 Zd 55
44390 Caharel 44 82 Yc 63
65190 Caharet 65 163 Ab 90
80132 Cahon 80 28 Be 48
46000 Cahors 46 150 Bc 82
46130 Cahus 46 138 Bf 79
11420 Cahuzac 11 165 Bf 89
47330 Cahuzac 47 136 Ad 81
81540 Cahuzac 81 165 Ca 88
32400 Cahuzac-sur-Adour 32 162 Zf 87
81140 Cahuzac-sur-Vère 81 151 Bf 85
32290 Cahuzéres 32 163 Aa 86
31560 Caignac 31 165 Be 89
12120 Caiholie, la 12 152 Cd 84
30740 Cailar, le 30 169 Eb 86
11240 Cailhau 11 165 Ca 90
11240 Cailhavel 11 165 Ca 90
34390 Cailho 34 166 Cf 87
34210 Cailhol 34 166 Ce 88
11140 Cailla 11 178 Cb 92
46140 Caillac 46 137 Bc 82
34550 Caillan 34 167 Dc 88
31420 Caillaouet 31 164 Af 89
33750 Caillau 33 135 Zd 79
40260 Caillaube 40 146 Ye 85
17120 Caillaud, le 17 122 Za 75
36500 Caillaudière 36 101 Bc 68
32190 Caillavet 32 163 Ab 86
06750 Caille 06 158 Ge 86
85410 Caillère-Saint-Hilaire, la 85 98 Za 69
16170 Cailletières, les 16 123 Zf 74
76460 Cailleville 76 36 Ae 50
31620 Caillol 31 150 Bc 85
36290 Caillonnière, la 36 100 Ba 67
45560 Caillot, le 45 87 Bf 61
36800 Caillots, les 36 101 Bc 68
02300 Caillouël 02 40 Da 51
27120 Caillouët 27 50 Bb 54
27120 Caillouet-Orgeville 27 50 Bb 55
59250 Cailloux, Triez- 59 30 Da 44
69270 Cailloux-sur-Fontaines 69M 130 Ef 73
76690 Cailly 76 37 Bb 51
27490 Cailly-sur-Eure 27 49 Bb 54
14480 Cainet 14 35 Zc 53
81390 Caïphe, le 81 151 Bf 86
11190 Cairac 11 178 Cb 91
84290 Cairanne 84 155 Ef 83
26620 Caire, la 26 144 Fd 81
04250 Caire, le 04 157 Ga 82
26120 Caires, les 26 143 Fa 79
14610 Cairon 14 35 Zd 53
60400 Caisnes 60 39 Da 51
30132 Caissargues 30 154 Ec 86
46140 Caix 46 137 Bb 82
80170 Caix 80 39 Cd 50
66300 Caixas 66 179 Ce 93
65500 Caixon 65 162 Aa 88
46160 Cajarc 46 138 Bf 82
31870 Calac 31 164 Bc 88
20224 Calacuccia CTC 182 Ka 94
13090 Calade, la 13 170 Fc 87
20138 Cala di Cigliu CTC 184 Ie 98
62100 Calais 62 27 Bf 43
46150 Calamane 46 137 Bc 81
56240 Calan 56 80 We 61
56240 Calan 56 79 Wf 62
26560 Calandre, le 26 156 Fd 83
22160 Calanhel 22 63 Wd 58
13520 Calans, les 13 169 Ef 86
20137 Cala Rossa CTC 185 Kc 99
13480 Calas 13 170 Fc 88
20224 Calasima CTC 180 If 95
15700 Calau 15 139 Cb 78
65190 Calavanté 65 163 Aa 89
20245 Calca CTC 182 Id 94
20111 Calcatoggio CTC 182 Ie 96
20111 Calcatoghju = Calcatoggio CTC 182 Ie 96
66600 Calce 66 179 Ce 92
12200 Calcomier 12 151 Bf 83
20131 Caldarello, Piianotolli- CTC 184 Ka 100
66760 Caldégas 66 178 Bf 94
33650 Calenta 33 135 Zc 81
20214 Calenzana CTC 180 If 93
24150 Calès 24 137 Ae 79
46350 Calès 46 138 Bd 80
47230 Calezun 47 148 Ab 83
64800 Calibet 64 174 Ze 90
47600 Calignac 47 148 Ac 84
61100 Caligny 61 47 Zc 56
20214 Calinzana = Calenzana CTC 180 If 93
64560 Calla 64 174 Zb 91
44160 Callac 44 81 Xf 64
56420 Callac 56 81 Xc 62
22160 Callac = Kallag 22 63 Wd 58
83830 Callas 83 172 Gd 87
40430 Callen 40 147 Zd 83
76270 Callengeville 76 37 Bd 50
27800 Calleville 27 49 Ae 53
76890 Calleville-les-Deux-Eglises 76 37 Ba 50
32190 Callian 32 163 Ab 87
83440 Callian 83 172 Ge 87
59270 Callicannes 59 30 Cd 44
12170 Calm, la 12 152 Cd 84
81430 Calm, la 81 151 Cc 85
66400 Calmeilles 66 179 Ce 93
12410 Calmejane 12 152 Ce 84
46120 Calméjanne 46 138 Bf 80
81260 Calmels 81 166 Cd 86
12400 Calmels-et-le-Viala 12 152 Ce 85
81350 Calmette 81 151 Cb 84
11340 Calmette, la 11 178 Ca 91
30190 Calmette, la 30 154 Eb 85
34330 Calmette, la 34 167 Cf 87
12450 Calmont 12 151 Cd 83
31560 Calmont 31 165 Bd 89
70240 Calmoutier 70 93 Gb 63
42240 Caloire 42 129 Eb 76
47430 Calonges 47 148 Ab 82
24410 Calonie, la 24 136 Ab 78
62160 Calonne 62 29 Ce 46
62260 Calonne-Ricouart 62 29 Cd 45
62350 Calonne-sur-la-Lys 62 29 Cd 45
22100 Calorguen 22 65 Xf 58
62170 Calotterie, la 62 28 Be 46
40090 Caloy, le 40 147 Zc 85
40090 Caloy, le 40 147 Zd 85
37460 Caltière, la 37 101 Bb 66
69300 Caluire-et-Cuire 69M 130 Ef 74
56310 Calvaire 56 79 Wf 61
44170 Calvernais, la 44 82 Yb 63
20260 Calvi CTC 180 Ie 93
12120 Calviac 12 152 Cc 83
46190 Calviac 46 138 Ca 79
47150 Calviac 47 136 Ae 81
24370 Calviac-en-Périgord 24 137 Bb 79
20270 Calviani CTC 183 Kc 96
12320 Calvignac 12 139 Cc 81
46160 Calvignac 46 138 Be 82
15340 Calvinet 15 139 Cc 80
30420 Calvisson 30 154 Eb 86
09120 Calzan 09 177 Be 90
20243 Calzarellu CTC 183 Kc 97
20123 Calzola CTC 182 If 98
13510 Camaisse 13 170 Fb 87
65500 Camalès 65 162 Aa 88
12440 Camalet 12 151 Cb 83
81330 Camalières 81 166 Cd 86
09290 Camarade 09 164 Bb 90
12360 Camarès 12 152 Cf 86
56250 Camaret 56 80 Xc 62
84850 Camaret sur-Aigues 84 155 Ef 83
29570 Camaret-sur-Mer 29 61 Vc 59
33750 Camarsac 33 135 Zd 80
81500 Cambards, les 81 165 Be 86
46140 Cambayrac 46 150 Bb 82
14230 Cambe, la 14 47 Yf 52
27170 Cambe, la 27 49 Ae 54
61160 Cambe, la 61 48 Aa 55
46340 Cambelève 46 137 Bb 81
31470 Cambernard 31 164 Bb 88
50200 Cambernon 50 46 Yd 54
81320 Cambert 81 166 Cf 86
33880 Cambes 33 135 Zd 80
46100 Cambes 46 138 Bf 81
47350 Cambes 47 136 Ab 81
14610 Cambes-en-Plaine 14 47 Zd 53
20244 Cambia CTC 183 Kb 94
31460 Cambiac 31 165 Be 88
12360 Cambias 12 167 Cf 86
81430 Cambieu 81 151 Cb 85
11240 Cambieure 11 165 Ca 90
62470 Camblain-Châtelain 62 29 Cc 46
62690 Camblain-L'Abbé 62 29 Cd 46
33360 Camblanes-et-Meynac 33 135 Zd 80
62690 Cambligneul 62 29 Cd 46
30170 Cambo 30 154 De 85
64250 Cambo-les-Bains 64 160 Yd 88
81990 Cambon 81 151 Cb 85
12400 Cambon, le 12 152 Ce 85
12500 Cambon, le 12 139 Cf 81
81430 Cambon-du-Temple 81 151 Cc 85
34330 Cambon-et-Salvergues 34 167 Cf 87
81470 Cambon-lès-Lavaur 81 165 Bf 87
24540 Cambou, le 24 137 Af 81
12260 Camboulan 12 138 Bf 81
12290 Camboulas 12 152 Cd 83
12160 Camboulazet 12 151 Cc 83
46100 Camboulit 46 138 Bf 81
81580 Cambounet-sur-le-Sor 81 165 Ca 87
81260 Cambournés 81 166 Cc 87
81260 Cambous 81 166 Cd 86
81360 Camboussié, la 81 166 Cb 86
22210 Cambout, le 22 64 Xc 60
11320 Camboyer 11 165 Be 88
59400 Cambrai 59 30 Db 47
14340 Cambremer 14 35 Aa 54
62149 Cambrin 62 29 Ce 45
02140 Cambron 02 41 Df 50
80132 Cambron 80 28 Be 48
60290 Cambronne-lès-Clermont 60 39 Cc 53
60170 Cambronne-les-Ribecourt 60 39 Cf 51
46100 Camburat 46 138 Bf 81
64520 Came 64 161 Yf 88
66300 Camelas 66 179 Ce 93
02300 Camelin 02 40 Da 51
40500 Camelot 40 147 Zc 86
61120 Camembert 61 48 Ab 55
44410 Camer 44 81 Xe 64
20238 Camera CTC 181 Kc 91
44410 Camerun 44 81 Xe 64
50570 Cametours 50 46 Ye 54
27470 Camfleur 27 49 Ad 54
33420 Camiac-et-Saint-Denis 33 135 Ze 80
62176 Camiers 62 28 Bd 45
46800 Caminel 46 150 Ba 83
33190 Camiran 33 135 Zf 81
22450 Camlez 22 63 We 56
81540 Cammazes, les 81 165 Ca 88
56130 Camoël 56 81 Xd 64
13011 Camoins, les 13 170 Fd 89
13011 Camoins-les-Bains 13 170 Fd 89
09500 Camon 09 178 Bf 90
80330 Camon Longueau 80 39 Cc 49
33830 Camontès 33 134 Za 82
64470 Camou-Cihigue 64 161 Za 90
64120 Camou-Mixe-Suhast 64 161 Yf 88
65410 Camous 65 175 Ac 91
63820 Camp, le 63 127 Cd 74
12560 Campagnac 12 152 Da 82
47470 Campagnac 47 149 Af 83
81140 Campagnac 81 151 Bf 84
24550 Campagnac-lès-Quercy 24 137 Bb 80
34230 Campagnan 34 167 Dc 87
32800 Campagne-d'Armagnac 32 148 Zf 85
24260 Campagne 24 137 Af 79
34160 Campagne 34 154 Ea 86
40090 Campagne 40 147 Zc 85
60640 Campagne 60 39 Cf 51
80132 Campagne 80 28 Be 48

A B C D E F G H I J K L M N O P Q R S T U V W X Y Z

Campagne | 251

11140 Campagne-de-Sault 11 178 Ca 92
62650 Campagne-lès-Boulonnais 62 28 Ca 45
62340 Campagne-lès-Guînes 62 27 Bf 43
62870 Campagne-lès-Hesdin 62 28 Bf 46
83690 Campagne-Neuve 83 171 Gb 87
09350 Campagne-sur-Arize 09 164 Bc 90
11260 Campagne-sur-Aude 11 178 Cb 91
12160 Campagnet 12 151 Cc 83
62380 Campagnette 62 29 Ca 44
14500 Campagnolles 14 47 Za 55
12160 Campan 12 151 Cc 83
65710 Campan 65 175 Ab 90
20229 Campana CTC 183 Kc 94
14260 Campandré-Valcongrain 14 47 Zc 55
13650 Campane, la 13 174 Fd 87
20227 Campanella CTC 183 Ka 96
65170 Camparan 65 175 Ac 91
32420 Campardon 32 163 Ae 88
44750 Campbon 44 81 Ya 64
34520 Camp-d'Alton, le 34 153 Dc 85
57570 Camp de Cattenom 57 44 Gb 52
06660 Camp-des-Fourches 06 158 Gf 82
60112 Campdeville 60 38 Ca 52
76390 Campdos, le 76 38 Bd 50
20215 Camp du Cap Sud CTC 181 Kd 93
83330 Camp-du-Castellet, le 83 171 Fe 89
67130 Camp du Struthof 67 60 Hb 58
14350 Campeaux 14 47 Za 55
60220 Campeaux 60 38 Be 51
76360 Campeaux, les 76 37 Af 51
35330 Campel 35 81 Xf 61
34390 Campels 34 167 Cf 87
27950 Campenard 27 50 Bc 54
56800 Campénéac 56 81 Xe 61
30750 Campestre-et-Luc 30 153 Dc 85
40090 Campet-et-Lamolère 40 147 Zc 85
11490 Campets, les 11 166 Cf 90
32200 Campezaygues 32 163 Ae 87
11230 Camp-Ferrier 11 178 Ca 91
72610 Campfleur 72 68 Aa 58
59133 Camphin-en-Carembault 59 30 Cf 45
59780 Camphin-en-Pévèle 59 30 Db 45
20270 Campi CTC 183 Kc 95
62170 Campigneulles-les-Grandes 62 28 Be 46
62170 Campigneulles-les-Petites 62 28 Be 46
14490 Campigny 14 34 Zb 53
27500 Campigny-la-Futelaye 27 36 Ad 53
20290 Campile CTC 181 Kc 94
65300 Campistrous 65 163 Ac 90
20252 Campitello CTC 181 Kb 93
34210 Camplong 34 166 Cd 88
34260 Camplong 34 167 Da 86
83250 Camp-Long 83 172 Gb 89
11200 Camplong-d'Aude 11 166 Cd 90
76340 Campneuseville 76 38 Bd 49
20142 Campo CTC 182 Ka 97
20229 Campo d'Onico CTC 183 Kb 94
64122 Campoito 64 160 Yb 88
66730 Campôme 66 178 Cc 93
20110 Campomoro, Belvédère- CTC 184 Ie 99
32300 Campouran 32 163 Ac 88
12460 Campouriez 12 139 Cd 80
66730 Campoussy 66 178 Cc 92
59570 Camp-Perdu, le 59 31 Df 47
34360 Camprafaud 34 167 Cf 88
20260 Camp Raffalli CTC 180 Ie 93
09300 Camp-Redon 09 178 Bf 91
34210 Campredon 34 166 Cd 88
60480 Camprémy 60 38 Cb 51
30750 Camprieu 30 153 Dc 84
50210 Camprond 50 34 Yd 54
28240 Camprond-en-Gâtine 28 69 Ba 58
34700 Camp-Rouch 34 153 Dc 86
19430 Camps 19 138 Bf 79
12370 Camps, les 12 152 Ce 85
34380 Camps, les 34 154 De 86
82370 Campsas 82 150 Bb 85
11230 Camp-Saure 11 178 Ca 91
24140 Campsegret 24 136 Ad 79
80540 Camps-en-Amiénois 80 38 Bf 49
83170 Camps-la-Source 83 171 Ga 88
11190 Camps-sur-L'Agly 11 178 Cc 91
33660 Camps-sur-l'Isle 33 135 Zf 78
11230 Camp-Sylvestre 11 178 Ca 91
64190 Camptort 64 161 Zb 89
20287 Campu CTC 181 Kc 91
12580 Campuac 12 139 Cd 81
20270 Campu a u Quarciu CTC 183 Kc 96
33750 Campugnan 33 135 Zc 77
20218 Campu Pianu CTC 181 Ka 93
20235 Campu Rossu = Campu Rosu CTC 181 Kb 94
20235 Campu Rosu CTC 181 Kb 94
65230 Campuzan 65 163 Ac 89
56330 Camros 56 80 Wf 61
11340 Camurac 11 178 Bf 92
39140 Camus, les 39 106 Fc 68
46140 Camy 46 137 Bb 82
46350 Camy 46 137 Bc 80
64490 Camy 64 174 Zc 91
12410 Canabières, les 12 152 Ce 84
12740 Canabols 12 152 Cd 82
12560 Canac 12 152 Da 82
81320 Canac 81 167 Cf 86
49250 Canada, le 49 84 Ze 64
83390 Canadel 83 171 Ga 89
20219 Canaglia CTC 183 Ka 96
20230 Canale-di-Verde CTC 183 Kc 95
09130 Canalès 09 164 Bc 89
12540 Canals 12 153 Db 85
82170 Canals 82 150 Bb 85
80670 Canaples 80 29 Cb 48
27400 Canappeville 27 49 Ba 54
14800 Canapville 14 36 Aa 53
61120 Canapville 61 48 Ab 55
19800 Canard 19 126 Bf 76
20217 Canari CTC 181 Kc 91
30350 Canaules-et-Argentières 30 154 Ea 85
06750 Canaux 06 158 Ge 86
20235 Canavaggia CTC 181 Kb 93
66360 Canaveilles 66 178 Cb 93
35260 Cancale = Kankaven 35 65 Ya 56
20146 Cancaraccia CTC 185 Kb 99
14230 Canchy 14 47 Za 53
80150 Canchy 80 28 Bf 47
47290 Cancon 47 136 Ad 81
46120 Cancros 46 138 Bf 80
40990 Candale 40 146 Yf 86
66260 Can Damon 66 179 Cd 94
12490 Candas 12 152 Cf 84
80750 Candas 80 29 Cb 48
64570 Candau 64 174 Zb 90
49440 Candé 49 83 Yf 63
32400 Candelle 32 162 Zf 87
37500 Candes-Saint-Martin 37 99 Aa 65
41120 Candé-sur-Beuvron 41 86 Bb 64
34130 Candillargues 34 168 Ea 87
40280 Candille 40 147 Zc 85
60310 Candor 60 39 Cf 51
40180 Candresse 40 161 Za 86
24300 Caneau, le 24 124 Ae 76
24200 Canéda, la 24 137 Bb 79
76260 Canehan 76 37 Bc 49
33610 Canéjean 33 134 Zc 80
20217 Canelle CTC 181 Kb 92
31310 Canens 31 164 Bb 89
40090 Canenx-et-Réaut 40 147 Zd 84
11200 Canet 11 166 Cf 89
33125 Canet 33 134 Zb 82
34800 Canet 34 167 Dc 87
12290 Canet-de-Salars 12 152 Ce 83
12560 Canet-d' Olt 12 152 Da 82
66140 Canet-en-Roussillon 66 179 Da 92
66140 Canet-Plage 66 179 Da 92
60600 Canettecourt 60 39 Cc 52
62270 Canettemont 62 29 Cc 47
81190 Canezac 81 151 Ca 83
37270 Cangé 37 85 Af 64
37530 Cangey 37 86 Ba 64
40400 Cangrand 40 146 Za 85
15220 Canhac 15 139 Cc 80
56310 Caniac 56 79 We 61
46240 Caniac-du-Causse 46 138 Bd 81
48500 Canilhac 48 152 Da 82
48500 Canilhac, Banassac- 48 152 Da 82
AD100 Canillo ◘ AND 177 Bd 93
50750 Canisy 50 46 Ye 54
80400 Canizy 80 39 Da 50
02800 Canlers 02 40 Db 50
62310 Canlers 62 29 Ca 46
12420 Canloin 12 139 Ce 79
60680 Canly 60 39 Ce 52
12170 Cannac 12 152 Cd 84
20290 Cannaja CTC 181 Kc 94
60310 Cannectancourt 60 39 Cf 51
20145 Cannella CTC 183 Kc 98
20151 Cannelle CTC 182 Ie 96
20238 Cannelle CTC 181 Kb 91
14100 Cannerie, la 14 48 Ac 54
06400 Cannes 06 173 Ha 87
20090 Cannes, les CTC 182 Ie 97
77130 Cannes-Ecluse 77 72 Cf 58
30260 Cannes-et-Clairan 30 154 Ea 85
80140 Cannessières 80 38 Be 49
32400 Cannet 32 162 Zf 87
06110 Cannet, le 06 173 Ha 87
83340 Cannet-des-Maures, le 83 172 Gc 88
20146 Canni CTC 185 Kb 99
60310 Canny-sur-Matz 60 39 Ce 51
60220 Canny-sur-Thérain 60 38 Be 51
66680 Canohès 66 179 Cf 93
14270 Canon 14 48 Zf 54
33950 Canon, le 33 134 Ye 80
09270 Canou, le 09 165 Bd 89
34700 Canourgue, la 34 153 Dc 86
48500 Canourgue, la 48 153 Db 82
46150 Canourgues 46 137 Bb 81
76450 Canouville 76 36 Ad 50
33340 Canquillac 33 122 Za 77
56540 Canquisquélen 56 79 We 61
48400 Cans et Cévennes 48 153 Dd 83
12150 Cantabel 12 152 Da 83
34380 Cantagrils 34 168 De 86
59267 Cantaing-sur-Escaut 59 30 Da 48
12470 Cantaloube 12 140 Cf 82
65150 Cantaous 65 163 Ac 90
06340 Cantaron 06 159 Hb 86
40210 Cantaure 40 146 Za 83
09700 Canté 09 165 Bd 89
31330 Cantegril 31 164 Bb 86
40210 Cantegrit 40 147 Zb 83
24510 Cantelaube 24 136 Ae 79
76380 Canteleu 76 37 Ba 52
80600 Canteleux 80 29 Cb 47
47150 Canteloube 47 137 Af 81
14370 Canteloup 14 35 Zf 54
50330 Canteloup 50 34 Yd 51
62380 Cantemerie 62 29 Ca 44
24130 Cante-Merle 24 136 Ac 79
33460 Cantenac, Margaux- 33 134 Zc 78
49460 Cantenay 49 83 Zc 63
49460 Cantenay-Epinard 49 83 Zc 63
14620 Cantepie 14 48 Zf 55
50500 Cantepie 50 46 Ye 53
49440 Canteries, les 49 83 Za 63
27420 Cantiers 27 50 Bd 53
80500 Cantigny 80 39 Cc 51
24530 Cantillac 24 124 Ad 76
59169 Cantin 59 30 Da 47
17380 Cantinauds, les 17 110 Zc 72
37370 Cantinière, la 37 85 Ad 63
32110 Cantiran 32 148 Zf 86
12230 Cantobre 12 153 Db 84
33760 Cantois 33 135 Ze 80
20122 Cantoli CTC 183 Ka 98
48320 Cantonnet 48 153 Dd 82
22480 Canuhuel 22 63 Wf 58
27500 Canurie, la 27 49 Ac 53
50580 Canville-la-Rocque 50 46 Yc 52
76560 Canville-les-Deux-Eglises 76 37 Af 50
76450 Cany-Barville 76 36 Ad 50
27300 Caorches-Saint-Nicolas 27 49 Ad 54
22300 Caouënnec-Lanvézéac 22 63 Wd 56
40170 Caoule 40 146 Ye 84
47510 Caoulet, le 47 149 Ad 83
80132 Caours 80 28 Bf 48
50620 Cap 50 46 Ye 53
20100 Capanella CTC 184 Ka 99
64130 Caparnia 64 161 Za 89
40170 Capas 40 146 Ye 84
15230 Capat, le 15 139 Ce 79
88152 Capavenir Vosges 88 76 Gc 59
64800 Capbis 64 162 Ze 90
40130 Capbreton 40 160 Yd 87
47420 Capchicot 47 148 Zf 83
29170 Cap-Coz 29 78 Wa 61
34300 Cap-d'Agde, le 34 168 Dd 89
06320 Cap-d'Ail 06 173 Hc 86
33113 Capdarrieux 33 147 Zd 82
33860 Cap-d' Avias, le 33 123 Zd 77
31370 Capdebat 31 164 Bb 88
47430 Cap-de-Bosc 47 148 Aa 82
40240 Cap-de-la-Hargue 40 148 Zf 85
40170 Cap-de-L'Homy 40 146 Yd 84
40350 Cap-de-Monpeyroux 40 161 Yf 87
46100 Capdenac 46 138 Ca 81
12700 Capdenac-Gare 12 138 Ca 81
12510 Capdenaguet 12 152 Cc 82
40210 Cap-de-Pin 40 146 Za 84
09140 Cap de Siguens 09 176 Ba 91
33113 Capdet 33 147 Zc 82
33121 Cap-de Ville 33 134 Yf 78
81250 Capdos 81 152 Cc 86
24540 Capdrot 24 137 Af 80
33125 Cap-du-Bos 33 134 Zc 82
47160 Cap-du-Bosc 47 148 Ab 83
32260 Cape, le 32 163 Ad 87
13104 Capeau 13 169 Ee 87
66750 Capellans, les 66 179 Da 93
12850 Capelle 12 152 Cc 82
59213 Capelle 59 31 Dd 47
02260 Capelle, la 02 41 Df 49
46000 Capelle, la 46 150 Bc 82
48500 Capelle, la 48 153 Db 82
81140 Capelle, la 81 150 Be 85
12260 Capelle-Balaguier, la 12 151 Bf 82
12240 Capelle-Bleys, la 12 151 Cb 83
12130 Capelle-Bonance, la 12 152 Da 82
12430 Capelle-Farcel, la 12 152 Cd 84
62690 Capelle-Fermont 62 29 Cd 46
62360 Capelle-lès-Boulogne, la 62 26 Be 44
27270 Capelle-les-Grands 27 49 Ac 54
62140 Capelle-lès-Hesdin 62 28 Bf 46
12140 Capelle-Neuve-Eglise 12 139 Ce 81
12450 Capelle-Saint-Martin, la 12 151 Cd 83
12450 Capelle-Viaur, la 12 152 Cd 83
13460 Capellière, la 13 169 Ed 87
11700 Capendu 11 166 Cd 89
76116 Capendu 76 37 Bb 52
31410 Capens 31 164 Bb 88
34310 Capestang 34 167 Da 89
24490 Capet 24 135 Zf 78
81260 Capette 81 166 Cd 86
33970 Cap Ferret 33 134 Ye 81
13310 Caphan 13 169 Ee 87
33550 Capian 33 135 Ze 80
20000 Capigliolo CTC 182 Id 97
83600 Capitou, le 83 172 Ge 88
33770 Caplanne 33 134 Za 81
40230 Caplet 40 160 Ye 86
33220 Caplong 33 136 Aa 80
12120 Caplongue 12 152 Cd 83
60120 Caply 60 38 Cb 51
06190 Cap-Martin 06 159 Hc 86
46170 Capmié 46 150 Bc 83
20236 Caporaline CTC 183 Kb 94
09400 Capoulet 09 177 Bd 92
57450 Cappel 57 57 Gf 54
32800 Cap-Pelat 32 148 Aa 85
59630 Cappelle-Brouck 59 27 Cb 43
59242 Cappelle-en-Pévèle 59 30 Db 45
59180 Cappelle-la-Grande 59 27 Cc 43
20113 Cappiciolo CTC 184 If 98
80340 Cappy 80 39 Ce 49
40410 Capsus 40 147 Zb 82
83400 Capte, la 83 172 Ga 90
33840 Captieux 33 147 Ze 83
20137 Capu CTC 185 Kb 98
33113 Capuron 33 147 Zc 82
76660 Capval 76 37 Bc 49
65130 Capvern 65 163 Ab 90
65130 Capvern-les-Bains 65 163 Ab 90
20124 Carabona CTC 185 Kb 98
22320 Caradeuc 22 64 Wf 58
31460 Caragoudes 31 165 Be 88
31460 Caraman 31 165 Be 87
66720 Caramany 66 179 Cd 92
20144 Caramontinu CTC 185 Kc 98
46600 Caran 46 138 Bc 79
29660 Carantec 29 62 Wa 56
50570 Carantilly 50 46 Ye 54
81100 Carauce 81 166 Cc 87
24540 Caravelle 24 137 Af 80
46160 Carayac 46 138 Bf 81
47500 Carayac 47 137 Af 81
09000 Caraybat 09 177 Bd 91
81530 Carayon 81 166 Cd 86
50190 Carbassue 50 46 Yd 53
49420 Carbay 49 82 Ye 62
20170 Carbini CTC 185 Ka 98
20167 Carbinica CTC 182 Ie 97
20228 Carbonacce CTC 181 Kc 91
33560 Carbon-Blanc 33 135 Zd 79
31390 Carbonne 31 164 Bb 89
20133 Carbuccia CTC 182 If 96
14740 Carcagny 14 34 Zc 53
11190 Carcanet 11 178 Cc 91
09460 Carcanières 09 178 Ca 92
11140 Carcanières-les-Bains 11 178 Ca 92
33121 Carcans 33 134 Yf 78
33121 Carcans-Plage 33 134 Ye 78
40400 Carcarès-Sainte-Croix 40 147 Zb 85
11000* Carcassonne 11 166 Cc 89
12120 Carcenac 12 152 Cd 83
12160 Carcenac-Peyralès 12 151 Cc 83
40400 Carcen-Ponson 40 147 Zb 85
83570 Carces 83 171 Gb 88
20229 Carcheto-Brustico CTC 183 Kc 94
20167 Carcopino, Sarrola- CTC 182 If 96
20167 Carcopinu, Sarrula = Carcopino, Sarrola- CTC 182 If 96
27400 Carcouet 27 49 Ba 54
35680 Carcraon 35 66 Ye 61
12340 Carcuac 12 139 Cd 82
46100 Cardaillac 46 138 Bf 80
04270 Cardaires, les 04 157 Ga 85
33410 Cardan 33 135 Zd 81
47290 Cardayres 47 136 Ad 81
31350 Cardeilhac 31 163 Ae 89
64360 Cardesse 64 161 Zc 89
30350 Cardet 30 154 Ea 84
20146 Cardetto CTC 185 Kb 99
20200 Cardo CTC 181 Kc 92
80260 Cardonette 80 39 Cc 49
47450 Cardonnet 47 149 Ad 83
80500 Cardonnois, le 80 39 Cc 51
14230 Cardonville 14 46 Yf 52
20190 Cardo-Torgia CTC 184 If 97
35190 Cardroc 35 65 Ya 59
20169 Cardu CTC 185 Ka 100
20218 Cardu CTC 181 Kb 94
44170 Cardunel 44 82 Yc 63
20190 Cardu Torgia = Cardo-Torgia CTC 184 If 97
14170 Carel 14 48 Zf 54
53120 Carelles 53 66 Za 58
82140 Carême 82 150 Be 84
56490 Carénan 56 64 Xc 60
62144 Carency 62 29 Ce 46
46110 Carennac 46 138 Be 79
50500 Carentan-les-Marais 50 46 Ye 53
47500 Carentas 47 137 Af 82
56910 Carentoir 56 81 Xf 62
22800 Carestremble 22 64 Xa 58
35120 Carfantin 35 65 Yb 57
22800 Carfot 22 64 Xa 58
20130 Cargèse CTC 182 Id 96
20130 Carghjese = Cargèse CTC 182 Id 96
20164 Cargiaca CTC 184 Ka 98
82340 Carhaule 82 149 Ae 84
22150 Caribet 22 64 Xb 58
08110 Carignan 08 42 Fb 51
33360 Carignan-de-Bordeaux 33 135 Zd 80
22130 Carimel 22 65 Xf 58
89360 Carisey 89 90 Df 61
38460 Carisieu 38 131 Fb 74
20115 Cariu CTC 182 Id 95
33720 Carjuzan 33 135 Zd 81
09130 Carla-Bayle 09 164 Bc 90
09300 Carla-de-Roquefort 09 177 Be 91
15130 Carlat 15 139 Cd 79
34600 Carlencas-et-Levas 34 167 Db 87
60170 Carlepont 60 39 Da 51
73630 Carlet 73 132 Gb 75
57490 Carling 57 57 Ge 53
11170 Carlipa 11 165 Ca 89
24590 Carlucet 24 137 Bb 79
46500 Carlucet 46 138 Bd 80
81990 Carlus 81 151 Ca 85
24370 Carlux 24 137 Bc 79
62830 Carly 62 28 Be 45
81400 Carmaux 81 151 Ca 84
81250 Carmenel 81 152 Cc 85
56480 Carmès 56 64 Wf 60
50390 Carmesnil 50 46 Yc 52
48210 Carnac 48 153 Dc 83
56470 Carnac 56 80 Wf 63
56340 Carnac-Plage 56 80 Wf 63
46140 Carnac-Rouffiac 46 150 Bb 82
30260 Carnas 30 154 Df 86
61100 Carneille, la 61 47 Zd 56
56230 Carnély 56 81 Xd 63
50240 Carnet 50 66 Yd 57
50330 Carneville 50 33 Yd 50
47800 Carnicot 47 136 Ac 81
59217 Carnières 59 30 Dc 47
59112 Carnin 59 30 Cf 45
04150 Carniol 04 156 Fd 85
22160 Carnoët 22 63 Wc 58
34280 Carnon-Plage 34 168 Df 87
30140 Carnoulès 30 154 Df 84
83660 Carnoules 83 171 Gb 89
13470 Carnoux en-Provence 13 171 Fd 89
59144 Carnoy 59 31 De 47
80300 Carnoy 80 39 Ce 49
29470 Caro 29 61 Vd 58
56140 Caro 56 81 Xe 61
64220 Caro 64 160 Ye 90
20290 Carogne CTC 181 Kc 94
09120 Carol 09 177 Bd 90
66760 Carol 66 177 Bf 93
09320 Carol, le 09 177 Bc 91
32300 Carole 32 163 Ac 87
50740 Carolles 50 46 Yc 56
84330 Caromb 84 155 Fa 84
29370 Caront-Lutin 29 78 Wa 60
22430 Caroual 22 64 Xc 57
44680 Carouère, la 44 96 Ya 66
20100 Carpatulia, Bergerie CTC 184 If 99
84200 Carpentras 84 155 Fa 84
20229 Carpineto CTC 183 Kc 94
14650 Carpiquet 14 35 Zd 53
40170 Carpit 40 146 Ye 85
20170 Carpulitanu Radici CTC 185 Ka 99
50480 Carquebut 50 46 Ye 52
44470 Carquefou 44 82 Yd 65
83320 Carqueiranne 83 171 Ga 90
22240 Carquois, la 22 64 Xd 57
34490 Carratiers, les 34 167 Da 88
76220 Carreaux, les 76 38 Bd 52
89130 Carreaux, les 89 89 Db 62
49530 Carrée, la 49 82 Ye 65
49390 Carrefour, le 49 84 Aa 64
50260 Carrefour, le 50 33 Yc 52
50860 Carrefour-de-Paris, le 50 46 Yf 55
73470 Carrel, le 73 131 Fe 75
81190 Carrelie, la 81 151 Cb 84
82140 Carrendier 82 150 Be 84
80700 Carrépuis 80 39 Ce 50
40310 Carrère 40 148 Aa 84
64160 Carrère 64 162 Ze 88
32170 Carrère, la 32 163 Ac 88
58350 Carrés, les 58 89 Db 65
64270 Carresse-Cassaber 64 161 Za 88
31430 Carretère 31 164 Ba 89
82000 Carreyrat 82 150 Bc 85
33680 Carreyre 33 134 Ye 79
46090 Carrières, les 46 137 Bc 81
55200 Carrières, les 55 55 Fd 56
78955 Carrières-sous-Poissy 78 51 Ca 55
47450 Carritor 47 149 Ad 83
13500 Carro 13 170 Fa 89
36180 Carroir 36 101 Bc 66
86200 Carroir, le 86 99 Aa 66
37240 Carroir-Jodel, le 37 100 Ae 66
01160 Carronnières, les 01 119 Fb 72
06510 Carros 06 159 Hb 86
45730 Carrouge, le 45 88 Cb 62
61320 Carrouges 61 67 Zf 57
18160 Carroux, la 18 102 Ca 68
49270 Carroye, le 49 83 Yf 65
74300 Carroz d'Arâches, les 74 120 Gd 72
13620 Carry-le-Rouet 13 170 Fa 89
33390 Cars 33 134 Zc 78
87230 Cars, les 87 125 Ba 74
15290 Carsac 15 139 Cb 79
24200 Carsac-Aillac 24 137 Bb 79
24610 Carsac-de-Gurson 24 136 Aa 79
30130 Carsan 30 155 Ed 83
27300 Carsix 27 49 Ae 54
68130 Carspach 68 95 Hb 63
20137 Cartalavone CTC 185 Ka 99
37350 Carte, la 37 100 Af 67
33390 Cartelègue 33 122 Zc 77
50270 Carteret 50 46 Yb 52
72800 Cartes, les 72 84 Aa 63
20244 Carticasi CTC 183 Kb 94
33990 Cartignac 33 122 Yf 77
59244 Cartignies 59 31 Df 48
80200 Cartigny 80 39 Da 49
14330 Cartigny-L'Epinay 14 47 Yf 53
34220 Cartouyre 34 166 Ce 88
28480 Cartrais, la 28 69 Af 59
56110 Carvarno 56 79 Wc 60
24170 Carves 24 137 Ba 80
14350 Carville 14 47 Za 55
79170 Carville 79 111 Zd 72
76190 Carville-la-Folletière 76 37 Ae 51
76560 Carville-Pot-de-Fer 76 36 Ae 50
62220 Carvin 62 30 Cf 46
20100 Casa CTC 185 Ka 99
20270 Casabertola CTC 183 Kc 96
20237 Casabianca CTC 181 Kc 94
20270 Casabianda CTC 183 Kd 96
20111 Casagliò = Casaglione CTC 182 Ie 96
20111 Casaglione CTC 182 Ie 96
20140 Casalabriva CTC 184 If 98
20215 Casalta CTC 181 Kc 94
20224 Casamaccioli CTC 182 Ka 95
20243 Casamozza CTC 183 Kc 97
20290 Casamozza CTC 181 Kc 93
20230 Casani CTC 183 Kd 95
20250 Casanova CTC 183 Kb 95
20235 Casa Pitti CTC 181 Kb 94
20620 Casatorra CTC 181 Kc 93
64360 Casaubieil 64 161 Zb 89
29390 Cascadec 29 79 Wb 61
11360 Cascastel-des-Corbières 11 179 Ce 91
46250 Cascavel 46 137 Bb 81
15120 Case, la 15 139 Cc 80
66130 Casefabre 66 179 Cd 93
40700 Casenave 40 161 Zc 87
13680 Caseneuve 13 170 Fb 87
84750 Caseneuve 84 156 Fc 85
64560 Caserne, la 64 174 Za 90
66600 Cases-de-Pène 66 179 Ce 92
20270 Casevecchie CTC 183 Kc 96
20147 Caspiu CTC 182 Id 95
64270 Cassaber 64 161 Yf 88
31420 Cassagnabère-Tournas 31 163 Ae 89
48400 Cassagnas 48 153 De 83
31260 Cassagne 31 164 Af 90
24120 Cassagne, la 24 137 Bb 78
32220 Cassagne, la 32 164 Af 88
46700 Cassagnes 46 137 Ba 81
66720 Cassagnes 66 179 Cd 92
12120 Cassagnes-Bégonhès 12 151 Cd 83
12340 Cassagnoles 12 152 Cf 82
30350 Cassagnoles 30 154 Ea 84
34210 Cassagnoles 34 166 Cd 88
32100 Cassaigne 32 148 Ac 85
11270 Cassaigne, la 11 165 Bf 89
11190 Cassaignes 11 178 Cb 91
56130 Cassan 56 81 Xe 63
30750 Cassanas 30 153 Dc 84
15340 Cassaniouze 15 139 Cc 80
20214 Cassano CTC 180 If 93
20214 Cassanu = Cassano CTC 180 If 93
32320 Cassebertats 32 163 Ac 87
59670 Cassel 59 27 Cc 44
40380 Cassen 40 146 Za 86
47440 Casseneuil 47 149 Ad 82
41310 Cassereau, le 41 85 Af 62
05600 Casses, les 05 145 Gd 81
11320 Cassés, les 11 165 Bf 88
05220 Casset, le 05 145 Gc 79

252 | Campagne-de-Sault

33190 Casseuil 33 135 Zf 81
63970 Cassière, la 63 128 Cf 74
15150 Cassiès 15 139 Cb 79
08160 Cassine, la 08 42 Ee 51
13260 Cassis 13 171 Fd 89
44390 Casson 44 82 Yc 64
47240 Cassou 47 149 Ae 83
12210 Cassuéjouls 12 139 Ce 80
33138 Cassy 33 134 Yf 80
29150 Cast 29 78 Vf 60
13910 Cast, le 13 155 Ee 86
20246 Casta CTC 181 Kb 93
20138 Castagna, la CTC 182 Ie 98
31310 Castagnac 31 164 Bc 89
47260 Castagnade, la 47 148 Ac 82
31260 Castagnède 31 176 Af 90
64270 Castagnède 64 161 Za 88
32350 Castagnère, la 32 163 Ac 87
20200 Castagnetu CTC 181 Kc 92
06670 Castagniers 06 159 Hb 86
40700 Castaignos-Souslens 40 161 Zb 87
47200 Castaing 47 136 Ab 81
40270 Castandet 40 147 Zd 86
82270 Castanède 82 150 Bc 83
12240 Castanet 12 151 Cb 83
81150 Castanet 81 151 Ca 85
81330 Castanet 81 152 Cc 86
82160 Castanet 82 151 Bf 83
34610 Castanet-le-Bas 34 167 Da 87
34610 Castanet-le-Haut 34 167 Cf 86
31320 Castanet-Tolosan 31 164 Bc 87
24100 Castang 24 136 Ac 80
24290 Castang 24 137 Ba 78
24370 Castang 24 137 Bc 79
46210 Castanie 46 138 Ca 80
11160 Castans 11 166 Cc 88
34630 Castans, les 34 167 Dc 88
11160 Castanviels 11 166 Cc 88
64170 Casteide-Cami 64 162 Zc 88
64370 Casteide-Candau 64 161 Zc 87
64460 Casteide-Doat 64 162 Zf 88
66360 Casteil 66 178 Cc 93
34570 Castel 34 168 De 86
80110 Castel 80 39 Cc 50
22560 Castel, le 22 63 Wc 56
65330 Castelbajac 65 163 Ac 89
31160 Castelbiague 31 176 Af 90
82100 Castelferrus 82 149 Ba 84
32170 Castelfranc 32 163 Ab 88
46140 Castelfranc 46 137 Bb 81
31230 Castelgaillard 31 164 Af 88
31780 Castelginest 31 164 Bc 86
32390 Casteljaloux 32 149 Ad 86
47700 Casteljaloux 47 148 Aa 83
07460 Casteljau 07 154 Eb 82
47340 Castella 47 149 Ae 83
04120 Castellane 04 157 Gd 85
06500 Castellar 06 159 Hc 86
04380 Castellard, le 04 157 Ga 83
20213 Castellare di Casinca CTC 181 Kc 94
20212 Castellare-di-Mercurio CTC 183 Kb 95
34200 Castellas, le 34 168 Dd 88
84400 Castellet 84 156 Fc 85
04170 Castellet, le 04 158 Gc 84
04700 Castellet, le 04 157 Ff 85
83330 Castellet, le 83 171 Fe 89
20222 Castello CTC 181 Kc 92
20228 Castello CTC 181 Kc 91
20235 Castello di Rustino CTC 181 Kb 94
20235 Castello di Rustinu = Castello di Rustino CTC 181 Kb 94
12800 Castelmary 12 151 Cb 83
31180 Castelmaurou 31 165 Bd 86
82210 Castelmayran 82 149 Ba 84
33540 Castelmoron-d'Albret 33 135 Zf 80
47260 Castelmoron-sur-Lot 47 148 Ac 82
12620 Castelmus 12 152 Cf 84
12800 Castelnau 12 151 Cb 83
33840 Castelnau 33 147 Zf 83
40410 Castelnau 40 147 Zb 82
32450 Castelnau-Barbarens 32 163 Ae 87
40360 Castelnau-Chalosse 40 161 Za 87
32320 Castelnau-d'Anglès 32 163 Ab 87
32500 Castelnau-d'Arbieu 32 149 Ae 85
11400 Castelnaudary 11 165 Bf 89
11700 Castelnau-d'Aude 11 166 Ce 89
32440 Castelnau-d'Auzan 32 148 Aa 85
47290 Castelnaud-de-Gratecambe 47 136 Ae 82
81260 Castelnau-de-Brassac 81 166 Cc 87
34120 Castelnau-de-Guers 34 167 Dc 88
81150 Castelnau-de-Lévis 81 151 Ca 85
12500 Castelnau-de-Mandailles 12 139 Cf 81
33480 Castelnau-de-Médoc 33 134 Zb 78
81140 Castelnau-de-Montmiral 81 150 Be 85
31620 Castelnau-d'Estrétefonds 31 150 Bc 86
24250 Castelnaud-la-Chapelle 24 137 Ba 80
09420 Castelnau-Durban 09 177 Bc 91
34170 Castelnau-le-Lez 34 168 Df 87
65230 Castelnau-Magnoac 65 163 Ad 89
46170 Castelnau-Montratier-Sainte Alauzie 46 150 Bc 83
12620 Castelnau-Pégayrols 12 152 Cf 84
31430 Castelnau-Picampeau 31 164 Ba 89
65700 Castelnau-Rivière-Basse 65 162 Zf 87
47180 Castelnau-sur-Gupie 47 136 Aa 81
32100 Castelnau-sur-L'Auvignon 32 148 Ac 85
40320 Castelnau-Tursan 40 162 Zd 87
30190 Castelnau-Valence 30 154 Eb 84
32290 Castelnavet 32 162 Aa 86
40700 Castelner 40 161 Zc 87
29280 Castel-Nevez 29 61 Vc 58
66300 Castelnou 66 179 Ce 93
12800 Castelpers 12 151 Cc 84
11300 Castelreng 11 178 Ca 90
82400 Castelsagrat 82 149 Af 83
32350 Castel-Saint-Louis 32 163 Ac 87
82100 Castelsarrasin 82 149 Ba 84
40330 Castel-Sarrazin 40 161 Zb 87
34320 Castelsec 34 167 Db 87
24220 Castels et Bézenac 24 137 Ba 79
24220 Castels et Bézenac 24 137 Ba 79
65350 Castelvieilh 65 163 Ab 89
33540 Castelviel 33 135 Zf 80
33380 Castendet 33 134 Za 81
31530 Castéra, le 31 164 Ba 86
82120 Castéra-Bouzet 82 149 Af 85
32700 Castéra-Lectourois 32 149 Ad 85
65350 Castéra-Lou 65 162 Aa 89
64460 Castéra-Loubix 64 162 Zf 88
09130 Castéras 09 164 Bc 90
32410 Castéra-Verduzan 32 148 Ac 86
31350 Castéra-Vignoles 31 163 Ae 89
32380 Castéron 32 149 Af 85
64260 Castet 64 162 Zd 90
64360 Castet 64 161 Zc 89
64300 Castétarbe 64 161 Zb 87
32340 Castet-Arrouy 32 149 Ae 85
64190 Castetbon 64 161 Zb 88
09320 Castet-d'Aleu 09 177 Bb 91
64300 Castétis 64 161 Zb 88
64190 Castetnau-Camblong 64 161 Zb 89
64300 Castetner 64 161 Zb 88
64330 Castetpugon 64 162 Ze 87
31390 Castets 31 164 Ba 88
40260 Castets 40 146 Yf 85
40300 Castets 40 161 Yf 87
33210 Castets-en-Dorthe 33 135 Zf 81
33210 Castets et Castillon 33 135 Ze 81
09350 Castex 09 164 Bb 89
31410 Castex 31 164 Bb 88
32170 Castex 32 163 Ab 88
32240 Castex-d'Armagnac 32 147 Zf 85
31430 Casties-Labrande 31 164 Ba 89
20218 Castifao CTC 181 Ka 93
20218 Castiglione CTC 181 Ka 94
65130 Castillon 65 163 Ab 90
47320 Castille 47 148 Ac 82
06500 Castillon 06 159 Hc 85
14490 Castillon 14 34 Zb 53
14570 Castillon 14 47 Zc 55
64350 Castillon 64 162 Zf 88
64370 Castillon 64 161 Zc 88
50510 Castillon, le 50 46 Yd 55
32190 Castillon-Debats 32 163 Ab 86
33210 Castillon-de-Castets 33 135 Zf 81
31110 Castillon-de-Larboust 31 175 Ad 92
31360 Castillon-de-Saint-Martory 31 164 Af 90
30210 Castillon-du-Gard 30 155 Ed 85
14140 Castillon-en-Auge 14 48 Aa 54
09800 Castillon-en-Couserans 09 176 Ba 91
33350 Castillon-la-Bataille 33 135 Zf 79
32360 Castillon-Massas 32 163 Ad 86
47330 Castillonnès 47 136 Ad 81
32490 Castillon-Savès 32 164 Af 87
33610 Castillonville 33 134 Za 80
14330 Castilly 14 34 Yf 53
32810 Castin 32 163 Ad 86
20218 Castineta CTC 181 Kb 94
20236 Castirla CTC 183 Ka 94
33114 Castor 33 134 Zb 81
63680 Castreix-Sancy 63 127 Ce 75
02680 Castres 02 40 Db 50
81100 Castres 81 166 Cb 87
33640 Castres-Gironde 33 135 Zd 80
34160 Castries 34 168 Df 86
12780 Castrieux 12 152 Cf 83
57510 Castviller 57 57 Gf 54
01110 Catagnolles, les 01 119 Fd 73
59178 Catarne 59 30 Dc 46
83490 Catchéou 83 172 Gd 87
59360 Cateau-Cambrésis, le 59 31 Dd 48
02420 Catelet, le 02 40 Db 48
76590 Catelier, le 76 37 Ba 50
76116 Catenay 76 37 Bb 51
60840 Catenoy 60 39 Cd 52
20220 Cateri CTC 180 If 93
20270 Caterragio CTC 183 Kd 96
18000 Cathédrale Saint-Étienne 18 102 Cc 66
33230 Catherineau 33 135 Zf 78
31110 Cathervielle 31 175 Ad 92
60360 Catheux 60 38 Ca 51
60640 Catigny 60 39 Cf 51
44530 Catiho 44 81 Xf 64
60130 Catillon-Fumechon 60 39 Cc 51
59360 Catillon-sur-Sambre 59 31 Dd 48
66500 Catllar 66 178 Cc 93
12130 Cats, les 12 140 Da 81
59148 Cattelet 59 30 Db 46
59217 Cattenières 59 30 Db 48
57570 Cattenom 57 44 Gb 52
50390 Catteville 50 46 Yc 52
32200 Cattonvielle 32 164 Af 87
46150 Catus 46 137 Bc 81
46400 Catusse, la 46 138 Bf 79
50500 Catz 50 46 Ye 53
82120 Caubel 82 149 Af 84
47160 Caubeyres 47 148 Aa 83
31480 Caubiac 31 164 Ba 86
64370 Caubin 64 161 Zc 88
64230 Caubios-Loos 64 162 Zd 88
47120 Caubon-Saint-Sauveur 47 136 Ab 81
32700 Cauboue 32 148 Ad 85
31110 Caubous 31 176 Ad 91
65230 Caubous 65 163 Ac 89
81200 Caucalières 81 166 Cb 87
12120 Caucart 12 152 Cc 83
62129 Cauchie 62 29 Cb 45
62158 Cauchie, la 62 29 Cd 47
62260 Cauchy-à-la-Tour 62 29 Cc 45
62150 Caucourt 62 29 Cd 46
19260 Caud 19 126 Be 75
56850 Caudan 56 79 Wd 62
76490 Caudebec-en-Caux 76 36 Ae 51
76320 Caudebec-lès-Elbeuf 76 49 Ba 53
11390 Caudebronde 11 166 Cb 88
47220 Caudecoste 47 149 Ae 84
47230 Cauderoue 47 148 Ab 84
59660 Caudescure 59 29 Cd 44
11230 Caudeval 11 165 Bf 90
34330 Caudezaures 34 166 Ce 87
66210 Caudiès-de-Conflent 66 178 Ca 93
11140 Caudiès-de-Fenouillèdes 11 178 Cc 92
33380 Caudos 33 134 Za 81
33490 Caudrot 33 135 Zf 81
59540 Caudry 59 30 Dc 48
34360 Cauduro 34 167 Cf 88
60290 Cauffry 60 39 Cc 53
27180 Caugé 27 49 Ba 54
31210 Cauhapé 31 163 Ad 90
31190 Caujac 31 164 Bc 89
02490 Caulaincourt 02 40 Da 49
76390 Caule-Sainte-Beuve, le 76 38 Bd 50
80290 Caulières 80 38 Bf 50
59191 Caullery 59 30 Dc 48
22350 Caulnes = Kaon 22 65 Xf 59
54800 Caulre 54 56 Ff 54
12560 Caumel 12 152 Da 82
02300 Caumont 02 40 Db 51
09160 Caumont 09 176 Ba 90
27310 Caumont 27 37 Af 52
32400 Caumont 32 162 Zf 86
33540 Caumont 33 135 Zf 80
62140 Caumont 62 29 Ca 47
82210 Caumont 82 149 Af 84
14240 Caumont-L'Eventé 14 47 Zb 54
14240 Caumont-sur-Aure 14 34 Za 54
84510 Caumont-sur-Durance 84 155 Ef 85
47430 Caumont-sur-Garonne 47 148 Ab 82
14220 Caumont-sur-Orne 14 47 Zd 55
40500 Cauna 40 147 Zc 86
81290 Caunan 81 166 Cb 87
34650 Caunas 34 167 Db 86
79190 Caunay 79 111 Aa 71
11160 Caunes-Minervois 11 166 Cd 89
34210 Caunette 34 166 Ce 88
11220 Caunettes-en-Val 11 166 Cd 90
11250 Caunette-sur-Lauquet 11 178 Cc 90
40250 Caupenne 40 161 Zb 86
32110 Caupenne-d-'Armagnac 32 148 Zf 86
33160 Caupian 33 134 Zb 79
50480 Cauquigny 50 33 Yd 52
51270 Caure, la 51 53 De 55
22530 Caurel 22 63 Wf 59
51110 Caurel 51 53 Ea 53
20117 Cauro CTC 182 If 97
59400 Cauroir 59 30 Db 47
08310 Cauroy 08 41 Ec 52
51220 Cauroy-lès-Hermonville 51 41 Df 52
62810 Cauroy, le 62 29 Cc 47
82500 Causé, le 82 149 Af 86
24150 Cause-de-Clérans 24 136 Ae 79
82300 Caussade 82 150 Bd 84
33180 Caussade, la 33 122 Za 77
65700 Caussade-Rivière 65 162 Aa 87
12260 Caussanels 12 138 Bf 82
09700 Caussatière, la 09 165 Bd 89
82290 Caussé 82 150 Bb 85
46110 Causse, le 46 138 Be 79
30750 Causse-Bégon 30 153 Dc 84
34380 Causse-de-la-Selle 34 153 Dd 86
12260 Causse-de-Saujac 12 138 Bf 82
12700 Causse-et-Diège 12 138 Ca 81
32100 Caussens 32 148 Ac 85
34490 Causses-et-Veyran 34 167 Da 88
82160 Causseviel 82 151 Bf 83
31560 Caussidières 31 165 Bd 88
48210 Caussignac 48 153 Dc 83
34600 Caussiniojouls 34 167 Da 87
06460 Caussols 06 173 Gf 86
09250 Caussou 09 177 Be 92
65110 Cauterets 65 175 Zf 91
19220 Cautine 19 138 Ca 78
36700 Cautronnières, les 36 100 Ba 67
30340 Cauvas 30 154 Eb 83
27350 Cauverville-en-Roumois 27 36 Ad 52
30430 Cauviac 30 154 Eb 83
14190 Cauvicourt 14 48 Ze 54
33690 Cauvignac 33 148 Zf 82
14270 Cauvigny 14 48 Zf 54
60730 Cauvigny 60 51 Cb 53
14770 Cauville 14 47 Zc 55
76930 Cauville 76 36 Aa 51
50390 Cauvinerie, la 50 46 Yc 52
19290 Caux 19 126 Ca 74
34720 Caux 34 167 Dc 87
46800 Caux 46 150 Ba 82
63680 Caux 63 127 Ce 76
11170 Caux-et-Sauzens 11 166 Cb 89
47470 Cauzac 47 149 Af 83
46110 Cavagnac 46 138 Bd 78
46700 Cavagnac 46 137 Ba 81
47250 Cavagnan 47 148 Aa 82
82160 Cavaille 82 150 Be 83
84300 Cavaillon 84 155 Fa 85
83240 Cavalaire-sur-Mer 83 172 Gd 89
44130 Cavalais 44 81 Ya 64
81350 Cavalarié, la 81 151 Cb 84
12230 Cavalerie, la 12 152 Da 84
83980 Cavalière 83 172 Gc 90
20132 Cavallara CTC 185 Kb 97
22140 Cavan 22 63 Wd 56
11570 Cavanac 11 166 Cb 89
19430 Cavanet 19 138 Ca 78
46210 Cavanie 46 138 Ca 80
47330 Cavarc 47 136 Ad 80
32190 Cavé, le 32 148 Ab 86
30820 Caveirac 30 154 Eb 86
34220 Cavenac 34 166 Ce 88
11510 Caves 11 179 Cf 91
37340 Caves, les 37 84 Ab 64
89100 Caves, les 89 72 Db 59
37140 Cave-Vandelet, la 37 84 Ab 64
33620 Cavignac 33 135 Zd 78
50620 Cavigny 50 46 Yf 53
30330 Cavillargues 30 155 Ed 84
60730 Cavillon 60 51 Cb 53
80310 Cavillon 80 38 Ca 49
62140 Cavron-Saint-Martin 62 28 Ca 46
20117 Cavru = Cauro CTC 182 If 97
20144 Cavu CTC 185 Kc 98
20227 Cavu CTC 183 Kb 96
33290 Caychac 33 134 Zc 79
09250 Caychax 09 177 Be 92
80800 Cayeux-en-Santerre 80 39 Cd 50
80410 Cayeux-sur-Mer 80 28 Bc 47
12550 Cayla, le 12 152 Cd 85
30480 Cayla, le 30 154 Df 84
34520 Caylar, le 34 153 Db 85
12400 Caylus 12 152 Ce 85
82160 Caylus 82 150 Be 83
12260 Cayrac 12 138 Ca 81
12450 Cayrac 12 152 Cd 83
82440 Cayrac 82 150 Bc 84
46230 Cayran, le 46 150 Bc 82
46160 Cayre, le 46 138 Bf 81
81350 Cayre, le 81 151 Cc 85
33930 Cayrehours 33 122 Yf 77
81260 Cayrélié, la 81 166 Cc 86
43510 Cayres 43 141 De 79
81990 Cayrie, la 81 151 Cb 85
82240 Cayriech 82 150 Bd 83
15290 Cayrols 15 139 Cb 80
12500 Cayrol, le 12 139 Ce 81
12490 Cayrou 12 152 Cd 83
12390 Cayrou, le 12 151 Cb 82
12740 Cayssac 12 152 Cd 82
12370 Cayzac 12 152 Cd 85
31230 Cazac 31 164 Af 88
46160 Cazal 46 138 Be 81
34210 Cazal, le 34 166 Ce 88
81360 Cazalie, la 81 166 Cb 86
33113 Cazalis 33 147 Zd 82
40700 Cazalis 40 161 Zc 87
40700 Cazalon 40 161 Zc 87
11270 Cazalrenoux 11 165 Bf 89
09000 Cazals 09 177 Bd 91
46250 Cazals 46 137 Bb 81
82140 Cazals 82 150 Be 84
12140 Cazals, les 12 139 Cd 81
09500 Cazals-des-Baylès 09 165 Bf 90
34460 Cazals-Vieil 34 167 Da 88
13116 Cazan 13 170 Fb 86
65370 Cazarilh 65 176 Ad 91
31580 Cazaril-Tambourès 31 163 Ad 89
33430 Cazats 33 135 Ze 82
32150 Cazaubon 32 148 Zf 85
40240 Cazaubon 40 147 Ze 84
40500 Cazaubon 40 161 Zc 86
33790 Cazaugitat 33 135 Aa 80
31160 Cazaunous 31 176 Ae 91
09120 Cazaux 09 177 Bd 90
09160 Cazaux 09 176 Ba 90
33260 Cazaux 33 134 Yf 81
32190 Cazaux-d'Anglès 32 163 Ab 87
65590 Cazaux-Debat 65 175 Ac 91
65240 Cazaux-Dessus 65 175 Ac 91
65240 Cazaux-Fréchet-Anéran-Camors 65 175 Ac 92
31440 Cazaux-Layrisse 31 176 Ad 91
32130 Cazaux-Savès 32 164 Af 87
32230 Cazaux-Villecomtal 32 163 Ab 88
09160 Cazavet 09 176 Ba 90
11420 Cazazils, les 11 165 Bf 90
33380 Caze 33 134 Za 81
46190 Caze, la 46 138 Ca 79
82300 Caze, la 82 150 Bc 84
34460 Cazedarnes 34 167 Da 88
12230 Cazejourdes 12 153 Db 85
34210 Cazelles 34 166 Ce 88
24220 Cazenac 24 137 Ba 79
09400 Cazenave 09 177 Be 91
32800 Cazeneuve 32 148 Aa 85
47110 Cazeneuve 47 149 Ad 82
31420 Cazeneuve-Montaut 31 164 Ae 89
31220 Cazères 31 164 Ba 89
40270 Cazères-sur-L'Adour 40 147 Ze 86
12200 Cazes, les 12 151 Bf 83
82110 Cazes-Mondenard 82 149 Bb 83
34270 Cazevieille 34 153 De 86
47370 Cazideroque 47 149 Af 82
11570 Cazilhac 11 166 Cc 89
34220 Cazilhac 34 166 Ce 88
34190 Cazilhac-Bas 34 153 De 85
34190 Cazilhac-Haut 34 153 De 85
46600 Cazillac 46 138 Bd 79
82110 Cazillac 82 149 Bb 83
34360 Cazo 34 167 Cf 88
12480 Cazotte, la 12 152 Ce 84
24370 Cazoulès 24 137 Bc 79
34120 Cazouls-d'Hérault 34 167 Dc 87
34370 Cazouls-lès-Béziers 34 167 Da 88
61330 Ceaucé 61 67 Zc 58
36200 Ceaulmont 36 113 Bd 69
19800 Céaux 19 126 Be 76
50220 Céaux 50 66 Yd 57
43270 Céaux-d'Allègre 43 141 De 77
86700 Ceaux-en-Couhé 86 111 Ab 71
86200 Ceaux-en-Loudun 86 99 Ab 66
34360 Cébazan 34 167 Cf 88
63118 Cébazat 63 128 Da 74
20137 Ceccia CTC 185 Kb 99
34270 Ceceles 34 154 Df 86
39240 Ceffia 39 119 Fd 71
52220 Ceffonds 52 74 Ee 58
12450 Ceignac 12 151 Cd 83
34260 Ceilhes-et-Rocozels 34 152 Da 86
05600 Ceillac 05 145 Ge 80
48170 Ceiller, le 48 141 De 80
63520 Ceilloux 63 128 Dd 75
46100 Ceint-d'Eau 46 138 Bf 81
54134 Ceintrey 54 76 Ga 57
29920 Célan 29 78 Wb 62
35170 Celar 35 65 Yb 61
30340 Celas 30 154 Eb 84
26770 Célas, le 26 155 Fa 82
18360 Celette, la 18 102 Cd 69
03600 Celle 03 115 Ce 71
19250 Celle 19 126 Ca 75
41360 Cellé 41 85 Ae 61
63620 Celle 63 127 Cc 73
18200 Celle, la 18 102 Cc 68
18160 Celle-Condé, la 18 102 Cb 68
23800 Celle-Dunoise, la 23 114 Be 71
71400 Celle-en-Morvan, la 71 105 Eb 66
16260 Cellefrouin 16 112 Ac 73
37350 Celle-Guenand, la 37 100 Af 67
78720 Celle-les-Bordes, la 78 50 Bf 57
86600 Celle-Lévescault 86 111 Ab 70
49330 Cellère 49 84 Zc 63
09000 Celles 09 177 Be 91
15170 Celles 15 140 Cf 78
15170 Celles 15 140 Cf 78
17520 Celles 17 123 Zd 75
24600 Celles 24 124 Ac 77
34800 Celles 34 167 Dc 86
37160 Celle-Saint-Avant, la 37 100 Ad 66
78170 Celle-Saint-Cloud, la 78 51 Ca 55
89116 Celle-Saint-Cyr, la 89 72 Db 61
52360 Celles-en-Bassigny 52 92 Fd 61
02330 Celles-lès-Condé 02 53 Dd 54
51260 Celle-sous-Chantemerle, la 51 73 De 57
23230 Celle-sous-Gouzon, la 23 114 Cb 71
02540 Celle-sous-Montmirail, la 02 52 Dc 55
02370 Celles-sur-Aisne 02 40 Dc 52
79370 Celles-sur-Belle 79 111 Ze 71
63250 Celles-sur-Durolle 63 128 Dd 73
10110 Celles-sur-Ource 10 74 Ec 60
88110 Celles-sur-Plaine 88 77 Gf 58
58440 Celle-sur-Loire, la 58 88 Cf 64
58700 Celle-sur-Nièvre, la 58 103 Db 65
63330 Cellette 63 115 Ce 72
85490 Cellette 85 110 Zc 70
23350 Cellette, la 23 114 Ca 70
16230 Cellettes 16 124 Aa 73
41120 Cellettes 41 86 Bc 63
30200 Cellettes, les 30 155 Ed 83
12380 Cellier, le 12 152 Cd 86
44850 Cellier, le 44 82 Yd 65
07590 Cellier-du-Luc 07 141 Df 80
03440 Cellière 03 115 Cf 69
73260 Celliers 73 132 Gc 76
42320 Cellieu 42 130 Ed 75
76520 Celloville 76 37 Ba 52
63200 Cellule 63 116 Da 73
18340 Celon 18 102 Cc 67
36200 Celon 36 113 Bc 69
13090 Celony 13 170 Fc 87
15500 Celoux 15 140 Db 78
52600 Celsoy 52 92 Fc 61
77930 Cély 77 71 Cd 58
70500 Cemboing 70 93 Ff 61
60210 Cempuis 60 38 Bf 51
12260 Cenac 12 151 Bf 82
33360 Cénac 33 135 Zd 80
43440 Cenac 43 128 Dd 77
46140 Cenac 46 150 Bb 82
86260 Cenan 86 100 Ae 69
70230 Cenans 70 93 Gb 64
30480 Cendras 30 154 Ea 84
63670 Cendre, le 63 128 Db 74
70500 Cendrecourt 70 93 Ff 61
25640 Cendrey 25 93 Gb 64
24380 Cendrieux 24 137 Ae 79
46330 Cènevières 46 138 Be 82
11170 Cenne-Monestiés 11 165 Ca 88
12360 Cenomes 12 152 Da 86
33150 Cenon 33 135 Zc 79
86530 Cenon-sur-Vienne 86 100 Ad 68
39250 Censeau 39 107 Ga 68
51300 Cense-des-Prés, la 51 54 Ed 55
21430 Censerey 21 105 Ec 65
89310 Censy 89 90 Ea 62
76590 Cent-Acres, les 76 37 Ba 50
09220 Centraux 09 177 Bd 92
12120 Centrès 12 151 Cc 84
20238 Centuri CTC 181 Kc 91
20238 Centuri-Port CTC 181 Kc 91
69840 Cenves 69D 118 Ed 71
31620 Cépet 31 164 Bc 86
11300 Cépie 11 166 Cb 90
45120 Cepoy 45 71 Ce 60
19200 Ceppe 19 126 Cb 75
34460 Ceps 34 167 Cf 87
32500 Céran 32 149 Ae 86
72330 Cérans 72 84 Aa 62
72330 Cérans-Foulletourte 72 84 Aa 62
20160 Cerasa CTC 182 Ie 96
66290 Cerbère 66 179 Da 94
18120 Cerbois 18 102 Ca 66
40370 Cerboueyre 40 146 Za 85
89200 Cerce, la 89 90 Df 64
16170 Cerceville 16 123 Aa 74
21320 Cercey 21 105 Ec 65
69220 Cercié 69D 118 Ee 72
74350 Cercier 74 120 Ga 72
24320 Cercles, La Tour-Blanche- 24 124 Ac 76
45520 Cercottes 45 70 Bf 61
17270 Cercoux 17 135 Ze 78
61500 Cercueil, le 61 68 Aa 57
10400 Cercy 10 72 Dc 58
71350 Cercy 71 106 Ef 67
58340 Cercy-la-Tour 58 104 Dd 67
01450 Cerdon 01 119 Fc 72
45620 Cerdon 45 87 Cc 63
36130 Céré 36 101 Be 67
40090 Cere 40 147 Zc 85
37460 Céré-la-Ronde 37 100 Bb 65
37390 Cérelles 37 85 Ae 63
50510 Cérences 50 46 Yd 55
04280 Céreste 04 156 Fd 85
66400 Céret 66 179 Ce 94
59680 Cerfontaine 59 31 Ea 47
42460 Cergne, la 42 117 Eb 72

A B C D E F G H I J K L M N O P Q R S T U V W X Y Z

Cergne, la | 253

95000 Cergy 95 51 Ca 54
33160 Cérillan 33 134 Zb 79
03350 Cérilly 03 103 Ce 69
21330 Cérilly 21 91 Ec 61
89320 Cérilly 89 73 Dd 59
01680 Cerin 01 131 Fd 74
31160 Cériros 31 176 Af 90
61000 Cerisé 61 68 Aa 58
77460 Cériseaux 77 71 Ce 59
50220 Cerisel 50 66 Ye 57
52320 Cerisières 52 75 Fa 59
89320 Cerisiers 89 72 Dc 60
80800 Cerisy 80 39 Cd 49
61100 Cerisy-Belle-Etoile 61 47 Zc 56
80140 Cérisy-Buleux 80 38 Be 49
50680 Cerisy-la-Forêt 50 34 Za 53
50210 Cerisy-la-Salle 50 46 Ye 54
79140 Cerizay 79 98 Zb 68
09230 Cérizols 09 164 Ba 90
02240 Cerizy 02 40 Db 50
76430 Cerlangue, la 76 36 Ac 51
08290 Cerleau, la 08 41 Ec 50
39110 Cernans 39 107 Ff 67
14290 Cernay 14 48 Ab 54
28120 Cernay 28 69 Bb 58
45190 Cernay 45 86 Bd 62
68700 Cernay 68 95 Hb 62
86140 Cernay 86 99 Ab 67
51800 Cernay-en-Dormois 51 54 Ee 53
78720 Cernay-la-Ville 78 51 Bf 56
25120 Cernay-L'Eglise 25 108 Ge 65
51420 Cernay-lès-Reims 51 53 Ea 53
77320 Cerneux 77 52 Dc 56
25210 Cerneux-Monnots, les 25 108 Ge 65
74350 Cernex 74 120 Ga 72
39250 Cerniébaud 39 107 Ga 68
08260 Cernion 08 41 Ec 50
73270 Cernix, les 73 133 Gd 74
73590 Cerniy, le 73 133 Gc 74
25240 Cernois, le 25 107 Ga 69
39240 Cernon 39 119 Fd 70
51240 Cernon 51 54 Ec 55
60190 Cernoy 60 39 Cd 52
45360 Cernoy-en-Berry 45 88 Cd 63
49310 Cernusson 49 98 Zd 65
91590 Cerny 91 71 Cb 58
02860 Cerny-en-Laonnois 02 40 De 52
02870 Cerny-lès-Bucy 02 40 Dd 51
19460 Céron 19 126 Be 77
71110 Céron 71 117 Df 71
33720 Cérons 33 135 Zd 81
78125 Cerqueuse 78 70 Be 57
14290 Cerqueux 14 48 Ac 55
45130 Cerqueux 45 70 Bd 61
49360 Cerqueux-de-Maulevrier, les 49 98 Zc 67
49310 Cerqueux-sous-Passavant 49 98 Zd 66
70000 Cerre-lès-Noroy 70 93 Gb 63
34420 Cers 34 167 Db 89
79290 Cersay 79 98 Zd 66
02220 Cerseuil 02 40 Dd 53
51700 Cerseuil 51 53 De 54
71390 Cersot 71 105 Ed 68
88300 Certaines 58 104 De 65
77840 Certigny 77 52 Da 54
88300 Certilleux 88 75 Fe 59
01240 Certines 01 119 Fb 72
87290 Cerveix, le 87 113 Bb 71
58210 Cervenon 58 89 Dd 64
58700 Cervenon 58 103 Db 66
74550 Cervens 74 120 Gc 71
05100 Cervières 05 145 Ge 79
42440 Cervières 42 129 De 73
74400 Cerville 54 56 Gb 56
20221 Cervione CTC 181 Kc 95
20221 Cervioni = Cervione CTC 181 Kc 95
55700 Cervisy 55 42 Fb 51
58800 Cervon 58 104 De 65
43380 Cerzat 43 128 Dc 78
79190 Cerzé 79 111 Aa 71
79400 Cerzeau 79 111 Ze 70
33830 Cès 33 134 Zb 81
39570 Cesancey 39 106 Fd 69
73200 Césarches 73 132 Gc 74
73530 César-Durand 73 132 Gb 77
05230 Césaris, les 05 144 Gb 81
45300 Césarville-Dossainville 45 71 Cb 59
09800 Cescau 09 176 Ba 91
64170 Cescau 64 162 Zc 88
14270 Cesny-aux-Vignes-Ouezy 14 48 Zf 54
14220 Cesny-Bois-Halbout 14 47 Zd 55
19410 Cessac 19 125 Bd 77
33760 Cessac 33 135 Ze 80
31290 Cessales 31 165 Be 88
55700 Cesse 55 42 Fa 51
01090 Cesseins 01 118 Ef 72
34460 Cessenon-sur-Orb 34 167 Da 88
73410 Cessens 73 132 Ff 74
34210 Cesseras 34 166 Ce 89
03500 Cesset 03 116 Db 71
27110 Cesseville 27 49 Af 53
21450 Cessey 21 91 Ed 63
25440 Cessey 25 107 Ff 66
21350 Cessey-lès-Vitteaux 21 91 Ed 64
21110 Cessey-sur-Tille 21 92 Fb 65
02320 Cessières 02 40 Dc 51
38110 Cessieu 38 131 Fc 75
22190 Cesson 22 64 Xb 57
77240 Cesson 77 71 Cd 57
35510 Cesson-Sévigné 35 65 Yc 60
01560 Cessort 01 118 Fa 70
77520 Cessoy-en-Montois 77 72 Da 57
01170 Cessy 01 120 Ga 71
58220 Cessy-les-Bois 58 89 Db 64
33610 Cestas 33 134 Zb 80
81150 Cestayrols 81 151 Bf 85
21440 Cestres 21 91 Ee 64
42110 Cétéraud 42 129 Ea 74
61260 Ceton 61 69 Ae 59
64490 Cette-Eygun 64 174 Zc 91
05400 Céüze 05 144 Ff 81
73730 Cevins 73 132 Gc 75
12340 Ceyrac 12 139 Ce 82
30170 Ceyrac 30 154 Df 85
34800 Ceyras 34 167 Dc 87
19130 Ceyrat 19 125 Bc 77
63122 Ceyrat 63 128 Da 74
13600 Ceyreste 13 171 Fd 89
23210 Ceyroux 23 114 Bd 72
63210 Ceyssat 63 127 Cf 74
63800 Ceyssat 63 128 Db 74
23200 Ceyvat 23 114 Ca 72
01250 Ceyzériat 01 119 Fb 71
01350 Ceyzérieu 01 131 Fe 73
33620 Cézac 33 135 Zd 78
46170 Cézac 46 150 Bc 82
85410 Cezais 85 98 Zb 69
32410 Cézan 32 148 Ac 86
30440 Cézas 30 153 De 85
42130 Cezay 42 129 Df 74
19290 Cezayrat 19 126 Ca 74
15230 Cézens 15 139 Cf 79
15160 Cézérat 15 127 Cf 77
39240 Cézia 39 119 Fd 70
89410 Cézy 89 72 Dc 61
10190 Chaast, le 10 73 Df 59
64570 Chabalgoïti 64 161 Zb 90
48250 Chabalier 48 141 De 81
79180 Chaban 79 111 Zd 70
16150 Chabanais 16 124 Ae 73
48500 Chabanes 48 140 Db 82
36370 Chabanet 36 113 Bb 70
06420 Chabanette 06 159 Hb 85
69440 Chabanière 69M 130 Ed 75
19550 Chabanne 19 126 Ca 77
23290 Chabanne 23 113 Bc 72
36310 Chabanne 36 113 Bb 70
63450 Chabanne 63 128 Da 75
03250 Chabanne, la 03 116 De 72
63600 Chabanne, la 63 129 Df 75
63820 Chabanne, la 63 127 Ce 74
48000 Chabannes 48 140 Dc 81
19170 Chabannes, les 19 126 Bf 75
70220 Chabannes, les 70 93 Gc 61
15320 Chabanol 15 140 Db 79
04140 Chabanon 04 157 Gb 82
42380 Chabany, le 42 129 Ea 76
15230 Chabasses 15 139 Ce 78
36800 Chabenet 36 101 Bc 69
04200 Chabert 04 157 Ga 83
07200 Chaberterie, la 07 142 Ec 81
05400 Chabestan 05 144 Fe 82
48600 Chabestras 48 141 Dd 80
26120 Chabeuil 26 143 Fa 79
30700 Chabian, le 30 154 Eb 84
45500 Chabinerie, la 45 88 Cd 63
16310 Chablanc 16 124 Ad 74
74160 Châble, le 74 120 Ga 72
89800 Chablis 89 90 De 62
44330 Chaboissière, les 44 97 Ye 65
38690 Châbons 38 131 Fc 76
17700 Chabosse 17 110 Zb 72
44220 Chabossière, la 44 96 Yb 65
61320 Chabossière, la 61 48 Zf 57
05260 Chabottes 05 144 Gb 81
05140 Chabottes, les 05 144 Fe 81
46500 Chabournac, le 46 138 Bc 79
86380 Chabournay 86 99 Ab 68
16150 Chabrac 16 112 Ae 73
19160 Chabrat 19 127 Cb 76
24120 Chabrat 24 137 Bb 78
63250 Chabreloche 63 129 De 73
63440 Chabrepine 63 115 Da 72
63580 Chabreyras 63 128 Dc 75
04000 Chabrières 04 157 Gb 84
19350 Chabrignac 19 125 Bc 77
36200 Chabrillac 15 140 Db 78
26400 Chabrillan 26 142 Ef 80
36320 Chabris 36 101 Bd 65
24130 Chabrouillas 24 136 Ac 79
49400 Chacé 49 99 Zf 65
10110 Chacenay 10 74 Ed 60
43510 Chacornac 43 141 Df 79
02200 Chacrise 02 52 Dc 53
19170 Chadebec 19 126 Ca 75
87500 Chadefaine 87 125 Bb 75
63320 Chadeleuf 63 128 Db 75
07160 Chadenac 07 142 Ec 79
17800 Chadenac 17 123 Zd 75
07150 Chadenède, la 07 142 Ec 82
48190 Chadenet 48 141 Dd 81
17260 Chadeniers 17 122 Zb 75
24700 Chadenne 24 136 Aa 78
43270 Chadernac 43 129 De 78
16120 Chadeuil 16 123 Zf 75
23800 Chadeurniat 23 113 Bd 70
19220 Chadiac 19 138 Ca 77
17520 Chadon 17 123 Zd 75
43150 Chadron 43 141 Df 79
16250 Chadurie 16 124 Aa 76
38290 Chaffard, le 38 131 Fa 74
85110 Chaffauds, les 85 97 Yf 68
04510 Chaffaut-Saint Jurson, le 04 157 Ga 84
25300 Chaffois 25 108 Gb 67
70400 Chagey 70 94 Ge 63
33860 Chagnas 33 123 Zc 77
79200 Chagnelle, la 79 99 Ze 68
38160 Chagneux 38 143 Fc 78
17139 Chagnolet 17 110 Yf 71
17770 Chagnon 17 123 Zd 73
42800 Chagnon 42 130 Ed 75
58120 Châgnon 58 104 Df 66
85710 Châgnon 85 96 Ya 67
08430 Chagny 08 42 Ee 51
71150 Chagny 71 105 Ee 67
72340 Chahaignes 72 85 Ad 62
53400 Chahains 61 67 Zf 57
28160 Chahuteau 28 69 Bb 59
21120 Chaignay 21 91 Fa 64
85770 Chaignée, la 85 110 Za 70
79190 Chaignepain 79 111 Zf 71
27120 Chaignes 27 50 Bc 54
19450 Chaillac 19 126 Be 76
36310 Chaillac 36 113 Bb 70
87200 Chaillac-sur-Vienne 87 125 Af 73
53420 Chailland 53 66 Za 59
04170 Chaillans, les 04 158 Gc 85
16380 Chaillat, le 16 124 Ac 75
17260 Chaillaud, le 17 122 Zb 75
17700 Chaillé 17 110 Zb 72
70290 Chaillée, la 70 94 Ge 62
85450 Chaillé-les-Marais 85 110 Yf 70
41120 Chailles 41 86 Bb 63
85310 Chaillé-sous-les-Ormeaux 85 97 Yd 69
39270* Chailleuse, la 39 106 Fd 69
17890 Chaillevette 17 122 Yf 74
02000 Chaillevois 02 40 Dd 51
89770 Chailley 89 73 De 60
05260 Chaillol 05 144 Gb 80
55210 Chaillon 55 55 Fd 55
28160 Chaillou, le 28 69 Af 59
61500 Chailloué 61 48 Ab 57
77930 Chailly-en-Bière 77 71 Cd 58
77120 Chailly-en-Brie 77 52 Da 56
45260 Chailly-en-Gâtinais 45 71 Cd 61
57365 Chailly-lès-Ennery 57 56 Gb 53
21320 Chailly-sur-Armançon 21 91 Ec 65
74540 Chainaz-les-Frasses 74 132 Ff 74
39120 Chaînée-des-Coupis 39 106 Fc 67
45380 Chaingy 45 87 Be 61
71570 Chaintré 71 118 Ee 71
77140 Chaintreauville 77 71 Ce 59
77460 Chaintreaux 77 72 Ce 59
51130 Chaintrix-Bierges 51 53 Ea 55
23500 Chairavaux 23 126 Cb 74
03190 Chaise 03 115 Ce 70
10500 Chaise 10 74 Ed 58
37240 Chaise 37 100 Ae 66
58230 Chaise 58 104 Ea 66
86300 Chaise 86 100 Ae 69
16220 Chaise, la 16 124 Ac 75
86320 Chaise, la 86 112 Ae 70
50370 Chaise-Baudouin, la 50 46 Ye 56
43160 Chaise-Dieu, la 43 129 De 77
27580 Chaise-Dieu-du-Theil 27 49 Ae 56
28250 Chaises, les 28 69 Ba 57
78125 Chaises, les 78 50 Be 57
85200 Chaix 85 110 Za 70
50600 Chaize, la 50 66 Yf 57
85220 Chaize-Giraud, la 85 96 Yb 69
85310 Chaize-le-Vicomte, la 85 97 Ye 68
73130 Chal 73 132 Gb 77
64410 Chalabart 64 162 Zd 87
11230 Chalabre 11 178 Ca 91
26510 Chalabrus 26 156 Fc 82
24380 Chalagnac 24 136 Ae 78
42600 Chalain-d'Uzore 42 129 Ea 74
55140 Chalaines 55 75 Fe 57
42600 Chalain-le-Comtal 42 129 Eb 75
16210 Chalais 16 123 Aa 77
36370 Chalais 36 113 Bb 69
85470 Chalais 85 110 Zb 70
86200 Chalais 86 99 Aa 67
01320 Chalamont 01 118 Fb 73
68490 Chalampé 68 95 Hd 62
40120 Chalan 40 148 Ze 83
52160 Chalancey 52 92 Fa 62
26470 Chalancon 26 143 Fc 81
86190 Chalandray 86 99 Zf 69
50540 Chalandrey 50 66 Ye 57
02270 Chalandry 02 40 Dd 50
08160 Chalandry-Elaire 08 42 Ee 50
61390 Chalange, le 61 68 Ab 57
04850 Chalannette, la 04 158 Ge 82
87500 Chalard, le 87 125 Ba 75
77171 Chalautre-la-Grande 77 72 Dc 57
77160 Chalautre-la-Petite 77 72 Db 57
77520 Chalautre-la-Reposte 77 72 Da 58
58140 Chalaux 58 90 Df 64
07570 Chalayes, les 07 142 Ec 79
48310 Chaldette, la 48 140 Da 80
49610 Chale 49 83 Zd 64
01480 Chaleins 01 118 Ee 72
24800 Chaleix 24 125 Af 75
07240 Chalencon 07 142 Ed 79
43130 Chalençon 43 129 Df 77
43220 Chalençonnoère, la 43 142 Ec 77
43530 Chales 43 129 Ea 77
39150 Chalesmes-Grand, les 39 107 Ga 68
39150 Chalesmes-Petit, les 39 107 Ff 68
05480 Chalet de l'Alpe du Villar d'Arène 05 145 Gc 79
73550 Chalet du Fruit 73 133 Gd 76
05800 Chalet-du-Gioberney 05 144 Gb 79
73210 Chalet-du-Palet 73 133 Ge 76
73550 Chalet-du-Saut 73 133 Gd 76
33480 Chalets, les 33 134 Zb 79
05100 Chalets-de-Ayes 05 145 Gd 79
05600 Chalets-de-Bramousse 05 145 Ge 80
74470 Chalets-de-Buchille 74 120 Gd 71
05350 Chalets-de-Clapeyto 05 145 Gd 80
05350 Chalets-de-Furands 05 145 Gd 80
73500 Chalets-de-la-Pelouse 73 145 Ge 77
73350 Chalets-de-la-Plagne 73 133 Ge 76
05100 Chalets-de-Laval 05 145 Gc 78
05350 Chalets-de-L'Eychaillon 05 145 Gd 80
05470 Chalets-de-Lombard 05 145 Gf 80
05100 Chalets-de-L'Orceyrette 05 145 Gd 80
05100 Chalets des Acle 05 145 Ge 78
73640 Chalets-des-Balmes 73 133 Gf 75
74740 Chalets-du-Fardelet 74 121 Ge 72
45120 Châlette-sur-Loing 45 71 Ce 60
10500 Chalette-sur-Voire 10 74 Ec 58
01230 Chaley 01 119 Fd 73
25220 Chalèze 25 93 Ga 65
25220 Chalezeule 25 107 Ga 65
15320 Chaliers 15 140 Db 79
54230 Chaligny 54 56 Ga 57
15170 Chalinargues 15 140 Cf 78
52600 Chalindrey 52 92 Fc 62
18130 Chalivoy-Milon 18 103 Ce 67
49440 Challain-la-Potherie 49 83 Yf 63
85300 Challans 85 96 Ya 67
15320 Challèles 15 140 Db 79
58420 Challement 58 89 Dd 65
08400 Challerange 08 42 Ee 53
01450 Challes 01 119 Fc 72
72250 Challes 72 85 Ac 61
73190 Challes-les-Eaux 73 132 Ff 75
28300 Challet 28 70 Bc 57
01630 Challex 01 120 Ff 71
16300 Challignac 16 123 Zf 76
74910 Challonges 74 119 Ff 72
58000 Challuy 58 103 Da 67
77650 Chalmaison 77 72 Db 58
42920 Chalmazel-Jeansagnière 42 129 Df 74
52160 Chalmessin 52 91 Fa 62
73530 Chalmieu, le 73 144 Gb 77
71140 Chalmoux 71 104 Df 69
26350 Chalon, le 26 143 Fa 78
49490 Chalonnes-sous-le-Lude 49 84 Ab 63
49290 Chalonnes-sur-Loire 49 83 Zb 64
17600 Chalons 17 122 Za 74
38122 Châlons 38 130 Ef 76
19200 Chalons-d'Aix 19 127 Cc 75
53470 Châlons-du-Maine 53 67 Zc 60
51000 Châlons-en-Champagne 51 54 Ec 55
51140 Châlons-sur-Vesle 51 53 Df 53
71100 Chalon-sur-Saône 71 106 Ef 68
70400 Châlonvillars-Mandrevillars 70 94 Ge 63
91780 Chalo-Saint-Mars 91 70 Ca 58
91740 Chalou-Moulineux 91 70 Ca 58
44330 Chalousière, la 44 97 Ye 66
05200 Chalp, la 05 145 Gd 81
05350 Chalp, la 05 145 Ge 80
38740 Chalp, la 38 144 Ff 79
05100 Chalps, les 05 145 Ge 79
51130 Chaltrait 51 53 Df 55
03150 Chalus 03 116 Dc 71
63340 Chalus 63 128 Db 76
63620 Chalus 63 127 Cc 73
87230 Châlus 87 125 Af 75
18390 Chalusse 18 102 Cc 66
63210 Chalusset 63 127 Ce 74
05470 Chalvet 05 145 Ge 80
15200 Chalvignac 15 127 Cb 77
52700 Chalvraines 52 75 Fc 59
58190 Chalvron 58 90 De 64
15170 Cham, la 15 140 Cf 78
33230 Chamadelle 33 135 Zf 78
88130 Chamagne 88 76 Gb 58
38460 Chamagnieu 38 131 Fa 74
63400 Chamalières 63 128 Da 74
43800 Chamalières-sur-Loire 43 129 Df 77
26150 Chamaloc 26 143 Fc 80
01340 Chamandre 01 118 Fb 70
60300 Chamant 60 51 Cd 53
91730 Chamarande 91 71 Cb 57
52000 Chamarandes-Choignes 52 75 Fa 60
26230 Chamaret 26 155 Ef 82
26470 Chamauche 26 143 Fb 81
42440 Chamba, la 42 129 De 74
21290 Chambain 21 91 Ef 62
43270 Chambarel 43 141 De 77
63200 Chambaron sur Morge 63 116 Da 73
43620 Chambaud 43 129 Ec 77
24120 Chambaudie, la 24 137 Bb 78
58150 Chambeau 58 89 Cf 65
21110 Chambeire 21 92 Fb 65
49220 Chambellay 49 83 Zb 62
42110 Chambeon 42 129 Eb 74
03370 Chambérat 03 115 Cc 70
23480 Chamberaud 23 114 Ca 72
19370 Chamberet 19 126 Be 75
39270 Chambéria 39 119 Fd 70
49260 Chambernou 49 98 Zd 66
82130 Chambert 82 150 Bc 84
33140 Chambéry 33 135 Zc 80
73000 Chambéry 73 132 Ff 75
89120 Chambeugle 89 89 Da 61
43000 Chambeyrac 43 141 Df 78
43270 Chambeyrac 43 129 De 77
43410 Chambezon 43 128 Db 76
19200 Chambige 19 126 Cb 75
71110 Chambilly 71 117 Ea 71
21250 Chamblanc 21 106 Fa 66
28630 Chamblay 28 70 Bd 58
36110 Chamblay 36 101 Bd 67
39380 Chamblay 39 107 Fe 67
42170 Chambles 42 129 Eb 76
03170 Chamblet 03 115 Ce 70
54890 Chambley-Bussières 54 56 Ff 54
60230 Chambly 60 51 Cb 54
21220 Chambœuf 21 106 Ef 65
42330 Chambœuf 42 129 Eb 75
27240 Chambois 27 49 Ba 55
61160 Chambois 61 48 Aa 56
71400 Chambois 71 105 Eb 66
63230 Chambois-Grand 63 127 Cf 74
63230 Chambois-Petit 63 127 Cf 74
21220 Chambolle-Musigny 21 106 Ef 65
15240 Chambon 15 127 Cd 76
17290 Chambon 17 110 Za 72
18190 Chambon 18 102 Cb 68
24270 Chambon 24 125 Bb 76
24290 Chambon 24 137 Ba 78
36210 Chambon 36 101 Bd 66
36270 Chambon 36 113 Bd 70
36320 Chambon 36 101 Bc 67
37290 Chambon 37 100 Ae 67
58240 Chambon 58 103 Da 68
07160 Chambon, le 07 142 Eb 79
15380 Chambon, le 15 127 Cc 77
19400 Chambon, le 19 138 Bf 78
26510 Chambon, le 26 156 Fc 82
30450 Chambon, le 30 154 Df 82
43300 Chambon, le 43 140 Db 78
43380 Chambon, le 43 140 Dc 78
48130 Chambon, le 48 140 Db 80
73530 Chambon, le 73 132 Gb 77
07140 Chambonas 07 154 Ea 82
23110 Chambonchard 23 115 Cd 71
42500 Chambon-Feugerolles, le 42 129 Eb 76
42440 Chambonie, la 42 129 De 74
45340 Chambon-la-Forêt 45 71 Cb 60
48600 Chambon-le-Château 48 141 Dd 79
43580 Chambonnet 43 141 Dd 79
07310 Chambonnet-Haut 07 142 Eb 79
07380 Chambons, les 07 141 Eb 81
23220 Chambon-Sainte-Croix 23 114 Be 70
41190 Chambon-sur-Cisse 41 86 Bb 63
63980 Chambon-sur-Dolore 63 128 Dd 76
63790 Chambon-sur-Lac 63 127 Cf 75
43400 Chambon-sur-Lignon, le 43 142 Eb 78
23170 Chambon-sur-Voueize 23 115 Cc 71
23240 Chamborand 23 113 Bd 72
27250 Chambord 27 49 Ad 55
27270 Chambord 27 49 Ad 55
41250 Chambord 41 86 Bd 63
87140 Chamborêt 87 113 Ba 72
30530 Chamborigaud 30 154 Df 83
70190 Chambornay-lès-Bellevaux 70 93 Ga 64
70150 Chambornay-lès-Pins 70 93 Ff 64
60240 Chambors 60 50 Be 53
69870 Chambost 69D 117 Ed 72
69870 Chambost-Allières 69D 117 Ed 72
69770 Chambost-Longessaigne 69M 129 Ec 74
73410 Chambotte, la 73 132 Ff 74
19450 Chamboulive 19 126 Be 76
43800 Chamboulive 43 129 Df 77
78240 Chambourcy 78 51 Ca 55
37310 Chambourg-sur-Indre 37 100 Af 65
05340 Chambran-Chalets 05 145 Gc 79
27120 Chambray 27 50 Bb 54
37170 Chambray-lès-Tours 37 85 Ae 64
15200 Chambre 15 127 Cc 77
58200 Chambre 58 89 Da 64
73130 Chambre, la 73 132 Gb 76
51170 Chambrecy 51 53 De 53
63580 Chambrefaite 63 128 Dc 76
50320 Chambres, les 50 46 Yd 56
85500 Chambretaud 85 97 Za 67
57170 Chambrey 57 57 Gc 56
72510 Chambriant 72 84 Aa 62
52700 Chambroncourt 52 75 Fc 58
79300 Chamboutet 79 98 Zd 67
23200 Chambroutière 23 114 Ca 73
02000 Chambry 02 40 Dd 51
77910 Chambry 77 52 Cf 55
86320 Chambu, la 86 112 Ae 70
63580 Chaméane 63 128 Dc 75
89430 Chamelard 89 90 Ea 61
69620 Chamelet 69D 117 Ed 73
01190 Chamerande 01 118 Ef 70
52210 Chameroy 52 92 Fa 61
02130 Chamery 02 53 Dd 53
51500 Chamery 51 53 Df 53
58350 Chamery 58 89 Db 65
07150 Chames 07 154 Ec 82
25380 Chamesey 25 108 Gd 65
25190 Chamesol 25 94 Ge 64
21400 Chamesson 21 91 Ed 62
05380 Chameyer 05 145 Gc 81
19330 Chameyrat 19 126 Be 77
18140 Chamignons, les 18 103 Cf 66
77260 Chamigny 77 52 Da 55
71510 Chamilly 71 105 Ee 67
53270 Chammes 53 67 Zd 60
19290 Chammet 19 126 Bf 74
58290 Chamnay 58 104 De 66
73350 Chamoeranger 73 133 Ge 76
39800 Chamole 39 107 Fe 67
38890 Chamon 38 131 Fc 75
13129 Chamone 13 169 Ee 88
74400 Chamonix-Mont-Blanc 74 121 Gf 73
21530 Chamont 21 90 Eb 64
17130 Chamouillac 17 123 Zd 77
02860 Chamouille 02 40 Dd 52
52410 Chamouilley 52 75 Fa 57
69930 Chamousset 69M 130 Ec 74
73390 Chamousset 73 132 Gb 75
89660 Chamoux 89 90 Dd 64
73390 Chamoux-sur-Gelon 73 132 Gb 75
10130 Chamoy 10 73 Df 60
55100 Champ 55 55 Fb 53
04320 Champ, le 04 158 Ge 85
73340 Champ, le 73 132 Ga 74
15350 Champagnac 15 127 Cc 76
17500 Champagnac 17 123 Zd 76
24600 Champagnac 24 124 Ab 77
43580 Champagnac 43 141 Dd 79
87380 Champagnac 87 125 Bb 75
24530 Champagnac-de-Belair 24 124 Ae 76
19320 Champagnac-la-Noaille 19 126 Ca 77
19320 Champagnac-la-Prune 19 126 Bf 77
87150 Champagnac-la-Rivière 87 125 Af 74
43440 Champagnac-le-Vieux 43 128 Dd 76
23190 Champagnat 23 114 Cb 72
71480 Champagnat 71 119 Fc 70
87120 Champagnat 87 126 Bf 74
63580 Champagnat-le-Jeune 63 128 Dc 76
01440 Champagné 01 118 Fb 71
07340 Champagne 07 130 Ee 77
07380 Champagne 07 141 Eb 80
17360 Champagne 17 123 Aa 77
17380 Champagné 17 110 Zc 73
17620 Champagne 17 122 Za 74
28410 Champagne 28 50 Bd 56
36220 Champagne 36 100 Af 68
39320 Champagne 39 119 Fc 70
58190 Champagne 58 90 Dd 64
72470 Champagné 72 68 Ab 60

254 I Cergy

69410 Champagne au-Mont d'Or 69M 130 Ee 74
01260 Champagne-en-Valromey 01 119 Fe 73
24320 Champagne-et-Fontaine 24 124 Ab 76
86510 Champagne-le-Sec 86 111 Ab 71
85450 Champagné-les-Marais 85 110 Yf 70
86400 Champagné-Lureau 86 112 Ab 71
16350 Champagne-Mouton 16 112 Ac 73
86160 Champagné-Saint-Hilaire 86 112 Ab 71
39600 Champagne-sur-Loue 39 107 Fe 66
95660 Champagne-sur-Oise 95 51 Cb 54
77430 Champagne-sur-Seine 77 72 Ce 58
21310 Champagne-sur-Vingeanne 21 92 Fc 64
73240 Champagneux 73 131 Fe 75
16250 Champagne-Vigny 16 123 Aa 75
25170 Champagney 25 107 Ff 65
39290 Champagney 39 106 Fd 65
70290 Champagney 70 94 Ge 62
38800 Champagnier 38 144 Fe 78
81120 Champagnol 81 151 Cb 86
17200 Champagnole 17 122 Yf 74
39300 Champagnole 39 107 Ff 68
17240 Champagnolles 17 122 Zc 75
21440 Champagny 21 91 Ee 64
42590 Champagny 42 129 Eb 73
73350 Champagny-en-Vanoise 73 133 Ge 76
71460 Champagny-sous-Uxelles 71 105 Ee 69
72110 Champaissant 72 68 Ac 59
18140 Champalais 18 103 Cf 65
58420 Champallement 58 104 Dc 65
04340 Champanastay 04 157 Gc 82
42600 Champanet 42 129 Ea 75
74500 Champanges 74 120 Gd 70
42990 Champas, le 42 129 Df 74
51270 Champaubert 51 53 De 55
16370 Champblanc 16 123 Zd 74
63680 Champ-Bourguet 63 127 Ce 75
02260 Champ-Bouvier 02 41 Df 49
28200 Champbuisson 28 69 Ba 60
58150 Champcelée 58 89 Da 65
05310 Champcella 05 145 Gd 80
77560 Champcenest 77 52 Db 56
61210 Champcerie 61 48 Ze 56
50320 Champcervon 50 46 Yd 56
24750 Champcevinel 24 124 Ae 77
89220 Champcevrais 89 88 Cf 62
50530 Champcey 50 46 Yd 56
43260 Champclause 43 141 Eb 78
30110 Champclauson 30 154 Ea 83
48000 Champclos 48 140 Dc 81
36600 Champcol 36 101 Bd 65
58230 Champcommeau 58 105 Eb 65
77560 Champcouelle 77 52 Dc 56
52330 Champcourt 52 74 Ef 59
91750 Champcueil 91 71 Cc 57
05190 Champdarène 05 157 Gb 82
38980 Champ-de-Chambaran 38 131 Fb 77
44860 Champ-de-Foire, le 44 97 Yc 66
86130 Champ-de-Grain 86 99 Ac 68
61320 Champ-de-la-Pierre, le 61 67 Ze 57
41310 Champ-Delay 41 86 Ba 62
79220 Champdeniers-Saint-Denis 79 111 Zd 70
77390 Champdeuil 77 51 Ce 57
42600 Champdieu 42 129 Ea 75
39500 Champdivers 39 106 Fc 66
21500 Champ-d'Oiseau 21 90 Ec 63
17430 Champdolent 17 110 Zb 73
27190 Champ-Dolent 27 49 Ba 55
27240 Champ-Dominel 27 49 Ba 55
01110 Champdor-Corcelles 01 119 Fd 72
21130 Champdôtre 21 106 Fb 65
36290 Champ-d'Ouf 36 100 Ba 68
88640 Champdray 88 77 Ge 60
14380 Champ-du-Boult 14 47 Yf 56
21210 Champeau 21 90 Ea 65
58210 Champeau 58 89 Dc 65
19400 Champeaux 19 138 Bf 78
35500 Champeaux 35 66 Ye 60
77720 Champeaux 77 72 Ce 57
79220 Champeaux 79 111 Zd 70
87330 Champeaux 87 112 Af 72
61120 Champeaux, les 61 48 Aa 55
24340 Champeaux-et-la-Chapelle-Pommier 24 124 Ad 76
61560 Champeaux-sur-Sarthe 61 68 Ac 57
23600 Champeix 23 114 Cb 71
63320 Champeix 63 128 Da 75
43580 Champels 43 141 Dd 79
67420 Champenay 67 77 Ha 58
36100 Champenoise, la 36 101 Be 67
54280 Champenoux 54 56 Gc 56
53640 Champéon 53 67 Zc 58
48210 Champerboux 48 153 Dc 82
63600 Champétières 63 129 De 75
50530 Champeux 50 46 Yc 56
70400 Champey 70 94 Ge 63
63720 Champeyroux 63 116 Db 73
54700 Champey-sur-Moselle 54 56 Ga 55
10700 Champfleury 10 73 Ea 57
51500 Champfleury 51 53 Ea 53
86100 Champ-Fleury 86 100 Ad 68
53370 Champfrémont 53 67 Zf 58
01410 Champfromier 01 119 Fe 71
18400 Champfrost 18 102 Cb 67
58230 Champgazon 58 104 Ea 65
53160 Champgénéteux 53 67 Zd 59
52130 Champ-Gerbeau 52 74 Ef 57
85210 Champgillon 85 97 Yf 69
10130 Champgiron 10 73 De 60
51310 Champguyon 51 53 Dd 56
61240 Champ-Haut 61 48 Ab 56
28300 Champhol 28 70 Bd 58
59740 Champiau 59 31 Ea 48
80700 Champien 80 39 Cf 50
38260 Champier 38 131 Fb 76
49330 Champigné 49 83 Zc 63
89350 Champignelles 89 89 Da 62
51150 Champigneul-Champagne 51 53 Eb 55
08250 Champigneulle 08 42 Ef 52
54250 Champigneulles 54 56 Ga 56
52150 Champigneulles-en-Bassigny 52 75 Fd 60
08430 Champigneul-sur-Vence 08 42 Ed 50
21230 Champignolles 21 105 Ed 66
27330 Champignolles 27 49 Ae 55
10200 Champignol-lez-Mondeville 10 74 Ee 60
49400 Champigny 49 99 Zf 65
51370 Champigny 51 53 Df 53
89340 Champigny 89 72 Da 59
41330 Champigny-en-Beauce 41 86 Bb 62
27220 Champigny-la-Futelaye 27 50 Bb 55
86170 Champigny-le-Sec 86 99 Aa 68
52200 Champigny-lès-Langres 52 92 Fc 61
52400 Champigny-sous-Varennes 52 92 Fd 61
10700 Champigny-sur-Aube 10 73 Ea 57
94500 Champigny-sur-Marne 94 51 Cd 56
37120 Champigny-sur-Veude 37 99 Ab 66
63230 Champille 63 127 Cf 74
36160 Champillet 36 114 Ca 69
51160 Champillon 51 53 Df 54
49520 Champiré 49 83 Za 62
07440 Champis 07 142 Ee 79
41100 Champlain 41 86 Bb 61
20213 Champlan CTC 181 Kc 94
91160 Champlan 91 51 Cb 56
51480 Champlat-et-Boujacourt 51 53 Df 54
73390 Champ-Laurent 73 132 Gb 75
89300 Champlay 89 72 Dc 61
71120 Champlecy 71 117 Eb 70
88600 Champ-le-Duc 88 77 Ge 59
58210 Champlemy 58 89 Dc 65
38190 Champ-les Adrets, le 38 132 Ff 77
08260 Champlin 08 41 Ec 49
58700 Champlin 58 104 Dc 65
70600 Champlitte 70 92 Fd 63
70600 Champlitte-la-Ville 70 92 Fd 63
25360 Champlive 25 93 Gb 65
55160 Champlon 55 55 Fd 54
43100 Champlong 43 128 Dc 77
63310 Champlong 63 116 Dc 72
37360 Champlonnière 37 85 Ad 63
89210 Champlost 89 73 De 60
16290 Champmillon 16 123 Aa 75
89420 Champmorlin 89 90 Ea 64
91150 Champmotteux 91 71 Cb 58
27160 Champ-Motteux, le 27 49 Af 55
87400 Champnétery 87 126 Bd 74
55100 Champneuville 55 55 Fb 53
16430 Champniers 16 124 Ab 74
86400 Champniers 86 112 Ac 71
24360 Champniers-et-Reilhac 24 124 Ae 74
05260 Champoléon 05 144 Gb 80
42430 Champoly 42 129 Df 73
61120 Champosoult 61 48 Aa 55
23800 Champotier 23 114 Be 71
55140 Champougny 55 75 Fe 57
25640 Champoux 25 93 Ga 64
21690 Champrenault 21 91 Ee 64
50800 Champrepus 50 46 Ye 55
01350 Champriond 01 119 Fe 73
58370 Champrobert 58 104 Df 67
28400 Champrond-en-Perchet 28 69 Af 59
91210 Champrosay 91 51 Cc 57
39230 Champrougier 39 106 Fd 67
03320 Champroux 03 103 Cf 68
02670 Champs 02 40 Db 51
42600 Champs 42 129 Ea 75
45310 Champs 45 70 Bd 61
54890 Champs 54 56 Ff 54
61190 Champs 61 68 Ad 57
63440 Champs 63 115 Da 72
86390 Champs 86 113 Af 70
87130 Champs 87 126 Bd 75
16500 Champs, les 16 112 Ae 72
23220 Champs, les 23 114 Bf 71
73220 Champs, les 73 132 Gb 76
87260 Champs, les 87 125 Bb 74
87230 Champsac 87 125 Af 74
23220 Champsanglard 23 114 Bf 71
50620 Champs-de-Losque, les 50 34 Ye 53
61700 Champsecret 61 67 Zc 57
19170 Champseix 19 126 Bf 75
28700 Champseru 28 70 Bd 58
17430 Champservé 17 110 Za 73
22630 Champs-Géraux, les 22 65 Ya 58
63220 Champsiaux 63 129 Dd 76
24470 Champs-Romain 24 124 Ae 75
15270 Champs-sur-Tarentaine-Marchal 15 127 Cd 76
89290 Champs-sur-Yonne 89 89 Dd 62
10140 Champ-sur-Barse 10 74 Ec 59
38560 Champ-sur-Drac 38 144 Fe 78
49380 Champ-sur-Layon, le 49 83 Zc 65
04660 Champtercier 04 157 Ga 84
49220 Champteussé-sur-Baconne 49 83 Zc 62
49270 Champtoceaux 49 82 Ye 64
49123 Champtocé-sur-Loire 49 83 Za 64
70100 Champtonnay 70 92 Fe 64
89710 Champvallon 89 89 Dc 61
39100 Champvans 39 106 Fc 66
70100 Champvans 70 92 Fd 64
25170 Champvans-les-Moulins 25 107 Ff 65
39800 Champvaux 39 107 Fe 68
43350 Champvert 43 141 Df 77
58300 Champvert 58 104 Dd 67
51700 Champvoisy 51 53 Dd 54
58400 Champvoux 58 103 Da 66
08240 Champy-Haut, le 08 42 Fa 52
38410 Chamrousse 38 144 Ff 78
48600 Chams 48 141 Dd 80
89300 Chamvres 89 72 Dc 61
48230 Chanac 48 140 Dc 82
19150 Chanac-les-Mines 19 126 Be 77
44119 Chanais 44 82 Yc 64
43170 Chanaleilles 43 140 Dc 79
63610 Chananeille 63 128 Cf 75
38150 Chanas 38 130 Ee 77
63530 Chanat-la-Mouteyre 63 128 Da 74
01420 Chanay 01 119 Fe 72
73310 Chanaz 73 132 Fe 74
37210 Chançay 37 85 Af 64
35680 Chancé 35 66 Yd 60
21440 Chanceaux 21 91 Ee 63
43000 Chanceaux 43 141 Df 78
37600 Chanceaux-près-Loches 37 100 Af 66
37390 Chanceaux-sur-Choisille 37 85 Ae 64
24650 Chancelade 24 124 Ad 77
63640 Chancelade 63 115 Cd 73
52100 Chancenay 52 55 Ef 56
70140 Chancey 70 92 Fe 65
40260 Chanchon 40 146 Ye 85
01590 Chancia 01 119 Fd 70
61300 Chandai 61 49 Ae 56
33860 Chandas 33 123 Zd 77
63610 Chandelière 63 128 Cf 76
28210 Chandelles 28 50 Bd 57
07230 Chandolas 07 154 Eb 82
42190 Chandon 42 117 Eb 72
73550 Chandon 73 133 Gd 76
41240 Chandry 41 86 Bd 61
07310 Chanéac 07 142 Eb 79
01990 Chaneins 01 118 Ef 72
04340 Chanenche, le 04 158 Gc 82
01360 Chânes 01 131 Fa 73
21340 Change 21 105 Ed 67
53810 Changé 53 67 Zb 60
72560 Changé 72 68 Ab 61
24640 Change, le 24 125 Af 77
52360 Changey 52 92 Fc 61
71360 Changey 71 105 Ed 67
77660 Changis-sur-Marne 77 52 Da 55
42310 Changy 42 117 Df 72
51300 Changy 51 54 Ee 56
71120 Changy 71 117 Eb 70
43100 Chaniat 43 128 Dc 77
17610 Chaniers 17 123 Zc 74
21330 Channay 21 90 Ec 61
37330 Channay-sur-Lathan 37 85 Ab 64
10340 Channes 10 90 Eb 61
50400 Channière, la 50 46 Yc 55
04420 Chanolles 04 157 Gc 84
23200 Chanon 23 114 Cb 71
63450 Chanonat 63 128 Da 74
26600 Chanos-Curson 26 142 Ef 78
43130 Chanou 43 141 Df 77
05700 Chanousse 05 156 Fd 82
45360 Chanoy 45 88 Ce 63
52260 Chanoy 52 92 Fb 61
01400 Chanoz-Châtenay 01 118 Fa 71
64500 Chantaco 64 160 Yc 88
18370 Chantafret 18 114 Cb 69
15140 Chantal-Péricot 15 139 Cb 78
19380 Chantarel 19 126 Be 78
23150 Chantaud 23 114 Ca 72
21210 Chanteau 21 90 Eb 65
45400 Chanteau 45 70 Bf 61
79420 Chantebuzin 79 111 Ze 69
45320 Chantecoq 45 72 Cf 60
19350 Chantecorps 19 125 Bb 77
79340 Chantecorps 79 111 Zf 70
25160 Chantegrue 25 107 Gb 68
54300 Chanteheux 54 77 Gd 57
19330 Chanteix 19 126 Bd 77
43380 Chantel 43 128 Dc 77
63650 Chantelause 63 128 Dd 73
03140 Chantelle 03 116 Da 71
05600 Chanteloub 05 145 Gd 80
05230 Chanteloube 05 144 Gb 81
23160 Chanteloube 23 113 Bc 70
23220 Chanteloube 23 114 Bf 71
27240 Chanteloup 27 49 Ba 55
27930 Chanteloup 27 50 Bb 54
35150 Chanteloup 35 65 Yc 61
50510 Chanteloup 50 46 Yd 55
58420 Chanteloup 58 104 Dd 65
72460 Chanteloup 72 68 Ab 60
77600 Chanteloup 77 52 Ce 55
79320 Chanteloup 79 98 Zc 68
86410 Chanteloup 86 112 Ad 70
49340 Chanteloup-les-Bois 49 98 Zb 66
78570 Chanteloup-les-Vignes 78 51 Ca 55
38740 Chantelouve 38 144 Ff 79
05330 Chantemerle 05 145 Gd 79
10500 Chantemerle 10 74 Ec 58
51260 Chantemerle 51 73 Dd 57
79320 Chantemerle 79 98 Zc 68
26600 Chantemerle-les-Blés 26 142 Ef 78
26230 Chantemerle-lès-Grignan 26 155 Ef 82
17470 Chantemerlière 17 111 Ze 72
58240 Chantenay-Saint-Imbert 58 103 Db 68
72430 Chantenay-Villedieu 72 84 Zf 61
42640 Chante-Oiseaux 42 117 Ea 72
35135 Chantepie 35 65 Yc 60
24350 Chantepoule 24 124 Ad 77
24190 Chantérac 24 136 Ac 77
55500 Chanteraine 55 55 Fc 56
15190 Chanterelle 15 127 Ce 76
48100 Chanteruéjols 48 140 Dc 81
70360 Chantes 70 93 Ff 63
38470 Chantesse 38 131 Fc 77
43300 Chanteuges 43 140 Dd 78
33114 Chantier 33 134 Zb 81
43000 Chantilhac 43 141 De 78
16360 Chantillac 16 123 Ze 77
60500 Chantilly 60 51 Cc 53
36270 Chantôme 36 113 Bd 70
41240 Chantôme 41 86 Bc 61
85110 Chantonnay 85 97 Yf 68
36150 Chantorin 36 101 Be 66
87160 Chantouant 87 113 Bb 70
88000 Chantraine 88 76 Gc 59
52700 Chantraines 52 75 Fb 59
25330 Chantrans 25 107 Ga 66
16270 Chantrezac 16 112 Ad 73
53300 Chantrigné 53 67 Zc 58
27640 Chanu 27 50 Bc 55
61800 Chanu 61 47 Zb 56
57580 Chanville 57 56 Gc 54
49750 Chanzeaux 49 83 Zc 65
41600 Chaon 41 87 Cb 63
54330 Chaouilley 54 76 Ga 58
10210 Chaource 10 73 Ea 60
02340 Chaourse 02 41 Df 50
05150 Chapaisse 05 156 Fd 82
71460 Chapaize 71 118 Ee 69
38530 Chapareillan 38 132 Ff 76
74210 Chaparon 74 132 Gb 74
64430 Chapatendéguia 64 160 Yd 89
48130 Chapchiniés 48 140 Db 81
63230 Chapdes-Beaufort 63 115 Cf 73
24320 Chapdeuil 24 124 Ac 76
24600 Chapdeuil, le 24 124 Ab 77
03340 Chapeau 03 116 Dd 70
59360 Chapeau-Rouge 59 31 De 48
48130 Chapeauroux 48 141 De 79
74540 Chapeiry 74 132 Ga 73
51290 Chapelaine 51 74 Ed 57
03380 Chapelaude, la 03 115 Cd 70
13010 Chapelette, la 13 170 Fc 89
24470 Chapellas 24 125 Af 75
40110 Chapelle 40 147 Zb 84
01160 Chapelle, la 01 119 Fb 72
03300 Chapelle, la 03 116 Dd 72
04140 Chapelle, la 04 157 Gb 82
04210 Chapelle, la 04 157 Ga 85
08200 Chapelle, la 08 42 Fa 50
16140 Chapelle, la 16 123 Aa 73
16300 Chapelle, la 16 123 Zf 76
17460 Chapelle, la 17 122 Zb 75
18340 Chapelle, la 18 102 Cc 67
19270 Chapelle, la 19 126 Bd 77
21340 Chapelle, la 21 105 Ed 66
23200 Chapelle, la 23 114 Ca 73
24260 Chapelle, la 24 137 Af 79
27560 Chapelle, la 27 49 Ac 53
31220 Chapelle, la 31 164 Ba 89
33240 Chapelle, la 33 135 Zd 79
35620 Chapelle, la 35 82 Yc 62
35800 Chapelle, la 35 65 Xf 57
36140 Chapelle, la 36 114 Be 70
38490 Chapelle, la 38 131 Fd 75
38620 Chapelle, la 38 131 Fe 76
44110 Chapelle, la 44 82 Yc 62
56460 Chapelle, la 56 81 Xd 61
63260 Chapelle, la 63 116 Da 72
64240 Chapelle, la 64 160 Ye 88
69650 Chapelle, la 69M 118 Ee 73
71340 Chapelle, la 71 117 Df 71
72130 Chapelle, la 72 68 Zf 59
73660 Chapelle, la 73 132 Gb 76
87110 Chapelle, la 87 125 Bb 74
87190 Chapelle, la 87 113 Bb 71
87380 Chapelle, la 87 125 Bc 75
88420 Chapelle, la 88 77 Gf 58
89340 Chapelle, la 89 72 Da 59
85150 Chapelle-Achard, la 85 97 Yc 69
63590 Chapelle-Agnon, la 63 128 Dd 75
53950 Chapelle-Anthenaise, la 53 67 Zb 60
24290 Chapelle-Aubareil, la 24 137 Bb 78
49110 Chapelle-Aubry, la 49 97 Za 65
53100 Chapelle-au-Grain, la 53 67 Zb 59
71130 Chapelle-au-Mans, la 71 104 Df 69
61100 Chapelle-au-Moine 61 47 Zc 56
53440 Chapelle-au-Riboul, la 53 67 Zd 59
88240 Chapelle-aux-Bois, la 88 76 Gb 60
19360 Chapelle-aux-Brocs, la 19 138 Bd 78
03230 Chapelle-aux-Chasses, la 03 104 Dd 68
72800 Chapelle-aux-Choux, la 72 85 Ab 63
35190 Chapelle-aux-Filtzméens, la 35 65 Yb 58
37130 Chapelle-aux-Naux, la 37 85 Ac 65
19120 Chapelle-aux-Saints 19 138 Be 79
23160 Chapelle-Baloue, la 23 113 Bd 70
44450 Chapelle-Basse-Mer, la 44 82 Yd 65
17400 Chapelle-Bâton, la 17 110 Zd 72
79220 Chapelle-Bâton, la 79 111 Ze 70
86250 Chapelle-Bâton, la 86 112 Ac 71
27260 Chapelle-Bayvel, la 27 48 Ac 53
86200 Chapelle-Bellouin, la 86 99 Ab 67
43270 Chapelle-Bertin, la 43 128 Dd 77
79200 Chapelle-Bertrand, la 79 99 Ze 69
61100 Chapelle-Biche, la 61 47 Zc 56
22350 Chapelle-Blanche, la 22 65 Xf 59
73110 Chapelle-Blanche, la 73 132 Ga 76
37240 Chapelle-Blanche-Saint-Martin, la 37 100 Ae 66
35330 Chapelle-Bouëxic, la 35 81 Ya 61
44850 Chapelle-Breton, la 44 82 Ye 64
19240 Chapelle-Brochas, la 19 125 Bc 77
50800 Chapelle-Cécelin, la 50 46 Yf 56
35630 Chapelle-Chaussée, la 35 65 Ya 59
53230 Chapelle-Craonnaise, la 53 83 Za 61
74360 Chapelle-d'Abondance 74 121 Ge 71
15300 Chapelle-d'Alagon, la 15 140 Cf 78
72300 Chapelle-d'Aligné, la 72 84 Ze 62
61140 Chapelle-d'Andaine, la 61 67 Zd 57
18380 Chapelle-d'Angillon, la 18 88 Cc 64
59930 Chapelle-d'Armentières, la 59 30 Cf 44
28700 Chapelle-d'Aunainville, la 28 70 Be 58
43120 Chapelle-d'Aurec, la 43 129 Eb 76
71240 Chapelle-de-Bragny, la 71 105 Ee 69
38110 Chapelle-de-la-Tour, la 38 131 Fc 75
69240 Chapelle-de-Mardore, la 69D 117 Ec 72
25240 Chapelle-des-Bois 25 107 Ga 69
35520 Chapelle-des-Fougereiz, la 35 65 Yb 59
44410 Chapelle-des-Marais, la 44 81 Xe 64
17100 Chapelle-des-Pots, la 17 123 Zc 74
38150 Chapelle-de-Surieu, la 38 130 Ef 76
88600 Chapelle-devant-Bruyères, la 88 77 Ge 59
25270 Chapelle-d'Huin 25 107 Gb 67
38580 Chapelle-du-Bard, la 38 132 Ga 76
72400 Chapelle-du-Bois, la 72 68 Ad 59
27930 Chapelle-du-Bois-des-Faulx, la 27 49 Ba 54
76590 Chapelle-du-Bourgay, la 76 37 Ba 50
01240 Chapelle-du-Châtelard, la 01 118 Fa 72
53320 Chapelle-du-Chêne, la 53 66 Za 60
72300 Chapelle-du-Chêne, la 72 84 Ze 62
50160 Chapelle-du-Fest, la 50 47 Za 54
49600 Chapelle-du-Genêt, la 49 97 Yf 65
35360 Chapelle-du Lou du Lac, la 35 65 Ya 59
71520 Chapelle-du-Mont-de-France, la 71 117 Ed 70
73370 Chapelle-du-Mont-du-Chat, la 73 132 Fe 74
29610 Chapelle-du-Mur, la 29 62 Wb 57
28200 Chapelle-du-Noyer, la 28 69 Bb 60
41290 Chapelle-Enchérie, la 41 86 Bb 62
14770 Chapelle-Engerbold, la 14 47 Zc 55
50570 Chapelle-en-Juger, la 50 33 Ye 54
42380 Chapelle-en-Lafaye, la 42 129 Df 76
60520 Chapelle-en-Serval, la 60 51 Cd 54
05800 Chapelle-en-Valgaudémar, la 05 144 Gb 80
38740 Chapelle-en-Valjouffrey, la 38 144 Ga 79
26420 Chapelle-en-Vercors, la 26 143 Fc 79
95420 Chapelle-en-Vexin, la 95 50 Be 53
35500 Chapelle-Erbrée, la 35 66 Yf 60
30700 Chapelle-et-Masmolène, la 30 155 Ed 84
24530 Chapelle-Faucher, la 24 124 Ae 76
51800 Chapelle-Felcourt, la 51 54 Ee 54
28500 Chapelle-Forainvilliers, la 28 50 Bd 56
28340 Chapelle-Fortin, la 28 49 Af 57
56200 Chapelle-Gaceline, la 56 81 Xf 62
79300 Chapelle-Gaudin, la 79 98 Zd 67
72310 Chapelle-Gaugain, la 72 85 Ae 62
27270 Chapelle-Gauthier, la 27 48 Ac 55
77720 Chapelle-Gauthier, la 77 72 Cf 57
43160 Chapelle-Geneste, la 43 129 De 76
44670 Chapelle-Glain, la 44 82 Ye 63
24350 Chapelle-Gonaguet, la 24 124 Ad 77
24320 Chapelle-Grésignac, la 24 124 Ac 76
28330 Chapelle-Guillaume, la 28 69 Af 60
27230 Chapelle-Hareng, la 27 48 Ac 54
14140 Chapelle-Haute-Grue, la 14 48 Aa 55
85220 Chapelle-Hermier, la 85 96 Yb 68
44330 Chapelle-Heulin, la 44 97 Yd 65
18150 Chapelle-Hugon, la 18 103 Cf 67
49420 Chapelle-Hullin, la 49 83 Yf 62
72310 Chapelle-Huon, la 72 85 Ae 61
51700 Chapelle-Hurlay, la 51 53 Dd 54
77540 Chapelle-Iger, la 77 52 Cf 57
35133 Chapelle-Janson, la 35 66 Yf 58
77760 Chapelle-la-Reine, la 77 71 Cd 59
79700 Chapelle-Largeau, la 79 98 Za 67
51260 Chapelle-Lasson, la 51 53 De 57
44260 Chapelle-Launay, la 44 81 Ya 64
15500 Chapelle-Laurent, la 15 140 Db 77
70300 Chapelle-lès-Luxeuil, la 70 93 Gc 62
27950 Chapelle-Longueville, la 27 50 Bc 54
63420 Chapelle-Marcousse, la 63 128 Da 76
24320 Chapelle-Montabourlet, la 24 124 Ac 76
87440 Chapelle-Montbrandeix, la 87 125 Af 75
02330 Chapelle-Monthodon, la 02 53 Dd 54
61400 Chapelle-Montligeon, la 61 69 Ad 58
18140 Chapelle-Montlinard, la 18 103 Cf 65
41320 Chapelle-Montmartin, la 41 87 Be 65
24300 Chapelle-Montmoreau, la 24 124 Ad 76
86470 Chapelle-Montreuil, la 86 111 Aa 69
86300 Chapelle-Morthemer 86 112 Ad 70
86210 Chapelle-Moulière, la 86 100 Ad 69
24120 Chapelle-Mouret, la 24 137 Bb 78
77320 Chapelle-Moutils, la 77 52 Dc 56
71500 Chapelle-Naude, la 71 106 Fb 69
22160 Chapelle-Neuve, la 22 63 Wd 58
56500 Chapelle-Neuve, la 56 80 Xa 61
45310 Chapelle-Onzerain, la 45 70 Bd 60
36500 Chapelle-Orthemale, la 36 101 Bc 67
85670 Chapelle-Palluau, la 85 97 Yc 68
24250 Chapelle-Péchaud, la 24 137 Ba 80
24340 Chapelle-Pommier, la 24 124 Ad 76
79190 Chapelle-Pouilloux, la 79 111 Aa 72
61500 Chapelle-Près-Sees, la 61 68 Aa 57
77370 Chapelle-Rablais, la 77 72 Cf 57
53150 Chapelle-Rainsouin, la 53 67 Zc 60
74800 Chapelle-Rambaud, la 74 120 Gb 72
27950 Chapelle-Réanville, la 27 50 Bc 54
44522 Chapelle-Rigaud, la 44 82 Ye 64
49120 Chapelle-Rousselin, la 49 98 Zb 65
28290 Chapelle-Royale 28 69 Ba 60
18800 Chapelles 18 103 Ce 66
53250 Chapelles 53 67 Zd 58
85160 Chapelles 85 96 Xf 68
87800 Chapelles 87 125 Bb 74
73700 Chapelles, les 73 133 Ge 75
58210 Chapelle-Saint-André, la 58 89 Dc 64
35140 Chapelle-Saint-Aubert, la 35 66 Ye 59
72650 Chapelle-Saint-Aubin, la 72 68 Aa 60
37190 Chapelle-Saint-Blaise, la 37 100 Ac 65
79240 Chapelle-Saint-Étienne, la 79 98 Zc 68
49410 Chapelle-Saint-Florent, la 49 83 Yf 65
72240 Chapelle Saint Fray, la 72 68 Aa 60

A B C D E F G H I J K L M N O P Q R S T U V W X Y Z

Chapelle Saint Fray, la | 255

19430 Chapelle-Saint-Géraud, la 19 138 Bf 78
24390 Chapelle-Saint Jean, la 24 125 Bb 77
79430 Chapelle-Saint-Laurent, la 79 98 Zd 68
10600 Chapelle-Saint-Luc, la 10 73 Ea 59
23250 Chapelle-Saint-Martial, la 23 114 Bf 72
79350 Chapelle-Saint-Martin 79 98 Zd 68
41500 Chapelle-Saint-Martin-en-Plaine, la 41 86 Bc 62
74410 Chapelle-Saint-Maurice 74 132 Ga 74
35660 Chapelle-Saint-Melaine, la 35 81 Ya 62
45380 Chapelle-Saint-Mesmin, la 45 87 Bf 61
27620 Chapelle-Saint-Ouen, la 27 50 Bd 54
70700 Chapelle-Saint-Quillain, la 70 93 Fe 64
72160 Chapelle-Saint-Rémy, la 72 68 Ac 60
24300 Chapelle-Saint-Robert, la 24 124 Ad 75
44370 Chapelle-Saint-Sauveur, la 44 83 Yf 64
71310 Chapelle-Saint-Sauveur, la 71 106 Fb 67
45210 Chapelle-Saint-Sépulcre, la 45 71 Cf 60
77160 Chapelle-Saint-Sulpice, la 77 72 Db 57
18570 Chapelle-Saint-Ursin, la 18 102 Cb 66
19130 Chapelle-Salamard 19 125 Bc 77
77610 Chapelles-Bourbon, les 77 52 Cf 56
79240 Chapelle-Seguin, la 79 98 Zc 69
61130 Chapelle-Souëf, la 61 68 Ad 59
71700 Chapelle-sous-Brancion, la 71 118 Ee 69
51270 Chapelle-sous-Orbais, la 51 53 De 55
07520 Chapelle-sous-Rochepaule, la 07 142 Ec 78
71190 Chapelle-sous-Uchon, la 71 105 Eb 67
19300 Chapelle-Spinasse 19 126 Ca 76
45230 Chapelle-sur-Aveyron, la 45 88 Cf 61
02570 Chapelle-sur-Chézy, la 02 52 Dc 55
69590 Chapelle-sur-Coise, la 69M 130 Ec 75
77580 Chapelle-sur-Crécy, la 77 52 Cf 55
71800 Chapelle-sur-Dun, la 71 117 Eb 71
76740 Chapelle-sur-Dun, la 76 37 Af 49
44240 Chapelle-sur-Erdre, la 44 82 Yc 65
39110 Chapelle-sur-Furieuse, la 39 107 Ff 67
37140 Chapelle-sur-Loire, la 37 99 Ab 65
89260 Chapelle-sur-Oreuse, la 89 72 Db 59
49500 Chapelle-sur-Oudon, la 49 83 Zb 62
63580 Chapelle-sur-Usson, la 63 128 Dc 76
50420 Chapelle-sur-Vire, la 50 46 Yf 54
23000 Chapelle-Taillefert, la 23 114 Bf 72
71470 Chapelle-Thècle, la 71 118 Fa 69
85210 Chapelle-Thémer, la 85 110 Za 69
79160 Chapelle-Thireuil, la 79 110 Zc 69
35590 Chapelle-Thouarault, la 35 65 Ya 60
35190 Chapelle-Trévinal, la 35 65 Ya 58
50370 Chapelle-Urée, la 50 46 Yf 56
10700 Chapelle-Vallon 10 73 Ea 58
89800 Chapelle-Vaupelteigne, la 89 90 De 61
41330 Chapelle-Vendômoise, la 41 86 Bb 62
24300 Chapelle-Verlaine, la 24 124 Ae 75
41270 Chapelle-Vicomtesse, la 41 69 Ba 61
61270 Chapelle-Viel, la 61 49 Ad 56
42410 Chapelle-Villars, la 42 130 Ee 76
86300 Chapelle-Viviers 86 112 Ae 70
39140 Chapelle-Voland 39 106 Fc 68
14290 Chapelle-Yvon, la 14 48 Ac 54
45270 Chapelon 45 71 Cd 60
16430 Chapelot 16 124 Aa 74
18250 Chapelotte, la 18 88 Cd 64
19320 Chapeloune, la 19 126 Ca 77
64420 Chaperot 64 162 Ze 89
78130 Chapet 78 50 Bf 55
71190 Chapey 71 105 Eb 67
07120 Chapias 07 142 Eb 82
73700 Chapieux, les 73 133 Ge 74
38110 Chapite, la 38 131 Fc 75
39300 Chapois 39 107 Ff 67
69970 Chaponnay 69M 130 Ef 75
63190 Chaponnier 63 128 Dc 73
69630 Chaponost 69M 130 Ee 74
19120 Chapoulie, la 19 138 Be 78
89560 Chapoux 89 89 Dc 63
05160 Chappas, les 05 145 Gc 81
03390 Chappes 03 115 Cf 70
08220 Chappes 08 41 Eb 51
10260 Chappes 10 73 Eb 59
63720 Chappes 63 128 Db 73
87270 Chaptelat 87 113 Bb 73
63260 Chaptuzat 63 116 Db 72
26350 Charaix, le 26 130 Fa 77
09120 Charameau 09 177 Bd 90
38490 Charancieu 38 131 Fd 75
01260 Charancin 01 119 Fd 73
87500 Charannat 87 125 Ba 75
38790 Charantonnay 38 131 Fa 75
86360 Charasse 86 100 Ac 69
38850 Charavines 38 131 Fd 76
08370 Charbeaux 08 42 Fb 51
67220 Charbes 67 60 Hb 58
05500 Charbillac 05 144 Ga 80
08130 Charbogne 08 42 Ed 51
71320 Charbonnat 71 105 Ea 68
49123 Charbonnerie, la 49 83 Za 64
16320 Charbonnier 16 124 Ab 76
23250 Charbonnier 23 114 Bf 73
43340 Charbonnier 43 141 De 79
63980 Charbonnier 63 128 Dd 75
28330 Charbonnières 28 69 Af 59
71260 Charbonnières 71 118 Ef 70
05200 Charbonnières, les 05 145 Gd 81
69260 Charbonnières-les-Bains 69M 130 Ee 74
25620 Charbonnières-les-Sapins 25 107 Gb 66
63410 Charbonnières-les-Varennes 63 115 Da 73
63410 Charbonnières-les-Vieilles 63 115 Cf 73
63340 Charbonnier-les-Mines 63 128 Db 76
88560 Charbonniers, les 88 94 Gf 61
39250 Charbonny 39 107 Ga 68
43270 Charbounouze 43 128 Dd 77
89113 Charbuy 89 89 Dc 62
70700 Charcenne 70 93 Fe 64
49320 Charcé-Saint-Ellier-sur-Aubance 49 84 Zd 64
53250 Charchigné 53 67 Zd 58
39260 Charchilla 39 119 Fe 70
39130 Charcier 39 107 Fe 69
23700 Chard 23 115 Cc 73
43270 Chardas 43 129 De 77
16500 Chardat 16 112 Ae 72
04200 Chardavon 04 157 Ff 83
04140 Chardavon-Bas 04 157 Gb 82
04140 Chardavon-Haut 04 157 Gb 82
48120 Chardenoux 48 140 Dc 80
87290 Chardent 87 113 Ba 72
08400 Chardeny 08 42 Ed 52
24420 Chardeuil 24 125 Af 77
16440 Chardin 16 123 Zf 75
55000 Chardogne 55 55 Fa 56
71700 Chardonnay 71 118 Ef 69
03600 Chardonneau 03 115 Ce 71
48500 Chardonnet 48 140 Db 82
03140 Chareil 03 116 Db 71
63490 Charel 63 128 Dc 75
21690 Charencey 21 91 Ee 64
61190 Charencey 61 49 Ae 57
39250 Charency 39 107 Ff 68
26310 Charens 26 143 Fd 81
87640 Charensannes 87 113 Bc 72
63640 Charensat 63 115 Cd 73
69220 Charentay 69D 118 Ee 72
17700 Charentenay 17 110 Zb 72
70130 Charentenay 70 93 Ff 63
89580 Charentenay 89 89 Dd 63
37390 Charentilly 37 85 Ad 64
18210 Charenton-du-Cher 18 103 Cd 68
94220 Charenton-le-Pont 94 51 Cc 56
18140 Charentonnay 18 103 Cf 66
38390 Charette 38 131 Fc 74
71270 Charette 71 106 Fb 67
54470 Charey 54 56 Ff 55
48800 Chareylasse 48 154 De 82
39130 Charézier 39 107 Fe 69
37530 Chargé 37 86 Ba 64
26190 Charge, la 26 143 Fb 79
70100 Chargey-lès-Grey 70 92 Fd 64
70170 Chargey-lès-Port 70 93 Ff 62
70000 Chariez 70 93 Ga 63
21140 Charigny 21 91 Ec 64
58400 Charité-sur-Loire, la 58 103 Da 65
01130 Charix 01 119 Fe 71
42155 Charizet 42 117 Df 73
31350 Charlas 31 163 Ae 89
58210 Charlay 58 89 Dc 64
12260 Charlet 12 138 Ca 82
13350 Charleval 13 170 Fb 86
27380 Charleval 27 37 Bc 52
51800 Charlevaux 51 54 Ef 53
51120 Charleville 51 53 De 56
08000 Charleville-Mézières 08 42 Ee 50
57220 Charleville-sous-Bois 57 56 Gc 53
42190 Charlieu 42 117 Eb 72
18350 Charly 18 103 Ce 67
69390 Charly 69M 130 Ee 75
74350 Charly 74 120 Ga 72
57640 Charly-Oradour 57 56 Gb 53
02310 Charly-sur-Marne 02 52 Db 55
16320 Charmant 16 124 Ab 76
25470 Charmauvillers 25 108 Gf 65
16140 Charmé 16 111 Aa 73
39230 Charme, la 39 107 Fd 67
45230 Charme, le 45 89 Cf 62
71100 Charmée, la 71 106 Ee 68
89190 Charmée, la 89 72 Dd 59
03110 Charmeil 03 116 Dc 72
02850 Charmel, le 02 53 Dd 54
15500 Charmensac 15 128 Da 77
77410 Charmentray 77 52 Ce 55
02800 Charmes 02 40 Dc 51
03800 Charmes 03 116 Db 72
21310 Charmes 21 92 Fc 64
52360 Charmes 52 92 Fc 61
88130 Charmes 88 76 Gb 58
52110 Charmes-en-L'Angle 52 75 Fa 58
54113 Charmes-la-Côte 54 56 Fe 57
52110 Charmes-la-Grande 52 74 Ef 58
70120 Charmes-Saint-Valbert 70 92 Fe 62
26260 Charmes-sur-L'Herbasse 26 143 Fa 78
07800 Charmes-sur-Rhône 07 142 Ee 79
73450 Charmette, la 73 145 Gc 78
74230 Charmette, la 74 132 Gc 73
70000 Charmoille 70 93 Ga 63
52260 Charmoilles 52 75 Fc 61
54360 Charmois 54 76 Gc 57
55700 Charmois 55 42 Fb 52
58500 Charmois 58 89 Dc 64
90140 Charmois 90 94 Gf 63
88460 Charmois-devant-Bruyères 88 77 Gd 59
88270 Charmois-L'Orgueilleux 88 76 Gb 60
25380 Charmonle 25 108 Ge 65
51330 Charmont 51 54 Ef 55
95420 Charmont 95 50 Be 54
45480 Charmont-en-Beauce 45 71 Ca 59
51330 Charmontois, les 51 55 Ef 55
10150 Charmont-sous-Barbuise 10 73 Eb 58
10290 Charmoy 10 73 Dd 58
52500 Charmoy 52 92 Fd 62
71710 Charmoy 71 105 Ec 68
89400 Charmoy 89 72 Dc 61
28250 Charmoy-Gontier, le 28 69 Bb 57
07340 Charnas 07 130 Ee 76
63290 Charnat 63 116 Dc 73
25440 Charnay 25 107 Ff 66
69380 Charnay 69D 118 Ee 73
58250 Charnay, le 58 104 De 68
71110 Charnay, les 71 117 Df 71
71800 Charnay-en-Vaux 71 117 Eb 70
71350 Charnay-lès-Chalon 71 106 Fa 67
71850 Charnay-lès-Mâcon 71 118 Ee 71
38140 Charnècles 38 131 Fd 76
19310 Charniac 19 125 Bb 77
37290 Charnizay 37 100 Af 67
39240 Charnod 39 119 Fc 71
08600 Charnois 08 42 Ee 48
03360 Charnoux 03 103 Ce 68
77580 Charnoy, le 77 52 Cf 55
01800 Charnoz 01 131 Fb 73
21350 Charny 21 91 Ec 64
77410 Charny 77 52 Ce 55
80290 Charny 80 38 Be 50
89120 Charny 89 89 Da 61
74110 Charny, le 74 121 Ge 72
10380 Charny-le-Bachot 10 73 Df 57
89120* Charny Orée de Puisaye 89 89 Da 61
55100 Charny-sur-Meuse 55 55 Fc 53
26450 Charois 26 143 Ef 81
71120 Charolles 71 117 Eb 70
18500 Châron 18 102 Cb 66
63640 Charonnet 63 115 Cd 72
36210 Charons, les 36 101 Bd 66
28120 Charonville 28 69 Bb 59
82370 Charos 82 150 Bc 85
17570 Charosson 17 122 Yf 74
18290 Chârost 18 102 Ca 67
24110 Charoux 24 124 Ac 77
85530 Charpe 85 97 Ye 66
24570 Charpenet 24 137 Bb 78
55270 Charpentry 55 55 Fa 53
26300 Charpey 26 143 Fa 79
38830 Charpieux, le 38 132 Ga 76
18260 Charpignon 18 88 Ce 64
28500 Charpont 28 50 Bc 56
85140 Charprais, la 85 97 Ye 68
85110 Charpre, le 85 97 Yf 69
25140 Charquemont 25 108 Ge 65
86170 Charrais 86 99 Ab 68
43300 Charraix 43 141 Dd 78
43800 Charraix 43 141 Df 78
16380 Charras 16 124 Ac 75
28220 Charray 28 69 Bb 61
64190 Charre 64 161 Za 89
86300 Charreau, le 86 100 Ad 69
71510 Charrecey 71 105 Ee 67
43130 Charrées 43 129 Ea 77
21170 Charrey-sur-Saône 21 106 Fa 66
21400 Charrey-sur-Seine 21 74 Ed 61
03250 Charrier 03 116 De 73
03330 Charrière, la 03 115 Da 71
58300 Charrin 58 104 Dd 68
64130 Charritte-de-Bas 64 161 Za 89
64470 Charritte-de-Haut 64 161 Za 90
64120 Charritte-Mixe 64 161 Yf 88
17230 Charron 17 110 Yf 71
23700 Charron 23 115 Cd 72
03140 Charroux 03 116 Da 71
86250 Charroux 86 112 Ac 72
87110 Charroux 87 125 Bb 74
95750 Chars 95 50 Bf 54
74430 Chars, les 74 120 Gd 71
45130 Charsonville 45 86 Bd 61
28130 Chartainvilliers 28 70 Bd 57
02400 Chartèves 02 53 Dd 54
49150 Chartrené 49 84 Zf 64
28000 Chartres 28 70 Bc 58
35131 Chartres-de-Bretagne 35 65 Yb 60
72340 Chartre-sur-le-Loir, la 72 85 Ad 62
77590 Chartrettes 77 71 Ce 58
72350 Chartreux, les 72 67 Ze 60
19600 Chartrier-Ferrière 19 138 Bc 78
77320 Chartronges 77 52 Db 56
19240 Chartroulle, la 19 125 Bc 77
13200 Chartrouse 13 169 Ee 88
17130 Chartuzac 17 123 Zd 76
38230 Charvieu Chavagneux 38 131 Fa 74
01230 Charvieux 01 131 Fd 73
74370 Charvonnex 74 120 Ga 73
85200 Charzais 85 110 Zb 70
79500 Charzay 79 111 Ze 71
48120 Charzel, le 48 140 Dc 80
63160 Chas 63 128 Db 74
19300 Chasalnoël 19 126 Bf 76
71240 Chasaux 71 106 Ef 68
15500 Chaselles 15 128 Da 77
07590 Chase-Neuve 07 141 Df 80
10210 Chaserey-Bas 10 73 Ea 61
10210 Chaserey-Haut 10 73 Ea 61
48600 Chases, les 48 141 Dd 80
85400 Chasnais 85 109 Ye 70
25580 Chasnans 25 108 Gb 66
58350 Chasnay 58 103 Db 65
35250 Chasné-sur-Illet 35 66 Yc 59
49370 Chasnière 49 83 Za 63
43700 Chaspinhac 43 141 Df 78
43320 Chaspuzac 43 141 De 78
87130 Chassagnas 87 126 Bd 75
87380 Chassagnas 87 125 Bd 75
01310 Chassagne 01 118 Fa 71
16410 Chassagne 16 124 Ab 75
63320 Chassagne 63 128 Da 76
21190 Chassagne-Montrachet 21 105 Ee 67
07140 Chassagnes 07 154 Eb 82
43230 Chassagnes 43 128 Dd 77
48700 Chassagnes 48 140 Dc 81
25290 Chassagne-Saint-Denis 25 107 Ga 66
23700 Chassagnette 23 115 Cd 73
42560 Chassagnieux 42 129 Ea 75
15190 Chassagny 15 127 Ce 77
69700 Chassagny 69M 130 Ee 75
39230 Chassague, la 39 106 Fc 67
24600 Chassaignes 24 124 Ab 77
19290 Chassain, le 19 126 Cb 75
19290 Chassaing, le 19 126 Ca 74
19300 Chassaing, le 19 126 Bf 76
23700 Chassaing, le 23 115 Cc 73
39360 Chassal 39 119 Fe 70
43350 Chassaleuil 43 141 Df 78
19190 Chassancet 19 138 Be 78
28480 Chassant 28 69 Ba 59
87120 Chassat 87 126 Be 74
19400 Chassat-de-Bourdet 19 138 Bf 78
04370 Chasse 04 158 Gd 83
72600 Chassé 72 68 Ab 58
50520 Chasseguey 50 66 Yf 57
36100 Chasseigne 36 101 Bf 67
86200 Chasseigne 86 99 Aa 67
86290 Chasseigne, la 86 113 Ba 70
71570 Chasselas 71 118 Ee 71
38470 Chasselay 38 131 Fc 77
69380 Chasselay d'Azergues 69M 130 Ee 73
02370 Chassemy 02 40 Dd 52
03510 Chassenard 03 117 Df 70
21230 Chassenay 21 105 Ec 66
63260 Chassenet 63 116 Db 73
36800 Chasseneuil 36 101 Bc 69
86360 Chasseneuil-du-Poitou 86 99 Ac 69
16310 Chasseneuil-sur-Bonnieure 16 124 Ac 74
16150 Chassenon 16 124 Ae 73
85240 Chassenon-le-Bourg 85 110 Zb 70
48250 Chasseradès 48 141 De 81
71340 Chassereux 71 117 Ea 71
10330 Chassericourt 10 74 Ed 57
38670 Chasse-sur-Rhône 38 130 Ee 75
21150 Chassey 21 91 Ec 64
39290 Chassey 39 92 Fd 65
55130 Chassey-Beaupré 55 75 Fc 58
71150 Chassey-le-Camp 71 105 Ee 67
70230 Chassey-lès-Moutbozon 70 93 Gc 63
70360 Chassey-lès-Scey 70 93 Ff 63
16350 Chassiecq 16 112 Ac 73
36160 Chassière 36 114 Ca 70
17260 Chassières, les 17 122 Zb 75
07110 Chassiers 07 142 Eb 81
69680 Chassieu 69M 130 Ef 74
89160 Chassignelles 89 90 Eb 62
03140 Chassignet 03 116 Db 71
38730 Chassignieu 38 131 Fd 76
43300 Chassignoles 43 140 Dc 78
36400 Chassignolles 36 114 Bf 69
43440 Chassignolles 43 128 Dc 76
86200 Chassigny 86 99 Zf 67
52190 Chassigny-Aisey 52 92 Fc 62
71170 Chassigny-sous-Dun 71 117 Eb 71
72540 Chassillé 72 67 Zf 60
36230 Chassin, le 36 101 Bf 69
02850 Chassins 02 53 Dd 54
26600 Chassis, les 26 142 Ee 78
63930 Chassonnerix 63 128 Dd 74
16120 Chassors 16 123 Zf 75
16200 Chassors 16 123 Ze 74
18800 Chassy 18 103 Cf 66
58110 Chassy 58 104 Dd 66
58270 Chassy 58 104 Dc 67
71130 Chassy 71 105 Ea 69
89110 Chassy 89 89 Dc 61
19160 Chastagner 19 126 Cb 76
19190 Chastagnol 19 138 Be 77
19390 Chastagnol 19 126 Bf 76
07110 Chastanet 07 141 Ea 81
19700 Chastanet, le 19 126 Be 76
19190 Chastang, le 19 138 Be 77
48300 Chastanier 48 141 De 80
43230 Chastanuel 43 141 Dd 78
19600 Chasteaux 19 138 Bc 78
43300 Chastel 43 140 Db 78
63690 Chastel, le 63 127 Cd 75
26340 Chastel-Arnaud 26 143 Fb 81
04320 Chastellet-lès-Sausses 04 158 Ge 85
89630 Chastellux-sur-Cure 89 90 Df 64
15240 Chastel-Merlhac 15 127 Cd 77
48000 Chastel-Nouvel 48 140 Dd 81
06470 Chastelonnette 06 158 Ge 84
03190 Chasteloy 03 115 Ce 69
89560 Chastenay 89 89 Dc 63
04120 Chasteuil 04 157 Gc 85
63680 Chastreix 63 127 Ce 75
63420 Chastrix 63 128 Da 76
58400 Chasue 58 103 Da 65
32190 Chat 32 163 Ab 86
16220 Chat, le 16 124 Ad 74
36200 Chataigne, la 36 113 Bd 69
16220 Châtaignier, le 16 124 Ac 74
85110 Châtaigneraie, la 85 97 Yf 69
85120 Châtaigneraie, la 85 98 Zb 69
85130 Châtaigneraie, la 85 97 Yf 67
19330 Chataignier, le 19 126 Be 77
23110 Châtaignier, le 23 115 Cc 72
87400 Châtaignier, le 87 126 Bd 74
36230 Châtaigniers, les 36 114 Be 69
23340 Chatain 23 126 Bf 74
23460 Chatain 23 114 Bf 73
86250 Chatain 86 112 Ac 72
87400 Chatain, le 87 125 Bc 74
87440 Chatain, le 87 124 Ae 75
16220 Chatain-Besson 16 124 Ad 74
28270 Châtaincourt 28 49 Bb 56
38142 Châtains 38 144 Ga 78
38110 Chatanay 38 131 Fc 75
88210 Châtas 88 77 Ha 58
71250 Château 71 118 Ed 70
04140 Château, le 04 157 Gb 83
04380 Château, le 04 157 Ga 83
05700 Château, le 05 144 Fd 82
53270 Château, le 53 67 Zd 61
56130 Château, le 56 81 Xe 63
04160 Château-Arnoux 04 157 Ga 84
38710 Château-Bas, le 38 144 Fe 80
16100 Châteaubernard 16 123 Ze 74
38650 Château-Bernard 38 143 Fd 79
77370 Châteaubleau 77 72 Da 57
44340 Château-Bougon 44 97 Yc 66
79310 Château-Bourdin 79 111 Zd 69
07300 Châteaubourg 07 142 Ef 78
35220 Châteaubourg 35 66 Yd 60
57340 Château-Bréhain 57 57 Gd 55
44110 Châteaubriant 44 82 Yd 62
56500 Châteaubriant 56 80 Xb 61
05200 Château-Caléyère 05 145 Gc 81
39210 Château-Chalon 39 107 Fd 68
87380 Château-Chervix 87 125 Bc 75
58120 Château-Chinon 58 104 Df 66
87120 Châteaucourt 87 126 Bf 74
61570 Château-d' Almenêches, le 61 48 Aa 56
05260 Château-d'Ancelle 05 144 Gb 81
61400 Château de la Pélonnière 61 68 Ad 58
46500 Château de Rocamadour 46 138 Bd 80
39150 Château-des-Prés 39 119 Ff 69
17480 Château-d'Oléron, le 17 122 Ye 73
26120 Châteaudouble 26 143 Fa 79
83300 Châteaudouble 83 172 Gc 87
58410 Château-du-Bois 58 89 Db 64
56460 Château du Crévy 56 81 Xd 61
72500 Château-du-Loir 72 85 Ac 62
28200 Châteaudun 28 70 Bb 60
25000 Château-Farine 25 107 Ff 65
04250 Châteaufort 04 157 Ga 83
78117 Châteaufort 78 51 Ca 56
85000 Château-Fromage 85 97 Yd 68
01500 Château-Gaillard 01 119 Fb 73
28310 Château Gaillard 28 70 Bf 60
86150 Château-Gaillard 86 112 Ad 71
18170 Château-Gaillard, le 18 102 Cb 68
04170 Château-Garnier 04 158 Gc 84
86350 Château-Garnier 86 112 Ac 71
63119 Châteaugay 63 128 Da 73
35410 Châteaugiron 35 66 Yc 60
13013 Château-Gombert 13 170 Fc 88
53200 Château-Gontier 53 83 Zb 62
70240 Château-Grenouille 70 93 Gb 63
85320 Château-Guibert 85 97 Ye 69
61310 Château Haras du Pin 61 48 Aa 56
59230 Château-L'Abbaye 59 30 Dc 46
70440 Château-Lambert, Haut-du-Them- 70 94 Ge 61
77570 Château-Landon 77 71 Ce 60
86370 Château-Larcher 86 112 Ab 70
37330 Château-la-Vallière 37 85 Ab 63
42240 Château-le-Bois 42 129 Eb 76
24460 Château-l'Évêque 24 124 Ae 77
29150 Châteaulin = Kastellin 29 62 Ve 59
35400 Château-Malo 35 65 Ya 57
38710 Château-Méa 38 144 Fe 80
18370 Châteaumeillant 18 114 Cb 69
24380 Château-Missier 24 137 Ae 78
85700 Châteaumur 85 98 Za 67
04300 Châteauneuf 04 156 Fe 85
21320 Châteauneuf 21 105 Ed 65
71740 Châteauneuf 71 117 Eb 71
73390 Châteauneuf 73 132 Gb 75
79240 Château-Neuf 79 98 Zc 68
83860 Châteauneuf 83 171 Fe 88
84190 Château-Neuf 84 155 Fa 83
85710 Châteauneuf 85 96 Ya 67
26110 Châteauneuf-de-Bordette 26 156 Fa 82
84470 Châteauneuf-de-Cadagne 84 155 Ef 85
06390 Châteauneuf-de-Contes 06 159 Hb 86
26330 Châteauneuf-de-Galaure 26 130 Ef 77
06470 Châteauneuf-d'Entraunes 06 158 Ge 84
48170 Châteauneuf-de-Randon 48 141 Dd 81
07240 Châteauneuf-de-Vernoux 07 142 Ed 79
35430 Châteauneuf-d'Ille-et-Villaine 35 65 Ya 57
05400 Châteauneuf-d'Oze 05 144 Ff 81
29520 Châteauneuf-du-Faou 29 78 Wb 59
84230 Châteauneuf-du-Pape 84 155 Ee 84
26780 Châteauneuf-du-Rhône 26 142 Ee 82
28170 Châteauneuf-en-Thymerais 28 69 Bb 57
06740 Châteauneuf-Grasse 06 173 Gf 86
87130 Châteauneuf-la-Forêt 87 126 Bd 74
13790 Châteauneuf-le-Rouge 13 171 Fd 88
63390 Châteauneuf-les-Bains 63 115 Cf 72
13220 Châteauneuf-les-Martigues 13 170 Fa 88
04200 Châteauneuf-Miravail 04 156 Fe 84
16120 Châteauneuf-sur-Charente 16 123 Zf 75
18190 Châteauneuf-sur-Cher 18 102 Cb 67
26300 Châteauneuf-sur-Isère 26 143 Ef 78
45110 Châteauneuf-sur-Loire 45 87 Cb 61
49330 Châteauneuf-sur-Sarthe 49 83 Zd 62
58350 Châteauneuf-Val-de-Bargis 58 89 Db 65
04200 Châteauneuf-Val-Saint-Donnat 04 157 Ff 84
49570 Châteaupanne 49 83 Za 64
87290 Châteauponsac 87 113 Bb 72
08360 Château-Porcien 08 41 Eb 51
05350 Château-Queyras 05 145 Ge 80
04270 Châteauredon 04 157 Gb 84
08120 Château-Regnault 08 42 Ed 49
13160 Châteaurenard 13 155 Ef 85
45220 Châteaurenard 45 88 Cf 61

256 | **Chapelle-Saint-Géraud, la**

44680 Chéméré 44 96 Ya 66
53340 Chéméré-le-Roi 53 67 Zd 61
41700 Chémery 41 86 Bc 64
57380 Chemery 57 57 Gd 55
08450 Chémery-Chéhéry 08 42 Ef 51
57320 Chémery-les-Deux 57 56 Gc 53
39240 Chemilla 39 119 Fd 70
01560 Chemillat 01 118 Fa 70
49120 Chemillé-en-Anjou 49 98 Zb 65
37370 Chemillé-sur-Dême 37 85 Ad 63
37460 Chemillé-sur-Indrois 37 100 Bb 66
61360 Chemilli 61 68 Ac 58
01300 Chemillieu 01 131 Fe 74
03210 Chemilly 03 116 Db 70
70360 Chemilly 70 93 Ga 63
89800 Chemilly-sur-Serein 89 90 Df 62
89250 Chemilly-sur-Yonne 89 89 Dd 61
39120 Chemin 39 106 Fb 67
52150 Chemin 52 75 Fd 59
28170 Chemin, le 28 69 Bb 57
51800 Chemin, le 51 55 Ef 54
58800 Chemin, le 58 89 De 65
07300 Cheminas 07 142 Ee 78
21400 Chemin-d'Aisey 21 91 Ed 62
14490 Chemin-de-Saint-Lô, le 14 34 Za 54
19320 Chemineaux, les 19 126 Bf 77
44470 Chemin-Nantais, le 44 82 Yd 65
57420 Cheminot 57 56 Ga 55
72540 Chemiré-en-Charnie 72 67 Ze 60
72210 Chemiré-le-Gaudin 72 84 Zf 61
49640 Chemiré-sur-Sarthe 49 84 Zd 62
88630 Chemisey 88 75 Fd 58
59147 Chemy 59 30 Cf 45
17120 Chenac-sur-Gironde 17 122 Zb 75
37350 Chênaie, la 37 100 Af 66
19120 Chenailler-Mascheix 19 138 Bf 78
73640 Chenal 73 133 Gf 75
73350 Chenal, la 73 133 Gd 76
25500 Chenalotte, la 25 108 Ge 66
69840 Chénas 69D 118 Ee 71
24410 Chenaud, Parcoul- 24 123 Aa 77
17120 Chênaumoine 17 122 Za 75
51140 Chenay 51 53 Df 53
72610 Chenay 72 68 Aa 58
79120 Chenay 79 111 Zf 71
37370 Chenaye, la 37 85 Ae 63
71340 Chenay-le-Châtel 71 117 Df 71
01300 Chêne 01 131 Fd 74
10700 Chêne 10 73 Eb 57
14410 Chêne 14 47 Zb 56
18140 Chêne 18 103 Cf 65
37120 Chêne 37 99 Ac 66
58140 Chêne 58 104 Df 65
44170 Chêne, le 44 82 Yb 63
84400 Chêne, le 84 156 Fc 85
88360 Chêne, le 88 94 Ge 61
89120 Chêne-Arnoult 89 89 Da 61
89520 Chêneau, le 89 89 Da 63
39120 Chêne Bernard 39 106 Fc 67
70400 Chenebier 70 94 Ge 63
02140 Chêne-Bourdon 02 41 Ea 49
25440 Chenecey-Buillon 25 107 Ff 66
86380 Cheneché 86 99 Ab 68
28170 Chêne-Chenu 28 70 Bb 57
14410 Chênedollé 14 47 Zb 55
61210 Chênedouit 61 47 Zd 56
74270 Chêne-en-Semine 74 119 Ff 72
49350 Chênehutte-Trèves-Cunault 49 84 Zf 65
69430 Chênelette 69D 118 Ec 71
37170 Chêne-Pendu 37 85 Ae 65
87520 Chêne-Pignier 87 112 Af 73
28160 Chêne-Pulvé, le 28 69 Ba 59
23130 Chénérailles 23 114 Cb 72
42380 Chenereilles 42 129 Ea 76
42560 Chenereilles 42 129 Ea 76
43190 Chenereilles 43 142 Eb 78
21440 Chêneroilles 21 91 Ee 64
18140 Chênes, les 18 103 Ce 66
39230 Chêne-Sec 39 106 Fc 67
83460 Chênes-Verts, les 83 172 Gc 88
16230 Chênet, le 16 124 Ab 73
86450 Chenevelles 86 100 Ad 68
72300 Chênevert 72 84 Ze 62
54122 Chenevières 54 77 Gd 57
70150 Chenevrey-et-Morogne 70 92 Fe 65
74520 Chênex 74 120 Ga 72
89700 Cheney 89 90 Df 61
28210 Chenicourt 28 50 Bd 57
54610 Chenicourt 54 56 Gb 55
36170 Chénier 36 113 Bc 70
54720 Chénières 54 43 Fe 52
85150 Chênières, les 85 96 Yb 69
23220 Chéniers 23 114 Be 70
51510 Cheniers 51 54 Eb 55
35270 Chenillé 35 65 Yb 58
49220 Chenillé-Champteussé 49 83 Zb 62
49220 Chenillé-Changé 49 83 Zc 62
88460 Cheniménil 88 77 Gd 60
27820 Chennebrun 27 49 Ae 56
10190 Chennegy 10 73 Df 59
28170 Chennevières 28 49 Ba 57
55500 Chennevières 55 55 Fc 57
95380 Chennevières-lès-Louvres 95 51 Cd 54
57580 Chenois 57 57 Gc 55
77160 Chenoise 77 72 Db 57
16460 Chenommet 16 111 Ab 73
16460 Chenon 16 111 Ab 73
37150 Chenonceaux 37 86 Ba 65
28360 Chenonville 28 70 Bc 58
77570 Chenou 77 71 Cd 60
87400 Chenour 87 125 Bc 74
21300 Chenôve 21 91 Ef 65
71390 Chenôves 71 105 Ee 68
45490 Chênoy, le 45 71 Cd 60
74140 Chens-sur-Léman 74 120 Gb 71
72500 Chenu 72 85 Ac 63
37380 Chenusson 37 85 Ae 63
89400 Cheny 89 72 Dd 61
17210 Chepniers 17 123 Ze 77
60120 Chepoix 60 39 Cc 51
51600 Cheppe, la 51 54 Ec 54
51240 Cheppes-la-Prairie 51 54 Ec 56
55270 Cheppy 55 55 Fa 53
91630 Cheptainville 91 71 Cb 57
51240 Chepy 51 54 Ec 55
80210 Chépy 80 28 Bd 48
15300 Cher, le 15 139 Cf 78
17290 Cher, le 17 110 Za 72
20146 Chera CTC 185 Kb 99
17610 Chérac 17 123 Zd 74
53400 Chérancé 53 83 Za 62
72170 Chérancé 72 68 Ab 59
64130 Chéraute 64 161 Za 89
17190 Chéray 17 109 Yd 73
03420 Cherbeix 03 115 Cd 71
17470 Cherbonnières 17 111 Zd 73
23260 Cherboucheix 23 127 Cb 74
50100* Cherbourg-en-Cotentin 50 33 Yc 51
64310 Cherchebruit 64 160 Yc 89
07170 Cherdenas 07 142 Ed 82
95510 Chérence 95 50 Be 54
50800 Chérence-le-Héron 50 46 Ye 56
50520 Chérences-le-Roussel 50 47 Yf 56
59152 Chéreng 59 30 Db 45
69380 Chères, les 69M 118 Ee 73
02860 Chérêt 02 40 De 51
62140 Chériennes 62 29 Ca 47
42430 Cherier 42 117 Df 73
79170 Chérigné 79 111 Zf 72
05160 Chérines 05 145 Gc 81
50220 Chéris, Ducey-, les 50 66 Ye 57
72610 Chérisay 72 68 Aa 58
57420 Chérisey 57 56 Gb 54
28500 Chérisy 28 50 Bc 56
62128 Chérisy 62 30 Cf 47
71250 Chérizet 71 118 Ed 69
88310 Cherménil 88 77 Gf 61
17460 Chermignac 17 122 Zc 74
02860 Chermizy-Ailles 02 40 De 52
87600 Chéronnac 87 124 Ae 74
27250 Chéronvilliers 27 49 Ae 56
89690 Chéroy 89 72 Da 59
49330 Cherré 49 83 Zc 62
72400 Cherré 72 69 Ad 59
72800 Cherré 72 84 Ab 63
72400 Cherreau 72 69 Ae 59
18300 Cherriers, les 18 88 Cd 65
35120 Cherrueix 35 65 Yb 57
17380 Chersoubro 15 139 Cd 78
24320 Cherval 24 124 Ac 76
79270 Cherve 79 110 Zd 71
24160 Cherveix 24 125 Af 76
24390 Cherveix-Cubas 24 125 Ba 77
16310 Cherves-Châtelars 16 124 Ad 74
16560 Cherves 16 124 Ab 74
36300 Cherves 36 100 Ba 68
16370 Cherves-Richemont 16 123 Zd 74
17380 Chervettes 17 110 Zb 72
79410 Cherveux 79 111 Zd 70
10110 Chervey 10 74 Ec 60
28210 Cherville 28 50 Bc 57
28700 Cherville 28 70 Be 58
51150 Cherville 51 53 Ea 54
69400 Chervinges 69D 118 Ee 73
18120 Chéry 18 102 Ca 66
02220 Chéry-Chartreuve 02 53 Dd 53
02000 Chéry-lès-Pouilly 02 40 Dd 51
02360 Chéry-lès-Rozoy 02 41 Ea 50
10120 Chesley 10 73 Ea 61
35120 Chesnardais, la 35 65 Yc 57
27160 Chesnay 27 49 Af 55
41130 Chesnay 41 87 Bd 64
50380 Chesnay 50 46 Yc 56
78150 Chesnay, le 78 51 Ca 56
22350 Chesnay-Barbot 22 65 Xe 59
79260 Chesnaye, la 79 111 Ze 70
08390 Chesne, le 08 42 Ee 51
27160 Chesne, le 27 49 Af 55
58410 Chesnois, le 58 89 Db 64
08270 Chesnois-Auboncourt 08 41 Ed 51
57245 Chesny 57 56 Gb 54
74270 Chessenaz 74 119 Ff 72
74230 Chesseney 74 120 Gb 73
69380 Chessy 69D 130 Ed 73
77700 Chessy 77 52 Ce 55
10130 Chessy-lès-Prés 10 73 Df 60
08400 Chestres 08 42 Ee 52
03120 Chételus 03 116 De 71
49400 Chétigné 49 99 Zf 65
74390 Chets-de-Lens 74 121 Ge 71
74390 Chets-de-Plaine-Dranse 74 121 Ge 71
89600 Chéu 89 73 De 61
57640 Cheuby 57 56 Gb 54
21310 Cheuge 21 92 Fc 64
89460 Cheuilly 89 90 De 62
14210 Cheux 14 35 Zc 54
03240 Chevagnes 03 104 Dd 69
71960 Chevagny-les-Chevrières 71 118 Ee 71
71220 Chevagny-sur-Guye 71 117 Ed 69
35250 Chevaigné 35 65 Yc 59
53250 Chevaigné-du-Maine 53 67 Zd 58
72610 Chevain, Saint-Paterne-, le 72 68 Aa 58
35460 Chevalais, la 35 66 Yc 58
84460 Cheval-Blanc 84 155 Fa 86
08230 Cheval-Blanc, le 08 41 Ed 49
59440 Cheval-Blanc, le 59 31 Df 48
17480 Chevalerie, la 17 122 Ye 73
72270 Chevalerie, la 72 84 Zf 62
69930 Chevaleron 69M 130 Ec 74
05700 Chevalet 05 156 Fe 83
74210 Chevaline 74 132 Gb 74
44810 Chevallerais, la 44 82 Yb 64
38340 Chevalon, le 38 131 Fd 77
03250 Cheval-Rigond 03 116 Dd 72
17210 Chevanceaux 17 123 Ze 77
21540 Chevannay 21 91 Ed 64
21220 Chevannes 21 106 Ef 66
45210 Chevannes 45 72 Cf 60
58250 Chevannes 58 104 De 67
58270 Chevannes 58 104 Dc 66
89240 Chevannes 89 89 Dc 62
89420 Chevannes 89 90 Ea 64
91750 Chevannes 91 71 Cc 57
58420 Chevannes-Changy 58 89 Dc 65
45410 Chevaux 45 70 Be 60
42920 Chevelière 42 129 Df 74
73170 Chevelu 73 132 Fe 74
02250 Chevennes 02 40 De 50
58160 Chevenon 58 103 Db 67
74500 Chevenoz 74 121 Gd 70
41700 Cheverny 41 86 Bc 64
70290 Chevestraye, la 70 94 Ge 62
08350 Cheveuges-Saint-Aignan 08 42 Ef 51
08250 Chevières 08 42 Ef 53
01370 Chevignat 01 119 Fc 71
25530 Chevigney 25 108 Gc 66
70140 Chevigney 70 92 Fd 64
25170 Chevigney-sur-L'Ognon 25 93 Ff 65
21140 Chevigny 21 90 Eb 63
21310 Chevigny 21 92 Fb 64
21600 Chevigny 21 106 Fa 65
39290 Chevigny 39 106 Fc 65
51130 Chevigny 51 53 Ea 55
58320 Chevigny 58 103 Da 66
21200 Chevigny-en-Valière 21 106 Ef 67
21800 Chevigny-Saint-Sauveur 21 92 Fa 65
01430 Chevillard 01 119 Fd 72
16120 Cheville 16 123 Zf 74
72350 Chevillé 72 67 Ze 61
52170 Chevillon 52 75 Fa 57
57530 Chevillon 57 56 Gc 54
89120 Chevillon 89 89 Db 61
45700 Chevillon-sur-Huillard 45 71 Cd 61
45520 Chevilly 45 70 Bf 60
74140 Chevilly 74 120 Gb 70
69210 Chevinay 69M 130 Ed 74
60150 Chevincourt 60 39 Cf 51
49150 Cheviré-le-Rouge 49 84 Ze 63
77760 Chevrainvilliers 77 71 Cd 59
86600 Chevraise, la 86 111 Aa 70
58800 Chevré 58 104 De 66
58250 Chèvre, la 58 104 De 67
79310 Chevreau 79 111 Ze 69
39190 Chevreaux 39 119 Fc 69
10160 Chevreaux, les 10 73 De 60
02000 Chevregny 02 40 Dd 52
90340 Chèvremont 90 94 Gf 63
42190 Chevrenay 42 117 Ea 71
16240 Chèvrerie, la 16 111 Aa 72
74470 Chèvrerie, la 74 120 Gd 71
02270 Chevresis 02 40 Dd 50
02270 Chevresis-lès-Dames 02 40 Dd 50
37140 Chevrette 37 84 Aa 65
58170 Chevrette 58 104 Df 68
85370 Chevrette 85 110 Yf 70
78460 Chevreuse 78 51 Ca 56
50600 Chèvreville 50 66 Yf 57
60440 Chèvreville 60 52 Cf 54
74520 Chevrier 74 119 Ff 72
38160 Chevrières 38 131 Fb 77
42140 Chevrières 42 130 Ec 75
60710 Chevrières 60 51 Ce 52
58500 Chevroches 58 89 Dd 64
44118 Chevrolière, la 44 97 Yc 66
73200 Chevronnet 73 132 Gc 74
39130 Chevrotaine 39 107 Ff 69
01190 Chevroux 01 118 Ef 70
18140 Chevroux 18 103 Cf 66
25870 Chevroz 25 93 Ff 64
77320 Chevru 77 52 Db 56
01170 Chevry 01 120 Ga 71
50420 Chevry 50 46 Yf 55
88100 Chevry 88 77 Gf 59
91400 Chevry2 91 51 Ca 56
77173 Chevry-Cossigny 77 51 Cd 56
77710 Chevry-en-Sereine 77 72 Cf 59
45210 Chevry-sous-le-Bignon 45 72 Cf 60
33640 Chey 33 135 Zd 80
79120 Chey 79 111 Zf 71
15270 Cheylade 15 127 Cd 76
15400 Cheylade 15 127 Ce 77
07160 Cheylard, le 07 142 Ec 79
26310 Cheylard, le 26 143 Fd 81
48300 Cheylard-L'Evêque 48 141 De 81
38570 Cheylas, le 38 132 Ff 76
43000 Cheyrac 43 141 Df 78
43500 Cheyrac 43 129 De 76
04150 Cheyran 04 156 Fd 84
07460 Cheyrès 07 154 Eb 82
24420 Cheyron, le 24 124 Ae 77
24530 Cheyrou, le 24 124 Ae 76
38550 Cheyssieu 38 130 Ef 76
18160 Chezal-Benoît 18 102 Ca 68
18130 Chezal-Chauvier 18 102 Cd 67
18300 Chezal-Reine 18 88 Ce 64
16480 Chez-Baudet 16 123 Zf 76
17240 Chez-Bizet 17 122 Zb 76
16480 Chez-Bobe 16 123 Zf 76
03320 Chez-Bois 03 103 Cf 68
17150 Chez-Bondut 17 122 Zc 76
17520 Chez-Bouchet 17 123 Zd 75
74490 Chez-Chométy 74 120 Gd 71
16250 Chez-Chotard 16 123 Zf 75
65120 Chèze 65 175 Zf 91
43520 Chèze, la 43 141 Eb 78
87240 Chèze, la 87 113 Bc 73
22210 Chèze, la = Kez 22 64 Xc 60
36800 Chézeau-Chrétien 36 101 Bb 68
52400 Chézeaux 52 92 Fd 61
36300 Chézeaux, les 36 100 Ba 69
86380 Chezeaux, les 86 99 Ac 68
03140 Chezelle 03 116 Da 71
03800 Chezelle 03 116 Db 72
36500 Chezelles 36 101 Bd 67
37220 Chézelles 37 99 Ac 66
38300 Chézeneuve 38 131 Fb 75
23700 Chézérade 23 115 Cd 72
01410 Chézery-Forens 01 119 Ff 71
71550 Chézet 71 105 Ea 66
87230 Chez-Eymard 87 125 Af 74
86510 Chez Fouché 86 111 Ab 71
16200 Chez-Froin 16 123 Ze 74
17100 Chez-Fruger 17 123 Zc 74
63120 Chez-Gagnat 63 128 Dc 74
17150 Chez-Gentet 17 123 Zd 76
16300 Chez-Grassin 16 123 Zf 76
17520 Chez-Grimard 17 123 Zd 75
74130 Chez-la-Jode 74 120 Gb 73
16190 Chez-le-Blais 16 123 Aa 76
58300 Chez-le-Bourg 58 104 Dc 68
58250 Chez-Legendre 58 104 De 68
16100 Chez-les-Rois 16 123 Zd 74
19210 Chez-le-Turc 19 125 Bc 76
87120 Chez-Lissandre 87 126 Be 74
16220 Chez-Manot 16 124 Ad 75
63810 Chez-Morissoux 63 127 Cd 75
87310 Chez-Moutaud 87 125 Af 74
17800 Chez-Nolin 17 123 Zc 75
17100 Chez-Portier 17 123 Zc 74
16350 Chez-Pouvaraud 16 112 Ac 73
17770 Chez-Quimand 17 123 Zd 74
86430 Chez-Range 86 112 Ae 71
16130 Chez-Richon 16 123 Ze 75
16450 Chez-Robinet 16 124 Ac 73
16260 Chez-Rozet 16 124 Ac 73
16360 Chez-Saillant 16 123 Zf 76
17460 Chez-Salignac 17 122 Zc 75
17100 Chez-Texier 17 122 Zc 74
16210 Chez-Tureau 16 123 Zf 77
16140 Chez-Veillon 16 123 Zf 73
87330 Chez-Vignan 87 112 Ae 71
03230 Chézy 03 104 Dc 69
02810 Chézy-en-Orxois 02 52 Db 54
02570 Chézy-sur-Marne 02 52 Dc 55
27120 Chiagnolles 27 50 Bc 54
20112 Chialza CTC 184 Ka 99
20169 Chiappili CTC 185 Kb 100
20230 Chiatra CTC 183 Kc 95
64600 Chiberta 64 160 Yc 87
83870 Chibron 83 171 Fe 89
79350 Chiché 79 98 Zd 68
14370 Chicheboville 14 35 Ze 54
89800 Chichée 89 90 Df 62
41100 Chicheray 41 86 Ba 61
89400 Chichery 89 89 Dd 61
51120 Chichey 51 53 De 56
38930 Chichilianne 38 143 Fd 80
89250 Chichy 89 73 Dd 61
40240 Chicot 40 148 Zf 85
57590 Chicourt 57 57 Gd 55
40120 Chicoy 40 148 Ze 84
20141 Chidazzu CTC 182 Ie 95
58170 Chiddes 58 104 Df 67
71220 Chiddes 71 117 Ed 70
63320 Chidrac 63 128 Da 75
94430 Chiennevières-sur-Marne 94 51 Cd 56
43580 Chier, le 43 141 De 79
02400 Chierry 02 52 Dc 54
17210 Chierzac 17 123 Ze 77
20228 Chiesa CTC 181 Kc 91
57070 Chieulles 57 56 Gb 54
26740 Chiffe 26 142 Ef 81
34210 Chiffre 34 166 Cd 88
20160 Chigliani CTC 182 Ie 95
19350 Chignac 19 125 Bb 76
23250 Chignal 23 114 Be 73
23000 Chignaroche 23 114 Bf 71
63910 Chignat 63 128 Db 74
49490 Chigné 49 84 Aa 63
16430 Chignolle, la 16 124 Ab 74
02120 Chigny 02 40 De 49
51500 Chigny-les-Roses 51 53 Ea 54
89190 Chigy 89 72 Dc 59
43380 Chilhac 43 140 Dc 78
16480 Chillac 16 123 Zf 76
79100 Chillas, le 79 99 Ze 67
37220 Chillaudières, les 37 100 Ac 66
16140 Chillé 16 111 Zf 73
39570 Chille 39 107 Fd 68
45170 Chilleurs-aux-Bois 45 71 Ca 60
49370 Chillon, le 49 83 Za 64
49110 Chillou 49 97 Yf 65
86260 Chillou 86 100 Ae 69
79600 Chillou, le 79 99 Zf 68
08260 Chilly 08 41 Ec 49
74270 Chilly 74 120 Ff 73
80170 Chilly 80 39 Ce 50
39570 Chilly-le-Vignoble 39 106 Fc 69
91420 Chilly-Mazarin 91 51 Cb 56
39110 Chilly-sur-Salins 39 107 Ff 67
38490 Chimilin 38 131 Fd 75
74450 Chinaillon, le 74 120 Gc 73
40120 Chinanin 40 147 Zd 84
86130 Chincé 86 99 Ac 68
73310 Chindrieux 73 132 Ff 74
19260 Chingeat 19 126 Be 75
37500 Chinon 37 99 Ab 66
20245 Chiorna CTC 182 Ie 94
20233 Chioso CTC 181 Kc 92
88520 Chipal, le 88 77 Ha 59
80800 Chipilly 80 39 Cd 49
70220 Chiquerie, la 70 93 Gc 61
16150 Chirac 16 112 Ad 73
48100 Chirac 48 140 Db 81
19160 Chirac-Bellevue 19 127 Cb 76
42114 Chirassimont 42 117 Eb 73
03330 Chirat-L'Église 03 115 Da 71
86190 Chiré-en-Montreuil 86 99 Aa 69
86340 Chiré-les-Bois 86 112 Ac 70
38850 Chirens 38 131 Fd 76
80250 Chirmont 80 39 Cc 50
07380 Chirols 07 142 Eb 80
18300 Chiron 18 103 Ce 65
17510 Chiron, la 17 111 Ze 73
69115 Chiroubles 69D 118 Ee 71
23500 Chiroux, le 23 126 Ca 74
63610 Chirouzes, les 63 128 Cf 76
60138 Chiry-Ourscamps 60 39 Cf 51
65800 Chis 65 162 Aa 89
20240 Chisa CTC 183 Kb 97
20240 Chisà = Chisa CTC 183 Kb 97
73350 Chiserette, la 73 133 Ge 76
23500 Chissac 23 126 Ca 74
41400 Chissay-en-Touraine 41 86 Ba 64
37150 Chisseaux 37 86 Ba 65
39240 Chisséria 39 119 Fd 70
71540 Chissey-en-Morvan 71 105 Eb 66
71460 Chissey-lès-Mâcon 71 118 Ee 69
39380 Chissey-sur-Loue 39 107 Fe 66
41350 Chîteau, le 41 86 Bc 63
41120 Chitenay 41 86 Bc 64
36800 Chitray 36 101 Bc 69
89530 Chitry 89 89 De 62
58800 Chitry-les-Mines 58 90 Dd 65
20121 Chiusa CTC 182 If 96
17510 Chives 17 111 Zf 73
21820 Chivres 21 106 Fa 67
58210 Chivres 58 89 Dc 64
02350 Chivres-en-Laonnais 02 41 Df 51
02880 Chivres-Val 02 40 Dc 52
02000 Chivy-lès-Étouvelles 02 40 Dd 51
79170 Chizé 79 111 Zd 72
20169 Chjappili = Chiappili CTC 185 Kb 100
20230 Chjatra = Chiatra CTC 183 Kc 95
20233 Chjosu u Chjusu = Chioso CTC 181 Kc 92
62920 Chocques 62 29 Cd 45
52190 Choilley-Dardenay 52 92 Fc 63
78460 Choisel 78 51 Ca 56
52240 Choiseul 52 75 Fd 60
39100 Choisey 39 106 Fc 66
59740 Choisies 59 31 Ea 47
48300 Choisinès, le 48 141 Df 80
19310 Choisne, la 19 125 Bc 77
74330 Choisy 74 120 Ga 73
60750 Choisy-au-Bac 60 39 Cf 52
77320 Choisy-en-Brie 77 52 Db 56
60190 Choisy-la-Victoire 60 39 Cd 52
94600 Choisy-le-Roi 94 51 Cc 56
49300 Cholet 49 98 Za 66
49220 Chollaie, la 49 83 Za 63
17360 Chollet 17 135 Zf 78
89100 Chollets, les 89 72 Db 59
38220 Cholonge 38 144 Fe 78
54200 Choloy-Ménillot 54 56 Fe 57
43500 Chomelix 43 129 De 77
07210 Chomérac 07 142 Ed 80
23700 Chomette, la 23 114 Cb 72
43230 Chomette, la 43 128 Dc 77
42660 Chomey 42 130 Ec 77
38121 Chonas-L'Amballan 38 130 Ee 76
55200 Chonville-Malaumont 55 55 Fc 56
08600 Chooz 08 42 Ee 48
36220 Chopinerie, la 36 100 Ba 68
31540 Choples 31 165 Bf 87
62360 Choquel, le 62 28 Bd 45
60380 Choqueuse 60 38 Bf 51
60360 Choqueuse-les-Bénards 60 38 Ca 51
38680 Choranche 38 143 Fc 78
21200 Chorey 21 106 Ef 66
05230 Chorges 05 144 Gb 81
63950 Choriol 63 127 Cd 75
73270 Chornais, le 73 133 Gd 75
24210 Chosedie, la 24 137 Af 77
63120 Chossière 63 128 Dd 74
07270 Chossons 07 142 Ee 78
14250 Chouain 14 34 Zc 53
35560 Chouannière, la 35 65 Yb 58
82800 Chouastrac 82 150 Bd 84
36100 Chouday 36 102 Ca 67
41170 Choue 41 69 Af 61
58110 Chougny 58 104 De 66
80340 Chouignolles 80 39 Ce 49
51530 Chouilly 51 53 Ea 54
01450 Chouin 01 119 Fc 72
17170 Choupeau 17 110 Za 71
63220 Choupeire 63 129 De 76
86110 Chouppes 86 99 Aa 68
24640 Chourgnac 24 125 Ba 77
15340 Chourlie, la 15 139 Cc 80
41700 Choussy 41 86 Bc 64
41500 Chousy 41 86 Bc 62
33570 Chouteau 33 135 Zf 79
03450 Chouvigny 03 115 Cf 72
39370 Choux 39 119 Fe 71
45290 Choux, les 45 88 Ce 62
02210 Chouy 02 52 Db 53
37140 Chouzé-sur-Loire 37 99 Aa 65
19290 Chouziou 19 126 Ca 74
41150 Chouzy-sur-Cisse 41 86 Bb 63
70700 Choye 70 93 Fe 64
74350 Chozal 74 120 Ga 72
38460 Chozeau 38 131 Fb 74
22340 C'hra, le 22 63 Wd 59
78660 Chraches 78 70 Be 57
76740 Chrashville-la-Rocqueville 76 37 Af 50
27800 Chrétienville 27 49 Ae 54
22300 Christ 22 63 Wc 56
28260 Christophes, les 28 50 Bc 56
45220 Chuelles 45 72 Cf 60
08130 Chuffilly-Roche 08 42 Ed 52
80340 Chuignes 80 39 Ce 49
28190 Chuisnes 28 69 Bb 58
16430 Churet 16 124 Ab 74
30200 Chusclan 30 155 Ee 84
42410 Chuyer 42 130 Ee 76
38200 Chuzelles 38 130 Ef 75
31350 Ciadoux 31 163 Ae 89
20134 Ciamannacce CTC 183 Ka 97
64120 Cibits 64 161 Yf 89
64500 Ciboure 64 160 Yb 88
76570 Cideville 76 37 Af 51
71350 Ciel 71 106 Fa 67
31110 Cier-de-Luchon 31 176 Ad 91
31510 Cier-de-Rivière 31 163 Ad 90
02130 Cierges 02 53 Dd 53
55270 Cierges-sous-Montfaucon 55 55 Fa 53

258 | Chéméré

03150 Ciernat 03 116 Dc 71
31440 Cierp-Gaud 31 176 Ad 91
27930 Cierrey 27 50 Bb 54
17520 Cierzac 17 123 Ze 75
46200 Cieurac 46 137 Bc 79
46230 Cieurac 46 150 Bd 82
47170 Cieuse 47 148 Ab 84
65200 Cieutat 65 163 Ab 90
87520 Cieux 87 113 Ba 73
58220 Ciez 58 89 Db 64
53300 Cigné 53 67 Zc 58
17290 Cigogne 17 110 Za 72
37310 Cigogné 37 86 Af 65
37240 Cigogne, la 37 100 Ae 66
36110 Cigognolles 36 101 Be 66
64470 Cihigue 64 161 Za 90
02250 Cilly 02 41 Df 50
18130 Cilly 18 103 Cd 67
26150 Cime, la 26 143 Fb 79
05600 Cime-du-Mélezet 05 145 Ge 81
73340 Cimeteret, le 73 132 Ga 74
37500 Cinais 37 99 Ab 66
03220 Cindré 03 116 Dd 71
61800 Cingallière, la 61 47 Zb 56
11360 Cingle, le 11 179 Ce 90
64520 Cinq-Cantons, les 64 161 Yf 88
59122 Cinq-Chemins, les 59 27 Cd 43
37130 Cinq-Mars-la-Pile 37 85 Ac 64
36170 Cinq-Routes, les 36 113 Bc 70
44270 Cinq-Routes, les 44 96 Yb 67
17460 Cinq-Timbres, les 17 122 Zb 75
39200 Cinquetral 39 119 Ff 70
60940 Cinqueux 60 39 Cd 53
31550 Cintegabelle 31 165 Bd 89
14680 Cintheaux 14 47 Ze 54
27160 Cintray 27 49 Af 56
28300 Cintray 28 69 Bc 58
35310 Cintré 35 65 Ya 60
70120 Cintrey 70 92 Fe 62
20238 Cinturi Portu = Centuri-Port CTC 181 Kc 91
13600 Ciotat, la 13 171 Fd 89
13600 Ciotat-Plage, la 13 171 Fd 89
06620 Cipières 06 158 Gf 86
20113 Cipiniellu CTC 184 If 98
20137 Cipponu CTC 185 Kb 99
61320 Ciral 61 67 Zf 58
37240 Ciran 37 100 Af 66
87380 Cirat 87 126 Bd 75
88270 Circourt 88 76 Gb 59
88300 Circourt-sur-Mouzon 88 75 Fe 59
17290 Ciré-d'Aunis 17 110 Za 72
20144 Cirendinu CTC 185 Kc 99
31110 Cirès 31 175 Ad 91
60660 Cires-lès-Mello 60 51 Cc 53
70190 Cirey 70 93 Ga 64
19800 Cireygeade, la 19 126 Bf 77
52700 Cirey-lès-Mareilles 52 75 Fb 59
21270 Cirey-lès-Pontailler 21 92 Fb 65
52110 Cirey-sur-Blaise 52 74 Ef 59
54480 Cirey-sur-Vezouze 54 77 Gf 57
52370 Cirfontaines-en-Azois 52 74 Ef 60
52230 Cirfontaines-en-Ornois 52 75 Fc 58
79140 Cirière 79 98 Zc 67
36300 Ciron 36 101 Bb 69
34800 Cirque de Mourèze 34 167 Dc 87
71420 Ciry-le-Noble 71 105 Eb 69
02220 Ciry-Salsogne 02 40 Dc 52
61230 Cisai-Saint-Aubin 61 48 Ac 56
59189 Ciseaux, les 59 29 Cc 44
89420 Cisery 89 90 Ea 63
33250 Cissac-Médoc 33 122 Zb 77
86170 Cissé 86 99 Ab 69
27220 Cissey 27 49 Bb 55
19250 Cisterne 19 126 Ca 75
63740 Cisternes-la-Forêt 63 127 Ce 74
63630 Cistrière 63 128 Dd 76
43160 Cistrières 43 128 Dd 77
68310 Cité-Amélie 68 95 Hb 62
13120 Cité-Biver 13 170 Fc 88
54640 Cité d'Arderny-Chevillon 54 43 Ff 53
42230 Cité-de-Beaulieu 42 129 Eb 76
36130 Cité-de-Brassioux 36 101 Be 67
20240 Cité de l'Air CTC 183 Kc 97
30960 Cité-de-L'Aubradou 30 154 Ea 83
84500 Cité de l'Usine 84 155 Ee 83
57730 Cité-de-Valmond 57 57 Ge 54
57500 Cité-Emile-Huchet 57 57 Ge 54
68260 Cité Fernand-Anna 68 95 Hc 62
68310 Cité-Graffenwald 68 95 Hb 62
57500 Cité Jeanne d'Arc 57 57 Ge 54
68270 Cité Jeune-Bois 68 95 Hb 62
80490 Citerne 80 38 Be 49
68310 Cité Rossallmend 68 95 Hb 62
70300 Citers 70 93 Gc 62
58470 Cités, les 58 103 Da 67
57500 Cité Sainte-Fontaine 57 57 Ge 53
57350 Cité Wendel 57 57 Gf 53
70700 Citey 70 93 Fe 64
33360 Citon 33 135 Zd 80
11160 Citou 11 166 Cd 88
77730 Citry 77 52 Db 55
86320 Civaux 86 112 Ad 70
42110 Civens 42 129 Eb 74
43320 Civeyrac 43 141 De 78
48200 Civeyrac 48 140 Db 80
27630 Civières 27 50 Bd 53
33920 Civrac-de-Blaye 33 135 Zd 78
33350 Civrac-de-Dordogne 33 135 Zf 80
33340 Civrac-en-Médoc 33 122 Za 76
18290 Civray 18 102 Cb 67
86400 Civray 86 112 Ab 72
37150 Civray-de-Touraine 37 86 Ba 64
86190 Civray-les-Essarts 86 99 Aa 69
37160 Civray-sur-Esves 37 100 Ae 66
36120 Civrenne 36 102 Bf 68
01390 Civrieux 01 118 Ef 73
69380 Civrieux-d'Azergues 69M 130 Ee 73
28200 Civry 28 70 Bc 60
21320 Civry-en-Montagne 21 91 Ed 65
78910 Civry-la-Forêt 78 50 Bd 55
89440 Civry-sur-Serein 89 90 Df 63
49700 Cizay-la-Madeleine 49 99 Ze 65
01250 Cize 01 119 Fc 71
39300 Cize 39 107 Ff 68
58270 Cizely 58 104 Dc 67
65230 Cizos 65 163 Ac 89
02000 Clacy-et-Thierret 02 40 Dd 51
24170 Cladech 24 137 Ba 80
24540 Cladech 24 137 Af 81
56250 Claies, les 56 81 Xc 62
14210 Claine, la 14 47 Zc 54
66530 Claira 66 179 Cf 92
34260 Clairac 34 167 Da 87
47320 Clairac 47 148 Ac 82
30260 Clairan 30 154 Ea 85
19150 Clairat 19 126 Be 77
49350 Clairay, le 49 84 Ze 64
23300 Clairbize 23 113 Bc 71
78120 Clairefontaine-en-Yvelines 78 70 Bf 57
61800 Clairefougère, Montsecret- 61 47 Zb 56
70200 Clairegoutte 70 94 Gd 63
88260 Clairey 88 76 Ga 60
59740 Clairfayts 59 31 Ea 48
02260 Clairfontaine 02 41 Df 49
54600 Clairlieu 54 56 Ga 57
62500 Clairmarais 62 27 Cb 44
71110 Clairmatin 71 117 Eb 71
60280 Clairoix 60 39 Cf 52
03450 Clairs, les 03 115 Da 72
49110 Clairtière, la 49 83 Za 65
12330 Clairvaux-d'Aveyron 12 151 Cc 82
39130 Clairvaux-les-Lacs 39 107 Fe 69
24160 Clairvivre 24 125 Bb 77
80540 Clairy-Saulchoix 80 38 Cb 49
76660 Clais 76 37 Bc 50
36500 Claise 36 101 Bc 68
16440 Claix 16 123 Aa 75
38640 Claix 38 144 Fe 78
17500 Clam 17 123 Zd 76
51130 Clamanges 51 53 Ea 56
92260 Clamart 92 51 Cb 56
02880 Clamecy 02 40 Dc 52
58500 Clamecy 58 89 Dd 64
11190 Clamenèes, les 11 178 Cb 91
12550 Clamensac 12 152 Cd 85
04250 Clamensane 04 157 Ga 83
21390 Clamerey 21 91 Ec 64
43360 Clamont 43 128 Db 77
58320 Clamour 58 103 Da 66
18800 Clanay 18 103 Ce 66
56500 Clandy, le 56 64 Xa 61
56920 Clandy, le 56 64 Xa 60
06420 Clans 06 159 Ha 85
70000 Clans 70 93 Ga 63
26130 Clansayes 26 155 Ee 82
55120 Claon, le 55 55 Ef 54
33950 Claouey 33 134 Ye 80
30430 Clap, le 30 154 Ec 83
12380 Claparède, la 12 152 Cd 86
12540 Clapier, le 12 153 Db 86
05600 Clapière 05 145 Ge 80
83400 Clapière, la 83 172 Ga 90
34830 Clapiers 34 168 Df 87
04200 Clapisse, la 04 157 Ff 83
04330 Clappe, la 04 157 Gb 84
66500 Clara 66 178 Cc 93
31210 Clarac 31 163 Ad 90
32390 Clarac 32 149 Ad 86
65190 Clarac 65 163 Ab 89
64330 Claracq 64 162 Ze 87
73420 Clarafond 73 132 Ff 75
74270 Clarafond 74 119 Ff 72
14130 Clarbec 14 35 Aa 53
65300 Clarens 65 163 Ac 90
30870 Clarensac 30 154 Eb 86
05110 Claret 05 157 Ff 82
34270 Claret 34 154 Df 85
73670 Clarets, les 73 132 Ff 76
24360 Clargour 24 124 Ad 75
62129 Clarques 62 29 Cb 45
22480 Clarté 22 63 Wf 58
22700 Clarté, la 22 63 Wd 56
59225 Clary 59 30 Dc 48
40320 Classun 40 162 Zd 86
31460 Clastre, la 31 165 Be 87
02440 Clastres 02 40 Db 50
83920 Clastron 83 172 Gd 88
76450 Clasville 76 36 Ad 50
11140 Clat, le 11 178 Cb 92
12780 Clau, la 12 152 Cf 83
88410 Claudon 88 76 Ga 60
86200 Claunay 86 99 Ab 67
12260 Claunhac 12 138 Ca 82
04530 Clausal 04 158 Ge 82
31470 Claussade 31 164 Ba 87
63330 Clautrier 63 115 Cd 72
15150 Claux, le 15 139 Cb 78
15400 Claux, le 15 127 Ce 78
19400 Claux, le 19 138 Bf 78
34190 Claux, le 34 153 Dd 85
05560 Claux, les 05 145 Ge 81
47140 Clauzade 47 149 Af 82
43170 Clauze, la 43 140 Dd 79
24620 Clauzel 24 137 Ba 79
43700 Clauzel, le 43 141 Df 79
12120 Clauzelles 12 152 Cd 83
38142 Clavans-en-Haut-Oisans 38 144 Ga 78
38142 Clavans-le-Haut 38 144 Ga 78
43220 Clavas 43 130 Ec 77
79420 Clavé 79 111 Ze 70
79400 Claveau 79 111 Ze 70
69870 Claveisolles 69D 118 Ec 72
63740 Claveix 63 127 Ce 74
46240 Clavel 46 138 Be 81
87120 Clavérolas 87 126 Be 74
23000 Clavérolles 23 114 Bf 71
17220 Clavette 17 110 Yf 72
26240 Claveyson 26 142 Ef 77
36120 Clavière 36 101 Be 68
63600 Clavière 63 129 De 75
15320 Clavières 15 140 Db 79
15320 Clavières-d'Outre 15 140 Db 79
83830 Claviers 83 172 Gd 87
46100 Clavies 46 138 Bf 81
27180 Claville 27 49 Ba 54
76690 Claville-Motteville 76 37 Bb 51
08460 Clavy-Warby 08 41 Ed 50
49610 Claye 49 83 Zc 64
85320 Claye, la 85 109 Ye 70
35590 Clayes 35 65 Ya 59
77410 Claye-Souilly 77 51 Ce 55
78450 Clayes-sous-Bois, les 78 51 Ca 56
54290 Clayeures 54 76 Gc 58
79300 Clazay 79 98 Zc 68
56580 Clebzur 56 64 Xb 60
14570 Clécy 14 47 Zd 55
29770 Cléden-Cap-Sizun 29 61 Vc 60
29270 Cléden-Poher 29 63 Wb 59
29233 Cléder 29 62 Vf 57
40320 Clèdes 40 162 Zd 87
83830 Clèdes, les 83 172 Gd 87
16320 Cledou, le 16 124 Ac 75
67160 Cleebourg 67 58 Hf 54
88230 Clefcy 88 77 Gf 59
52240 Clefmont 52 75 Fd 60
74230 Clefs, les 74 132 Gb 73
49150 Clefs-Val d'Anjou 49 84 Zf 63
27490 Clef Vallée d'Eure 27 49 Bb 54
56620 Cléguer 56 79 Wd 61
56480 Cléguerec = Klegereg 56 79 Wf 60
38930 Clelles-en-Trièves 38 144 Fd 80
61130 Clémance 61 69 Ad 59
85440 Clémantlnière, la 85 109 Yc 70
37460 Clémencerie, la 37 100 Ba 65
21220 Clémencey 21 106 Ef 65
63320 Clémensat 63 128 Da 75
63540 Clémensat 63 128 Da 74
63310 Clémenter 63 116 Db 73
54610 Clémery 54 56 Gb 55
18410 Clémont 18 88 Cb 63
21490 Clénay 21 92 Fa 64
62650 Clenleu 62 28 Bf 45
76410 Cléon 76 37 Ba 53
26450 Cleon-d'Andran 26 142 Ef 81
42110 Cleppé 42 129 Eb 74
17270 Clérac 17 135 Ze 77
24150 Clérans 24 136 Ad 79
44450 Cleray, le 44 97 Yd 65
14230 Clerbosq, les 14 34 Yf 53
40460 Clerc, le 40 134 Yf 82
17350 Cléré 17 122 Zb 73
36700 Cléré-du-Bois 36 100 Ba 67
37340 Cléré-les-Pins 37 85 Ac 64
76690 Clères 76 37 Ba 51
49560 Cléré-sur-Layon 49 98 Zd 66
10390 Clérey 10 73 Eb 59
88630 Clérey-la-Côte 88 76 Fe 58
54330 Clérey-sur-Brénon 54 76 Ga 57
44850 Clergerie, la 44 82 Yd 64
19320 Clergoux 19 126 Bf 77
26260 Clérieux 26 143 Ef 78
89190 Clérimois, les 89 72 Dc 59
88240 Clerjus, le 88 76 Gb 61
63720 Clerlande 63 116 Db 73
71520 Clermain 71 118 Ed 70
09420 Clermont 09 177 Bb 90
40180 Clermont 40 161 Za 87
60600 Clermont 60 39 Cc 52
74270 Clermont 74 119 Ff 73
72200 Clermont-Créans 72 84 Zf 62
24140 Clermont-de-Beauregard 24 136 Ad 79
24160 Clermont-d'Excideuil 24 125 Ba 76
55120 Clermont-en-Argonne 55 55 Fa 54
14430 Clermont-en-Auge 14 35 Zf 53
63000* Clermont-Ferrand 63 128 Da 74
31810 Clermont-le-Fort 31 164 Bc 88
02340 Clermont-lès-Fermes 02 41 Df 50
34800 Clermont-L'Hérault 34 167 Dc 87
32300 Clermont-Pouyguillès 32 163 Ad 88
32600 Clermont-Savès 32 164 Ba 87
47270 Clermont-Soubiran 47 149 Ae 84
11250 Clermont-sur-Lauquet 11 178 Cc 90
25330 Cléron 25 107 Ga 66
62890 Clerques 62 27 Bf 44
43160 Clersange 43 128 Dd 77
25340 Clerval 25 94 Gc 64
21270 Cléry 21 92 Fc 65
73460 Cléry 73 132 Gb 75
95420 Cléry-en-Vexin 95 50 Bf 54
55110 Cléry-Grand 55 42 Fa 52
55110 Cléry-Petit 55 42 Fb 52
45370 Cléry-Saint-André 45 87 Be 62
80200 Cléry-sur-Somme 80 39 Cf 49
01960 Clés, les 01 118 Fa 71
51260 Clesles 51 73 De 57
56450 Clesse 56 80 Xc 63
71260 Clessé 71 118 Ee 70
79350 Clessé 79 98 Zd 68
71130 Clessy 71 117 Ea 69
30410 Clet 30 154 Ea 83
62380 Cléty 62 29 Cb 45
56140 Cleu, la 56 81 Xe 62
29390 Cleumérien 29 79 Wb 60
76450 Cleuville 76 36 Ad 50
14370 Cléville 14 35 Zf 54
76640 Cléville 76 36 Ad 51
28300 Clévilliers 28 69 Bc 57
33540 Cleyrac 33 135 Zf 80
01230 Cleyzieu 01 119 Fc 73
88700 Clézentaine 88 77 Gd 58
54113 Clézilles 54 76 Ff 57
92110 Clichy 92 51 Cb 55
04370 Clignon 04 158 Gd 83
67510 Climbach 67 58 Hf 54
52700 Clinchamp 52 75 Fc 59
14320 Clinchamps-sur-Oroe 14 47 Zd 54
17240 Clion 17 123 Zc 76
36700 Clion 36 101 Bb 67
44210 Clion-sur-Mer, le 44 96 Xf 66
26270 Cliousclat 26 142 Ef 80
59279 Clipon, le 59 27 Cb 42
76640 Cliponville 76 36 Ad 50
21150 Clirey 21 91 Ed 64
08090 Cliron 08 42 Ed 50
44350 Clis 44 81 Xd 64
17600 Clisse, la 17 122 Zb 74
44190 Clisson 44 97 Ye 66
50330 Clitourps 50 33 Yd 51
28240 Cloche, la 28 69 Af 58
59470 Cloche, la 59 27 Cc 43
29360 Clohars-Carnoët 29 79 Wc 62
29950 Clohars-Fouesnant 29 78 Vf 61
29190 Cloître-Pleyben, le 29 62 Wa 59
29410 Cloître-Saint-Thégonnec 29 62 Wb 58
21230 Clomot 21 105 Ec 65
38550 Clonas-sur-Varèze 38 130 Ee 76
62560 Cloquant 62 29 Ca 45
16120 Clos, le 16 123 Zf 76
35210 Clos, le 35 66 Ye 59
38550 Clos, le 38 130 Ee 76
44530 Clos, le 44 81 Xf 64
05150 Clos d'Antouret 05 143 Fc 82
84220 Clos-de-Filliol 84 156 Fb 85
37210 Closeaux, les 37 85 Ae 64
77370 Clos-Fontaine 77 72 Da 57
51120 Clos-le-Roi, le 51 53 Dd 56
22550 Clos-Noël, le 22 64 Xd 57
38520 Clot-d'en-Haut, le 38 144 Gb 79
34710 Clotinières 34 167 Da 89
04400 Clot-Meyran 04 158 Gd 82
17360 Clotte, la 17 135 Zf 78
05100 Clottet, le 05 145 Ge 79
87360 Clotures, les 87 113 Ba 71
57185 Clouange-sur-Orne 57 56 Ga 53
86600 Cloué 86 111 Aa 70
16410 Cloulas 16 124 Ab 75
41700 Clouseau, le 41 86 Bc 64
71960 Cloux, le 71 118 Ee 70
03600 Cloux, les 03 115 Ce 71
18170 Cloux, les 18 102 Cb 68
85430 Clouzeaux, Aubigny-, les 85 97 Yc 69
28220 Cloyes-les-Trois-Rivières 28 69 Bb 60
28220 Cloyes-sur-le-Loir 28 69 Bb 61
51300 Cloyes-sur-Marne 51 54 Ed 57
07270 Cluac 07 142 Ed 79
04420 Clucheret, le 04 157 Gb 83
39110 Clucy 39 107 Ff 67
23270 Clugnat 23 114 Ca 71
36340 Cluis 36 114 Be 69
04330 Clumanc 04 157 Gc 84
71250 Cluny 71 118 Ed 70
23210 Cluptat 23 114 Bd 72
40990 Clusatdit 40 146 Yf 86
74220 Clusaz, la 74 120 Gc 73
01460 Cluse, la 01 119 Fd 71
05250 Cluse, la 05 144 Ff 81
25300 Cluse, la 25 108 Gc 67
03190 Cluseau, le 03 115 Cd 69
25300 Cluse-et-Mijoux, la 25 108 Gc 67
74300 Cluses 74 120 Gd 72
79190 Clussais 79 111 Aa 71
71270 Clux-Villeneuve 71 106 Fb 67
24530 Cluzeau 24 124 Ae 76
03250 Cluzel 03 116 Dd 72
12200 Cluzel, le 12 151 Ca 83
46090 Cluzel, le 46 150 Bc 82
24800 Cluzelet, le 24 125 Af 76
63640 Cluzet 63 115 Ce 73
29246 Coadigou 29 63 Wc 58
29390 Coadigou 29 78 Wb 60
29390 Coadry 29 78 Wb 60
22970 Coadut 22 63 We 57
06390 Coaraze 06 159 Hb 85
64800 Coarraze 64 162 Ze 89
22140 Coatascorn 22 63 We 56
29140 Coat-Canton 29 78 Wb 61
56520 Coat-Coff 56 79 Wd 62
29640 Coatélan 29 62 Wb 57
56520 Coatermalo 56 79 Wd 62
22390 Coat-Forn 22 63 We 58
29400 Coativellec 29 62 Vf 57
22160 Coatleau 22 63 Wc 58
29870 Coat-Méal 29 61 Vc 57
29140 Coat-Meur 29 78 Wb 61
29460 Coat-Nant 29 62 Ve 58
29340 Coat-Pin 29 79 Wb 62
22480 Coat-Piquet 22 63 We 58
29640 Coat-Quéau 29 63 Wb 58
22450 Coatréven 22 63 Wd 56
29670 Cobalon 29 62 Wa 57
26400 Cobonne 26 143 Fa 80
59830 Cobrieux 59 30 Db 45
36500 Cocandière, la 36 101 Bb 67
09200 Coch, le 09 176 Bb 91
05260 Coche, la 05 144 Gb 80
77440 Cocheral 77 52 Da 54
61310 Cochère, la 61 48 Aa 56
57800 Cocheren 57 57 Gf 54
38112 Cochet 38 143 Fc 78
10240 Coclois 10 74 Ec 58
80510 Cocquerel 80 28 Bf 48
18120 Cocuas, les 18 102 Ca 66
47250 Cocumont 47 148 Aa 82
12460 Cocural 12 139 Ce 80
48400 Cocurès, Bédouès- 48 153 Dd 82
30920 Codognan 30 169 Eb 86
30200 Codolet 30 155 Ee 84
51170 Coëmy 51 53 De 53
35134 Coësmes 35 82 Yd 61
56230 Coët-Bihan 56 81 Xd 63
22240 Coëtbily 22 64 Xd 57
56120 Coët-Bugat 56 80 Xc 61
22210 Coëtlogon 22 64 Xc 60
22400 Coëtmieux 22 64 Xc 58
56540 Coët-Milin 56 79 Wd 60
56310 Coët-Organ 56 80 We 61
46240 Cœur-de-Causse 46 138 Bd 80
23250 Cœurgne 23 114 Be 72
58210 Cœurs 58 89 Dc 65
85220 Coëx 85 96 Yb 68
77320 Coffery 77 52 Db 56
35380 Coganne 35 65 Xf 60
20160 Coggia CTC 182 Ie 96
35460 Coglès 35 66 Yd 58
39130 Cogna 39 107 Fe 69
16100 Cognac 16 123 Ze 74
87310 Cognac-la-Forêt 87 125 Ba 73
58130 Cognan 58 103 Db 66
03110 Cognat-Lyonne 03 116 Db 72
28120 Cogné 28 69 Bb 58
72310 Cogners 72 85 Ad 61
38350 Cognet 38 144 Fe 79
26110 Cognets, les 26 156 Fa 82
70230 Cognières 70 93 Gb 64
38470 Cognin-les-Gorges 38 143 Fc 77
20123 Cognocoli-Monticchi CTC 182 If 98
63990 Cognol 63 129 De 75
63300 Cognord 63 116 Dc 73
18130 Cogny 18 103 Cd 67
69640 Cogny 69D 118 Ed 73
83310 Cogolin 83 172 Gd 89
24500 Cogulot 24 136 Ac 80
43100 Cohade 43 128 Dc 76
02130 Cohan 02 53 Dd 53
02270 Cohartille 02 40 De 50
63310 Cohat, le 63 116 Db 73
73400 Cohennoz 73 133 Gc 74
22800 Cohiniac 22 64 Xa 58
52600 Cohons 52 92 Fc 62
44530 Coiffy 44 81 Xf 64
52400 Coiffy-le-Bas 52 92 Fe 61
52400 Coiffy-le-Haut 52 92 Fe 61
19170 Coignac 19 126 Be 75
53100 Coignardière, la 53 67 Zb 59
32270 Coignax 32 163 Ae 86
80560 Coigneux 80 29 Cd 48
78310 Coignières 78 50 Bf 56
50250 Coigny 50 33 Yd 53
33210 Coimères 33 135 Ze 82
26140 Coinaud 26 130 Ef 77
45310 Coinces 45 70 Be 60
88100 Coinches 88 77 Ha 59
54370 Coincourt 54 57 Gd 56
02210 Coincy 02 52 Dc 54
57530 Coincy 57 56 Gb 54
49270 Coindassière, la 49 82 Ye 65
79100 Coindrie, la 79 99 Ze 67
36130 Coings 36 101 Be 67
02360 Coingt 02 41 Ea 50
57420 Coin-lès-Cuvry 57 56 Ga 54
57420 Coin-sur-Seille 57 56 Ga 54
33540 Coirac 33 135 Ze 80
38110 Coiranne 38 131 Fc 75
38220 Coirelle, la 38 144 Fe 78
69590 Coise 69M 130 Ec 75
73800 Coise 73 132 Ga 75
39200 Coiserette 39 119 Ff 70
70400 Coisevaux 70 94 Ge 63
39240 Coisia, Thoirette- 39 119 Fd 71
44460 Coisnauté 44 81 Ya 63
19170 Coissac 19 126 Bf 75
80260 Coisy 80 39 Cb 49
17330 Coivert 17 111 Zd 72
60420 Coivrel 60 39 Cd 51
51270 Coizard-Joches 51 53 Df 56
73500 Col, le 73 133 Gd 77
47450 Colayrac-Saint-Cirq 47 149 Ad 83
22480 Coldabry 22 63 Wf 58
09300 Col-del-Teil 09 178 Bf 91
62142 Colembert 62 27 Bf 44
89150 Coleuvrat 89 72 Da 60
01270 Coligny 01 119 Fc 70
80560 Colincamps 80 29 Cd 48
89700 Collan 89 90 Df 61
58800 Collancelle, la 58 104 Dd 65
15400 Collandres 15 127 Cd 77
27190 Collandres-Quincarnon 27 49 Af 55
15300 Collanges 15 127 Ce 78
63220 Collanges 63 129 De 76
63340 Collanges 63 128 Db 76
63940 Collanges 63 129 Dd 76
17210 Collardeau 17 123 Ze 77
43230 Collat 43 128 Dd 77
83440 Colle, la 83 172 Gd 86
83630 Colle, la 83 171 Gb 86
77090 Collégien 77 51 Ce 55
47320 Colleignes 47 148 Ac 83
89100 Collemiers 89 72 Db 60
69660 Collonges-au-Mont-d'Or 69M 130 Ef 74
83440 Colle-Noire, la 83 172 Ge 87
59680 Colleret 59 31 Ea 47
06480 Colle-sur-Loup, le 06 173 Ha 86
05260 Collet 05 144 Gb 81
42130 Collet 42 129 Df 74
73300 Collet 73 132 Gb 77
05250 Collet, le 05 144 Ff 80
44760 Collet, le 44 96 Xf 66
38580 Collet d'Allevard, le 38 132 Ga 76
48160 Collet-de-Dèze, le 48 154 Df 83
27500 Colletot 27 36 Ad 52
76400 Colleville 76 36 Ac 50
14880 Colleville-Montgomery 14 47 Ze 53
14710 Colleville-sur-Mer 14 47 Za 52
30210 Collias 30 154 Ec 85
02860 Colligis 02 40 Dd 52
57530 Colligny-Maizery 57 56 Gb 54
62180 Colline-Beaumont 62 28 Be 46
22330 Collinée = Koedlinez 22 64 Xc 59
66190 Collioure 66 179 Da 93
83610 Collobrières 83 172 Gb 89
71250 Collonge 71 118 Ed 70
71700 Collonge 71 118 Ee 69
71460 Collonge-en-Charollais 71 105 Ed 69
71360 Collonge-la-Madeleine 71 105 Ed 67
01550 Collonges 01 119 Ff 72
19500 Collonges-la-Rouge 19 138 Bd 78
21220 Collonges-lès-Bevy 21 106 Ef 65

Collonges-lès-Bevy | 259

21110 Collonges-lès-Premières 21 106 Fb 65
74160 Collonges-sous-Salève 74 120 Ga 72
06910 Collongues 06 158 Gf 85
65350 Collongues 65 163 Aa 89
29530 Collorec 29 62 Wb 59
30190 Collorgues 30 154 Eb 84
68000 Colmar 68 60 Hc 60
76690 Colmare 76 37 Bb 51
04370 Colmars 04 158 Gd 83
57320 Colmen 57 44 Gd 52
58350 Colméry 58 89 Db 64
76550 Colmesnil-Mannevil 76 37 Ba 49
54260 Colmey 54 43 Fd 52
52160 Colmier-le-Bas 52 91 Ef 62
52160 Colmier-le-Haut 52 91 Ef 62
06420 Colniane, la 06 159 Hb 84
30460 Colognac 30 154 De 84
32430 Cologne 32 164 Af 86
06670 Colomars 06 159 Hb 86
81170 Colombarie, la 81 151 Bf 84
05300 Colombe 05 156 Fe 82
38690 Colombe 38 131 Fc 76
41160 Colombe, la 41 86 Bc 61
50800 Colombe, la 50 46 Ye 55
48000 Colombèche, la 48 140 Dd 81
23400 Colombeix 23 114 Be 73
10200 Colombé-la-Fosse 10 74 Ee 59
70200 Colombe-lès-Bithaine 70 93 Gc 62
10200 Colombé-le-Sec 10 74 Ee 59
70000 Colombe-lès-Vesoul 70 93 Gb 63
14460 Colombelles 14 47 Ze 53
92700 Colombes 92 51 Cb 55
71370 Colombey 71 106 Ef 68
54170 Colombey-les-Belles 54 76 Ff 57
52240 Colombey-lès-Choiseul 52 75 Fd 60
03600 Colombier 03 115 Ce 71
21360 Colombier 21 105 Ee 65
24480 Colombier 24 137 Af 80
24560 Colombier 24 136 Ad 80
30200 Colombier 30 155 Ed 84
42220 Colombier 42 130 Ed 76
43500 Colombier 43 129 De 76
59118 Colombier 59 30 Da 44
70000 Colombier 70 93 Gb 63
18340 Colombier, le 18 102 Cc 67
19120 Colombier, le 19 138 Be 78
26160 Colombier, le 26 142 Ee 82
36170 Colombier, le 36 113 Bc 69
25260 Colombier-Châtelot 25 94 Gd 64
25500 Colombière 25 108 Gd 66
71800 Colombier-en-Brionnais 71 117 Ec 70
34390 Colombières-sur-Orb 34 167 Da 87
25260 Colombier-Fontaine 25 94 Ge 64
07430 Colombier-le-Cardinal 07 130 Ee 77
07270 Colombier-le-Jeune 07 142 Ee 78
07410 Colombier-le-Vieux 07 142 Ee 78
17460 Colombiers 17 123 Zc 75
18200 Colombiers 18 102 Cd 68
34440 Colombiers 34 167 Da 89
61250 Colombiers 61 68 Aa 58
86490 Colombiers 86 99 Ac 68
69124 Colombier-Saugnieu 69M 131 Fa 74
53120 Colombiers-du-Plessis 53 66 Za 58
14480 Colombiers-sur-Seulles 14 35 Zc 53
12240 Colombiès 12 151 Cc 82
20167 Colombina CTC 182 If 97
14710 Colombrières 14 34 Za 53
50700 Colomby 50 33 Yd 52
14610 Colomby-Anguerny 14 47 Zd 53
14610 Colomby-sur-Thaon 14 47 Zd 53
31770 Colomiers 31 164 Bc 87
01300 Colomieu 01 131 Fd 74
61340 Colonard-Corubert 61 69 Ad 58
23800 Colondannes 23 113 Bd 71
02120 Colonfay 02 40 De 49
37390 Colonie, la 37 85 Ad 64
65400 Colonies, les 65 174 Ze 91
39800 Colonne 39 107 Fd 67
26130 Colonzelle 26 155 Ef 82
71580 Colots, les 71 106 Fc 69
56350 Colpo 56 80 Xb 62
88490 Colroy-la-Grande 88 77 Ha 59
67420 Colroy-la-Roche 67 77 Hb 58
28300 Coltainville 28 70 Bd 58
15170 Coltines 15 140 Cf 78
24120 Coly 24 137 Bb 78
34980 Combaillaux 34 168 De 86
15220 Combaldie, la 15 139 Cb 79
43160 Combalibœuf 43 128 Da 77
30250 Combas 30 154 Ea 85
12800 Combe 12 151 Cc 83
30200 Combe 30 155 Ed 84
42830 Combe 42 116 De 73
63320 Combe 63 128 Da 76
15130 Combe, la 15 139 Cd 80
19270 Combe, la 19 126 Bd 77
24290 Combe, la 24 137 Bb 78
26170 Combe, la 26 156 Fc 83
38300 Combe, la 38 131 Fb 75
38650 Combe, la 38 143 Fd 79
48100 Combe, la 48 140 Db 80
63260 Combe, la 63 116 Db 72
73300 Combe, la 73 132 Gb 77
73610 Combe, la 73 132 Fe 75
74330 Combe, la 74 120 Ga 73
74970 Combe, la 74 120 Gc 72
87140 Combe, la 87 113 Bb 72
70120 Combeaufontaine 70 93 Ff 62
25650 Combe-Benoit 25 108 Gd 67
04530 Combe-Brémond 04 145 Gf 81
25500 Combe-d'Abondance 25 108 Gd 66
39400 Combe-de-Morbier, la 39 107 Ga 69
26110 Combe-de-Sauve, la 26 155 Fa 82
81640 Combefa 81 151 Ca 84
05140 Combe-Fère 05 144 Fd 81
34520 Combefère 34 153 Db 85
34360 Combejean 34 167 Cf 88
34220 Combeliobert 34 166 Ce 88
63570 Combelle, la 63 128 Db 76
09420 Combelongue 09 177 Bb 91
48100 Combe-Maury 48 140 Dc 81
24600 Comberanche-et-Epeluche 24 124 Ab 77
70000 Comberjon 70 93 Gb 63
82600 Comberouger 82 149 Ba 85
21200 Combertault 21 106 Ef 67
34240 Combes 34 167 Da 87
01130 Combes, les 01 119 Fe 71
01570 Combes, les 01 118 Ef 70
05100 Combes, les 05 145 Gd 79
05110 Combes, les 05 157 Ff 82
07130 Combes, les 07 142 Ee 79
23500 Combes, les 23 114 Cb 73
42440 Combes, les 42 129 De 74
48600 Combes, les 48 140 Dd 80
73450 Combes, les 73 133 Gc 77
74210 Combes, les 74 132 Gb 74
74210 Combes, les 74 132 Gb 74
87340 Combes, les 87 113 Bc 72
87600 Combes, les 87 125 Af 74
46240 Combescure 46 138 Bd 80
81360 Combessié, la 81 151 Cb 86
63600 Combest 63 129 De 76
82800 Combettes 82 150 Bd 84
16320 Combiers 16 124 Ac 76
21700 Comblanchien 21 106 Ef 66
80360 Combles 80 39 Cf 48
55000 Combles-en-Barrois 55 55 Fa 56
35330 Comblessac 35 81 Xf 61
45800 Combleux 45 87 Bf 61
51700 Comblizy 51 53 De 54
61400 Comblot 61 68 Ad 58
74920 Combloux 74 121 Gd 73
27170 Combon 27 49 Af 54
86460 Combourg 86 112 Ad 72
35270 Combourg = Komborn 35 65 Yb 58
35210 Combourtillé 35 66 Ye 59
26120 Combovin 26 143 Fa 79
12170 Combradet 12 151 Cc 85
63380 Combrailles 63 127 Cd 73
79140 Combrand 79 98 Zb 67
14220 Combray 14 47 Zd 55
42840 Combre 42 117 Eb 72
49520 Combrée 49 83 Yf 62
28480 Combres 28 69 Ba 59
43130 Combres 43 129 Df 77
43160 Combres 43 128 Dd 77
43590 Combres 43 129 Ea 77
19250 Combressol 19 126 Cb 76
55160 Combres-sous-les-Côtes 55 55 Fd 54
12370 Combret 12 152 Ce 85
43300 Combret 43 141 Dd 78
48340 Combret 48 140 Da 81
48800 Combret 48 141 Df 82
87400 Combret 87 126 Bd 74
45530 Combreux 45 71 Cb 61
19320 Combrignac 19 126 Ca 77
88490 Combrimont 88 77 Ha 59
29120 Combrit 29 78 Vf 61
63460 Combronde 63 115 Da 73
12240 Combrouze 12 151 Cb 83
87210 Combrun 87 113 Ba 71
77380 Combs-la-Ville 77 51 Cd 57
74230 Comburce 74 132 Gc 73
71990 Comelle, la 71 105 Ea 67
87160 Comergnac 87 113 Bb 71
66500 Comes 66 178 Cc 92
46190 Comiac 46 138 Bf 79
11700 Comigne 11 166 Cd 89
09320 Cominac 09 177 Bb 91
59560 Comines 59 30 Da 44
71500 Commagne, la 71 106 Fa 69
71400 Commaille, la 71 105 Eb 67
29450 Commana 29 62 Wa 58
21320 Commarin 21 105 Ed 65
21320 Comme, la 21 91 Ec 65
58430 Comme, la 58 104 Df 66
61200 Commeaux 61 48 Zf 56
38260 Commelle 38 131 Fb 76
42120 Commelle 42 117 Ea 73
39140 Commenailles 39 106 Fc 68
02300 Commenchon 02 40 Da 50
40210 Commensacq 40 147 Zb 83
03600 Commentry 03 115 Ce 71
95450 Commeny 95 50 Bf 54
85220 Commequiers 85 96 Ya 68
53470 Commer 53 67 Zc 59
55200 Commercy 55 55 Fd 56
19300 Commerly 19 126 Bf 76
72560 Commerreries, les 72 68 Ac 61
72600 Commerveil 72 68 Ac 59
14520 Commes 14 47 Zb 52
89430 Commissey 89 90 Ea 61
45700 Commodité, la 45 88 Ce 61
39250 Communailles-en-Montagne 39 107 Ga 68
62910 Communal, le 62 27 Ca 44
69360 Communay 69M 130 Ef 75
71220 Commune 71 117 Eb 69
37110 Commune, la 37 85 Ae 63
30190 Commune de Sainte-Anastasie 30 154 Eb 85
28290 Commune nouvelle d'Arrou 28 69 Ba 60
18150 Communes, les 18 103 Ce 67
42123 Communes, les 42 117 Ea 73
24200 Compagnoles 24 137 Bb 79
63610 Compains 63 127 Cf 76
76440 Compainville 76 37 Bd 51
32260 Compans 32 163 Ad 88
77290 Compans 77 51 Cd 55
23700 Compas, le 23 115 Cc 73
23460 Compeix, le 23 114 Bf 73
51510 Compertrix 51 54 Ec 55
35330 Compessy 35 81 Ya 61
12520 Compeyre 12 152 Da 84
60200 Compiègne 60 39 Ce 52
19800 Compiène 19 126 Bf 76
89140 Compigny 89 72 Db 58
17132 Compin, le 17 122 Za 75
44310 Compointrie, la 44 96 Yb 66
12350 Compolibat 12 151 Cb 82
73630 Compôte, la 73 132 Gb 74
12100 Comprégnac 12 152 Cf 84
87140 Compreignac 87 113 Bb 73
07120 Comps 07 154 Eb 82
12450 Comps 12 152 Cd 83
19290 Comps 19 126 Ca 74
30300 Comps 30 155 Ed 85
33710 Comps 33 135 Zc 78
12120 Comps-la-Grand-Ville 12 152 Cd 83
83840 Comps-sur-Artuby 83 172 Gd 86
33460 Comte 33 134 Zb 79
62150 Comté, la 62 29 Cd 46
32410 Comte, le 32 148 Ac 86
82200 Comtesse, la 82 149 Ba 83
11340 Comus 11 178 Bf 92
17150 Conac 17 122 Zb 76
43580 Conac 43 141 Dd 79
41290 Conan 41 86 Bb 62
01230 Conand 01 119 Fc 73
66500 Conat 66 178 Cc 93
20135 Conca CTC 185 Kc 98
29900 Concarneau = Konk-Kerne 29 78 Wa 61
02160 Concevreux 02 40 De 52
19350 Concèze 19 125 Bc 76
04400 Conche, la 04 158 Ge 82
48240 Conchès 48 153 Df 83
77600 Conches 77 51 Ce 55
85560 Conches, les 85 109 Yd 70
27190 Conches-en-Ouche 27 49 Af 55
04400 Conchette, la 04 158 Gd 82
27170 Conchez 27 49 Ae 54
64330 Conchez-de-Béarn 64 162 Ze 87
20228 Conchigliu CTC 181 Kc 91
62180 Conchil-le-Temple 62 28 Bd 46
07200 Conchy, la 07 142 Ec 80
60490 Conchy-les-Pots 60 39 Ce 51
62270 Conchy-sur-Canche 62 29 Cb 47
43370 Concis 43 141 Df 79
12520 Conclus 12 152 Da 83
46310 Concorès 46 137 Bc 81
56430 Concoret 56 65 Xe 60
46260 Concots 46 150 Bd 82
30450 Concoules 30 154 Df 82
12740 Concourès 12 152 Cd 82
49700 Concourson-sur-Layon 49 98 Zd 65
36300 Concremiers 36 100 Ba 69
18260 Concressault 18 88 Cd 64
41370 Concriers 41 86 Bc 62
16700 Condac 16 111 Ab 72
34220 Condades 34 166 Ce 88
71480 Condal 71 119 Fb 70
01430 Condamine 01 119 Fd 72
39570 Condamine 39 106 Fc 69
42230 Condamine 42 129 Eb 76
48210 Condamine, la 48 153 Dd 83
04530 Condamine-Châtelard, la 04 145 Ge 82
12500 Condamines 12 140 Cf 81
15190 Condat 15 127 Ce 76
46110 Condat 46 138 Bd 79
47500 Condat 47 137 Af 81
63380 Condat-en-Combraille 63 127 Cd 73
63490 Condat-lès-Montboissier 63 128 Dd 75
19140 Condat-sur-Ganaveix 19 126 Bd 76
24530 Condat-sur-Trincou 24 124 Ae 76
24570 Condat-sur-Vézère 24 137 Bb 78
87920 Condat-sur-Vienne 87 125 Bb 74
19170 Condau 19 126 Bf 75
34330 Condax 34 166 Cd 87
18160 Condé 18 102 Cb 68
36100 Condé 36 102 Bf 67
36230 Condé 36 102 Bf 69
61110 Condeau 61 69 Af 58
95450 Condécourt 95 50 Bf 54
55000 Condé-en-Barrois 55 55 Fa 55
02330 Condé-en-Brie 02 53 Dd 54
14110 Condé-en-Normandie 14 47 Zc 55
01400 Condeissiat 01 118 Fa 72
81800 Condel 81 150 Bd 86
08250 Condé-lès-Autry 08 54 Ef 53
08360 Condé-lès-Herpy 08 41 Eb 51
57220 Condé-Northen 57 56 Gc 54
16360 Condéon 16 123 Zf 76
39240 Condes 39 119 Fd 70
52000 Condes 52 75 Fa 60
77450 Condé-Sainte-Libiaire 77 52 Ce 55
02370 Condé-sur-Aisne 02 40 Dc 52
61110 Condé-sur-Huisne 61 69 Af 58
14270 Condé-sur-Ifs 14 48 Zf 54
27160 Condé-sur-Iton 27 49 Af 55
59163 Condé-sur-L'Escaut 59 31 Dd 46
51150 Condé-sur-Marne 51 53 Eb 54
14110 Condé-sur-Noireau 14 47 Zc 55
27290 Condé-sur-Risle 27 36 Ad 53
61250 Condé-sur-Sarthe 61 68 Aa 58
14400 Condé-sur-Seulles 14 34 Zc 53
02190 Condé-sur-Suippe 02 41 Df 52
78113 Condé-sur-Vesgre 78 50 Bd 56
50890 Condé-sur-Vire 50 46 Yf 54
62360 Condette 62 28 Bd 45
47500 Condezaygues 47 137 Af 82
32100 Condom 32 148 Ac 85
12470 Condom-d'Aubrac 12 139 Cf 81
81320 Condomines 81 166 Ce 86
26110 Condorcet 26 155 Fb 82
47290 Condou 47 136 Ad 81
02700 Condren 02 40 Db 51
69420 Condrieu 69M 130 Ee 76
74220 Confins, les 74 120 Gc 73
70170 Conflandey 70 93 Ga 62
73790 Conflans 73 132 Gc 74
54800 Conflans-en-Jarnisy 54 56 Ff 53
78700 Conflans-Sainte-Honorine 78 51 Ca 55
72120 Conflans-sur-Anille 72 69 Ae 61
70800 Conflans-sur-Lanterne 70 93 Gb 62
45700 Conflans-sur-Loing 45 72 Ce 61
51260 Conflans-sur-Seine 51 73 De 57
16500 Confolens 16 112 Ae 72
38740 Confolens 38 144 Ff 79
19200 Confolent-Port-Dieu 19 127 Cc 75
01200 Confort 01 119 Fe 72
22140 Confort 22 63 We 56
29790 Confort 29 78 Vd 60
70120 Confracourt 70 93 Ff 62
01310 Confrançon 01 118 Fa 71
72170 Congé-les-Guérets 72 68 Aa 59
30111 Congénies 30 154 Ea 86
91740 Congerville-Thionville 91 70 Bf 58
72290 Congé-sur-Orne 72 68 Ab 59
77440 Congis-sur-Thérouanne 77 52 Cf 54
53800 Congrier 53 83 Yf 62
51270 Congy 51 53 De 55
58150 Congy 58 89 Cf 65
28200 Conie-Molitard 28 70 Bc 60
43510 Conil 43 141 De 79
11200 Conilhac-Corbières 11 166 Ce 89
11190 Conilhac-de-la-Montagne 11 178 Cb 91
36800 Conives 36 101 Bc 69
73310 Conjux 73 132 Fe 74
56000 Conleau 56 80 Xb 63
72240 Conlie 72 68 Zf 60
39570 Conliège 39 107 Fd 69
12170 Connac 12 152 Cd 84
43350 Connac 43 141 De 78
08450 Connage 08 42 Ef 51
43160 Connangles 43 128 Dd 77
51230 Connantray-Vaurefroy 51 53 Ea 56
51230 Connantre 51 53 Df 56
30330 Connaux 30 155 Ed 84
15150 Conne 15 138 Ca 79
24100 Conne-de-Bergerac, la 24 136 Ad 80
24560 Conne-de-Labarde 24 136 Ad 80
81190 Connelié 81 151 Ca 84
27430 Connelles 27 50 Bb 53
72160 Connerré 72 68 Ac 60
12410 Connes 12 152 Ce 83
62350 Connet-Malo, le 62 29 Cd 45
24300 Connezac 24 124 Ad 75
02330 Connigis 02 53 Dd 54
87510 Conore 87 113 Ba 73
34380 Conque, la 34 153 De 86
44290 Conquereuil 44 82 Yb 63
12320 Conques-en-Rouergue 12 139 Cc 81
11600 Conques-sur-Orbiel 11 166 Cc 89
29217 Conquet, le 29 61 Vb 58
12290 Conquettes 12 152 Ce 83
17150 Consac 17 122 Zc 76
06510 Conségudes 06 158 Ha 85
55110 Consenvoye 55 55 Fb 53
52700 Consigny 52 75 Fc 60
54870 Cons-la-Grandville 54 43 Fe 52
74270 Cons-Sainte-Colombe 74 132 Gb 74
46090 Constans 46 137 Bc 81
33480 Constantenins 33 134 Za 78
55230 Constantine-Ferme 55 43 Fd 52
04150 Contadour, le 04 156 Fd 84
80300 Contalmaison 80 39 Ce 48
46200 Contaloube 46 138 Bd 80
74130 Contamines, les 74 120 Gc 73
74270 Contamine-Sarzin 74 120 Ff 72
74170 Contamines-Montjoie, les 74 133 Ge 74
74130 Contamine-sur-Arve 74 120 Gc 72
24210 Contarie, la 24 137 Ba 77
51330 Contault 51 54 Ee 55
33990 Contaut, le 33 122 Yf 77
80560 Contay 80 39 Cc 48
39300 Conte 39 107 Ga 68
17120 Conteneuil 17 122 Za 75
31550 Contery 31 164 Bc 89
06390 Contes 06 159 Hb 86
62990 Contes 62 28 Bf 46
53100 Contest 53 67 Zc 59
14540 Conteville 14 48 Ze 54
27210 Conteville 27 36 Ac 52
60360 Conteville 60 38 Ca 51
62130 Conteville 62 29 Cb 46
76390 Conteville 76 38 Bd 50
76450 Conteville 76 36 Ad 49
80370 Conteville 80 29 Ca 47
62126 Conteville-lez-Boulogne 62 26 Be 44
57340 Conthil 57 57 Gd 55
24400 Contie, la 24 136 Ac 79
82330 Contie, la 82 151 Bf 83
49330 Contigné 49 84 Zc 62
03500 Contigny 03 116 Db 70
72600 Contilly 72 68 Ac 58
37340 Continvoir 37 85 Ab 64
40170 Contis-les-Marais 40 146 Ye 84
40170 Contis-Plage 40 146 Ye 84
80500 Contoire 80 39 Cd 50
63160 Contournat 63 128 Db 74
47390 Contras 47 149 Ad 84
09230 Contrazy 09 177 Bb 90
17470 Contré 17 111 Ze 72
80160 Contre 80 38 Ca 50
70160 Contréglise 70 93 Ga 62
76400 Contremoulins 76 36 Ac 50
18130 Contres 18 102 Cc 67
41700 Contres 41 86 Bc 64
72110 Contres-en-Vairais 72 68 Ac 59
08400 Contreuve 08 42 Ed 52
01300 Contrevoz 01 131 Fd 74
88140 Contrexéville 88 76 Ff 59
50660 Contrières 50 46 Yd 55
55800 Contrisson 55 54 Ef 56
29300 Controal 29 79 Wc 61
80160 Conty 80 38 Ca 50
57480 Contz-les-Bains 57 44 Gc 52
48800 Conzes 48 141 Df 81
01300 Conzieu 01 131 Fd 74
69210 Conzy 69D 130 Ed 73
51320 Coole 51 54 Ec 56
51510 Coolus 51 54 Ec 55
85260 Copechagnière, la 85 97 Yd 67
95770 Copierres 95 50 Be 54
59279 Coppenaxfort 59 27 Cb 43
74350 Copponex 74 120 Ga 72
34360 Copujol 34 166 Ce 88
14130 Coquainvilliers 14 35 Ab 53
50500 Coquebourg 50 46 Ye 52
62231 Coquelles 62 26 Be 43
48210 Coquenas 48 153 Db 83
24450 Coquille, la 24 125 Af 75
28630 Corancez 28 70 Bd 58
58120 Corancy 58 104 Df 66
29370 Coray 29 78 Wb 60
36290 Corbançon 36 101 Bb 68
20256 Corbara CTC 180 If 93
82370 Corbarieu 82 150 Bc 85
69960 Corbas 69M 130 Ef 74
62112 Corbehem 62 30 Da 46
51320 Corbeil 51 74 Ec 57
60110 Corbeil-Cerf 60 51 Ca 53
91250 Corbeil-Essonnes 91 71 Cc 57
45490 Corbeilles 45 71 Cd 60
38630 Corbelin 38 131 Fd 75
44330 Corbellières, les 44 97 Ye 66
70320 Corbenay 70 93 Gb 61
02820 Corbeny 02 41 De 52
66130 Corbère 66 179 Cd 93
64350 Corbère-Abères 64 162 Zf 88
66130 Corbère-les-Cabanes 66 179 Ce 93
21250 Corberon 21 106 Ef 66
80800 Corbie 80 39 Cd 49
19210 Corbier 19 125 Bc 76
74650 Corbier 74 132 Ga 73
70300 Corbière, la 70 94 Gc 62
86310 Corbière, la 86 100 Ae 69
04220 Corbières 04 156 Fe 86
30570 Corbières 30 153 De 84
58800 Corbigny 58 89 De 65
53700 Corbinière, la 53 67 Ze 59
56200 Corblaie, la 56 81 Xe 62
40120 Corbleu 40 147 Zd 85
14340 Corbon, Notre-Dame-d'Estrées- 14 35 Zf 54
01420 Corbonod 01 119 Fe 73
56480 Corboulo, le 56 79 Wf 59
91410 Corbreuse 91 70 Bf 57
50490 Corbuchon 50 33 Yc 54
89260 Corceaux 89 72 Dc 58
58360 Corcelle 58 104 Df 67
71250 Corcelle 71 118 Ed 69
25640 Corcelle-Mieslot 25 93 Gb 64
01290 Corcelles 01 118 Ef 71
01340 Corcelles 01 118 Fb 71
21550 Corcelles 21 106 Ef 66
58180 Corcelles 58 103 Da 67
70400 Corcelles 70 94 Gd 63
71760 Corcelles 71 104 Df 68
01110 Corcelles, Champdor- 01 119 Fd 72
69220 Corcelles-en-Beaujolais 69D 118 Ee 72
25410 Corcelles-Ferrières 25 107 Fe 65
21190 Corcelles-les-Arts 21 106 Ee 67
21910 Corcelles-lès-Cîteaux 21 106 Fa 65
21160 Corcelles-les-Monts 21 91 Ef 65
21540 Corcelotte 21 91 Ed 64
88430 Corcieux 88 77 Gf 59
17270 Corcin 17 135 Ze 78
47150 Corconat 47 136 Ae 82
25410 Corcondray 25 107 Fe 65
30260 Corconne 30 154 Df 85
44650 Corcoué-sur-Logne 44 97 Yc 67
02600 Corcy 02 52 Db 53
36290 Cordasserie, la 36 100 Ba 67
49640 Cordé 49 84 Zd 62
72140 Cordé 72 68 Zf 59
38710 Cordéac 38 144 Ff 80
14100 Cordebugle 14 48 Ac 54
89113 Cordeil 89 89 Dc 61
42123 Cordelle 42 117 Ea 73
87310 Cordelle, la 87 125 Af 73
44360 Cordemais 44 82 Ya 65
22170 Corderie, la 22 64 Xa 57
33480 Cordes 33 134 Za 78
71540 Cordesse 71 105 Ec 66
81170 Cordes-sur-Ciel 81 151 Bf 84
14700 Cordey 14 48 Ze 55
61570 Cordey 61 48 Aa 56
84490 Cordiers, les 84 156 Fc 85
01120 Cordieux 01 118 Fa 73
25170 Cordiron 25 93 Fe 65
74700 Cordon 74 120 Gd 73
77166 Cordon 77 51 Ce 57
07000 Cordon-Blanc 07 142 Ed 80
70190 Cordonnet 70 93 Ff 64
15100 Coren 15 140 Da 78
63730 Corent 63 128 Da 75
23220 Côrets, les 23 114 Bf 70
51210 Corfélix 51 53 De 55
45310 Corfeu 45 70 Bd 60
21250 Corgengoux 21 106 Ef 67
52500 Corgirnon 52 92 Fc 62
24800 Corgnac-sur l'Isle 24 125 Af 76
21700 Corgoloin 21 106 Ef 66
17130 Corignac 17 123 Zd 77
36230 Corlay 36 101 Bf 68
22320 Corlay = Korle 22 63 Wf 59
01110 Corlier 01 119 Fc 72
28140 Cormainville 28 70 Bd 60
01110 Cormaranche-en-Bugey 01 119 Fd 73
89420 Cormarin 89 90 Ea 63
71460 Cormatin 71 118 Ee 69
17600 Corme-Ecluse 17 122 Za 75
27260 Cormeilles 27 48 Ac 53
60120 Cormeilles 60 38 Cb 51
95240 Cormeilles-en-Par 95 51 Cb 55
95830 Cormeilles-en-Vexin 95 51 Ca 54
79360 Cormenier, le 79 110 Zd 71
41170 Cormenon 41 69 Af 61
41120 Cormeray 41 86 Bc 64
50170 Cormeray 50 66 Yd 57
17600 Corme-Royal 17 122 Zb 74
37320 Cormery 37 85 Af 65
72400 Cormes 72 69 Ae 59

260 | Collonges-lès-Premières

01370 Courmangoux 01 119 Fc 71
45260 Cour-Marigny, la 45 88 Cd 61
51390 Courmas 51 53 Df 53
61110* Cour-Maugis sur Huisne 61 69 Ae 58
02200 Courmelles 02 52 Db 52
51360 Courmelois 51 53 Eb 54
41230 Courmemin 41 87 Bd 64
61310 Courménil 61 48 Ab 56
06620 Courmes 06 173 Ha 86
02130 Courmont 02 53 Dd 54
70400 Courmont 70 94 Gd 63
11300 Cournanel 11 178 Cb 90
46300 Cournazac 46 137 Bc 80
40460 Courneilley 40 134 Yf 82
87380 Courneix 87 125 Bc 75
34220 Courniou 34 166 Ce 88
63450 Cournols 63 128 Da 75
56230 Cournon 56 81 Xf 62
63800 Cournon-d'Auvergne 63 128 Db 74
34660 Cournonsec 34 168 De 87
34660 Cournonterral 34 168 De 87
12150 Cournuéjouls 12 152 Cf 82
83840 Cournuelle, la 83 172 Gc 86
85170 Courollière, la 85 97 Yc 68
16400 Couronne, la 16 123 Aa 75
13500 Couronne-Carro, la 13 170 Fa 88
55260 Courouvre 55 55 Fc 55
89260 Couroy 89 72 Dc 59
77540 Courpalay 77 52 Cf 57
17400 Courpeteau 17 111 Zd 73
63120 Courpière 63 128 Dd 74
17130 Courpignac 17 123 Zd 77
77390 Courquetaine 77 52 Ce 56
42940 Courreau, le 42 129 Df 75
32330 Courrensan 32 148 Ab 85
44330 Courrères, les 44 97 Ye 65
16410 Courrière 16 124 Ab 75
14220 Courrière, la 14 47 Zd 55
62710 Courrières 62 30 Cf 46
81340 Courris 81 151 Cc 85
71110 Courroule 71 117 Ea 71
60112 Courroy 60 38 Ca 51
83120 Courruères 83 172 Gd 89
30500 Courry 30 154 Ea 83
46090 Cours 46 138 Bd 81
47360 Cours 47 149 Ad 83
58200 Cours 58 88 Cf 64
69470 Cours 69D 117 Eb 72
89310 Cours 89 90 Ea 62
56230 Cours, le 56 81 Xc 62
46210 Cours, les 46 138 Ca 80
24430 Coursac 24 136 Ad 78
46320 Coursac 46 138 Be 81
03380 Coursage 03 115 Cd 71
25380 Cour-Saint-Maurice 25 108 Ge 65
10130 Coursan-en-Othe 10 73 Df 60
33580 Cours-de-Monségur 33 136 Aa 81
24520 Cours-de-Pile 24 136 Ad 79
06140 Coursegoules 06 158 Ha 86
62240 Courset 62 28 Bf 45
14470 Courseulles-sur-Mer 14 47 Zd 52
12190 Coursière, la 12 139 Ce 81
50240 Coursinière, la 50 66 Yd 57
79220 Cours-la-Véquière 79 111 Zd 70
33690 Cours-les-Bains 33 148 Zf 82
18320 Cours-les-Barres 18 103 Da 66
02380 Courson 02 40 Dc 52
14380 Courson 14 46 Yf 55
89560 Courson-les-Carrières 89 89 Dd 63
91680 Courson-Monteloup 91 71 Ca 57
41500 Cour-sur-Loire 41 86 Bc 63
77560 Courtacon 77 52 Db 56
63250 Courtade, la 63 129 De 73
51480 Courtagnon 51 53 Df 54
28290 Courtalain 28 69 Ba 60
09320 Courtal-de-Lers 09 177 Bc 92
12800 Courtalesque 12 151 Cc 83
10130 Courtaoult 10 73 Df 60
11230 Courtauly 11 178 Ca 90
10400 Courtavant 10 73 Dd 57
68480 Courtavon 68 95 Hb 64
25470 Courtefontaine 25 94 Gf 65
39700 Courtefontaine 39 107 Fe 66
27130 Courteilles 27 49 Ba 56
61210 Courteilles 61 48 Ze 56
19340 Courteix 19 127 Cc 75
25530 Courtelain-et-Salans 25 108 Gc 65
90100 Courtelevant 90 94 Ha 63
80500 Courtemanche 80 39 Cd 51
45320 Courtemaux 45 72 Cf 60
51800 Courtémont 51 54 Ee 54
02850 Courtemont-Varennes 02 53 Dd 54
38510 Courtenay 38 131 Fc 74
45320 Courtenay 45 72 Da 60
10260 Courtenot 10 74 Eb 60
10270 Courteranges 10 73 Eb 59
10250 Courteron 10 74 Ec 60
01560 Courtes 01 118 Fa 70
70600 Courtesoult-et-Gatey 70 92 Fd 63
77580 Courte-Soupe 77 52 Da 55
63120 Courtesserre 63 128 Dc 74
11240 Courtète, la 11 165 Ca 90
60300 Courteuil 60 51 Cd 53
84350 Courthézon 84 155 Ef 84
51700 Courthiézy 51 53 Dd 54
32330 Courties 32 162 Aa 87
60350 Courtieux 60 40 Da 52
72300 Courtillers 72 84 Ze 62
12400 Courtilles 12 152 Ce 85
36230 Courtillets, les 36 101 Bf 69
50220 Courtils 50 66 Yd 57
23100 Courtine, la 23 127 Cb 74
15100 Courtines 15 140 Cf 78
10400 Courtioux 10 72 Dc 57
63190 Courtioux, les 63 128 Dc 74
51460 Courtisols 51 54 Ed 55
21120 Courtivron 21 91 Ef 63
45700 Courtoin 45 88 Ce 61
89100 Courtois-sur-Yonne 89 72 Db 59
61390 Courtomer 61 48 Ac 57
77390 Courtomer 77 52 Cf 57
77650 Courton 77 72 Db 57
14100 Courtonne-la-Meurdrac 14 48 Ab 54
14290 Courtonne-les-Deux-Eglises 14 48 Ac 54
02820 Courtrizy-et-Fussigny 02 40 De 51
77115 Courtry 77 71 Ce 57
77181 Courtry 77 51 Cd 55
46240 Courty 46 138 Bd 81
14260 Courvaudon 14 47 Zc 54
25560 Courvières 25 107 Ga 67
51170 Courville 51 53 De 53
72140 Courville 72 67 Zf 60
28190 Courville-sur-Eure 28 69 Bb 58
03370 Courzat 03 114 Cc 70
69690 Courzieu 69M 130 Ed 74
39190 Cousance 39 119 Fc 69
55500 Cousances-aux-Bois 55 55 Fc 56
55170 Cousances-les-Forges 55 75 Fa 57
55500 Cousances-lès-Triconville 55 55 Fc 56
19800 Cousin 19 126 Be 76
12550 Cousinie, la 12 152 Cd 85
60730 Cousnicourt 60 51 Cb 53
59149 Cousolre 59 31 Ea 47
09120 Coussa 09 177 Be 90
87240 Coussa, la 87 113 Bc 73
87500 Coussac-Bonneval 87 125 Bb 75
47200 Coussan 47 136 Aa 82
65350 Coussan 65 163 Ab 89
63470 Coussat 63 127 Cc 74
86110 Coussay 86 99 Ab 67
86270 Coussay-les-Bois 86 100 Ae 68
33660 Cousseau 33 135 Aa 78
10210 Coussegrey 10 73 Ea 61
12310 Coussergues 12 152 Cf 82
88630 Coussey 88 75 Fe 58
18210 Coust 18 102 Cd 68
11190 Coustaussa 11 178 Cb 91
84220 Coustellet 84 156 Fa 85
34330 Coustorgues 34 166 Ce 87
11220 Coustouge 11 179 Ce 90
66260 Coustouges 66 179 Cd 94
14430 Coustranville 14 35 Zf 53
12350 Cout, la 12 151 Cb 82
40170 Cout, le 40 146 Yf 84
64270 Cout, le 64 161 Za 88
50230 Coutainville, Agon- 50 46 Yc 54
50200 Coutances 50 46 Yd 54
35210 Coutancière, la 35 66 Ye 59
03330 Coutansouze 03 115 Da 71
49800 Coutardière 49 84 Zd 64
89440 Coutarnoux 89 90 Df 63
43260 Couteaux 43 141 Ea 79
01500 Coutelieu 01 119 Fc 73
85710 Coutellerie, la 85 96 Ya 67
09500 Coutens 09 165 Be 90
02140 Coutenval 02 41 Ea 50
61410 Couterne 61 67 Zd 57
21560 Couternon 21 92 Fa 65
13540 Couteron 13 170 Fc 87
43230 Couteuges 43 128 Dc 77
77580 Coutevroult 77 52 Cf 55
70400 Couthenans 70 94 Ge 63
47700 Couthures 47 148 Aa 83
47180 Couthures-sur-Garonne 47 135 Aa 81
59310 Coutiches 59 30 Db 46
79340 Coutières 79 111 Zf 69
85200 Coutigny 85 110 Za 70
05700 Coutilles, les 05 156 Fd 82
42460 Coutouvre 42 117 Eb 72
33230 Coutras 33 135 Zf 78
28400 Coutretot 28 69 Af 59
22250 Coutûme, la 22 65 Xe 58
19170 Couturas 19 126 Be 75
16460 Couture 16 112 Ab 73
24240 Couture 24 136 Ab 80
86380 Couture 86 99 Ab 68
18370 Couture, la 18 114 Cb 70
62136 Couture, la 62 29 Ce 45
85320 Couture, la 85 109 Ye 69
27750 Couture-Boussey, la 27 50 Bc 55
79110 Couture-d'Argenson 79 111 Zf 73
62158 Couturelle 62 29 Cd 47
24320 Coutures 24 124 Ac 77
33580 Coutures 33 135 Aa 81
49320 Coutures 49 84 Zd 64
57170 Coutures 57 57 Gc 56
82210 Coutures 82 149 Af 85
82400 Coutures 82 149 Af 83
41800 Couture-sur-Loir 41 85 Ae 62
50680 Couvains 50 34 Yf 54
61550 Couvains 61 49 Ad 55
04200 Couvent, le 04 156 Fe 84
14250 Couvert 14 47 Zb 53
12230 Couvertoirade, la 12 153 Db 85
55290 Couvertpuis 55 75 Fb 57
10200 Couvignon 10 74 Ed 59
50690 Couville 50 33 Yb 51
55800 Couvonges 55 55 Fa 56
02220 Couvrelles 02 53 Dc 52
02600 Couvres-et-Valsery 02 52 Da 52
02270 Couvron-et-Aumencourt 02 40 Dd 51
51300 Couvrot 51 54 Ed 56
07000 Coux 07 142 Ed 80
17130 Coux 17 123 Zd 77
17530 Coux 17 122 Yf 74
24220 Coux-et-Bigaroque-Mouzens 24 137 Af 79
18140 Couy 18 103 Ce 66
40430 Couyalas 40 147 Zc 83
35320 Couyère, la 35 82 Yc 61
24400 Couyet 24 136 Ab 78
33121 Couyras 33 134 Yf 78
33121 Couyrasseau 33 134 Yf 78
24150 Couze-et-Saint-Front 24 136 Ae 80
87270 Couzeix 87 125 Bb 73
16330 Couziers 16 124 Aa 74
37500 Couziers 37 99 Aa 66
03160 Couzon 03 103 Da 69
52190 Couzon-sur-Coulange 52 92 Fb 63
46500 Couzou 46 138 Bd 80
31480 Cox 31 149 Ba 86
62560 Coyecques 62 29 Cb 45
60580 Coye-la-Forêt 60 51 Cc 54
02600 Coyolles 02 52 Da 53
39200 Coyrière 39 119 Ff 70
39260 Coyron 39 119 Fe 69
54210 Coyviller 54 76 Gb 57
38460 Cozance 38 131 Fb 74
17120 Cozes 17 122 Zb 75
20148 Cozzano CTC 183 Ka 97
23100 Crabanat 23 126 Ca 74
31430 Crabères 31 164 Ba 89
40410 Crabette, la 40 146 Za 82
32420 Crabots 32 163 Ae 88
82800 Craboula 82 150 Bd 84
56950 Crac'h 56 79 Xa 63
38300 Crachier 38 131 Fb 75
89660 Crai 89 90 Dd 64
89480 Crain 89 89 Dd 63
57590 Craincourt 57 56 Gb 55
42210 Craintilleux 42 129 Eb 75
88140 Crainvilliers 88 76 Fe 60
17170 Cramahé 17 110 Za 71
02130 Cramaille 02 52 Dc 53
39600 Cramans 39 107 Fe 66
51530 Cramant 51 53 Df 55
86190 Cramard 86 99 Aa 69
87380 Cramarigeas 87 125 Bc 75
87600 Cramaud 87 125 Af 74
35580 Crambert, le 35 65 Ya 60
17170 Cramchaban 17 110 Zb 71
61220 Craménil 61 47 Zd 56
60660 Cramoisy 60 51 Cc 53
80370 Cramont 80 29 Ca 48
09120 Crampagna 09 177 Bd 90
62179 Cran-aux-Oufs 62 26 Bd 43
37350 Crançay, le 37 100 Af 67
10100 Crancey 10 73 Dd 57
39570 Crançot 39 107 Fd 68
15250 Crandelles 15 139 Cc 79
56150 Crann 56 80 Wf 61
72240 Crannes 72 68 Zf 60
72540 Crannes-en-Champagne 72 68 Zf 61
01320 Crans 01 118 Fb 73
39300 Crans 39 107 Ff 68
12110 Cransac 12 139 Cb 81
74380 Cranves-Sales 74 120 Gb 71
53400 Craon 53 83 Za 61
86110 Craon 86 99 Aa 68
02160 Craonne 02 40 De 52
60310 Crapeaumesnil 60 39 Ce 51
69290 Craponne 69M 130 Ee 74
43500 Craponne-sur-Arzon 43 129 Df 77
74140 Crapons, les 74 120 Gc 71
38210 Cras 38 131 Fc 77
46360 Cras 46 138 Bd 81
12170 Crassous 12 152 Cd 84
12400 Crassous 12 152 Cf 85
01340 Cras-sur-Reyssouze 01 118 Fb 71
67310 Crastatt 67 58 Hc 57
32270 Crastes 32 163 Ae 86
33680 Crastieu, le 33 134 Yf 79
27400 Crasville 27 49 Ba 53
50630 Crasville 50 34 Yd 51
76450 Crasville-la-Mallet 76 36 Ae 50
83260 Crau, la 83 171 Ga 90
14240 Crauville 14 34 Zb 54
17260 Cravans 17 122 Zb 75
45190 Cravant 45 86 Bd 62
89460 Cravant 89 89 De 62
37500 Cravant-les-Côteaux 37 99 Ac 66
32110 Cravencères 32 148 Aa 86
78270 Cravent 78 50 Bc 55
71460 Cray 71 118 Ec 69
46100 Crayssac 46 138 Bf 81
46150 Crayssac 46 137 Bb 81
59279 Craywick 59 27 Cb 43
01200 Craz 01 119 Fe 72
03300 Crcuzjer-le-Vieux 03 116 Dc 71
72200 Cré 72 84 Zf 62
29440 Creac'h 29 62 Vf 57
29390 Creac'h Courant 29 78 Wb 60
22610 Creac'h Maout 22 63 Wf 55
29880 Créach-Pont 29 62 Vd 57
50710 Créances 50 46 Yc 53
21320 Créancey 21 105 Ed 65
52120 Créancey 52 74 Ef 60
58210 Créantay 58 89 Db 64
21120 Crécey-sur-Tille 21 92 Fa 63
23290 Créchat 23 113 Bc 72
79260 Crèche, la 79 111 Ze 70
27190 Crèches 27 49 Af 54
71680 Crêches-sur-Saône 71 118 Ee 71
22720 Crec'h Metern 22 63 Wf 58
63700 Créchol 63 115 Ce 71
03150 Créchy 03 116 Dc 71
62120 Crecques 62 29 Cb 45
02380 Crécy-au-Mont 02 40 Db 52
28500 Crécy-Couvé 28 50 Bb 56
80150 Crécy-en-Ponthieu 80 28 Bf 47
77580 Crécy-la-Chapelle 77 52 Cf 55
02270 Crécy-sur-Serre 02 40 Dd 50
56580 Crédin 56 64 Xb 60
46330 Crégols 46 138 Be 82
77124 Crégy-lès-Meaux 77 52 Cf 55
22950 Créhac, le 22 64 Xb 58
57690 Créhange 57 57 Gd 54
57385 Créhange-Citex 57 57 Gd 54
22130 Créhen 22 65 Xe 57
60100 Creil 60 51 Cc 53
34370 Creissan 34 167 Da 88
84800 Crémade, la 84 155 Fa 85
62240 Crémarest 62 28 Be 44
42260 Crémeaux 42 117 Df 73
56800 Créménan 56 81 Xd 61
80700 Crémery 80 39 Ce 50
38460 Crémieu 38 131 Fb 74
86450 Crémille 86 100 Ae 68
74150 Crempigny 74 119 Ff 73
46230 Cremps 46 150 Bd 82
39260 Crenans 39 119 Fe 70
52000 Crenay 52 75 Fa 60
10150 Creney-près-Troyes 10 73 Ea 59
50170 Crenne, la 50 66 Yd 57
61200 Crennes 61 48 Aa 56
53700 Crennes-sur-Fraubée 53 67 Ze 58
29390 Crénorien 29 78 Wb 60
33670 Créon 33 135 Zd 80
40240 Créon-d'Armagnac 40 148 Zf 85
71490 Créot 71 105 Ed 67
28200 Crépainville 28 69 Bb 60
21500 Crépand 21 90 Eb 63
54170 Crépey 54 76 Ff 57
23290 Crépiat 23 113 Bd 72
69140 Crépieux 69M 130 Ef 74
02300 Crépigny 02 40 Da 51
03300 Crépin 03 116 Dc 72
55150 Crépion 55 55 Fc 53
77440 Crépoil 77 52 Da 54
26350 Crépol 26 143 Fa 77
14480 Crépon 14 35 Zc 53
01470 Crept 01 131 Fc 74
02870 Crépy 02 40 Dd 51
62310 Crépy 62 29 Cb 46
60800 Crépy-en-Valois 60 52 Cf 53
62310 Créquy 62 29 Ca 46
34920 Crès, le 34 168 Df 87
70100 Cresancey 70 92 Fd 64
10320 Crésantignes 10 73 Ea 60
50370 Cresnays, les 50 46 Yf 56
63310 Cresneuil 63 116 Db 73
22120 Crésouard 22 64 Xc 58
44310 Crespelière, la 44 96 Yb 66
12290 Crespiaguet 12 152 Ce 83
30260 Crespian 30 154 Ea 85
78121 Crespières 78 50 Bf 55
12800 Crespin 12 151 Cb 84
59154 Crespin 59 31 Dd 46
81350 Crespin 81 151 Cb 84
81350 Crespinet 81 151 Cb 85
10500 Crespy-le-Neuf 10 74 Ed 58
17360 Cressac 17 123 Zf 77
87190 Cressac 87 113 Bb 71
16250 Cressac-Saint-Génis 16 123 Aa 76
03240 Cressanges 03 116 Da 70
23140 Cressat 23 114 Ca 72
17160 Cressé 17 111 Ze 73
12640 Cresse, la 12 152 Da 83
46600 Cressensac 46 138 Bd 78
27440 Cressenville 27 50 Bc 52
14440 Cresserons 14 47 Zd 53
14430 Cresseveuille 14 48 Aa 53
39270 Cressia 39 119 Fc 69
01350 Cressin-Rochefort 01 132 Fe 74
17380 Cresson 17 110 Zb 73
14420 Cressonière, la 14 47 Zd 55
60190 Cressonsacq 60 39 Cd 52
76720 Cressy 76 37 Ba 50
80190 Cressy-Omencourt 80 39 Cf 50
71760 Cressy-sur-Somme 71 104 Df 68
26400 Crest 26 143 Fa 80
63450 Crest, le 63 128 Da 74
63320 Creste 63 128 Da 75
12140 Crestes 12 139 Cc 81
84110 Crestet 84 155 Fa 83
07270 Crestet, le 07 142 Ed 78
27110 Crestot 27 49 Af 53
82220 Crestou 82 150 Bb 84
73590 Crest-Voland 73 133 Gd 74
01550 Crêt 01 120 Ff 72
24360 Crête, la 24 124 Ad 75
94000 Créteil 94 51 Cc 56
01130 Crêtet, le 01 119 Fe 71
27250 Crétil, le 27 49 Ae 56
27240 Créton 27 49 Ba 55
39200 Crêt Pourri, le 39 119 Ff 70
38570* Crêts en Belledonne 38 132 Ff 76
50250 Cretteville 50 46 Yd 52
55210 Creuë 55 55 Fe 55
58250 Creuille 58 104 De 67
14480 Creully 14 35 Zc 53
14480 Creully sur Seulles 14 47 Zc 53
80480 Creuse 80 38 Ca 49
71200 Creusot, le 71 105 Ec 68
57150 Creutzwald 57 57 Ge 53
58500 Creux 58 89 Dd 64
22100 Creux, le 22 65 Xf 58
45130 Creux, le 45 87 Bd 61
56420 Creux, le 56 80 Xc 61
26140 Creux-de-la-Thine, le 26 130 Ee 77
69460 Creuze, la 69D 118 Ed 72
03300 Creuzier-le-Neuf 03 116 Dc 71
45520 Creuzy 45 70 Bf 60
70400 Crevans-et-la-Chapelle-lès-Granges 70 94 Gd 63
03410 Crevant 03 115 Cd 70
36130 Crevant 36 101 Be 67
36140 Crevant 36 114 Bf 70
63350 Crevant-Laveine 63 116 Dc 73
54290 Crévéchamps 54 76 Gb 57
27490 Crèvecœur 27 50 Bb 54
60360 Crèvecœur-le-Grand 60 38 Ca 51
60420 Crèvecœur-le-Petit 60 39 Cd 51
59258 Crèvecœur-sur-l'Escaut 59 30 Db 48
14340 Crèvecour-en-Auge 14 35 Aa 54
77610 Crèvecour-en-Brie 77 52 Cf 56
70240 Creveney 70 93 Gb 62
54110 Crévic 54 56 Gc 57
38510 Crevières 38 131 Fc 74
35320 Crévin 35 82 Yc 61
76750 Crevon 76 37 Bb 51
05200 Crévoux 05 145 Gd 81
24100 Crevsse 24 136 Ad 79
73260 Crey, le 73 132 Gc 76
05140 Creyers 05 144 Fd 81
38510 Creys-et-Pusignieu 38 131 Fc 74
24350 Creyssac 24 124 Ad 77
46600 Creysse 46 138 Bd 79
07000 Creysseilles 07 142 Ed 80
81990 Creyssens 81 151 Cb 85
24380 Creyssensac-et-Pissot 24 136 Ad 78
18190 Crézancay 18 102 Cc 68
02650 Crézancy 02 53 Dd 54
18300 Crézancy-en-Sancerre 18 88 Ce 65
62610 Crézeeques 62 27 Bf 44
87620 Crezeunet 87 125 Ba 74
79110 Crézières 79 111 Zf 72
03240 Criards, les 03 116 Db 70
12360 Cribas 12 152 Cf 86
14430 Cricqueville-en-Auge 14 35 Zf 53
14450 Cricqueville-en-Bessin 14 47 Za 52
13610 Cride, la 13 170 Fc 87
76910 Criel-Plage 76 28 Bb 48
76910 Criel-sur-Mer 76 37 Bb 48
58270 Criens 58 104 Dc 66
40260 Criéré 40 146 Yf 85
09700 Crieu 09 165 Be 90
58110 Crieur 58 104 De 66
17700 Crignolée, la 17 110 Zb 72
39130 Crillat 39 107 Fe 69
60112 Crillon 60 38 Bf 51
84410 Crillon-le-Brave 84 156 Fa 84
21800 Crimolois 21 92 Fa 65
29180 Crinquellic 29 78 Ve 60
54300 Crion 54 57 Gd 57
76850 Crique, la 76 37 Bb 50
27110 Criquebeuf-la-Campagne 27 49 Ba 53
27340 Criquebeuf-sur-Seine 27 49 Ba 53
14600 Criquebœuf 14 36 Aa 52
27110 Criquetot 27 49 Ba 54
76540 Criquetot-le-Mauconduit 76 36 Ad 50
76280 Criquetot-L'Esneval 76 36 Ab 51
76590 Criquetot-sur-Longueville 76 37 Ba 50
76760 Criquetot-sur-Ouville 76 37 Af 50
76390 Criquiers 76 38 Be 50
50310 Crisbec 50 33 Ye 52
77390 Crisenoy 77 71 Ce 57
60400 Crisolles 60 39 Da 51
37220 Crissay-sur-Manse 37 100 Ac 66
72140 Crissé 72 68 Zf 59
39100 Crissey 39 106 Fc 66
71530 Crissey 71 106 Ef 68
20126 Cristinacce CTC 182 If 95
81260 Cristol 81 166 Cd 87
14250 Cristot 14 47 Zc 53
16300 Criteuil-la-Magdeleine 16 123 Ze 75
76680 Critot 76 37 Bb 51
54120 Criviller 54 77 Ge 58
84490 Croagnes 84 156 Fb 85
56560 Croajou 56 79 Wc 60
29420 Croas-ar-Born 29 62 Wa 57
29940 Croas-Avalou 29 78 Wa 61
29910 Croaz-Hent-Bouillet 29 78 Wa 61
29260 Croaz-Kerduff 29 62 Vd 57
29890 Croazou 29 62 Vd 57
29430 Croazu 29 62 Ve 57
36160 Crobonne 36 114 Ca 70
20237 Croce CTC 181 Kc 94
20140 Croce, Moca- CTC 182 Ka 98
73340 Crochère, la 73 132 Ga 75
24150 Crocherie 24 136 Ad 79
53380 Crochetières, les 53 66 Za 59
59380 Crochte 59 27 Cc 43
20290 Crocicchia CTC 181 Kc 94
23260 Crocq 23 127 Cc 73
60120 Crocq, le 60 38 Cb 51
14620 Crocy 14 48 Zf 55
29180 Croëzou, le 29 78 Ve 60
61200 Crogny 61 48 Zf 56
33990 Crohot-de-France, le 33 134 Ye 78
33121 Crohot-des-Cavales, le 33 134 Ye 78
43580 Croisances 43 141 Dd 79
62130 Croisette 62 29 Cb 46
56350 Croisette, la 56 81 Xe 63
59230 Croisette, la 59 30 Dc 46
74560 Croisette, la 74 120 Gb 72
88340 Croisette, la 88 94 Gc 61
61260 Croisettes, les 61 69 Ae 59
76870 Croisettes, les 76 38 Bd 51
44490 Croisic, le 44 81 Xc 65
48600 Croisières 48 141 Dd 79
19430 Croisille 19 138 Bf 78
27190 Croisille, la 27 49 Af 55
14220 Croisilles 14 47 Zd 55
28210 Croisilles 28 50 Bc 56
61230 Croisilles 61 48 Ab 56
62128 Croisilles 62 30 Cf 47
87130 Croisille-sur-Briance, la 87 126 Bd 75
54300 Croismare 54 77 Gd 57
29470 Croisquer 29 62 Ve 58
50380 Croissant, le 50 46 Yc 56
29246 Croissant-Marie-Jaffré 29 63 Wc 58
14370 Croissanville 14 35 Zf 54
77183 Croissy-Beaubourg 77 51 Cd 56
78560 Croissy-sur-Seine 78 51 Ca 55
60120 Croissy-sur-Selle 60 38 Cb 50
56540 Croisty, le 56 79 Wd 60
18350 Croisy 18 103 Ce 67
76780 Croisy-sur-Andelle 76 37 Bc 52
27120 Croisy-sur-Eure 27 50 Bc 54
59170 Croix 59 30 Da 44
90100 Croix 90 94 Gf 64
19260 Croix, la 19 126 Be 75
20137 Croix, la CTC 185 Kb 98
44210 Croix, la 44 96 Xf 66
44650 Croix, la 44 97 Yc 67
46200 Croix, la 46 138 Bc 79
49400 Croix, la 49 84 Ze 65
71170 Croix, la 71 117 Eb 71
71500 Croix, la 71 106 Fa 69
73800 Croix, la 73 132 Ga 76
85350 Croix, la 85 96 Xe 68
85450 Croix, la 85 110 Yf 70
56120 Croix, les 56 64 Xc 61
56920 Croixanvec 56 64 Xa 60
08400 Croix-au-Bois, la 08 42 Ee 52
23190 Croix-au-Bost, la 23 114 Cb 72
22380 Croix-aux-Merles, la 22 64 Xe 57
88520 Croix-aux-Mines, la 88 77 Ha 59
50240 Croix-Avranchin, la 50 66 Yd 57

262 | Courmangoux

62136 Croix-Barbet 62 29 Ce 45
22200 Croix-Blanche 22 63 Wf 57
32700 Croix-Blanche, la 32 149 Ad 84
46240 Croix-Blanche, la 46 138 Bd 81
47340 Croix-Blanche, la 47 149 Ae 83
59223 Croix-Blanche, la 59 30 Da 44
71960 Croix-Blanche, la 71 118 Ee 70
49630 Croix-Boujuau, la 49 84 Zd 64
45520 Croix-Briquet, la 45 70 Bf 60
22320 Croix-Burlot, la 22 64 Wf 58
59222 Croix-Caluyau 59 31 Dd 48
72320 Croix-Champagne 72 69 Af 60
22600 Croix-Chanvril, la 22 64 Xb 59
17220 Croix-Chapeau 17 110 Yf 72
61190 Croix-Chemin, le 61 69 Ae 57
17330 Croix-Comtesse, la 17 110 Zd 72
73390 Croix-d'Aiguebelle, la 73 132 Gb 75
76660 Croixdalle 76 37 Bc 50
42122 Croix-de-Bard, la 42 129 Eb 73
56390 Croix-de-Bois 56 80 Xa 62
49250 Croix-de-Bois-Maudet, la 49 84 Zf 64
72500 Croix-de-Bonlieu, la 72 85 Ac 62
13310 Croix-de-Crau 13 170 Ef 87
03130 Croix-de-la-Fée, la 03 117 De 71
19270 Croix-de-la-Maleyire 19 125 Bd 77
63980 Croix-de-la-Paix 63 128 Dd 76
49400 Croix-de-la-Voulte, la 49 84 Zf 65
71220 Croix-de-Mornay, la 71 117 Ec 69
46300 Croix-de-Pech 46 137 Bb 80
53220 Croix-de-Pierre, la 53 66 Za 58
22960 Croix-de-Piruit, la 22 64 Xb 58
35350 Croix-Desilles, la 35 65 Ya 57
44430 Croix-des-Landes, la 44 82 Ye 65
71450 Croix-des-Mâts, la 71 105 Ec 68
49270 Croix-des-Victoires 49 83 Yf 65
15120 Croix-de-Thérondels, la 15 139 Cc 80
03460 Croix-de-Vaux, la 03 103 Db 69
85800 Croix-de-Vie 85 96 Ya 68
33380 Croix-d'Hins 33 134 Za 80
56490 Croix-d'Iff, la 56 64 Xc 60
59181 Croix-du-Bac 59 30 Ce 44
19300 Croix-du-Bourg 19 126 Ca 76
28480 Croix-du-Perche, la 28 69 Ba 59
42370 Croix-du-Sud, la 42 117 Df 72
77370 Croix-en-Brie, la 77 72 Da 57
51600 Croix-en-Champagne, la 51 54 Ed 54
62130 Croix-en-Ternois 62 29 Cb 46
37150 Croix-en-Touraine, la 37 86 Af 64
02110 Croix-Fonsommes 02 40 Dc 49
56230 Croix-Galle, la 56 81 Xd 62
26620 Croix-Haute, la 26 144 Fe 80
56120 Croix-Helléan, la 56 81 Xd 61
53380 Croixille, la 53 66 Yf 59
50260 Croix-Jacob 50 33 Yc 51
22130 Croix-Janet, la 22 65 Xe 57
03110 Croix-Jardot, la 03 116 Db 71
35720 Croix-Juhel, la 35 65 Ya 58
87130 Croix-Lattée, la 87 126 Bd 74
76190 Croix-Mare 76 37 Af 51
44130 Croix-Michéon, la 44 82 Ya 64
80400 Croix-Moligneaux 80 39 Da 50
50260 Croix-Morain, la 50 33 Yb 52
29410 Croix-Neuve 29 62 Wa 57
22340 Croix-Neuve, la 22 63 Wd 59
29190 Croix-Nu 29 62 Wa 59
29640 Croixp-de-Pierre, la 29 62 Wb 57
80290 Croixrault 80 38 Bf 50
71140 Croix-Récy 71 104 De 68
85390 Croix-Renard, le 85 98 Zb 69
03120 Croix-Rouge 03 116 Dd 72
12800 Croix-Rouge 12 151 Cc 83
13013 Croix-Rouge 13 170 Fc 88
27160 Croix-Rouge 27 49 Ae 56
29640 Croix-Rouge 29 63 Wb 58
03510 Croix-Rouge, la 03 117 Df 70
31570 Croix-Rouge, la 31 165 Be 87
36250 Croix-Rouge, la 36 101 Bd 68
24580 Croix-Ruchal, la 24 137 Ba 78
77123 Croix-Saint-Jérôme, la 77 71 Cd 58
27490 Croix-Saint-Leufroy, la 27 50 Bb 54
63250 Croix-Saint-Martin 63 129 De 73
87210 Croix-sur-Gartempe, la 87 113 Af 72
02210 Croix-sur-Ourcq, la 02 52 Dc 53
06260 Croix-sur-Roudoule, la 06 158 Gf 85
83420 Croix-Valmer, la 83 172 Gd 89
63390 Croizet 63 115 Ce 72
63410 Croizet 63 115 Cf 73
42540 Croizet-sur-Gand 42 117 Eb 73
38920 Crolles 38 132 Ff 77
50220 Crollon 50 66 Yd 57
87160 Cromac 87 113 Bb 70
70190 Cromary 70 93 Ga 64
56190 Cromenach 56 81 Xc 63
87150 Cromière 87 124 Ae 74
71760 Crona 71 104 Df 68
71140 Cronat 71 104 De 68
43300 Cronce 43 140 Dc 78
67000 Cronenbourg 67 60 He 57
74230 Cropt, le 74 132 Gb 73
53170 Cropte, la 53 67 Zd 61
76720 Cropus 76 37 Ba 50
44590 Croquemais 44 82 Yb 63
09400 Croquié 09 177 Bd 91
19200 Cros 19 127 Cc 76
23290 Cros 23 113 Bd 71
30170 Cros 30 154 De 85
63810 Cros 63 127 Cd 76
05500 Cros, le 05 144 Ga 81
12370 Cros, le 12 152 Ce 86
30120 Cros, le 30 153 Dd 85
34520 Cros, le 34 153 Dc 85
43150 Cros, le 43 141 Df 79
43340 Cros, le 43 141 De 79
46100 Cros, le 46 138 Bf 81
46190 Cros, le 46 138 Ca 79
46260 Cros, le 46 150 Be 83
48160 Cros, le 48 154 Df 83
63210 Cros, le 63 127 Ce 75
63600 Cros, le 63 129 De 76
87190 Cros, le 87 113 Bb 71
48230 Cros-Bas, le 48 153 Db 82
06800 Cros-de-Cagnes 06 173 Hb 87
07510 Cros-de-Géorand 07 141 Ea 80
15150 Cros-de-Montvert 15 138 Ca 78
83340 Cros-de-Mouton 83 172 Gb 89
15130 Cros-de-Ronesque 15 139 Cd 79
43230 Crose-Marie 43 128 Dd 77
25340 Crosey-le-Grand 25 94 Gd 64
25340 Crosey-le-Petit 25 94 Gc 64
48400 Crosgarnon 48 153 Dd 83
70220 Croslières 70 94 Gc 61
72200 Crosmières 72 84 Zf 62
91560 Crosne 91 51 Cc 56
44160 Crossac 44 81 Xe 64
43600 Crossacs 43 129 Eb 77
18340 Crosses 18 102 Cd 66
27110 Crosville-la-Vienne 27 49 Af 54
50360 Crosville-sur-Douve 50 33 Yd 52
76590 Crosville-sur-Scie 76 37 Ba 50
73640 Crôt, le 73 133 Gf 75
89450 Crot, le 89 90 De 64
71990 Crot-au-Meunier, le 71 105 Ea 67
58000 Crot-de-Savigny 58 103 Db 67
37380 Crotelles 37 85 Af 63
39300 Crotenay 39 107 Fe 68
27530 Croth 27 50 Bc 55
80550 Crotoy, le 80 28 Bd 47
05200 Crots 05 145 Gc 81
71190 Crots, les 71 105 Eb 68
58300 Crots-Maillots, les 58 104 Dc 68
40410 Crotte, la 40 147 Zb 83
58220 Crotte, la 58 89 Db 64
07150 Crottes 07 154 Ec 82
83310 Crottes 83 172 Gc 89
83700 Crottes 83 172 Ge 88
84390 Crottes 84 156 Fc 84
45170 Crottes-en-Pithiverais 45 70 Ca 60
01290 Crottet 01 118 Ef 71
35290 Crouais, le 35 65 Xf 59
14400 Crouay 14 34 Zb 53
37320 Croule, le 37 85 Ae 65
14140 Croupte, la 14 48 Ab 54
64350 Crouseilles 64 162 Zf 87
07530 Crouset, le 07 142 Ec 80
53600 Crousille, la 53 67 Zd 60
32230 Crousse 32 162 Aa 87
86240 Croutelle 86 112 Ab 69
10130 Croûtes, les 10 73 Df 61
60350 Croutoy 60 39 Da 52
61120 Croûttes 61 48 Aa 55
02310 Crouttes-sur-Marne 02 52 Db 55
11190 Croux 11 178 Cb 91
02880 Crouy 02 40 Dc 52
60530 Crouy-en-Thelle 60 51 Cb 53
80310 Crouy-Saint-Pierre 80 38 Ca 49
41220 Crouy-sur-Cosson 41 86 Bd 63
77840 Crouy-sur-Ourcq 77 52 Da 54
07690 Crouzet 07 130 Ed 77
87220 Crouzet 87 125 Bc 74
12110 Crouzet, le 12 139 Cb 81
25240 Crouzet, le 25 107 Ga 68
43150 Crouzet, le 43 141 Ea 79
43170 Crouzet, le 43 140 Dd 79
43170 Crouzet, le 43 141 Dd 79
48190 Crouzet, le 48 141 De 82
48700 Crouzet, le 48 140 Dc 80
48700 Crouzet, le 48 140 Dc 81
25270 Crouzet-Migette 25 107 Ga 67
48700 Crouzet-Plo, le 48 140 Dc 80
12470 Crouzets, les 12 140 Cf 81
09230 Crouzette, la 09 176 Ba 90
31310 Crouzettes, les 31 164 Bb 90
81260 Crouzettes, les 81 166 Cd 87
47150 Crouzillac 47 136 Ae 82
63700 Crouzille, la 63 115 Ce 71
87240 Crouzille, la 87 113 Bb 73
37220 Crouzilles 37 100 Ac 66
43150 Crouziols 43 141 Ea 79
15200 Crouzit 15 127 Cb 77
23160 Crozant 23 113 Bd 70
03410 Crozardais 03 115 Cd 70
84400 Crozat, le 84 156 Fc 84
23500 Croze 23 126 Cb 74
48130 Crozes 48 140 Db 80
12230 Crozes, les 12 153 Dc 84
34800 Crozes, les 34 167 Db 87
81320 Crozes, les 81 166 Ce 87
26600 Crozes-Hermitage 26 142 Ef 78
01170 Crozet 01 120 Ff 71
01300 Crozet 01 131 Fd 74
01851 Crozet, le 01 119 Fb 70
42310 Crozet, le 42 117 Df 71
39260 Crozets, les 39 119 Fe 70
12210 Crozillac 12 139 Ce 81
29160 Crozon = Kraozon 29 61 Vd 59
36140 Crozon-sur-Vauvre 36 114 Bf 70
07350 Cruas 07 142 Ee 81
28270 Crucey 28 49 Ba 56
41100 Crucheray 41 86 Ba 62
21500 Cruchy 21 90 Eb 62
20166 Cruciata CTC 184 Ie 97
20160 Cruciate CTC 182 Ie 96
37230 Crucifix, le 37 85 Ad 64
20133 Crucoli CTC 182 If 96
56410 Crucuno 56 80 Wf 63
86200 Crué 86 99 Ab 66
53800 Crue, la 53 83 Yf 62
36310 Cruet 36 113 Bb 70
73550 Cruet 73 133 Gd 76
73800 Cruet 73 132 Ga 75
87360 Cruet 87 113 Ba 71
74410 Cruet, le 74 132 Ga 74
21360 Crugey 21 105 Ee 65
51170 Crugny 51 53 De 53
56420 Cruguël 56 80 Xc 61
04230 Cruis 04 157 Ff 84
61300 Crulai 61 49 Ae 56
53600 Crun 53 67 Zd 59
12330 Cruou 12 139 Cc 82
26460 Crupies 26 143 Fa 81
02120 Crupilly 02 40 De 49
11200 Cruscades 11 166 Ce 89
74350 Cruseilles 74 120 Ga 72
54680 Crusnes 54 43 Ff 52
12190 Crussac 12 139 Cd 81
30360 Cruviers-Lascours 30 154 Eb 84
18800 Crux 18 103 Ce 66
58330 Crux-la-Ville 58 104 Dd 66
71260 Cruzille 71 118 Ee 69
01290 Cruzilles-lès-Mépillat 01 118 Ef 71
81330 Cruzis 81 166 Cc 86
34310 Cruzy 34 167 Cf 88
89740 Cruzy-le-Châtel 89 90 Eb 61
89390 Cry 89 90 Eb 62
43170 Cubelles 43 141 Dd 78
63220 Cubelles 63 129 De 76
48190 Cubières 48 141 De 82
11190 Cubières-sur-Cinoble 11 178 Cc 91
48190 Cubiérettes 48 141 De 82
24640 Cubjac-Auvézère-Val d'Ans 24 125 Af 77
19520 Cublac 19 137 Bb 78
43200 Cublaise 43 129 Ea 77
69550 Cublize 69D 117 Ec 72
33620 Cubnezais 33 135 Zd 78
86300 Cubord 86 112 Ad 70
59230 Cubray 59 30 Dc 46
25680 Cubrial 25 93 Gc 64
25680 Cubry 25 93 Gc 64
70160 Cubry-lès-Faverney 70 93 Ga 62
70130 Cubry-lès-Soing 70 93 Ff 63
33240 Cubzac-les-Ponts 33 135 Zd 79
32240 Cucassé 32 147 Zf 85
77160 Cucharmoy 77 72 Db 57
51480 Cuchery 51 53 De 54
66720 Cuchous 66 179 Cd 92
62780 Cucq 62 28 Bd 46
11350 Cucugnan 11 179 Cd 91
84160 Cucuron 84 156 Fc 86
29540 Cudef 29 79 Wb 60
33430 Cudos 33 147 Ze 82
89116 Cudot 89 72 Db 61
06910 Cuébris 06 158 Ha 85
03140 Cueillat 03 116 Db 71
36120 Cueille, la 36 101 Be 68
35340 Cueillerais, la 35 66 Yd 59
18800 Cueilly 18 103 Ce 66
32300 Cuélas 32 163 Ac 88
83390 Cuers 83 171 Ga 89
01340 Cuet 01 118 Fa 71
02880 Cuffies 02 40 Db 52
18150 Cuffy 18 103 Da 67
85610 Cugand 85 97 Ye 66
13780 Cuges-les-Pins 13 171 Fe 89
31270 Cugnaux 31 164 Bb 87
17220 Cugné 17 110 Za 72
70700 Cugney 70 92 Fe 64
02480 Cugny 02 40 Da 50
77690 Cugny 77 71 Ce 59
35270 Cuguen 35 65 Yc 58
31210 Cuguron 31 163 Ad 90
62960 Cuhem 62 29 Cb 45
86110 Cuhon 86 99 Aa 68
61200 Cui 61 48 Zf 56
60130 Cuignières 60 39 Cc 52
61200 Cuigny 61 48 Zf 56
60850 Cuigny-en-Bray 60 38 Be 52
53540 Cuillé 53 66 Yf 61
38530 Cuiller, la 38 132 Ff 76
09420 Cuillère 09 177 Bb 91
76390 Cuillère 76 38 Be 50
62149 Cuinchy 62 29 Ce 45
59553 Cuincy 59 30 Da 46
31210 Cuing, le 31 163 Ad 90
42460 Cuinzier 42 117 Eb 72
02350 Cuirieux 02 40 De 50
02220 Cuiry-Housse 02 53 Dc 53
02160 Cuiry-lès-Chaudardes 02 40 De 52
02360 Cuiry-lès-Iviers 02 41 Ea 50
51530 Cuis 51 53 Df 55
71480 Cuiseaux 71 119 Fc 70
60350 Cuise-la-Motte 60 39 Da 52
21310 Cuiserey 21 92 Fb 64
71290 Cuisery 71 118 Fa 69
39190 Cuisia 39 119 Fc 69
01370 Cuisiat 01 119 Fc 71
51700 Cuisles 51 53 De 54
61250 Cuissai 61 68 Aa 58
55270 Cuisy 55 55 Fb 53
77165 Cuisy 77 52 Ce 54
02200 Cuisy-en-Almont 02 40 Db 52
46230 Cujoul, le 46 150 Bd 83
18270 Culan 18 114 Cc 69
35500 Culaudière, la 35 66 Yf 59
74490 Culaz, la 74 120 Gc 71
73630 Cul-du-Bois, le 73 132 Gb 74
49370 Culée, la 49 83 Za 63
21230 Culêtre 21 105 Ed 66
89450 Culêtre 89 90 De 64
55000 Culey 55 55 Fb 56
14220 Culey-le-Patry 14 47 Zc 55
63350 Culhat 63 128 Db 73
38300 Culin 38 131 Fb 75
71460 Culles-les-Roches 71 105 Ed 69
14480 Cully 14 35 Zc 53
52600 Culmont 52 92 Fc 62
50500 Culot 50 33 Ye 53
01350 Culoz 01 132 Fe 73
70150 Cult 70 92 Fe 65
48230 Cultures 48 140 Dc 82
20167 Culumbina = Colombina CTC 182 If 97
42890 Culvé 42 129 Df 74
51480 Cumières 51 53 Df 54
11410 Cumiès 11 165 Bf 89
24410 Cumond 24 124 Ab 77
82500 Cumont 82 149 Af 85
81990 Cunac 81 151 Cb 85
49350 Cunault 49 84 Ze 65
58210 Cuncy-lès-Varzy 58 89 Dc 64
24240 Cunèges 24 136 Ac 80
55110 Cunel 55 55 Fa 52
90150 Cunelières 90 94 Gf 63
27240 Cunelle, la 27 49 Ba 56
10360 Cunfin 10 74 Ed 60
63590 Cunlhat 63 128 Dd 75
12230 Cuns, les 12 153 Db 84
49150 Cuon 49 84 Zf 64
51400 Cuperly 51 54 Ec 54
11380 Cupserviès 11 166 Cc 88
47220 Cuq 47 149 Ae 84
16390 Cuq, le 16 124 Ab 77
81470 Cuq-Toulza 81 165 Bf 87
64360 Cuqueron 64 161 Zc 89
16210 Curac 16 123 Aa 77
46270 Curade, la 46 138 Ca 80
12410 Curan 12 152 Cf 83
05110 Curbans 05 157 Ga 82
20256 Curbara = Corbara CTC 180 If 93
71800 Curbigny 71 117 Eb 71
86120 Curçay-sur-Dive 86 99 Zf 66
80190 Curchy 80 39 Cf 50
71470 Curciat 71 118 Fa 69
01560 Curciat-Dongalon 01 118 Fa 70
71130 Curdin 71 104 Df 69
17700 Curé 17 110 Zb 72
89450 Cure 89 90 De 64
52300 Curel-Autigny 52 75 Fa 58
19500 Curemonte 19 138 Be 79
72240 Cures 72 68 Zf 60
50170 Curey 50 66 Yd 57
59990 Curgies 59 31 Dd 47
71400 Curgy 71 105 Ec 67
73190 Curienne 73 132 Ga 75
12210 Curières 12 139 Cf 81
12340 Curlande 12 152 Ce 82
21220 Curley 21 106 Ef 65
80360 Curlu 80 39 Ce 49
24450 Curmont 24 125 Af 75
24800 Curmont 24 125 Af 76
52330 Curmont 52 74 Ef 59
05110 Curnerie, la 05 157 Ga 82
29880 Curnic, le 29 61 Vd 57
26110 Curnier 26 156 Fb 82
83670 Curnière, la 83 171 Ga 87
87380 Cursac 87 125 Bd 75
20270 Cursigliese CTC 183 Kc 95
01310 Curtafond 01 118 Fa 71
01440 Curtaringe 01 118 Fb 71
71340 Curtil, le 71 117 Df 71
38580 Curtillard, le 38 132 Ga 77
73270 Curtillets, les 73 133 Gd 74
21380 Curtil-Saint-Seine 21 91 Ef 64
71520 Curtil-sous-Buffières 71 117 Ed 70
71460 Curtil-sous-Burnand 71 105 Ed 69
21220 Curtil-Vergy 21 106 Ef 65
38510 Curtin 38 131 Fc 75
33125 Curton 33 135 Zc 82
27700 Curverville 27 50 Bc 53
86600 Curzay-sur-Vonne 86 111 Aa 70
85540 Curzon 85 109 Ye 70
20147 Curzu CTC 182 Ie 95
25110 Cusance 25 93 Gc 65
86120 Cusay 86 99 Aa 66
25680 Cuse-et-Adrisans 25 93 Gc 64
52190 Cusey 52 92 Fc 63
12600 Cussac 12 139 Ce 79
15430 Cussac 15 140 Cf 79
19200 Cussac 19 126 Cb 76
24480 Cussac 24 137 Af 79
33460 Cussac 33 134 Zb 78
87150 Cussac 87 125 Af 74
43370 Cussac-sur-Loire 43 141 Df 79
12160 Cussan 12 151 Cc 83
10210 Cussangy 10 73 Ea 60
37240 Cussay 37 100 Ae 66
31700 Cussecs 31 164 Bb 87
03170 Cusséjat 03 115 Cd 70
12360 Cusses 12 152 Cf 86
03300 Cusset 03 116 Dc 72
21580 Cussey-les-Forges 21 92 Fa 63
25440 Cussey-sur-Lison 25 107 Ff 66
25870 Cussey-sur-L'Ognon 25 93 Ff 64
21700 Cussigny 21 106 Ef 66
14280 Cussy 14 35 Zd 53
14400 Cussy 14 47 Zb 53
58470 Cussy 58 103 Db 67
71550 Cussy-en-Morvan 71 105 Ea 66
21360 Cussy-la-Colonne 21 105 Ed 66
21230 Cussy-le-Châtel 21 105 Ed 66
89420 Cussy-les-Forges 89 90 Ea 64
54670 Custines 54 56 Ga 56
74540 Cusy 74 132 Ga 74
89160 Cusy 89 90 Ea 62
20250 Cuticci CTC 183 Ka 94
77520 Cutrelles 77 72 Da 58
02600 Cutry 02 52 Db 52
54720 Cutry 54 43 Fe 52
60400 Cuts 60 40 Da 51
57260 Cutting 57 57 Gf 55
20167 Cuttoli-Corticchiato CTC 182 If 97
20167 Cuttuli Curtichjatu = Cuttoli-Corticchiato CTC 182 If 97
39170 Cuttura 39 119 Fe 70
32150 Cutxan 32 148 Zf 85
74350 Cuvat 74 120 Ga 73
70800 Cuve 70 93 Gb 61
60620 Cuvergnon 60 52 Cf 53
14840 Cuverville 14 35 Ze 53
76280 Cuverville 76 36 Ab 51
76260 Cuverville-sur-Yères 76 37 Bc 49
50670 Cuves 50 46 Yf 56
52240 Cuves 52 75 Fc 60
39250 Cuvier 39 107 Ga 68
59268 Cuvillers 59 30 Db 47
60490 Cuvilly 60 39 Ce 51
80400 Cuvilly 80 39 Da 50
57420 Cuvry 57 56 Ga 54
11390 Cuxac-Cabardès 11 166 Cb 88
11590 Cuxac-Coursan d'Aude 11 167 Cf 89
60310 Cuy 60 39 Cf 51
89140 Cuy 89 72 Db 59
76220 Cuy-Saint-Fiacre 76 38 Be 51
46270 Cuzac 46 138 Ca 81
46600 Cuzance 46 138 Bd 79
44160 Cuziac 44 81 Xe 64
01300 Cuzieu 01 131 Fe 74
42330 Cuzieu 42 129 Eb 75
47500 Cuzorn 47 137 Af 81
46500 Cuzoul 46 138 Be 80
82160 Cuzoul, le 82 151 Bf 83
58190 Cuzy 58 90 Dd 64
58800 Cuzy 58 90 De 65
71320 Cuzy 71 104 Ea 68
20148 Cuzzà = Cozzano CTC 183 Ka 97
59285 Cygne, le 59 27 Cc 43
02220 Cys-la-Commune 02 40 Dd 52
59830 Cysoing 59 30 Db 45

D

04190 Dabisse 04 157 Ff 85
57850 Dabo = Dagsburg 57 58 Hb 57
67120 Dachstein 67 60 Hd 57
03110 Dacs, les 03 116 Db 71
24250 Daglan 24 137 Bb 80
16210 Dagnaud 16 123 Aa 77
01120 Dagneux 01 131 Fa 73
77320 Dagny 77 52 Db 56
02140 Dagny-Lambercy 02 41 Ea 50
55500 Dagonville 55 55 Fc 56
57850 Dagsburg = Dabo 57 58 Hb 57
49800 Daguenière, la 49 84 Zd 64
46500 Dagues 46 138 Bd 80
12360 Daguette, la 12 167 Da 86
67310 Dahlenheim 67 60 Hd 57
22370 Dahouët 22 64 Xc 57
33420 Daignac 33 135 Ze 80
08140 Daigny 08 42 Ef 50
52110 Daillancourt 52 74 Ef 59
73150 Daille, la 73 133 Gf 76
52240 Daillecourt 52 75 Fd 60
57580 Dain-en-Saulnois 57 56 Gc 54
62000 Dainville 62 29 Ce 47
55130 Dainville-Bertheléville 55 75 Fd 58
29252 Dalar 29 62 Wa 57
46260 Dalat 46 150 Be 82
57550 Dalem 57 57 Gd 53
57340 Dalhain 57 57 Gd 55
67770 Dalhunden 67 59 Hf 56
04400 Dalis, les 04 158 Gd 82
63460 Dallages, les 63 115 Da 73
43580 Dallas 43 141 De 78
62830 Dalles 62 28 Be 45
63111 Dallet 63 128 Db 74
02680 Dallon 02 40 Db 50
19430 Dalmasane 19 138 Bf 78
34650 Dalmerie, la 34 152 Da 86
09120 Dalou 09 177 Bd 90
57320 Dalstein 57 44 Gc 53
06470 Daluis 06 158 Ge 84
88330 Damas-aux-Bois 88 77 Gc 58
88270 Damas-et-Bettegney 88 76 Gb 59
47160 Damazan 47 148 Ab 83
67110 Dambach 67 58 Hd 54
67650 Dambach-la-Ville 67 60 Hc 59
25150 Dambelin 25 94 Ge 64
70200 Dambenoît-lès-Colombes 70 93 Gc 62
88320 Damblain 88 75 Fd 60
14620 Damblainville 14 48 Zf 55
28140 Dambron 28 70 Bf 60
54360 Damelevières 54 76 Gc 57
37110 Dame-Marie-les-Bois 37 86 Ba 63
27160 Dame-Marie 27 49 Af 56
61130 Dame-Marie 61 68 Ad 58
60210 Daméraucourt 60 38 Bf 50
71620 Damerey 71 106 Ef 67
51480 Damery 51 53 Df 54
80700 Damery 80 39 Ce 50
25520 Dames-aux-Cordiers, la 25 108 Gc 66
56750 Damgan 56 80 Xc 63
61250 Damigny 61 68 Aa 58
55400 Damloup 55 55 Fc 53
02470 Dammard 02 52 Db 54
28360 Dammarie 28 70 Bc 58
45420 Dammarie-en-Puisaye 45 88 Cf 63
77190 Dammarie-les-Lys 77 71 Cd 57
45230 Dammarie-sur-Loing 45 88 Cf 62
55500 Dammarie-sur-Saulx 55 75 Fb 57
77230 Dammartin-en-Goële 77 51 Ce 54
78111 Dammartin-en-Serve 78 50 Bd 55
25110 Dammartin-les-Templiers 25 93 Gb 65
39290 Dammartin-Marpain 39 107 Fd 65
52140 Dammartin-sur-Meuse 52 75 Fd 61
77163 Dammartin-sur-Tigeaux 77 52 Cf 56
59680 Damousies 59 31 Ea 47
08090 Damouzy 08 42 Ee 50
39500 Damparis 39 106 Fc 66
02300 Dampcourt 02 40 Da 51
10240 Dampierre 10 74 Ec 57
14350 Dampierre 14 47 Za 54
18160 Dampierre 18 102 Ca 67
28800 Dampierre 28 70 Bc 59
39700 Dampierre 39 107 Fe 66
52360 Dampierre 52 75 Fc 61
51400 Dampierre-au-Temple 51 54 Ec 54
76220 Dampierre-en-Bray 76 38 Bd 51
71310 Dampierre-en-Bresse 71 106 Fb 68
45570 Dampierre-en-Burly 45 88 Cd 62
18260 Dampierre-en-Crot 18 88 Cd 64
18310 Dampierre-en-Graçay 18 102 Bf 65
21350 Dampierre-en-Montagne 21 91 Ed 64
78720 Dampierre-en-Yvelines 78 51 Bf 56
21310 Dampierre-et-Flée 21 92 Fc 64
36190 Dampierre-Gargilesse 36 113 Bd 69
51330 Dampierre-le-Château 51 54 Ee 54
25490 Dampierre-les-Bois 25 94 Gf 63
70800 Dampierre-lès-Conflans 70 93 Gb 61
76510 Dampierre-Saint-Nicolas 76 37 Bb 49

Dampierre-Saint-Nicolas | 263

17610 Dompierre-sur-Charente 17 123 Zd 74
58420 Dompierre-sur-Héry 58 89 Dd 65
17139 Dompierre-sur-Mer 17 110 Yf 71
39270 Dompierre-sur-Mont 39 119 Fd 69
58350 Dompierre-sur-Nièvre 58 103 Db 65
01240 Dompierre-sur-Veyle 01 118 Fb 72
85170 Dompierre-sur-Yon 85 97 Yd 68
07260 Dompnac 07 141 Ea 81
25510 Domprel 25 108 Gc 65
51300 Dompremy 51 54 Ee 56
54490 Domprix 54 43 Fe 53
87120 Domps 87 126 Be 75
88700 Domptail 88 77 Gd 58
54290 Domptail-en-L'Air 54 76 Gb 57
02310 Domptin 02 52 Db 54
80620 Domqueur 80 29 Ca 48
55500 Domrémy-aux-Bois 55 55 Fc 56
55240 Domrémy-la-Canne 55 55 Fe 53
52270 Domrémy-Landéville 52 75 Fb 58
88630 Domrémy-la-Pucelle 88 75 Fe 58
01270 Domsure 01 119 Fb 70
88500 Domvallier 88 76 Ga 59
80150 Domvast 80 28 Bf 47
59272 Don 59 30 Cf 45
08350 Donchery 08 42 Ef 50
88700 Doncières 88 77 Gd 58
55160 Doncourt-aux-Templiers 55 55 Fe 54
54800 Doncourt-lès-Conflans 54 56 Ff 54
54620 Doncourt-lès-Longuyon 54 43 Fe 52
52150 Doncourt-sur-Meuse 52 75 Fd 60
47470 Dondas 47 149 Af 83
44480 Donges 44 81 Xf 65
12780 Donhès-Basses, les 12 152 Cf 83
12780 Donhès-Hautes, les 12 152 Cf 83
33480 Donissan 33 134 Zb 78
52300 Donjeux 52 75 Fa 58
57590 Donjeux 57 56 Gc 55
03130 Donjon, le 03 116 De 70
34360 Donnadieu 34 167 Cf 88
18210 Donnais, les 18 103 Ce 68
56360 Donnant 56 80 We 65
30200 Donnat 30 155 Ed 83
14220 Donnay 14 47 Zd 55
81170 Donnazac 81 151 Bf 84
57810 Donnelay 57 57 Ge 56
28200 Donnemain-Saint-Mamès 28 69 Bc 60
52800 Donnemarie 52 75 Fc 60
77520 Donnemarie-Dontilly 77 72 Da 58
10330 Donnement 10 74 Ec 57
67170 Donnenheim 67 58 Hd 56
48170 Donnepau 48 141 Dd 81
45450 Donnery 45 87 Ca 61
31450 Donneville 31 165 Bd 88
50350 Donneville-les-Bains 50 46 Yc 55
33860 Donnezac 33 123 Zd 77
38930 Donnière 38 143 Fd 80
11200 Donos 11 166 Ce 90
23700 Dontreix 23 115 Cd 73
51490 Dontrien 51 54 Ec 53
33410 Donzac 33 135 Ze 81
82340 Donzac 82 149 Ae 84
40360 Donzacq 40 161 Zb 87
23480 Donzeil, le 23 114 Bf 72
19270 Donzenac 19 125 Bd 77
26290 Donzère 26 155 Ee 82
58220 Donzy 58 89 Da 64
71250 Donzy-le-National 71 118 Ed 70
71250 Donzy-le-Pertuis 71 118 Ee 70
58220 Donzy-le-Pré 58 89 Da 64
63220 Doranges 63 128 Dd 76
90400 Dorans 90 94 Gf 63
63300 Dorat 63 116 Dc 73
87210 Dorat, le 87 113 Ba 71
04250 Dorats, les 04 157 Gb 82
33138 Dorats, les 33 134 Yf 80
61110 Dorceau 61 69 Ae 58
45680 Dordives 45 71 Ce 60
58460 Dordres 58 89 Db 64
49600 Doré, le 49 97 Ye 65
53190 Dorée, la 53 66 Za 58
63220 Dore-L'Eglise 63 129 De 76
26120 Dorelons, les 26 143 Ef 79
02450 Dorengt 02 40 De 49
59500 Dorignies 59 30 Da 46
67120 Dorlisheim 67 60 Hc 57
51700 Dormans 51 53 Dd 54
77130 Dormelles 77 72 Cf 59
69720 Dormont 69M 130 Fa 74
24120 Dornac, la 24 137 Bc 78
07160 Dornas 07 142 Ec 79
58530 Dornecy 58 89 Dd 64
58390 Dornes 58 103 Dc 68
57130 Dornot, Ancy- 57 56 Ga 54
66760 Dorres 66 178 Bf 94
57720 Dorst 57 58 Hc 54
01590 Dortan 01 119 Fd 71
57690 Dorviller 57 57 Gd 54
10220 Dosches 10 73 Eb 59
10700 Dosnon 10 73 Eb 57
45300 Dossainville, Césarville- 45 71 Cb 59
29250 Dossen 29 62 Vf 56
67117 Dossenheim-Kochersberg 67 58 Hd 57
67330 Dossenheim-sur-Zinsel 67 58 Hc 56
49750 Doua 49 83 Zc 65
36300 Douadic 36 100 Ba 68
59553 Douai 59 30 Da 46
74470 Douai, la 74 120 Gd 71
27120 Douains 27 50 Bc 54
06660 Douans 06 158 Gf 83
13740 Douard, le 13 170 Fb 88
29100 Douarnenez 29 78 Ve 60
50800 Doublière, la 50 46 Ye 55
25300 Doubs 25 108 Gc 67
39700 Doubs 39 107 Fe 66
49640 Doucé 49 84 Zd 63
72170 Doucelles 72 68 Ab 59
34610 Douch 34 167 Cf 87
24350 Douchapt 24 124 Ac 77
02590 Douchy 02 40 Da 50
62116 Douchy-lès-Ayette 62 29 Ce 47
59282 Douchy-les-Mines 59 30 Dc 47
45220 Douchy-Montcorbon 45 72 Da 61
39130 Doucier 39 107 Fe 69
73260 Doucy 73 132 Gc 75
73630 Doucy-en-Bauges 73 132 Gb 74
62830 Doudeauville 62 28 Bf 45
76220 Doudeauville 76 38 Be 51
27150 Doudeauville-en-Vexin 27 38 Bd 53
80140 Doudelainville 80 38 Be 48
76560 Doudeville 76 36 Ae 50
47210 Doudrac 47 136 Ae 81
77510 Doue 77 52 Da 55
49700 Doué-en-Anjou 49 98 Ze 66
49700 Doué-la-Fontaine 49 98 Ze 65
46140 Douelle 46 137 Bc 82
33125 Douence 33 134 Zc 81
14250 Douesnots, les 14 34 Zb 54
14450 Douet, le 14 46 Yf 52
44530 Douettée, la 44 81 Ya 63
17100 Douhet, le 17 123 Zc 74
35420 Douillet 35 66 Yf 57
72130 Douillet 72 68 Zf 59
80400 Douilly 80 39 Da 50
33380 Douils, les 33 134 Za 81
52270 Doulaincourt-Saucourt 52 75 Fb 59
25330 Doulaize 25 107 Ff 66
55110 Doulcon 55 42 Fa 52
19220 Doulet 19 138 Ca 78
52110 Doulevant-le-Château 52 74 Ef 58
52130 Doulevant-le-Petit 52 74 Ef 58
33350 Doulezon 33 135 Zf 80
59940 Doulieu, le 59 29 Ce 44
43500 Doulioux 43 129 Df 77
80600 Doullens 80 29 Cc 48
19320 Doumail 19 126 Bf 77
12290 Doumazergues 12 152 Ce 83
08220 Doumely-Bégny 08 41 Eb 51
16380 Doumérac 16 124 Ac 75
87300 Doumezy 87 113 Ba 72
15200 Doumis 15 126 Cb 77
64450 Doumy 64 162 Zd 88
88220 Dounoux 88 76 Gc 60
04000 Dourbes, les 04 157 Gb 84
04330 Dourbettes, les 04 157 Gb 84
30750 Dourbies 30 153 Dc 84
35450 Dourdain 35 66 Yd 59
91410 Dourdan 91 70 Ca 57
57500 Dourd'hal 57 57 Gd 54
29252 Dourduff-en-Mer, le 29 62 Wa 57
62119 Dourges 62 30 Cf 46
81110 Dourgne 81 165 Ca 88
44190 Dourie, la 44 97 Ye 66
62870 Douriez 62 28 Bf 47
24350 Dourle 24 124 Ad 77
59440 Dourlers 59 31 Df 47
22560 Dourlin 22 63 Wc 56
05310 Dourmillouse 05 145 Gc 80
81340 Dourn, le 81 152 Cc 84
87230 Dournazac 87 125 Af 75
39110 Dournon 39 107 Ff 67
79600 Douron 79 99 Zf 67
04330 Douroulles 04 157 Gc 84
12120 Dours 12 152 Cd 83
65350 Dours 65 162 Aa 89
49460 Doussai, le 49 84 Zc 63
74210 Doussard 74 132 Gb 74
58800 Doussas 58 104 De 65
86140 Doussay 86 99 Ab 67
44650 Douteries, les 44 97 Yc 67
74140 Douvaine 74 120 Gb 71
80200 Douvieux 80 39 Da 49
24140 Douville 24 136 Ad 79
14430 Douville-en-Auge 14 48 Zf 53
27380 Douville-sur-Andelle 27 50 Bb 52
01370 Douvre, le 01 119 Fc 71
76630 Douvrend 76 37 Bb 49
01500 Douvres 01 119 Fc 73
14440 Douvres-la-Délivrande 14 47 Zd 53
62138 Douvrin 62 30 Ce 45
49260 Douvy 49 99 Zf 66
08300 Doux 08 41 Ec 51
79390 Doux 79 99 Aa 68
85200 Doux 85 110 Zb 70
85170 Doux, la 85 97 Yd 68
28220 Douy 28 69 Bb 60
77139 Douy-la-Ramée 77 52 Cf 54
47330 Douzains 47 136 Ad 81
12600 Douzalbats 12 139 Ce 79
16290 Douzat 16 123 Aa 74
15430 Douze 15 140 Cf 79
24330 Douze, la 24 137 Af 78
11700 Douzens 11 166 Cd 89
48150 Douzes, les 48 153 Db 83
07570 Douzet 07 142 Ec 78
40240 Douzevieille 40 147 Ze 85
24190 Douzillac 24 136 Ac 78
08140 Douzy 08 42 Fa 50
42600 Dovezy 42 129 Df 75
50250 Doville 50 33 Yc 53
03250 Doyat 03 116 Dd 72
39250 Doye 39 107 Ga 68
39400 Doye, la 39 120 Ff 70
03170 Doyet 03 115 Ce 70
14430 Dozulé 14 35 Zf 53
69220 Dracé 69D 118 Ee 72
37800 Draché 37 100 Ad 66
67160 Drachenbronn-Birlenbach 67 58 Hf 55
21350 Dracy 21 91 Ed 64
89130 Dracy 89 89 Db 62
21230 Dracy-Chalas 21 105 Ec 66
71640 Dracy-le-Fort 71 105 Ee 68
71490 Dracy-lès-Couches 71 105 Ed 67
71400 Dracy-Saint-Loup 71 105 Ec 66
50530 Dragey-Ronthon 50 46 Yd 56
83300 Draguignan 83 172 Gc 87
74550 Draillant 74 120 Gc 71
49530 Drain 49 82 Ye 64
04420 Draix 04 157 Gc 84
08220 Draize 08 41 Ec 51
21270 Drambon 21 92 Fc 64
39240 Dramelay 39 119 Fd 70
83530 Dramont, le 83 172 Gf 88
93700 Drancy 93 51 Cc 55
50250 Dranguerie, la 50 46 Yd 53
76870 Dranville 76 38 Bd 50
06340 Drap 06 173 Hb 86
76890 Draqueville 76 37 Af 50
02130 Dravegny 02 53 Dd 53
91210 Draveil 91 51 Cc 56
73270 Dray, la 73 133 Gd 74
21540 Drée 21 91 Ee 64
71360 Drée, la 71 105 Ed 67
44530 Drefféac 44 81 Xf 64
58220 Dreigny 58 89 Db 65
24700 Dreilles 24 136 Ab 78
15190 Dreils 15 127 Cf 76
31280 Drémil 31 165 Bd 87
60790 Drenne, la 60 51 Ca 53
29860 Drennec, le 29 62 Vd 57
44630 Dreny 44 81 Ya 63
60170 Dreslincourt 60 39 Cf 51
22780 Dresnay, le 22 63 Wd 57
36120 Dressais, le 36 101 Be 68
63850 Dressondeix 63 127 Ce 76
73410 Dressy 73 132 Ff 74
80470 Dreuil-lès-Amiens 80 38 Cb 49
80540 Dreuil-lès-Molliens 80 38 Ca 49
28100 Dreux 28 50 Bc 56
18200 Drevant 18 102 Cd 68
71670 Drevin 71 105 Ed 67
31380 Drian 31 165 Bd 86
08310 Dricourt 08 41 Ed 52
80240 Driencourt 80 39 Da 49
48150 Drigas 48 153 Dc 83
03250 Drigeard 03 116 De 72
15700 Drignac 15 139 Cc 77
55110 Drillancourt 55 55 Fb 53
59630 Drincham 59 27 Cb 43
65380 Drincles 65 162 Aa 90
62560 Drionville 62 29 Ca 45
62320 Drocourt 62 30 Cf 46
78440 Drocourt 78 50 Be 54
27320 Droisy 27 49 Ba 56
74270 Droisy 74 119 Ff 73
54800 Droitaumont 54 56 Fe 54
25380 Droitfontaine 25 94 Ge 65
03120 Droiturier 03 116 De 71
60440 Droizelles 60 52 Ce 54
02210 Droizy 02 52 Dc 53
01250 Drom 01 119 Fc 71
80640 Dromesnil 80 38 Bf 49
59114 Droogland 59 27 Cd 43
76460 Drosay 76 36 Ae 50
51290 Drosnay 51 74 Ed 57
41270 Droué 41 69 Ba 60
28230 Droue-sur-Drouette 28 70 Be 57
35130 Drouges 35 82 Ye 61
30160 Drouilhèdes 30 154 Ea 83
36800 Drouillé 36 101 Bb 69
87300 Drouilles 87 113 Ba 72
51300 Drouilly 51 54 Ed 56
10170 Droupt-Saint-Basle 10 73 Df 58
10170 Droupt-Sainte-Marie 10 73 Df 58
54370 Drouville 54 56 Gc 56
87190 Droux 87 113 Ba 72
52220 Droyes 52 74 Ee 57
14130 Drubec 14 48 Aa 53
27230 Drucourt 27 48 Ac 54
31480 Drudas 31 149 Ba 86
12510 Druelle 12 151 Cd 82
15140 Drugeac 15 139 Cc 77
01160 Druillat 01 119 Fb 72
12350 Drulhe 12 138 Ca 82
67320 Drulingen 67 57 Hb 55
73420 Drumettaz-Clarafond 73 132 Ff 75
67410 Drusenheim 67 59 Hf 56
14340 Druval, Beaufour- 14 48 Aa 53
37190 Druyé 37 85 Ad 65
89560 Druyes-les-Belles-Fontaines 89 89 Dc 63
58160 Druy-Parigny 58 103 Dc 67
45370 Dry 45 87 Be 62
22160 Dualult 22 63 Wd 58
47400 Dubédat 47 136 Ab 82
49123 Duberie, la 49 83 Za 64
12210 Duc, le 12 140 Cf 81
50220 Ducey-Les Chéris 50 66 Ye 57
76480 Duclair 76 37 Af 52
48140 Ducs, les 48 140 Dc 79
60800 Ducy 60 52 Ce 53
14250 Ducy-Sainte-Marguerite 14 34 Zc 53
69850 Duerne 69M 130 Ed 74
21510 Duesme 21 91 Ee 63
32170 Duffort 32 163 Ac 88
82160 Duges 82 151 Bf 83
93440 Dugny 93 51 Cc 55
55100 Dugny-sur-Meuse 55 55 Fc 54
40140 Duha 40 160 Ye 86
40800 Duhort-Bachen 40 162 Ze 86
11350 Duilhac-sous-Peyrepertuse 11 179 Cd 91
74410 Duingt 74 132 Gb 74
62161 Duisans 62 29 Ce 47
73610 Dullin 73 131 Fe 75
71240 Dulphey 71 118 Ef 69
40430 Dumène 40 147 Zd 83
40500 Dumes 40 161 Zc 86
09600 Dun 09 177 Be 90
72160 Duneau 72 68 Ad 60
82340 Dunes 82 149 Ae 84
62215 Dunes-d'Oye, les 62 27 Ca 42
36310 Dunet 36 113 Bb 70
14710 Dungy 14 47 Za 53
43220 Dunières 43 129 Ec 77
07360 Dunière-sur-Eyrieux 07 142 Ed 80
59140 Dunkerque 59 27 Cc 42
23800 Dun-le-Palestel 23 114 Bd 71
36210 Dun-le-Poëlier 36 101 Be 65
58230 Dun-les-Places 58 90 Ea 65
18130 Dun-sur-Auron 18 102 Cd 67
58110 Dun-sur-Grandry 58 104 De 66
55110 Dun-sur-Meuse 55 42 Fb 52
67270 Duntzenheim 67 58 Hd 56
40160 Dupouy 40 146 Yf 83
67120 Duppigheim 67 60 Hd 57
31230 Duprat 31 164 Af 88
58350 Duprés, les 58 89 Db 64
32810 Duran 32 163 Ad 86
47420 Durance 47 148 Aa 84
86300 Durands, les 86 112 Ae 70
32230 Duransan 32 162 Aa 87
06670 Duranus 06 159 Hb 85
27230 Duranville 27 49 Ad 54
47120 Duras 47 136 Ab 80
86100 Durauderie, la 86 100 Ad 67
46700 Duravel 46 137 Ba 81
23480 Durazat 23 114 Ca 72
65130 Durban 65 163 Ab 90
81140 Durban 81 151 Bf 85
11360 Durban-Corbières 11 179 Ce 91
46320 Durbans 46 138 Be 80
09240 Durban-sur-Arize 09 177 Bc 90
05140 Durbon 05 144 Fe 81
61100 Durcet 61 47 Zd 56
03310 Durdat 03 115 Ce 71
03310 Durdat-Larequille 03 115 Ce 71
72270 Dureil 72 84 Zf 61
12170 Durenque 12 152 Cd 84
33620 Duret 33 135 Zd 78
32260 Duret, le 32 148 Aa 85
09130 Durfort 09 164 Bc 89
81540 Durfort 81 165 Ca 88
30170 Durfort-et-Saint-Martin-de-Sossenac 30 154 Df 85
82390 Durfort-Lacapelette 82 150 Ba 83
32260 Durhan 32 163 Ad 87
01370 Durlande 01 119 Fb 71
68480 Durlinsdorf 68 95 Hb 64
68480 Durmenach 68 95 Hc 63
63700 Durmignat 63 115 Cf 71
25580 Durnes 25 107 Gb 66
67270 Durningen 67 58 Hd 56
67360 Durrenbach 67 58 He 55
68320 Durrenentzen 68 60 Hd 60
67320 Durstel 67 57 Hb 55
49430 Durtal 49 84 Ze 62
63830 Durtol 63 128 Da 74
02480 Dury 02 40 Da 50
62156 Dury 62 30 Da 47
80480 Dury 80 38 Cb 49
24270 Dussac 24 125 Ba 76
58800 Dussy 58 104 De 65
67120 Duttlenheim 67 60 Hd 57
60800 Duvy 60 52 Cf 53
55230 Duzey 55 43 Fd 52
89360 Dyé 89 90 Df 61
71800 Dyo 71 117 Eb 70

E

33220 Ealues, les 33 136 Aa 80
35640 Eancé 35 82 Ye 62
02480 Eaucourt 02 40 Da 50
80580 Eaucourt-sur-Somme 80 28 Bf 48
31600 Eaunes 31 164 Bc 88
79130 Eaux, les 79 98 Zd 69
64440 Eaux-Bonnes 64 174 Zd 91
04420 Eaux-Chaudes, les 04 158 Gc 83
64440 Eaux-Chaudes, les 64 174 Zd 91
10130 Eaux-Puiseaux 10 73 Df 60
32800 Eauze 32 148 Aa 85
21190 Ebaty 21 105 Ee 67
44750 Ebaupin, l' 44 81 Ya 64
59173 Ebblinghem 59 27 Cc 44
17770 Ebéon 17 123 Zd 73
67470 Eberbach-Seltz 67 59 Ia 55
67110 Eberbach-Wœrth 67 58 He 55
67600 Ebersheim 67 60 Hc 59
67600 Ebersmunster 67 60 Hd 59
57320 Ebersviller 57 56 Gc 53
38880 Ebertière 38 143 Fd 77
25380 Ebey 25 94 Gd 65
57220 Eblange 57 57 Gc 53
02350 Ebouleau 02 41 Df 50
16140 Ebréon 16 111 Aa 73
03450 Ébreuil 03 116 Da 72
57980 Ebring 57 57 Gf 54
62170 Ebruyères 62 28 Be 46
08300 Écaille, l' 08 41 Eb 52
59176 Écaillon 59 30 Db 46
14270 Écajeul 14 48 Zf 54
76750 Écalles 76 37 Bb 51
76190 Écalles-Alix 76 37 Ae 51
20217 E Canelle = Canelle CTC 181 Kb 92
20238 E Canelle = Cannelle CTC 181 Kb 91
20151 E Cannelle = Cannelle CTC 182 If 96
27290 Ecaquelon 27 49 Ae 53
20228 E Carbunacce = Carbonacce CTC 181 Kc 91
27170 Ecardenville-la-Campagne 27 49 Af 54
27490 Ecardenville-sur-Eure 27 50 Bb 54
44460 Ecare, l' 44 81 Ya 63
20270 E Case Vechje = Casevecchie CTC 183 Kc 96
60210 Ecâtelet 60 38 Bf 51
62360 Ecault 62 28 Bd 45
50310 Ecausseville 50 33 Yd 52
27110 Ecauville 27 49 Af 54
20117 Eccica-Suarella CTC 182 If 97
59740 Eccles 59 31 Ea 47
39270 Echailla 39 119 Fd 70
45390 Echainvilliers 45 71 Cb 59
69700 Echalas 69M 130 Ee 75
16170 Echallat 16 123 Zf 74
01130 Echallon 01 119 Fe 71
21510 Echalot 21 91 Ef 63
61440 Echalou 61 47 Zd 56
05460 Echalp, l' 05 145 Gf 80
18400 Echalusse, l' 18 102 Cb 67
77440 Échampeu 77 52 Da 54
07310 Echamps 07 141 Eb 79
63980 Echandelys 63 128 Dd 75
21540 Echannay 21 91 Ee 65
91540 Echarcon 91 71 Cc 57
69870 Echarmeaux, les 69D 117 Ec 72
49300 Echasserie, l' 49 98 Zb 66
03330 Échassières 03 115 Cf 71
61370 Echauffour 61 48 Ac 56
25440 Echay 25 107 Ff 66
17800 Echebrune 17 123 Zd 75
08150 Echelle, l' 08 41 Ec 50
80700 Échelle, l' 80 39 Ce 50
51210 Echelle-le-Franc, l' 51 53 Dd 55
28140 Echelles 28 70 Be 60
73360 Echelles, les 73 131 Fe 76
10350 Échemines 10 73 Df 58
49150 Echemiré 49 84 Ze 63
25550 Echenans 25 94 Ge 63
70400 Echenans 70 94 Ge 63
52230 Echenay 52 75 Fb 58
01170 Échenevex 01 120 Ga 71
21170 Echenon 21 106 Fb 66
70000 Echenoz-la-Méline 70 93 Ga 63
70000 Echenoz-le-Sec 70 93 Ga 63
68160 Echery 68 60 Ha 59
01700 Echets, les 01 130 Ef 73
70100 Echevanne 70 92 Fe 64
21120 Echevannes 21 92 Fb 63
25580 Echevannes 25 107 Gb 66
21420 Echevronne 21 106 Ef 66
21110 Echigey 21 106 Fb 65
49150 Echigné 49 84 Ze 63
17620 Echillais 17 110 Za 73
45390 Echilleuses 45 71 Cc 60
73700 Échines, les 73 133 Ge 75
62360 Echinghem 62 28 Bd 44
79410 Echiré 79 111 Zd 70
38130 Echirolles 38 144 Fe 78
16230 Echoisy 16 124 Aa 73
79110 Echorigné 79 111 Ze 72
77830 Echou 77 72 Cf 58
77830 Échouboulains 77 72 Cf 58
24410 Echourgnac 24 136 Ab 78
67201 Eckbolsheim 67 60 He 57
67550 Eckwersheim 67 58 He 56
28350 Eclache, l' 28 49 Ba 56
63470 Eclache, l' 63 127 Ce 74
51800 Eclaires 51 55 Fa 54
10200 Éclance 10 74 Ed 59
39700 Eclans-Nenon 39 107 Fd 66
52290 Éclaron-Braucourt-Sainte-Livière 52 74 Ef 57
07370 Eclassan 07 130 Ee 78
18190 Ecléneuil 18 102 Cb 67
39600 Ecleux 39 107 Fe 66
62770 Eclimeux 62 29 Cb 46
55270 Eclisfontaine 55 55 Fa 53
38300 Eclose-Badinières 38 131 Fb 75
83560 Eclou, l' 83 171 Ff 86
42380 Eclunes 42 129 Ea 76
05300 Ecluse, l' 05 156 Fe 82
87160 Ecluse, l' 87 113 Bb 71
28500 Ecluzelles 28 50 Bc 56
08300 Ecly 08 41 Eb 51
42670 Ecoche 42 117 Eb 72
62144 Écoivres 62 29 Ce 46
62270 Ecoivres 62 29 Cb 47
04360 Ecole 04 157 Gb 86
27130 Ecole 27 49 Af 56
73630 École 73 132 Gb 75
29590 Ecole d'Agriculture du Nivot 29 62 Vf 59
25480 Ecole-Valentin 25 93 Ff 65
51290 Ecollemont 51 54 Ee 57
41290 Ecoman 41 86 Bb 61
72220 Ecommoy 72 85 Ab 62
01560 Ecopets, les 01 118 Fa 70
50480 Ecoquenéauville 50 34 Ye 52
01550 Ecorans 01 119 Ff 72
61270 Ecorcel 61 49 Ad 56
25140 Ecorces, les 25 108 Ge 65
76550 Ecorchebœuf 76 37 Ba 49
61160 Ecorches 61 48 Aa 55
27480 Ecorcheval 27 37 Bd 52
08130 Ecordal 08 42 Ed 51
72120 Ecorpain 72 85 Ad 61
21150 Ecorsaint 21 91 Ed 64
27630 Ecos 27 50 Bd 54
25150 Ecot 25 94 Ge 64
42600 Ecotay-L'Olme 42 129 Ea 75
74360 Ecotex 74 121 Gd 71
41160 Ecotière, l' 41 86 Ba 61
52700 Ecot-la-Combe 52 75 Fc 59
14170 Ecots 14 48 Aa 55
62850 Ecottes 62 27 Bf 44
86450 Ecoubesse 86 100 Ae 68
61150 Écouché-les-Vallées 61 48 Zf 56
85200 Ecoué 85 110 Za 70
95440 Écouen 95 51 Cc 54
49000 Ecouflant 49 84 Zc 63
27440 Ecouis 27 37 Bc 53
62860 Ecourt-Saint-Quentin 62 30 Da 47
62128 Écoust-Saint-Mein 62 30 Cf 47
61250 Écouves 61 68 Aa 57
55600 Ecouviez 55 43 Fc 51
25640 Ecouvotte, l' 25 93 Gb 64
17770 Ecoyeux 17 123 Zc 74
62190 Ecquedecques 62 29 Cc 45
62990 Ecquemicourt 62 28 Bf 46
27110 Ecquetot 27 49 Ba 53
76930 Ecqueville 76 35 Aa 51
78920 Ecquevilly 78 50 Bf 55
76110 Ecrainville 76 36 Ab 51
14710 Ecrammeville 14 47 Za 53
06460 Ecre, l' 06 173 Gf 86
77820 Ecrennes, les 77 71 Cf 57
76890 Ecrépigny 76 37 Ba 50

A B C D E F G H I J K L M N O P Q R S T U V W X Y Z

Ecrépigny | 265

F

11260 Fa 11 178 Cb 91
09230 Fabas 09 164 Ba 90
31230 Fabas 31 164 Af 89
81430 Fabas 81 151 Cb 85
82170 Fabas 82 150 Bc 85
65170 Fabian 65 175 Ab 92
07380 Fabras 07 142 Eb 81
12410 Fabrègue, la 12 152 Cf 83
34690 Fabrègues 34 168 De 87
48110 Fabrègues 48 153 De 83
12290 Fabrèque, la 12 152 Ce 83
05200 Fabres, les 05 145 Gc 82
11200 Fabrezan 11 166 Ce 90
12160 Fabrie, la 12 151 Cc 83
81190 Fabrié, la 81 151 Ca 84
87200 Fabrique, la 87 112 Af 73
58270 Faches 58 104 Dd 67
59155 Faches-Thumesnil 59 30 Da 45
58430 Fâchin 58 104 Df 66
33380 Facture 33 134 Za 81
34340 Fadèze, la 34 167 Dd 88
83510 Fadons, les 83 172 Gc 88
46360 Fage 46 138 Bd 81
11500 Fage, la 11 178 Ca 91
12270 Fage, la 12 151 Bf 83
15400 Fage, la 15 127 Cd 77
43100 Fage, la 43 128 Db 77
48170 Fage, la 48 141 Dd 81
48310 Fage-Montivernoux, la 48 140 Da 80
15500 Fageole, la 15 140 Da 78
09240 Fages 09 177 Bc 91
24590 Fages 24 137 Bb 79
46140 Fages 46 137 Bb 81
47200 Faget 47 136 Ab 81
31460 Faget, le 31 165 Be 87
64400 Faget, le 64 161 Zc 89
32450 Faget-Abbatial 32 163 Ae 87
48500 Fagette, la 48 152 Da 82
51510 Fagnières 51 54 Eb 55
08090 Fagnon 08 42 Ed 50
54120 Fagnoux 54 77 Ge 58
63550 Fagot 63 116 Dd 73
70100 Fahy-lès-Autrey 70 92 Fc 63
72510 Faigne, la 72 84 Ab 62
63940 Faillargues 63 129 De 76
04420 Faillefeu 04 158 Gc 83
02700 Faillouël 02 40 Db 50
57640 Failly 57 56 Gb 54
27240 Failly, le 27 49 Bb 55
25250 Faimbe 25 94 Gd 64
21500 Fain-lès-Montbard 21 91 Ec 63
21500 Fain-lès-Moutiers 21 90 Eb 63
27120 Fains 27 50 Bc 55
28150 Fains-la-Folie 28 70 Bd 59
55000 Fains-Véel 55 55 Fa 56
15320 Fairollettes 15 140 Db 79
08270 Faissault 08 41 Ed 51
48140 Faissinet-Langlade 48 140 Dc 79
01560 Faissolles 01 118 Fa 70
11220 Fajac-en-Val 11 166 Cc 90
11410 Fajac-la-Ralenque 11 165 Be 89
48400 Fajole, la 48 153 Dd 83
46300 Fajoles 46 137 Bc 80
43170 Fajolette, la 43 140 Dd 79
11140 Fajolle, la 11 178 Bf 92
82210 Fajolles 82 149 Ba 85
08400 Falaise 08 42 Ee 52
14700 Falaise 14 48 Ze 55
27940 Falaise, la 27 50 Bc 53
78410 Falaise, la 78 50 Be 55
63113 Falaitouze 63 127 Ce 76
57550 Falck 57 57 Gd 53
33760 Faleyras 33 135 Ze 80
31540 Falga 31 165 Bf 88
81800 Falgade 81 150 Bd 85
15380 Falgoux, le 15 139 Cd 78
24260 Falgueyras 24 137 Af 79
24560 Falgueyrat 24 136 Ad 80
24510 Falgueyret 24 137 Ae 79
12170 Falguières 12 151 Cc 84
82000 Falguières 82 150 Bc 84
12130 Falguières, les 12 140 Da 82
06950 Falicon 06 173 Hb 86
48000 Falisson, le 48 153 Dc 82
15230 Falitoux 15 139 Cf 79
62118 Falkwiller 68 94 Ha 62
38480 Fallamieux 38 131 Fd 75
76340 Fallencourt 76 37 Bd 49
25580 Fallerans 25 108 Gb 66
85670 Falleron 85 96 Yb 67
39700 Falletans 39 107 Fd 66
88200 Fallières 88 77 Gd 60
70110 Fallon 70 94 Gc 63
80250 Faloise, la 80 39 Cc 50
47220 Fals 47 149 Ae 84
46600 Falsemoyer 46 137 Bc 79
80190 Falvy 80 39 Cf 50
59300 Famars 59 30 Dd 47
62760 Famechon 62 29 Cc 48
80290 Famechon 80 38 Ca 50
57290 Fameck 57 56 Ga 53
14290 Familly 14 48 Ac 55
62118 Fampoux 62 30 Cf 47
52500 Fanay 87 113 Bc 72
15200 Fanc, le 15 127 Cb 77
66760 Fanès 66 178 Bf 94
71510 Fangey 71 105 Ed 68
71490 Fangy 71 105 Ec 67
11270 Fanjeaux 11 165 Ca 89
24290 Fanlac 24 137 Ba 78
63690 Fanostre 63 127 Cd 75
77515 Fans, les 77 52 Db 55
36170 Fant 36 113 Bc 70
12150 Fantayrou 12 152 Da 82
29690 Fao, le 29 62 Wb 58
29460 Faou, le 29 62 Ve 59
56500 Faouët 56 80 Xb 61
22290 Faouët, le 22 63 Wf 56
56320 Faouët, Le 56 79 Wd 60
52500 Faraincourt 52 92 Fd 62
13129 Faraman 13 169 Ee 88
01800 Faramans 01 118 Fa 73
38260 Faramans 38 131 Fb 76
62580 Farbus 62 30 Ce 46
17150 Farceaux 27 50 Bd 53
24450 Fardoux 24 125 Af 75
26510 Fare, la 26 156 Fc 83
57450 Farébersviller = Pfarrebersweiler 57 57 Gf 54
05500 Fare-en-Cros, la 05 144 Ga 81
01480 Fareins 01 118 Ee 72
13580 Fare-les-Oliviers, la 13 170 Fb 87
05500 Farelles, les 05 144 Ga 81
77515 Faremoutiers 77 52 Cf 56
07190 Fargatte, la 07 142 Ed 79
12200 Fargayrolles 12 151 Ca 83
19390 Farge, la 19 126 Be 76
42470 Farge, la 42 117 Eb 73
63930 Farge, la 63 129 De 74
19210 Fargeas 19 125 Bc 76
87260 Fargeas 87 125 Bc 74
01550 Farges 01 119 Ff 71
15300 Farges 15 140 Cf 78
19600 Farges 19 138 Bc 78
23200 Farges 23 114 Ca 73
45240 Farges 45 87 Bf 62
63770 Farges 63 115 Ce 73
23500 Farges, les 23 126 Ca 74
24290 Farges, les 24 137 Bb 78
18200 Farges-Allichamps 18 102 Cc 68
18800 Farges-en-Septaine 18 103 Cd 66
71150 Farges-lès-Chalon 71 106 Ee 67
71700 Farges-lès-Mâcon 71 118 Ef 69
02700 Fargniers 02 40 Db 51
82130 Fargue 82 149 Bb 84
82220 Fargue 82 150 Bc 84
24620 Fargue, la 24 137 Ba 79
15290 Fargues 15 138 Ca 79
33210 Fargues 33 135 Ze 81
40500 Fargues 40 162 Zd 86
46800 Fargues 46 149 Bb 82
33370 Fargues-Saint-Hilaire 33 135 Zd 80
47700 Fargues-sur-Ourbise 47 148 Aa 83
81100 Farguettes, les 81 166 Ca 87
81190 Farguettes, les 81 151 Cb 84
43370 Farigoules 43 141 De 78
34450 Farinette-Plage 34 167 Dc 89
20253 Faringule = Farinole CTC 181 Kc 92
20253 Farinole CTC 181 Kc 92
84100 Farjons, les 84 155 Ee 83
83210 Farlède, la 83 171 Ga 90
42320 Farnay 42 130 Ed 76
12550 Farret 12 152 Cd 85
15230 Farreyre 15 139 Ce 79
12200 Farrou 12 151 Ca 82
57450 Farschviller 57 57 Gf 54
72470 Fatines 72 68 Ac 60
27210 Fatouvill-Grestain 27 36 Ab 52
02120 Faty 02 40 De 49
04140 Fau, le 04 157 Gc 82
07160 Fau, le 07 142 Ec 79
12780 Fau, le 12 152 Cf 83
15140 Fau, le 15 139 Cd 78
46210 Fau, le 46 138 Ca 80
82000 Fau, le 82 150 Bc 85
32720 Faubourg, le 32 162 Ze 86
02000 Faubourg-de-Leuilly 02 40 Dd 51
81120 Fauch 81 151 Cb 86
62450 Faucherias 24 136 Ae 78
74130 Faucigny 74 120 Gc 72
70310 Faucogney-et-la-Mer 70 94 Gd 61
88460 Faucompierre 88 77 Ge 60
04400 Faucon 04 158 Ge 82
26470 Faucon 26 143 Fb 81
84110 Faucon 84 156 Fa 83
88700 Fauconcourt 88 77 Gd 58
04250 Faucon-du-Caire 04 157 Ga 82
26120 Fauconnières 26 143 Ef 79
26120 Faucons, les 26 143 Fa 79
02320 Faucoucourt 02 40 Dc 51
02270 Faucouzy 02 40 Dd 50
48130 Fau-de-Peyre 48 140 Db 80
82500 Faudoas 82 149 Af 86
31410 Fauga, le 31 164 Bb 88
31600 Faugarouse 31 164 Bb 88
19600 Faugère 19 138 Bd 78
07230 Faugères 07 141 Ea 82
34600 Faugères 34 167 Db 87
79270 Faugerit 79 110 Zc 71
14100 Fauguernon 14 48 Ab 53
47400 Fauguerolles 47 148 Ab 82
47400 Fauillet 47 148 Ab 82
77320 Faujus 77 52 Db 56
57570 Faulbach 57 44 Gb 52
14130 Faulq, le 14 48 Ab 53
57380 Faulquemont 57 57 Gd 54
57690 Faulquemont-Citex 57 57 Gd 54
54760 Faulx 54 56 Gb 56
59310 Faumont 59 30 Da 46
81240 Faumontagne 81 166 Cd 88
09140 Faup 09 176 Ba 92
62560 Fauquembergues 62 29 Ca 45
62840 Fauquissart 62 30 Ce 45
33550 Faure 33 135 Zd 80
05190 Faure, la 05 144 Gb 82
38740 Faures, les 38 144 Ga 79
43520 Faurie 43 141 Eb 78
05140 Faurie, la 05 144 Fe 81
19130 Faurie, la 19 125 Bc 77
19190 Faurie, la 19 138 Be 78
19510 Faurie, la 19 126 Bd 75
24560 Faurilles 24 136 Ae 80
82190 Fauroux 82 149 Ba 83
42600 Faury 42 129 Ea 75
81340 Faussergues 81 151 Cc 84
28120 Fausserville 28 69 Bb 58
20135 Fautea CTC 185 Kc 98
85460 Faute-sur-Mer, la 85 109 Ye 70
37350 Fauvellière, la 37 100 Af 67
21110 Fauverney 21 106 Fa 65
87520 Fauvette, la 87 113 Ba 73
63390 Fauvielle, la 63 115 Ce 72
76640 Fauville-en-Caux 76 36 Ad 51
50250 Fauvrerie, la 50 46 Yd 53
08270 Faux 08 41 Ed 51
19340 Faux 19 127 Cc 75
24560 Faux 24 136 Ad 80
48320 Faux 48 153 Dd 82
23170 Faux, le 23 114 Cc 71
35550 Faux, le 35 81 Xf 62
42440 Faux, le 42 129 De 74
43230 Faux, le 43 128 Dd 77
27400 Faux, les 27 49 Bb 54
48120 Faux, les 48 140 Dc 80
58330 Faux, les 58 104 Dd 66
51230 Faux-Fresnay 51 53 Df 57
23340 Faux-la-Montagne 23 126 Bf 74
23400 Faux-Mazuras 23 114 Be 73
51320 Faux-Vésigneul 51 54 Ec 56
10290 Faux-Villecerf 10 73 De 59
34210 Fauzan 34 166 Ce 88
20140 Favalella CTC 184 Ie 98
20212 Favalello CTC 183 Kb 95
15310 Favard 15 139 Cc 78
19330 Favars 19 126 Be 77
19600 Favars 19 138 Bc 78
34220 Favayroles 34 166 Cd 88
30110 Favède, la 30 154 Ea 83
45130 Favelles 45 70 Bd 61
49380 Faveraye 49 98 Zc 65
49380 Faveraye-Mâchelles 49 98 Zd 65
18360 Faverdines 18 102 Cc 69
45420 Faverelles 45 88 Cf 63
38510 Faverge 38 131 Fc 74
42940 Faverge 42 129 Df 74
38110 Faverges-de-la-Tour 38 131 Fd 75
74210 Faverges-Seythenex 74 132 Gb 74
85220 Faverie, la 85 96 Yb 68
70160 Faverney 70 93 Ga 62
90100 Faverois 90 94 Ha 63
63630 Faverol 63 128 Dd 76
02600 Faverolles 02 52 Db 53
15230 Faverolles 15 139 Cf 79
15320 Faverolles 15 140 Da 79
28140 Faverolles 28 70 Be 60
28210 Faverolles 28 50 Bd 56
36360 Faverolles 36 101 Bc 65
52260 Faverolles 52 75 Fb 61
61600 Faverolles 61 47 Ze 56
80500 Faverolles 80 39 Cd 51
51170 Faverolles-et-Coëmy 51 53 De 53
27190 Faverolles-la-Campagne 27 49 Af 54
21290 Faverolles-lès-Lucey 21 91 Ef 61
41400 Faverolles-sur-Cher 41 86 Bb 65
30122 Faveyrolle 30 153 De 84
12480 Faveyrolles 12 152 Ce 85
39250 Favière 39 107 Ga 68
83230 Favière 83 172 Gc 90
04420 Favière, la 04 158 Gc 83
28170 Favières 28 69 Bb 57
54115 Favières 54 76 Ff 58
77220 Favières 77 52 Ce 56
80120 Favières 80 28 Bd 47
01130 Favillon, le 01 119 Fe 71
20135 Favone CTC 183 Kc 98
41120 Favras 41 86 Bc 64
16600 Favrauds, les 16 124 Ab 74
51300 Favresse 51 54 Ee 56
62450 Favreuil 62 30 Cf 48
27230 Favril, le 27 49 Ad 53
28120 Favril, le 28 69 Bb 59
28190 Favril, le 28 69 Ba 58
59550 Favril, le 59 31 De 48
78200 Favrneux 78 50 Bd 55
61390 Fay 61 48 Ac 57
72550 Fay 72 68 Aa 60
80200 Fay 80 39 Ce 49
71290 Fay, la 71 106 Fa 69
36170 Fay, le 36 113 Bc 70
36230 Fay, le 36 101 Be 69
71580 Fay, le 71 106 Fb 68
80270 Fay, le 80 38 Be 49
44850 Fayau, le 44 82 Yd 64
45450 Fay-aux-Loges 45 87 Ca 61
46100 Faycelles 46 138 Bf 81
44130 Fay-de-Bretagne 44 82 Yb 64
63550 Faydit 63 116 Dd 73
05300 Faye 05 157 Ff 82
24600 Faye 24 124 Ab 77
41100 Faye 41 86 Bb 62
71550 Faye 71 105 Eb 66
16700 Faye, la 16 111 Aa 72
19510 Faye, la 19 126 Bd 75
24750 Faye, la 24 136 Ae 78
42660 Faye, la 42 130 Ec 77
63640 Faye, la 63 115 Ce 73
63980 Faye, la 63 128 Dd 75
71410 Faye, la 71 105 Eb 68
71520 Faye, la 71 117 Ec 70
79140 Faye, la 79 98 Zc 67
49380 Faye-d'Anjou 49 84 Zc 65
60730 Fayel 60 38 Cb 53
27380 Fayel, le 27 37 Bc 52
27480 Fayel, le 27 37 Bd 52
79350 Faye-L'Abbesse 79 98 Zd 68
37120 Faye-la-Vineuse 37 99 Ac 67
24300 Fayemarteau 24 124 Ac 75
83440 Fayence 83 172 Ge 87
39800 Fay-en-Montagne 39 107 Fe 68
63480 Fayes, les 63 129 De 74
79160 Faye-sur-Ardin 79 110 Zc 70
02100 Fayet 02 40 Db 49
03250 Fayet 03 116 De 73
12360 Fayet 12 152 Cf 86
63590 Fayet 63 128 Dd 75
63610 Fayet 63 128 Cf 76
15100 Fayet, le 15 140 Da 79
15190 Fayet, le 15 127 Cf 76
38540 Fayet, le 38 130 Fa 75
74190 Fayet, le 74 121 Ge 73
63160 Fayet-le-Château 63 128 Dc 74
63630 Fayet-Ronaye 63 128 Dd 76
71160 Fayette, la 71 117 Df 69
46120 Fayfol 46 138 Bf 80
52500 Fayl-Billot 52 92 Fd 62
26240 Fay-le-Clos 26 130 Ef 77
60240 Fay-les-Etangs 60 50 Bf 53
10290 Fay-lès-Marcilly 10 73 Dd 58
77167 Faÿ-lès-Nemours 77 71 Ce 59
70200 Faymont 70 94 Gd 63
88340 Faymont 88 77 Gd 61
85240 Faymoreau 85 110 Zc 69
84570 Fayol 84 156 Fb 84
01190 Fayolle 01 118 Ef 70
24600 Fayolle 24 124 Ac 77
63220 Fayolle, la 63 129 De 76
63660 Fayolle, la 63 129 Df 75
03250 Fayot 03 116 De 72
89570 Fays, le 89 73 De 60
60510 Fay-Saint-Quentin, le 60 38 Cb 52
10320 Fays-la-Chapelle 10 73 Ea 60
81600 Fayssac 81 151 Bf 85
43430 Fay-sur-Lignon 43 141 Eb 79
63660 Fayt, le 63 129 Df 75
64570 Féas 64 161 Zb 90
62960 Febvin-Palfart 62 29 Cb 45
76400 Fécamp 76 36 Ac 50
59247 Féchain 59 30 Db 47
63420 Féchal 63 128 Da 76
90100 Fêche-l'Eglise 90 94 Gf 63
73230 Féclaz, la 73 132 Ff 75
54115 Fécocourt 54 76 Ga 58
70120 Fédry 70 93 Ff 63
28290 Fée 28 69 Bb 60
18350 Feez 18 103 Ce 67
67640 Fegersheim 67 60 He 58
44460 Fégréac 44 81 Xf 63
74160 Feigères 74 120 Ga 72
60800 Feigneux 60 52 Cf 53
01570 Feillens 01 118 Ef 70
09420 Feillet 09 177 Bb 91
05230 Fein, le 05 144 Gb 81
41120 Feings 41 86 Bc 64
61400 Feings 61 68 Ad 57
35440 Feins 35 65 Yc 59
45230 Feins-en-Gâtinais 45 88 Cf 62
73260 Feissons-sur-Isère 73 133 Gc 75
73350 Feissons-sur-Salins 73 133 Gd 76
61160 Fel 61 48 Aa 56
12140 Fel, le 12 139 Cc 81
20234 Felce CTC 183 Kc 94
68640 Feldbach 68 95 Hb 63
68540 Feldkirch 68 95 Hb 61
35300 Felger = Fougères 35 66 Ye 58
35390 Felgerieg = Grand-Fougeray 35 82 Yb 62
20225 Feliceto CTC 180 If 93
20225 Felicetu = Feliceto CTC 180 If 93
07340 Félines 07 130 Ee 77
26160 Félines 26 143 Fa 81
43160 Félines 43 129 De 77
63320 Félines 63 128 Da 75
82160 Félines 82 150 Be 83
34210 Félines-Minervois 34 166 Cd 89
11330 Félines-Termenès 11 179 Cd 91
24520 Félix, les 24 136 Ad 80
59740 Felleries 59 31 Ea 48
68470 Fellering 68 94 Gf 61
23500 Felletin 23 114 Cb 73
66730 Felluns 66 178 Cc 92
90110 Felon 90 94 Gf 62
46270 Felzins 46 138 Ca 81
86700 Fémolant 86 112 Ab 71
24490 Fénage, la 24 135 Aa 78
59179 Fenain 59 30 Db 46
21600 Fénay 21 106 Fa 65
11400 Fendeille 11 165 Bf 89
06580 Fénerier, le 06 173 Gf 87
63440 Fénérol 63 115 Da 72
79450 Fénery 79 98 Zd 68
57930 Fénétrange = Finstingen 57 57 Ha 55
36500 Fenets, les 36 101 Bc 68
49460 Feneu 49 83 Zc 63
19110 Feneyrol 19 127 Cc 76
43380 Feneyroles 43 128 Dc 77
43160 Feneyrolles 43 128 Dd 77
82140 Féneyrols 82 150 Be 84
63570 Fenier 63 128 Db 76
01710 Fénières 01 120 Ff 71
23100 Féniers 23 126 Ca 74
17350 Fenioux 17 110 Zc 73
79160 Fenioux 79 110 Zd 69
88320 Fenneciere, la 88 75 Fe 60
54540 Fenneviller 54 77 Gf 58
81600 Fénols 81 151 Ca 85
85800 Fenouiller, le 85 96 Ya 68
04110 Fenouillet 04 156 Fd 85
31150 Fenouillet 31 164 Bc 86
66220 Fenouillet 66 178 Cc 92
11240 Fenouillet-du-Razès 11 165 Ca 90
20212 Feo CTC 183 Kb 95
85210 Féole 85 97 Yf 69
86400 Féolle, la 86 112 Ab 71
08170 Fépin 08 42 Ee 48
86160 Férabœuf 86 112 Ac 70
50260 Férage, le 50 33 Yc 52
24320 Féraillon 24 124 Ac 76
78770 Féranville 78 50 Be 55
47150 Feratie 47 137 Ae 81
81340 Feraudie, la 81 151 Cc 84
44660 Fercé 44 82 Yd 62
72430 Fercé-sur-Sarthe 72 84 Zf 61
33820 Ferchaud 33 122 Zc 77
60730 Fercourt 60 38 Cb 53
88360 Ferdrupt 88 94 Ge 61
02800 Fère, la 02 40 Dc 51
51270 Fèrebrianges 51 53 Df 55
51230 Fère-Champenoise 51 53 Df 56
08290 Férée, la 08 41 Eb 50
02130 Fère-en-Tardenois 02 53 Dd 53
56130 Férel 56 81 Xd 64
47240 Féréol 47 149 Ae 83
63680 Férérolles 63 127 Ce 75
07140 Féreyrolles 07 141 Df 81
62260 Ferfay 62 29 Cc 45
77133 Féricy 77 72 Ce 58
59169 Férin 59 30 Da 47
20290 Ferlaggia CTC 181 Kc 94
48120 Ferluc 48 140 Dc 80
28500 Fermaincourt 28 50 Bc 56
50840 Fermanville 50 33 Yd 50
32600 Ferme-des-Loups 32 164 Ba 87
58160 Fermeté, la 58 103 Db 67
04340 Fermeyer 04 157 Gb 82
05260 Fermons, les 05 144 Gb 80
54870 Fermont 54 43 Fd 52
47320 Fernand 47 148 Ab 82
01280 Ferney-Voltaire 01 120 Ga 71
63620 Fernoël 63 127 Cc 74
74220 Fernuy, le 74 120 Gc 73
45150 Férolles 45 87 Ca 61
77150 Férolles-Attilly 77 51 Cd 56
59610 Féron 59 31 Ea 48
02140 Féronval 02 40 De 49
62250 Ferques 62 26 Be 44
11200 Ferrals-les-Corbières 11 166 Ce 90
34210 Ferrals-les-Montagnes 34 166 Cd 88
11240 Ferran 11 165 Ca 90
40270 Ferran 40 147 Zd 86
79800 Ferrandière, la 79 111 Zf 70
26120 Ferrands, les 26 143 Fa 79
26570 Ferrassières 26 156 Fc 84
35420 Ferré, le 35 66 Ye 58
47330 Ferrensac 47 136 Ad 81
63660 Ferréol 63 129 Df 76
65370 Ferrère 65 175 Ad 91
06510 Ferres, les 06 158 Ha 85
33820 Ferrés, les 33 122 Zc 77
68480 Ferrette 68 95 Hb 64
28350 Ferrette, la 28 49 Bb 56
10400 Ferreux-Quincey 10 73 Dd 58
02270 Ferrière 02 40 Dd 50
03440 Ferrière 03 115 Cf 70
19600 Ferrière 19 137 Bc 78
06750 Ferrière, la 06 158 Ge 86
22210 Ferrière, la 22 64 Xc 60
24240 Ferrière, la 24 136 Ac 80
37110 Ferrière, la 37 85 Ae 63
38580 Ferrière, la 38 132 Ga 77
56930 Ferrière, la 56 64 Xa 61
85280 Ferrière, la 85 97 Ye 68
86390 Ferrière, la 86 112 Af 71
86160 Ferrière-Airoux, la 86 112 Ac 71
14350 Ferrière-au-Doyen, la 14 47 Zb 54
61380 Ferrière-au-Doyen, la 61 49 Ac 57
61450 Ferrière-aux-Etangs, la 61 47 Zc 57
61500 Ferrière-Béchet, la 61 68 Aa 57
61420 Ferrière-Bochard, la 61 68 Zf 58
49500 Ferrière-de-Flée, la 49 83 Za 62
79390 Ferrière-en-Parthenay, la 79 99 Zf 69
52300 Ferrière-et-Lafolie 52 75 Fa 58
14350 Ferrière-Harang, la 14 47 Za 55
59680 Ferrière-la-Grande 59 31 Df 47
59680 Ferrière-la-Petite 59 31 Ea 47
37350 Ferrière-Larçon 37 100 Af 67
17170 Ferrières 17 110 Za 71
21530 Ferrières 21 90 Ea 64
45210 Ferrières 45 72 Ce 60
50640 Ferrières 50 66 Za 57
54210 Ferrières 54 76 Gb 57
60420 Ferrières 60 39 Cd 51
65560 Ferrières 65 174 Ze 90
74370 Ferrières 74 120 Ga 73
80470 Ferrières 80 38 Cb 49
81260 Ferrières 81 166 Cc 87
89480 Ferrières 89 89 Dc 63
77164 Ferrières de Forrières 77 51 Ce 56
76220 Ferrières-en-Bray 76 38 Be 52
27190 Ferrières-Haut-Clocher 27 49 Af 54
61390 Ferrières-la-Verrerie 61 48 Ac 57
25470 Ferrières-le-Lac 25 94 Gf 65
25410 Ferrières-les-Bois 25 107 Fe 65
70130 Ferrières-lès-Ray 70 93 Fe 63
70360 Ferrières-lès-Scey 70 93 Ga 63
34190 Ferrières-les-Verreries 34 154 De 85
34360 Ferrières-Poussarou 34 167 Cf 88
27270 Ferrières-Saint-Hilaire 27 49 Ad 54
15170 Ferrières-Saint-Mary 15 128 Da 77
03250 Ferrières-sur-Sichon 03 116 Dd 72
37600 Ferrière-sur-Beaulieu 37 100 Ba 66
27760 Ferrière-sur-Risle, la 27 49 Ae 55
63290 Ferriers, les 63 116 Dc 73
43300 Ferrussac 43 140 Dc 78
48150 Ferrussac 48 153 Dc 84
25330 Fertans 25 107 Ga 66
36360 Fertay 36 101 Bc 66
36260 Ferté, la 36 102 Ca 66
39600 Ferté, la 39 107 Fd 67
91590 Ferté-Alais, la 91 71 Cc 58
41210 Ferté-Beauharnais, la 41 87 Bf 63
72400 Ferté-Bernard, la 72 69 Ad 59
02270 Ferté-Chevresis, la 02 40 Dd 50
61470* Ferté-en-Ouche, la 61 48 Ac 55
61550 Ferté-Frenel, la 61 49 Ad 55
77320 Ferté-Gaucher, la 77 52 Db 56
03340 Ferté-Hauterive, la 03 116 Dc 70
41300 Ferté-Imbault, la 41 87 Bf 64
89110 Ferté-Loupière, la 89 89 Db 61
61600 Ferté-Macé, la 61 67 Zd 57
02460 Ferté-Milon, la 02 52 Da 53
45240 Ferté-Saint-Aubin, la 45 87 Bf 62
41220 Ferté-Saint-Cyr, la 41 87 Be 63
76440 Ferté-Saint-Samson, la 76 37 Bd 51
77260 Ferté-sous-Jouarre, la 77 52 Da 55
08370 Ferté-sur-Chiers, la 08 42 Fb 51
28340 Ferté-Vidame, la 28 69 Af 57
28220 Ferté-Villeneuil, la 28 69 Bc 61
58270 Fertrève 58 104 Dd 67
68160 Fertrupt 68 77 Hb 59
82150 Férussac 82 149 Af 83
50420 Fervaches 50 46 Yf 55

14140 Fervaques 14 48 Ab 54
80500 Fescamps 80 39 Ce 51
25490 Fesches-le-Châtel 25 94 Gf 63
02450 Fesmy-le-Sart 02 31 De 48
43270 Fespescle 43 141 De 78
28270 Fessanvilliers-Mattanvilliers 28 49 Ba 56
68740 Fessenheim 68 95 Hd 61
67117 Fessenheim-le-Bas 67 58 Hd 57
25470 Fessevillers 25 94 Gf 65
74890 Fessy 74 120 Gc 71
24410 Festalemps 24 124 Ab 77
11300 Festes-et-Saint-André 11 178 Ca 91
02840 Festieux 02 40 De 51
51700 Festigny 51 53 De 54
89480 Festigny 89 89 Dd 63
38119 Festinière, la 38 144 Fe 79
62149 Festubert 62 29 Ce 45
74500 Féternes 74 120 Gd 70
39240 Fétigny 39 119 Fd 70
03130 Fétrez, le 03 116 De 71
08160 Feuchères 08 42 Ee 50
78810 Feucherolles 78 51 Bf 55
62223 Feuchy 62 30 Cf 47
47230 Feugarolles 47 148 Ac 83
19470 Feugeas 19 126 Be 76
50190 Feugères 50 34 Ye 54
27170 Feugérolles 27 49 Ae 54
10150 Feuges 10 73 Ea 58
50360 Feugrey, le 50 46 Yd 52
27110 Feuguerolles 27 49 Ba 54
14320 Feuguerolles-Bully 14 35 Zd 54
14240 Feuguerolles-sur-Seulles 14 34 Zb 54
11510 Feuilla 11 179 Cf 91
16380 Feuillade 16 124 Ac 75
44320 Feuillardais, le 44 96 Ya 65
18320 Feuillarde 18 103 Cf 66
21130 Feuillée, la 21 106 Fc 65
29690 Feuillée, la 29 62 Wa 58
80200 Feuillères 80 39 Cf 49
28170 Feuilleuse 28 69 Ba 57
50190 Feuillie, la 50 33 Yd 53
76220 Feuillie, la 76 37 Bd 52
60960 Feuquières 60 38 Bf 51
80210 Feuquières-en-Vimeu 80 28 Bd 48
70100 Feurg 70 92 Fc 64
42110 Feurs 42 129 Eb 74
36160 Feusines 36 114 Ca 69
29242 Feuteunvelen 29 61 Uf 58
44110 Feuvrais, la 44 82 Yd 62
18300 Feux 18 103 Cf 65
23140 Feuyas 23 114 Ca 71
57280 Fèves 57 56 Ga 53
57420 Féy 57 56 Ga 54
73260 Fey, le 73 133 Gc 76
46300 Feydedie, la 46 137 Bc 80
15160 Feydit 15 128 Da 77
54470 Fey-en-Haye 54 56 Ff 55
38830 Feyjoux, le 38 132 Ga 76
19290 Feyssac 19 126 Ca 74
19340 Feyt 19 127 Cc 74
19320 Feyt, le 19 126 Bf 77
23250 Feyte, la 23 114 Bf 72
87220 Feytiat 87 125 Bb 74
69320 Feyzin 69M 130 Ef 74
18300 Fez 18 103 Ce 65
81500 Fiac 81 165 Bf 86
81490 Fiallesuch 81 166 Cc 87
87150 Fiateau 87 125 Af 74
20117 Fica CTC 182 If 97
20237 Ficaghja = Ficaja CTC 181 Kc 94
20237 Ficaja CTC 181 Kc 94
16330 Fichère, la 16 123 Aa 74
62173 Ficheux 62 29 Ce 47
64410 Fichous-Riumayou 64 162 Zd 88
27190 Fidelaire, le 27 49 Ae 55
39800 Fied, le 39 107 Fe 68
85310 Fief, le 85 109 Ye 69
86450 Fief-Batard 86 100 Ad 68
80670 Fieffes-Montrelet 80 29 Cb 48
62134 Fiefs 62 29 Cb 45
49600 Fief-Sauvin, le 49 97 Yf 65
62132 Fiennes 62 27 Be 44
20228 Fieno CTC 181 Kc 91
80750 Fienvillers 80 29 Cb 48
85680 Fier, le 85 96 Xe 67
14190 Fierville-Bray 14 48 Ze 54
50580 Fierville-les-Mines 50 33 Yb 52
14130 Fierville-les-Parcs 14 48 Ab 53
24140 Fieu, le 24 136 Ac 79
33230 Fieu, le 33 135 Zf 78
02110 Fieulaine 02 40 Dc 49
47600 Fieux 47 148 Ac 84
33850 Fieuzal 33 134 Zc 80
89110 Fièvres, les 89 89 Db 61
19800 Fieyre, la 19 126 Bf 76
20135 Figa CTC 185 Kc 98
12540 Figairol, le 12 153 Db 85
83830 Figanières 83 172 Gc 87
20200 Figarella CTC 181 Kc 92
13123 Figarès 13 169 Ec 87
30440 Figaret 30 153 Dd 85
06450 Figaret-d'Utella, le 06 159 Hb 85
20230 Figareto CTC 181 Kd 94
20114 Figari CTC 185 Ka 100
31260 Figarol 31 164 Af 90
46100 Figeac 46 138 Ca 81
12430 Figeaguet 12 152 Ce 84
87500 Figeas 87 125 Bc 76
17800 Figers 17 123 Zc 75
15380 Fignac 15 127 Cd 77
88410 Fignévelle 88 76 Ff 61
80500 Fignières 80 39 Cd 50
20138 Figoni CTC 184 Ie 98
13510 Figons, les 13 170 Fc 87
47250 Figuès 47 148 Aa 82
12330 Fijaguet 12 152 Cc 82
02000 Filain 02 40 Dd 52
70230 Filain 70 93 Gb 63
18370 Filaine, la 18 114 Cb 69
47110 Filhol 47 149 Ad 82
20140 Filitosa CTC 184 If 98
72210 Fillé 72 84 Aa 61
33840 Fille, la 33 148 Zf 83
74370* Fillière 74 120 Gb 73
54560 Fillières 54 43 Ff 52
62770 Fillièvres 62 29 Ca 47
74250 Fillinges 74 120 Gc 72
66820 Fillols 66 178 Cc 93
74140 Filly 74 120 Gc 71
57320 Filstroff 57 44 Gd 53
88600 Fiménil 88 77 Ge 59
66320 Finestret 66 178 Cd 93
82700 Finhan 82 150 Bb 85
48220 Finialette 48 153 De 82
20090 Finosello, le CTC 182 Ie 97
81440 Finotes 81 165 Cb 86
80360 Fins 80 30 Da 48
25500 Fins, les 25 108 Gd 66
57930 Finstingen = Fénétrange 57 57 Ha 55
58230 Fiole, la 58 104 Df 66
74500 Fion, le 74 121 Gd 71
19300 Fioux 19 126 Ca 76
27210 Fiquefleur-Equainville 27 36 Ab 52
54800 Fiquelmont 54 56 Fe 53
24450 Firbeix 24 125 Af 75
14100 Firfol 14 48 Ab 54
12300 Firmi 12 139 Cb 81
42700 Firminy 42 129 Eb 76
67110 Fischeracker 67 58 Hd 54
51170 Fismes 51 40 De 53
71260 Fissy 71 118 Ee 70
01260 Fitignieu 01 119 Fe 73
38490 Fitilieu 38 131 Fd 75
11510 Fitou 11 179 Cf 91
60600 Fitz-James 60 39 Cc 52
57570 Fixem 57 44 Gb 52
21220 Fixin 21 106 Ef 65
43320 Fix-Saint-Geneys 43 141 De 78
08450 Flaba 08 42 Ef 51
55150 Flabas 55 55 Fc 53
54260 Flabeuville 54 43 Fd 52
72210 Flacé 72 68 Aa 61
21490 Flacey 21 92 Fa 64
28800 Flacey 28 69 Bc 60
71580 Flacey-en-Bresse 71 106 Fc 69
85190 Flachausières, les 85 96 Yb 68
38530 Flachère, la 38 132 Ff 76
38690 Flachères 38 131 Fb 76
44270 Flachou, le 44 96 Yb 67
88120 Flaconnières 88 77 Gd 60
78200 Flacourt 78 50 Bd 55
89190 Flacy 89 73 Dd 59
25330 Flagey 25 107 Ga 66
52250 Flagey 52 92 Fb 62
21640 Flagey-Echézeaux 21 106 Ef 66
21130 Flagey-lès-Auxonne 21 106 Fc 66
12300 Flagnac 12 139 Cb 81
25640 Flagney-Rigney 25 93 Gb 64
70000 Flagy 70 93 Gb 62
71250 Flagy 71 118 Ed 70
77940 Flagy 77 72 Cf 59
08260 Flaignes-Havys 08 41 Ec 50
74300 Flaine 74 121 Ge 72
54110 Flainval 54 76 Gc 57
76740 Flainville 76 37 Af 49
63940 Flaittes 63 129 De 75
50340 Flamanville 50 33 Ya 51
76970 Flamanville 76 37 Af 51
76450 Flamanvillette 76 36 Ae 50
32340 Flamarens 32 149 Ae 84
77114 Flamboin 77 72 Db 58
05700 Flamenche, la 05 156 Fe 82
02260 Flamengrie, la 02 41 Df 48
59570 Flamengrie, la 59 31 De 47
76270 Flaments-Frétils 76 38 Bd 50
21130 Flammerans 21 106 Fc 65
52110 Flammerécourt 52 75 Fa 58
27310 Flancourt-Catelon 27 49 Ae 52
27310 Flancourt-Crescy-en-Roumois 27 37 Ae 53
80120 Flandre 80 28 Be 47
25390 Flangebouche 25 108 Gc 66
84410 Flassan 84 156 Fb 84
83340 Flassans-sur-Issole 83 171 Gb 88
55600 Flassigny 55 43 Fc 52
58420 Flassy 58 104 Dd 65
57320 Flastroff 57 44 Gd 52
63500 Flat, Aulhat- 63 128 Db 75
80200 Flaucourt 80 39 Cf 49
24240 Flaugeac 24 136 Ac 80
46170 Flaugnac, Saint-Paul- 46 150 Bc 83
46320 Flaujac-Gare 46 138 Be 80
46090 Flaujac-Poujols 46 150 Bd 82
33350 Flaujagues 33 135 Aa 80
59440 Flaumont-Waudrechies 59 31 Df 48
81530 Flausines 81 152 Cd 86
30700 Flaux 30 154 Ed 84
12440 Flauzins 12 151 Ca 83
60590 Flavacourt 60 50 Be 52
07000 Flaviac 07 142 Ee 80
87230 Flavignac 87 125 Ba 74
21160 Flavignerot 21 91 Ef 65
02120 Flavigny 02 40 Dd 49
18350 Flavigny 18 103 Ce 67
51190 Flavigny 51 53 Ea 55
57130 Flavigny 57 56 Ff 54
54630 Flavigny-sur-Moselle 54 76 Gb 57
21150 Flavigny-sur-Ozerain 21 91 Ed 63
12450 Flavin 12 152 Cd 83
02520 Flavy-le-Martel 02 40 Db 50
60640 Flavy-le-Meldeux 60 39 Da 50
01350 Flaxieu 01 131 Fe 74
68720 Flaxlanden 68 95 Hb 62
17290 Flay 17 110 Za 72
24600 Flayac 24 124 Ac 77
23260 Flayat 23 127 Cc 74
83780 Flayosc 83 172 Gc 87
83300 Flayosquet, le 83 172 Gc 87
16730 Fléac 16 123 Aa 75
17800 Fléac-sur-Seugne 17 123 Zc 75
72200 Flèche, la 72 84 Zf 62
62960 Fléchin 62 29 Cb 45
80240 Fléchin 80 40 Da 49
62145 Fléchinelle 62 29 Cb 45
13520 Fléchons, les 13 169 Ef 86
60120 Fléchy 60 38 Cb 51
49500 Flée 49 83 Za 62
72500 Flée 72 85 Ac 62
08200 Fleigneux 08 42 Ef 50
57635 Fleisheim 57 57 Ha 56
86300 Fleix 86 112 Ae 69
24130 Fleix, le 24 136 Ab 79
36700 Fléré-la-Rivière 36 100 Ba 66
61100 Flers 61 47 Zc 56
62270 Flers 62 29 Cb 47
80360 Flers 80 30 Ce 48
80160 Flers-sur-Noye 80 38 Cb 50
59267 Flesquières 59 30 Da 48
80260 Flesselles 80 29 Cb 49
57690 Flétrange 57 57 Gd 54
59270 Flêtre 59 30 Cd 44
58170 Fléty 58 104 Df 68
12800 Fleur, la 12 151 Cc 84
16200 Fleurac 16 123 Zf 74
24580 Fleurac 24 137 Ba 78
32500 Fleurance 32 149 Ad 85
86350 Fleuransan 86 112 Ad 71
23320 Fleurat 23 113 Be 71
37530 Fleuray 37 86 Ba 63
62840 Fleurbaix 62 30 Cf 45
61200 Fleuré 61 48 Zf 56
86340 Fleuré 86 112 Ad 70
21320 Fleurey 21 91 Ec 65
70160 Fleurey-lès-Faverney 70 93 Ga 62
70120 Fleurey-lès-Lavoncourt 70 93 Fe 63
70800 Fleurey-lès-Saint-Loup 70 93 Gb 61
21410 Fleurey-sur-Ouche 21 91 Ef 65
28190 Fleurfontaine 28 69 Bb 58
69820 Fleurie 69D 118 Ee 71
03140 Fleuriel 03 116 Db 71
74800 Fleuries, les 74 120 Gb 72
69210 Fleurieux-sur-L'Arbresle 69M 130 Ed 73
89260 Fleurigny 89 72 Dc 59
60700 Fleurines 60 51 Cd 53
35133 Fleurtigné 35 66 Yf 58
71260 Fleurville 71 118 Ef 70
02600 Fleury 02 52 Da 53
11560 Fleury 11 167 Da 89
41500 Fleury 41 86 Bc 62
50800 Fleury 50 46 Ye 55
54800 Fleury 54 56 Ff 53
57420 Fleury 57 56 Gb 54
60240 Fleury 60 51 Bf 53
62134 Fleury 62 29 Cb 46
77540 Fleury 77 52 Cf 57
79110 Fleury 79 111 Ze 72
80160 Fleury 80 38 Ca 50
77930 Fleury-en-Bière 77 71 Cd 58
27480 Fleury-la-Forêt 27 37 Bd 52
71340 Fleury-la-Montagne 71 117 Ea 71
51480 Fleury-la-Rivière 51 53 Df 54
58110 Fleury-la-Tour 58 104 Dd 67
89113 Fleury-la-Vallée 89 89 Dc 61
45400 Fleury-les-Aubrais 45 87 Bf 61
91700 Fleury-Mérogis 91 51 Cc 57
55250 Fleury-sur-Aire 55 55 Fa 54
27380 Fleury-sur-Andelle 27 37 Bc 52
58240 Fleury-sur-Loire 58 103 Db 67
14123 Fleury-sur-Orne 14 35 Zd 54
01470 Flévieu 01 131 Fc 74
08250 Fléville 08 55 Ef 53
54710 Fléville-devant-Nancy 54 56 Gb 57
54150 Fléville-Lixières 54 56 Fe 53
57365 Flévy 57 56 Gb 53
78910 Flexanville 78 50 Be 55
67310 Flexbourg 67 60 Hc 57
71390 Fley 71 105 Ed 68
89800 Fleys 89 90 Df 62
58190 Flez 58 90 Dd 64
58210 Flez 58 89 Dc 64
58190 Flez-Cuzy 58 90 Dd 64
86460 Flier 86 112 Ad 72
08380 Fligny 08 41 Eb 49
38380 Flin 38 132 Fe 77
54122 Flin 54 77 Gd 58
59148 Flines-lez-Raches 59 30 Db 46
78790 Flins-Neuve-Église 78 50 Bd 55
78410 Flins-sur-Seine 78 50 Bf 55
27380 Flipou 27 37 Bb 53
54470 Flirey 54 56 Ff 55
80420 Flixecourt 80 38 Ca 48
08160 Flize 08 42 Ee 50
85300 Flocellière, la 85 96 Yb 67
85700 Flocellière, la 85 98 Za 68
57580 Flocourt 57 56 Gc 55
76260 Flocques 76 28 Bc 48
05300 Flogère, la 05 156 Fe 83
89360 Flogny-la-Chapelle 89 73 Df 61
08600 Flohimont 08 42 Ef 48
08200 Floing 08 42 Ef 50
12200 Floirac 12 151 Bf 83
17120 Floirac 17 122 Zb 76
46600 Floirac 46 138 Bd 79
47360 Floiras 47 149 Ad 83
28100 Flonville 28 50 Bc 56
33270 Florac 33 135 Zc 79
48600 Florac 48 141 De 80
48400 Florac Trois Rivières 48 153 Dd 83
57190 Florange 57 44 Ga 53
88130 Florémont 88 76 Gb 58
33380 Florence 33 134 Za 81
34510 Florensac 34 167 Dc 88
48600 Florensac 48 141 De 80
51800 Florent-en-Argonne 51 54 Ef 54
39320 Florentia 39 119 Fc 70
81150 Florentin 81 151 Ca 85
12140 Florentin-la-Capelle 12 139 Cd 81
46700 Floressas 46 150 Ba 82
83690 Florielle 83 172 Gc 87
33290 Florimond 33 135 Zc 79
90100 Florimont 90 94 Ha 63
24250 Florimont-Gaumier 24 137 Bb 80
64350 Floris 64 162 Zf 88
52130 Flornoy 52 74 Ef 57
38300 Flosaille 38 131 Fb 75
17630 Flotte, la 17 109 Ye 71
50690 Flottemanville-Hague 50 33 Yb 51
46090 Flottes 46 150 Bc 82
33190 Floudès 33 135 Zf 81
11800 Floure 11 166 Cc 89
72800 Flourière, la 72 84 Aa 62
59440 Floursies 59 31 Df 47
59219 Floyon 59 31 Df 48
73590 Flumet 73 133 Gd 74
02590 Fluquières 02 40 Da 50
01140 Fluriex 01 118 Ee 72
80540 Flury 80 38 Ca 49
58210 Fly 58 89 Dc 64
55400 Foameix-Ornel 55 55 Fd 53
20100 Foce CTC 184 Ka 99
20100 Foce di Bilia CTC 184 If 99
20212 Focicchia CTC 183 Kb 95
20100 Foci di Bila = Foce di Bilia CTC 184 If 99
18500 Foëcy 18 102 Ca 65
22800 Fœil, le 22 64 Xa 58
29252 Foën, le 29 62 Wb 57
63970 Fohet 63 128 Da 75
02140 Foigny 02 41 Df 49
22600 Foil-Marreuc 22 64 Xb 59
08600 Foisches 08 42 Ee 48
12260 Foissac 12 138 Ca 81
30700 Foissac 30 154 Eb 84
01340 Foissiat 01 118 Fb 70
21230 Foissy 21 105 Ed 66
89450 Foissy-lès-Vézelay 89 90 De 64
89190 Foissy-sur-Vanne 89 72 Dd 59
42260 Foive 42 117 Ea 73
09000 Foix 09 177 Bd 91
37150 Foix 37 86 Ba 65
23270 Folbeix 23 114 Ca 71
31290 Folcarde 31 165 Be 88
07140 Folcheran 07 154 Ea 82
20213 Folelli CTC 181 Kd 94
02670 Folembray 02 40 Db 51
68220 Folgensbourg 68 95 Hc 63
22400 Folgoat 22 63 Wf 57
29260 Folgoët, le 29 62 Vd 57
14710 Folie, la 14 34 Za 53
27220 Folie, la 27 50 Bb 55
52500 Folie, la 52 92 Fd 62
89160 Folie, la 89 90 Eb 62
28150 Folie-Herbault, la 28 70 Bd 59
80170 Folies 80 39 Ce 50
77140 Foljuif 77 71 Ce 59
57600 Folkling 57 57 Gf 54
78520 Follainville-Dennemont 78 50 Be 54
87250 Folles 87 113 Bc 72
41240 Folletière, la 41 86 Bc 61
76190 Folletière, la 76 36 Ae 51
14290 Folletière-Abenon, la 14 48 Ac 55
27190 Folleville 27 49 Af 54
27230 Folleville 27 49 Ad 54
56580 Folleville 56 64 Xb 60
80250 Folleville 80 39 Cc 50
50320 Folligny 50 46 Yd 56
76660 Folny 76 37 Bc 49
57200 Folpersviller 57 57 Ha 54
57730 Folschviller 57 57 Ge 54
87380 Fombeaux 87 125 Bc 75
19410 Fombiardes, les 19 125 Bc 76
24220 Fomboise 24 136 Ac 80
88390 Fomerey 88 76 Gc 59
79340 Fomperron 79 111 Zf 70
31140 Fonbeauzard 31 164 Bc 86
12190 Fonbillou 12 139 Cd 81
21260 Foncegrive 21 92 Fa 63
80700 Fonches 80 39 Ce 50
39520 Foncine-le-Bas 39 107 Ga 69
39460 Foncine-le-Haut 39 107 Ga 69
81430 Foncouvete 81 151 Cb 85
62111 Foncquevillers 62 29 Cd 48
12540 Fondamente 12 152 Da 85
38580 Fond-de-France, le 38 132 Ga 77
32810 Fond-du-Bois 32 163 Ad 86
33220 Fondefière 33 136 Ab 80
58500 Fondelin 58 89 Dc 64
37230 Fondettes 37 85 Ad 64
62140 Fondeval, le 62 28 Bf 47
37140 Fondis, les 37 84 Aa 65
70190 Fondremand 70 93 Ga 64
12150 Fonds, les 12 152 Da 82
86460 Fonfadour, la 86 112 Ad 72
58350 Fonfaye 58 89 Db 65
19170 Fonfreyde 19 126 Ca 75
18150 Fonfrin 18 103 Cf 67
24170 Fongalop 24 137 Af 80
47260 Fongrave 47 149 Ad 82
76280 Fonguesemare 76 36 Ab 50
24400 Fonmoure 24 136 Ac 78
82000 Fonneuve 82 150 Bc 84
24500 Fonroque 24 136 Ac 80
07200 Fons 07 142 Ec 81
30730 Fons 30 154 Eb 85
46100 Fons 46 138 Bf 81
31130 Fonsegrives 31 165 Bd 87
02110 Fonsommes 02 40 Dc 49
31470 Fonsorbes 31 164 Bb 87
87440 Fonsoumagne 87 124 Ae 74
30580 Fons-sur-Lussan 30 154 Eb 83
16170 Fontafie 16 124 Ad 73
38350 Fontagnieu 38 144 Ff 79
25660 Fontain 25 107 Ga 65
10200 Fontaine 10 74 Ee 59
24320 Fontaine 24 124 Ac 76
27320 Fontaine 27 50 Bb 56
28500 Fontaine 28 50 Bc 56
38600 Fontaine 38 131 Fe 77
45130 Fontaine 45 87 Bd 61
59330 Fontaine 59 31 Df 47
73460 Fontaine 73 132 Gb 75
77570 Fontaine 77 71 Ce 60
79190 Fontaine 79 111 Ab 72
83630 Fontaine 83 171 Ga 86
85560 Fontaine 85 109 Yd 70
86130 Fontaine 86 99 Ac 69
90150 Fontaine 90 94 Ha 63
50500 Fontaine, la 50 33 Ye 53
76480 Fontaine, la 76 37 Af 52
73600 Fontaine, Salins- 73 133 Gd 76
59550 Fontaine-au-Bois 59 31 Dd 48
51210 Fontaine-au-Bron 51 53 Dd 55
59157 Fontaine-au-Pire 59 30 Dc 48
27600 Fontaine-Bellenger 27 50 Bb 53
77300 Fontainebleau 77 71 Ce 58
60360 Fontaine-Bonneleau 60 38 Ca 51
39140 Fontainebrux 39 106 Fc 68
60300 Fontaine-Châalis 60 51 Ce 53
17510 Fontaine-Chalendray 17 111 Ze 73
32360 Fontaine-Chaude 32 148 Ac 86
53350 Fontaine-Couverte 53 83 Yf 61
51120 Fontaine-Denis-Nuisy 51 53 De 57
84800 Fontaine-de-Vaucluse 84 156 Fa 85
76440 Fontaine-en-Bray 76 37 Bc 50
51800 Fontaine-en-Dormois 51 54 Ee 53
14790 Fontaine-Etoupefour 14 35 Zd 54
77480 Fontaine-Fourches 77 72 Dc 58
21610 Fontaine-Française 21 92 Fc 63
49250 Fontaine-Guérin 49 84 Ze 64
14220 Fontaine-Halbout 14 47 Zd 55
14610 Fontaine-Henry 14 35 Zd 53
27490 Fontaine-Heudebourg 27 49 Bb 54
27470 Fontaine-L'Abbé 27 49 Ae 54
89100 Fontaine-la-Gaillarde 89 72 Dc 59
28190 Fontaine-la-Guyon 28 69 Bb 58
27230 Fontaine-la-Louvet 27 48 Ac 54
76290 Fontaine-la-Mallet 76 36 Aa 51
27550 Fontaine-la-Soret 27 49 Ae 54
60690 Fontaine-Lavaganne 60 38 Bf 51
76690 Fontaine-le-Bourg 76 37 Ba 51
86240 Fontaine-le-Comte 86 112 Ab 69
76740 Fontaine-le-Dun 76 37 Af 50
48400 Fontaine-le-Mazet 48 153 Dd 83
14190 Fontaine-le-Pin 14 47 Ze 55
77590 Fontaine-le-Port 77 71 Ce 58
61160 Fontaine-les-Bassets 61 48 Aa 55
62134 Fontaine-lès-Boulans 62 29 Cb 46
80340 Fontaine-lès-Cappy 80 39 Ce 49
02680 Fontaine-lès-Clercs 02 40 Db 50
25340 Fontaine-lès-Clerval 25 94 Gd 64
41800 Fontaine-les-Côteaux 41 85 Ae 62
62128 Fontaine-lès-Croisilles 62 30 Cf 47
21121 Fontaine-lès-Dijon 21 91 Fa 64
80140 Fontaine-le-Sec 80 38 Be 49
10280 Fontaine-les-Grès 10 73 Df 58
62550 Fontaine-lès-Hermans 62 29 Cc 45
70800 Fontaine-lès-Luxeuil 70 93 Gc 61
28170 Fontaine-les-Ribouts 28 50 Bb 57
02140 Fontaine-lès-Vervins 02 41 Df 49
62390 Fontaine-L'Etalon 62 29 Ca 47
10150 Fontaine-Luyères 10 73 Eb 58
10400 Fontaine-Mâcon 10 72 Dd 58
49140 Fontaine-Milon 49 84 Ze 63
02110 Fontaine-Notre-Dame 02 40 Dc 49
59400 Fontaine-Notre-Dame 59 30 Da 48
41270 Fontaine-Raoul 41 69 Ba 61
71150 Fontaines 71 105 Ee 67
89130 Fontaines 89 89 Db 62
89150 Fontaines 89 72 Da 59
85200 Fontaines, Doix lès 85 110 Zb 70
22170 Fontaines, les 22 64 Xa 57
50340 Fontaines, les 50 33 Yb 51
60480 Fontaine-Saint-Lucien 60 38 Ca 51
72330 Fontaine-Saint-Martin, la 72 84 Aa 62
21450 Fontaines-en-Duesmois 21 91 Ed 63
41250 Fontaines-en-Sologne 41 86 Bd 63
28240 Fontaine-Simon 28 69 Ba 57
21330 Fontaines-les-Sèches 21 90 Ec 62
27120 Fontaine-sous-Jouy 27 50 Bb 54
77560 Fontaine-sous-Montaiguillon 77 72 Dd 57
80500 Fontaine-sous-Montdidier 80 39 Cd 51
76160 Fontaine-sous-Préaux 76 37 Bb 52
55110 Fontaines-Saint-Clair 55 42 Fb 52
69270 Fontaines-Saint-Martin 69M 130 Ef 73
52170 Fontaines-sur-Marne 52 75 Fa 57
69270 Fontaines-sur-Saône 69M 130 Ef 73
51160 Fontaine-sur-Ay 51 53 Ea 54
51320 Fontaine-sur-Coole 51 54 Ec 56
80150 Fontaine-sur-Maye 80 28 Bf 47
02110 Fontaine-Uterte 02 40 Dc 49
74570 Fontaine-Vive 74 120 Gb 72
77370 Fontains 77 72 Da 57
06540 Fontan 06 159 Hd 84
34310 Fontanche 34 167 Cf 88
AD600 Fontaneda ◘ AND 177 Bc 94
12640 Fontaneilles 12 152 Da 83
15230 Fontanes 15 139 Cf 79
30250 Fontanès 30 154 Ea 86
34270 Fontanès 34 154 Df 86
42140 Fontanès 42 130 Ec 75
46230 Fontanes 46 150 Bc 83
48300 Fontanes, Naussac- 48 141 De 80
11140 Fontanès-de-Sault 11 178 Ca 92
46240 Fontanes-du-Causse 46 138 Bd 81
15140 Fontanges 15 139 Cd 78
21390 Fontangy 21 90 Ec 64
23110 Fontanières 23 115 Cd 72
05200 Fontaniers, les 05 145 Gc 81
38120 Fontanil-Cornillon 38 131 Fe 77
42600 Fontannes 42 129 Ea 75
43100 Fontannes 43 128 Dc 77
43320 Fontannes 43 141 De 78
43500 Fontannes 43 129 De 77
48700 Fontans 48 140 Dc 80
10110 Fontarce 10 74 Ed 60
30580 Fontarèches 30 154 Ec 84
47310 Fontarède 47 148 Ac 84
23110 Fontauble 23 115 Cc 72
17200 Fontbedeau 17 122 Za 74

A B C D E F G H I J K L M N O P Q R S T U V W X Y Z

Fontbedeau | 269

81260 Fontbelle 81 166 Cc 87
36150 Fontbon 36 101 Be 66
07240 Fontbonne 07 142 Ed 79
81140 Fontbonne 81 150 Be 84
83320 Fontbrun 83 171 Ga 90
83630 Font-Castellan 83 171 Gb 86
43300 Fontchave 43 140 Dc 78
63970 Fontclairant 63 127 Cf 74
16230 Fontclaireau 16 111 Ab 73
63630 Fontcourbe 63 128 Dd 76
11700 Fontcouverte 11 166 Ce 89
17100 Fontcouverte 17 122 Zc 74
66300 Fontcouverte 66 179 Cd 93
73300 Fontcouverte 73 132 Gb 77
83149 Font-Couverte 83 171 Ff 88
26110 Font-de-Barrat 26 155 Fa 83
31160 Font-de-la-Vielle 31 176 Af 90
34150 Font-du-Griffe, la 34 167 Dc 86
76890 Fontelaye, la 76 37 Af 50
61420 Fontenai-les-Louvets 61 68 Zf 57
37370 Fontenaille 37 85 Ad 63
14400 Fontenailles 14 47 Zb 53
77370 Fontenailles 77 72 Cf 57
89480 Fontenailles 89 89 Dc 63
89560 Fontenailles 89 89 Dc 63
61200 Fontenai-sur-Orne 61 48 Zf 56
18330 Fontenay 18 87 Cb 65
27510 Fontenay 27 50 Bd 53
36150 Fontenay 36 101 Be 66
36400 Fontenay 36 102 Ca 69
50140 Fontenay 50 66 Yf 57
71120 Fontenay 71 117 Eb 70
76290 Fontenay 76 35 Ab 51
79100 Fontenay 79 99 Ze 67
88600 Fontenay 88 77 Gd 59
10400 Fontenay-de-Bossery 10 72 Dc 58
95190 Fontenay-en-Parisis 95 51 Cc 54
85200 Fontenay-le-Comte 85 110 Zb 70
78330 Fontenay-le-Fleury 78 51 Ca 56
14320 Fontenay-le-Marmion 14 47 Zd 54
14250 Fontenay-le-Pesnel 14 47 Zc 53
91640 Fontenay-lès-Briis 91 71 Ca 57
91540 Fontenay-le-Vicomte 91 71 Cc 57
78200 Fontenay-Mauvoisin 78 50 Bd 55
89800 Fontenay-près-Chablis 89 90 De 61
89450 Fontenay-près-Vézelay 89 90 De 64
78440 Fontenay-Saint-Père 78 50 Be 54
89660 Fontenay-sous-Fouronnes 89 89 Dd 63
28140 Fontenay-sur-Conie 28 70 Bd 60
28630 Fontenay-sur-Eure 28 70 Bc 58
45210 Fontenay-sur-Loing 45 71 Ce 60
50310 Fontenay-sur-Mer 50 34 Ye 52
72350 Fontenay-sur-Vègre 72 84 Ze 61
60380 Fontenay-Torcy 60 38 Be 51
77610 Fontenay-Trésigny 77 52 Cf 56
16300 Fonteneaux, les 16 123 Ze 76
77460 Fonte-Neilles 77 71 Ce 59
02170 Fontenelle 02 41 Df 48
08260 Fontenelle 08 41 Eb 49
16170 Fontenelle 16 123 Zf 74
21610 Fontenelle 21 92 Fc 63
24700 Fontenelle 24 135 Aa 78
89140 Fontenelle 89 72 Da 59
90340 Fontenelle 90 94 Gf 63
35560 Fontenelle, la 35 66 Yc 58
37530 Fontenelle, la 37 86 Af 64
41270 Fontenelle, la 41 69 Ba 60
02540 Fontenelle-en-Brie 02 53 Dc 55
25340 Fontenelle-Montby 25 93 Gc 64
25210 Fontenelles, les 25 108 Ge 65
88240 Fontenelles, les 88 76 Gb 61
14380 Fontenermont 14 46 Yf 56
17400 Fontenet 17 111 Zd 73
71430 Fontenette 71 117 Ea 69
16230 Fontenille 16 111 Aa 73
24480 Fontenille 24 137 Af 79
63320 Fontenille 63 128 Da 75
79110 Fontenille 79 111 Zf 72
89660 Fontenille 89 89 De 63
31470 Fontenilles 31 164 Bb 87
24550 Fontenilles-d'Aigueparse 24 137 Ba 81
70190 Fontenis, les 70 93 Ga 64
70210 Fontenois-la-Ville 70 93 Ga 61
70230 Fontenois-lès-Montbozon 70 93 Gb 64
25130 Fontenottes, les 25 108 Gd 66
89120 Fontenouilles 89 89 Da 61
02290 Fontenoy 02 40 Db 52
89520 Fontenoy 89 89 Db 63
54122 Fontenoy-la-Joûte 54 77 Gd 58
88240 Fontenoy-le-Château 88 76 Gb 61
54840 Fontenoy-sur-Moselle 54 56 Ff 56
39130 Fontenu 39 107 Fe 68
39110 Fonteny 39 107 Ff 67
57590 Fonteny 57 57 Gc 55
34320 Fontès 34 167 Dc 87
24510 Fontesteyenie 24 137 Af 79
33190 Fontet 33 135 Zf 81
71160 Fontête 71 117 De 69
10360 Fontette 10 74 Ed 60
21540 Fontette 21 91 Ee 64
19170 Fontevialle 19 126 Be 75
49590 Fontevraud-L'Abbaye 49 99 Aa 65
63122 Fontfreide 63 128 Da 74
05350 Fontgillarde 05 145 Gf 80
36220 Fontgombault 36 100 Af 68
36230 Fontguenand 36 101 Bd 65
04230 Fontienne 04 156 Fe 84
11310 Fontiers-Cabardès 11 166 Cb 88
30000 Fontilles, les 30 154 Ec 85
11360 Fontjoncouse 11 179 Ce 90
63310 Fontmarcel 63 128 Cf 75
19120 Fontmerle 19 138 Bf 79
86250 Fontmoran 86 112 Ac 71
86290 Fontmorond 86 113 Ba 70
42130 Fontobé 42 129 Ea 74
60510 Fontomettes, les 60 38 Bf 52
19190 Fontourcy 19 138 Be 78
57650 Fontoy 57 43 Ga 52
66360 Fontpédrouse 66 178 Cb 93
03160 Font-Picard, la 03 115 Cf 69
86300 Fontprévoir 86 112 Ae 69
66210 Fontrabiouse 66 178 Ca 93
65220 Fontrailles 65 163 Ac 88
81260 Fontrieu 81 166 Cd 87
66120 Font-Romeu 66 178 Bf 93
05100 Fonts, les 05 145 Ge 79
48500 Fonts, les 48 153 Db 82
17150 Fontsablouse 17 122 Zc 76
63210 Fontsalive 63 127 Cf 75
07250 Fonts-du-Pouzin, les 07 142 Ee 80
38740 Font-Turbat 38 144 Gb 79
10190 Fontvannes 10 73 Df 59
13990 Fontvieille 13 169 Ee 86
23300 Font-Vieillé 23 113 Bc 71
28210 Fonville 28 50 Bc 56
57600 Forbach 57 57 Gf 53
29430 Forban 29 62 Ve 56
83136 Forcalqueiret 83 171 Ga 88
04300 Forcalquier 04 156 Fe 85
53260 Forcé 53 67 Zb 60
11270 Force, la 11 165 Ca 89
24130 Force, la 24 136 Ac 79
54330 Forcelles-Saint-Gorgon 54 76 Ga 58
54930 Forcelles-sous-Gugney 54 76 Ga 58
32170 Forcets 32 163 Ab 88
80560 Forceville 80 29 Cd 48
80140 Forceville-en-Vimeu 80 38 Be 49
52700 Forcey 52 75 Fc 60
20259 Forcili CTC 180 If 93
20190 Forciolo CTC 184 Ka 97
74200 Forclaz, la 74 120 Gd 71
58330 Forcy 58 104 Dc 65
08220 Forest 08 41 Eb 51
04140 Forest, le 04 157 Gb 83
04200 Forest, le 04 157 Ff 84
05560 Forest, le 05 145 Gd 81
05700 Forest, le 05 144 Fe 82
56550 Forest, le 56 79 Wf 62
02590 Foreste 02 40 Da 50
62560 Forestel 62 29 Ca 45
59222 Forest-en-Cambrésis 59 31 Dd 48
80960 Foresterie, la 87 125 Ba 75
51120 Forestière, la 51 53 Dd 57
80150 Forest-L'Abbaye 80 28 Be 47
04250 Forest-Lacour 04 157 Ga 82
29800 Forest-Landerneau, la 29 62 Ve 58
80120 Forest-Montiers 80 28 Be 47
05260 Forest-Saint-Julien 05 144 Ga 81
59510 Forest-sur-Marque 59 30 Db 45
03420 Forêt, la 03 115 Cd 71
13104 Forêt, la 13 169 Ee 87
14330 Forêt, la 14 34 Yf 53
17460 Forêt, la 17 122 Zb 74
21290 Forêt, la 21 91 Ef 62
23400 Forêt, la 23 113 Bd 73
24380 Forêt, la 24 137 Ae 78
24590 Forêt, la 24 137 Bc 78
24700 Forêt, la 24 136 Aa 78
27180 Forêt, la 27 49 Af 54
33660 Forêt, la 33 135 Aa 78
36310 Forêt, la 36 113 Bb 70
49640 Forêt, la 49 84 Zd 62
53700 Forêt, la 53 67 Ze 59
54480 Forêt, la 54 77 Gf 57
58500 Forêt, la 58 89 Dc 64
63740 Forêt, la 63 127 Ce 74
71360 Forêt, la 71 105 Ed 67
83670 Forêt, la 83 171 Ff 87
88240 Forêt, la 88 76 Gb 60
61210 Forêt-Auvray, la 61 47 Zd 56
89310 Forêt-Bréault 89 90 Df 62
10130 Forêt-Chenu 10 73 Df 60
02510 Forêt d'Andigny 02 40 Dd 48
16240 Forêt-de-Tessé, la 16 111 Aa 72
27220 Forêt-du-Parc, la 27 50 Bb 55
23360 Forêt-du-Temple, la 23 114 Bf 70
29940 Forêt-Fouesnant, la 29 78 Wa 61
27510 Forêt-la-Folie 27 50 Bd 53
91410 Forêt-le-Roi, la 91 70 Ca 58
01340 Forêts, les 01 118 Fa 70
91150 Forêt-Sainte-Croix, la 91 71 Cb 58
79380 Forêt-sur-Sèvre, la 79 98 Zc 68
77165 Forfry 77 52 Cf 54
58160 Forge 58 103 Db 67
71220 Forge 71 117 Ec 69
09110 Forge, la 09 178 Bf 92
14350 Forge, la 14 47 Za 55
24580 Forge, la 24 137 Ba 78
44520 Forge, la 44 82 Yd 63
47700 Forge, la 47 148 Aa 83
87440 Forge, la 87 124 Ae 74
88530 Forge, la 88 77 Ge 60
24630 Forge-des-Feynières 24 125 Ba 75
88270 Forge-de-Thunimont, la 88 76 Gb 60
50680 Forge Fallot, la 50 34 Yf 53
87200 Forgeix 87 112 Ae 73
17290 Forges 17 110 Za 72
19380 Forgès 19 138 Bf 78
49700 Forges 49 99 Ze 65
58310 Forges 58 89 Db 64
61250 Forges 61 68 Aa 58
08270 Forges, les 08 41 Ec 51
17430 Forges, les 17 110 Zb 73
21120 Forges, les 21 91 Fa 63
22460 Forges, les 22 64 Xb 59
23160 Forges, les 23 113 Bd 70
23230 Forges, les 23 114 Cb 71
23450 Forges, les 23 114 Be 70
40160 Forges, les 40 146 Za 83
42720 Forges, les 42 117 Ea 72
49370 Forges, les 49 83 Za 63
50480 Forges, les 50 33 Ye 52
50500 Forges, les 50 46 Yd 53
56120 Forges, les 56 64 Xc 60
76170 Forges, les 76 36 Ac 51
79340 Forges, les 79 111 Zf 69
88390 Forges, les 88 76 Gc 59
89160 Forges, les 89 90 Eb 62
35380 Forges-de-Paimpont, les 35 65 Xf 61
35640 Forges-la-Forêt 35 82 Ye 61
91470 Forges-les-Bains 91 51 Ca 57
76440 Forges-les-Eaux 76 37 Bd 51
55110 Forges-sur-Meuse 55 55 Fb 53
23220 Forgette, la 23 114 Bf 70
23160 Forgevielle 23 113 Bd 71
31370 Forgues 31 164 Ba 88
63600 Forie, la 63 129 De 75
63890 Forie, la 63 128 Dd 75
21460 Forléans 21 90 Eb 64
14340 Formentin 14 35 Aa 53
60220 Formerie 60 38 Be 51
14710 Formigny 14 47 Za 52
14710 Formigny La Bataille 14 47 Za 52
66210 Formiguères 66 178 Ca 93
74490 Fornets, les 74 120 Gd 71
79230 Fors 79 111 Zd 71
68320 Forschwihr 68 60 Hc 60
29460 Forsqully 29 62 Vf 58
67480 Forstfeld 67 59 Ia 55
67580 Forstheim 67 58 He 55
29710 Fort, le 29 78 Ve 60
77320 Fortail 77 52 Db 56
41360 Fortan 41 86 Af 61
31560 Fortanié 31 165 Bd 89
62162 Fort-Bâtard 62 27 Ca 43
56270 Fort-Bloqué, le 56 79 Wd 62
11330 Fort de Razouls 11 178 Cc 91
39150 Fort-du-Plasne 39 107 Ff 69
62270 Fortel-en-Artois 62 29 Cb 47
52150 Fortelle, la 52 75 Fc 59
17700 Fortenuzay 17 110 Zb 71
38590 Forteresse, la 38 131 Fc 77
67480 Fort-Louis 67 59 Ia 56
80120 Fort-Mahon-Plage 80 28 Bd 46
59430 Fort-Mardyck 59 27 Cb 42
27210 Fort-Moville 27 48 Ac 52
62370 Fort-Saint-Jean, le 62 27 Ca 43
15300 Fortuniez 15 127 Cf 77
62730 Fort-Vert, le 62 27 Bf 43
31440 Fos 31 176 Ae 91
34320 Fos 34 167 Db 87
46310 Fos 46 137 Bc 81
56120 Fossac 56 64 Xc 61
09130 Fossat, le 09 164 Bc 89
48800 Fossat, le 48 141 Df 81
08240 Fossé 08 42 Fa 52
41330 Fossé 41 86 Bb 63
58430 Fosse 58 104 Ea 66
66220 Fosse 66 178 Cc 92
30800 Fosse, la 30 169 Ec 87
53100 Fosse, la 53 67 Zb 59
62136 Fosse, la 62 29 Ce 45
72430 Fosse, la 72 84 Zf 61
85630 Fosse, la 85 96 Xe 67
88240 Fosse, la 88 76 Gb 61
76440 Fossé, le 76 38 Bd 51
08430 Fosse-à-L'Eau, la 08 41 Ed 50
49700 Fosse-Bellay 49 99 Ze 65
10100 Fosse-Corduan, la 10 73 Dd 58
41100 Fosse-Courtin, la 41 85 Af 61
49540 Fosse-de-Tigné, la 49 98 Zd 65
24210 Fossemagne 24 137 Af 78
80160 Fossemanant 80 38 Cb 50
60620 Fosse-Martin 60 52 Cf 54
44170 Fossé-Neuf, le 44 82 Yb 63
85600 Fossé-Neuf, le 85 97 Ye 67
49150 Fosse-Porée 49 84 Zf 63
88100 Fosses 88 77 Gf 59
95470 Fosses 95 51 Cd 54
10360 Fosses, les 10 74 Ed 60
23700 Fosses, les 23 115 Cd 72
79360 Fosses, les 79 111 Zd 72
79800 Fosses, les 79 111 Zf 70
60530 Fosse-Saint-Clair, la 60 51 Cb 53
33190 Fossés-et-Baleyssac 33 135 Aa 81
08380 Fosses-Rousseaux 08 41 Eb 49
83980 Fossette, la 83 172 Gc 90
60540 Fosseuse 60 51 Cb 53
62810 Fosseux 62 29 Cd 47
57590 Fossieux 57 56 Gb 55
02650 Fossoy 02 53 Dc 54
89140 Fossoy 89 72 Da 59
13270 Fos-sur-Mer 13 170 Ef 88
50680 Fotelaie, la 50 34 Yf 53
41310 Fouasserie, la 41 85 Af 62
42400 Fouay 42 130 Ec 76
03230 Foubrac 03 116 Dc 69
89520 Foucards, les 89 89 Db 63
76340 Foucarmont 76 37 Bd 49
76640 Foucart 76 36 Ad 51
50480 Foucarville 50 34 Ye 52
80340 Foucaucourt-en-Santerre 80 39 Ce 49
80140 Foucaucourt-Hors-Nesle 80 38 Be 49
55250 Foucaucourt-sur-Thabas 55 55 Fa 54
16620 Foucaud 16 123 Aa 77
44670 Foucaudais, la 44 82 Ye 63
53160 Foucault 53 67 Zd 59
18240 Fouchards, les 18 88 Cf 64
70160 Fouchécourt 70 93 Ff 62
88320 Fouchécourt 88 76 Ff 60
25620 Foucherans 25 107 Ga 66
39100 Foucherans 39 106 Fc 66
10260 Fouchères 10 74 Eb 60
77171 Fouchères 77 72 Dc 57
55500 Fouchères-aux-Bois 55 55 Fb 57
45320 Foucherolles 45 72 Da 60
89150 Fouchgres 89 72 Da 59
88650 Fouchifol 88 77 Ha 59
67220 Fouchy 67 60 Hb 59
27220 Foucrainville 27 50 Bb 55
03390 Foucrière, la 03 115 Cf 70
67130 Fouday 67 77 Hb 58
49124 Foudon 49 84 Zd 64
29170 Fouenant = Fouesnant 29 78 Vf 61
80440 Fouenchamps 80 39 Cc 50
70600 Fouent-le-Bas 70 92 Fe 63
70600 Fouent-Saint-Andoche 70 92 Fd 63
29170 Fouesnant 29 78 Vf 61
73540 Fouette, la 73 132 Gc 75
62130 Foufflin-Ricametz 62 29 Cc 46
54570 Foug 54 56 Fe 56
31160 Fougaron 31 176 Af 91
09300 Fougax-et-Barrineuf 09 178 Bf 91
50530 Fougeray, le 50 46 Yd 56
49150 Fougeré 49 84 Zf 63
85480 Fougeré 85 97 Ye 69
86160 Fougeré 86 112 Ab 71
73230 Fougère, la 73 132 Ga 75
33230 Fougereau 33 135 Aa 78
37290 Fougereau 37 100 Ba 67
19560 Fougères 19 126 Bd 77
35300 Fougères = Felger 35 66 Ye 58
41120 Fougères-sur-Bièvres 41 86 Bc 64
56200 Fougerêts, les 56 81 Xe 62
79150 Fougereuse, la 79 98 Zd 66
17380 Fougerolle 17 110 Zb 73
36170 Fougerolles 36 113 Bb 70
36230 Fougerolles 36 114 Bf 69
37140 Fougerolles 37 84 Ab 65
70220 Fougerolles 70 93 Gc 61
70220 Fougerolles-le-Château 70 93 Gc 61
89520 Fougilet 89 89 Dc 63
33220 Fougueyrolles 33 136 Ab 79
12270 Fouillade, la 12 151 Ca 83
88490 Fouillaupré 88 77 Hb 59
36500 Fouillereau 36 101 Bd 67
05130 Fouillouse 05 144 Ga 82
26300 Fouillouse 26 142 Ef 79
42480 Fouillouse, la 42 129 Eb 75
86370 Fouilloux 86 111 Ab 70
16140 Fouilloux, le 16 123 Aa 73
17270 Fouilloux, le 17 123 Zf 77
04530 Fouillouze 04 145 Ge 81
80800 Fouilloy 80 39 Cc 49
60220 Fouilly 60 38 Be 50
77390 Foujou 77 72 Ce 57
52800 Foulain 52 75 Fb 60
15130 Foulan 15 139 Cc 79
60250 Foulanges 60 51 Cb 53
47370 Foulanou 47 149 Af 82
47510 Foulayronnes 47 149 Ad 83
27210 Foulbec 27 36 Ac 52
57830 Foulcrey 57 57 Gf 57
24380 Fouleix 24 136 Ae 79
39230 Foulenay 39 106 Fc 67
57220 Fouligny 57 57 Gd 54
15400 Foulioux 15 139 Cd 77
60190 Foulliese 60 39 Cd 52
14240 Foulognes 14 34 Zb 54
36200 Foulon 36 101 Bd 69
50680 Foulons, les 50 34 Yf 53
30750 Foulquarie, la 30 153 Db 84
87190 Foulventour 87 113 Bb 71
08260 Foulzy 08 41 Ec 49
43430 Foumourette 43 141 Eb 78
16410 Fouquebrune 16 124 Ab 75
62232 Fouquereuil 62 29 Cd 45
60510 Fouquerolles 60 38 Cb 52
80170 Fouquescourt 80 39 Ce 50
16140 Fouqueure 16 111 Aa 73
27370 Fouqueville 27 49 Af 53
62640 Fouquières 62 30 Cf 46
62232 Fouquières-les-Béthune 62 29 Cd 45
14540 Four 14 35 Ze 54
38080 Four 38 131 Fb 75
43290 Four 43 142 Eb 78
36370 Four, le 36 113 Bb 70
31550 Fourane, la 31 164 Bc 89
17450 Fouras 17 110 Yf 73
35800 Fourberie, la 35 65 Xf 57
44420 Fourbihan 44 81 Xd 64
32250 Fourcès 32 148 Ab 85
58600 Fourchambault 58 103 Da 66
71120 Fourche, la 71 117 Ec 70
14620 Fourches 14 48 Zf 55
36130 Fourches 36 101 Be 68
66300 Fourches 66 179 Ce 93
63940 Fourcheval 63 129 De 76
89400 Fourchotte, la 89 72 Dc 60
80290 Fourcigny 80 38 Be 50
62380 Fourdebecques 62 29 Ca 44
02870 Fourdrain 02 40 Dc 51
80310 Fourdrinoy 80 38 Ca 49
07290 Fourel 07 142 Ed 78
32600 Fourès 32 164 Ba 87
25440 Fourg 25 107 Fe 66
27630 Fourges 27 50 Bd 54
63420 Fourges 63 128 Da 76
25300 Fourgs, les 25 108 Gc 67
34700 Fourille, la 34 167 Db 86
03140 Fourilles 03 116 Db 71
03140 Fourillette 03 116 Da 71
46100 Fourmagnac 46 138 Bf 81
59440 Fourmanoir 59 31 Df 48
27500 Fourmetot 27 36 Ad 52
59610 Fourmies 59 41 Ea 48
33250 Fournas 33 122 Zb 77
89320 Fournaudin 89 73 Dd 60
17250 Fourne 17 122 Zb 74
23200 Fourneaux 23 114 Ca 72
42470 Fourneaux 42 117 Eb 73
45380 Fourneaux 45 87 Be 61
50420 Fourneaux 50 46 Yf 55
73500 Fourneaux 73 145 Gd 77
89210 Fourneaux 89 73 Dd 60
45210 Fourneaux, les 45 72 Cf 60
14700 Fourneaux-le-Val 14 48 Ze 55
48310 Fournels 48 140 Da 80
41310 Fournerie, la 41 85 Af 63
11380 Fournès 11 166 Cc 88
30210 Fournès 30 155 Ed 85
11600 Fournes-Cabardès 11 166 Cc 88
59134 Fournes-en-Weppes 59 30 Cf 45
73230 Fournet 73 132 Ff 75
87120 Fournet, le 87 126 Bf 74
25140 Fournet-Blancheroche 25 108 Ge 65
25390 Fournets, les 25 108 Gd 66
46230 Fournets, les 46 150 Bd 82
25390 Fournets-Luisans 25 108 Gd 66
14600 Fourneville 14 36 Ab 52
81210 Fournials, les 81 165 Cb 86
12200 Fourniès 12 151 Ca 82
36220 Fournioux 36 100 Af 68
60130 Fournival 60 39 Cc 52
19170 Fournol 19 126 Ca 75
63980 Fournols 63 128 Dd 75
15600 Fournoulès, St.-Constant 15 139 Cb 80
89560 Fouronnes 89 89 Dd 63
30300 Fourques 30 169 Ed 86
43340 Fourques 43 141 Df 79
47200 Fourques-sur-Garonne 47 148 Aa 82
82400 Fourquet 82 149 Af 83
78112 Fourqueux 78 51 Ca 55
31450 Fourquevaux 31 165 Bd 87
63690 Fourroux 63 127 Cd 75
33390 Fours 33 134 Zc 77
58250 Fours 58 104 De 68
27630 Fours-en-Vexin 27 50 Bd 53
11190 Fourtou 11 178 Cc 91
34800 Fouscais 34 167 Dc 87
85240 Foussais-Payré 85 110 Zb 69
30700 Foussargues 30 154 Eb 84
90150 Foussemagne 90 94 Ha 63
31430 Fousseret, le 31 164 Ba 89
16200 Foussignac 16 123 Zf 74
04120 Foux, la 04 158 Ge 86
83310 Foux, la 83 172 Gd 89
83390 Foux, la 83 171 Ga 89
04260 Foux-d'Allos, la 04 158 Gd 83
44520 Fouy, le 44 82 Yd 63
34480 Fouzilhon 34 167 Db 87
57420 Foville 57 56 Gb 55
83670 Fox-Amphoux 83 171 Ga 87
49560 Foye 49 98 Zd 66
17240 Foye, la 17 122 Zb 76
36150 Foye, la 36 101 Bf 66
79200 Foye, la 79 98 Ze 69
79360 Foye-Monjault, la 79 110 Zc 71
50260 Foyer, le 50 33 Yc 52
56660 Foz, le 56 80 Xb 61
34700 Fozières 34 167 Dc 86
20116 Fozzaninco CTC 183 Ka 98
20143 Fozzano CTC 184 Ka 99
20116 Fozzinacu = Fozzaninco CTC 183 Ka 98
19310 Frabet 19 125 Bb 77
89160 Frace 89 90 Eb 62
05100 Fraches, les 05 145 Ge 79
74130 Frachets, les 74 120 Gc 72
17270 Fradon 17 123 Ze 77
89520 Fragnes, les 89 89 Db 63
71530 Fragnes-La Loyère 71 106 Ef 67
58370 Fragny 58 104 Df 67
71400 Fragny 71 105 Eb 67
71330 Fragny-en-Bresse 71 106 Fc 68
70400 Frahier-et-Chatebier 70 94 Ge 63
24400 Fraicherode 24 136 Ab 78
85110 Fraigne 85 97 Yf 68
85200 Fraigneau 85 110 Za 70
21580 Fraignot-et-Vesvrotte 21 91 Ef 63
08220 Fraillicourt 08 41 Ea 50
54300 Fraimbois 54 77 Gd 57
88320 Frain 88 76 Ff 60
33860 Fraineau 33 123 Zc 77
28360 Frainville 28 70 Bd 58
88700 Fraipertuis 88 77 Ge 59
90150 Frais 90 94 Gf 63
23480 Frais, le 23 114 Ca 72
39700 Fraisans 39 107 Fe 66
59500 Frais-Marais 59 30 Da 46
54930 Fraisnes-en-Saintois 54 76 Ga 58
15270 Fraisse 15 127 Cd 76
24130 Fraisse 24 136 Ab 79
43500 Fraisse 43 129 Df 77
47360 Fraisse 47 149 Ad 83
81530 Fraïsse 81 152 Cd 86
12290 Fraisse, la 12 152 Ce 83
12350 Fraisse, la 12 151 Ca 82
43170 Fraisse, la 43 140 Dd 79
63980 Fraisse, la 63 128 Dd 75
11600 Fraisse-Cabardès 11 166 Cb 89
11360 Fraissé-des-Corbières 11 179 Cf 91
63880 Fraisses 63 128 Dd 75
38650 Fraisses, les 38 143 Fd 79
34330 Fraisse-sur-Agout 34 166 Ce 87
81340 Fraissines 81 152 Cc 85
12130 Fraissinet 12 152 Da 82
15100 Fraissinet 15 140 Da 78
48100 Fraissinet 48 140 Db 81
48140 Fraissinet-Chazalais 48 140 Dc 79
48400 Fraissinet-de-Fourques 48 153 Dd 83
48220 Fraissinet-de-Lozère 48 153 De 82
48210 Fraissinet-de-Poujols 48 153 Dc 83
12290 Fraissinhes 12 152 Cd 83
48310 Fraissinoux 48 140 Da 80
15700 Fraissy 15 139 Cb 78
88230 Fraize 88 77 Gf 59
10110 Fralignes 10 74 Ec 60
28250 Framboisière, la 28 69 Ba 57
25140 Frambouhans 25 108 Ge 65
25300 Frambourg, le 25 108 Gc 67
62130 Framecourt 62 29 Cb 47
80131 Framerville-Rainecourt 80 39 Ce 49
80140 Framicourt 80 38 Be 49
70600 Framont 70 92 Fd 63
52220 Frampas 52 74 Ee 57
62179 Framzelle 62 26 Bd 43
57670 Francaltroff 57 57 Ge 55
20236 Francardo CTC 183 Kb 94
20236 Francardu = Francardo CTC 183 Kb 94
31460 Francarville 31 165 Be 87
60480 Francastel 60 38 Ca 51
41190 Françay 41 86 Ba 63
31100 Francazal 31 164 Bc 87
31260 Francazal 31 176 Af 90
47600 Francescas 47 148 Ac 84
44440 Franchaud 44 82 Yd 64
01090 Francheleins 01 118 Ee 72
03160 Franchesse 03 103 Da 69

270 | Fontbelle

08140 Francheval 08 42 Fa 50
70200 Franchevelle 70 94 Gc 62
18220 Francheville 18 103 Ce 66
21440 Francheville 21 91 Ef 64
27160 Francheville 27 49 Af 56
27220 Francheville 27 49 Bb 55
39230 Francheville 39 106 Fd 67
51240 Francheville 51 54 Ed 55
54200 Francheville 54 56 Ff 56
61570 Francheville 61 48 Zf 57
69340 Francheville 69M 130 Ee 74
08000 Francheville, la 08 42 Ee 50
29810 Franchise, la 29 61 Vb 58
60190 Francières 60 39 Ce 52
80690 Franciers 80 28 Bf 48
36110 Francillon 36 101 Bd 67
26400 Francillon-sur-Roubion 26 143 Fa 81
02760 Francilly-Selency 02 40 Db 49
73800 Francin 73 132 Ga 75
15230 Francio, la 15 139 Ce 79
74910 Franclens 74 119 Fe 72
79260 François 79 111 Zd 70
31420 Francon 31 164 Af 89
15380 Franconeche 15 139 Cd 78
54830 Franconville 54 77 Gc 58
95130 Franconville 95 51 Cb 54
46090 Francoulès 46 138 Bc 81
47290 Francoulon 47 136 Ad 82
70180 Francourt 70 92 Fe 63
28700 Francourville 28 70 Bd 58
33570 Francs 33 135 Zf 79
23800 Francs, les 23 114 Be 71
37150 Francueil 37 86 Ba 65
85300 Frandière 85 96 Ya 67
85630 Frandière, la 85 96 Xf 67
25170 Franey 25 93 Fe 65
74270 Frangy 74 120 Ff 72
68130 Franken 68 95 Hc 63
80210 Franleu 80 28 Bd 48
25770 Franois 25 107 Ff 65
88200 Franould 88 77 Gd 60
30640 Franquevau 30 169 Ec 87
31210 Franquevielle 31 163 Ad 90
02140 Franqueville 02 40 De 50
27800 Franqueville 27 49 Ae 53
80620 Franqueville 80 29 Ca 48
76520 Franqueville-Saint-Pierre 76 37 Bb 52
11370 Franqui, la 11 179 Da 91
01480 Frans 01 118 Ee 73
28120 Fransache 28 69 Bb 59
80700 Fransart 80 39 Ce 50
23480 Fransèches 23 114 Ca 72
80620 Fransu 80 29 Ca 48
80160 Fransures 80 38 Cb 50
80800 Franvillers 80 39 Cd 49
21170 Franxault 21 106 Fb 66
88490 Frapelle 88 77 Ha 59
33230 Frappier, le 33 135 Aa 78
57790 Fraquelfing 57 57 Gf 57
15600 Fraquier 15 139 Cb 80
39250 Fraroz 39 107 Ga 68
58270 Frasnay-Reugny 58 104 Dd 67
25560 Frasne 25 107 Ga 67
39290 Frasne 39 106 Fd 65
39130 Frasnée, la 39 119 Fe 69
70700 Frasne-le-Château 70 93 Ff 64
39130 Frasnois, le 39 107 Ff 69
59530 Frasnoy 59 31 De 47
74300 Frasse, la 74 120 Gd 72
20157 Frasseto CTC 182 Ka 97
20121 Frassetu CTC 182 If 96
20270 Frassiccia CTC 183 Kc 96
20230 Fratta CTC 183 Kd 95
57200 Frauenberg 57 57 Ha 54
81170 Frausseilles 81 151 Bf 84
10200 Fravaux 10 74 Ed 59
33125 Frayot, le 33 134 Zb 81
52130 Frays 52 75 Fa 58
12600 Fraysse 12 139 Cd 80
81430 Fraysse 81 151 Cc 85
12370 Fraysse, le 12 152 Ce 86
12410 Fraysse, le 12 152 Ce 83
19380 Fraysse, le 19 138 Bf 77
19430 Fraysse, le 19 138 Ca 78
26230 Fraysse, le 26 142 Ef 82
43260 Fraysse, le 43 141 Ea 78
15800 Fraysse-Haut 15 139 Cd 79
12130 Frayssinède, la 12 140 Da 81
46310 Frayssinet 46 138 Bc 81
12230 Frayssinet-Bas, le 12 153 Db 85
46250 Frayssinet-le-Gélat 46 137 Ba 81
46400 Frayssinhes 46 138 Bf 79
04250 Frayssinie, la 04 157 Ga 82
28160 Frazé 28 69 Ba 59
76660 Fréauville 76 37 Bc 50
88630 Frebécourt 88 75 Fe 58
39570 Frébuans 39 106 Fc 69
40190 Frêche, le 40 147 Ze 85
65220 Fréchède 65 163 Ab 88
80260 Fréchencourt 80 39 Cc 49
65130 Fréchendets 65 163 Ab 90
31360 Fréchet, le 31 164 Af 89
57480 Freching 57 44 Gc 52
47600 Fréchou 47 148 Ab 84
65190 Fréchou-Fréchet 65 163 Aa 89
67130 Fréconrupt 67 77 Hb 58
52360 Frécourt 52 75 Fc 61
57530 Frécourt 57 56 Gc 54
28140 Frécul 28 70 Be 60
65170 Frédançon 65 175 Ab 92
70200 Frédéric-Fontaine 70 94 Gd 63
23700 Frédeval 23 115 Cd 73
36180 Frédille 36 101 Bc 66
87620 Fregefont 87 125 Ba 74
81300 Frégère, la 81 151 Ca 86
28480 Frégigny 28 69 Af 58
47360 Frégimont 47 148 Ac 83
32490 Frégouville 32 164 Af 87
22240 Fréhel 22 64 Xd 57
49440 Freigné 49 83 Yf 63
56800 Freique, le 56 64 Xd 61
05310 Freissinières 05 145 Gd 80
05000 Freissinouse, la 05 144 Ga 81
57320 Freistroff 57 57 Gc 53
15310 Freix-Anglards 15 139 Cc 78
81990 Fréjairolles 81 151 Cb 85
81570 Fréjeville 81 165 Ca 87
05240 Fréjus 05 145 Gd 79
83600 Fréjus 83 172 Ge 88
68240 Fréland 68 77 Hb 59
85170 Frelandière, la 85 97 Yd 68
59236 Frelinghien 59 30 Cf 44
41120 Frelonnière, la 41 86 Bb 64
95450 Frémainville 95 50 Bf 54
95830 Frémécourt 95 51 Ca 54
54450 Fréménil 54 77 Ge 57
55200 Fréméréville-sous-les-Côtes 55 55 Fd 56
57590 Frémery 57 57 Gc 55
57660 Frémestroff 57 57 Ge 54
62450 Frémicourt 62 30 Cf 48
88600 Fremifontaine-la-Basse 88 77 Ge 59
80260 Frémont 80 38 Cb 49
80160 Frémontiers 80 38 Ca 50
54450 Frémonville 54 77 Gf 57
76170 Frenaye, la 76 36 Ad 51
76680 Frénaye, la 76 37 Bb 50
76750 Frénaye, la 76 37 Bc 51
62630 Frencq 62 28 Be 45
72510 Frêne, le 72 84 Aa 62
33820 Fréneau 33 122 Zb 77
17160 Fréneau 17 123 Ze 73
61500 Fréneaux 61 48 Ab 57
79250 Frêne-Chabot, le 79 98 Zc 67
88500 Frenelle-la-Grande 88 76 Ga 58
88500 Frenelle-la-Petite 88 76 Ga 58
61800 Frênes 61 47 Zb 56
76410 Freneuse 76 37 Ba 53
78840 Freneuse 78 50 Bd 54
27290 Freneuse-sur-Risle 27 49 Ae 53
73500 Freney, le 73 133 Gd 77
38142 Freney-d'Oisans, le 38 144 Ga 78
60640 Fréniches 60 39 Da 50
08200 Frénois 08 42 Ef 50
21120 Frénois 21 91 Ef 63
88270 Frénois 88 76 Ga 59
14630 Frénouville 14 35 Ze 54
95740 Frépillon 95 51 Cb 54
15170 Frerissinet 15 140 Cf 78
76270 Fresles 76 37 Bc 50
28220 Freslonnière, la 28 69 Ba 60
61230 Fresnaie-Fayel, la 61 48 Ab 55
35111 Fresnais, la 35 65 Ya 57
10200 Fresnay 10 74 Ee 59
51230 Fresnay 51 53 Df 57
27480 Fresnay, le 27 37 Bc 52
61210 Fresnaye-au-Sauvage, la 61 48 Ze 56
44580 Fresnay-en-Retz 44 96 Ya 66
72600 Fresnaye-sur-Chédouet, la 72 68 Ab 58
28360 Fresnay-le-Comte 28 70 Bc 59
28300 Fresnay-le-Gilmert 28 70 Bc 57
76850 Fresnay-le-Long 76 37 Ba 51
61120 Fresnay-le-Samson 61 48 Ab 55
45300 Fresnay-les-Chaumes 45 71 Cb 59
28310 Fresnay-L'Évêque 28 70 Be 59
72130 Fresnay-sur-Sarthe 72 68 Aa 59
45300 Fresne 45 71 Cb 59
80120 Fresne 80 28 Be 46
27190 Fresne, le 27 49 Af 55
51240 Fresne, le 51 54 Ed 55
76260 Fresne, le 76 37 Bc 48
60240 Fresneaux-Montchevreuil 60 51 Ca 53
14480 Fresne-Camilly, le 14 35 Zd 53
27260 Fresne-Cauverville 27 48 Ac 53
14700 Fresné-la-Mère 14 48 Zf 55
27700 Fresne-l'Archevêque 27 50 Bc 53
60240 Fresne-Léguillon 60 51 Bf 53
76520 Fresne-le-Plan 76 37 Bb 52
50850 Fresne-Poret, le 50 47 Zb 56
02380 Fresnes 02 40 Dc 51
21500 Fresnes 21 91 Ec 63
41700 Fresnes 41 86 Bc 64
89310 Fresnes 89 90 Df 62
94260 Fresnes 94 51 Cb 56
70130 Fresne-Saint-Mamès 70 93 Ff 63
55260 Fresnes-au-Mont 55 55 Fc 55
57170 Fresnes-en-Saulnois 57 56 Gc 55
02130 Fresnes-en-Tardenois 02 53 Dd 54
55160 Fresnes-en-Woëvre 55 55 Fd 54
62490 Fresnes-lès-Montauban 62 30 Cf 46
51110 Fresnes-lès-Reims 51 53 Ea 52
80320 Fresnes-Mazancourt 80 39 Cf 49
52400 Fresnes-sur-Apance 52 76 Ff 61
59970 Fresnes-sur-Escaut 59 31 Dd 46
77410 Fresnes-sur-Marne 77 52 Ce 55
80140 Fresnes-Tilloloy 80 38 Be 49
49123 Fresne-sur-Loire, Ingrandes-, le 49 83 Za 64
80140 Fresneville 80 38 Be 49
27220 Fresney 27 50 Bb 55
14680 Fresney-le-Puceux 14 47 Zd 54
14220 Fresney-le-Vieux 14 47 Zd 54
62150 Fresnicourt 62 29 Cd 46
60310 Fresnières 60 39 Ce 51
55600 Fresnois 55 43 Fc 51
54260 Fresnois-la-Montagne 54 43 Fd 52
62770 Fresnoy 62 29 Ca 46
80140 Fresnoy 80 38 Be 49
80290 Fresnoy-au-Val 80 38 Ca 49
52400 Fresnoy-en-Bassigny 52 75 Fd 60
80110 Fresnoy-en-Chaussée 80 39 Cd 50
62580 Fresnoy-en-Gohelle 62 30 Cf 46
60530 Fresnoy-en-Thelle 60 51 Cb 53
76660 Fresnoy-Folny 76 37 Bc 49
10270 Fresnoy-le-Château 10 73 Eb 59
02230 Fresnoy-le-Grand 02 40 Dc 49
60800 Fresnoy-le-Luat 60 52 Ce 53
02100 Fresnoy-le-Petit 02 40 Db 49
80700 Fresnoy-lès-Roye 80 39 Ce 50
46260 Frespech 46 151 Bf 82
47140 Frespech 47 149 Ae 83
76270 Fresques 76 37 Bc 50
76570 Fresquiennes 76 37 Ba 51
30170 Fressac 30 154 Df 85
59234 Fressain 59 30 Db 47
02800 Fressancourt 02 40 Dc 51
15380 Fressange 15 127 Cc 77
15260 Fressanges 15 140 Cf 79
43320 Fressanges 43 141 Dd 78
70270 Fresse 70 94 Gd 62
23130 Fresse, la 23 114 Cb 72
23450 Fresselines 23 113 Be 70
23130 Fressenède 23 114 Cb 72
80390 Fressenneville 80 28 Bd 48
88160 Fresse-sur-Moselle 88 94 Ge 61
59268 Fressies 59 30 Db 47
62140 Fressin 62 29 Ca 46
79370 Fressines 79 111 Ze 71
42440 Fressinie, la 42 129 De 74
42380 Fressonnet 42 129 Ea 76
60420 Frestoy, le 60 39 Cd 51
50310 Fresville 50 34 Yd 52
29160 Fret, le 29 61 Vc 59
37600 Fretay 37 100 Af 66
91140 Fretay 91 51 Cb 56
23270 Freteix 23 114 Ca 70
63380 Freteix 63 115 Cd 73
73250 Fréterive 73 132 Gb 75
41160 Fréteval 41 86 Bb 61
62185 Fréthun 62 27 Be 43
70130 Fretigney-et-Velloreille 70 93 Ff 64
59710 Fretin Ennevelin 59 30 Da 45
60380 Frétoy 60 38 Bf 51
77320 Frétoy 77 52 Db 56
60640 Frétoy-le-Château 60 39 Cf 51
71440 Frette 71 106 Fa 69
38260 Frette, la 38 131 Fc 76
80140 Frettecuisse 80 38 Be 49
80220 Frettemeule 80 38 Bd 48
71270 Fretterans 71 106 Fb 67
70600 Frettes 70 92 Fd 62
95530 Frette-sur-Seine, la 95 51 Cb 55
27430 Fretteville 27 50 Bb 53
08290 Fréty, le 08 41 Eb 50
76510 Freulleville 76 37 Bb 50
62270 Frévent 62 29 Cb 47
27170 Fréville 27 49 Ae 54
76190 Fréville 76 37 Ae 51
88350 Fréville 88 75 Fd 59
45270 Fréville-du-Gâtinais 45 71 Cc 60
62127 Frévillers 62 29 Cd 46
57660 Freybouse 57 57 Ge 54
43170 Freycenet 43 141 Dd 79
43190 Freycenet 43 142 Eb 78
43200 Freycenet 43 141 Eb 78
43340 Freycenet 43 141 De 80
43420 Freycenet 43 141 Df 80
43150 Freycenet-la-Cuche 43 141 Ea 79
43150 Freycenet-la-Tour 43 141 Ea 79
09300 Freychenet 09 177 Be 91
63710 Freydefond 63 128 Cf 75
07190 Freydier, le 07 142 Ec 80
19320 Freygnac 19 138 Bf 78
57800 Freyming-Merlebach 57 57 Ge 54
48320 Freysinel, le 48 153 Dc 82
19390 Freysselines 19 126 Bf 76
07000 Freyssenet 07 142 Ed 80
07600 Freyssenet 07 142 Eb 80
19250 Freyte 19 126 Cb 75
09400 Freyte, la 09 177 Bc 91
81440 Frezouls 81 166 Ca 86
28240 Friaize 28 69 Ba 58
25160 Friard 25 108 Gb 67
14290 Friardel, La Vespière- 14 48 Ac 54
80460 Friaucourt 80 28 Bc 48
87250 Friaudour 87 113 Bb 72
54800 Friauville 54 56 Ff 54
57810 Fribourg 57 57 Gf 56
73350 Friburge 73 133 Ge 76
80290 Fricamps 80 38 Bf 50
79360 Fricaudière, la 79 110 Zd 72
17250 Frichebois 17 122 Zb 73
76690 Frichemesnil 76 37 Ba 51
80300 Fricourt 80 29 Ce 49
15110 Fridefont 15 140 Da 79
67490 Friedolsheim 67 58 Hc 56
59750 Frieglies 59 31 Df 47
13460 Friélouse 13 169 Ed 87
02700 Frières-Faillouël 02 40 Db 50
68580 Friesen 68 95 Ha 63
67860 Friesenheim 67 60 He 59
51300 Frignicourt 51 54 Ed 56
30630 Frigoulet 30 154 Ec 83
28140 Frileuse, la 28 70 Bd 60
50800 Friloux, le 50 46 Ye 56
18390 Fringale 18 102 Cd 66
77640 Fringale, la 77 52 Da 55
31660 Friques, les 31 150 Bd 86
80132 Frireulle 80 28 Bd 48
80340 Frise 80 39 Ce 49
88260 Frison, la 88 76 Ga 60
43160 Frissonnet 43 128 Dd 77
36310 Frissonnette, la 36 113 Bb 70
50340 Fritot 50 33 Yb 52
80130 Friville-Escarbotin 80 28 Bd 48
88440 Frizon 88 76 Gc 59
76400 Froberville 76 36 Ab 50
60000 Frocourt 60 38 Ca 52
68720 Frœningen 68 95 Hb 62
67360 Frœschwiller 67 58 He 55
38190 Froges 38 132 Ff 77
80370 Frohen-le-Grand 80 29 Cb 47
80370 Frohen-le-Petit 80 29 Cb 47
67290 Frohmuhl 67 58 Hb 55
70300 Froideconche 70 93 Gc 62
39250 Froidefontaine 39 107 Ga 68
90140 Froidefontaine 90 94 Gf 63
50760 Froide-Rue, la 50 34 Ye 51
02260 Froidestrées 02 41 Df 49
70200 Froideterre 70 94 Gd 62
25190 Froidevaux 25 94 Ge 65
22410 Froideville, la 22 64 Xa 57
39230 Froideville, Vincent- 39 106 Fc 68
85300 Froidfond 85 96 Yb 67
53170 Froid-Fonds 53 83 Zc 61
60930 Froidmont 60 38 Cb 52
02270 Froidmont-Cohartille 02 40 De 50
55120 Froidos 55 55 Fa 54
48700 Froid-Viala 48 140 Dc 81
80120 Froise 80 28 Bd 47
21150 Frôlois 21 91 Ed 63
54160 Frolois 54 76 Ga 57
26470 Fromagère, la 26 156 Fc 82
49670 Fromagère, la 49 98 Zc 65
08600 Fromelennes Rancennes 08 42 Ee 48
59249 Fromelles 59 30 Cf 45
87250 Fromental 87 113 Bc 72
12510 Fromentals 12 151 Cc 82
61210 Fromentel 61 47 Ze 56
62850 Fromentel 62 28 Bf 44
51210 Fromentières 51 53 De 55
53200 Fromentières 53 83 Zc 61
85550 Fromentine 85 96 Xf 67
55100 Fromeréville-les-Vallons 55 55 Fb 54
55400 Fromezey 55 55 Fd 53
77760 Fromont 77 71 Cd 59
08370 Fromy 08 42 Fb 51
52320 Froncles 52 75 Fa 59
70130 Frondey, les 70 93 Ff 64
67680 Fronholtz 67 60 Hc 58
12600 Frons 12 139 Ce 79
12800 Frons 12 151 Cc 83
31440 Fronsac 31 176 Ad 91
33126 Fronsac 33 135 Ze 79
19290 Fronsergues 19 126 Ca 74
30450 Frontal, le 30 154 Ea 82
33760 Frontenac 33 135 Zf 80
46160 Frontenac 46 138 Bf 81
71270 Frontenard 71 106 Fa 67
69620 Frontenas 69D 118 Ed 73
03380 Frontenat 03 115 Cc 70
03420 Frontenat 03 115 Ce 71
71580 Frontenaud 71 119 Fb 69
79270 Frontenay-Rohan-Rohan 79 110 Zc 71
86330 Frontenay-sur-Dive 86 99 Aa 67
88210 Frontenelle, la 88 77 Gf 58
73460 Frontenex 73 132 Gb 75
74210 Frontenex 74 132 Gb 74
34110 Frontignan 34 168 De 88
31510 Frontignan-de-Comminges 31 176 Ad 91
34110 Frontignan-Plage 34 168 De 88
31230 Frontignan-Savès 31 164 Af 88
57245 Frontigny 57 56 Gb 54
31620 Fronton 31 150 Bc 85
38290 Frontonas 38 131 Fb 75
87800 Frontouin 87 125 Ba 75
52300 Fronville 52 75 Fa 58
44320 Frossay 44 96 Ya 65
85320 Frosse 85 110 Ye 69
60480 Frossy 60 38 Cb 51
70200 Frotey-lès-Lure 70 94 Gd 63
70000 Frotey-lès-Vesoul 70 93 Gb 63
28120 Frou, le 28 69 Bb 58
54390 Frouard 54 56 Ga 56
40560 Frouas 40 146 Ye 85
95690 Frouville 95 51 Ca 54
34380 Frouzet 34 153 De 86
31270 Frouzins 31 164 Bb 87
54290 Froville 54 76 Gc 58
80150 Froyelles 80 28 Bf 47
86190 Frozes 86 99 Aa 69
80490 Frucourt 80 28 Be 49
43250 Frugères-les-Mines 43 128 Db 76
62310 Fruges 62 29 Ca 45
43230 Frugières-le-Pin 43 128 Dc 77
29242 Frugullou 29 61 Uf 58
40110 Fruit, le 40 147 Zb 85
65110 Fruitière, la 65 175 Zf 91
36190 Frulon 36 113 Be 69
28190 Fruncé 28 69 Bb 58
76780 Fry 76 37 Bd 51
22260 Fry Quemper 22 63 Wf 56
25390 Fuans 25 108 Gd 66
77470 Fublaines 77 52 Cf 55
43150 Fugères 43 141 Df 79
04240 Fugeret, le 04 158 Gd 84
53190 Fugerolles-du-Plessis 53 66 Za 58
38350 Fugière 38 144 Fe 79
49270 Fuilet, le 49 83 Yf 65
66820 Fuilla 66 178 Cc 93
71960 Fuissé 71 118 Ee 71
85110 Fuiteau, le 85 97 Yf 69
10200 Fuligny 10 74 Ee 59
68210 Fulleren 68 95 Ha 63
76560 Fultot 76 36 Ae 50
89160 Fulvy 89 90 Ea 62
30500 Fumades-les-Bains, les 30 154 Eb 83
08170 Fumay 08 42 Ee 49
29600 Fumé, le 29 62 Wb 57
27170 Fumechon 27 49 Ae 54
76260 Fumechon 76 37 Bc 49
27930 Fumeçon 27 49 Ba 55
17450 Fumée, la 17 110 Yf 72
84400 Fumeirasse 84 156 Fc 85
47500 Fumel 47 137 Af 82
14590 Fumichon 14 48 Ac 53
87120 Fumouse 87 126 Bf 74
63350 Fumoux, les 63 116 Dc 73
67700 Furchhausen 67 58 Hc 56
20190 Furciolu = Forciolo CTC 184 Ka 97
67117 Furdenheim 67 60 Hd 57
38210 Fures 38 131 Fc 77
20600 Furiani CTC 181 Kc 93
86170 Furigny 86 99 Ab 68
05400 Furmeyer 05 144 Ff 81
31260 Furne 31 164 Af 90
23290 Fursac 23 113 Bd 72
87370 Fursannes 87 113 Bc 72
58110 Fusilly 58 104 De 66
63260 Fusse 63 116 Db 72
21700 Fussey 21 106 Ef 66
18110 Fussy 18 102 Cc 66
58800 Fussy 58 104 Dd 65
32400 Fustérouau 32 162 Aa 86
09130 Fustié, le 09 164 Bc 90
31430 Fustignac 31 164 Af 89
55120 Futeau 55 55 Fa 54
13710 Fuveau 13 171 Fd 88
37340 Fuye 37 85 Ab 64
86140 Fuye, la 86 99 Ab 67
20143 Fuzzà = Fozzano CTC 184 Ka 98
72610 Fyé 72 68 Aa 59
89800 Fyé 89 90 De 62

G

40350 Gaas 40 161 Yf 87
82700 Gabachoux 82 150 Ba 85
33410 Gabarnac 33 135 Ze 81
40310 Gabarret 40 148 Aa 85
64440 Gabas 64 174 Zd 91
64160 Gabaston 64 162 Ze 88
64120 Gabat 64 161 Yf 88
09200 Gabats, les 09 176 Ba 90
46500 Gabautet 46 138 Be 80
84390 Gabelle, la 84 156 Fb 84
34320 Gabian 34 167 Db 87
87380 Gabie-de-la-Poule, la 87 125 Bc 75
24210 Gabillou 24 125 Ba 77
88370 Gabiotte, la 88 76 Gc 60
33860 Gablezac 33 123 Zd 77
09290 Gabre 09 164 Bc 90
12340 Gabriac 12 152 Ce 82
34380 Gabriac 34 153 De 86
48110 Gabriac 48 153 De 83
48100 Gabrias 48 140 Dc 81
36220 Gabriau 36 100 Ba 68
16190 Gabrielle, la 16 123 Zf 76
61230 Gacé 61 48 Ab 56
58300 Gachat 58 104 Dd 68
85470 Gachère, la 85 96 Ya 69
24410 Gâcherie, la 24 124 Ab 77
87230 Gacherie, la 87 125 Ba 75
72800 Gachetière 72 84 Aa 63
50600 Gachetière, la 50 66 Yf 57
56200 Gacilly, La 56 81 Xf 62
58140 Gâcogne 58 104 Df 65
03300 Gacon 03 116 Dd 72
17480 Gaconnière 17 109 Ye 73
85170 Gaconnière, la 85 97 Yc 67
95450 Gadancourt 95 50 Bf 54
17270 Gadebourg 17 123 Ze 77
27120 Gadencourt 27 50 Bc 55
33690 Gadine 33 148 Zf 82
35290 Gaël 35 65 Xe 60
83170 Gaëtans, les 83 171 Ga 88
47440 Gaffarot 47 136 Ad 82
87290 Gaffary 87 113 Bb 72
24240 Gageac-et-Rouillac 24 136 Ac 80
13200 Gageron 13 169 Ed 87
12630 Gages-le-Haut 12 152 Ce 82
81190 Gagets, les 81 151 Ca 84
12310 Gagnac 12 152 Cf 82
46130 Gagnac-sur-Cère 46 138 Bf 79
31150 Gagnac-sur-Garonne 31 164 Bc 86
63660 Gagnère 63 129 Df 75
30160 Gagnières 30 154 Ea 83
93220 Gagny 93 51 Cd 55
58700 Gagy 58 103 Db 65
41160 Gahandière, la 41 86 Bc 61
35490 Gahard 35 66 Yc 59
64780 Gahardou 64 160 Ye 89
09800 Gaiey 09 176 Af 91
30260 Gailhan 30 154 Ea 85
81600 Gaillac 81 151 Bf 85
12310 Gaillac-d'Aveyron 12 152 Cf 82
46160 Gaillac Monastère 46 138 Be 82
31550 Gaillac-Toulza 31 164 Bc 89
65400 Gaillagos 65 174 Ze 91
33340 Gaillan-en-Médoc 33 122 Za 77
40210 Gaillard 40 146 Za 83
27440 Gaillardbois-Cressenville 27 50 Bc 52
76740 Gaillarde 76 37 Af 49
83380 Gaillarde, la 83 172 Ge 88
05200 Gaillards, les 05 145 Gd 81
37290 Gaillards, les 37 100 Af 67
76870 Gaillefontaine 76 38 Bd 51
40090 Gaillères 40 147 Zd 85
27600 Gaillon 27 50 Bc 54
78250 Gaillon-sur-Montcient 78 50 Bf 54
40140 Gaillou-de-Pountaout 40 160 Yd 86
33260 Gaillouneys 33 134 Ye 81
16500 Gain 16 112 Ae 72
53220 Gainé 53 66 Yf 58
76700 Gainneville 76 36 Ab 51
12740 Gajac 12 152 Cd 82
33430 Gajac 33 147 Zf 82
11300 Gaja-et-Villedieu 11 165 Cb 90
11270 Gaja-la-Selve 11 165 Bf 89
09190 Gajan 09 176 Ba 90
30730 Gajan 30 154 Eb 85
87330 Gajoubert 87 112 Ae 72
32600 Galabart 32 164 Ba 87
65710 Galade 65 175 Ab 91
12400 Galamans 12 152 Ce 85
62770 Galametz 62 29 Ca 47
65330 Galan 65 163 Ac 89
47190 Galapian 47 148 Ac 83
49620 Galardières, les 49 83 Za 65
34160 Galargues 34 154 Ea 86
84800 Galas 84 155 Fa 85
65330 Galave, la 65 163 Ac 89
31330 Galembrun 31 150 Ba 86
12210 Galens, les 12 139 Ce 81

Galens, les | 271

06590 Galère, la 06 173 Gf 88
83270 Galère, la 83 171 Fe 90
20245 Galéria CTC 182 Id 94
46090 Galessie 46 138 Bd 82
65330 Galez 65 163 Ac 89
68990 Galfingue 68 95 Hb 62
12220 Galgan 12 139 Cb 81
59229 Galghouck, le 59 27 Cc 42
33133 Galgon 33 135 Ze 79
32160 Galiax 32 162 Aa 87
31510 Galié 31 176 Ad 91
47340 Galimas 47 149 Ae 83
11140 Galinagues 11 178 Ca 92
24620 Galinat 24 137 Ba 79
34220 Galinié 34 166 Cd 88
24550 Galinier, le 24 137 Ba 81
81500 Galiniers 81 151 Bf 86
26410 Gallands, les 26 143 Fc 81
28320 Gallardon 28 70 Be 57
30660 Gallargues-le-Monteux 30 168 Ea 86
84100 Galle, la 84 155 Ee 83
45170 Gallerand 45 71 Cb 60
35270 Gallerie, la 35 65 Yb 58
60360 Gallet, le 60 38 Ca 51
30600 Gallician 30 169 Eb 87
36210 Galliers, les 36 87 Be 65
33580 Gallochet 33 136 Aa 81
78490 Galluis 78 50 Be 56
57530 Galonnière, la 57 57 Gd 54
40550 Galoppe 40 146 Ye 85
80220 Gamaches 80 37 Bd 49
27150 Gamaches-en-Vexin 27 50 Bd 53
40380 Gamarde-les-Bains 40 161 Za 86
64220 Gamarthe 64 161 Yf 89
21190 Gamay 21 105 Ee 67
78950 Gambais 78 50 Be 56
78490 Gambaiseuil 78 50 Be 56
50480 Gambosville 50 33 Yd 52
67760 Gambsheim 67 58 Hf 56
30410 Gammal 30 154 Ea 83
63380 Gamy 63 127 Cd 74
64290 Gan 64 162 Zd 89
04230 Ganas 04 156 Fe 84
76220 Gancourt-Saint-Étienne 76 38 Be 51
82100 Gandalou 82 149 Ba 84
61420 Gandelain 61 67 Zf 58
81700 Gandels 81 165 Bf 88
02810 Gandelu 02 52 Db 54
91720 Gandevilliers 91 71 Cb 58
63640 Gandichoux 63 115 Ce 73
24330 Gandilie, la 24 137 Af 78
82270 Gandoules 82 150 Bc 83
57570 Gandren 57 44 Gb 52
24270 Gandumas 24 125 Ba 76
34190 Ganges 34 153 De 85
46170 Ganic 46 150 Bc 83
03800 Gannat 03 116 Db 72
03230 Gannay-sur-Loire 03 104 Dd 68
60120 Gannes 60 39 Cc 51
63750 Gannes, les 63 127 Cd 75
33430 Gans 33 135 Zf 82
62910 Ganspette 62 27 Ca 44
31160 Ganties 31 163 Af 90
67400 Ganzau, la 67 60 He 57
76400 Ganzeville 76 36 Ac 50
13170 Gaotte, la 13 170 Fc 88
83250 Gaouby, les 83 172 Gb 90
29160 Gaoulac'h 29 61 Vc 59
05000 Gap 05 144 Ga 81
80150 Gapennes 80 28 Bf 47
05190 Gapian 05 144 Gb 81
61390 Gâprée 61 48 Ab 57
84570 Gaps, les 84 156 Fb 84
31480 Garac 31 164 Ba 86
78890 Garancières 78 50 Be 56
28700 Garancières-en-Beauce 28 70 Bf 58
28500 Garancières-en-Drouais 28 50 Bb 56
63970 Garandie, la 63 127 Cf 75
85300 Garanger 85 96 Yb 68
16410 Garat 16 124 Ab 75
06500 Garavan 06 159 Hd 86
64130 Garaybie 64 161 Yf 90
32490 Garbic 32 164 Af 87
04510 Garce 04 157 Ga 84
14540 Garcelles-Secqueville 14 47 Ze 54
57100 Garche 57 44 Gb 52
92380 Garches 92 51 Cb 55
58600 Garchizy 58 103 Da 66
58150 Garchy 58 89 Da 65
47130 Garcine, la 47 148 Ac 83
28480 Gardais 28 69 Ba 59
13120 Gardanne 13 170 Fc 88
03120 Garde 03 116 De 71
04340 Garde 04 157 Gb 82
15110 Garde 15 140 Cf 80
16270 Garde 16 124 Ad 73
18290 Garde 18 102 Cb 67
24340 Garde 24 124 Ac 75
24600 Garde 24 124 Ac 77
38520 Garde 38 144 Ga 78
48200 Garde 48 140 Db 79
63220 Garde 63 129 Df 76
63310 Garde 63 116 Dc 73
82400 Garde 82 149 Af 83
86400 Garde 86 112 Ab 71
04120 Garde, la 04 158 Gd 86
06390 Garde, la 06 159 Hc 86
07100 Garde, la 07 130 Ed 77
12170 Garde, la 12 152 Cd 84
12260 Garde, la 12 151 Bf 82
23600 Garde, la 23 114 Cb 71
24210 Garde, la 24 137 Ba 78
63760 Garde, la 63 127 Cd 74
79170 Garde, la 79 111 Zd 72
83130 Garde, la 83 171 Ga 90
26700 Garde-Adhémar, la 26 155 Ee 82
05300 Garde-Colombe 05 156 Fe 82
24700 Gardedeuil 24 136 Aa 78
18300 Gardefort 18 88 Ce 65
83680 Garde-Freinet, la 83 172 Gc 89
33350 Gardegan-et-Tourtirac 33 135 Zf 79
48800 Garde-Guérin, la 48 141 Df 82
16320 Garde-le-Pontaroux 16 124 Ab 75
12200 Gardelle, la 12 151 Bf 82
48140 Gardelle, la 48 140 Dc 80
77130 Gardeloup 77 72 Cf 58
65320 Gardères 65 162 Zf 89
49120 Gardes, les 49 98 Zb 66
63590 Gardette, la 63 128 Dd 75
82150 Gardette, la 82 149 Af 82
81190 Garde-Viaur, la 81 151 Ca 83
11250 Gardie 11 166 Cb 90
48600 Gardilles, les 48 141 Dd 80
33113 Gardit 33 135 Zc 82
36180 Gardon-Frit, le 36 101 Bb 66
24680 Gardonne 24 136 Ab 79
31290 Gardouch 31 165 Be 88
20270 Gare, la CTC 183 Kc 96
22720 Gare, la 22 63 We 58
22780 Gare, la 22 63 Wc 57
29180 Gare, la 29 78 Vf 60
33430 Gare, la 33 135 Ze 82
40120 Gare, la 40 147 Ze 84
70500 Gare, la 70 93 Ff 61
87230 Gare, la 87 125 Ba 75
19800 Gare-de-Corrèze, la 19 126 Bf 77
29300 Gare-de-la-Forêt, la 29 79 Wc 61
33830 Gare-de-Lugos, la 33 146 Za 82
19800 Gare-d'Eyrein, la 19 126 Bf 76
22120 Gare-d'Yffiniac, la 22 64 Xc 58
40420 Garein 40 147 Zc 84
19400 Garel 19 138 Bf 78
27180 Garel 27 49 Ba 55
27220 Garencières 27 50 Bb 55
71360 Garenne, la 71 105 Ed 67
89140 Garenne, la 89 72 Db 58
27780 Garennes-sur-Eure 27 50 Bc 55
49610* Garennes sur Loire, les 49 84 Zc 64
77890 Garentreville 77 71 Cd 59
83136 Garéoult 83 171 Ga 89
31220 Gargaillous 31 164 Ba 89
33114 Gargails, les 33 134 Zb 81
63350 Gargantias 63 128 Dc 73
82100 Garganvillar 82 149 Ba 85
12120 Garagaros 12 151 Cc 83
31620 Gargas 31 150 Bc 86
84400 Gargas 84 156 Fc 85
78440 Gargenville 78 50 Be 55
95140 Garges-lès-Gonesse 95 51 Cc 55
36190 Gargilesse-Dampierre 36 113 Bd 69
31220 Gariat 31 164 Ba 89
31380 Garidech 31 165 Bd 86
82500 Gariès 82 149 Ba 86
33420 Gariga 33 135 Ze 80
18140 Garigny 18 103 Cf 66
64130 Garindein 64 161 Za 89
31110 Garin de-Larboust 31 175 Ad 92
24380 Garissoux, les 24 136 Ae 79
29610 Garlan 29 62 Wb 57
64450 Garlède-Mondebat 64 162 Zd 88
47600 Garlies 47 148 Ac 84
64330 Garlin 64 162 Ze 87
02170 Garmouzet 02 41 Df 48
30760 Garn, le 30 154 Ec 83
85710 Garnache, la 85 96 Yb 67
03230 Garnat-sur-Engièvre 03 104 Dd 69
05260 Garnauds, les 05 144 Gb 80
28500 Garnay 28 50 Bc 56
01140 Garnerans 01 118 Ef 71
85370 Garnerie, la 85 110 Za 70
12190 Garnie, la 19 138 Be 78
63980 Garnisson 63 128 Dd 75
83220 Garonne, la 83 171 Ga 90
30128 Garons 30 154 Ec 86
64410 Garos 64 162 Zd 87
09400 Garrabet 09 177 Bd 91
32260 Garrane 32 163 Ad 87
32220 Garravet 32 164 Af 88
57820 Garrebourg 57 58 Hb 56
44650 Garrelière, la 44 97 Yc 67
64160 Garreta 64 160 Ye 89
81700 Garrevaques 81 165 Bf 88
15190 Garrey 15 127 Cf 76
40180 Garrey 40 161 Za 86
12390 Garric, la 12 139 Cb 82
15130 Garric, le 15 139 Cc 79
81450 Garric, le 81 151 Ca 84
12450 Garrigous 12 152 Cd 83
24620 Garrigue 24 137 Ba 79
33910 Garrigue, la 33 135 Ze 78
34210 Garrigue, la 34 166 Ce 88
34360 Garrigue, la 34 166 Ce 88
30190 Garrigues 30 154 Eb 85
34160 Garrigues 34 154 Ea 86
81500 Garrigues 81 165 Be 86
82800 Garrigues 82 150 Bd 84
64120 Garris 64 161 Yf 88
12170 Garrissous 12 152 Cd 84
83830 Garron 83 172 Gd 87
32600 Garros, le 32 164 Af 87
40110 Garrosse 40 146 Za 84
06850 Gars 06 158 Ge 85
37150 Gars, les 37 86 Ba 65
09310 Garsan 09 177 Be 93
29190 Gars-ar-Goff 29 62 Wa 59
36600 Garsenland 36 101 Bd 66
23320 Gartempe 23 114 Be 72
33990 Garthieu, le 33 134 Yf 78
28320 Gas 28 70 Bd 57
79230 Gascougnolle 79 111 Zd 71
23500 Gasne-Claire 23 126 Ca 74
27620 Gasny 27 50 Bd 54
11200 Gasparets 11 166 Ce 90
82400 Gasques 82 149 Af 84
33650 Gassies 33 135 Zc 81
83580 Gassin 83 172 Gd 89
14380 Gast, le 14 46 Yf 56
40160 Gastes 40 146 Yf 83
15320 Gastier, le 15 140 Db 79
53540 Gastines 53 66 Yf 61
35430 Gastines, les 35 65 Ya 57
72300 Gastines-sur-Erve 72 84 Zd 61
77370 Gastins 77 52 Da 57
33460 Gaston 33 134 Zb 78
83120 Gastons, les 83 172 Gd 88
22210 Gastry 22 64 Xc 60
28300 Gasville 28 70 Bd 58
17270 Gat, le 17 123 Zf 77
23800 Gat, le 23 114 Bd 71
87320 Gatebourg 87 112 Af 71
17470 Gâtebourse 17 111 Ze 72
28170 Gâtelles 28 69 Bb 57
39120 Gatey 39 106 Fc 67
70600 Gatey 70 92 Fd 63
50150 Gathemo 50 47 Za 56
17150 Gâtine, la 17 123 Zc 76
49600 Gâtine, la 49 97 Yf 65
28380 Gâtines, les 28 49 Bb 56
35270 Gâts, les 35 65 Ya 58
85170 Gâts, les 85 97 Yd 68
85480 Gats, les 85 97 Ye 68
50760 Gatteville-le-Phare 50 33 Ye 50
06510 Gattières 06 159 Hb 86
30700 Gattigues 30 154 Eb 84
48150 Gatuzières 48 153 Dc 83
40190 Gaube 40 147 Ze 85
28140 Gaubert 28 70 Bd 60
79210 Gaubertière, la 79 110 Zc 72
45340 Gaubertin 45 71 Cc 60
57600 Gaubiving 57 57 Gf 54
85130 Gaubretière, la 85 97 Yf 67
33920 Gauchere, la 33 135 Zd 78
18260 Gaucherie, la 18 88 Cd 64
41250 Gaucherie, la 41 86 Bc 64
24230 Gauchers, les 24 135 Aa 79
62130 Gauchin 62 29 Cc 46
62150 Gauchin-Légal 62 29 Cd 46
62130 Gauchin-Verloingt 62 29 Cb 46
02430 Gauchy 02 40 Db 50
27930 Gauciel 27 50 Bb 54
28400 Gaudaine, la 28 69 Af 59
06610 Gaude, la 06 173 Ha 86
60210 Gaudechart 60 38 Bf 51
04340 Gaudeissard 04 158 Gc 82
65370 Gaudent 65 176 Ad 91
38660 Gaudes, les 38 132 Ff 77
19210 Gaudie, la 19 125 Bc 76
62760 Gaudiempré 62 29 Cd 47
35520 Gaudière, la 35 65 Yb 59
37390 Gaudières, les 37 85 Ae 64
09700 Gaudiès 09 165 Be 89
35190 Gaudinais, la 35 65 Ya 58
31800 Gaudines 31 163 Ae 90
18380 Gaudins, les 18 88 Cc 65
03110 Gaudons, les 03 116 Db 72
32380 Gaudonville 32 149 Af 85
32810 Gaudoux 32 163 Ad 86
83690 Gaudran, le 83 171 Gb 87
28310 Gaudreville 28 70 Bf 58
24540 Gaugeac 24 137 Af 80
30330 Gaujac 30 155 Ed 84
32220 Gaujac 32 164 Ae 88
47200 Gaujac 47 136 Aa 82
40330 Gaujacq 40 161 Zb 87
32420 Gaujan 32 163 Ae 88
81340 Gaulène 81 151 Cc 84
41270 Gault-du-Perche, le 41 69 Af 60
28800 Gault-Saint-Denis, le 28 70 Bc 59
51210 Gault-Soigny, le 51 53 Dd 56
63700 Gaumes, les 63 115 Ce 71
24250 Gaumier 24 137 Bb 80
31590 Gauré 31 165 Bd 87
33710 Gauriac 33 134 Zc 78
33240 Gauriaguet 33 135 Zd 78
65670 Gaussan 65 163 Ac 89
22150 Gausson 22 64 Xb 59
87520 Gautaud, le 87 125 Ba 73
71230 Gautherets, les 71 105 Eb 69
19300 Gautherie, la 19 126 Ca 76
26400 Gauthiers 26 143 Fa 80
58200 Gauthiers 58 88 Cf 64
33500 Gauthiers, les 33 135 Ze 79
17100 Gautiers, les 17 122 Zb 74
49170 Gautraie, la 49 83 Zb 64
35450 Gautrais, la 35 66 Yd 59
17360 Gautreau, le 17 135 Ze 78
17650 Gautrie, la 17 109 Yd 72
27130 Gauville 27 49 Af 56
61550 Gauville 61 49 Ad 56
80290 Gauville 80 38 Be 50
27930 Gauville-la-Campagne 27 49 Ba 54
45630 Gauvins, les 45 88 Ce 63
85220 Gauvrière, la 85 96 Yb 68
81290 Gaux, les 81 166 Cb 87
09290 Gauziats 09 164 Bb 90
46120 Gauzinie, la 46 138 Bf 80
65120 Gavarnie-Gèdre 65 175 Zf 92
32390 Gavarret-sur-Aulouste 32 149 Ad 86
47150 Gavaudun 47 137 Af 81
50430 Gaverie, la 50 33 Yc 53
12620 Gaverlac 12 152 Cf 83
38220 Gavet 38 144 Ff 78
20218 Gavignano CTC 181 Kb 94
20218 Gavignanu = Gavignano CTC 181 Kb 94
57570 Gavisse 57 44 Gb 52
50450 Gavray 50 46 Yd 55
44130 Gâvre, le 44 82 Yb 63
62580 Gavrelle 62 30 Cf 47
14210 Gavrus 14 35 Zc 54
65320 Gayan 65 162 Aa 89
81340 Gaycre 81 151 Cc 85
40210 Gaye 40 146 Yf 83
51120 Gaye 51 53 De 56
04250 Gayne, le 04 157 Ga 83
64350 Gayon 64 162 Ze 88
82110 Gayraud 82 149 Ba 83
31370 Gayrimont 31 164 Af 88
63310 Gays, les 63 116 Dc 72
82210 Gayssanès 82 149 Af 84
32480 Gazaupouy 32 148 Ac 84
65250 Gazave 65 175 Ac 90
32230 Gazax-et-Baccarisse 32 163 Ab 87
34330 Gazel, le 34 166 Cd 87
15300 Gazelle, la 15 127 Cf 77
43130 Gazelle, la 43 129 Df 77
78125 Gazéran 78 50 Be 57
47200 Gazette, la 47 136 Ab 81
56200 Gazilieg = La Gacilly 56 81 Xf 62
33610 Gazinet 33 134 Zb 80
65100 Gazost 65 175 Aa 90
48230 Gazy 48 153 Db 82
71350 Géanges 71 106 Ef 67
71700 Geatay 71 118 Ee 69
40320 Geaune 40 162 Zd 87
17250 Geay 17 122 Zb 73
79330 Geay 79 98 Ze 67
57430 Geblingen = Le Val-de-Guéblange 57 57 Gf 55
65120 Gèdre, Gavarnie- 65 175 Aa 92
49250 Gée 49 84 Ze 64
32720 Gée-Rivière 32 162 Ze 86
50560 Geffosses 50 33 Yc 54
14230 Géfosse-Fontenay 14 46 Yf 52
31510 Gège 31 176 Ad 90
36240 Gehée 36 101 Bd 66
68690 Geishouse 68 94 Ha 61
68510 Geispitzen 68 95 Hc 62
67118 Geispolsheim 67 60 Hd 57
67310 Geissweg 67 60 Hc 57
68600 Geiswasser 68 60 Hd 61
67270 Geiswiller 67 58 Hc 56
54120 Gélacourt 54 77 Ge 58
13400 Gélade, la 13 170 Fc 89
10100 Gélannes 10 73 De 58
54115 Gélaucourt 54 76 Ff 58
09160 Gèle 09 176 Ba 90
40630 Gelère, la 40 147 Zb 83
24580 Gélie, la 24 137 Af 78
28630 Gellainville 28 70 Bd 58
12700 Gelle 12 138 Ca 81
32290 Gellenave 32 162 Aa 86
54110 Gellenoncourt 54 56 Gc 56
63740 Gelles 63 127 Ce 74
25240 Gellin 25 107 Gb 68
40090 Geloux 40 147 Zc 85
40300 Geloux 40 160 Ye 87
57260 Gelucourt 57 57 Ge 56
88270 Gelvécourt-et-Adompt 88 76 Gb 59
61130 Gémages 61 68 Ad 59
88520 Gemaingoutte 88 77 Ha 59
21120 Gemeaux 21 92 Fa 64
33480 Gémeillan 33 134 Za 79
13420 Gémenos 13 171 Fd 89
45310 Gémigny 45 70 Be 61
31380 Gémil 31 165 Bd 86
73200 Gémilly 73 132 Gc 75
88170 Gemmelaincourt 88 76 Ff 59
25250 Gémonval 25 94 Gd 63
54115 Gémonville 54 76 Ff 58
17260 Gémozac 17 122 Zb 75
16170 Genac 16 123 Aa 74
95420 Genainville 95 50 Be 54
28190 Genainvilliers 28 69 Bc 58
28800 Genarville 28 69 Bc 59
33790 Génas 33 136 Aa 80
69740 Genas 69M 130 Ef 74
54150 Génaville 54 56 Ff 53
21140 Genay 21 90 Eb 63
69730 Genay 69M 118 Ef 73
79170 Genay 79 111 Ze 72
86160 Gençay 86 112 Ac 70
86230 Gençay 86 99 Ab 67
41130 Gendretière, la 41 87 Bd 65
88140 Gendreville 88 75 Fe 59
39350 Gendrey 39 107 Fe 65
49220 Gené 49 83 Zb 63
03380 Génébrière, la 03 115 Cc 70
82230 Génébrières 82 150 Bc 85
59242 Genech 59 30 Db 45
71420 Génelard 71 105 Eb 69
63340 Genelières 63 128 Da 76
30510 Générac 30 169 Ec 86
33920 Générac 33 135 Zc 77
30140 Générargues 30 154 Df 84
65150 Générest 65 175 Ad 90
11270 Generville 11 165 Bf 89
28630 Génerville 28 70 Bd 58
61140 Geneslay 61 67 Zd 57
87500 Geneste, la 87 125 Bb 76
07530 Genestelle 07 142 Ec 80
19300 Genestine, la 19 126 Ca 76
44140 Geneston 44 97 Yc 66
63150 Genestoux, le 63 127 Ce 75
53940 Genest-Saint-Isle, le 53 66 Za 60
36160 Genet 36 114 Ca 70
37260 Genetay, le 37 100 Ad 65
71290 Genête, la 71 118 Fa 69
23800 Genêtes, les 23 113 Bd 71
42990 Genetey, le 42 129 De 74
17360 Génétouze, la 17 123 Zf 77
85190 Génétouze, la 85 97 Yc 68
23160 Genêts 23 113 Bc 70
50530 Genêts 50 46 Yd 56
18210 Genêts, les 18 102 Cd 68
61270 Genettes, les 61 49 Ad 57
25870 Geneuille 25 93 Ff 65
02110 Genève 02 40 Db 49
42380 Geneviecq 42 129 Ea 76
49350 Genevraie, la 49 84 Ze 65
61240 Genevraie, la 61 48 Ab 56
77580 Génevray 77 52 Cf 56
38450 Genevray, le 38 143 Fd 78
77690 Genevraye, la 77 71 Ce 59
70240 Genevreuille 70 93 Gc 62
70240 Genevrey 70 93 Gb 62
52500 Genevrières 52 92 Fd 62
52320 Genevroye, la 52 75 Fa 59
25250 Geney 25 94 Gd 64
87400 Geneytouse, la 87 125 Bc 74
95650 Génicourt 95 51 Ca 54
55000 Génicourt-sous-Condé 55 55 Fa 55
55320 Génicourt-sur-Meuse 55 55 Fc 54
85580 Génie, le 85 109 Ye 71
37460 Genillé 37 100 Ba 65
24160 Génis 24 125 Ba 77
33420 Génissac 33 135 Ze 79
01200 Génissiat 01 119 Fe 72
26750 Génissieux 26 143 Fa 78
21110 Genlis 21 106 Fb 65
25660 Gennes 25 107 Ga 65
62390 Gennes-Ivergny 62 29 Ca 47
53200 Gennes-sur-Glaize 53 83 Zc 61
35370 Gennes-sur-Seiche 35 66 Yf 61
49350 Gennes-Val-de-Loire 49 84 Ze 64
49490 Genneteil 49 84 Aa 63
03400 Gennetines 03 104 Dc 69
79150 Genneton 79 98 Zd 66
76550 Gennetuit 76 37 Af 49
14600 Genneville 14 36 Ab 52
92270 Genne-Villiers 92 51 Cb 55
39240 Genod 39 119 Fd 70
30450 Génolhac 30 154 Df 82
28150 Genonville 28 70 Bd 59
31510 Génos 31 176 Ae 91
65240 Génos 65 175 Ac 92
16270 Genouillac 16 124 Ad 73
23350 Genouillac 23 114 Bf 70
17430 Genouillé 17 110 Zb 72
86250 Genouillé 86 112 Ac 72
01090 Genouilleux 01 118 Ee 72
18310 Genouilly 18 101 Bf 65
21390 Genouilly 21 90 Eb 64
71460 Genouilly 71 105 Ed 69
52400 Genrupt 52 92 Fe 61
32220 Gensac 32 164 Af 88
33890 Gensac 33 135 Aa 80
65140 Gensac 65 162 Aa 88
82120 Gensac 82 149 Af 85
31350 Gensac-de-Boulogne 31 163 Ad 89
16130 Gensac-la-Pallue 16 123 Ze 75
31310 Gensac-sur-Garonne 31 164 Ba 89
83170 Gensiés, les 83 171 Ff 88
16130 Genté 16 123 Ze 75
35150 Genteg 35 66 Yd 61
80800 Gentelles 80 39 Cc 49
35270 Gentière, la 35 65 Yb 58
03420 Gentioux, le 03 115 Cd 71
23340 Gentioux-Pigerolles 23 126 Bf 74
60400 Genvry 60 39 Cf 51
09100 George 09 165 Bd 90
03450 Georges, les 03 116 Da 72
86310 Georgets 86 112 Af 69
71410 Georgets, les 71 105 Eb 68
01100 Géovreisset 01 119 Fd 71
50850 Ger 50 47 Zb 56
64530 Ger 64 162 Zf 89
39110 Geraise 39 107 Ff 67
71330 Gérand 71 106 Fb 68
03120 Géranton 03 116 De 72
35500 Gérard 35 66 Ye 60
35560 Gerardais, le 35 66 Yc 58
27240 Gerarderie, la 27 49 Af 55
50810 Gérardière, la 50 47 Yf 54
88400 Gérardmer 88 77 Gf 60
10220 Géraudot 10 74 Eb 59
55130 Gérauvilliers 55 75 Fd 57
55130 Gerauvilliers 55 75 Fd 57
73470 Gerbaix 73 131 Fe 75
42590 Gerbe 42 117 Ea 73
57170 Gerbécourt 57 57 Gd 55
54740 Gerbécourt-et-Haplemont 54 76 Ga 58
88430 Gerbépal 88 77 Gf 60
60380 Gerberoy 60 38 Bf 51
54830 Gerbéviller 54 77 Gd 58
55110 Gercourt-et-Drillantcourt 55 55 Fb 53
02140 Gercy 02 41 Df 50
31440 Ger de Boutx 31 176 Ae 91
64160 Gerderest 64 162 Ze 88
64260 Gère-Béleston 64 174 Zd 90
02260 Gergny 02 41 Df 49
63670 Gergovie 63 128 Da 74
21410 Gergueil 21 106 Ee 65
56140 Gerguy 56 81 Xe 61
71590 Gergy 71 106 Ef 67
21700 Gerland 21 106 Fa 66
13490 Gerle 13 171 Fd 87
65240 Germ 65 175 Ac 92
01250 Germagnat 01 119 Fc 71
42940 Germagneux 42 129 Df 75
71460 Germagny 71 105 Ed 68
02590 Germaine 02 40 Da 50
51160 Germaine 51 53 Ea 54
52160 Germaines 52 91 Fa 62
28500 Germainville 28 50 Bc 56
52150 Germainvilliers 52 75 Fd 60
52230 Germay 52 75 Fc 58
71640 Germdles 71 105 Ee 68
25510 Germéfontaine 25 108 Gc 65
58800 Germenay 58 89 Dd 65
24210 Germenie, la 24 125 Ba 77
16140 Germeville 16 111 Zf 73
86200 Germier 86 99 Aa 66
17520 Germignac 17 123 Zd 75
33320 Germignan 33 134 Zb 79
39380 Germigney 39 107 Fe 66
70100 Germigney 70 92 Fd 64
28140 Germignonville 28 70 Be 59
51390 Germigny 51 53 Df 53
89600 Germigny 89 73 De 61
45110 Germigny-des-Prés 45 88 Cb 61
77910 Germigny-L'Evêque 77 52 Cf 55
18150 Germigny-L'Exempt 18 103 Cf 67
77840 Germigny-sous-Coulombs 77 52 Da 54
58320 Germigny-sur-Loire 58 103 Da 66
51130 Germinon 51 53 Ea 55
54170 Germiny 54 76 Ff 57
52230 Germisay 52 75 Fc 58
71520 Germolles-sur-Grosne 71 118 Ed 71
25640 Germondans 25 93 Gb 64
79220 Germond-Rouvre 79 111 Zd 70
08240 Germont 08 42 Ef 52
45480 Germonville 45 70 Bf 59

272 | Galère, la

54740 Germonville 54 76 Gb 58
08440 Gernelle 08 42 Ee 50
19500 Gernes 19 138 Bd 78
02160 Gernicourt 02 41 Df 52
05310 Géro 05 145 Gd 80
88220 Géroménil 88 77 Gc 60
64400 Géronce 64 161 Zb 89
18350 Gérots, les 18 103 Cf 67
76540 Gerponville 76 36 Ad 50
14430 Gerrots 14 35 Zf 53
24480 Gers, le 24 137 Af 79
16440 Gersac 16 123 Aa 75
27770 Gersey 27 50 Bb 55
67150 Gerstheim 67 60 He 58
67140 Gertwiller 67 60 Hc 58
39570 Geruge 39 107 Fd 69
34380 Gervais 34 153 Dd 86
13090 Gervais, les 13 170 Fc 87
26600 Gervans 26 142 Ef 78
76790 Gerville 76 36 Ab 50
50430 Gerville-la-Forêt 50 46 Yd 53
47410 Gervinie 47 136 Ad 81
62530 Gervins 62 29 Cd 46
55000 Géry 55 55 Fb 56
63360 Gerzat 63 128 Da 74
70500 Gésincourt-Oboncourt 70 93 Ff 62
53150 Gesnes 53 67 Zc 60
55110 Gesnes-en-Argonne 55 55 Fa 53
72130 Gesnes-le-Gandelin 72 68 Aa 58
08700 Gespunsart 08 42 Ee 50
31510 Gesset 31 176 Ae 90
64190 Gestas 64 161 Za 88
49600 Gesté 49 97 Yf 65
56530 Gestel 56 79 Wd 62
09220 Gestiès 09 177 Bd 92
53370 Gesvres 53 67 Zf 58
44190 Gétigné 44 97 Ye 66
74260 Gets, les 74 121 Ge 72
65100 Geu 65 175 Zf 90
67170 Geudertheim 67 58 He 56
64370 Géus-d'Arzacq 64 162 Zc 88
64400 Géüs-d'Oloron 64 161 Zb 89
35850 Gévézé 35 65 Yb 59
70500 Gevigney-et-Mercey 70 93 Ff 62
55200 Geville 55 55 Fe 56
39570 Gevingey 39 106 Fd 69
73300 Gévoudaz 73 132 Gb 77
25270 Gevresin 25 107 Ga 67
21220 Gevrey-Chambertin 21 106 Ef 65
21520 Gevrolles 21 74 Ee 61
39100 Gevry 39 106 Fc 66
01170 Gex 01 120 Ga 70
26750 Geyssans 26 143 Fa 78
80600 Gézaincourt 80 29 Cb 48
65100 Gez-ez-Angles 65 162 Aa 90
70700 Gezier-et-Fontenelay 70 93 Ff 64
54380 Gézoncourt 54 56 Ff 55
20121 Ghigliazza CTC 182 If 96
20228 Ghilloni Suprana CTC 181 Kc 91
20240 Ghisonaccia CTC 183 Kc 96
20240 Ghisonaccia Gare CTC 183 Kc 96
20227 Ghisoni CTC 183 Kb 96
59530 Ghissignies 59 31 Dd 47
20240 Ghisunaccia = Ghisonaccia CTC 183 Kc 96
20100 Ghjunchetu = Giuncheto CTC 184 If 99
59254 Ghyvelde 59 27 Cd 42
20143 Giacomoni CTC 184 Ka 98
20170 Gialla CTC 185 Kb 99
06540 Giandola, la 06 159 Hd 85
20171 Giannuccio CTC 184 Ka 99
63620 Giat 63 127 Cc 74
17270 Gibeau, le 17 135 Zf 77
54112 Gibeaumeix 54 75 Fe 57
31560 Gibel 31 165 Be 89
02440 Gibercourt 02 40 Db 50
55150 Gibercy 55 43 Fc 53
37340 Giberdière, la 37 85 Ac 64
10500 Giberie, la 10 74 Ed 58
48100 Gibertés, le 48 140 Db 81
14730 Giberville 14 47 Ze 53
19150 Gibiat 19 126 Be 77
19300 Gibiat 19 126 Ca 76
71800 Gibles 71 117 Ec 71
03210 Gibons, les 03 116 Db 70
17160 Gibourne 17 111 Ze 73
23700 Gibreix 23 115 Cd 72
40380 Gibret 40 161 Zb 86
17160 Gicq, le 17 111 Ze 73
22650 Giclais, la 22 65 Xe 57
44440 Gicquelière, la 44 82 Yd 63
45520 Gidy 45 70 Bf 61
61210 Giel-Gourteilles 61 48 Ze 56
45500 Gien 45 88 Cd 62
83400 Giens 83 172 Ga 90
58230 Gien-sur-Cure 58 105 Ea 66
38610 Gières 38 144 Fe 77
73590 Giettaz, la 73 133 Gd 73
50160 Gieville 50 47 Za 54
41130 Gièvres 41 87 Be 65
52210 Giey-sur-Aujon 52 91 Fa 61
74210 Giez 74 132 Gb 74
51290 Giffaumont-Champaubert 51 74 Ee 57
91440 Gif-sur-Yvette 91 51 Ca 56
83420 Gigaro 83 172 Gd 89
34770 Gigean 34 168 De 88
16400 Giget 16 124 Aa 75
47300 Giget 47 149 Ae 82
20170 Giglio CTC 185 Kb 98
34150 Gignac 34 167 Dd 87
46600 Gignac 46 138 Bc 78
84400 Gignac 84 156 Fd 85
13180 Gignac-la-Nerthe 13 170 Fb 88
63340 Gignat 63 128 Db 76
88320 Gignéville 88 76 Ff 60
88390 Gigney 88 76 Gc 59
21200 Gigny 21 106 Ef 66
39320 Gigny 39 119 Fc 70
89160 Gigny 89 90 Eb 62
51290 Gigny-Bussy 51 74 Ed 57
71240 Gigny-sur-Saône 71 106 Ef 69
84190 Gigondas 84 155 Ef 84
04250 Gigors 04 157 Ga 82
26400 Gigors 26 143 Fa 80
46150 Gigouzac 46 137 Bc 81
81530 Gijounet 81 166 Cd 86
76630 Gilcourt 76 37 Bb 49
06830 Gilette 06 159 Hb 85
07270 Gilhoc-sur-Ormèze 07 142 Ee 79
52330 Gillancourt 52 74 Ef 60
35160 Gillard, le 35 65 Ya 60
31190 Gillard-Tournié 31 164 Bc 88
52230 Gillaumé 52 75 Fc 58
28260 Gilles 28 50 Bd 55
40210 Gillet 40 146 Yf 83
33730 Gillets, les 33 147 Ze 82
25650 Gilley 25 108 Gc 66
52500 Gilley 52 92 Fd 62
17590 Gillieux, le 17 109 Yc 71
39250 Gillois 39 107 Ga 68
38260 Gillonnay 38 131 Fb 76
12340 Gillorgues 12 152 Ce 82
21640 Gilly-lès-Citeaux 21 106 Ef 65
73200 Gilly-sur-Isère 73 132 Gc 75
71160 Gilly-sur-Loire 71 116 De 69
60129 Gilocourt 60 52 Cf 53
82500 Gimat 82 149 Af 85
32340 Gimbrède 32 149 Ae 84
67370 Gimbrett 67 58 Hd 56
13200 Gimeaux 13 169 Ed 87
63200 Gimeaux 63 115 Da 73
55260 Gimécourt 55 55 Fc 55
19800 Gimel-les-Cascades 19 126 Bf 77
16130 Gimeux 16 123 Zd 75
54170 Gimeys 54 56 Ff 57
42140 Gimond, la 42 130 Ec 75
18250 Gimonets, les 18 88 Cd 65
32200 Gimont 32 164 Af 87
58470 Gimouille 58 103 Da 67
65220 Gimous 65 163 Ab 88
61310 Ginai 61 48 Ab 56
82330 Ginals 82 151 Bf 83
83560 Ginasservis 83 171 Ff 86
80360 Ginchy 80 39 Cf 48
11140 Gincla 11 178 Cb 92
55400 Gincrey 55 55 Fd 53
46250 Gindou 46 137 Bb 81
11120 Ginestas 11 167 Cf 89
12160 Gineste 12 152 Cc 83
12120 Ginestet 12 151 Cc 84
24130 Ginestet 24 136 Ac 79
34610 Ginestet 34 167 Cf 86
07660 Ginestet, le 07 141 Df 80
12170 Ginestous 12 152 Cd 84
48260 Ginestouse, la 48 140 Cf 81
67270 Gingsheim 67 58 Hd 56
12140 Ginolhac 12 139 Cd 81
46300 Ginouillac 46 138 Bd 80
46320 Ginouillac 46 138 Be 81
46130 Gintrac 46 138 Be 79
40120 Ginx, le 40 147 Zd 84
20237 Giocatojo CTC 181 Kc 94
51130 Gionges 51 53 Df 55
18000 Gionne 18 102 Cc 66
15130 Giou-de-Mamou 15 139 Cc 79
23500 Gioux 23 126 Ca 74
63690 Gioux 63 127 Cd 75
63810 Gioux 63 127 Cd 76
20134 Giovicacce CTC 183 Ka 97
20100 Giovighi CTC 184 Ka 99
58700 Gipy 58 103 Dc 65
48170 Giraldès 48 141 Dd 80
88390 Girancourt 88 76 Gb 60
33133 Girard 33 135 Ze 79
33790 Girard 33 135 Aa 80
73660 Girard, le 73 132 Gb 76
36290 Girardetterie, la 36 101 Bb 67
37600 Girardière, la 37 100 Af 66
86210 Girardière, la 86 100 Ad 68
05700 Girards, les 05 156 Fe 82
18110 Girards, les 18 102 Cb 65
18300 Girarmes, les 18 88 Cf 65
41210 Giraudière 41 87 Be 63
53470 Giraudière, la 53 67 Zb 59
36120 Giraudons, les 36 102 Bf 68
03120 Girauds, les 03 116 Dd 71
08460 Giraumont 08 41 Ed 50
54780 Giraumont 54 56 Ff 54
60150 Giraumont 60 39 Ce 52
55200 Girauvoisin 55 55 Fd 56
07800 Girbaud 07 142 Ee 79
88500 Gircourt-lès-Viéville 88 76 Gb 58
88600 Girecourt-sur-Durbion 88 77 Gd 59
70210 Girefontaine 70 93 Gb 61
77120 Giremoutiers 77 52 Da 55
12240 Giret 12 151 Cb 83
32600 Girette, la 32 164 Ba 87
15310 Girgols 15 139 Cc 78
38140 Girin 38 131 Fc 77
54830 Giriviller 54 77 Gc 58
81260 Girmanes, les 81 166 Cd 87
88150 Girmont 88 76 Gc 59
88340 Girmont-Val-d'Ajol 88 77 Gd 61
20147 Girolata CTC 182 Id 94
45120 Girolles 45 71 Ce 60
89200 Girolles 89 90 Df 63
90200 Giromagny 90 94 Ge 62
01130 Giron 01 119 Fe 71
88170 Gironcourt-sur-Vraine 88 76 Ff 59
07160 Girond 07 142 Ec 79
08260 Girondelle 08 41 Ec 49
33190 Gironde-sur-Dropt 33 135 Zf 81
28170 Gironville 28 50 Bc 57
77890 Gironville 77 71 Cd 59
55200 Gironville-sous-les-Côtes 55 55 Fe 56
91720 Gironville-sur-Essonne 91 71 Cc 58
31160 Girosp 31 176 Ae 90
85150 Girouard, le 85 109 Yc 69
81500 Giroussens 81 150 Be 86
15140 Giroux 15 139 Cc 78
36150 Giroux 36 101 Bf 66
20147 Girulatu = Girolata CTC 182 Id 94
85340 Girvière, la 85 109 Ya 69
58700 Giry 58 103 Dc 65
27330 Gisay-la-Coudre 27 49 Ad 55
32200 Giscaro 32 164 Af 87
33840 Giscos 33 148 Ze 83
50190 Gislarderie, la 50 46 Yd 53
27140 Gisors 27 50 Be 53
12360 Gissac 12 152 Cf 85
21350 Gissey-le-Vieil 21 91 Ec 65
21150 Gissey-sous-Flavigny 21 91 Ed 63
21410 Gissey-sur-Ouche 21 91 Ee 65
71190 Gissy 71 105 Ea 67
89140 Gisy-les-Nobles 89 72 Db 59
73210 Gitte, la 73 133 Gd 75
20251 Giuncaggio CTC 183 Kc 95
20100 Giuncheto CTC 184 If 99
18600 Givardon 18 103 Ce 67
03190 Givarlais 03 115 Cd 70
84500 Givaudan 84 155 Ee 83
18340 Givaudins 18 102 Cc 66
62149 Givenchy 62 29 Ce 45
62580 Givenchy-en-Gohelle 62 30 Ce 46
62810 Givenchy-le-Noble 62 29 Cc 47
58330 Giverdy 58 104 Dc 66
27620 Giverny 27 50 Bd 54
27560 Giverville 27 49 Ad 53
08600 Givet 08 42 Ee 48
08200 Givonne 08 42 Ef 50
69700 Givors 69M 130 Ee 75
45300 Givraines 45 71 Cc 60
85800 Givrand 85 96 Ya 68
55500 Givrauval 55 55 Fb 57
85540 Givre, le 85 109 Yd 70
03410 Givrette 03 115 Cd 70
17260 Givrezac 17 122 Zc 75
39240 Givria 39 119 Fd 70
08220 Givron 08 41 Eb 51
08130 Givry 08 41 Ed 52
71640 Givry 71 105 Ee 68
89200 Givry 89 90 De 63
57670 Givrycourt 57 57 Gf 55
51330 Givry-en-Argonne 51 54 Ef 55
51130 Givry-lès-Loisy 51 53 Df 55
46150 Gizard 46 137 Bb 81
51800 Gizaucourt 51 54 Ee 54
86340 Gizay 86 112 Ac 70
37340 Gizeux 37 84 Ab 64
39190 Gizia 39 119 Fc 69
46240 Gizot 46 138 Bd 81
02350 Gizy 02 40 De 51
50470 Glacerie, la 50 33 Yc 51
05340 Glacier Blanc 05 145 Gc 79
83136 Glacières, les 83 171 Fe 88
59132 Glageon 59 31 Ea 48
60129 Glaignes 60 52 Cf 53
25340 Glainans 25 94 Gd 64
63160 Glaine-Montaigut 63 128 Dc 74
08200 Glaire 08 42 Ef 50
05400 Glaise 05 144 Fe 81
33620 Glaive, la 33 135 Ze 78
05800 Glaizil, le 05 144 Ff 80
25360 Glamondans 25 93 Gb 65
02400 Gland 02 52 Dc 54
42740 Gland 42 129 Eb 76
89740 Gland 89 90 Eb 62
26410 Glandage 26 143 Fd 80
77167 Glandelles 77 71 Ce 59
79290 Glandes 79 98 Ze 66
41200 Glandier 41 87 Be 64
19230 Glandier, le 19 125 Bc 76
01300 Glandieu 01 131 Fd 74
87500 Glandon 87 125 Bb 76
02810 Glandons, les 02 52 Db 54
53110 Glandsemé 53 67 Zd 58
46130 Glanes 46 138 Bf 79
44390 Glanet 44 82 Yc 64
87380 Glanges 87 125 Bc 74
51300 Glannes 51 54 Ed 56
21250 Glanon 21 106 Fa 66
14950 Glanville 14 48 Aa 53
73340 Glapigny 73 132 Ga 74
82500 Glatens 82 149 Af 85
36210 Glatigny 36 101 Be 65
50250 Glatigny 50 33 Yc 53
57530 Glatigny 57 56 Gc 54
60650 Glatigny 60 38 Bf 52
46160 Glaudet 46 138 Bf 81
25310 Glay 25 94 Gf 64
69210 Glay 69M 130 Ed 73
44580 Glémerie, la 44 96 Ya 66
56200 Glénac 56 81 Xf 62
15150 Glénat 15 139 Cb 79
63460 Glenat 63 116 Da 72
79330 Glénay 79 98 Ze 67
12780 Glène, la 12 152 Da 83
23380 Glénic 23 114 Bf 71
02160 Glennes 02 40 De 52
86200 Glénouze 86 99 Zf 67
19220 Gleny 19 138 Ca 78
11360 Gléon 11 179 Cf 90
25190 Glère 25 94 Gf 64
56350 Gléré 56 81 Xf 63
36140 Glésolle, la 36 114 Be 70
81330 Glevade, la 81 166 Cc 86
12780 Gleysenove 12 152 Cf 83
38580 Gleyzin 38 132 Ga 76
50620 Glinel, le 50 46 Ye 53
27190 Glisolles 27 49 Ba 55
80440 Glisy 80 39 Cc 49
76750 Gloe, la 76 37 Bc 51
22110 Glomel 22 63 Wd 59
62120 Glomenghem 62 29 Cc 45
35550 Glonais, la 35 81 Ya 62
54122 Glonville 54 77 Ge 58
85430 Glorandière, la 85 109 Yd 69
66320 Glorianes 66 179 Cd 93
14100 Glos 14 48 Ab 54
61550 Glos-la-Ferrière 61 49 Ad 55
27290 Glos-sur-Risle 27 49 Ae 53
38250 Glovettes, les 38 143 Fd 78
29190 Glugéau 29 62 Vf 58
46600 Gluges 46 138 Bd 79
07190 Gluiras 07 142 Ed 79
07300 Glun 07 142 Ee 78
58370 Glux-en-Glenne 58 104 Ea 67
32100 Goalard, le 32 148 Ab 85
29470 Goarem-Coz 29 62 Ve 58
82500 Goas 82 149 Af 86
29690 Goashalec 29 62 Wb 58
29460 Goasven 29 62 Ve 58
21540 Godan 21 91 Ed 64
50300 Godefroy, la 50 46 Ye 56
85600 Godelinières, les 85 97 Ye 66
60420 Godenvillers 60 39 Cd 51
76110 Goderville 76 36 Ac 51
24460 Godet, le 24 124 Ae 77
59270 Godewaersvelde 59 30 Cd 44
50500 Godillerie, la 50 34 Yd 53
49310 Godinière, la 49 98 Zc 66
61240 Godisson 61 48 Ab 56
63850 Godivelle, la 63 127 Cf 76
88410 Godoncourt 88 76 Ff 60
28800 Godonville 28 70 Bc 60
03370 Goélat 03 115 Cc 70
67320 Gœrlingen 67 57 Ha 56
67360 Gœrsdorf 67 58 He 55
64400 Goès 64 161 Zc 89
57620 Goetzenbruck 57 58 Hc 55
59169 Gœulzin 59 30 Da 47
07700 Gogne 07 154 Ed 82
54450 Gogney 54 77 Gf 57
59600 Gognies-Chaussée 59 31 Df 46
50300 Gohannière, la 50 46 Ye 56
14400 Goherrerie, la 14 34 Zb 53
49320 Gohier 49 84 Zd 64
28160 Gohory 28 69 Bb 59
57420 Goin 57 56 Gb 55
42110 Goincet 42 129 Ea 74
60000 Goincourt 60 38 Ca 52
13610 Goirands, les 13 170 Fc 87
33910 Goizet 33 135 Ze 79
60640 Golancourt 60 39 Da 50
87130 Golas 87 126 Be 74
88190 Golbey 88 76 Gc 59
68760 Goldbach-Altenbach 68 94 Ha 61
82400 Golfech 82 149 Af 84
06220 Golfe-Juan 06 173 Ha 87
12140 Golinhac 12 139 Cd 81
45330 Gollainville 45 71 Cc 59
50390 Golleville 50 33 Yc 52
22390 Golloth, le 22 63 We 58
33220 Golse 33 136 Ab 79
41310 Gombergean 41 86 Ba 63
57220 Gomelange 57 57 Gc 53
22230 Gomené 22 64 Xd 59
64420 Gomer 64 162 Ze 89
91400 Gometz-la-Ville 91 51 Ca 56
91940 Gometz-le-Châtel 91 51 Ca 56
62121 Gomiécourt 62 30 Ce 48
12400 Gommaric 12 152 Cf 85
62111 Gommecourt 62 29 Cd 48
78270 Gommecourt 78 50 Bd 54
59144 Gommegnies 59 31 De 47
22290 Gommenec'h 22 63 Wf 57
68210 Gommersdorf 68 94 Ha 63
28310 Gommerville 28 70 Bf 58
76430 Gommerville 76 36 Ac 51
21400 Gomméville 21 74 Ec 61
28140 Gommiers 28 70 Be 60
02120 Gomont 02 40 De 49
08190 Gomont 08 41 Ea 51
52150 Gonaincourt 52 75 Fd 59
72600 Gonardière, la 72 68 Ab 58
38290 Gonas 38 131 Fa 74
38570 Goncelin 38 132 Ff 76
52150 Goncourt 52 75 Fd 59
87500 Gondandeix 87 125 Ba 75
62570 Gondardenne 62 29 Cb 44
59147 Gondecourt 59 30 Cf 45
25680 Gondenans-les-Moulins 25 93 Gc 64
25340 Gondenans-Montby 25 94 Gc 64
16200 Gondeville 16 123 Zf 74
73660 Gondran 73 132 Gb 76
54800 Gondrecourt-Aix 54 56 Fe 53
55130 Gondrecourt-le-Château 55 75 Fd 57
45340 Gondreville 45 71 Cc 60
45490 Gondreville 45 71 Cd 60
54840 Gondreville 54 56 Ff 56
57640 Gondreville 57 56 Gc 53
60117 Gondreville 60 52 Cf 53
57815 Gondrexange 57 57 Gf 56
54450 Gondrexon 54 77 Ge 57
32330 Gondrin 32 148 Ab 85
17100 Gonds, les 17 122 Zc 74
95500 Gonesse 95 51 Cc 55
65350 Gonez 65 163 Ab 89
83590 Gonfaron 83 172 Gb 89
50190 Gonfreville 50 46 Yd 53
76110 Gonfreville-Caillot 76 36 Ac 51
76700 Gonfreville-l'Orcher 76 35 Ab 51
61550 Gonfrière, la 61 49 Ac 56
56440 Gonnec 56 80 Wf 61
59231 Gonnelieu 59 30 Da 48
76730 Gonnetot 76 37 Af 50
50560 Gonneville 50 46 Yc 54
14810 Gonneville-en-Auge 14 48 Ze 53
76280 Gonneville-la-Mallet 76 36 Ab 51
50330 Gonneville-Le Theil 50 33 Yd 51
14600 Gonneville-sur-Honfleur 14 36 Ab 52
14510 Gonneville-sur-Mer 14 48 Zf 53
76590 Gonneville-sur-Scie 76 37 Ba 50
25360 Gonsans 25 108 Gb 65
47400 Gontaud-de-Nogaret 47 136 Ab 82
24310 Gonterie-Boulouneix, la 24 124 Ad 76
33330 Gontey 33 135 Ze 79
70400 Gonvillars 70 94 Gd 63
76560 Gonzeville 76 37 Ae 50
40180 Goos 40 161 Za 86
06500 Gorbio 06 159 Hc 86
24250 Gorce, la 24 137 Bb 80
63640 Gorce, la 63 115 Cd 73
63660 Gorce, la 63 129 Df 75
17120 Gorces, les 17 122 Zb 75
54730 Gorcy 54 43 Fe 51
84220 Gordes 84 155 Fb 85
80690 Gorenflos 80 29 Ca 48
38190 Gorge, la 38 132 Ff 77
38510 Gorge, la 38 131 Fc 74
44190 Gorges 44 97 Ye 66
50190 Gorges 50 46 Yd 53
80370 Gorges 80 29 Cb 48
48210* Gorges du Tarn Causses 48 153 Dc 82
59253 Gorgue, la 59 29 Ce 45
88270 Gorhey 88 76 Gb 59
33540 Gornac 33 135 Ze 81
85110 Gornieres, les 85 97 Yf 68
34190 Gorniès 34 153 Dd 85
62660 Gorre 62 29 Ce 45
87310 Gorre 87 125 Af 74
29460 Gorrequer 29 62 Ve 58
29870 Gorréquer 29 61 Vc 57
29550 Gorré-Toulhoat 29 78 Ve 59
01190 Gorrevod 01 118 Ef 70
53120 Gorron 53 66 Zb 58
87800 Gorsas 87 125 Ba 75
46210 Gorses 46 138 Ca 80
56250 Gorvello, le 56 80 Xc 63
57680 Gorze 57 56 Ga 54
81320 Gos 81 166 Ce 86
35140 Gosné 35 66 Yd 59
57930 Gosselming 57 57 Ha 56
63300 Gosson 63 128 Dd 73
42440 Got, le 42 129 De 74
64130 Gotein-Libarrenx 64 161 Za 89
67700 Gottenhouse 67 58 Hc 56
67490 Gottesheim 67 58 Hc 56
01100 Gottetaz, le 01 119 Fd 71
77114 Gouaix 77 72 Db 58
33840 Goualade 33 147 Zf 83
65240 Gouaux 65 175 Ac 91
31110 Gouaux-de-Larboust 31 175 Ac 92
31110 Gouaux-de-Luchon 31 176 Ad 91
40600 Goubern 40 146 Yf 82
49450 Gouberte, la 49 97 Yf 66
50330 Gouberville 50 33 Ye 50
76630 Gouchaupré 76 37 Bb 49
44470 Gouchère, la 44 82 Yd 65
50620 Goucherie, la 50 33 Ye 53
82270 Goudal 82 150 Bc 83
30630 Goudargues 30 154 Ec 83
02820 Goudelancourt-lès-Berrieux 02 41 Df 52
02350 Goudelancourt-lès-Pierrepont 02 41 Df 50
22290 Goudelin 22 64 Wf 57
13008 Goudes, les 13 170 Fc 89
43150 Goudet 43 141 Df 79
31230 Goudex 31 164 Af 88
65190 Goudon 65 163 Ab 89
40250 Goudosse 40 147 Zb 86
46240 Goudou 46 138 Bd 81
32600 Goudourvielle 32 164 Ba 87
82400 Goudourville 82 149 Af 84
50190 Goudrie, la 50 34 Yd 54
88630 Gouécourt 88 75 Fe 58
29370 Gouélet 29 78 Wa 60
36100 Gouers 36 102 Ca 67
29950 Gouesnac'h 29 78 Vf 61
35350 Gouesnière, la 35 65 Ya 57
29850 Gouesnou 29 62 Vd 58
86320 Gouex 86 112 Ae 70
56730 Gouézan 56 80 Xb 63
29190 Gouézec 29 78 Wa 59
61160* Gouffern en Auge 61 48 Aa 56
67270 Gougenheim 67 58 Hd 56
25680 Gouhelans 25 93 Gc 64
70110 Gouhenans 70 94 Gc 63
16150 Gouîe, la 16 112 Ae 73
28310 Gouillons 28 70 Bf 58
31160 Gouillou 31 176 Ae 90
09600 Gouiric 09 177 Be 90
03340 Gouise 03 116 Dc 70
46250 Goujounac 46 137 Bb 81
73480 Goula, la 73 133 Ha 77
27390 Goulafrière, la 27 48 Ac 55
60650 Goulancourt 60 38 Be 52
24460 Goulandie, la 24 124 Ae 76
63950 Goulandre, la 63 127 Cd 75
47310 Goulard 47 149 Ad 83
25450 Goule, la 25 108 Gf 65
76950 Goule, le 76 37 Bb 50
46310 Goulème 46 137 Bc 80
61150 Goulet 61 48 Zf 56
27600 Goulet, le 27 50 Bc 54
76640 Goulet, le 76 36 Ad 51
29160 Goulien 29 61 Vc 59
29770 Goulien 29 61 Vc 60
09220 Goulier 09 177 Bd 92
44850 Goulière, la 44 82 Yd 64
19430 Goulles 19 138 Ca 78
21520 Goulles, les 21 91 Ef 61
09140 Goulos 09 177 Bb 91
70270 Goulotte, la 70 94 Gd 62
65220 Goulous 65 163 Ac 89
58230 Gouloux 58 104 Ea 65
84220 Goult 84 156 Fb 85
29890 Goulven 29 62 Ve 57
47110 Gouneau 47 148 Ad 82
46300 Gouny 46 138 Bc 80
27150 Goupilière 27 37 Bd 52
87500 Goupillas 87 125 Bb 75
14210 Goupillières 14 47 Zd 54
27170 Goupillières 27 49 Ae 54
76570 Goupillières 76 37 Af 51
78770 Goupillières 78 50 Be 55
37290 Goupillières, les 37 100 Af 67
72150 Goupillières, les 72 85 Ad 61
27170 Goupil-Othon 27 49 Ae 54

A B C D E F G H I J K L M N O P Q R S T U V W X Y Z

Goupil-Othon | 273

55230 Gouraincourt 55 55 Fd 53
22330 Gouray, le 22 64 Xd 59
40990 Gourbera 40 146 Yf 86
50480 Gourbesville 50 33 Yd 52
09400 Gourbit 09 177 Bd 91
60220 Gourchelles 60 38 Be 50
31210 Gourdan-Polignan 31 163 Ad 90
15230 Gourdièges 15 139 Cf 79
06620 Gourdon 06 173 Gf 86
19170 Gourdon 19 126 Bf 75
46300 Gourdon 46 137 Bc 80
71300 Gourdon 71 105 Ec 69
19170 Gourdon-Murat 19 126 Bf 75
24750 Gourdoux 24 124 Ae 77
64440 Gourette 64 174 Ze 91
50750 Gourfaleur 50 46 Yf 54
51230 Gourgançon 51 53 Ea 56
79200 Gourgé 79 99 Ze 68
70120 Gourgeon 70 93 Ff 62
42240 Gourgois 42 129 Eb 76
48170 Gourgons 48 141 Dd 81
31160 Gourgue 31 176 Af 91
65130 Gourgue 65 163 Ab 90
56800 Gourhel 56 81 Xd 61
56110 Gourin 56 79 Wc 60
29710 Gourlizon 29 78 Ve 60
40370 Gournau 40 146 Yf 85
27120 Gournay 27 50 Bc 54
36230 Gournay 36 101 Be 69
62560 Gournay 62 29 Ca 45
76700 Gournay 76 36 Ab 51
76970 Gournay 76 37 Ae 50
79110 Gournay 79 111 Zf 72
76220 Gournay-en-Bray 76 38 Be 52
27580 Gournay-le-Guérin 27 49 Ae 56
60190 Gournay-sur-Aronde 60 39 Ce 52
03310 Gournet 03 115 Ce 71
27380 Gournets 27 37 Bc 52
05160 Gournier 05 144 Gb 81
61120 Gourquesalles 61 48 Ab 55
33660 Gours 33 135 Aa 79
16140 Gours, les 16 111 Zf 73
15170 Gourt 15 128 Cf 77
11410 Gourvieille 11 165 Be 88
16170 Gourville 16 123 Zf 74
78660 Gourville 78 70 Be 57
17490 Gourvillette 17 111 Ze 73
52170 Gourzon 52 75 Fa 57
29510 Goussagtel 29 78 Vf 60
28410 Goussainville 28 50 Bd 56
95190 Goussainville 95 51 Cc 54
02130 Goussancourt 02 53 De 53
30630 Goussargues 30 154 Ec 83
81640 Goussaudié, la 81 151 Ca 84
40465 Gousse 40 146 Za 86
78930 Goussonville 78 50 Be 55
19300 Goute, la 19 126 Bf 76
63230 Goutelle, la 63 127 Ce 73
09210 Goutemajou 09 164 Bb 89
31310 Goutevernisse 31 164 Bb 89
12390 Goutrens 12 151 Cc 82
24320 Gout-Rossignol 24 124 Ac 76
40400 Gouts 40 147 Zb 86
82150 Gouts 82 149 Ba 82
63880 Goutte, la 63 129 De 74
42990 Goutte-Claire 42 129 Df 74
88560 Goutte-du-Rieux 88 94 Gf 61
23320 Gouttes 23 114 Be 71
48130 Gouttes 48 140 Db 80
03290 Gouttes, les 03 116 De 70
88650 Gouttes, les 88 77 Gf 59
79300 Gouttieville 79 98 Zd 68
27410 Gouttières 27 49 Ae 54
63390 Gouttières 63 115 Ce 72
32500 Goutz 32 149 Ae 86
47250 Goutz 47 148 Aa 82
56480 Gouvello, la 56 79 Wf 59
82140 Gouvern 82 150 Be 84
77400 Gouvernes 77 51 Ce 55
62123 Gouves 62 29 Cd 47
50420 Gouvets 50 46 Yf 55
60270 Gouvieux 60 51 Cc 53
27240 Gouville 27 49 Af 55
50560 Gouville-sur-Mer 50 33 Yc 54
14680 Gouvix 14 47 Ze 54
38510 Gouvoux 38 131 Fc 74
17380 Goux 17 110 Zc 72
17800 Goux 17 123 Zd 75
32400 Goux 32 162 Zf 87
39100 Goux 39 106 Fd 66
49490 Goux, les 49 84 Aa 64
25150 Goux-lès-Dambelin 25 94 Ge 64
25520 Goux-les-Usiers 25 108 Gb 67
25440 Goux-sous-Landet 25 107 Ff 66
02420 Gouy 02 40 Db 48
76520 Gouy 76 37 Ba 52
62123 Gouy-en-Artois 62 29 Cd 47
62127 Gouy-en-Ternois 62 29 Cc 47
60120 Gouy-les-Groseillers 60 38 Cb 50
80640 Gouy-L'Hôpital 80 38 Bf 49
62870 Gouy-Saint-André 62 28 Bf 46
62530 Gouy-Servins 62 29 Cd 46
62112 Gouy-sous-Bellonne 62 30 Da 47
95450 Gouzangrez 95 50 Bf 54
64300 Gouze 64 161 Zb 88
59231 Gouzeaucourt 59 30 Da 48
31310 Gouzens 31 164 Bb 89
63410 Gouzet 63 115 Cf 73
23230 Gouzon 23 114 Cb 71
63300 Gouzon 63 128 Dd 74
23230 Gouzougnat 23 114 Cb 72
35580 Goven 35 65 Ya 60
54330 Goviller 54 76 Ga 58
56160 Govran 56 79 Wf 60
67210 Goxwiller 67 60 Hc 58
80700 Goyencourt 80 39 Ce 50
31120 Goyrans 31 164 Bc 88
34790 Grabels 34 168 De 87
22630 Grabuisson 22 65 Ya 58
18310 Graçay 18 101 Bf 66
47300 Grâce, la 47 149 Ae 82
22200 Grâces 22 63 We 57
22460 Grâce-Uzel 22 64 Xb 59
04530 Grach, le 04 145 Ge 82
48130 Grach, le 48 140 Db 81
70700 Grachaux 70 93 Ff 64
40560 Gracian 40 146 Yd 85
33990 Gracieuse, la 33 134 Yf 78
23500 Gradeix 23 126 Ca 74
20123 Gradello CTC 182 Ie 98
33170 Gradignan 33 134 Zc 80
87150 Grafeuil 87 124 Af 74
72150 Graffardières, les 72 85 Ac 61
52150 Graffigny-Chemin 52 75 Fd 59
49150 Grafinière, la 49 84 Zf 64
19190 Grafouillière, la 19 138 Be 78
31380 Gragnague 31 165 Bd 86
74430 Graidon 74 120 Gd 71
65170 Grailhen 65 175 Ac 91
86500 Graillé 86 112 Ae 70
76430 Graimbouville 76 36 Ab 51
76370 Graincourt 76 37 Bb 49
62147 Graincourt-lès-Havrincourt 62 30 Da 48
27380 Grainville 27 37 Bc 52
14190 Grainville-Langannerie 14 47 Ze 54
76450 Grainville-la-Teinturière 76 36 Ad 50
14210 Grainville-sur-Odon 14 35 Zc 54
76116 Grainville-sur-Ry 76 37 Bb 52
76110 Grainville-Ymauville 76 36 Ac 51
18500 Graire 18 102 Cb 66
37270 Grais, le 37 85 Af 65
61600 Grais, le 61 67 Ze 57
12420 Graissac 12 139 Ce 80
12420 Graissac 12 139 Ce 80
34260 Graissessac 34 167 Da 86
42220 Graix 42 130 Ed 76
47370 Gral, le 47 149 Af 82
17920 Grallet, le 17 122 Yf 74
46500 Gramat 46 138 Be 80
11240 Gramazie 11 165 Ca 90
84240 Grambois 84 156 Fd 86
42140 Grammond 42 130 Ec 75
70110 Grammont 70 94 Gd 63
12160 Gramond 12 151 Cc 83
19320 Gramont 19 138 Ca 77
32550 Gramont 32 163 Ad 87
82120 Gramont 82 149 Ae 85
20100 Granaccia = Granace CTC 184 Ka 99
20100 Granace CTC 184 Ka 99
20100 Granajola CTC 184 Ka 99
21580 Grancey-le-Château-Neuvelle 21 91 Fa 62
21570 Grancey-sur-Durce 21 74 Ed 60
89100 Granchette 89 72 Db 59
76660 Grancourt 76 37 Bc 49
88350 Grand 88 75 Fc 58
01260 Grand-Abergement, le 01 119 Fd 72
17290 Grand-Agère 17 110 Za 72
44520 Grand-Auverné 44 82 Ye 63
83230 Grand-Avis 83 172 Gc 90
89116 Grand-Bailly, le 89 89 Db 61
37420 Grand Ballet 37 99 Ab 65
89520 Grand-Banny, le 89 89 Db 63
59550 Grand-Béart 59 31 De 48
85130 Grand-Belon 85 97 Ye 67
05460 Grand Belvedere 05 145 Gf 80
19290 Grand-Billoux 19 126 Ca 75
28800 Grand-Bois 28 69 Bb 59
59219 Grand Bois 59 31 Df 48
18310 Grand-Boisfort, le 18 101 Bf 66
13104 Grand-Boisviel 13 169 Ee 87
18360 Grand-Bord, le 18 102 Cc 69
74450 Grand-Bornand, le 74 120 Gc 73
33680 Grand-Bos 33 134 Yf 79
23240 Grand-Bourg, le 23 113 Bd 72
27520 Grand Bourgtheroulde 27 49 Af 53
24350 Grand Brassac 24 124 Ac 77
59178 Grand-Bray 59 30 Dc 46
13310 Grand-Brays 13 170 Ef 86
16300 Grand-Breuil, le 16 123 Ze 75
86480 Grand-Breuil, le 86 111 Aa 70
19410 Grand-Brugeron 19 125 Bc 76
87130 Grand-Bueix 87 126 Bd 74
30300 Grand-Cabane, la 30 169 Ec 86
27270 Grand-Camp 27 49 Ad 54
76170 Grand-Camp 76 36 Ad 51
14450 Grandcamp-Maisy 14 34 Yf 52
40400 Grand-Candeles 40 146 Za 86
83340 Grand Candumy 83 171 Gb 88
24150 Grand-Castang 24 136 Ae 79
13830 Grand Caunet 13 171 Fd 89
50370 Grand-Celland 50 46 Ye 56
27410 Grandchain 27 49 Ad 54
08270 Grandchamp 08 41 Ec 51
19380 Grandchamp 19 138 Bf 78
52600 Grandchamp 52 92 Fc 62
58110 Grand-Champ 58 104 Dd 66
72610 Grandchamp 72 68 Ab 59
89350 Grandchamp 89 89 Da 62
56390 Grand-Champ = Gregam 56 80 Xa 62
14140 Grandchamp-le-Château 14 48 Aa 54
44119 Grandchamps-des-Fontaines 44 82 Yc 64
25200 Grand-Charmont 25 94 Ge 63
39260 Grand-Châtel 39 119 Fe 70
86150 Grand-Chaume 86 112 Ad 71
25390 Grand-Chaux 25 108 Gd 65
28150 Grand-Chavernay, le 28 70 Bd 59
19270 Grand-Chemin 19 126 Bd 77
33550 Grand-Chemin, le 33 135 Zd 80
73260 Grand-Cœur 73 133 Gd 75
63300 Grand-Cognet 63 128 Dd 74
30110 Grand-Combe, la 30 154 Ea 83
25570 Grand' Combe-Châteleu 25 108 Gd 66
25210 Grand'Combe-des-Bois 25 108 Ge 66
25210 Grand-Communal, le 25 108 Ge 65
01250 Grand-Corent 01 119 Fc 71
40110 Grand-Coulin 40 146 Yf 84
33680 Grand-Courgas, le 33 134 Yf 79
76530 Grand-Couronne 76 37 Ba 52
80300 Grandcourt 80 29 Ce 48
33950 Grand-Crohot-Océan 33 134 Ye 80
42320 Grand-Croix, la 42 130 Ed 75
77510 Grand-Doucy 77 52 Db 55
87140 Grande, la 87 113 Bb 72
23140 Grande Balleyte 23 114 Ca 72
81140 Grande-Baraque, la 81 150 Be 84
83143 Grande-Bastide 83 171 Ff 88
83560 Grande-Bastide, la 83 171 Fe 87
83640 Grande-Bastide, la 83 171 Fe 88
84460 Grande Bastide, la 84 155 Fa 86
13530 Grande-Boise, la 13 171 Fe 88
18240 Grande-Borne, la 18 88 Ce 64
58220 Grande-Brosse, la 58 89 Da 64
05200 Grande-Cabane 05 145 Gc 82
88410 Grande-Catherine, la 88 76 Ga 60
08230 Grande-Chaudière 08 41 Ed 49
86330 Grande-Chaussée 86 99 Aa 67
85260 Grande-Chevasse, la 85 97 Yd 67
19290 Grande-Combe 19 126 Ca 74
17420 Grande-Côte, la 17 122 Yf 75
70120 Grandecourt 70 93 Ff 63
85690 Grande-Croix 85 96 Xf 67
02140 Grande Denteuse, la 02 41 Df 50
33680 Grande-Escoure 33 134 Yf 79
88490 Grande-Fosse 88 77 Ha 58
88240 Grande-Fosse, la 88 76 Gb 60
79120 Grande-Foye, la 79 111 Zf 71
87800 Grande-Garde, la 87 125 Bb 75
17600 Grande Gorce, la 17 122 Za 75
89770 Grande Jaronnée, la 89 73 Dd 60
89150 Grande-Justice, la 89 72 Da 59
37800 Grande-Maison 37 100 Ad 65
36500 Grande-Maison, la 36 101 Bb 67
27160 Grande-Mare, la 27 49 Af 56
86290 Grande-Mothe, la 86 113 Ba 70
34280 Grande-Motte, la 34 168 Ea 87
59710 Grande-Ennetières 59 30 Da 45
18290 Grand-Entrevin, le 18 102 Cb 67
77130 Grande-Paroisse, la 77 72 Cf 58
18170 Grande-Pra, la 18 102 Cb 69
70140 Grande-Résie, la 70 92 Fd 64
83111 Grande-Rimande, la 83 172 Gc 87
77150 Grande-Romaine, la 77 51 Cd 56
27350 Grande Rue, la 27 36 Ad 52
50700 Grande-Rue, la 50 33 Yd 51
10170 Grandes-Chapelles, les 10 73 Ea 58
76540 Grandes-Dalles, les 76 36 Ac 50
04530 Grande-Serenne 04 145 Ge 81
51400 Grandes-Loges, les 51 54 Eb 54
37370 Grandes Maisons, les 37 85 Ad 62
76520 Grandes Masures, les 76 37 Bb 52
76530 Grand Essart, le 76 49 Ba 52
38490 Grandes-Ternes, les 38 131 Fd 75
76950 Grandes-Ventes, les 76 37 Bb 50
59760 Grande-Synthe 59 27 Cb 42
68150 Grande-Verrerie, La 68 60 Hb 59
71990 Grande-Verrière, la 71 105 Ea 67
37340 Grande-Vignellerie, la 37 85 Ab 64
85670 Grande-Villeneuve, la 85 97 Yc 67
63320 Grandeyrolles 63 128 Da 75
54260 Grand-Failly 54 43 Fd 52
70220 Grand-Fays, le 70 93 Gc 61
59244 Grand-Fayt 59 31 De 48
47240 Grandfonds 47 149 Ae 83
24700 Grand-Fonmassonnade 24 136 Aa 78
25320 Grandfontaine 25 107 Ff 65
67130 Grandfontaine 67 60 Ha 58
25510 Grandfontaine-sur-Creuse 25 108 Gc 65
59153 Grand-Fort-Philippe 59 27 Ca 42
35390 Grand-Fougeray = Felgerieg 35 82 Yb 62
60680 Grandfresnoy 60 39 Cd 52
45760 Grand Gharmoy, le 45 70 Ca 61
24300 Grand-Gillou 24 124 Ad 75
58350 Grand-Guichy 58 89 Da 65
08250 Grandham 08 54 Ef 53
50700 Grand-Hameau 50 33 Yc 52
14520 Grand Hameau, le 14 47 Za 52
88420 Grand-Himbaumont, le 88 77 Gf 58
33490 Grand-Housteau, le 33 135 Ze 81
28120 Grandhoux 28 69 Ba 59
86220 Grandins, les 86 100 Ad 67
86200 Grand-Insay, le 86 99 Aa 66
89200 Grand-Island, le 89 90 Df 64
23460 Grand-Janoit, le 23 114 Bf 73
33230 Grand-Jard, le 33 135 Ze 78
17350 Grandjean 17 122 Zc 73
28200 Grand-Juday, le 28 69 Bb 60
85670 Grand'Landes 85 97 Yc 68
18150 Grand-Laubray, le 18 103 Da 67
80132 Grand Lavuers 80 28 Be 48
37150 Grandlay 37 86 Af 65
33840 Grand-Lèbe 33 148 Ze 83
38690 Grand-Lemps, le 38 131 Fc 76
40210 Grand-Ligautenx 40 146 Yf 83
04210 Grand-Logisson, le 04 157 Ga 85
89300 Grand-Longueron, le 89 72 Dc 61
72150 Grand-Lucé, le 72 85 Ac 61
33480 Grand-Ludey 33 134 Za 78
02350 Grandlup-et-Fay 02 40 De 51
16450 Grand Madieu, le 16 112 Ac 73
18400 Grand-Malleray, le 18 102 Cb 67
12330 Grand-Mas 12 139 Cc 82
14170 Grandmesnil 14 48 Aa 55
18110 Grand-Millanfroid, le 18 88 Cb 65
59380 Grand Millebrugghe 59 27 Cb 43
79600 Grand-Moiré, le 79 99 Ze 67
71360 Grand-Moloy 71 105 Ec 66
50570 Grand-Moulin, le 50 33 Ye 53
83670 Grand-Nans 83 171 Ga 87
73260 Grand Naves 73 133 Gd 75
23240 Grand-Nérat 23 113 Bd 71
50600 Grandparigny 50 66 Yf 57
44850 Grand-Pâtis, le 44 82 Yd 64
16500 Grand-Peaupiquet 16 112 Ad 73
03350 Grand-Pernier 03 103 Ce 69
24440 Grand-Peyssou 24 137 Af 80
33950 Grand-Piquey, le 33 134 Ye 80
23360 Grand-Plaix, le 23 114 Be 70
36120 Grand-Plessis, le 36 102 Bf 68
70320 Grand-Poirmont 70 76 Gc 61
85480 Grand-Poiron, le 85 97 Ye 69
89113 Grand-Ponceau, le 89 89 Dc 61
13129 Grand-Ponche, le 13 169 Ed 88
86360 Grand-Pont 86 99 Ac 69
85230 Grand-Pont, le 85 96 Xf 67
08250 Grandpré 08 54 Ef 52
51480 Grand-Pré 51 53 Df 54
37350 Grand-Pressigny, le 37 100 Ae 67
53210 Grand-Puits, le 53 67 Zc 60
77720 Grandpuits-Bailly-Carrois 77 72 Cf 57
71350 Grand-Pussey 71 106 Ef 67
42290 Grand-Quartier, le 42 130 Ec 75
76140 Grand-Quevilly, le 76 37 Ba 52
13460 Grand-Radeau, le 13 169 Ec 88
57175 Grandrange 57 56 Ga 53
56440 Grand-Resto 56 80 Wf 61
48600 Grandrieu 48 141 Dd 80
02360 Grandrieux 02 41 Eb 50
63600 Grandrif 63 129 De 75
44660 Grand-Rigné, le 44 82 Yd 62
42940 Grand-Ris 42 129 Df 74
69870 Grandris 69D 117 Ec 72
19270 Grand-Roche 19 125 Bd 77
68160 Grand-Rombach 68 60 Hb 59
13460 Grand-Romieu 13 169 Ed 87
02210 Grand-Rozoy 02 52 Dc 53
60400 Grandrû 60 40 Da 51
62810 Grand-Rullecourt 62 29 Cc 47
88210 Grandrupt 88 77 Ha 58
88240 Grandrupt-de-Bains 88 76 Gb 60
58110 Grandry 58 104 De 66
58290 Grandry 58 104 De 66
40420 Grand-Sablis 40 147 Zd 84
23220 Grandsagne 23 114 Be 71
19300 Grandsaigne 19 126 Bf 76
27680 Grand-Saint-Aubin, le 27 36 Ad 52
80490 Grandsart 80 38 Bf 48
87160 Grands-Chézeaux, les 87 113 Bc 70
84400 Grands-Cléments, les 84 156 Fc 85
59232 Grand-Sec-Bois 59 29 Cd 44
71600 Grand-Sélore 71 117 Ea 70
82600 Grand-Selve 82 149 Ba 85
26530 Grand-Serre, le 26 131 Fa 77
83920 Grands-Esclans 83 172 Gd 87
45220 Grands-Moreaux, les 45 89 Da 61
42370 Grands-Murcins, les 42 117 Df 72
57560 Grand-Soldat 57 60 Ha 57
18240 Grand-Sort, le 18 88 Cf 64
41210 Grand-Soupeau, le 41 87 Bf 63
58400 Grand-Soury, le 58 103 Da 66
30300 Grands-Patis, les 30 169 Ed 86
12320 Grand-Vabre 12 139 Cc 81
15260 Grandval 15 140 Da 79
63890 Grandval 63 128 Dd 75
23250 Grandvallée 23 114 Be 73
37110 Grand-Vallée, la 37 85 Af 63
48260 Grandvals 48 140 Da 80
88230 Grand-Valtin, le 88 77 Gf 60
71430 Grandvaux 71 117 Eb 69
03320 Grand-Veau 03 103 Cf 68
70190 Grandvelle-et-le-Perrenot 70 93 Ff 63
02120 Grand-verly 02 40 Dd 49
42111 Grand-Vernay 42 129 Df 74
85330 Grand-Viel, le 85 96 Xe 66
56360 Grand-Village 56 80 We 65
85140 Grand Village 85 97 Ye 68
17270 Grand-Village, le 17 135 Ze 77
33860 Grand-Village, le 33 123 Zc 77
37530 Grand-Village, le 37 86 Ba 64
17370 Grand-Village-Plage, le 17 122 Ye 73
18120 Grand-Villalin 18 102 Ca 66
90600 Grandvillars 90 94 Gf 63
10700 Grandville 10 73 Eb 57
22120 Grandville 22 64 Xc 57
77720 Grandvillé 77 52 Cf 57
08700 Grandville, la 08 42 Ee 50
44170 Grandville, la 44 82 Yc 63
28310 Grandville-Gaudreville 28 70 Bf 58
88600 Grandvillers 88 77 Ge 59
03350 Grand-Villers, le 03 115 Cd 69
27240 Grandvilliers 27 49 Ba 56
60210 Grandvilliers 60 38 Bf 51
89700 Grand-Virey, le 89 90 Ea 61
17470 Grand-Virollet 17 111 Zd 73
02170 Grand-Wez, le 02 40 De 49
26400 Grâne 26 142 Ef 80
46170 Granéjouls 46 150 Bc 82
46140 Granels, les 46 150 Bb 82
30750 Granerie, la 30 153 Db 84
11500 Granès 11 178 Cb 91
33450 Graney 33 135 Zd 79
63690 Grange 63 127 Cd 75
16350 Grange, la 16 112 Ac 72
17700 Grange, la 17 110 Zb 71
24640 Grange, la 24 125 Af 77
25380 Grange, la 25 94 Ge 65
31330 Grange, la 31 164 Bb 86
33290 Grange, la 33 135 Zc 79
33430 Grange, la 33 147 Ze 82
63630 Grange, la 63 128 Dd 76
83111 Grange, la 83 172 Gc 87
17770 Grange-à-Robin, la 17 123 Zd 73
88260 Grange-au-Bois, la 88 76 Ga 60
60190 Grange au Diable 60 39 Cd 52
89510 Grange-au-Doyen, la 89 72 Dc 60
10300 Grange-au-Rez 10 73 Df 59
51800 Grange aux-Bois, la 51 54 Ef 54
57070 Grange-aux-Bois, la 57 56 Gb 54
87520 Grange-de-Beuil, la 87 113 Ba 73
39600 Grange-de-Vaivre 39 107 Ff 66
89260 Grange-le-Bocage 89 72 Dc 59
10300 Grange-L'Evêque 10 73 Df 59
58350 Grange-Mouton, la 58 103 Db 65
40990 Grangeon 40 146 Ye 86
89500 Grange-Pourrain 89 72 Dc 60
45390 Grangermont 45 71 Cc 59
07500 Granges 07 142 Ef 79
71390 Granges 71 105 Ee 68
88220 Granges 88 76 Gc 60
03500 Granges, les 03 116 Db 70
05700 Granges, les 05 144 Fd 82
10210 Granges, les 10 73 Ea 60
10510 Granges, les 10 73 De 57
21150 Granges, les 21 91 Ec 63
24350 Granges, les 24 124 Ad 77
24400 Granges, les 24 136 Ab 78
26110 Granges, les 26 156 Fb 83
26150 Granges, les 26 143 Fc 80
26170 Granges, les 26 156 Fc 83
36200 Granges, les 36 113 Bd 69
43320 Granges, les 43 141 De 78
46110 Granges, les 46 138 Be 79
52220 Granges, les 52 74 Ee 58
56190 Granges, les 56 81 Xd 63
65100 Granges, les 65 162 Zf 90
73210 Granges, les 73 133 Ge 75
73440 Granges, les 73 133 Gd 76
74470 Granges, les 74 120 Gd 71
82140 Granges, les 82 150 Bd 84
85340 Granges, les 85 96 Ya 69
88640 Granges-Aumontzey 88 77 Ge 60
24390 Granges-d'Ans 24 125 Ba 77
31110 Granges-d'Astau 31 175 Ad 92
04150 Granges de Dauban 04 156 Fd 84
31110 Granges-de-Labach 31 176 Ad 92
06450 Granges-de-la-Brasque 06 159 Hb 84
06430 Granges-de-la-Pie 06 159 Hd 84
25360 Granges-de-Vienney 25 107 Gb 65
06450 Granges-du-Colonel 06 159 Hc 84
65170 Granges-du-Moudang 65 175 Ab 92
25440 Granges-du-Sapin 25 107 Ff 66
39250 Granges-du-Sillet, les 39 107 Ga 68
26290 Granges-Gontardes, les 26 155 Ee 82
70270 Granges-Guenin, les 70 94 Gd 62
70400 Granges-la-Ville 70 94 Gd 63
70400 Granges-le-Bourg 70 94 Gd 63
91410 Granges-le-Roi, les 91 70 Ca 57
26600 Granges-les-Beaumont 26 143 Ef 78
25300 Granges-Narboz 25 108 Gb 67
88220 Granges-Richard, les 88 76 Gc 60
51260 Granges-sur-Aube 51 73 Df 57
39210 Granges-sur-Baume 39 107 Fd 68
47260 Granges-sur-Lot 47 148 Ac 82
88640 Granges-sur-Vologne 88 77 Ge 60
89520 Grangette 89 89 Db 63
31310 Grangette, la 31 164 Bb 89
25160 Grangettes, les 25 108 Gb 67
14160 Grangues 14 48 Zf 53
73210 Granier 73 133 Gd 75
30170 Graniers 30 154 Df 85
38490 Granieu 38 131 Fd 75
05100 Granon 05 145 Gd 79
04110 Granons, les 04 156 Fd 85
13450 Grans 13 170 Fa 87
50400 Granville 50 46 Yc 55
79360 Granzay-Gript 79 110 Zd 71
07260 Granzial 07 141 Ea 81
41100 Grapperie, la 41 86 Ba 62
07700 Gras 07 155 Ed 82
25790 Gras, les 25 108 Gd 67
12120 Grascazes 12 151 Cc 84
16380 Grassac 16 124 Ac 75
06130 Grasse 06 173 Gf 87
67350 Grassendorf 67 58 Hd 56
34420 Grassette, la 34 167 Dc 88
85150 Grassière 85 96 Yb 69
38380 Grassotière, la 38 131 Fe 76
27210 Grasville 27 36 Ac 52
23500 Gratade, la 23 126 Ca 74
63210 Gratade, la 63 127 Ce 75
20147 Gratelle CTC 182 Id 95
20250 Gratelle CTC 182 Ka 95
87310 Grateloube 87 125 Af 74
40120 Grateloup 40 147 Zd 84
47400 Grateloup 47 148 Ac 82
31430 Gratens 31 164 Ba 89
31150 Gratentour 31 164 Bc 86
27220 Gratheuil 27 50 Bb 55
80500 Gratibus 80 39 Cd 50
33910 Gratien 33 135 Ze 78
24130 Grationie, la 24 136 Ab 79
50200 Gratot 50 46 Yc 54
51800 Gratreuil 51 54 Ee 53
02360 Gratreux 02 41 Eb 50
80680 Grattepanche 80 38 Cb 50
25620 Gratteris, le 25 107 Ga 65
70170 Grattery 70 93 Ga 62
53100 Grattoir, le 53 66 Zb 58
34300 Grau-d'Agde, le 34 167 Dc 89
30240 Grau-du-Roi, le 30 168 Ea 87
67320 Graufthal 67 58 Hb 56
46500 Graules 46 138 Bd 80
24340 Graulges, les 24 124 Ac 76
81300 Graulhet 81 151 Bf 86
09420 Grausse, la 09 177 Bb 90
51190 Grauves 51 53 Df 55
88300 Graux 88 76 Ff 58
76270 Graval 76 37 Bd 50
12260 Grave 12 138 Bf 82
33230 Grave 33 135 Zf 78
05320 Grave, la 05 144 Gb 78
06440 Grave, la 06 159 Hc 86
24490 Grave, la 24 135 Aa 78
39190 Graveleuse 39 119 Fc 69
59820 Gravelines 59 27 Ca 43
17290 Gravelle, la 17 110 Za 72
53410 Gravelle, la 53 66 Yf 60
01160 Gravelles 01 119 Fc 72
57130 Gravelotte 57 56 Ga 54
50720 Gravengerie, la 50 66 Za 57
14350 Graverie, la 14 47 Za 55
63440 Graverolles, les 63 115 Cf 72
27110 Graveron-Sémerville 27 49 Af 54
04250 Graves 04 157 Ga 82
12200 Graves 12 151 Bf 82
16120 Graves 16 123 Zf 75

274 | Gouraincourt

03500 Graves, les 03 116 Db 71
13690 Graveson 13 155 Ee 85
24400 Gravette, la 24 136 Ac 78
41170 Gravier 41 69 Af 61
18150 Gravier, le 18 103 Cf 67
61310 Gravière, la 61 48 Ab 56
83340 Gravière, la 83 171 Gb 88
07140 Gravières 07 154 Ea 82
27930 Gravigny 27 49 Ba 54
24130 Gravillac 24 136 Ac 79
74300 Gravin 74 120 Gd 72
77118 Gravon 77 72 Da 58
35480 Gravot 35 82 Ya 62
70100 Gray 70 92 Fd 64
33590 Grayan-et-L'Hôpital 33 122 Yf 76
39320 Graye-et-Charnay 39 119 Fc 70
14470 Graye-sur-Mer 14 47 Zd 53
70100 Gray-la-Ville 70 92 Fd 64
47270 Grayssas 47 149 Af 83
31190 Grazac 31 164 Bc 89
43200 Grazac 43 129 Eb 77
81800 Grazac 81 150 Bd 85
53440 Grazay 53 67 Zd 59
20218 Grazianaccia CTC 181 Ka 94
48120 Grazières-Mages 48 140 Dc 80
46160 Gréalou 46 138 Bf 81
13850 Gréasque 13 171 Fd 88
56840 Gréavo 56 80 Xb 63
80140 Grebault-Mesnil 80 38 Be 48
64240 Gréciette 64 160 Ye 88
80400 Grécourt 80 39 Cf 50
39290 Gredisans 39 106 Fd 66
35380 Grée, la 35 81 Xf 61
44410 Grée, la 44 81 Xe 63
56120 Grée-Saint-Laurent, le 56 64 Xd 61
72320 Gréez-sur-Roc 72 69 Ae 60
11250 Greffeil 11 166 Cc 90
01440 Greffets, les 01 118 Fb 71
78120 Greffiers 78 70 Bf 57
56140 Greffins, les 56 81 Xe 62
56390 Gregam = Grand-Champ 56 80 Xa 62
76370 Grèges 76 37 Ba 49
63380 Grégottier 63 115 Ce 73
77166 Grégy-sur-Yerres 77 51 Cd 56
24800 Grelière 24 125 Ba 76
57170 Grémecey 57 56 Gc 56
60380 Grémevillers 60 38 Bf 51
88240 Grémifontaine 88 76 Gb 60
55150 Gremilly 55 55 Fc 53
76970 Grémonville 76 37 Ae 50
31330 Grenade 31 150 Bb 86
40270 Grenade-sur-l'Adour 40 147 Zd 86
21540 Grenand-lès-Sombernon 21 91 Ee 65
52500 Grenant 52 92 Fd 62
62760 Grenas 62 29 Cc 47
38540 Grenay 38 131 Fa 75
62160 Grenay 62 29 Ce 46
67190 Grendelbruch 67 60 Hb 58
87800 Grenerie, la 87 125 Ba 75
17740 Grenettes, les 17 109 Yd 72
45480 Greneville-en-Beauce 45 71 Ca 59
43450 Grenier-Montgon 43 128 Db 77
63410 Greniers, les 63 115 Cf 73
42510 Grénieux 42 129 Ea 74
57660 Gréning 57 57 Gf 55
38000 Grenoble 38 131 Fe 77
58420 Grenois 58 89 Dd 65
16150 Grenord 16 124 Ae 73
34190 Grenouillet 34 153 Dd 85
24320 Grenouillier 24 124 Ac 76
35270 Grenouillière, la 35 65 Yb 58
53940 Grenoux 53 66 Za 60
14540 Grentheville 14 35 Ze 54
68960 Grentzingen 68 95 Hb 63
76630 Greny 76 37 Bb 49
44530 Grény, le 44 81 Ya 63
06620 Gréolières 06 158 Gf 86
06620 Gréolières-les-Neiges 06 158 Gf 85
04800 Gréoux-les-Bains 04 157 Ff 86
31190 Grépiac 31 164 Bc 88
31480 Grés, le 31 164 Ba 86
27320 Gres, les 27 50 Bb 56
33570 Grésard 33 135 Zf 79
13750 Grès-Hauts 13 155 Fa 86
21150 Grésigny-Sainte-Reine 21 91 Ed 63
49700 Grésille, la 49 98 Zd 65
73240 Gresin 73 131 Fd 75
42460 Gresle, la 42 117 Eb 72
26560 Gresse 26 156 Fc 83
38650 Gresse-en-Vercors 38 143 Fd 79
12230 Gressentis 12 153 Dc 85
78550 Gressey 78 50 Bd 55
44390 Gressin, le 44 82 Yd 64
67190 Gresswiller 67 60 Hc 57
77410 Gressy 77 51 Ce 55
73100 Grésy-sur-Aix 73 132 Ff 74
73460 Grésy-sur-Isère 73 132 Gb 75
35690 Gretais, la 35 66 Yc 59
77220 Gretz-Armainvilliers 77 52 Ce 56
70130 Greucourt 70 93 Ff 63
76810 Greuville 76 37 Af 50
88630 Greux 88 75 Fe 58
17330 Grève 17 111 Zd 72
44310 Grève, la 44 97 Yc 66
52220 Grève, la 52 74 Ee 58
76480 Greve, la 76 37 Af 52
85140 Grève, la 85 97 Ye 68
17170 Grève-sur-Mignon, la 17 110 Zb 71
50440 Gréville-Hague 50 33 Yb 50
62450 Grévillers 62 30 Ce 48
71700 Grevilly 71 118 Ee 69
07000 Greytus 07 142 Ec 80
60210 Grez 60 38 Bf 51
82270 Grez 82 150 Bd 83
72140 Grez, le 72 67 Zf 59
17120 Grézac 17 122 Za 75
46350 Grezal 46 137 Bc 80
24250 Grèze, la 24 137 Bb 80
24250 Grézelle 24 137 Ba 80
46700 Grézels 46 137 Ba 82
53290 Grez-en-Bouère 53 84 Zc 61
11000 Grèzes 11 166 Cb 89
24120 Grèzes 24 137 Bc 78
43170 Grèzes 43 140 Dc 79
46320 Grèzes 46 138 Be 81
48100 Grèzes 48 140 Dc 81
46140 Grèzes, les 46 150 Bb 82
47250 Grézet-Cavagnan 47 148 Aa 82
65440 Grézian 65 175 Ac 91
69290 Grézieu-la-Varenne 69M 130 Ee 74
69610 Grézieu-le-Marché 69M 130 Ec 75
42600 Grézieux-le-Fromental 42 129 Ea 75
33420 Grézillac 33 135 Ze 80
49320 Grézillé 49 84 Zd 65
49220 Grez-Neuville 49 83 Zb 63
42260 Grézolles 42 129 Df 73
77880 Grez-sur-Loing 77 71 Ce 59
12170 Griac 12 152 Cd 84
02100 Gricourt 02 40 Db 49
01290 Grièges 01 118 Ef 71
85360 Grière, la 85 109 Yd 70
67240 Gries 67 58 He 56
67110 Griesbach 67 58 He 55
68140 Griesbach-au-Val 68 77 Hb 60
67330 Griesbach-le-Bastberg 67 58 Hc 56
67870 Griesheim-près-Molsheim 67 60 Hd 57
67370 Griesheim-sur-Souffel 67 58 He 57
15220 Griffeuilles 15 139 Cc 79
20200 Grigione CTC 181 Kc 92
26230 Grignan 26 155 Ef 82
76850 Grigneuseville 76 37 Bb 51
24110 Grignols 24 136 Ad 78
33690 Grignols 33 148 Zf 82
21150 Grignon 21 91 Ec 63
45260 Grignon 45 88 Cc 61
73200 Grignon 73 132 Gc 75
37160 Grignon, le 37 100 Ad 66
88410 Grignoncourt 88 76 Ff 61
51800 Grigny 51 55 Fa 54
62140 Grigny 62 29 Ca 46
62650 Grigny 62 28 Bf 45
69520 Grigny 69M 130 Ee 75
91350 Grigny 91 51 Cc 57
44170 Grigonnais, la 44 82 Yb 63
57245 Grigy 57 56 Gb 54
15700 Grillère, la 15 139 Cb 77
89240 Grilletière, la 89 89 Dc 62
84600 Grillon 84 155 Ef 82
01220 Grilly 01 120 Ga 71
12200 Grimals, les 12 151 Bf 82
33910 Grimard 33 135 Ze 78
55400 Grimaucourt-en-Woëvre 55 55 Fd 53
55500 Grimaucourt-près-Sampigny 55 55 Fc 56
83310 Grimaud 83 172 Gd 89
82230 Grimaudié, la 82 150 Bd 85
86330 Grimaudière, la 86 99 Aa 68
89310 Grimault 89 90 Df 63
14220 Grimbosq 14 47 Zd 54
50450 Grimesnil 50 46 Yd 55
82160 Grimmaudie, la 82 151 Bf 83
54115 Grimonviller 54 76 Ga 58
50590 Grimouville 50 46 Yc 54
62760 Grincourt-lès-Pas 62 29 Cc 47
57480 Grindorff 57 44 Gd 52
15130 Grinhac 15 139 Cd 79
12630 Grioudas 12 152 Ce 82
79150 Gripière, la 79 98 Zc 66
65710 Gripp 65 175 Ab 91
58130 Grippe, la 58 103 Db 66
17620 Gripperie-Saint-Symphorien, la 17 122 Za 74
50320 Grippon, le 50 46 Yd 56
54290 Gripport 54 76 Gb 58
79360 Gript 79 110 Zd 71
86700 Gris 86 112 Ab 71
54380 Griscourt 54 56 Ga 55
21330 Griselles 21 90 Ec 61
45210 Griselles 45 72 Ce 60
20218 Grisgione CTC 181 Kb 94
20200 Grisgioni = Grigione CTC 181 Kc 92
59600 Grisoëlle, la 59 31 Df 47
02210 Grisolles 02 52 Dc 54
82170 Grisolles 82 150 Bb 86
40430 Grison 40 147 Zd 83
14170 Grisy 14 48 Zf 54
95810 Grisy-les-Plâtres 95 51 Ca 54
77166 Grisy-Suisnes 77 51 Cd 56
77480 Grisy-sur-Seine 77 72 Db 58
38300 Grive, la 38 131 Fb 75
24170 Grives 24 137 Ba 80
80250 Grivesnes 80 39 Cc 50
80700 Grivillers 80 39 Ce 51
38460 Grivoux 38 131 Fc 74
08400 Grivy-Loisy 08 42 Ed 52
48220 Grizac 48 153 De 82
56700 Groac'h Carnet 56 79 We 62
29520 Groas-Brenn 29 78 Wa 60
46110 Groches 46 138 Be 79
67470 Grœttwiller 67 59 Ia 55
48170 Grofau 48 141 De 81
62600 Groffliers 62 28 Bd 46
28190 Grognault 28 69 Bb 58
16200 Groie, la 16 123 Ze 74
28630 Groindreville 28 70 Bc 58
63790 Groire 63 128 Cf 75
85110 Grois, les 85 97 Yf 68
59360 Groise, la 59 31 De 48
18140 Groises 18 103 Ce 65
01100 Groissiat 01 119 Fd 71
74570 Groisy 74 120 Ga 72
56590 Groix 56 79 Wd 63
24250 Groléjac 24 137 Bb 80
19320 Grolier, le 19 126 Ca 77
16490 Grolière, la 16 112 Ac 72
16360 Grolle, la 16 123 Ze 76
85190 Grolle, la 85 97 Yc 69
18800 Gron 18 103 Ce 66
89100 Gron 89 72 Db 60
02140 Gronard 02 41 Df 50
17100 Gros-, le 17 123 Zc 74
84220 Gros, les 84 155 Fb 85
57520 Grosbliederstroff 57 57 Gf 53
21540 Grosbois-en-Montagne 21 91 Ed 65
21250 Grosbois-lès-Tichey 21 106 Fb 66
17100 Gros-Bonnet, le 17 123 Zc 74
16380 Grosbot 16 124 Ac 75
16570 Grosbot 16 123 Aa 74
85440 Grosbreuil 85 109 Yc 69
19320 Gros-Chastang 19 126 Bf 77
71220 Gros-Chigy, le 71 118 Ed 69
79220 Groseillers, les 79 111 Zd 69
62134 Groseillier, le 62 29 Cb 45
04330 Gros-Jas 04 157 Gb 85
36160 Groslards, les 36 114 Ca 70
95410 Groslay 95 51 Cb 55
01680 Groslée-Saint-Benoît 01 131 Fd 74
27170 Grosley-sur-Risle 27 49 Ae 54
63140 Grosliers, les 63 115 Da 73
28170 Groslu-Saint-Ange 28 49 Bb 57
90200 Grosmagny 90 94 Gf 62
90100 Grosne 90 94 Ha 63
23350 Grospeaux 23 114 Bf 70
07120 Grospierres 07 154 Eb 82
57410 Gros-Réderching 57 57 Hb 54
78490 Grosrouvre 78 50 Be 56
54470 Grosrouvres 54 56 Ff 56
20100 Grossa CTC 184 If 99
55140 Grossaincourt 55 75 Fe 58
20128 Grosseto-Prugna CTC 184 If 97
79150 Grossinière, la 79 98 Zc 66
47110 Grossis 47 149 Ad 82
27220 Grossœuvre 27 49 Bb 55
18600 Grossouvre 18 103 Cf 67
57660 Grostenquin 57 57 Ge 55
27370 Gros-Theil, le 27 49 Af 53
16170 Grosville 16 123 Zf 74
50340 Grosville 50 33 Yb 51
73360 Grotte, la 73 132 Fe 76
09400 Grotte de Niaux 09 177 Bd 92
01450 Grotte du Cerdon 01 119 Fc 72
38390 Grottes de la Balme 38 131 Fc 73
31260 Grottes de Marsoulas 31 164 Af 90
09400 Grotte Soudour 09 177 Bd 91
29880 Grouannec, le 29 61 Vd 57
80600 Grouches-Luchuel 80 29 Cc 47
45380 Groue, la 45 87 Be 61
02110 Grougis 02 40 Dd 49
81600 Groulrère, la 81 150 Be 85
18240 Grouseau, le 18 88 Cf 64
50610 Groussey 50 46 Yc 56
72610 Groutel 72 68 Aa 58
18200 Groutte, la 18 102 Cd 68
86100 Groyes, les 86 100 Ae 68
24350 Groze, la 24 124 Ad 77
07270 Grozon 07 142 Ee 79
39800 Grozon 39 107 Fe 67
76760 Gruchet 76 37 Af 50
76210 Gruchet-le-Valasse 76 36 Ac 51
76810 Gruchet-Saint-Siméon 76 37 Af 50
14740 Gruchy 14 35 Zd 53
50440 Gruchy 50 33 Yb 50
40210 Grué 40 146 Za 83
08380 Gruerie, la 08 41 Ec 49
85580 Grues 85 109 Ye 70
40410 Gruey 40 147 Zb 83
88240 Gruey-lès-Surance 88 76 Gb 60
74540 Gruffy 74 132 Ga 74
49520 Grugé-L'Hôpital 49 83 Yf 62
02680 Grugies 02 40 Db 50
76690 Grugny 76 37 Ba 51
11430 Gruissan 11 167 Da 90
11430 Gruissan-Plage 11 167 Db 90
76440 Grumesnil 76 38 Be 51
24380 Grun 24 136 Ad 78
57510 Grundviller 57 57 Gf 54
63490 Gruns, les 63 128 Dc 75
80700 Gruny 80 39 Ce 50
71760 Grury 71 104 Df 68
59152 Gruson 59 30 Db 45
39190 Grusse 39 106 Fd 69
68320 Grussenheim 68 60 Hc 60
20128 Grussetu-Prugnu = Grosseto-Prugna CTC 184 If 97
74170 Gruvaz, la 74 133 Ge 73
08430 Gruyères 08 42 Ed 50
33590 Gua, la 33 122 Yf 76
17600 Gua, le 17 122 Za 74
38450 Gua, le 38 144 Fd 78
20160 Guagno CTC 182 If 95
20125 Guagno les Bains CTC 182 If 95
20160 Guagnu = Guagno CTC 182 If 95
28260 Guainville 28 50 Bc 55
20200 Guaitella CTC 181 Kc 92
20245 Guaitella u Fangu CTC 180 Ie 94
20121 Guarchetta CTC 182 Ka 96
20220 Guardiola CTC 180 If 93
20128 Guargualé CTC 184 If 97
24370 Guarrigues, les 24 137 Bb 79
04150 Gubian 04 156 Fd 85
65170 Guchan 65 175 Ac 91
65240 Guchen 65 175 Ac 91
09120 Gudas 09 177 Be 90
47220 Gudech 47 149 Ad 84
52320 Gudmont-Villiers 52 75 Fa 58
79270 Gué 79 110 Zc 71
86380 Gué, le 86 99 Ab 68
57510 Guebenhouse 57 57 Gf 54
68420 Gueberschwihr 68 60 Hb 60
57260 Guébestroff 57 57 Ge 56
57260 Guéblange-lès-Dieuze 57 57 Ge 56
57260 Guébling 57 57 Ge 55
68500 Guebwiller 68 95 Hb 61
72230 Guécélard 72 84 Aa 61
17540 Gué-d'Alleré, le 17 110 Za 71
61130 Gué-de-la-Chaîne, le 61 68 Ad 58
49390 Gué-de-Lauet, le 49 84 Aa 64
72320 Gué-de-Launay 72 69 Ae 60
28700 Gué-de-Longroi, le 28 70 Be 57
49650 Gué-de-Louet, le 49 84 Af 65
72500 Gué-de-Mézières, le 72 85 Ac 63
49150 Guédéniau, le 49 84 Zf 64
49390 Gué-de-Ray 49 84 Aa 64
85770 Gué-de Velluire, le 85 110 Za 70
08230 Gué-d'Hossus 08 41 Ed 49
41100 Gué-du-Loir, le 41 86 Af 62
56120 Guégon 56 81 Xc 61
35111 Guéhairie, la 35 65 Yb 57
50210 Guéhébert 50 46 Yd 55
56420 Guéhenno 56 80 Xc 61
85640 Gué-Jourdain, le 85 97 Yf 68
57310 Guélange 57 56 Gb 53
56300 Gueltas 56 79 Wf 60
56920 Gueltas 56 64 Xb 60
72110 Guémançais 72 68 Ac 59
62128 Guémappe 62 30 Cf 47
68970 Guémar 68 60 Hc 59
44290 Guémené-Penfao 44 82 Ya 63
56160 Guémené-sur-Scorff 56 79 We 60
80430 Guémicourt 80 38 Be 50
49490 Gué-Morin 49 84 Ab 64
62370 Guemps 62 27 Bf 43
62890 Guémy 62 27 Bf 44
29190 Guénaléguen 29 62 Wa 59
71190 Guenand 71 105 Eb 67
57310 Guénange 57 44 Gb 53
22140 Guénézan 22 63 We 57
29180 Guengat 29 78 Ve 60
56150 Guénin 56 79 Xa 61
56920 Guénolay 56 64 Xa 60
44290 Guénouvry 44 82 Yb 63
22350 Guenroc 22 65 Xf 59
44530 Guenrouet 44 81 Ya 63
57470 Guenviller 57 57 Ge 54
72130 Gué-Ory 72 68 Zf 59
61160 Guêprei 61 48 Zf 55
56380 Guer 56 81 Xf 61
44350 Guérande 44 81 Xd 65
27310 Guérard 27 37 Ae 52
77580 Guérard 77 52 Cf 56
81710 Guéraudarre, la 81 165 Cb 87
80500 Guerbigny 80 39 Cd 50
37350 Guerche, la 37 100 Ae 67
86420 Guerche, la 86 99 Ab 67
35130 Guerche-de-Bretagne, la 35 66 Ye 61
18150 Guerche-sur-L'Aubois, la 18 103 Cf 67
77760 Guercheville 77 71 Cd 59
89113 Guerchy 89 89 Dc 61
01090 Guéreins 01 118 Ee 72
23000 Guéret 23 114 Bf 71
71620 Guerfand 71 106 Fa 68
22210 Guerfiac 22 64 Xc 60
58330 Guérignaults 58 104 Dd 66
58130 Guérigny 58 103 Db 66
56660 Guérihuel, le 56 80 Xb 62
47250 Guèrin 47 148 Aa 82
63310 Guerinet, le 63 116 Dc 72
85680 Guerinière, la 85 96 Xe 67
04400 Guérins, les 04 158 Gd 82
22530 Guerlédan 22 64 Xa 59
29650 Guerlesquin 29 63 Wc 57
57260 Guermange 57 57 Ge 56
77600 Guermantes 77 51 Ce 55
29410 Guern 29 62 Wa 57
56310 Guern 56 79 Wf 60
27160 Guernanville 27 49 Af 55
78520 Guernes 78 50 Bd 54
56130 Guernet 56 81 Xd 64
56500 Guernic 56 80 Xa 61
29160 Guernigenet 29 62 Vd 59
29410 Guernigou 29 62 Wa 58
56190 Guerno, le 56 81 Xd 63
27720 Guerny 27 50 Be 53
14400 Guéron 14 47 Zb 53
53290 Guérouillère, la 53 84 Zc 62
27160 Guéroulde, la 27 49 Af 56
55000 Guerpont 55 55 Fb 56
71160 Guerreaux, les 71 117 Df 69
29400 Guerruas 29 62 Vf 57
57320 Guerstling 57 44 Gd 53
57880 Guerting 57 57 Gd 53
56400 Guerveur 56 80 Wf 62
76340 Guerville 76 37 Bd 49
78930 Guerville 78 50 Be 55
80150 Gueschart 80 28 Ca 47
59287 Guesnain 59 30 Da 46
86420 Guesnes 86 99 Aa 67
57380 Guessling-Hémering 57 57 Gd 54
56190 Guet, le 56 81 Xd 63
40170 Guetch 40 146 Ye 84
64210 Guéthary 64 160 Yc 88
89570 Guette 89 73 De 60
21430 Guette, la 21 105 Eb 65
36500 Guette, la 36 101 Bb 67
80360 Gueudecourt 80 30 Cf 48
45480 Gueudreville 45 70 Ca 59
45480 Gueudreville 45 71 Ca 60
71130 Gueugnon 71 104 Ea 69
76890 Gueures 76 37 Af 49
50360 Gueutteville 50 33 Yd 52
76890 Gueutteville 76 37 Ba 51
76460 Gueutteville-les-Grès 76 36 Ae 49
51390 Gueux 51 53 Df 53
68210 Guevenatten 68 94 Ha 62
68116 Guewenheim 68 94 Ha 62
33240 Gueynard 33 135 Zd 78
11230 Gueytes-et-Labastide 11 165 Ca 90
24310 Gueyzat 24 124 Ad 76
47170 Gueyze 47 148 Aa 84
80400 Gugnécourt 88 77 Gd 59
54930 Gugney 54 76 Ga 58
88450 Gugney-aux-Aulx 88 76 Gb 59
39190 Gugniots, les 39 119 Fc 69
33620 Guiard 33 135 Zd 78
64250 Guibelarte 64 160 Yd 89
53110 Guiberdière, la 53 67 Zd 58
80430 Guibermesnil 80 38 Bf 49
05220 Guiberts, les 05 145 Gd 79
35460 Guiborel 35 66 Yd 58
44440 Guibretière, la 44 82 Ye 64
44680 Guibretière, la 44 96 Yb 66
27930 Guichainville 27 49 Bb 55
64520 Guiche 64 160 Ye 87
71220 Guiche, la 71 117 Ec 69
35580 Guichen = Gwizien 35 65 Yb 61
85130 Guicherie, la 85 97 Yf 67
29410 Guiclan 29 62 Wa 57
71130 Guide, le 71 117 Df 69
56520 Guidel 56 79 Wc 62
56520 Guidel-Plages 56 79 Wc 62
57720 Guiderkirch 57 58 Hb 54
45230 Guidus, les 45 88 Cf 61
72380 Guierche, la 72 68 Ab 60
60480 Guignecourt 60 38 Ca 52
16140 Guignefolle 16 111 Zf 73
80540 Guignemicourt 80 38 Cb 49
35580 Guignen 35 82 Ya 61
77390 Guignes 77 52 Ce 57
45300 Guigneville 45 71 Cb 59
91590 Guigneville-sur-Essonne 91 71 Cc 58
02190 Guignicourt 02 41 Df 52
08430 Guignicourt-sur-Vence 08 42 Ed 50
45480 Guignonville 45 71 Ca 59
62140 Guigny 62 28 Ca 47
50160 Guilberville 50 47 Za 55
29820 Guilers 29 61 Vc 58
29710 Guiler-sur-Goyen 29 78 Vd 60
86120 Guilgaudrie, la 86 99 Aa 66
64270 Guilhat 64 161 Za 88
07500 Guilherand 07 142 Ef 79
33420 Guillac 33 135 Ze 80
56800 Guillac 56 81 Xd 61
31420 Guillanat 31 164 Af 89
22470 Guillardon 22 63 Wf 56
82240 Guillau 82 150 Bd 84
80170 Guillaucourt 80 39 Cd 49
06470 Guillaumes 06 158 Gf 84
33720 Guillaumes, les 33 135 Zc 81
03390 Guillaumets, les 03 115 Cf 71
44360 Guillaumière, la 44 96 Yb 65
46330 Guillayne 46 150 Bd 82
40090 Guillemensous 40 147 Zc 84
33720 Guillemin 33 135 Zc 81
47170 Guillemont 47 148 Ab 84
80360 Guillemont 80 39 Ce 48
32730 Guilleri 32 163 Ab 88
03250 Guillermie, la 03 116 Dd 73
03120 Guillermin 03 116 Dd 71
91690 Guillerval 91 70 Ca 58
14630 Guillerville 14 35 Ze 54
05600 Guillestre 05 145 Gd 81
28310 Guilleville 28 70 Be 59
56490 Guilliers 56 64 Xd 60
29300 Guilligomarc'h 29 79 Wd 61
32720 Guillon 32 162 Ze 86
89420 Guillon 89 90 Ea 63
25110 Guillon-les-Bains 25 93 Gc 65
28140 Guillonville 28 70 Bd 60
33720 Guillos 33 135 Zc 81
58240 Guillot, le 58 103 Da 68
79420 Guillotière, la 79 111 Zf 69
50500 Guillotterie, la 50 34 Yd 53
32600 Guilloutets, les 32 164 Ba 86
24380 Guilloux, les 24 136 Ae 78
18220 Guilly 18 102 Cd 66
36150 Guilly 36 101 Be 66
45600 Guilly 45 88 Cb 62
29246 Guilly, le 29 63 Wc 58
29730 Guilvinec = Ar-Gelveneg 29 78 Ve 62
29620 Guimaëc 29 63 Wb 56
76630 Guimécourt 76 37 Bb 49
76340 Guimerville 76 38 Be 49
29400 Guimiliau 29 62 Wa 58
61700 Guimondières, les 61 67 Zb 57
35350 Guimorais, la 35 65 Ya 56
16300 Guimps 16 123 Ze 76
40140 Guin 40 160 Yd 86
64390 Guinarthe-Parenties 64 161 Za 88
08130 Guincourt 08 42 Ed 51
52300 Guindrecourt-aux-Ormes 52 75 Fa 58
52330 Guindrecourt-sur-Blaise 52 74 Ef 59
44450 Guineau, le 44 82 Yd 65
62130 Guinecourt 62 29 Cb 46
47350 Guine-du-Bois 47 136 Ac 81
62340 Guînes 62 27 Bf 43
22200 Guingamp = Gwengamp 22 63 Wf 57
57690 Guinglange 57 57 Gd 54
57220 Guinkirchen 57 56 Gc 53
31330 Guinot 31 164 Bb 86
57670 Guinzeling 57 57 Gf 55
83310 Guiols, les 83 172 Gc 89
29490 Guipavas 29 62 Vd 58
35440 Guipel 35 65 Yb 59
78125 Guiperreux 78 50 Be 57
29290 Guipronvel 29 61 Vc 58
29290 Guipronvel, Milizac- 29 61 Vc 58
35480 Guipry-Messac 35 82 Ya 62
58420 Guipy 58 104 Dd 65
46270 Guirande 46 138 Ca 81
19800 Guirande, la 19 126 Bf 77
33230 Guirande, la 33 135 Ze 78
34300 Guirandette, la 34 167 Dc 89
33125 Guirdeyre 33 135 Zc 81
32490 Guironne, la 32 164 Af 87
40200 Guirosse 40 146 Ye 83
95450 Guiry-en-Vexin 95 50 Bf 54
26460 Guisand 26 143 Fb 81
57415 Guisberg 57 58 Hb 54
60640 Guiscard 60 39 Da 51
56560 Guiscriff 56 79 Wc 60
02120 Guise 02 40 Dd 49
27700 Guiseniers 27 50 Bc 53
57410 Guising 57 58 Hb 54
16430 Guissalle 16 124 Aa 74
29880 Guissény 29 62 Vd 57
50410 Guistain, le 50 46 Ye 55
62140 Guisy 62 28 Ca 46
81220 Guitalens 81 165 Ca 87
20153 Guitera-les-Bains CTC 183 Ka 97
17500 Guitinières 17 123 Zc 76
78440 Guitrancourt 78 50 Be 54
33230 Guîtres 33 135 Ze 78
27510 Guitry 27 50 Bd 53

Guitry | 275

22350 Guitté 22 65 Xf 59
03430 Guittonnière, la 03 115 Ce 70
03300 Guittons, les 03 116 Dc 71
02300 Guivry 02 40 Da 51
80290 Guizancourt 80 38 Bf 50
80400 Guizancourt 80 39 Da 50
65230 Guizerix 65 163 Ac 89
33470 Gujan-Mestras 33 134 Yf 81
20170 Guldaricciu CTC 185 Ka 98
29510 Gulvain 29 78 Wa 60
67110 Gumbrechtshoffen 67 58 Hd 55
88220 Guménil 88 77 Gc 60
10400 Gumery 10 72 Dc 58
26470 Gumiane-Haut 26 143 Fb 81
42560 Gumières 42 129 Df 75
19320 Gumond 19 126 Bf 77
19600 Gumond 19 125 Bc 78
67110 Gundershoffen 67 58 Hd 55
68250 Gundolsheim 68 95 Hb 61
67320 Gungwiller 67 57 Ha 55
46250 Gunies, les 46 137 Ba 81
68140 Gunsbach 68 77 Hb 60
67360 Gunstett 67 58 He 55
57405 Guntzviller 57 57 Ha 56
02300 Guny 02 40 Db 51
31440 Guran 31 176 Ad 91
16320 Gurat 16 124 Ab 76
77520 Gurcy-le-Châtel 77 72 Da 58
20169 Gurgazu CTC 185 Kb 100
89250 Gurgy 89 89 Dd 61
21290 Gurgy-la-Ville 21 91 Ef 61
21290 Gurgy-le-Château 21 91 Ef 62
64400 Gurmençon 64 161 Zd 90
03350 Gurp, le 33 122 Yf 76
73640 Gurraz, la 73 133 Gf 75
64190 Gurs 64 161 Zb 89
22390 Gurunhuel 22 63 We 57
29510 Gurvennou 29 78 Wa 60
60310 Gury 60 39 Ce 51
55400 Gussainville 55 55 Fe 53
59570 Gussignies 59 31 De 46
78280 Guyancourt 78 51 Ca 56
25580 Guyans-Durnes 25 107 Gb 66
25390 Guyans-Vennes 25 108 Gd 66
85300 Guy-Ayraud, le 85 96 Ya 68
02160 Guyencourt 02 41 Df 52
80240 Guyencourt-Saulcourt 80 40 Da 49
80250 Guyencourt-sur-Noye 80 39 Cc 50
85260 Guyonnière, la 85 97 Yc 67
85600 Guyonnière, la 85 97 Ye 67
52400 Guyonvelle 52 92 Fe 61
81260 Guyor 81 166 Cc 87
81260 Guzanes 81 166 Cc 87
34820 Guzargues 34 168 Df 86
09140 Guzet-Neige 09 177 Bb 92
22570 Gwareg = Gouarec 22 63 We 59
56000 Gwened = Vannes 56 80 Xb 63
22200 Gwengamp = Guingamp 22 63 Wf 57
56380 Gwen-Porc'hoed = Guer 56 81 Xf 61
35130 Gwerc'h-Breizh = La Guerche-de-Bretagne 35 66 Ye 61
29490 Gwipavaz = Guipavas 29 62 Vd 58
29830 Gwitalmeze = Ploudalmézeau 29 61 Vc 57
35500 Gwitreg = Vitré 35 66 Ye 60
35580 Gwizien = Guichen 35 65 Yb 61
70700 Gy 70 93 Fe 64
54113 Gye 54 76 Ff 57
41230 Gy-en-Sologne 41 86 Bd 64
10250 Gyé-sur-Seine 10 74 Ec 60
45220 Gy-les-Nonains 45 71 Cf 61
89580 Gy-L'évêque 89 89 Dd 62

H

62123 Habarcq 62 29 Cd 47
40290 Habas 40 161 Za 87
64400 Habas 64 161 Zc 89
88230 Habeaurupt 88 77 Ha 60
74420 Habère-Lullin 74 120 Gc 71
74420 Habère-Poche 74 120 Gc 71
19150 Habilis 19 126 Bf 77
27220 Habit, l' 27 50 Bc 55
85220 Habites, les 85 96 Yb 68
54120 Hablainville 54 77 Ge 57
27600 Habloville 27 50 Bc 54
61210 Habloville 61 48 Ze 56
54580 Habonville 54 56 Ff 53
57340 Haboudange 57 57 Gd 55
68440 Habsheim 68 95 Hc 62
65230 Hachan 65 163 Ac 89
59530 Hachette 59 31 De 48
68650 Hachimette 68 77 Hb 60
52150 Hâcourt 52 75 Fd 60
27150 Hacqeville 27 50 Bd 53
60240 Hadancourt-le-Haut-Clocher 60 50 Bf 53
88330 Hadigny-lès-Verrières 88 77 Gc 59
88220 Hadol 88 77 Gc 60
55210 Hadonville-lès-Lachaussée 55 56 Fe 54
67700 Haegen 67 58 Hc 56
88270 Hagécourt 88 76 Ga 59
65700 Hagedet 65 162 Zf 87
57570 Hagen 57 44 Gb 52
67500 Hagenbach 68 95 Ha 63
68220 Hagenthal-le-Bas 68 95 Hc 63
68220 Hagenthal-le-Haut 68 95 Hc 63
32730 Haget 32 163 Aa 88
64370 Hagetaubin 64 161 Zc 87
40700 Hagetmau 40 161 Zc 87
54470 Hagéville 54 56 Ff 54
88300 Hagnéville-et-Roncourt 88 76 Fe 59
08430 Hagnicourt 08 42 Ed 51
57300 Hagondange 57 56 Gb 53
50440* Hague, la 50 33 Yb 51
67500 Haguenau 67 58 He 56
49440 Haie, la 49 83 Yf 63
41100 Haie-de-Champ 41 86 Ba 61
49370 Haie-Diot, la 49 83 Za 63
35560 Haie-d'Irée, la 35 65 Yc 58
35450 Haie d'Izé 35 66 Ye 59
44690 Haie-Fouassière, la 44 97 Yd 66
49190 Haie-Longue, la 49 83 Zb 64
59360 Haie-Menneresse, la 59 30 Dd 48
44390 Haie-Pacoret, la 44 82 Yc 64
89100 Haie-Pélegrine, la 89 72 Db 60
53390 Haie-Rouge, la 53 82 Ye 61
17540 Haies 17 110 Za 72
69420 Haies 69M 130 Ee 75
22350 Haies, les 22 65 Xf 59
41160 Haies, les 41 86 Bb 61
53300 Haie-Traversaine, la 53 67 Zc 58
54290 Haigneville 54 76 Gc 58
65200 Hailla, la 65 163 Ab 90
88330 Haillainville 88 77 Gc 58
33160 Haillan, le 33 134 Zb 79
80440 Hailles 80 39 Cc 50
62940 Haillicourt 62 29 Cd 46
17160 Haimps 17 123 Ze 73
86310 Haims 86 112 Af 69
60380 Haincourt 60 38 Be 51
50120 Hainneville 50 33 Yb 51
60490 Hainvillers 60 39 Ce 51
55000 Haironville 55 55 Fa 56
62138 Haisnes 62 30 Ce 45
14290 Halbouldière, la 14 48 Ab 55
60210 Haleine 60 38 Bf 50
61410 Haleine 61 67 Zd 57
62830 Halinghen 62 28 Be 45
36190 Halle 36 113 Be 69
80490 Hallencourt 80 38 Bf 49
59320 Hallennes-lez-Haubourdin 59 30 Cf 45
57690 Hallering 57 57 Gd 54
80200 Halles 80 39 Cf 49
69610 Halles, les 69M 130 Ec 74
72500 Halles, les 72 85 Ab 63
55700 Halles-sous-les-Côtes 55 42 Fa 52
52100 Hallignicourt 52 54 Ef 57
62570 Hallines 62 29 Cb 44
57570 Halling 57 44 Gb 52
57220 Halling-lès-Boulay 57 57 Gd 54
80250 Hallivillers 80 38 Cb 50
80640 Hallivillers 80 38 Bf 49
28160 Hallonière, la 28 69 Ba 60
40430 Hallot, le 40 147 Zc 83
76780 Hallotière, la 76 37 Bc 51
54450 Halloville 54 77 Gf 57
60210 Halloy 60 38 Bf 51
62760 Halloy 62 29 Cc 48
80670 Halloy-lès-Pernois 80 29 Cb 48
80320 Hallu 80 39 Ce 50
59250 Halluin 59 30 Da 44
57480 Halstroff 57 44 Gc 52
08600 Ham 08 42 Ee 48
80400 Ham 80 39 Da 50
14430 Ham, le 14 35 Zf 53
50310 Ham, le 50 33 Yd 52
53250 Ham, le 53 67 Zd 58
88340 Hamanxard 88 94 Gd 61
14220 Hamars 14 47 Zc 55
50340 Ham-au-Conte 50 33 Yb 52
57910 Hambach 57 57 Ha 54
53160 Hambers 53 67 Zd 59
62118 Hamblain-les-Prés 62 30 Cf 47
50450 Hambye 50 46 Ye 55
53140 Hameau, le 53 67 Ze 58
50270 Hameau-Bonnard 50 33 Yb 52
14370 Hameau-de-Franqueville 14 35 Ze 54
50120 Hameau-de-la-Mer, le 50 33 Yb 51
59279 Hameau-des-Dunes 59 27 Cb 42
50260 Hameau-du-Mesnil 50 33 Yc 52
50310 Hameau-du-Nord 50 33 Ye 52
14710 Hameau-Minet 14 47 Yf 53
14210 Hameau-Neuf 14 34 Zc 54
76780 Hameaux, les 76 37 Bc 52
20166 Hameaux de P. Buselica, les CTC 184 Ie 97
59151 Hamel 59 30 Da 47
80300 Hamel 80 29 Cd 48
60210 Hamel, le 60 38 Bf 51
76660 Hamel, le 76 37 Bb 49
80800 Hamel, le 80 39 Cd 49
50410 Hamel-aux-Hervy 50 46 Ye 55
80800 Hamelet 80 39 Cd 49
27160 Hamelet, le 27 49 Ae 55
80120 Hamelet, le 80 28 Bd 47
50730 Hamelin 50 66 Ye 57
62121 Hamelincourt 62 30 Ce 47
62190 Ham-en-Artois 62 29 Cc 45
62340 Hames-Boucles 62 27 Bf 43
08090 Ham-lès-Moines 08 42 Ed 50
54330 Hammeville 54 76 Ga 58
22650 Hamonais, le 22 65 Xf 57
54470 Hamonville 54 56 Fe 56
10500 Hampigny 10 74 Ed 58
57170 Hampont 57 57 Gd 55
57880 Ham-sous-Varsberg 57 57 Gd 53
54760 Han 54 56 Gb 55
79110 Hanc 79 111 Zf 72
28130 Hanches 28 70 Bd 57
80135 Hanchy 80 29 Ca 48
80240 Hancourt 80 39 Da 49
54620 Han-devant-Pierrepont 54 43 Fe 52
55230 Handeville 55 43 Fd 52
67117 Handschuheim 67 60 Hd 57
80110 Hangard 80 39 Cd 50
67980 Hangenbieten 67 60 Hd 57
80134 Hangest-en-Santerre 80 39 Cd 50
80310 Hangest-sur-Somme 80 38 Ca 49
57370 Hangviller 57 58 Hb 56
55600 Han-lès-Juvigny 55 43 Fc 52
60650 Hannaches 60 38 Be 52
02510 Hannapes 02 40 Dd 49
08290 Hannappes 08 41 Eb 50
62111 Hannescamps 62 29 Cd 47
57590 Hannocourt 57 56 Gc 55
08160 Hannogne-Saint-Martin 08 42 Ee 50
08220 Hannogne-Saint-Rémy 08 41 Ea 51
55210 Hannonville-sous-les-Côtes 55 55 Fd 54
54800 Hannonville-Suzémont 54 56 Ff 54
76450 Hanouard, la 76 36 Ad 50
51800 Hans 51 54 Ee 54
55300 Han-sur-Meuse 55 55 Fd 55
57580 Han-sur-Nied 57 56 Gc 55
59496 Hantay 59 30 Cf 45
29460 Hanvec 29 62 Vf 59
57230 Hanviller 57 58 Hc 54
60650 Hanvoile 60 38 Bf 51
62124 Haplincourt 62 30 Cf 48
62650 Happe 62 28 Bf 45
02480 Happencourt 02 40 Db 50
28480 Happonvilliers 28 69 Ba 59
56440 Haquéla 56 80 We 62
02600 Haramont 02 52 Da 53
08450 Haraucourt 08 42 Ef 51
54110 Haraucourt 54 56 Gc 57
57630 Haraucourt-sur-Seille 57 57 Gd 56
55110 Haraumont 55 55 Fb 52
62390 Haravesnes 62 29 Ca 47
95640 Haravilliers 95 51 Ca 53
51800 Harazée, la 51 54 Ef 53
80131 Harbonnières 80 39 Ce 49
27160 Harboudière, la 27 49 Af 56
54450 Harbouey 54 77 Gf 57
28200 Harbouville 28 70 Bc 60
76560 Harcanville 76 36 Ae 50
88300 Harchéchamp 88 76 Fe 58
54480 Harcholins, les 54 77 Ha 57
02140 Harcigny 02 41 Df 50
27800 Harcourt 27 49 Ae 53
08150 Harcy 08 41 Ed 49
88700 Hardancourt 88 77 Gd 58
53640 Hardanges 53 67 Zd 58
80360 Hardecourt-aux-Bois 80 39 Ce 49
62152 Hardelot-Plage 62 28 Bd 45
88240 Hardémont 88 76 Gb 60
60140 Hardencourt 60 51 Cd 52
27120 Hardencourt-Cocherel 27 50 Bb 54
61370 Hardière, la 61 48 Ac 56
59670 Hardifort 59 27 Cc 44
62132 Hardinghen 62 26 Be 44
50690 Hardinvast 50 33 Yc 51
60120 Hardivillers 60 38 Cb 51
60240 Hardivillers-en-Vexin 60 50 Bf 53
08150 Hardoncelle 08 41 Ed 50
08220 Hardoye, la 08 41 Eb 50
78250 Hardricourt 78 50 Bf 54
57230 Hardt 57 58 Hd 54
40140 Hardy 40 160 Yd 86
27370 Harengère, la 27 49 Af 53
40110 Harenoin 40 146 Yf 84
88800 Haréville 88 76 Ga 59
76610 Harfleur 76 36 Aa 51
37530 Hargandière, la 37 86 Ba 64
57550 Hargarten-aux-Mines 57 57 Gd 53
78790 Hargeville 78 50 Be 55
55000 Hargeville-sur-Chée 55 55 Fb 55
02420 Hargicourt 02 40 Db 49
80500 Hargicourt 80 39 Cd 50
08170 Hargnies 08 42 Ee 48
59138 Hargnies 59 31 Df 47
45320 Haricot, les 45 72 Cf 60
62380 Harlettes 62 28 Ca 44
02100 Harly 02 40 Db 49
52230 Harméville 52 75 Fc 58
72290 Harmonerie, la 72 68 Ab 60
88300 Harmonville 88 76 Ff 58
22320 Harmoye, la 22 63 Xa 58
62440 Harnes 62 30 Cf 46
88270 Harol 88 76 Gb 60
54740 Haroué 54 76 Gb 58
03420 Harpe, l' 03 115 Cd 71
80560 Harponville 80 39 Cd 48
57340 Harprich 57 57 Gd 55
27700 Harquency 27 50 Bc 53
57870 Harreberg 57 57 Hb 56
52150 Harréville-lès-Chanteurs 52 75 Fd 59
40430 Harribey 40 147 Zc 82
08240 Harricourt 08 42 Ef 52
52330 Harricourt 52 74 Ef 59
88240 Harsault 88 76 Gb 60
67260 Harskirchen 67 57 Ha 55
22230 Hartelois, le 22 64 Xd 59
02210 Hartennes-et-Taux 02 52 Dc 53
68500 Hartmannswiller 68 95 Hb 61
57870 Hartzviller 57 57 Ha 56
28120 Harville 28 69 Bb 58
28200 Harville 28 70 Bc 60
55160 Harville 55 55 Fe 54
02140 Hary 02 41 Df 50
57850 Haselbourg 57 57 Hb 56
59178 Hasnon 59 30 Dc 46
64240 Hasparren 64 160 Ye 88
57230 Haspelschiedt 57 58 Hc 54
59198 Haspres 59 30 Dc 47
40300 Hastingues 40 161 Yf 87
44110 Hatais, la 44 82 Yc 62
58230 Hâte-au-Sergent, l' 58 105 Ea 65
88240 Hatrey, Le 88 76 Ga 60
54800 Hatrize 54 56 Ff 53
64480 Hatsou 64 160 Yd 88
67690 Hatten 67 59 Hf 55
80700 Hattencourt 80 39 Ce 50
76640 Hattenville 76 36 Ad 51
57790 Hattigny 57 57 Gf 57
67330 Hattmatt 67 58 Hc 56
55210 Hattonchâtel 55 55 Fd 55
55210 Hattonville 55 55 Fe 55
14250 Hattot-les-Bagues 14 34 Zc 54
68420 Hattstatt 68 60 Hb 60
65200 Hauban 65 162 Aa 90
59320 Haubourdin 59 30 Da 45
57280 Hauconcourt 57 56 Gb 53
60112 Haucourt 60 38 Bf 51
62156 Haucourt 62 30 Cf 47
76440 Haucourt 76 38 Bd 51
02420 Haucourt, le 02 40 Db 49
59191 Haucourt-en-Cambrésis 59 30 Dc 48
55230 Haucourt-la-Rigole 55 43 Fe 53
54860 Haucourt-Moulaine 54 43 Fe 52
55100 Haudainville 55 55 Fc 54
55130 Haudelaincourt 55 75 Fc 57
55160 Haudiomont 55 55 Fd 54
60510 Haudivillers 60 38 Cb 52
88240 Haudompré 88 76 Gc 60
54830 Haudonville 54 77 Gd 57
53140 Haudre 53 67 Ze 57
08090 Haudrecy 08 42 Ed 50
76390 Haudricourt 76 38 Be 50
02260 Haudroy 02 41 Df 49
59121 Haulchin 59 30 Dc 47
32550 Haulies 32 163 Ae 87
08800 Haulmé 08 42 Ee 49
55210 Haumont-lès-Lachaussée 55 56 Fe 54
40250 Hauriet 40 161 Zb 86
68130 Hausgauen 68 95 Hb 63
76440 Haussez 76 38 Be 51
51300 Haussignémont 51 54 Ee 56
51320 Haussimont 51 53 Eb 56
54290 Haussonville 54 76 Gb 57
59294 Haussy 59 30 Dc 47
65400 Hautacam 65 175 Zf 91
65150 Hautaget 65 175 Ac 90
63210 Haut-Angle 63 127 Ce 74
20276 Haut Asco CTC 180 If 94
38690 Haut-Biol 38 131 Fc 75
03190 Haut-Bocage 03 115 Ce 70
27120 Haut-Boisset, le 27 50 Bc 55
60210 Hautbos 60 38 Bf 51
22400 Haut-Boulay 22 64 Xd 57
18310 Haut-Bourg 18 101 Bf 65
79140 Haut-Bourg, le 79 98 Zc 67
33990 Haut-Bré 33 134 Za 77
53400 Haut-Breuil, le 53 83 Za 61
89570 Haut-Chainq 89 73 De 60
61700 Haut-Chapelle, la 61 67 Zb 57
10270 Haut-Chêne, le 10 74 Eb 59
57400 Haut-Clocher 57 57 Gf 56
22320 Haut-Corlay, le 22 63 Wf 59
39200 Haut-Crêt 39 120 Ff 70
64800 Haut-de-Bosdarros 64 162 Ze 89
64290 Haut-de-Gan 64 162 Zd 89
14170 Haut-de-Tôtes, le 14 48 Zf 55
14420 Haut-de-Villiers 14 47 Ze 55
14240 Haut-Digny, le 14 34 Za 54
70440 Haut-du-Them-Château-Lambert 70 94 Ge 61
62144 Haute-Avesnes 62 29 Cd 47
37360 Haute-Barde, la 37 85 Ad 63
05140 Haute Beaume, la 05 144 Fd 81
72400 Haute-Biche 72 68 Ad 59
03500 Haute Brenne 03 116 Db 70
19220 Haute-Brousse 19 138 Ca 78
80460 Hautebut 80 28 Bc 48
72170 Haut-Éclair 72 68 Zf 59
62130 Hautecloque 62 29 Cb 46
04250 Haute-Combe, la 04 157 Gb 82
39130 Hautecour 39 119 Fe 69
73600 Hautecour 73 133 Gd 75
55400 Hautecourt-lès-Broville 55 55 Fd 53
01250 Hautecourt-Romanèche 01 119 Fc 72
04380 Haute-Duyes 04 157 Ga 83
37320 Hautée 37 100 Ae 65
60690 Haute-Épine 60 38 Ca 51
02540 Haute-épine, la 02 52 Dc 55
19400 Hautefage 19 138 Bf 78
47340 Hautefage-la-Tour 47 149 Ae 83
24300 Hautefaye 24 124 Ac 75
71600 Hautefond 71 117 Eb 70
60350 Hautefontaine 60 39 Da 52
24390 Hautefort 24 125 Ba 77
44115 Haute-Goulaine 44 97 Yd 65
57100 Haute-Ham 57 44 Gb 52
95780 Haute-Isle 95 50 Bd 54
57480 Haute-Kontz 57 44 Gb 52
73620 Hauteluce 73 133 Gd 74
77580 Haute-Maison, la 77 52 Cf 55
62890 Haute Pannée 62 27 Ca 44
57570 Haute-Parthe 57 44 Gb 52
44320 Haute-Perche 44 96 Ya 66
25580 Hautepierre-le-Châtelet 25 108 Gb 66
57570 Haute-Rentgen 57 44 Gb 52
01640 Hauterive 01 119 Fc 72
03270 Hauterive 03 116 Dc 72
28170 Hauterive 28 69 Bb 57
59230 Hauterive 59 30 Dc 46
61250 Hauterive 61 68 Ab 58
70190 Hauterive 70 93 Ff 64
81100 Hauterive 81 166 Cb 87
89250 Hauterive 89 89 Dd 61
25650 Hauterive-la-Flesse 25 108 Gc 67
26390 Hauterives 26 130 Fa 77
69610 Haute-Rivoire 69M 130 Ec 74
21150 Hauteroche 21 91 Ed 64
39177 Hauteroche 39 107 Fe 68
89260 Hautes-Bergeries, les 89 72 Dc 59
81140 Haute-Serre 81 150 Be 84
26570 Hautes-Ferrassières 26 156 Fc 84
57480 Haute Sierck 57 44 Gc 52
37130 Hautes-Martinières, les 37 85 Ab 64
08800 Hautes-Rivières, les 08 42 Ef 49
70400 Hautes-Valettes, les 70 94 Gd 63
01560 Hautes-Varennes 01 118 Fa 70
47400 Hautesvignes 47 136 Ac 82
35250 Haute-Touche, la 35 65 Yb 59
35500 Haute-Touche, la 35 66 Ye 59
07200 Haute-Valette 07 141 Eb 81
70800 Hautevelle 70 93 Gb 61
04140 Haute-Vernet, le 04 157 Gc 83
83340 Haute Verrerie, la 83 172 Gc 88
02810 Hautevesnes 02 52 Db 54
43800 Haute-Vialle 43 141 Df 78
57690 Haute-Vigneulles 57 57 Gd 54
02120 Hauteville 02 40 Dd 49
08300 Hauteville 08 41 Eb 51
50270 Hauteville 50 33 Yb 52
51290 Hauteville 51 54 Ee 57
62810 Hauteville 62 29 Cd 47
73390 Hauteville 73 132 Gb 75
44660 Haute-Ville, la 44 82 Yc 62
78113 Hauteville, la 78 50 Bd 56
88700 Haute-Ville, la 88 77 Ge 59
21121 Hauteville-Ahuy 21 91 Fa 64
73700 Hauteville-Gondon 73 133 Ge 75
50570 Hauteville-la-Guichard 50 34 Ye 54
21121 Hauteville-lès-Dijon 21 91 Ef 64
01110 Hauteville-Lompnes 01 119 Fd 73
74150 Hauteville-sur-Fier 74 120 Ff 73
50590 Hauteville-sur-Mer 50 46 Yc 55
50590 Hauteville-sur-Mer-Plage 50 46 Yc 55
80600 Haute-Visée 80 29 Cb 47
53410 Haut-Feil 53 66 Yf 60
18220 Haut-Fouillet 18 103 Ce 65
43170 Haut-Hontès 43 140 Dc 79
78510 Hautil, l' 78 51 Ca 54
02140 Haution 02 41 Df 49
40280 Haut-Mauco 40 147 Zc 86
50390 Hautmesnil 50 46 Yc 52
59330 Hautmont 59 31 Df 47
82500 Hautmont 82 149 Af 85
17360 Haut-Mont, le 17 123 Zf 77
88240 Hautmougey 88 76 Gb 60
65150 Haut-Nistos 65 175 Ac 91
76450 Hautot-l'Auvray 76 36 Ae 50
76190 Hautot-le-Vatois 76 36 Ae 51
76190 Hautot-Saint-Sulpice 76 36 Ae 50
76550 Hautot-sur-Mer 76 37 Ba 49
76113 Hautot-sur-Seine 76 37 Af 52
62830 Haut-Pichot 62 28 Be 45
81200 Hautpoul 81 166 Cc 88
40410 Haut-Richet 40 147 Zb 83
62190 Haut-Rieux 62 29 Cc 45
08800 Hauts-Buttés, les 08 42 Ee 49
49600 Hauts-Champs, les 49 97 Ye 65
49330 Hauts d'Anjou, les 49 83 Zc 62
39400 Hauts de Bienne 39 120 Ff 69
55000 Hauts-de-Chée, les 55 55 Fb 55
52250 Hauts-de-Vingeanne, les 52 92 Fb 62
52600 Hauts-le-Palliy 52 92 Fc 62
68780 Haut Soultzbach, le 68 94 Ha 62
04140 Hauts-Savornins 04 157 Gc 82
14250 Hauts-Vents, les 14 34 Zc 53
50390 Hauts-Vents, les 50 33 Yd 52
50390 Hautteville-Bocage 50 33 Yd 52
01260 Haut Valromey 01 119 Fe 72
21121 Haut-Val-Suzon 21 91 Ef 64
50620 Haut-Vernay, le 50 46 Ye 53
51160 Hautvillers 51 53 Df 54
80132 Hautvillers-Ouville 80 28 Be 47
27350 Hauville 27 36 Ae 52
08310 Hauviné 08 54 Ec 53
33550 Haux 33 135 Zd 80
64470 Haux 64 174 Za 90
57650 Havange 57 43 Ff 52
28410 Havelu 28 50 Bd 56
59255 Haveluy 59 30 Dc 46
80670 Havernas 80 29 Cb 48
59660 Haverskerque 59 29 Cd 45
14240 Havetot 14 34 Zb 54
76600 Havre, le 76 36 Aa 52
62147 Havrincourt 62 30 Da 48
08260 Havys 08 41 Ec 50
57700 Hayange 57 43 Ff 53
08170 Haybes 08 42 Ee 48
28410 Haye, la 28 50 Bd 56
41270 Haye, la 41 69 Ba 60
50450 Haye, la 50 46 Ye 55
76780 Haye, la 76 37 Bd 52
88270 Haye, la 88 76 Gb 60
50250* Haye, la 50 46 Yc 53
27350 Haye-Aubrée, la 27 36 Ae 52
50410 Haye-Bellefond, la 50 46 Ye 55
27800 Haye-de-Calleville, la 27 49 Ae 53
50270 Haye-d'Ectot, la 50 33 Yb 52
27350 Haye-de-Routot, la 27 36 Ae 52
50250 Haye-du-Puits, la 50 33 Yc 53
27370 Haye-du-Theil, la 27 49 Af 53
27400 Haye-le-Comte, la 27 49 Ba 53
27400 Haye-Malherbe, la 27 49 Ba 53
50320 Haye-Pesnel, la 50 46 Yd 56
57530 Hayes 57 56 Gc 53
41800 Hayes, les 41 85 Ae 62
27330 Haye-Saint-Sylvestre, la 27 49 Ad 55
02260 Hayettes, les 02 41 Df 48
92340 Hay-les-Roses, l' 92 51 Cb 56
59268 Haynecourt 59 30 Da 47
39120 Hays, les 39 106 Fc 67
40200 Haza 40 146 Yf 83
59190 Hazebrouck 59 27 Cd 44
57430 Hazembourg 57 57 Gf 55
33125 Hazéra 33 134 Zc 81
59114 Hazewinde, l' 59 27 Cd 44
65120 Hèas 65 175 Aa 92
95640 Heaulme, le 95 51 Bf 54
53220 Heaumes, les 53 66 Za 58
41160 Héauville 41 69 Bb 61
50340 Héauville 50 33 Yb 51
27150 Hébécourt 27 38 Be 52
80680 Hébécourt 80 38 Cb 50
50180 Hébécrevon 50 33 Ye 54
76740 Héberville 76 37 Ae 50
62111 Hébuterne 62 29 Cd 48
65250 Hèches 65 175 Ac 90
68210 Hecken 68 95 Ha 62
57510 Heckenransbach 57 57 Gf 54
57320 Heckling 57 57 Gd 53
27800 Hecmanville 27 49 Ad 53
27120 Hécourt 27 50 Bc 55
60380 Hécourt 60 38 Be 51
27110 Hectomare 27 49 Af 53
80560 Hédauville 80 29 Cd 48
35630 Hédé Hazou 35 65 Yb 59
95690 Hédouville 95 51 Ca 54
67360 Hegeney 67 58 He 55
68220 Hégenheim 68 95 Hd 63
64990 Héguia 64 160 Yd 88
67390 Heidolsheim 67 60 Hd 59

276 | Guitté

68720 Heidwiller 68 95 Hb 63
67190 Heiligenberg 67 60 Hc 57
67140 Heiligenstein 67 60 Hc 58
57560 Heille 57 57 Ha 57
54180 Heillecourt 54 56 Gb 57
60250 Heilles 60 51 Cb 52
80800 Heilly 80 39 Cd 49
51300 Heiltz-le-Houtier 51 54 Ee 56
51340 Heiltz-le-Maurupt 51 54 Ee 56
51340 Heiltz-l'Evêque 51 54 Ee 56
68560 Heimersdorf 68 95 Hb 63
68990 Heimsbrunn 68 95 Hb 62
55220 Heippes 55 55 Fb 55
68600 Heiteren 68 60 Hd 61
68130 Heiwiller 68 95 Hb 63
59171 Hélesmes 59 30 Dc 46
64640 Hélette 64 160 Ye 89
62570 Helfaut 62 29 Cb 44
68510 Helfrantzkirch 68 95 Hc 63
56120 Helléan 56 64 Xd 61
59800 Hellemmes 59 30 Da 45
29510 Hellen 29 78 Wa 60
27240 Hellenvilliers 27 49 Ba 56
57930 Hellering-lès-Fénétrange 57 57 Ha 56
57850 Hellert 57 58 Hb 56
29640 Helles 29 63 Wc 58
29620 Hellès, le 29 63 Wb 57
50340 Helleville 50 33 Yb 51
57660 Hellimer 57 57 Ge 55
57920 Helling 57 44 Gc 53
57810 Hellocourt 57 57 Ge 56
61250 Héloup 61 68 Aa 58
57220 Helstroff 57 57 Gc 54
59510 Hem 59 30 Db 45
50700 Hémevez 50 33 Yd 52
60190 Hémévillers 60 39 Ce 52
80600 Hem-Hardinval 80 29 Cb 48
34700 Hémiès, les 34 167 Db 86
57690 Hémilly 57 57 Gd 54
57830 Heming 57 57 Gf 56
59247 Hem-Lenglet 59 30 Db 47
62730 Hemmes, les 62 27 Bf 43
22600 Hémonstoir 22 64 Xb 60
59390 Hempempont, l' 59 30 Db 44
54370 Hénaménil 54 57 Gd 56
22550 Hénanbihen 22 64 Xd 57
22400 Hénansal 22 64 Xd 57
56700 Henbont 56 79 We 62
64700 Hendaye 64 160 Yb 88
64700 Hendaye-Plage 64 160 Yb 88
62182 Hendecourt-lès-Cagnicourt 62 30 Cf 47
62175 Hendecourt-les-Ransart 62 29 Ce 47
80300 Hénencourt 80 29 Cd 49
68960 Henflingen 68 95 Hb 63
22450 Hengoat 22 63 We 56
67440 Hengwiller 67 58 Hc 56
62110 Hénin-Beaumont 62 30 Cf 46
62128 Héninel 62 30 Cf 47
62128 Hénin-sur-Cojeul 62 30 Cf 47
56800 Henlé 56 64 Xd 61
48300 Henn, l' 48 141 De 80
56700 Hennebont 56 79 Wd 62
88270 Hennecourt 88 76 Gb 59
55160 Hennemont 55 55 Fd 54
14360 Hennequeville 14 36 Aa 52
62142 Henneveux 62 27 Bf 44
88260 Hennezel 88 76 Ga 60
27700 Hennezis 27 50 Bc 53
60220 Hennicourt 60 38 Be 50
22150 Hénon 22 64 Xb 58
60119 Hénonville 60 51 Ca 53
76840 Hénouville 76 37 Af 52
62650 Hénoville 62 28 Bf 45
18250 Henrichemont 18 88 Cd 65
57820 Henridorff 57 57 Hb 56
57450 Henriville 57 57 Gf 54
78320 Henriville 78 50 Bf 56
03470 Henry, les 03 116 De 70
29710 Hent-Meur 29 78 Ve 60
62760 Hénu 62 29 Cd 48
29670 Henvic 29 62 Wa 57
24270 Hépital, l' 24 125 Ba 76
57635 Hérange 57 57 Hb 56
48150 Herans 48 153 Dc 83
64480 Hérauritz 64 160 Yd 88
64640 Hérauritz 64 160 Ye 89
53300 Herbaine 53 67 Zc 58
16490 Herbaudie 16 112 Ad 72
85330 Herbaudière, l' 85 96 Xd 66
41190 Herbault 41 86 Ba 63
88470 Herbaville 88 77 Gf 59
77760 Herbeauvilliers 77 71 Cc 59
80200 Herbécourt 80 39 Cf 49
19550 Herbeil, l' 19 126 Ca 77
62129 Herbelles 62 29 Cb 45
38650 Herbelon 38 144 Fd 79
85260 Herbergement, l' 85 97 Yd 67
08370 Herbeuval 08 43 Fc 51
55210 Herbeuville 55 55 Fd 54
78580 Herbeville 78 50 Bf 55
54450 Herbéviller 54 77 Ge 57
38320 Herbeys 38 144 Fe 78
85500 Herbiers, les 85 97 Yf 67
44410 Herbignac 44 81 Xe 64
59530 Herbignies 59 31 De 47
08270 Herbigny 08 41 Eb 51
41500 Herbilly 41 86 Bd 62
62650 Herbinghen 62 27 Bf 44
10700 Herbisse 10 53 Ea 57
67260 Herbitzheim 67 57 Ha 54
95220 Herblay 95 51 Ca 55
67230 Herbsheim 67 60 Hd 58
53120 Hercé 53 66 Za 58
60112 Herchies 60 38 Ca 52
36160 Héréat 36 114 Ca 70
32450 Heréchou 32 163 Ae 87
60120 Hérelle, la 60 39 Cc 51
50660 Hérenguerville 50 46 Yc 55
34600 Hérépian 34 167 Da 87
65700 Hères 65 162 Aa 87
59570 Hergies 59 31 De 46
59199 Hergnies 59 30 Dd 46
88130 Hergugney 88 76 Gb 58
44810 Héric 44 82 Yc 64
44390 Héricher, le 44 82 Yc 64
77850 Héricy 77 71 Ce 58
62130 Héricourt 62 29 Cb 46
70400 Héricourt 70 94 Ge 63
76560 Héricourt-en-Caux 76 36 Ae 50
60380 Héricourt-sur-Thérain 60 38 Be 51
02500 Herie, la 02 41 Ea 49
02120 Hérie-La-Viéville, la 02 40 Dd 50
54300 Hériménil 54 77 Gc 57
25310 Hérimoncourt 25 94 Gf 64
59195 Hérin 59 30 Dc 46
14670 Heriot 14 35 Zf 54
80260 Hérissart 80 39 Cc 48
03190 Hérisson 03 115 Ce 69
79130 Hérisson 79 98 Zd 68
80340 Herlevillers 80 39 Ce 49
62158 Herlière, la 62 29 Cd 47
59134 Herlies 59 30 Cf 45
62130 Herlincourt 62 29 Cb 46
62130 Herlin-le-Sec 62 29 Cb 46
62650 Herly 62 28 Bf 45
80190 Herly 80 39 Cf 50
09000 Herm, l' 09 177 Be 91
12440 Herm, l' 12 151 Cb 83
15700 Herm, l' 15 139 Cb 78
40990 Herm, l' 40 146 Yf 86
43200 Herm, l' 43 141 Ea 78
48600 Herm, l' 48 141 De 80
76730 Hermanville 76 37 Af 50
14880 Hermanville-sur-Mer 14 47 Ze 53
48340 Hermaux, les 48 140 Da 81
62690 Hermaville 62 29 Cd 47
77114 Hermé 77 72 Dc 58
57790 Hermelange 57 57 Ha 56
62132 Hermelinghen 62 27 Bf 44
85570 Hermenault, l' 85 110 Za 69
63470 Herment 63 127 Cd 74
83910 Hermentaires, les 83 171 Fe 87
78125 Hermeray 78 50 Be 57
67250 Hermerswiller 67 58 Hf 55
60370 Hermes 60 38 Cb 52
12330 Hermets, les 12 139 Cc 82
76280 Hermeville 76 36 Ab 51
55400 Herméville-en-Woëvre 55 55 Fd 53
62147 Hermies 62 30 Da 48
53380 Hermillon 53 66 Yf 59
73300 Hermillon 73 132 Gc 77
62150 Hermin 62 29 Cd 46
11000 Herminis 11 166 Cb 89
11190 Hermita 11 178 Cc 91
05000 Hermitage, l' 05 144 Ga 81
22250 Hermitage, l' 22 65 Xe 59
35590 Hermitage, l' 35 65 Yb 60
22150 Hermitage-Lorge, l' 22 64 Xb 59
43440 Hermitagne, l' 43 128 Dd 77
87270 Hermiterie, l' 87 125 Bb 73
37110 Hermites, les 37 85 Ae 63
61260 Hermitière, l' 61 68 Ad 59
14100 Hermival-les-Vaux 14 48 Ab 53
51220 Hermonville 51 53 Df 52
62130 Hernicourt 62 29 Cb 46
57580 Herny 57 57 Gc 54
86290 Herolles, les 86 113 Bb 70
76780 Héron, le 76 37 Bc 52
76750 Héronchelles 76 37 Bc 51
95300 Hérouville 95 51 Ca 54
14200 Hérouville-Saint-Clair 14 47 Ze 53
14850 Hérouvillette 14 48 Ze 53
88600 Herpelmont 88 77 Ge 59
53440 Herperie, la 53 67 Zc 59
16200 Herpes 16 123 Ze 74
51460 Herpine 51 54 Ee 55
51460 Herpont 51 54 Ee 55
08360 Herpy-L'Arlésienne 08 41 Eb 51
27430 Herqueville 27 50 Bb 53
50440 Herqueville 50 33 Ya 50
31160 Herran 31 176 Af 91
40160 Herran 40 146 Yf 83
40310 Herré 40 148 Zf 84
57380 Herrenwald 57 57 Gd 54
64680 Herrère 64 162 Zc 89
65560 Herrère, la 65 174 Ze 90
32100 Herret 32 148 Ac 85
59147 Herrin 59 30 Cf 45
67850 Herrlisheim 67 58 Hf 56
68420 Herrlisheim-près-Colmar 68 60 Hb 60
18140 Herry 18 103 Cf 65
34330 Hers, les 34 166 Ce 87
67130 Hersbach 67 60 Hb 58
54440 Herserange 54 43 Fe 51
62530 Hersin-Coupigny 62 29 Cd 46
57815 Hertzing 57 57 Gf 56
36240 Hervault 36 101 Bb 66
62179 Hervelinghen 62 26 Be 43
22100 Herviais, le 22 65 Xf 58
28150 Herville 28 70 Be 59
80240 Hervilly 80 40 Da 49
58800 Héry 58 89 Dd 65
73400 Héry 73 132 Gc 74
89550 Héry 89 90 Dd 61
74540 Héry-sur-Alby 74 132 Ga 74
59470 Herzeele 59 27 Cd 43
80240 Hesbécourt 80 40 Da 49
80290 Hescamps 80 38 Bf 50
62196 Hesdigneul 62 29 Cd 45
62360 Hesdigneul-lès-Boulogne 62 28 Be 45
62140 Hesdin 62 29 Ca 46
62360 Hesdin-L'Abbé 62 28 Be 44
62720 Hesdres 62 26 Be 44
68220 Hésingue 68 95 Hd 63
62990 Hesmond 62 28 Bf 46
76660 Hesmy 76 37 Bc 49
57640 Hessange 57 56 Gb 53
57400 Hesse 57 57 Ha 56
67390 Hessenheim 67 60 Hd 59
57320 Hestroff 57 56 Gc 53
59740 Hestrud 59 31 Ea 47
62550 Hestrus 62 29 Cb 46
79150 Hétivault 79 98 Zc 67
60360 Hétomesnil 60 38 Ca 51
57330 Hettange-Grande 57 44 Ga 52
68600 Hettenschlag 68 60 Hc 60
67114 Hetzlader 67 60 He 58
27630 Heubécourt-Haricourt 27 50 Bd 54
62134 Heuchin 62 29 Cb 46
80270 Heucourt-Croquoison 80 38 Bf 49
27400 Heudebouville 27 50 Bb 53
76260 Heudelimont 76 37 Bc 48
27860 Heudicourt 27 50 Bd 52
80122 Heudicourt 80 40 Da 48
55210 Heudicourt-sous-les-Côtes 55 55 Fe 55
27230 Heudreville-en-Lieuvin 27 49 Ad 53
27400 Heudreville-sur-Eure 27 49 Bb 54
40180 Heugas 40 161 Yf 87
76720 Heugleville-sur-Scie 76 37 Ba 50
36180 Heugnes 36 101 Bc 66
61470 Heugon 61 48 Ac 55
32700 Heuguère 32 149 Ad 84
50200 Heugueville-sur-Sienne 50 46 Yc 54
52600 Heuilley-Cotton 52 92 Fc 62
52600 Heuilley-le-Grand 52 92 Fc 62
21270 Heuilley-sur-Saône 21 92 Fc 65
14430 Heuland 14 35 Aa 53
47700 Heulies 47 148 Zf 82
63210 Heume-L'Eglise 63 127 Ce 74
27950 Heunière, la 27 50 Bc 54
27700 Heuqueville 27 50 Bc 53
76280 Heuqueville 76 36 Aa 51
32380 Heure-et-Bartens 32 149 Ae 85
62575 Heuringhem 62 29 Cb 44
89320 Heurtebise 89 72 Dd 60
14140 Heurtevent 14 48 Aa 55
50640 Heussé 50 66 Za 57
67150 Heussern 67 60 Hd 58
51110 Heutrégiville 51 41 Eb 53
32100 Heux 32 148 Ab 85
80370 Heuzecourt 80 29 Cb 47
60380 Hévécourt 60 38 Be 51
55290 Hévilliers 55 75 Fc 57
01460 Heyriat 01 119 Fc 71
38540 Heyrieux 38 131 Fa 75
62310 Hézecques 62 29 Cb 45
56450 Hézo, le 56 80 Xb 63
65380 Hibarette 65 162 Aa 90
38118 Hières-sur-Amby 38 131 Fb 74
08320 Hierges 08 42 Ee 48
80370 Hiermont 80 29 Ca 47
72430 Hierray 72 84 Ze 61
16290 Hiersac 16 123 Aa 74
17320 Hiers-Brouage 17 122 Yf 73
16490 Hiesse 16 112 Ad 72
50480 Hiesville 50 46 Ye 52
14170 Hiéville 14 48 Zf 54
54490 Higny 54 43 Fe 52
64160 Higuères-Souye 64 162 Ze 88
65200 Hiis 65 162 Aa 90
49700 Hilay 49 98 Zd 65
57400 Hilbesheim 57 57 Ha 56
17770 Hillairets, les 17 123 Zd 73
40160 Hillan 40 146 Ye 83
31310 Hillet 31 164 Bb 90
32300 Hillet 32 163 Ad 87
09120 Hillette, la 09 164 Bc 90
22120 Hillion 22 64 Xc 57
32300 Hillougros 32 163 Ac 88
67600 Hilsenheim 67 60 Hd 59
57510 Hilsprich 57 57 Gf 54
57570 Himeling 57 44 Gb 52
02440 Hinacourt 02 40 Db 50
57220 Hinckange 57 56 Gc 53
67150 Hindisheim 67 60 Hd 58
68580 Hindlingen 68 95 Ha 63
62232 Hinges 62 29 Cd 45
22100 Hinglé, le 22 65 Xf 58
22100 Hinglé-les-Granits, le 22 65 Xf 58
44170 Hingué 44 82 Yb 63
67290 Hinsbourg 67 58 Hb 55
57510 Hinsing 57 57 Gf 55
67260 Hinsingen 67 57 Gf 55
67360 Hinterfeld 67 58 He 55
40180 Hinx 40 161 Za 86
47360 Hiot 47 149 Ad 83
67150 Hipsheim 67 60 He 58
57510 Hirbach 57 57 Gf 54
35120 Hirel 35 65 Yb 57
22960 Hirel, le 22 64 Xb 58
67320 Hirschland 67 57 Ha 55
68560 Hirsingue 68 95 Hb 63
02500 Hirson 02 41 Ea 49
68118 Hirtzbach 68 95 Hb 63
67220 Hirtzelbach 67 60 Hb 59
68740 Hirtzfelden 68 95 Hc 61
31260 His 31 164 Af 90
31210 Hite, la 31 163 Ad 90
32460 Hitère, la 32 162 Ze 86
09230 Hitte 09 164 Ba 90
65190 Hitte 65 163 Aa 90
67270 Hochfelden 67 58 Hd 56
68720 Hochstatt 68 95 Hb 62
67170 Hochstett 67 58 He 56
62650 Hocqueliers 62 28 Bf 45
80210 Hocquélus 80 28 Bd 48
02340 Hocquet, le 02 41 Ea 50
50320 Hocquigny 50 46 Yd 56
80490 Hocquincourt 80 28 Bf 49
62850 Hocquinghen 62 27 Bf 44
60650 Hodenc-en-Bray 60 38 Bf 52
60430 Hodenc-L'Evêque 60 51 Ca 52
76340 Hodeng-au-Bosc 76 38 Be 49
76780 Hodenger 76 38 Bd 51
76780 Hodeng-Hodenger 76 38 Bd 51
95420 Hodent 95 50 Be 54
57410 Hœlling 57 58 Hb 54
67250 Hœlschloch 67 58 He 55
67800 Hœnheim 67 58 He 57
67720 Hœrdt 67 58 He 56
54370 Hoéville 54 56 Gc 56
67250 Hoffen 67 58 Hf 55
27910 Hogues, les 27 37 Bc 52
14700 Hoguette, la 14 48 Zf 55
67170 Hohatzenheim 67 58 Hd 56
67310 Hohengœft 67 58 Hc 57
67270 Hohfrankenheim 67 58 Hd 56
68140 Hohrod 68 77 Ha 60
68140 Hohrodberg 68 77 Ha 60
67140 Hohwald, le 67 60 Hb 58
67220 Hohwarth 67 60 Hc 58
67250 Hohwiller 67 58 Hf 55
57380 Holacourt 57 57 Gc 55
57410 Holbach 57 58 Hc 54
57730 Holbach 57 57 Ge 54
88470 Hollande, la 88 77 Gf 58
57220 Holling 57 57 Gc 53
63470 Holmes, les 63 127 Cd 74
02760 Holnon 02 40 Db 49
59143 Holque 59 27 Cb 43
67230 Holtzbad 67 60 Hd 58
67810 Holtzheim 67 60 Hd 57
68320 Holtzwihr 68 60 Hc 60
57510 Holving 57 57 Gf 54
48400 Hom, l' 48 153 Dc 83
14220 Hom, le 14 47 Zc 55
02720 Homblières 02 40 Dc 49
80400 Homblieux 80 39 Cf 50
57470 Hombourg 57 57 Ge 54
68490 Hombourg 68 95 Hc 62
57920 Hombourg-Budange 57 56 Gc 53
82800 Hombrails 82 150 Bd 84
61290 Hôme-Chamondot, l' 61 69 Ae 57
54310 Homecourt 54 56 Ff 53
14390 Home-sur-Mer, la 14 48 Zf 53
37320 Hommais, l' 37 85 Ae 65
57405 Hommarting 57 57 Ha 56
58120 Homme, l' 58 104 Df 66
53320 Hommeau, l' 53 66 Yf 61
26740 Homme-d'Armes, l' 26 142 Ee 81
57870 Hommert 57 57 Hb 56
37340 Hommes 37 85 Ab 64
50620 Hommet-d'Arthenay, le 50 33 Ye 53
11200 Homps 11 166 Ce 89
32120 Homps 32 149 Af 86
81130 Homps, les 81 151 Ca 84
59190 Hondeghem 59 27 Cd 44
77510 Hondevilliers 77 52 Db 55
27400 Hondouville 27 49 Ba 54
59122 Hondschoote 59 27 Cd 43
14600 Honfleur 14 36 Ab 52
27310 Honguemare-Guenouville 27 37 Ae 52
59980 Honnechy 59 30 Dc 48
59266 Honnecourt-sur-Escaut 59 30 Db 48
82130 Honor-de-Cos, l' 82 150 Bc 84
57670 Honskirch 57 57 Gf 55
40190 Hontanx 40 147 Ze 86
28150 Honville 28 70 Be 58
01150 Hôpital, l' 01 131 Fb 73
15130 Hôpital, l' 15 139 Cc 79
15140 Hôpital, l' 15 139 Cc 78
15250 Hôpital, l' 15 139 Cb 79
19300 Hôpital, l' 19 126 Ca 76
19400 Hôpital, l' 19 138 Bf 78
22120 Hôpital, l' 22 64 Xb 58
22550 Hôpital, l' 22 64 Xe 57
24600 Hôpital, l' 24 124 Ac 77
33590 Hôpital, l' 33 122 Yf 76
46500 Hôpital, l' 46 138 Be 80
57490 Hôpital, l' = Spittel 57 57 Ge 54
12170 Hôpital-Bellegarde, l' 12 152 Cd 84
29460 Hôpital-Camfrout 29 62 Ve 59
64270 Hôpital-d'Orion, l' 64 161 Za 88
25620 Hôpital-du-Grosbois, l' 25 107 Gb 65
42210 Hôpital-le-Grand, l' 42 129 Eb 75
71600 Hôpital-le-Mercier, l' 71 117 Ea 70
64130 Hôpital-Saint-Blaise, l' 64 161 Zb 89
46600 Hôpital-Saint-Jean 46 138 Bd 78
25340 Hôpital-Saint-Lieffroy, l' 25 94 Gc 64
42130 Hôpital-sous-Rochefort, l' 42 129 Df 74
85250 Hopitaud, l' 85 97 Ye 67
22430 Hôpitaux, les 22 64 Xd 57
25370 Hôpitaux-Neufs, les 25 108 Gc 68
25370 Hôpitaux-Vieux, les 25 108 Gc 68
58350 Hopitot, l' 58 103 Db 65
27210 Hopsores, le 27 48 Ac 53
64130 Hoquy 64 161 Za 89
37260 Horaie, la 37 85 Ad 65
68180 Horbourg-Wihr 68 60 Hc 60
59111 Hordain 59 30 Db 47
40390 Horgave 40 160 Ye 87
08430 Horgne, la 08 42 Ee 51
65310 Horgues 65 162 Aa 89
59171 Hornaing 59 30 Dc 46
80640 Hornoy-le-Bourg 80 38 Bf 49
53640 Horps, le 53 67 Zd 58
63950 Hors 63 127 Ce 75
40700 Horsarrieu 40 161 Zc 86
52600 Hortes 52 92 Fd 61
73500 Hortière, l' 73 133 Ge 77
80250 Hortoy, l' 80 38 Cb 50
55130 Horville-en-Ornois 55 75 Fc 58
44410 Hoscas 44 81 Xe 64
27570 Hosmes, l' 27 49 Ba 56
63980 Hospeux, l' 63 128 Dc 75
31110 Hospice de France 31 176 Ad 92
04150 Hospitalet, l' 04 156 Fe 84
12510 Hospitalet, l' 12 151 Cc 82
42680 Hospitalet, l' 42 129 Eb 76
46500 Hospitalet, l' 46 138 Bd 80
48110 Hospitalet, l' 48 153 Dd 83
12230 Hospitalet-du-Larzac, l' 12 153 Db 85
09390 Hospitalet-près-L'Andorre, l' 09 177 Be 93
40150 Hossegor 40 160 Yd 87
64120 Hosta 64 161 Yf 90
66300 Hostalets, les 66 179 Ce 93
57510 Hoste-Bas 57 57 Gf 54
57510 Hoste-Haut 57 57 Gf 54
04000 Hostelleries, les 04 157 Gb 84
33125 Hostens 33 134 Zc 82
43200 Hostes, les 43 141 Eb 78
01110 Hostiaz 01 119 Fd 73
26730 Hostun 26 143 Fb 78
50570 Hôtel-d'Artenay, l' 50 34 Ye 54
22550 Hôtel-Juhel, l' 22 64 Xd 57
14100 Hôtellerie, l' 14 48 Ac 54
53160 Hôtellerie, l' 53 67 Zd 59
53410 Hôtellerie, l' 53 66 Yf 59
49500 Hôtellerie-de-Flée, l' 49 83 Za 62
61120 Hotellerie-Farault, l' 61 48 Aa 55
01260 Hotonnes 01 119 Fe 73
14430 Hotot-en-Auge 14 35 Zf 53
57720 Hottviller 57 58 Hc 54
15590 Houade 15 139 Cd 78
56170 Houat 56 80 Xa 64
57850 Hoube, la 57 58 Hb 57
14340 Houblonnière, la 14 35 Aa 54
74310 Houches, les 74 121 Ge 73
62620 Houchin 62 29 Cd 46
59570 Houdain 59 31 De 47
62150 Houdain 62 29 Cd 46
78550 Houdan 78 50 Bd 56
60710 Houdancourt 60 51 Cd 52
55230 Houdelaucourt-sur-Othain 55 43 Fe 53
54330 Houdelmont 54 76 Ga 57
54180 Houdemont 54 56 Gb 57
76740 Houdetot 76 36 Ae 50
08190 Houdilcourt 08 41 Ea 52
40140 Houdin 40 146 Ye 86
61270 Houdonnière, la 61 49 Ad 56
54330 Houdreville 54 76 Ga 57
88170 Houécourt 88 76 Ff 59
32440 Houeillère 32 148 Aa 85
47420 Houeillès 47 148 Aa 83
50480 Houesville 50 46 Ye 52
27400 Houetteville 27 49 Ba 54
88300 Houéville 88 76 Fe 58
65330 Houeydets 65 163 Ac 90
32460 Houga, le 32 148 Ze 86
40120 Houga, le 40 147 Zd 83
33980 Houguey, le 33 134 Za 80
16110 Houillères, les 16 124 Ac 74
78800 Houilles 78 51 Ca 55
57830 Houillons 57 57 Gf 56
27120 Houlbec-Cocherel 27 50 Bc 54
27370 Houlbec-près-le-Gros-Theil 27 49 Ae 53
08090 Houldizy 08 42 Ee 50
16200 Houlette 16 123 Ze 74
59236 Houlette, la 59 30 Cf 44
14510 Houlgate 14 48 Zf 53
62910 Houlle 62 27 Cb 44
76770 Houlme, le 76 37 Ba 51
86250 Houmaillerie, l' 86 112 Ab 72
36500 Houme 36 101 Bc 68
17137 Houmeau, l' 17 110 Ye 71
31530 Hounédis 31 164 Bb 86
11240 Hounoux 11 165 Ca 90
64220 Hountto 64 160 Ye 90
55170 Houpette, la 55 55 Fa 57
59263 Houplin 59 30 Da 45
59116 Houplines 59 30 Cf 44
76770 Houppeville 76 37 Ba 51
40420 Hourats 40 147 Zc 84
65350 Hourc 65 163 Aa 89
65330 Hourcaud 65 163 Ac 89
80410 Hourdel, le 80 28 Bd 47
33930 Hourean 33 122 Yf 76
51140 Hourges 51 53 De 53
47420 Hourquey 47 147 Zf 83
40110 Hourre 40 146 Za 84
64420 Hours 64 162 Ze 89
40410 Hourson 40 146 Zb 82
33990 Hourtin 33 122 Yf 77
33990 Hourtin-Plage 33 122 Yf 77
31370 Hourton 31 164 Ba 88
33160 Hourton 33 134 Zb 79
40410 Hourtoy 40 147 Zb 82
02140 Houry 02 41 Df 50
33610 House, la 33 134 Zc 80
44440 Houssaie, la 44 82 Ye 63
35460 Houssais, la 35 66 Yd 58
40630 Houssats, les 40 147 Zb 83
41800 Houssay 41 86 Af 62
53360 Houssay 53 83 Zb 61
41310 Houssay, le 41 85 Af 62
27220 Houssaye 27 50 Bc 55
27410 Houssaye 27 49 Ae 55
41250 Houssaye 41 86 Bd 64
22120 Houssaye, la 22 64 Xb 58
50200 Houssaye, la 50 33 Yd 54
76690 Houssaye-Bérenger, la 76 37 Ba 51
77610 Houssaye-en-Brie, la 77 52 Cf 56
53110 Housseau-Bretignolles, le 53 67 Zc 58
68125 Houssen 68 60 Hc 60
88700 Housseras 88 77 Ge 59
02250 Housset 02 40 De 50
54930 Housséville 54 76 Ga 58
88220 Houssière, la 88 76 Gc 60
88430 Houssière, la 88 77 Gf 59
62870 Houssoye 62 28 Be 46
60390 Houssoye, la 60 38 Bf 52
60112 Houssoy-le-Farcy 60 38 Ca 52
25300 Houtaud 25 108 Gb 67
59470 Houtkerque 59 27 Cd 43
50250 Houtteville 50 46 Yd 52
27440 Houville-en-Vexin 27 50 Bc 53
28700 Houville-la-Branche 28 70 Bd 58
62270 Houvin-Houvigneul 62 29 Cc 47
28130 Houx 28 70 Bd 57
88640 Houx 88 77 Ge 60
44522 Houx, la 44 82 Ye 64
44170 Houx, le 44 82 Yd 63
59492 Hoymille 59 27 Cc 43
25680 Huanne-Montmartin 25 93 Gc 64
50580 Huanville 50 46 Yc 52
50800 Huardière, la 50 46 Ye 55

A B C D E F G H I J K L M N O P Q R S T U V W X Y Z

Huardière, la | 277

58420 Hubans 58 89 Dd 65
50800 Huberdière, la 50 46 Ye 55
62630 Hubersent 62 28 Be 45
88410 Hubert, le 88 76 Ga 60
14540 Hubert-Folie 14 47 Ze 54
50700 Huberville 50 33 Yd 51
19800 Hublange 19 126 Be 77
62140 Huby-Saint-Leu 62 29 Ca 46
12380 Hucaloup 12 152 Cd 86
80132 Huchenneville 80 28 Be 48
40560 Huchet 40 146 Yd 85
21110 Huchey 21 106 Fb 65
62130 Huclier 62 29 Cc 46
50510 Hudimesnil 50 46 Yd 55
54110 Hudiviller 54 76 Gc 57
07590 Huédour 07 141 Df 81
29690 Huelgoat 29 62 Wb 58
27930 Huest 27 49 Bb 54
45520 Huêtre 45 70 Be 60
41320 Huets, les 41 101 Be 65
33680 Huga, le 33 134 Ye 78
70150 Hugier 70 92 Fe 65
76570 Hugleville-en-Caux 76 37 Af 51
07320 Hugons 07 142 Eb 79
12150 Huguiès 12 152 Da 83
71500 Huichards, les 71 106 Fb 69
49430 Huillé 49 84 Ze 63
52150 Huilliécourt 52 75 Fd 60
21230 Huilly 21 105 Ec 65
71290 Huilly-sur-Seille 71 106 Fa 69
51300 Huiron 51 54 Ed 56
58140 Huis-Bobin, l' 58 90 Df 64
58140 Huis-Bouché, l' 58 90 Df 65
58230 Huis-Gaumont, l' 58 104 Ea 65
58230 Huis-Laurent, l' 58 90 Ea 65
37420 Huismes 37 99 Ab 65
50170 Huisnes-sur-Mer 50 66 Yd 57
41310 Huisseau-en-Beauce 41 86 Ba 62
41350 Huisseau-sur-Cosson 41 86 Bc 63
45130 Huisseau-sur-Mauves 45 87 Be 61
69550 Huissel-Saint-Claude 69D 117 Eb 73
53970 Huisserie, l' 53 67 Zb 60
62410 Hulluch 62 30 Ce 46
57820 Hultehouse 57 58 Hb 56
51320 Humbauville 51 54 Ec 57
52290 Humbécourt 52 74 Ef 57
62158 Humbercamps 62 29 Cd 47
80600 Humbercourt 80 29 Cc 47
62650 Humbert 62 28 Bf 45
52700 Humberville 52 75 Fc 59
18250 Humbligny 18 103 Cd 65
37310 Humeau 37 100 Ae 65
62130 Humerœuille 62 29 Cb 46
52200 Humes-Jorquenay 52 92 Fb 61
62130 Humières 62 29 Cb 46
72230 Hunaudières, les 72 68 Ab 61
68150 Hunawihr 68 60 Hb 59
57990 Hundling 57 57 Gf 54
68130 Hundsbach 68 95 Hb 63
78120 Hunière, la 78 70 Bf 57
68128 Huningue 68 95 Hd 63
67250 Hunspach 67 58 Hf 55
57480 Hunting 57 44 Gb 52
31210 Huos 31 163 Ad 90
12460 Huparlac 12 139 Ce 80
80140 Huppy 80 38 Be 48
88210 Hurbache 88 77 Gf 58
33190 Hure 33 135 Zf 81
70210 Hurecourt 70 93 Ga 61
48150 Hures 48 153 Dc 83
48150 Hures-la-Parade 48 153 Dc 83
03380 Huriel 03 115 Cc 70
71870 Hurigny 71 118 Ee 70
35490 Hurlais, la 35 65 Yc 59
67730 Hurst 67 60 Hc 59
02500 Hurtebise 02 41 Eb 50
67117 Hurtigheim 67 60 Hd 57
37270 Husseau 37 85 Af 64
68420 Husseren-les-Châteaux 68 60 Hb 60
68470 Husseren-Wesserling 68 94 Gf 61
54590 Hussigny-Godbrange 54 43 Ff 52
50640 Husson 50 66 Za 57
53250 Hussonière, la 53 67 Zd 58
22800 Hutte, la 22 64 Xa 58
72130 Hutte, la 72 68 Aa 59
88540 Hutte, la 88 94 Gf 61
22330 Hutte-à-L'Anguille, la 22 64 Xc 59
67270 Huttendorf 67 58 Hd 56
67230 Huttenheim 67 60 Hd 58
41400 Hutterie, la 41 86 Ba 64
17650 Huttes, les 17 109 Yd 72
33123 Huttes, les 33 122 Yf 75
48300 Huttes, les 48 141 De 80
61150 Huttière, la 61 48 Ze 56
03600 Hyds 03 115 Ce 71
04170 Hyèges 04 157 Gc 85
25450 Hyémondans 25 94 Gd 64
80320 Hyencourt-le-Grand 80 39 Ce 50
80320 Hyencourt-le-Petit 80 39 Cf 50
50660 Hyenville 50 46 Yd 55
83400 Hyères 83 172 Ga 90
83400 Hyères-Plage 83 172 Ga 90
70190 Hyet 70 93 Ga 64
25110 Hyèvre-Paroisse 25 94 Gc 64
88500 Hymont 88 76 Ga 59
80320 Hypercourt 80 39 Cf 50
37460 Hys 37 100 Ba 65

I

60880 Iaux 60 39 Ce 52
20125 I Bagni di Guagnu = Guagno les Bains CTC 182 If 95
20153 I Bagni di Vuttera = Bains de Guitera CTC 183 Ka 97
64120 Ibarre 64 161 Yf 89
64120 Ibarrolle 64 161 Yf 89
64310 Ibarron 64 160 Yc 88
57830 Ibigny 57 57 Gf 57
65420 Ibos 65 162 Aa 89
67640 Ichtratzheim 67 60 He 58
77890 Ichy 77 71 Cd 59
64130 Idaux-Mendy 64 161 Za 89
32300 Idrac-Respaillès 32 163 Ac 87
64320 Idron-Lée-Ousse-Sendets 64 162 Ze 89
18170 Ids-Saint-Roch 18 102 Cb 68
20246 Ifana CTC 181 Ka 92
35750 Iffendic 35 65 Xf 60
47800 Iffour 47 136 Ac 81
35630 Iffs, les 35 65 Ya 59
20169 i Frasselli CTC 185 Ka 100
14123 Ifs 14 35 Zd 54
85390 Ifs, les 85 98 Zb 68
14270 Ifs-sur-Laizon 14 48 Zf 54
20213 i Fulelli = Folelli CTC 181 Kd 94
61130 Igé 61 68 Ad 59
71960 Igé 71 118 Ee 70
08200 Iges 08 42 Ef 50
80800 Ignaucourt 80 39 Cd 50
09110 Ignaux 09 177 Be 92
54450 Igney 54 57 Ge 57
88150 Igney 88 76 Gc 59
18350 Ignol 18 103 Cf 67
70700 Igny 70 93 Fe 64
91370 Igny 91 51 Cb 56
51700 Igny-Comblizy 51 53 De 54
64800 Igon 64 162 Ze 90
71540 Igornay 71 105 Ec 66
27460 Igoville 27 37 Ba 53
71340 Iguerande 71 117 Ea 71
09300 Ihat 09 177 Be 91
64640 Iholoy 64 161 Ye 89
39150 Ilay 39 107 Ff 69
81640 Ilchardié 81 151 Ca 84
17190 Ile, l' 17 109 Yd 73
17310 Ileau, l' 17 109 Yd 73
56780 Ile-aux-Kerno 56 80 Xa 63
79210 Ile-Bapaume, l' 79 110 Zc 71
37220 Île-Bouchard, l' 37 99 Ac 66
29120 Île Chevalier 29 78 Ve 61
44720 Ile-d'Aignac 44 81 Xe 64
17123 Ile-d'Aix 17 110 Ye 72
17430 Ile-d'Albe, l' 17 110 Za 72
83230 Île de Bagaud 83 172 Gc 90
22870 Ile-de-Bréhat 22 63 Wf 55
44720 Ile-de-Fédrun 44 81 Xe 64
85770 Ile-d'Elle, l' 85 110 Za 71
44720 Ile-de-Mazin 44 81 Xe 64
44720 Ile-de-Ménac 44 81 Xe 64
29259 Île de Molène 29 61 Va 58
44550 Ile-d'Errand 44 81 Xf 64
17750 Ile-d'Étaules, l' 17 122 Yf 74
85340 Ile-d'Olonne, l' 85 109 Yb 69
20220 Ile Rousse, l' CTC 180 If 93
37420 Ile-Saint-Martin 37 85 Ab 65
29980 Île Tudy 29 78 Vf 61
65590 Ilhan 65 175 Ac 91
64120 Ilharre 64 161 Yf 88
11380 Ilhes, les 11 166 Cc 88
65410 Ilhet 65 175 Ac 91
65370 Ilheu 65 176 Ad 91
57110 Illange 57 44 Gb 53
33720 Illats 33 135 Zd 81
29810 Illen 29 61 Vb 58
66130 Ille-sur-Têt 66 179 Cd 92
33380 Illet, l' 33 134 Za 81
27290 Illeville-sur-Montfort 27 36 Ae 53
68720 Illfurth 68 95 Hb 62
68970 Illhaeusern 68 60 Hc 59
01140 Illiat 01 118 Ef 71
09220 Illier-et-Laramade 09 177 Bd 92
28120 Illiers-Combray 28 69 Bb 59
27770 Illiers-L'Evêque 27 50 Bb 56
59480 Illies 59 30 Ce 45
22230 Illifaut 22 64 Xd 60
38200 Illins 38 130 Ef 75
67400 Illkirch-Graffenstaden 67 60 He 57
76390 Illois 76 38 Bd 50
52150 Illoud 52 75 Fd 59
68960 Illtal 68 95 Hb 63
08200 Illy 08 42 Ef 50
68110 Illzach 68 95 Hc 62
06420 Ilonse 06 158 Ha 84
14480 Ily 14 35 Zd 53
63740 Imbauds, les 63 127 Ce 74
28500 Imbermais 28 50 Bc 56
84220 Imberts, les 84 156 Fa 85
76760 Imbleville 76 37 Af 50
88170 Imbrécourt 88 76 Fe 58
30200 Imbres, les 30 155 Ed 84
67330 Imbsheim 67 58 Hc 56
08240 Imécourt 08 42 Ef 52
57310 Imeldange 57 44 Gb 53
57400 Imling 57 57 Ha 56
44600 Immaculée, l' 44 81 Xe 65
54150 Immonville 54 56 Ff 53
58160 Imphy 58 103 Db 67
08300 Inaumont 08 41 Eb 51
76520 Incarville 76 37 Ba 52
76117 Incheville 76 37 Bc 48
59540 Inchy 59 30 Dc 48
62860 Inchy-en-Artois 62 30 Da 47
62770 Incourt 62 29 Ca 46
25470 Indevillers 25 94 Gf 65
18160 Ineuil 18 102 Cb 68
05500 Infournas, les 05 144 Ga 80
80220 Infray 80 38 Bd 49
43150 Infruits, les 43 141 Ea 79
12230 Infruts, les 12 153 Db 85
67270 Ingenheim 67 58 Hd 56
68040 Ingersheim 68 60 Hb 60
62129 Inghem 62 29 Cb 44
57970 Inglange 57 56 Gb 52
67250 Ingolsheim 67 58 Hf 55
76460 Ingouville 76 36 Ae 49
36300 Ingrandes 36 100 Af 69
86220 Ingrandes 86 100 Ad 67
37140 Ingrandes-de-Touraine 37 85 Ab 65
49123 Ingrandes-Le Fresne sur Loire 49 83 Za 64
45450 Ingrannes 45 71 Cb 61
45140 Ingré 45 87 Be 61
27600 Ingremare 27 49 Bb 53
56240 Inguiniel 56 79 We 61
67340 Ingwiller 67 58 Hc 55
12850 Inières 12 152 Cd 83
01200 Injoux-Génissiat 01 119 Fe 72
67880 Innenheim 67 60 Hd 58
01680 Innimond 01 131 Fd 74
55700 Inor 55 42 Fa 51
48500 Inos 48 152 Da 83
63330 Insacq 63 115 Cd 72
57670 Insming 57 57 Gf 55
33840 Insos 33 147 Ze 82
57670 Insviller 57 57 Gf 55
07400 Intras 07 142 Ed 82
76630 Intraville 76 37 Bb 49
07310 Intres 07 142 Ec 79
28310 Intréville 28 70 Bf 59
01580 Intriat 01 119 Fd 71
45300 Intville-la-Guétard 45 71 Cb 59
58800 Inty 58 89 Dd 65
80580 Inval 80 28 Be 48
80430 Inval-Boiron 80 38 Be 49
45300 Invault 45 71 Cc 59
45300 Invilliers 45 71 Cc 60
62170 Inxent 62 28 Be 45
56650 Inzinzac-Lochrist 56 80 We 61
20234 i Perelli = Perelli CTC 183 Kc 95
55220 Ippécourt 55 55 Fb 54
61190 Irai 61 49 Ae 56
79600 Irais 79 99 Zf 67
89290 Irancy 89 89 De 62
64560 Iraty 64 174 Yf 90
55600 Iré-le-Sec 55 43 Fc 52
69540 Irigny 69M 130 Ee 74
64780 Irissarry 64 160 Ye 89
80300 Irles 80 29 Ce 48
67310 Irmstedt 67 60 Hc 57
35850 Irodouër 35 65 Ya 59
02510 Iron 02 40 Dd 49
15100 Ironde 15 140 Da 79
64220 Irouléguy 64 160 Ye 89
27930 Irreville 27 49 Bb 54
29460 Irvillac 29 62 Ve 58
65240 Is 65 175 Ac 91
62330 Isbergues 62 29 Cc 45
88320 Isches 88 76 Fe 60
04170 Iscle, l' 04 158 Gd 85
45620 Isdes 45 87 Cb 62
58290 Isenay 58 104 De 67
52140 Is-en-Bassigny 52 75 Fc 60
50540 Isigny-le-Buat 50 66 Yf 57
14230 Isigny-sur-Mer 14 46 Yf 53
57320 Ising 57 56 Gc 53
21210 Island 21 105 Eb 65
89200 Island 89 90 Df 64
87170 Isle 87 125 Bb 74
22160 Isle, l' 22 63 Wd 58
50290 Isle, l' 50 46 Yc 55
56130 Isle, l' 56 81 Xd 63
95290 Isle-Adam, l' 95 51 Cb 54
32270 Isle-Arné, l' 32 163 Ae 87
17250 Isleau, l' 17 122 Zb 74
10240 Isle-Aubigny 10 74 Eb 57
10800 Isle-Aumont 10 73 Ea 59
32380 Isle-Bouzon, l' 32 149 Ae 85
38080 Isle-d'Abeau, l' 38 131 Fb 75
32300 Isle-de-Noé, l' 32 163 Ac 87
31230 Isle-en-Dodon, l' 31 163 Af 88
03360 Isle-et-Bardais 03 103 Ce 68
32600 Isle-Jourdain, l' 32 164 Ba 87
86150 Isle-Jourdain, l' 86 112 Ae 71
33640 Isle-Saint-Georges 33 135 Zd 80
14690 Isles-Bardel, les 14 47 Zd 55
77440 Isles-les-Meldeuses 77 52 Da 55
89630 Isles-Ménéfrier, les 89 90 Df 64
51110 Isles-sur-Suippe 51 41 Eb 52
84800 Isle-sur-la-Sorgue, l' 84 155 Fa 85
25250 Isle-sur-le-Doubs, l' 25 94 Gd 64
51290 Isle-sur-Marne 51 54 Ee 57
89440 Isle-sur-Serein, l' 89 90 Ea 63
55120 Islettes, les 55 55 Fa 54
04000 Isnards, les 04 157 Gb 84
76230 Isneauville 76 37 Ba 52
05150 Isnières, les 05 156 Fc 82
06420 Isola 06 158 Ha 83
06420 Isola 2000 06 159 Ha 83
20230 Isolaccio, Taglio- CTC 181 Kc 94
20243 Isolaccio-di-Fiumorbo CTC 183 Kb 96
52190 Isômes 52 92 Fb 63
48320 Ispagnac 48 153 Dd 82
62360 Isques 62 28 Bd 44
12190 Issac 12 139 Cd 81
24400 Issac 24 136 Ac 78
33160 Issac 33 134 Zb 79
83380 Issambres, les 83 172 Ge 88
33460 Issan 33 134 Zb 78
08440 Issancourt-et-Rumel 08 42 Ee 50
07660 Issanlas 07 141 Ea 80
25550 Issans 25 94 Ge 63
09100 Issards, les 09 165 Be 90
63940 Issards, les 63 129 De 76
07470 Issarlès 07 141 Ea 79
28160 Issay 28 69 Bb 59
44520 Issé 44 82 Yd 63
11400 Issel 11 165 Bf 88
46500 Issendolus 46 138 Be 80
67330 Issenhausen 67 58 Hd 56
68500 Issenheim 68 95 Hb 61
46320 Issepts 46 138 Bf 80
03120 Isserpent 03 116 Dd 72
63270 Isserteaux 63 128 Dc 75
63380 Isserts, les 63 115 Cd 73
43100 Isseuge 43 128 Dc 76
24560 Issigeac 24 136 Ad 80
30760 Issirac 30 154 Ec 83
63500 Issoire 63 128 Db 75
64570 Issor 64 161 Zd 90
78440 Issou 78 50 Be 55
36100 Issoudun 36 102 Bf 67
23130 Issoudun-Letrieix 23 114 Ca 72
21120 Is-sur-Tille 21 92 Fa 63
31450 Issus 31 164 Bd 88
51150 Issy 51 53 Eb 54
92130 Issy-les-Moulineaux 92 51 Cb 56
71760 Issy-L'Evêque 71 104 Df 68
38970 Istiers, les 38 144 Ff 79
51190 Istres-et-Bury, les 51 53 Ea 55
64240 Isturits 64 160 Ye 88
20220 Isula Rossa = L'Ile Rousse CTC 180 If 93
41370 Isy 41 86 Bd 62
02240 Itancourt 02 40 Dc 50
09140 Itès 09 177 Bb 92
86240 Iteuil 86 112 Ab 70
67117 Ittenheim 67 60 Hd 57
68160 Ittenheim la Petite-Liepvre 68 60 Ha 59
67680 Itterswiller 67 60 Hc 58
91760 Itteville 91 71 Cc 57
64250 Itxassou 64 160 Yd 89
81170 Itzac 81 151 Bf 84
62810 Ivergny 62 29 Cc 47
77165 Iverny 77 52 Ce 55
02360 Iviers 02 41 Ea 50
27110 Iville 27 49 Af 53
55270 Ivoiry 55 55 Fa 53
60141 Ivors 60 52 Da 53
39110 Ivory 39 107 Ff 67
88600 Ivoux 88 77 Ge 59
18380 Ivoy-le-Pré 18 88 Cc 64
17380 Ivraie 17 110 Zb 72
39110 Ivrey 39 107 Ff 67
21340 Ivry-en-Montagne 21 105 Ed 66
27540 Ivry-la-Bataille 27 50 Bc 55
60173 Ivry-le-Temple 60 51 Ca 53
94200 Ivry-sur-Seine 94 51 Cc 56
59141 Iwuy 59 30 Db 47
65370 Izaourt 65 176 Ad 90
31160 Izaut-de-L'Hôtel 31 176 Ae 90
65250 Izaux 65 163 Ac 90
53160 Izé 53 67 Ze 59
38140 Izeaux 38 131 Fc 76
62490 Izel-lès-Équerchin 62 30 Cf 46
62690 Izel-les-Hameaux 62 29 Cd 47
01430 Izenave 01 119 Fd 72
56130 Izernac 56 81 Xe 63
01580 Izernore 01 119 Fd 71
38160 Izeron 38 143 Fc 78
64260 Izeste 64 162 Zd 90
21110 Izeure 21 106 Fa 65
21110 Izier 21 92 Fb 65
01300 Izieu 01 131 Fd 75
33450 Izon 33 135 Zd 79
32400 Izotges 32 162 Zf 87
45480 Izy 45 70 Ca 60

J

24380 Jabaux 24 136 Ae 78
43370 Jabier 43 141 De 79
77450 Jablines 77 52 Ce 55
87370 Jabreilles-les-Bordes 87 113 Bd 72
83840 Jabron 83 158 Gc 86
15110 Jabrun 15 140 Cf 80
34830 Jacou 34 168 Df 87
09320 Jacoy 09 177 Bc 91
65350 Jacque 65 163 Ab 89
45320 Jacqueminière, la 45 72 Da 61
59310 Jacques-Varlet 59 30 Db 46
38630 Jacquet, le 38 131 Fd 75
77760 Jacqueville 77 71 Cd 59
05100 Jadis, le 05 145 Gd 78
95850 Jagny-sous-Bois 95 51 Cc 54
87160 Jagon, le 87 113 Bc 70
43340 Jagonzac 43 141 De 79
77440 Jaignes 77 52 Da 55
26300 Jaillans 26 143 Fb 78
49500 Jaillette, la 49 83 Zb 62
01120 Jailleux 01 130 Fa 73
49220 Jaille-Yvon, la 49 83 Zb 62
54200 Jaillon 54 56 Ff 56
58110 Jailly 58 104 Dd 66
58330 Jailly 58 104 Dc 66
21150 Jailly-les-Moulins 21 91 Ed 64
88300 Jainvillotte 88 75 Fe 59
07510 Jalades, les 07 141 Ea 80
81260 Jaladieu 81 166 Cd 87
19220 Jaladis 19 138 Ca 78
23270 Jalesches 23 114 Ca 71
15200 Jaleyrac 15 127 Cc 77
03220 Jaligny-sur-Besbre 03 116 Dd 70
01260 Jalinard 01 119 Fd 72
23340 Jallagnat 23 126 Bf 74
49510 Jallais 49 98 Za 65
21250 Jallanges 21 106 Fa 67
28200 Jallans 28 69 Bc 60
57590 Jallaucourt 57 56 Gc 55
25170 Jallerange 25 107 Fe 65
15150 Jalles 15 139 Cb 79
20122 Jallicu CTC 183 Ka 98
18300 Jalognes 18 103 Ce 65
71250 Jalogny 71 118 Ed 70
51150 Jâlons 51 53 Eb 54
87460 Jalouneix 87 126 Bd 74
74470 Jambaz 74 120 Gd 71
42600 Jambin 42 129 Ea 75
71640 Jambles 71 105 Ee 68
46260 Jamblusse 46 150 Be 83
78440 Jambville 78 50 Bf 54
60240 Jaméricourt 60 50 Bf 53
55600 Jametz 55 43 Fc 52
65220 Jammets 65 163 Ab 88
09140 Jammets, les 09 177 Bb 92
87800 Janailhac 87 125 Bb 75
23250 Janaillat 23 114 Be 72
57410 Janau 57 58 Hb 54
21310 Jancigny 21 92 Fc 64
08430 Jandun 08 41 Ed 50
33125 Janic 33 135 Zc 81
49170 Janière, la 49 83 Zb 64
38280 Janneyrias 38 131 Fa 74
87400 Janouzeix 87 125 Bc 74
44170 Jans 44 82 Yc 63
19700 Jante, la 19 126 Be 76
14670 Janville 14 35 Zf 54
28310 Janville 28 70 Bf 59
60150 Janville 60 39 Cf 52
76450 Janville 76 36 Ad 49
91510 Janville-sur-Juine 91 71 Cb 57
51210 Janvilliers 51 53 Dd 55
51390 Janvry 51 53 Df 53
91640 Janvry 91 51 Ca 57
35150 Janzé 35 66 Yd 61
12230 Jaoul, le 12 153 Dc 84
38270 Jarcieu 38 130 Ef 76
17210 Jarculet, le 17 123 Ze 77
17460 Jard, la 17 122 Zc 75
41000 Jarday 41 86 Bb 63
33920 Jard-de-Bourdillas, le 33 123 Zd 77
19300 Jardin, le 19 126 Ca 77
86800 Jardres 86 112 Ad 69
85520 Jard-sur-Mer 85 109 Yc 70
19390 Jarenne 19 126 Be 76
45150 Jargeau 45 87 Ca 61
85600 Jarie, la 85 97 Ye 66
23130 Jarige, la 23 114 Cb 72
26620 Jarjatte, la 26 144 Fe 80
05130 Jarjayes 05 144 Ga 81
17800 Jarlac 17 123 Zc 74
88550 Jarménil 88 77 Gd 60
16200 Jarnac 16 123 Ze 74
33620 Jarnac 33 135 Ze 78
17520 Jarnac-Champagne 17 123 Zd 75
23140 Jarnages 23 114 Ca 71
18140 Jarnay 18 103 Cf 65
22480 Jarnay 22 63 Wf 58
17220 Jarne, la 17 110 Yf 72
69640 Jarnioux 69D 118 Ed 73
58230 Jarnois, le 58 90 Ea 64
42460 Jarnosse 42 117 Eb 72
54800 Jarny 54 56 Ff 54
24630 Jarousse, la 24 125 Ba 75
71480 Jarrey 71 119 Fc 69
17220 Jarrie, la 17 110 Yf 72
85170 Jarrie, la 85 97 Yd 68
17330 Jarrie-Audouin, la 17 110 Zd 72
38560 Jarrie-les-Chaberts 38 144 Fe 78
73300 Jarrier 73 132 Gb 77
44590 Jarrier, le 44 82 Yc 63
24210 Jarripigier, le 24 137 Ba 78
25650 Jarrons, les 25 108 Gd 66
85120 Jarrousselière, la 85 98 Zb 68
15300 Jarry, le 15 139 Cf 78
50720 Jarry, le 50 66 Za 57
18260 Jars 18 88 Ce 64
18260 Jarsot 18 88 Ce 64
73630 Jarsy 73 132 Gb 75
23400 Jartaud 23 114 Be 73
54140 Jarville-la-Malgrange 54 56 Gb 56
86170 Jarzay 86 99 Aa 68
49140 Jarzé Villages 49 84 Ze 63
42110 Jas 42 129 Eb 74
84410 Jas, le 84 156 Fb 84
04230 Jas-de-Berle 04 156 Fe 84
13170 Jas-de-Rhodes 13 170 Fb 88
83920 Jas-d'Esclans 83 172 Gd 87
83870 Jas-des-Marquands, le 83 171 Ff 89
84410 Jas-des-Melettes 84 156 Fb 84
70800 Jasney 70 93 Gb 61
01480 Jassans-Riottier 01 118 Ee 73
79120 Jassay 79 111 Aa 70
13430 Jasse 13 170 Ef 86
19290 Jasse 19 126 Ca 74
46250 Jasse 46 137 Ba 81
12100 Jasse, la 12 152 Da 84
30560 Jasse-de-Bernard, la 30 154 Ea 84
10330 Jasseines 10 74 Ec 57
42740 Jasserie, la 42 130 Ed 76
01250 Jasseron 01 119 Fb 71
64190 Jasses 64 161 Zb 89
44830 Jasson 44 96 Yb 65
83250 Jassons, les 83 171 Gb 90
63420 Jassy 63 128 Cf 76
64480 Jatxou 64 160 Yd 88
10200 Jaucourt 10 74 Ed 59
33590 Jau-Dignac-et-Loirac 33 122 Za 76
85110 Jaudonnière, la 85 97 Za 69
28250 Jaudrais 28 69 Ba 57
24320 Jaufrenie, la 24 124 Ab 76
33610 Jauge 33 134 Zb 80
21410 Jaugey 21 105 Ee 65
33114 Jaugut 33 134 Zb 81
07380 Jaujac 07 142 Eb 81
16560 Jauldes 16 124 Ab 74
89360 Jaulges 89 73 De 61
02850 Jaulgonne 02 53 Dd 54
37120 Jaulnay 37 99 Ac 67
77480 Jaulnes 77 72 Db 58
54470 Jaulny 54 56 Ff 55
60350 Jaulzy 60 39 Da 52
65150 Jaunac 65 176 Ad 90
86130 Jaunay-Clan 86 99 Ac 68
03700 Jaunet, le 03 116 Db 72
78113 Jaunière, la 78 50 Be 56
24400 Jaunies, les 24 136 Ab 79
24100 Jaure 24 136 Ad 79
24140 Jaure 24 136 Ad 78
04850 Jausier 04 158 Ge 82
04240 Jaussiers 04 158 Ge 85
12350 Jaux 12 151 Cb 82
72110 Jauzé 72 68 Ac 59
43100 Javaugues 43 128 Dc 77
07270 Javelat, la 07 142 Ed 78
35133 Javené 35 66 Ye 59
87520 Javerdat 87 113 Af 73

278 | Hubans

24300 Javerlhac-et-la-Chapelle-Saint-Robert 24 124 Ad 75
04420 Javie, la 04 157 Gc 83
48130 Javols 48 140 Dc 80
79320 Javrelière, la 79 98 Zc 68
16100 Javrezac 16 123 Zd 74
17120 Javrezac 17 122 Za 75
53250 Javron-les-Chapelles 53 67 Zd 58
43230 Jax 43 141 Dd 77
64220 Jaxu 64 161 Ye 89
40120 Jay, le 40 147 Zd 84
24590 Jayac 24 137 Bc 78
01340 Jayat 01 118 Fa 70
63260 Jayet 63 116 Db 72
86600 Jazeneuil 86 111 Aa 70
17260 Jazennes 17 122 Zc 75
40250 Jeanbidaou 40 147 Zb 86
25210 Jean-Chevaux, les 25 108 Ge 66
17360 Jeancoiin 17 123 Zf 78
38190 Jean Collet 38 132 Ff 77
02490 Jeancourt 02 40 Da 49
47290 Jean-d'Ardot 47 136 Ad 81
32330 Jeandaugé 32 148 Ab 85
40200 Jean-de-Crabe 40 146 Yf 83
54114 Jeandelaincourt 54 56 Gb 55
54800 Jeandelize 54 56 Fe 54
84400 Jean-Jean 84 156 Fc 85
88700 Jeanménil 88 77 Ge 58
40270 Jeanpierre 40 147 Zc 86
42920 Jeansagnière, Chalmazel- 42 129 Df 74
63410 Jeansol 63 115 Cf 73
33650 Jeansotte 33 135 Zd 81
02140 Jeantes 02 41 Ea 50
33113 Jeantie 33 135 Zc 81
40560 Jeantot 40 146 Ye 85
36100 Jean-Varenne 36 101 Bf 67
58140 Jeaux 58 104 Df 65
68320 Jebsheim 68 60 Hc 60
32360 Jegun 32 148 Ac 86
24410 Jemaye-Ponteyraud, la 24 136 Ab 77
86290 Jemelle 86 113 Ba 69
24700 Jenduffe 24 136 Aa 79
59144 Jenlain 59 31 Dd 47
03800 Jenzat 03 116 Db 72
02510 Jérusalem 02 40 Dd 49
88260 Jésonville 88 76 Ga 60
10140 Jessains 10 74 Ed 59
67440 Jetterswiller 67 58 Hc 56
68130 Jettingen 68 95 Hc 63
73500 Jeu, le 73 145 Gd 78
78270 Jeufosse 78 50 Bd 54
10320 Jeugny 10 73 Ea 60
89110 Jeuilly 89 89 Db 62
36120 Jeu-les-Bois 36 101 Be 68
36240 Jeu-Maloches 36 101 Bc 66
59460 Jeumont 59 31 Ea 47
19150 Jeune 19 126 Bf 77
33780 Jeune-Soulac 33 122 Yf 75
39360 Jeurre 39 119 Fe 70
19110 Jeux 19 127 Cc 76
88000 Jeuxey 88 77 Gc 59
21460 Jeux-lès-Bard 21 90 Eb 63
54740 Jevoncourt 54 76 Gb 58
54700 Jezainville 54 56 Ga 55
65240 Jézeau 65 175 Ac 91
07110 Joannas 07 142 Eb 81
42380 Joansiecq 42 129 Df 76
82140 Joany-et-Roubert 82 150 Be 83
63990 Job 63 129 De 75
50440 Jobourg 50 33 Ya 50
66320 Joch 66 178 Cd 93
54240 Jœf 54 56 Ga 53
42155 Jœuvre 42 117 Ea 73
50310 Joganville 50 34 Yd 52
89300 Joigny 89 72 Dc 61
08700 Joigny-sur-Meuse 08 42 Ee 49
52300 Joinville 52 75 Fa 58
51310 Joiselle 51 53 Dd 56
59530 Jolimetz 59 31 De 47
54300 Jolivet 54 77 Gd 57
63210 Jollere 63 127 Ce 74
69330 Jonage 69M 130 Fa 74
34650 Joncelets 34 153 Db 86
34650 Joncels 34 167 Db 86
66360 Joncet 66 178 Cb 93
03140 Jonchère 03 116 Db 71
18110 Jonchère, la 18 102 Cc 66
85540 Jonchère, la 85 109 Yd 70
21430 Jonchères 21 105 Eb 65
26310 Jonchères 26 143 Fc 81
87340 Jonchère-Saint-Maurice, la 87 113 Bc 72
53190 Joncherets, les 53 66 Za 58
43340 Joncherette 43 141 De 80
90100 Joncherey 90 94 Ha 63
52000 Jonchery 52 75 Fa 60
51600 Jonchery-sur-Suippe 51 54 Ec 54
51140 Jonchery-sur-Vesle 51 53 De 53
26170 Jonchiers, les 26 156 Fb 83
02420 Joncourt 02 40 Db 49
10330 Joncreuil 10 74 Ed 57
71460 Joncy 71 105 Ed 69
73170 Jongieux 73 132 Fe 74
27410 Jonquerets-de-Livet, les 27 49 Ad 54
84450 Jonquerettes 84 155 Ef 85
51700 Jonquery 51 53 De 54
04150 Jonquet, le 04 156 Fd 84
27210 Jonquets, les 27 36 Ab 53
02120 Jonqueuse 02 40 Dd 49
11220 Jonquières 11 179 Ce 90
34725 Jonquières 34 167 Dc 86
60680 Jonquieres 60 39 Ce 52
81440 Jonquières 81 165 Ca 87
84150 Jonquières 84 155 Ef 84
30300 Jonquières-Saint-Vincent 30 155 Ed 86
69330 Jons 69M 131 Fa 74
48150 Jontanels 48 153 Dc 83
08130 Jonval 08 42 Ed 51
70500 Jonvelle 70 93 Ff 61
28800 Jonville 28 70 Bd 59
50760 Jonville 50 33 Ye 51
55160 Jonville-en-Woëvre 55 56 Fe 54
28320 Jonvilliers 28 70 Be 57
17500 Jonzac 17 123 Zd 76
74520 Jonzier-Epagny 74 120 Ff 72
42660 Jonzieux 42 129 Ec 77
71110 Jonzy 71 117 Ea 71
54620 Joppécourt 54 43 Fe 52
19150 Jordes, les 19 126 Be 77
31810 Jordi 31 164 Bc 88
33125 Jordis 33 134 Zc 81
17260 Jorignac 17 122 Zb 75
28190 Jornad 28 69 Bb 58
14170 Jort 14 48 Zf 55
88500 Jorxey 88 76 Gb 59
43230 Josat 43 128 Dd 77
64190 Josbaig, Préchacq- 64 161 Zb 89
56120 Josilin = Josslin 56 81 Xc 61
41370 Josnes 41 86 Bd 62
33138 Jossaume 33 134 Za 80
40230 Josse 40 160 Ye 87
56120 Josselin 56 81 Xc 61
21820 Jossigny 21 106 Fa 67
77600 Jossigny 77 52 Ce 55
74200 Jotty, le 74 120 Gd 71
12600 Jou 12 139 Ce 79
87890 Jouac 87 113 Bb 70
02220 Jouaignes 02 53 Dd 53
89310 Jouancy 89 90 Ea 62
33113 Jouanhaut 33 147 Zc 82
40210 Jouanicot 40 146 Yf 84
31800 Jouanicou 31 163 Ad 90
41290 Jouannière, la 41 86 Bc 61
40170 Jouanon 40 146 Ye 84
07190 Jouanvins 07 142 Ec 79
86340 Jouarenne 86 112 Ab 70
77640 Jouarre 77 52 Da 55
78760 Jouars-Pontchartrain 78 50 Bf 56
54800 Jouaville 54 56 Ff 54
24380 Joubertie 24 136 Ad 78
89120 Joubins, les 89 89 Db 61
84220 Joucas 84 156 Fb 85
09100 Joucla 09 165 Bd 90
11140 Joucou 11 178 Ca 92
71480 Joudes 71 119 Fc 70
54490 Joudreville 54 56 Fe 53
86200 Joué 86 99 Ab 66
61320 Joué-du-Bois 61 67 Ze 57
61150 Joué-du-Plain 61 48 Zf 56
72540 Joué-en-Charnie 72 67 Ze 60
49670 Joué-Étiau 49 98 Zc 65
72380 Joué-L'Abbé 72 68 Ab 60
37300 Joué-lès-Tours 37 85 Ad 64
12800 Jouels 12 151 Cb 83
32190 Jouéou 32 148 Ab 86
64490 Jouers 64 174 Zc 91
44440 Joué-sur-Erdre 44 82 Yd 64
18320 Jouet-sur-L'Aubois 18 103 Cf 66
31110 Jouéu 31 176 Ad 92
21230 Jouey 21 105 Ec 66
25370 Jougne 25 108 Gc 68
34490 Jougrand 34 167 Da 88
39100 Jouhe 39 106 Fc 66
79110 Jouhé 79 111 Aa 72
86500 Jouhet 86 112 Af 70
23220 Jouillat 23 114 Bf 71
35133 Jouillère, la 35 66 Ye 59
86300 Joumé 86 112 Ae 69
34330 Jounié, le 34 166 Cd 87
13490 Jouques 13 171 Fd 87
12440 Jouqueviel 12 151 Ca 83
47480 Jourda 47 149 Ae 83
17360 Jourdain 17 123 Zf 77
32120 Jourdain 32 149 Af 86
12480 Jourdanie, la 12 152 Ce 84
40120 Jourets 40 147 Zd 84
87800 Jourgnac 87 125 Bb 74
58140 Jourland 58 90 Df 65
01250 Journans 01 119 Fc 72
85320 Journée 85 110 Ye 69
86290 Journet 86 113 Af 70
15270 Journiac 15 127 Cd 76
19370 Journiac 19 126 Be 75
24260 Journiac 24 137 Af 79
62850 Journy 62 27 Bf 44
15170 Joursac 15 140 Da 78
21340 Jours-en-Vaux 21 105 Ed 66
21450 Jours-lès-Baigneux 21 91 Ed 63
86350 Joussé 86 112 Ac 71
85300 Jousselandière, la 85 96 Yb 67
15800 Jou-sur-Monjou 15 139 Cd 79
27260 Jouveaux, Morainville- 27 48 Ac 53
39220 Jouvencelles, les 39 120 Ff 70
71290 Jouvençon 71 118 Fa 69
81530 Jouvens 81 152 Cd 85
74550 Jouvernesinaz 74 120 Gd 71
74200 Jouvernex 74 120 Gc 71
69170 Joux 69D 117 Ec 73
74230 Joux 74 132 Gc 73
74500 Joux, la 74 121 Ge 70
74520 Joux, la 74 120 Ff 72
36170 Joux, le 36 113 Bc 70
89440 Joux-la-Ville 89 90 Df 63
18600 Jouy 18 103 Cf 68
28300 Jouy 28 70 Bd 57
89150 Jouy 89 72 Cf 60
91650 Jouy 91 71 Ca 57
57130 Jouy-aux-Arches 57 56 Ga 54
55120 Jouy-en-Argonne 55 55 Fb 54
78350 Jouy-en-Josas 78 51 Cb 56
45480 Jouy-en-Pithiverais 45 71 Ca 60
77970 Jouy-le-Châtel 77 52 Da 57
95620 Jouy-le-Comte 95 51 Cb 54
95280 Jouy-le-Moutier 95 51 Ca 54
45370 Jouy-le-Potier 45 87 Be 62
51390 Jouy-lès-Reims 51 53 Df 53
78200 Jouy-Mauvoisin 78 50 Bd 55
60240 Jouy-sous-Thelle 60 38 Bf 53
27120 Jouy-sur-Eure 27 50 Bb 54
77320 Jouy-sur-Morin 77 52 Db 56
07260 Joyeuse 07 141 Eb 82
15130 Joyeuse, la 15 139 Cd 79
01800 Joyeux 01 118 Fa 73
63350 Joze 63 128 Db 73
63460 Jozerand 63 116 Da 72
06160 Juan-les-Pins 06 173 Ha 87
14250 Juaye-Mondaye 14 34 Zb 53
88630 Jubainville 88 76 Fe 58
49510 Jubaudière, la 49 98 Za 65
55120 Jubécourt 55 55 Fa 54
32160 Jù-Belloc 32 162 Aa 87
AD100 Juberri □ AND 177 Bc 94
53160 Jublains 53 67 Zd 59
29100 Juch, le 29 78 Ve 60
87230 Judie, la 87 125 Af 74
74250 Juffly 74 120 Gc 71
33420 Jugazan 33 135 Zf 80
12200 Juge, le 12 151 Bf 82
19500 Jugeals-Nazareth 19 138 Bd 78
63380 Jugie, la 63 115 Cd 73
87500 Jugie, la 87 125 Bc 76
87800 Jugie, la 87 125 Bb 75
35134 Jugon 35 82 Yd 61
22270 Jugon-les-Lacs = Lanyugon 22 64 Xe 58
71240 Jugy 71 106 Ef 69
39140 Juhans 39 107 Fd 68
17770 Juicq 17 123 Zc 73
71440 Juif 71 106 Fa 68
16190 Juignac 16 124 Ab 76
49640 Juigné 49 84 Zd 62
49460 Juigné-Bené 49 83 Zc 63
44670 Juigné-des-Moutiers 44 82 Ye 62
49610 Juigné-sur-Loire 49 83 Zd 64
72300 Juigné-sur-Sarthe 72 84 Ze 61
27250 Juignettes 27 49 Ad 55
19350 Juillac 19 125 Bb 77
32230 Juillac 32 162 Aa 87
33890 Juillac 33 135 Aa 80
46140 Juillac 46 137 Bb 82
16130 Juillac-le-Coq 16 123 Ze 75
64350 Juillacq 64 162 Zf 88
16320 Juillaguet 16 124 Ab 76
65290 Juillan 65 162 Aa 89
16230 Juillé 16 111 Aa 73
72170 Juillé 72 68 Aa 59
79170 Juillé 79 111 Ze 72
21210 Juillenay 21 90 Eb 64
32200 Juilles 32 164 Ae 87
50220 Juilley 50 66 Yd 57
21140 Juilly 21 91 Ec 64
77230 Juilly 77 51 Ce 54
66360 Jujols 66 178 Cb 93
01640 Jujurieux 01 119 Fc 72
48140 Julianges 48 140 Db 79
16200 Julienne 16 123 Ze 74
88120 Julienrupt 88 77 Ge 60
69840 Juliénas 69D 118 Ee 71
43500 Jullianges 43 129 De 77
69840 Jullié 69D 118 Ee 71
42130 Jullieux 42 129 Ea 74
50610 Jullouville 50 46 Yc 56
71390 Jully-lès-Buxy 71 105 Ee 68
10260 Jully-sur-Sarce 10 74 Eb 60
65100 Julos 65 162 Zf 90
55120 Julvécourt 55 55 Fb 54
28800 Jumainville 28 70 Bd 60
78580 Jumeauville 78 50 Be 55
28200 Jumeaux 28 69 Bc 60
63570 Jumeaux 63 128 Dc 76
79600 Jumeaux, le 79 99 Zf 68
80250 Jumel 80 39 Cc 50
27220 Jumelles 27 49 Bb 55
49120 Jumellière, la 49 83 Zb 65
20100 Jumenta Grossa CTC 184 If 99
65410 Jumet 65 175 Ac 91
76480 Jumièges 76 37 Ae 52
02160 Jumigny 02 40 De 52
24530 Jumilhac 24 124 Ae 76
24630 Jumilhac-le-Grand 24 125 Ba 76
09400 Junac 09 177 Bd 92
30250 Junas 30 154 Ea 86
89700 Junay 89 90 Df 61
65100 Juncalas 65 175 Aa 90
68500 Jungholtz 68 95 Hb 61
15120 Junhac 15 139 Cc 80
46150 Junies, les 46 137 Bb 81
08310 Juniville 08 41 Ec 52
09130 Junquière, la 09 164 Bc 89
72500 Jupilles 72 85 Ac 62
30120 Jurade, la 30 153 Dd 85
64110 Jurançon 64 162 Zd 89
45340 Juranville 45 71 Cd 60
42430 Juré 42 129 Df 73
15500 Jureuge 15 128 Da 77
16250 Jurignac 16 123 Zf 75
23600 Jurigny 23 114 Cb 70
14260 Jurques 14 47 Zb 54
31110 Jurvielle 31 175 Ac 92
02200 Jury 02 40 Dc 52
57245 Jury 57 56 Gb 54
36500 Juscop 36 101 Bc 67
79230 Juscorps 79 111 Zd 71
47180 Jusix 47 135 Aa 81
15250 Jussac 15 139 Cc 79
43130 Jussac 43 129 Ea 77
88640 Jussarupt 88 77 Ge 60
17130 Jussas 17 123 Zd 77
63310 Jussat 63 116 Dc 73
63450 Jussat 63 128 Da 74
51340 Jussecourt-Minecourt 51 54 Ee 56
70500 Jussey 70 93 Ff 62
02480 Jussy 02 40 Db 50
57130 Jussy 57 56 Ga 54
58220 Jussy 58 89 Db 64
74930 Jussy 74 120 Gb 72
89290 Jussy 89 89 Dd 62
18130 Jussy-Champagne 18 103 Cd 67
18140 Jussy-le-Chaudrier 18 103 Cf 66
32190 Justian 32 148 Ab 86
08270 Justine-Herbigny 08 41 Eb 51
09700 Justiniac 09 164 Bc 89
50720 Jutigny 50 67 Zb 57
77650 Jutigny 77 72 Db 58
88500 Juvaincourt 88 76 Ga 59
10310 Juvancourt 10 74 Ee 60
10140 Juvanzé 10 74 Ed 59
49330 Juvardeil 49 84 Zc 63
57630 Juvelize 57 57 Gd 56
53380 Juvigné 53 66 Yf 59
60112 Juvignes 60 38 Ca 51
02880 Juvigny 02 40 Db 52
51150 Juvigny 51 54 Eb 54
55170 Juvigny-en-Perthois 55 75 Fa 57
50520 Juvigny les Vallées 50 46 Yf 56
50520 Juvigny-le-Tertre 50 47 Yf 56
61140 Juvigny-sous-Andaine 61 67 Zc 57
55600 Juvigny-sur-Loison 55 43 Fc 52
61200 Juvigny-sur-Orne 61 48 Aa 56
14250 Juvigny-sur-Seulles 14 34 Zc 54
61140* Juvigny Val d'Andaine 61 67 Zc 57
57590 Juville 57 56 Gc 55
07600 Juvinas 07 142 Eb 80
02190 Juvincourt-et-Damary 02 41 Df 52
91260 Juvisy-sur-Orge 91 51 Cc 56
28200 Juvrainville 28 70 Bd 60
54370 Juvrecourt 54 57 Gd 56
64120 Juxue 64 161 Yf 89
08190 Juzancourt 08 41 Eb 52
10500 Juzanvigny 10 74 Ed 58
52330 Juzennecourt 52 74 Ef 59
31540 Juzes 31 165 Be 88
31110 Juzet-de-Luchon 31 176 Ad 92
31160 Juzet-d'Izaut 31 176 Ae 91
78820 Juziers 78 50 Bf 55

K

67160 Kaidenbourg 67 59 Ia 55
50380 Kairon 50 46 Yc 56
50380 Kairon-Plage 50 46 Yc 56
57480 Kalembourg 57 44 Gc 52
57412 Kalhausen 57 57 Ha 54
22160 Kallag = Callac 22 63 Wd 58
67240 Kaltenhouse 67 58 Hf 56
57480 Kaltweiller 57 44 Gc 52
57330 Kanfen 57 44 Ga 52
35260 Kankaven = Cancale 35 65 Ya 56
22350 Kaon = Caulnes 22 65 Xf 59
68510 Kappelen 68 95 Hc 63
57430 Kappelkinger 57 57 Gf 55
22340 Karhaez Plougêr 22 63 Wc 59
29890 Karrec'h Hir 29 62 Vd 57
22170 Kastelladdren = Châtelaudren 22 63 Xa 57
35220 Kastell-Bourc'h = Châteaubourg 35 66 Yd 60
35410 Kastell-Geron = Châteaugiron 35 66 Yc 60
29150 Kastellin = Châteaulin 29 62 Ve 59
29250 Kastell-Paol = Saint-Pol-de-Léon 29 62 Wa 56
35430 Kastel-Noez = Châteauneuf-d'Ille-et-Villaine 35 65 Ya 57
64430 Katalinaenea 64 160 Yd 90
68230 Katzenthal 68 60 Hb 60
67480 Kauffenheim 67 59 Ia 55
68240 Kaysersberg Vignoble 68 60 Hb 60
57920 Kédange-sur-Canner 57 56 Gc 53
67250 Keffenach 67 58 Hf 55
29880 Kélerdut 29 61 Vc 57
68680 Kembs 68 95 Hd 62
29000 Kemper = Quimper 29 78 Vf 61
29300 Kemperle = Quimperlé 29 79 Wc 61
57920 Kemplich 57 44 Gc 53
56250 Kerabus 56 80 Xb 62
29410 Keradalan 29 62 Wa 58
29250 Keradenec 29 62 Vf 56
29180 Kéradily 29 78 Vf 60
29640 Keradily 29 63 Wc 58
29340 Kéraël 29 79 Wc 61
56240 Keraize 56 79 We 61
29470 Keralcun 29 62 Vd 59
22820 Keralio 22 63 We 56
29470 Keraliou 29 62 Vd 58
29390 Kerallé 29 78 Wb 60
29850 Kérallenoc 29 61 Vd 58
29830 Kéraloret 29 61 Vc 57
22810 Keramanac'h 22 63 Wd 57
22390 Kerambuan 22 63 Wd 58
29000 Kerancloarec 29 78 Vf 60
29140 Kerancornec 29 78 Wb 61
29460 Kérancurru 29 62 Vf 59
56240 Kerandal 56 79 We 61
29530 Kerandouaré 29 62 Wa 59
29100 Kerandraon 29 61 Vd 60
29770 Kerandraon 29 61 Vc 60
29390 Kérandréo 29 78 Wb 60
56440 Kerandué 56 80 Wf 61
29920 Kerangall 29 78 Wb 62
22300 Keranglas 22 63 Wc 56
29390 Keranglay 29 78 Wb 60
29640 Keranguéven 29 62 Wb 57
29860 Kerangueven 29 62 Vd 57
22480 Ker-Anna 22 63 Wf 58
56480 Keranroué 56 79 Wf 60
29930 Keranperchec 29 78 Wb 61
29380 Keranquelven 29 79 Wb 61
29420 Keranton 29 62 Wa 57
56630 Kerantonze 56 79 Wd 59
29870 Kerantour 29 61 Vc 57
56860 Kerarden 56 80 Xb 63
29860 Keraredeau 29 61 Vd 57
29770 Keraudierne 29 61 Vc 60
22300 Keraudy 22 63 Wc 57
22300 Kerauzen 22 63 Wd 57
29190 Keravon 29 62 Vf 59
29630 Kerbabu 29 62 Wa 56
57460 Kerbach 57 57 Gf 54
22720 Kerbaëlen 22 63 Wf 57
29530 Kerbalaun 29 62 Wa 59
29120 Kerbascol 29 78 Ve 61
29160 Kerbastun 29 62 Vd 59
29560 Kerbéron 29 62 Ve 59
29460 Kerbiaouen 29 62 Ve 58
29520 Kerbiliguet 29 78 Wa 59
56560 Kerbiquet 56 79 Wb 60
29246 Kerbizien 29 63 Wb 59
29410 Kerbizien 29 62 Wb 58
22300 Kerblat 22 63 Wd 56
56310 Kerboharn 56 79 We 61
29150 Kerbolé 29 78 Vf 59
22610 Kerbors 22 63 We 56
85350 Ker-Bossy 85 96 Xd 68
29241 Kerboulic 29 63 Wb 56
44410 Kerbourg 44 81 Xd 64
29250 Kerbrat 29 62 Vf 56
29690 Kerbrat 29 63 Wb 59
56930 Kerbrégent 56 79 Wf 61
29890 Kerbrézant 29 62 Vd 57
44420 Kercabellec 44 81 Xd 64
22410 Kercadoret 22 64 Xa 56
56730 Kercambre 56 80 Xa 64
85350 Ker-Châlon 85 96 Xd 68
56400 Kercohan 56 81 Xc 63
22310 Kercoz 22 63 Wc 56
29860 Kerdalaes 29 62 Vd 57
56520 Kerdalhué 56 79 Wd 62
29910 Kerdallé 29 78 Wa 62
22720 Kerdanielou 22 63 Wf 58
29430 Kerdanné 29 62 Ve 56
29800 Kerdaoulas 29 62 Ve 58
56700 Kerdavid 56 80 We 62
56150 Kerdéhel 56 79 Xa 61
29410 Kerdéland 29 62 Wa 57
29880 Kerdelant 29 62 Vd 57
29370 Kerden 29 78 Wa 60
29470 Kerdéniel 29 61 Vd 58
29500 Kerdévot 29 78 Wa 60
29430 Kerdézant 29 62 Ve 57
29500 Kerdilès 29 78 Wa 61
29260 Kerdivès 29 62 Ve 57
29310 Kerdonars 29 79 Wd 61
29246 Kerdoncuff 29 63 Wb 59
56550 Kerdonnerch 56 80 We 63
56330 Kerdosso 56 80 Wf 62
29350 Kerdoualen 29 78 Wb 62
22110 Kerdouc'h 22 63 Wd 59
29310 Kerdoudu 29 79 Wc 61
22480 Kerdrain 22 63 Wf 58
56480 Kerdréan 56 79 Wf 60
56400 Kerdrec'h 56 80 Xa 63
29630 Kerdrein 29 62 Wb 56
29160 Kerdreux 29 61 Vc 59
56390 Kerdroguen 56 80 Xb 62
29920 Kerdruc 29 78 Wb 62
56530 Kerdual 56 79 Wd 62
29150 Kérédan 29 62 Vf 59
22580 Kérégal 22 64 Xa 56
29690 Kerelcun 29 62 Wb 58
29430 Ker-Emma 29 62 Ve 57
29630 Kerénot 29 62 Wb 56
29810 Kerescart 29 61 Vb 58
29390 Kerescun 29 78 Wb 60
29800 Kérézellec 29 62 Ve 58
56760 Kerfalher 56 81 Xc 64
29350 Kerfany-les-Pins 29 79 Wb 62
22330 Kerfiac 22 64 Xc 59
29280 Kerfily 29 61 Vc 58
29970 Kerfinous 29 78 Wa 60
29233 Kerfissien 29 62 Vf 56
56370 Kerfontaine 56 80 Xb 64
22500 Kerfot 22 63 Wf 56
56920 Kerfourn 56 64 Xb 60
29540 Kerfranc 29 78 Wb 59
29140 Kerfrancès 29 78 Wb 61
29410 Kerfrecq 29 62 Wa 58
29690 Kergadiou 29 62 Wb 59
22390 Kergaër 22 63 We 57
56300 Kergal 56 64 Xa 60
56500 Kergal 56 80 Xb 61
29410 Kergalein 29 62 Wa 58
56270 Kergantic 56 79 Wd 62
29150 Kergaradec 29 78 Vf 60
29370 Kergariou 29 78 Wa 60
29840 Kergastel 29 61 Vb 57
56500 Kergauthier 56 80 Xa 61
56500 Kergilet 56 80 Xa 61
29350 Kerglien 29 79 Wb 62
29160 Kerglintin 29 61 Vc 59
29270 Kergloff 29 63 Wc 59
29350 Kerglouanou 29 79 Wb 62
56680 Kergo 56 80 We 62
29430 Kergoarat 29 62 Ve 56
29150 Kergoat 29 62 Ve 59
29180 Kergoat 29 78 Ve 60
29860 Kergoat 29 61 Vd 58
56110 Kergoat 56 79 Wc 60
56320 Kergoat 56 79 Wd 60
29270 Kergoff 29 63 Wc 59
29400 Kergoff 29 62 Ve 57
29880 Kergoff 29 61 Vc 57
29260 Kergolestroc 29 62 Vd 57
22320 Kergonan 22 64 Xa 59
29810 Kergonan 29 61 Vb 58
56620 Kergonan 56 79 Wd 61
29260 Kergongar 29 62 Ve 57
29380 Kergonval 29 78 Wb 61
22480 Kergoten 22 63 We 59
29420 Kergoulouarn 29 62 Vf 57
29970 Kergréac'h 29 78 Wa 60
22570 Kergrenel 22 63 Wf 59
29410 Kergrenn 29 62 Wa 58
29400 Kergréven 29 62 Vf 58
22290 Kergrist 22 63 Wf 56
22500 Kergrist 22 63 Wf 56
56300 Kergrist 56 64 Xa 60
22110 Kergrist-Moëlou 22 63 We 59
29260 Kergroas 29 62 Ve 57
56150 Kergroix 56 79 Wf 61

A B C D E F G H I J K L M N O P Q R S T U V W X Y Z

Kergroix I 279

56330 Kergroix 56 79 Wf 62
29260 Kergûaoc 29 62 Vd 57
29260 Kerguélen 29 62 Ve 57
29720 Kerguellec 29 78 Vd 61
29590 Kerguellen 29 62 Vf 59
56650 Kerguer 56 80 We 61
56240 Kerguescanff 56 79 Wd 61
56370 Kerguet 56 80 Xb 63
29250 Kerguiduff 29 62 Vf 57
56660 Kerguillerme 56 80 Xb 62
29260 Kergunic 29 62 Vd 57
22340 Kerguz 22 63 Wd 59
56770 Kerguzul 56 79 Wd 60
22170 Kerhamon 22 64 Wf 57
56420 Kerhello 56 80 Xb 61
22720 Kerhenry 22 63 We 58
56500 Kerhero 56 80 Xa 61
29270 Kerhervé 29 63 Wb 59
29170 Kerho 29 78 Wa 61
29530 Kerhoaden 29 62 Wa 59
29540 Kerholen 29 79 Wb 59
22200 Kerhonn 22 63 We 57
29810 Kerhornou 29 61 Vb 58
56510 Kerhostin 56 80 Wf 63
29233 Kérider 29 62 Ve 56
22660 Kériec 22 63 Wd 56
22480 Kerien 22 63 We 58
56920 Kériffé 56 64 Xb 60
29530 Kériffin 29 62 Wb 59
29160 Kerifloch 29 61 Vc 59
56370 Kerignard 56 80 Xb 63
29490 Kérigoualch 29 62 Vd 58
56240 Kérihuel 56 79 We 61
29410 Kerilly 29 62 Wa 57
22320 Kerimard 22 64 Wf 59
56500 Kerimars 56 80 Xb 61
29217 Kerinou 29 61 Vb 58
56350 Kério 56 64 Xb 60
29510 Kériou 29 78 Wa 60
56470 Kerisper 56 80 Wf 63
22500 Kerity 22 63 Wf 56
29760 Kérity 29 78 Vd 62
29530 Kerivarc'h 29 62 Wb 59
29860 Kérivinoc 29 61 Vc 57
29460 Kerivoal 29 62 Ve 58
29290 Kerivot 29 61 Vc 58
29430 Kerizinen 29 62 Ve 57
29280 Kerjean 29 61 Vc 58
56640 Kerjouanno 56 80 Xa 63
29400 Kerlaer 29 62 Ve 57
29830 Kerlanou 29 61 Vb 57
29100 Kerlaz 29 78 Ve 60
56160 Kerlénant 56 79 We 60
29200 Kerléo 29 61 Vc 58
29190 Kerlesquin 29 62 Vf 59
56920 Kerlezan 56 64 Xb 60
29420 Kerlidou 29 62 Vf 57
56620 Kerliff 56 79 Wd 62
29910 Kerlin 29 78 Wa 62
57480 Kerling-lès-Sierck 57 44 Gc 52
29390 Kerliou 29 78 Wb 60
29233 Kerlissien 29 62 Vf 57
56160 Kerlividic 56 79 We 60
29350 Kerliviou 29 79 Wb 62
29450 Kerlodezan 29 62 Vf 58
56420 Kerlois 56 80 Xb 61
29890 Kerlouan 29 62 Vd 57
22480 Kerlouët 22 63 We 58
22500 Kerloury 22 63 Wf 56
22610 Kermagen 22 63 Wf 55
29910 Kermao 29 78 Wa 61
29890 Kermarguel 29 62 Vd 57
22580 Kermaria 22 64 Xa 56
29930 Kermaria 29 78 Ve 61
22450 Kermaria-Sulard 22 63 Wd 56
29410 Kermat 29 62 Wa 57
56500 Kermaux 56 64 Xa 61
29660 Kermen 29 62 Wa 57
29920 Kermen 29 78 Wb 62
22320 Kermenguy 22 63 Wf 59
29100 Kermenguy 29 78 Ve 60
29250 Kermenguy 29 62 Vf 57
29710 Kermenguy 29 78 Vd 60
29870 Kermenguy 29 61 Vc 57
29840 Kermerrien 29 61 Vb 58
22140 Kermeur 22 63 Wd 56
29640 Kermeur 29 62 Wb 58
29770 Kermeur 29 61 Vc 60
29490 Kermeur-Saint-Yves 29 62 Vd 58
22200 Kermilon 22 63 Wf 57
56500 Kermoisan 56 80 Xb 61
56370 Kermoizan 56 80 Xb 63
22140 Kermoroc'h 22 63 We 57
22740 Kermouster 22 63 Wf 56
22140 Kernalégan 22 63 Wd 57
44780 Kernan 44 81 Xf 63
29150 Kernaou 29 78 Vf 60
56540 Kernascléden 56 79 We 60
56450 Kernau 56 80 Xc 63
56410 Kerné 56 79 Wf 64
29410 Kernelecq 29 62 Wa 58
29252 Kernéléhen 29 62 Wa 57
56670 Kerner 56 79 We 62
56640 Kerners 56 80 Xa 63
29390 Kernescop 29 78 Wb 60
56150 Kernestic 56 79 Wf 61
29140 Kernével 29 78 Wb 61
29510 Kernévez 29 78 Wa 60
29690 Kernévez 29 62 Wa 58
29690 Kernévez 29 62 Wb 58
29830 Kernevez 29 61 Vc 57
29430 Kernic 29 62 Ve 57
29470 Kernie 29 61 Vd 58
29260 Kernilis 29 62 Vd 57
29510 Kerninou 29 78 Wa 60
29470 Kernisi 29 62 Vd 58
29510 Kernon 29 78 Vf 60
29400 Kernonen 29 62 Vf 58
29440 Kernoter 29 62 Vf 57
29310 Kernouarn 29 79 Wc 61
29260 Kernouës 29 62 Vd 57
56800 Kernoul 56 64 Xd 60
44420 Kero 44 81 Xc 64
22290 Kerognan 22 63 Wf 56
22340 Keroguiou 22 63 Wd 59
29420 Kerohantiou 29 62 Vf 57
29250 Keromnes 29 62 Vf 56
29970 Kéroret 29 78 Wa 60
29400 Kéroual 29 62 Vf 58
29290 Keroudy 29 61 Vc 58
29710 Kerougou 29 78 Ve 60
29860 Kérouné 29 61 Vd 57
29840 Keroustat 29 61 Vb 57
29590 Kerouzarc'h 29 62 Ve 59
22160 Kerouzérien 22 63 Wd 58
22580 Kerouziel 22 64 Xa 56
56220 Kerpaillard 56 81 Xd 62
56260 Kerpape 56 79 Wd 62
56740 Kerpenhir 56 80 Xa 63
22480 Kerpert 22 63 Wf 58
57830 Kerprich-aux-Bois 57 57 Gf 56
56730 Kerpont 56 80 Xa 63
29660 Kerprigent 29 62 Wa 57
29590 Kerrec 29 62 Ve 59
29600 Kerret 29 62 Wa 57
29640 Kerrgorre 29 62 Wb 58
56500 Kerrob 56 80 Xb 61
29400 Kerroch 29 62 Vf 58
56270 Kerroc'h 56 79 Wd 62
22450 Kerrod 22 63 We 56
56590 Kerrohet 56 79 Wd 63
22170 Kerronniou 22 63 Wf 57
22780 Kerroué 22 63 Wc 57
29780 Kerruc 29 61 Vd 61
29700 Kersabiec 29 78 Ve 61
29630 Kersaint 29 62 Wb 56
29830 Kersaint 29 61 Vb 57
29860 Kersaint-Plabennec 29 62 Vd 58
56800 Kersamson 56 64 Xd 60
29160 Kersaniou 29 62 Vd 59
29800 Kersaos 29 62 Vd 58
29350 Kersauz 29 79 Wc 62
29630 Kersco 29 62 Wb 57
22540 Kerscoul 22 63 Wd 57
56240 Kerscoulic 56 79 Wd 61
29160 Kerséguénou 29 61 Vc 59
22480 Kersolec 22 63 We 58
56400 Kerstran 56 80 Wf 62
29710 Kerstridic 29 78 Vd 61
29420 Kertanguy 29 62 Vf 57
29610 Kertanguy 29 62 Wb 57
56130 Kertouard 56 81 Xd 63
44410 Kertrait 44 81 Xd 64
22410 Kertugal 22 64 Xa 57
67230 Kertzfeld 67 60 Hd 58
56310 Kervalan 56 79 We 61
56400 Kervaly 56 80 Xa 62
29710 Kervargon 29 78 Ve 61
56360 Kervarijon 56 80 Wf 65
56680 Kervarlay 56 79 We 62
29390 Kervars 29 78 Wb 60
29830 Kervasdué 29 61 Vc 57
29630 Kervebel 29 62 Wa 56
22140 Kervec 22 63 We 57
22560 Kervégan 22 63 Wc 56
56530 Kervégant 56 79 Wd 62
56550 Kervéhél 56 80 Xb 61
29550 Kervel 29 78 Ve 60
22290 Kervélard 22 63 Xa 57
29630 Kervélégant 29 62 Wb 57
29690 Kervélen 29 62 Wb 59
29830 Kerveltec 29 61 Vc 57
29520 Kerven 29 78 Wa 60
29790 Kerven 29 61 Vc 60
29410 Kervenarc'hant 29 62 Wa 57
56870 Kervenir 56 80 Xa 63
56270 Kervenois 56 79 Wd 62
29890 Kerverven 29 62 Vd 56
29710 Kerveyen 29 78 Vd 61
29590 Kervez 29 62 Vf 59
29410 Kervian 29 62 Wa 58
29550 Kervigen 29 78 Ve 60
56700 Kervignac 56 80 We 62
56500 Kervihan 56 80 Xa 61
56360 Kervilahouen 56 80 We 65
29290 Kerviniou 29 61 Vc 58
29520 Kerviniou 29 62 Wa 60
56560 Kerviniou 56 79 Wc 60
22200 Kerviou 22 63 We 57
29390 Kervir 29 78 Wb 60
29610 Kervolaugar 29 62 Wb 57
29000 Kervouyec 29 78 Vf 60
56750 Kervoyal 56 81 Xc 63
56170 Kervozès 56 79 We 64
29380 Kervran 29 79 Wb 61
56760 Kervraud 56 81 Xc 64
56440 Kervréhan 56 79 Wf 62
22300 Kervren 22 63 Wd 56
22530 Keryhouée 22 64 Wf 59
29190 Keryvarc'h 29 62 Wa 59
29520 Keryvon-Bourg 29 78 Wa 59
56110 Kerzallec 56 79 Wb 60
29233 Kerzean 29 62 Vf 57
29470 Kerziou 29 62 Vd 58
67260 Keskastel 67 57 Ha 55
67930 Kesseldorf 67 59 Ia 55
67730 Kestenholz = Châtenois 67 60 Hc 59
56530 Kevenn = Quéven 56 79 Wd 62
22210 Kez = La Chèze 22 64 Xc 60
56170 Kiberen = Quiberon 56 79 Wf 64
67270 Kienheim 67 58 Hd 56
68240 Kientzheim 68 60 Hb 60
67750 Kientzville 67 60 Hc 59
68480 Kiffis 68 95 Hc 64
59122 Killem 59 27 Cd 43
59122 Killem-Linde 59 27 Cd 43
67840 Kilstett 67 58 Hf 56
67350 Kindwiller 67 58 Hd 55
68390 Kingersheim 68 95 Hc 62
22800 Kintin = Quintin 22 64 Xa 58
67600 Kintzheim 67 60 Hc 59
13530 Kirbon 13 171 Fd 88
67520 Kirchheim 67 60 Hc 57
88400 Kirchompré 88 77 Gf 60
67320 Kirrberg 67 57 Ha 56
67330 Kirrwiller 67 58 Hd 56
57935 Kirsch-lès-Luttange 57 56 Gb 53
57480 Kirsch-lès-Sierck 57 44 Gc 52
57480 Kirschnaumen 57 44 Gc 52
57430 Kirviller 57 57 Gf 55
56230 Kistreberzh = Questrembert 56 81 Xd 63
57480 Kitzing 57 44 Gc 52
57920 Klang 57 44 Gc 53
56480 Klegereg = Cléguérec 56 79 Wf 60
57740 Kleindal 57 57 Gd 54
67370 Kleinfrankenheim 67 58 Hd 57
67440 Kleingœft 67 58 Hc 56
57410 Kleinmühle 57 58 Hb 54
22160 Klempétu 22 63 Wc 58
67530 Klingenthal 67 60 Hc 58
68220 Knœringue 68 95 Hc 63
67310 Knœrsheim 67 58 Hc 56
57240 Knutange 57 56 Ga 52
22330 Koedlinez = Colinnée 22 64 Xc 59
57100 Kœking 57 44 Gb 52
67000* Koenigshoffen 67 60 He 57
57970 Kœnigsmacker 57 44 Gb 52
68480 Kœstlach 68 95 Hb 63
68510 Kœtzingue 68 95 Hc 63
55300 Kœur-la-Petite 55 55 Fc 55
67230 Kogenheim 67 60 Hd 58
67120 Kolbsheim 67 60 Hd 57
35270 Komborn = Combourg 35 65 Yb 58
29900 Konk-Kerne = Concarneau 29 78 Wa 61
22320 Korle = Corlay 22 63 Wf 59
55300 Kour-la-Grande 55 55 Fc 55
67150 Krafft 67 60 He 58
29160 Kraozon = Crozon 29 61 Vd 59
67118 Kratz 67 60 He 57
67880 Krautergersheim 67 60 Hd 58
67170 Krautwiller 67 58 He 56
94270 Kremlin-sur-Seine, le 94 51 Cc 56
59190 Kreule, la 59 27 Cd 44
67170 Kriegsheim 67 58 He 56
68820 Kruth 68 94 Gf 61
59470 Kruystraete, la 59 27 Cd 43
67660 Kuhlendorf 67 58 Hf 55
68320 Kunheim 68 60 Hd 60
57970 Kuntzig 57 56 Gb 52
67240 Kurtzenhouse 67 58 He 56
67520 Kuttolsheim 67 58 Hd 57
67250 Kutzenhausen 67 58 Hf 55

L

49360 La, la 49 98 Zb 66
64300 Laà-Mondrans 64 161 Zb 88
32170 Laas 32 163 Ab 88
45300 Laas 45 71 Cb 60
64390 Laàs 64 161 Za 88
29710 Lababan 29 78 Vd 61
31440 Labach 31 176 Ae 91
24560 Labadie 24 136 Ad 80
32700 Labadie 32 149 Ad 85
24550 Labardamier 24 137 Ba 81
33460 Labarde 33 134 Zc 78
33730 Labardin 33 147 Ze 82
68910 Labaroche 68 77 Hb 60
47290 Labarque 47 136 Ad 81
09000 Labarre 09 177 Bd 91
32250 Labarrère 32 148 Aa 85
32260 Labarthe 32 163 Ad 88
46090 Labarthe 46 137 Bc 81
47150 Labarthe 47 136 Ae 82
64290 Labarthe 64 162 Zd 89
82220 Labarthe 82 150 Bb 83
65140 Labarthe, Trouley- 65 163 Ab 89
31800 Labarthe-Inard 31 163 Af 90
31800 Labarthe-Rivière 31 163 Ae 90
31860 Labarthe-sur-Lèze 31 164 Bc 88
32400 Labarthète 32 162 Zf 87
65200 Labassère 65 162 Aa 90
40260 Labaste 40 146 Ye 85
07600 Labastide 07 142 Eb 80
32140 Labastide 32 163 Ad 88
65130 Labastide 65 175 Ab 90
31450 Labastide-Beauvoir 31 165 Be 88
64170 Labastide-Cézéracq 64 162 Zc 88
40700 Labastide-Chalosse 40 161 Zc 87
64240 Labastide-Clairence 64 160 Ye 88
31370 Labastide-Clermont 31 164 Ba 88
11320 Labastide-d'Anjou 11 165 Bf 88
40240 Labastide-d'Armagnac 40 148 Ze 85
81150 Labastide-de-Lévis 81 151 Ca 85
81120 Labastide-Dénat 81 151 Cb 85
82240 Labastide-de-Penne 82 150 Bd 83
12540 Labastide-des-Fonts 12 153 Db 85
07150 Labastide-de-Virac 07 154 Ec 82
46210 Labastide-du-Haut-Mont 46 138 Ca 79
82100 Labastide-du-Temple 82 149 Bb 84
46150 Labastide-du-Vert 46 137 Bb 81
11220 Labastide-en-Val 11 166 Cc 90
11380 Labastide-Esparbairenque 11 166 Cc 88
81400 Labastide-Gabausse 81 151 Ca 84
46090 Labastide-Marnhac 46 150 Bc 82
64170 Labastide-Monréjeau 64 162 Zc 88
46240 Labastide-Murat 46 138 Bd 81
31230 Labastide-Paumès 31 164 Af 89
81270 Labastide-Rouairoux 81 166 Cd 88
82370 Labastide-Saint-Pierre 82 150 Bc 85
31620 Labastide-Saint-Sernin 31 164 Bc 86
32130 Labastide-Savès 32 164 Af 87
31600 Labastidette 31 164 Bb 88
64270 Labastide-Villefranche 64 161 Yf 88
09000 Labat 09 177 Be 91
65400 Labat-de-Bun 65 174 Ze 91
46120 Labathude 46 138 Bf 80
07570 Labatie-d'Andaure 07 142 Ec 78
32360 Labâtisse 32 163 Ac 86
64530 Labatmale 64 162 Zf 89
09700 Labatut 09 164 Bd 89
40300 Labatut 40 161 Za 87
64460 Labatut 64 162 Zf 88
65700 Labatut-Rivière 65 162 Aa 87
43320 Labauche 43 141 De 78
44500 La-Baule-Escoublac 44 81 Xd 65
30700 Labaume 30 154 Ec 84
95690 Labbeville 95 51 Ca 54
32270 Labbubée 32 163 Ae 86
11400 Labécède-Lauragais 11 165 Ca 88
31670 Labège 31 165 Bd 87
34700 Labeil 34 153 Db 86
32300 Labéjan 32 163 Ad 87
32350 Labenne 32 163 Ac 87
40530 Labenne 40 160 Yd 87
40530 Labenne-Océan 40 160 Yd 87
46090 Labéraudie 46 137 Bc 82
25270 Labergement-du-Navois 25 107 Ga 67
21110 Labergement-Foigney 21 106 Fb 65
21130 Labergement-lès-Auxonne 21 106 Fc 66
21820 Labergement-lès-Seurre 21 106 Fa 67
25160 Labergement-Sainte-Marie 25 108 Gb 68
60310 Laberlière 60 39 Ce 51
31530 Labesque 31 164 Ba 86
87600 Labesse 87 124 Ae 74
15120 Labesserette 15 139 Cc 80
63690 Labessette 63 127 Cd 76
81300 Labessière-Candeil 81 151 Ca 86
64120 Labets-Biscay 64 161 Yf 88
55160 Labeuville 55 56 Fe 54
62122 Labeuvrière 62 29 Cd 45
64300 Labeyrie 64 161 Zc 87
34600 la-Billière 34 167 Da 87
12360 Labiras 12 152 Da 86
07230 Lablachère 07 141 Eb 82
80500 Laboissière-en-Santerre 80 39 Ce 51
60570 Laboissière-en-Thelle 60 51 Ca 53
80430 Laboissière-Saint-Martin 80 38 Be 49
19330 Laborde 19 126 Bd 77
47210 Laborde 47 136 Ae 81
65130 Laborde 65 175 Ab 90
89000 Laborde 89 90 Dd 62
26560 Laborel 26 156 Fd 83
09420 Laborie 09 177 Bb 91
19330 Laborie 19 126 Bd 77
47800 Laborie 47 136 Ac 81
60590 Labosse 60 50 Bf 52
40210 Labouheyre 40 146 Za 83
07110 Laboule 07 141 Eb 81
24440 Labouquerie 24 137 Ae 80
04420 Labouret, le 04 157 Gb 83
82100 Labourgade 82 149 Ba 85
62113 Labourse 62 29 Ce 45
23220 Laboutant 23 114 Bf 70
81120 Laboutarie 81 151 Ca 86
43800 Labraud 43 129 Df 78
47350 Labretonie 47 136 Ac 82
33460 Labric 33 134 Zc 79
32120 Labrihe 32 149 Af 86
40420 Labrit 40 147 Zc 84
15380 Labro 15 127 Cc 77
31510 Labroquère 31 176 Ad 90
45330 Labrosse 45 71 Cc 59
15130 Labrousse 15 139 Cd 79
24590 Labrousse 24 137 Bb 78
87190 Labrousse 87 113 Ba 71
87440 Labrousse 87 124 Ae 75
87600 Labrousse 87 125 Af 73
62140 Labroye 62 28 Bf 47
81290 Labruguière 81 166 Cb 87
21250 Labruyère 21 106 Fa 66
60140 Labruyère 60 39 Cd 52
31190 Labruyère-Dorsa 31 164 Bc 88
54800 Labry 54 56 Ff 53
62700 Labuissière 62 29 Cd 46
46230 Laburgade 46 150 Bd 82
62150 La-Bussière 62 29 Cd 46
11130 Lac, le 11 179 Cf 90
12160 Lac, le 12 152 Cc 83
15170 Lac, le 15 128 Cf 77
19270 Lac, le 19 125 Bd 77
40160 Lac, le 40 146 Yf 82
71110 Lac, le 71 117 Ea 71
83340 Lac, le 83 172 Gb 88
87230 Lac, le 87 125 Af 75
81240 Lacabarède 81 166 Cd 88
64300 Lacadée 64 161 Zc 87
40320 Lacajunte 40 162 Zd 87
12210 Lacalm 12 139 Cf 80
81200 Lacalmille 81 166 Cb 88
46190 Lacam-d'Ourcet 46 138 Ca 79
34360 Lacan 34 166 Ce 88
33680 Lacanau 33 134 Yf 79
33380 Lacanau-de-Mios 33 134 Za 81
33680 Lacanau-Océan 33 134 Ye 78
21230 Lacanche 21 105 Ed 66
15230 Lacapelle-Barrès 15 139 Ce 79
47150 Lacapelle-Biron 47 137 Af 81
46700 Lacapelle-Cabanac 46 137 Ba 82
15120 Lacapelle-del-Fraisse 15 139 Cc 80
15130 Lacapelle-en-Vézie 15 139 Cc 80
82160 Lacapelle-Livron 82 150 Be 83
46120 Lacapelle-Marival 46 138 Bf 80
81340 Lacapelle-Pinet 81 151 Cc 84
81170 Lacapelle-Ségalar 81 151 Bf 84
15150 Lacapelle-Viescamp 15 139 Cb 79
64220 Lacarre 64 161 Yf 89
64470 Lacarry-Arhan-Charritte-de-Haut 64 174 Za 90
32300 Lacassagne 32 163 Ac 87
65140 Lacassagne 65 162 Aa 88
82160 Lacau 82 151 Bf 83
31390 Lacaugne 31 164 Bb 89
81230 Lacaune 81 166 Ce 86
32400 Lacaussade 32 162 Zf 86
47150 Lacaussade 47 137 Ae 81
09160 Lacave 09 176 Ba 90
46200 Lacave 46 138 Bd 79
40260 Lacay 40 146 Yf 85
81330 Lacaze 81 166 Cd 86
12800 Lac-Blanc 12 151 Cc 83
15270 Lac de Crégut 15 127 Cd 76
07470 Lac-d'Issarlès, le 07 141 Ea 80
69640 Lacenas 69D 118 Ed 73
47360 Lacenne 47 149 Ad 83
47360 Lacépède 47 148 Ac 83
05100 Lacha 05 145 Gd 78
24390 Lachabroulie 24 125 Ba 77
16300 Lachaise 16 123 Ze 75
55120 Lachalade 55 54 Ef 53
57730 Lachambre 57 57 Ge 54
48100 Lachamp 48 140 Dc 81
07530 Lachamp-Raphaël 07 142 Eb 80
33990 Lachanau 33 122 Yf 78
47350 Lachapelle 47 136 Ab 81
54120 Lachapelle 54 77 Ge 58
80290 Lachapelle 80 38 Bf 50
82120 Lachapelle 82 149 Af 85
85120 La-Chapelle-aux-Lys 85 98 Zc 69
60650 Lachapelle-aux-Pots 60 38 Bf 52
46200 Lachapelle-Auzac 46 138 Bc 79
71570 Lachapelle-de-Guinchay, la 71 118 Ee 71
52330 Lachapelle-en-Blaisy 52 74 Ef 59
07470 Lachapelle-Graillouse 07 141 Ea 80
60730 Lachapelle-Saint-Pierre 60 51 Cb 53
07200 Lachapelle-sous-Aubenas 07 142 Ec 81
07310 Lachapelle-sous-Chanéac 07 142 Eb 79
90300 Lachapelle-sous-Chaux 90 94 Ge 62
60380 Lachapelle-sous-Gerberoy 60 38 Bf 51
90360 Lachapelle-sous-Rougemont 90 94 Gf 62
69480 Lachassagne 69D 118 Ee 73
74540 Lachat 74 132 Ga 74
05100 Lachau 05 145 Ge 79
26560 Lachau 26 156 Fd 83
19380 Lachaud 19 138 Be 78
19510 Lachaud 19 126 Be 75
23340 Lachaud 23 126 Bf 74
23460 Lachaud 23 114 Bf 73
87120 Lachaud 87 126 Be 74
05250 Lachaup 05 144 Fe 80
55210 Lachaussée 55 56 Fe 54
60480 Lachaussée-du-Bois-d'écu 60 38 Cb 51
63290 Lachaux 63 116 Dd 73
58420 Laché 58 104 Dd 65
60190 Lachelle 60 39 Ce 52
51120 Lachy 51 53 De 56
46600 Lacisque 46 138 Bc 79
18310 Laclaire, le 18 102 Bf 65
71800 Laclayette 71 117 Eb 71
87290 Laclotre 87 113 Bb 72
90150 Lacollonge 90 94 Gf 63
11310 Lacombe 11 166 Cb 88
19170 Lacombe 19 126 Bf 74
81320 Lacombe 81 166 Ce 86
64360 Lacommande 64 162 Zc 89
09130 Lacoste 09 164 Bc 90
24520 Lacoste 24 136 Ad 79
34800 Lacoste 34 167 Dc 87
40190 Lacoste 40 147 Ze 85
84480 Lacoste 84 156 Fb 86
05500 Lacoue 05 144 Ga 80
81500 Lacougotte-Cadoul 81 165 Be 87
24270 Lacour 24 125 Ba 76
82190 Lacour 82 149 Af 83
21210 Lacour-d'Arcenay 21 90 Eb 64
09200 Lacourt 09 176 Bb 91
82290 Lacourt-Saint-Pierre 82 150 Bb 85
01110 Lacoux 01 119 Fd 73
23220 Lacoux 23 114 Bf 71
87210 Lacoux 87 113 Ba 71
64170 Lacq 64 161 Zc 88
40120 Lacquy 40 147 Ze 85
40700 Lacrabe 40 161 Zc 87
62830 Lacres 62 28 Be 45
52700 Lacrête 52 75 Fb 59
81470 Lacroisille 81 165 Bf 87
57320 Lacroix 57 44 Gc 52
12600 Lacroix-Barrez 12 139 Cd 80
31120 Lacroix-Falgarde 31 164 Bc 88
60610 Lacroix-Saint-Ouen 60 39 Ce 52
55300 Lacroix-sur-Meuse 55 55 Fd 55
24380 Lacropte 24 137 Ae 78
71700 Lacrost 71 118 Ef 69
81210 Lacrouzette 81 166 Cc 87
15500 Lacroze 15 128 Da 77
36400 Lacs 36 102 Ca 69
89270 Lac-Sauvin 89 90 De 63
23270 Ladapeyre 23 114 Ca 71
33760 Ladaux 33 135 Ze 80
12490 Ladepeyre 12 152 Ce 84
11250 Ladern-sur-Lauquet 11 166 Cc 90
24330 Ladeuil 24 137 Af 78
32230 Ladevèze-Rivière 32 162 Aa 87
32230 Ladevèze-Ville 32 162 Aa 87
12800 Ladignac 12 139 Ce 79
46320 Ladignac 46 138 Be 80
87500 Ladignac-le-Long 87 125 Ba 75
19150 Ladignac-sur-Rondelles 19 126 Bf 77
43100 Ladignat 43 128 Db 77
43100 Ladignat 43 128 Dc 77
81310 Ladin 81 150 Be 85
15120 Ladinhac 15 139 Cd 80
46400 Ladirat 46 138 Bf 80
16120 Ladiville 16 123 Zf 75
21550 Ladoix-Serrigny 21 106 Ef 66
45270 Ladon 45 71 Cd 60
33124 Lados 33 135 Zf 82
63980 Ladoux 63 128 Dc 75

280 I Kergroix

39210 Ladoye-sur-Seille 39 107 Fe 68
87460 Ladrat 87 126 Be 73
89110 Laduz 89 89 Dc 61
89110 Laduz 89 89 Dc 61
77720 Lady 77 72 Cf 57
11420 Lafage 11 165 Bf 89
48200 la-Fage-Saint-Julien 48 140 Db 80
19320 Lafage-sur-Sombre 19 126 Ca 77
07700 Lafare 07 142 Ed 82
84190 Lafare 84 155 Fa 84
24460 Lafarerie 24 124 Ae 77
19370 Lafarge 19 126 Bd 75
24800 Lafarge 24 125 Af 75
87800 Lafarge 87 125 Ba 75
43490 Lafarre 43 141 Df 79
23800 Lafat 23 113 Bd 70
52700 Lafauche 52 75 Fd 59
15310 Lafaurge 15 139 Cc 78
16310 Lafaurie 16 124 Ad 74
03500 Laféline 03 116 Db 70
52500 Laferté-sur-Amance 52 92 Fe 61
52120 Laferté-sur-Aube 52 74 Ee 60
15130 Lafeuillade-en-Vézie 15 139 Cc 80
43500 Laffarge 43 129 De 77
07520 Laffarre 07 142 Ed 78
02880 Laffaux 02 40 Dc 52
63840 Laffix 63 129 Df 76
38220 Laffrey 38 144 Fe 78
07140 Lafigère 07 154 Ea 82
65700 Lafitole 65 162 Aa 88
82340 Lafitte 82 149 Af 84
82700 Lafitte 82 149 Ba 85
47320 Lafitte-sur-Lot 47 148 Ac 82
31360 Lafitte-Toupière 31 164 Af 89
31390 Lafitte-Vigordane 31 164 Ba 89
52300 Lafolie 52 75 Fa 58
19250 Lafond 19 126 Ca 75
17570 Lafont 17 122 Yf 74
33460 Lafont 33 135 Zc 79
40200 Lafont 40 146 Ye 83
69870 Lafont 69D 118 Ec 72
33710 Lafosse 33 135 Zc 78
47240 Lafox 47 149 Ae 83
82130 Lafrançaise 82 150 Bb 84
60510 Lafraye 60 38 Cb 52
80430 Lafresguimont-Saint-Martin 80 38 Be 50
57560 Lafrimbolle 57 77 Ha 57
47380 Lagaillardie 47 136 Ac 81
64520 Lagaillardie 64 160 Ye 88
34150 Lagamas 34 167 Dd 86
09500 Lagarde 09 178 Bf 90
12150 Lagarde 12 152 Da 82
15310 Lagarde 15 139 Cc 78
31230 Lagarde 31 164 Ae 88
31290 Lagarde 31 165 Be 88
32500 Lagarde 32 149 Ad 86
32700 Lagarde 32 149 Ad 85
57810 Lagarde 57 57 Ge 56
65320 Lagarde 65 162 Aa 89
84400 Lagarde-d'Apt 84 156 Fc 85
19150 Lagarde-Enval 19 126 Be 77
32300 Lagarde-Hachan 32 163 Ac 88
46220 Lagardelle 46 137 Bb 82
31870 Lagardelle-sur-Lèze 31 164 Bc 88
84290 Lagarde-Paréol 84 155 Ef 83
32310 Lagardère 32 148 Ab 85
16300 Lagarde-sur-le-Né 16 123 Ze 75
81110 Lagardiolle 81 165 Ca 87
47190 Lagarrigue 47 148 Ac 83
40430 Lagassey 40 147 Zd 83
40500 Lagastet 40 147 Zc 86
40430 Lagavarre 40 147 Zd 83
47210 Lage-Haute 47 136 Ae 81
79200 Lageon 79 99 Ze 68
87230 Lagérat 87 125 Af 74
77460 Lagerville 77 72 Ce 59
51170 Lagery 51 53 De 53
10210 Lagesse 10 73 Ea 60
06340 Laghet 06 159 Hc 86
19500 Lagleygeolle 19 138 Be 78
19600 Lagleygeolles 19 138 Bd 78
40410 Lagleyre 40 147 Zc 82
40090 Laglorieuse 40 147 Zd 85
12340 Lagnac 12 139 Cd 82
84800 Lagnes 84 156 Fa 85
54200 Lagney 54 56 Ff 56
62159 Lagnicourt-Marcel 62 30 Cf 48
01150 Lagnieu 01 119 Fc 73
73170 Lagnieu 73 132 Fe 74
60310 Lagny 60 39 Cf 51
60330 Lagny-le-Sec 60 52 Ce 54
36100 Lagnys, les 36 101 Be 67
77400 Lagny-sur-Marne 77 51 Ce 55
20290 Lago CTC 181 Kc 93
29460 Lagonna-Daoulas 29 62 Ve 59
64150 Lagor 64 161 Zc 88
07150 Lagorce 07 154 Ec 82
33230 Lagorce 33 135 Zf 78
17140 Lagord 17 109 Yf 71
64800 Lagos 64 162 Ze 89
31190 Lagraçe-Dieu 31 164 Bc 88
19430 Lagrange 19 138 Bf 78
40240 Lagrange 40 148 Zf 85
65300 Lagrange 65 163 Ac 90
81260 Lagrange 81 166 Cd 87
11220 Lagrasse 11 166 Cd 90
32190 Lagraulas 32 148 Ab 86
40090 Lagraulet 40 147 Zb 85
32330 Lagraulet-du-Gers 32 148 Ab 85
31480 Lagraulet-Saint Nicolas 31 149 Ba 86
19700 Lagraulière 19 126 Bd 76
81150 Lagrave 81 151 Bf 85
12360 Lagraverie 12 152 Cf 86
47400 Lagrùère 47 148 Ab 82
19150 Laguenne 19 126 Be 77
82250 Laguépie 82 151 Bf 84
64470 Laguinge-Restoue 64 161 Za 90
12210 Laguiole 12 139 Cf 80
32170 Lagujan-Mazous 32 163 Ab 88
33990 Lagunan 33 122 Za 77
33340 Lagune 33 122 Za 77
33340 Lagune, la 33 122 Za 76
47180 Lagupie 47 136 Aa 81
31370 Lahage 31 164 Ba 88
64120 Laharanne 64 161 Yf 88
40110 Laharie 40 146 Yf 84
52000 Laharmand 52 75 Fa 60
32130 Lahas 32 164 Af 87
80290 Lahaye-Saint-Romain 80 38 Bf 50
55260 Lahaymeix 55 55 Fc 55
55300 Lahayville 55 56 Fe 55
40270 Lahemme 40 147 Zd 86
55800 Laheycourt 55 55 Fa 55
31310 Lahitère 31 164 Bb 90
32810 Lahitte 32 163 Ae 87
40160 Lahitte 40 146 Yf 82
65130 Lahitte 65 163 Ab 90
65220 Lahitte 65 163 Ac 89
65700 Lahitte-Toupière 65 162 Zf 88
64990 Lahonce 64 160 Yd 88
64270 Lahontan 64 161 Za 87
40250 Lahosse 40 161 Zb 86
64150 Lahourcase 64 161 Zc 88
80800 Lahoussoye 80 39 Cc 49
08800 Laifour 08 42 Ee 49
53200 Laigné 53 83 Zb 61
17170 Laigne, la 17 110 Zb 71
17400 Laigne, la 17 110 Zc 73
72220 Laigné-en-Belin 72 85 Ab 61
35133 Laignelet 35 66 Yf 58
21330 Laignes 21 90 Ec 61
60290 Laigneville 60 51 Cc 53
02140 Laigny 02 41 Df 49
35890 Laillé 35 65 Yb 61
72220 Laillé 72 85 Ac 62
87340 Lailloux 87 113 Bc 72
89190 Lailly 89 72 Dd 59
45740 Lailly-en-Val 45 87 Be 62
79440 Laimière, la 79 98 Zc 68
55800 Laimont 55 55 Fa 55
89560 Lain 89 89 Dc 63
10120 Laines-aux-Bois 10 73 Df 59
33230 Lainier 33 135 Ze 78
39320 Lains 39 119 Fc 70
89520 Lainsecq 89 89 Db 63
78440 Lainville 78 50 Be 54
42550 Lair 42 129 Df 76
79100 Laire 79 99 Zf 67
62960 Laires 62 29 Cb 45
11330 Lairière 11 178 Cc 90
85280 Lairière 85 97 Ye 68
85400 Lairoux 85 109 Ye 70
73350 Laisonnay 73 133 Ge 76
12310 Laissac-Sévérac-L'Eglise 12 152 Ce 82
73800 Laissaud 73 132 Ga 76
25820 Laissey 25 93 Gb 65
74490 Laitraz 74 120 Gd 71
54770 Laître-sous-Amance 54 56 Gb 56
71240 Laives 71 106 Ef 69
54720 Laix 54 43 Fe 52
01290 Laiz 01 118 Ef 71
71870 Laizé 71 118 Ee 70
14320 Laize-Clinchamps 14 35 Zd 54
14320 Laize-la-Ville 14 47 Zd 54
71190 Laizy 71 105 Eb 67
24320 Lajard 24 124 Ac 77
24260 Lajerthe 24 137 Af 78
48120 Lajo 48 140 Dc 79
39310 Lajoux 39 120 Ff 70
61320 Lalacelle 61 67 Zf 58
82400 Lalande 82 149 Af 84
89130 Lalande 89 89 Db 62
33500 Lalande-de-Pomerol 33 135 Ze 79
60590 Lalande-en-Son 60 38 Be 52
60850 Lalandelle 60 38 Bf 52
47330 Lalandusse 47 136 Ad 81
32500 Lalanne 32 149 Ae 86
40090 Lalanne 40 147 Zd 85
65230 Lalanne 65 163 Ad 89
32140 Lalanne-Arqué 32 163 Ad 89
65220 Lalanne-Trie 65 163 Ac 89
67220 Lalaye 67 60 Hb 59
12420 Lalbaret 12 139 Ce 80
46230 Lalbenque 46 150 Bd 82
30140 Lale 30 154 Df 84
31530 Lalenne 31 164 Ba 87
61170 Laleu 61 68 Ac 57
80270 Laleu 80 38 Bf 49
07380 Lalevade-d'Ardèche 07 142 Eb 81
71240 Lalheue 71 106 Ee 69
24150 Lalinde 24 136 Ae 79
24700 Lalinde 24 136 Ab 79
46320 Laliniè 46 138 Be 80
03450 Lalizolle 03 115 Da 72
59167 Lallaing 59 30 Db 46
26150 Lallet 26 143 Fb 80
35320 Lalleu 35 82 Yc 61
41400 Lalleu 41 86 Bb 64
38930 Lalley 38 144 Fe 80
01130 Lalleyriat, Le Poizat- 01 119 Fe 72
07510 Lalligie 07 141 Ea 80
12160 Lalo 12 151 Cc 83
12350 Lalo 12 151 Ca 82
12560 Lalo 12 140 Da 82
15130 Lalo 15 139 Cd 79
08460 Lalobbe 08 41 Ec 50
54115 Lalœf 54 76 Ga 58
36400 Lalœuf 36 102 Bf 69
64350 Lalongue 64 162 Ze 88
64350 Lalonquère 64 162 Zf 88
64450 Lalonquette 64 162 Ze 88
19220 Lalot 19 126 Ca 77
65310 Laloubère 65 162 Aa 89
31800 Lalouret-Laffiteau 31 163 Ae 89
07520 Lalouvesc 07 142 Ed 78
02170 Lalouzy 02 31 De 48
40465 Laluque 40 146 Za 85
20218 Lama CTC 181 Kb 93
90170 Lamadeleine-Val-des-Anges 90 94 Gf 62
46090 Lamagdelaine 46 138 Bc 82
82360 Lamagistère 82 149 Ae 84
32260 Lamaguère 32 163 Ae 88
03380 Lamaids 03 115 Cc 71
79600 Lamairé 79 99 Zf 68
63120 Lamalle 63 128 Dd 74
34240 Lamalou-les-Bains 34 167 Da 87
52310 Lamancines 52 75 Fa 59
82160 Lamandine 82 150 Bd 83
66230 Lamanère 66 178 Cd 94
13113 Lamanon 13 170 Fa 86
29410 Lamarc'h 29 62 Wa 58
88320 Lamarche 88 76 Fe 60
55210 Lamarche-en-Woëvre 55 56 Fe 55
21760 Lamarche-sur-Saône 21 92 Fc 65
21440 Lamargelle 21 91 Ef 63
52160 Lamargelle-aux-Bois 52 91 Fa 62
80290 Lamaronde 80 38 Bf 50
33460 Lamarque 33 134 Zb 78
47400 Lamarque 47 148 Ab 82
64530 Lamarque-Pontacq 64 162 Zf 89
65220 Lamarque-Rustaing 65 163 Ab 89
71480 Lamarre 71 119 Fc 70
31600 Lamasquère 31 164 Bb 88
07270 Lamastre 07 142 Ed 79
53400 Lamath 54 76 Gc 57
46190 Lamativie 46 138 Ca 79
24410 Lamaure 24 123 Aa 77
47110 Lamaurelle 47 149 Ad 82
64460 Lamayou 64 162 Zf 88
81340 Lamayoux 81 151 Cc 84
11340 Lamayrède 11 178 Ca 91
81660 Lamays 81 166 Cc 87
32300 Lamazère 32 163 Ac 87
19160 Lamazière-Basse 19 126 Cb 76
19340 Lamazière-Haute 19 127 Cc 74
57410 Lambach 57 58 Hc 54
29420 Lambader 29 62 Vf 57
29780 Lambadu 29 61 Vd 60
22400 Lambal = Lamballe 22 64 Xc 58
22400 Lamballe = Lambal 22 64 Xc 58
56330 Lambel 56 80 Wf 61
56320 Lambélléguic 56 79 Wc 60
29810 Lamber 29 61 Vb 58
02140 Lambercy 02 41 Ea 50
59130 Lambersart 59 30 Da 45
87500 Lambertie 87 125 Bb 75
86460 Lambertière 86 112 Ac 72
33480 Lamberts, les 33 134 Za 78
50160 Lamberville 50 47 Za 54
76730 Lamberville 76 37 Ba 50
13410 Lambesc 13 170 Fb 87
56440 Lambézégan 56 80 Wf 61
29570 Lambézen 29 61 Vc 59
28340 Lamblore 28 49 Af 57
26400 Lambres 26 143 Fa 80
62120 Lambres 62 29 Cc 45
59500 Lambres-lez-Douai 59 30 Da 46
70500 Lambrey 70 93 Ff 62
04170 Lambruisse 04 157 Gc 84
65140 Laméac 65 163 Ab 89
60600 Lamécourt 60 39 Cc 52
30110 Lamelouze 30 154 Df 83
58300 Lamenay-sur-Loire 58 104 Dd 68
88380 Laménil 88 77 Gc 60
40270 Lamensans 40 147 Zd 86
16300 Lamérac 16 123 Ze 76
46330 Lamerlie 46 138 Be 81
55250 Lamermont 55 55 Fa 55
81390 Lames 81 151 Bf 86
08130 Lametz 08 42 Ee 51
81120 Lamillarié 81 151 Ca 85
76730 Lammerville 76 37 Af 50
72320 Lamnay 72 69 Ae 60
19510 Lamongerie 19 126 Bd 75
81260 Lamontélarié 81 166 Cd 87
63570 Lamontgie 63 128 Db 76
47310 Lamontjoie 47 149 Ad 84
24520 Lamonzie-Montastruc 24 136 Ad 79
24680 Lamonzie-Saint-Martin 24 136 Ac 79
60260 Lamorlaye 60 51 Cc 54
55300 Lamorville 55 55 Fd 55
09290 Lamothe 09 177 Bb 90
32120 Lamothe 32 163 Af 86
32800 Lamothe 32 148 Aa 85
40250 Lamothe 40 147 Zc 86
43100 Lamothe 43 128 Dc 77
82130 Lamothe-Capdeville 82 150 Bc 84
46240 Lamothe-Cassel 46 138 Bd 81
82500 Lamothe-Cumont 82 149 Af 85
47800 Lamothe-d'Alles 47 136 Ac 81
52330 Lamothe-en-Blaisy 52 74 Ef 59
46350 Lamothe-Fénelon 46 137 Bc 79
47150 Lamothefey 47 136 Ae 82
32500 Lamothe-Goas 32 149 Ad 85
33190 Lamothe-Landerron 33 135 Aa 81
24230 Lamothe-Montravel 24 135 Aa 79
33660 Lamothe-Soudanne 33 135 Aa 78
33450 Lamotte 33 135 Zd 79
41600 Lamotte-Beuvron 41 87 Ca 63
80450 Lamotte-Brebière 80 39 Cc 49
80150 Lamotte-Buleux 80 28 Bf 47
80800 Lamotte-Warfusée 80 39 Cd 49
55700 Lamouilly 55 42 Fb 51
39310 Lamoura 39 120 Ff 70
47210 Lamoure 47 136 Ae 81
24800 Lamouretie 24 125 Af 76
29242 Lampaul 29 61 Uf 58
29400 Lampaul-Guimiliau 29 62 Vf 58
29810 Lampaul-Plouarzel 29 61 Vb 58
29830 Lampaul-Ploudalmézeau 29 61 Vc 57
67450 Lampertheim 67 58 He 57
67250 Lampertsloch 67 58 He 55
17270 Lampiat 17 123 Zf 77
63113 Lamur 63 127 Ce 76
43210 Lamure 43 129 Ea 77
69590 Lamure 69M 130 Ed 75
69870 Lamure-sur-Azergues 69D 118 Ec 72
33113 Lanan 33 147 Zd 83
25360 Lanans 25 94 Gc 65
07660 Lanarce 07 141 Ea 80
29860 Lanarvily 29 62 Vd 57
07200 Lanas 07 142 Ec 81
22860 Lancerf 22 63 Wf 56
57245 Lanceumont 57 56 Gb 54
28190 Lancey 28 69 Bb 58
38190 Lancey 38 132 Ff 77
71460 Lancharre 71 118 Ee 69
36200 Lanchâtra 38 144 Ga 79
80230 Lanchères 80 28 Bd 48
80620 Lanches 80 29 Ca 48
73210 Lanches, les 73 133 Ge 75
02590 Lanchy 02 40 Da 50
69220 Lancié 69D 118 Ee 71
22770 Lancieux 22 65 Xf 57
38510 Lancin 38 131 Fc 74
28290 Lancisière 28 69 Ba 60
41190 Lancôme 41 86 Ba 63
08250 Lançon 08 54 Ef 53
32700 Lançon 32 149 Ad 85
65240 Lancon 65 175 Ac 91
13680 Lançon-Provence 13 170 Fa 87
36500 Lancosme 36 101 Bc 68
51120 Lancourt 51 53 De 57
45120 Lancy 45 71 Ce 60
34270 Lancyre 34 154 Df 86
57830 Landange 57 57 Gf 56
29160 Landaoudec 29 61 Vc 59
59310 Landas 59 30 Db 46
56690 Landaul 56 80 Wf 62
88300 Landaville-le-Bas 88 75 Fe 59
88300 Landaville-le-Haut 88 76 Fe 59
35450 Landavran 35 66 Ye 60
14330 Lande 14 34 Yf 53
15310 Lande 15 139 Cc 78
22100 Lande 22 65 Xf 58
36160 Lande 36 114 Ca 69
44650 Lande 44 97 Yc 67
50590 Lande 50 46 Yc 55
50670 Lande 50 46 Yf 56
60110 Lande 60 51 Cb 53
82240 Lande 82 150 Bd 83
24700 Lande, la 24 135 Aa 79
36130 Lande, la 36 101 Be 67
36170 Lande, la 36 113 Bb 69
79200 Lande, la 79 99 Ze 68
82200 Lande, la 82 150 Ba 84
86110 Lande, la 86 99 Zf 68
86700 Lande, la 86 112 Ab 71
35133 Landéan 35 66 Yf 58
22140 Landebaëron 22 63 We 57
22130 Landébia 22 64 Xd 57
22980 Landec, la 22 65 Xe 58
49150 Lande Chasles, la 49 84 Zf 64
54360 Landécourt 54 76 Gc 57
29870 Landéda 29 61 Vc 57
50800 Lande-d'Airou, la 50 46 Ye 56
50700 Lande-de-Beaumont 50 33 Yc 51
33240 Lande-de-Fronsac, la 33 135 Zd 79
61320 Lande-de-Goult, la 61 68 Zf 57
61210 Lande-de-Lougé, la 61 48 Ze 56
29930 Landédéo 29 78 Wb 61
22630 Lande-du-Tournay, la 22 65 Xf 58
50500 Lande-Godard, la 50 34 Ye 53
22400 Landéhen 22 64 Xc 58
29530 Landeleau 29 63 Wb 59
28190 Landelles 28 69 Bb 58
44110 Landelles, les 44 82 Yd 62
14380 Landelles-et-Coupigny 14 47 Za 55
14110 Landemeure 14 47 Zc 55
49270 Landemont 49 82 Ye 65
61100 Lande-Patry, la 61 47 Zc 56
27410 Landepereuse 27 49 Ad 54
29800 Landerneau 29 62 Vd 58
35140 Landeronde 35 66 Yc 59
85150 Landeronde 85 97 Yc 69
33790 Landerrouat 33 136 Aa 80
33540 Landerrouet-sur-Ségur 33 135 Zf 81
68380 Landersen 68 77 Ha 61
67700 Landersheim 67 58 Hc 56
09300 Landes 09 177 Be 91
17380 Landes 17 110 Zc 73
36800 Landes 36 101 Bc 69
46120 Landes, les 46 138 Bf 80
49170 Landes, les 49 83 Zb 64
60590 Landes, les 60 38 Be 52
61350 Landes, les 61 66 Za 57
72170 Landes, les 72 68 Zf 59
72270 Landes, les 72 84 Aa 61
85710 Landes, les 85 96 Yb 67
27210 Lande-Saint-Léger, la 27 48 Ac 53
61100 Lande-Saint-Siméon, la 61 47 Zd 56
14330 Landes-du-Rosey, les 14 47 Yf 53
85130 Landes-Genusson, les 85 97 Yf 67
41190 Landes-les-Gaulois 41 86 Bb 63
14310 Landes-sur-Ajon 14 47 Zc 54
14240 Lande-sur-Drôme, la 14 47 Za 54
61290 Lande-sur-Eure, la 61 69 Af 57
76390 Landes-Vieilles-et-Neuves 76 38 Bd 50
85430 Landette, la 85 97 Yc 69
56690 Landévant 56 80 We 62
14500 Lande-Vaumont, la 14 47 Za 56
29560 Landévennec 29 62 Ve 59
85220 Landevieille 85 96 Yb 69
52270 Landéville 52 75 Fb 58
15160 Landeyrat 15 127 Cf 77
02120 Landifay-et-Bertaignemant 02 40 Dd 50
61100 Landigou 61 47 Zd 56
27350 Landin, le 27 36 Ae 52
33720 Landiras 33 135 Zd 81
61100 Landisacq 61 47 Zc 56
29510 Landivigen 29 78 Wa 60
29400 Landivisiau = Landivizio 29 62 Vf 57
29400 Landivizio = Landivisiau 29 62 Vf 57
53190 Landivy 53 66 Yf 58
63380 Landogne 63 127 Cd 73
57530 Landonvillers 57 56 Gc 54
31800 Landorthe 31 163 Ae 90
43340 Landos 43 141 De 79
87100 Landouge 87 125 Bb 73
33230 Landournerie 33 135 Ze 78
02140 Landouzy-la-Cour 02 41 Df 49
02140 Landouzy-la-Ville 02 41 Ea 49
77370 Landoy 77 72 Db 57
17290 Landrais 17 110 Za 72
88240 Landre, la 88 76 Gb 61
30770 Landre, le 30 153 Dd 85
44320 Landreau, le 44 96 Xf 65
44430 Landreau, le 44 97 Ye 65
59550 Landrecies 59 31 De 48
55100 Landrecourt-Lempire 55 55 Fc 54
22220 Landreger = Treguier 22 63 We 56
54380 Landremont 54 56 Ga 55
57530 Landremont 57 56 Gc 54
54970 Landres 54 43 Fe 53
08240 Landres-et-Saint-Georges 08 42 Fa 52
25530 Landresse 25 94 Gc 65
62250 Landrethun-le-Nord 62 26 Be 43
62610 Landrethun-lès-Ardres 62 27 Bf 44
29510 Landrévarzec 29 78 Vf 60
08240 Landreville 08 42 Fa 52
10110 Landreville 10 74 Ec 60
08600 Landrichamps 08 42 Ee 48
02380 Landricourt 02 40 Dc 51
51290 Landricourt 51 74 Ee 57
57340 Landroff 57 57 Gd 55
49600 Landronnière 49 97 Yf 65
73210 Landry 73 133 Ge 75
68440 Landser 68 95 Hc 62
29510 Landudal 29 78 Wa 60
29710 Landudec 29 78 Vd 60
22160 Landugen 22 63 Wd 58
35360 Landujan 35 65 Ya 59
29840 Landunvez 29 61 Vb 57
77140 Landy, le 77 71 Ce 59
37140 Lane, le 37 84 Ab 65
65190 Lanespède 65 163 Ab 89
56600 Lanester = Lannarstêr 56 79 Wd 62
11330 Lanet 11 178 Cc 91
52400 Laneuvelle 52 92 Fe 61
54280 Laneuvelotte 54 56 Gb 56
54370 Laneuveville-aux-Bois 54 77 Gd 57
54570 Laneuveville-derrière-Foug 54 56 Fe 56
54740 Laneuveville-devant-Bayon 54 76 Gb 58
54410 Laneuveville-devant-Nancy 54 56 Gb 57
57590 Laneuveville-en-Saulnois 57 56 Gc 55
57790 Laneuveville-lès-Lorquin 57 57 Ha 57
55130 Laneuville 55 75 Fc 57
57640 Laneuville 57 56 Gc 53
52170 Laneuville-à-Bayard 52 75 Fa 57
52220 Laneuville-à-Rémy 52 74 Ef 58
52100 Laneuville-au-Pont 52 54 Ef 57
55190 Laneuville-au-Rupt 55 55 Fd 56
52230 Laneuville-aux-Bois 52 75 Fc 58
60190 Laneuvilleroy 60 39 Cd 52
55700 Laneuville-sur-Meuse 55 42 Fa 52
22800 Lanfains 22 64 Xa 58
29810 Lanfeust 29 61 Vb 58
54760 Lanfroicourt 54 56 Gb 56
22360 Langaeg = Langueux 22 64 Xb 58
29530 Langalet 29 62 Wa 59
35850 Langan 35 65 Ya 59
22150 Langast 22 64 Xc 59
57400 Langatte 57 57 Gf 56
22460 Langaury 22 64 Xa 58
88170 Langchamp-sous-Châtenois 88 76 Fe 59
04200 Lange 04 156 Fe 84
36600 Langé 36 101 Bd 66
43300 Langeac 43 140 Dc 78
37130 Langeais 37 85 Ac 65
16320 Langely 16 124 Ab 76
37390 Langennerie 37 85 Ae 64
67360 Langensoultzbach 67 58 He 55
29440 Langeoguer 29 62 Vf 57
40460 Langeot 40 134 Yf 81
18600 Langeron 18 103 Cf 68
58240 Langeron 58 103 Da 68
45290 Langesse 45 88 Cd 62
28220 Langey 28 69 Bb 60
74890 Langin 74 120 Gc 71
19100 Langlade 19 137 Bc 78
24360 Langlade 24 124 Ad 74
24590 Langlade 24 137 Bb 79
30980 Langlade 30 154 Eb 86
34220 Langlade 34 166 Ce 87
43170 Langlade 43 140 Dd 78
87460 Langlard 87 126 Be 74
29360 Langlazic 29 79 Wc 62
56860 Langle 56 80 Xb 63
44130 Langlechais 44 82 Yb 63
23320 Langledure 23 114 Be 71
88130 Langley 88 76 Gb 58
58250 Langlois 58 104 De 68
22450 Langoat 22 63 We 56
56160 Langoëlan 56 79 We 60
48300 Langogne 48 141 Df 80
33550 Langoiran 33 135 Zd 80
29510 Langolen 29 78 Wa 60
56690 Langombrac'h 56 80 Wf 62
33210 Langon 33 135 Ze 81
35660 Langon 35 82 Ya 62
41320 Langon 41 87 Be 65
73730 Langon 73 132 Gc 75
85370 Langon, le 85 110 Za 70
56630 Langonnet 56 79 Wd 60
35630 Langouet 35 65 Yb 59
22330 Langourla 22 64 Xd 59
52200 Langres Corlée 52 92 Fb 61
56400 Langroix 56 80 Xa 62
56400 Langroix 56 80 We 62
22490 Langrolay-sur-Rance 22 65 Xf 57
14750 Langrune-sur-Mer 14 47 Zd 53
22980 Languédias 22 65 Xe 58
22130 Languénan 22 65 Xf 57
44440 Langueurs 44 82 Yd 63

Langueurs | 281

22360 Langueux = Langaeg 22 64 Xb 58
80190 Languevoisin 80 39 Cf 50
56440 Languidic 56 79 Wf 62
57810 Languimberg 57 57 Gf 56
44390 Languin 44 82 Yc 64
29720 Languivoa 29 78 Ve 61
03150 Langy 03 116 Dc 71
35720 Lanhélin 35 65 Yb 58
22110 Lanhellen 22 63 Wd 59
55400 Lanhères 55 55 Fe 53
29890 Lanhir 29 62 Vd 57
29430 Lanhouarneau 29 62 Ve 57
29530 Lanignac 29 62 Wb 59
47700 Lanin, le 47 148 Aa 83
57660 Laning 57 57 Ge 54
22570 Laniscat 22 63 Wf 59
02000 Laniscourt 02 40 Dd 51
22290 Lanleff 22 63 Wf 56
29610 Lanleya 29 63 Wb 57
22580 Lanloup 22 63 Xa 56
60650 Lanlu 60 38 Bf 52
22300 Lanmérin 22 63 Wd 56
22800 Lanmeur 29 79 Wb 61
56480 Lanmeur 56 79 Wf 59
29620 Lanmeur = Lanneur 29 63 Wb 57
22610 Lanmodez 22 63 Wf 55
29530 Lannac'h 29 63 Wb 59
56600 Lannarstêr = Lanester 56 79 Wd 62
59310 Lannay 59 30 Db 45
65380 Lanne 65 162 Aa 90
29640 Lannéanou 29 63 Wb 58
22290 Lannebert 22 64 Wf 57
29880 Lannebeur 29 61 Vd 57
64350 Lannecaube 64 162 Ze 88
29190 Lannédern 29 62 Wa 59
64570 Lanne-en-Barétous 64 161 Zb 90
64350 Lannegrasse 64 162 Zf 88
29340 Lannéguy 29 79 Wb 62
29190 Lannelec 29 62 Wa 59
32240 Lannemaignan 32 147 Ze 85
65300 Lannemezan 65 163 Ac 90
56270 Lannénec 56 79 Wc 62
32190 Lannepax 32 148 Ab 86
64300 Lanneplaà 64 161 Zb 88
28200 Lanneray 28 69 Bb 60
31160 Lannes 31 176 Af 90
47170 Lannes 47 148 Ab 84
52260 Lannes 52 75 Fb 61
65190 Lannès 65 163 Ab 89
32550 Lannes, les 32 163 Ad 87
32110 Lanne-Soubiran 32 162 Zf 86
29400 Lanneuffret 29 62 Ve 58
29260 Lanneunval 29 62 Vd 57
29620 Lanneur = Lanmeur 29 63 Wb 57
29233 Lanneusfeld 29 62 Vf 57
22620 Lannevez 22 63 Wf 56
22570 Lannilien 29 61 Vc 59
29870 Lannilis = Lanniliz 29 61 Vc 57
29870 Lanniliz = Lannilis 29 61 Vc 57
22300 Lannion = Lannuon 22 63 Wd 56
29340 Lann-Lothan 29 78 Wb 62
56440 Lann-Menhir 56 80 Wf 61
29260 Lannoazoc 29 62 Vd 57
22290 Lannolon = Lannvollon 22 63 Xa 57
29860 Lannon 29 62 Vd 58
22350 Lannouée 22 65 Xe 58
59390 Lannoy 59 30 Db 45
60220 Lannoy-Cuillère 60 38 Be 50
29790 Lannuign 29 61 Vc 60
56110 Lannuon 56 63 Wc 60
22300 Lannuon = Lannion 22 63 Wd 56
29430 Lannurien 29 62 Ve 57
32400 Lannux 32 162 Ze 87
20244 Lano CTC 183 Kb 94
15270 Lanobre 15 127 Cd 76
29380 Lanorgar 29 79 Wc 61
33770 Lanot 33 134 Za 81
24270 Lanouaille 24 125 Ba 76
56120 Lanouée 56 64 Xc 60
19300 Lanour 19 126 Bf 76
09130 Lanoux 09 164 Bc 90
24150 Lanquais 24 136 Ae 80
52800 Lanques-sur-Rognon 52 75 Fc 60
76210 Lanquetot 76 36 Ad 51
22220 Lanrelas 22 64 Xe 59
29900 Lanriec 29 78 Wa 61
35270 Lanrigan 35 65 Yb 58
22480 Lanrivain 22 63 We 58
29290 Lanrivoaré 29 61 Vc 58
22170 Lanrodec 22 64 Wf 57
71380 Lans 71 106 Ef 68
13150 Lansac 13 155 Ed 86
33710 Lansac 33 135 Zc 78
66720 Lansac 66 179 Cd 92
22340 Lansalaün 22 63 Wd 59
34130 Lansargues 34 168 Ea 87
38250 Lans-en-Vercors 38 143 Fd 78
73480 Lanslebourg-Mont-Cenis 73 133 Gf 77
73480 Lanslevillard 73 133 Gf 77
31570 Lanta 31 165 Bd 87
10210 Lantages 10 73 Eb 60
18130 Lantan 18 103 Cd 67
54150 Lantéfontaine 54 56 Ff 53
01430 Lantenay 01 119 Fd 72
21370 Lantenay 21 91 Ef 64
25170 Lantenne-Vertière 25 107 Fe 65
70200 Lantenot 70 94 Gc 62
70270 Lanterne-et-les-Armonts, la 70 94 Gd 62
19190 Lanteuil 19 138 Bd 78
22210 Lanthenac 22 64 Xc 60
43320 Lanthenas 43 141 De 78
21250 Lanthes 21 106 Fb 67
14480 Lantheuil 14 35 Zc 53
22410 Lantic 22 64 Xa 57
56190 Lantiern 56 81 Xd 63
69430 Lantignié 69D 118 Ed 72
56120 Lantillac 56 80 Xc 61
21140 Lantilly 21 91 Ec 63
16200 Lantin 16 123 Zf 74
33138 Lanton 33 134 Yf 80
06450 Lantosque 06 159 Hb 85
22830 Lantran 22 65 Ya 59
43260 Lantriac 43 141 Ea 78
58250 Lanty 58 104 Df 68
52120 Lanty-sur-Aube 52 74 Ee 60
20244 Lanu = Lano CTC 183 Kb 94
30750 Lanuéjols 30 153 Dc 84
48000 Lanuéjols 48 141 Dd 81
12350 Lanuéjouls 12 151 Ca 82
65190 Lanusse 65 163 Ab 90
22100 Lanvallay 22 65 Xf 58
29880 Lanvaon 29 61 Vc 57
56240 Lanvaudan 56 80 We 61
22420 Lanvellec 22 63 Wc 57
29550 Lanvelliau 29 62 Vd 60
29290 Lanvenec 29 61 Vc 58
56320 Lanvénégen 56 79 Wc 61
29160 Lanvéoc 29 61 Vd 59
29233 Lanveur 29 62 Vf 57
56440 Lanveur 56 80 Wf 61
22300 Lanvézéac 22 63 Wd 56
22800 Lanvia 22 64 Xa 58
22470 Lanvian 22 63 Wf 56
29150 Lanvian 29 62 Ve 59
29800 Lanviguer 29 62 Ve 58
16140 Lanville 16 123 Aa 73
22290 Lanvollon 22 63 Xa 57
29460 Lanvoy 29 62 Ve 59
29470 Lanvrizan 29 62 Vd 58
22270 Lanyugon = Jugon-les-Lacs 22 64 Xe 58
46200 Lanzac 46 138 Bc 79
02000 Laon 02 40 Dd 51
28270 Laons 28 49 Bb 56
47230 Laou 47 148 Ab 84
83330 Laouque 83 171 Fe 89
03120 Lapalisse 03 116 Dd 71
84840 Lapalud 84 155 Ee 83
18340 Lapan 18 102 Cb 67
12150 Lapanouse 12 152 Da 82
12230 Lapanouse-de-Cernon 12 152 Da 85
47260 Laparade 47 148 Ac 82
81640 Laparrouquial 81 151 Ca 84
56550 Lapaul 56 79 Wf 62
20233 Lapedina CTC 181 Kc 91
09400 Lapège 09 177 Bd 92
63390 Lapeize 63 115 Ce 72
82240 Lapenche 82 150 Bd 83
65220 Lapène 65 163 Ac 89
09500 Lapenne 09 165 Be 90
50600 Lapenty 50 66 Yf 57
47800 Laperche 47 136 Ac 81
26210 Laperouse-Mornay 26 130 Ef 77
21450 Laperrière 21 91 Ee 63
21170 Laperrière-sur-Saône 21 106 Fc 66
40240 Lapeyrade 40 148 Zf 84
12400 Lapeyre 12 152 Cf 85
40090 Lapeyre 40 147 Zd 85
65220 Lapeyre 65 163 Ac 89
31310 Lapeyrère 31 164 Bb 89
81310 Lapeyrière 81 150 Be 85
82170 Lapeyrière 82 150 Bb 85
01330 Lapeyrouse 01 118 Ef 73
63700 Lapeyrouse 63 115 Cf 71
31180 Lapeyrouse-Fossat 31 165 Bd 86
15120 Lapeyrugue 15 139 Cd 80
24800 Lapeyzie 24 125 Ba 76
33190 Lapierre 33 135 Zf 81
47500 Lapile 47 137 Ba 81
64120 Lapiste 64 161 Yf 89
16270 Laplaud 16 112 Ad 73
19550 Lapleau 19 126 Cb 77
47310 Laplume 47 149 Ad 84
46140 Lapoujade 46 137 Bc 82
24510 Lapouleille 24 136 Ad 79
33370 Lapourcaud 33 135 Zf 79
68650 Lapoutroie 68 60 Ha 60
33620 Lapouyade 33 135 Ze 78
02150 Lappion 02 41 Df 51
11390 Laprade 11 166 Cb 88
16390 Laprade 16 124 Ab 77
11390 Laprade-Basse 11 166 Cb 88
11140 Lapradelle 11 178 Cb 92
43500 Laprat 43 129 Df 77
35640 Lâpre 35 82 Yd 61
03250 Laprugne 03 116 De 73
63270 Laps 63 128 Db 74
87380 Laps 87 125 Bc 75
43200 Lapte 43 129 Eb 77
62122 Lapugnoy 62 29 Cd 45
57530 Laquenexy 57 56 Gb 54
63820 Laqueuille 63 127 Ce 75
63820 Laqueuille-Gare 63 127 Ce 75
11560 Laquirou 11 167 Da 89
09200 Lara 09 176 Ba 90
05300 Laragne-Montéglin 05 157 Fe 83
69590 Larajasse 69M 130 Ed 75
46260 Laramière 46 151 Bf 82
31700 Laran 31 164 Bb 87
65670 Laran 65 163 Ac 89
40250 Larbey 40 161 Zb 86
24130 Larbogne 24 136 Ab 79
60400 Larbroye 60 39 Cf 51
31800 Larcan 31 163 Ae 89
09310 Larcat 09 177 Bd 92
17520 Larceau-les-Corbinaux 17 123 Zd 75
43800 Larcenac 43 141 Df 78
64120 Larceveau-Arros-Cibits 64 161 Yf 89
53220 Larchamp 53 66 Yf 58
61800 Larchamp 61 47 Zb 56
77760 Larchant 77 71 Cd 59
04530 Larche 04 158 Gf 82
19600 Larche 19 137 Bc 78
47210 Larche 47 137 Ae 80
46240 Larcher 46 138 Bd 80
33650 Larchey 33 135 Zc 80
21580 Larçon 21 91 Ef 63
24530 Lardailler 24 124 Ae 76
82330 Lardailles 82 151 Bf 83
12240 Lardayrolles 12 151 Cc 83
39300 Larderet, le 39 107 Ff 68
35450 Larderie, la 35 66 Ye 59
60110 Lardières 60 51 Ca 53
05110 Lardier-et-Valença 05 157 Ff 82
04230 Lardiers 04 156 Fe 84
87260 Lardimalie 87 125 Bc 75
24570 Lardin-Saint-Lazare, le 24 137 Bb 78
91510 Lardy 91 71 Cb 57
81290 Larécuquèle 81 166 Cb 87
11700 Laredorte 11 166 Cd 89
32150 Larée 32 148 Zf 85
31480 Laréole 31 164 Ba 86
19170 Larfeuil 19 126 Bf 75
19170 Larfeuil 19 126 Bf 75
79240 Largeasse 79 98 Zd 68
07110 Largentière 07 142 Eb 81
85220 Largerie, la 85 96 Yb 68
03130 Larges, les 03 117 Df 70
39130 Largillay-Marsonnay 39 119 Fe 69
68580 Largitzen 68 95 Hb 63
02600 Largny-sur-Automne 02 52 Da 53
22970 Largoat 22 63 We 57
04150 Largue, le 04 156 Fe 84
70230 Larians-et-Munans 70 93 Gb 64
46270 Larive 46 139 Cb 80
24150 Larives 24 137 Ae 79
33290 Larivière 33 134 Zc 79
90150 Larivière 90 94 Gf 62
52400 Larivière-Arnoncourt 52 75 Fe 60
31230 Larjo 31 163 Ae 88
31530 Larmont 31 164 Bb 87
56550 Larmor 56 80 We 62
56690 Larmor 56 79 Wf 62
56870 Larmor-Baden 56 80 Xa 63
56260 Larmor-Plage 56 79 Wd 62
30700 Larnac 30 154 Ec 84
33340 Larnac 33 122 Za 76
26600 Larnage 26 142 Ef 78
46160 Larnagol 46 138 Be 82
12290 Larnaldesq 12 152 Ce 83
07220 Larnas 07 155 Ed 82
09310 Larnat 09 177 Bd 92
39140 Larnaud 39 106 Fc 68
25720 Larnod 25 107 Ff 65
24440 Larocal 24 136 Ae 80
43360 Laroche 43 128 Db 77
58370 Larochemillay 58 104 Ea 67
19340 Laroche-près-Feyt 19 127 Cd 74
89400 Laroche-Saint-Cydroine 89 72 Dc 61
85000 La-Roche-sur-Yon 85 97 Yd 68
63690 Larodde 63 127 Cd 75
64110 Laroin 64 162 Zd 89
54950 Laronxe 54 77 Gd 57
12360 Laroque 12 152 Cf 86
24550 Laroque 24 137 Ba 80
33410 Laroque 33 135 Ze 81
33910 Laroque 33 135 Ze 78
34190 Laroque 34 153 De 85
15150 Laroquebrou 15 139 Cb 79
11330 Laroque-de-Fa 11 179 Cd 91
66740 Laroque-des-Albères 66 179 Cf 93
46090 Laroque-des-Arcs 46 138 Bc 82
09600 Laroque-d'Olmes 09 177 Bf 91
47340 Laroque-Timbaut 47 149 Ae 83
15250 Laroquevieille 15 139 Cc 78
47410 Larougie 47 136 Ac 81
59219 Larouillies 59 31 Df 48
24800 Laroulandie 24 125 Af 75
32360 Larrama 32 163 Ad 86
64120 Larrandaberry 64 161 Za 89
64560 Larrau 64 174 Za 90
82500 Larrazet 82 149 Ba 85
24120 Larre 24 125 Bb 77
56230 Larré 56 81 Xc 62
61250 Larré 61 68 Aa 58
32100 Larressingle 32 148 Ab 85
64480 Larressore 64 160 Yd 88
29840 Larret 29 61 Vb 57
33660 Larret 33 135 Zf 78
70600 Larret 70 92 Fd 63
64410 Larreule 64 162 Zd 88
65700 Larreule 65 162 Aa 88
21330 Larrey 21 91 Ec 61
29160 Larrial 29 61 Vc 59
64120 Larribar-Sorhapuru 64 161 Yf 89
65400 Larribet 65 174 Ze 91
31160 Larrigau 31 176 Af 90
74500 Larringes 74 120 Gd 70
40270 Larrivière 40 147 Zd 86
39360 Larrivoire 39 119 Fe 70
31580 Larroque 31 163 Ad 89
32700 Larroque 32 149 Ad 85
65230 Larroque 65 163 Ac 89
81140 Larroque 81 150 Be 84
81270 Larroque 81 166 Cd 88
32480 Larroque-Engalin 32 149 Ad 85
32410 Larroque-Saint-Sernin 32 148 Ac 86
32100 Larroque-sur-L'Osse 32 148 Ab 85
46160 Larroque-Toirac 46 138 Bf 81
64130 Larrory 64 161 Za 89
32220 Larroucau 32 164 Ae 88
32800 Larroudé 32 148 Aa 85
32450 Larrouly 32 163 Ae 87
32500 Larroumiouac 32 149 Ad 85
40200 Larrousseau 40 146 Yf 83
64490 Larry 64 174 Zc 91
24400 Lartige 24 136 Ab 78
87400 Lartige 87 125 Bd 74
32290 Lartigue 32 162 Aa 86
32450 Lartigue 32 163 Ae 87
33220 Lartigue 33 136 Ab 79
33840 Lartigue 33 148 Zf 83
40090 Lartigue 40 147 Zd 86
33680 Laruau 33 134 Yf 79
64440 Laruns 64 174 Zd 91
33620 Laruscade 33 135 Zd 78
24170 Larzac 24 137 Ba 80
51290 Larzicourt 51 54 Ee 57
02580 Larzille 02 41 Df 49
32190 Las 32 163 Ab 86
33127 Las, le 33 134 Za 80
30460 Lasalle 30 153 Df 84
65190 las Barthes 65 163 Ab 89
12500 Lasbinals 12 139 Ce 81
11400 Lasbordes 11 165 Ca 89
64270 Lasbordes 64 161 Za 88
46800 Lasbouygues 46 149 Bb 82
12470 Lasbros 12 139 Cf 81
40420 Lasbroudes 40 147 Zd 84
46800 Lascabanes 46 150 Bb 82
09200 las Cabesses 09 177 Bb 91
23170 Lascau 23 115 Cc 71
23500 Lascaud-Maury 23 126 Ca 73
23500 Lascaus 23 127 Cb 74
19130 Lascaux 19 125 Bc 76
65700 Lascazères 65 162 Zf 87
63122 Laschamp 63 128 Cf 74
64450 Lasclaveries 64 162 Ze 88
24800 las Combas 24 125 Af 76
13360 Lascours 13 171 Fd 88
09800 Lascoux 09 176 Af 91
16450 Lascoux 16 112 Ad 73
87290 Lascoux 87 113 Bb 72
24700 Laser 24 135 Aa 78
24270 las Fargeas 24 125 Ba 76
09240 Lasfittes 09 177 Bc 90
48130 Lasfonds 48 140 Db 80
16490 Lasfont 16 112 Ad 72
81300 Lasgraisses 81 151 Ca 86
66480 las Illas 66 179 Ce 94
65350 Laslades 65 163 Ab 89
40240 Laslangaches 40 148 Ze 84
15190 Lasparet 15 127 Ce 76
32250 Laspeyres 32 148 Ab 85
47270 Laspeyres 47 149 Ae 84
81190 las Planques 81 151 Cb 84
64330 Lasque 64 162 Zf 87
18220 Lass 18 102 Cd 65
11600 Lassac 11 166 Cc 89
65670 Lassales 65 163 Ac 89
64520 Lassarrade 64 160 Ye 88
53110 Lassay-les-Châteaux 53 67 Zd 58
41230 Lassay-sur-Croisne 41 87 Bd 64
49490 Lasse 49 84 Aa 63
64220 Lasse 64 160 Ye 90
32550 Lasséran 32 163 Ad 87
09230 Lassere 09 164 Bb 90
44370 Lasseron 44 83 Za 64
01250 Lasserra 01 119 Fc 71
64300 Lasserrade 64 161 Zb 88
24310 Lasserre 24 124 Ad 77
32350 Lasserre 32 163 Ac 86
32400 Lasserre 32 162 Ze 87
47420 Lasserre 47 148 Aa 83
47600 Lasserre 47 148 Ac 84
64350 Lasserre 64 162 Zf 87
11270 Lasserre-de-Prouille 11 165 Ca 89
31530 Lasserre-Pradère 31 164 Bb 87
64290 Lasseube 64 162 Zd 89
32550 Lasseube-Propre 32 163 Ad 87
32430 Lasseubes 32 164 Af 86
64290 Lasseubetat 64 162 Zd 89
63160 Lassias 63 128 Db 74
10500 Lassicourt 10 74 Ec 58
60310 Lassigny 60 39 Ce 51
14740 Lasson 14 35 Zd 53
89570 Lasson 89 73 De 60
18160 Lassout 18 102 Ca 68
12500 Lassouts 12 139 Cf 82
81260 Lassouts 81 166 Cd 87
09310 Lassur 09 177 Be 92
33113 Lassus 33 147 Zd 82
88240 Lassus 88 76 Gc 61
14770 Lassy 14 47 Zb 55
35580 Lassy 35 65 Ya 61
50250 Lastelle 50 46 Yd 53
09200 Lastès 09 177 Bb 91
19240 Lasteyrie 19 125 Bc 77
15500 Lastic 15 140 Db 78
63760 Lastic 63 127 Cd 74
15500 Lastiguet 15 140 Db 78
11490 Lastours 11 179 Cf 90
46800 Lastours 46 150 Ba 82
82440 Lastours 82 150 Bc 84
87800 Lastours 87 125 Ba 75
47500 Lastreilles 47 137 Af 81
16190 Lataiteau 16 124 Ab 76
26110 Latards, les 26 155 Fb 82
60490 Lataule 60 39 Ce 51
83870 Latay, le 83 171 Ff 89
39300 Latet, le 39 107 Ff 68
39250 Latette, la 39 107 Ga 68
15100 Latga 15 140 Cf 78
87190 Lathière 87 113 Ba 71
74210 Lathuile 74 132 Gb 74
86390 Lathus-Saint-Rémy 86 112 Af 71
86190 Latillé 86 99 Aa 69
02210 Latilly 02 52 Db 54
45430 Latingy 45 87 Ca 61
31800 Latoue 31 163 Ae 89
46400 Latouille-Lentillac 46 138 Bf 79
12540 Latour 12 152 Da 85
31310 Latour 31 164 Bb 89
43700 Latour 43 141 Df 78
66200 Latour-Bas-Elne 66 179 Da 93
66760 Latour-de-Carol 66 178 Bf 94
66720 Latour-de-France 66 179 Cd 92
55160 Latour-en-Woëvre 55 56 Fe 54
24800 Latrade 24 125 Ba 76
31310 Latrape 31 164 Bb 89
52120 Latrecey-Ormoy 52 74 Ef 61
33360 Latresne 33 135 Zd 80
40800 Latrille 40 162 Ze 87
19160 Latronche 19 126 Cb 77
46210 Latronquière 46 138 Ca 80
18120 Lats, les 18 102 Ca 66
60240 Lattainville 60 50 Be 53
87310 Latterie 87 125 Af 74
34970 Lattes 34 168 Df 87
06850 Lattes, les 06 158 Ge 86
62810 Lattre-Saint-Quentin 62 29 Cd 47
34520 Latude 34 153 Dc 85
72300 laTuilerie 72 84 Ze 62
32110 Lau 32 148 Zf 86
34390 Lau, le 34 167 Da 87
67580 Laubach 67 58 He 55
31160 Laubague 31 176 Ae 91
24130 Laubanie 24 136 Ac 79
19250 Laubard 19 126 Ca 75
48300 Laubarnès 48 141 De 81
67190 Laubenheim 67 60 Hc 58
48170 Laubert 48 141 Dd 81
16170 Laubertière 16 123 Zf 74
48700 Laubespin 48 140 Dc 81
15320 Laubie, la 15 140 Db 79
48000 Laubies, les 48 153 Dd 82
48700 Laubies, les 48 140 Dc 80
64230 Laubiosse 64 162 Zd 88
04330 Laubre 04 157 Gc 84
79350 Laubreçais 79 98 Zd 67
10270 Laubressel 10 73 Eb 59
41140 Laubrière 41 86 Bc 65
53540 Laubrières 53 66 Yf 61
09200 Lauch 09 177 Bb 91
80700 Laucourt 80 39 Ce 50
03300 Laudemarière 03 116 Dc 71
76220 Laudencourt 76 38 Be 51
24290 Laudigerie 24 137 Ba 78
28250 Laudigerie 28 69 Ba 57
32420 Laudine 32 164 Ae 88
24420 Laudinie 24 125 Af 77
24210 Laudonnie 24 125 Ba 77
57385 Laudrefang 57 57 Gd 54
30290 Laudun 30 155 Ed 84
47360 Laugnac 47 149 Ad 83
50380 Laugny 50 46 Yd 56
33340 Laujac 33 122 Za 76
32110 Laujuzan 32 148 Zf 86
33210 Laulan 33 135 Zd 81
50430 Laulne 50 33 Yd 53
34700 Laulo 34 167 Dc 86
46200 Laumède 46 138 Bd 79
48230 Laumède 48 153 Dc 82
21150 Laumes, les 21 91 Ec 63
57480 Laumesfeld 57 44 Gc 52
46500 Laumière 46 138 Be 80
85710 Laumière, la 85 96 Ya 67
19190 Laumont 19 138 Be 78
31330 Launac 31 149 Bb 86
34690 Launac-Saint-André 34 168 De 87
31140 Launaguet 31 164 Bc 86
22210 Launay 22 64 Xc 60
22240 Launay 22 64 Xd 57
36500 Launay 36 101 Bc 67
36600 Launay 36 101 Bd 65
44640 Launay 44 96 Yb 65
45190 Launay 45 86 Bd 61
79100 Launay 79 99 Ze 67
53410 Launay-Villiers 53 66 Yf 60
06470 Launes, les 06 158 Gf 84
08430 Launois-sur-Vence 08 41 Ed 51
02210 Launoy 02 52 Dc 53
57480 Launstroff 57 44 Gc 52
26740 Laupie, la 26 142 Ef 81
30750 Laupies 30 153 Dc 84
30750 Laupiettes 30 153 Dc 84
11400 Laurabuc-et-Mireval 11 165 Bf 89
11270 Laurac 11 165 Bf 89
32130 Laurac 32 164 Ae 87
07110 Laurac-en-Vivarais 07 142 Eb 81
32330 Lauraët 32 148 Ab 85
11300 Lauraguel 11 165 Cb 90
12250 Lauras 12 152 Cf 85
13180 Laure 13 170 Fb 88
40250 Laurède 40 147 Zb 86
11800 Laure-Minervois 11 166 Cd 89
22230 Laurenan 22 64 Xc 59
34480 Laurens 34 167 Db 87
81200 Laurens 81 166 Cb 88
24330 Laurent 24 136 Ae 78
42830 Laurent 42 116 De 73
19400 Laurent, le 19 138 Bf 78
03250 Laurents, les 03 116 De 72
47150 Laures 47 136 Ae 81
46210 Lauresses 46 138 Ca 80
34270 Lauret 34 154 Df 85
40320 Lauret 40 162 Zd 87
15500 Laurie 15 128 Da 77
46140 Laurie, la 46 149 Bb 82
59630 Laurier, le 59 27 Cb 43
87500 Lauriéras 87 125 Bb 75
87370 Laurière 87 113 Bc 72
84360 Lauris 84 170 Fb 86
33680 Lauros 33 134 Yf 79
34700 Lauroux 34 153 Db 86
05100 Laus, le 05 145 Ge 79
12600 Laussac 12 139 Ce 79
47230 Lausseignan 47 148 Ab 83
82140 Laussier 82 150 Be 84
43150 Laussonne 43 141 Ea 79
47150 Laussou 47 137 Ae 81
04340 Lautaret 04 157 Gb 82
43620 Lautat 43 129 Eb 77
68610 Lautenbach 68 60 Ha 61
68610 Lautenbachzell 68 95 Ha 61
67630 Lauterbourg 67 59 Ib 55
24420 Lauterie 24 125 Af 77
88520 Lauterupt 88 77 Ha 59
86300 Lauthiers 86 100 Ae 69
31370 Lautignac 31 164 Ba 88
16200 Lautrait 16 123 Zf 74
81440 Lautrec 81 165 Ca 86
89630 Lautreville 89 90 Df 64
24510 Lauturie 24 136 Ae 79
19270 Lauvinerie 19 126 Bd 77
33230 Lauvirat 33 135 Zf 78
68290 Lauw 68 94 Ha 62
59553 Lauwin 59 30 Da 46
26510 Laux-Montaux 26 156 Fd 83
56190 Lauzach 56 81 Xc 63
83340 Lauzade, la 83 172 Gb 88
87120 Lauzat 87 126 Bf 74
06450 Lauze, la 06 159 Hc 84

282 | **Langueux**

24380 Lauzellie 24 136 Ae 78
46270 Lauzeral 46 138 Ca 81
82110 Lauzerte 82 150 Ba 83
31650 Lauzerville 31 165 Bd 87
46360 Lauzès 46 138 Bd 81
05220 Lauzet, le 05 145 Gc 78
05310 Lauzet, le 05 145 Gd 80
04340 Lauzet-Ubaye, le 04 157 Gc 82
17137 Lauzières 17 110 Ye 71
17260 Lauzignac 17 122 Zc 75
23450 Lauzine 23 113 Be 70
47410 Lauzun 47 136 Ac 81
60120 Lavacquerie 60 38 Ca 50
12360 Lavagne 12 152 Da 86
48500 Lavagne, la 48 153 Db 82
34150 Lavagnes, les 34 153 Dc 86
09110 Lavail 09 178 Bf 92
81260 Lavaissière 81 166 Cc 86
07210 Laval 07 142 Ed 80
07250 Laval 07 142 Ee 80
12360 Laval 12 152 Da 85
19250 Laval 19 126 Ca 75
19290 Laval 19 126 Ca 75
24590 Laval 24 137 Bc 78
31290 Laval 31 165 Bd 88
38190 Laval 38 132 Ff 77
42131 Laval 42 130 Ec 76
53000 Laval 53 67 Zb 60
63700 Laval 63 115 Ce 72
81140 Laval 81 150 Be 85
81340 Laval 81 152 Cc 85
24260 Lavalade 24 137 Ae 79
24540 Lavalade 24 137 Af 80
48600 Laval-Atger 48 141 De 80
26150 Laval-d'Aix 26 143 Fc 80
07590 Laval-d'Aurelle 07 141 Df 81
38350 Lavaldens 38 144 Ff 79
08260 Laval-d'Estrebay 08 41 Ec 50
08800 Laval-Dieu 08 42 Ee 49
48500 Laval-du-Tarn 48 153 Dc 82
77148 Laval-en-Brie 77 72 Cf 58
02860 Laval-en-Laonnois 02 40 Dd 51
11290 Lavalette 11 166 Cb 89
31590 Lavalette 31 165 Bd 87
34700 Lavalette 34 167 Db 86
19330 Lavalgrière 19 126 Be 77
29140 Lavalhars 29 78 Wb 61
66690 Lavall 66 179 Cf 93
16310 Lavallade 16 124 Ad 74
63320 Lavalle 63 128 Da 75
55260 Lavallée 55 55 Fc 56
08150 Laval-Morency 08 41 Ec 50
12380 Laval-Roquecezière 12 152 Cd 86
30760 Laval-Saint Roman 30 155 Ed 83
43440 Laval-sur-Doulon 43 128 Dd 76
19550 Laval-sur-Luzège 19 126 Cb 77
51600 Laval-sur-Tourbe 51 54 Ee 54
88600 Laval-sur-Vologne 88 77 Ge 59
74400 Lavancher, le 74 121 Gf 73
01590 Lavancia-Epercy 01 119 Fe 71
20246 Lavandaghju = Lavandaju CTC 181 Kb 93
20246 Lavandaju CTC 181 Kb 93
83980 Lavandou, le 83 172 Gc 90
39700 Lavangeot 39 107 Fd 66
51110 Lavannes 51 41 Eb 53
39700 Lavans-lès-Dole 39 107 Fd 66
39170 Lavans-lès-Saint-Claude 39 119 Fe 70
25440 Lavans-Quingey 25 107 Ff 66
39240 Lavans-sur-Valouse 39 119 Fd 70
25580 Lavans-Vuillafans 25 107 Gb 66
02450 Lavaqueresse 02 40 De 49
47230 Lavardac 47 148 Ab 83
32360 Lavardens 32 149 Ad 86
41800 Lavardin 41 85 Af 62
72240 Lavardin 72 68 Aa 60
72390 Lavaré 72 69 Ad 60
38710 Lavars 38 144 Fe 79
20222 Lavasina CTC 181 Kc 92
19300 Lavastre, la 19 126 Bf 76
15260 Lavastrie 15 140 Da 79
20225 Lavatoggio CTC 180 If 93
10150 Lavau 10 73 Ea 59
41370 Lavau 41 86 Bd 62
89170 Lavau 89 88 Cf 63
16700 Lavaud 16 111 Ab 72
23800 Lavaud 23 114 Be 71
79320 Lavaud 79 98 Zc 68
85320 Lavaud 85 109 Ye 69
87130 Lavaud 87 126 Bd 74
87270 Lavaud 87 113 Bb 73
43100 Lavaudieu 43 128 Dc 77
23600 Lavaufranche 23 114 Cb 71
58140 Lavault 58 104 Df 65
58230 Lavault-de-Frétoy 58 104 Ea 66
03100 Lavault-Sainte Anne 03 115 Cd 71
19250 Lavaur 19 126 Ca 75
24550 Lavaur 24 137 Ba 81
81500 Lavaur 81 165 Be 86
24400 Lavaure 24 136 Ac 78
82240 Lavaurette 82 150 Be 83
03410 Lavaury 03 115 Cc 71
86470 Lavausseau 86 111 Aa 69
44260 Lavau-sur-Loire 44 81 Ya 65
89630 Lavauts, les 89 90 Ea 65
71120 Lavaux 71 117 Eb 70
23150 Lavaveix-les-Mines 23 114 Ca 72
33690 Lavazan 33 148 Zf 82
36340 Laveau 36 114 Be 69
15300 Laveissenet 15 139 Cf 78
15300 Laveissière 15 139 Ce 78
09300 Lavelanet 09 177 Bf 91
31220 Lavelanet-de-Comminges 31 164 Ba 89
88600 Laveline-devant-Bruyères 88 77 Ge 59
88640 Laveline-du-Houx 88 77 Ge 60
72310 Lavenay 72 85 Ae 62
12100 Lavencas 12 152 Da 84
29260 Lavengat 29 62 Vd 57
62840 Laventie 62 30 Ce 45
13117 Lavéra 13 170 Fa 88
32230 Laveraët 32 163 Ab 87
46340 Lavercantière 46 137 Bb 81
18800 Laverdines 18 103 Ce 66
56450 Laverdon 56 80 Xc 63
12800 Lavergne 12 151 Cb 83
15190 Lavergne 15 127 Ce 76
19700 Lavergne 19 126 Be 76
24270 Lavergne 24 125 Ba 76
46500 Lavergne 46 138 Be 80
47800 Lavergne 47 136 Ac 81
72500 Lavernat 72 85 Ab 62
25170 Lavernay 25 107 Fe 65
12150 Lavernhe 12 152 Da 83
31410 Lavernose-Lacasse 31 164 Bb 88
52140 Lavernoy 52 92 Fd 61
86340 Laverré 86 112 Ab 70
60210 Laverrière 60 38 Ca 50
02600 Laversine 02 52 Db 52
60510 Laversines 60 38 Cb 52
34880 Lavérune 34 168 De 87
38520 Lavey, la 38 144 Gb 79
26240 Laveyron 26 130 Ee 77
48250 Laveyrune 48 141 Df 81
24130 Laveyssière 24 136 Ac 79
63570 Lavialle 63 128 Dc 76
42560 Lavieu 42 129 Ea 75
80300 Laviéville 80 39 Cd 49
15300 Lavigerie 15 139 Ce 78
24330 Lavignac 24 137 Af 78
87230 Lavignac 87 125 Ba 74
40160 Lavigne 40 146 Za 83
06470 Lavigné, le 06 158 Gf 84
55300 Lavignéville 55 55 Fd 55
70120 Lavigney 70 93 Fe 62
39210 Lavigny 39 107 Fd 68
20230 Lavilanella CTC 183 Kd 94
74800 Lavillat 74 120 Gb 72
07660 Lavillatte 07 141 Df 80
52000 Laville-aux-Bois 52 75 Fb 60
07170 Lavilledieu 07 142 Ec 81
81360 Lavilledieu 81 151 Cc 86
52140 Lavilleneuve 52 75 Fd 60
52120 Lavilleneuve-au-Roi 52 74 Ef 60
52330 Lavilleneuve-aux-Fresnes 52 74 Ef 59
60240 Lavillertertre 60 50 Bf 53
55170 Lavincourt 55 55 Fa 57
07530 Laviolle 07 142 Eb 80
25510 Laviron 25 108 Gd 65
82120 Lavit 82 149 Af 85
03250 Lavoine 03 116 De 73
44240 Lavoir, le 44 82 Yc 64
70120 Lavoncourt 70 93 Fe 63
74470 Lavouet, le 74 120 Gd 71
01350 Lavours 01 132 Fe 74
43380 Lavoûte-Chilhac 43 140 Dc 78
43800 Lavoûte-sur-Loire 43 141 Df 78
86800 Lavoux 86 100 Ad 69
55120 Lavoye 55 55 Fa 54
20127 Lavu Donacu CTC 183 Ka 98
80250 Lawarde-Mauger-L'Hortoy 80 38 Cb 50
12160 Lax 12 152 Cc 83
64250 Laxia 64 160 Yd 89
54520 Laxou 54 56 Ga 56
42470 Lay 42 117 Eb 73
38730 Layat 38 131 Fc 76
21520 Layer-sur-Roche 21 91 Ee 61
64190 Lay-Lamidou 64 161 Zb 89
32220 Laymont 32 164 Af 88
30750 Layolle 30 153 Dc 84
47390 Layrac 47 149 Ad 84
31340 Layrac-sur-Tarn 31 150 Bd 85
65380 Layrisse 65 162 Aa 90
40410 Lays 40 147 Zb 82
54690 Lay-Saint-Christophe 54 56 Gb 56
54570 Lay-Saint-Rémy 54 56 Fe 56
71270 Lays-sur-le-Doubs 71 106 Fb 67
29520 Laz 29 78 Wa 60
48190 Lazalier 48 141 De 81
18120 Lazenay 18 102 Ca 66
05300 Lazer 05 157 Ff 82
20290 Lazzarotti CTC 181 Kc 93
80560 Léalvillers 80 29 Cd 48
14340 Léaupartie 14 48 Aa 53
01200 Léaz 01 119 Ff 72
68660 Leberau = Liepvre 68 60 Hb 59
90100 Lebetain 90 94 Gf 64
54740 Lebeuville 54 76 Gb 58
62990 Lebiez 62 28 Bf 46
40140 Leborde 40 161 Ye 86
32810 Leboulin 32 163 Ae 86
12170 Lebous 12 152 Cd 84
81140 Lèbre, la 81 150 Be 85
46800 Lebreil 46 149 Bb 83
62124 Lebucquière 62 30 Cf 48
14140 Lécaude 14 35 Aa 54
59226 Lecelles 59 30 Dc 46
85540 le-Champ Saint-Père 85 109 Yd 69
65250 Léchan 65 175 Ac 90
21250 Lechâtelet 21 106 Fa 66
32270 Léchaux 32 163 Ae 86
02200 Léchelle 02 40 Db 53
62124 Léchelle 62 30 Cf 48
77171 Léchelle 77 72 Dc 57
73260 Lechères, la 73 132 Gc 75
24400 Lèches, les 24 136 Ac 79
73130 Léchet 73 132 Gb 77
29730 Léchiagat 29 78 Ve 62
59259 Lécluse 59 30 Da 47
52140 Lécourt 52 75 Fd 60
35133 Lécousse 35 66 Ye 58
30250 Lecques 30 154 Ea 85
83270 Lecques, les 83 171 Fe 89
39260 Lect 39 119 Fe 70
32700 Lectoure 32 149 Ad 85
64220 Lecumberry 64 161 Yf 90
31580 Lécussan 31 163 Ad 90
81340 Lédas-et-Penthiès 81 151 Cc 84
47300 Lédat 47 149 Ae 82
21390 Ledavrée 21 91 Ec 64
30210 Lédenon 30 155 Ed 85
12170 Lédergues 12 151 Cc 84
59143 Lederzeele 59 27 Cb 44
64400 Ledeuix 64 161 Zc 89
30350 Lédignan 30 154 Ea 85
62380 Ledinghem 62 28 Bf 45
59470 Ledringhem 59 27 Cc 43
64320 Lée 64 162 Ze 89
64320 Lée-Ousse-Sendets 64 162 Ze 89
59115 Leers 59 30 Db 44
64490 Lées-Athas 64 174 Zc 91
22250 Léez, le 22 65 Xe 59
62630 Lefaux 62 28 Bd 45
14700 Leffard 14 47 Ze 55
08310 Leffincourt 08 41 Ed 52
70600 Leffond 70 92 Fc 63
52210 Leffonds 52 75 Fa 61
59240 Leffrinckoucke 59 27 Cc 42
59495 Leffrinckoucke-Village 59 27 Cc 42
29460 Léflez, les 29 62 Vf 58
62790 Leforest 62 30 Da 46
87120 Légaud 87 126 Be 74
31440 Lège 31 176 Ad 91
44650 Legé 44 97 Yc 67
33950 Lège-Cap-Ferret 33 134 Yf 80
58250 Legendre 58 104 De 68
88270 Légéville-et-Bonfays 88 76 Ga 59
56690 Légevin 56 79 Wf 62
60420 Léglantiers 60 39 Cd 52
39240 Légna 39 119 Fd 70
69620 Légny 69D 118 Ed 73
31490 Léguevin 31 164 Bb 87
24340 Léguillac-de-Cercles 24 124 Ad 76
24110 Léguillac-de-L'Auche 24 124 Ad 77
22100 Léhon 22 65 Xf 58
03320 Leige 03 103 Cf 68
86400 Leigné 86 112 Ab 71
42380 Leignecq 42 129 Ea 76
86450 Leigné-les-Bois 86 100 Ae 68
86300 Leignes-sur-Fontaine 86 112 Ae 69
86230 Leigné-sur-Usseau 86 100 Ac 67
42130 Leigneux 42 129 Df 74
68800 Leimbach 68 94 Ha 62
55210 Leintrey 54 57 Ge 57
67250 Leiterswiller 67 58 Hf 55
88120 Lejole 88 77 Ge 60
01410 Lélex 01 120 Ff 71
32400 Lelin-Lapujolle 32 162 Zf 86
57660 Lelling 57 57 Ge 54
50570 Le-Lozon, Marigny- 50 34 Ye 54
54740 Lemainville 54 76 Gb 57
67510 Lembach 67 58 He 54
82200 Lembenne 82 150 Ba 84
57620 Lemberg 57 58 Hc 54
24350 Lembertie 24 124 Ad 77
40360 Lembeye 40 161 Za 87
64350 Lembeye 64 162 Zf 88
24100 Lembras 24 136 Ad 79
02140 Lemé 02 40 De 49
64450 Lème 64 162 Zd 88
54740 Leménil-Mitry 54 76 Gb 58
37120 Léméré 37 99 Ac 66
57970 Lemestroff 57 44 Gc 52
88300 Lemmecourt 88 75 Fe 59
55220 Lemmes 55 55 Fb 54
57590 Lemoncourt 57 56 Gc 55
81700 Lempaut 81 165 Ca 87
43410 Lempdes 43 128 Db 76
63370 Lempdes 63 128 Db 74
02420 Lempire 02 40 Db 49
55100 Lempire-aux-Bois 55 55 Fb 54
15350 Lempret 15 127 Cc 76
07610 Lemps 07 142 Ee 78
26510 Lemps 26 156 Fc 82
63190 Lempty 63 128 Db 74
24800 Lempzours 24 124 Ae 76
57580 Lemud 57 56 Gc 54
39110 Lemuy 39 107 Ff 67
14770 Lénault 14 47 Zc 55
03130 Lenax 03 117 De 71
18310 Lenay 18 101 Bf 66
86140 Lencloître 86 99 Ab 68
45410 Lencorne 45 70 Be 60
40120 Lencouacq 40 147 Zd 84
46800 Lendou-en-Quercy 46 149 Bb 83
64300 Lendresse 64 161 Zb 88
35380 Lénéheuc 35 65 Xf 60
86500 Lenest 86 112 Af 70
57720 Lengelsheim 57 58 Hc 54
50450 Lengronne 50 46 Yd 55
51230 Lenharrée 51 53 Ea 56
57670 Léning 57 57 Ge 55
52140 Lénizeul 52 75 Fd 60
12130 Lenne 12 152 Cf 82
29190 Lennon 29 62 Wa 59
54110 Lenoncourt 54 56 Gb 57
62800 Lens 62 30 Ce 46
26210 Lens-Lestang 26 130 Fa 77
01240 Lent 01 118 Fb 72
63710 Lenteuges 63 128 Da 75
34480 Lenthérie 34 167 Da 87
83111 Lentier 83 172 Gc 87
47290 Lentignac 47 136 Ad 81
42155 Lentigny 42 117 Df 73
46330 Lentillac-Lauzès 46 138 Bd 81
46100 Lentillac-Saint-Blaise 46 138 Ca 81
07200 Lentillères 07 142 Eb 81
10330 Lentilles 10 74 Ed 58
69210 Lentilly 69M 130 Ed 74
12170 Lentin 12 151 Cc 84
38270 Lentiol 38 131 Fa 77
20252 Lento CTC 181 Kb 93
33480 Lentre 43 128 Dc 77
20252 Lentu = Lento CTC 181 Kb 93
46300 Léobard 46 137 Bb 80
33210 Léogeats 33 135 Zd 81
33850 Léognan 33 135 Zc 80
82000 Léojac 82 150 Bc 84
27150 Léomesnil 27 50 Bc 53
40550 Léon 40 146 Ye 85
26190 Léoncel 26 143 Fb 79
23200 Léon-le-Franc 23 114 Cb 72
43410 Léotoing 43 128 Db 76
31260 Leoudary 31 164 Af 90
06260 Léouve 06 158 Gf 84
45480 Léouville 45 70 Ca 59
26510 Léoux 26 143 Fb 82
17500 Léoville 17 123 Zd 76
88360 Lépange 88 77 Gd 61
88600 Lépanges-sur-Vologne 88 77 Ge 59
24490 Léparon 24 123 Aa 78
44320 le-Pas-Bochet 44 96 Ya 65
23170 Lépaud 23 115 Cc 71
36210 Lépina 36 101 Bd 65
23150 Lépinas 23 114 Bf 72
10120 Lépine 10 73 Ea 59
62170 Lépine 62 28 Be 46
73610 Lépin-le-Lac 73 132 Fe 75
85770 le-Pont-aux-Chèvres 85 110 Za 70
08150 Lépron-les-Vallées 08 41 Ec 50
90200 Lepuix-Gy 90 94 Ge 62
90100 Lepuix-Neuf 90 94 Ha 63
30580 Lèque, la 30 154 Ec 83
09600 Léran 09 178 Bf 91
44420 Lerat 44 81 Xc 64
09220 Lercoul 09 177 Bd 92
18240 Léré 18 88 Cf 64
64270 Léren 64 161 Yf 87
42600 Lérigneux 42 129 Df 75
33840 Lerm-et-Musset 33 147 Zf 83
22120 Lermot 22 64 Xb 57
49260 Lernay 49 99 Zf 66
55200 Lérouville 55 55 Fd 56
88260 Lerrain 88 76 Ga 60
44270 Lerrière 44 96 Yb 67
21440 Léry 21 91 Ef 63
27690 Léry 27 49 Bb 53
63210 Léry 63 127 Ce 74
02260 Lerzy 02 41 Df 49
43300 Lesbinières 43 140 Dc 78
80360 Lesbœufs 80 30 Cf 48
53120 Lesbois 53 67 Zb 58
33730 Lesbordes 33 135 Zd 82
40110 Lesbordes 40 146 Yf 84
11340 Lescale 11 178 Ca 91
64230 Lescar 64 162 Zd 89
56250 Lescastel 56 80 Xc 62
74320 Leschaux 74 132 Ga 74
02170 Leschelles 02 40 De 49
73340 Lescheraines 73 132 Ga 74
39170 Leschères 39 119 Fe 70
52110 Leschères-sur-le-Blaiseron 52 75 Fa 58
77320 Lescherolles 77 52 Dc 56
01560 Lescheroux 01 118 Fa 70
26310 Lesches-en-Diois 26 143 Fd 81
29770 Lescleden 29 61 Vb 60
77450 Lesches 77 52 Ce 55
29770 Lescoff 29 61 Vb 60
29790 Lescogan 29 61 Vd 60
05500 les-Combes 05 144 Ga 80
29740 Lesconil 29 78 Ve 62
22570 Lescouët-Gouarec 22 79 We 60
09100 Lescousse 09 165 Bd 90
81110 Lescout 81 165 Ca 87
64490 Lescun 64 174 Zc 91
31220 Lescuns 31 164 Ba 89
09420 Lescure 09 177 Bb 90
15300 Lescure 15 139 Cf 78
81380 Lescure-d'Albigeois 81 151 Cb 85
12440 Lescure-Jaoul 12 151 Ca 83
65140 Lescurry 65 162 Aa 88
59258 Lesdain 59 30 Db 48
02100 Lesdins 02 40 Db 49
02220 Lesges 02 53 Dd 53
40400 Lesgor 40 146 Za 85
40630 Lesgoudies 40 147 Zb 84
08390 les-Grandes-Armoises 08 42 Ef 51
16500 Lésignac 16 112 Ae 73
77150 Lésigny 77 51 Cd 56
86270 Lésigny 86 100 Ae 67
22800 Leslay, le 22 63 Xa 58
63730 les-Martres-de-Veyro 63 128 Db 74
71140 Lesme 71 104 De 69
27160 Lesme, le 27 49 Af 55
54700 Lesménils 54 56 Ga 55
10500 Lesmont 10 74 Ec 58
29260 Lesneven 29 62 Ve 57
59610 Les-Noires-Terres 59 41 Ea 48
56230 Lesnoyal 56 81 Xd 62
82270 Lesparre 82 150 Bc 83
33340 Lesparre-Médoc 33 122 Za 77
09300 Lesparrou 09 178 Bf 91
40200 Lespecier 40 146 Ye 84
07660 Lespéron 07 141 Df 80
40260 Lesperon 40 146 Yf 85
62190 Lespesses 62 29 Cc 45
24490 Lespic 24 135 Aa 78
64350 Lespielle 64 162 Zf 88
34710 Lespignan 34 167 Db 89
24380 Lespinasse 24 136 Ae 78
24480 Lespinasse 24 136 Ae 80
11160 Lespinassière 11 166 Cd 88
12800 Lespinassolle 12 151 Cb 84
43160 Lespinasson 43 129 De 77
19500 Lespinassou 19 138 Be 78
62990 Lespinoy 62 28 Bf 46
43300 Lespitallet 43 141 Dd 78
31160 Lespiteau 31 163 Ae 90
29410 Lespodou 29 62 Wa 57
65710 Lesponne 65 175 Aa 90
64160 Lespourcy 64 162 Zf 88
31350 Lespugue 31 163 Ae 89
29860 Lesquelen 29 62 Vd 58
33113 Lesquerde 33 147 Zd 83
66220 Lesquerde 66 179 Cd 92
29170 Lesquidic 29 78 Vf 61
02120 Lesquielles-Saint-Germain 02 40 Dd 49
59810 Lesquin 59 30 Da 45
40410 Lesquire 40 147 Zb 82
29520 Lesren 29 62 Wa 60
16500 Lessac 16 112 Ae 72
15340 Lessal 15 139 Cb 80
71440 Lessard-en-Bresse 71 106 Fa 68
14140 Lessard-et-le-Chêne 14 48 Aa 54
71530 Lessard-le-National 71 106 Ef 67
50430 Lessay 50 46 Yc 53
57580 Lesse 57 57 Gd 55
85490 Lesson 85 110 Zc 70
71470 Lessot 71 118 Fb 69
71590 Lessu 71 106 Ef 67
57160 Lessy 57 56 Ga 54
40370 Lestage 40 146 Za 85
40630 Lestage 40 147 Zb 84
40110 Lestajaou 40 146 Yf 84
29860 Lestanet 29 62 Vd 57
24500 Lestang 24 136 Ac 80
76730 Lestanville 76 37 Af 50
19170 Lestards 19 126 Bf 75
64800 Lestelle-Bétharram 64 162 Ze 90
31360 Lestelle-de Saint-Martury 31 164 Af 90
16420 Lesterps 16 112 Ae 72
33550 Lestiac 33 135 Zd 80
43300 Lestigeollet 43 140 Dc 78
24240 Lestignac 24 136 Ac 80
41500 Lestiou 41 86 Bd 62
43300 Lestival 43 140 Dc 78
43300 Lestival 43 140 Dc 78
19370 Lestivalerie 19 126 Be 75
29500 Lestonan 29 78 Vf 60
80160 l ,Estox 80 38 Cb 50
19500 Lestrade 19 138 Bd 78
23400 Lestrade 23 114 Be 73
47700 Lestrade 47 148 Zf 82
63300 Lestrade 63 128 Dd 74
12430 Lestrade-et-Thouels 12 152 Cd 84
23700 Lestrades 23 115 Cc 72
50310 Lestre 50 34 Yd 51
22160 Lestrédiec 22 63 Wc 58
62136 Lestrem 62 29 Ce 45
29450 Lestrémélard 29 62 Vf 58
29260 Lestreonec 29 62 Ve 58
29550 Lestrevet 29 78 Vd 59
56400 Lestréviau 56 80 Xa 63
29600 Lestrézec 29 62 Wb 57
29120 Lestriguiou 29 78 Vd 62
29100 Lestrivin 29 78 Vd 60
40400 Lestronques 40 147 Zb 86
29710 Lestuyen 29 78 Vd 61
29790 Lesven 29 61 Vc 60
29780 Lesvénez 29 61 Vd 60
29440 Lesvéoc 29 62 Ve 57
08210 Létanne 08 42 Fa 51
03360 Lételon 03 102 Cd 69
28700 Lethuin 28 70 Bf 58
20160 Letia CTC 182 If 95
69620 Létra 69D 117 Ed 73
71290 Letrey 71 106 Fa 69
54610 Létricourt 54 56 Gb 55
23130 Létrieix 23 114 Cb 72
40170 Lette, la 40 146 Ye 84
27910 Letteguives 27 37 Bb 52
57560 Lettenbach 57 77 Ha 57
74320 Lettraz 74 132 Ga 73
51320 Lettrée 51 54 Eb 56
20242 Lettu Majo CTC 183 Kc 96
29950 Letty, le 29 78 Vf 61
62250 Leubringhen 62 26 Be 43
11250 Leuc 11 166 Cb 90
15120 Leucamp 15 139 Cd 80
11370 Leucate 11 179 Da 91
11370 Leucate-Plage 11 179 Da 91
52190 Leuchey 52 92 Fb 62
91630 Leudeville 91 71 Cb 57
77320 Leudon 77 72 Da 57
77320 Leudon-en-Brie 77 52 Db 56
85210 Leue, la 85 97 Yf 69
21290 Leuglay 21 91 Ee 62
21150 Leugny 21 91 Ed 64
79100 Leugny 79 99 Zf 67
86220 Leugny 86 100 Ae 67
86330 Leugny 86 99 Aa 68
89130 Leugny 89 89 Dc 62
29390 Leuhan 29 78 Wb 60
02380 Leuilly-sous-Coucy 02 40 Dc 52
33480 Leujean 33 134 Zb 79
62500 Leuline 62 27 Cb 44
62500 Leulinghem 62 27 Ca 44
62250 Leulinghen 62 26 Be 44
76660 Leuqueue, la 76 37 Bc 49
29880 Leuré 29 61 Vd 57
52700 Leurville 52 75 Fc 59
02880 Leury 02 40 Dc 52
74120 Leutaz 74 133 Gd 74
67480 Leutenheim 67 59 Ia 55
91310 Leuville-sur-Orge 91 71 Cb 57
51700 Leuvrigny 51 53 De 54
18210 Leux, la 18 103 Ce 67
40250 Leuy, le 40 147 Zc 86
58330 Leuzat 58 104 Dc 66
02500 Leuze 02 41 Ea 49
30110 Levade, la 30 154 Ea 83
48310 Levades, les 48 140 Da 80
28700 Levainville 28 70 Be 58
59620 Leval 59 31 De 47
90110 Leval 90 94 Gf 62
52140 Le-Val-de-Musée 52 75 Fd 61
53120 Levaré 53 66 Za 58
28170 Levasville 28 50 Bb 57
52150 Levécourt 52 75 Fd 60
81570 Levéjac 81 165 Ca 87
77710 Levelay 77 72 Ce 59
06670 Levens 06 159 Hb 85
02420 Levergies 02 40 Db 49
21200 Levernois 21 106 Ef 67
28300 Lèves 28 70 Bc 58
79190 Levescault 79 111 Aa 72
33220 Lèves-et-Thoumeyragues, les 33 136 Ab 80

A
B
C
D
E
F
G
H
I
J
K
L
M
N
O
P
Q
R
S
T
U
V
W
X
Y
Z

29140 Locunduff 29 78 Wb 60
29310 Locunolé 29 79 Wd 61
56310 Locunolé 56 80 We 61
56160 Locuon 56 79 We 60
06450 Loda 06 159 Hb 85
03130 Loddes 03 116 De 71
31800 Lodes 31 163 Ae 89
34700 Lodève 34 167 Db 86
58250 Lodey, le 58 104 De 68
29750 Lodonnec 29 78 Ve 62
25930 Lods 25 107 Gb 66
68680 Loechle 68 95 Hd 63
70100 Lœuilley 70 92 Fc 64
80160 Lœuilly 80 38 Cb 50
29380 Logan 29 79 Wb 61
36800 Loge, la 36 101 Bc 68
41300 Loge, la 41 87 Ca 64
62140 Loge, la 62 29 Ca 46
63700 Loge, la 63 115 Cf 71
70100 Loge, la 70 92 Fd 64
89160 Loge, la 89 90 Eb 62
10140 Loge-aux-Chèvres, la 10 74 Ec 59
85120 Loge-Fougereuse 85 98 Zb 69
68280 Logelheim 68 60 Hc 60
10210 Loge-Pomblin, la 10 73 Ea 60
08230 Loge-Rosette, la 08 41 Ec 49
18140 Loges 18 103 Cf 65
18320 Loges 18 103 Cf 66
36400 Loges 36 102 Ca 68
52500 Loges 52 92 Fc 62
77720 Loges 77 72 Da 57
80700 Loges 80 39 Ce 51
85240 Loges 85 110 Zb 70
87240 Loges 87 113 Bc 73
87330 Loges 87 112 Af 72
89320 Loges 89 73 Dd 60
03220 Loges, les 03 116 Dd 70
14240 Loges, les 14 47 Zb 54
41300 Loges, les 41 87 Ca 64
49150 Loges, les 49 84 Zf 63
49390 Loges, les 49 84 Aa 64
58110 Loges, les 58 104 Dc 66
72440 Loges, les 72 68 Ad 61
76790 Loges, les 76 36 Ab 50
85140 Loges, les 85 97 Ye 68
36330 Loges-Brûlées, les 36 101 Be 69
36340 Loges-de-Bonavois, les 36 101 Be 69
36120 Loges-de-Champ, les 36 101 Be 68
58390 Loges-des-Bruyères 58 103 Db 68
78350 Loges-en-Josas, les 78 51 Ca 56
50600 Loges-Marchis, les 50 66 Yf 57
10210 Loges-Margueron, les 10 73 Ea 60
14700 Loges-Saulces, les 14 47 Ze 55
50800 Loges-sur-Brécey, les 50 46 Yf 56
83670 Logis 83 171 Ga 87
13490 Logis-d'Anne, le 13 171 Fd 87
13114 Logis-de-la-Colle 13 171 Fd 88
17430 Logis-du-Péré 17 110 Zb 73
84460 Logis-Neuf 84 156 Fa 86
13190 Logis-Neuf, le 13 170 Fc 88
26740 Logis-Neuf, le 26 142 Ee 81
37460 Logny 37 100 Ba 66
08150 Logny-Bogny 08 41 Ec 50
02500 Logny-lès-Aubenton 02 41 Eb 50
08220 Logny-lès-Chaumont 08 41 Eb 51
29590 Logonna-Quimerch 29 62 Vf 59
22390 Logoray 22 63 We 58
56190 Logorenhe 56 81 Xc 63
01630 Logras 01 119 Ff 71
30610 Logrian-Florian 30 154 Ea 85
28200 Logron 28 69 Bb 60
22480 Logueltas 22 63 Wf 58
22620 Loguivy 22 63 Wf 56
22300 Loguivy-lès-Lannion 22 63 Wd 56
22780 Loguivy-Plougras 22 63 Wd 57
56500 Logunec'h = Locminé 56 80 Xa 61
35550 Lohéac 35 82 Ya 61
64120 Lohitzun-Oyhercq 64 161 Za 89
67290 Lohr 67 58 Hb 55
22160 Lohuec 22 63 Wc 58
53200 Loigné-sur-Mayenne 53 83 Zb 61
28140 Loigny-la-Bataille 28 70 Be 60
33590 Loirac 33 122 Za 76
34700 Loiras 34 167 Dc 86
17540 Loiré 17 110 Za 71
49440 Loiré 49 83 Za 63
71290 Loire 71 106 Ef 69
49140* Loire-Authion 49 84 Zd 64
44370 Loireauxence 44 83 Yf 64
17870 Loire-les-Marais 17 110 Za 73
72310* Loir en Vallée 72 85 Ad 62
17470 Loiré-sur-Nie 17 111 Ze 73
69700 Loire-sur-Rhône 69M 130 Ee 75
53320 Loiron-Ruillé 53 66 Za 60
61400 Loisail 61 68 Ad 57
61400 Loisé 61 68 Ad 57
55000 Loisey-Culey 55 55 Fb 56
39320 Loisia 39 119 Fc 70
73170 Loisieux 73 131 Fe 75
74140 Loisin 74 120 Gb 71
74930 Loisinges-le-Châtelet 74 120 Gb 72
55230 Loison 55 43 Fd 53
62990 Loison-sur-Créquoise 62 28 Bf 46
28160 Loisville 28 69 Bb 59
54700 Loisy 54 56 Ga 55
71290 Loisy 71 106 Fa 69
51130 Loisy-en-Brie 51 53 Df 55
51300 Loisy-sur-Marne 51 54 Ed 56
51220 Loivre 51 53 Df 52
17111 Loix 17 109 Yd 71
79110 Loizé 79 111 Zf 72
71470 Loizette 71 118 Fa 69
63250 Lojardie 63 129 De 74
29390 Loj-Goar 29 78 Wb 60
41300 Lojon 41 87 Ca 65
29290 Lokournan 29 61 Vc 58
24510 Lol 24 136 Ae 79
45300 Lolainville 45 71 Cb 59
50530 Lolif 50 46 Yd 56
24540 Lolme 24 137 Af 80
28800 Lolon 28 70 Bc 60
25440 Lombard 25 107 Ff 66
39230 Lombard 39 106 Fd 68
40460 Lombard 40 134 Yf 82
87220 Lombardie 87 125 Bc 74
40460 Lombard-Méoule 40 134 Yf 82
26400 Lombards, les 26 143 Ef 81
81120 Lombers 81 151 Ca 86
32220 Lombez 32 164 Af 88
64160 Lombia 64 162 Zf 89
24310 Lombraud 24 124 Ad 76
02300 Lombray 02 40 Da 51
65150 Lombrès 65 175 Ac 90
45700 Lombreuil 45 71 Cd 61
72450 Lombron 72 68 Ac 60
56240 Lomelec 56 80 We 61
56270 Lomener 56 79 Wd 62
59160 Lomme 59 30 Da 45
57650 Lommerange 57 43 Ff 53
78270 Lommoye 78 50 Bd 55
65130 Lomné 65 175 Ab 90
70200 Lomont 70 94 Gd 63
70200 Lomontot 70 94 Gd 63
25110 Lomont-sur-Crête 25 94 Gc 64
12200 Lompla 12 151 Bf 83
01680 Lompnas 01 131 Fd 74
01260 Lompnieu 01 119 Fd 73
40630 Lompré 40 147 Zc 84
59840 Lompret 59 30 Cf 44
86170 Lonchard 86 99 Ab 69
64410 Lonçon 64 162 Zd 88
50430 Londe, la 50 33 Yc 53
61160 Londe, la 61 48 Zf 56
76500 Londe, la 76 49 Af 53
83250 Londe-les-Maures, la 83 172 Gb 90
24320 Londet 24 124 Ac 77
16700 Londigny 16 111 Aa 72
76660 Londinières 76 37 Bc 50
29100 Lonévry 29 78 Ve 60
18600 Long 18 103 Cf 67
19500 Long 19 138 Be 78
80510 Long 80 28 Bf 48
31410 Longages 31 164 Bb 88
12480 Longagnes, les 12 152 Cd 84
35190 Longaulnay 35 65 Ya 59
60380 Longavesne 60 38 Be 51
80240 Longavesnes 80 39 Da 49
46500 Longayries 46 138 Be 80
15150 Longayroux 15 139 Cb 78
21110 Longchamp 21 92 Fb 65
52240 Longchamp 52 75 Fc 60
63340 Longchamp 63 128 Da 76
88000 Longchamp 88 77 Gd 59
02120 Longchamps 02 40 Dd 49
27150 Longchamps 27 38 Bd 52
55260 Longchamps-sur-Aire 55 55 Fb 55
10310 Longchamp-sur-Aujon 10 74 Ee 60
39400 Longchaumois 39 120 Ff 70
39250 Longcochon 39 107 Ga 68
10260 Long-du-Bois 10 73 Ea 59
27160 Long-du-Bois, le 27 49 Ae 56
03350 Longe, la 03 115 Ce 69
21110 Longeault 21 106 Fb 65
52250 Longeau-Percey 52 92 Fb 62
55500 Longeaux 55 55 Fc 57
23000 Longechaud 23 114 Be 71
25690 Longechaux 25 108 Gc 66
38690 Longechenal 38 131 Fc 76
01110 Longecombe 01 119 Fd 73
21110 Longecourt-en-Plaine 21 106 Fa 65
21230 Longecourt-lès-Culêtre 21 105 Ed 66
38930 Longefont 38 143 Fd 80
73210 Longefoy 73 133 Gd 75
25690 Longemaison 25 108 Gc 66
71270 Longepierre 71 106 Fb 67
49710 Longeron, le 49 97 Yf 66
88270 Longeroye 88 76 Gb 60
69420 Longes 69M 130 Ee 75
69770 Longessaigne 69M 130 Ec 74
51240 Longevas 51 54 Ec 55
70110 Longevelle 70 94 Gc 63
70700 Longevelle 70 93 Fe 64
25380 Longevelle-lès-Russey 25 108 Gd 65
25260 Longevelle-sur-Doubs 25 94 Gd 64
17230 Longèves 17 110 Za 71
85200 Longèves 85 110 Za 70
25330 Longeville 25 107 Gb 66
55000 Longeville-en-Barrois 55 55 Fb 56
57740 Longeville-lès-Saint-Avold 57
57 Gd 54
25370 Longevilles-Hautes 25 108 Gb 68
25370 Longevilles-Mont-d'Or 25 108 Gb 68
10170 Longeville-sur-Aube 10 73 Df 57
52220 Longeville-sur-la-Laines 52 74 Ee 58
85560 Longeville-sur-Mer 85 109 Yd 70
10320 Longeville-sur-Mogne 10 73 Ea 60
62240 Longfossé 62 28 Be 45
70310 Longine, la 70 94 Gd 61
91160 Longjumeau 91 51 Cb 56
54810 Longlaville 54 43 Fe 51
76440 Longmesnil 76 38 Bd 51
72540 Longnes 72 68 Zf 60
78980 Longnes 78 50 Bd 55
61290 Longny-au-Perche 61 69 Ae 57
61290 Longny les Villages 61 69 Ae 57
77230 Longperrier 77 51 Cd 54
02600 Longpont 02 52 Db 53
91310 Longpont-sur-Orge 91 51 Cb 57
43380 Longpral 43 140 Dc 78
41310 Longpré 41 86 Af 63
80510 Longpré-les-Corps-Saints 80
38 Bf 48
10140 Longpré-le-Sec 10 74 Ed 59
44470 Longrais 44 82 Yd 64
14250 Longraye 14 34 Zb 54
16240 Longré 16 111 Zf 72
76260 Longroy 76 37 Bc 49
04400 Longs, les 04 158 Ge 83
59127 Longsart 59 30 Db 48
10240 Longsols 10 74 Eb 58
59190 Longue-Croix 59 27 Cc 44
53200 Longuefuye 53 83 Zc 61
81710 Longuegineste 81 165 Ca 87
76860 Longueil 76 37 Af 49
60150 Longueil-Annel 60 39 Cf 52
60126 Longueil-Sainte-Marie 60 39 Ce 52
49160 Longué-Jumelles 49 84 Zf 64
27130 Longuelune 27 49 Ba 56
49770 Longuenée-en-Anjou 49 83 Zb 63
62219 Longuenesse 62 27 Cb 44
61320 Longuenoë 61 68 Zf 57
10100 Longueperle 10 73 Dd 58
76750 Longuerue 76 37 Bb 51
02140 Longue-Rue-de-Haut 02 41 Ea 50
63270 Longues 63 128 Db 75
95450 Longuesse 95 50 Bf 54
14400 Longues-sur-Mer 14 47 Zb 52
88200 Longuet 88 77 Gd 60
80360 Longueval 80 39 Ce 48
02160 Longueval-Barbonval 02 40 Dd 52
14230 Longueville 14 47 Za 52
47200 Longueville 47 136 Ab 82
50290 Longueville 50 46 Yc 55
62142 Longueville 62 27 Bf 44
77650 Longueville 77 72 Db 57
59570 Longueville, la 59 31 Df 47
76590 Longueville-sur-Scie 76 37 Ba 50
80600 Longuevillette 80 29 Cb 48
12100 Longuiers 12 152 Da 84
54260 Longuyon 54 43 Fd 52
21700 Longvay 21 106 Ef 66
19160 Longvert 19 127 Cc 76
48500 Longviala 48 152 Da 82
21600 Longvic 21 91 Fa 65
57160 Longville-lès-Metz 57 56 Ga 54
14310 Longvillers 14 47 Zc 54
62630 Longvillers 62 28 Be 45
80370 Longvillers 80 29 Ca 48
78730 Longvilliers 78 70 Bf 57
08400 Longwé 08 42 Ee 52
54440 Longwy 54 43 Fe 51
39120 Longwy-sur-le-Doubs 39 106 Fc 67
19290 Lonjy, le 19 126 Ca 75
19110 Lonjard, le 19 127 Cc 76
61700 Lonlay-L'Abbaye 61 67 Zb 57
61600 Lonlay-le-Tesson 61 67 Zd 57
23110 Lonlevade 23 115 Cd 72
12200 Lonnac 12 151 Ca 83
16230 Lonnes 16 111 Aa 73
08150 Lonny 08 42 Ed 50
61250 Lonrai 61 68 Aa 58
39000 Lons-le-Saunier 39 107 Fd 68
19250 Lontrade 19 126 Ca 75
17520 Lonzac 17 123 Zd 75
19470 Lonzac, le 19 126 Be 76
03260 Lonzat, le 03 116 Dc 71
31510 Lôo 31 176 Ae 90
59630 Looberghe 59 27 Cb 43
59279 Loon-Plage 59 27 Cb 43
59120 Loos 59 30 Da 45
64230 Loos 64 162 Zd 88
62750 Loos-en-Gohelle 62 30 Ce 46
89300 Looze 89 72 Dc 61
56390 Lopabu 56 80 Xa 62
64780 Lopeinea 64 160 Ye 89
29590 Lopérec 29 62 Vf 59
29470 Loperhet 29 62 Ve 58
56390 Loperhet 56 80 Xa 62
56410 Loperhet 56 80 We 63
20139 Lopigna CTC 182 If 96
29420 Lopréden 29 62 Wa 57
29530 Loqueffret 29 62 Wa 59
29242 Loqueltas 29 61 Uf 58
56680 Loquénin 56 79 We 62
62850 Loquin-Haut 62 27 Bf 44
02190 Lor 02 41 Ea 51
71270 Lorances, les 71 106 Fb 68
25390 Loray 25 108 Gc 66
15320 Lorcières 15 140 Db 79
09250 Lordat 09 177 Be 92
61330 Loré 61 67 Zc 58
67430 Lorentzen 67 57 Hb 55
16170 Loret 16 123 Zf 74
20215 Loreto-di-Casinca CTC 181 Kc 94
20165 Loreto-di-Tallano CTC 184 Ka 98
29380 Loretta 29 78 Wb 61
42420 Lorette 42 130 Ed 75
59163 Lorette 59 31 Dd 46
50510 Loreur, le 50 46 Yd 55
41200 Loreux 41 87 Be 64
27640 Lorey 27 50 Bc 55
45490 Lorey 45 71 Cd 60
54290 Lorey 54 76 Gb 58
50570 Lorey, le 50 34 Ye 54
41370 Lorges 41 86 Bc 62
62840 Lorgies 62 30 Ce 45
83510 Lorgues 83 172 Gc 88
35150 Loriais 35 66 Yd 61
20244 Loriani CTC 183 Kb 94
33670 Lorient 33 135 Zd 80
56100 Lorient An Oriant 56 79 Wd 62
03500 Loriges 03 116 Dc 71
17240 Lorignac 17 122 Zb 76
79190 Lorigné 79 111 Aa 72
43100 Lorillot 43 128 Db 77
84870 Loriol-du-Comtat 84 155 Fa 84
26270 Loriol-sur-Drôme 26 142 Ee 80
23160 Lorioux 23 113 Bd 71
43360 Lorlanges 43 128 Db 76
27480 Lorleau 27 37 Bd 52
60110 Lormaison 60 51 Ca 53
28210 Lormaye 28 50 Bd 57
58140 Lormes 58 90 De 65
33310 Lormont 33 135 Zc 79
19410 Lornac 19 125 Bd 76
74150 Lornay 74 119 Ff 73
54290 Loromontzey 54 76 Gc 58
35133 Loroux, le 35 66 Yf 58
49390 Loroux, le 49 84 Zf 64
44430 Loroux-Bottereau, le 44 97 Yd 65
09190 Lorp 09 176 Ba 90
09190 Lorp-Sentaraille 09 176 Ba 90
57790 Lorquin 57 57 Gf 56
22640 Lorrain, le 22 64 Xd 58
45230 Lorrains, les 45 88 Ce 61
77710 Lorrez-le-Bocage 77 72 Cf 59
45260 Lorris 45 88 Cd 61
57050 Lorry-lès-Metz 57 56 Ga 54
57420 Lorry-Mardigny 57 56 Ga 55
60130 Lorteil 60 39 Cc 52
65250 Lortet 65 175 Ac 90
22230 Loscouët-sur-Meu 22 65 Xe 59
76430 Loslière 76 36 Ac 51
21170 Losne 21 106 Fb 66
29150 Lospars 29 62 Vf 59
37140 Lossay 37 85 Ab 65
40240 Losse 40 148 Zf 84
19500 Lostanges 19 138 Be 78
56250 Losthuel 56 80 Xc 63
29160 Lost-Marc'h 29 61 Vc 59
62610 Lostrat 62 27 Ca 43
57670 Lostroff 57 57 Gf 55
56220 Lot, le 56 81 Xe 63
29300 Lothéa 29 79 Wc 61
29190 Lothey 29 78 Vf 59
36330 Lothiers 36 101 Bd 68
62240 Lottinghen 62 28 Bf 44
56700 Lotuën 56 79 We 62
72300 Louailles 72 84 Ze 62
77560 Louan 77 53 Dc 57
22700 Louannec 22 63 Wd 56
37320 Louans 37 100 Ae 65
77560 Louan-Villegruis-Fontaine 77
72 Dc 57
22540 Louargat 22 63 Wd 57
02600 Louâtre 02 52 Db 53
65100 Loubajac 65 162 Zf 90
79700 Loubande 79 98 Za 67
07110 Loubaresse 07 141 Eb 81
15320 Loubaresse 15 140 Db 79
15320 Loubaresse 15 140 Db 79
12220 Loubatie 12 138 Ca 82
09350 Loubaut 09 164 Bb 89
63680 Loubazet 63 127 Ce 75
32110 Loubédat 32 162 Aa 86
64160 Loubée 64 162 Ze 88
24550 Loubejac 24 137 Ba 81
82130 Loubéjac 82 150 Bc 84
09120 Loubens 09 177 Bd 90
33190 Loubens 33 135 Zf 81
31460 Loubens-Lauragais 31 165 Be 87
09800 Loubères, les 09 176 Af 91
81190 Louberquet 81 151 Ca 84
81170 Loubers 81 151 Bf 84
32300 Loubersan 32 163 Ac 88
09420 Loubersenac 09 177 Bb 90
16270 Loubert 16 112 Ad 73
47120 Loubès-Bernac 47 136 Ab 80
63410 Loubeyrat 63 115 Da 73
64300 Loubieng 64 161 Zb 88
87420 Loubier, le 87 113 Af 73
12740 Loubière, la 12 152 Ce 82
09000 Loubières 09 177 Bd 90
19520 Loubignac 19 137 Bb 78
79110 Loubigné 79 111 Zf 72
79800 Loubigné 79 111 Zf 70
79110 Loubillé 79 111 Zf 72
64460 Loubix 64 162 Zf 88
46130 Loubressac 46 138 Be 79
17780 Loubresse 17 122 Yf 73
48240 Loubreyroux 48 154 Df 83
61150 Loucé 61 48 Zf 56
14250 Loucelles 14 47 Zc 53
33125 Louchats 33 135 Zc 81
52500 Loucheroy 52 92 Fd 62
04120 Louches 04 157 Gb 85
62610 Louches 62 27 Ca 44
70600 Louches, les 70 92 Fc 63
03500 Louchy-Montfand 03 116 Db 71
65200 Loucrup 65 162 Aa 90
22600 Loudéac = Loudieg 22 64 Xb 59
65510 Loudenvielle 65 175 Ac 92
43320 Loudes 43 141 De 78
31580 Loudet 31 163 Ad 90
22600 Loudieg = Loudéac 22 64 Xb 59
15430 Loudier 15 140 Cf 78
15100 Loudières 15 140 Db 78
15700 Loudiès 15 126 Cb 78
23340 Loudouéneix 23 126 Bf 74
57670 Loudrefing 57 57 Gf 55
86200 Loudun 86 99 Aa 66
72540 Loué 72 67 Zf 61
33290 Louens 33 134 Zb 79
40380 Louer 40 146 Za 86
03430 Louère 03 115 Cf 69
49700 Louerre 49 84 Ze 65
21520 Louesme 21 91 Ee 61
89350 Louesme 89 89 Da 62
37370 Louestault, Beaumont- 37 85 Ad 63
60380 Loueuse 60 38 Be 51
65290 Louey 65 162 Aa 89
18330 Louf-du-Houx, la 18 87 Ca 65
61150 Lougé-sur-Maire 61 48 Ze 56
47290 Lougratte 47 136 Ad 81
25260 Lougres 25 94 Ge 64
71500 Louhans 71 106 Fb 69
64250 Louhossoa 64 160 Yd 89
19310 Louignac 19 125 Bb 77
79600 Louin 79 99 Zf 68
40170 Louise 40 146 Ye 85
44110 Louisfert 44 82 Yd 62
13129 Louisiana, la 13 169 Ee 88
65350 Louit 65 162 Aa 89
70230 Loulans-Verchamp 70 93 Gb 64
28190 Loulappe 28 69 Bb 58
17330 Loulay 17 110 Zc 72
31190 Loulé 31 164 Bc 89
47170 Loulle 47 148 Aa 84
39300 Loulle 39 107 Ff 68
40310 Lou Maïsouot 40 148 Zf 84
18120 Loumet 18 102 Ca 65
64360 Loune-Laheuguère 64 162 Zc 89
86130 Louneuil 86 99 Ab 68
64370 Loup 64 161 Zc 87
28240 Loupe, la 28 69 Ba 58
02130 Loupeigne 02 53 Dd 53
57510 Loupershouse 57 57 Gf 54
33370 Loupes 33 135 Zd 80
53700 Loupfougères 53 67 Zd 58
11300 Loupia 11 165 Ca 90
12700 Loupiac 12 138 Ca 81
15700 Loupiac 15 139 Cc 78
33410 Loupiac 33 135 Ze 81
46260 Loupiac 46 151 Bf 82
46350 Loupiac 46 138 Bc 80
46700 Loupiac 46 137 Ba 81
81800 Loupiac 81 150 Be 86
33190 Loupiac-de-la-Réole 33 135 Zf 81
34140 Loupian 34 168 Dd 88
28140 Loupille 28 70 Bd 60
72210 Louplande 72 68 Aa 61
55300 Loupmont 55 55 Fe 55
55800 Louppy-le-Château 55 55 Fa 55
55000 Louppy-sur-Chée 55 55 Fa 55
55600 Louppy-sur-Loison 55 43 Fc 52
10400 Louptière-Thénard, la 10 72 Dc 58
59156 Lourches 59 30 Dc 47
31510 Lourde 31 176 Ad 91
65100 Lourdes 65 162 Zf 90
64570 Lourdios-Ichere 64 174 Zc 90
36140 Lourdoueix-Saint-Michel 36
114 Be 70
23360 Lourdoueix-Saint-Pierre 23
114 Be 70
03110 Lourdy 03 116 Dc 71
64420 Lourenties 64 162 Zf 89
65370 Loures-Barousse 65 176 Ad 90
49700 Louresse-Rochemenier 49 98 Ze 65
40800 Lourine 40 162 Ze 86
35270 Lourmais 35 65 Yb 58
84160 Lourmarin 84 156 Fc 86
35230 Lourme 35 65 Yc 61
71250 Lournand 71 118 Ed 70
65380 Louroes 65 162 Zf 89
36400 Lourouer-Saint-Laurent 36 102 Ca 69
37240 Louroux, le 37 100 Ae 66
49370 Louroux-Béconnais, le 49 83 Za 63
03350 Louroux-Bourbonnais 03 115 Cf 69
03600 Louroux-de-Beaune 03 115 Cf 71
03330 Louroux-de-Bouble 03 115 Cf 71
03190 Louroux-Hodement 03 115 Ce 70
40250 Lourquen 40 161 Zb 86
32140 Lourties-Monbrun 32 163 Ad 88
45470 Loury 45 70 Ca 61
40460 Louse 40 134 Yf 82
85640 Lousigny 85 97 Yf 68
32230 Louslitges 32 163 Aa 87
32290 Loussous-Débat 32 162 Aa 87
40090 Loustalet 40 147 Zc 85
40120 Loustalot 40 147 Zd 84
32490 Loustaou 32 164 Af 87
47170 Loustaunau 47 148 Aa 84
35330 Loutehel 35 81 Xf 61
57220 Loutremange 57 56 Gc 54
57720 Loutzviller 57 58 Hc 54
23100 Louvage 23 126 Ca 74
14170 Louvagny 14 48 Zf 55
49500 Louvaines 49 83 Zb 62
39350 Louvatange 39 107 Fe 65
78430 Louveciennes 78 51 Ca 55
52130 Louvemont 52 74 Ef 57
80560 Louvencourt 80 29 Cd 48
39320 Louvenne 39 119 Fc 70
51400 Louvercy, Livry- 51 54 Eb 54
08390 Louvergny 08 42 Ee 51
53950 Louverné 53 67 Zb 60
39210 Louverot, le 39 107 Fd 68
27190 Louversay 27 49 Af 55
62147 Louverval 62 30 Da 48
76490 Louvetot 76 36 Ae 51
76850 Louvetot 76 37 Bb 50
64260 Louvie-Juzon 64 162 Zd 90
22350 Louvière, la 22 65 Xf 58
11410 Louvière-Lauragais, la 11 165 Be 89
14710 Louvières 14 47 Za 52
52800 Louvières 52 75 Fb 60
61160 Louvières-en-Auge 61 48 Aa 55
27400 Louviers 27 49 Bb 53
64440 Louvie-Soubiron 64 174 Zd 90
53210 Louvigné 53 67 Zc 60
35680 Louvigné-de-Bais 35 66 Ye 60
35420 Louvigné-du-Désert 35 66 Yf 58
35420 Louvigneg an-Dezerezh 35 66 Yf 58
59530 Louvignies 59 31 Dd 47
14111 Louvigny 14 35 Zd 54
57420 Louvigny 57 56 Gb 55
64410 Louvigny 64 162 Zd 87
72600 Louvigny 72 68 Ab 58
59830 Louvil 59 30 Db 45
28150 Louville-la-Chenard 28 70 Be 59
28500 Louvilliers-en-Drouais 28 50 Bb 56
28250 Louvilliers-lès-Perche 28 49 Ba 57
51150 Louvois 51 53 Ea 54
80250 Louvrechy 80 39 Cc 50
95380 Louvres 95 51 Cd 54
59720 Louvroil 59 31 Df 47
27650 Louye 27 50 Bb 56
16100 Louzac-Saint-André 16 123 Zd 74
52220 Louze 52 74 Ee 58
72600 Louzes 72 68 Ab 58
17160 Louzignac 17 123 Ze 73
79100 Louzy 79 99 Ze 66
74330 Lovagny 74 120 Ga 73
55500 Loxéville 55 55 Fc 56
35290 Loya, le 35 65 Xe 60
56800 Loyat 56 64 Xd 61
39380 Loye, la 39 107 Fd 66
74890 Loyer 74 120 Gc 71
71530 Loyère, Fragnes-, la 71 106 Ee 67
01800 Loyes 01 119 Fb 73
43450 Loyes, les 43 128 Db 76
18170 Loye-sur-Arnon 18 102 Cc 69
01360 Loyettes 01 131 Fb 74
45190 Loynes 45 86 Bd 62
17330 Lozay 17 110 Zc 72

A
B
C
D
E
F
G
H
I
J
K
L
M
N
O
P
Q
R
S
T
U
V
W
X
Y
Z

Lozay | 285

60600 Maimbeville 60 39 Cd 52
45630 Maimbray 45 88 Cf 63
77760 Mainbervilliers 77 71 Cc 59
85320 Mainborgère, la 85 109 Ye 69
18300 Mainbré 18 88 Ce 64
08220 Mainbresson 08 41 Eb 50
08220 Mainbressy 08 41 Eb 50
78720 Maincourt 78 50 Bf 56
77950 Maincy 77 71 Ce 57
33160 Main-d'Estève, la 33 134 Zb 79
89160 Maine, la 89 90 Eb 62
16260 Maine, le 16 124 Ac 73
24170 Maine, le 24 137 Ba 80
24460 Maine, le 24 125 Af 76
17610 Maine-Allain, le 17 123 Zc 74
17890 Maine-Auriou, le 17 122 Yf 74
16230 Maine-de-Boixe 16 124 Ab 73
17260 Maine-Fleuret 17 122 Zc 75
16590 Maine-Joizeau 16 124 Ab 74
24400 Maine-Lava 24 136 Ab 79
76440 Mainemare 76 37 Bc 51
16130 Maine-Neuf, le 16 123 Zd 75
28160 Maineuf 28 69 Ba 59
16250 Mainfonds 16 123 Aa 75
59233 Maing 59 30 Dc 47
27150 Mainneville 27 38 Be 52
23700 Mainsat 23 114 Cc 72
62870 Maintenay 62 28 Be 46
28130 Maintenon 28 70 Bd 57
28270 Mainterne 28 49 Ba 56
76660 Maintru 76 37 Bb 50
54150 Mainville 54 56 Ff 53
57380 Mainvillers 57 57 Gd 54
28300 Mainvilliers 28 70 Bc 58
45330 Mainvilliers 45 71 Cb 59
16200 Mainxe 16 123 Ze 75
16380 Mainzac 16 124 Ac 75
79190 Mairé 79 111 Aa 72
86270 Mairé 86 100 Ae 67
79230 Mairé-Bas 79 111 Zd 71
21500 Mairie, la 21 90 Ec 63
12260 Mairinhagues 12 151 Bf 82
08140 Mairy 08 42 Fa 51
54150 Mairy-Mainville 54 56 Ff 53
51240 Mairy-sur-Marne 51 54 Ec 55
44690 Maisdon-sur-Sèvre 44 97 Yd 66
21400 Maisey-le-Duc 21 91 Ee 61
25290 Maisières-Notre-Dame 25 107 Ga 66
80220 Maisnières 80 38 Bd 48
62130 Maisnil 62 29 Cc 46
62380 Maisnil 62 29 Ca 45
59134 Maisnil, le 59 30 Cf 45
62380 Maisnil-Boutry, le 62 28 Bf 45
62620 Maisnil-lès-Ruitz 62 29 Cd 46
39260 Maisod 39 119 Fe 70
59190 Maison-Blanche, la 59 27 Cc 44
44850 Maison-Blanche 44 82 Yd 65
35760 Maison-Blanche, la 35 65 Yc 60
42130 Maison-Blanche, la 42 129 Ea 74
63190 Maison-Blanche, la 63 128 Dc 74
71570 Maison-Blanche, la 71 118 Ee 71
62310 Maisoncelle 62 29 Ca 46
79600 Maisoncelle 79 99 Zf 68
08450 Maisoncelle-et-Villers 08 42 Ef 51
52240 Maisoncelles 52 75 Fd 60
72440 Maisoncelles 72 85 Ad 61
60112 Maisoncelle-Saint-Pierre 60 38 Ca 51
53170 Maisoncelles-du-Maine 53 67 Zc 61
77570 Maisoncelles-en-Gâtinais 77 71 Cd 59
14500 Maisoncelles-la-Jordan 14 47 Za 56
14310 Maisoncelles-Pelvey 14 47 Zb 54
60480 Maisoncelle-Tuilerie 60 38 Cb 51
10140 Maison-des-Champs 10 74 Ed 59
70230 Maison-des-Vaux, la 70 93 Gb 63
89420 Maison-Dieu 89 90 Ea 63
58190 Maison-Dieu, la 58 90 Dd 64
60590 Maisonettes, les 60 50 Bf 52
23800 Maison-Feyne 23 113 Be 70
20214 Maison forest. de Bonifatu CTC 180 Ie 94
57230 Maison Forestière Biesenberg 57 58 Hd 54
57230 Maison Forestière Dauenthal 57 58 Hd 54
57230 Maison Forestière Erlenmoos 57 58 Hd 54
24140 Maison-Jeannette 24 136 Ad 78
61110 Maison-Maugis 61 69 Ae 58
04530 Maison-Méane 04 158 Gf 82
18170 Maisonnais 18 102 Cb 69
87440 Maisonnais-sur-Tardoire 87 124 Ae 74
40090 Maisonnave 40 147 Zc 85
79500 Maisonnay 79 111 Zf 71
07230 Maison-Neuve 07 154 Eb 82
16410 Maison-Neuve 16 124 Ac 75
19400 Maison-Neuve 19 138 Ca 78
35500 Maison-Neuve 35 66 Yf 60
40240 Maison-Neuve 40 147 Ze 84
67130 Maison-Neuve 67 77 Hb 57
86170 Maisonneuve 86 99 Aa 68
53320 Maison-Neuve, la 53 66 Za 60
33138 Maisonnieu 33 134 Yf 80
23150 Maisonnisses 23 114 Bf 72
20242 Maison Pierraggi CTC 183 Kc 96
80150 Maison-Ponthieu 80 29 Ca 47
80135 Maison-Roland 80 29 Ca 48
23600 Maison-Rouge 23 114 Cb 70
24800 Maison-Rouge 24 125 Af 76
59530 Maison-Rouge 59 31 De 47
63210 Maison-Rouge 63 127 Cf 75
77370 Maison-Rouge 77 72 Da 57
41300 Maison-Rouge, la 41 87 Ca 64
11330 Maisons 11 179 Cd 91
14400 Maisons 14 47 Zb 53
28700 Maisons 28 70 Bf 58
18200 Maisons, les 18 102 Cc 68
19170 Maisons, les 19 126 Ca 75
24160 Maisons, les 24 125 Af 76
94700 Maisons-Alfort 94 51 Cc 56
25650 Maisons-du-Bois 25 108 Gc 67
51300 Maisons-en-Champagne 51 54 Ec 56
67220 Maisonsgoutte 67 60 Hb 58
78600 Maisons-Laffitte 78 51 Ca 55
10210 Maisons-lès-Chaource 10 73 Eb 60
10200 Maisons-lès-Soulaines 10 74 Ee 59
10130 Maisons-Rouges, les 10 73 Df 60
72800 Maisons-Rouges, les 72 84 Ab 62
63230 Maisons-Rouges-les-Fontêtes, les 63 127 Cf 74
24590 Maisons-Selves 24 137 Bb 78
79600 Maisontiers 79 98 Ze 68
91720 Maisse 91 71 Cc 58
02490 Maissemy 02 40 Db 49
64360 Maissonave 64 161 Zc 89
14450 Maisy 14 46 Yf 52
54370 Maixe 54 56 Gc 57
54470 Maizerais 54 56 Fe 55
55160 Maizeray 55 55 Fe 54
71460 Maizeray 71 105 Ed 69
57530 Maizeroy 57 56 Gc 54
57530 Maizery, Colligny- 57 56 Gc 54
14210 Maizet 14 47 Zd 54
55300 Maizey 55 55 Fd 55
58150 Maizière 58 89 Da 65
14190 Maizières 14 48 Zf 54
52300 Maizières 52 75 Fa 58
54550 Maizières 54 76 Ga 57
62127 Maizières 62 29 Cc 47
70190 Maizières 70 93 Ga 64
10510 Maizières-la-Grande-Paroisse 10 73 De 57
10500 Maizières-lès-Brienne 10 74 Ed 58
57280 Maizières-lès-Metz 57 56 Ga 53
57810 Maizières-lès-Vic 57 57 Ge 56
52500 Maizières-sur-Amance 52 92 Fd 62
42750 Maizilly 42 117 Eb 71
36170 Maizotin 36 113 Bc 70
02160 Maizy 02 40 De 52
82160 Majac 82 151 Be 83
04270 Majastres 04 157 Gb 85
46160 Majourals 46 138 Be 81
32730 Malabat 32 163 Ab 88
81490 Malacan 81 166 Cc 87
56330 Malachappe 56 80 Wf 62
70190 Malachère, la 70 93 Ga 64
28140 Maladrerie, la 28 70 Be 60
89710 Maladrerie, la 89 89 Dc 61
01340 Malafretaz 01 118 Fa 71
24210 Malagnac 24 137 Ba 78
74580 Malagny 74 120 Ga 72
17620 Malaigre 17 122 Yf 73
21410 Mâlain 21 91 Ee 65
88140 Malaincourt 88 76 Fe 59
52150 Malaincourt-sur-Meuse 52 75 Fd 60
87520 Malaise, la 87 113 Af 73
55270 Malancourt 55 55 Fb 53
57360 Malancourt-la-Montagne 57 56 Ga 53
08370 Malandry 08 42 Fb 51
39700 Malange 39 107 Fd 65
19150 Malangle 19 126 Be 77
16500 Malanguin 16 112 Ae 72
25330 Malans 25 107 Ga 66
70140 Malans 70 92 Fd 65
56220 Malansac 56 81 Xe 62
63250 Malaptie, la 63 129 De 74
07140 Malarce-sur-la-Thines 07 154 Ea 82
91470 Malassis 91 51 Ca 57
56140 Malastraed = Malestroit 56 81 Xd 62
46600 Malastrèges 46 138 Bd 79
26780 Malataverne 26 142 Ee 82
30580 Malataverne 30 154 Ec 83
43200 Malataverne 43 141 Ea 77
16300 Malatret 16 123 Zf 76
84340 Malaucène 84 156 Fa 83
57590 Malaucourt-sur-Seille 57 56 Gc 55
55200 Malaumont 55 55 Fc 56
35330 Malaunay 35 81 Xf 61
35460 Malaunay 35 66 Yd 58
76770 Malaunay 76 37 Ba 51
82200 Malause 82 149 Af 84
64410 Malaussanne 64 162 Zd 87
06710 Malaussène 06 158 Ha 85
63200 Malauzat 63 128 Da 73
48100 Malavielle 48 140 Db 81
54560 Malavillers 54 43 Ff 52
71460 Malay 71 118 Ee 69
12220 Malayal 12 139 Cb 81
89100 Malay-le-Grand 89 72 Dc 59
89100 Malay-le-Petit 89 72 Dc 59
15230 Malbo 15 139 Ce 79
07140 Malbosc 07 154 Ea 82
07140 Malbosquet 07 154 Ea 82
70200 Malbouhans 70 94 Gd 62
48270 Malbouzon, Prinsuéjols- 48 140 Da 80
25620 Malbrans 25 107 Ga 66
25160 Malbuisson 25 108 Gb 68
18130 Malçay 18 102 Cd 67
19340 Malcornet 19 127 Cc 74
57560 Malcôte 57 77 Ha 57
61260 Mâle 61 69 Ae 59
04000 Malefiance 04 157 Gb 83
09500 Malegoude 09 165 Bf 90
19360 Malemort 19 138 Bd 77
84570 Malemort-du-Comtat 84 156 Fa 84
48210 Malène, la 48 153 Db 83
19290 Malepouge 19 126 Ca 75
33133 Maleret 33 135 Ze 79
44390 Malescot 44 82 Yc 63
45330 Malesherbes 45 71 Cc 59
45300* Malesherbois, le 45 71 Cc 59
19160 Malesoute 19 126 Ca 76
56140 Malestroit = Malastraed 56 81 Xd 62
40400 Malet 40 147 Zb 85
61290 Malétable 61 69 Ae 57
86160 Maleuf 86 112 Ab 70
63840 Maleval 63 129 Df 76
07660 Malevielle 07 141 Df 80
12350 Maleville 12 151 Ca 82
48500 Maleville 48 153 Db 82
19300 Maleyre 19 126 Ca 76
43230 Malgascon 43 141 Dd 78
15140 Malgorse 15 139 Cc 78
30600 Malgue, la 30 169 Eb 87
56300 Malguénac 56 79 Wf 60
14260 Malherbe-sur-Ajon 14 47 Zc 54
22640 Malhourne, la 22 64 Xd 58
36340 Malicornay 36 114 Bd 69
03600 Malicorne 03 115 Ce 71
37310 Malicorne 37 100 Ae 65
89120 Malicorne 89 89 Da 62
72270 Malicorne-sur-Sarthe 72 84 Zf 62
48120 Malige, la 48 140 Dc 80
49540 Maligné 49 98 Zd 65
21230 Maligny 21 105 Ed 66
89800 Maligny 89 90 De 61
04350 Malijai 04 157 Ga 84
59127 Malincourt 59 30 Db 48
63510 Malintrat 63 128 Db 74
26120 Malissard 26 143 Ef 79
37230 Malitourne 37 85 Ad 64
13115 Mallabré 13 171 Fe 86
16120 Mallaville 16 123 Zf 75
04230 Mallefougasse 04 157 Ff 84
54670 Malleloy 54 56 Ga 56
04510 Mallemoisson 04 157 Ga 84
13370 Mallemort 13 170 Fb 86
09120 Malléon 09 177 Be 90
19500 Mallepeyre 19 138 Bd 78
23260 Malleret 23 127 Cb 74
23600 Malleret-Boussac 23 114 Ca 70
39190 Mallerey 39 106 Fc 69
15100 Mallesaignes 15 140 Cf 79
07320 Malleval 07 142 Ec 78
38470 Malleval 38 143 Fc 78
42520 Malleval 42 130 Ee 76
24200 Mallevergne 24 137 Bb 79
17360 Malleville 17 135 Zf 77
76450 Malleville-les-Grès 76 36 Ad 50
27800 Malleville-sur-le-Bec 27 49 Ae 53
16110 Malleyrand 16 124 Ac 74
85590 Mallièvre 85 98 Za 67
38460 Mallin 38 131 Fb 74
57480 Malling 57 44 Gb 52
03250 Mallot, le 03 116 De 72
14350 Malloué 14 47 Za 55
57130 Malmaison 57 56 Ga 54
02190 Malmaison, la 02 41 Df 51
54150 Malmaison, la 54 56 Ff 53
68550 Malmerspach 68 94 Ha 61
08450 Malmy 08 42 Ef 51
51800 Malmy 51 54 Ee 53
63320 Malnon, le 63 128 Da 75
85300 Malnoue 85 96 Ya 67
59240 Malo-les-Bains 59 27 Cc 42
14280 Mâlon 14 35 Zd 53
13090 Malouesse, la 13 170 Fc 88
30450 Malous-et-Elze 30 154 Ea 82
27300 Malouy 27 49 Ad 54
80250 Malpart 80 39 Cc 50
25160 Malpas 25 108 Gb 68
31380 Malpas 31 150 Bd 86
43370 Malpas 43 141 Df 79
82160 Malpérie 82 150 Be 83
12800 Malphettes 12 151 Cc 84
63490 Malpie 63 128 Dc 75
59570 Malplaquet 59 31 Df 47
46400 Malpuch 46 138 Bf 80
11300 Malras 11 165 Cb 90
43800 Malrevers 43 141 Df 78
05460 Malrif 05 145 Gf 80
52140 Malroy 52 75 Fd 61
57640 Malroy 57 56 Gb 53
89520 Malrue, la 89 89 Db 63
19290 Malsagne 19 126 Ca 74
71140 Maltat 71 104 De 68
58150 Maltaverne 58 88 Cf 64
73390 Maltaverne 73 132 Gb 75
14930 Maltot 14 35 Zd 54
50760 Maltot 50 33 Ye 51
23220 Malval 23 114 Bf 70
70400 Malval 70 94 Gd 63
43210 Malvalette 43 129 Ea 76
87250 Malvat 87 113 Bc 71
02140 Malvaux 02 41 Ea 50
90200 Malvaux 90 94 Gf 62
11600 Malves-en-Minervois 11 166 Cc 89
11120 Malvesi 11 167 Cf 89
31510 Malvezie 31 176 Ae 90
16290 Malvieille 16 123 Zf 74
63980 Malvielle 63 129 Dd 75
43160 Malvières 43 129 De 76
11300 Malviès 11 165 Cb 90
38510 Malville 38 131 Fc 74
44260 Malville 44 82 Ya 64
70120 Malvillers 70 93 Fe 62
89120 Malvrain 89 89 Da 61
56480 Malvran 56 63 Wf 59
54220 Malzéville 54 56 Gb 56
43340 Malzieu, le 43 141 Df 80
48140 Malzieu-Forain, le 48 140 Dc 79
48140 Malzieu-Ville, le 48 140 Dc 79
02120 Malzy 02 40 De 49
25150 Mambouhans 25 94 Gd 64
43190 Mamea 43 141 Eb 78
87500 Mameix 87 125 Bb 75
72600 Mamers 72 68 Ac 58
62120 Mametz 62 29 Cb 45
80300 Mametz 80 29 Ce 49
54470 Mamey 54 56 Ff 55
25620 Mamirolle 25 107 Ga 65
80360 Manancourt 80 39 Cf 48
26160 Manas 26 143 Ef 81
32170 Manas-Bastanous 32 163 Ac 88
22540 Manaty, le 22 63 We 57
54150 Mance 54 56 Ff 53
50540 Mancellière, la 50 66 Yf 57
50750 Mancellière-sur-Vire, la 50 46 Yf 54
25250 Mancenans 25 94 Gd 64
34210 Mancès 34 166 Cd 88
71240 Mancey 71 106 Ee 69
28700 Manchainville 28 70 Be 58
45300 Manchecourt 45 71 Cc 59
32370 Manciet 32 148 Aa 86
54790 Mancieulles 54 56 Ff 53
31360 Mancioux 31 164 Af 90
49350 Mancotiers, les 49 84 Ze 64
51530 Mancy 51 53 Df 55
57640 Mancy 57 56 Gb 53
24560 Mandacou 24 136 Ad 80
30120 Mandagout 30 153 Dd 84
12500 Mandailles 12 152 Cf 81
15590 Mandailles-Saint-Julien 15 139 Cd 78
30480 Mandajors 30 154 Df 84
74350 Mandallaz 74 120 Ga 73
79190 Mandegault 79 111 Zf 72
06210 Mandelieu-La-Napoule 06 173 Gf 87
63630 Mandelles 63 128 Dd 76
21190 Mandelot 21 105 Ee 66
23800 Mandement, le 23 113 Bd 71
57480 Manderen 57 44 Gc 52
25350 Mandeure 25 94 Gf 64
27370 Mandeville 27 49 Ba 53
14710 Mandeville-en-Bessin 14 47 Za 53
30170 Mandiargues 30 154 Df 85
83690 Mandins, les 83 172 Gb 87
88650 Mandray 88 77 Gf 59
27130 Mandres 27 49 Af 56
54470 Mandres-aux-Quatres-Tours 54 56 Fe 55
55290 Mandres-en-Barrois 55 75 Fc 58
52800 Mandres-la-Côte 52 75 Fb 60
94520 Mandres-les-Roses 94 51 Cd 56
88800 Mandres-sur-Vair 88 76 Ff 59
20200 Mandriale CTC 181 Kc 92
20167 Mandriolo CTC 182 Ie 96
20167 Mandriolu = Mandriolo CTC 182 Ie 96
30129 Manduel 30 154 Ec 86
04300 Mane 04 156 Fe 85
31260 Mane 31 164 Af 90
56440 Mané-er-Ven 56 80 We 61
76133 Manéglise 76 36 Ab 51
29300 Mane-Guégan 29 79 Wc 61
56680 Manéguen 56 79 We 62
76590 Manéhouville 76 37 Ba 50
32140 Manent-Montané 32 163 Ad 88
14340 Manerbe 14 35 Ab 53
35430 Manezelaban 35 65 Xf 59
58430 Manges, les 58 104 Df 66
55130 Mangiennes 55 43 Fd 52
63270 Manglieu 63 128 Dc 75
54290 Mangonville 54 76 Gb 58
12160 Manhac 12 152 Cc 83
15220 Manhes 15 139 Cb 79
55160 Manheulles 55 55 Fd 54
33210 Manhot 33 135 Zd 81
57590 Manhoué 57 56 Gc 56
02300 Manicamp 02 40 Db 51
34620 Manière, la 34 167 Da 88
74230 Manigod 74 132 Gc 73
62810 Manin 62 29 Cd 47
87380 Manin 87 125 Bd 75
38650 Maninaire 38 143 Fd 79
62650 Maninghem 62 28 Bf 45
62250 Maninghen-Henne 62 26 Be 44
69800 Manissieux 69M 130 Ef 74
21430 Manlay 21 105 Ec 66
76110 Mannevil-la-Goupil 76 36 Ac 51
76460 Manneville-ès-Plains 76 36 Ae 49
14130 Manneville-la-Pipard 14 48 Ab 53
27210 Manneville-la-Raoult 27 36 Ab 52
27500 Manneville-sur-Risle 27 36 Ad 52
76290 Mannevillette 76 35 Ab 51
40410 Mano 40 147 Zb 82
24370 Manobre 24 137 Bb 80
14400 Manoir, le 14 47 Zc 53
27460 Manoir, les 27 37 Bb 53
76510 Manoir-du-Val 76 37 Bb 50
52700 Manois 52 75 Fc 59
57100 Manom 57 44 Gb 52
65220 Manoncères 65 163 Ac 89
54210 Manoncourt-en-Vermois 54 76 Gb 57
54385 Manoncourt-en-Woëvre 54 56 Ff 56
54610 Manoncourt-sur-Seille 54 56 Ga 55
54385 Manonville 54 56 Ff 56
54300 Manonviller 54 77 Gd 57
04100 Manosque 04 156 Fe 86
16500 Manot 16 112 Ad 73
28240 Manou 28 69 Af 57
58210 Manou 58 89 Db 64
08400 Manre 08 54 Ed 53
43130 Mans 43 129 Df 77
71800 Mans 71 117 Eb 70
72000 Mans, le 72 68 Ab 60
19520 Mansac 19 137 Bc 77
65140 Mansan 65 163 Ab 88
23400 Mansat-la-Courrière 23 114 Be 73
27410 Manselles 27 49 Ae 55
32120 Mansempuy 32 164 Ae 86
32310 Mansencôme 32 148 Ac 85
40560 Mansenes 40 146 Yd 85
46110 Mansergues 46 138 Be 79
09500 Manses 09 165 Be 90
72510 Mansigné 72 84 Aa 62
16230 Mansle 16 124 Ab 73
20245 Manso CTC 182 Ie 94
63122 Manson 63 128 Da 74
82120 Mansonville 82 149 Af 84
68210 Manspach 68 94 Ha 63
40700 Mant 40 162 Zc 87
26140 Mantaille 26 130 Ef 77
22450 Mantallot 22 63 We 56
20123 Mantarellu CTC 182 If 98
28700 Mantarville 28 70 Bf 58
58270 Mantelet 58 103 Dc 66
01560 Mantenay-Montlin 01 118 Fa 70
38350 Mantes-en-Ratier 38 144 Fe 79
78200 Mantes-la-Jolie 78 50 Be 55
78711 Mantes-la-Ville 78 50 Be 55
66360 Mantet 66 178 Cb 94
64300 Mantette 64 161 Zb 88
05400 Manteyer 05 144 Ff 81
37240 Manthelan 37 100 Ae 66
27240 Manthelon 27 49 Ba 55
26210 Manthes 26 130 Fa 77
41240 Manthierville 41 70 Bc 61
61350 Mantilly 61 67 Zb 57
70100 Mantoche 70 92 Fd 64
39230 Mantry 39 107 Fd 68
88240 Manufacture, la 88 76 Gb 61
14117 Manvieux 14 47 Zc 52
87150 Manvin 87 125 Af 74
57380 Many 57 57 Gd 54
41320 Many, le 41 87 Bf 65
57420 Many-aux-Bois 57 56 Ga 55
24110 Manzac-sur-Vern 24 136 Ad 78
63410 Manzat 63 115 Cf 73
01570 Manziat 01 118 Ef 70
56430 Maoron = Mauron 56 64 Xe 60
83510 Mappe 83 172 Gb 88
12480 Mappen 12 152 Ce 85
62360 Maquinghen 62 28 Be 44
52260 Marac 52 92 Fb 61
54300 Marainviller 54 77 Gd 57
88130 Marainville-sur-Madon 88 76 Gb 58
62360 Marais, le 62 28 Be 44
74230 Marais, le 74 132 Gc 74
91530 Marais, le 91 71 Ca 57
03170 Marais, les 03 115 Ce 71
39400 Marais, les 39 120 Ga 69
14620 Marais-la-Chapelle, le 14 48 Zf 55
85350 Marais-Salé 85 96 Xe 68
27680 Marais-Vernier 27 36 Ac 52
32190 Marambat 32 148 Ab 86
20600 Marana CTC 181 Kc 93
20290 Marana, la CTC 181 Kd 93
16290 Marange 16 123 Aa 74
39270 Marangea 39 119 Fd 70
57535 Marange-Silvange 57 56 Ga 53
57690 Marange-Zondrage 57 57 Gd 54
17230 Marans 17 110 Za 71
49500 Marans 49 83 Za 63
33230 Maransin 33 135 Ze 78
47230 Maransin, le 47 148 Ab 84
62170 Marant 62 28 Bf 46
52370 Maranville 52 74 Ef 60
08460 Maranwez 08 41 Ec 50
79100 Maranzais 79 99 Zf 67
70110 Marast 70 93 Gc 63
63480 Marat 63 129 De 75
55000 Marats, les 55 55 Fb 55
52310 Marault 52 75 Fa 59
24620 Maraurie 24 137 Af 79
34370 Maraussan 34 167 Da 88
24400 Maraval 24 136 Ac 78
83260 Maraval 83 171 Ga 89
31450 Maravals 31 165 Bd 88
32120 Maravat 32 149 Ae 86
41320 Maray 41 101 Bf 65
10160 Maraye-en-Othe 10 73 Df 60
68420 Marbach 68 60 Hb 60
54820 Marbache 54 56 Ga 56
59440 Marbaix 59 31 Df 48
27110 Marbeuf 27 49 Af 54
52320 Marbéville 52 75 Fa 59
44140 Marbœuf 44 97 Yc 66
09230 Marbois 09 176 Bb 90
27160 Marbois 27 49 Af 55
55300 Marbotte 55 55 Fd 55
28200 Marboué 28 70 Bb 60
01851 Marboz 01 119 Fb 70
31440 Marbre 31 176 Ad 91
33180 Marbuzet 33 122 Zb 77
08260 Marby 08 41 Ec 50
09220 Marc 09 177 Bc 92
65110 Marcadau 65 174 Ze 92
18170 Marçais 18 102 Cc 68
37500 Marçay 37 99 Ab 66
86370 Marçay 86 111 Ab 70
35133 Marcé 35 66 Ye 58
41800 Marcé 41 85 Ae 62
49140 Marcé 49 84 Ze 63
74210 Marceau 74 132 Gb 74
61570 Marcei 61 48 Aa 57
80800 Marcelcave 80 39 Cd 49
14740 Marcelet 14 35 Zd 53
74250 Marcellaz 74 120 Gc 72
74150 Marcellaz-Albanais 74 132 Ff 73
21350 Marcellois 21 91 Ed 64
47200 Marcellus 47 135 Aa 82
33620 Marcenais 33 135 Zd 78
03260 Marcenat 03 116 Dc 71
15150 Marcenat 15 139 Cb 78
15190 Marcenat 15 127 Ce 77
63530 Marcenat-Moullet 63 115 Da 73
21330 Marcenay 21 91 Ec 61
42140 Marcenod 42 130 Ec 75
24590 Marces 24 137 Bb 79
37160 Marcé-sur-Esves 37 100 Ad 66
66320 Marcevol 66 178 Cd 92
50300 Marcey-les-Grèves 50 46 Yd 56
61290 Marchainville 61 69 Ae 57
02350 Marchais 02 40 De 51
91410 Marchais 91 70 Ca 57
91820 Marchais 91 71 Cc 58
41160 Marchais, le 41 86 Ba 61
41300 Marchais, les 41 87 Ca 63
89120 Marchais, les 89 73 Dd 59
89120 Marchais-Beton 89 89 Da 61
02540 Marchais-en-Brie 02 53 Dc 55
15270 Marchal 15 127 Cd 76
01680 Marchamp 01 131 Fd 74
69430 Marchampt 69D 118 Ed 72
44390 Marchanderie, la 44 82 Yd 64
21270 Marchandeuil 21 92 Fc 64
15400 Marchastel 15 127 Ce 77
48260 Marchastel 48 140 Da 81
25360 Marchaux-Chaudefontaine 25 93 Ga 65
41190 Marché 41 86 Ba 63
33910 Marche, la 33 135 Ze 79
58400 Marche, la 58 103 Da 66
28260 Marchefroy 28 50 Bd 55

A B C D E F G H I J K L M N O P Q R S T U V W X Y Z

Marchefroy | 287

80200 Marchélepot 80 39 Cf 49
61170 Marchemaisons 61 68 Ab 57
77230 Marchémoret 77 52 Ce 54
44140 Marché-Neuf, le 44 97 Yd 66
41370 Marchenoir 41 86 Bc 62
33380 Marcheprime 33 134 Za 80
08270 Marchéroménil 08 41 Ec 51
26300 Marches 26 143 Fa 79
45290 Marches, les 45 88 Ce 62
73800 Marches, les 73 132 Ga 76
77510 Marchés, les 77 52 Db 55
20130 Marchese CTC 182 Id 96
21430 Marcheseuil 21 105 Ec 66
50190 Marchésieux 50 33 Ye 53
70310 Marchessant, le 70 94 Gd 61
28120 Marchéville 28 69 Bb 58
80150 Marcheville 80 28 Bf 47
55160 Marchéville-en-Woëvre 55 55 Fe 54
28410 Marchezais 28 50 Bd 56
59870 Marchiennes 59 30 Db 46
41700 Marchigny 41 86 Bc 64
59990 Marchipont 59 31 De 46
01100 Marchon 01 119 Fe 71
15320 Marchot 15 140 Db 78
44540 Marchy 44 82 Ye 63
32230 Marciac 32 163 Aa 87
38350 Marcieu 38 144 Fe 79
59149 Marcignies 59 31 Eb 47
71110 Marcigny 71 117 Ea 71
21390 Marcigny-sous-Thil 21 91 Ec 64
43350 Marcilhac 43 141 De 78
46160 Marcilhac-sur-Célé 46 138 Be 81
16500 Marcillac 16 112 Ae 72
24700 Marcillac 24 136 Aa 78
33860 Marcillac 33 123 Zc 77
19320 Marcillac-la-Croisille 19 126 Ca 77
19500 Marcillac-la-Croze 19 138 Be 78
16140 Marcillac-Lanville 16 123 Aa 73
24200 Marcillac-Saint-Quentin 24 137 Bb 79
12330 Marcillac-Vallon 12 139 Cc 82
63440 Marcillat 63 115 Da 72
03420 Marcillat-en-Combraille 03 115 Cd 71
53440 Marcillé-la-Ville 53 67 Zd 59
35560 Marcillé-Raoul 35 65 Yc 58
35240 Marcillé-Robert 35 66 Yd 61
01150 Marcilleux 01 131 Fb 74
38260 Marcilloles 38 131 Fb 76
18140 Marcilly 18 103 Ce 66
42130 Marcilly 42 129 Ea 74
45340 Marcilly 45 71 Cc 60
50220 Marcilly 50 66 Ye 57
58270 Marcilly 58 104 Dc 67
58800 Marcilly 58 104 De 65
61130 Marcilly 61 68 Ad 59
77139 Marcilly 77 52 Cf 54
89200 Marcilly 89 90 Df 63
69380 Marcilly-d'Azergues 69M 130 Ee 73
41100 Marcilly-en-Beauce 41 86 Ba 62
41210 Marcilly-en-Gault 41 87 Bf 64
45240 Marcilly-en-Villette 45 87 Ca 62
27320 Marcilly-la-Campagne 27 49 Bb 55
71120 Marcilly-la-Gueurce 71 117 Eb 70
42130 Marcilly-le-Châtel 42 129 Ea 74
10290 Marcilly-le-Hayer 10 73 Dd 58
71390 Marcilly-lès-Buxy 71 105 Ed 68
21350 Marcilly-lès-Vitteaux 21 91 Ed 64
21320 Marcilly-Ogny 21 105 Ec 65
52360 Marcilly-Plesnoy 52 92 Fd 61
27810 Marcilly-sur-Eure 27 50 Bc 56
37330 Marcilly-sur-Maulne 37 85 Ab 63
51260 Marcilly-sur-Seine 51 73 De 57
21120 Marcilly-sur-Tille 21 92 Fa 63
37800 Marcilly-sur-Vienne 37 100 Ad 66
62730 Marck 62 27 Bf 43
67390 Marckolsheim 67 60 Hd 59
19150 Marc-la-Tour 19 126 Bf 77
19150 Marc-le-Vieux 19 126 Bf 77
42210 Marclopt 42 129 Eb 75
40190 Marcoge 40 147 Ze 85
59159 Marcoing 59 30 Db 48
15220 Marcolès 15 139 Cc 80
63380 Marcollange 63 127 Cd 73
38270 Marcollin 38 131 Fa 77
07190 Marcols-les-Eaux 07 142 Ec 80
72340 Marçon 72 85 Ad 62
62140 Marconne 62 29 Ca 46
62140 Marconnelle 62 28 Ca 46
74140 Marcorens 74 120 Gb 71
11120 Marcorignan 11 167 Cf 89
91460 Marcoussis 91 51 Cb 57
27520 Marcouville 27 49 Af 53
04420 Marcoux 04 157 Gb 84
42130 Marcoux 42 129 Ea 74
19300 Marcouyeux 19 126 Ca 77
08250 Marcq 08 42 Ef 53
78770 Marcq 78 50 Be 55
59700 Marcq-en-Barœul 59 30 Da 44
59252 Marcq-en-Ostrevent 59 30 Db 47
02720 Marcy 02 40 Dc 49
19170 Marcy 19 126 Ca 75
58130 Marcy 58 103 Db 66
58210 Marcy 58 89 Dc 65
69480 Marcy 69D 118 Ee 73
69280 Marcy-L'Etoile 69M 130 Ee 74
02250 Marcy-sous-Marle 02 40 De 50
36220 Mardelle, la 36 100 Ba 68
41130 Mardelles, les 41 86 Bc 65
45170 Mardelles, les 45 70 Bf 60
51530 Mardeuil 51 53 Df 54
45430 Mardié 45 87 Ca 61
57420 Mardigny 57 56 Ga 55
61230 Mardilly 61 48 Ab 55
52200 Mardor 52 92 Fb 61
69240 Mardore 69D 117 Ec 72
59279 Mardyck 59 27 Cb 42
27940 Mare, la 27 50 Bb 53
35540 Mare, la 35 65 Ya 57
37290 Mare, la 37 100 Ae 68
45300 Mareau-aux-Bois 45 71 Cb 60
45370 Mareau-aux-Prés 45 87 Be 61
40350 Maréchal 40 161 Za 87
58190 Maréchal, le 58 89 De 65
33180 Maréchale, la 33 122 Zb 77
14240 Maréchaux, les 14 34 Zb 54
77560 Maréchère 77 52 Db 57
60540 Mare-d'Ovillers, la 60 51 Cb 53
50270 Mare-du-Parc, la 50 33 Yb 52
72540 Mareil-en-Champagne 72 67 Ze 61
95850 Mareil-en-France 95 51 Cc 54
23150 Mareille 23 114 Bf 72
78490 Mareil-le-Guyon 78 50 Bf 56
52700 Mareilles 52 75 Fb 59
72200 Mareil-sur-Loir 72 84 Aa 62
78124 Mareil-sur-Mauldre 78 50 Bf 55
36160 Marembert, le 36 114 Ca 70
62990 Marenla 62 28 Bf 46
17320 Marennes 17 122 Yf 74
69970 Marennes 69M 130 Ef 75
17560 Marennes-Plage 17 122 Yf 74
72110 Mare-Pineau, la 72 68 Ac 59
27160 Mares 27 49 Af 55
85490 Mares 85 110 Zc 70
14230 Mares, les 14 47 Yf 53
27500 Mares, les 27 49 Ac 52
72170 Mareschè 72 68 Aa 59
59990 Maresches 59 31 Dd 47
62990 Maresquel-Ecquemicourt 62 28 Bf 46
50770 Maresquière, la 50 33 Yc 54
62550 Marest 62 29 Cc 46
32490 Marestaing 32 164 Ba 87
17160 Marestay 17 123 Ze 73
02300 Marest-Dampcourt 02 40 Da 51
80500 Marestmontiers 80 39 Cd 50
60490 Marest-sur-Matz 60 39 Ce 51
62630 Maresville 62 28 Be 45
77560 Marêts, les 77 52 Db 56
63290 Marette 63 116 Dd 73
59238 Maretz 59 30 Dc 48
63710 Mareuge 63 127 Cf 75
63850 Mareuge, la 63 127 Ce 76
63340 Mareugheol 63 128 Da 76
16170 Mareuil 16 123 Zf 74
33210 Mareuil 33 135 Zd 81
80132 Mareuil-Caubert 80 28 Bf 48
51270 Mareuil-en-Brie 51 53 De 55
02130 Mareuil-en-Dôle 02 53 Dd 53
24340 Mareuil en Périgord 24 124 Ac 76
60490 Mareuil-la-Motte 60 39 Ce 51
51700 Mareuil-le-Port 51 53 De 54
77100 Mareuil-lès-Meaux 77 52 Cf 55
18290 Mareuil-sur-Arnon 18 102 Ca 67
51160 Mareuil-sur-Ay 51 53 Ea 54
41110 Mareuil-sur-Cher 41 86 Bb 65
85320 Mareuil-Sur-Lay-Dissais 85 109 Ye 69
60890 Mareuil-sur-Ourca 60 52 Da 54
88320 Marey 88 76 Ff 60
21700 Marey-lès-Fussey 21 106 Ef 66
21120 Marey-sur-Tille 21 92 Fa 63
51170 Marfaux 51 53 Df 54
02140 Marfontaine 02 40 De 50
33570 Margagne, la 33 135 Zf 79
34600 Margal 34 167 Da 87
12440 Margat 12 151 Cb 83
33460 Margaux-Cantenac 33 134 Zb 78
95580 Margency 95 51 Cb 55
19200 Margerides 19 127 Cc 76
26230 Margerie 26 155 Ef 82
15400 Margerie, la 15 127 Cd 77
42560 Margerie-Chantagret 42 129 Ea 75
51290 Margerie-Hancourt 51 74 Ed 57
26260 Margès 26 143 Fa 78
70600 Margilley 70 92 Fd 63
02880 Margival 02 40 Dc 52
08370 Margny 08 43 Fc 51
51210 Margny 51 53 Dd 55
60310 Margny-aux-Cerises 60 39 Cf 50
60200 Margny-lès-Compiègne 60 39 Ce 52
60490 Margny-sur-Matz 60 39 Ce 51
74350 Margolliets, les 74 120 Gb 72
28400 Margon 28 69 Ae 58
34320 Margon 34 167 Db 88
32290 Margouët-Meymes 32 162 Aa 86
83440 Margoutons, les 83 172 Ge 87
48500 Marguefré, le 48 153 Db 82
50410 Margueray 50 46 Ye 55
16250 Marguerie, la 16 123 Zf 75
30320 Marguerittes 30 154 Ec 85
33220 Margueron 33 136 Ab 80
32150 Marguestau 32 148 Zf 85
83670 Margui 83 171 Ga 87
33830 Marguit 33 134 Zb 81
08370 Margut 08 42 Fb 51
08270 Margy 08 41 Ec 51
33650 Marheuil, le 33 134 Zc 80
07160 Mariac 07 142 Ec 79
32170 Mariachous 32 163 Ac 88
33830 Marian 33 146 Za 82
41230 Mariaville 41 87 Be 64
54800 Mariaville 54 56 Fe 54
80360 Maricourt 80 39 Ce 49
84410 Maridats, les 84 155 Fb 84
06420 Marie 06 158 Ha 84
81240 Mariech, le 81 166 Cc 87
57455 Marienthal 57 57 Ge 54
67500 Marienthal 67 58 He 56
17200 Maries, les 17 122 Za 75
57420 Marieulles 57 56 Ga 54
80560 Marieux 80 29 Cc 48
17800 Marignac 17 123 Zd 75
30700 Marignac 30 154 Eb 84
31440 Marignac 31 176 Ad 91
82500 Marignac 82 149 Af 85
26150 Marignac-en-Diois 26 143 Fc 80
31430 Marignac-Lasclares 31 164 Ba 89
31220 Marignac-Laspeyres 31 164 Af 89
20141 Marignana CTC 182 Ie 95
13700 Marignane 13 170 Fb 88
39240 Marigna-sur-Valouse 39 119 Fd 70
49330 Marigné 49 83 Zc 62
49410 Marigné 49 83 Za 65
72220 Marigné-Laillé 72 85 Ac 62
53200 Marigné-Peuton 53 83 Zb 61
74970 Marignier 74 120 Gd 72
01300 Marignieu 01 131 Fe 74
03210 Marigny 03 103 Db 69
21400 Marigny 21 91 Ed 61
39130 Marigny 39 107 Fe 68
51230 Marigny 51 53 Df 57
58160 Marigny 58 103 Db 67
71300 Marigny 71 105 Ec 68
79360 Marigny 79 111 Zd 71
86380 Marigny-Brizay 86 99 Ac 68
86370 Marigny-Chémereau 86 111 Ab 70
58140 Marigny-la-Ville 58 90 Df 64
21150 Marigny-le-Cahouët 21 91 Ec 64
10350 Marigny-le-Châtel 10 73 De 58
58140 Marigny-L'Eglise 58 90 Df 64
50570 Marigny-Le-Lozon 50 33 Ye 54
21200 Marigny-lès-Reullée 21 106 Ef 67
45760 Marigny-les-Usages 45 70 Ca 61
37120 Marigny-Marmande 37 100 Ac 67
74150 Marigny-Saint-Marcel 74 132 Ff 74
58800 Marigny-sur-Yonne 58 90 Dd 65
16110 Marillac-le-Franc 16 124 Ac 74
49410 Marillais, le 49 83 Yf 64
01440 Marillat 01 118 Fb 71
85240 Marillet 85 110 Zc 69
33430 Marimbault 33 147 Ze 82
57810 Marimont 57 57 Ge 56
24800 Marimont, les 24 125 Af 76
57670 Marimont-lès-Bénestroff 57 57 Ge 55
12260 Marin 12 151 Bf 82
74200 Marin 74 120 Gd 70
20233 Marina d'Ampuglia = Marine de Pietracorbara CTC 181 Kc 91
20287 Marina de Meria = Marine di Meria CTC 181 Kc 91
20240 Marina di a Scaffa Rossa = Marine di Scaffa Rossa CTC 185 Kc 97
20145 Marina di Cala d'Oru = Marine de Cala d'Oru CTC 183 Kc 98
20253 Marina di Faringule = Marine de Farinole CTC 181 Kb 92
20137 Marina di Fiori CTC 185 Kb 99
20228 Marina di Giottani = Marine de Giottani CTC 181 Kb 91
20111 Marina di Pévani CTC 182 Ie 96
20260 Marina di Sant'Ambrosgiu = Marine de Sant'Ambroggio CTC 180 Ie 93
20233 Marina di Siscu = Marine de Sisco CTC 181 Kc 92
20213 Marina di Sorbo CTC 181 Kd 94
20213 Marina di Sorbu = Marina di Sorbo CTC 181 Kd 94
20145 Marina di u Manichinu = Marine de Manichinu CTC 185 Kc 97
20240 Marina di u Sulaghju = Marine de Solaro CTC 183 Kc 97
20166 Marina Viva CTC 182 Ie 97
20217 Marinca CTC 181 Kb 91
40210 Mariné 40 146 Za 83
30460 Marine, la 30 154 De 84
20230 Marine de Bravone CTC 183 Kd 95
20145 Marine de Cala d'Oru CTC 183 Kc 98
20256 Marine de Davia CTC 180 Ie 93
20253 Marine de Farinole CTC 181 Kb 92
20228 Marine de Giottani CTC 181 Kb 91
20145 Marine de Manichinu CTC 185 Kc 97
20233 Marine de Pietracorbara CTC 181 Kc 91
20260 Marine de Sant'Ambroggio CTC 180 Ie 93
20228 Marine de Scalo CTC 181 Kb 91
20228 Marine de Scalo = Marina di Scalu CTC 181 Kb 91
20233 Marine de Sisco CTC 181 Kc 92
20240 Marine de Solaro CTC 183 Kc 97
20287 Marine di Meria CTC 181 Kc 91
20240 Marine di Scaffa Rossa CTC 185 Kc 97
95640 Marines 95 51 Bf 54
20253 Marines du Soleil, les CTC 181 Kb 92
42140 Maringes 42 130 Ec 74
71140 Maringes 71 104 De 69
63350 Maringues 63 116 Db 73
85480 Marinière, la 85 97 Ye 69
03270 Mariol 03 116 Dc 72
44540 Mariolle, la 44 83 Yf 63
43440 Marion 43 128 Dc 76
33690 Marions 33 148 Zf 82
57530 Marivaux 57 56 Gc 53
02300 Marizelle 02 40 Db 51
71220 Marizy, Le Rousset- 71 117 Ec 69
02470 Marizy-Sainte-Geneviève 02 52 Db 53
02470 Marizy-Saint-Mard 02 52 Db 53
83440 Marjoris, les 83 172 Ge 87
68470 Markstein, le 68 94 Ha 61
44117 Marland 44 81 Xe 65
36290 Marlanges 36 101 Bb 67
15240 Marlat 15 127 Cc 77
70500 Marlay 70 93 Fe 62
02250 Marle 02 40 De 50
73190 Marle 73 132 Ga 75
08290 Marlemont 08 41 Ec 50
67520 Marlenheim 67 60 Hc 57
74210 Marlens 74 132 Gc 74
80290 Marlers 80 38 Bf 50
77610 Marles-en-Brie 77 52 Cf 56
62170 Marles-sur-Canche 62 28 Be 46
48120 Marlet, le 48 140 Dc 80
23430 Marlhac 23 113 Bd 73
42660 Marlhes 42 130 Ec 77
19700 Marliac 19 126 Be 76
31550 Marliac 31 164 Bc 89
21110 Marliens 21 106 Fb 65
59680 Marlière 59 31 Df 47
01240 Marlieux 01 118 Fa 72
74270 Marlioz 74 120 Ga 72
17290 Marlonges 17 110 Za 72
57155 Marly 57 56 Ga 54
59770 Marly 59 31 Dd 46
02120 Marly-Gomont 02 40 De 49
95670 Marly-la-Ville 95 51 Cc 54
78160 Marly-le-Roi 78 51 Ca 55
71760 Marly-sous-Issy 71 104 Df 68
71420 Marly-sur-Arroux 71 105 Ea 69
18500 Marmagne 18 102 Cb 66
21500 Marmagne 21 90 Ec 63
71710 Marmagne 71 105 Ec 67
43300 Marmaisse 43 140 Dc 78
47200 Marmande 47 136 Aa 82
15250 Marmanhac 15 139 Cc 78
58330 Marmantray 58 104 Dd 66
89420 Marmeaux le Pâtis 89 90 Ea 63
52120 Marmesse 52 74 Ef 60
03630 Marmignolles 03 115 Cd 70
46250 Marminiac 46 137 Bb 81
63410 Marmoizoux 63 115 Cf 73
12200 Marmon 12 151 Ca 83
47220 Marmont-Pachas 47 149 Ad 84
11110 Marmorières 11 167 Da 89
61240 Marmouillé 61 48 Ab 56
16370 Marmounier 16 123 Ze 74
67440 Marmoutier 67 58 Hc 56
24220 Marnac 24 137 Ba 80
69240 Marnand 69D 117 Eb 72
38980 Marnans 38 131 Fb 77
81170 Marnaves 81 151 Bf 84
18300 Marnay 18 103 Cf 65
37190 Marnay 37 85 Ac 65
70150 Marnay 70 93 Fe 65
71240 Marnay 71 106 Ef 68
86160 Marnay 86 112 Ac 70
52800 Marnay-sur-Marne 52 75 Fb 60
10400 Marnay-sur-Seine 10 73 Dd 57
74460 Marnaz 74 120 Gd 72
44270 Marne, la 44 96 Yb 67
61550 Marnefer 61 49 Ad 55
77185 Marne-la-Valle 77 51 Cd 55
79600 Marnes 79 99 Zf 67
39270 Marnézia 39 107 Fd 69
43200 Marnhac 43 129 Ea 78
12540 Marnhagues 12 152 Da 85
12540 Marnhagues-et-Latour 12 152 Da 85
27330 Marnières, les 27 49 Ae 55
36290 Marnoux 36 101 Bb 68
39110 Marnoz 39 107 Fe 67
62161 Marœuil 62 29 Ce 47
59550 Maroilles 59 31 De 48
41210 Marolle-en-Sologne, la 41 87 Be 63
14100 Marolles 14 48 Ac 54
28410 Marolles 28 50 Bd 56
41330 Marolles 41 86 Bb 63
51300 Marolles 51 54 Ed 56
58700 Marolles 58 104 Dc 65
60890 Marolles 60 52 Da 53
91150 Marolles-en-Beauce 91 71 Cb 58
77120 Marolles-en-Brie 77 52 Da 56
94440 Marolles-en-Brie 94 51 Cd 56
91630 Marolles-en-Hurepoix 91 71 Cb 57
10110 Marolles-lès-Bailly 10 74 Ec 59
72260 Marolles-les-Braults 72 68 Ab 59
28400 Marolles-les-Buis 28 69 Af 58
72120 Marolles-lès-Saint-Calais 72 85 Ae 61
10130 Marolles-sous-Lignières 10 73 Df 61
77130 Marolles-sur-Seine 77 72 Da 58
72600 Marollette 72 68 Ac 58
42560 Marols 42 129 Ea 76
76150 Maromme 76 37 Ba 52
33720 Maron 33 135 Zd 81
36120 Mâron 36 101 Bf 68
54230 Maron 54 56 Ga 57
88270 Maroncourt 88 76 Ga 59
24410 Marot 24 136 Ab 78
47800 Marot 47 136 Ac 81
19170 Marouby 19 126 Bf 75
22400 Maroué 22 64 Xc 58
17340 Marouillet, le 17 110 Yf 72
16420 Marousse, le 16 112 Af 72
39290 Marpain 39 92 Fd 65
40330 Marpaps 40 161 Zb 87
59164 Marpent 59 31 Ea 47
35220 Marpiré 35 66 Yd 60
80240 Marquaix 80 39 Da 49
24620 Marquay 24 137 Ba 79
62127 Marquay 62 29 Cc 46
48500 Marquayres 48 153 Db 82
23250 Marque 23 114 Be 72
33180 Marque 33 122 Zb 77
65800 Marque-Debat 65 162 Aa 89
31390 Marquefave 31 164 Bb 89
60490 Marqueglise 60 39 Ce 51
11410 Marquein 11 165 Be 89
65350 Marquerie 65 163 Ab 89
76390 Marques 76 38 Be 50
40190 Marquestau 40 147 Ze 86
59252 Marquette-en-Ostrevent 59 30 Db 47
59520 Marquette-lez-Lille 59 30 Da 44
08390 Marquigny 08 42 Ee 51
59274 Marquillies 59 30 Cf 45
62860 Marquion 62 30 Da 47
40550 Marquis 40 146 Yd 85
62250 Marquise 62 26 Be 44
80700 Marquivillers 80 39 Ce 50
66320 Marquixanes 66 178 Cc 93
32420 Marrast 32 163 Ae 88
89200 Marrault 89 90 Df 64
37370 Marray 37 85 Ae 63
55100 Marre 55 55 Fb 53
39210 Marre, la 39 107 Fe 68
83670 Marreliers, les 83 171 Ff 87
13105 Marres, les 13 170 Fc 88
40110 Marrouat 40 147 Zb 85
12200 Marroule 12 151 Bf 82
24170 Marroux, les 24 137 Ba 80
07320 Mars 07 142 Eb 78
30120 Mars 30 153 Dd 84
42750 Mars 42 117 Eb 72
87380 Mars 87 125 Bc 75
01410 Mars, les 01 120 Ff 71
23700 Mars, les 23 115 Cc 73
11140 Marsa 11 178 Ca 92
16110 Marsac 16 124 Ac 74
16570 Marsac 16 123 Aa 74
19210 Marsac 19 125 Bc 76
23210 Marsac 23 113 Bd 72
33460 Marsac 33 134 Zb 78
47320 Marsac 47 148 Ac 82
47360 Marsac 47 149 Ad 83
65500 Marsac 65 162 Aa 88
82120 Marsac 82 149 Ae 85
63940 Marsac-en-Livradois 63 129 De 76
44170 Marsac-sur-Don 44 82 Yb 63
24430 Marsac-sur-l'Isle 24 124 Ad 77
45300 Marsainvilliers 45 71 Cb 59
03390 Marsais 03 115 Cf 70
17700 Marsais 17 110 Zc 72
85570 Marsais-Sainte-Radégonde 85 110 Za 69
57630 Marsal 57 57 Gd 56
81430 Marsal, Bellegarde- 81 151 Cb 85
24540 Marsalès 24 137 Af 80
19200 Marsalouse, la 19 127 Cc 75
32270 Marsan 32 163 Ae 87
45700 Marsan 45 71 Cd 61
24750 Marsaneix 24 137 Ae 78
51260 Marsangis 51 73 Df 57
89500 Marsangy 89 72 Db 60
21160 Marsannay-la-Côte 21 91 Ef 65
21380 Marsannay-le-Bois 21 92 Fa 64
26740 Marsanne 26 142 Ef 81
33620 Marsas 33 135 Zd 78
65200 Marsas 65 175 Ab 90
63200 Marsat 63 128 Da 73
26260 Marsaz 26 143 Ef 78
03220 Marseigne 03 116 Dd 70
32170 Marseillan 32 163 Ab 88
34340 Marseillan 34 167 Dd 88
65350 Marseillan 65 163 Ab 89
34340 Marseillan-Plage 34 167 Dd 89
13001* Marseille 13 170 Fc 89
60690 Marseille-en-Beauvaisis 60 38 Bf 51
18320 Marseilles-lès-Aubigny 18 103 Da 66
11800 Marseillette 11 166 Cd 89
23800 Marseuil 23 114 Be 71
15320 Marsillac 15 140 Db 79
33112 Marsillan 33 122 Za 78
34590 Marsillargues 34 168 Eb 87
23270 Marsillat 23 114 Ca 71
23700 Marsillat 23 115 Cc 72
16240 Marsillé 16 111 Aa 73
17137 Marsilly 17 110 Yf 71
57530 Marsilly 57 56 Gb 54
86260 Marsilly 86 100 Af 69
54800 Mars-la-Tour 54 56 Ff 54
63610 Marsol 63 128 Cf 76
32700 Marsolan 32 149 Ad 85
51240 Marson 51 54 Ed 55
01340 Marsonnas 01 118 Fa 70
39240 Marsonnas 39 119 Fc 71
55190 Marson-sur-Barboure 55 55 Fc 57
65400 Marsous 65 174 Ze 91
57700 Marspich 57 56 Ga 52
81150 Marssac-sur-Tarn 81 151 Ca 85
08400 Mars-sous-Bourcq 08 42 Ed 52
58240 Mars-sur-Allier 58 103 Da 67
87130 Martageix 87 125 Bd 75
27150 Martagny 27 38 Bd 53
80460 Martaigneville 80 28 Bc 48
47250 Martaillac 47 148 Aa 82
71700 Martailly-lès-Brancion 71 118 Ee 69
80140 Martainneville 80 38 Be 48
14220 Martainville 14 47 Zd 55
27210 Martainville 27 36 Ac 53
76116 Martainville-Epreville 76 37 Bb 52
86330 Martaizé 86 99 Aa 67
58700 Martangy 58 103 Dc 66
33125 Martat, le 33 134 Zc 81
36700 Marteau 36 101 Bb 67
19250 Marteaux, les 19 126 Ca 76
63410 Marteaux, les 63 115 Cf 73
46600 Martel 46 138 Bd 79
83470 Martelle 83 171 Ff 88
38510 Marteray, le 38 131 Fc 75
12240 Martes, les 12 151 Cb 83
32550 Martet 32 163 Ac 87
10500 Marthaux 10 74 Ec 58
54330 Marthemont 54 76 Ga 57
62120 Marthes 62 29 Cb 45
57340 Marthille 57 57 Gd 55
34220 Marthomis 34 166 Ce 87
16380 Marthon 16 124 Ac 75
73400 Marthou 73 132 Gc 74
24590 Marthres 24 137 Bb 79
63330 Marthuret 63 115 Ce 72
12200 Martiel 12 151 Bf 82
39260 Martigna 39 119 Fe 70
46700 Martignac 46 137 Ba 81
84100 Martignan 84 155 Ee 84
30360 Martignargues 30 154 Eb 84
33127 Martignas-sur-Jalle 33 134 Zb 79
01100 Martignat 01 119 Fd 71
63250 Martignat 63 128 Dd 73
49540 Martigné-Briand 49 98 Zd 65
35640 Martigné-Ferchaud 35 82 Ye 62
53470 Martigné-sur Mayenne 53 67 Zc 59
02500 Martigny 02 41 Ea 49
50600 Martigny 50 66 Yf 57
76880 Martigny 76 37 Ba 49
86170 Martigny 86 99 Ab 69
02860 Martigny-Courpierre 02 40 De 52
71220 Martigny-le-Comte 71 117 Ec 69
88320 Martigny-les-Bains 88 76 Fe 60
88300 Martigny-lès-Gerbonvaux 88 76 Fe 58
14700 Martigny-sur-L'Ante 14 47 Ze 55
13500 Martigues 13 170 Fa 88
33650 Martillac 33 135 Zc 80
88430 Martimpré 88 77 Gf 60
56130 Martinais 56 81 Xe 63
76270 Martincamp 76 37 Bc 50

288 | Marchélepot

54380 Martincourt 54 56 Ff 55
60112 Martincourt 60 38 Bf 51
55700 Martincourt-sur-Meuse 55 42 Fb 51
76370 Martin-Église 76 37 Ba 49
23250 Martineiche 23 114 Be 73
50190 Martinerie, la 50 46 Yc 53
85150 Martinet 85 96 Yb 68
85700 Martinet 85 98 Zb 68
30960 Martinet, le 30 154 Ea 83
12800 Martinie, la 12 151 Cb 84
81250 Martinie, la 81 152 Cd 85
17220 Martinière 17 110 Za 72
44640 Martinière 44 96 Yb 65
50660 Martinière 50 46 Yc 55
17600 Martinière, la 17 122 Zb 74
45210 Martinière, la 45 72 Cf 61
79600 Martinière, la 79 99 Ze 68
32350 Martinique, la 32 163 Ac 87
62450 Martinpuich 62 30 Ce 48
39150 Martins 39 107 Ff 69
05260 Martins, les 05 144 Gb 80
59113 Martinsart 59 30 Da 45
80300 Martinsart 80 29 Cd 48
50690 Martinvast 50 33 Yb 51
88410 Martinvelle 88 76 Ff 61
50000 Martinville 50 34 Yf 54
82110 Martissan 82 150 Bb 83
36220 Martizay 36 100 Ba 68
49490 Martoisière 49 84 Aa 63
15800 Martons 15 139 Cd 79
71960 Martoret, le 71 118 Ee 70
27340 Martot 27 49 Ba 53
14740 Martragny 14 47 Zc 53
83840 Martre, la 83 158 Gd 86
33760 Martres 33 135 Ze 80
63430 Martres-d'Artières, les 63 128 Db 73
31210 Martres-de-Rivière 31 163 Ad 90
63720 Martres-sur-Morge 63 116 Db 73
31220 Martres-Tolesane 31 164 Ba 89
86290 Martreuil 86 113 Ba 70
12550 Martrin 12 152 Cd 85
21320 Martrois 21 91 Ed 65
17270 Martron 17 123 Zf 77
09500 Marty 09 165 Bf 90
29800 Martyre, la 29 62 Vf 58
23400 Martyrs, les 23 113 Bd 73
11390 Martys, les 11 166 Cb 88
81440 Martys, les 81 151 Ca 86
30870 Maruéjols 30 154 Eb 86
30350 Maruéjols-lès-Gardon 30 154 Ea 84
87440 Marval 87 124 Ae 75
08400 Marvaux-Vieux 08 54 Ee 53
48100 Marvejols 48 140 Db 81
25250 Marvelise 25 94 Gd 63
55600 Marville 55 43 Fc 52
28170 Marville-les-Bois 28 69 Bb 57
28500 Marville-Moutiers-Brûlé 28 50 Bc 56
67500 Marxenhouse 67 58 He 56
71300 Mary 71 105 Ec 69
77440 Mary-sur-Marne 77 52 Da 54
56130 Marzan 56 81 Xe 63
19300 Marzeix 19 126 Bf 76
23700 Marzelle, la 23 115 Cd 73
44680 Marzelle, la 44 96 Yb 66
49610 Marzelle, la 49 83 Zc 64
85110 Marzelle, la 85 97 Yf 68
81500 Marzens 81 165 Be 87
12490 Marzials 12 152 Cf 84
43450 Marzun 43 128 Da 76
58180 Marzy 58 103 Da 67
06910 Mas, le 06 158 Gf 85
16310 Mas, le 16 124 Ad 74
18270 Mas, le 18 114 Cb 69
19170 Mas, le 19 126 Be 75
19220 Mas, le 19 126 Ca 77
19230 Mas, le 19 125 Bc 76
24700 Mas, le 24 136 Ab 78
32350 Mas, le 32 163 Ac 86
48250 Mas, le 48 141 De 81
63200 Mas, le 63 116 Da 73
63330 Mas, le 63 115 Ce 72
63550 Mas, le 63 116 Dd 73
19700 Masaleix 19 126 Bd 76
48110 Masaribal 48 153 De 83
66650 Mas-Atxer 66 179 Da 94
34520 Mas-Audran 34 153 Db 85
13460 Mas-Bade 13 169 Ec 87
23400 Masbaraud-Mérignat 23 114 Be 73
34260 Mas-Blanc, le 34 167 Db 87
13103 Mas-Blanc-des-Alpilles 13 155 Ee 86
30800 Mas-Blanquet 30 169 Ec 87
26620 Mas-Bourget 26 144 Fe 80
30740 Mas-Bourrie 30 169 Eb 87
11380 Mas-Cabardès 11 166 Cc 88
64330 Mascaraàs-Haron 64 162 Ze 87
32230 Mascaras 32 163 Ab 87
65190 Mascaras 65 163 Ab 89
31460 Mascarville 31 165 Be 87
13800 Mas-Chauvet, le 13 169 Ef 87
19120 Mascheix 19 138 Be 78
19170 Mas-Chevalier, le 19 126 Ca 75
46350 Masclat 46 137 Bc 79
87360 Mascornu, le 87 113 Ba 71
64370 Mascouette 64 161 Zc 87
12400 Mascourbe 12 152 Cf 85
47430 Mas-d' Agenais, le 47 148 Ab 82
13200 Mas-d'Agon 13 169 Ed 87
34700 Mas-d'Alary 34 167 Db 86
13800 Mas-d'Amphoux, le 13 170 Ef 87
34230 Mas-d'Arnaud 34 168 Dd 87
23100 Mas-d'Artige, le 23 126 Cb 74
32700 Mas-d'Auvignon 32 148 Ad 85
09290 Mas-d'Azil, le 09 164 Bc 90
13310 Mas-de-Aulnes 13 169 Ee 87
46330 Mas-de-Bassoul 46 150 Be 82
34380 Mas-de-Bouis 34 153 De 86
13200 Mas-de-Cabassolle 13 169 Ed 87
34520 Mas-de-Calmels 34 153 Dc 85
46150 Mas-de-Camp 46 137 Bc 81
30800 Mas-de-Capette 30 169 Ec 87
34160 Mas-de-Carrat 34 168 Df 86
30220 Mas-de-Chaberton 30 169 Eb 87
46320 Mas-de-Chaupet 46 138 Be 81
11570 Mas-de-Cours 11 166 Cc 90
13200 Mas de Grille 13 169 Ec 86
46260 Mas-de-Guiralet 46 150 Be 82
34520 Mas-de-Jourdes 34 153 Dc 86
13104 Mas de Lanau 13 169 Ee 87
30580 Mas-de-la-Vieille-église, la 30 154 Ec 84
13200 Mas de la Ville 13 169 Ed 87
19380 Masdelbos 19 138 Bf 78
34380 Mas-de-Londres 34 153 De 86
34160 Mas-de-Martin 34 154 Df 86
46160 Mas-de-Pégourié 46 138 Bf 81
13310 Mas de Pernes 13 169 Ee 87
46150 Mas-de-Peyrou 46 137 Bb 81
13460 Mas de Pioch 13 169 Ec 87
12230 Mas-de-Pomier 12 153 Db 85
13200 Mas-de-Pontevès 13 169 Ed 87
46090 Mas-de-Proupo 46 138 Bd 81
30300 Mas de Ranguy 30 155 Ed 86
30600 Mas-des-Iscles 30 169 Ec 87
87170 Mas-des-Landes, le 87 125 Ba 74
12360 Mas-de-Soulier 12 152 Cf 85
34590 Mas-Desports 34 168 Ea 87
43190 Mas-de-Tence, le 43 142 Ec 78
48210 Masdeval 48 153 Dc 83
46230 Mas-de-Vers 46 150 Bd 82
13200 Mas-de-Vert 13 169 Ed 86
13460 Mas-d'Icard 13 169 Ec 88
13104 Mas-d'Icart 13 169 Ee 87
30110 Mas-Dieu, le 30 154 Ea 83
48190 Mas-d'Orcières 48 141 De 82
87300 Mas-du-Bost 87 112 Af 71
30220 Mas-du-Bousquet 30 168 Eb 87
07700 Mas du Gras 07 155 Ed 82
13200 Mas-du-Pont-de-Pousty 13 169 Ed 87
12230 Mas-du-Pré 12 153 Db 85
13200 Mas-du-Tort 13 169 Ed 86
48370 Masel-Rosade 48 153 De 83
68290 Masevaux-Niederbruck 68 94 Gf 62
87220 Mas-Gauthier 87 125 Bb 74
30770 Mas-Gauzin 30 153 Dc 85
13200 Mas-Giraud 13 169 Ee 87
23460 Masgrangeas 23 126 Bf 74
82600 Mas-Grenier 82 149 Bb 85
12540 Mas-Hugonenq 12 153 Db 86
38190 Mas-Julien, le 38 132 Ff 77
64300 Maslacq 64 161 Zb 88
46600 Maslaton 46 138 Bd 79
30122 Mas-Lautal 30 153 De 84
87130 Masléon 87 126 Bd 74
41250 Maslives 41 86 Bc 63
24380 Maslusson 24 137 Ae 78
23320 Masmeau 23 114 Be 71
48220 Masméjan 48 154 De 82
07590 Masméjean 07 141 Df 81
30700 Masmolène 30 155 Ed 84
34210 Masnaguine 34 166 Cd 88
12400 Mas-Nau 12 152 Cf 85
81530 Masnau-Massuguiès, le 81 152 Cd 86
30600 Mas-Neuf 30 169 Eb 87
59241 Masnières 59 30 Db 48
59176 Masny 59 30 Db 46
66320 Masos, les 66 178 Cc 93
66100 Mas-Palégry 66 179 Cf 93
64120 Masparraute 64 161 Yf 88
87120 Maspecout, le 87 126 Be 74
47370 Masquières 47 149 Ba 82
12540 Mas-Raynal, le 12 153 Db 85
01700 Mas-Rillier, le 01 130 Ef 74
23110 Masroudier, le 23 115 Cc 72
32360 Massa 32 148 Ac 86
11330 Massac 11 179 Cd 91
17490 Massac 17 123 Ze 73
87510 Massac 87 113 Bb 73
81500 Massac-Séran 81 165 Bf 87
63210 Massages 63 127 Ce 74
63210 Massagettes 63 127 Ce 74
81110 Massaguel 81 166 Ca 88
48210 Mas-Saint-Chély 48 153 Dc 83
11400 Mas-Saintes-Puelles 11 165 Bf 89
79150 Massais 79 98 Zd 66
81250 Massals 81 151 Cd 85
AD400 Massana, la ◘ AND 177 Bd 93
13920 Massane 13 170 Fa 88
30350 Massanes 30 154 Ea 84
89440 Massangis 89 90 Df 63
07310 Massas 07 142 Eb 79
47340 Massas, la 47 149 Ae 82
09320 Massat 09 177 Bc 91
18120 Massay 18 102 Bf 66
86510 Massay 86 111 Aa 71
46150 Masse, la 46 137 Bb 81
12100 Massebiau 12 152 Da 84
48500 Massegros, le 48 153 Db 83
48500 Massegros Causses Gorges 48 153 Db 83
33690 Masseilles 33 148 Zf 82
47140 Masseis 47 149 Ae 83
63220 Massélèbre 63 129 De 76
30170 Masselle 30 153 Df 85
13460 Mas Sénébier 13 169 Ec 87
44290 Masserac 44 81 Ya 62
19510 Masseret 19 125 Bd 75
24130 Masseries, les 24 136 Ab 79
46330 Masseries, les 46 138 Bd 82
58420 Masserons, les 58 89 Dc 65
32140 Masseube 32 163 Ad 88
48400 Massevaques 48 153 Dd 83
15500 Massiac 15 128 Db 77
24490 Massias, le 24 135 Aa 78
43150 Massibrand 43 141 Ea 79
17270 Massicot 17 123 Ze 78
38620 Massieu 38 131 Fd 76
51800 Massiges 51 54 Ee 53
16310 Massignac 16 124 Ad 74
01300 Massignieu-de-Rives 01 132 Fe 74
21350 Massigny-lès-Vitteaux 21 91 Ed 64
30000 Massillan 30 154 Ec 85
30140 Massillargues 30 154 Df 84
71250 Massilly 71 118 Ee 70
21400 Massingy 21 91 Ed 61
74150 Massingy 74 132 Ff 74
21140 Massingy-lès-Semur 21 91 Ec 63
86170 Massognes 86 99 Aa 68
06710 Massoins 06 158 Ha 85
74140 Massongy 74 120 Gb 71
44160 Massonnais, la 44 81 Xf 64
05230 Massots 05 144 Gb 81
23460 Massoubrot, le 23 126 Be 74
47140 Massoulès 47 149 Af 82
21330 Massoult 21 91 Ec 62
19170 Massoutre 19 126 Bf 75
28800 Massuère 28 70 Bc 59
33790 Massugas 33 136 Aa 80
71250 Massy 71 118 Ed 70
76270 Massy 76 37 Bc 50
91300 Massy 91 51 Cb 56
59172 Mastaing 59 30 Db 47
46340 Mas-Teulat 46 137 Bb 80
13104 Mas-Thibert, le 13 169 Ee 87
64300 Mastrot 64 161 Zb 87
07590 Mas-Vendran 07 141 Df 80
01580 Matafelon-Granges 01 119 Fd 71
63440 Matas 63 115 Da 72
47800 Matelis 47 136 Ac 81
34270 Matelles, les 34 168 De 86
66210 Matemale 66 178 Ca 93
17160 Matha 17 123 Ze 73
40090 Matha 40 147 Zc 85
82200 Mathaly 82 149 Ba 84
42260 Mathaude, la 42 117 Df 73
25700 Mathay 25 94 Ge 64
49140 Matheflon 49 84 Zd 63
39600 Mathenay 39 107 Fe 67
17570 Mathes, les 17 122 Yf 74
14920 Mathieu 14 47 Zd 53
31470 Mathieu 31 164 Bb 88
73460 Mathiez, le 73 132 Gc 75
40560 Mathiouic 40 146 Ye 85
07270 Mathon 07 142 Ed 79
74340 Mathonex 74 121 Ge 72
03190 Mathonnière 03 115 Ce 69
52300 Mathons 52 75 Fa 58
76450 Mathonville 76 36 Ae 50
76590 Mathonville 76 37 Bb 50
76680 Mathonville 76 37 Bc 51
73310 Mathy 73 119 Fe 73
51300 Matignicourt-Goncourt 51 54 Ee 56
22550 Matignon 22 64 Xe 57
80400 Matigny 80 39 Da 50
40320 Matilas 40 162 Ze 87
51510 Matougues 51 54 Eb 55
71520 Matour 71 117 Ec 71
83780 Matourne 83 172 Gc 87
20270 Matra CTC 183 Kc 95
74440 Matringes 74 120 Gd 72
62310 Matringhem 62 29 Ca 45
88500 Mattaincourt 88 76 Ga 59
15110 Matte, la 15 140 Cf 80
37260 Mattés, les 37 85 Ad 65
85270 Mattes, les 85 96 Ya 68
54830 Mattexey 54 77 Gd 58
20123 Mattiolo CTC 182 If 98
08110 Matton-et-Clemency 08 42 Fb 51
67510 Mattstall 67 58 He 55
67150 Matzenheim 67 60 Hd 58
82500 Maubec 82 149 Af 86
84660 Maubec 84 156 Fa 85
12100 Maubert 12 153 Db 84
08260 Maubert-Fontaine 08 41 Ec 49
59600 Maubeuge 59 31 Df 47
43200 Mauborg 43 129 Ea 77
05250 Maubourg 05 144 Ff 80
33160 Maubourguet 33 134 Za 79
65700 Maubourguet 65 162 Aa 88
18390 Maubranches 18 102 Cd 66
23240 Maubrant 23 113 Bd 71
33121 Maubuisson 33 134 Yf 78
79600 Maucarrière, la 79 99 Ze 68
91730 Mauchamps 91 71 Cb 57
76680 Maucomble 76 37 Bb 50
64160 Maucor 64 162 Ze 88
80170 Maucourt 80 39 Ce 50
55400 Maucourt-sur-Orne 55 55 Fd 53
95420 Maudétour-en-Vexin 95 50 Be 54
61110 Maufaise, la 61 69 Ae 58
19460 Maugein 19 126 Be 77
49110* Mauges-sur-Loire 49 83 Za 64
74550 Maugny 74 120 Gc 71
34130 Mauguio 34 168 Ea 87
52140 Maulain 52 75 Fd 60
79100 Maulais 79 99 Ze 67
55500 Maulan 55 55 Fb 56
86200 Maulay 86 99 Ab 67
59158 Maulde 59 30 Dc 45
78580 Maule 78 50 Bf 55
72650 Maule, la 72 68 Aa 60
79700 Mauléon 79 98 Zb 67
65370 Mauléon-Barousse 65 176 Ad 91
32240 Mauléon-d'Armagnac 32 147 Zf 85
64130 Mauléon-Licharre 64 161 Za 89
60480 Maulers 60 38 Ca 51
78550 Maulette 78 50 Bd 56
49360 Maulévrier 49 98 Zb 66
76490 Maulévrier-Sainte-Gertrude 76 36 Ae 51
32400 Maulichères 32 162 Zf 86
89740 Maulnes 89 90 Eb 61
28150 Mauloup 28 70 Bd 59
87800 Maumond 87 125 Bb 75
19300 Maumont 19 126 Ca 76
44540 Maumusson 44 83 Yf 64
82120 Maumusson 82 149 Af 85
32400 Maumusson-Laguian 32 162 Zf 87
89190 Mauny 89 72 Dd 58
22630 Mauny, le 22 65 Ya 58
10320 Maupas 10 73 Ea 60
32240 Maupas 32 147 Zf 85
76580 Maupas, le 76 37 Ae 52
83390 Maupas, le 83 171 Ga 89
77120 Mauperthuis 77 52 Da 56
50410 Maupertuis 50 46 Ye 55
58110 Maupertuis 58 104 Dd 66
50330 Maupertus-sur-Mer 50 33 Yd 51
06910 Maupoil 06 158 Ge 85
88260 Maupotel 88 76 Gb 60
86460 MaupRévoir 86 112 Ad 71
76440 Mauquency 76 37 Bc 51
23380 Mauques 23 114 Bf 71
13130 Mauran 13 170 Fa 87
31220 Mauran 31 164 Ba 89
32230 Maurar 32 163 Ab 87
47380 Maurasse 47 136 Ad 82
31870 Maurat 31 164 Bc 88
04140 Maure 04 157 Gc 83
42130 Maure 42 129 Df 74
04400 Maure, la 04 158 Gd 82
46200 Maure, le 46 138 Bc 79
78780 Maurecourt 78 51 Ca 55
35330 Maure-de-Bretagne 35 81 Ya 61
13600 Mauregard 13 171 Fd 89
77990 Mauregard 77 51 Cd 54
02820 Mauregny-en-Haye 02 40 De 51
34370 Maureilhan 34 167 Da 88
66480 Maureillas-las-Illas 66 179 Ce 94
04330 Maurelière, la 04 157 Gc 85
12400 Maurelle, la 12 152 Ce 84
31290 Mauremont 31 165 Be 88
12260 Maurenque, la 12 151 Bf 82
24140 Maurens 24 136 Ac 79
31540 Maurens 31 165 Be 88
32200 Maurens 32 164 Af 87
78310 Maurepas 78 50 Bf 56
80360 Maurepas 80 39 Cf 49
31190 Mauressac 31 164 Bc 89
30350 Mauressargues 30 154 Ea 85
32350 Mauret 32 163 Ac 86
77390 Maurevert 77 52 Ce 57
06210 Maure-Vieil 06 173 Gf 87
31460 Maureville 31 165 Be 87
12620 Mauriac 12 152 Cf 83
15200 Mauriac 15 127 Cc 77
33540 Mauriac 33 135 Zf 80
33840 Mauriac 33 147 Ze 83
47120 Maurice 47 136 Ab 80
47260 Maurice 47 136 Ac 82
19300 Maurie, la 19 126 Ca 76
40320 Mauries 40 162 Ze 87
32310 Mauriet 32 162 Zf 86
04530 Maurin 04 145 Ge 81
34970 Maurin 34 168 Df 87
15110 Maurines 15 140 Da 79
06540 Maurioun 06 159 Hc 84
59980 Maurois 59 30 Dc 48
56430 Mauron 56 64 Xe 60
12350 Mauron, le 12 151 Ca 82
32380 Mauroux 32 149 Ae 85
46700 Mauroux 46 149 Ba 82
40270 Maurrin 40 147 Zd 86
15600 Maurs 15 139 Cb 80
67440 Maursmünster = Marmoutier 67 58 Hc 56
51340 Maurupt-le-Montois 51 54 Ef 56
09290 Maury 09 177 Bc 90
12800 Maury 12 151 Cc 83
66460 Maury 66 179 Cd 92
20259 Mausoléo CTC 180 Ka 93
12360 Maussac 12 152 Cf 86
19250 Maussac 19 126 Ca 76
19250 Maussac-Gare 19 126 Ca 76
13520 Maussane-les-Alpilles 13 169 Ee 86
70230 Maussans 70 93 Gb 64
03700 Maussans, les 03 116 Dc 72
64360 Mautalen 64 161 Zc 89
33138 Mautans 33 134 Za 80
23190 Mautes 23 114 Cc 73
40420 Mautoire 40 147 Zc 84
55190 Mauvages 55 75 Fd 57
43100 Mauvagnat 43 128 Dc 77
31190 Mauvaisin 31 165 Bd 88
07300 Mauves 07 142 Ee 78
61400 Mauves-sur-Huisne 61 68 Ad 58
44470 Mauves-sur-Loire 44 82 Yd 65
31230 Mauvezin 31 164 Af 88
32120 Mauvezin 32 149 Ae 86
40240 Mauvezin-d'Armagnac 40 148 Zf 85
09160 Mauvezin-de-Prat 09 176 Af 90
09230 Mauvezin-de-Sainte-Croix 09 164 Bb 90
47200 Mauvezin-sur-Gupie 47 136 Aa 81
36370 Mauvières 36 113 Ba 69
21510 Mauvilly 21 91 Ee 62
41370 Mauvoy 41 86 Bc 62
58700 Mauvrain 58 103 Da 65
24150 Maux 24 136 Ae 79
58290 Maux 58 104 De 66
65130 Mauxjean 65 163 Ab 90
17320 Mauzac 17 122 Yf 74
31410 Mauzac 31 164 Bb 88
31560 Mauzac 31 165 Bd 88
24150 Mauzac-et-Grand-Castang 24 137 Ae 79
24260 Mauzens-et-Miremont 24 137 Af 79
79210 Mauzé-sur-le-Mignon 79 110 Zb 71
33230 Mauzet 33 135 Zf 78
79100 Mauzé-Thouarsais 79 98 Ze 67
63160 Mauzun 63 128 Dc 74
24800 Mavaleix 24 125 Af 75
41500 Maves 41 86 Bc 62
21190 Mavilly-Mandelot 21 105 Ee 66
57140 Maxe, la 57 56 Gb 53
35380 Maxent 35 65 Xf 61
54320 Maxéville 54 56 Ga 56
88630 Maxey-sur-Meuse 88 75 Fe 58
55140 Maxey-sur-Vaise 55 75 Fd 57
74500 Maxilly-Petite-Rive 74 120 Gd 70
74500 Maxilly-sur-Lac 74 120 Gd 70
21270 Maxilly-sur-Saône 21 92 Fc 64
46090 Maxou 46 137 Bc 81
57660 Maxstadt 57 57 Ge 54
24420 Mayac 24 125 Af 77
33930 Mayan 33 122 Yf 76
79100 Mayé 79 99 Zf 66
42111 Mayen 42 129 Df 74
77145 May-en-Multien 77 52 Da 54
53100 Mayenne 53 67 Zc 59
24400 Mayet 24 136 Ab 78
72360 Mayet 72 85 Ab 62
03800 Mayet-d'Ecole, le 03 116 Db 72
03250 Mayet-de-Montagne, le 03 116 De 72
42370 Mayeuvre 42 117 Df 72
40250 Maylis 40 161 Zb 86
12340 Maymac 12 152 Ce 82
40160 Maynage 40 146 Yf 83
39190 Maynal 39 119 Fc 69
04250 Maynard 04 157 Ga 83
33770 Mayne, le 33 134 Za 81
47150 Mayne-de-Bosq 47 136 Ae 81
33121 Mayne-Pauvre 33 134 Yf 78
48150 Maynial, le 48 153 Db 83
43210 Mayol 43 129 Eb 76
83340 Mayons, les 83 172 Gc 89
02800 Mayot 02 40 Dc 50
12550 Mayous, les 12 152 Cd 85
46200 Mayrac 46 138 Bd 79
12390 Mayran 12 151 Cc 82
63420 Mayrand, la 63 128 Da 76
31110 Mayrègne 31 175 Ad 91
07270 Mayres 07 142 Ee 79
07330 Mayres 07 141 Ea 81
63220 Mayres 63 129 De 76
38350 Mayres-Savel 38 144 Fe 79
11420 Mayreville 11 165 Bf 89
12310 Mayrinhac 12 152 Cf 82
12600 Mayrinhac 12 139 Ce 80
46500 Mayrinhac-le-Francal 46 138 Bd 79
46500 Mayrinhac-Lentour 46 138 Be 80
11220 Mayronnes 11 178 Cd 90
49122 May-sur-Evre, le 49 98 Za 66
14320 May-sur-Orne 14 35 Zd 54
44410 Mayun 44 81 Xe 64
07570 Mazabrard 07 142 Ec 78
08400 Mazagran 08 42 Ed 52
63780 Mazal, le 63 115 Cf 73
19170 Mazaleyrat, les 19 126 Bf 75
43520 Mazalibrand 43 141 Eb 78
81200 Mazamet 81 166 Cc 88
63330 Mazan 63 115 Cd 72
84380 Mazan 84 156 Fa 84
41100 Mazangé 41 86 Af 62
07510 Mazan-L'Abbaye 07 141 Ea 80
13008 Mazargues 13 170 Fc 89
19170 Mazau, le 19 126 Bf 75
83136 Mazaugues 83 171 Ff 88
86200 Mazault 86 99 Aa 67
63230 Mazaye 63 127 Cf 74
19390 Mazeau 19 126 Bf 76
85420 Mazeau, le 85 110 Zb 70
87340 Mazeaud, le 87 113 Bc 72
87380 Mazeaud, le 87 125 Bc 75
43190 Mazeaux 43 142 Eb 78
43220 Mazeaux, les 43 130 Ec 77
23170 Mazeiras 23 114 Cc 72
23150 Mazeirat 23 114 Bf 72
23000 Mazeire, la 23 114 Bf 72
23140 Mazeires, les 23 114 Ca 72
24460 Mazel 24 124 Ae 77
30570 Mazel, le 30 153 Dc 84
48190 Mazel, le 48 141 De 82
48700 Mazel, le 48 140 Dc 80
48210 Mazel-Bouissy, le 48 153 Db 82
88150 Mazeley 88 76 Gc 59
43520 Mazelgirard 43 142 Eb 78
43340 Mazemblard 43 141 De 79
49630 Mazé-Milon 49 84 Ze 64
71510 Mazenay 71 105 Ed 67
23260 Mazendreau, le 23 114 Cc 73
63340 Mazérat 63 128 Da 76
17400 Mazeray 17 110 Zc 73
23400 Mazère 23 114 Bd 72
37460 Mazère, la 37 101 Bb 66
09270 Mazères 09 165 Be 89
32450 Mazères 32 163 Ae 87
33210 Mazères 33 135 Ze 82
47370 Mazères 47 149 Ba 82
65700 Mazères 65 162 Zf 87
82110 Mazères 82 149 Bb 83
65150 Mazères-de-Neste 65 163 Ad 90
64110 Mazères-Lezons 64 162 Zd 89
31260 Mazères-sur-Salat 31 164 Af 90
23130 Mazergue, la 23 127 Cc 74
03800 Mazerier 03 116 Db 72
87130 Mazermaud 87 125 Bc 74
08430 Mazerny 08 42 Ed 51
09500 Mazeroles 09 177 Be 90
33390 Mazerolle 33 134 Zc 78
36170 Mazerolle 36 113 Bc 70
16310 Mazerolles 16 124 Ad 74
17800 Mazerolles 17 122 Zc 75
40090 Mazerolles 40 147 Zd 85
64230 Mazerolles 64 162 Zd 88
65220 Mazerolles 65 163 Ab 88
86320 Mazerolles 86 112 Ad 70
11240 Mazerolles-du-Razès 11 165 Ca 90
25170 Mazerolles-le-Salin 25 107 Ff 65
46270 Mazers, le 46 138 Ca 80
54280 Mazerulles 54 56 Gc 56
12130 Mazes 12 140 Cf 81
30750 Mazes, les 30 153 Dc 84
46090 Mazet, le 46 150 Bd 82
48100 Mazet, le 48 140 Dc 81
63390 Mazet, le 63 115 Cd 72
87150 Mazet, le 87 125 Af 74
87470 Mazet, le 87 126 Be 74
43520 Mazet-Saint Voy 43 141 Eb 78
86110 Mazeuil 86 99 Aa 68
48200 Mazeyrac 48 140 Db 79
43230 Mazeyrat-Aurouze 43 128 Dd 77
43300 Mazeyrat-d'Allier 43 140 Dd 78
24550 Mazeyrolles 24 137 Ba 80

Mazeyrolles | 289

39600 Mesnay 39 107 Fe 67
51370 Mesneux, les 51 53 Df 53
76270 Mesnières-en-Bray 76 37 Bc 50
14270 Mesnil 14 48 Ze 54
27430 Mesnil 27 50 Bb 53
27570 Mesnil 27 49 Ba 56
28800 Mesnil 28 70 Bc 60
45110 Mesnil 45 87 Cb 61
50190 Mesnil 50 33 Ye 53
51230 Mesnil 51 53 Df 56
60240 Mesnil 60 50 Bf 53
80300 Mesnil 80 29 Cd 48
14210 Mesnil, le 14 47 Zd 54
27300 Mesnil, le 27 49 Ad 54
50500 Mesnil, le 50 46 Yd 53
50580 Mesnil, le 50 46 Yb 52
50660 Mesnil, le 50 46 Yc 55
50520 Mesnil-Adelée, le 50 46 Yf 56
50450 Mesnil-Amand, le 50 46 Yd 55
77990 Mesnil-Amelot, le 77 51 Cd 54
50570 Mesnil-Amey, le 50 33 Ye 54
50620 Mesnil-Angot, le 50 34 Ye 53
50510 Mesnil-Aubert, le 50 46 Yd 55
95720 Mesnil-Aubry, le 95 51 Cc 54
14260 Mesnil-au-Grain, le 14 47 Zc 54
50110 Mesnil-au-Val, le 50 33 Yc 51
14260 Mesnil-Auzouf, le 14 47 Zb 55
14140 Mesnil-Bacley, le 14 48 Aa 55
14380 Mesnil-Benoist, le 14 47 Za 55
50540 Mesnil-Bœufs, le 50 66 Yf 57
27110 Mesnil-Broquet, le 27 49 Af 54
80200 Mesnil-Bruntel 80 39 Cf 49
50490 Mesnilbus, le 50 34 Yd 54
14380 Mesnil-Caussois, le 14 47 Yf 55
14380 Mesnil-Clinchamps 14 47 Za 55
60210 Mesnil-Conteville, le 60 38 Ca 50
76390 Mesnil-David 76 38 Bd 50
14860 Mesnil-de-Bures, le 14 48 Ze 53
80620 Mesnil-Domqueur 80 29 Ca 48
50320 Mesnil-Drey, le 50 46 Yd 56
14140 Mesnil-Durand, le 14 48 Aa 54
76460 Mesnil-Durdent, les 76 36 Ae 50
80360 Mesnil-en-Arrouaise 80 30 Cf 48
76910 Mesnil-en-Caux 76 37 Bb 48
24710* Mesnil-en-Ouche 24 49 Ad 54
60530 Mesnil-en-Thelle, le 60 51 Cb 53
49410 Mesnil-en-Vallée, le 49 83 Za 64
76240 Mesnil-Esnard, le 76 37 Ba 52
14100 Mesnil-Eudes, le 14 35 Ab 54
80140 Mesnil-Eudin 80 38 Be 49
50570 Mesnil-Eury, le 50 33 Ye 54
76660 Mesnil-Follemprise 76 37 Bb 50
27930 Mesnil-Fuquet, le 27 49 Ba 54
50450 Mesnil-Garnier, le 50 46 Ye 55
50510 Mesnilgé 50 46 Yc 55
14140 Mesnil-Germain, le 14 48 Ab 54
27660 Mesnil-Gilbert, le 27 50 Be 53
50670 Mesnil-Gilbert, le 50 46 Yf 56
14100 Mesnil-Guillaume, le 14 48 Ab 54
27190 Mesnil-Hardray, le 27 49 Af 55
50750 Mesnil-Hermann, le 50 46 Yf 54
50450 Mesnil-Hue, le 50 46 Ye 55
27400 Mesnil-Jourdain, les 27 49 Ba 53
10700 Mesnil-la-Comtesse 10 73 Eb 58
50600 Mesnillard, le 50 66 Yf 57
80190 Mesnil-le-Petit 80 39 Cf 50
78600 Mesnil-le-Roi, le 78 51 Ca 55
10240 Mesnil-Lettre 10 74 Eb 58
76780 Mesnil-Lieubray, le 76 37 Bd 51
76440 Mesnil-Mauger 76 37 Bd 50
14270 Mesnil-Mauger, le 14 48 Aa 54
27620 Mesnil-Milon, les 27 50 Bd 54
50860 Mesnil-Opac, le 50 46 Yf 54
50220 Mesnil-Ozenne, le 50 46 Ye 57
76570 Mesnil-Panneville 76 37 Af 51
14740 Mesnil-Patry, le 14 35 Zc 53
27110 Mesnil-Péan 27 49 Ba 54
27910 Mesnil-Perruel, le 27 37 Bc 52
91580 Mesnil-Racoin 91 71 Cb 58
50520 Mesnil-Rainfray, le 50 46 Yf 56
76520 Mesnil-Raoul 76 37 Bb 52
50420 Mesnil-Raoult, le 50 46 Yf 54
76260 Mesnil-Réaume, le 76 37 Bc 49
14380 Mesnil-Robert, le 14 47 Za 55
50450 Mesnil-Rogues 50 46 Yd 55
27390 Mesnil-Rousset 27 49 Ad 55
50000 Mesnil-Rouxelin, le 50 34 Yf 54
76560 Mesnil-Rury, le 76 37 Af 50
27250 Mesnils, les 27 49 Ae 55
76730 Mesnils, les 76 37 Af 50
78320 Mesnil-Saint-Denis, le 78 51 Bf 56
60120 Mesnil-Saint-Firmin, le 60 39 Cc 51
80500 Mesnil-Saint-Georges 80 39 Cd 51
02720 Mesnil-Saint-Laurent 02 40 Dc 50
10190 Mesnil-Saint-Loup 10 73 De 59
10140 Mesnil-Saint-Père 10 74 Ec 59
50410 Mesnil-Sauvage, le 50 46 Yf 55
10220 Mesnil-Sellières 10 73 Eb 58
28260 Mesnil-Simon, le 28 50 Bd 55
14140 Mesnil-Simon, le 14 48 Aa 54
76480 Mesnil-sous-Jumièges, les 76 37 Af 52
55160 Mesnil-sous-les-Côtes 55 55 Fd 54
27150 Mesnil-sous-Vienne 27 38 Be 52
27160* Mesnils-sur-Iton 27 49 Af 56
54740 Mesnils-sur-Madon 54 76 Gb 58
14130 Mesnil-sur-Blangy, le 14 48 Ab 53
60130 Mesnil-sur-Bulles, le 60 39 Cc 52
27650 Mesnil-sur-L'Estrée 27 50 Bb 56
51190 Mesnil-sur-Oger, le 51 53 Ea 55
50540 Mesnil-Thébault, le 50 66 Ye 57
60240 Mesnil-Theribus, le 60 51 Bf 53
28250 Mesnil-Thomas, le 28 69 Ba 57
14220 Mesnil-Touffay, le 14 47 Ze 54
50520 Mesnil-Tôve, le 50 47 Yf 56
76470 Mesnil-Val 76 28 Bb 48
10300 Mesnil-Vallon 10 73 Df 59
50620 Mesnil-Véneron, le 50 34 Ye 53
27440 Mesnil-Verclives 27 37 Bc 53
50570 Mesnil-Vigot, le 50 34 Ye 54
50450 Mesnil-Villeman, le 50 46 Ye 55
14690 Mesnil-Villement, le 14 47 Zd 55
39130 Mesnois 39 107 Fe 69
78490 Mesnuls, les 78 50 Bf 56
29420 Mespaul 29 62 Vf 57
81140 Mespel 81 150 Be 84
64370 Mesplede 64 161 Zc 88
03370 Mesples 03 114 Cc 70
46250 Mespouillé 46 137 Ba 81
12220 Mespoulières 12 139 Cb 81
91150 Mespuits 91 71 Cb 58
44420 Mesquer 44 81 Xd 64
44410 Mesquery 44 81 Xd 64
17130 Messac 17 123 Ze 76
35480 Messac, Guipry- 35 82 Yb 62
86330 Messais 86 99 Aa 67
21220 Messanges 21 106 Ef 66
40660 Messanges 40 146 Yd 86
40660 Messanges-Plage 40 146 Yd 86
45190 Messas 45 87 Bd 62
79120 Messé 79 111 Aa 71
61440 Messei 61 47 Zc 56
54850 Messein 54 76 Ga 57
63750 Messeix 63 127 Cd 75
49260 Messemé 49 98 Ze 66
86200 Messemé 86 99 Ab 66
19300 Messence 19 126 Ca 76
74140 Messery 74 120 Gb 70
16700 Messeux 16 112 Ac 72
71390 Messey-le-Bois 71 105 Ee 69
71390 Messey-sur-Grosne 71 105 Ee 69
39270 Messia 39 119 Fd 70
39570 Messia-sur-Sorne 39 106 Fd 69
21380 Messigny-et-Vantoux 21 91 Fa 64
69510 Messimy 69M 130 Ee 74
01480 Messimy-sur-Saône 01 118 Ee 72
08110 Messincourt 08 42 Fa 50
43200 Messinhac 43 141 Ea 78
10190 Messon 10 73 Df 59
74440 Messy 74 120 Gd 72
77410 Messy 77 51 Ce 55
33540 Mesterrieux 33 135 Zf 81
19200 Mestes 19 127 Cb 75
14330 Mestry 14 34 Za 53
58400 Mesves-sur-Loire 58 103 Cf 65
71190 Mesvres 71 105 Eb 67
25370 Métabief 25 108 Gc 68
16200 Métairies, les 16 123 Zf 74
59270 Météren 59 30 Ce 44
84570 Méthamis 84 156 Fb 84
53100 Metière, la 53 67 Zb 59
80270 Métigny 80 38 Bf 49
01400 Métras, les 01 118 Ef 71
57970 Métrich 57 44 Gb 52
57410 Metschbruch 57 57 Hb 54
57370 Metting 57 57 Hb 56
37390 Mettray 37 85 Ad 64
57000 Metz 57 56 Gb 54
62124 Metz-en-Couture 62 30 Da 48
68380 Metzeral 68 77 Ha 61
57920 Metzeresche 57 56 Gb 53
57940 Metzervisse 57 44 Gb 53
57980 Metzing 57 57 Gf 54
58190 Metz-le-Compte 58 90 Dd 64
10210 Metz-Robert 10 73 Ea 60
74370 Metz-Tessy, Épagny 74 120 Ga 73
56890 Meucon 56 80 Xb 62
92140 Meudon 92 51 Cb 56
89520 Meugnes 89 89 Db 63
21700 Meuilley 21 106 Ef 66
78250 Meulan 78 50 Bf 54
53380 Meule, la 53 66 Za 59
76510 Meulers 76 37 Bb 49
14290 Meulles 14 48 Ab 55
21510 Meulson 21 91 Ee 62
77760 Meun 77 71 Cd 58
36100 Meunet-Planches 36 102 Bf 67
36150 Meunet-sur-Vatan 36 101 Bf 66
45130 Meung-sur-Loire 45 87 Be 62
74300 Meuniers, les 74 120 Gd 72
72170 Meurcé 72 68 Ab 59
62410 Meurchin 62 30 Cf 46
70300 Meurcourt 70 93 Gb 62
50510 Meurdraquière, la 50 46 Yd 55
58110 Meuré 58 104 Dd 66
52310 Meures 52 75 Fa 59
02160 Meurival 02 40 De 52
17120 Meursac 17 122 Zb 75
21200 Meursanges 21 106 Ef 67
21450 Meursauge 21 91 Ed 63
21190 Meursault 21 105 Ee 67
10200 Meurville 10 74 Ed 59
52140 Meuse 52 75 Fd 61
41130 Meusnes 41 101 Bc 65
17800 Meussac 17 123 Zd 75
39260 Meussia 39 119 Fe 70
14960 Meuvaines 14 47 Zc 53
41150 Meuves 41 86 Ba 64
52240 Meuvy 52 75 Fd 60
17500 Meux 17 123 Zd 76
60880 Meux, le 60 39 Ce 52
87380 Meuzac 87 125 Bc 75
28130 Mévoisins 28 70 Bd 57
26560 Mévouillon 26 156 Fc 83
01800 Meximieux 01 118 Fb 73
54135 Mexy 54 43 Fe 52
57070 Mey 57 56 Gb 54
65170 Méyabat 65 175 Ab 92
68890 Meyenheim 68 95 Hc 61
57410 Meyerhof 57 58 Hb 54
38700 Meylan 38 131 Fe 77
47170 Meylan 47 148 Aa 84
42210 Meylieu 42 129 Eb 75
19250 Meymac 19 126 Ca 75
26300 Meymans 26 143 Fa 78
12340 Meynac 12 139 Cd 82
24220 Meynard 24 137 Af 79
30840 Meynes 30 155 Ed 85
15230 Meynial, le 15 139 Cf 79
19160 Meynie, la 19 126 Ca 76
33830 Meynieu, le 33 147 Zb 82
46200 Meyraguet 46 138 Bd 79
24220 Meyrals 24 137 Ba 79
33470 Meyran 33 134 Yf 81
30410 Meyrannes 30 154 Eb 83
13650 Meyrargues 13 170 Fd 87
07380 Meyres 07 142 Eb 80
13590 Meyreuil 13 170 Fc 88
01250 Meyriat 01 119 Fc 72
38300 Meyrié 38 131 Fb 75
05350 Meyriès, les 05 145 Ge 80
38440 Meyrieu-les-Étanges 38 131 Fb 75
42380 Meyrieux 42 129 Eb 76
73170 Meyrieux-Trouet 73 132 Fe 75
19800 Meyrignac-l'Église 19 126 Bf 76
43170 Meyronne 43 140 Dc 78
46200 Meyronne 46 138 Bd 79
04530 Meyronnes 04 145 Ge 82
48150 Meyrueis 48 153 Dc 83
69610 Meys 69M 130 Ec 74
19560 Meysonnade, la 19 126 Bd 77
19500 Meyssac 19 138 Be 78
07400 Meysse 07 142 Ee 81
38440 Meyssiès 38 130 Fa 76
87800 Meyze, la 87 125 Bb 75
69330 Meyzieu 69M 130 Fa 74
53600 Mézangers 53 67 Zd 59
34140 Mèze 34 168 Dd 88
34390 Mézeilles 34 167 Cf 87
04270 Mézel 04 157 Gb 85
63115 Mezel 63 128 Db 74
46110 Mézels 46 138 Be 79
81800 Mézens 81 150 Bd 86
12310 Mezerac 12 152 Cf 82
81260 Mezerac 81 166 Cd 87
72270 Mézeray 72 84 Zf 62
43800 Mézères 43 129 Ea 78
01660 Mézériat 01 118 Fa 71
80600 Mézerolles 80 29 Cb 47
11410 Mézerville 11 165 Be 89
07660 Mézeyrac 07 141 Df 80
43150 Mezeyrac 43 141 Ea 79
14270 Mézidon-Canon 14 48 Zf 54
14270 Mézidon Vallée d'Auge 14 48 Zf 54
04200 Mezien 04 157 Ga 83
35520 Mézière, la 35 65 Yb 59
10130 Mézières 10 73 Df 60
28800 Mézières 28 70 Bc 59
41240 Mézières 41 69 Bc 61
41330 Mézières 41 86 Bc 62
45410 Mézières 45 70 Bf 60
72290 Mézières 72 68 Ab 59
50480 Mézières, les 50 33 Ye 52
28160 Mézières-au-Perche 28 69 Bb 59
36290 Mézières-en-Brenne 36 101 Bb 68
28500 Mézières-en-Drouais 28 50 Bc 56
80110 Mézières-en-Santerre 80 39 Cd 50
27510 Mézières-en-Vexin 27 50 Bd 53
45370 Mézières-lez-Clery 45 87 Be 62
72240 Mézières-sous-Lavardin 72 68 Aa 60
35140 Mézières-sur-Coueson 35 66 Yd 59
87330 Mézières-sur-Issoire 87 112 Af 72
02240 Mézières-sur-Oise 02 40 Dc 50
78970 Mézières-sur-Seine 78 50 Be 55
07530 Mézilhac 07 142 Ec 80
89130 Mézilles 89 89 Db 62
47170 Mézin 47 148 Ab 84
77570 Mézin 77 71 Ce 60
90120 Méziré 90 94 Gf 63
40170 Mézos 40 146 Yf 84
78250 Mézy-sur-Seine 78 50 Bf 54
20140 Mezzana CTC 184 If 98
20230 Mezzana, Poggio- CTC 183 Kc 94
20230 Mezzana, U Poghju- = Mezzana, Poggio- CTC 183 Kc 94
20214 Mezzanodi CTC 180 Ie 94
20167 Mezzavia CTC 182 Ie 97
58140 Mhère 58 104 Df 65
58210 Mhers 58 89 Dc 64
48140 Mialanes 48 140 Dc 79
19430 Mialaret 19 138 Bf 78
24450 Mialet 24 125 Af 75
30140 Mialet 30 154 Df 84
64410 Mialos 64 162 Zd 88
80132 Miannay 80 28 Be 48
65400 Miaous 65 174 Ze 91
24560 Micalie, la 24 136 Ae 80
31310 Micas 31 164 Bb 90
42640 Michaude, la 42 117 Df 72
58420 Michaugues 58 89 Dd 65
58230 Michaux, les 58 90 Ea 65
68700 Michelbach, Aspach- 68 94 Ha 62
68730 Michelbach-le-Bas 68 95 Hc 63
68220 Michelbach-le-Haut 68 95 Hc 63
89140 Michery 89 72 Db 59
03600 Michet 03 115 Cf 71
36150 Michots, les 36 101 Be 66
33330 Micoulau 33 135 Zf 79
31350 Micous 31 163 Ae 89
88630 Midrevaux 88 75 Fd 58
39250 Mièges 39 107 Ga 68
32170 Miélan 32 163 Ab 88
70440 Miellin, Servance- 70 94 Ge 62
76340 Mienval 76 38 Bd 49
50150 Mière, la 50 47 Za 56
28480 Miermaigne 28 69 Af 59
19220 Miermont 19 138 Ca 78
46500 Miers 46 138 Be 79
39800 Miéry 39 107 Fe 68
67580 Mietesheim 67 58 Hd 55
62650 Mieurles 62 28 Bf 45
74440 Mieussy 74 120 Gd 72
61250 Mieuxcé 61 68 Aa 58
64800 Mifaget 64 162 Ze 90
28160 Mifoucher 28 69 Bb 59
24160 Migaudie, la 24 125 Af 77
79150 Migaudon 79 98 Zd 67
28800 Migaudry 28 70 Bc 59
89580 Migé 89 89 Dd 62
89400 Migennes 89 72 Dd 61
19320 Miginiac 19 126 Bf 77
20243 Migliacciaru CTC 183 Kc 97
09400 Miglos 09 177 Bd 92
70110 Mignafans 70 94 Gd 63
86550 Mignaloux-Beauvoir 86 112 Ac 69
38350 Mignanne 38 144 Fe 79
20240 Mignataja CTC 183 Kc 97
70400 Mignavillers 70 94 Gd 63
36800 Migné 36 101 Bb 68
86440 Migné-Auxances 86 99 Ab 69
41190 Mignerary 41 86 Ba 62
45490 Mignères 45 71 Cd 60
45490 Mignerette 45 71 Cd 60
54540 Mignéville 54 77 Ge 57
28630 Mignières 28 70 Bc 58
24190 Mignots, les 24 136 Ac 78
39250 Mignovillard 39 107 Ga 68
33850 Mignoy 33 134 Zc 80
36260 Migny 36 102 Ca 66
58210 Migny 58 89 Dc 64
17330 Migré 17 110 Zc 72
17770 Migron 17 123 Zd 74
09460 Mijanès 09 178 Ca 92
01410 Mijoux 01 120 Ff 70
56700 Miledec 56 80 We 62
20090 Milelli, les CTC 182 Ie 97
72650 Milesse, la 72 68 Aa 60
46300 Milhac 46 137 Bc 80
24330 Milhac-d'Auberoche 24 137 Af 78
24470 Milhac-de-Nontron 24 124 Ae 76
87440 Milhaguet 87 124 Ae 75
81170 Milhars 81 151 Bf 84
31160 Milhas 31 176 Ae 91
30540 Milhaud 30 154 Eb 86
81130 Milhavet 81 151 Ca 84
29290 Milizac-Guipronvel 29 61 Vc 58
24150 Millac 24 136 Ae 79
24370 Millac 24 137 Bc 79
86150 Millac 86 112 Ae 71
59143 Millam 59 27 Cb 43
41200 Millançay 41 87 Be 64
40600 Millas 40 146 Yf 82
66170 Millas 66 179 Ce 92
12100 Millau 12 152 Da 84
34620 Millau 34 167 Da 88
58170 Millay 58 104 Ea 67
76260 Millebosc 76 37 Bc 49
11800 Millegrand 11 166 Cc 89
78940 Millemont 78 50 Be 56
80300 Millencourt 80 29 Cd 49
80135 Millencourt-en-Ponthieu 80 28 Bf 48
27240 Millerette, la 27 49 Ba 55
50190 Milleries, le 50 46 Yd 53
78790 Millerus, les 78 50 Bd 55
21140 Millery 21 90 Eb 63
54670 Millery 54 56 Ga 56
69390 Millery 69M 130 Ee 75
13090 Milles, les 13 170 Fc 87
17270 Millet 17 123 Ze 77
49122 Millet, le 49 98 Za 66
19290 Millevaches 19 126 Ca 75
86160 Millière, la 86 112 Ab 71
50190 Millières 50 46 Yd 53
52240 Millières 52 75 Fc 60
30124 Milliérines 30 153 De 84
01680 Millieu 01 131 Fd 74
71400 Milliore 71 105 Eb 67
95510 Millonets, les 95 50 Be 54
36310 Milloux 36 113 Bb 70
18350 Milly 18 103 Ce 66
50600 Milly 50 66 Yf 57
89800 Milly 89 90 De 62
91490 Milly-la-Forêt 91 71 Cc 58
71960 Milly-Lamartine 71 118 Ee 70
49350 Milly-le-Meugon 49 84 Ze 65
55110 Milly-sur-Bradon 55 42 Fb 52
60112 Milly-sur-Thérain 60 38 Ca 51
78470 Milon-la-Chapelle 78 51 Ca 56
31230 Milor 31 163 Ae 89
44130 Miltais, la 44 82 Yb 64
20140 Miluccia CTC 184 If 98
40350 Mimbaste 40 161 Za 87
61160 Mimbeville 61 48 Aa 56
13105 Mimet 13 170 Fd 88
21230 Mimeure 21 105 Ec 66
40200 Mimizan 40 146 Ye 83
40200 Mimizan-Plage 40 146 Ye 83
32290 Mimort 32 162 Aa 86
51800 Minaucourt-le-Mesnil-lès-Hurlus 51 54 Ee 53
63310 Minaux, les 63 116 Dc 73
63350 Minaux, les 63 116 Dc 73
44250 Mindin 44 81 Xf 65
29246 Mine, la 29 63 Wc 58
36150 Mineaux 36 101 Be 66
39700 Minerais, les 39 107 Fe 65
34210 Minerve 34 166 Ce 88
20228 Minerviu CTC 181 Kb 91
63880 Mines, les 63 129 Dd 74
29390 Miné Tréouzal 29 78 Wb 60
19130 Mingedeloup 19 125 Bb 77
65140 Mingot 65 163 Ab 88
62690 Mingoval 62 29 Cd 46
35540 Miniac-Morvan 35 65 Ya 57
35190 Miniac-sous-Becherei 35 65 Ya 59
36170 Minière, la 36 113 Bb 69
27190 Minières, les 27 49 Af 55
28700 Minières, les 86 111 Ab 70
35400 Minihic, le 35 65 Xf 56
35870 Minihic-sur-Rance, le 35 65 Xf 57
22220 Minihy-Tréguier 22 63 We 56
36120 Minimes, les 36 102 Bf 68
74270 Minizier 74 120 Ff 72
40260 Minjouay 40 146 Yf 85
64400 Minone 64 161 Zb 90
54385 Minorville 54 56 Ff 56
21510 Minot 21 91 Ef 62
29710 Minven 29 78 Ve 61
67270 Minversheim 67 58 Hd 56
24610 Minzac 24 135 Aa 79
81250 Miolles 81 152 Cd 85
43500 Miollet 43 129 Df 77
20200 Miomo CTC 181 Kc 92
20200 Miomu = Miomo CTC 181 Kc 92
01390 Mionnay 01 118 Ef 73
69780 Mions 69M 130 Ef 75
33380 Mios 33 134 Za 81
64450 Miossens-Lanusse 64 162 Ze 88
63740 Miouze, la 63 127 Ce 74
38690 Mi-Plaine 38 131 Fc 76
69800 Mi-Plaine 69M 130 Ef 74
83510 Miquelets, les 83 172 Gb 88
83550 Miquelette, la 83 172 Gc 88
34500 Miquelle, la 34 167 Db 89
40120 Miquelot 40 147 Ze 84
12240 Miquels 12 151 Cb 82
40170 Miquéou 40 146 Ye 85
04510 Mirabeau 04 157 Ga 84
84120 Mirabeau 84 171 Fd 86
26320 Mirabeaux, les 26 143 Ef 79
07170 Mirabel 07 142 Ed 81
82440 Mirabel 82 150 Bc 84
26110 Mirabel-aux-Baronnies 26 155 Fa 83
26400 Mirabel-et-Blacons 26 143 Fa 80
40410 Mirador 40 147 Zb 82
32340 Miradoux 32 149 Ae 85
31100 Mirail, le 31 164 Bc 87
06590 Miramar 06 173 Gf 88
13140 Miramas 13 170 Fa 87
13140 Miramas-le-Vieux 13 170 Fa 87
17150 Mirambeau 17 122 Zc 76
17270 Mirambeau 17 135 Ze 78
31230 Mirambeau 31 164 Af 88
32300 Miramont-d'Astarac 32 163 Ac 87
31800 Miramont-de-Comminges 31 163 Ae 90
47800 Miramont-de-Guyenne 47 136 Ac 81
82190 Miramont-de-Quercy 82 149 Ba 83
65380 Miramontès 65 162 Zf 89
32390 Miramont-Latour 32 149 Ae 86
40320 Miramont-Sensacq 40 162 Ze 87
32190 Miran 32 148 Ab 86
16410 Mirande 16 124 Ac 75
32300 Mirande 32 163 Ac 87
81190 Mirandol-Bourgnounac 81 151 Ca 84
32350 Mirannes 32 163 Ac 87
80300 Miraumont 80 29 Ce 48
83570 Miraval 83 171 Ga 88
11380 Miraval-Cabardès 11 166 Cc 88
52320 Mirbel 52 75 Fa 59
37510 Miré 37 85 Ad 65
49330 Miré 49 83 Zd 62
86110 Mirebau 86 99 Ab 68
21310 Mirebeau-sur-Bèze 21 92 Fb 64
39570 Mirebel 39 107 Fe 68
88500 Mirecourt 88 76 Ga 59
63730 Mirefleurs 63 128 Db 74
24260 Miremont 24 137 Af 79
31190 Miremont 31 164 Bc 88
63380 Miremont 63 115 Cc 73
11120 Mirepeisset 11 167 Cf 89
64800 Mirepeix 64 162 Ze 89
09500 Mirepoix 09 165 Bf 90
32390 Mirepoix 32 163 Ae 86
31340 Mirepoix-sur-Tarn 31 150 Bd 86
34110 Mireval 34 168 De 87
15110 Mirial, le 15 140 Da 79
01700 Miribel 01 130 Ef 74
26350 Miribel 26 131 Fa 77
38450 Miribel-Lanchâtre 38 144 Fd 79
38380 Miribel-les-Echelles 38 131 Fe 76
26270 Mirmande 26 142 Ee 80
71480 Miroir, le 71 119 Fc 69
73640 Miroir, le 73 133 Gf 75
80260 Mirvaux 80 39 Cc 48
76210 Mirville 76 36 Ac 51
31550 Mis 31 165 Bd 88
26310 Miscon 26 143 Fd 81
27930 Miserey 27 50 Bb 54
25480 Miserey-Salines 25 93 Ff 65
01600 Misérieux 01 118 Ee 73
80320 Misery 80 39 Cf 49
89480 Misery 89 89 Dd 63
04200 Mison 04 157 Ff 83
02800 Missancourt 02 40 Dc 51
79100 Missé 79 99 Ze 67
81300 Missècle 81 165 Bf 86
11580 Missègre 11 178 Cc 90
21210 Missery 21 90 Ec 65
44780 Missillac 44 81 Xf 64
56140 Missiriac 56 81 Xd 61
40290 Misson 40 161 Za 87
14210 Missy, Noyers- 14 35 Zc 54
02200 Missy-aux-Bois 02 52 Db 52
02350 Missy-lès-Pierrepont 02 40 De 51
02880 Missy-sur-Aisne 02 40 Dc 52
33680 Mistre 33 134 Yf 79
77130 Misy-sur-Yonne 77 72 Da 58
83920 Mitan, le 83 172 Gd 88
36800 Mitatis, les 36 101 Bd 69
77290 Mitry-Mory 77 51 Cd 55
67360 Mitschdorf 67 58 He 55
78125 Mittainville 78 50 Bd 56
28190 Mittainvilliers 28 69 Bb 57
67140 Mittelbergheim 67 60 Hc 58
57370 Mittelbronn 57 58 Hb 56
67170 Mittelhausen 67 58 Hd 56
67170 Mittelschaeffolsheim 67 58 Hd 56
68630 Mittelwihr 68 60 Hb 60
18110 Mitterand 18 87 Cc 65
57930 Mittersheim 57 57 Gf 55
68380 Mittlach 68 77 Ha 61
67206 Mittelhausbergen 67 60 He 57
14170 Mittois 14 48 Aa 54
33690 Mitton 33 148 Zf 82
68470 Mitzach 68 94 Ha 61
64520 Mixe 64 161 Ye 88
28120 Mizeray 28 69 Bc 59
01140 Mizériat 01 118 Ef 71
42110 Mizérieux 42 129 Eb 74
38142 Mizoën 38 144 Ga 78
50250 Mobecq 50 46 Yc 53
20140 Moca-Croce CTC 182 Ka 98
45700 Mocquepoix 45 88 Ce 61
32300 Mocuhès 32 163 Ac 87

Mocuhès | 291

73500 Modane 73 133 Ge 77
84330 Modène 84 156 Fa 84
29350 Moëlan-sur-Mer 29 79 Wc 62
29190 Moënnec, le 29 62 Wa 59
59122 Moëres, les 59 27 Cd 42
68480 Mœrnach 68 95 Hb 63
52100 Moëslains 52 74 Ef 57
51120 Mœurs-Verdey 51 53 De 56
62147 Mœuvres 62 30 Da 48
17780 Moëze 17 110 Yf 73
70200 Moffans-et-Vacheresse 70 94 Gd 63
88220 Moge, la 88 76 Gb 60
55400 Mogeville 55 55 Fd 53
14770 Mogisière, la 14 47 Zc 55
01140 Mogneneins 01 118 Ee 72
55800 Mognéville 55 55 Fa 56
60140 Mogneville 60 39 Cc 53
71500 Mogny 71 106 Fa 69
29250 Moguériec 29 62 Vf 56
08110 Mogues 08 42 Fb 51
56490 Mohon 56 64 Xc 60
38440 Moidieu-Détourbe 38 130 Fa 75
50170 Moidrey 50 66 Yc 57
69330 Moifono 69M 131 Fa 74
35650 Moigné 35 65 Yb 60
63560 Moignons, les 63 115 Cf 72
91490 Moigny-sur-Ecole 91 71 Cc 58
70110 Moimay 70 93 Gc 63
17360 Moinet 17 135 Ze 78
54580 Moineville 54 56 Ff 53
17500 Moings 17 123 Zd 76
79390 Moinie, la 79 99 Zf 68
28700 Moinville-la-Jeulin 28 70 Be 58
38430 Moirans 38 131 Fd 77
39260 Moirans-en-Montagne 39 119 Fe 70
47310 Moirax 47 149 Ad 84
47800 Moirax 47 136 Ac 81
69620 Moiré 69D 118 Ed 73
51800 Moiremont 51 54 Ef 54
01350 Moiret 01 119 Fe 73
28200 Moireville 28 70 Bc 60
55150 Moirey-Flabas-Crépion 55 55 Fc 53
39570 Moiron 39 107 Fd 69
08370 Moiry 08 42 Fb 51
58490 Moiry 58 103 Da 67
86500 Moisais 86 111 Ab 70
44520 Moisdon-la-Rivière 44 82 Yd 63
77950 Moisenay 77 71 Ce 57
80200 Moislains 80 39 Cf 49
15130 Moissac 15 139 Cd 79
15170 Moissac 15 140 Cf 78
15170 Moissac 15 140 Da 78
82200 Moissac 82 149 Ba 84
87500 Moissac 87 125 Bb 76
43440 Moissac-Bas 43 128 Dd 77
83630 Moissac-Bellevue 83 171 Ga 87
48110 Moissac-Vallée-Française 48 153 De 83
82190 Moissaguet 82 149 Ba 83
87400 Moissannes 87 126 Bd 73
63190 Moissat 63 128 Dc 74
63190 Moissat-Bas 63 128 Dc 74
95570 Moisselles 95 51 Cc 54
39290 Moissey 39 106 Fd 65
38270 Moissieu-sur-Dolon 38 130 Ef 76
78840 Moisson 78 50 Be 54
14220 Moissonnière, la 14 47 Zd 54
77550 Moissy-Cramayel 77 51 Cd 57
58190 Moissy-Moulinot 58 89 De 65
27320 Moisville 27 49 Bb 55
41160 Moisy 41 86 Bb 61
20270 Moita CTC 183 Kc 95
50270 Moitiers-d'Allonne, les 50 33 Yb 52
50360 Moitiers-en-Bauptois 50 46 Yd 52
21510 Moitron 21 91 Ee 62
72170 Moitron-sur-Sarthe 72 68 Aa 59
51240 Moivre 51 54 Ed 55
54760 Moivrons 54 56 Gb 56
20100 Mola CTC 184 If 99
56230 Molac 56 81 Xd 62
76220 Molagnies 76 38 Be 51
02110 Molain 02 40 Dd 48
39800 Molain 39 107 Fe 68
39600 Molamboz 39 107 Fe 67
11420 Molandier 11 165 Be 89
04400 Molanès 04 158 Gd 82
38114 Molard, le 38 132 Ga 78
71290 Molard, le 71 106 Fa 69
73480 Môlard, le 73 133 Gf 76
31230 Molas 31 163 Ae 88
39500 Molay 39 106 Fc 66
70120 Molay 70 92 Fe 62
89310 Môlay 89 90 Df 62
14330 Molay, le 14 47 Za 53
14330 Molay-Littry, le 14 47 Za 53
46170 Molayrette, la 46 150 Bc 83
18320 Môle, la 18 103 Da 66
81660 Mole, la 81 166 Cc 87
83310 Môle, la 83 172 Gc 89
28200 Moléans 28 69 Bc 60
15500 Molèdes 15 128 Da 77
73260 Molençon 73 133 Gd 75
65130 Molère, Benqué- 65 163 Ab 90
21330 Molesmes 21 90 Ec 61
89560 Molesmes 89 89 Dc 63
12330 Molet 12 139 Cd 81
48800 Molette, la 48 141 Df 81
73800 Molettes, les 73 132 Ga 76
48110 Molezon 48 153 De 83
53540 Molhiac 63 129 Df 76
60220 Moliens 60 38 Be 50
07270 Molière 07 142 Ed 78
53200 Molière 53 83 Zb 62
36300 Molière, la 36 100 Ba 69
46300 Molière, la 46 137 Bc 80
80410 Molière, la 80 28 Bd 47
13450 Molières 13 170 Ef 87
24480 Molières 24 137 Ae 80
46120 Molières 46 138 Bf 80
82220 Molières 82 150 Bc 83
91470 Molières, les 91 51 Ca 56
30120 Molières-Cavaillac 30 153 Dd 85
26150 Molières-Glandaz 26 143 Fc 80
30410 Molières-sur-Ceze 30 154 Ea 83
40660 Moliets-et-Maa 40 146 Yd 85
40660 Moliets-Plage 40 146 Yd 85
88240 Molieu, le 88 76 Gc 61
02100 Molinchart 02 40 Dd 51
20233 Moline CTC 181 Kc 92
05500 Molines en-Champsaur 05 144 Ga 80
05350 Molines-en-Queyras 05 145 Gf 80
03510 Molinet 03 117 Df 70
41190 Molineuf 41 86 Bb 63
39360 Molinges 39 119 Fe 70
62330 Molinghem 62 29 Cc 45
20128 Molini CTC 184 Ie 97
89190 Molinons 89 72 Dd 59
21340 Molinot 21 105 Ed 66
10500 Molins-sur-Aube 10 74 Ec 58
28200 Molitard 28 70 Bc 60
66500 Molitg-les-Bains 66 178 Cc 93
70240 Mollans 70 93 Gc 63
26170 Mollans-sur-Ouvèze 26 155 Fb 83
73300 Mollard, le 73 132 Gc 77
68470 Mollau 68 94 Gf 61
49260 Mollay 49 99 Zf 65
24700 Molle, la 24 136 Aa 78
13940 Mollegès 13 155 Ef 86
03300 Molles 03 116 Dd 72
18260 Mollets, les 18 88 Cd 64
11410 Molleville 11 165 Bf 89
80260 Molliens-au-Bois 80 39 Cc 49
80540 Molliens-Dreuil 80 38 Ca 49
06420 Mollières 06 159 Hb 84
73720 Molliessoulaz 73 132 Gc 74
67190 Mollkirch 67 60 Hc 57
01800 Mollon 01 119 Fb 73
15500 Molompize 15 128 Da 77
89700 Molosmes 89 90 Ea 61
87130 Molou 87 126 Bd 75
21120 Moloy 21 91 Ef 63
21210 Molphey 21 90 Eb 64
39250 Molpré 39 107 Ga 68
57670 Molring 57 57 Ge 55
67120 Molsheim 67 60 Hc 57
20218 Moltifao CTC 181 Ka 94
20218 Moltifau = Moltifao CTC 181 Ka 94
39310 Molunes, les 39 120 Ff 70
57330 Molvange 57 43 Ga 52
64230 Momas 64 162 Zd 88
33710 Mombrier 33 135 Zc 78
65360 Momères 65 162 Aa 89
57220 Momerstroff 57 57 Gd 54
12210 Mommaton 12 139 Cf 80
67670 Mommenheim 67 58 Hd 56
24700 Momtpon-Ménestérol 24 136 Aa 78
40700 Momuy 40 161 Zc 87
64350 Momy 64 162 Zf 88
20171 Monacia d'Aullène CTC 184 Ka 99
20229 Monacia-d'Orezza CTC 183 Kc 94
98000* Monaco ◘ MC 173 Hc 86
98000 Monaco-Ville ◘ MC 173 Hc 86
73640 Monal, le 73 133 Gf 75
02000 Monampteuil 02 40 Dd 52
17120 Monards, les 17 122 Za 75
64160 Monassut-Audiracq 64 162 Ze 88
12000 Monastère, le 12 152 Cd 82
12190 Monastère, le 12 139 Ce 81
48100 Monastier-Pins-Moriès, le 48 140 Db 81
43150 Monastier-sur-Gazeille, le 43 141 Df 79
63790 Monaux 63 127 Cf 75
39230 Monay 39 107 Fd 67
33570 Monbadon 33 135 Zf 79
47290 Monbahus 47 136 Ad 81
47340 Monbalen 47 149 Ae 83
47320 Monbarbat 47 148 Ac 82
32420 Monbardon 32 163 Ae 88
24240 Monbazillac 24 136 Ac 80
47370 Monbeau 47 149 Af 82
82170 Monbéqui 82 150 Bb 85
32130 Monblanc 32 164 Af 88
24240 Monbos 24 136 Ac 80
47510 Monbran 47 149 Ad 83
32600 Monbrun 32 164 Ba 87
20214 Moncale CTC 180 If 93
24250 Moncalou 24 137 Bb 80
12130 Moncan 12 140 Da 81
32300 Moncassin 32 163 Ac 88
47700 Moncassin 47 148 Aa 83
31160 Moncaup 31 176 Ae 91
64350 Moncaup 64 162 Zf 88
47310 Moncaut 47 148 Ad 84
45740 Monçay 45 87 Be 62
64130 Moncayolle-Larrory-Mendibieu 64 161 Za 89
49800 Monceau 49 84 Zd 64
03380 Monceau, le 03 114 Cc 71
02270 Monceau-le-Neuf 02 40 Dd 50
02270 Monceau-lès-Leups 02 40 Dc 50
02840 Monceau-le-Waast 02 40 De 51
59620 Monceau-Saint-Waast 59 31 Df 47
02120 Monceau-sur-Oise 02 40 De 49
19170 Monceaux 19 126 Bf 75
60940 Monceaux 60 39 Cd 53
14100 Monceaux, les 14 35 Aa 54
23270 Monceaux, les 23 114 Ca 71
61290 Monceaux-au-Perche 61 69 Ae 58
14400 Monceaux-en-Bessin 14 47 Zb 53
60220 Monceaux-l'Abbaye 60 38 Be 50
58190 Monceaux-le-Comte 58 90 Dd 65
19400 Monceaux-sur-Dordogne 19 138 Bf 78
72230 Moncé-en-Belin 72 84 Ab 61
72260 Moncé-en-Saosnois 72 68 Ac 59
88630 Moncel 88 75 Fe 58
08140 Moncelle, la 08 42 Ef 50
54300 Moncel-lès-Lunéville 54 77 Gd 57
54280 Moncel-sur-Seille 54 56 Gc 56
88630 Moncel-sur-Vair 88 75 Fe 58
51290 Moncetz-L'Abbaye 51 54 Ed 57
51470 Moncetz-Longevas 51 54 Ec 55
25870 Moncey 25 93 Ga 64
76340 Monchaux-Soreng 76 38 Bd 49
59224 Monchaux-sur-Écaillon 59 30 Dc 47
59283 Moncheaux 59 30 Da 46
80120 Moncheaux 80 28 Bd 47
62270 Moncheaux-lès-Frévent 62 29 Cc 47
59234 Monchecourt 59 30 Db 47
80220 Monchelet 80 38 Bd 48
62270 Monchel-sur-Canche 62 29 Cb 47
37310 Monchenin 37 100 Af 65
24160 Monchenit 24 125 Ba 77
57420 Moncheux 57 56 Gc 55
62123 Monchiet 62 29 Cd 47
62111 Monchy-au-Bois 62 29 Cd 47
62127 Monchy-Breton 62 29 Cc 46
62134 Monchy-Cayeux 62 29 Cb 46
60113 Monchy-Humières 60 39 Ce 52
80200 Monchy-Lagache 80 39 Da 49
62118 Monchy-le-Preux 62 30 Cf 47
76340 Monchy-le-Preux 76 38 Bd 49
60290 Monchy-Saint-Eloy 60 51 Cc 53
76260 Monchy-sur-Eu 76 28 Bc 49
64330 Moncla 64 162 Ze 87
32150 Monclar 32 148 Zf 85
47380 Monclar 47 149 Ad 82
82230 Monclar-de-Quercy 82 150 Bd 85
32300 Monclar-sur-Losse 32 163 Ab 87
25170 Moncley 25 93 Ff 65
08270 Monclin 08 41 Ed 51
22510 Moncontour 22 64 Xb 58
86330 Moncontour 86 99 Zf 67
32260 Moncorneil-Grazan 32 163 Ad 88
29510 Moncouar 29 78 Vf 60
19410 Moncoulon 19 125 Bc 77
57810 Moncourt 57 57 Gd 56
79320 Moncoutant-sur-Sèvre 79 98 Zc 68
46090 Moncoutié 46 138 Bc 81
47600 Moncrabeau 47 148 Ac 84
61800 Moncy 61 47 Zb 56
12330 Mondalazac 12 139 Cd 82
31220 Mondavezan 31 164 Ba 89
14250 Mondaye 14 34 Zb 53
32160 Mondebat 32 162 Aa 87
64450 Mondebat 64 162 Zd 87
57300 Mondelange 57 56 Gb 53
51120 Mondement-Montgivroux 51 53 De 56
82110 Mondenard 82 149 Bb 83
44450 Monderie, la 44 82 Yd 65
60400 Mondescourt 60 40 Da 51
91690 Mondésir 91 70 Ca 58
28170 Mondétour 28 50 Bb 57
35370 Mondevert 35 66 Yf 60
14120 Mondeville 14 47 Ze 53
91590 Mondeville 91 71 Cc 58
62760 Mondicourt 62 29 Cc 47
08430 Mondigny 08 42 Ed 50
31350 Mondilhan 31 163 Ae 89
31420 Mondine 31 163 Ae 89
40800 Mondine 40 162 Ze 87
86230 Mondion 86 100 Ac 67
25680 Mondon 25 93 Gb 64
31700 Mondonville 31 164 Bb 86
28150 Mondonville-Sainte-Barbe 28 70 Be 59
28700 Mondonville-Saint-Jean 28 70 Be 58
41170 Mondoubleau 41 69 Af 61
43500 Mondoulioux 43 129 Df 77
31850 Mondouzil 31 165 Bd 87
84430 Mondragon 84 155 Ee 83
14210 Mondrainville 14 35 Zc 54
55220 Mondrecourt 55 55 Fb 55
02500 Mondrepuis 02 41 Ea 49
77570 Mondreville 77 71 Cd 60
78980 Mondreville 78 50 Bd 55
35680 Mondron 35 66 Ye 60
43260 Monedeyres 43 141 Ea 78
64360 Monein 64 161 Zc 89
31370 Monès 31 164 Ba 88
09130 Monesple 09 164 Bc 90
03140 Monestier 03 116 Da 71
07690 Monestier 07 130 Ed 77
24240 Monestier 24 136 Ab 80
26110 Monestier, le 26 156 Fb 82
26340 Monestier, le 26 143 Fb 81
63890 Monestier, le 63 129 Dd 75
38970 Monestier-d'Ambel 38 144 Ff 80
38650 Monestier-de-Clermont 38 144 Fe 79
38930 Monestier-du-Percy, le 38 144 Fd 80
19340 Monestier-Merlines 19 127 Cc 75
19110 Monestier-Port-Dieu 19 127 Cd 76
81640 Monestiés 81 151 Ca 84
31560 Monestrol 31 165 Be 88
03500 Monétay-sur-Allier 03 116 Db 70
03470 Monétay-sur-Loire 03 117 De 70
89470 Monéteau 89 89 Dd 61
05110 Monêtier-Allemont 05 157 Ff 82
05220 Monêtier-les-Bains, le 05 145 Gd 79
24130 Monfaucon 24 136 Ab 79
24140 Monfaucon 24 136 Ad 78
65140 Monfaucon 65 162 Aa 88
32260 Monferran-Plavès 32 163 Ad 88
32490 Monferran-Savès 32 164 Af 87
47150 Monflanquin 47 136 Ae 81
32120 Monfort 32 149 Ae 86
35160 Monforzh = Montfort 35 65 Ya 60
72300 Monfrou 72 84 Ze 61
40200 Mongaillard 40 146 Ye 83
47230 Mongaillard 47 148 Ab 83
33480 Mongarnl 33 134 Zb 79
32220 Mongausy 32 163 Ae 87
33190 Mongauzy 33 135 Aa 81
09300 Monges 09 177 Be 91
11100 Monges 11 167 Da 90
63740 Monges 63 127 Ce 74
40700 Monget 40 162 Zc 87
33240 Mongie, la 33 135 Ze 78
65200 Mongie, la 65 175 Ab 91
86300 Mongodar, la 86 112 Ae 70
32240 Monguilhem 32 148 Ze 85
53500 Monhages, les 53 66 Zb 59
47160 Monheurt 47 148 Ab 82
72260 Monhoudou 72 68 Ab 59
08260 Mon-Idée 08 41 Ec 49
84390 Monieux 84 156 Fc 84
71160 Monins, les 71 117 De 69
43580 Monistrol-d'Allier 43 141 Dd 79
43120 Monistrol-sur-Loire 43 129 Eb 77
22510 Monkontour = Moncontour 22 64 Xb 58
32140 Monlaur-Bernet 32 163 Ad 88
41290 Monlavy 41 86 Bb 61
65670 Monléon-Magnoac 65 163 Ad 89
43270 Monlet 43 129 De 77
32230 Monlezun 32 163 Ab 88
32240 Monlezun-d'Armagnac 32 147 Zf 86
15120 Monlogis 15 139 Cd 80
65670 Monlong 65 163 Ac 89
12240 Monloube 12 151 Ca 83
47160 Monluc 47 148 Ab 83
24560 Monmadalès 24 136 Ad 80
24560 Monmarvès 24 136 Ad 80
12100 Monna, le 12 152 Da 84
61470 Monnai 61 48 Ac 55
37380 Monnaie 37 85 Ae 63
63710 Monne 63 128 Cf 75
02400 Monneaux 02 52 Db 54
23320 Monnéger 23 114 Be 71
57920 Monneren 57 56 Gc 52
72300 Monnerie, la 72 84 Zd 61
63650 Monnerie-le-Montel, la 63 128 Dd 73
91930 Monnerville 91 70 Ca 58
02470 Monnes 02 52 Db 54
48100 Monnet 48 140 Db 81
39320 Monnetay 39 119 Fd 70
74410 Monnetier 74 132 Ga 74
74560 Monnetier-Mornex 74 120 Gb 72
39300 Monnet-la-Ville 39 107 Fe 68
39150 Monnets, les 39 107 Ga 69
60240 Monneville 60 51 Bf 53
39100 Monnières 39 106 Fc 66
44690 Monnières 44 97 Yd 66
82200 Monniés 82 150 Ba 84
30170 Monoblet 30 154 Df 84
82140 Monpalach 82 150 Bd 83
79100 Monpalais 79 99 Zf 67
32170 Monpardiac 32 163 Ab 88
24540 Monpazier 24 137 Af 80
64350 Monpezat 64 162 Zf 87
24170 Monplaisant 24 137 Af 80
02390 Monplaisir 02 40 Dd 50
31590 Monplaisir 31 165 Bd 87
41170 Mon-Plaisir 41 85 Af 61
33410 Monprimblanc 33 135 Ze 81
16140 Mons 16 123 Zf 73
17160 Mons 17 123 Zd 74
30340 Mons 30 154 Eb 84
31280 Mons 31 165 Bd 87
32270 Mons 32 163 Ae 86
34390 Mons 34 167 Cf 87
63310 Mons 63 116 Dc 72
69330 Mons 69M 131 Fa 74
83440 Mons 83 172 Ge 86
87310 Mons 87 125 Af 74
19220 Mons, le 19 138 Ca 77
19550 Mons, le 19 126 Cb 77
63600 Mons, le 63 129 De 75
24440 Monsac 24 136 Ae 80
24560 Monsaguel 24 136 Ad 80
80210 Mons-Boubert 80 28 Be 48
24340 Monsec 24 124 Ad 76
33580 Monségur 33 135 Aa 81
40700 Monségur 40 162 Zc 87
47150 Monségur 47 137 Af 82
64460 Monségur 64 162 Zf 88
15240 Monselie, le 15 127 Cd 77
47500 Monsempron-Libos 47 137 Af 82
59370 Mons-en-Barœul 59 30 Da 45
80200 Mons-en-Chaussée 80 39 Da 49
02000 Mons-en-Laonnois 02 40 Dd 51
77520 Mons-en-Montois 77 72 Da 58
59246 Mons-en-Pévèle 59 30 Da 46
33240 Monsieur-Dubois 33 135 Zd 78
85110 Monsireigne 85 97 Za 68
69860 Monsols 69D 117 Ed 71
24450 Monssigoux 24 125 Ba 75
38122 Monsteroux-Milieu 38 130 Ef 76
80160 Monsures 80 38 Cb 50
67700 Monswiller 67 58 Hc 56
36500 Mont 36 101 Bb 67
64300 Mont 64 161 Zc 88
74230 Mont 74 132 Gc 74
01400 Mont, le 01 118 Ef 72
23200 Mont, le 23 114 Cb 73
23600 Mont, le 23 114 Ca 70
42560 Mont, le 42 129 Ea 76
43170 Mont, le 43 140 Dc 79
50390 Mont, le 50 33 Yc 52
62910 Mont, le 62 27 Ca 44
63610 Mont, le 63 128 Cf 75
70290 Mont, le 70 94 Ge 62
74310 Mont, le 74 121 Ge 73
74360 Mont, le 74 121 Ge 71
74740 Mont, le 74 121 Ge 72
87460 Mont, le 87 126 Bd 74
88210 Mont, le 88 77 Ha 58
61160 Montabard 61 48 Zf 56
72500 Montabon 72 85 Ac 62
50410 Montabots 50 46 Yf 55
89150 Montacher-Villegardin 89 72 Da 59
13190 Montade, la 13 170 Fc 88
34600 Montades, les 34 167 Db 87
32220 Montadet 32 164 Af 88
34310 Montady 34 167 Da 89
09240 Montagagne 09 177 Bc 91
04500 Montagnac 04 157 Ga 86
12560 Montagnac 12 152 Cf 82
30350 Montagnac 30 154 Ea 85
34530 Montagnac 34 167 Dc 88
43270 Montagnac 43 141 De 78
43370 Montagnac 43 141 Df 79
48170 Montagnac 48 141 Dd 80
24210 Montagnac-d'Auberoche 24 125 Af 77
24140 Montagnac-la-Crempse 24 136 Ad 79
47600 Montagnac-sur-Auvignon 47 148 Ac 84
47150 Montagnac-sur-Lède 47 137 Af 81
39160 Montagna-le-Reconduit 39 119 Fc 70
39320 Montagna-le-Templier 39 119 Fc 70
32170 Montagnan 32 163 Ac 88
81110 Montagnarie, la 81 165 Ca 88
01250 Montagnat 01 119 Fb 71
33570 Montagne 33 135 Zf 79
38160 Montagne 38 143 Fb 78
05400 Montagne, la 05 144 Ff 81
05400 Montagne, la 05 144 Ff 81
05700 Montagne, la 05 144 Fd 82
44620 Montagne, la 44 96 Yb 65
70310 Montagne, la 70 94 Gd 61
71760 Montagne, la 71 104 Df 68
91150 Montagne, la 91 71 Cb 58
80540 Montagne-Fayel 80 38 Bf 49
73400 Montagnes, les 73 132 Gc 74
81200 Montagnés, les 81 166 Cb 88
42560 Montagneux 42 129 Df 75
70140 Montagney 70 92 Fd 65
01470 Montagnieu 01 131 Fc 74
38110 Montagnieu 38 131 Fc 75
12360 Montagnol 12 152 Da 85
73000 Montagnole 73 132 Ff 75
01990 Montagnuex 01 118 Ef 72
42840 Montagny 42 117 Eb 72
69700 Montagny 69M 130 Ee 75
73000 Montagny 73 132 Ff 75
73340 Montagny 73 132 Ga 74
73350 Montagny 73 133 Gd 76
60240 Montagny-en-Vexin 60 50 Be 53
21200 Montagny-lès-Beaune 21 106 Ef 67
71390 Montagny-lès-Buxy 71 105 Ee 68
74600 Montagny-les-Lanches 74 132 Ga 73
21250 Montagny-lès-Seurre 21 106 Fb 66
71500 Montagny-près-Louhans 71 106 Fb 69
60950 Montagny-Sainte-Félicité 60 52 Ce 54
71520 Montagny-sur-Grosne 71 118 Ed 70
33190 Montagoudin 33 135 Zf 81
24350 Montagrier 24 124 Ac 77
48340 Montagudet 48 140 Da 82
82110 Montagudet 82 149 Ba 83
48340 Montagut 48 152 Da 82
64410 Montagut 64 162 Zc 87
19300 Montaignac 19 126 Bf 76
19300 Montaignac Saint-Hippolyte 19 126 Ca 76
50700 Montaigou-la-Brisette 50 33 Yd 51
02820 Montaigu 02 41 De 51
39570 Montaigu 39 107 Fd 69
48310 Montaigu 48 140 Da 79
53160 Montaigu 53 67 Zd 59
79120 Montaigu 79 111 Ab 71
85600 Montaigu 85 97 Ye 67
82150 Montaigu-de-Quercy 82 149 Ba 82
03130 Montaiguët-en-Forez 03 116 De 71
03150 Montaigu-le-Blin 03 116 Dd 71
50450 Montaigu-les-Bois 50 46 Ye 55
12360 Montaigut 12 152 Cf 85
63700 Montaigut 63 115 Ce 71
81320 Montaigut 81 167 Cf 86
23320 Montaigut-le-Blanc 23 114 Be 72
63320 Montaigut-le-Blanc 63 128 Da 75
31530 Montaigut-sur-Save 31 164 Bb 86
47120 Montaillac 47 136 Ab 80
72120 Montaillé 72 85 Ae 61
73460 Montailleur 73 132 Gb 75
79370 Montaillon 79 111 Ze 71
09110 Montaillou 09 178 Bf 92
73130 Montaimont 73 132 Gc 76
39210 Montain 39 107 Fd 68
82100 Montain 82 149 Ba 85
28150 Montainville 28 70 Bd 59
78124 Montainville 78 50 Bf 55
66110 Montalba-d'Amélie 66 179 Ce 94
66130 Montalba-le-Château 66 179 Cd 92
79190 Montalembert 79 111 Aa 72
23400 Montaletang 23 114 Be 73
78440 Montalet-le-Bois 78 50 Be 54
38390 Montalieu-Vercieu 38 131 Fc 74
33930 Montalivet-les-Bains 33 122 Yf 76
89290 Montallery 89 89 De 62
30120 Montals 30 153 Dd 84
82270 Montalzat 82 150 Bc 83
05140 Montamat 05 144 Fd 81
32220 Montamat 32 163 Af 88
58250 Montambert 58 104 De 68
46310 Montamel 46 137 Bc 81
86360 Montamisé 86 99 Ac 69
14260 Montamy 14 47 Zb 55
69250 Montanay 69M 130 Ef 73
24110 Montanceix 24 136 Ad 78
25190 Montancy 25 94 Ha 64
25190 Montandon 25 94 Gf 65
18170 Montandré 18 102 Cb 68
73300 Montandré 73 132 Gc 77
50240 Montanel 50 66 Yd 58
64460 Montaner 64 162 Zf 88
10220 Montangon 10 74 Ec 58
87290 Montannaud 87 113 Bb 72
81600 Montans 81 151 Bf 85
58110 Montapas 58 104 Dd 66
03230 Montapeine 03 104 Dd 69
24800 Montardie 24 125 Ba 76
09230 Montardit 09 164 Bb 90
64121 Montardon 64 162 Zd 88
24350 Montardy 24 124 Ac 77
24130 Montarel 24 136 Ab 79
30700 Montaren-et-Saint-Médiers 30 154 Ec 84
19700 Montargis 19 126 Be 76
45200 Montargis 45 71 Ce 61

292 | Modane

77250 Montarlot 77 71 Cf 58
70600 Montarlot-lès-Champlitte 70 92 Fd 63
70190 Montarlot-lès-Rioz 70 93 Ff 64
09200 Montarna 09 176 Ba 91
34570 Montarnaud 34 168 De 87
58250 Montaron 58 104 De 67
58360 Montarons, les 58 104 De 67
47380 Montastruc 47 136 Ad 82
65330 Montastruc 65 163 Ac 89
82130 Montastruc 82 150 Bb 84
31380 Montastruc-la-Conseillère 31 165 Bd 86
42830 Montat 42 116 De 73
46090 Montat 46 150 Bc 82
58140 Montat, le 58 90 Df 64
60160 Montataire 60 51 Cc 53
26170 Montauban 26 156 Fd 83
82000 Montauban 82 150 Bc 84
35360 Montauban-de-Bretagne 35 65 Xf 59
31110 Montauban-de-Luchon 31 176 Ad 92
80300 Montauban-de-Picardie 80 39 Ce 48
34160 Montaud 34 168 Df 86
38210 Montaud 38 131 Fd 77
53220 Montaudin 53 66 Za 58
70270 Montaujeux, le 70 94 Gd 62
26110 Montaulieu 26 156 Fb 82
10270 Montaulin 10 73 Eb 59
27400 Montaure 27 49 Ba 53
63380 Montaurier 63 127 Cd 73
11410 Montauriol 11 165 Be 89
31280 Montauriol 31 165 Bd 87
47330 Montauriol 47 136 Ad 81
66300 Montauriol 66 179 Ce 93
83440 Montauroux 83 172 Ge 87
09160 Montaut 09 164 Ba 90
09700 Montaut 09 165 Bd 89
24560 Montaut 24 136 Ad 80
31310 Montaut 31 164 Bb 90
32300 Montaut 32 163 Ac 88
40500 Montaut 40 161 Zc 86
47210 Montaut 47 136 Ae 81
64800 Montaut 64 162 Ze 90
33121 Montaut, le 33 134 Yf 78
12170 Montautat 12 151 Cd 84
32810 Montaut-les-Créneaux 32 163 Ad 86
35210 Montautour 35 66 Yf 59
54700 Montauville 54 56 Ga 55
40410 Montauzey 40 147 Zb 82
59360 Montay 59 31 Dd 48
47500 Montayral 47 137 Af 82
24230 Montazeau 24 136 Aa 79
81330 Montazel 81 166 Cd 86
11190 Montazels 11 178 Cb 91
21500 Montbard 21 90 Ec 63
05350 Montbardon 05 145 Ge 80
82110 Montbarla 82 149 Ba 83
39380 Montbarrey 39 107 Fd 66
45340 Montbarrois 45 71 Cc 60
82700 Montbartier 82 150 Bb 85
12220 Montbazens 12 139 Cb 82
34560 Montbazin 34 168 De 87
37250 Montbazon 37 85 Ae 65
09500 Montbel 09 165 Bf 90
09600 Montbel 09 178 Bf 91
48170 Montbel 48 141 De 81
25600 Montbéliard 25 94 Ge 63
25210 Montbéliardot 25 108 Gd 65
71260 Montbellet 71 118 Ef 70
25650 Montbenoît 25 108 Gc 67
62350 Mont-Bernanchon 62 29 Cd 45
31230 Montbernard 31 163 Ae 89
31140 Montberon 31 164 Bc 86
44140 Montbert 44 97 Yd 66
38230 Montbertand 38 131 Fa 74
21460 Montberthault 21 90 Ea 64
14350 Mont-Bertrand 14 47 Za 55
82290 Montbeton 82 150 Bb 84
12160 Montbétou 12 152 Cc 83
03340 Montbeugny 03 116 Dc 69
72380 Montbizot 72 68 Ab 60
55270 Montblainville 55 55 Fa 53
04320 Montblanc 04 158 Ge 85
31230 Mont-Blanc 31 164 Ae 89
34290 Montblanc 34 167 Dc 88
45290 Montblin 45 88 Ce 61
70700 Montboillon 70 93 Ff 64
14190 Montboint 14 48 Ze 55
28800 Montboissier 28 69 Bc 59
63490 Montboissier 63 128 Dc 75
66110 Montbolo 66 179 Cd 94
43370 Montbonnet 43 141 De 79
38330 Montbonnot 38 132 Fe 77
54111 Mont-Bonvillers 54 43 Ff 53
23400 Montboucher 23 113 Be 73
26740 Montboucher-sur-Jabron 26 142 Ee 81
15190 Montboudif 15 127 Ce 76
90500 Montbouton 90 94 Gf 64
45230 Montbouy 45 88 Ce 61
16620 Montboyer 16 123 Aa 77
70230 Montbozon 70 93 Gb 64
43550 Montbrac 43 141 Ea 79
22550 Montbran 22 64 Xd 57
05140 Montbrand 05 144 Fe 81
55140 Montbras 55 75 Fe 57
50410 Montbray 50 46 Yf 55
51500 Montbré 51 53 Ea 53
02110 Montbrehain 02 40 Dc 49
26770 Montbrison 26 155 Fa 82
42600 Montbrison 42 129 Ea 75
16220 Montbron 16 124 Ac 75
57415 Montbronn 57 58 Hb 55
87160 Montbrugnaud 87 113 Bb 71
46160 Montbrun 46 138 Bf 81
48210 Montbrun 48 153 Dd 82
73300 Montbrunal 73 132 Gb 77
31310 Montbrun-Bocage 31 164 Bb 90
11700 Montbrun-des-Corbières 11 166 Ce 89
31450 Montbrun-Lauragais 31 165 Bd 88
26570 Montbrun-les-Bains 26 156 Fc 83
25340 Montby 25 94 Gc 64
09500 Montcabirol 09 177 Be 90
46700 Montcabrier 46 137 Ba 81
81500 Montcabrier 81 165 Be 87
09220 Montcalm 09 177 Bc 92
30600 Montcalme 30 169 Eb 87
24230 Montcaret 24 135 Aa 79
38890 Montcarra 38 131 Fc 75
50560 Montcarville 50 33 Yc 54
76690 Mont-Cauvaire 76 37 Ba 51
62170 Montcavrel 62 28 Be 45
38300 Montceau 38 131 Fc 75
21360 Montceau-et-Echarnant 21 105 Ed 66
71300 Montceau-les-Mines 71 105 Ec 68
01090 Montceaux 01 118 Ee 72
77470 Montceaux 77 52 Cf 55
77151 Montceaux-lès-Provins 77 52 Dc 56
10260 Montceaux-lès-Vaudes 10 73 Ea 60
71110 Montceaux-L'Etoile 71 117 Ea 70
71240 Montceaux-Ragny 71 106 Ef 69
63460 Montcel 63 115 Da 72
73100 Montcel 73 132 Ff 74
02540 Mont-Cel-Enger 02 52 Dc 55
71710 Montcenis 71 105 Ec 68
01310 Montcet 01 118 Fa 71
70000 Montcey 70 93 Gb 63
38220 Montchaboud 38 144 Fe 78
02860 Montchâlons 02 40 De 51
14350 Montchamp 14 47 Zb 55
15100 Montchamp 15 140 Db 78
48700 Montchamp 48 140 Dc 80
71210 Montchanin 71 105 Ec 68
15320 Mont-Chanson 15 140 Da 79
43500 Montchany 43 129 Df 76
58370 Montcharlon 58 104 Df 67
52400 Montcharvot 52 92 Fe 61
50660 Montchaton 50 46 Yc 54
16300 Montchaude 16 123 Ze 76
14350 Montchauvet 14 47 Zb 55
78790 Montchauvet 78 50 Bd 55
73210 Montchavin 73 133 Ge 75
26350 Montchenu 26 130 Fa 77
23270 Montcheny 23 114 Bf 71
08250 Montcheutin 08 54 Ee 53
61170 Montchevral 61 68 Ac 57
36140 Montchevrier 36 114 Bf 70
71450 Montchevrier 71 105 Ec 68
48100 Montchiroux 48 140 Dc 81
01340 Montcindroux 01 118 Fa 70
04140 Montclar 04 157 Gc 82
11250 Montclar 11 166 Cb 90
12550 Montclar 12 152 Cd 85
43230 Montclard 43 128 Dd 77
31220 Montclar-de-Comminges 31 164 Ba 89
31290 Montclar-Lauragais 31 165 Be 88
26400 Montclar-sur-Gervanne 26 143 Fa 80
46250 Montcléra 46 137 Bb 81
05700 Montclus 05 156 Fe 82
30630 Montclus 30 154 Ec 83
63330 Montcocu 63 115 Ce 71
03130 Montcombroux-les-Mines 03 116 De 70
03130 Montcombroux-Vieux-Bourg 03 116 De 70
71500 Montcony 71 106 Fb 68
23190 Montcor 23 114 Cc 73
45220 Montcorbon, Douchy- 45 72 Da 61
02340 Montcornet 02 41 Ea 50
08090 Montcornet 08 42 Ed 50
42380 Montcoudiol 42 129 Ea 76
02400 Montcourt 02 52 Dc 54
70500 Montcourt 70 93 Ff 61
77140 Montcourt-Fromonville 77 71 Ce 59
71620 Montcoy 71 106 Ef 68
45700 Montcresson 45 88 Ce 61
01380 Mont-Crozier 01 118 Ef 71
50490 Montcuit 50 34 Yd 54
38230 Montcul 38 131 Fb 74
46800 Montcuq-en-Quercy-Blanc 46 149 Bb 82
39260 Montcusel 39 119 Fd 70
08090 Montcy-Notre-Dame 08 42 Ee 50
30120 Montdardier 30 153 Dd 85
32140 Mont-d'Astarac 32 163 Ad 89
05600 Mont-Dauphin 05 145 Gd 81
77320 Montdauphin 77 52 Dc 55
38860 Mont-de-Lans 38 144 Ga 78
25210 Mont-de-Laval 25 108 Gd 65
76190 Mont-de-L'If 76 37 Ae 51
32170 Mont-de-Marrast 32 163 Ac 88
40000 Mont-de-Marsan 40 147 Zd 85
71130 Montdemot 71 104 Ea 69
73870 Mont-Denis 73 132 Gc 77
59690 Mont-de-Péruwelz 59 31 Dd 46
88410 Mont-de-Savillon 88 76 Ff 60
73400 Mont-Dessus 73 132 Gc 74
55110 Mont-devt-Sassey 55 42 Fb 52
57670 Montdidier 57 57 Ge 55
80500 Montdidier 80 39 Cd 51
64330 Mont-Disse 64 162 Zf 87
35120 Mont-Dol 35 65 Yb 57
63240 Mont-Dore 63 127 Ce 75
70210 Montdoré 70 93 Ga 61
02390 Mont-d'Origny 02 40 Dd 49
46230 Montdoumerc 46 150 Bd 83
81440 Montdragon 81 151 Ca 86
39260 Mont-du-Cerf 39 119 Fe 70
02500 Mont-du-Faux, le 02 41 Ea 50
20290 Monte CTC 181 Kc 94
41150 Monteaux 41 86 Ba 64
20138 Monte Biancu CTC 184 Ie 98
50310 Montebourg 50 33 Yd 52
23600 Montebras 23 114 Cb 71
98000 Monte Carlo □ MC 173 Hc 86
82700 Montech 82 150 Bb 85
25190 Montécheroux 25 94 Ge 64
59258 Montecouvez 59 30 Db 48
20245 Monte Estremo CTC 182 Ie 94
02600 Montefontaine 02 40 Da 53
20214 Montegrosso CTC 180 Ie 93
40190 Montégut 40 147 Ze 85
65150 Montégut 65 163 Ad 90
32730 Montégut-Arros 32 163 Ab 88
31430 Montégut-Bourjac 31 164 Af 89
09200 Montégut-en-Couserans 09 176 Ba 91
31540 Montégut-Lauragais 31 165 Bf 88
09120 Montégut-Plantaurel 09 164 Bd 90
32220 Montégut-Savès 32 164 Af 88
03800 Monteignet-sur-L'Andelot 03 116 Db 72
15240 Monteil 15 127 Cd 77
15700 Monteil 15 139 Cb 78
19170 Monteil 19 126 Ca 74
23220 Monteil 23 114 Bf 71
23320 Monteil 23 114 Be 72
24680 Monteil 24 136 Ac 80
43380 Monteil 43 140 Db 77
43700 Monteil 43 141 Df 78
79600 Monteil 79 99 Ze 67
87200 Monteil 87 112 Ae 73
24390 Monteil, le 24 125 Bb 77
36370 Monteil, le 36 113 Bb 70
43340 Monteil, le 43 141 De 79
23460 Monteil-au-Vicomte, la 23 114 Bf 73
14270 Monteille 14 35 Aa 54
12290 Monteillets 12 152 Cf 83
12160 Monteils 12 151 Cc 83
12200 Monteils 12 151 Bf 83
12380 Monteils 12 152 Cd 85
30360 Monteils 30 154 Eb 84
30630 Monteils 30 154 Ec 83
46330 Monteils 46 138 Be 81
48400 Monteils 48 153 Dd 82
82300 Monteils 82 150 Bd 83
63480 Monteix, le 63 129 De 75
63700 Monteix, les 63 115 Cf 71
63740 Montel, le 63 127 Ce 74
89210 Monteland, le 89 73 Dd 60
23700 Montel-au-Temple, le 23 115 Cc 73
63380 Montel-de-Gelat 63 115 Cd 73
26760 Montéléger 26 142 Ef 79
26120 Montélier 26 143 Fa 79
26200 Montélimar 26 142 Ee 81
01800 Montellier, le 01 118 Fa 73
30580 Montellier, le 30 154 Eb 84
09240 Montels 09 177 Bc 90
34310 Montels 34 167 Da 89
81140 Montels 81 151 Bf 85
23700 Montely 23 115 Cc 72
20214 Montemaggiore CTC 180 If 93
16310 Montembœuf 16 124 Ad 74
57480 Montenach 57 44 Gc 52
53500 Montenay 53 66 Za 59
17130 Montendre 17 123 Zd 77
73390 Montendry 73 132 Gb 75
62123 Montenescourt 62 29 Cd 47
56380 Monteneuf 56 81 Xe 61
77320 Montenils 77 53 Dc 55
25260 Montenois 25 94 Ge 64
58700 Montenoison 58 104 Dc 65
54760 Montenoy 54 56 Gb 56
80540 Montenoy 80 38 Bf 49
60810 Montépilloy 60 51 Ce 53
51320 Montépreux 51 53 Ea 56
86430 Monterbean 86 112 Ae 71
56250 Monterblanc 56 80 Xb 62
45260 Montereau 45 88 Cd 61
77130 Montereau-Fault-Yonne 77 72 Cf 58
77950 Montereau-sur-le-Jard 77 71 Ce 57
35160 Monterfil 35 65 Ya 60
41400 Monteriou 41 86 Ba 65
76680 Montérolier 76 37 Bc 51
20128 Monte Rosso CTC 182 If 97
20128 Monte Rossu = Monte Rosso CTC 182 If 97
74470 Monterrebout 74 120 Gc 71
56800 Monterrein 56 81 Xd 61
56800 Montertelot 56 81 Xd 61
12160 Montes 12 152 Cc 83
66200 Montescot 66 179 Cf 93
82200 Montescot 82 150 Ba 84
02440 Montescourt-Lizerolles 02 40 Db 50
31260 Montespan 31 163 Af 90
47130 Montesquieu 47 148 Ac 83
82200 Montesquieu 82 149 Ba 83
09200 Montesquieu-Avantès 09 176 Bb 90
66740 Montesquieu-des-Albères 66 179 Cf 93
31230 Montesquieu-Guittaut 31 163 Ae 88
31450 Montesquieu-Lauragais 31 165 Bd 88
31310 Montesquieu-Volvestre 31 164 Bb 89
32320 Montesquiou 32 163 Ab 87
70270 Montessaux 70 94 Gd 62
52500 Montesson 52 92 Fe 62
64300 Montestrucq 64 161 Zb 88
32390 Montestruc-sur-Gers 32 149 Ad 86
24450 Montet 24 125 Af 75
24560 Montet 24 136 Ad 80
42220 Montet 42 130 Ed 77
03240 Montet, le 03 115 Da 70
58110 Mont-et-Marré 58 104 Dd 66
47120 Monteton 47 136 Ab 81
05460 Montette, la 05 145 Gf 79
84170 Monteux 84 155 Ef 84
77144 Montévrain 77 52 Ce 55
70140 Montey-Besuche 70 92 Fe 65
38770 Monteynard 38 144 Fe 79
70130 Montey-sur-Saône 70 92 Fe 63
30170 Montèzes, les 30 154 Df 85
12460 Montézic 12 139 Cd 80
09350 Montfa 09 164 Bb 90
38940 Montfalcon 38 131 Fb 77
48340 Montfalgoux 48 140 Da 81
50760 Montfarville 50 34 Ye 51
25660 Montfaucon 25 107 Ga 65
30150 Montfaucon 30 155 Ee 84
46240 Montfaucon 46 138 Bd 80
49230 Montfaucon 49 97 Yf 66
55270 Montfaucon 55 55 Fa 53
43290 Montfaucon-en-Velay 43 129 Eb 77
84140 Montfavet 84 155 Ef 85
87400 Montfayon 87 113 Bc 73
93370 Montfermail 93 51 Cd 55
82270 Montfermier 82 150 Bc 83
63230 Montfermy 63 127 Ce 73
31590 Montferran 31 165 Bd 86
11320 Montferrand 11 165 Be 88
63510 Montferrand 63 128 Da 74
24440 Montferrand-du-Périgord 24 137 Af 80
26510 Montferrand-la-Fare 26 156 Fc 82
25320 Montferrand-le-Château 25 107 Ff 65
38620 Montferrat 38 131 Fd 76
83131 Montferrat 83 172 Gc 87
66150 Montferrer 66 179 Cd 94
09300 Montferrier 09 177 Be 91
34980 Montferrier-sur-Lez 34 168 Df 86
71300 Montferroux 71 105 Ec 69
10130 Montfey 10 73 Df 60
14490 Montfiquet 14 34 Za 53
01250 Montfleur 01 119 Fc 71
07470 Montflor 07 141 Df 80
25650 Montflovin 25 108 Gc 67
04600 Montfort 04 157 Ff 84
24200 Montfort 24 137 Bb 79
25440 Montfort 25 107 Ff 66
35160 Montfort 35 65 Ya 60
49700 Montfort 49 99 Ze 65
64190 Montfort 64 161 Za 88
73160 Montfort 73 132 Ff 75
40380 Montfort-en-Chalosse 40 161 Za 86
78490 Montfort-l'Amaury 78 50 Be 56
72450 Montfort-le-Gesnois 72 68 Ac 60
83570 Montfort-sur-Argens 83 171 Ga 88
11140 Montfort-sur-Boulzane 11 178 Cb 92
27290 Montfort-sur-Risle 27 49 Ad 53
12380 Montfranc 12 152 Cd 85
23500 Montfranc, le 23 126 Ca 74
81600 Montfrays 81 151 Bf 85
23110 Montfrialoux 23 115 Cc 72
30490 Montfrin 30 155 Ed 85
26560 Montfroc 26 156 Fd 83
04110 Montfuron 04 156 Fe 86
63350 Montgacon 63 116 Db 73
09330 Montgaillard 09 177 Bd 91
11350 Montgaillard 11 179 Cd 91
32190 Montgaillard 32 163 Ab 87
40500 Montgaillard 40 162 Zd 86
65200 Montgaillard 65 162 Aa 90
81630 Montgaillard 81 150 Bd 85
82120 Montgaillard 82 149 Af 85
31260 Montgaillard-de-Salies 31 164 Af 90
31290 Montgaillard-Lauragais 31 165 Be 88
31350 Montgaillard-sur-Save 31 163 Ae 89
86210 Montgamé 86 100 Ad 68
05230 Montgardin 05 144 Gb 81
50250 Montgardon 50 33 Yc 53
37160 Mont-Garni 37 100 Ae 67
61150 Montgaroult 61 48 Zf 56
09160 Montgauch 09 176 Ba 90
61360 Montgaudry 61 68 Ac 58
31410 Montgazin 31 164 Bb 89
31560 Montgeard 31 165 Bd 88
77230 Montgé-en-Goële 77 52 Ce 54
73130 Montgellafrey 73 132 Gb 76
05100 Montgenèvre 05 145 Ge 79
51260 Montgenost 51 73 Dd 57
60420 Montgérain 60 39 Cd 51
35760 Montgermont 35 65 Yb 60
91230 Montgeron 91 51 Cc 56
95650 Montgeroult 95 51 Ca 54
35520 Montgerval 35 65 Yb 59
73210 Montgésin 73 133 Gd 75
25111 Montgesoye 25 107 Gb 66
46150 Montgesty 46 137 Bb 81
81470 Montgey 81 165 Bf 87
63890 Montghéol 63 128 Dd 75
19210 Montgibaud 19 125 Bc 75
73220 Montgilbert 73 132 Gb 75
73210 Montgirod 73 133 Gd 75
73700 Montgirod 73 133 Ge 75
31450 Montgiscard 31 165 Bd 88
36400 Montgivray 36 102 Bf 69
02600 Montgobert 02 40 Da 53
63600 Montgolfier 63 129 De 75
08390 Montgon 08 42 Ee 51
50540 Montgothier 50 66 Ye 57
38830 Montgoutoux 38 132 Ga 76
11240 Montgradail 11 165 Bf 90
31370 Montgras 31 164 Ba 88
15190 Montgreleix 15 127 Cf 76
01230 Montgriffon 01 119 Fc 72
15110 Montgros 15 140 Cf 80
26170 Montguers 26 156 Fc 83
10300 Montgueux 10 73 Df 59
49500 Montguillon 49 83 Zb 62
24500 Montguyard 24 136 Ac 80
17270 Montguyon 17 123 Ze 77
55320 Monthairons, les 55 55 Fc 54
28800 Montharville 28 70 Bb 59
35420 Monthault 35 66 Ye 57
41200 Monthault 41 87 Be 64
11240 Monthaut 11 165 Ca 90
21190 Monthelie 21 105 Ee 67
51530 Monthelon 51 53 Df 55
71400 Monthelon 71 105 Eb 67
02860 Monthenault 02 40 De 52
77580 Monthérand 77 52 Cf 56
52330 Montheries 52 74 Ef 59
60790 Montherlant 60 51 Ca 53
08800 Monthermé 08 42 Ee 49
02400 Monthiers 02 52 Db 54
01390 Monthieux 01 118 Ef 73
73200 Monthion 73 132 Gc 75
37110 Monthodon 37 85 Af 63
86210 Monthoiron 86 100 Ad 68
08400 Monthois 08 42 Ee 53
39800 Montholier 39 107 Fd 67
77750 Monthomé 77 52 Db 55
41120 Monthou-sur-Bièvre 41 86 Bb 64
41400 Monthou-sur-Cher 41 86 Bb 64
50200 Monthuchon 50 46 Yd 54
02330 Monthurel 02 53 Dd 54
88800 Monthureux-le-Sec 88 76 Ga 59
88410 Monthureux-sur-Saône 88 76 Ff 60
77122 Monthyon 77 52 Ce 54
06500 Monti 06 159 Hc 86
24450 Montibus, le 24 125 Af 75
20123 Monticchi CTC 182 If 98
20220 Monticello CTC 180 If 93
10270 Montiéramey 10 74 Eb 59
36130 Montierchaume 36 101 Be 67
52220 Montier-en-Der 52 74 Ee 58
10200 Montier-en-L'Isle 10 74 Ed 59
17620 Montierneuf 17 122 Za 73
60190 Montiers 60 39 Cd 52
55290 Montiers-sur-Saulx 55 75 Fb 57
32420 Monties 32 163 Ad 88
33230 Montigaud 33 135 Ze 78
12320 Montignac 12 139 Cc 81
17800 Montignac 17 123 Zc 75
24290 Montignac 24 137 Ba 78
24320 Montignac 24 124 Ab 76
24700 Montignac 24 136 Ab 78
33760 Montignac 33 135 Ze 80
48210 Montignac 48 153 Dc 83
65690 Montignac 65 162 Aa 89
16330 Montignac-Charente 16 124 Aa 74
47800 Montignac-de-Lauzun 47 136 Ac 81
16390 Montignac-le-Coq 16 124 Ab 76
47350 Montignac-Toupinerie 47 136 Ac 81
30190 Montignargues 30 154 Eb 85
23140 Montignat 23 114 Ca 71
16170 Montigné 16 123 Zf 74
79370 Montigné 79 111 Ze 71
53970 Montigné-le-Brillant 53 66 Zb 60
49430 Montigné-lès-Rairies 49 84 Ze 63
49230 Montigné-sur-Moine 49 97 Yf 66
14210 Montigny 14 47 Zc 54
18250 Montigny 18 103 Ce 65
45170 Montigny 45 71 Ca 60
50540 Montigny 50 66 Yf 57
51700 Montigny 51 53 De 54
54540 Montigny 54 77 Ge 57
72600 Montigny 72 68 Ab 58
76380 Montigny 76 37 Af 52
79380 Montigny 79 98 Zc 68
80240 Montigny 80 40 Da 49
89630 Montigny 89 90 Df 64
58130 Montigny-aux-Amognes 58 103 Db 66
55110 Montigny-devant-Sassey 55 42 Fa 52
02110 Montigny-en-Arrouaise 02 40 Dc 49
59225 Montigny-en-Cambrésis 59 30 Dc 48
62640 Montigny-en-Gohelle 62 30 Cf 46
58120 Montigny-en-Morvan 58 104 Df 66
59182 Montigny-en-Ostrevent 59 30 Db 46
02810 Montigny-l'Allier 02 52 Da 54
89230 Montigny-la-Resle 89 89 De 61
78180 Montigny-le-Bretonneux 78 51 Ca 56
28120 Montigny-le-Chartif 28 69 Ba 59
02250 Montigny-le-Franc 02 41 Df 50
28220 Montigny-le-Gennelon 28 69 Bb 60
77480 Montigny-le-Guesdier 77 72 Db 58
77520 Montigny-Lencoup 77 72 Da 58
02290 Montigny-Lengrain 02 40 Da 52
52140 Montigny-le-Roi 52 75 Fc 61
39600 Montigny-lèsArsures 39 107 Fe 67
70500 Montigny-lès-Cherlieu 70 93 Fe 62
02330 Montigny-lès-Condé 02 53 Dd 55
95370 Montigny-les-Cormeilles 95 51 Cb 55
80370 Montigny-les-Jongleurs 80 29 Ca 47
57160 Montigny-lès-Metz 57 56 Ga 54
10130 Montigny-les-Monts 10 73 Df 60
55140 Montigny-lès-Vaucouleurs 55 75 Fd 57
70000 Montigny-lès-Vesoul 70 93 Ga 63
21500 Montigny-Montfort 21 90 Ec 63
21610 Montigny-Mornay-Villeneuve-sur-Vingeanne 21 92 Fc 63
21390 Montigny-Saint-Barthélemy 21 90 Eb 64
02250 Montigny-sous-Marle 02 40 De 50
21140 Montigny-sur-Armançon 21 90 Ec 64
21520 Montigny-sur-Aube 21 74 Ee 61
28270 Montigny-sur-Avre 28 49 Ba 56
58340 Montigny-sur-Canne 58 104 Dd 67
54870 Montigny-sur-Chiers 54 43 Fe 52
39300 Montigny-sur-L'Ain 39 107 Fe 68
80260 Montigny-sur-L'Hallue 80 39 Cc 49
77690 Montigny-sur-Loing 77 71 Ce 58
08170 Montigny-sur-Meuse 08 42 Ee 48
08430 Montigny-sur-Vence 08 42 Ed 51
51140 Montigny-sur-Vesle 51 40 De 53
49250 Montil, le 49 84 Ze 64
72150 Montillés, les 72 85 Ac 61
71520 Montillet 71 118 Ed 71
49310 Montilliers 49 98 Zc 65
89660 Montillot 89 89 De 63
03000 Montilly 03 103 Db 69
42720 Montilly 42 117 Ea 71
61100 Montilly-sur-Noireau 61 47 Zc 56
17800 Montils 17 123 Zc 75
77370 Montils 77 72 Cf 57
41120 Montils, les 41 86 Bb 64
36230 Montipouret 36 101 Bf 69
11800 Montirat 11 166 Cc 89
81190 Montirat 81 151 Ca 84
28240 Montireau 28 69 Ba 58
32200 Montiron 32 163 Af 87
76290 Montivilliers 76 35 Ab 51
74800 Montizel 74 120 Gb 72
89200 Montjalin 89 90 Df 63
11230 Montjardin 11 178 Ca 91
30750 Montjardin 30 153 Dc 84
12490 Montjaux 12 152 Cf 84
60240 Montjavoult 60 50 Be 53
05150 Montjay 05 156 Fd 82
71310 Montjay 71 106 Fb 68
77410 Montjay-la-Tour 77 51 Ce 55
16240 Montjean 16 111 Aa 72

Montjean I 293

26110 Poët-Sigillat, le 26 156 Fb 82
80240 Pœuilly 80 40 Da 49
64230 Poey-de-Lescar 64 162 Zd 88
64400 Poey-d'Oloron 64 161 Zc 89
03800 Poëzat 03 116 Db 72
20114 Poggiale CTC 185 Ka 99
20218 Poggio CTC 181 Kb 94
20224 Poggio CTC 182 If 94
20275 Poggio CTC 181 Kc 91
20240 Poggio-di-Nazza CTC 183 Kb 96
20250 Poggio-di-Venaco CTC 183 Kb 95
20232 Poggio-d'Oletta CTC 181 Kc 93
20169 Poggio d'Olmo CTC 185 Kb 100
20144 Poggioli CTC 185 Kc 98
20125 Poggiolo CTC 182 If 95
20237 Poggio-Marinaccio CTC 181 Kc 94
20230 Poggio-Mezzana CTC 183 Kc 94
51240 Pogny 51 54 Ec 55
39570 Poids-de-Fiole 39 107 Fd 69
50190 Poignavanderie, la 50 46 Yd 53
77160 Poigny 77 72 Db 57
78125 Poigny-la-Forêt 78 50 Be 56
58170 Poil 58 104 Ea 67
89630 Poil-Chevré 89 90 Ea 64
08190 Poilcourt-Sydney 08 41 Ea 52
34310 Poilhes 34 167 Da 89
86500 Poilieu 86 112 Ae 70
72350 Poillé-sur-Vègre 72 84 Ze 61
35420 Poilley 35 66 Ye 58
50220 Poilley 50 66 Ye 57
51170 Poilly 51 53 De 53
45500 Poilly-lez-Gien 45 88 Cd 62
89310 Poilly-sur-Serein 89 90 Df 62
89110 Poilly-sur-Tholon 89 89 Dc 61
17470 Poimier, le 17 111 Zd 72
89800 Poinchy 89 90 De 62
21330 Poinçon-lès-Larrey 21 91 Ec 61
36330 Poinçonnet, le 36 101 Be 68
77470 Poincy 77 52 Cf 55
85710 Poinière, la 85 96 Ya 67
52160 Poinsenot 52 91 Fa 62
52500 Poinson-lès-Fayl 52 92 Fd 62
52160 Poinson-lès-Grancey 52 91 Ef 62
52800 Poinson-lès-Nogent 52 75 Fc 61
72510 Point-du-Jour, le 72 84 Aa 62
33980 Pointe 33 134 Za 80
49080 Pointe 49 83 Zc 64
06440 Pointe, la 06 159 Hc 86
56140 Pointe, la 56 81 Xe 62
82200 Pointe, la 82 149 Ba 84
85330 Pointe de L' Herbaudière 85 96 Xe 66
56190 Pointe-de-Pen-Lan 56 81 Xc 63
61220 Pointel 61 47 Zd 56
45150 Pointes, les 45 87 Ca 61
09160 Pointis 09 164 Ba 90
31210 Pointis-de-Rivière 31 163 Ad 90
31800 Pointis-Inard 31 163 Ae 90
39290 Pointre 39 106 Fd 65
25440 Pointvillers 25 107 Ff 66
28310 Poinville 28 70 Bf 59
85770 Poiré-sur-Velluire, le 85 110 Za 70
85170 Poiré-sur-Vie, le 85 97 Yc 68
61430 Poirier 61 47 Zc 56
22400 Poirier, le 22 64 Xc 57
62890 Poirier, le 62 27 Bf 44
49770 Poiriers, les 49 83 Zb 63
86400 Poiriers, les 86 111 Ab 72
36140 Poirond 36 114 Be 70
58230 Poirot 58 104 Df 66
85230 Poirot, le 85 96 Xf 67
85440 Poiroux, le 85 109 Yc 69
45130 Poiseaux 45 70 Bd 61
52360 Poiseul 52 92 Fc 61
21440 Poiseul-la-Grange 21 91 Ee 63
21450 Poiseul-la-Ville-et-Laperrière 21 91 Ed 63
21120 Poiseul-lès-Saulx 21 91 Ef 63
58130 Poiseux 58 103 Db 66
58370 Poiseux 58 104 Df 67
18200 Poisieux 18 102 Cc 68
18290 Poisieux 18 102 Ca 66
41270 Poislay, le 41 69 Ba 60
41240 Poisly 41 86 Bd 61
39160 Poisoux 39 119 Fc 70
19330 Poissac 19 126 Be 77
58130 Poisson 58 103 Db 66
71600 Poisson 71 117 Ea 70
52230 Poissons 52 75 Fb 58
78300 Poissy 78 51 Ca 55
28300 Poisvilliers 28 70 Bc 57
74330 Poisy 74 120 Ga 73
44440 Poitevinière, la 44 82 Ye 63
49510 Poitevinière, la 49 98 Za 65
23140 Poitière Marsat 23 114 Ca 71
86000 Poitiers 86 99 Ac 69
39130 Poitte 39 119 Fe 69
10700 Poivres 10 54 Eb 56
51460 Poix 51 54 Ed 55
80290 Poix-de-Picardie 80 38 Bf 50
59218 Poix-du-Nord 59 31 Dd 47
08430 Poix-Terron 08 42 Ed 51
01130 Poizat-Lalleyriat, le 01 119 Fe 72
86220 Poizay 86 100 Ad 67
38460 Poizieu 38 131 Fb 74
70210 Polaincourt-et-Clairefontaine 70 93 Ga 61
31430 Polastron 31 164 Af 89
32130 Polastron 32 163 Af 87
17700 Poléon 17 110 Zb 72
60690 Polhoy 60 38 Bf 51
38210 Poliénas 38 131 Fc 77
03310 Polier 03 115 Cd 71
15260 Polignac 15 140 Da 79
17210 Polignac 17 123 Ze 77
43000 Polignac 43 141 Df 78
35320 Poligné 35 82 Yb 61
05500 Poligny 05 144 Ga 80
10110 Poligny 10 74 Eb 59
39800 Poligny 39 107 Fe 67
77167 Poligny 77 71 Ce 59
62370 Polincove 62 27 Ca 43
10110 Polisot 10 74 Ec 60
12330 Polissat 12 139 Cd 81
10110 Polisy 10 74 Ec 60
66300 Politg 66 179 Ce 93
86200 Polka, la 86 99 Ab 66
66450 Pollestres 66 179 Cf 93
01800 Pollet 01 131 Fa 74
01310 Polliat 01 118 Fa 71
01350 Pollieu 01 131 Fe 74
69290 Pollionnay 69M 130 Ed 74
15800 Polminhac 15 139 Cd 79
19220 Polprat 19 138 Ca 77
73500 Polsets Chalets 73 133 Gd 77
20229 Polveroso CTC 183 Kc 94
51110 Pomacle 51 53 Ea 52
12150 Pomairols 12 152 Cf 83
38120 Pomaray 38 131 Fe 77
46250 Pomarède 46 137 Bb 81
09140 Pomarède, la 09 177 Bb 92
11400 Pomarède, la 11 165 Bf 88
48190 Pomaret 48 141 De 82
40360 Pomarez 40 161 Zb 87
11250 Pomas 11 166 Cb 90
12160 Pomayret 12 151 Cc 82
12130 Pomayrols 12 140 Da 82
09420 Pombole 09 177 Bb 91
24100 Pombonne 24 136 Ad 79
24160 Pomélie, la 24 125 Ba 76
42240 Pomerley 42 129 Ea 76
33500 Pomerol 33 135 Ze 79
34810 Pomérols 34 167 Dc 88
48300 Pomeyrols 48 141 De 80
69590 Pomeys 69M 130 Ec 75
32430 Pominet 32 164 Af 86
61200 Pommainville 61 48 Zf 56
21630 Pommard 21 106 Ee 66
81250 Pommardelle 81 152 Cc 85
28140 Pommay 28 70 Bd 60
47170 Pomme-d'Or, la 47 148 Ab 84
62760 Pommera 62 29 Cc 47
79190 Pommeraie, la 79 111 Aa 71
85700 Pommeraie-sur-Sèvre, la 85 98 Zb 67
28120 Pommeray 28 69 Bb 58
14100 Pommeraye, la 14 35 Ab 54
14690 Pommeraye, la 14 47 Zd 55
49360 Pommeraye, la 49 98 Zc 67
49620 Pommeraye, la 49 83 Za 64
76750 Pommeraye, la 76 37 Bb 51
22120 Pommeret 22 64 Xc 58
59360 Pommereuil 59 31 Dd 48
60590 Pommereux 60 38 Bf 53
76440 Pommereux 76 38 Bd 51
76680 Pommeréval 76 37 Bb 50
19290 Pommerie, la 19 126 Ca 74
53400 Pommerieux 53 83 Za 62
57420 Pommérieux 57 56 Gb 55
22450 Pommerit-Jaudy 22 63 We 56
22200 Pommerit-le-Vicomte 22 63 Wf 57
77515 Pommeuse 77 52 Da 56
82400 Pommevic 82 149 Af 84
24340 Pommier 24 124 Ad 76
38280 Pommier 38 131 Fa 74
46600 Pommier 46 138 Bd 79
62111 Pommier 62 29 Cd 47
71120 Pommier 71 117 Ec 70
23300 Pommier, le 23 113 Bc 71
23400 Pommier, le 23 114 Be 72
23400 Pommier, le 23 126 Be 73
38260 Pommier-de-Beaurepaire 38 131 Fa 76
02200 Pommiers 02 40 Db 52
12320 Pommiers 12 139 Cc 81
30120 Pommiers 30 153 Dd 85
36190 Pommiers 36 114 Bd 69
42260 Pommiers 42 129 Ea 74
69480 Pommiers 69D 118 Ee 73
38340 Pommiers-la-Placette 38 131 Fd 77
17130 Pommiers-Moulons 17 123 Zd 77
70240 Pomoy 70 93 Gc 63
79200 Pompaire 79 99 Ze 69
44410 Pompas 44 81 Xd 64
33730 Pompéjac 33 147 Ze 82
31450 Pompertuzat 31 165 Bd 88
54340 Pompey 54 56 Ga 56
43170 Pompeyrin 43 140 Dc 79
32130 Pompiac 32 164 Ba 87
47330 Pompiac 47 136 Ad 81
48110 Pompidou, le 48 153 Dd 83
49350 Pompierre 49 84 Ze 65
88300 Pompierre 88 75 Fe 59
25340 Pompierre-sur-Doubs 25 94 Gd 64
04140 Pompiéry 04 157 Gc 82
47230 Pompiey 47 148 Ab 83
33370 Pompignac 33 135 Zd 79
30170 Pompignan 30 153 Df 85
82170 Pompignan 82 150 Bb 86
47420 Pompogne 47 148 Aa 83
79100 Pompois 79 98 Ze 66
24240 Pomport 24 136 Ac 80
64370 Pomps 64 162 Zc 88
40160 Poms 40 146 Yf 82
72340 Poncé-sur-le-Loir 72 85 Ad 62
36260 Poncet-la-Ville 36 102 Bf 66
71640 Poncey 71 105 Ee 68
21130 Poncey-lès-Athée 21 106 Fc 65
33220 Ponchapt 33 136 Ab 79
62390 Ponchel, le 62 29 Ca 47
80150 Ponches-Estruval 80 28 Bf 47
60430 Ponchon 60 51 Cb 52
01450 Poncin 01 119 Fc 72
42110 Poncins 42 129 Ea 74
33190 Pondaurat 33 135 Zf 81
24430 Pondemaux 24 136 Ad 78
36230 Ponderon, le 36 101 Bf 69
16440 Pondeville 16 123 Zf 75
56300 Pondivi = Pontivy 56 79 Xa 60
35720 Pondolay 35 65 Ya 58
18210 Pondy, le 18 103 Cd 68
26150 Ponet-et-Saint Auban 26 143 Fb 80
31210 Ponlat-Taillebourg 31 163 Ad 90
62270 Ponnières 62 29 Cb 47
12140 Pons 12 139 Cd 80
15400 Pons 15 127 Cd 77
17800 Pons 17 123 Zc 75
32300 Ponsampère 32 163 Ac 88
32300 Ponsan-Soubiran 32 163 Ac 88
26240 Ponsas 26 130 Ef 78
23250 Ponsat 23 114 Bf 72
40400 Ponson 40 146 Zb 85
64460 Ponson-Debat-Pouts 64 162 Zf 89
64460 Ponson-Dessus 64 162 Zf 89
38350 Ponsonnas 38 144 Fe 79
09800 Pont, le 09 176 Af 91
17600 Pont, le 17 122 Za 74
21130 Pont, le 21 106 Fb 65
42260 Pont, le 42 117 Df 73
45640 Pont, le 45 87 Ca 61
50770 Pont, le 50 46 Yc 53
79210 Pont, le 79 110 Zc 71
02270 Pont-à-Bucy 02 40 Dc 50
64530 Pontacq 64 162 Zf 89
17640 Pontaillac 17 122 Yf 75
21270 Pontailler-sur-Saône 21 92 Fc 65
26150 Pontaix 26 143 Fb 80
43170 Pontajou 43 140 Dc 79
87200 Pont-à-la-Planche 87 112 Af 73
02500 Pont-à-L'Écu 02 41 Ea 49
86120 Pontalon 86 99 Aa 66
73300 Pontamafrey 73 132 Gc 77
59710 Pont-à-Marcq 59 30 Da 45
54700 Pont-à-Mousson 54 56 Ga 55
02160 Pont-Arcy 02 40 Dd 52
23250 Pontarion 23 114 Bf 73
25300 Pontarlier 25 108 Gc 67
60520 Pontarmé 60 51 Cd 54
22650 Pont-Arson 22 65 Xe 57
63190 Pont-Astier 63 128 Dc 73
89200 Pontaubert 89 90 Df 64
27500 Pont-Audemer 27 36 Ad 52
56440 Pont-Augen 56 80 Wf 61
28140 Pontault 28 70 Bd 60
94510 Pontault-Combault 94 51 Cd 56
63380 Pontaumur 63 127 Ce 73
50250 Pont-Auny 50 46 Yd 53
27290 Pont-Authou 27 49 Ae 53
50390 Pont-aux-Moines, le 50 33 Yc 52
29930 Pont-Aven 29 78 Wb 61
62880 Pont-à-Vendin 62 30 Cf 46
02160 Pontavert 02 41 De 52
14380 Pont-Bellanger 14 47 Za 55
53500 Pontbellon 53 66 Yf 59
44640 Pont-Béranger, le 44 96 Yb 66
50380 Pont-Bleu, le 50 46 Yc 56
37130 Pont-Boutard 37 85 Ab 64
50750 Pont-Brocard, le 50 46 Ye 54
46340 Pont-Carral 46 137 Bb 80
77135 Pontcarré 77 51 Ce 56
70360 Pontcey 70 93 Ga 63
61120 Pontchardon 61 48 Ab 55
38530 Pontcharra 38 132 Ga 76
69490 Pontcharra-sur-Turdine 69D 118 Ec 73
23260 Pontcharraud 23 127 Cb 73
85150 Pont-Chartran, le 85 109 Yb 69
44160 Pontchâteau 44 81 Xf 64
36800 Pont-Chrétien-Chabenet 36 101 Bc 69
46150 Pontcirq 46 137 Bb 81
29190 Pont-Coblant 29 78 Wa 59
22650 Pont-Cornou 22 65 Xe 57
19500 Pont-Coudert, le 19 138 Bd 78
29790 Pont-Croix 29 61 Vd 60
16110 Pont-d'Agris, le 16 124 Ab 74
01160 Pont-d'Ain 01 119 Fc 72
21390 Pont-d'Aisy 21 90 Eb 64
43580 Pont-d'Alleyras, le 43 141 Dd 79
03380 Pont-d'Any 08 41 Ec 49
62610 Pont d'Ardres, le 62 27 Bf 43
83510 Pont-d'Argens 83 172 Gc 88
44410 Pont-d'Armes 44 81 Xd 64
68520 Pont d'Aspach 68 95 Ha 62
59173 Pont-d'Asquin 59 29 Cc 44
30340 Pont-d'Avène, le 30 154 Ea 83
26160 Pont-de-Barret 26 143 Fa 81
73330 Pont-de-Beauvoisin, le 73 131 Fe 75
07000 Pont-de-Boyon, le 07 142 Ed 80
29590 Pont-de-Buis-lès-Quimerch 29 62 Vf 59
24250 Pont-de-Cause 24 137 Ba 80
38230 Pont-de-Chéruy 38 131 Fb 74
38800 Pont-de-Claix, le 38 144 Fe 78
63920 Pont-de-Dore 63 128 Dc 73
13460 Pont-de-Gau 13 169 Ec 88
50250 Pont-de-Glatigny, le 50 33 Yc 53
07380 Pont-de-Labeaume 07 142 Eb 81
33220 Pont-de-la-Beauze 33 136 Ab 80
20244 Pont de Lano CTC 183 Kb 94
27340 Pont-de-L'Arche 27 49 Ba 53
09140 Pont-de-la-Taule 09 177 Bb 92
33730 Pont-de-la-Trave 33 147 Zd 82
26260 Pont-de-L'Herbasse 26 142 Ef 78
26600 Pont-de-L'Isère 26 142 Ef 78
63560 Pont-de-Menat 63 115 Cf 72
80480 Pont-de-Metz 80 38 Cb 49
48220 Pont-de-Montvert, le 48 153 De 82
59850 Pont-de-Nieppe 59 30 Cf 44
21410 Pont-de-Pany 21 91 Ee 65
20251 Pont de Piedicorte CTC 183 Kb 95
21130 Pont-de-Pierre 21 106 Fc 65
70130 Pont-de-Planches, le 70 93 Ff 63
39130 Pont-de-Poitte 39 107 Fe 69
46310 Pont-de-Rhodes 46 138 Bc 81
25150 Pont-de-Roide 25 94 Ge 64
37260 Pont-de-Ruan 37 85 Ad 65
59177 Pont-de-Sains 59 31 Ea 48
12290 Pont-de-Salars 12 152 Ce 83
01200 Pont-des-Pierres 01 119 Fe 72
01190 Pont-de-Vaux 01 118 Ef 70
01290 Pont-de-Veyle 01 118 Ef 71
30440 Pont-d'Herault 30 153 Dd 85
39110 Pont-d'Héry 39 107 Ff 67
44170 Pont-d'Indre, le 44 82 Yc 63
21360 Pont-d'Ouche 21 105 Ee 65
14690 Pont-d'Ouilly 14 47 Zd 55
62215 Pont d'Oye 62 27 Ca 43
60127 Pontdron 60 52 Cf 53
70210 Pont-du-Bois 70 76 Ga 61
47480 Pont-du-Casse 47 149 Ae 83
20133 Pont d'Ucciani, le CTC 182 If 96
19320 Pont du Chambon 19 126 Ca 77
63430 Pont-du-Château 63 128 Db 74
29260 Pont-du-Chatel 29 62 Ve 57
05260 Pont-du-Fossé 05 144 Gb 80
85230 Pont-du-Fresne, le 85 96 Ya 66
74490 Pont-du-Giffre 74 120 Gc 72
62370 Pont-du-Halot 62 27 Ca 43
30750 Pont-du-Lingas 30 153 Dc 84
56390 Pont-du-Luc 56 80 Xb 62
64800 Pont-du-Moulin 64 162 Ze 90
39300 Pont-du-Navoy 39 107 Fe 68
13250 Pont-du-Raud, le 13 170 Fa 87
20218 Ponte à a Leccia = Ponte Leccia CTC 181 Kb 94
29430 Pontéalet 29 62 Ve 57
20236 Ponte Castirla CTC 183 Ka 94
14110 Pontécoulant 14 47 Zc 55
66300 Ponteilla 66 179 Ce 93
43150 Ponteils 43 141 Df 79
30450 Ponteils-et-Brésis 30 154 Df 82
63970 Ponteix 63 128 Da 75
29790 Pontekroaz = Pont-Croix 29 61 Vd 60
20218 Ponte Leccia CTC 181 Kb 94
42550 Pontempeyrat 42 129 Df 76
20235 Ponte Novu CTC 181 Kb 94
38680 Pont-en-Royans 38 143 Fc 78
40200 Pontenx-les-Forges 40 146 Yf 83
14110 Pont-Erambourg 14 47 Zc 55
19130 Ponterie, la 19 125 Bc 77
20235 Ponte Rosso CTC 181 Kb 94
20235 Ponte Rossu = Ponte Rosso CTC 181 Kb 94
13090 Pontès 13 170 Fc 87
44522 Pont-Esnaud 44 82 Ye 64
07320 Pontet, le 07 142 Ec 79
15130 Pontet, le 15 139 Cc 79
33390 Pontet, le 33 122 Zc 77
73110 Pontet, le 73 132 Gb 76
84130 Pontet, le 84 155 Ef 85
21140 Pont-et-Massène 21 90 Ec 64
25240 Pontets, les 25 107 Gb 68
38780 Pont-Évêque 38 130 Ef 75
83670 Pontevès 83 171 Ga 87
24410 Ponteyraud, La Jemaye- 24 124 Ab 77
14380 Pont-Farcy 14 46 Yf 55
51490 Pontfaverger-Moronvilliers 51 54 Eb 53
14430 Pontfol 14 35 Aa 54
63230 Pontgibaud 63 127 Cf 74
44770 Pont-Giraud 44 96 Xe 66
28190 Pontgouin 28 69 Ba 58
61220 Pont-Guillaume, le 61 67 Zd 57
50880 Pont-Hébert 50 46 Yf 53
21470 Pont-Hémery 21 106 Fb 66
78730 Ponthévrard 78 70 Bf 57
77310 Ponthierry 77 71 Cd 57
01110 Ponthieu 01 131 Fd 73
51300 Ponthion 51 54 Ee 56
80860 Ponthoile 80 28 Be 47
29650 Ponthou, le 29 63 Wc 57
72290 Ponthouin 72 68 Ab 59
39170 Ponthoux 39 119 Fe 70
64460 Pontiacq-Viellepinte 64 162 Zf 88
32350 Pontic 32 163 Ac 87
20169 Ponti di a Nava CTC 185 Kb 100
49150 Pontigné 49 84 Zf 63
89230 Pontigny 89 89 De 61
41500 Pontijou 41 86 Bb 62
05160 Pontis 05 145 Gc 81
56300 Pontivy = Pondivi 56 79 Xa 60
85470 Pont-Jaunay, le 85 96 Ya 68
29120 Pont-l'Abbe 29 78 Ve 61
50360 Pont-L'Abbé 50 33 Yd 52
17250 Pont-L'Abbé-d'Arnoult 17 122 Za 74
52120 Pont-la-Ville 52 74 Ef 60
85600 Pont-Legé, le 85 97 Ye 67
88260 Pont-lès-Bonfays 88 76 Ga 59
25110 Pont-les-Moulins 25 93 Gc 65
14130 Pont-L'Évêque 14 35 Ab 53
41400 Pontlevoy 41 86 Bb 64
29810 Pont-L'Hôpital 29 61 Vc 58
40120 Pont-Long, le 40 148 Ze 83
53220 Pontmain 53 66 Yf 58
08350 Pont-Maugis 08 42 Ef 50
19800 Pont-Maure 19 126 Bf 76
22390 Pont-Melvez 22 63 We 58
29620 Pont-Menou 29 63 Wb 57
29390 Pont-Meur 29 79 Wb 60
29120 Pont-'N-Abad = Pont-l'Abbe 29 78 Ve 61
12390 Pont-Neuf, le 12 151 Cb 82
80115 Pont-Noyelles 80 39 Cc 49
04800 Pontoise 04 157 Fe 86
95520 Pontoise 95 51 Ca 54
60400 Pontoise-lès-Noyon 60 39 Da 51
40465 Pontonx-sur-L'Adour 40 146 Za 86
50170 Pontorson 50 66 Yc 57
24150 Pontours 24 136 Ae 79
71270 Pontoux 71 106 Fa 67
57420 Pontoy 57 56 Gb 54
35131 Pont-Péan 35 65 Yb 60
57380 Pontpierre 57 57 Gd 54
60700 Pontpoint 60 51 Cd 53
35580 Pont-Réan 35 65 Yb 60
17350 Pontreau, le 17 110 Zb 73
80580 Pont-Rémy 80 28 Bf 48
22260 Pontrev = Pontrieux 22 63 Wf 56
22260 Pontrieux 22 63 Wf 56
59253 Pont-Riqueul 59 29 Ce 45
14250 Pont-Roc, le 14 34 Zc 53
04340 Pont romain 04 157 Gc 82
87260 Pont-Roy 87 125 Bc 75
13370 Pont-Royal 13 170 Fb 86
02490 Pontru 02 40 Db 49
02490 Pontruet 02 40 Db 49
50300 Ponts 50 46 Yd 56
60700 Pont-Sainte-Maxence 60 51 Cd 53
30130 Pont-Saint-Esprit 30 155 Ed 83
24140 Pont-Saint-Mamet 24 136 Ad 79
02380 Pont-Saint-Mard 02 40 Db 52
10150 Pont-Saint-Marie 10 73 Ea 59
44860 Pont-Saint-Martin 44 97 Yc 66
87300 Pont-Saint-Martin 87 112 Af 71
27360 Pont-Saint-Pierre 27 37 Bb 53
54550 Pont-Saint-Vincent 54 76 Ga 57
43330 Pont-Salomon 43 129 Eb 76
05000 Pont-Sarrazin 05 144 Ga 81
56620 Pont-Scorff 56 79 Wd 61
49130 Ponts-de-Cé, les 49 84 Zc 64
02250 Pontséricourt 02 41 Df 50
76260 Ponts-et-Marais 76 28 Bc 48
22400 Ponts-Neufs 22 64 Xc 57
14480 Ponts sur Seulles 14 35 Zc 53
70110 Pont-sur-l'Ognon 70 93 Gc 63
88500 Pont-sur-Madon 88 76 Ga 58
59138 Pont-sur-Sambre 59 31 Df 47
10400 Pont-sur-Seine 10 73 Dd 57
89190 Pont-sur-Vanne 89 72 Dc 59
89140 Pont-sur-Yonne 89 72 Db 59
69240 Pont-Trambouze 69D 117 Eb 72
47380 Pont-Trancat 47 136 Ad 82
28630 Pont-Tranche-Fétu 28 69 Bc 58
72510 Pontvallain 72 84 Ab 62
52130 Pont-Varin 52 74 Ef 57
15290 Pontverny 15 138 Ca 79
53400 Pont-Vien, le 53 83 Za 61
81440 Pont-Vieux, le 81 151 Ca 86
23130 Ponty 23 114 Ca 72
58140 Ponty 58 90 De 65
34230 Popian 34 167 Dd 87
80700 Popincourt, Dancourt- 80 39 Ce 51
20218 Popolasca CTC 181 Ka 94
56380 Porcaro 56 81 Xe 61
86320 Porcelaine, la 86 112 Ae 70
13104 Porcelette 13 169 Ee 88
57890 Porcelette 57 57 Gd 54
44520 Porche, le 44 82 Ye 63
54800 Porcher 54 56 Fe 54
33660 Porchères 33 135 Aa 78
86160 Porcherie, la 86 112 Ab 71
87380 Porcherie, la 87 125 Bd 75
28200 Porcheronville 28 70 Bd 61
60390 Porcheux 60 50 Bf 52
78440 Porcheville 78 50 Be 55
84120 Porchière 84 156 Fe 86
38390 Porcieu-Amblagnieu 38 131 Fc 74
58140 Porcmignon 58 90 Df 65
22590 Pordic 22 64 Xb 57
20137 Poretta CTC 185 Kb 99
20222 Poretto CTC 181 Kc 92
33680 Porge, le 33 134 Yf 79
33680 Porge-Océan, le 33 134 Ye 79
29260 Porléach 29 62 Ve 57
58330 Pornas 58 104 Dc 66
44210 Pornic 44 96 Xf 66
44380 Pornichet 44 81 Xd 65
60400 Porquéricourt 60 39 Cf 51
83400 Porquerolles 83 172 Gb 91
37330 Porrerie, la 37 85 Ab 63
20215 Porri CTC 181 Kc 94
29242 Porsguen 29 61 Uf 58
29280 Porsmilin 29 61 Vb 58
29810 Porsmoguer 29 61 Vb 58
29360 Porsmoric 29 79 Wc 62
29840 Porspoder 29 61 Vb 57
01460 Port 01 119 Fd 72
09320 Port, le 09 177 Bc 91
33680 Port, le 33 134 Yf 79
85440 Port, le 85 109 Yc 70
66760 Porta 66 177 Bf 93
20237 Porta, la CTC 181 Kc 94
16330 Portal, le 16 123 Aa 74
34300 Port-Ambonne 34 167 Dd 89
83390 Portanière, la 83 171 Gb 89
83390 Portaniere, la 83 171 Gb 89
44420 Port-au-Loup 44 81 Xc 64
20245 Porta Vecchia CTC 180 Ie 94
50580 Portbail 50 46 Yb 52
66420 Port-Barcarès 66 179 Da 92
22610 Port-Béni 22 63 We 55
22710 Port-Blanc 22 63 We 55
56870 Port-Blanc 56 80 Xa 63
37140 Port-Boulet, le 37 99 Aa 65
53410 Port-Brillet 53 66 Za 60
30240 Port-Camargue 30 168 Ea 87
34420 Port-Cassafières 34 167 Dc 89
83400 Port-Cros 83 172 Gc 90
37140 Port-d'Ablevois, le 37 99 Ab 65
83270 Port-d'Alon 83 171 Fd 90
81500 Port-d'Ambres 81 165 Be 86
70160 Port-d'Atelier-Amance 70 93 Ga 62
13110 Port-de-Bouc 13 170 Ef 88
33340 Port-de-By 33 122 Za 76
20221 Port de Campoloro CTC 183 Kd 94
17150 Port-de-Cônac 17 122 Zb 76
33420 Port-de-Génissac 33 135 Ze 79
33590 Port-de-Goulée 33 122 Za 76
33290 Port-de-Grattequina 33 135 Zc 79
01680 Port-de-Groslée 01 131 Fd 74
85540 Port-de-la-Claye 85 109 Ye 70
33460 Port-de-Lamarque 33 134 Zb 78
33340 Port-de-Lamena 33 122 Zb 76
85350 Port-de-la-Meule 85 96 Xd 68
40300 Port-de-Lanne 40 161 Ye 87
83250 Port-de-Miramare 83 172 Gb 90
AD200 Port d'Envalira □ AND 177 Be 93
17350 Port-d'Envaux 17 122 Zb 73
09110 Port-de-Pailhères 09 178 Bf 92
47140 Port-de-Penne 47 149 Ae 82
86220 Port-de-Piles 86 100 Ad 66
33590 Port-de-Richard 33 122 Za 76
63290 Port-de-Ris 63 116 Dc 73
35660 Port-de-Roche 35 82 Ya 62

Port-de-Roche | 303

11250 Preixan 11 166 Cb 90
49370 Préjean, le 49 83 Zb 63
38450 Prélenfrey 38 144 Fd 78
58800 Préliechy 58 104 Dd 65
42130 Prélion 42 129 Df 74
05120 Prelles 05 145 Gd 79
70600 Prélot, le 70 92 Fc 63
58140 Prélouis 58 104 Df 65
34390 Prémain 34 166 Cf 87
39220 Prémanon 39 120 Ga 70
21700 Premeaux-Prissey 21 106 Ef 66
58700 Prémery 58 103 Db 65
59840 Premesques 59 30 Cf 45
01300 Prémeyzel 01 131 Fd 74
21110 Premières 21 106 Fb 65
10170 Prémierfait 10 73 Ea 57
25580 Premiers Sapins, les 25 108 Gb 66
73130 Premier-Villard, le 73 132 Gb 77
03410 Prémilhat 03 115 Cd 71
24800 Prémillac 24 125 Af 76
01110 Prémillieu 01 131 Fd 73
02110 Prémont 02 40 Dc 48
02320 Prémontré 02 40 Dc 51
36260 Prenay 36 102 Ca 66
41370 Prenay 41 86 Bd 62
46270 Prendeignes 46 138 Ca 80
07110 Prends-toi-gardes 07 142 Eb 81
32190 Préneron 32 163 Ab 86
22210 Prénessaye, la 22 64 Xc 59
21370 Prenois 21 91 Ef 64
41240 Prénouvellon 41 70 Bd 61
39150 Prénovel 39 119 Ff 69
54530 Prény 54 56 Ff 55
36220 Pré-Picault 36 100 Af 68
73530 Pré-Plan 73 132 Gb 77
58360 Préporché 58 104 Df 67
61190 Préportin 61 68 Ad 57
35330 Pré-Quérat, le 35 81 Ya 61
26560 Pré-Rond 26 156 Fd 83
26310 Prés 26 143 Fd 81
05290 Prés, les 05 145 Gc 80
43150 Présailles 43 141 Ea 79
28800 Pré-Saint-Evroult 28 70 Bc 59
28800 Pré-Saint-Martin 28 70 Bc 59
89144 Prés-du-Bois, les 89 90 De 61
59990 Préseau 59 31 Dd 47
25550 Présentevillers 25 94 Ge 63
31570 Préserville 31 165 Bd 87
05800 Près-Hauts, la 05 144 Ga 80
46200 Présignac 46 137 Bc 79
39270 Présilly 39 119 Fd 69
74160 Présilly 74 120 Ga 72
42123 Presle 42 117 Ea 73
70230 Presle 70 93 Gb 63
73110 Presle 73 132 Ga 76
18360 Presle, la 18 102 Cc 69
14410 Presles 14 47 Zb 55
38680 Presles 38 143 Fc 78
95590 Presles 95 51 Cb 54
77220 Presles-en-Brie 77 52 Ce 56
02370 Presles-et-Boves 02 40 Dd 52
02860 Presles-et-Thierny 02 40 Dd 51
18380 Presly 18 87 Cc 64
45260 Presnoy 45 71 Cd 61
43100 Pressac 43 128 Dc 77
86460 Pressac 86 112 Ad 72
27940 Pressagny-le-Val 27 50 Bc 54
27510 Pressagny-L'Orgueilleux 27 50 Bc 54
45130 Pressailles 45 70 Bd 61
86800 Pressec 86 112 Ad 69
19150 Presset 19 126 Be 77
01370 Pressiat 01 119 Fc 71
16150 Pressignac 16 124 Ae 74
24150 Pressignac-Vicq 24 136 Ae 79
52500 Pressigny 52 92 Fd 62
79390 Pressigny 79 99 Zf 68
45290 Pressigny-les-Pins 45 88 Ce 61
38480 Pressins 38 131 Fd 75
18340 Pressoir, le 18 102 Cc 67
79200 Pressoux, le 79 99 Ze 68
62550 Pressy 62 29 Cc 46
74300 Pressy 74 120 Gd 72
71220 Pressy-sous-Dondin 71 117 Ed 70
22120 Prest, le 22 64 Xb 58
66230 Preste, la 66 178 Cc 94
39110 Pretin 39 107 Ff 67
50250 Prétot-Sainte-Suzanne 50 46 Yd 53
76560 Prétot-Vicquemare 76 37 Af 50
14140 Prêtreville 14 48 Ab 54
80290 Prettemolle 80 38 Bf 50
71290 Préty 71 118 Ef 69
55250 Pretz-en-Argonne 55 55 Fa 55
18370 Preugne, la 18 102 Cb 69
36400 Preugné, la 36 114 Ca 69
18120 Preuilly 18 102 Cb 66
86360 Preuilly 86 99 Ab 69
85250 Preuilly, le 85 97 Ye 67
36220 Preuilly-la-Ville 36 100 Af 68
37290 Preuilly-sur-Claise 37 100 Af 67
62650 Preures 62 28 Bf 45
67250 Preuschdorf 67 58 He 55
76660 Preuseville 76 38 Bd 49
54490 Preutin-Higny 54 56 Fe 52
59288 Preux-au-Bois 59 31 Dd 48
59144 Preux-au-Sart 59 31 De 47
72400 Préval 72 68 Ad 59
18300 Prévant 18 88 Cf 65
72110 Prévelles 72 68 Ac 60
48800 Prévenchères 48 141 Df 81
18370 Préveranges 18 114 Cb 70
01280 Prévessin-Moëns 01 120 Ga 71
12120 Préviala 12 152 Cd 83
49420 Prévière, la 49 83 Ye 62
60360 Prévillers 60 38 Bf 51
77470 Prévilliers 77 52 Cf 55
12350 Prévinquières 12 151 Cb 82
57590 Prévocourt 57 56 Gc 55
22770 Prévotais, la 22 65 Xf 57
59840 Prévôté, la 59 30 Cf 44
27220 Prey 27 49 Bb 55
88600 Prey 88 77 Ge 59
24460 Preyssac-d'Agonac 24 124 Ae 77
24160 Preyssac-d'Excideuil 24 125 Ba 76
08290 Prez 08 41 Ec 50
52700 Prez-sous-Lafauche 52 75 Fc 59
52170 Prez-sur-Marne 52 75 Fa 57
20245 Prezzuna CTC 180 Ie 94
79210 Priaires 79 110 Zc 72
01160 Priay 01 119 Fb 73
36400 Priche 36 114 Ca 69
20230 Pricoju CTC 183 Kd 95
66130 Prieuré de Serrabone (romane) 66 179 Cd 93
02470 Priez 02 52 Db 54
17160 Prignac 17 123 Zd 74
33710 Prignac-et-Marcamps 33 135 Zd 78
33340 Prignac-en-Médoc 33 122 Za 77
06850 Prignolet, le 06 158 Ge 85
44760 Prigny 44 96 Ya 66
24130 Prigonrieux 24 136 Ac 79
20260 Prigugio CTC 180 Ie 93
38270 Primarette 38 130 Fa 76
08250 Primat 08 42 Ee 52
12450 Primaube, la 12 152 Cd 83
17810 Primaudières, les 17 122 Zb 74
29770 Primelin 29 61 Vc 60
18400 Primelles 18 102 Cb 67
29630 Primel-Trégastel 29 62 Wb 56
86420 Prinçay 86 99 Ab 67
35210 Princé 35 66 Yf 59
44680 Princé 44 96 Ya 66
56230 Prince, la 56 81 Xc 62
79210 Prin-Deyrançon 79 110 Zc 71
72800 Pringé 72 84 Aa 62
51300 Pringy 51 54 Ed 56
74370 Pringy 74 120 Ga 73
77310 Pringy 77 71 Cd 57
18110 Prinquette, la 18 102 Cb 65
44260 Prinquiau 44 81 Xf 64
48100 Prinsuéjols-Malbouzon 48 140 Db 80
85170 Printemps, le 85 97 Yc 68
67490 Printzheim 67 58 Hc 56
34360 Priou, le 34 167 Cf 88
73710 Prioux, les 73 133 Ge 76
02140 Prisces 02 41 Df 50
59550 Prisches 59 31 De 48
33990 Prise, la 33 122 Yf 77
36370 Prissac 36 113 Bb 69
24580 Prisse 24 137 Af 78
71960 Prissé 71 118 Ee 71
79360 Prissé-la-Charrière 79 110 Zd 72
33730 Privaillet 33 147 Zd 82
07000 Privas 07 142 Ed 80
30630 Privat 30 154 Ec 83
18370 Privez 18 102 Cb 69
12350 Privezac 12 151 Cb 82
12700 Prix 12 138 Ca 81
37240 Prix 37 100 Ae 66
56320 Priziac 56 79 Wd 60
71800 Prizy 71 117 Eb 70
22510 Probrien, le 22 64 Xc 58
74110 Prodains 74 121 Ge 71
12370 Prohencoux 12 152 Ce 86
70310 Proiselière-et-Langle, la 70 93 Gd 62
24200 Proissans 24 137 Bb 79
02120 Proisy 02 40 De 49
02120 Proix 02 40 Dd 49
32400 Projan 32 162 Ze 87
42560 Prolanges 42 129 Df 75
21230 Promenois 21 105 Ec 65
46260 Promilhanes 46 150 Be 82
38520 Promontoire 38 144 Gb 79
63200 Prompsat 63 115 Da 73
71380 Prondevaux 71 106 Ef 68
63470 Prondines 63 127 Ce 74
60190 Pronleroy 60 39 Cd 52
47370 Pronquière, la 47 149 Af 82
62860 Pronville 62 30 Da 47
26170 Propiac 26 155 Fb 83
69790 Propières 69D 117 Ec 71
20110 Propriano CTC 184 If 98
51400 Prosnes 51 54 Eb 53
36370 Prots, les 36 113 Bb 69
28410 Prouais 28 50 Bd 56
44320 Prouaud, le 44 96 Xf 65
34220 Prouilhe 34 166 Cd 87
51140 Prouilly 51 53 Df 53
01150 Proulieu 01 131 Fb 73
31360 Proupiary 31 163 Af 90
31210 Proupriary 31 163 Ad 90
37160 Prouray 37 100 Ad 66
14110 Proussy 14 47 Zc 55
02190 Prouvais 02 41 Df 52
35490 Prouverie, la 35 65 Yc 59
80370 Prouville 80 29 Ca 48
59121 Prouvy 59 30 Dc 47
89130 Proux, les 89 89 Db 62
18140 Prouze, la 18 103 Cf 66
80160 Prouzel 80 38 Cb 50
74700 Provence, la 74 120 Gd 73
25380 Provenchère 25 94 Gd 65
70170 Provenchère 70 93 Ga 62
18120 Provenchère, la 18 102 Bf 66
88490 Provenchères-et-Colroy 88 77 Ha 59
88260 Provenchères-lès-Darney 88 76 Ff 60
88490 Provenchères-sur-Fave 88 77 Ha 59
52320 Provenchères-sur-Marne 52 75 Fa 59
52140 Provenchères-sur-Meuse 52 75 Fd 60
45520 Provenchérie, la 45 70 Be 60
89200 Provency 89 90 Df 63
10200 Proverville 10 74 Ee 59
38120 Proveysieux 38 131 Fe 77
33480 Providence, la 33 134 Za 78
59267 Proville 59 30 Db 48
59185 Provin 59 30 Cf 45
77160 Provins 77 72 Db 57
02190 Proviseux-et-Plesnoy 02 41 Ea 52
35580 Provostais, la 35 65 Yb 61
44440 Provostière, la 44 82 Yd 63
80340 Proyart 80 39 Ce 49
28270 Prudemanche 28 49 Ba 56
46130 Prudhomat 46 138 Be 79
20128 Prugna, Grosseto- CTC 184 If 97
11140 Prugnanes 11 178 Cc 92
03370 Prugne, la 03 115 Cd 70
12360 Prugnes-les-Eaux 12 152 Cf 86
10190 Prugny 10 73 Df 59
49220 Pruillé 49 83 Zc 63
72700 Pruillé-le-Chétif 72 68 Aa 61
72150 Pruillé-L'Eguillé 72 85 Ac 61
12320 Pruines 12 139 Cd 81
63590 Prulhière, la 63 128 Dc 75
86430 Prun 86 112 Ae 71
34190 Prunarède, la 34 153 Dc 85
30750 Prunaret 30 153 Dc 84
51360 Prunay 51 53 Eb 53
10350 Prunay-Belleville 10 73 De 58
41310 Prunay-Cassereau 41 86 Af 62
78660 Prunay-en-Yvelines 78 70 Be 57
28360 Prunay-le-Gillon 28 70 Bd 58
78910 Prunay-le-Temple 78 50 Be 55
36200 Prune, la 36 113 Bd 69
17800 Prunelas, le 17 123 Zd 75
20290 Prunelli di Casacconi CTC 181 Kc 93
20243 Prunelli-di-Fiumorbo CTC 183 Kb 96
63580 Prunerette, la 63 128 Dc 76
03410 Prunet 03 115 Cd 70
07110 Prunet 07 142 Eb 81
15130 Prunet 15 139 Cc 80
31460 Prunet 31 165 Be 87
66130 Prunet 66 179 Cd 93
81190 Prunet 81 151 Cb 84
20232 Pruneta CTC 181 Kc 93
20221 Prunete CTC 183 Kd 95
48210 Prunets 48 153 Dc 82
28140 Pruneville 28 70 Bd 60
36290 Prung 36 100 Ba 68
36200 Prunget 36 101 Bd 69
12210 Prunhes, les 12 140 Cf 80
05230 Prunières 05 145 Gb 81
38350 Prunières 38 144 Fe 79
48200 Prunières 48 140 Dc 80
36120 Pruniers 36 102 Ca 68
49080 Pruniers 49 83 Zc 64
86500 Pruniers 86 112 Ae 70
41200 Pruniers-en-Sologne 41 87 Be 65
20114 Pruno CTC 185 Ka 99
20167 Pruno CTC 182 Ie 97
20213 Pruno CTC 181 Kc 94
20114 Pruno = U Prunu CTC 185 Ka 99
89120 Prunoy 89 89 Da 61
12160 Pruns 12 151 Cc 83
12290 Pruns 12 152 Ce 83
15150 Pruns 15 139 Cb 78
63260 Pruns 63 116 Db 72
20213 Prunu = Pruno CTC 181 Kc 94
20110 Prupia = Propriano CTC 184 If 98
21400 Prusly-sur-Ource 21 91 Ed 61
10210 Prusy 10 73 Ea 61
58160 Prye 58 103 Db 67
85320 Pû, le 85 109 Yf 69
67290 Puberg 67 58 Hb 55
33840 Publanc 33 147 Ze 83
74500 Publier 74 120 Gd 70
39570 Publy 39 107 Fd 69
72450 Puce, la 72 68 Ac 60
09800 Pucelle, la 09 176 Af 91
44390 Puceul 44 82 Yc 63
33610 Puch 33 134 Zb 80
33830 Puch 33 147 Zb 82
09460 Puch, le 09 178 Ca 92
33540 Puch, le 33 135 Zf 80
33650 Puch, le 33 135 Zc 81
27150 Puchay 27 50 Bd 52
47160 Puch-d'Agenais 47 148 Ab 83
76340 Puchervin 76 37 Bd 49
64260 Pucheux 64 162 Zd 90
80560 Puchevillers 80 29 Cc 48
33113 Pudaou, le 33 135 Zc 82
33112 Pudos 33 134 Za 78
12150 Puech 12 152 Da 83
30580 Puech, la 30 154 Eb 84
12290 Puech, le 12 152 Ce 83
12390 Puech, le 12 151 Cc 82
34700 Puech, le 34 167 Db 86
34150 Puéchabon 34 168 Dd 86
12290 Puech-Arnal, le 12 152 Ce 83
81100 Puech-Auriol 81 166 Cb 87
12340 Puech-Gros 12 139 Cd 82
12270 Puechiguier 12 151 Bf 83
82250 Puech-Mignon 82 151 Bf 84
81470 Puéchoursi 81 165 Bf 87
30610 Puechredon 30 154 Ea 85
12390 Puechs 12 151 Cc 82
30140 Puechs, les 30 154 Df 84
52220 Puellemontier 52 74 Ee 58
28140 Puerthe 28 70 Bd 60
84360 Puget 84 156 Fb 86
06260 Puget-Rostange 06 158 Gf 85
31250 Pugets 31 165 Ca 88
83480 Puget-sur-Argens 83 172 Ge 88
06260 Puget-Théniers 06 158 Gf 85
83390 Puget-Ville 83 171 Ga 89
25720 Pugey 25 107 Ff 65
01510 Pugieu 01 131 Fd 74
11400 Puginier 11 165 Bf 88
49440 Pugle, la 49 83 Yf 63
33710 Pugnac 33 135 Zd 78
79320 Pugny 79 98 Zc 68
73100 Pugny-Chatenod 73 132 Ff 74
11700 Puichéric 11 166 Cd 89
88210 Puid, le 88 77 Ha 58
23200 Puids, les 23 114 Cb 73
34230 Puilacher 34 167 Dd 87
11140 Puilaurens 11 178 Cb 92
17138 Puilboreau 17 110 Yf 71
08370 Puilly-et-Charbeaux 08 42 Fb 51
42110 Puilly-lès-Feurs 42 129 Eb 74
87140 Puimenier 87 113 Bb 72
04700 Puimichel 04 157 Ga 85
34480 Puimisson 34 167 Db 88
04410 Puimoisson 04 157 Ga 85
79350 Puiravault 79 98 Ze 68
86250 Puiraveau 86 112 Ac 71
10130 Puiseaux 10 73 Df 60
45390 Puiseaux 45 71 Cc 59
45480 Puiselet 45 70 Ca 59
77140 Puiselet 77 71 Cd 59
91150 Puiselet-le-Marais 91 71 Cb 58
76660 Puisenval 76 37 Bc 49
21400 Puiset, le 21 91 Ee 62
28310 Puiset, le 28 70 Bf 59
49600 Puiset-Doré, le 49 97 Yf 65
08270 Puiseux 08 41 Ed 51
28170 Puiseux 28 50 Bc 57
60850 Puiseux-en-Bray 60 38 Be 52
95380 Puiseux-en-France 95 51 Cc 54
95380 Puiseux-en-France le Village 95 51 Cc 54
02600 Puiseux-en-Retz 02 52 Da 53
60540 Puiseux-le-Hauberger 60 51 Cb 53
51500 Puisieulx 51 53 Ea 53
62116 Puisieux 62 29 Ce 48
77139 Puisieux 77 52 Cf 54
02120 Puisieux-et-Clanlieu 02 40 De 49
34480 Puissalicon 34 167 Db 88
28250 Puissaye, la 28 69 Af 57
33570 Puisseguin 33 135 Zf 79
34620 Puisserguier 34 167 Da 88
21400 Puits 21 91 Ec 62
17400 Puits, le 17 110 Zd 73
76780 Puits, le 76 37 Bc 52
62170 Puits-Bérault, le 62 28 Be 46
86200 Puits-d'Ardanne 86 99 Aa 67
13126 Puits-d'Auzon, le 13 171 Fe 87
45630 Puits-d'Avenat 45 88 Ce 63
89310 Puits-de-Bon 89 90 Df 62
89800 Puits-de-Courson 89 90 De 62
83560 Puits-de-Rians, le 83 171 Fe 87
52340 Puits-des-Mèzes, le 52 75 Fb 60
10140 Puits-et-Nuisement 10 74 Ed 59
76113 Puits-Fouquet, les 76 37 Af 52
77171 Puits-Froux 77 72 Dc 57
60480 Puits-la-Vallée 60 38 Cb 51
85480 Puits-Pellerin, le 85 97 Ye 69
11340 Puivert 11 178 Ca 91
32600 Pujaudran 32 164 Ba 87
30131 Pujaut 30 155 Ee 84
65500 Pujo 65 162 Aa 88
12380 Pujol, le 12 152 Cd 86
13390 Pujol, le 13 171 Fd 88
11160 Pujol-de-Bosc 11 166 Cc 88
40190 Pujo-le-Plan 40 147 Zd 85
33350 Pujols 33 135 Zf 80
47300 Pujols 47 149 Ae 82
81310 Pujols 81 150 Be 85
09100 Pujols, les 09 165 Be 90
33210 Pujols-sur-Ciron 33 135 Zd 81
31160 Pujos 31 176 Ae 90
32290 Pujos 32 163 Ab 86
71460 Puley, le 71 105 Ed 68
21190 Puligny-Montrachet 21 105 Ee 67
27130 Pullay 27 49 Af 56
54160 Pulligny 54 76 Ga 57
54115 Pulney 54 76 Ga 58
54425 Pulnoy 54 56 Gb 56
85390 Pulteau 85 98 Za 69
63230 Pulvériès 63 115 Cf 73
68840 Pulversheim 68 95 Hb 61
56330 Pulvigner 56 79 Wf 62
80320 Punchy 80 39 Ce 50
20240 Punta CTC 183 Kc 97
65230 Puntous 65 163 Ac 89
63490 Pupidon 63 128 Dc 75
39600 Pupillin 39 107 Fe 67
08110 Pure 08 42 Fb 50
20290 Purettone CTC 181 Kc 93
70160 Purgerot 70 93 Ff 62
20166 Purtichju = Porticcio CTC 182 Ie 97
20137 Purtivechju = Porto-Vecchio CTC 185 Kb 99
70000 Pusey 70 93 Ga 63
69330 Pusignan 69M 131 Fa 74
38510 Pusignieu 38 131 Fc 74
33125 Pussac 33 135 Zc 81
91740 Pussay 91 70 Bf 58
37800 Pussigny 37 100 Ad 67
73260 Pussy 73 132 Gc 75
70000 Pusy-et-Épenoux 70 93 Ga 62
61210 Putanges-le-Lac 61 47 Ze 56
61210 Putanges-Pont-Écrepin 61 48 Ze 56
27170 Puthenaye, la 27 49 Af 54
01420 Puthier 01 119 Fe 73
88120 Putières 88 77 Gd 60
13109 Putis, les 13 170 Fc 88
14430 Putot-en-Auge 14 35 Zf 53
14740 Putot-en-Bessin 14 35 Zc 53
88270 Puttegney 88 76 Gb 60
57510 Puttelange-aux-Lacs = Püttlingen 57 57 Gf 54
57570 Puttelange-lès-Thionville 57 44 Gb 52
57170 Puttigny 57 57 Gd 55
57510 Püttlingen = Puttelange-aux-Lacs 57 57 Gf 54
54115 Puxe 54 76 Ff 58
54800 Puxe 54 56 Fe 54
54800 Puxieux 54 56 Ff 54
03800 Puy, la 03 116 Da 72
16420 Puy, le 16 112 Ae 73
24210 Puy, le 24 137 Ba 78
25640 Puy, le 25 93 Gb 64
33580 Puy, le 33 135 Aa 81
42155 Puy, le 42 117 Df 73
42210 Puy, le 42 129 Eb 75
50540 Puy, le 50 66 Ye 57
77460 Puy, le 77 72 Ce 59
87500 Puy, le 87 125 Ba 75
05290 Puy-Aillaud 05 145 Gc 79
63230 Puy-à-L'Ane 63 127 Ce 74
40230 Puyau 40 160 Ye 87
33190 Puybarban 33 135 Zf 81
16270 Puybareau 16 124 Ad 73
19100 Puybaret 19 138 Bc 78
81390 Puybegon 81 151 Bf 86
24300 Puybegout 24 124 Ad 75
85110 Puybelliard 85 97 Yf 68
24460 Puyblanc 24 124 Ae 77
46320 Puy-Blanc 46 138 Bf 81
46130 Puybrun 46 138 Be 79
81440 Puycalvel 81 165 Ca 86
32120 Puycasquier 32 163 Ae 86
87330 Puycatelin 87 112 Af 71
81140 Puycelsi 81 150 Be 85
23350 Puy-Cesset 23 114 Ca 70
24460 Puychantu 24 124 Ae 76
16210 Puychaud 16 123 Aa 77
48400 Puychauzier 48 153 Dd 83
87230 Puyconnieux, le 87 125 Af 75
31190 Puydaniel 31 164 Bc 88
19120 Puy-d'Arnac 19 138 Be 78
65220 Puydarrieux 65 163 Ac 89
33720 Puy-de-Cornac 33 135 Zd 81
24310 Puy-de-Fourches 24 124 Ad 77
85240 Puy-de-Serre 85 110 Zc 69
17290 Puydrouard 17 110 Za 72
63980 Puy du-Sapt 63 128 Dd 75
86260 Puye, la 86 100 Ae 69
43000 Puy-en-Velay, le 43 141 Df 78
23380 Puy-Gaillard 23 114 Bf 71
82120 Puygaillard-de-Lomagne 82 149 Af 85
82800 Puygaillard-de-Quercy 82 150 Bd 84
17490 Puygard 17 123 Zf 74
26160 Puygiron 26 142 Ef 81
81990 Puygouzon 81 151 Cb 85
73190 Puygros 73 132 Ga 75
24240 Puyguilhem 24 136 Ac 80
63290 Puy-Guillaume 63 116 Dc 73
19300 Puyhabilier 19 126 Ca 77
79160 Puyhardy 79 110 Zc 69
24310 Puy-Henry 24 124 Ad 76
46260 Puyjourdes 46 151 Bf 82
19410 Puy-Juge 19 125 Bc 76
87380 Puy-la-Brune 87 125 Bc 75
82160 Puylagarde 82 151 Bf 83
19190 Puy-la-Mouche 19 138 Bd 78
82240 Puylaroque 82 150 Bd 83
81700 Puylaurens 81 165 Ca 87
48250 Puylaurent 48 141 Df 81
32220 Puylausic 32 164 Af 88
63820 Puy-Lavèze 63 127 Ce 74
46700 Puy-l'Evêque 46 137 Ba 81
86170 Puy-Lonchard 86 99 Ab 69
13114 Puyloubier 13 171 Fe 87
63230 Puy-Maladroit 63 127 Ce 73
23130 Puy-Malsignat 23 114 Cb 72
24410 Puymangou, Saint-Aulaye- 24 123 Aa 77
87290 Puymarron 87 113 Bb 72
31230 Puymaurin 31 163 Ae 88
84110 Puyméras 84 156 Fa 83
87500 Puy-Merle 87 125 Ba 75
47350 Puymiclan 47 136 Ab 81
47270 Puymirol 47 149 Ae 83
17400 Puymoreau 17 110 Zc 72
15190 Puymoreau 87 125 Af 74
87260 Puymoret 87 125 Bc 74
23140 Puy-Mouillera 23 114 Ca 71
16400 Puymoyen 16 124 Ab 75
19800 Puynèdre 19 126 Be 76
33660 Puynormand 33 135 Aa 79
49260 Puy-Notre-Dame, le 49 99 Ze 66
40320 Puyol-Cazalet 40 162 Zd 87
64270 Puyoô 64 161 Za 87
16310 Puyponchet 16 124 Ac 74
24400 Puyrajou 24 136 Ab 78
17700 Puyravault 17 110 Zb 72
79100 Puyravault 79 99 Zf 67
85450 Puyravault 85 110 Yf 70
03250 Puyravel 03 116 Dd 72
19510 Puy-Razit 19 126 Bd 75
16230 Puyréaux 16 124 Ab 73
24340 Puyrenier 24 124 Ac 76
13540 Puyricard 13 170 Fc 87
37420 Puy-Rigaud 37 99 Aa 65
17380 Puyrolland 17 110 Zc 72
76200 Puys 76 37 Ba 49
05100 Puy-Saint-André 05 145 Gd 79
49300 Puy-Saint-Bonnet, le 49 98 Za 67
13610 Puy-Sainte-Réparade, le 13 170 Fc 87
05200 Puy-Saint-Eusèbe 05 145 Gc 81
63470 Puy-Saint-Gulmier 63 127 Cd 74
87190 Puy-Saint-Jean, le 87 113 Bb 71
26450 Puy-Saint-Martin 26 143 Ef 81
05100 Puy-Saint-Pierre 05 145 Gd 79
05290 Puy-Saint-Vincent 05 145 Gc 80
79390 Puysan 79 99 Zf 68
85200 Puy-Sec 85 110 Zb 70
32390 Puységur 32 149 Ad 86
24160 Puyssegeney 24 125 Ba 76
31480 Puysségur 31 164 Ba 86
47800 Puysserampion 47 136 Ab 81
66210 Puyvalador 66 178 Ca 93
24260 Puyvendran 24 137 Af 79
84160 Puyvert 84 156 Fc 86
17220 Puyvineux 17 110 Za 72
74130 Puze 74 120 Gc 72
86170 Puzé 86 99 Ab 68
80320 Puzeaux 80 39 Ce 50
57590 Puzieux 57 56 Gc 55
88500 Puzieux 88 76 Ga 58
66360 Py 66 178 Cc 94
12240 Py, le 12 151 Cb 83
33460 Pyis, le 33 134 Zb 78
33115 Pyla-sur-Mer 33 134 Ye 81
27370 Pyle, la 27 49 Af 53
66210 Pyrénées 2000 66 178 Ca 93
31490 Pyroutet 31 164 Bb 87
80300 Pys 80 29 Ce 48

A B C D E F G H I J K L M N O P Q R S T U V W X Y Z

39700 Romagne 39 107 Fd 66
86700 Romagne 86 112 Ab 71
08220 Romagne, la 08 41 Eb 50
49740 Romagne, la 49 97 Yf 66
55110 Romagne-Gesnes 55 42 Fa 53
55150 Romagne-sous-les-Côtes 55 43 Fc 53
38480 Romagnieu 38 131 Fd 75
50140 Romagny 50 66 Za 57
68210 Romagny 68 94 Ha 63
25680 Romain 25 93 Gc 64
39350 Romain 39 107 Fe 65
51140 Romain 51 53 De 52
54360 Romain 54 76 Gc 57
88320 Romain-aux-Bois 88 75 Fe 60
80860 Romaine 80 28 Be 47
70130 Romaine, la 70 93 Ff 63
52150 Romain-sur-Meuse 52 75 Fd 59
75019 Romainville 75 51 Cc 55
27240 Roman 27 49 Ba 55
01250 Romanèche 01 119 Fc 71
71570 Romanèche-Thorins 71 118 Ee 71
20167 Romanetti CTC 182 Ie 97
15160 Romaniargues 15 127 Cf 77
07790 Romanieux 07 142 Ed 77
01400 Romans 01 118 Fa 72
79260 Romans 79 111 Ze 70
26100 Romans-sur-Isère 26 143 Fa 78
67310 Romanswiller 67 58 Hc 57
17120 Romarin, le 17 122 Zb 74
17520 Romas 17 123 Zd 75
71600 Romay 71 117 Ea 70
17510 Romazières 17 111 Ze 73
35490 Romazy 35 65 Yd 58
68660 Rombach-le-Franc 68 60 Hb 59
57120 Rombas 57 56 Ga 53
59990 Rombies-et-Marchipont 59 31 Dd 46
19470 Rome 19 126 Be 76
37190 Rome 37 85 Ad 65
16460 Romefort 16 124 Ab 73
17250 Romegoux 17 122 Zb 73
57930 Romelfing 57 57 Ha 56
58110 Romenay 58 104 Dd 66
71470 Romenay 71 118 Fa 69
77640 Romeny 77 52 Da 55
02310 Romeny-sur-Marne 02 52 Dc 55
44440 Romerai, la 44 82 Yd 63
59730 Romeries 59 30 Dd 47
51480 Romery 51 53 Df 54
60220 Romescamps 60 38 Be 50
47250 Romestaing 47 148 Aa 82
05000 Romette 05 144 Ga 81
12440 Romette 12 151 Cb 83
26150 Romeyer 26 143 Fc 80
43400 Romières 43 142 Eb 78
32480 Romieu, la 32 148 Ac 85
51170 Romigny 51 53 De 53
12430 Romiguière, la 12 152 Ce 84
46270 Romiguière, la 46 138 Ca 81
34650 Romiguières 34 153 Db 86
35850 Romillé 35 65 Ya 59
27170 Romilly 27 49 Af 54
41270 Romilly 41 69 Ba 61
28220 Romilly-sur-Aigre 28 69 Bb 61
27610 Romilly-sur-Andelle 27 50 Bb 52
10100 Romilly-sur-Seine 10 73 De 57
74300 Romme 74 120 Gd 72
88700 Romont 88 77 Gd 58
41200 Romorantin-Lanthenay 41 87 Be 64
07250 Rompoi 07 142 Ee 80
21290 Romprey 21 91 Ef 62
61160 Rônai 61 48 Zf 56
63630 Ronaye 63 128 Dd 76
28800 Ronce, la 28 69 Bc 59
17390 Ronce-les-Bains 17 122 Yf 74
10130 Roncenay 10 73 Df 60
27240 Roncenay-Authenay, le 27 49 Ba 55
50210 Roncey 50 46 Yd 55
70250 Ronchamp 70 94 Gd 62
77320 Ronchat 73 133 Gd 75
25440 Ronchaux 25 107 Ff 66
39130 Ronchaux, les 39 119 Fe 70
02130 Ronchères 02 53 Dd 54
89170 Ronchères 89 89 Da 63
76440 Roncherolles-en-Bray 76 37 Bc 51
76160 Roncherolles-sur-le-Vivier 76 37 Bb 52
59790 Ronchin 59 30 Da 45
76390 Ronchois 76 38 Bd 50
22150 Roncière, la 22 64 Xb 59
57860 Roncourt 57 56 Ga 53
88300 Roncourt 88 76 Fe 59
59223 Roncq 59 30 Da 44
17170 Ronde, la 17 110 Zb 71
36260 Ronde, la 36 101 Bf 66
36500 Ronde, la 36 101 Bb 67
79380 Ronde, la 79 98 Zc 68
40270 Rondebœuf 40 147 Zd 86
25240 Rondefontaine 25 107 Ga 68
50490 Ronde-Haye, la 50 33 Yd 54
27290 Rondemare 27 49 Ad 52
45130 Rondonneau 45 87 Bd 61
20130 Rondulinu CTC 182 Id 96
81120 Ronel 81 151 Cb 86
61100 Ronfeugerai 61 47 Zd 56
34610 Rongas 34 167 Da 86
03430 Rongère 03 115 Cf 70
18220 Rongère 18 102 Cc 65
71380 Rongère, la 71 106 Ef 68
87260 Rongère, la 87 125 Bc 74
10530 Rongères 03 116 Dc 71
36160 Rongères 36 114 Ca 69
24380 Ronlet, le 24 136 Ae 78
03420 Ronnet 03 115 Ce 71
69550 Ronno 69D 117 Ec 73
60600 Ronquerolles 60 39 Cc 52
95340 Ronquerolles 95 51 Cb 53
62129 Rons 62 29 Cb 44
40400 Ronsacq 40 147 Zb 85
16320 Ronsenac 16 124 Ab 76
12410 Ronsignac 12 152 Cf 84
80740 Ronssoy 80 40 Da 49
69510 Rontalon 69M 130 Ed 75
50530 Ronthon 50 46 Yd 56
64110 Rontignon 64 162 Ze 89
55160 Ronvaux 55 55 Fd 54
24490 Ronze, la 24 135 Aa 78
79370 Ronze, la 79 111 Ze 71
63470 Ronzet 63 127 Cd 74
15100 Ronzière, la 15 140 Db 78
42470 Ronzières 42 117 Eb 73
63320 Ronzières 63 128 Da 75
52310 Roôcourt-la-Côte 52 75 Fa 59
59286 Roost-Warendin 59 30 Da 46
90380 Roppe 90 94 Gf 62
67480 Roppenheim 67 59 Ia 55
68480 Roppentzwiller 68 95 Hc 63
57230 Roppeviller 57 58 Hd 54
12540 Roquaubel, la 12 151 Da 85
12560 Roque, la 12 152 Da 82
34290 Roque, la 34 167 Db 88
84190 Roque-Alric, la 84 155 Fa 84
14340 Roque-Bainard, la 14 48 Aa 53
06450 Roquebillière 06 159 Hb 84
06450 Roquebillière-Vieux 06 159 Hb 84
46270 Roque-Bouillac, la 46 139 Cb 81
34460 Roquebrun 34 167 Da 87
06190 Roquebrune 06 159 Hc 86
32190 Roquebrune 32 163 Ab 86
33580 Roquebrune 33 135 Aa 81
83520 Roquebrune-sur-Argens 83 172 Gd 88
83136 Roquebrussanne, la 83 171 Ff 88
81330 Roquecave 81 152 Cc 86
82150 Roquecor 82 149 Af 83
81170 Roquecourbe 81 151 Bf 84
81210 Roquecourbe 81 166 Cb 87
11700 Roquecourbe-Minervois 11 166 Cd 89
13640 Roque-d'Anthéron, la 13 170 Fb 86
30440 Roquedur 30 153 Dd 85
46240 Roquedure 46 138 Bc 80
83840 Roque-Esclapon, la 83 172 Gd 86
11380 Roquefère 11 166 Cc 88
11340 Roquefeuil 11 178 Bf 92
09300 Roquefixade 09 177 Be 91
12320 Roquefort 12 139 Cc 81
13830 Roquefort 13 171 Fd 89
32390 Roquefort 32 149 Ad 86
40120 Roquefort 40 147 Ze 84
47310 Roquefort 47 149 Ad 83
11140 Roquefort-de-Sault 11 178 Cb 92
11540 Roquefort-des-Corbières 11 179 Cf 91
13830 Roquefort-la-Bédoule 13 171 Fd 89
06330 Roquefort-les-Pins 06 173 Ha 86
31360 Roquefort-sur-Garonne 31 164 Af 90
12250 Roquefort-sur-Soulzon 12 152 Cf 85
24250 Roque-Gageac, la 24 137 Bb 80
12200 Roque-Jammé, la 12 151 Bf 83
32810 Roquelaure 32 163 Ad 86
32430 Roquelaure-Saint-Aubin 32 164 Af 86
30150 Roquemaure 30 155 Ee 84
81800 Roquemaure 81 150 Bd 86
24130 Roquepine 24 136 Ac 79
32100 Roquepine 32 148 Ac 85
34650 Roqueredonde 34 153 Db 86
31570 Roques 31 165 Bd 87
32310 Roques 32 148 Ab 85
34800 Roques 34 167 Db 87
46140 Roques, les 46 150 Bb 82
84260 Roques, les 84 155 Ef 84
12100 Roque-Sainte-Marguerite, la 12 153 Db 84
31380 Roquesérière 31 165 Bd 86
34320 Roquessels 34 167 Db 87
06910 Roquesteron 06 158 Ha 85
30200 Roque-sur-Cèze, la 30 155 Ed 83
84210 Roque-sur-Pernes 84 155 Fa 85
11300 Roquetaillade 11 178 Cb 91
12490 Roquetaillade 12 152 Cf 84
62120 Roquetoire 62 29 Cc 44
12850 Roquette 12 152 Cd 82
24330 Roquette 24 137 Af 77
27700 Roquette 27 50 Bc 53
12230 Roquette, la 12 153 Dc 84
83670 Roquette, la 83 171 Ga 87
31120 Roquettes 31 164 Bc 88
06550 Roquette-sur-Siagne, la 06 173 Gf 87
06670 Roquette-sur-Var, la 06 159 Hb 85
22230 Roquetton 22 64 Xc 59
13360 Roquevaire 13 171 Fd 88
81470 Roquevidal 81 165 Bf 87
64130 Roquiague 64 161 Za 89
33220 Roquille, la 33 136 Ab 80
68590 Rorschwihr 68 60 Hc 59
79700 Rorthais 79 98 Zb 67
22190 Rosaires, les 22 64 Xb 57
05150 Rosans 05 156 Fc 82
28410 Rosay 28 50 Bd 56
39190 Rosay 39 119 Fc 69
51340 Rosay 51 54 Ee 56
76680 Rosay 76 37 Bb 50
78790 Rosay 78 50 Be 55
28360 Rosay-au-Val 28 70 Bd 58
27790 Rosay-sur-Lieure 27 37 Bc 52
20121 Rosazia CTC 182 If 96
57800 Rosbruck 57 57 Gf 54
29570 Roscanvel 29 61 Vc 59
22390 Roscaradec 22 63 We 58
56500 Roscoët-Fily, le 56 64 Xb 61
29680 Roscoff 29 62 Wa 56
18110 Rose 18 102 Cc 65
13013 Rose, la 13 170 Fc 89
14740 Rosel 14 35 Zd 53
68128 Rosenau 68 95 Hd 63
67490 Rosenwiller 67 58 Hc 56
67560 Rosenwiller 67 60 Hc 57
49250 Roseray 49 84 Ze 64
50500 Roserie, la 50 33 Ye 53
56360 Roserière 56 80 Wf 64
13110 Roseron 13 170 Ef 88
58340 Roses, les 58 104 Dd 68
25410 Roset-Fluans 25 107 Fe 66
70000 Rosey 70 93 Ga 63
71390 Rosey 71 105 Ee 68
67560 Rosheim 67 60 Hc 58
17520 Rosier 17 123 Zd 75
05100 Rosier, le 05 145 Ge 79
18300 Rosière 18 103 Cf 65
38780 Rosière 38 130 Ef 76
70310 Rosière, la 70 94 Gd 61
73550 Rosière, la 73 133 Gd 76
73700 Rosière, la 73 133 Gf 75
07260 Rosières 07 142 Eb 82
18400 Rosières 18 102 Cb 67
43800 Rosières 43 141 Df 78
60440 Rosières 60 52 Ce 53
54110 Rosières-aux-Salines 54 76 Gb 57
55000 Rosières-devant-Bar 55 55 Fb 56
55130 Rosières-en-Blois 55 75 Fd 57
54385 Rosières-en-Haye 54 56 Ff 56
80170 Rosières-en-Santerre 80 39 Ce 50
10430 Rosières-près-Troyes 10 73 Ea 59
25190 Rosières-sur-Barbèche 25 94 Gd 65
70500 Rosières-sur-Mance 70 93 Fe 61
63230 Rosiers 63 127 Ce 74
77167 Rosiers 77 72 Ce 59
49350 Rosiers, les 49 84 Ze 64
19300 Rosiers-d'Egletons 19 126 Ca 76
19350 Rosiers-de-Juillac 19 125 Bb 77
34610 Rosis 34 167 Da 87
36300 Rosnay 36 101 Bb 68
51390 Rosnay 51 53 Df 53
85320 Rosnay 85 109 Ye 69
10500 Rosnay-L'Hôpital 10 74 Ec 58
29590 Rosnoën 29 62 Ve 59
93250 Rosny-sous-Bois 93 51 Cd 55
78710 Rosny-sur-Seine 78 50 Bd 55
60140 Rosoy 60 51 Cc 52
89100 Rosoy 89 72 Db 60
60620 Rosoy-en-Multien 60 52 Cf 54
45210 Rosoy-le-Vieil 45 72 Cf 60
52600 Rosoy-sur-Amance 52 92 Fd 62
22300 Rospez 22 63 Wd 56
20242 Rospigliani CTC 183 Kb 95
29140 Rosporden 29 78 Wa 61
22570 Rosquelfen 22 63 Wf 59
20167 Rossa = Piscia CTC 182 Ie 96
26310 Rossas 26 143 Fd 82
72470 Rossay 72 68 Ac 61
86200 Rossay 86 99 Aa 67
20227 Rosse CTC 183 Kb 96
57780 Rosselange 57 56 Ga 53
67230 Rossfeld 67 60 Hd 58
24320 Rossignol 24 124 Ac 76
24380 Rossignol 24 136 Ae 78
01510 Rossillon 01 131 Fd 74
10220 Rosson 10 73 Eb 59
20144 Rossu CTC 185 Kb 98
74350 Rossy 74 120 Ga 72
46150 Rostassac 46 137 Bb 81
29560 Rostegoff 29 62 Vd 59
67290 Rosteig 67 58 Hc 55
29160 Rostellec 29 61 Vc 59
27300 Rostes 27 49 Ae 54
29470 Rostiviec 29 62 Ve 58
22110 Rostrenen 22 63 We 59
44420 Rostu, le 44 81 Xd 64
73210 Rosuel 73 133 Ge 75
59230 Rosult 59 30 Dc 46
25380 Rosureux 25 108 Ge 65
39190 Rotalier 39 106 Fc 69
60360 Rotangy 60 38 Ca 51
57910 Roth 57 57 Ha 54
67570 Rothau 67 77 Hb 58
67340 Rothbach 67 58 Hd 55
35400 Rothéneuf 35 65 Ya 56
73110 Rotherens 73 132 Ga 76
10500 Rothière, la 10 74 Ed 58
60690 Rothois 60 38 Bf 51
39270 Rothonay 39 119 Fd 69
60130 Rotibéquet 60 39 Cc 52
91870 Rotoir, le 91 70 Ca 58
61210 Rotours, les 61 48 Ze 56
14980 Rots 14 35 Zd 53
67160 Rott 67 58 Hf 54
20270 Rottani CTC 183 Kc 96
67170 Rottelsheim 67 58 He 56
26470 Rottier 26 143 Fc 82
49630 Rouages, les 49 84 Zd 64
04240 Rouaine 04 158 Gd 85
04240 Rouainette 04 158 Gd 85
81240 Rouairoux 81 166 Cd 88
44640 Rouans 44 96 Ya 65
22230 Rouarie, la 22 64 Xd 59
53390 Rouaudière, la 53 82 Ye 62
88210 Rouaux, le 88 77 Ha 58
59100 Roubaix 59 30 Db 44
47260 Roubertou 47 148 Ad 82
11200 Roubia 11 166 Ce 89
83510 Roubine 83 172 Gc 88
06420 Roubion 06 158 Ha 84
14260 Roucamps 14 47 Zc 55
17800 Rouchave 17 123 Zd 75
04250 Rouchaye, la 04 157 Gb 83
15230 Rouches 15 139 Ce 79
41300 Rouches, les 41 87 Ca 63
85270 Rouches, les 85 96 Ya 68
87130 Rouchoux 87 126 Bd 75
37130 Rouchouze, la 37 85 Ac 64
15190 Roucoule 15 127 Ce 76
59169 Roucourt 59 30 Da 47
12780 Roucous, le 12 152 Cf 83
02160 Roucy 02 41 De 52
23380 Roudeau 23 114 Bf 71
15150 Roudettes 15 138 Ca 79
31330 Roudiè 31 164 Bb 86
87620 Roudie, la 87 125 Ba 74
33340 Roudillac 33 122 Yf 77
89520 Roudons, les 89 89 Db 63
56110 Roudouallec 56 79 Wb 60
22820 Roudour, le 22 63 We 55
29260 Roudouhil 29 62 Vd 57
52320 Rouécourt 52 75 Fa 59
31160 Rouède 31 176 Af 90
61700 Rouellé 61 67 Zb 57
14260 Rouelle, la 14 47 Zc 54
52160 Rouelles 52 92 Fa 62
76130 Rouen 76 37 Ba 52
12140 Rouens 12 139 Cd 80
36300 Rouère, la 36 100 Bb 69
72610 Rouessé-Fontaine 72 68 Aa 59
72140 Rouessé-Vassé 72 67 Ze 60
12800 Rouet 12 151 Cc 84
34380 Rouet 34 153 De 86
13620 Rouet-Plage, le 13 170 Fb 88
11120 Roueyre, la 11 167 Cf 88
72140 Rouez 72 67 Zf 60
68250 Rouffach 68 60 Hb 61
39350 Rouffange 39 107 Fe 65
87380 Rouffardie 87 125 Bc 75
15130 Rouffiac 15 139 Cd 79
15150 Rouffiac 15 138 Ca 78
16210 Rouffiac 16 123 Aa 75
16210 Rouffiac 16 123 Aa 77
17800 Rouffiac 17 123 Zd 74
46140 Rouffiac 46 149 Bb 82
81150 Rouffiac 81 151 Ca 85
11250 Rouffiac-d'Aude 11 166 Cb 90
11350 Rouffiac-des-Corbières 11 179 Cd 91
31180 Rouffiac-Tolosan 31 165 Bd 87
19250 Rouffiat 19 126 Ca 75
19800 Rouffiat 19 126 Bf 76
17130 Rouffignac 17 123 Zd 76
24240 Rouffignac-de-Sigoulès 24 136 Ac 80
24580 Rouffignac-Saint-Cernin-de-Reilhac 24 137 Af 78
50800 Rouffigny, Villedieu-les-Poêles- 50 46 Ye 56
46300 Rouffilhac 46 137 Bc 80
24370 Rouffillac 24 137 Bb 79
19160 Roufflanges 19 126 Cb 77
51130 Rouffy 51 53 Ea 55
61210 Roufigny 61 48 Ze 56
09420 Rougé 09 177 Bc 91
31870 Rouge 31 164 Bb 88
44660 Rougé 44 82 Yd 62
61260 Rouge, la 61 69 Ae 59
59190 Rouge-Croix 59 30 Cd 44
62840 Rouge-Croix 62 29 Ce 45
62390 Rougefay 62 29 Cb 47
90200 Rougegoutte 90 94 Gf 62
76220 Rouge-Mare 76 38 Bd 52
45300 Rougemont 45 71 Cb 60
01110 Rougemont 01 119 Fd 72
21500 Rougemont 21 90 Eb 62
25680 Rougemont 25 93 Gc 64
27350 Rougemontiers 27 36 Ae 52
90110 Rougemont-le-Château 90 94 Gf 62
25640 Rougemontot 25 93 Gb 64
41230 Rougeou 41 86 Bd 64
27110 Rouge-Perriers 27 49 Af 54
24390 Rougerie, la 24 125 Ba 77
24800 Rougerie, la 24 125 Af 76
02140 Rougeries 02 40 De 50
13500 Rouges, les 13 170 Fa 88
88600 Rouges-Eaux, les 88 77 Ge 59
48500 Rougesparets 48 153 Db 82
15290 Rouget-Pers, le 15 139 Cb 79
52500 Rougeux 52 92 Fd 62
83170 Rougier 83 171 Ff 88
04140 Rougiers, les 04 157 Gb 82
88100 Rougiville 88 77 Gf 59
16320 Rougnac 16 124 Ac 75
23700 Rougnat 23 115 Cd 72
25440 Rouhe 25 107 Ff 66
16330 Rouhénac 16 124 Aa 74
57520 Rouhling 57 57 Ha 54
63970 Rouilhas-Haut 63 128 Da 74
16170 Rouillac 16 123 Zf 74
22250 Rouillac 22 64 Xd 59
63970 Rouillas-Bas 63 128 Da 74
86480 Rouillé 86 111 Aa 70
36110 Rouillecoustant 36 101 Bd 66
10800 Rouillerot 10 73 Ea 59
88140 Rouillie, la 88 76 Fe 60
41160 Rouillis, le 41 86 Ba 61
72270 Rouillis, les 72 84 Zf 62
59158 Rouillon 59 30 Dd 45
72700 Rouillon 72 68 Aa 60
37500 Rouilly 37 99 Ab 66
77160 Rouilly 77 72 Db 57
08230 Rouilly, le 08 41 Ec 49
10220 Rouilly-Sacey 10 74 Eb 58
10800 Rouilly-Saint-Loup 10 73 Ea 59
04420 Rouine, la 04 157 Gc 84
34320 Roujan 34 167 Db 87
12720 Roujarie, la 12 153 Db 83
12230 Roujerie, la 12 153 Dc 85
35390 Roulais, la 35 82 Yb 62
31530 Roulan 31 164 Ba 86
25640 Roulans 25 93 Gb 65
18220 Roulier, le 18 102 Cd 65
88220 Roulier, le 88 77 Gc 60
88460 Roulier, le 88 77 Gd 59
72600 Roullée 72 68 Ab 58
11290 Roullens 11 166 Cb 90
03380 Roullet, le 03 115 Cc 71
16440 Roullet-Saint-Estèphe 16 123 Aa 75
14500 Roullours 14 47 Za 56
87920 Roulouzat 87 125 Bb 74
47800 Roumagne 47 136 Ac 81
81150 Roumanou 81 151 Bf 85
76480 Roumare 76 37 Af 51
49400 Rou-Marson 49 99 Zf 65
16270 Roumazières-Loubert 16 124 Ad 73
33125 Rouméguos 33 134 Zc 81
15290 Roumégoux 15 139 Cb 79
81120 Roumégoux 81 151 Cb 86
81350 Roumegoux 81 151 Cc 84
09500 Roumengoux 09 165 Bf 90
31540 Roumens 31 165 Bf 88
07240 Roumezoux 07 142 Ed 79
19200 Roumignac 19 126 Cb 75
04500 Roumoules 04 157 Ga 86
67480 Rountzenheim 67 59 Ia 56
57220 Roupeldange 57 57 Gc 53
61320 Rouperroux 61 67 Zf 57
72110 Rouperroux-le-Coquet 72 68 Ac 59
29250 Roupiouenan 29 62 Vf 57
15230 Roupons 15 139 Ce 79
02590 Roupy 02 40 Db 50
33125 Rouquet 33 134 Zb 81
24500 Rouquette 24 136 Ac 80
12200 Rouquette, la 12 151 Bf 83
33220 Rouquette, la 33 136 Ab 79
34700 Rouquette, la 34 167 Dc 86
33550 Rouquey 33 135 Zd 80
82370 Rouqueyral 82 150 Bd 85
46120 Rouqueyroux 46 138 Ca 80
81260 Rouquié 81 166 Cd 87
06420 Roure 06 158 Ha 84
63230 Roure 63 127 Ce 74
43260 Roure, le 43 141 Df 78
06260 Rourebel 06 158 Gf 85
79130 Rourie, la 79 98 Zc 69
06650 Rourpet 06 173 Ha 86
59131 Rousies 59 31 Ea 47
86310 Roussac 86 100 Af 69
87140 Roussac 87 113 Bb 72
22100 Roussais, la 22 65 Xf 58
85600 Roussais, les 85 97 Yd 66
48210 Roussao 48 153 Dc 82
13390 Roussargue 13 171 Fd 89
26230 Roussas 26 155 Ee 82
49450 Roussay 49 97 Yf 66
63220 Roussay 63 129 De 76
81140 Roussayrolles 81 150 Be 84
12780 Rousseaup 12 152 Cf 83
18110 Rousseaux 18 102 Cc 65
33860 Rousseaux, les 33 122 Zc 77
82400 Roussel 82 149 Ba 84
24540 Roussel, le 24 137 Af 81
17700 Rousselière, la 17 110 Zb 72
60660 Rousseloy 60 51 Cc 53
89500 Roussemeau 89 72 Db 60
12220 Roussenac 12 151 Cb 82
62870 Roussent 62 28 Be 46
49370 Rousserie, la 49 83 Za 63
48400 Rousses 48 153 Dd 83
05160 Rousses, les 05 145 Gc 81
39220 Rousses, les 39 120 Ga 70
05110 Rousset 05 157 Ff 82
05190 Rousset 05 144 Gb 82
12260 Rousset 12 138 Ca 82
13790 Rousset 13 171 Fd 88
26420 Rousset 26 143 Fc 79
27570 Rousset, le 27 49 Ba 56
26770 Rousset-les-Vignes 26 155 Fa 82
71220 Rousset-Marizy, le 71 117 Ec 69
38420 Roussets, les 38 132 Ff 77
76440 Rousseville 76 38 Bd 51
27270 Roussière 27 49 Ad 55
85670 Roussière 85 96 Yb 68
85280 Roussière, la 85 97 Yd 68
79250 Roussières, les 79 98 Zc 67
26510 Roussieux 26 156 Fc 82
91470 Roussigny 91 51 Ca 57
16360 Roussillères, les 16 123 Ze 76
38150 Roussillon 38 130 Ee 76
84220 Roussillon 84 156 Fb 85
71550 Roussillon-en-Morvan 71 105 Ea 66
15230 Roussinches, les 15 139 Ce 78
16310 Roussines 16 124 Ad 74
36170 Roussines 36 113 Bc 70
89500 Rousson 89 72 Db 60
15130 Roussy 15 139 Cd 80
57330 Roussy-le-Bourg 57 44 Gb 52
57330 Roussy-le-Village 57 44 Gb 52
26470 Roustans, les 26 143 Fc 81
04140 Route, la 04 157 Gc 83
72610 Route, la 72 68 Aa 59
77220 Route, la 77 52 Ce 56
25410 Routelle, Osselle- 25 107 Ff 65
76560 Routes 76 36 Ae 50
11240 Routier 11 165 Ca 90
60850 Routis, les 60 38 Be 52
27350 Routot 27 36 Ae 52
53370 Rouvadin 53 67 Ze 58
12150 Rouvayre, la 12 152 Da 83
43170 Rouve, le 43 140 Dc 79
24350 Rouveille 24 124 Ac 77
24270 Rouveire 24 125 Bb 76
11260 Rouvenac 11 178 Ca 91
22150 Rouvenaie, la 22 64 Xa 59
87500 Rouverat 87 125 Bb 75
24390 Rouverel 24 125 Bb 77
12130 Rouveret 12 140 Da 82
54610 Rouves 54 56 Gb 55
19310 Rouvet, le 19 137 Bb 77
63980 Rouvet, le 63 128 Dd 75
48200 Rouveyret 48 140 Db 79
30190 Rouvière 30 154 Eb 85
30170 Rouvière, la 30 154 De 84
48000 Rouvière, la 48 141 Dd 81
48230 Rouvière, la 48 153 Dc 82
48800 Rouvière, la 48 141 Df 82
83560 Rouvières, les 83 171 Ff 86
34260 Rouvignac 34 152 Da 86
34460 Rouvigno 34 167 Da 87
60800 Rouville 60 52 Cf 53
76210 Rouville 76 36 Ac 51
60190 Rouvillers 60 39 Cd 52
21340 Rouvray 21 105 Ed 66
21530 Rouvray 21 90 Ea 64
27120 Rouvray 27 50 Bc 54
89230 Rouvray 89 89 De 61
28170 Rouvray, le 28 69 Bb 57
76440 Rouvray-Catillon 76 37 Bc 51
28310 Rouvray-Saint-Denis 28 70 Bf 59
45310 Rouvray-Sainte-Croix 45 70 Be 60
28150 Rouvray-Saint-Florentin 28 70 Bd 59
37310 Rouvre 37 100 Af 65
79220 Rouvre 79 111 Zd 70

A B C D E F G H I J K L M N O P Q R S T U V W X Y Z

Rouvre | 309

S

16120 Saint Amant-de-Graves 16 123 Zf 75
16190 Saint-Amant-de-Montmoreau 16 124 Aa 76
16170 Saint-Amant-de-Nouère 16 123 Aa 74
63890 Saint-Amant-Roche-Savine 63 128 Dd 75
63450 Saint-Amant-Tallende 63 128 Da 74
68550 Saint-Amarin 68 94 Ha 61
71240 Saint-Ambreuil 71 106 Ef 68
29690 Saint-Ambroise 29 63 Wb 58
18290 Saint-Ambroix 18 102 Ca 67
30500 Saint-Ambroix 30 154 Eb 83
88120 Saint-Amé 88 77 Gd 60
56890 Saint-Amon 56 80 Xb 62
39160 Saint-Amour 39 119 Fc 70
63610 Saint-Anastaise 63 128 Cf 76
81500 Saint-Anathole 81 150 Be 86
58150 Saint-Andelain 58 88 Cf 65
26150 Saint-Andéol 26 143 Fb 80
26240 Saint-Andéol 26 130 Ef 78
38650 Saint-Andéol 38 143 Fd 79
07170 Saint-Andéol-de-Berg 07 142 Ed 81
48160 Saint-Andéol-de-Clerguemort 48 154 Df 83
48160 Saint-Andéol-de-Clerguemort 48 154 Df 83
07160 Saint-Andéol-de-Fourchades 07 142 Eb 79
07600 Saint-Andéol-de-Vals 07 142 Ec 80
21530 Saint-Andeux 21 90 Ea 64
13670 Saint-Andiol 13 155 Ef 85
70600 Saint-Andoche 70 92 Fe 63
11300 Saint-André 11 178 Ca 91
14250 Saint-André 14 34 Zb 53
16100 Saint-André 16 123 Zd 74
31420 Saint-André 31 163 Af 89
32200 Saint-André 32 163 Af 87
32330 Saint-André 32 148 Ab 85
38530 Saint-André 38 132 Ff 76
47270 Saint-André 47 149 Ae 83
59520 Saint-André 59 30 Da 44
66690 Saint-André 66 179 Cf 93
73500 Saint-André 73 133 Gd 77
81220 Saint-André 81 165 Bf 87
81250 Saint-André 81 151 Cc 85
24200 Saint-André-d'Allas 24 137 Ba 79
42370 Saint-André-d'Apchon 42 117 Df 72
01380 Saint-André-de-Bâgé 01 118 Ef 71
74420 Saint-André-de-Boëge 74 120 Gc 71
50500 Saint-André-de-Bohon 50 34 Ye 53
61220 Saint-André-de-Briouze 61 47 Ze 56
34190 Saint-André-de-Buèges 34 153 Dd 85
43130 Saint-André-de-Chalençon 43 129 Df 77
01390 Saint-André-de-Corcy 01 118 Ef 73
07460 Saint-André-de-Cruzières 07 154 Eb 83
33240 Saint-André-de-Cubzac 33 135 Zd 79
24190 Saint-André-de-Double 24 136 Ab 78
49450 Saint-André-de-la-Marche 49 97 Za 66
48240 Saint-André-de-Lancize 48 154 De 83
27220 Saint-André-de-l'Eure 27 50 Bb 55
17260 Saint-André-de-Lidon 17 122 Zb 75
30570 Saint-André-de-Majencoules 30 153 Dd 84
05200 Saint-André-d'Embrun 05 145 Gd 81
61440 Saint-André-de-Messei 61 47 Zc 56
12270 Saint-André-de-Najac 12 151 Ca 83
11200 Saint-André-de-Roquelongue 11 166 Cf 90
30630 Saint-André-de-Roquepertuis 30 154 Ec 83
05150 Saint-André-de-Rosans 05 156 Fd 82
34725 Saint-André-de-Sangonis 34 167 Dd 87
22630 Saint-André-des-Eaux 22 65 Xf 58
44117 Saint-André-des-Eaux 44 81 Xe 65
40390 Saint-André-de-Seignanx 40 160 Yd 87
30940 Saint-André-de-Valborgne 30 153 De 84
12720 Saint-André-de-Vézines 12 153 Db 84
14130 Saint-André-d'Hébertot 14 36 Ab 53
01290 Saint-André-d' Huiriat 01 118 Ef 71
30330 Saint-André-d'Olérargues 30 154 Ec 84
33490 Saint-André-du-Bois 33 135 Ze 81
55220 Saint-André-en-Barrois 55 55 Fb 54
71440 Saint-André-en-Bresse 71 106 Fa 69
58140 Saint-André-en-Morvan 58 90 Df 64
38680 Saint-André-en-Royans 38 143 Fc 78
89420 Saint-André-en-Terre-Plaine 89 90 Ea 64
07690 Saint-André-en-Vivarais 07 142 Ec 78
60480 Saint-André-Farivillers 60 38 Cb 51
85250 Saint-André-Goule-d'Oie 85 97 Ye 67
07230 Saint-André-Lachamp 07 141 Eb 81
69440 Saint-André-la-Crôte 69M 130 Ed 75
01240 Saint-André-le-Bouchoux 01 118 Fa 72
69700 Saint-André-le-Château 69M 130 Ee 75
63310 Saint-André-le-Coq 63 116 Db 73
71220 Saint-André-le-Désert 71 117 Ed 70
38490 Saint-André-le-Gaz 38 131 Fd 75
42210 Saint-André-le-Puy 42 129 Eb 75
04170 Saint-André-les-Alpes 04 157 Gd 85
10120 Saint-André-les-Vergers 10 73 Ea 59
76690 Saint-André-sur-Cailly 76 37 Bb 51
14320 Saint-André-sur-Orne 14 35 Zd 54
79380 Saint-André-sur-Sèvre 79 98 Zb 68
01960 Saint-André-sur-Vieux-Jonc 01 118 Fa 72
85260 Saint-André-Treize-Voies 85 97 Yd 67
76930 Saint-Andrieux 76 36 Aa 51
33390 Saint-Androny 33 122 Zb 77
16230 Saint-Angeau 16 124 Ab 73
03170 Saint-Angel 03 115 Ce 70
19200 Saint-Angel 19 126 Cb 75
24300 Saint-Angel 24 124 Ae 76
63410 Saint-Angel 63 115 Cf 73
77710 Saint-Ange-le-Vieil 77 72 Cf 59
63660 Saint-Anthème 63 129 Df 75
21540 Saint-Anthot 21 91 Ed 65
04530 Saint-Antoine 04 145 Ge 81
05340 Saint-Antoine 05 145 Gc 79
06670 Saint Antoine 06 159 Hb 86
15220 Saint-Antoine 15 139 Cc 80
17240 Saint-Antoine 17 122 Zc 76
18350 Saint-Antoine 18 103 Ce 67
19270 Saint-Antoine 19 125 Bd 77
20167 Saint Antoine CTC 182 If 96
20240 Saint Antoine CTC 183 Kc 96
22610 Saint-Antoine 22 63 Wf 55
25370 Saint-Antoine 25 108 Gc 68
32340 Saint-Antoine 32 149 Af 84
33240 Saint-Antoine 33 135 Zd 78
24410 Saint-Antoine-Cumond 24 124 Ab 77
24330 Saint-Antoine-d'Auberoche 24 137 Af 78
24230 Saint-Antoine-de-Breuilh 24 136 Aa 79
47340 Saint-Antoine-de-Ficalba 47 149 Ae 82
81100 Saint-Antoine-de-la-Verdarié 81 166 Cb 87
33790 Saint-Antoine-du-Queyret 33 135 Aa 80
37360 Saint-Antoine-du-Rocher 37 85 Ad 64
38160 Saint-Antoine-l'Abbaye 38 143 Fb 77
76170 Saint-Antoine-la-Forêt 76 36 Ac 51
33660 Saint-Antoine-sur-l'Isle 33 135 Aa 78
13015 Saint Antonie 13 170 Fc 88
22480 Saint-Antoine 22 63 We 58
06260 Saint-Antonin 06 158 Gf 85
32120 Saint-Antonin 32 164 Ae 86
81120 Saint-Antonin-de-Lacalm 81 151 Cb 86
27250 Saint-Antonin-de-Sommaire 27 49 Ae 56
83510 Saint-Antonin-du-Var 83 172 Gb 87
82140 Saint-Antonin-Noble-Val 82 150 Be 84
36100 Saint-Aoustrille 36 102 Bf 67
36120 Saint-Août 36 102 Bf 68
05160 Saint Apollinaire 05 145 Gc 81
21850 Saint-Apollinaire 21 92 Fa 64
69170 Saint-Appolinaire 69D 117 Ec 73
07240 Saint-Appolinaire-de-Rias 07 142 Ed 79
38160 Saint-Appolinard 38 131 Fb 77
42520 Saint Appolinard 42 130 Ed 76
24110 Saint-Aquilin 24 124 Ac 77
61380 Saint-Aquilin-de-Corbion 61 49 Ad 57
27120 Saint-Aquilin-de-Pacy 27 50 Bb 54
31430 Saint-Araille 31 164 Af 88
32170 Saint-Arailles 32 163 Ac 88
32350 Saint-Arailles 32 163 Ac 87
43300 Saint-Arcons-d'Allier 43 140 Dd 78
43420 Saint-Arcons-de-Barges 43 141 Df 79
35230 Saint-Armel 35 65 Yc 60
56310 Saint-Armel 56 79 We 61
56450 Saint-Armel 56 80 Xb 63
64160 Saint-Armou 64 162 Ze 88
66220 Saint-Arnac 66 179 Cd 92
47480 Saint-Arnaud 47 149 Ae 83
14800 Saint-Arnoult 14 48 Aa 52
41800 Saint-Arnoult 41 85 Af 62
60220 Saint-Arnoult 60 38 Be 51
76490 Saint-Arnoult 76 36 Ae 51
28190 Saint-Arnoult-des-Bois 28 69 Bb 58
78730 Saint-Arnoult-en-Yvelines 78 70 Bf 57
32300 Saint-Arroman 32 163 Ad 88
65250 Saint-Arroman 65 175 Ac 90
82210 Saint Arroumex 82 149 Af 85
82220 Saint-Arthémie 82 150 Bb 83
24110 Saint-Astier 24 136 Ad 78
47120 Saint Astier 47 136 Ab 80
04600 Saint-Auban 04 157 Ff 84
06850 Saint-Auban 06 158 Ge 85
05400 Saint-Auban-d'Oze 05 144 Ff 82
26170 Saint-Auban-sur-L'Ouvèze 26 156 Fc 83
59188 Saint-Aubert 59 30 Dc 47
61210 Saint-Aubert-sur-Orne 61 47 Ze 56
02300 Saint-Aubin 02 40 Db 51
10400 Saint-Aubin 10 73 Dd 58
21190 Saint-Aubin 21 105 Ee 67
22270 Saint-Aubin 22 64 Xd 58
27410 Saint-Aubin 27 49 Ae 55
32460 Saint-Aubin 32 147 Ze 86
36100 Saint-Aubin 36 102 Ca 67
39410 Saint-Aubin 39 106 Fb 66
40250 Saint-Aubin 40 161 Zb 86
47150 Saint-Aubin 47 137 Af 82
49420 Saint-Aubin 49 83 Ye 62
56420 Saint-Aubin 56 80 Xc 61
59440 Saint-Aubin 59 31 Df 47
62170 Saint-Aubin 62 28 Bd 46
76220 Saint-Aubin 76 38 Be 52
86330 Saint-Aubin 86 99 Aa 67
89630 Saint-Aubin 89 90 Ea 64
91190 Saint-Aubin 91 51 Ca 56
62223 Saint-Aubin, Anzin- 62 29 Ce 47
76520 Saint-Aubin-Celloville 76 37 Ba 52
89110 Saint-Aubin-Château-Neuf 89 89 Db 62
61170 Saint-Aubin-d'Appenai 61 68 Ac 57
14970 Saint-Aubin-d'Arquenay 14 47 Ze 53
35250 Saint-Aubin-d'Aubigné = Saint-Albin-Elvinieg 35 65 Yc 59
79700 Saint-Aubin-de-Baubigné 79 98 Zb 67
33820 Saint-Aubin-de-Blaye 33 123 Zc 77
61470 Saint-Aubin-de-Bonneval 61 48 Ac 55
33420 Saint Aubin-de-Branne 33 135 Ze 80
24500 Saint-Aubin-de-Cadelech 24 136 Ac 80
61560 Saint-Aubin-de-Courteraie 61 68 Ac 57
27110 Saint-Aubin-d'Ecrosville 27 49 Af 54
24560 Saint-Aubin-de-Lanquais 24 136 Ad 80
72130 Saint-Aubin-de-Locquenay 72 68 Aa 59
49190 Saint-Aubin-de-Luigné 49 83 Zc 65
33160 Saint-Aubin-de-Médoc 33 134 Zb 79
14380 Saint-Aubin-des-Bois 14 46 Yf 56
28300 Saint-Aubin-des-Bois 28 69 Bc 58
27230 Saint-Aubin-de-Scellon 27 49 Ac 53
44110 Saint-Aubin-des-Châteaux 44 82 Yd 62
58190 Saint-Aubin-des-Chaumes 58 90 De 64
72400 Saint-Aubin-des-Coudrais 72 68 Ad 59
61340 Saint-Aubin-des-Grois 61 69 Ad 58
27410 Saint-Aubin-des-Hayes 27 49 Ae 54
35500 Saint-Aubin-des-Landes 35 66 Ye 60
85130 Saint-Aubin-des-Ormeaux 85 97 Yf 67
50380 Saint-Aubin-des-Préaux 50 46 Yc 56
50240 Saint-Aubin-de-Terregatte 50 66 Ye 57
35140 Saint-Aubin-du-Cormier 35 66 Yd 59
53700 Saint-Aubin-du-Désert 53 67 Ze 59
35410 Saint-Aubin-du-Pavail 35 66 Yd 60
49500 Saint-Aubin-du-Pavoil 49 83 Za 62
50490 Saint-Aubin-du-Perron 50 33 Yd 54
79300 Saint-Aubin-du-Plain 79 98 Zd 67
27270 Saint-Aubin-du-Thenney 27 49 Ac 54
27930 Saint-Aubin-du-Vieil-Evreux 27 49 Bb 54
60650 Saint-Aubin-en-Bray 60 38 Bf 52
71430 Saint-Aubin-en-Charollais 71 117 Eb 70
76160 Saint-Aubin-Epinay 76 37 Bb 52
53120 Saint-Aubin-Fosse-Louvain 53 66 Zb 58
85210 Saint-Aubin-la-Plaine 85 110 Yf 69
76510 Saint-Aubin-le-Cauf 76 37 Bb 49
79450 Saint-Aubin-le-Cloud 79 98 Zd 69
37370 Saint-Aubin-le-Dépeint 37 85 Ac 63
27410 Saint-Aubin-le-Guichard 27 49 Ae 54
03160 Saint-Aubin-le-Monial 03 115 Da 69
76410 Saint-Aubin-lès-Elbeuf 76 49 Ba 53
58130 Saint-Aubin-les-Forges 58 103 Db 66
27300 Saint-Aubin-le-Vertueux 27 49 Ad 54
80540 Saint-Aubin-Montenoy 80 38 Bf 49
80430 Saint-Aubin-Rivière 80 38 Be 49
76430 Saint-Aubin-Routot 76 36 Ab 51
60600 Saint-Aubin-sous-Erquery 60 39 Cc 52
55500 Saint-Aubin-sur-Aire 55 55 Fc 56
27600 Saint-Aubin-sur-Gaillon 27 50 Bb 54
71140 Saint-Aubin-sur-Loire 71 116 De 69
14750 Saint-Aubin-sur-Mer 14 47 Zd 52
76740 Saint-Aubin-sur-Mer 76 37 Af 49
27680 Saint-Aubin-sur-Quillebeuf 27 36 Ad 52
76550 Saint-Aubin-sur-Scie 76 37 Ba 49
89300 Saint-Aubin-sur-Yonne 89 72 Dc 60
17570 Saint-Augustin 17 122 Yf 74
19390 Saint-Augustin 19 126 Bf 76
77515 Saint-Augustin 77 52 Da 56
62120* Saint Augustin 62 29 Cb 45
49170 Saint-Augustin-des-Bois 49 83 Zb 64
19130 Saint-Aulaire 19 125 Bc 77
16300 Saint-Aulais-la-Chapelle 16 123 Zf 76
24230 Saint-Aulaye-de-Breuilh 24 136 Aa 80
24410 Saint Aulaye-Puymangou 24 124 Aa 77
09500 Saint-Aulin 09 165 Bf 90
34130 Saint-Aunès 34 168 Df 87
32160 Saint-Aunix-Lengros 32 162 Aa 87
38960 Saint Aupre 38 131 Fe 76
46170 Saint-Aureil 46 150 Bb 83
43380 Saint-Austremoine 43 140 Dc 78
87310 Saint-Auvent 87 125 Af 74
85540 Saint-Avaugourd-des-Landes 85 109 Yd 69
56890 Saint-Ave = Saint-Trve 56 80 Xb 62
10390 Saint-Aventin 10 73 Eb 59
31110 Saint-Aventin 31 176 Ad 92
37550 Saint-Avertin 37 85 Ae 64
16210 Saint-Avit 16 123 Aa 77
26330 Saint Avit 26 130 Ef 77
40090 Saint-Avit 40 147 Zd 85
41170 Saint-Avit 41 69 Af 60
47150 Saint-Avit 47 137 Af 81
47350 Saint-Avit 47 136 Ab 81
53120 Saint-Avit 53 67 Zb 58
63380 Saint-Avit 63 127 Cd 73
81110 Saint-Avit 81 165 Ca 87
82200 Saint-Avit 82 149 Ba 84
33220 Saint-Avit-de-Soulège 33 136 Aa 80
23200 Saint-Avit-de-Tardes 23 114 Cb 73
24260 Saint-Avit-de-Vialard 24 137 Af 79
32700 Saint-Avit-Frandat 32 149 Ad 85
23480 Saint-Avit-le-Pauvre 23 114 Ca 73
28120 Saint-Avit-les-Guespières 28 69 Bb 59
24540 Saint-Avit-Rivière 24 137 Af 80
33220 Saint-Avit-Saint-Nazaire 33 136 Ab 79
24440 Saint-Avit-Sénieur 24 137 Ae 80
57500 Saint-Avold 57 57 Ge 54
73130 Saint-Avre 73 132 Gb 76
45130 Saint-Ay 45 87 Be 61
59163 Saint-Aybert 59 31 Dd 46
22130 Saint-Ayes 22 64 Xe 57
83370 Saint-Aygulf 83 172 Ge 88
63500 Saint-Babel 63 128 Db 75
73190 Saint Baldoph 73 132 Ff 75
02290 Saint-Bandry 02 40 Db 52
39120 Saint-Baraing 39 106 Fc 67
87330 Saint-Barbant 87 112 Af 71
23260 Saint-Bard 23 115 Cc 73
63380 Saint-Bard 63 115 Cd 73
26260 Saint-Bardoux 26 143 Ef 78
26400 Saint-Bardoux 26 142 Ef 80
06140 Saint-Barnabe 06 173 Gf 86
13012 Saint Barnabe 13 170 Fc 89
22410 Saint-Barnabé 22 64 Xa 57
22600 Saint-Barnabé 22 64 Xb 60
04340 Saint-Barthélemy 04 157 Gc 82
34260 Saint-Barthélémy 34 167 Da 86
35750 Saint-Barthélemy 35 65 Xf 60
38270 Saint-Barthélemy 38 131 Fa 76
38450 Saint-Barthélemy 38 143 Fd 78
40390 Saint-Barthélemy 40 160 Ye 87
45520 Saint-Barthélemy 45 70 Bf 60
50140 Saint-Barthélemy 50 47 Za 56
56150 Saint-Barthélemy 56 79 Wf 61
70270 Saint-Barthélemy 70 94 Gd 62
76930 Saint-Barthélemy 76 36 Aa 51
77320 Saint-Barthélemy 77 52 Dc 56
82440 Saint-Barthélémy 82 150 Bc 84
47350 Saint-Barthélemy-d'Agenais 47 136 Ac 81
24700 Saint-Barthélemy-de-Bellegarde 24 136 Ab 78
24360 Saint Barthélemy-de-Bussière 24 124 Ae 75
26240 Saint-Barthélemy-de-Vals 26 142 Ef 77
07270 Saint-Barthélemy-Grozon 07 142 Ed 79
07160 Saint-Barthélemy-le-Meil 07 142 Ec 79
07300 Saint-Barthélemy-le-Plain 07 142 Ee 78
42110 Saint-Barthélemy-Lestra 42 129 Ec 74
38220 Saint-Barthélmy-de-Séchilienne 38 144 Fe 78
07270 Saint-Basile 07 142 Ed 79
88260 Saint-Baslemont 88 76 Ff 60
18160 Saint-Baudel 18 102 Cb 67
53100 Saint-Baudelle 53 67 Zc 59
58180 Saint-Baudière 58 103 Da 67
81660 Saint-Baudille 81 166 Cc 87
38118 Saint-Baudille-de-la-Tour 38 131 Fc 74
38710 Saint-Baudille-et-Pipet 38 144 Fe 80
37310 Saint-Bauld, Tauxigny- 37 100 Af 65
54470 Saint-Baussant 54 56 Fe 55
09120 Saint-Bauzeil 09 165 Bd 90
30730 Saint-Bauzély 30 154 Eb 85
48000 Saint-Bauzile 48 140 Dc 82
07210 Saint-Bauzille 07 142 Ee 80
34500 Saint-Bauzille 34 167 Db 88
34230 Saint-Bauzille-de-la-Sylve 34 167 Dd 87
34160 Saint-Bauzille-de-Montmel 34 154 Df 86
34190 Saint-Bauzille-de-Putois 34 153 De 85
14140 Saint-Bazile 14 48 Aa 55
87150 Saint-Bazile 87 124 Ae 74
19320 Saint-Bazile-de-la-Roche 19 126 Bf 78
19500 Saint-Bazile-de-Meyssac 19 138 Be 78
31440 Saint-Béat 31 176 Ae 91
12540 Saint-Beaulize 12 152 Da 85
82150 Saint-Beauzeil 82 149 Af 82
12620 Saint-Beauzély 12 152 Cf 84
81140 Saint-Beauzile 81 151 Be 84
43100 Saint-Beauzire 43 128 Db 77
63360 Saint-Beauzire 63 128 Db 73
30350 Saint-Bénézet 30 154 Ea 85
01190 Saint-Bénigne 01 118 Ef 70
59360 Saint-Benin 59 30 Dd 48
58270 Saint-Benin-d'Azy 58 104 Dc 66
58330 Saint-Benin-de-Bois 58 104 Dc 66
28290 Saint-Benoist 28 69 Ba 60
85540 Saint-Benoist-sur-Mer 85 109 Yd 70
10160 Saint-Benoist-sur-Vanne 10 73 De 59
04240 Saint-Benoit 04 158 Ge 85
11230 Saint-Benoît 11 178 Ca 90
47200 Saint Benoit 47 136 Ab 82
50240 Saint-Benoît 50 66 Ye 57
72210 Saint-Benoit 72 84 Aa 61
78610 Saint-Benoît 78 50 Bf 56
81400 Saint-Benoît 81 151 Ca 84
82200 Saint-Benoît 82 149 Ba 84
86280 Saint-Benoît 86 112 Ac 69
01300 Saint-Benoît, Groslée- 01 131 Fd 74
81120 Saint-Benoît-de-Frédefonds 81 151 Ca 85
27450 Saint-Benoît-des-Ombres 27 49 Ad 53
35114 Saint-Benoît-des-Ondes 35 65 Ya 57
14130 Saint-Benoît-d' Hébertot 14 36 Ab 53
36170 Saint-Benoît-du-Sault 36 113 Bc 70
26340 Saint-Benoit-en-Diois 26 143 Fb 81
55210 Saint-Benoît-en-Woëvre 55 56 Fe 55
88700 Saint-Benoît-la-Chipotte 88 77 Ge 58
37500 Saint-Benoît-la-Forêt 37 99 Ab 65
45730 Saint-Benoît-sur-Loire 45 88 Cb 62
10180 Saint-Benoît-sur-Seine 10 73 Ea 58
43300 Saint-Berain 43 141 Dd 78
71300 Saint-Bérain-sous-Sanvignes 71 105 Eb 68
71510 Saint-Bérain-sur-Dheune 71 105 Ed 68
01600 Saint-Bernard 01 118 Ee 73
10310 Saint-Bernard 10 74 Ee 59
21700 Saint-Bernard 21 106 Fa 66
38660 Saint-Bernard 38 132 Ff 77
57220 Saint-Bernard 57 56 Gc 53
68720 Saint-Bernard 68 95 Hb 62
73520 Saint-Béron 73 131 Fe 75
53940 Saint-Berthevin 53 66 Za 60
53220 Saint-Berthevin-la-Tannière 53 66 Za 58
13129 Saint-Bertrand 13 169 Ed 88
31510 Saint-Bertrand-de-Comminges 31 176 Ad 90
72220 Saint-Biez-en-Belin 72 85 Ab 62
22800 Saint-Bihy 22 63 Xa 58
06670 Saint-Blaise 06 159 Hb 86
22120 Saint-Blaise 22 64 Xc 58
22170 Saint-Blaise 22 64 Xa 57
74350 Saint-Blaise 74 120 Ga 72
82230 Saint-Blaise 82 150 Bd 85
88420 Saint-Blaise 88 77 Gf 58
38140 Saint-Blaise-du-Buis 38 131 Fd 76
67420 Saint-Blaise-la-Roche 67 77 Hb 58
32140 Saint-Blancard 32 163 Ad 88
80960 Saint-Blimont 80 28 Bd 48
52700 Saint-Blin-Semilly 52 75 Fc 59
64300 Saint-Boès 64 161 Zb 87
41330 Saint-Bohaire 41 86 Bb 63
71390 Saint-Boil 71 105 Ee 69
54290 Saint-Boingt 54 76 Gc 58
01300 Saint-Bois 01 131 Fd 74
28330 Saint-Bomer 28 69 Ae 59
61700 Saint-Bômer-les-Forges 61 67 Zc 57
51310 Saint-Bon 51 52 Dc 56
16300 Saint-Bonnet 16 123 Zf 76
38090 Saint-Bonnet 38 131 Fa 75
46600 Saint-Bonnet 46 137 Bc 79
19150 Saint-Bonnet-Avalouze 19 126 Bf 77
87260 Saint-Bonnet-Briance 87 125 Bc 74
87300 Saint-Bonnet-de-Bellac 87 112 Af 71
38840 Saint-Bonnet-de-Chavagne 38 143 Fb 78
15190 Saint-Bonnet-de-Condat 15 127 Ce 77
71340 Saint-Bonnet-de-Cray 71 117 Ea 71
03390 Saint-Bonnet-de-Four 03 115 Cf 71
26330 Saint-Bonnet-de-Galaure 26 130 Ef 77
71220 Saint-Bonnet-de-Joux 71 117 Ec 70
48600 Saint-Bonnet-de-Montauroux 48 141 De 80
69720 Saint-Bonnet-de-Mure 69M 130 Ef 74
03800 Saint-Bonnet-de-Rochefort 03 116 Da 72
15140 Saint-Bonnet-de-Salers 15 127 Cc 78
69790 Saint-Bonnet-des-Bruyères 69D 117 Ec 71
42310 Saint-Bonnet-des-Quarts 42 117 Df 72
26350 Saint-Bonnet-de-Valclérieux 26 131 Fa 77
71430 Saint-Bonnet-de-Vieille-Vigne 71 117 Eb 69
30210 Saint-Bonnet-du-Gard 30 155 Ed 85
19380 Saint-Bonnet-Elvert 19 126 Bf 78
71310 Saint-Bonnet-en-Bresse 71 106 Fb 67
05500 Saint-Bonnet-en-Champsaur 05 144 Ga 80
19130 Saint-Bonnet-la-Rivière 19 125 Bc 77
48600 Saint-Bonnet-Laval 48 141 Dd 80
63630 Saint-Bonnet-le-Bourg 63 128 Dd 76
63630 Saint-Bonnet-le-Chastel 63 128 Dd 76
42380 Saint-Bonnet-le-Château 42 129 Ea 76
42940 Saint-Bonnet-le-Courreau 42 129 Df 75
43290 Saint-Bonnet-le-Froid 43 142 Ec 78
19410 Saint-Bonnet-L'Enfantier 19 125 Bd 77
63800 Saint-Bonnet-lès-Allier 63 128 Db 74
42330 Saint-Bonnet-les-Oules 42 129 Eb 75
19430 Saint-Bonnet-les-Tours-de-Merle 19 138 Ca 78
69870 Saint Bonnet-le-Troncy 69D 117 Ec 72
19200 Saint-Bonnet-près-Bort 19 127 Cc 75
63210 Saint-Bonnet-près-Orcival 63 127 Cf 74
63200 Saint-Bonnet-près-Riom 63 116 Da 73
17150 Saint-Bonnet-sur-Gironde 17 122 Zc 76
03330 Saint-Bonnet-Tison 03 116 Da 71
03360 Saint-Bonnet-Tronçais 03 103 Ce 69
58700 Saint-Bonnot 58 103 Db 65
73120 Saint-Bon-Tarentaise 73 133 Gd 76
18300 Saint-Boulze 18 88 Cf 65
71120 Saint-Brancher 71 117 Ec 70
89630 Saint-Brancher 89 90 Df 64
37320 Saint-Branchs 37 100 Ae 65
22800 Saint-Brandan 22 64 Xa 58
30500 Saint-Brès 30 154 Eb 83
32120 Saint-Brès 32 149 Ae 86
34670 Saint-Brès 34 168 Ea 87
30440 Saint-Bresson 30 153 Dd 85
70280 Saint-Bresson 70 93 Gd 61
46120 Saint-Breussou 46 138 Bf 80
44250 Saint-Brevin-les-Pins 44 96 Xf 65
44250 Saint-Brevin-L'Océan 44 96 Xe 65
35800 Saint-Briac-sur-Mer 35 65 Xf 57
16100 Saint-Brice 16 123 Ze 74
33540 Saint-Brice 33 135 Zf 80
50300 Saint-Brice 50 46 Ye 56
53290 Saint-Brice 53 83 Zd 61
61700 Saint-Brice 61 67 Zc 57
77160 Saint-Brice 77 72 Db 57
95350 Saint Brice 95 51 Cc 54
51370 Saint-Brice-Courcelles 51 53 Df 53
50730 Saint-Brice-de-Landelles 50 66 Yf 57
35460 Saint-Brice-en-Coglès 35 66 Yd 58
61150 Saint-Brice-sous-Rânes 61 48 Ze 56
87200 Saint-Brice-sur-Vienne 87 125 Af 73
22000 Saint-Brieg = Saint-Brieuc 22 64 Xb 57
22000 Saint-Brieuc 22 64 Xb 57

Saint-Brieuc | 311

82410 Saint-Étienne-de-Tulmont 82 150 Bc 84
03300 Saint-Étienne-de-Vicq 03 116 Dd 71
47210 Saint-Étienne-de-Villeréal 47 136 Ae 81
81310 Saint-Étienne-de-Vionan 81 150 Be 85
40300 Saint-Étienne-d'Orthe 40 161 Ye 87
01370 Saint-Étienne-du-Bois 01 119 Fb 71
85670 Saint-Étienne-du-Bois 85 97 Yc 68
13103 Saint-Étienne-du-Grès 13 155 Ee 86
76800 Saint-Étienne-du-Rouvray 76 37 Ba 52
48000 Saint-Étienne-du-Valdonnez 48 153 Dd 82
27430 Saint-Étienne-du-Vauvray 27 49 Bb 53
43420 Saint-Étienne-du-Vigan 43 141 Df 80
71370 Saint-Étienne-en-Bresse 71 106 Fa 68
35460 Saint-Étienne-en-Coglès 35 66 Ye 58
05250 Saint-Étienne-en-Dévoluy 05 144 Ff 80
34260 Saint-Étienne-Estréchoux 34 167 Da 87
79360 Saint-Étienne-la-Cigogne 79 110 Zc 72
19160 Saint-Étienne-la-Geneste 19 127 Cc 76
27450 Saint-Étienne-L'Allier 27 49 Ad 53
43260 Saint-Étienne Lardeyrol 43 141 Df 78
14950 Saint-Étienne-la-Thillaye 14 35 Aa 53
69460 Saint-Étienne-la-Varenne 69D 118 Ed 72
05130 Saint-Étienne-le-Laus 05 144 Ga 81
42130 Saint-Étienne-le-Molard 42 129 Ea 74
04230 Saint-Étienne-les-Orgues 04 156 Fe 84
88200 Saint-Étienne-lès-Remiremont 88 77 Gd 60
60350 Saint-Étienne-Roilaye 60 39 Da 52
27920 Saint-Étienne-sous-Bailleul 27 50 Bc 54
10700 Saint-Étienne-sous-Barbuise 10 73 Ea 57
43450 Saint-Étienne-sur-Blesle 43 128 Da 77
01140 Saint-Étienne-sur-Chalaronne 01 118 Ef 72
01190 Saint-Étienne-sur-Reyssouze 01 118 Ef 70
51110 Saint-Étienne-sur-Suippe 51 41 Ea 52
80200 Saint-Étienne-sur-Suippe 80 39 Cf 49
63580 Saint-Étienne-sur-Usson 63 128 Dc 75
48330 Saint-Étienne-Vallée-Française 48 153 Df 83
22480 Sainte-Tréphine 22 63 Wf 59
56300 Sainte-Tréphine 56 79 Xa 60
24160 Sainte-Trie 24 125 Bb 77
20137 SainteTrinité CTC 185 Kb 99
02330 Saint-Eugène 02 53 Dd 54
14130 Saint-Eugène 14 35 Aa 53
17520 Saint-Eugène 17 123 Ze 75
71320 Saint-Eugène 71 105 Eb 68
24640 Saint-Eulalie-d'Ans 24 125 Ba 77
26190 Saint-Eulalie-en-Royans 26 143 Fc 78
52100 Saint-Eulien 52 54 Ef 56
26170 Saint-Euphème-sur-Ouvèze 26 156 Fc 83
51390 Saint-Euphraise-et-Clairizet 51 53 Df 53
21140 Saint-Euphrône 21 91 Ec 64
71210 Saint-Eusèbe 71 105 Ec 68
74150 Saint-Eusèbe 74 120 Ff 73
05500 Saint-Eusèbe-en-Champsaur 05 144 Ga 80
74410 Saint-Eustache 74 132 Ga 74
76210 Saint-Eustache-la-Forêt 76 36 Ac 51
16190 Saint-Eutrope 16 124 Aa 76
22800 Saint-Eutrope 22 64 Xa 58
29640 Saint-Eutrope 29 62 Wb 57
56350 Saint-Eutrope 56 81 Xe 63
47210 Saint-Eutrope-de-Born 47 136 Ae 81
11120 Sainte-Valière 11 166 Cf 89
29170 Saint-Evarzec 29 78 Vf 61
08130 Sainte-Vaubourg 08 42 Ed 52
79100 Sainte-Verge 79 99 Ze 66
89310 Sainte-Vertu 89 90 Df 62
61230 Saint-Evroult-de-Montfort 61 48 Ab 56
61550 Saint-Evroult-Notre-Dame-du-Bois 61 48 Ac 56
12550 Saint-Exupère 12 152 Cd 85
33190 Saint-Exupéry 33 135 Zf 81
19200 Saint-Exupéry-les-Roches 19 127 Cc 75
89170 Saint-Fargeau 89 89 Da 63
77310 Saint-Fargeau-Ponthierry 77 71 Cd 57
03420 Saint-Fargeol 03 115 Cd 72
64110 Saint-Faust 64 162 Zd 89
07410 Saint-Félicien 07 142 Ed 78
66170 Saint-Féliu-d'Amont 66 179 Ce 92
66170 Saint-Féliu-d'Avall 66 179 Ce 92
03260 Saint-Félix 03 116 Dc 71
16480 Saint-Félix 16 123 Aa 76
17330 Saint-Félix 17 110 Zc 72
46100 Saint-Félix 46 138 Ca 81
46800 Saint Félix 46 150 Ba 83
60370 Saint-Félix 60 38 Cb 52
74540 Saint-Félix 74 132 Ff 74
24340 Saint-Félix-de-Bourdoilles 24 124 Ad 76
33540 Saint-Félix-de-Foncaude 33 135 Zf 81
34520 Saint-Félix-de-l'Héras 34 153 Db 85
34725 Saint-Felix-de-Lodez 34 167 Dc 87
12320 Saint-Félix-de-Lunel 12 139 Cd 81
30140 Saint-Félix-de-Pallières 30 154 Df 84
24260 Saint-Félix-de-Reillac-et-Mortemart 24 137 Af 78
09120 Saint-Félix-de-Rieutord 09 177 Be 90
12400 Saint-Félix-de-Sorgues 12 152 Cf 85
09500 Saint-Félix-de-Tournegat 09 165 Be 90
24510 Saint-Félix-de-Villadeix 24 136 Ae 79
31540 Saint-Félix-Lauragais 31 165 Bf 88
08360 Saint-Fergeux 08 41 Eb 51
33580 Saint-Ferme 33 135 Aa 80
31250 Saint-Ferréol 31 165 Ca 88
31350 Saint-Ferréol 31 163 Ae 88
74210 Saint-Ferréol 74 132 Gb 74
43330 Saint-Ferréol-d'Aurore 43 129 Eb 76
63600 Saint-Ferréol-des-Côtes 63 129 De 75
26110 Saint-Ferréol-Trente-Pas 26 156 Fb 82
11500 Saint-Ferriol 11 178 Cb 91
22720 Saint-Fiacre 22 63 Wf 58
56320 Saint-Fiacre 56 79 Wd 60
77470 Saint-Fiacre 77 52 Cf 55
44690 Saint-Fiacre-sur-Maine 44 97 Yd 66
56310 Saint-Ficare 56 79 Wf 61
23000 Saint-Fiel 23 114 Bf 71
05800 Saint-Firmin 05 144 Ga 80
54930 Saint-Firmin 54 76 Ga 58
58270 Saint-Firmin 58 104 Dc 66
71670 Saint-Firmin 71 105 Ec 67
80550 Saint-Firmin 80 28 Bd 47
45220 Saint-Firmin-des-Bois 45 72 Cf 61
41100 Saint-Firmin-des-Prés 41 86 Ba 61
45200 Saint-Firmin-des-Vignes 45 71 Ce 61
45360 Saint-Firmin-sur-Loire 45 88 Ce 63
04850 Saint-Flavi 04 158 Ge 82
10350 Saint-Flavy 10 73 De 58
20217 Saint Florent CTC 181 Kb 92
45600 Saint-Florent 45 88 Cc 62
85310 Saint-Florent-des-Bois 85 97 Ye 69
89600 Saint-Florentin 89 73 De 60
49410 Saint-Florent-le-Vieil 49 83 Yf 64
30960 Saint-Florent-sur-Auzonnet 30 154 Ea 83
18400 Saint-Florent-sur-Cher 18 102 Cb 67
63320 Saint-Floret 63 128 Da 75
62350 Saint-Floris 62 29 Cd 45
15100 Saint-Flour 15 140 Da 78
31470 Saint-Flour 31 164 Bb 87
63520 Saint-Flour 63 128 Dd 74
63840 Saint-Flour 63 129 De 76
48300 Saint-Flour-de-Mercoire 48 141 De 80
37600 Saint-Flovier 37 100 Ba 67
50310 Saint-Floxel 50 34 Yd 52
62370 Saint-Folquin 62 27 Ca 43
69190 Saint-Fons 69M 130 Ef 74
71400 Saint-Forgeot 71 105 Eb 66
69490 Saint-Forgeux 69D 130 Ec 73
42640 Saint-Forgeux-Lespinasse 42 117 Df 72
53200 Saint-Fort 53 83 Zb 62
17240 Saint-Fort-sur-Gironde 17 122 Zb 76
16130 Saint-Fort-sur-le-Né 16 123 Ze 75
07360 Saint-Fortunat-sur-Eyrieux 07 142 Ee 80
16140 Saint-Fraigne 16 111 Zf 73
61350 Saint-Fraimbault 61 67 Zb 58
53300 Saint-Fraimbault-de-Prières 53 67 Zc 58
31230 Saint-Frajou 31 163 Af 88
58330 Saint-Franchy 58 104 Dc 66
83860 Saint François 83 171 Fe 88
73340 Saint-François-de-Sales 73 132 Ga 74
57320 Saint-François-Lacroix 57 56 Gc 52
73130 Saint-François-Longchamp 73 132 Gc 76
29260 Saint-Frégant 29 62 Vd 57
19200 Saint-Fréjoux 19 127 Cc 75
48170 Saint-Frézal-d'Albuges 48 141 De 81
48240 Saint-Frézal-de-Ventalon 48 154 Df 83
11800 Saint-Frichoux 11 166 Cd 89
72150 Saint-Frimbault 72 85 Ad 62
23500 Saint-Frion 23 126 Cb 73
50620 Saint-Fromond 50 46 Yf 53
16460 Saint-Front 16 112 Ab 73
24150 Saint Front 24 136 Ae 80
43550 Saint-Front 43 141 Ea 79
47120 Saint-Front 47 136 Ab 80
24460 Saint-Front-d'Alemps 24 124 Ae 77
24400 Saint-Front-de-Pradoux 24 136 Ac 78
24300 Saint-Front-la-Rivière 24 124 Ae 76
47500 Saint-Front-sur-Lémance 47 137 Af 81
24300 Saint-Front-sur-Nizonne 24 124 Ad 76
17780 Saint-Froult 17 110 Yf 73
85250 Saint-Fulgent 85 97 Ye 67
61130 Saint-Fulgent-des-Ormes 61 68 Ac 59
80680 Saint-Fuscien 80 39 Cb 49
14480 Saint-Gabriel-Brécy 14 47 Zc 53
48700 Saint-Gal 48 140 Dc 80
67440 Saint-Gall 67 58 Hb 56
56610 Saint-Galles 56 80 Xb 63
42330 Saint Galmier 42 129 Eb 75
63440 Saint-Gal-sur-Sioule 63 115 Da 72
70130 Saint-Gand 70 93 Ff 63
68570 Saint-Gangolf 68 77 Hb 61
35550 Saint-Ganton 35 82 Ya 62
14130 Saint-Gatien-des-Bois 14 48 Ab 52
31800 Saint Gaudens 31 163 Ae 90
86400 Saint-Gaudent 86 112 Ab 72
11270 Saint-Gaudéric 11 165 Bf 90
53360 Saint-Gault 53 83 Zb 61
36800 Saint-Gaultier 36 101 Bc 69
33340 Saint-Gaux 33 122 Za 77
81390 Saint-Gauzens 81 165 Bf 86
40190 Saint Gein 40 147 Ze 85
79410 Saint-Gelais 79 111 Zd 70
22570 Saint-Gelven 22 63 Wf 59
30630 Saint Gély 30 154 Ec 83
34980 Saint-Gély-du-Fesc 34 168 De 86
49500 Saint-Gemmes-d'Andigné 49 83 Za 62
79500 Saint-Génard 79 111 Zf 71
87510 Saint-Gence 87 113 Ba 73
79600 Saint-Généroux 79 99 Zf 67
63122 Saint-Genès-Champanelle 63 128 Da 74
63850 Saint-Genès-Champespe 63 127 Ce 76
33390 Saint-Genès-de-Blaye 33 122 Zc 78
33350 Saint-Genès-de-Castillon 33 135 Zf 79
33240 Saint-Genès-de-Fronsac 33 135 Zd 78
33670 Saint-Genès-de-Lombaud 33 135 Zd 80
63260 Saint-Genès-du-Retz 63 116 Db 72
63580 Saint-Genès-la-Tourette 63 128 Dc 75
03310 Saint-Genest 03 115 Cd 71
19500 Saint-Genest 19 138 Be 78
51310 Saint-Genest 51 53 Dc 57
88700 Saint Genest 88 77 Gd 58
86140 Saint-Genest-d'Ambière 86 99 Ac 68
07230 Saint-Genest-de-Beauzon 07 141 Ea 82
81440 Saint-Genest-de-Contest 81 151 Ca 86
42530 Saint-Genest-Lerpt 42 129 Ec 76
42660 Saint-Genest-Malifaux 42 130 Ec 76
87260 Saint-Genest-sur-Roselle 87 125 Bc 74
43350 Saint-Geneys-près-Saint-Paulien 43 129 De 78
02810 Saint-Gengoulph 02 52 Db 54
58370 Saint-Gengoult 58 104 Df 67
71260 Saint-Gengoux-de-Scissé 71 118 Ee 70
71460 Saint-Gengoux-le-National 71 105 Ed 69
07460 Saint-Geniés 07 154 Eb 83
24590 Saint-Geniès 24 137 Bb 79
31180 Saint-Geniès-Bellevue 31 164 Bc 86
30150 Saint-Geniès-de-Comolas 30 155 Ee 84
30190 Saint-Geniès-de-Malgoire 30 154 Eb 85
12190 Saint-Geniès-des-Ers 12 139 Cd 81
34160 Saint-Geniès-des-Mourgues 34 168 Ea 86
34610 Saint-Geniès-de-Varensal 34 167 Da 86
34480 Saint-Geniès-le-Bas 34 167 Db 88
04200 Saint Geniez 04 157 Ga 83
12100 Saint-Geniez-de-Bertrand 12 152 Da 84
12130 Saint-Geniez-d'Olt et d'Aubrac 12 140 Cf 82
05300 Saint-Genis 05 156 Fe 82
05300 Saint Genis 05 156 Fe 82
17240 Saint-Genis-de-Saintonge 17 123 Zc 76
66740 Saint-Génis-des-Fontaines 66 179 Cf 93
16570 Saint-Genis-d'Hiersac 16 123 Aa 74
33760 Saint-Genis-du-Bois 33 135 Ze 80
69610 Saint-Genis-L'Argentière 69M 130 Ec 74
69230 Saint-Genis-Laval 69M 130 Ee 74
69290 Saint-Genis-les-Ollières 69M 130 Ee 74
01630 Saint-Genis-Pouilly 01 120 Ga 71
01380 Saint-Genis-sur-Menthon 01 118 Fa 71
42800 Saint-Genis-Terrenoire 42 130 Ed 75
73240 Saint-Genix-sur-Guiers 73 131 Fd 75
36500 Saint-Genou 36 101 Bc 67
37510 Saint-Genouph 37 85 Ad 64
84210 Saint-Gens 84 156 Fa 85
47250 Saint-Gény 47 148 Aa 82
26250 Saint-Genys 26 142 Ef 80
38620 Saint-Geoire-en-Valdaine 38 131 Fd 76
38590 Saint-Geoirs 38 131 Fc 77
35430 Saint-George 35 65 Ya 57
08240 Saint-Georges 08 55 Ef 52
15140 Saint-Georges 15 139 Cd 78
16700 Saint-Georges 16 112 Ab 73
19510 Saint-Georges 19 125 Bc 76
24220 Saint-Georges 24 137 Af 79
32430 Saint-Georges 32 164 Af 86
33570 Saint-Georges 33 135 Zf 79
35490 Saint-Georges 35 66 Yd 58
47370 Saint Georges 47 149 Af 82
54380 Saint-Georges 54 56 Ga 56
56320 Saint-Georges 56 79 Wc 60
57830 Saint-Georges 57 57 Gf 57
62770 Saint-Georges 62 29 Ca 46
82240 Saint-Georges 82 150 Bd 83
89150 Saint-Georges 89 72 Da 59
25340 Saint-Georges-Armont 25 94 Gd 64
24130 Saint-Georges-Blancaneix 24 136 Ac 79
53100 Saint-Georges-Buttavent 53 67 Zb 59
61600 Saint-Georges-d'Annebecq 61 48 Ze 57
14260 Saint-Georges-d' Aunay 14 47 Zb 54
43230 Saint-Georges-d'Aurac 43 128 Dd 78
42510 Saint-Georges-de-Baroille 42 129 Ea 73
50500 Saint-Georges-de-Bohon 50 33 Ye 53
35140 Saint-Georges-de-Chesné 35 66 Ye 59
38450 Saint-Georges-de-Commiers 38 144 Fe 78
17240 Saint-Georges-de-Cubillac 17 123 Zd 76
17110 Saint-Georges-de-Didonne 17 122 Za 75
35610 Saint-Georges-de-Gréhaigne 35 66 Yc 57
72150 Saint-Georges-de-la-Couée 72 85 Ad 61
50270 Saint-Georges-de-la-Rivière 50 46 Yb 52
48500 Saint-Georges-de-Lévéjac 48 153 Db 83
50370 Saint-Georges-de-Livoye 50 46 Ye 56
50680 Saint-Georges-d'Elle 50 34 Za 54
17470 Saint-Georges-de-Longuepierre 17 111 Zd 72
12100 Saint-Georges-de-Luzençon 12 152 Cf 84
63780 Saint-Georges-de-Mons 63 115 Cf 73
85600 Saint-Georges-de-Montaigu 85 97 Ye 67
24140 Saint-Georges-de-Montclard 24 136 Ad 79
79400 Saint-Georges-de-Noisné 79 111 Ze 70
85150 Saint-Georges-de-Pointindoux 85 97 Yc 69
18200 Saint-Georges-de-Poisieux 18 102 Cc 68
35420 Saint-Georges-de-Reintembault 35 66 Ye 57
69830 Saint-Georges-de-Reneins 69D 118 Ee 72
79210 Saint-Georges-de-Rex 79 110 Zc 71
50720 Saint-Georges-de-Rouelley 50 67 Zb 57
17150 Saint-Georges-des-Agoûts 17 122 Zc 76
17810 Saint-Georges-des-Côteaux 17 122 Zb 74
49120 Saint-Georges-des-Gardes 49 98 Zb 66
61100 Saint-Georges-des-Groseillers 61 47 Zc 56
73220 Saint-Georges-des-Hurtières 73 132 Gb 75
38790 Saint-Georges-d'Espérance 38 131 Fa 75
49350 Saint-Georges-des-Sept-Voies 49 84 Ze 64
17190 Saint-Georges-d'Oléron 17 109 Ye 73
34680 Saint-Georges-d'Orques 34 168 De 87
17700 Saint-Georges-du-Bois 17 110 Zb 72
49250 Saint-Georges-du-Bois 49 84 Ze 64
72700 Saint-Georges-du-Bois 72 68 Aa 61
27560 Saint-Georges-du-Mesnil 27 49 Ad 53
72700 Saint-Georges-du-Plain 72 68 Aa 61
72110 Saint-Georges-du-Rosay 72 68 Ad 59
27450 Saint-Georges-du-Vièvre 27 49 Ad 53
14140 Saint-Georges-en-Auge 14 48 Aa 55
42990 Saint-Georges-en-Couzan 42 129 Df 74
42610 Saint-Georges-Haute-Ville 42 129 Ea 75
43500 Saint-Georges-Lagricol 43 129 Df 77
23250 Saint-Georges-la-Pouge 23 114 Bf 73
53480 Saint-Georges-le-Fléchard 53 67 Zc 60
72130 Saint-Georges-le-Gaultier 72 67 Zf 59
86130 Saint-Georges-les-Baillargeaux 86 99 Ac 68
07800 Saint-Georges-les-Bains 07 142 Ee 79
87160 Saint-Georges-les-Landes 87 113 Bc 70
50000 Saint-Georges-Montcocq 50 34 Yf 54
27710 Saint-Georges-Motel 27 50 Bc 56
23500 Saint-Georges-Nigremont 23 127 Cb 73
63800 Saint-Georges-sur-Allier 63 128 Db 74
36100 Saint-Georges-sur-Arnon 36 102 Ca 67
89000 Saint-Georges-sur-Baulche 89 89 Dd 62
41400 Saint-Georges-sur-Cher 41 86 Ba 65
53600 Saint-Georges-sur-Erve 53 67 Ze 59
28190 Saint-Georges-sur-Eure 28 69 Bc 58
76690 Saint-Georges-sur-Fontaine 76 37 Bb 51
59820 Saint-Georges-sur-L'Aa 59 27 Cb 43
18100 Saint-Georges-sur-la-Prée 18 102 Bf 65
49700 Saint-Georges-sur-Layon 49 98 Zd 65
49170 Saint-Georges-sur-Loire 49 83 Zb 64
18110 Saint-Georges-sur-Moulon 18 102 Cc 65
01400 Saint-Georges-sur-Renon 01 118 Fa 72
40380 Saint-Geours-d'Auribat 40 146 Za 86
40230 Saint-Geours-de-Maremne 40 160 Ye 86
56920 Saint-Gerand 56 64 Xa 60
03340 Saint-Gérand-de-Vaux 03 116 Dc 70
03150 Saint-Gérand-le-Puy 03 116 Dd 71
81310 Saint-Gérard-d'Armissart 81 150 Be 85
47120 Saint-Géraud 47 136 Aa 81
81350 Saint-Géraud 81 151 Cb 84
24700 Saint Géraud-de-Crops 24 136 Ab 79
07170 Saint-Germain 07 142 Ec 81
10120 Saint-Germain 10 73 Ea 59
12100 Saint Germain 12 152 Da 84
22550 Saint-Germain 22 64 Xe 57
26390 Saint-Germain 26 130 Fa 77
27150 Saint-Germain 27 37 Bd 52
29710 Saint-Germain 29 78 Ve 61
37600 Saint-Germain 37 100 Ba 66
49640 Saint-Germain 49 84 Zd 62
54290 Saint Germain 54 76 Gc 58
70200 Saint-Germain 70 94 Gd 62
73700 Saint-Germain 73 133 Ge 75
69650 Saint-Germain-au-Mont-d'Or 69M 130 Ee 73
23160 Saint-Germain-Beaupré 23 113 Bd 71
58300 Saint-Germain-Chassenay 58 104 Dc 68
53240 Saint-Germain-d'Anxure 53 67 Zb 59
72800 Saint-Germain-d'Arcé 72 85 Ab 63
61470 Saint-Germain-d' Aunay 61 48 Ac 55
24170 Saint-Germain-de-Belvès 24 137 Ba 80
18340 Saint-Germain-de-Bois 18 102 Cc 67
48370 Saint-Germain-de-Calberte 48 154 De 83
61370 Saint-Germain-d'Echaffour 61 48 Ac 56
61240 Saint-Germain-de-Clairefeuille 61 48 Ab 56
16500 Saint-Germain-de-Confolens 16 112 Ae 72
53700 Saint-Germain-de-Coulamer 53 67 Ze 59
14240 Saint-Germain-d'Ectot 14 34 Zb 54
27220 Saint-Germain-de-Fresney 27 50 Bb 55
33490 Saint-Germain-de-Grave 33 135 Ze 81
01130 Saint-Germain-de-Joux 01 119 Fe 71
61130 Saint-Germain-de-la-Coudre 61 68 Ad 59
78640 Saint-Germain-de-la-Grange 78 50 Bf 55
33240 Saint-Germain-de-la-Rivière 33 135 Ze 79
53200 Saint-Germain-de-L'Hommel 53 83 Zb 61
14100 Saint-Germain-de-Livet 14 48 Ab 54
50810 Saint-Germain-d'Elle 50 34 Za 54
79200 Saint-Germain-de-Longue-Chaume 79 98 Zd 68
17500 Saint-Germain-de-Lusignan 17 123 Zd 76
17700 Saint-Germain-de-Marencennes 17 110 Zb 72
61560 Saint-Germain-de-Martigny 61 68 Ac 57
21530 Saint-Germain-de-Modéon 21 90 Ea 64
16380 Saint-Germain-de-Montbron 16 124 Ac 75
14140 Saint-Germain-de-Montgommery 14 48 Ab 55
27370 Saint-Germain-de-Pasquier 27 49 Ba 53
85110 Saint-Germain-de-Prinçay 85 97 Yf 68
03140 Saint-Germain-de-Salles 03 116 Db 71
27930 Saint-Germain-des-Angles 27 49 Ba 54
58210 Saint-Germain-des-Bois 58 89 Dd 64
89630 Saint-Germain-des Champs 89 90 Df 64
76750 Saint-Germain-des-Essourts 76 37 Bb 51
03260 Saint-Germain-des-Fossés 03 116 Dc 71
61110 Saint-Germain-des-Grois 61 69 Ae 58
24160 Saint-Germain-des-Prés 24 125 Af 76
45220 Saint-Germain-des-Prés 45 71 Cf 61
49170 Saint-Germain-des-Prés 49 83 Zb 64
81700 Saint-Germain-des-Prés 81 165 Ca 87
71600 Saint-Germain-des-Rives 71 117 Ea 70
33340 Saint-Germain-d'Esteuil 33 122 Za 77
50440 Saint-Germain-des-Vaux 50 33 Ya 50
76590 Saint-Germain-d'Etables 76 37 Bb 49
14500 Saint-Germain-de-Tallevende 14 47 Za 56
50700 Saint-Germain-de-Tournebut 50 33 Yd 51
50480 Saint-Germain-de-Varreville 50 33 Ye 52
17500 Saint-Germain-de-Vibrac 17 123 Ze 76
46310 Saint-Germain-du-Bel-Air 46 137 Bc 81
71330 Saint-Germain-du-Bois 71 106 Fb 68
61000 Saint-Germain-du-Corbéis 61 68 Aa 58
14110 Saint-Germain-du-Crioult 14 47 Zc 55
14230 Saint-Germain-du-Pert 14 46 Yf 52
35370 Saint-Germain-du-Pinel 35 66 Yf 60
71370 Saint-Germain-du-Plain 71 106 Ef 68
33750 Saint-Germain-du-Puch 33 135 Ze 79
18390 Saint-Germain-du-Puy 18 102 Cc 66
24190 Saint-Germain-du-Salembre 24 136 Ac 78
17240 Saint-Germain-du-Seudre 17 122 Zc 75
48340 Saint-Germain-du-Teil 48 140 Db 82
72200 Saint-Germain-du-Val 72 84 Zf 62
71800 Saint-Germain-en-Brionnais 71 117 Eb 70
35133 Saint-Germain-en-Coglès 35 66 Ye 58
78100 Saint-Germain-en-Laye 78 51 Ca 55
39300 Saint-Germain-en-Montagne 39 107 Ff 68
24520 Saint-Germain-et-Mons 24 136 Ad 79
14280 Saint-Germain-la-Blanche-Herbe 14 35 Zd 53

314 | **Saint-Étienne-de-Tulmont**

27230 Saint-Germain-la-Campagne 27 48 Ac 54
73410 Saint-Germain-la-Chambotte 73 132 Ff 74
28300 Saint-Germain-la-Gâtine 28 70 Bc 57
85390 Saint-Germain-L'Aiguiller 85 98 Za 68
42670 Saint-Germain-la-Montagne 42 117 Ec 71
14700 Saint-Germain-Langot 14 47 Ze 55
60650 Saint-Germain-la-Poterie 60 38 Bf 52
43700 Saint-Germain-Laprade 43 141 Df 78
42260 Saint-Germain-Laval 42 129 Ea 74
77130 Saint-Germain-Laval 77 72 Cf 58
51240 Saint-Germain-la-Ville 51 54 Ec 55
19290 Saint-Germain-Lavolps 19 126 Cb 75
77950 Saint-Germain-Laxis 77 71 Ce 57
90110 Saint-Germain-le-Châtelet 90 94 Gf 62
53240 Saint-Germain-le-Fouilloux 53 67 Zb 60
28190 Saint-Germain-le-Gaillard 28 69 Bb 58
50340 Saint-Germain-le-Gaillard 50 33 Yb 52
53240 Saint-Germain-le-Guillaume 53 66 Zb 59
19250 Saint-Germain-le-Lièvre 19 126 Cb 75
63340 Saint-Germain-Lembron 63 128 Db 76
21510 Saint-Germain-le-Rocheux 21 91 Ee 62
39210 Saint-Germain-lès-Arlay 39 107 Fd 68
91180 Saint-Germain-les-Arpajon 91 71 Cb 57
87380 Saint-Germain-les-Belles 87 125 Bc 75
71390 Saint-Germain-lès-Buxy 71 105 Ee 68
91250 Saint-Germain-lès-Corbeil 91 51 Cc 57
01300 Saint-Germain-les-Paroisses 01 131 Fd 74
42640 Saint-Germain-Lespinasse 42 117 Df 72
21500 Saint-Germain-lès-Senailly 21 90 Eb 63
19330 Saint-Germain-les-Vergnes 19 126 Bd 77
14190 Saint-Germain-le-Vasson 14 47 Ze 54
61390 Saint-Germain-le-Vieux 61 68 Ab 57
63630 Saint-Germain-L'Herm 63 128 Dd 76
08190 Saint-Germainmont 08 41 Ea 51
69210 Saint-Germain-Nuelles 69M 130 Ed 73
63470 Saint-Germain-près-Herment 63 127 Cd 74
21690 Saint-Germain-source-Seine 21 91 Ee 64
76690 Saint-Germain-sous-Cailly 76 37 Bb 51
77169 Saint-Germain-sous-Doue 77 52 Da 55
50190 Saint-Germains-sur-Sèves 50 46 Yd 53
27320 Saint-Germain-sur-Avre 27 50 Bb 56
50430 Saint-Germain-sur-Ay 50 46 Yc 53
50430 Saint-Germain-sur-Ay-Plage 50 46 Yc 53
80430 Saint-Germain-sur-Bresle 80 38 Be 50
76270 Saint-Germain-sur-Eaulne 76 37 Bd 50
77930 Saint-Germain-sur-École 77 71 Cd 58
35250 Saint-Germain-sur-Ille 35 65 Yc 59
55140 Saint-Germain-sur-Meuse 55 55 Fe 57
49230 Saint-Germain-sur-Moine 49 97 Yf 66
77860 Saint-Germain-sur-Morin 77 52 Cf 55
01240 Saint-Germain-sur-Renon 01 118 Fa 72
72130 Saint-Germain-sur-Sarthe 72 68 Aa 59
37500 Saint-Germain-sur-Vienne 37 99 Aa 65
27500 Saint-Germain-Village 27 36 Ad 52
32400 Saint-Germé 32 162 Zf 86
60850 Saint-Germer-de-Fly 60 38 Be 52
31290 Saint-Germier 31 165 Be 88
32200 Saint-Germier 32 164 Af 86
79340 Saint-Germier 79 111 Zf 70
81210 Saint-Germier 81 166 Cb 86
81220 Saint-Germier 81 165 Bf 87
43360 Saint-Géron 43 128 Db 76
15150 Saint-Gérons 15 139 Cb 79
16700 Saint-Gervais 16 112 Ac 73
30200 Saint-Gervais 30 155 Ed 83
33240 Saint-Gervais 33 135 Zd 78
38470 Saint-Gervais 38 131 Fc 77
85230 Saint-Gervais 85 96 Xf 67
87600 Saint-Gervais 87 124 Ae 74
95420 Saint-Gervais 95 50 Be 53
63390 Saint-Gervais-d'Auvergne 63 115 Ce 72
61160 Saint-Gervais-des-Sablons 61 48 Aa 55
72120 Saint-Gervais-de-Vic 72 85 Ae 61
61500 Saint-Gervais-du-Perron 61 68 Aa 57
72220 Saint-Gervais-en-Belin 72 85 Ab 61
71350 Saint-Gervais-en-Vallière 71 106 Ef 67
41350 Saint-Gervais-la-Forêt 41 86 Bc 63
74170 Saint-Gervais-les-Bains 74 121 Ge 73
86230 Saint-Gervais-les-Trois-Clochers 86 99 Ac 67
63880 Saint-Gervais-sous-Meymont 63 128 Dd 74
71490 Saint-Gervais-sur-Couches 71 105 Ed 67
34610 Saint-Gervais-sur-Mare 34 167 Da 87
26160 Saint-Gervais-sur-Roubion 26 142 Ef 81
30320 Saint-Gervasy 30 154 Ec 85
63340 Saint-Gervazy 63 128 Db 76
24400 Saint-Géry 24 136 Ab 79
81800 Saint-Géry 81 150 Be 86
46330 Saint-Géry-Vers 46 138 Bd 82
24330 Saint-Geyrac 24 137 Af 78
51510 Saint-Gibrien 51 54 Eb 55
22800 Saint-Gildas 22 64 Wf 58
56730 Saint-Gildas-de-Rhuys 56 80 Xa 63
44530 Saint-Gildas-des-Bois 44 81 Xf 63
17310 Saint-Gilles 17 109 Yd 73
22940 Saint-Gilles 22 64 Xa 58
30800 Saint-Gilles 30 169 Ec 86
35590 Saint-Gilles 35 65 Yb 60
36170 Saint-Gilles 36 113 Bc 70
49520 Saint-Gilles 49 83 Yf 62
50180 Saint-Gilles 50 33 Ye 54
51170 Saint-Gilles 51 53 De 53
56560 Saint-Gilles 56 79 Wc 60
71510 Saint-Gilles 71 105 Ed 67
85800 Saint-Gilles-Croix-de-Vie 85 96 Ya 68
76490 Saint-Gilles-de-Crétot 76 36 Ad 51
76430 Saint-Gilles-de-la-Neuville 76 36 Ac 51
61700 Saint-Gilles-des-Marais 61 67 Zb 57
22330 Saint-Gilles-du-Mené 22 64 Xc 59
22290 Saint-Gilles-les-Bois 22 63 Wf 57
87130 Saint-Gilles-les-Forêts 87 126 Be 75
22480 Saint-Gilles-Pligeaux 22 63 Wf 58
22530 Saint-Gilles-Vieux-Marché 22 63 Xa 59
07580 Saint-Gineis-en-Coiron 07 142 Ed 81
13007 Saint Giniez 13 170 Fc 89
73410 Saint-Girod 73 132 Ff 74
09200 Saint-Girons 09 176 Ba 91
64300 Saint-Girons 64 161 Za 87
33920 Saint-Girons-d'Aiguevives 33 135 Zc 78
40560 Saint-Girons-en-Marensin 40 146 Ye 85
40560 Saint-Girons-Plage 40 146 Yd 85
64390 Saint-Gladie-Arrive-Munein 64 161 Za 88
22510 Saint-Glen 22 64 Xc 58
29520 Saint-Goazes 29 62 Wb 60
02410 Saint-Gobain 02 40 Dc 51
02700 Saint Gobain 02 40 Db 51
02140 Saint-Gobert 02 40 De 50
56120 Saint-Gobrien 56 81 Xc 61
64400 Saint-Goin 64 161 Zb 89
45500 Saint-Gondon 45 88 Cd 62
35630 Saint-Gondran 35 65 Ya 59
22820 Saint-Gonery 22 63 We 56
35750 Saint-Gonlay 35 65 Xf 60
56920 Saint-Gonnery 56 64 Xb 60
40120 Saint-Gor 40 147 Ze 84
56350 Saint-Gorgon 56 81 Xe 63
88700 Saint-Gorgon 88 77 Gd 59
25520 Saint-Gorgon-Main 25 108 Gb 66
22330 Saint-Gouéno 22 64 Xc 59
41310 Saint-Gourgon 41 86 Ba 63
16700 Saint-Gourson 16 112 Ab 73
23430 Saint-Goussaud 23 113 Bd 72
56400 Saint-Goustan 56 80 Xa 63
56580 Saint-Gouvry 56 64 Xb 60
06450 Saint-Grat 06 159 Hc 84
12200 Saint-Grat 12 151 Bf 83
80260 Saint-Gratien 80 39 Cc 49
95210 Saint Gratien 95 51 Cb 55
58340 Saint-Gratien-Savigny 58 104 De 67
56220 Saint-Gravé 56 81 Xe 62
12150 Saint-Grégoire 12 152 Da 83
35760 Saint-Grégoire 35 65 Yb 60
47330 Saint-Grégoire 47 136 Ad 81
81350 Saint-Grégoire 81 151 Cb 85
17240 Saint-Grégoire-d'Ardennes 17 123 Zd 75
27450 Saint-Grégoire-du-Vièvre 27 49 Ad 53
32110 Saint-Griède 32 162 Zf 86
16230 Saint-Groux 16 111 Aa 73
22530 Saint-Guen 22 64 Xa 59
56000 Saint-Guen 56 80 Xb 62
56600 Saint-Guénaël 56 79 Wd 62
56620 Saint-Guénaël 56 79 Wd 61
22660 Saint-Guénole 22 63 Wd 56
29390 Saint-Guénolé 29 78 Wb 61
29760 Saint-Guénolé 29 78 Vd 62
22170 Saint-Guignan 22 64 Wf 57
22150 Saint-Guihen 22 64 Xb 58
34150 Saint-Guilhem-le-Désert 34 167 Dd 86
38650 Saint-Guillaume 38 143 Fd 79
44160 Saint-Guillaume 44 81 Xf 64
35430 Saint-Guinoux 35 65 Ya 57
32450 Saint-Guiraud 32 163 Ae 87
34725 Saint-Guiraud 34 167 Dc 86
56460 Saint-Guyomard 56 81 Xc 62
43340 Saint-Haon 43 141 De 79
42370 Saint-Haon-le-Châtel 42 117 Df 72
42370 Saint-Haon-le-Vieux 42 117 Df 72
42570 Saint Héand 42 129 Ec 75
22100 Saint-Helen 22 65 Ya 58
21690 Saint-Hélier 21 91 Ee 64
76680 Saint-Hellier 76 37 Bb 50
46000 Saint-Henri 46 137 Bc 81
44800 Saint-Herblain 44 97 Yc 65
44150 Saint-Herblon 44 83 Yf 64
29530 Saint-Herbot 29 62 Wb 59
63340 Saint-Hérent 63 128 Da 76
22970 Saint-Hernin 22 63 Wf 57
29270 Saint-Hernin 29 63 Wc 59
22440 Saint-Hervé 22 64 Xb 57
22460 Saint-Hervé 22 64 Xb 59
56110 Saint-Hervé 56 79 Wc 59
56160 Saint-Hervezen 56 79 We 60
03440 Saint-Hilaire 03 115 Da 70
05260 Saint-Hilaire 05 144 Gb 81
11250 Saint-Hilaire 11 166 Cb 90
12290 Saint-Hilaire 12 152 Cd 83
23240 Saint-Hilaire 23 113 Bd 71
25640 Saint-Hilaire 25 93 Gb 64
31410 Saint-Hilaire 31 164 Bb 88
34530 Saint-Hilaire 34 167 Dd 88
43390 Saint-Hilaire 43 128 Dc 76
46230 Saint-Hilaire 46 150 Bd 83
56930 Saint-Hilaire 56 79 Wf 61
63330 Saint-Hilaire 63 115 Cd 72
80620 Saint-Hilaire 80 29 Ca 48
82000 Saint-Hilaire 82 150 Bb 84
91780 Saint-Hilaire 91 70 Ca 58
51400 Saint-Hilaire-au-Temple 51 54 Ec 54
87260 Saint-Hilaire-Bonneval 87 125 Bc 74
62120 Saint-Hilaire-Cottes 62 29 Cc 45
42380 Saint-Hilaire-Cusson-la-Valmitte 42 129 Ea 76
34160 Saint-Hilaire-de-Beauvoir 34 154 Ea 86
38460 Saint-Hilaire-de-Brens 38 131 Fb 74
30560 Saint-Hilaire-de-Brethmas 30 154 Ea 84
61220 Saint-Hilaire-de-Briouze 61 47 Ze 56
44680 Saint-Hilaire-de-Chaléons 44 96 Ya 66
44190 Saint-Hilaire-de-Clisson 44 97 Ye 66
18100 Saint-Hilaire-de-Court 18 102 Ca 65
82390 Saint-Hilaire-de-Durfort 82 149 Ba 83
18320 Saint-Hilaire-de-Gondilly 18 103 Cf 66
38260 Saint-Hilaire-de-la-Côte 38 131 Fb 76
33190 Saint-Hilaire-de-la-Noaille 33 135 Aa 81
48160 Saint-Hilaire-de-Lavit 48 153 Df 83
85600 Saint-Hilaire-de-Loulay 85 97 Ye 66
47450 Saint-Hilaire-de-Lusignan 47 149 Ad 83
49300 Saint-Hilaire-de-Mortagne 49 97 Za 67
85270 Saint-Hilaire-de-Riez 85 96 Ya 68
35140 Saint-Hilaire-des-Landes 35 66 Yd 58
85240 Saint-Hilaire-des-Loges 85 110 Zc 70
24140 Saint-Hilaire-d'Estissac 24 136 Ad 78
17770 Saint-Hilaire-de-Villefranche 17 123 Zc 73
85120 Saint-Hilaire-de-Voust 85 98 Zc 69
30210 Saint-Hilaire-d'Ozilhan 30 155 Ed 85
17500 Saint-Hilaire-du-Bois 17 123 Zd 76
33540 Saint-Hilaire-du-Bois 33 135 Zf 81
49310 Saint-Hilaire-du-Bois 49 98 Zc 66
85410 Saint-Hilaire-du-Bois 85 97 Za 69
50600 Saint-Hilaire-du-Harcouët 50 66 Yf 57
53380 Saint-Hilaire-du-Maine 53 66 Za 59
38840 Saint-Hilaire-du-Rosier 38 143 Fb 78
18160 Saint-Hilaire-en-Lignières 18 102 Cb 68
58120 Saint-Hilaire-en-Morvan 58 104 Df 66
55160 Saint-Hilaire-en-Woëvre 55 55 Fe 54
19550 Saint-Hilaire-Foissac 19 126 Ca 77
58300 Saint-Hilaire-Fontaine 58 104 Dd 68
63440 Saint-Hilaire-la-Croix 63 115 Da 72
85440 Saint-Hilaire-la-Forêt 85 109 Yc 70
61500 Saint-Hilaire-la-Gérard 61 68 Aa 57
41160 Saint-Hilaire-la-Gravelle 41 86 Bb 61
79210 Saint-Hilaire-la-Palud 79 110 Zb 71
23150 Saint-Hilaire-la-Plaine 23 114 Bf 72
87190 Saint-Hilaire-la-Treille 87 113 Bb 71
23250 Saint-Hilaire-le-Château 23 114 Bf 73
61400 Saint-Hilaire-le-Châtel 61 68 Ad 57
51600 Saint-Hilaire-le-Grand 51 54 Ec 53
72160 Saint-Hilaire-le-Lierru 72 68 Ad 60
51490 Saint-Hilaire-le-Petit 51 54 Ec 53
45320 Saint-Hilaire-les-Andrésis 45 72 Da 60
19170 Saint-Hilaire-les-Courbes 19 126 Be 75
63380 Saint-Hilaire-les-Monges 63 127 Cd 74
87800 Saint-Hilaire-les-Places 87 125 Ba 75
85480 Saint-Hilaire-le-Vouhis 85 97 Yf 68
59292 Saint-Hilaire-lez-Cambrai 59 30 Dc 47
19160 Saint-Hilaire-Luc 19 126 Cb 76
50500 Saint-Hilaire-Petitville 50 46 Ye 53
19560 Saint-Hilaire-Peyroux 19 126 Bd 77
49400 Saint-Hilaire-Saint-Florent 49 84 Zf 65
45160 Saint-Hilaire-Saint-Mesmin 45 87 Be 61
42190 Saint-Hilaire-sous-Charlieu 42 117 Eb 72
10100 Saint-Hilaire-sous-Romilly 10 73 Dd 57
36370 Saint-Hilaire-sur-Benaize 36 113 Ba 69
61340 Saint-Hilaire-sur-Erre 61 69 Ae 59
59440 Saint-Hilaire-sur-Helpe 59 31 Df 48
45700 Saint-Hilaire-sur-Puiseaux 45 88 Ce 61
61270 Saint-Hilaire-sur-Risle 61 49 Ac 56
28220 Saint-Hilaire-sur-Yerre 28 69 Bb 60
19400 Saint-Hilaire-Taurieux 19 138 Bf 78
78125 Saint-Hilarion 78 50 Be 57
77160 Saint-Hilliers 77 52 Db 57
12140 Saint-Hippolyte 12 139 Cd 80
13280 Saint-Hippolyte 13 169 Ee 87
15400 Saint-Hippolyte 15 127 Ce 77
17430 Saint-Hippolyte 17 110 Za 73
25190 Saint-Hippolyte 25 94 Ge 65
37600 Saint-Hippolyte 37 100 Ba 66
63140 Saint-Hippolyte 63 115 Da 73
66510 Saint-Hippolyte 66 179 Cf 92
71460 Saint-Hippolyte 71 118 Ed 69
30360 Saint-Hippolyte-de-Caton 30 154 Eb 84
30700 Saint-Hippolyte-de-Montaigue 30 154 Ec 84
30170 Saint-Hippolyte-du-Fort 30 153 Df 85
84330 Saint Hippolyte-le-Gravoron 84 155 Fa 84
38350 Saint-Honoré 38 144 Fe 79
76590 Saint-Honoré 76 37 Ba 50
83250 Saint-Honoré 83 172 Gb 90
58360 Saint-Honoré-les-Bains 58 104 Df 67
43260 Saint-Hostien 43 141 Ea 78
22390 Saint-Houameau 22 63 We 58
56160 Saint-Houarno 56 79 We 60
57640 Saint-Hubert 57 56 Gc 53
72360 Saint-Hubert 72 85 Ac 62
84390 Saint-Hubert 84 156 Fb 84
78690 Saint-Hubert-le-Roi 78 50 Bf 56
82240 Saint-Hugues 82 150 Bd 83
71460 Saint-Huruge 71 105 Ed 69
14130 Saint-Hymer 14 35 Ab 53
39240 Saint Hymetière 39 119 Fd 70
68590 Saint Hyppolyte = Sankt Pilt 68 60 Hc 59
22570 Saint-Igeaux 22 63 Wf 59
12260 Saint-Igest 12 151 Ca 82
31800 Saint-Ignan 31 163 Ae 90
63720 Saint-Ignat 63 116 Db 73
82330 Saint-Igne 82 151 Bf 83
22270 Saint-Igneuc 22 64 Xd 58
18800 Saint-Igny 18 103 Ce 66
71170 Saint-Igny-de-Roche 71 117 Eb 71
69790 Saint-Igny-de-Vers 69D 117 Ec 71
22360 Saint-Illan 22 64 Xb 57
15310 Saint-Illide 15 139 Cb 78
78980 Saint-Illiers-la-Ville 78 50 Bd 55
78980 Saint-Illiers-le-Bois 78 50 Bd 55
51160 Saint-Imoges 51 53 Df 54
60410 Saintines 60 52 Ce 53
62250 Saint-Inglevert 62 26 Be 43
33990 Saint Isidore 33 122 Yf 77
53940 Saint-Isle 53 66 Za 60
38330 Saint-Ismier 38 132 Fe 77
12480 Saint-Izaire 12 152 Ce 85
04330 Saint-Jacques 04 157 Gc 85
22290 Saint-Jacques 22 63 Wf 56
22400 Saint-Jacques 22 64 Xc 57
29380 Saint-Jacques 29 79 Wb 61
76510 Saint-Jacques-d'Aliermont 76 37 Bb 49
63230 Saint-Jacques-d'Ambur 63 115 Ce 73
35136 Saint-Jacques-de-la-Landes 35 65 Yb 60
50390 Saint-Jacques-de-Néhou 50 33 Yc 52
69860 Saint-Jacques-des-Arrêts 69D 118 Ed 71
15800 Saint-Jacques-des-Blats 15 139 Ce 78
41800 Saint-Jacques-des-Guérets 41 85 Ae 62
79100 Saint-Jacques-de-Thouars 79 99 Ze 67
05800 Saint-Jacques-en-Valgodemard 05 144 Ga 80
76160 Saint-Jacques-sur-Darnetal 76 37 Bb 52
22750 Saint-Jacut-de-la-Mer 22 65 Xe 57
22330 Saint-Jacut-du-Mené 22 64 Xd 59
56220 Saint-Jacut-les-Pins 56 81 Xe 62
22380 Saint-Jaguel 22 65 Xe 57
19700 Saint-Jal 19 126 Bd 76
36190 Saint-Jallet 36 113 Bd 70
22100 Saint-James 22 65 Xf 58
50240 Saint-James 50 66 Ye 57
64160 Saint-Jammes 64 162 Ze 88
59270 Saint-Jans-Cappel 59 30 Ce 44
06210 Saint Jean 06 172 Gf 87
06420 Saint Jean 06 159 Hb 85
06550 Saint-Jean 06 173 Gf 87
12170 Saint-Jean 12 151 Cc 84
12400 Saint-Jean 12 152 Ce 85
13150 Saint Jean 13 169 Ee 86
20251 Saint Jean CTC 183 Kb 95
22200 Saint-Jean 22 63 We 57
22340 Saint-Jean 22 63 Wd 59
22860 Saint-Jean 22 63 Wf 56
27260 Saint-Jean 27 48 Ac 53
29390 Saint-Jean 29 78 Wb 60
29390 Saint-Jean 29 79 Wb 60
31240 Saint-Jean 31 164 Bd 87
34290 Saint-Jean 34 167 Db 88
46700 Saint-Jean 46 137 Ba 82
47200 Saint-Jean 47 136 Aa 82
54470 Saint-Jean 54 56 Ff 55
56230 Saint-Jean 56 81 Xd 63
56440 Saint-Jean 56 80 Wf 61
84390 Saint-Jean 84 156 Fc 84
53270 Saint Jean, Blandouet- 53 67 Zd 60
58270 Saint-Jean-aux-Amognes 58 103 Dc 66
08220 Saint-Jean-aux-Bois 08 41 Eb 50
60350 Saint-Jean-aux-Bois 60 52 Cf 52
29860 Saint-Jean-Balanant 29 62 Vd 57
42650 Saint-Jean-Bonnefonds 42 130 Ec 76
56660 Saint-Jean-Brévelay 56 80 Xb 61
06230 Saint-Jean-Cap-Ferrat 06 173 Hb 86
07240 Saint-Jean-Chambre 07 142 Ed 79
76430 Saint-Jean-d'Abbetot 76 36 Ac 51
12250 Saint-Jean-d'Alcapiès 12 152 Cf 85
12250 Saint-Jean-d'Alcas 12 152 Da 85
17400 Saint-Jean-d'Angély 17 110 Zc 73
17620 Saint-Jean-d' Angle 17 122 Za 74
69220 Saint-Jean-d'Ardières 69D 118 Ee 72
73530 Saint-Jean-d'Arves 73 132 Gb 77
73230 Saint-Jean-d'Arvey 73 132 Ff 75
72380 Saint-Jean-d'Assé 72 68 Aa 60
43500 Saint-Jean-d'Aubrigoux 43 129 De 76
74430 Saint-Jean-d'Aulps 74 121 Gd 71
38480 Saint-Jean-d'Avelanne 38 131 Fe 75
11360 Saint-Jean-de-Barrou 11 179 Cf 91
57930 Saint-Jean-de-Bassel 57 57 Gf 56
73440 Saint-Jean-de-Belleville 73 133 Gc 76
85210 Saint-Jean-de-Beugné 85 110 Yf 69
33420 Saint-Jean-de-Blaignac 33 135 Zf 80
44640 Saint-Jean-de-Boiseau 44 96 Yb 65
10320 Saint-Jean-de-Bonneval 10 73 Ea 60
21410 Saint-Jean-de-Bouf 21 105 Ee 65
38440 Saint-Jean-de-Bournay 38 131 Fa 75
45800 Saint-Jean-de-Braye 45 87 Bf 61
34380 Saint-Jean-de-Buèges 34 153 Dd 86
82500 Saint-Jean-de-Cauquessac 82 149 Ba 85
30360 Saint-Jean-de-Ceyrargues 30 154 Eb 84
73170 Saint-Jean-de-Chevelu 73 132 Fe 74
24800 Saint-Jean-de-Côle 24 125 Af 76
82400 Saint Jean-de-Cornac 82 149 Ba 84
34160 Saint-Jean-de-Cornies 34 168 Ea 86
73160 Saint-Jean-de-Couz 73 132 Fe 76
30610 Saint-Jean-de-Crieulon 30 154 Df 85
34270 Saint-Jean-de-Cuculles 34 153 Df 86
50620 Saint-Jean-de-Daye 50 46 Yf 53
47120 Saint-Jean-de-Duras 47 136 Ab 80
76170 Saint-Jean-de-Folleville 76 36 Ad 51
34150 Saint-Jean-de-Fos 34 167 Dd 86
27150 Saint-Jean-de-Frenelles 27 50 Bc 53
01630 Saint-Jean-de-Gonville 01 120 Ff 71
81250 Saint-Jean-de-Jeannes 81 151 Cc 86
34700 Saint-Jean-de-la-Blaquière 34 167 Dc 86
49130 Saint-Jean-de-la-Croix 49 83 Zc 64
61340 Saint-Jean-de-la-Forêt 61 68 Ad 58
50300 Saint-Jean-de-la-Haize 50 46 Yd 56
72510 Saint-Jean-de-la-Motte 72 84 Aa 62
76210 Saint-Jean-de-la-Neuville 76 36 Ac 51
73250 Saint-Jean-de-la-Porte 73 132 Ga 75
50270 Saint-Jean-de-la-Rivière 50 46 Yb 52
45140 Saint-Jean-de-la-Ruelle 45 87 Bf 61
46260 Saint-Jean-de-Laur 46 151 Bf 82
40380 Saint-Jean-de-Lier 40 146 Za 86
49070 Saint-Jean-de-Linières 49 83 Zc 64
17170 Saint-Jean-de-Liversay 17 110 Za 71
14100 Saint-Jean-de-Livet 14 48 Ab 54
50810 Saint-Jean-d'Elle 50 47 Yf 54
12170 Saint-Jean-Delnous 12 152 Cc 84
21170 Saint-Jean-de-Losne 21 106 Fb 66
64500 Saint-Jean-de-Luz 64 160 Yc 88
81350 Saint-Jean-de-Marcel 81 151 Cb 84
40230 Saint-Jean-de-Marsacq 40 160 Ye 87
30430 Saint-Jean-de-Maruéjols-et-Avéjan 30 154 Eb 83
73300 Saint-Jean-de-Maurienne 73 132 Gc 77
82240 Saint-Jean-de-Mazérac 82 150 Bd 83
34360 Saint-Jean-de-Minervois 34 166 Cf 88
38430 Saint-Jean-de-Moirans 38 131 Fd 76
85160 Saint-Jean-de-Monts 85 96 Xf 68
27180 Saint-Jean-de-Morsent 27 49 Ba 54
07300 Saint-Jean-de-Muzols 07 142 Ee 78
43320 Saint-Jean-de-Nay 43 141 De 78
01800 Saint-Jean-de-Niost 01 131 Fb 73
11260 Saint-Jean-de-Paracol 11 178 Ca 91
82220 Saint-Jean-de-Perges 82 150 Bb 83
28170 Saint-Jean-de-Rebervilliers 28 69 Bb 57
81500 Saint-Jean-de-Rives 81 165 Be 86
86330 Saint-Jean-de-Sauves 86 99 Aa 67
50680 Saint-Jean-de-Savigny 50 34 Za 53
50810 Saint-Jean-des-Baisants 50 47 Za 54
61800 Saint-Jean-des-Bois 61 47 Zb 56
50320 Saint-Jean-des-Champs 50 46 Yd 56
72320 Saint-Jean-des-Echelles 72 69 Ae 60
81630 Saint-Jean-de-Senespe 81 150 Bd 85
30350 Saint-Jean-de-Serres 30 154 Ea 85
14350 Saint-Jean-des-Essartiers 14 47 Za 54
74450 Saint-Jean-de-Sixt 74 120 Gc 73
49370 Saint-Jean-des-Marais 49 83 Zb 63
49320 Saint-Jean-des-Mauvrets 49 83 Zd 64
28240 Saint-Jean-des-Murgers 28 69 Af 58
63520 Saint-Jean-des-Ollières 63 128 Dc 75
24140 Saint-Jean-d'Estissac 24 136 Ad 78
69380 Saint-Jean-des-Vignes 69D 130 Ed 73
74250 Saint Jean-de-Tholome 74 120 Gc 72
47270 Saint-Jean-de-Thurac 47 149 Ae 84
01390 Saint-Jean-de-Thurigneux 01 118 Ef 73
69700 Saint-Jean-de-Touslas 69M 130 Ed 75
39160 Saint-Jean-d'Etreux 39 119 Fc 70
71490 Saint-Jean-de-Trézy 71 105 Ed 67
30960 Saint-Jean-de-Valériscle 30 154 Ea 83
81210 Saint-Jean-de-Vals 81 166 Cb 86
51330 Saint-Jean-devant-Possesse 51 54 Ee 55
38220 Saint-Jean-de-Vaulx 38 144 Fe 78
34430 Saint-Jean-de-Védas 34 168 De 87
09000 Saint-Jean-de-Verges 09 177 Bd 90
24140 Saint-Jean-d' Eyraud 24 136 Ac 79
38710 Saint-Jean-d'Herans 38 144 Fe 79
63190 Saint-Jean-d' Heurs 63 128 Dc 74
33127 Saint-Jean-d'Illac 33 134 Zb 80
88210 Saint-Jean-d'Ormont 88 77 Gf 59
72430 Saint-Jean-du-Bois 72 84 Zf 61
82120 Saint-Jean-du-Bouzet 82 149 Af 85
12230 Saint-Jean-du-Bruel 12 153 Dc 84
76150 Saint-Jean-du-Cardonnay 76 37 Ba 51
09800 Saint-Jean-du-Castillonnais 09 176 Af 91
50140 Saint-Jean-du-Corail 50 66 Za 57
50370 Saint-Jean-du-Corail-des-Bois 50 46 Ye 56
04320 Saint-Jean-du-Désert 04 158 Ge 85
29630 Saint-Jean-du-Doigt 29 62 Wb 56
09100 Saint-Jean-du-Falga 09 165 Bd 90
30270 Saint-Jean-du-Gard 30 154 Df 84
88600 Saint-Jean-du-Marché 88 77 Ge 60
30140 Saint-Jean-du-Pin 30 154 Ea 84
27270 Saint-Jean-du-Thenney 27 48 Ac 54

A
B
C
D
E
F
G
H
I
J
K
L
M
N
O
P
Q
R
S
T
U
V
W
X
Y
Z

Saint-Jean-du-Thenney | 315

81600 Saint-Jean-du-Vigan 81 151 Bf 86
26190 Saint-Jean-en-Royans 26 143 Fb 78
63490 Saint-Jean-en-Val 63 128 Dc 75
41160 Saint-Jean-Froidmentel 41 69 Bb 61
22170 Saint-Jean-Kerdaniel 22 64 Wf 57
57370 Saint-Jean-Kourtzerode 57 57 Hb 56
69550 Saint-Jean-la-Bussière 69D 117 Eb 73
43510 Saint-Jean-Lachalm 43 141 De 79
48170 Saint-Jean-la-Fouillouse 48 141 De 80
46400 Saint-Jean-Lagineste 46 138 Bf 80
56350 Saint-Jean-la-Poterie 56 81 Xf 63
06450 Saint-Jean-la-Rivière 06 159 Hb 85
66300 Saint-Jean-Lasseille 66 179 Cf 93
42440 Saint-Jean-la-Vêtre 42 129 De 74
14770 Saint-Jean-le-Blanc 14 47 Zc 55
45650 Saint-Jean-le-Blanc 45 87 Bf 61
07580 Saint-Jean-le-Centenier 07 142 Ed 81
32550 Saint-Jean-le-Comtal 32 163 Ad 87
12410 Saint-Jean-le-Froid 12 152 Ce 84
71000 Saint-Jean-le-Priche 71 118 Ef 70
55400 Saint-Jean-lès-Buzy 55 55 Fe 53
77660 Saint-Jean-les-Deux-Jumeaux 77 52 Cf 55
46400 Saint-Jean-Lespinasse 46 138 Bf 79
50530 Saint-Jean-le-Thomas 50 46 Yc 56
01640 Saint-Jean-le-Vieux 01 119 Fc 72
38420 Saint-Jean-le-Vieux 38 132 Ff 77
64220 Saint-Jean-le-Vieux 64 160 Ye 90
87260 Saint-Jean-Ligoure 87 125 Bb 74
46270 Saint-Jean-Mirabel 46 138 Ca 81
04270 Saint Jeannet 04 157 Ga 85
06640 Saint Jeannet 06 173 Ha 86
64220 Saint-Jean-Pied-de-Port 64 160 Ye 89
28400 Saint-Jean-Pierre-Fixte 28 69 Ae 59
66490 Saint-Jean-Pla-de-Corts 66 179 Ce 93
64330 Saint-Jean-Pougde 64 162 Ze 87
32190 Saint-Jean-Poutge 32 163 Ac 86
57510 Saint-Jean-Rohrbach 57 57 Gf 54
07160 Saint-Jean-Roure 07 142 Ec 79
37600 Saint-Jean-Saint-Germain 37 100 Ba 66
42155 SaintJean-Saint-Maurice-sur-Loire 42 117 Ea 73
05260 Saint-Jean-Saint Nicolas 05 144 Gb 80
67700 Saint-Jean-Saverne 67 58 Hc 56
42560 Saint-Jean-Soleymieux 42 129 Ea 75
35140 Saint-Jean-sur-Couesnon 35 66 Yd 59
53270 Saint-Jean-sur-Erve 53 67 Zd 60
53240 Saint-Jean-sur-Mayenne 53 67 Zb 60
51240 Saint-Jean-sur-Moivre 51 54 Ed 55
01560 Saint-Jean-sur-Reyssouze 01 118 Fa 70
51600 Saint-Jean-sur-Tourbe 51 54 Ee 54
01290 Saint-Jean-sur-Veyle 01 118 Ef 71
35220 Saint-Jean-sur-Vilaine 35 66 Yd 60
29120 Saint-Jean-Trolimon 29 78 Ve 61
18370 Saint-Jeanvrin 18 102 Cb 69
74490 Saint-Jeoire 74 120 Gc 72
73190 Saint-Jeoire-Prieuré 73 132 Ff 75
01640 Saint-Jérôme 01 119 Fc 72
81140 Saint-Jérome 81 150 Be 85
07320 Saint-Jeure-d'Andaure 07 142 Ec 78
07290 Saint-Jeure-d'Ay 07 142 Ee 78
43200 Saint-Jeures 43 141 Eb 78
63160 Saint-Jilien-de-Coppel 63 128 Db 74
44720 Saint-Joachim 44 81 Xe 64
42590 Saint-Jodard 42 129 Ea 73
55130 Saint-Joire 55 75 Fc 57
50250 Saint-Jores 50 46 Yd 53
74410 Saint-Jorioz 74 132 Ga 74
31790 Saint-Jory 31 164 Bc 86
24800 Saint-Jory-de-Chalais 24 125 Af 76
24160 Saint-Jory-las-Bloux 24 125 Af 76
13015 Saint-Joseph 13 170 Fc 88
22330 Saint-Joseph 22 64 Xd 59
29710 Saint-Joseph 29 78 Ve 61
44300 Saint-Joseph 44 82 Yc 65
50700 Saint-Joseph 50 33 Yc 51
86390 Saint-Joseph 86 113 Ba 70
38134 Saint-Joseph-de-Rivière 38 131 Fe 76
07530 Saint Joseph-des-Barics 07 142 Ec 80
69910 Saint-Joseph-en-Beaujolais 69D 118 Ed 71
42800 Saint Josepll 42 130 Ed 75
62170 Saint-Josse 62 28 Bd 46
35260 Saint-Jouan 35 65 Ya 56
22350 Saint-Jouan-de-L'Isle 22 65 Xf 59
35430 Saint-Jouan-des-Guérets 35 65 Ya 57
14430 Saint-Jouin 14 35 Zf 53
76280 Saint-Jouin-Bruneval 76 36 Aa 51
61360 Saint-Jouin-de-Blavou 61 68 Ac 58
79600 Saint-Jouin-de-Marnes 79 99 Zf 67
79380 Saint-Jouin-de-Milly 79 98 Zc 68
87510 Saint-Jouvent 87 113 Bb 73
25360 Saint-Juan 25 93 Gc 65
22630 Saint-Judoce 22 65 Ya 58
12460 Saint-Juéry 12 139 Ce 80
12550 Saint-Juéry 12 152 Ce 85
48310 Saint-Juéry 48 140 Da 80
81990 Saint-Juéry 81 151 Cb 85
85210 Saint-Juire-Champgillon 85 97 Yf 69
31540 Saint-Julia 31 165 Bf 88
11500 Saint-Julia-de-Bec 11 178 Cb 91
11200 Saint-Julien 11 167 Cf 90
12170 Saint-Julien 12 151 Cd 84
12290 Saint-Julien 12 152 Ce 83
12340 Saint-Julien 12 139 Cd 81
13012 Saint-Julien 13 170 Fc 89
21490 Saint-Julien 21 92 Fa 64
22210 Saint-Julien 22 64 Xc 59
22940 Saint-Julien 22 64 Xb 58
25210 Saint-Julien 25 108 Ge 65
26530 Saint-Julien 26 131 Fa 77
30340 Saint-Julien 30 154 Ea 83
31220 Saint-Julien 31 164 Ba 89
31550 Saint-Julien 31 164 Bc 89
39320 Saint-Julien 39 119 Fc 70
47700 Saint-Julien 47 148 Ab 83
51460 Saint-Julien 51 54 Ed 55
63320 Saint-Julien 63 128 Da 75
69640 Saint-Julien 69D 118 Ed 72
70120 Saint-Julien 70 92 Fe 62
81350 Saint Julien 81 151 Cb 84
82200 Saint-Julien 82 149 Ba 84
83560 Saint Julien 83 171 Ff 86
88410 Saint-Julien 88 76 Ff 60
19110 Saint-Julien, Sarroux- 19 127 Cc 76
19220 Saint-Julien-aux-Bois 19 138 Ca 78
33250 Saint-Julien-Beychevelle 33 122 Zb 78
07310 Saint-Julien-Boutières 07 142 Ec 79
43260 Saint-Julien-Chapteuil 43 141 Ea 78
43500 Saint-Julien-d'Ance 43 129 Df 77
40240 Saint-Julien-d'Armagnac 40 147 Zf 85
48400 Saint-Julien-d'Arpaon 48 153 De 83
04270 Saint-Julien-d'Asse 04 157 Ga 85
24310 Saint-Julien-de-Bourdeilles 24 124 Ad 76
11270 Saint-Julien-de-Briola 11 165 Bf 90
30500 Saint-Julien-de-Cassagnes 30 154 Eb 83
41400 Saint-Julien-de-Chédon 41 86 Bb 65
71800 Saint-Julien-de-Civry 71 117 Eb 70
44450 Saint-Julien-de-Concelles 44 97 Yd 65
24140 Saint-Julien-de-Crempse 24 136 Ad 79
09500 Saint-Julien-de-Gras-Capou 09 177 Bf 90
71110 Saint-Julien-de-Jonzy 71 117 Ea 71
15590 Saint-Julien-de-Jordanne 15 139 Cd 78
27600 Saint-Julien-de-la-Liegue 27 50 Bb 54
24370 Saint-Julien-de-Lampon 24 137 Bc 79
30440 Saint-Julien-de-la-Nef 30 153 De 85
17400 Saint-Julien-de-l'Escap 17 110 Zd 73
38122 Saint-Julien-de-L'Herms 38 131 Fa 76
14290 Saint-Julien-de-Mailloc 14 48 Ab 54
12320 Saint-Julien-de-Malnon 12 139 Cc 81
34210 Saint-Julien-de-Molières 34 166 Cd 88
30760 Saint-Julien-de-Peyrolas 30 155 Ed 83
12300 Saint-Julien-de-Piganiol 12 139 Cb 81
38134 Saint-Julien-de-Raz 38 131 Fd 76
43300 Saint-Julien-des-Chazes 43 141 Dd 78
53140 Saint-Julien-des-Eglantiers 53 67 Ze 58
85150 Saint-Julien-des-Landes 85 96 Yb 69
48160 Saint-Julien-des-Points 48 154 Df 83
47510 Saint-Julien-de-Terre-Fosse 47 149 Ad 83
15600 Saint-Julien-de-Toursac 15 139 Cb 80
44670 Saint-Julien-de-Vouvantes 44 82 Ye 63
24500 Saint-Julien-d'Eymet 24 136 Ac 80
42260 Saint-Julien-d'Oddes 42 129 Df 73
07190 Saint-Julien-du-Gua 07 142 Ec 80
43200 Saint-Julien-du-Pinet 43 141 Ea 78
81440 Saint-Julien-du-Puy 81 151 Ca 86
89330 Saint-Julien-du-Sault 89 72 Db 60
07200 Saint-Julien-du Serre 07 142 Ec 81
53110 Saint-Julien-du-Terroux 53 67 Zd 58
48190 Saint-Julien-du-Tournel 48 141 De 82
04170 Saint-Julien-du-Verdon 04 158 Gd 85
05140 Saint-Julien-en-Beauchêne 05 144 Fe 81
40170 Saint-Julien-en-Born 40 146 Ye 84
05500 Saint-Julien-en-Champsaur 05 144 Ga 81
74160 Saint-Julien-en-Genevois 74 120 Ga 72
26150 Saint-Julien-en-Quint 26 143 Fb 79
07000 Saint-Julien-en-Saint-Alban 07 142 Ee 80
26420 Saint-Julien-en-Vercors 26 143 Fc 78
81340 Saint-Julien-Gaulène 81 151 Cb 85
07160 Saint-Julien-Labrousse 07 142 Ed 79
63390 Saint-Julien-la-Geneste 63 115 Ce 72
23110 Saint-Julien-la-Genête 23 115 Cc 72
86800 Saint-Julien-L'Ars 86 112 Ad 69
42440 Saint-Julien-la-Vêtre 42 129 De 74
23130 Saint-Julien-le-Châtel 23 114 Cb 72
14140 Saint-Julien-le-Faucon 14 48 Aa 54
72240 Saint-Julien-le-Pauvre 72 68 Zf 60
19430 Saint-Julien-le-Pèlerin 19 138 Ca 78
87460 Saint-Julien-le-Petit 87 126 Be 74
07240 Saint-Julien-le-Roux 07 142 Ee 79
54470 Saint Julien-lès-Gorze 54 56 Ff 54
57000 Saint-Julien-lès-Metz 57 56 Gb 54
25550 Saint-Julien-lès-Montbéliard 25 94 Ge 63
30340 Saint-Julien-les-Rosiers 30 154 Ea 83
10800 Saint-Julien-les-Villas 10 73 Ea 59
19210 Saint-Julien-le-Vendômois 19 125 Bb 76
19500 Saint-Julien-Maumont 19 138 Be 78
43220 Saint-Julien-Molhesabate 43 130 Ec 77
42220 Saint-Julien-Molins-Molette 42 130 Ed 77
73870 Saint-Julien-Mont-Denis 73 132 Gc 77
63820 Saint-Julien-Puy-Lareze 63 127 Ce 75
55200 Saint-Julien-sous-les-Côtes 55 55 Fd 56
69690 Saint-Julien-sur-Bibost 69M 130 Ed 74
14130 Saint-Julien-sur-Calonne 14 48 Ab 53
41320 Saint-Julien-sur-Cher 41 87 Be 65
71210 Saint-Julien-sur-Dheune 71 105 Ed 68
01560 Saint-Julien-sur-Reyssouze 01 118 Fa 70
61170 Saint-Julien-sur-Sarthe 61 68 Ac 58
01540 Saint-Julien-sur Veyle 01 118 Ef 71
07690 Saint-Julien-Vocance 07 142 Ed 77
87200 Saint-Junien 87 112 Af 73
87300 Saint-Junien-les-Combes 87 113 Ba 72
23400 Saint-Junier-la-Bregère 23 126 Be 73
57420 Saint-Jure 57 56 Gb 55
04410 Saint Jurs 04 157 Gb 85
01250 Saint-Just 01 119 Fb 71
07700 Saint-Just 07 155 Ed 83
13014 Saint-Just 13 170 Fc 89
15320 Saint-Just 15 140 Db 79
18340 Saint-Just 18 102 Cd 67
24320 Saint-Just 24 124 Ad 76
27950 Saint-Just 27 50 Bc 54
34400 Saint-Just 34 168 Ea 87
35550 Saint-Just 35 81 Ya 62
63600 Saint-Just 63 129 De 76
38540 Saint-Just-Chaleyssin 38 130 Ef 75
69870 Saint-Just-d'Avray 69D 117 Ec 72
38680 Saint-Just-de-Claix 38 143 Fb 78
42990 Saint-Just-en-Bas 42 129 Df 74
60130 Saint-Just-en-Chaussée 60 39 Cc 51
42430 Saint-Just-en-Chevalet 42 117 Df 73
42740 Saint-Just-en-Doizieux 42 130 Ed 76
11500 Saint-Just-et-le-Bézu 11 178 Cb 91
30580 Saint-Just-et-Vacquières 30 154 Eb 84
64120 Saint-Just-Ibarre 64 161 Yf 89
32230 Saint-Justin 32 162 Aa 88
40240 Saint-Justin 40 147 Ze 85
42540 Saint-Just-la-Pendue 42 117 Eb 73
87590 Saint-Just-le-Martel 87 125 Bc 73
17320 Saint-Just-Luzac 17 122 Yf 74
43240 Saint-Just-Malmont 43 129 Eb 76
43100 Saint-Just-près-Brioude 43 128 Dc 77
42170 Saint-Just-Saint-Rambert 42 129 Eb 76
51260 Saint-Just-Sauvage 51 73 De 57
42170 Saint-Just-sur-Loire 42 129 Eb 75
22630 Saint-Juvat 22 65 Xf 58
08250 Saint-Juvin 08 42 Ef 53
36500 Saint-Lactencin 36 101 Bc 67
69220 Saint-Lager 69D 118 Ee 72
07210 Saint-Lager-Bressac 07 142 Ee 80
39230 Saint-Lamain 39 107 Fd 68
14570 Saint-Lambert 14 47 Zc 55
78470 Saint-Lambert 78 51 Ca 56
49750 Saint-Lambert-du-Lattay 49 83 Zc 65
08130 Saint-Lambert-et-Mont-de-Jeux 08 42 Ed 52
49070 Saint-Lambert-la-Potherie 49 83 Zb 64
61160 Saint-Lambert-sur-Dive 61 48 Aa 56
61400 Saint-Langis-lès-Mortagne 61 68 Ad 57
65700 Saint-Lanne 65 162 Zf 87
86200 Saint-Laon 86 99 Zf 67
09800 Saint-Lary 09 176 Af 91
32360 Saint-Lary 32 163 Ad 86
31350 Saint-Lary-Boujean 31 163 Ae 89
65170 Saint-Lary-Soulan 65 175 Ab 92
38840 Saint-Lattier 38 143 Fb 78
22230 Saint-Launeuc 22 64 Xd 59
63350 Saint-Laure 63 116 Db 73
05130 Saint-Laurent 05 144 Ff 82
08090 Saint-Laurent 08 42 Ee 50
11320 Saint-Laurent 11 165 Be 88
18330 Saint-Laurent 18 102 Cb 65
19130 Saint-Laurent 19 125 Bc 77
22140 Saint-Laurent 22 63 We 57
22150 Saint-Laurent 22 64 Xb 58
22240 Saint-Laurent 22 64 Xd 57
22580 Saint-Laurent 22 64 Xa 56
23000 Saint-Laurent 23 114 Bf 71
28240 Saint-Laurent 28 69 Ba 58
31230 Saint-Laurent 31 163 Ae 89
33790 Saint-Laurent 33 136 Aa 80
40250 Saint-Laurent 40 161 Zb 86
42340 Saint-Laurent 42 129 Eb 75
47130 Saint-Laurent 47 148 Ac 83
56400 Saint-Laurent 56 79 Wf 63
56800 Saint-Laurent 56 81 Xd 61
58150 Saint-Laurent 58 89 Cf 64
59114 Saint-Laurent 59 30 Cd 43
74800 Saint-Laurent 74 120 Gc 72
81310 Saint-Laurent 81 151 Bf 86
82200 Saint-Laurent 82 149 Ba 84
82270 Saint-Laurent 82 150 Bc 83
88000 Saint-Laurent 88 76 Gc 60
89500 Saint-Laurent 89 72 Db 60
62223 Saint-Laurent-Blagny 62 30 Ce 47
64160 Saint-Laurent-Bretagne 64 162 Ze 88
43100 Saint-Laurent-Chabreuges 43 128 Dc 77
69440 Saint-Laurent-d'Agny 69M 130 Ee 75
30220 Saint-Laurent-d'Aigouze 30 169 Eb 87
71210 Saint-Laurent-d'Andenay 71 105 Ed 68
33240 Saint Laurent-d'Arce 33 135 Zd 78
61500 Saint-Laurent-de-Beauménil 61 68 Aa 57
16190 Saint-Laurent-de-Belzagot 16 124 Aa 76
76700 Saint-Laurent-de-Brévedent 76 36 Ab 51
30200 Saint-Laurent-de-Carnols 30 155 Ed 83
66260 Saint-Laurent-de-Cerdans 66 179 Cd 94
16450 Saint-Laurent-de-Céris 16 112 Ac 73
69930 Saint-Laurent-de-Chamousset 69M 130 Ec 74
16100 Saint Laurent-de-Charente 16 123 Zd 74
14220 Saint-Laurent-de-Condel 14 47 Zd 54
50670 Saint-Laurent-de-Cuves 50 46 Yf 56
40390 Saint-Laurent-de-Gosse 40 160 Ye 87
86410 Saint-Laurent-de-Jourdes 86 112 Ad 70
17380 Saint-Laurent-de-la-Barrière 17 110 Zb 72
11220 Saint-Laurent-de-la-Cabrerisse 11 166 Ce 90
73440 Saint-Laurent-de-la-Côte 73 133 Gc 76
22190 Saint-Laurent-de-la-Mer 22 64 Xb 57
49290 Saint-Laurent-de-la-Plaine 49 83 Zb 65
17450 Saint-Laurent-de-la-Prée 17 110 Yf 73
66250 Saint-Laurent-de-la-Salanque 66 179 Cf 92
85410 Saint-Laurent-de-la-Salle 85 110 Za 69
12620 Saint-Laurent-de-Lévézou 12 152 Cf 83
37330 Saint-Laurent-de-Lin 37 85 Ab 63
82800 Saint-Laurent-de-Maynet 82 150 Bd 84
69720 Saint Laurent-de-Mure 69M 130 Fa 74
48100 Saint-Laurent-de-Muret 48 140 Db 81
65150 Saint-Laurent-de-Neste 65 163 Ac 90
30126 Saint-Laurent-des-Arbres 30 155 Ee 84
49270 Saint-Laurent-des-Autels 49 82 Ye 65
24510 Saint-Laurent-des-Bâtons 24 136 Ae 79
27220 Saint-Laurent-des-Bois 27 50 Bb 55
41240 Saint-Laurent-des-Bois 41 86 Bc 61
16480 Saint-Laurent-des-Combes 16 123 Aa 76
33330 Saint Laurent-des-Combes 33 135 Zf 79
27270 Saint-Laurent-des-Grès 27 48 Ac 55
24400 Saint-Laurent-des-Hommes 24 136 Ab 78
53290 Saint-Laurent-des-Mortiers 53 83 Zc 62
24100 Saint-Laurent-des-Vignes 24 136 Ac 80
50240 Saint-Laurent-de-Terregatte 50 66 Ye 57
48400 Saint-Laurent-de-Trèves 48 153 Dd 83
69670 Saint-Laurent-de-Vaux 69M 130 Ed 74
48310 Saint-Laurent-de-Veyrès 48 140 Da 80
69620 Saint-Laurent-d'Oingt 69D 118 Ed 73
12560 Saint-Laurent d'Olt 12 152 Da 82
26350 Saint-Laurent-d'Onay 26 143 Fa 77
33540 Saint-Laurent-du-Bois 33 135 Zf 81
05500 Saint-Laurent-du-Cros 05 144 Ga 81
49410 Saint-Laurent-du-Mottay 49 83 Za 64
07800 Saint-Laurent-du-Pape 07 142 Ee 80
33190 Saint-Laurent-du-Plan 33 135 Zf 81
38380 Saint-Laurent-du-Pont 38 131 Fe 76
61470 Saint-Laurent-du-Tencement 61 48 Ac 55
06700 Saint-Laurent-du-Var 06 173 Hb 86
04500 Saint Laurent du-Verdon 04 171 Ga 86
38350 Saint-Laurent-en-Beaumont 38 144 Ff 79
71800 Saint-Laurent-en-Brionnais 71 117 Eb 71
76560 Saint-Laurent-en-Caux 76 37 Af 50
37380 Saint-Laurent-en-Gâtines 37 85 Ae 63
39150 Saint-Laurent-en-Grandvaux 39 120 Ff 69
26190 Saint-Laurent-en-Royans 26 143 Fb 78
42210 Saint-Laurent-la-Conche 42 129 Eb 74
28210 Saint-Laurent-la-Gâtine 28 50 Bd 56
39570 Saint-Laurent-la-Roche 39 106 Fd 69
24170 Saint-Laurent-la-Vallée 24 137 Ba 80
30330 Saint-Laurent-la-Vernède 30 154 Ec 84
30440 Saint-Laurent-le-Minier 30 153 Dd 85
07590 Saint-Laurent-les-Bains 07 141 Df 81
87240 Saint-Laurent-les-Églises 87 113 Bc 73
46400 Saint-Laurent-les-Tours 46 138 Bf 79
46800 Saint-Laurent-Lolmie 46 150 Bb 83
33112 Saint-Laurent-Médoc 33 134 Zb 78
41220 Saint-Laurent-Nouan 41 86 Bd 62
07170 Saint-Laurent-sous-Coiron 07 142 Ec 81
87310 Saint-Laurent-sur-Gorre 87 125 Af 74
24330 Saint-Laurent-sur-Manoire 24 137 Ae 78
14710 Saint-Laurent-sur-Mer 14 47 Za 52
55150 Saint-Laurent-sur-Othain 55 43 Fd 52
56140 Saint-Laurent-sur-Oust 56 81 Xe 62
01750 Saint-Laurent-sur-Saône 01 118 Ef 71
85290 Saint-Laurent-sur-Sèvre 85 98 Za 67
79160 Saint-Laurs 79 110 Zc 69
58350 Saint-Lay 58 103 Db 65
22210 Saint-Leau 22 64 Xc 60
06260 Saint-Léger 06 158 Ge 84
14740 Saint-Léger 14 47 Zc 53
17800 Saint-Léger 17 122 Zc 75
47140 Saint-Léger 47 149 Af 82
47160 Saint Léger 47 148 Ab 83
53480 Saint-Léger 53 67 Zd 60
62128 Saint-Léger 62 30 Cf 47
68210 Saint-Léger 68 94 Ha 63
86380 Saint-Léger 86 99 Ac 68
60170 Saint-Léger-aux-Bois 60 39 Cf 52
76340 Saint-Léger-aux-Bois 76 38 Bd 50
23300 Saint-Léger-Bridereix 23 113 Bd 71
33113 Saint-Léger-de-Balson 33 147 Zd 82
58120 Saint-Léger-de-Fougeret 58 104 Df 66
21210 Saint-Léger-de-Fourches 21 105 Ea 65
79500 Saint-Léger-de-la-Martinière 79 111 Zf 71
86120 Saint-Léger-de-Montbrillais 86 99 Zf 66
79100 Saint-Léger-de-Montbrun 79 99 Zf 66
48100 Saint-Léger-de-Peyre 48 140 Db 81
27300 Saint-Léger-de-Rôtes 27 49 Ad 54
28700 Saint-Léger-des-Aubées 28 70 Be 58
49170 Saint-Léger-des-Bois 49 83 Zb 64
35270 Saint-Léger-des-Prés 35 65 Yc 58
58300 Saint-Léger-des-Vignes 58 104 Dc 67
33540 Saint Léger-de-Vignague 33 135 Zf 80
71360 Saint-Léger-du-Bois 71 105 Ec 66
14430 Saint-Léger-Dubosq 14 35 Zf 53
76160 Saint-Léger-du-Bourg-Denis 76 37 Ba 52
27520 Saint-Léger-du-Gennetey 27 49 Ae 53
48140 Saint-Léger-du-Malzieu 48 140 Db 79
84390 Saint-Léger-du-Ventoux 84 156 Fb 83
60155 Saint-Léger-en-Bray 60 38 Ca 52
78610 Saint-Léger-en-Yvelines 78 50 Be 56
87340 Saint-Léger-la-Montagne 87 113 Bc 72
23000 Saint-Léger-le-Guéretois 23 114 Be 72
18140 Saint-Léger-le-Petit 18 103 Da 66
80560 Saint-Léger-lès-Authie 80 29 Cd 48
80780 Saint-Léger-lès-Domart 80 29 Ca 48
05260 Saint-Léger-les-Melèzes 05 144 Gb 81
44710 Saint-Léger-les-Vignes 44 96 Yb 66
87190 Saint-Léger-Magnazeix 87 113 Bb 71
10800 Saint-Léger-Près-Troyes 10 73 Ea 59
71990 Saint-Léger-sous-Beuvray 71 105 Ea 67
10500 Saint-Léger-sous-Brienne 10 74 Ed 58
49280 Saint-Léger-sous-Cholet 49 98 Za 66
71520 Saint-Léger-sous-la-Bussière 71 118 Ed 71
10330 Saint-Léger-sous-Margerie 10 74 Ec 57
80140 Saint-Léger-sur-Bresle 80 38 Be 49
71510 Saint-Léger-sur-Dheune 71 105 Ed 67
42155 Saint-Léger-sur-Roanne 42 117 Df 72
61170 Saint-Léger-sur-Sarthe 61 68 Ac 57
03130 Saint-Léger-sur-Vouzance 03 117 Df 70
21270 Saint-Léger-Triey 21 92 Fc 65
89630 Saint-Léger-Vauban 89 90 Ea 64
86290 Saint-Léomer 86 113 Af 70
03220 Saint-Léon 03 116 De 70
22460 Saint-Léon 22 64 Xa 59
31560 Saint-Léon 31 165 Bd 88
33670 Saint-Léon 33 135 Ze 80
36190 Saint-Léon 36 114 Bd 70
47160 Saint-Léon 47 148 Ab 83
57870 Saint-Leon 57 57 Ha 57
28140 Saint-Léonard 28 70 Be 59
32380 Saint-Léonard 32 149 Ae 85
35120 Saint-Léonard 35 65 Yb 58
50300 Saint-Léonard 50 46 Yd 56
51500 Saint-Léonard 51 53 Ea 53
62360 Saint-Léonard 62 28 Bd 44
76400 Saint-Léonard 76 36 Ac 50
88650 Saint-Léonard 88 77 Gf 59
87400 Saint-Léonard-de-Noblat 87 125 Bc 73
72130 Saint-Léonard-des-Bois 72 68 Zf 58
61390 Saint-Léonard-des-Parcs 61 48 Ab 57
41370 Saint-Léonard-en-Beauce 41 86 Bc 61
24560 Saint Léon-d'Issigeac 24 136 Ae 80
12780 Saint-Léons 12 152 Cf 83
24110 Saint-Léon-sur-L'Isle 24 136 Ad 78
24290 Saint-Léon-sur-Vézère 24 137 Ba 78
03160 Saint-Léopardin 03 103 Da 68
03160 Saint-Léopardin-d'Augy 03 103 Da 68
56430 Saint-Léry 56 65 Xe 60
60340 Saint-Leu-d'Esserent 60 51 Cc 53
95320 Saint-Leu-la-Forêt 95 51 Cb 54
65500 Saint-Lézer 65 162 Aa 88
49120 Saint-Lézin 49 98 Zb 65
81120 Saint-Lieux-Lafenasse 81 151 Cb 86
81500 Saint-Lieux-lès-Lavour 81 150 Be 86
79000 Saint-Liguaire 79 110 Zc 71
79420 Saint-Lin 79 111 Ze 69
04330 Saint Lions 04 157 Gc 85
09140 Saint-Lizier 09 177 Bb 92
09190 Saint-Lizier 09 176 Ba 90
32220 Saint-Lizier-du-Planté 32 164 Af 88
43380 Saint-Ilpize 43 128 Dc 77
50000 Saint-Lô 50 34 Yf 54
50580 Saint-Lô-d'Ourville 50 46 Yb 52
44530 Saint-Lomer 44 81 Xf 64
72600 Saint-Longis 72 68 Ac 58
40300 Saint-Lon-les-Mines 40 161 Yf 87
22130 Saint-Lormel 22 65 Xe 57
39230 Saint-Lothain 39 107 Fd 68

316 | Saint-Jean-du-Vigan

37500 Saint-Louand 37 99 Ab 65
32220 Saint-Loube 32 164 Af 88
33690 Saint-Loubert 33 148 Zf 82
33450 Saint-Loubès 33 135 Zd 79
40320 Saint-Loubouer 40 162 Zd 86
14310 Saint-Louet-sur-Seulles 14 34 Zc 54
50420 Saint-Louet-sur-Vire 50 47 Za 55
34510 Saint-Louis 34 167 Dc 88
44440 Saint-Louis 44 82 Ye 64
57820 Saint-Louis 57 57 Hb 56
57970 Saint-Louis 57 44 Gb 52
68300 Saint-Louis 68 95 Hd 63
33440 Saint-Louis-de-Montferrand 33 135 Zc 79
11500 Saint-Louis-et-Parahou 11 178 Cb 91
68300 Saint-Louis-la-Chaussée 68 95 Hd 63
57620 Saint-Louis-lès-Bitche = Münzthal 57 58 Hc 55
03150 Saint-Loup 03 116 Dc 70
17380 Saint-Loup 17 110 Zc 73
23130 Saint-Loup 23 114 Cb 72
28360 Saint-Loup 28 70 Bc 59
36400 Saint-Loup 36 102 Ca 69
39120 Saint-Loup 39 106 Fb 66
41320 Saint-Loup 41 101 Bf 65
50300 Saint-Loup 50 46 Ye 56
51120 Saint-Loup 51 53 De 56
58200 Saint-Loup 58 89 Da 64
69490 Saint-Loup 69D 118 Ec 73
82340 Saint-Loup 82 149 Af 84
31140 Saint-Loup-Cammas 31 164 Bc 86
08300 Saint-Loup-Champagne 08 41 Eb 52
10100 Saint-Loup-de-Buffigny 10 73 Dd 58
14340 Saint-Loup-de-Fribois 14 35 Aa 54
71350 Saint-Loup-de-la-Salle 71 106 Ef 67
77650 Saint-Loup-de-Naud 77 72 Db 57
18190 Saint-Loup-des-Chaumes 18 102 Cc 68
45340 Saint-Loup-des-Vignes 45 71 Cc 60
71240 Saint-Loup-de-Varennes 71 106 Ef 68
89330 Saint-Loup-d'Ordon 89 72 Da 60
53290 Saint-Loup-du-Dorat 53 84 Zd 61
53300 Saint-Loup-du-Gast 53 67 Zc 58
31350 Saint-Loup-en-Comminges 31 163 Ad 89
14400 Saint-Loup-Hors 14 47 Zb 53
79600 Saint-Loup-Lamaire 79 99 Zf 68
70100 Saint-Loup-Nantouard 70 92 Fe 64
52210 Saint-Loup-sur-Aujon 52 92 Fa 61
70800 Saint Loup-sur-Semouse 70 93 Gb 61
08130 Saint-Loup-Terrier 08 42 Ed 51
61570 Saint-Loyer-des-Champs 61 48 Aa 56
22110 Saint-Lubin 22 63 We 59
22210 Saint-Lubin 22 64 Xc 59
28270 Saint-Lubin-de-Cravant 28 49 Ba 56
28410 Saint-Lubin-de-la-Haye 28 50 Bd 56
28330 Saint-Lubin-des-cinq-Fonds 28 69 Af 59
28350 Saint-Lubin-des-Joncherets 28 49 Bb 56
41190 Saint-Lubin-en-Vergonnois 41 86 Bb 63
27930 Saint-Luc 27 50 Bb 55
28210 Saint-Lucien 28 50 Bd 57
76780 Saint-Lucien 76 37 Bc 51
51300 Saint-Lumier-en-Champagne 51 54 Ed 56
51340 Saint-Lumier-la-Populeuse 51 54 Ee 56
44190 Saint-Lumine-de-Clisson 44 97 Yd 66
44310 Saint-Lumine-de-Coutais 44 96 Yb 66
35800 Saint-Lunaire 35 65 Xf 57
28190 Saint-Luperce 28 69 Bb 58
39170 Saint-Lupicin 39 119 Fe 70
10350 Saint-Lupien 10 73 De 58
10180 Saint-Lyé 10 73 Ea 58
45170 Saint-Lyé-la-Forêt 45 70 Bf 60
44410 Saint-Lyphard 44 81 Xe 64
31470 Saint-Lys 31 164 Bb 87
49260 Saint-Macaire-du-Bois 49 98 Ze 66
49450 Saint-Macaire-en-Mauges 49 97 Za 66
27210 Saint-Maclou 27 36 Ac 52
76890 Saint-Maclou-de-Folleville 76 37 Ba 50
76110 Saint-Maclou-la-Brière 76 36 Ac 51
86400 Saint-Macoux 86 111 Ab 72
22350 Saint-Maden 22 65 Xf 59
82800 Saint-Mafre 82 150 Bd 84
33125 Saint Magne 33 134 Zc 81
33350 Saint-Magne-de-Castillon 33 135 Zf 79
63330 Saint-Maigner 63 115 Ce 72
17520 Saint-Maigrin 17 123 Ze 76
04300 Saint-Maime 04 156 Fe 85
23200 Saint-Maixant 23 114 Cb 73
33490 Saint-Maixant 33 135 Ze 81
72320 Saint-Maixent 72 69 Ad 60
79160 Saint-Maixent-de-Beugné 79 110 Zc 69
79400 Saint-Maixent-l'Ecole 79 111 Ze 70
85220 Saint-Maixent-sur-Vie 85 96 Yb 68
28170 Saint-Maixme-Hauterive 28 69 Bb 57
35400 Saint-Malo 35 65 Xf 57
35620 Saint Malo 35 82 Yc 62
56380 Saint-Malo-de-Beignon 56 81 Xf 61
44550 Saint-Malo-de-Guersac 44 81 Xe 64
50200 Saint-Malo-de-la-Lande 50 46 Yc 54
35480 Saint-Malo-de-Phily 35 82 Yb 61
56490 Saint-Malo-des-Trois-Fontaines 56 64 Xd 60
85590 Saint-Malô-du-Bois 85 98 Za 67
58350 Saint-Malo-en-Donziois 58 89 Db 65
35400 Saint-Malou = Saint-Malo 35 65 Xf 57
26300 Saint Mamans 26 143 Fa 78
69860 Saint-Mamert 69D 118 Ed 71
30730 Saint-Mamert-du-Gard 30 154 Eb 85
31110 Saint-Mamet 31 176 Ad 92
15220 Saint-Mamet-la-Salvetat 15 139 Cb 79
77670 Saint-Mammès 77 72 Ce 58
17470 Saint-Mandé-sur-Brédoire 17 111 Ze 72
83430 Saint-Mandrier-sur-Mer 83 171 Ff 90
14380 Saint-Manvieu-Bocage 14 47 Za 56
14740 Saint-Manvieu-Norrey 14 35 Zd 53
15320 Saint-Marc 15 140 Db 79
22400 Saint-Marc 22 64 Xc 57
36300 Saint-Marc 36 100 Ba 68
44600 Saint-Marc 44 96 Xe 65
79160 Saint-Marc 79 110 Zd 69
83310 Saint-Marc 83 172 Gc 89
23200 Saint-Marc-à-Frongier 23 114 Ca 73
66110 Saint-Marcal 66 179 Cd 93
23460 Saint-Marc-à-Loubaud 23 126 Ca 73
35120 Saint-Marcan 35 65 Yc 57
41170 Saint-Marc-du-Cor 41 69 Af 61
08160 Saint-Marceau 08 42 Ee 50
72170 Saint-Marceau 72 68 Aa 59
01390 Saint-Marcel 01 118 Ef 73
08460 Saint-Marcel 08 41 Ed 50
12320 Saint-Marcel 12 139 Cc 81
13011 Saint-Marcel 13 170 Fc 89
27950 Saint-Marcel 27 50 Bc 54
36200 Saint-Marcel 36 101 Bd 69
54800 Saint Marcel 54 56 Ff 54
56140 Saint-Marcel 56 81 Xd 62
70500 Saint-Marcel 70 93 Fe 62
71380 Saint-Marcel 71 106 Ef 68
73440 Saint-Marcel 73 133 Gd 76
73600 Saint-Marcel 73 133 Gd 75
81170 Saint-Marcel 81 151 Bf 84
38080 Saint-Marcel-Bel-Accueil 38 131 Fb 75
07700 Saint-Marcel-d'Ardèche 07 155 Ed 83
30330 Saint-Marcel-de-Careinet 30 154 Ec 84
42122 Saint-Marcel-de-Félines 42 129 Eb 73
30122 Saint-Marcel-de-Fontfouillouse 30 153 De 84
24510 Saint-Marcel-du-Périgord 24 136 Ae 79
42430 Saint-Marcel-d'Urfé 42 129 Df 73
03420 Saint-Marcel-en-Marcillat 03 115 Cd 72
03390 Saint-Marcel-en-Murat 03 115 Da 71
71460 Saint-Marcelin-de-Cray 71 117 Ed 69
69170 Saint-Marcel L'Eclairé 69D 130 Ec 73
07100 Saint-Marcel-lès-Annonay 07 130 Ed 77
26740 Saint-Marcel-lès-Sauzet 26 142 Ee 81
26320 Saint-Marcel-lès-Valence 26 143 Ef 79
35600 Saint-Marcellin 35 81 Xf 62
38160 Saint-Marcellin 38 143 Fb 78
42680 Saint-Marcellin-en-Forez 42 129 Eb 76
31590 Saint-Marcel-Paulel 31 165 Bd 87
11120 Saint-Marcel-sur-Aude 11 167 Cf 89
31800 Saint-Marcet 31 163 Ae 89
13100 Saint-Marc-Jaumegarde 13 170 Fd 87
79310 Saint-Marc-la-Lande 79 111 Zd 69
35460 Saint-Marc-le-Blanc 35 66 Yd 58
24540 Saint-Marcory 24 137 Af 80
14330 Saint-Marcouf 14 34 Za 53
50310 Saint-Marcouf 50 33 Ye 52
35140 Saint-Marc-sur-Couesnon 35 66 Yd 59
21450 Saint-Marc-sur-Seine 21 91 Ed 62
02220 Saint-Mard 02 40 Dd 52
17700 Saint-Mard 17 110 Zb 72
54290 Saint-Mard 54 76 Gb 57
77230 Saint-Mard 77 51 Ce 54
80700 Saint-Mard 80 39 Ce 50
61400 Saint-Mard-de-Reno 61 68 Ad 57
71640 Saint-Mard-de-Vaux 71 105 Ee 68
51130 Saint-Mard-lès-Rouffy 51 53 Ea 55
76730 Saint-Mards 76 37 Ba 50
27500 Saint-Mards-de-Blacarville 27 36 Ad 52
27230 Saint-Mards-de-Fresne 27 48 Ac 54
10160 Saint-Mards-en-Othe 10 73 De 59
51800 Saint-Mard-sur-Auve 51 54 Ee 54
51330 Saint-Mard-sur-le-Mont 51 54 Ef 55
27150 Saint-Marie-de-Vatimesnil 27 50 Bd 53
23600 Saint-Marien 23 114 Cb 70
33620 Saint-Mariens 33 135 Zd 78
36200 Saint-Marin 36 101 Bc 69
43260 Saint-Marsal 43 141 Ea 78
79380 Saint-Marsault 79 98 Zc 68
44680 Saint-Mars-de-Coutais 44 96 Yb 66
72440 Saint-Mars-de-Locquenay 72 85 Ac 61
61350 Saint-Mars-d'Ergenne 61 67 Zb 57
85110 Saint-Mars-des-Pres 85 97 Za 68
72220 Saint-Mars-d'Outillé 72 85 Ab 61
44850 Saint-Mars-du-Désert 44 82 Yd 64
53700 Saint-Mars-du-Désert 53 67 Zf 59
77320 Saint-Mars-en-Brie 77 52 Db 56
72470 Saint-Mars-la-Brière 72 68 Ac 60
44540 Saint-Mars-la-Jaille 44 82 Ye 63
85590 Saint-Mars-la-Réorthe 85 98 Za 67
72290 Saint-Mars-sous-Ballon 72 68 Ab 59
53300 Saint-Mars-sur-Colmont 53 67 Zb 58
53220 Saint-Mars-sur-la-Futaie 53 66 Yf 58
77320 Saint-Mars-Vieux-Maisons 77 52 Db 56
07310 Saint-Martial 07 142 Eb 79
12800 Saint-Martial 12 151 Cc 84
15110 Saint-Martial 15 140 Da 79
16190 Saint-Martial 16 123 Aa 76
16210 Saint-Martial 16 124 Aa 77
17330 Saint-Martial 17 110 Zd 72
23600 Saint-Martial 23 114 Cb 71
30440 Saint-Martial 30 153 De 84
33220 Saint-Martial 33 136 Ab 80
33490 Saint-Martial 33 135 Ze 81
34360 Saint-Martial 34 166 Ce 88
46800 Saint-Martial 46 150 Bb 82
81100 Saint-Martial 81 165 Cb 87
24160 Saint-Martial-d'Albarède 24 125 Ba 77
24700 Saint Martial-d' Artenset 24 136 Ab 78
19150 Saint-Martial-de-Gimel 19 126 Bf 77
24250 Saint-Martial-de-Nabirat 24 137 Bb 80
24300 Saint-Martial-de-Valette 24 124 Ad 75
17500 Saint-Martial-de-Vitaterne 17 123 Zd 76
19400 Saint-Martial-Entraygues 19 138 Bf 78
24390 Saint-Martial-Laborie 24 125 Ba 77
23150 Saint-Martial-le-Mont 23 114 Ca 72
23100 Saint-Martial-le-Vieux 23 127 Cb 74
87330 Saint-Martial-sur-Isop 87 112 Af 71
17520 Saint-Martial-sur-Né 17 123 Zd 75
24320 Saint-Martial-Viveyrol 24 124 Ac 76
04200 Saint-Martin 04 156 Fe 83
04290 Saint-Martin 04 157 Ga 84
12100 Saint-Martin 12 152 Da 84
12310 Saint-Martin 12 152 Ce 82
17600 Saint-Martin 17 122 Za 74
23320 Saint-Martin 23 114 Be 71
24680 Saint-Martin 24 136 Ac 79
31160 Saint-Martin 31 164 Af 90
32300 Saint-Martin 32 163 Ac 87
32300 Saint-Martin 32 163 Ac 87
34150 Saint-Martin 34 168 Dd 87
34700 Saint-Martin 34 167 Dc 86
47350 Saint-Martin 47 136 Ab 81
47430 Saint-Martin 47 148 Ab 82
48000 Saint-Martin 48 140 Dd 81
50410 Saint-Martin 50 46 Yf 55
51460 Saint-Martin 51 54 Ed 55
54450 Saint-Martin 54 77 Ge 57
56200 Saint-Martin 56 81 Xe 62
64390 Saint-Martin 64 161 Za 88
64640 Saint-Martin 64 161 Yf 89
65360 Saint-Martin 65 162 Aa 90
66220 Saint-Martin 66 178 Cc 92
66480 Saint-Martin 66 179 Cf 94
67220 Saint-Martin 67 60 Hb 58
69770 Saint-Martin 69M 130 Ec 74
76680 Saint-Martin 76 37 Bb 50
81390 Saint-Martin 81 165 Bf 86
81600 Saint-Martin 81 151 Bf 85
82160 Saint-Martin 82 151 Be 83
82240 Saint-Martin 82 150 Bd 83
83460 Saint-Martin 83 172 Gc 88
83520 Saint-Martin 83 172 Gd 88
83560 Saint-Martin 83 171 Ff 87
76340 Saint-Martin-au-Bosc 76 38 Bd 50
76760 Saint-Martin-aux-Arbres 76 37 Af 51
60420 Saint-Martin-aux-Bois 60 39 Cd 51
76450 Saint-Martin-aux-Buneaux 76 36 Ad 50
51240 Saint-Martin-aux-Champs 51 54 Ec 56
14800 Saint-Martin-aux-Chartrains 14 36 Aa 53
71118 Saint-Martin-Belle-Roche 71 118 Ef 70
74370 Saint-Martin-Bellevue 74 120 Ga 73
62280 Saint-Martin-Boulogne 62 26 Bd 44
15140 Saint-Martin-Cantalès 15 139 Cb 78
23460 Saint-Martin-Château 23 126 Be 73
77560 Saint-Martin-Chennetron 77 72 Dc 57
62240 Saint-Martin-Choquel 62 28 Bf 44
47700 Saint-Martin-Curton 47 148 Aa 82
45110 Saint-Martin-d'Abbat 45 87 Cb 61
51530 Saint-Martin-d'Ablois 51 53 Df 54
26330 Saint-Martin-d'Août 26 130 Ef 77
64640 Saint-Martin-d'Arberoue 64 160 Ye 88
49150 Saint-Martin-d'Arcé 49 84 Zf 63
07700 Saint-Martin-d'Ardèche 07 155 Ed 83
32110 Saint-Martin-d'Armagnac 32 162 Zf 86
64780 Saint-Martin-d'Arrossa 64 160 Ye 89
17270 Saint-Martin-d'Ary 17 123 Ze 77
50190 Saint-Martin-d'Aubigny 50 33 Yd 54
50310 Saint-Martin-d'Audoville 50 33 Yd 51
18110 Saint-Martin-d'Auxigny 18 102 Cc 65
71390 Saint-Martin-d'Auxy 71 105 Ed 68
34520 Saint-Martin-d'Azirou 34 153 Dd 86
01510 Saint-Martin-de-Bavel 01 131 Fe 73
47270 Saint-Martin-de-Beauville 47 149 Ae 83
73440 Saint-Martin-de-Belleville 73 133 Gd 76
79230 Saint-Martin-de-Bernegoue 79 111 Zd 71
14290 Saint-Martin-de-Bienfaite-la-Cressonnière 14 48 Ac 54
14710 Saint-Martin-de-Blagny 14 34 Za 53
42155 Saint-Martin-de-Boisy 42 117 Df 72
50750 Saint-Martin-de-Bonfossé 50 46 Ye 54
76840 Saint-Martin-de-Boscherville 76 37 Af 52
10100 Saint-Martin-de-Bossenay 10 73 De 58
48160 Saint-Martin-de-Boubaux 48 154 Df 83
50290 Saint-Martin-de-Bréhal 50 46 Yc 55
78660 Saint-Martin-de-Bréthencourt 78 70 Bf 57
04800 Saint-Martin-de-Brômes 04 157 Ff 86
82240 Saint-Martin-de-Caissac 82 150 Bd 83
81360 Saint-Martin-de-Calmes 81 166 Cb 86
09000 Saint-Martin-de-Caralp 09 177 Bd 91
84750 Saint-Martin-de-Castillon 84 156 Fd 85
38930 Saint-Martin-de-Celles 38 144 Fd 79
50210 Saint-Martin-de-Cenilly 50 46 Ye 55
50150 Saint-Martin-de-Chaulieu 50 47 Za 56
71490 Saint-Martin-de-Commune 71 105 Ed 67
53160 Saint-Martin-de-Connée 53 67 Ze 59
30124 Saint-Martin-de-Corconac 30 154 De 84
17360 Saint-Martin-de-Coux 17 135 Zf 78
13310 Saint-Martin-de-Crau 13 169 Ee 87
71460 Saint-Martin-de-Croix 71 105 Ed 69
14320 Saint-Martin-de-Fontenage 14 35 Zd 54
85200 Saint-Martin-de-Fraigneau 85 110 Zb 70
14170 Saint-Martin-de-Fresnay 14 48 Aa 55
24800 Saint-Martin-de-Fressengeas 24 125 Af 76
43150 Saint-Martin-de-Fugères 43 141 Df 79
32480 Saint-Martin-de-Goyne 32 149 Ad 84
24610 Saint-Martin-de-Gurçon 24 136 Aa 79
40390 Saint-Martin-de-Hinx 40 160 Ye 87
17400 Saint-Martin-de-Juillers 17 111 Zd 73
87200 Saint-Martin-de-Jussac 87 125 Af 73
84760 Saint-Martin-de-la-Brasque 84 156 Fd 86
81630 Saint-Martin-de-la-Cesquière 81 150 Be 85
38650 Saint-Martin-de-la-Cluze 38 144 Fd 79
17330 Saint-Martin-de-la-Coudre 17 110 Zc 72
14100 Saint-Martin-de-la-Lieue 14 48 Ab 54
21210 Saint-Martin-de-la-Mer 21 105 Eb 65
36110 Saint-Martin-de-Lamps 36 101 Bd 67
50730 Saint-Martin-de-Landelles 50 66 Ye 57
48110 Saint-Martin-de-Lansuscle 48 153 De 83
49160 Saint-Martin-de-la-Place 49 84 Zf 65
73140 Saint-Martin-de-la-Porte 73 132 Gc 77
34390 Saint-Martin-de-L'Arçon 34 167 Cf 87
32380 Saint-Martin-de-las-Oumettes 32 149 Af 85
33910 Saint-Martin-de-Laye 33 135 Ze 78
12130 Saint-Martin-de-Lenne 12 152 Cf 82
33540 Saint-Martin-de-Lerm 33 135 Zf 81
76190 Saint Martin de l'If 76 36 Ae 51
71740 Saint-Martin-de-Lixy 71 117 Eb 71
34380 Saint-Martin-de-Londres 34 153 De 86
79100 Saint-Martin-de-Mâcon 79 99 Zf 66
14100 Saint-Martin-de-Mailloc 14 48 Ab 54
14700 Saint-Martin-de-Mieux 14 48 Ze 55
28130 Saint-Martin-de-Nigelles 28 70 Bd 57
40240 Saint-Martin-de-Noët 40 147 Ze 84
79110 Saint-Martin-d'Entraigues 79 111 Zf 72
06470 Saint-Martin-d'Entraunes 06 158 Ge 84
05120 Saint-Martin-de-Queyrières 05 145 Gd 79
17410 Saint-Martin-de-Ré 17 109 Yd 71
24600 Saint-Martin-de-Ribérac 24 124 Ac 77
79400 Saint-Martin-de-Saint-Maixent 79 111 Ze 70
71220 Saint-Martin-de-Salencey 71 117 Ed 69
14220 Saint-Martin-de-Sallen 14 47 Zc 55
79290 Saint-Martin-de-Sanzay 79 99 Ze 66
14350 Saint-Martin-des-Besaces 14 47 Za 54
41800 Saint-Martin-des-Bois 41 85 Ae 62
18140 Saint-Martin-des-Champs 18 103 Cf 66
29600 Saint-Martin-des-Champs 29 62 Wa 57
50300 Saint-Martin-des-Champs 50 46 Yd 56
77320 Saint-Martin-des-Champs 77 52 Dc 56
77560 Saint-Martin-des-Champs 77 72 Dc 57
78790 Saint-Martin-des-Champs 78 50 Be 55
89170 Saint-Martin-des-Champs 89 89 Da 63
24140 Saint-Martin-des-Combes 24 136 Ad 79
40390 Saint-Martin-de-Seignanx 40 160 Yd 87
14400 Saint-Martin-des-Entrées 14 47 Zb 53
33490 Saint-Martin-de-Sescas 33 135 Zf 81
12410 Saint-Martin-des-Faux 12 152 Ce 83
85570 Saint-Martin-des-Fontaines 85 110 Za 69
03230 Saint-Martin-des-Lais 03 104 Dd 68
61320 Saint-Martin-des-Landes 61 67 Zf 57
72400 Saint-Martin-des-Monts 72 68 Ad 60
85140 Saint-Martin-des-Noyers 85 97 Ye 68
63600 Saint-Martin-des-Olmes 63 129 De 75
61380 Saint-Martin-des-Pézerits 61 49 Ac 57
63570 Saint-Martin-des-Plains 63 128 Db 76
22320 Saint-Martin-des-Prés 22 64 Xa 59
11220 Saint-Martin-des-Puits 11 179 Cd 90
26140 Saint-Martin-des-Rosiers 26 130 Ef 77
85130 Saint-Martin-des-Tilleuls 85 97 Yf 67
42620 Saint-Martin-d'Estréaux 42 116 De 71
14500 Saint-Martin-de-Tallevende 14 47 Za 55
63210 Saint-Martin-de-Tours 63 127 Ce 74
07310 Saint Martin de-Valamas 07 142 Ec 79
30520 Saint-Martin-de-Valgalgues 30 154 Ea 84
50480 Saint-Martin-de-Varreville 50 33 Ye 52
46360 Saint-Martin-de-Vers 46 138 Bd 81
53290 Saint-Martin-de-Ville-Anglose 53 83 Zd 62
47210 Saint-Martin-de-Villeréal 47 137 Ae 81
11300 Saint-Martin-de-Villereglan 11 166 Cb 90
38320 Saint-Martin-d'Hères 38 132 Fe 78
58130 Saint-Martin-d'Heuille 58 103 Db 66
63580 Saint-Martin-d'Ollières 63 128 Dc 76
14350 Saint-Martin-Don 14 47 Za 55
40090 Saint-Martin-d'Oney 40 147 Zc 85
89330 Saint-Martin-d'Ordon 89 72 Db 60
09100 Saint-Martin-d'Oydes 09 164 Bc 89
76133 Saint-Martin-du-Bec 76 35 Ab 51
33910 Saint-Martin-du-Bois 33 135 Ze 78
49500 Saint-Martin-du-Bois 49 83 Zb 62
77320 Saint-Martin-du-Boschet 77 52 Dc 56
16700 Saint-Martin-du-Clocher 16 111 Aa 72
87510 Saint-Martin-du-Fault 87 113 Bb 73
49170 Saint-Martin-du-Fouilloux 49 83 Zb 64
79420 Saint-Martin-du-Fouilloux 79 99 Zf 69
01430 Saint-Martin-du-Frêne 01 119 Fd 72
32200 Saint-Martin-du-Hour 32 164 Af 86
71110 Saint-Martin-du-Lac 71 117 Ea 71
12100 Saint-Martin-du-Larzac 12 152 Da 84
53800 Saint-Martin-du-Limet 53 83 Yf 62
76290 Saint-Martin-du-Manoir 76 36 Ab 51
14140 Saint-Martin-du-Mesnil-Oury 14 48 Aa 54
01160 Saint-Martin-du-Mont 01 119 Fb 72
21440 Saint-Martin-du-Mont 21 91 Ee 64
71580 Saint-Martin-du-Mont 71 106 Fb 69
76750 Saint-Martin-du-Plessis 76 37 Bc 51
33540 Saint-Martin-du-Puy 33 135 Zf 80
58140 Saint-Martin-du-Puy 58 90 Df 65
81140 Saint-Martin-d'Urbens 81 150 Be 84
38410 Saint-Martin-d'Uriage 38 144 Ff 78
71460 Saint-Martin-du-Tartre 71 105 Ed 69
89100 Saint-Martin-du-Tertre 89 72 Db 59
27300 Saint-Martin-du-Tilleul 27 49 Ad 54
06670 Saint-Martin-du-Var 06 159 Hb 86
61130 Saint-Martin-du-Vieux-Bellême 61 68 Ad 58
76160 Saint-Martin-du-Vivier 76 37 Ba 52
77630 Saint-Martin-en-Bière 77 71 Cd 58
71620 Saint-Martin-en-Bresse 71 106 Fa 68
76370 Saint-Martin-en-Campagne 76 37 Bb 49
71350 Saint-Martin-en-Gâtinois 71 106 Fa 67
69850 Saint-Martin-en-Haut 69M 130 Ed 75
26420 Saint-Martin-en-Vercors 26 143 Fc 78
32450 Saint-Martin-Gimois 32 163 Ae 87
50690 Saint-Martin-Gréard 50 33 Yc 51
03380 Saint Martinien 03 115 Cc 70
07400 Saint-Martin-l'Inférieur 07 142 Ee 81
46330 Saint-Martin-Labouval 46 138 Be 82
27930 Saint-Martin-la-Campagne 27 49 Ba 54
33390 Saint-Martin-Lacaussade 33 134 Zc 78
78520 Saint-Martin-la-Garenne 78 50 Be 54
61320 Saint-Martin-L'Aiguillon 61 67 Ze 57
11400 Saint-Martin-Lalande 11 165 Ca 89
19320 Saint-Martin-la-Méanne 19 126 Bf 78
71460 Saint-Martin-la-Patrouille 71 105 Ed 69
42800 Saint-Martin-la-Plaine 42 130 Ed 75
86350 Saint-Martin-L'Ars 86 112 Ad 71
85210 Saint-Martin-Lars-en-Sainte-Hermine 85 97 Za 69
42260 Saint-Martin-la-Sauveté 42 129 Df 73
24400 Saint-Martin-L'Astier 24 136 Ac 78
37270 Saint-Martin-le-Beau 37 85 Af 64
50800 Saint-Martin-le-Bouillant 50 46 Ye 56
01310 Saint-Martin-le-Châtel 01 118 Fa 71
76260 Saint-Martin-le-Gaillard 76 37 Bc 49
34500 Saint-Martin-le Grand 34 167 Db 89
50260 Saint-Martin-le-Hébert 50 33 Yc 51
87360 Saint-Martin-le-Mault 87 113 Bb 70
60000 Saint-Martin-le-Nœud 60 38 Ca 52
24300 Saint-Martin-le-Pin 24 124 Ad 75
46700 Saint-Martin-le-Redon 46 137 Ba 81
04300 Saint-Martin-les-Eaux 04 156 Fe 85
52200 Saint-Martin-lès-Langres 52 92 Fb 61
79500 Saint-Martin-lès-Melles 79 111 Zf 71
81140 Saint-Martin-L'Espinas 81 150 Be 85
04140 Saint-Martin-lès-Seyne 04 157 Gb 82
42110 Saint-Martin-Lestra 42 129 Ec 74
11170 Saint-Martin-le-Vieil 11 165 Ca 89
87700 Saint-Martin-le-Vieux 87 125 Ba 74
62500 Saint-Martin-lez-Tatinghem 62 27 Cb 44
51490 Saint-Martin-L'Heureux 51 54 Ec 53
76270 Saint-Martin-L'Hortier 76 37 Bc 50
60700 Saint-Martin-Longueau 60 51 Cd 52
11500 Saint-Martin-Lys 11 178 Cb 92
76680 Saint-Martin-Osmonville 76 37 Bb 51
47180 Saint-Martin-Petit 47 135 Aa 81
76370 Saint-Martin-Plage 76 37 Ba 49
02110 Saint-Martin-Rivière 02 31 Dd 48
23430 Saint-Martin-Sainte-Catherine 23 113 Bd 73
27450 Saint-Martin-Saint-Firmin 27 49 Ad 53
19210 Saint-Martin-Sepert 19 125 Bc 76
71640 Saint-Martin-sous-Montaigu 71 105 Ee 68
15230 Saint-Martin-sous-Vigouroux 15 139 Ce 79
89700 Saint-Martin-sur-Armançon 89 90 Ea 61

A B C D E F G H I J K L M N O P Q R S T U V W X Y Z
Saint-Martin-sur-Armançon | 317

74700 Saint-Martin-sur-Arve 74 121 Gd 73
62128 Saint-Martin-sur-Cojeul 62 30 Cf 47
59213 Saint-Martin-sur-Ecaillon 59 30 Dd 47
73130 Saint-Martin-sur-la-Chambre 73 132 Gb 76
52120 Saint-Martin-sur-la-Renne 52 74 Ef 60
07400 Saint-Martin-sur-Lavezon 07 142 Ed 81
51520 Saint-Martin-sur-le-Pré 51 54 Ec 55
58150 Saint-Martin-sur-Nohain 58 88 Cf 64
45500 Saint-Martin-sur-Ocre 45 88 Cd 63
89110 Saint-Martin-sur-Ocre 89 89 Dc 62
89110 Saint-Martin-sur-Ocre 89 89 Dc 62
89260 Saint-Martin-sur-Oreuse 89 72 Dc 59
89120 Saint-Martin-sur-Ouanne 89 89 Da 61
87400 Saint-Martin-Terressus 87 113 Bc 73
15140 Saint-Martin-Valmeroux 15 139 Cc 78
06450 Saint-Martin-Vésubie 06 159 Hb 84
31360 Saint-Martory 31 164 Af 90
16260 Saint-Mary 16 124 Ac 73
15170 Saint-Mary-le-Gros 15 128 Da 77
15500 Saint-Mary-le-Plain 15 128 Da 77
51490 Saint-Masmes 51 41 Eb 53
29217 Saint-Mathieu 29 61 Vb 59
29600 Saint-Mathieu 29 62 Wb 57
56520 Saint-Mathieu 56 79 Wd 62
87440 Saint-Mathieu 87 124 Ae 74
34270 Saint-Mathieu-de-Tréviers 34 153 Df 86
22590 Saint-Mathurin 22 64 Xa 57
85150 Saint-Mathurin 85 109 Yb 69
19430 Saint-Mathurin-Léobazel 19 138 Ca 78
49250 Saint-Mathurin-sur-Loire 49 84 Ze 64
46800 Saint-Matré 46 150 Ba 82
22600 Saint-Maudan 22 64 Xb 60
56120 Saint-Maudé 56 81 Xc 61
22980 Saint-Maudez 22 65 Xe 58
29510 Saint-Maudez 29 78 Wa 60
35750 Saint-Maugan 35 65 Xf 60
80140 Saint-Maulvis 80 38 Bf 49
18270 Saint-Maur 18 102 Cb 69
32300 Saint-Maur 32 163 Ac 88
36250 Saint-Maur 36 101 Bd 68
39570 Saint-Maur 39 107 Fd 69
60190 Saint-Maur 60 39 Ce 51
60210 Saint-Maur 60 38 Bf 51
83560 Saint-Maur 83 172 Gc 89
50800 Saint-Maur-des-Bois 50 46 Yf 56
94210 Saint-Maur-des-Fossés 94 51 Cd 56
06460 Saint Maurice 06 158 Gf 86
12380 Saint-Maurice 12 152 Cd 85
12540 Saint-Maurice 12 152 Da 85
17130 Saint-Maurice 17 123 Zd 76
22310 Saint-Maurice 22 63 Wc 57
22320 Saint-Maurice 22 64 Wf 59
22400 Saint-Maurice 22 64 Xc 57
22600 Saint-Maurice 22 64 Xb 60
52200 Saint-Maurice 52 92 Fc 61
56240 Saint-Maurice 56 79 We 61
58300 Saint-Maurice 58 104 Dc 68
58330 Saint-Maurice 58 104 Dd 66
63270 Saint-Maurice 63 128 Db 74
67220 Saint-Maurice 67 60 Hc 59
70700 Saint-Maurice 70 93 Ff 64
79150 Saint-Maurice 79 98 Zc 66
81310 Saint-Maurice 81 151 Bf 86
82130 Saint-Maurice 82 150 Bb 84
54540 Saint-Maurice-aux-Forges 54 77 Gf 57
89190 Saint-Maurice-aux-Riches-Hommes 89 72 Dd 58
25260 Saint-Maurice-Colombier 25 94 Gd 64
39130 Saint-Maurice-Crillat 39 119 Fe 69
07200 Saint-Maurice-d'Ardèche 07 142 Ec 81
01700 Saint-Maurice de Beynost 01 130 Ef 73
30360 Saint-Maurice-de-Cazevieille 30 154 Eb 84
01800 Saint-Maurice-de-Gourdans 01 131 Fb 74
47290 Saint-Maurice-de-Lestapel 47 136 Ad 81
43200 Saint-Maurice-de-Lignon 43 129 Ea 77
01500 Saint-Maurice-de-Rémens 01 119 Fb 73
43810 Saint-Maurice-de-Roche 43 129 Df 77
73240 Saint-Maurice-de-Rotherens 73 131 Fe 75
71260 Saint-Maurice-de-Satonnay 71 118 Ee 70
71460 Saint-Maurice-des-Champs 71 105 Ed 69
16500 Saint-Maurice-des-Lions 16 112 Ae 73
85120 Saint-Maurice-des-Noues 85 98 Zb 69
17500 Saint-Maurice-de-Tavernole 17 123 Zd 76
76330 Saint-Maurice-d'Etelan 76 36 Ad 52
48220 Saint-Maurice-de-Ventalon 48 154 De 83
07170 Saint-Maurice-d'Ibie 07 142 Ec 81
61600 Saint-Maurice-du-Désert 61 67 Zd 57
50270 Saint-Maurice-en-Cotentin 50 33 Yb 52
42240 Saint-Maurice-en-Gourgois 42 129 Eb 76
46120 Saint-Maurice-en-Quercy 46 138 Bf 80
71620 Saint-Maurice-en-Rivière 71 106 Fa 67
38930 Saint-Maurice-en-Trièves 38 144 Fe 80
05800 Saint-Maurice-en-Valgodemard 05 144 Ga 80
86160 Saint-Maurice-la-Clouère 86 112 Ac 70
23300 Saint-Maurice-la-Souterraine 23 113 Bc 71
85390 Saint-Maurice-le-Girard 85 98 Zb 69
87800 Saint-Maurice-les-Brousses 87 125 Bb 74
61190 Saint-Maurice-lès-Charencey 61 49 Ae 57
71740 Saint-Maurice-lès-Châteauneuf 71 117 Eb 71
71490 Saint-Maurice-lès-Couches 71 105 Ed 67
89110 Saint-Maurice-le-Vieil 89 89 Dc 62
38550 Saint-Maurice-L'Exil 38 130 Ee 76
91530 Saint-Maurice-Montcouronne 91 71 Ca 57
34190 Saint-Maurice-Navacelles 34 153 Dd 85
23260 Saint-Maurice-près-Crocq 23 127 Cb 73
63330 Saint-Maurice-près-Pionsat 63 115 Cd 72
28240 Saint-Maurice-Saint-Germain 28 69 Ba 58
55210 Saint-Maurice-sous-les-Côtes 55 55 Fe 54
40270 Saint-Maurice-sur-Adur 40 147 Zd 86
45230 Saint-Maurice-sur-Aveyron 45 88 Cf 61
69440 Saint-Maurice-sur-Dargoire 69M 130 Ed 75
26110 Saint-Maurice-sur-Eygues 26 155 Fa 83
45700 Saint-Maurice-sur-Fessard 45 71 Cd 61
61110 Saint-Maurice-sur-Huisne 61 69 Ae 58
42155 Saint-Maurice-sur-Loire 42 117 Ea 73
88700 Saint-Maurice-sur-Mortagne 88 77 Gd 58
88560 Saint-Maurice-sur-Moselle 88 94 Ge 61
21610 Saint-Maurice-sur-Vingeanne 21 92 Fc 63
89110 Saint-Maurice-Thizouaille 89 89 Dc 62
47270 Saint-Maurin 47 149 Af 83
83560 Saint-Maurin 83 171 Fe 87
28800 Saint-Maur-sur-le-Loir 28 70 Bc 60
54130 Saint Max 54 56 Gb 56
80140 Saint-Maxent 80 38 Be 48
30700 Saint-Maximin 30 154 Ec 85
38530 Saint-Maximin 38 132 Ga 76
60740 Saint-Maximin 60 51 Cc 53
83470 Saint-Maximin-la-Sainte-Baume 83 171 Ff 88
79410 Saint-Maxire 79 110 Zd 70
26510 Saint-May 26 156 Fb 82
22320 Saint-Mayeux 22 64 Wf 59
24380 Saint-Mayme-de-Péreyrol 24 136 Ad 78
87130 Saint-Méard 87 125 Bd 74
24600 Saint-Méard-de-Drône 24 124 Ac 77
24610 Saint-Méard-de-Gurçon 24 136 Ab 79
16300 Saint-Médard 16 123 Zf 75
17500 Saint-Médard 17 123 Zd 76
31360 Saint-Médard 31 163 Ae 90
32300 Saint-Médard 32 163 Ac 88
36700 Saint-Médard 36 101 Bb 67
46150 Saint-Médard 46 137 Bb 81
47130 Saint-Médard 47 148 Ac 83
47130 Saint-Médard 47 149 Ad 82
57260 Saint-Médard 57 57 Gd 56
64370 Saint-Médard 64 161 Zc 87
79370 Saint-Médard 79 111 Ze 71
17220 Saint-Médard-d'Aunis 17 110 Za 72
33230 Saint-Médard-de-Guizières 33 135 Zf 78
24400 Saint-Médard-de-Mussidan 24 136 Ac 78
46400 Saint-Médard-de-Presque 46 138 Bf 79
24160 Saint-Médard-d'Excideuil 24 125 Ba 76
33650 Saint-Médard-d'Eyrans 33 135 Zc 80
42330 Saint-Médard-en-Foerz 42 129 Eb 75
33160 Saint Médard-en-Jalles 33 134 Zb 79
23200 Saint-Médard-la-Rochette 23 114 Ca 72
46210 Saint-Médard-Nicourby 46 138 Ca 80
35250 Saint-Médard-sur-Ille 35 65 Yc 59
16170 Saint-Médart 16 123 Zf 73
12360 Saint-Méen 12 166 Cf 86
29260 Saint-Méen 29 62 Ve 57
56380 Saint-Méen 56 81 Xe 61
35290 Saint-Méen-le-Grand 35 65 Xe 59
40310 Saint Meille 40 148 Aa 84
35220 Saint-Melaine 35 66 Yd 60
49610 Saint-Melaine-sur-Aubance 49 83 Zd 64
07260 Saint-Mélany 07 141 Ea 81
22980 Saint-Méloir 22 65 Xe 58
35350 Saint-Meloir-des-Ondes 35 65 Ya 57
16720 Saint-Même-les-Carrières 16 123 Zf 75
44270 Saint-Même-le-Tenu 44 96 Yb 66
51000 Saint-Memmie 51 54 Ec 55
51460 Saint-Memmie 51 54 Ed 55
88170 Saint-Menge 88 76 Ff 59
08200 Saint-Menges 08 42 Ef 50
03210 Saint-Menoux 03 103 Da 69
19320 Saint-Merd-de-Lapleau 19 126 Ca 77
23100 Saint-Merd-la-Breuille 23 127 Cc 74
19170 Saint-Merd-les-Oussines 19 126 Ca 75
56300 Saint-Mérec 56 79 Xa 60
77720 Saint-Méry 77 72 Ce 57
27370 Saint-Meslin-du-Bosc 27 49 Af 53
77410 Saint-Mesmes 77 51 Ce 55
10280 Saint-Mesmin 10 73 Df 58
21540 Saint-Mesmin 21 91 Ed 64
24270 Saint-Mesmin 24 125 Bb 76
85700 Saint-Mesmin 85 98 Zb 68
19330 Saint-Mexant 19 126 Bd 77
32700 Saint-Mézard 32 149 Ad 84
35500 Saint-M'Hervé 35 66 Yf 59
35360 Saint-M'Hervon 35 65 Xf 59
71460 Saint-Micaud 71 105 Ed 68
02830 Saint-Michel 02 41 Ea 49
09100 Saint-Michel 09 164 Bd 90
12100 Saint-Michel 12 152 Da 84
22110 Saint-Michel 22 79 Wd 59
29880 Saint-Michel 29 61 Vc 57
31220 Saint Michel 31 164 Ba 89
32300 Saint-Michel 32 163 Ac 88
34520 Saint-Michel 34 153 Dc 85
37290 Saint-Michel 37 100 Af 67
38650 Saint-Michel 38 144 Fd 79
40550 Saint-Michel 40 146 Ye 85
45340 Saint-Michel 45 71 Cc 60
46090 Saint-Michel 46 138 Bd 81
52190 Saint-Michel 52 92 Fb 62
64220 Saint-Michel 64 160 Ye 90
82340 Saint-Michel 82 149 Af 84
44730 Saint-Michel-Chef-Chef 44 96 Xf 65
07160 Saint-Michel-d'Aurence 07 142 Ec 79
46110 Saint-Michel-de-Bannières 46 138 Be 79
33840 Saint-Michel-de-Castelnau 33 148 Zf 83
07360 Saint-Michel-de-Chabrillanoux 07 142 Ed 79
05260 Saint-Michel-de-Chaillol 05 144 Gb 80
72440 Saint-Michel-de-Chavaignes 72 68 Ad 60
48160 Saint-Michel-de-Dèze 48 154 Df 83
24400 Saint-Michel-de-Double 24 136 Ab 78
53290 Saint-Michel-de-Feins 53 83 Zc 62
33126 Saint Michel-de-Fronsac 33 135 Ze 79
12400 Saint-Michel-de-Landesque 12 152 Ce 85
11410 Saint-Michel-de-Lanès 11 165 Be 89
50490 Saint-Michel-de-la-Pierre 50 33 Yd 54
33190 Saint-Michel-de-Lapujade 33 135 Aa 81
53350 Saint-Michel-de-la-Roë 53 83 Yf 61
81530 Saint-Michel-de-Léon 81 151 Cc 86
14140 Saint-Michel-de-Livet 14 48 Aa 54
66130 Saint-Michel-de-Llotes 66 179 Cd 93
73140 Saint-Michel-de-Maurienne 73 133 Gc 77
24230 Saint-Michel-de-Montaigne 24 135 Aa 79
50670 Saint-Michel-de-Montjoie 50 46 Yf 56
22980 Saint-Michel-de-Plélan 22 65 Xe 58
33720 Saint-Michel-de-Rieufret 33 135 Zd 81
24490 Saint-Michel-de-Rivière 24 135 Zf 78
12230 Saint-Michel-de-Rouviac 12 153 Db 84
38590 Saint-Michel-de-Saint-Geoirs 38 131 Fc 77
83920 Saint-Michel-d'Esclans 83 172 Gd 87
50610 Saint-Michel-des-Loups 50 46 Yc 56
30200 Saint-Michel-d'Euzet 30 155 Ed 83
81140 Saint-Michel-de-Vax 81 150 Be 84
23480 Saint-Michel-de-Veisse 23 114 Ca 73
24380 Saint-Michel-de-Villadeix 24 136 Ae 79
18390 Saint-Michel-de-Volangis 18 102 Cc 66
76440 Saint-Michel-d'Halescourt 76 38 Be 51
44522 Saint-Michel-du-Bois 44 83 Yf 64
38350 Saint-Michel-en-Beaumont 38 144 Ff 79
36290 Saint-Michel-en-Brenne 36 100 Ba 68
22300 Saint-Michel-en-Grève 22 63 Wc 56
85580 Saint-Michel-en-L'Herm 85 109 Ye 70
40550 Saint-Michel-Escalus 40 146 Ye 85
49420 Saint-Michel-et-Chanveaux 49 83 Yf 62
81340 Saint-Michel-Labadié 81 151 Cc 84
85200 Saint-Michel-le-Cloucq 85 110 Zb 70
24490 Saint-Michel-l'Ecluse 24 135 Aa 78
61600 Saint-Michel-les-Andaines 61 67 Zd 57
38650 Saint-Michel-les-Portes 38 143 Fd 79
04870 Saint-Michel-l'Observatoire 04 156 Fe 85
46130 Saint-Michel-Loubéjou 46 138 Bf 79
85700 Saint-Michel-Mont-Mercure 85 98 Za 68
62650 Saint-Michel-sous-Bois 62 28 Bf 45
37130 Saint-Michel-sur-Loire 37 85 Ac 65
88470 Saint-Michel-sur-Meurthe 88 77 Gf 59
42410 Saint-Michel-sur-Rhône 42 130 Ee 76
26750 Saint-Michel-sur-Savasse 26 143 Fa 78
62130 Saint-Michel-sur-Ternoise 62 29 Cc 46
61300 Saint-Michel-Tubœuf 61 49 Ae 56
55300 Saint-Mihiel 55 55 Fd 55
13920 Saint-Mitre-les-Remparts 13 170 Fa 88
44350 Saint-Molf 44 81 Xd 64
56300 Saint-Molvan 56 79 Wf 60
59143 Saint-Momelin 59 27 Cb 44
32400 Saint-Mont 32 162 Zf 87
07220 Saint-Montant 07 155 Ed 82
89270 Saint-Moré 89 90 De 63
23400 Saint-Moreil 23 126 Be 73
08400 Saint-Morel 08 54 Ee 52
33650 Saint-Morillon 33 135 Zd 81
38190 Saint-Mury-Monteymond 38 132 Ff 77
63460 Saint-Myon 63 116 Da 73
67530 Saint-Nabor 67 60 Hc 58
88200 Saint-Nabord 88 77 Gd 60
10700 Saint-Nabord-sur-Aube 10 73 Eb 57
17600 Saint-Nadeau 17 122 Za 74
82370 Saint-Nauphary 82 150 Bc 85
30200 Saint-Nazaire 30 155 Ed 83
36800 Saint-Nazaire 36 101 Bb 69
38330 Saint-Nazaire 38 132 Ff 77
44600 Saint-Nazaire 44 81 Xe 65
47410 Saint-Nazaire 47 136 Ac 81
66570 Saint-Nazaire 66 179 Cf 92
11120 Saint-Nazaire-d'Aude 11 167 Cf 89
34490 Saint-Nazaire-de-Ladarez 34 167 Da 87
34400 Saint-Nazaire-de-Pézan 34 168 Ea 87
82190 Saint Nazaire-de-Valentane 82 149 Ba 83
26190 Saint-Nazaire-en-Royans 26 143 Fb 78
26340 Saint-Nazaire-le-Désert 26 143 Fb 81
17780 Saint-Nazaire-sur-Charente 17 110 Yf 73
33490 Saint-Nectaire 33 135 Ze 81
63710 Saint-Nectaire 63 128 Cf 75
24520 Saint-Nexans 24 136 Ad 80
29550 Saint-Nic 29 62 Ve 59
80190 Saint-Nicaise-le-Grand 80 39 Cf 50
22160 Saint-Nicodème 22 63 Wd 58
22220 Saint-Nicolas 22 63 We 56
22450 Saint-Nicolas 22 63 We 56
22960 Saint-Nicolas 22 64 Xb 58
56110 Saint-Nicolas 56 79 Wc 60
62223 Saint-Nicolas 62 30 Ce 47
90110 Saint-Nicolas 90 94 Gf 62
02410 Saint-Nicolas-aux-Bois 02 40 Dc 51
87230 Saint-Nicolas-Courbefy 87 125 Ba 75
76510 Saint-Nicolas-d'Aliermont 76 37 Bb 49
27160 Saint-Nicolas-d'Attez 27 49 Af 56
76940 Saint-Nicolas-de-Bliquetuit 76 36 Ae 51
37140 Saint-Nicolas-de-Bourgueil 37 84 Aa 65
85470 Saint-Nicolas-de-Brem 85 96 Ya 69
47220 Saint-Nicolas-de-la-Balerme 47 149 Ae 84
82210 Saint Nicolas-de-la-Grave 82 149 Ba 84
76490 Saint-Nicolas-de-la-Haie 76 36 Ad 51
76170 Saint-Nicolas-de-la-Taille 76 36 Ac 51
38500 Saint-Nicolas-de-Macherin 38 131 Fd 76
50250 Saint-Nicolas-de-Pierrepont 50 33 Yc 53
54210 Saint-Nicolas-de-Port 54 56 Gb 57
44460 Saint-Nicolas-de-Redon 44 81 Xf 63
03250 Saint-Nicolas-des-Biefs 03 116 De 72
50370 Saint-Nicolas-des-Bois 50 46 Ye 56
61250 Saint-Nicolas-des-Bois 61 68 Aa 58
56930 Saint-Nicolas-des-Eaux 56 79 Wf 61
61550 Saint-Nicolas-des-Laitiers 61 48 Ac 55
37110 Saint-Nicolas-des-Motets 37 86 Ba 63
61550 Saint-Nicolas-de-Sommaire 61 49 Ad 56
74170 Saint-Nicolas-de-Véroce 74 133 Ge 73
27370 Saint-Nicolas-du-Bosc 27 49 Af 53
22480 Saint-Nicolas-du-Pélem 22 63 Wf 59
56910 Saint-Nicolas-du-Tertre 56 81 Xe 62
57700 Saint-Nicolas-en-Forêt 57 43 Ga 53
10400 Saint-Nicolas-la-Chapelle 10 72 Dc 57
73590 Saint-Nicolas-la-Chapelle 73 133 Gc 74
21700 Saint-Nicolas-lès-Cîteaux 21 106 Fa 66
50400 Saint-Nicolas-près-Granville 50 46 Yc 55
38410 Saint-Nizier 38 132 Ff 78
69870 Saint-Nizier-d'Azergues 69D 117 Ec 72
42380 Saint-Nizier-de-Fornas 42 129 Ea 76
38250 Saint-Nizier-du-Moucherotte 38 144 Fd 77
01560 Saint-Nizier-le-Bouchoux 01 118 Fa 70
01320 Saint-Nizier-le-Désert 01 118 Fa 72
42190 Saint-Nizier-sous-Charlieu 42 117 Ea 72
71190 Saint-Nizier-sur-Arroux 71 105 Ea 68
56300 Saint-Nizon 56 79 Wf 60
56250 Saint-Nolff 56 80 Xc 62
78860 Saint-Nom-la-Bretèche 78 51 Ca 55
22480 Saint-Norgant 22 63 We 58
29440 Saint-Oerrien 29 62 Ve 57
73100 Saint-Offenge 73 132 Ga 74
39570 Saint-Oidier 39 106 Fd 68
14220 Saint-Omer 14 47 Zd 55
44130 Saint-Omer 44 82 Ya 64
62500 Saint-Omer 62 27 Cb 44
62162 Saint-Omer-Capelle 62 27 Ca 43
60860 Saint-Omer-en-Chaussée 60 38 Ca 51
38490 Saint Ondras 38 131 Fd 75
35290 Saint-Onen-la-Chapelle 35 65 Xe 59
82200 Saint-Onge 82 149 Bb 84
27680 Saint-Opportune-la-Marne 27 36 Ad 52
23100 Saint-Oradoux-de-Chirouze 23 127 Cb 74
23260 Saint-Oradoux-près-Crocq 23 127 Cc 73
32120 Saint-Orens 32 164 Af 86
31650 Saint-Orens-de-Gameville 31 165 Bd 87
32100 Saint-Orens-Pouy-Petit 32 148 Ac 85
32300 Saint-Ost 32 163 Ac 88
76590 Saint-Ouen 76 37 Ba 50
80610 Saint-Ouen 80 29 Ca 48
85480 Saint-Ouen 85 97 Yf 69
93400 Saint-Ouen 93 51 Cc 55
27160 Saint-Ouen-d'Attez 27 49 Af 56
17230 Saint-Ouen-d'Aunis 17 110 Yf 71
61130 Saint-Ouën-de-la-Cour 61 68 Ad 58
27330 Saint-Ouen-de-Mancelles 27 49 Ad 55
72130 Saint-Ouen-de-Mimbré 72 68 Aa 59
27370 Saint-Ouen-de-Pontcheuil 27 49 Af 53
35140 Saint-Ouen-des-Alleux 35 66 Yd 59
14350 Saint-Ouen-des-Besaces 14 47 Za 54
27680 Saint-Ouen-des-Champs 27 36 Ad 52
61560 Saint-Ouen-de-Sécherouvre 61 68 Ac 57
53410 Saint-Ouën-des-Toits 53 66 Za 60
53150 Saint-Ouën-des-Vallons 53 67 Zc 59
27310 Saint-Ouen-de-Thouberville 27 37 Af 52
51320 Saint-Ouen-Domprot 51 74 Ec 57
76890 Saint-Ouen-du-Breuil 76 37 Ba 51
14670 Saint-Ouen-du-Mesnil-Oger 14 35 Zf 54
27670 Saint-Ouen-du-Tilleul 27 49 Af 53
72220 Saint-Ouen-en-Belin 72 84 Ab 62
77720 Saint-Ouen-en-Brie 77 72 Cf 57
72350 Saint-Ouen-en-Champagne 72 67 Ze 61
35460 Saint-Ouen-la-Rouërie 35 66 Yd 58
95310 Saint-Ouen-l'Aumône 95 51 Ca 54
61410 Saint-Ouen-le-Brisoult 61 67 Zd 57
14140 Saint-Ouen-le-Houx 14 48 Ab 55
76730 Saint-Ouen-le-Mauger 76 37 Af 50
14340 Saint-Ouen-le-Pin 14 35 Aa 54
88140 Saint-Ouen-lès-Parey 88 76 Fe 59
37530 Saint-Ouen-les-Vignes 37 86 Af 64
28260 Saint-Ouen-Marchefroy 28 50 Bd 55
76630 Saint-Ouen-sous-Bailly 76 37 Bb 49
87300 Saint-Ouen-sur-Gartempe 87 113 Ba 72
61300 Saint-Ouen-sur-Iton 61 49 Ae 56
58160 Saint-Ouen-sur-Loire 58 103 Db 67
61150 Saint-Ouen-sur-Maire 61 48 Ze 56
77750 Saint-Ouen-sur-Morin 77 52 Db 55
10170 Saint-Oulph 10 73 Df 57
47600 Saint-Ourens 47 148 Ac 84
04530 Saint-Ours 04 145 Ge 82
04530 Saint Ours 04 145 Ge 82
63230 Saint-Ours 63 127 Cf 73
73410 Saint-Ours 73 132 Ff 74
18310 Saint-Outrille 18 101 Be 66
50300 Saint-Ovin 50 46 Ye 56
73260 Saint-Oyen 73 133 Gc 75
71260 Saint-Oyen-Montbellet 71 118 Ef 70
22430 Saint-Pabu 22 64 Xd 57
29830 Saint-Pabu 29 61 Vc 57
76480 Saint-Paër 76 37 Af 51
14670 Saint-Pair 14 48 Ze 53
14340 Saint-Pair-du-Mont 14 35 Aa 54
50380 Saint-Pair-sur-Mer 50 46 Yc 56
03370 Saint-Palais 03 114 Cb 70
18110 Saint-Palais 18 102 Cc 65
33820 Saint Palais 33 122 Zc 77
64120 Saint-Palais 64 161 Yf 89
17210 Saint-Palais-de-Négrignac 17 123 Ze 77
17800 Saint-Palais-de-Phiolin 17 122 Zc 75
16300 Saint-Palais-du-Né 16 123 Ze 75
17420 Saint-Palais-sur-Mer 17 122 Yf 75
46110 Saint-Palavy 46 138 Bd 78
43620 Saint-Pal-de-Mons 43 129 Eb 77
43160 Saint-Pal-de-Senouire 43 128 Dd 77
04150 Saint-Pancrace 04 156 Fd 84
24530 Saint Pancrace 24 124 Ae 76
73300 Saint-Pancrace 73 132 Gb 77
11330 Saint-Pancrasse 11 178 Cc 91
38660 Saint-Pancrasse 38 132 Ff 77
54730 Saint-Pancré 54 43 Fd 51
40180 Saint-Pandelon 40 161 Yf 86
46800 Saint-Pantaléon 46 150 Bb 82
71400 Saint-Pantaléon 71 105 Eb 67
84220 Saint-Pantaléon 84 156 Fb 85
19160 Saint-Pantaléon-de-Lapleau 19 126 Cb 77
19600 Saint-Pantaléon-de-Larche 19 137 Bc 78
26770 Saint-Pantaléon-les-Vignes 26 155 Fa 82
24640 Saint-Pantaly-d'Ans 24 125 Af 77
11400 Saint-Papoul 11 165 Ca 89
33870 Saint-Pardon 33 135 Ze 79
33210 Saint-Pardon-de-Comques 33 135 Ze 81
17400 Saint-Pardoult 17 111 Zd 73
23110 Saint-Pardoux 23 114 Cc 72
63440 Saint-Pardoux 63 115 Da 72
63680 Saint-Pardoux 63 127 Ce 75
79310 Saint-Pardoux 79 98 Ze 69
87250 Saint-Pardoux 87 113 Bb 72
47410 Saint Pardoux-Bourgougnague 47 136 Ac 81
19210 Saint-Pardoux-Corbier 19 125 Bc 76
23260 Saint-Pardoux-d'Arnet 23 114 Cc 73
24600 Saint-Pardoux-de-Drône 24 124 Ac 77
47200 Saint-Pardoux-du-Breuil 47 136 Ab 82
24170 Saint-Pardoux-et-Vielvic 24 137 Af 80
47800 Saint-Pardoux-Isaac 47 136 Ac 81
19320 Saint-Pardoux-la-Croisille 19 126 Bf 77
24470 Saint-Pardoux-la-Rivière 24 124 Ae 76

318 | Saint-Martin-sur-Arve

19200 Saint-Pardoux-le-Neuf 19 127 Cb 75
23200 Saint-Pardoux-le-Neuf 23 114 Cb 73
23150 Saint-Pardoux-les-Cards 23 114 Ca 72
19200 Saint-Pardoux-le-Vieux 19 127 Cb 75
19270 Saint-Pardoux-L'Ortigier 19 126 Bd 77
23400 Saint-Pardoux-Morterolles 23 114 Be 73
34230 Saint-Pargoire 34 167 Dd 87
58300 Saint-Parize-en-Viry 58 103 Dc 68
58490 Saint-Parize-le-Châtel 58 103 Db 67
10410 Saint-Parres-aux-Tertres 10 73 Ea 59
10260 Saint-Parres-lès-Vaudes 10 73 Eb 59
12300 Saint-Parthem 12 139 Cb 81
47290 Saint-Pastour 47 136 Ad 82
83340 Saint Pastour 83 172 Gb 88
65400 Saint-Pastous 65 175 Zf 90
31350 Saint-Patatin 31 163 Ae 89
72610 Saint-Paterne-Le Chevain 72 68 Aa 58
37370 Saint-Paterne-Racan 37 85 Ac 63
77178 Saint-Pathus 77 52 Ce 54
37130 Saint-Patrice 37 85 Ab 65
50190 Saint-Patrice-de-Claids 50 33 Yd 53
61600 Saint-Patrice-du-Désert 61 67 Ze 57
04530 Saint-Paul 04 145 Ge 81
06570 Saint-Paul 06 173 Ha 86
19150 Saint-Paul 19 126 Bf 77
22470 Saint-Paul 22 63 Xa 56
31550 Saint-Paul 31 164 Bc 89
33390 Saint-Paul 33 135 Zc 78
60650 Saint-Paul 60 38 Ca 52
61100 Saint-Paul 61 47 Zc 56
65150 Saint-Paul 65 163 Ac 90
73170 Saint-Paul 73 132 Fe 74
76580 Saint-Paul 76 37 Ae 52
81360 Saint-Paul 81 151 Cc 86
81530 Saint-Paul 81 151 Cd 86
84750 Saint-Paul 84 156 Fd 85
87260 Saint-Paul 87 125 Bc 74
88170 Saint-Paul 88 76 Ff 59
03110 Saint-Paul, les 03 116 Db 71
02300 Saint-Paul-aux-Bois 02 40 Db 51
81220 Saint-Paul-Cap-de-Joux 81 165 Bf 87
32190 Saint-Paul-de-Baïse 32 148 Ac 86
82390 Saint-Paul-de-Burgues 82 149 Bb 83
66220 Saint-Paul-de-Fenouillet 66 178 Cd 92
27800 Saint-Paul-de-Fourques 27 49 Ae 53
09000 Saint-Paul-de-Jarrat 09 177 Bd 91
81140 Saint-Paul-de-Mamiac 81 150 Be 84
15140 Saint-Paul-de-Salers 15 139 Cd 78
24380 Saint-Paul-de-Serre 24 136 Ad 78
12250 Saint-Paul-des-Fonts 12 152 Da 85
15250 Saint-Paul-des-Landes 15 139 Cb 79
82400 Saint-Paul-d'Espis 82 149 Af 84
43420 Saint-Paul-de-Tartas 43 141 Df 80
01240 Saint-Paul-de-Varax 01 118 Fa 72
38760 Saint-Paul-de-Varces 38 144 Fd 78
46400 Saint-Paul-de-Vern 46 138 Bf 79
42590 Saint-Paul-de-Vézelin 42 129 Ea 73
38140 Saint-Paul-d'Izeaux 38 131 Fc 77
31110 Saint-Paul-d'Oueil 31 176 Ad 91
49310 Saint-Paul-du-Bois 49 98 Zc 66
14490 Saint-Paul-du-Vernay 14 34 Zb 53
42600 Saint-Paul-d'Uzore 42 129 Ea 74
40200 Saint-Paul-en-Born 40 146 Yf 83
74500 Saint-Paul-en-Chablais 74 120 Gd 70
83440 Saint-Paul-en-Forêt 83 172 Ge 87
79240 Saint-Paul-en-Gâtine 79 98 Zc 69
42740 Saint-Paul-en-Jarez 42 130 Ed 76
85500 Saint-Paul-en-Pareds 85 97 Za 68
11320 Saint-Paulet 11 165 Bf 88
30130 Saint-Paulet-de-Caisson 30 155 Ed 83
09000 Saint-Paulet-de-Jarrat 09 177 Bd 91
34570 Saint-Paul-et-Valmalle 34 168 De 87
46170 Saint-Paul-Flaugnac 46 150 Bc 83
43350 Saint-Paulien 43 141 De 78
30480 Saint-Paul-la-Coste 30 154 Df 84
24800 Saint-Paul-la-Roche 24 125 Ba 76
48600 Saint-Paul-le-Froid 48 141 Dd 80
72130 Saint-Paul-le-Gaultier 72 67 Zf 59
07460 Saint-Paul-le-Jeune 07 154 Ea 82
40990 Saint-Paul-lès-Dax 40 161 Yf 86
13115 Saint-Paul-lès-Durance 13 171 Fe 86
30330 Saint-Paul-les-Font 30 155 Ed 84
26750 Saint-Paul-les-Romans 26 143 Fa 78
24320 Saint-Paul-Lizonne 24 124 Ab 77
85670 Saint-Paul-Mont-Penit 85 97 Yc 68
73730 Saint-Paul-sur-Isère 73 132 Gc 75
59430 Saint-Paul-sur-Mer 59 27 Cc 42
27500 Saint-Paul-sur-Risle 27 49 Ad 52
31530 Saint-Paul-sur-Save 31 164 Bb 86
26130 Saint-Paul-Trois-Châteaux 26 155 Ee 82
04270 Saint Paulus 04 157 Gb 85
72190 Saint-Pavace 72 68 Ab 60
31480 Saint-Pé 31 164 Ba 86
32190 Saint-Pé 32 163 Ab 86
31510 Saint-Pé-d'Ardet 31 176 Ae 91
65270 Saint-Pé-de-Bigorre 65 162 Zf 90
31350 Saint-Pé-Delbosc 31 163 Ae 89
64270 Saint-Pé-de-Léren 64 161 Yf 88
64400 Saint-Pée-d'en-Bas 64 161 Zb 89
64400 Saint-Pée-d'en-Haut 64 161 Zb 89
64310 Saint-Pée-sur-Nivelle 64 160 Yc 88
28290 Saint-Pellerin 28 69 Ba 60
50500 Saint-Pellerin 50 46 Ye 53
35380 Saint-Péran 35 65 Xf 60
58270 Saint-Péraville 58 103 Db 66
45480 Saint-Péravy-Epreux 45 70 Bf 59
45310 Saint-Péravy-la-Colombe 45 70 Be 60
07130 Saint-Péray 07 142 Ef 79
40090 Saint Perdon 40 147 Zc 85
24560 Saint-Perdoux 24 136 Ad 80
46100 Saint-Perdoux 46 138 Ca 80
35430 Saint-Père 35 65 Ya 57
58200 Saint-Père 58 88 Cf 64
89450 Saint-Père 89 90 De 64
44320 Saint-Père-eb-Retz 44 96 Xf 65
45600 Saint-Père-sur-Loire 45 88 Cc 62
58110 Saint-Péreuse 58 104 De 66
35190 Saint-Pern 35 65 Ya 59
56350 Saint-Perreux 56 81 Xf 62
47170 Saint-Pé-Saint-Simon 47 148 Aa 84
22720 Saint-Péver 22 63 Wf 58
33330 Saint-Pey-d'Armens 33 135 Zf 79
33350 Saint-Pey-de-Castets 33 135 Zf 80
82160 Saint-Peyronis 82 150 Be 83
10130 Saint-Phal 10 73 Ea 60
36110 Saint-Phalier 36 101 Bd 67
37340 Saint-Philbert 37 84 Aa 64
85660 Saint-Philbert-de-Bouaine 85 97 Yc 67
44310 Saint-Philbert-de-Grand-Lieu 44 97 Yc 66
14130 Saint-Philbert-des-Champs 14 48 Ab 53
49160 Saint-Philbert-du-Peuple 49 84 Zf 64
85110 Saint-Philbert-du-Pont-Charrault 85 97 Za 69
49600 Saint-Philbert-en-Mauges 49 97 Yf 66
61430 Saint-Philbert-sur-Orne 61 47 Zd 55
27290 Saint-Philbert-sur-Risle 27 49 Ad 53
14130 Saint-Philibert 14 36 Aa 52
21220 Saint-Philibert 21 106 Fa 65
29910 Saint-Philibert 29 78 Wb 62
56470 Saint-Philibert 56 79 Wf 63
73670 Saint Philibert 73 132 Ff 76
33350 Saint-Philippe-d'Aiguille 33 135 Zf 79
33220 Saint-Philippe-du-Seignal 33 136 Ab 80
22100 Saint-Piat 22 65 Ya 58
28130 Saint-Piat 28 70 Bd 57
02140 Saint-Pierre 02 41 De 50
04300 Saint-Pierre 04 157 Ff 85
04420 Saint-Pierre 04 157 Gc 83
06260 Saint-Pierre 06 158 Gf 85
09140 Saint-Pierre 09 177 Bb 91
12400 Saint-Pierre 12 152 Ce 85
14250 Saint-Pierre 14 34 Zc 53
15350 Saint-Pierre 15 127 Cc 76
26340 Saint-Pierre 26 143 Fb 80
31590 Saint-Pierre 31 165 Bd 87
32430 Saint-Pierre 32 149 Af 86
38850 Saint-Pierre 38 131 Fd 76
39150 Saint-Pierre 39 120 Ff 69
47270 Saint-Pierre 47 149 Af 83
51510 Saint-Pierre 51 54 Eb 55
56740 Saint-Pierre 56 80 Wf 63
59219 Saint-Pierre 59 31 Df 48
62380 Saint-Pierre 62 29 Ca 44
67140 Saint-Pierre 67 60 Hc 58
81390 Saint-Pierre 81 151 Bf 86
82300 Saint-Pierre 82 150 Bd 83
83560 Saint-Pierre 83 171 Ff 86
84600 Saint-Pierre 84 155 Fa 82
08310 Saint-Pierre-à-Arnes 08 54 Ec 53
79290 Saint-Pierre-à-Champ 79 98 Zd 66
02600 Saint-Pierre-Aigle 02 40 Db 53
05300 Saint-Pierre-Avez 05 156 Fe 83
14950 Saint-Pierre-Azif 14 35 Aa 53
23460 Saint-Pierre-Bellevue 23 114 Bf 73
76890 Saint-Pierre-Bénouville 76 37 Af 50
67220 Saint-Pierre-Bois 67 60 Hc 59
59630 Saint-Pierre-Brouck 59 27 Cb 43
14700 Saint-Pierre-Canivet 14 48 Ze 55
23430 Saint-Pierre-Chérignat 23 113 Bd 73
63320 Saint-Pierre-Colamine 63 128 Cf 75
73250 Saint-Pierre-d'Albigny 73 132 Ga 75
73170 Saint-Pierre-d'Alvey 73 131 Fe 75
17700 Saint-Pierre-d'Amilly 17 110 Zb 71
05140 Saint-Pierre-d'Argençon 05 144 Fe 81
50270 Saint-Pierre-d'Arthéglise 50 33 Yb 52
32290 Saint-Pierre-d'Aubézies 32 163 Aa 87
33490 Saint-Pierre-d'Aurillac 33 135 Ze 81
27950 Saint-Pierre-d'Autils 27 50 Bc 54
38830 Saint-Pierre-d'Avellard 38 132 Ga 76
27920 Saint-Pierre-de-Bailleul 27 50 Bc 54
33760 Saint Pierre-de-Bat 33 135 Ze 80
73220 Saint-Pierre-de-Belleville 73 132 Gb 76
12400 Saint-Pierre-de-Bétirac 12 152 Ce 85
42520 Saint-Pierre-de-Bœuf 42 130 Ee 76
38870 Saint-Pierre-de-Bressieux 38 131 Fb 77
47160 Saint Pierre-de-Buzet 47 148 Ab 83
47380 Saint-Pierre-de-Caubel 47 136 Ad 82
27390 Saint-Pierre-de-Cernières 27 49 Ad 55
69780 Saint-Pierre-de-Chandieu 69M 130 Fa 75
38380 Saint-Pierre-de-Chartreuse 38 132 Fe 76
38160 Saint-Pierre-de-Chérennes 38 143 Fc 78
72500 Saint-Pierre-de-Chevillé 72 85 Ac 63
24330 Saint-Pierre-de-Chignac 24 137 Af 78
47270 Saint-Pierre-de-Clairac 47 149 Ae 83
24800 Saint-Pierre-de-Côle 24 124 Ae 76
07450 Saint-Pierre-de-Colombier 07 142 Eb 80
81330 Saint-Pierre-de-Combejac 81 152 Cd 86
38450 Saint-Pierre-de-Commiers 38 144 Fe 78
27260 Saint-Pierre-de-Cormeilles 27 48 Ac 53
73310 Saint-Pierre-de-Curtille 73 132 Fe 74
24450 Saint-Pierre-de-Frugie 24 125 Ba 75
23290 Saint-Pierre-de-Fursac 23 113 Bd 72
73360 Saint-Pierre-de-Genebroz 73 131 Fe 76
36260 Saint-Pierre-de-Jards 36 102 Bf 66
17400 Saint-Pierre-de-Juillers 17 111 Zd 73
34520 Saint-Pierre-de-la-Fage 34 153 Dc 86
31570 Saint-Pierre-de-Lages 31 165 Bd 87
66210 Saint-Pierre-dels-Forcats 66 178 Ca 94
86260 Saint-Pierre-de-Maille 86 100 Af 68
14290 Saint-Pierre-de-Mailloc 14 48 Ab 54
76113 Saint-Pierre-de-Manneville 76 37 Af 52
38350 Saint-Pierre-de-Méaroz 38 144 Fe 79
81170 Saint-Pierre-de-Mercens 81 151 Bf 84
82190 Saint-Pierre-de-Nazac 82 149 Ba 83
48340 Saint-Pierre-de-Nogaret 48 140 Da 82
61800 Saint-Pierre-d'Entremont 61 47 Zc 56
73670 Saint-Pierre-d'Entremont 73 132 Ff 76
35720 Saint-Pierre-de-Plesguen 35 65 Ya 58
09000 Saint-Pierre-de-Rivière 09 177 Bd 91
27800 Saint-Pierre-de-Salerne 27 49 Ad 53
72430 Saint-Pierre-des-Bois 72 67 Zf 61
12360 Saint-Pierre-des-Cats 12 167 Cf 86
11220 Saint-Pierre-des-Champs 11 179 Cd 90
37700 Saint-Pierre-des-Corps 37 85 Ae 64
79700 Saint-Pierre-des-Echaubrognes 79 98 Zb 67
50810 Saint-Pierre-de-Semilly 50 47 Yf 54
27370 Saint-Pierre-des-Fleurs 27 49 Af 53
14100 Saint-Pierre-des-Ifs 14 35 Ab 54
27450 Saint-Pierre-des-Ifs 27 49 Ad 53
76660 Saint-Pierre-des-Jonquières 76 37 Bc 49
53500 Saint-Pierre-des-Landes 53 66 Yf 59
53370 Saint-Pierre-des-Nids 53 67 Zf 58
61550 Saint-Pierre-des-Sommaire 61 49 Ad 56
72600 Saint-Pierre-des-Ormes 72 68 Ac 59
73800 Saint-Pierre-de-Soucy 73 132 Ga 76
48150 Saint-Pierre-des-Tripiers 48 153 Db 83
83690 Saint-Pierre-de-Tourtour 83 172 Gc 87
81330 Saint-Pierre-de-Trivisy 81 151 Cc 86
76480 Saint-Pierre-de-Varengeville 76 37 Af 51
71670 Saint-Pierre-de-Varennes 71 105 Ed 67
84330 Saint-Pierre-de-Vassols 84 156 Fa 84
86400 Saint-Pierre-d'Exideuil 86 112 Ab 72
24130 Saint-Pierre-d'Eyraud 24 136 Ab 79
64990 Saint-Pierre-d'Irube 64 160 Yd 88
17310 Saint-Pierre-d'Oléron 17 109 Ye 73
27370 Saint-Pierre-du-Bosguérard 27 49 Af 53
14700 Saint-Pierre-du-Bû 14 48 Ze 55
43810 Saint-Pierre-du-Champ 43 129 Df 77
85120 Saint-Pierre-du-Chemin 85 98 Zb 68
14260 Saint-Pierre-du-Fresne 14 47 Zb 54
14670 Saint-Pierre-du-Jonquet 14 35 Zf 53
72150 Saint-Pierre-du-Lorouër 72 85 Ad 62
27330 Saint-Pierre-du-Mesnil 27 49 Ad 55
14450 Saint-Pierre-du-Mont 14 47 Za 52
58210 Saint-Pierre-du-Mont 58 89 Dc 64
17270 Saint-Pierre-du-Palais 17 135 Zf 77
91280 Saint-Pierre-du-Perray 91 71 Cd 57
61790 Saint-Pierre-du-Regard 61 47 Zc 55
50800 Saint-Pierre-du-Tronchet 50 46 Ye 56
27210 Saint-Pierre-du-Val 27 36 Ac 52
27100 Saint-Pierre-du-Vauvray 27 49 Bb 53
50330 Saint-Pierre-Église 50 33 Yd 50
14170 Saint-Pierre-en-Auge 14 48 Zf 55
74800 Saint-Pierre-en-Faucigny 74 120 Gc 72
76540 Saint-Pierre-en-Port 76 36 Ac 50
76260 Saint-Pierre-en-Val 76 37 Bc 48
21230 Saint-Pierre-en-Vaux 21 105 Ed 66
49350 Saint-Pierre-en-Vaux 49 84 Ze 64
60850 Saint-Pierre-ès-Champs 60 38 Be 52
43260 Saint-Pierre-Eynac 43 141 Ea 78
53410 Saint-Pierre-la-Cour 53 66 Yf 60
63480 Saint-Pierre-la-Bourlhonne 63 129 De 74
61110 Saint-Pierre-la-Bruyère 61 69 Ae 58
46090 Saint-Pierre-Lafeuille 46 137 Bc 81
27600 Saint-Pierre-la-Garenne 27 50 Bc 54
50530 Saint-Pierre-Langers 50 46 Yd 56
42190 Saint-Pierre-la-Noaille 42 117 Ea 71
69210 Saint-Pierre-la-Palud 69M 130 Ed 74
61310 Saint-Pierre-la-Rivière 61 48 Ab 56
07400 Saint-Pierre-la-Roche 07 142 Ed 81
42620 Saint-Pierre-Laval 42 116 De 71
14770 Saint-Pierre-la-Vieille 14 47 Zc 55
76640 Saint-Pierre-Lavis 76 36 Ad 51
23600 Saint-Pierre-le-Bost 23 114 Cb 70
63230 Saint-Pierre-le-Chastel 63 127 Cf 74
07140 Saint-Pierre-le-Déchausselat 07 141 Ea 82
58240 Saint-Pierre-le-Moutier 58 103 Da 68
53000 Saint-Pierre-le-Potier 53 67 Zb 60
60350 Saint-Pierre-lès-Bitry 60 40 Da 52
18170 Saint-Pierre-les-Bois 18 102 Cb 69
76320 Saint-Pierre-lès-Elbeuf 76 49 Ba 53
18210 Saint-Pierre-les-Etieux 18 102 Cd 68
77140 Saint-Pierre-lès-Nemours 77 71 Ce 59
71520 Saint-Pierre-le-Vieux 71 117 Ed 71
76740 Saint-Pierre-le-Vieux 76 37 Af 49
85420 Saint-Pierre-le-Vieux 85 110 Zb 70
76740 Saint-Pierre-le-Viger 76 37 Af 50
82160 Saint-Pierre-Livron 82 150 Be 83
02250 Saint-Pierremont 02 41 Df 50
08240 Saint-Pierremont 08 42 Ef 52
88700 Saint-Pierremont 88 77 Gd 58
49110 Saint-Pierre-Montlimart 49 83 Yf 65
56510 Saint-Pierre-Quiberon 56 79 Wf 63
63210 Saint-Pierre-Roche 63 127 Ce 74
14170 Saint-Pierre-sur-Dives 14 48 Zf 54
07520 Saint-Pierre-sur-Doux 07 142 Ec 78
47120 Saint-Pierre-sur-Dropt 47 136 Ab 81
53270 Saint-Pierre-sur-Erve 53 67 Zd 60
11560 Saint-Pierre-sur-Mer 11 167 Db 89
53160 Saint-Pierre-sur-Orthe 53 67 Ze 59
08430 Saint-Pierre-sur-Vence 08 42 Ee 50
14350 Saint-Pierre-Tarentaine 14 47 Zb 55
46160 Saint-Pierre-Toirac 46 138 Bf 81
07190 Saint-Pierreville 07 142 Ec 80
55230 Saint-Pierrevillers 55 43 Fe 52
03160 Saint-Plaisir 03 103 Cf 69
31580 Saint-Plancard 31 163 Ad 89
50400 Saint-Planchers 50 46 Yc 56
36190 Saint-Plantaire 36 113 Be 70
71520 Saint-Point 71 118 Ed 70
25160 Saint-Point-Lac 25 108 Gb 68
50670 Saint-Pois 50 46 Yf 56
53540 Saint-Poix 53 66 Yf 61
29250 Saint-Pol-de-Léon 29 62 Wa 56
42260 Saint-Polgues 42 117 Df 73
62130 Saint-Pol-sur-Ternoise 62 29 Cc 46
11300 Saint-Polycarpe 11 178 Cb 90
79160 Saint-Pompain 79 110 Zc 70
24170 Saint-Pompont 24 137 Ba 80
15500 Saint-Poncy 15 128 Db 78
04140 Saint-Pons 04 157 Gc 82
04400 Saint-Pons 04 158 Gd 82
06620 Saint Pons 06 158 Gf 84
07580 Saint-Pons 07 142 Ed 81
26110 Saint-Pons 26 155 Fb 82
34230 Saint-Pons-de-Mauchiens 34 167 Dd 87
34220 Saint-Pons-de-Thomières 34 166 Ce 88
30330 Saint-Pons-la-Calm 30 155 Ed 84
03110 Saint-Pont 03 116 Db 72
17250 Saint-Porchaire 17 122 Zb 74
79300 Saint-Porchaire 79 98 Zd 67
82700 Saint-Porquier 82 149 Bb 84
22550 Saint-Pôtan 22 64 Xe 57
10120 Saint-Pouange 10 73 Ea 59
03230 Saint-Pourçain-Malchère 03 116 Dd 69
03290 Saint-Pourçain-sur-Besbre 03 116 Dd 70
03500 Saint-Pourçain-sur-Sioule 03 116 Db 71
88500 Saint Prancher 88 76 Ff 58
88420 Saint-Prayel 88 77 Gf 58
43230 Saint-Préjet-Armandon 43 128 Dd 77
43580 Saint-Préjet-d'Allier 43 141 Dd 79
28300 Saint-Prest 28 70 Bd 58
16130 Saint Preuil 16 123 Ze 75
07000 Saint-Priest 07 142 Ed 80
23110 Saint-Priest 23 114 Cc 72
42560 Saint-Priest 42 129 Ea 75
63600 Saint-Priest 63 129 De 76
69800 Saint-Priest 69M 130 Ef 74
63310 Saint-Priest-Bramefant 63 116 Dc 72
03800 Saint-Priest-d'Andelot 03 116 Db 72
19800 Saint-Priest-de-Gimel 19 126 Bf 77
63640 Saint-Priest-des-Champs 63 115 Ce 73
42270 Saint-Priest-en-Jarrez 42 130 Ec 76
03390 Saint-Priest-en-Murat 03 115 Cf 70
23300 Saint-Priest-la-Feuille 23 113 Bd 71
18370 Saint-Priest-la-Marche 18 114 Cb 70
23240 Saint-Priest-la-Plaine 23 113 Bd 71
42830 Saint-Priest-la-Prugne 42 116 De 73
42590 Saint-Priest-la-Roche 42 117 Ea 73
42440 Saint-Priest-la-Vêtre 42 129 De 74
87290 Saint-Priest-le-Betoux 87 113 Bb 71
24450 Saint-Priest-les-Fougères 24 125 Ba 75
87120 Saint-Priest-les-Vergnes 87 126 Be 74
87800 Saint-Priest-Ligoure 87 125 Bb 75
87700 Saint-Priest-sous-Aixe 87 125 Ba 74
87480 Saint-Priest-Taurion 87 113 Bc 73
38370 Saint-Prim 38 130 Ee 76
07200 Saint-Privat 07 142 Ec 81
12150 Saint-Privat 12 152 Da 83
12370 Saint-Privat 12 152 Ce 85
19220 Saint-Privat 19 138 Ca 78
24420 Saint-Privat 24 125 Af 77
34700 Saint-Privat 34 167 Dc 86
43580 Saint-Privat-d'Allier 43 141 Dd 79
30430 Saint-Privat-de-Champclos 30 154 Ec 83
24410 Saint-Privat-des-Prés 24 124 Ab 77
30340 Saint-Privat-des-Vieux 30 154 Ea 84
48240 Saint-Privat-de-Vallongue 48 153 Df 83
43380 Saint-Privat-du-Dragon 43 128 Dc 77
48140 Saint-Privat-du-Fau 48 140 Dc 79
24410 Saint Privat en Périgord 24 124 Ab 77
57855 Saint-Privat-la-Montagne 57 56 Ga 53
71390 Saint-Privé 71 105 Ed 68
89220 Saint-Privé 89 89 Da 62
03120 Saint-Prix 03 116 Dd 71
07270 Saint-Prix 07 142 Ed 79
71800 Saint-Prix 71 117 Eb 70
71990 Saint-Prix 71 104 Ea 67
21230 Saint-Prix-lès-Arnay 21 105 Ec 66
46300 Saint-Projet 46 138 Bc 80
82160 Saint-Projet 82 150 Be 83
15140 Saint-Projet-de-Salers 15 139 Cd 78
16110 Saint-Projet-Saint-Constant 16 124 Ac 74
85110 Saint-Prouant 85 97 Za 68
45750 Saint-Pryvé-Saint-Mesmin 45 87 Bf 61
32310 Saint Puy 32 148 Ac 85
59730 Saint-Python 59 30 Dc 47
17800 Saint-Quantin-de-Rançanne 17 122 Zc 75
22170 Saint-Quay 22 63 Xa 57
22700 Saint-Quay-Perros 22 63 Wd 56
22410 Saint-Quay-Portrieux 22 64 Xb 57
17490 Saint-Quen 17 123 Zf 73
44440 Saint-Quen 44 82 Ye 63
26110 Saint Quenin 26 156 Fb 83
02100 Saint-Quentin 02 40 Db 49
16420 Saint-Quentin 16 112 Ae 72
24200 Saint-Quentin 24 137 Bb 79
50810 Saint-Quentin 50 34 Za 54
71220 Saint-Quentin 71 118 Ec 69
76630 Saint-Quentin-au-Bosc 76 37 Bb 49
33750 Saint-Quentin-de-Baron 33 135 Ze 80
61360 Saint-Quentin-de-Blavou 61 68 Ac 58
33220 Saint Quentin-de-Caplong 33 136 Aa 80
16210 Saint-Quentin-de-Chalais 16 123 Aa 77
27270 Saint-Quentin-des-Isles 27 49 Ad 54
60380 Saint-Quentin-des-Prés 60 38 Be 51
47330 Saint-Quentin-du-Dropt 47 136 Ad 80
49110 Saint-Quentin-en-Mauges 49 83 Za 65
80120 Saint-Quentin-en-Tourmont 80 28 Bd 47
38070 Saint-Quentin-Fallavier 38 131 Fa 75
23500 Saint-Quentin-la-Chabanne 23 126 Ca 73
80880 Saint-Quentin-la-Motte-Croix-au-Bailly 80 28 Bc 48
30700 Saint-Quentin-la-Poterie 30 154 Ec 84
09500 Saint-Quentin-la-Tour 09 178 Bf 90
08220 Saint-Quentin-le-Petit 08 41 Ea 51
49150 Saint-Quentin-lès-Beaurepaire 49 84 Zf 63
61800 Saint-Quentin-les-Chardonnets 61 47 Zb 56
51300 Saint-Quentin-les-Marais 51 54 Ed 56
41800 Saint-Quentin-lès-Troo 41 85 Ae 62
51120 Saint-Quentin-le-Verger 51 73 De 57
16150 Saint-Quentin-sur-Charente 16 124 Ae 73
51240 Saint-Quentin-sur-Coole 51 54 Eb 55
37310 Saint-Quentin-sur-Indrois 37 100 Ba 65
38210 Saint-Quentin-sur-Isère 38 131 Fd 77
50220 Saint-Quentin-sur-le-Homme 50 46 Ye 57
58150 Saint-Quentin-sur-Nohain 58 89 Da 64
63490 Saint-Quentin-sur-Sauxillanges 63 128 Dc 75
33112 Saint-Queyran 33 134 Za 78
56500 Saint-Quidy 56 80 Xa 61
22940 Saint-Quihouet 22 64 Xb 58
63440 Saint-Quintin-sur-Sioule 63 115 Da 72
09700 Saint-Quirc 09 164 Bd 89
57560 Saint-Quirin 57 77 Ha 57
24210 Saint-Rabier 24 137 Ba 77
71800 Saint-Racho 71 117 Ec 71
26140 Saint-Rambert-d'Albon 26 130 Ee 77
01230 Saint-Rambert-en-Bugey 01 119 Fc 73
42170 Saint-Rambert-sur-Loire 42 129 Eb 76
46270 Saint-Rame 46 138 Ca 81
12580 Saint-Rames 12 139 Cd 81
56380 Saint-Raoul 56 81 Xf 61
24160 Saint-Raphaël 24 125 Ba 77
33480 Saint-Raphaël 33 134 Zb 79
83700 Saint Raphaël 83 172 Ge 88
42660 Saint-Regis-du-Coin 42 130 Ec 77
37530 Saint-Règle 37 86 Ba 64
07700 Saint-Remèze 07 154 Ed 82
54740 Saint Remimont 54 76 Gb 58
88800 Saint-Remimont 88 76 Ff 59
57140 Saint-Remis 57 56 Ga 53
01310 Saint-Rémy 01 118 Fb 71
03370 Saint-Rémy 03 114 Cc 70
12200 Saint-Rémy 12 151 Ca 82
12430 Saint-Rémy 12 152 Ce 84
14570 Saint-Rémy 14 47 Zc 55
19290 Saint-Rémy 19 127 Cb 75
21500 Saint-Rémy 21 90 Eb 63
24700 Saint-Rémy 24 136 Ab 79
46090 Saint-Rémy 46 150 Bc 82
70160 Saint-Rémy 70 93 Ga 61
71100 Saint-Rémy 71 106 Ef 68
76340 Saint-Rémy 76 38 Bd 49
79310 Saint-Rémy 79 111 Ze 69
79410 Saint-Rémy 79 110 Zc 70
88480 Saint-Rémy 88 77 Ge 58
62870 Saint-Rémy-au-Bois 62 28 Bf 46
54290 Saint-Rémy-aux-Bois 54 76 Gc 58
02210 Saint-Rémy-Blanzy 02 52 Db 53
76260 Saint-Remy-Boscrocourt 76 37 Bc 48
59620 Saint-Rémy-Chaussée 59 31 Df 47
63440 Saint-Rémy-de-Blot 63 115 Cf 72
63500 Saint-Rémy-de-Chargnat 63 128 Db 75
15110 Saint-Rémy-de-Chaudes-Aigues 15 140 Da 80
73660 Saint-Rémy-de-Maurienne 73 132 Gb 76
12210 Saint-Rémy-de-Montpeyroux 12 139 Ce 81
13210 Saint-Rémy-de-Provence 13 155 Ee 86
15140 Saint-Rémy-de-Salers 15 139 Cc 78
72140 Saint-Rémy-de-Sillé 72 67 Zf 59
50580 Saint-Rémy-des-Landes 50 33 Yc 53
72600 Saint-Rémy-des-Monts 72 68 Ac 59
59330 Saint-Rémy-du-Nord 59 31 Df 47
35560 Saint-Rémy-du-Plain 35 65 Yc 58
72600 Saint-Rémy-du-Val 72 68 Ab 58
51290 Saint-Rémy-en-Bouzemont-Saint-Genest-et-Isson 51 54 Ed 57
60130 Saint Remy en l'Eau 60 39 Cc 52
49110 Saint-Rémy-en-Mauges 49 83 Yf 65
86390 Saint-Rémy-en-Montmorillon 86 112 Af 71
03110 Saint-Rémy-en-Rollat 03 116 Dc 71
55160 Saint-Rémy-la-Calonne 55 55 Fd 54
77320 Saint-Rémy-la-Vanne 77 52 Db 56

Saint-Rémy-la-Vanne | 319

71230 Saint-Vallier 71 105 Ec 69
88270 Saint-Vallier 88 76 Gb 59
06460 Saint-Vallier-de-Thiey 06 172 Gf 86
52200 Saint-Vallier-sur-Marne 52 92 Fc 61
79330 Saint-Varent 79 99 Ze 67
81800 Saint-Vast 81 150 Be 86
23320 Saint-Vaury 23 114 Be 71
62350 Saint-Venant 62 29 Cd 45
29510 Saint-Venec 29 78 Vf 60
43580 Saint-Vénérand 43 141 De 79
58310 Saint-Vérain 58 89 Da 64
04250 Saint-Véran 04 157 Ga 83
05350 Saint-Véran 05 145 Gf 80
12100 Saint-Véran 12 153 Db 84
84220 Saint-Véran 84 156 Fb 85
84330 Saint-Véran 84 155 Fa 84
38160 Saint-Vérand 38 143 Fb 77
69620 Saint Vérand 69D 117 Ed 73
71570 Saint-Vérand 71 118 Ee 71
43440 Saint-Vert 43 128 Dd 76
19240 Saint-Viance 19 125 Bc 77
41210 Saint-Viâtre 41 87 Bf 63
44320 Saint-Viaud 44 96 Xf 65
72130 Saint-Victeur 72 68 Aa 59
03410 Saint-Victor 03 115 Cd 70
07410 Saint-Victor 07 142 Ee 78
13200 Saint-Victor 13 169 Ed 87
19200 Saint-Victor 19 127 Cc 76
24350 Saint-Victor 24 124 Ac 77
43150 Saint-Victor 43 141 Df 79
47470 Saint-Victor 47 149 Af 83
76760 Saint-Victor 76 37 Af 51
81800 Saint-Victor 81 150 Be 86
28240 Saint-Victor-de-Buthon 28 69 Af 58
27300 Saint-Victor-de-Chrétienville 27
49 Ad 54
30500 Saint-Victor-de-Malcap 30 154 Eb 83
38510 Saint-Victor-de-Morestel 38
131 Fd 74
27800 Saint-Victor-d'Epine 27 49 Ad 53
61290 Saint-Victor-de-Reno 61 69 Ae 57
30700 Saint-Victor-des Oules 30 154 Ec 84
23000 Saint-Victor-en-Marche 23 114 Be 72
13730 Saint-Victoret 13 170 Fb 88
12400 Saint-Victor-et-Melvieu 12 152 Ce 84
76890 Saint-Victor-l'Abbaye 76 37 Ba 50
30290 Saint-Victor-la-Coste 30 155 Ed 84
63790 Saint-Victor-la-Rivière 63 128 Cf 75
43140 Saint Victor-Malescours 43
129 Eb 77
63550 Saint-Victor-Montvianeix 63
116 Dd 73
09100 Saint-Victor-Rouzaud 09 165 Bd 90
43500 Saint-Victor-sur-Arlanc 43 129 De 76
27130 Saint-Victor-sur-Avre 27 49 Af 56
21410 Saint-Victor-sur-Ouche 21 105 Ee 65
42630 Saint-Victor-sur-Rhins 42 117 Eb 72
87420 Saint-Victurnien 87 125 Ba 73
43320 Saint-Vidal 43 141 De 78
40190 Saint-Vidou 40 147 Ze 85
27930 Saint-Vigor 27 50 Bb 54
14700 Saint-Vigor-de-Mieux 14 48 Ze 55
14770 Saint-Vigor-des-Mézerets 14
47 Zc 55
50420 Saint-Vigor-des-Monts 50 46 Yf 55
76430 Saint-Vigor-d'Ymonville 76 36 Ac 52
14400 Saint-Vigor-le-Grand 14 47 Zb 53
07700 Saint-Vincent 07 155 Ed 82
12370 Saint-Vincent 12 152 Ce 86
15380 Saint-Vincent 15 127 Cd 77
20272 Saint Vincent CTC 183 Kc 95
31290 Saint-Vincent 31 165 Be 88
35350 Saint-Vincent 35 65 Ya 56
43800 Saint-Vincent 43 141 Df 78
47320 Saint-Vincent 47 148 Ac 83
56160 Saint-Vincent 56 79 We 61
63320 Saint-Vincent 63 128 Da 75
64800 Saint-Vincent 64 162 Zf 90
82300 Saint-Vincent 82 150 Bc 84
82330 Saint-Vincent 82 151 Bf 83
71430 Saint-Vincent-Bragny 71 117 Ea 69
76430 Saint-Vincent-Cramesnil 76 36 Ac 51
34730 Saint-Vincent-de-Barbeyrargues 34
168 Df 86
07210 Saint-Vincent-de-Barrès 07
142 Ee 81
42120 Saint-Vincent-de-Boisset 42
117 Ea 72
24190 Saint-Vincent-de-Connezac 24
124 Ac 78
24220 Saint-Vincent-de-Cosse 24
137 Ba 79
07360 Saint-Vincent-de-Durfort 07
142 Ed 80
47310 Saint-Vincent-de-Lamontjoie 47
149 Ad 84
38660 Saint-Vincent-de-Mercuze 38
132 Ff 76
33440 Saint-Vincent-de-Paul 33 135 Zd 79
40990 Saint-Vincent-de-Paul 40 161 Yf 86
33420 Saint Vincent-de-Pertignas 33
135 Zf 80
69240 Saint-Vincent-de-Reins 69D
117 Ec 72
27950 Saint-Vincent-des-Bois 27 50 Bc 54
44590 Saint-Vincent-des-Landes 44
82 Yd 63
71250 Saint-Vincent-des-Prés 71 118 Ed 70
72600 Saint-Vincent-des-Prés 72 68 Ac 59
40230 Saint-Vincent-de-Tyrosse 40
160 Ye 87
34390 Saint-Vincent-d'Olargues 34
167 Cf 87
27230 Saint-Vincent-du-Boulay 27 49 Ac 54
72150 Saint-Vincent-du-Lorouër 72
85 Ac 62
46400 Saint-Vincent-du-Pendit 46 138 Bf 79
71440 Saint-Vincent-en-Bresse 71
106 Fa 68
24410 Saint-Vincent-Jalmoutiers 24
124 Ab 77
79500 Saint-Vincent-la-Châtre 79 111 Zf 71
26300 Saint-Vincent-la-Commanderie 26
143 Fa 79
27270 Saint-Vincent-la-Rivière 27 49 Ac 55
04340 Saint-Vincent-les-Forts 04 157 Gc 82
82400 Saint-Vincent-Lespinasse 82
149 Af 84
85480 Saint-Vincent-Puymaufrais 85
97 Yf 69
46140 Saint-Vincent-Rive-d'Olt 46
137 Bb 82
85110 Saint-Vincent-Sterlanges 85 97 Yf 68
85540 Saint-Vincent-sur-Graon 85
109 Yd 69
04200 Saint-Vincent-sur-Jabron 04
156 Fe 83
85520 Saint-Vincent-sur-Jard 85 109 Yc 70
24420 Saint Vincent-sur-l'Isle 24 125 Af 77
56350 Saint-Vincent-sur-Oust 56 81 Xf 62
89430 Saint-Vinnemer 89 90 Ea 62
25410 Saint-Vit 25 107 Fe 65
34600 Saint-Vital 34 167 Da 87
73460 Saint Vital 73 132 Gb 75
47500 Saint Vite 47 137 Af 82
18360 Saint-Vitte 18 115 Cd 69
87380 Saint-Vitte-sur-Briance 87 125 Bd 75
39290 Saint-Vivant-en-Amaou 39 106 Fc 66
17220 Saint-Vivien 17 110 Yf 72
24230 Saint-Vivien 24 136 Aa 79
24310 Saint-Vivien 24 124 Ad 77
47210 Saint-Vivien 47 136 Ad 81
33920 Saint Vivien-de-Blaye 33 135 Zc 78
33590 Saint-Vivien-de-Médoc 33 122 Yf 76
33580 Saint-Vivien-de-Monségur 33
136 Aa 81
03220 Saint-Voir 03 116 Dd 70
22120 Saint-Volon 22 64 Xb 58
29440 Saint-Vougay 29 62 Vf 57
51340 Saint-Vrain 51 54 Ee 56
91770 Saint-Vrain 91 71 Cb 57
22230 Saint-Vran 22 64 Xd 59
01150 Saint-Vulbas 01 131 Fb 74
59570 Saint-Waast 59 31 De 47
62990 Saint-Wandrille 62 28 Bf 45
76490 Saint-Wandrille-Rançon 76 36 Ae 51
95470 Saint-Witz 95 51 Cd 54
17138 Saint-Xandre 17 110 Yf 71
12540 Saint-Xist 12 152 Da 85
34260 Saint-Xist 34 167 Da 86
40400 Saint-Yaguen 40 147 Zb 85
71600 Saint-Yan 71 117 Ea 70
56660 Saint-Yann-Brevele =
Saint-Jean-Brévelay 56 80 Xb 61
19140 Saint-Ybard 19 125 Bd 76
09210 Saint-Ybars 09 164 Bc 89
03270 Saint-Yorre 03 116 Dc 72
32320 Saint-Yors 32 163 Ab 87
23460 Saint-Yrieix-la-Montagne 23
126 Ca 73
87500 Saint-Yrieix-la-Perche 87 125 Bb 75
19300 Saint-Yrieix-le-Déjalat 19 126 Bf 76
23150 Saint-Yrieix-les-Bois 23 114 Bf 72
87700 Saint-Yrieix-sous-Aixe 87 125 Ba 73
16710 Saint Yrieix-sur-Charente 16
124 Aa 74
71460 Saint-Ythaire 71 118 Ed 69
56310 Saint-Yves 56 79 We 61
63500 Saint-Yvoine 63 128 Db 75
29140 Saint-Yvy 29 78 Wa 61
33920 Saint-Yzan-de-Soudiac 33 135 Zd 78
33340 Saint Yzans-de-Médoc 33 122 Zb 77
83640 Saint-Zacharie 83 171 Fe 88
28700 Sainville 28 70 Bf 58
86420 Saires 86 99 Ab 67
61220 Saires-la-Verrerie 61 47 Zd 56
11310 Saissac 11 165 Cb 88
80540 Saisseval 80 38 Ca 49
71360 Saisy 71 105 Ed 67
95270 Sait-Martin-du-Tertre 95 51 Cc 54
79400 Saivres 79 111 Ze 70
81710 Saïx 81 165 Cb 87
86120 Saix 86 99 Aa 66
05400 Saix, le 05 144 Fe 82
39110 Saizenay 39 107 Ff 67
54380 Saizerais 54 56 Ga 56
58190 Saizy 58 89 De 64
31370 Sajas 31 164 Ba 88
34360 Salabert 34 167 Cf 88
24160 Salagnac 24 125 Bb 77
38890 Salagnon 38 131 Fc 75
30120 Salagosse 30 153 Dd 84
85340 Salaire, la 85 96 Yb 69
38150 Salaise-sur-Sanne 38 130 Ee 76
24590 Salamonie, la 24 137 Bc 79
39700 Salans 39 107 Fe 66
87130 Salas 87 125 Bc 74
34800 Salasc 34 167 Db 87
20242 Salastracu CTC 183 Kb 96
09140 Salau 09 176 Bb 92
33160 Salaunes 33 134 Zb 79
07150 Salaves 07 154 Ec 82
01270 Salavre 01 119 Fc 70
42550 Salayes 42 129 Df 76
30760 Salazac 30 155 Ed 83
40170 Salbert 40 146 Yf 84
90350 Salbert 90 94 Ge 62
35320 Sal-Breizh = Le Sel-de-Bretagne 35
82 Yc 61
41300 Salbris 41 87 Ca 64
67420 Salcée, la 67 60 Ha 58
34700 Salces 34 153 Dc 86
48100 Salces, les 48 140 Da 81
81360 Salclas 81 166 Cc 86
20246 Saleccia CTC 181 Kb 92
65370 Saléchan 65 176 Ad 91
31260 Saleich 31 176 Af 90
17510 Saleignes 17 111 Ze 72
66280 Saleilles 66 179 Cf 93
09220 Saleix 09 177 Bc 92
34700 Salèlles 34 167 Dc 86
07140 Salelles, les 07 154 Ea 82
07170 Salelles, les 07 142 Ec 82
48230 Salelles, les 48 140 Db 82
68240 Salem 68 77 Hb 59
15250 Salemagne 15 139 Cc 79
60400 Salency 60 39 Da 51
50430 Salenel 50 33 Yc 53
67440 Salenthal 67 58 Hc 57
05300 Saléon 05 156 Fe 83
05300 Salérans 05 156 Fe 83
31230 Salerm 31 164 Ae 89
83690 Salernes 83 172 Gb 87
15140 Salers 15 139 Cc 78
74150 Sales 74 132 Ff 73
81240 Sales 81 166 Cd 88
15260 Salès, le 15 140 Da 79
24590 Sales, les 24 137 Bc 78
59218 Salesches 59 31 Dd 47
12600 Salesse 12 139 Cd 80
23260 Salesse 23 127 Cc 74
15430 Salesse, la 15 140 Cf 78
82330 Salesse, la 82 151 Bf 83
81240 Salesses 81 166 Cc 87
15190 Salesses, les 15 127 Cf 76
48170 Salesses, les 48 141 De 81
63120 Salet 63 128 Dd 74
38970 Salette-Fallavaux, la 38 144 Ff 79
26160 Salettes 26 142 Ef 81
43150 Salettes 43 141 Df 79
24460 Saleuil 24 124 Ae 77
80480 Saleux 80 38 Cb 49
48400 Salgas 48 153 Dd 83
12470 Salgues 12 139 Cf 81
19380 Salgues 19 138 Bf 78
46090 Salgues 46 150 Bc 82
48700 Salhens 48 140 Dc 80
20121 Salice CTC 182 If 96
20218 Saliceto CTC 183 Kb 94
33260 Salie, la 33 134 Ye 81
48400 Saliège 48 153 De 82
13200 Saliers 13 169 Ec 87
81990 Saliès 81 151 Ca 85
64270 Salies-de-Béarn 64 161 Za 88
31260 Salies-du-Salat 31 164 Af 90
04290 Salignac 04 157 Ff 84
33240 Salignac 33 135 Zd 78
17130 Salignac-de-Mirambeau 17
123 Zd 76
24590 Salignac-Eyvigues 24 137 Bb 79
17800 Salignac-sur-Charente 17 123 Zd 74
39350 Saligney 39 107 Fd 65
58190 Saligny 58 89 Dd 64
85170 Saligny 85 97 Yd 68
89100 Saligny 89 72 Dc 59
18800 Saligny-le-Vif 18 103 Ce 66
03470 Saligny-sur-Roudon 03 116 De 70
65120 Saligos 65 175 Zf 91
65120 Saligos 65 175 Zf 91
15700 Saligoux 15 139 Cb 77
40200 Salin 40 146 Ye 83
13200 Salin-de-Badon 13 169 Ed 88
13129 Salin-de-Giraud 13 169 Ee 88
30340 Salindres 30 154 Ea 83
14670 Saline 14 48 Ze 53
56730 Saline, la 56 80 Xa 63
30250 Salinelles 30 154 Ea 86
09220 Salines 09 177 Bc 92
77148 Salins 77 72 Da 58
83400 Salins-d'Hyères, les 83 171 Gb 90
73600 Salins-Fontaine 73 133 Gd 76
39110 Salins-les-Bains 39 107 Ff 67
64360 Saliou 64 162 Zc 89
21580 Salives 21 91 Ef 63
06910 Salagriffon 06 158 Gf 85
74700 Sallanches 74 120 Gd 73
87800 Sallas 87 125 Ba 74
62680 Sallaumines 62 30 Cf 46
20000 Sallcia CTC 182 Id 97
05100 Sallé 05 145 Gd 78
05240 Salle, la 05 145 Gd 79
49330 Salle, la 49 83 Zc 62
71260 Salle, la 71 118 Ef 70
81340 Salle, la 81 151 Cc 84
82160 Salle, la 82 150 Be 83
88470 Salle, la 88 77 Ge 59
33370 Salleboeuf 33 135 Zd 79
63270 Sallèdes 63 128 Db 75
49310 Salle-de-Vihiers, la 49 98 Zc 66
38350 Salle-en-Beaumont, la 38 144 Ff 79
49110 Salle-et-Chapelle-Aubry 49 97 Za 65
11600 Sallèles-Cabardès 11 166 Cc 89
11590 Sallèles-d'Aude 11 167 Cf 89
14240 Sallen 14 34 Zb 54
80230 Sallenelle 80 28 Bd 47
14121 Sallenelles 14 48 Ze 53
32550 Salleneuve 32 163 Ad 87
74270 Sallenôves 74 120 Ff 72
85300 Sallertaine 85 96 Ya 67
01160 Salles 01 119 Fb 72
03140 Salles 03 116 Db 71
24480 Salles 24 137 Af 80
26310 Salles 26 143 Fc 81
33770 Salles 33 134 Za 81
47150 Salles 47 137 Af 81
65400 Salles 65 175 Zf 90
79800 Salles 79 111 Zf 70
81640 Salles 81 151 Ca 84
86300 Salles 86 112 Ad 70
23340 Salles, les 23 126 Bf 74
30570 Salles, les 30 153 Dd 84
42440 Salles, les 42 129 De 73
48600 Salles, les 48 141 De 80
65360 Salles-Adour 65 162 Aa 89
69460 Salles-Arbuissonnas-en-Beaujolais
69D 118 Ed 72
12260 Salles-Courbatiés 12 138 Ca 82
12410 Salles-Curan 12 152 Ce 83
16130 Salles-d'Angles 16 123 Ze 75
32370 Salles-d'Armagnac 32 148 Zf 86
11110 Salles-d'Aude 11 167 Da 89
16300 Salles-de-Barbezieux 16 123 Zf 76
24170 Salles-de-Belvès 24 137 Af 80
33350 Salles-de-Castillon, les 33 135 Zf 79
16700 Salles-de-Villefagnan 16 111 Aa 73
30110 Salles-du-Gardon, les 30 154 Ea 83
31110 Salles-et-Pratviel 31 176 Ad 92
12330 Salles-la-Source 12 151 Cd 82
16190 Salles-Lavalette 16 124 Ab 76
87440 Salles-Lavauguyon, les 87 124 Ae 74
17470 Salles-lès-Aulnay 17 111 Ze 72
64300 Salles-Mongiscard 64 161 Za 88
64300 Sallespisse 64 161 Zb 87
26770 Salles-sous-Bois 26 155 Ef 82
31390 Salles-sur-Garonne 31 164 Bb 89
11410 Salles-sur-L'Hers 11 165 Be 89
17220 Salles-sur-Mer 17 110 Yf 72
83630 Salles-sur-Verdon, les 83 157 Gb 86
64400 Sallet-de-Haut 64 161 Zb 89
26150 Sallières 26 143 Fc 80
74150 Sallongy 74 120 Ff 73
55000 Salmagne 55 55 Fb 56
21690 Salmaise 21 91 Ed 64
67160 Salmbach 67 59 Ia 55
12120 Salmiech 12 152 Cd 83
63230 Salmondèche 63 127 Ce 73
76116 Salmonville 76 37 Bb 52
59496 Salomé 59 30 Cf 45
87330 Salomon 87 112 Af 72
10700 Salon 10 53 Ea 57
24290 Salon 24 137 Ba 79
24380 Salon 24 136 Ae 78
13300 Salon-de-Provence 13 170 Fa 87
20246 Salone CTC 181 Kb 93
19510 Salon-la-Tour 19 125 Bd 75
57170 Salonnes 57 57 Gc 56
71250 Salornay-sur-Guye 71 118 Ed 69
80480 Salouël 80 38 Cb 49
63440 Salpaleine 63 115 Da 72
62500 Salperwick 62 27 Cb 44
09800 Salsein 09 176 Ba 91
66600 Salses-le-Chateau 66 179 Cf 91
11600 Salsigne 11 166 Cc 89
42110 Salt-en-Donzy 42 129 Eb 74
09270 Saltré, la 09 165 Be 89
20146 Salvadilevo CTC 185 Kb 99
20146 Salvadilevu = Salvadilevo CTC
185 Kb 99
81100 Salvages, les 81 166 Cb 87
81320 Salvaget 81 166 Ce 87
12400 Salvagnac 12 152 Ce 85
81630 Salvagnac 81 150 Be 85
12260 Salvagnac-Cajarc 12 138 Bf 82
74740 Salvagny 74 121 Ge 72
09100 Salvayre 09 165 Bd 89
62380 Salvecques 62 29 Ca 45
30450 Salveplane 30 154 Df 82
81190 Salveredonde 81 151 Ca 84
34330 Salvergues 34 167 Cf 87
12230 Salvetat 12 153 Db 85
15220 Salvetat 15 139 Cb 80
24480 Salvetat 24 137 Af 80
82270 Salvetat, la 82 150 Bc 83
82230 Salvetat-Belmontet, la 82 150 Bd 85
31460 Salvetat-Lauragais, la 31 165 Be 87
12440 Salvetat-Peyralès, la 12 151 Cb 83
31880 Salvetat-Saint-Gilles, la 31 164 Bb 87
34330 Salvetat-sur-Agout, la 34 166 Ce 87
11140 Salvezines 11 178 Cb 92
46150 Salvezou 46 137 Bc 81
46340 Salviac 46 137 Bb 80
11390 Salvis, les 11 166 Cb 88
42110 Salvizinet 42 129 Eb 74
20117 Salvolaccia CTC 182 If 97
11330 Salza 11 178 Cc 91
30770 Salze, le 30 153 Dc 85
43230 Salzuit 43 128 Dc 77
40320 Samadet 40 162 Zd 87
31350 Saman 31 163 Ae 89
32140 Samaran 32 163 Ad 88
32130 Samatan 32 164 Af 88
13310 Samatane, la 13 170 Ef 87
32230 Samazan 32 162 Aa 88
47250 Samazan 47 148 Aa 82
43220 Sambin 41 86 Bb 64
89160 Sambourg 89 90 Ea 62
13200 Sambuc, le 13 169 Ed 87
04140 Sambue, la 04 157 Gc 83
59310 Saméon 59 30 Dc 46
62830 Samer 62 28 Be 45
21170 Samerey 21 106 Fc 66
64520 Sames 64 161 Yf 87
87460 Samis 87 125 Be 74
86200 Sammarçolles 86 99 Aa 66
77260 Sammeron 77 52 Da 55
74340 Samoëns 74 121 Ge 72
01580 Samognat 01 119 Fd 71
55100 Samogneux 55 55 Fc 53
77920 Samois-sur-Seine 77 71 Ce 58
33710 Samonac 33 135 Zc 78
12150 Samonta, le 12 152 Da 83
77210 Samoreau 77 71 Ce 58
31420 Samouillan 31 164 Af 89
02840 Samoussy 02 40 De 51
07100 Samoyas 07 130 Ed 77
39100 Sampans 39 106 Fc 66
55300 Sampigny 55 55 Fd 56
71150 Sampigny-lès-Maranges 71
105 Ed 67
20134 Sampolo CTC 183 Ka 97
20227 Sampolu CTC 183 Kb 96
20134 Sampolu = Sampolo CTC 183 Ka 97
07120 Sampzon 07 154 Ec 82
25440 Samson 25 107 Ff 66
35730 Samsonnais, la 35 65 Xf 57
64350 Samsons-Lion 64 162 Zf 88
20270 Samuletu CTC 183 Kc 96
56360 Samzun 56 80 Wf 65
31220 Sana 31 164 Ba 89
20167 San Antone = Saint Antoine CTC
182 If 96
83110 Sanary sur-Mer 83 171 Fe 90
19350 Sanas 19 125 Bb 77
20167 San Benedettu CTC 182 Ie 97
71000 Sancé 71 118 Ee 70
58420 Sancenay 58 104 Dc 65
18140 Sancergues 18 103 Cf 66
18300 Sancerre 18 88 Ce 65
25430 Sancey 25 94 Gd 65
25430 Sancey-le-Grand 25 94 Gd 65
25430 Sancey-le-Long 25 94 Gd 65
28800 Sancheville 28 70 Bd 59
88390 Sanchey 88 76 Gc 59
01370 Sanciat 01 119 Fc 71
20137 San Ciprianu CTC 185 Kc 99
18600 Sancoins 18 103 Cf 68
27150 Sancourt 27 38 Be 52
59268 Sancourt 59 30 Db 47
80400 Sancourt 80 39 Da 50
54560 Sancy 54 56 Ff 52
58800 Sancy 58 89 De 65
77580 Sancy 77 52 Cf 55
02880 Sancy-les-Cheminots 02 40 Dc 52
77320 Sancy-lès-Provins 77 52 Dc 56
67230 Sand 67 60 Hd 58
20213 San Damiano CTC 183 Kc 94
28120 Sandarville 28 69 Bc 58
88170 Sandaucourt 88 76 Ff 59
20213 San Diamianu = San Damiano CTC
183 Kc 94
45640 Sandillon 45 87 Ca 61
38710 Sandon 38 144 Fe 80
76430 Sandouville 76 36 Ab 52
78520 Sandrancourt 78 50 Bd 54
01400 Sandrans 01 118 Ef 72
44410 Sandun 44 81 Xd 64
24400 Saneuil 24 136 Ab 78
20217 San Fiurenzu = Saint-Florent CTC
181 Kb 92
62231 Sangatte 62 26 Be 43
20213 San-Gavino-d'Ampugnani CTC
181 Kc 94
20170 San-Gavino-di-Carbini CTC
185 Ka 98
20243 San Gavino-di-Fiumorbo CTC
183 Kb 97
20246 San-Gavino-di-Tenda CTC 181 Kb 93
20140 San Ghjorghju = San Giorgio CTC
182 If 98
20230 San Ghjulianu = San Giuliano CTC
183 Kd 95
20251 San Ghjuvanni = St Jean CTC
183 Kb 95
20230 San Ghjuvanni di Moriani = San
Giovanni-di-Moriani CTC 183 Kc 94
20246 San Giavanu di Tenda =
San-Gavino-di-Tenda CTC 181 Kb 93
20140 San Giorgio CTC 182 If 98
20230 San Giovanni-di-Moriani CTC
183 Kc 94
20114 San Giovano CTC 185 Ka 99
20114 San Giovanu = San Giovano CTC
185 Ka 99
20230 San Giuliano CTC 183 Kd 95
40110 Sangla, la 40 146 Za 84
85110 Sangle, la 85 97 Yf 68
18170 Sanglier 18 102 Cb 68
57640 Sangry-lès-Vigy 57 56 Gb 53
58700 Sangué 58 103 Dc 66
36120 Sanguille 36 101 Be 68
40460 Sanguinet 40 134 Yf 82
07110 Sanilhac 07 142 Eb 81
24660 Sanilhac 24 136 Ae 78
30700 Sanilhac-Sagriès 30 154 Ec 85
30440 Sanissac 30 153 De 84
15110 Sanivalo 15 140 Cf 80
58110 Sanizy 58 104 Dd 66
68590 Sankt Pilt = Saint Hyppolyte 68
60 Hc 59
20244 San Lorenzo = San Lorenzu CTC
183 Kb 94
20244 San Lorenzu = San Lorenzo CTC
183 Kb 94
20200 San-Martino-di-Lota CTC 181 Kc 92
20115 San Martinu CTC 182 Id 95
23110 Sannat 23 115 Cc 72
23190 Sannegrand 23 114 Cc 73
14940 Sannerville 14 48 Ze 53
84240 Sannes 84 156 Fc 86
20230 San Nicolao CTC 183 Kc 94
20230 San Niculaiu = San Nicolao CTC
183 Kc 94
20246 San Pancraziu CTC 181 Kb 92
83380 San-Peïre-sur-Mer 83 172 Ge 88
20233 San Pellegrinu CTC 181 Kd 94
20167 San Petru CTC 182 If 96
20251 San Petru Fagu CTC 183 Kc 95
20214 San Quilcu CTC 180 Ie 94
57530 Sanry-sur-Nied 57 56 Gc 54
66360 Sansa 66 178 Cb 93
15130 Sansac-de-Marmiesse 15 139 Cc 79
15120 Sansac-Veinazès 15 139 Cc 80
79270 Sansais 79 110 Zc 71
32260 Sansan 32 163 Ad 87
21230 Sansange 21 105 Ec 66
33840 Sansin 33 148 Ze 83
43320 Sanssac-L'Eglise 43 141 De 78
03150 Sanssat 03 116 Dc 71
88260 Sans-Vallois 88 76 Ga 60
AD500 Santa Coloma ▫ AND 177 Bc 94
71460 Santagny 71 105 Ed 69
35250 Saint-Albin-Elvinieg =
Saint-Aubin-d'Aubigné 35 65 Yc 59
20114 Santa Lucia CTC 185 Ka 100
20250 Santa Lucia-di-Mercurio CTC
183 Kb 95
20250 Santa Lucia di Merculiu =
Santa-Lucia-di-Mercurio CTC
183 Kb 95
20230 Santa-Lucia-di-Moriani CTC
183 Kc 94
20144 Santa Lucia di Portivechju =
Sainte-Lucie-de-Porto-Vecchio CTC
185 Kc 98
20169 Sant'Amanza CTC 185 Kb 100

Sant'Amanza | 321

20110 Santa Margarita CTC 184 If 99
20200 Santa Maria di Lota CTC 181 Kc 92
20143 Santa-Maria-Figaniella CTC 184 Ka 98
20221 Santa-Maria-Poggio CTC 183 Kc 94
20221 Santa Maria-Poghju = Santa-Maria-Poggio CTC 183 Kc 94
20190 Santa-Maria-Siché CTC 182 If 97
20112 Sant'Andréa CTC 185 Ka 98
20212 Sant'Andrea-di-Bozio CTC 183 Kb 95
20221 Sant'Andrea-di-Cotone CTC 183 Kc 95
20151 Sant'Andréa-d'Orcino CTC 182 Ie 96
20151 Sant'Andrea-d'Orcinu = Sant'Andréa-d'Orcino CTC 182 Ie 96
39380 Santans 39 107 Fd 66
20233 Sant'Antone CTC 181 Kc 92
20240 Sant'Antone = Saint Antoine CTC 183 Kc 96
20220 Sant'Antonino CTC 180 If 93
20220 Sant'Antoniu = Sant'Antonino CTC 180 If 93
20236 Santa Régina CTC 183 Ka 94
20220 Santa-Reparata-di-Balagna CTC 180 If 93
20230 Santa-Reparata-di-Moriani CTC 183 Kc 94
20228 Santa Severa CTC 181 Kc 91
20228 Santa Suvera = Santa Severa CTC 181 Kc 91
45170 Santeau 45 71 Ca 60
29250 Santec 29 62 Vf 56
21590 Santenay 21 105 Ee 67
41190 Santenay 41 86 Ba 63
52160 Santenoge 52 91 Ef 62
94440 Santeny 94 51 Cd 56
59211 Santes 59 30 Cf 45
28700 Santeuil 28 70 Be 58
95640 Santeuil 95 50 Bf 54
12420 Santignac 12 139 Ce 80
89420 Santigny 89 90 Ea 63
28310 Santilly 28 70 Bf 60
71460 Santilly 71 105 Ee 69
28310 Santilly-le-Vieux 28 70 Bf 60
AD600 Sant Julià de Lòria ◘ AND 177 Bc 94
25340 Santoche 25 93 Gd 64
05000 Santons, les 05 144 Ga 81
20246 Santo-Pietro-di-Tenda CTC 181 Kb 93
20250 Santo Pietro-di-Venaco CTC 183 Kb 95
21340 Santosse 21 105 Ed 66
18240 Santranges 18 88 Ce 63
29410 Sant-Tegoneg = Saint-Thegonnec 29 62 Wa 57
20246 Santu Petru di Tenda = Santo-Pietro-di-Tenda CTC 181 Kb 93
20250 Santu Petru di Venacu = Santo Pietro-di-Venaco CTC 183 Kb 95
12200 Sanvensa 12 151 Ca 83
20220 San Vicensu CTC 180 If 93
89310 Sanvigne 89 90 Ea 62
71410 Sanvignes-les-Mines 71 105 Eb 68
86600 Sanxay 86 111 Zf 70
79150 Sanzay 79 98 Zd 67
54200 Sanzey 54 56 Ff 56
49260 Sanziers 49 99 Ze 66
14330 Saon 14 47 Za 53
25660 Saône 25 107 Ga 65
14330 Saonnet 14 47 Za 53
06540 Saorge 06 159 Hd 85
72600 Saosnes 72 68 Ab 59
26400 Saou 26 143 Fa 81
64360 Saou 64 162 Zc 89
61470 Sap, le 61 48 Ac 55
61230 Sap-André, le 61 48 Ac 56
20100 Saparale CTC 184 If 99
20100 Saparella CTC 184 If 99
20138 Saparella Sottana CTC 182 Ie 98
20138 Saparella Suttana = Saparella Sottana CTC 182 Ie 98
20242 Saparelle CTC 183 Kb 96
20122 Saparellu CTC 183 Ka 98
63710 Sapchat 63 128 Cf 75
61120* Sap-en-Auge 61 48 Ab 55
73130 Sapey, le 73 132 Ga 77
04250 Sapie, la 04 157 Ga 83
52100 Sapignicourt 52 54 Ee 57
62121 Sapignies 62 30 Cf 48
35470 Sapin, le 35 82 Yb 61
08160 Sapogne-et-Feuchères 08 42 Ee 51
08370 Sapogne-sur-Marche 08 42 Fb 51
39300 Sapois 39 107 Ff 68
88120 Sapois 88 77 Ge 60
02130 Saponay 02 53 Dc 53
70210 Saponcourt 70 93 Ga 61
74230 Sappey, le 74 120 Gb 73
74350 Sappey, le 74 120 Gb 72
38700 Sappey-en-Chartreuse 38 132 Fe 77
09320 Saraillé 09 177 Bb 91
32450 Saramon 32 163 Ae 87
45770 Saran 45 70 Bf 61
25330 Saraz 25 107 Ff 67
40120 Sarbazan 40 147 Ze 84
72360 Sarcé 72 85 Ab 62
61200 Sarceaux 61 48 Zf 56
95200 Sarcelles 95 51 Cc 54
38700 Sarcenas 38 131 Fe 77
43200 Sarcenas 43 130 Ec 77
63870 Sarcenat 63 128 Da 74
52800 Sarcey 52 75 Fb 60
69490 Sarcey 69M 130 Ed 73
52000 Sarcicourt 52 75 Fa 60
81400 Sarclars 81 151 Cb 84
32420 Sarcos 32 163 Ae 88
60210 Sarcus 60 38 Bf 50
51170 Sarcy 51 53 De 53
30260 Sardan 30 154 Ea 85
23220 Sardé 23 114 Be 70
20134 Sardegna CTC 183 Kb 97
23250 Sardent 23 114 Bf 72
73500 Sardières 73 133 Ge 77
38260 Sardieu 38 131 Fb 76
58270 Sardolles 58 103 Dc 67
63260 Sardon 63 116 Db 73
38114 Sardonne 38 144 Ga 78
58800 Sardy-lès-Epiry 58 104 De 65
58530 Sardy-les-Forges 58 90 Dd 64
64310 Sare 64 160 Yc 89
09290 Saret, le 09 177 Bb 90
72190 Sargé-lès-le-Mans 72 68 Ab 60
41170 Sargé-sur-Braye 41 85 Af 61
23400 Sargnat 23 113 Bd 73
19510 Sargueix, le 19 126 Bd 75
09120 Sarguet 09 177 Bd 90
65230 Sariac-Magnoac 65 163 Ad 89
20145 Sari di Solenzara CTC 185 Kc 97
20151 Sari-d'Orcino CTC 182 Ie 96
20151 Sari d'Orcinu = Sari-d'Orcino CTC 182 Ie 96
77176 Sarigny-le-Temple 77 71 Cd 57
65130 Sarlabous 65 163 Ab 90
24270 Sarlande 24 125 Ba 76
43530 Sarlanges 43 129 Ea 77
24200 Sarlat-la-Canéda 24 137 Bb 79
24420 Sarliac-sur-l'Isle 24 125 Af 77
43200 Sarlis 43 129 Ea 78
81170 Sarmases 81 151 Bf 84
43100 Sarniat 43 128 Dc 76
65390 Sarniguet 65 162 Aa 89
60210 Sarnois 60 38 Bf 50
51260 Saron-sur-Aube 51 73 De 57
31160 Sarous 31 164 Af 90
65370 Sarp 65 176 Ad 90
63490 Sarpoil 63 128 Dc 76
64300 Sarpourenx 64 161 Zb 88
07110 Sarrabasche 07 141 Eb 81
09220 Sarradeil 09 177 Bd 92
65120 Sarradets 65 175 Zf 92
20127 Sarra di Scopamena = Serra-di-Scopamène CTC 185 Ka 98
32400 Sarragachies 32 162 Zf 86
25240 Sarrageois 25 107 Gb 68
32170 Sarraguzan 32 163 Ab 88
63250 Sarraix, les 63 116 Dd 73
57430 Sarralbe = Saaralben 57 57 Ha 55
57400 Sarraltroff 57 57 Ha 56
15270 Sarran 15 127 Cd 76
19800 Sarran 19 126 Bf 76
40310 Sarran 40 148 Aa 85
64490 Sarrance 64 174 Zc 90
65410 Sarrancolin 65 175 Ac 91
32120 Sarrant 32 149 Af 86
07370 Sarras 07 130 Ee 77
64220 Sarrasquette 64 161 Yf 90
09800 Sarrat 09 176 Ba 91
31160 Sarrat 31 163 Ae 90
65710 Sarrat de Bon 65 175 Ab 91
84390 Sarraud 84 156 Fc 84
24800 Sarrazac 24 125 Ba 76
46600 Sarrazac 46 138 Bd 78
40500 Sarraziet 40 162 Zd 86
18140 Sarré 18 103 Cf 65
57400 Sarrebourg 57 57 Ha 56
31350 Sarrecave 31 163 Ad 89
58170 Sarrée, la 58 104 Df 68
57200 Sarreguemines = Saargemünd 57 57 Ha 54
57905 Sarreinsming 57 57 Ha 54
31350 Sarremezan 31 163 Ae 89
05340 Sarret, le 05 145 Gc 79
05700 Sarret, le 05 156 Fe 82
12240 Sarrette, la 12 151 Cb 82
67260 Sarre-Union 67 57 Ha 55
57400 Sarrewald 57 57 Ha 56
67260 Sarrewerden 67 57 Ha 55
21350 Sarrey 52 75 Fc 60
65140 Sarriac-Bigorre 65 162 Aa 88
84260 Sarrians 84 155 Ef 84
49800 Sarrigné 49 84 Zd 63
89110 Sarrigny 89 89 Dc 61
39270 Sarrogna 39 119 Fd 70
20167 Sarrola-Carcopino CTC 182 If 96
40800 Sarron 40 162 Ze 87
60700 Sarron 60 39 Cd 53
40430 Sarroucas 40 147 Zc 83
65600 Sarrouilles 65 162 Aa 89
48200 Sarroul 48 140 Db 80
19110 Sarroux-Saint-Julien 19 127 Cc 76
20167 Sarrula-Carcopinu = Sarrola-Carcopino CTC 182 If 96
51520 Sarry 51 54 Ec 55
71110 Sarry 71 117 Ea 71
89310 Sarry 89 90 Ea 62
62450 Sars, le 62 30 Ce 48
59145 Sarsbarras, le 59 31 De 47
62810 Sars-le-Bois 62 29 Cc 47
59216 Sars-Poteries 59 31 Ea 47
59550 Sart, le 59 31 De 48
59660 Sart, le 59 29 Cd 45
20100 Sartè = Sartène CTC 184 If 99
20100 Sartène CTC 184 If 99
88300 Sartes 88 75 Fe 59
50530 Sartilly-Baie-Bocage 50 46 Yd 56
33125 Sarton 33 135 Zc 82
62760 Sarton 62 29 Cc 48
78500 Sartrouville 78 51 Ca 55
88650 Sarupt 88 77 Gf 59
36230 Sarzay 36 101 Bf 69
56370 Sarzeau = Sarzhav 56 80 Xb 63
56370 Sarzhav = Sarzeau 56 80 Xb 63
41310 Sasnières 41 86 Af 62
21230 Sasoge 21 105 Ed 66
71390 Sassangy 71 105 Ed 68
41700 Sassay 41 86 Bc 64
59145 Sassegnies 59 31 De 47
38360 Sassenage 38 131 Fd 77
71530 Sassenay 71 106 Ef 68
76730 Sassetot-le-Malgardé 76 37 Af 50
76540 Sassetot-le-Mauconduit 76 36 Ad 50
76450 Sasseville 76 36 Ae 50
27930 Sassey 27 49 Bb 54
73640 Sassière, la 73 133 Gf 75
36120 Sassierges-Saint-Germain 36 101 Bf 68
65120 Sassis 65 175 Zf 91
14170 Sassy 14 48 Zf 55
69580 Sathonay-Camp 69M 130 Ef 74
69580 Sathonay-Village 69M 130 Ef 73
07290 Satillieu 07 142 Ed 78
58320 Sating 58 103 Da 66
38290 Satolas-et-Bonce 38 131 Fa 74
34400 Saturargues 34 168 Ea 86
48150 Saubert 48 153 Dc 83
40230 Saubion 40 160 Yd 86
32370 Sauboires 32 148 Aa 85
64420 Saubole 64 162 Zf 89
33730 Saubotte, la 33 135 Zd 82
40230 Saubrigues 40 160 Ye 87
40180 Saubusse 40 161 Ye 87
33650 Saucats 33 135 Zc 81
64400 Saucède 64 161 Zb 89
28250 Saucelle, la 28 49 Ba 57
88470 Sauceray 88 77 Gf 59
61700 Saucerie, la 61 67 Zb 57
25380 Saucet, le 25 108 Gd 65
76630 Sauchay-le-Bas 76 37 Bb 49
76630 Sauchay-le-Haut 76 37 Bb 49
62860 Sauchy-Cauchy 62 30 Da 47
62860 Sauchy-Lestrée 62 30 Da 47
12480 Sauclière, la 12 152 Cd 85
12230 Sauclières 12 153 Dc 85
52270 Saucourt-sur-Rognon 52 75 Fb 58
62860 Saudemont 62 30 Da 47
51120 Saudoy 51 53 De 56
35360 Saudraie, la 35 65 Xf 59
56430 Saudrais, la 56 64 Xe 60
22150 Saudrette, la 22 64 Xb 58
52230 Saudron 52 75 Fb 58
55000 Saudrupt 55 55 Fa 56
12430 Sauganne 12 152 Cd 84
08460 Sauge-aux-Bois, la 08 41 Ec 51
39130 Saugeot 39 107 Fe 69
41130 Saugirard 41 87 Bd 65
41200 Saugirard 41 87 Bd 65
40410 Saugnacq-et-Muret 40 147 Zb 82
69124 Saugnieu 69M 131 Fa 74
33920 Saugon 33 135 Zc 77
43170 Saugues 43 140 Dd 79
64470 Sauguis-Saint-Étienne 64 161 Za 90
18290 Saugy 18 102 Ca 67
89240 Sauilly 89 89 Dc 62
12260 Saujac 12 138 Bf 82
17600 Saujon 17 122 Za 74
05110 Saulce, la 05 157 Ga 82
28330 Saulce, le 28 69 Af 59
08130 Saulces-Champenoises 08 41 Ed 52
08270 Saulces-Monclin 08 41 Ec 51
26270 Saulce-sur-Rhône 26 142 Ee 80
03500 Saulcet 03 116 Db 71
02310 Saulchery 02 52 Db 55
62870 Saulchoy 62 28 Bf 46
60360 Saulchoy, le 60 38 Ca 51
80910 Saulchoy-sur-Davenescourt 80 39 Cd 50
10200 Saulcy 10 74 Ee 59
88210 Saulcy, le 88 77 Ha 58
88580 Saulcy-sur-Meurthe 88 77 Gf 59
49500 Saule, le 49 83 Za 63
79420 Saule, le 79 111 Ze 69
25580 Saules 25 107 Gb 66
71390 Saules 71 105 Ee 69
86500 Saulgé 86 112 Af 70
49320 Saulgé-L'Hôpital 49 84 Zd 65
53340 Saulges 53 67 Zd 61
16420 Saulgond 16 112 Ae 73
19110 Sauliac 19 127 Cc 76
46330 Sauliac-cur-Célé 46 138 Be 81
19170 Saulière, la 19 126 Ca 75
19400 Saulières 19 138 Bf 78
21210 Saulieu 21 90 Eb 65
52500 Saulles 52 92 Fd 62
36290 Saulnay 36 101 Bb 67
41100 Saulnerie, la 41 86 Af 62
54650 Saulnes 54 43 Fe 51
58240 Saulnière 58 103 Db 68
28500 Saulnières 28 50 Bb 57
35320 Saulnières 35 82 Yc 61
70400 Saulnot 70 94 Gd 63
57140 Saulny 57 56 Ga 54
12580 Saulodes 12 139 Cd 81
21910 Saulon-la-Chapelle 21 106 Fa 65
21910 Saulon-la-Rue 21 106 Fa 65
10400 Saulsotte, la 10 72 Dd 57
84390 Sault 84 156 Fc 84
59990 Saultain 59 31 Dd 46
01150 Sault-Brénaz 01 131 Fc 73
50800 Saultchevreuil-du-Tronchet 50 46 Ye 56
64300 Sault-de-Navailles 64 161 Zb 87
08300 Sault-lès-Rethel 08 41 Ec 52
08190 Sault-Saint-Rémy 08 41 Ea 52
62158 Saulty 62 29 Cd 47
70240 Saulx 70 93 Gb 62
55500 Saulx-en-Barrois 55 55 Fc 56
55160 Saulx-en-Woëvre 55 55 Fd 54
54115 Saulxerotte 54 76 Ff 58
21120 Saulx-le-Duc 21 91 Fa 63
91160 Saulx-les-Chartreux 91 51 Cb 56
78650 Saulx-Marchais 78 50 Bf 55
52140 Saulxures 52 75 Fd 61
67420 Saulxures 67 77 Ha 58
88140 Saulxures-lès-Bulgnéville 88 76 Fe 59
54420 Saulxures-lès-Nancy 54 56 Gb 56
54170 Saulxures-lès-Vannes 54 76 Fe 57
88290 Saulxures-sur-Moselotte 88 77 Ge 61
18360 Saulzais-le-Potier 18 102 Cc 69
03800 Saulzet 03 116 Db 72
63540 Saulzet-le-Chaud 63 128 Da 74
63970 Saulzet-le-Froid 63 127 Cf 75
59227 Saulzoir 59 30 Dc 47
04150 Saumane 04 156 Fe 84
84800 Saumane-de-Vaucluse 84 155 Fa 85
47420 Sauméjan 47 148 Zf 83
04420 Saume-Longe 04 157 Gc 83
28800 Saumeray 28 69 Bb 59
45310 Saumery 45 70 Be 61
47600 Saumont 47 148 Ac 84
76440 Saumont-la-Poterie 76 38 Bd 51
33680 Saumos 33 134 Za 79
49400 Saumur 49 99 Zf 65
87230 Saumur 87 125 Ba 75
37110 Saunay 37 86 Af 63
23000 Saunière, la 23 114 Bf 72
71350 Saunières 71 106 Fa 67
40420 Sauque 40 147 Zc 84
60112 Sauqueuse-Saint-Lucien 60 38 Ca 51
76550 Sauqueville 76 37 Ba 49
79200 Saurais 79 99 Zf 69
09400 Saurat 09 177 Bd 91
63390 Sauret-Besserve 63 115 Ce 73
63320 Saurier 63 128 Da 75
47700 Saurine 47 148 Zf 83
74210 Saury 74 132 Gb 74
44110 Sausay, la 44 82 Yc 62
68390 Sausheim 68 95 Hc 62
65120 Saussa 65 175 Zf 92
61100 Saussaie, la 61 47 Zd 56
34570 Saussan 34 168 De 87
28260 Saussay 28 50 Bc 55
76760 Saussay 76 37 Af 51
28160 Saussay, le 28 69 Bb 59
27370 Saussaye, la 27 49 Af 53
28400 Saussaye, la 28 69 Af 59
27150 Saussay-la-Champagne 27 37 Bd 53
50700 Saussemesnil 50 33 Yd 51
81350 Saussenac 81 151 Cb 85
88270 Saussenot 88 76 Gb 60
31460 Saussens 31 165 Be 87
04320 Sausses 04 158 Ge 84
06910 Sausses, les 06 158 Gf 86
07450 Sausses, les 07 141 Eb 80
65150 Sausset 65 175 Ac 90
13960 Sausset-les-Pins 13 170 Fa 89
06470 Saussette, la 06 158 Ge 84
08130 Sausseuil 08 41 Ed 51
76270 Sausseuse-Mare 76 37 Bd 50
76110 Sausseuzemare-en-Caux 76 36 Ac 50
50200 Saussey 50 46 Yd 54
24240 Saussignac 24 136 Ab 80
34160 Saussines 34 154 Ea 86
21380 Saussy 21 91 Ef 64
09300 Sautel 09 177 Be 91
33210 Sauternes 33 135 Zd 81
63410 Sauterre 63 115 Cf 73
34270 Sauteyrargues 34 154 Df 85
44880 Sautron 44 82 Yb 65
33680 Sautuges 33 134 Za 79
63220 Sauvades, les 63 129 De 76
51260 Sauvage 51 73 De 57
58130 Sauvage 58 103 Db 66
52220 Sauvage-Magny 52 74 Ee 58
22230 Sauvagere, la 22 64 Xc 59
61600 Sauvagère, la 61 67 Zd 57
15300 Sauvages 15 139 Cf 77
69170 Sauvages, les 69D 117 Ec 73
16310 Sauvagnac 16 124 Ad 74
19270 Sauvagnac 19 126 Bd 77
24270 Sauvagnac 24 125 Bb 76
87340 Sauvagnac 87 113 Bc 72
47340 Sauvagnas 47 149 Ae 83
63470 Sauvagnat 63 127 Cd 74
63500 Sauvagnat-Sainte-Marthe 63 128 Db 75
32240 Sauvagnère 32 148 Zf 85
25170 Sauvagney 25 93 Ff 65
64230 Sauvagnon 64 162 Zd 88
03430 Sauvagny 03 115 Ce 70
43100 Sauvagny 43 128 Db 77
42990 Sauvain 42 129 Df 74
24320 Sauvanie, la 24 124 Ac 76
04140 Sauvans, les 04 157 Gb 83
07460 Sauvas 07 154 Ea 83
15240 Sauvat 15 127 Cc 77
30610 Sauve 30 154 Df 85
33670 Sauve, la 33 135 Ze 80
24150 Sauvebœf 24 136 Ae 79
83260 Sauvebonne 83 171 Ga 89
64150 Sauvelade 64 161 Zb 88
07200 Sauveplantade 07 142 Ec 81
01220 Sauverny 01 120 Ga 71
63840 Sauvessanelle 63 129 Df 76
63840 Sauvessanges 63 129 Df 76
84220 Sauvestres, les 84 156 Fb 85
63660 Sauvetas, la 63 129 Df 75
32500 Sauvetat, la 32 149 Ad 85
43340 Sauvetat, la 43 141 Df 79
47500 Sauvetat, la 47 137 Af 81
63730 Sauvetat, la 63 128 Db 75
47270 Sauvetat-de-Savères, la 47 149 Ae 83
47800 Sauvetat-du-Dropt, la 47 136 Ac 81
47150 Sauvetat-sur-Lède, la 47 136 Ae 82
30150 Sauveterre 30 155 Ee 84
32220 Sauveterre 32 164 Af 88
48210 Sauveterre 48 153 Dc 82
65700 Sauveterre 65 162 Aa 88
81240 Sauveterre 81 166 Cd 88
82110 Sauveterre 82 150 Bb 83
64390 Sauveterre-de Béarn 64 161 Za 88
31510 Sauveterre-de-Comminges 31 176 Ae 90
33540 Sauveterre-de-Guyenne 33 135 Zf 80
12800 Sauveterre-de-Rouergue 12 151 Cb 83
47500 Sauveterre-la-Lémance 47 137 Ba 81
47220 Sauveterre-Saint-Denis 47 149 Ae 84
19200 Sauvette-d'Aix, la 19 127 Cc 75
65120 Sauveur 65 175 Zf 91
32300 Sauviac 32 163 Ac 88
33430 Sauviac 33 148 Ze 82
34410 Sauvian 34 167 Db 89
63120 Sauviat 63 128 Dd 74
87400 Sauviat-sur-Vige 87 113 Bd 73
16480 Sauvignac 16 123 Zf 77
70100 Sauvigney-lès-Gray 70 92 Fe 64
70140 Sauvigney-lès-Pesmes 70 92 Fd 65
55140 Sauvigny 55 75 Fe 57
58270 Sauvigny 58 104 Dd 67
58800 Sauvigny 58 90 Dd 65
89420 Sauvigny-le-Beuréal 89 90 Ea 64
89200 Sauvigny-le-Bois 89 90 Df 63
58160 Sauvigny-les-Bois 58 103 Db 67
08390 Sauville 08 42 Ee 51
88140 Sauville 88 75 Fe 60
80110 Sauvillers-Mongival 80 39 Cc 50
32220 Sauvimont 32 164 Af 88
89480 Sauvin, la 89 89 Db 63
58270 Sauvry 58 104 Dc 67
46800 Saux 46 149 Ba 82
65100 Saux 65 162 Zf 90
82110 Saux 82 150 Bb 83
63490 Sauxillanges 63 128 Dc 75
81320 Sauyères 81 166 Ce 87
17470 Sauzaie 17 111 Zd 72
17138 Sauzaie, la 17 110 Yf 71
85470 Sauzaie, la 85 96 Ya 69
44390 Sauzais, le 44 82 Yc 63
58290 Sauzay 58 104 De 67
58460 Sauzay 58 89 Dc 64
06470 Sauze 06 158 Ge 84
04400 Sauze, le 04 158 Ge 82
05160 Sauze, le 05 144 Gb 82
81140 Sauze, le 81 150 Be 84
17190 Sauzelle 17 109 Ye 73
36220 Sauzelles 36 100 Ba 69
04330 Sauzeries, les 04 157 Gc 84
26740 Sauzet 26 142 Ee 81
30190 Sauzet 30 154 Eb 85
46140 Sauzet 46 150 Bb 82
63420 Sauzet 63 128 Da 76
87360 Sauzet 87 113 Ba 71
79190 Sauzé-Vaussais 79 111 Aa 72
06470 Sauze-Vieux 06 158 Ge 84
81630 Sauzière-Saint-Jean, la 81 150 Bd 85
11260 Sauzils, les 11 178 Ca 91
58380 Sauzin, le 58 104 Dc 68
56360 Sauzon 56 80 We 64
46090 Savanac 46 138 Bd 82
17290 Savarit 17 110 Zb 72
31800 Savarthès 31 163 Ae 90
07430 Savas 07 130 Ee 77
38440 Savas 38 130 Fa 75
38440 Savas-Mépin 38 131 Fa 76
26740 Savasse 26 142 Ee 81
74230 Savataz, la 74 132 Gc 74
18380 Savaterie, la 18 88 Cd 64
58230 Savault 58 104 Df 65
76680 Saveaumare 76 37 Bb 51
16240 Saveille 16 111 Zf 72
30440 Savel, le 30 153 De 84
58230 Savelot 58 104 Df 65
23430 Savenas 23 113 Bd 73
44260 Savenay 44 81 Ya 64
58110 Savenay 58 104 De 66
82600 Savenès 82 149 Bb 86
23000 Savennes 23 114 Bf 72
63750 Savennes 63 127 Cc 75
49170 Savennières 49 83 Zc 64
09700 Saverdun 09 165 Bd 89
31370 Savères 31 164 Ba 88
87310 Savergnac 87 125 Af 74
57720 Savernaz 74 120 Gc 72
67700 Saverne = Zabern 67 58 Hc 56
77820 Saveteux 77 72 Ce 57
61420 Savette, la 61 68 Zf 57
80470 Saveuse 80 38 Cb 49
71460 Savianges 71 105 Ed 68
10600 Savières 10 73 Df 58
39240 Savigna 39 119 Fd 70
12200 Savignac 12 151 Bf 82
12400 Savignac 12 152 Cf 85
33124 Savignac 33 135 Zf 81
47120 Savignac-de-Duras 47 136 Ab 80
33910 Savignac-de-l'Isle 33 135 Ze 79
24260 Savignac-de-Miremont 24 137 Af 79
24300 Savignac-de-Nontron 24 124 Ae 75
24270 Savignac-Lédrier 24 125 Bb 76
24420 Savignac-les-Églises 24 125 Af 77
09110 Savignac-les-Ormeaux 09 177 Be 92
32130 Savignac-Mona 32 164 Ba 88
47150 Savignac-sur-Leyze 47 137 Ae 82
11330 Savignan 11 178 Cc 91
30350 Savignargues 30 154 Ea 85
86400 Savigné 86 112 Ab 72
72460 Savigné-l'Evêque 72 68 Ab 60
72800 Savigné-sous-le-Lude 72 84 Aa 63
37340 Savigné-sur-Lathan 37 85 Ab 64
42140 Savigneux 42 130 Ec 75
42600 Savigneux 42 129 Ea 75
01480 Savigneyux 01 118 Ef 72
60650 Savignies 60 38 Bf 52
03190 Savigny 03 115 Cd 70
50210 Savigny 50 34 Yd 54
52500 Savigny 52 92 Fd 62
69210 Savigny 69M 130 Ed 74
74520 Savigny 74 120 Ff 72
88130 Savigny 88 76 Gb 58
71580 Savigny-en-Revermont 71 106 Fc 69
18240 Savigny-en-Sancerre 18 88 Ce 64
18390 Savigny-en-Septaine 18 102 Cd 66
89420 Savigny-en-Terre-Plaine 89 90 Ea 64
37420 Savigny-en-Véron 37 99 Aa 65
21420 Savigny-lès-Beaune 21 106 Ee 66
21380 Savigny-le-Sec 21 91 Fa 64
86800 Savigny-Lévescault 86 112 Ac 69
50640 Savigny-le-Vieux 50 66 Yf 57
58170 Savigny-Poil-Fol 58 104 Df 68
86140 Savigny-sous-Faye 86 99 Ab 67
21540 Savigny-sous-Mâlain 21 91 Ee 65
08400 Savigny-sur-Aisne 08 42 Ee 52
51170 Savigny-sur-Ardes 51 53 De 53

322 | Santa Margarita

05700 Serres 05 156 Fe 82
07310 Serres 07 142 Eb 79
11190 Serres 11 178 Cb 91
17132 Serres 17 122 Za 75
43270 Serres 43 141 De 77
47120 Serres 47 136 Ab 81
48500 Serres 48 153 Db 83
54370 Serres 54 57 Gc 56
84200 Serres 84 155 Fa 84
64121 Serres-Castet 64 162 Zd 88
24500 Serres-et-Montguyard 24 136 Ac 80
40700 Serres-Gaston 40 162 Zc 87
40700 Serreslous-et-Arribans 40 161 Zc 87
64160 Serres-Morlaàs 64 162 Ze 89
64170 Serres-Sainte-Marie 64 161 Zc 88
09000 Serres-sur-Arget 09 177 Bd 91
63690 Serrette 63 127 Cd 75
64570 Serreuille 64 161 Zb 90
20147 Serriera CTC 182 Ie 95
38550 Serrières 38 130 Ee 77
54610 Serrières 54 56 Gb 55
71960 Serrières 71 118 Ee 71
01470 Serrières-de-Briord 01 131 Fc 74
73310 Serrières-en-Chautagne 73 132 Ff 73
89700 Serrigny 89 90 Df 61
71310 Serrigny-en-Bresse 71 106 Fa 68
77700 Serris 77 52 Ce 55
40110 Serroun 40 146 Za 85
54560 Serrouville 54 43 Ff 52
18190 Serruelles 18 102 Cc 67
16410 Sers 16 124 Ab 75
46210 Sers, le 46 138 Ca 80
67130 Serva, la 67 60 Hb 58
38470 Servagère, la 38 131 Fc 78
02700 Servais 02 40 Dc 51
02160 Serval 02 40 De 52
82140 Servanac 82 150 Be 83
70440 Servance-Miellin 70 94 Ge 62
24410 Servanches 24 136 Aa 78
63560 Servant 63 115 Cf 72
01960 Servas 01 118 Fa 72
30340 Servas 30 154 Eb 84
63610 Serveix 63 127 Cf 75
22300 Servel 22 63 Wd 56
48700 Serverette 48 140 Dc 80
26600 Serves-sur-Rhône 26 142 Ee 78
34290 Servian 34 167 Db 88
19290 Servières 19 126 Bf 74
43170 Servières 43 140 Dc 79
43450 Servières 43 128 Db 77
48000 Servières 48 140 Dc 81
19220 Servières-le-Château 19 138 Ca 78
30700 Serviers-et-Labaume 30 154 Ec 84
34260 Serviès 34 167 Da 86
48190 Serviès 48 141 De 82
81220 Serviès 81 165 Ca 87
11220 Serviès-en-Val 11 166 Cd 90
01560 Servignat 01 118 Fa 70
70240 Servigney 70 93 Gb 62
50200 Servigny 50 46 Yd 54
57530 Servigny-lès-Raville 57 56 Gc 54
57640 Servigny-lès-Sainte-Barbe 57 56 Gb 54
28410 Serville 28 50 Bc 56
03120 Servilly 03 116 Dd 71
25430 Servin 25 94 Gc 65
89140 Servins 89 72 Dc 59
08150 Servion 08 41 Ed 50
16390 Servolle 16 124 Ab 76
50170 Servon 50 66 Yd 57
77170 Servon 77 51 Cd 56
51800 Servon-Melzicourt 51 54 Ef 53
35530 Servon-sur-Vitaine 35 66 Yd 60
74310 Servoz 74 121 Ge 73
08270 Sery 08 41 Ec 51
18220 Séry 18 103 Cd 65
89270 Sery 89 89 De 63
02240 Séry-lès-Mézières 02 40 Dc 50
60800 Séry-Magneval 60 52 Cf 53
51170 Serzy-et-Prin 51 53 De 53
67770 Sessenheim 67 59 Hf 56
34200 Sète 34 168 De 88
43220 Setoux, les 43 130 Ec 77
62380 Setques 62 29 Ca 44
58230 Settons, les 58 104 Ea 65
52500 Seuchey 52 92 Fc 62
95270 Seugy 95 51 Cc 54
04340 Seuil 04 157 Gc 82
08300 Seuil 08 41 Ec 52
84120 Seuil, le 84 171 Fd 86
19520 Seuil-Bas 19 137 Bc 77
55250 Seuil-d'Argonne 55 55 Fa 55
19520 Seuil-Haut 19 137 Bc 77
03260 Seuillet 03 116 Dc 71
14260* Seulline 14 47 Zb 54
41120 Seur 41 86 Bc 63
17770 Seure, le 17 123 Zd 74
21250 Seurre 21 106 Fa 67
71440 Seurres, les 71 106 Fa 68
07100 Seux 07 130 Ed 77
80540 Seux 80 38 Ca 49
88200 Seux 88 77 Gd 60
46160 Seuzac 46 138 Be 82
55300 Seuzey 55 55 Fd 55
12330 Seveirac 12 152 Cc 82
42460 Sevelinges 42 117 Eb 72
90400 Sevenans 90 94 Gf 63
23110 Sévennes 23 115 Cd 72
12240 Sever 12 151 Cb 83
44530 Sévérac 44 81 Xf 63
12150 Sévérac d'Aveyron 12 152 Da 83
12150 Sévérac-le-Château 12 152 Da 83
12310 Sévérac-L'Eglise, Laissac- 12 152 Cf 82
44210 Severie, la 44 96 Xf 66
28140 Sevestreville 28 70 Be 59
70130 Seveux 70 92 Fe 63
22250 Sévignac 22 64 Xd 59
64260 Sévignacq-Meyracq 64 162 Zd 90
64160 Sévignacq-Thèze 64 162 Ze 88
34370 Sévignao 34 167 Da 88
61200 Sevigny 61 48 Zf 56
08230 Sévigny-la-Forêt 08 41 Ec 49
08220 Sévigny-Waleppe 08 41 Ea 51
76850 Sévis 76 37 Ba 50
61150 Sevrai 61 48 Zf 56
93190 Sevran 93 51 Cd 55
74250 Sevraz 74 120 Gc 72
49230 Sèvremoine 49 97 Ye 66
84700 Sèvremont 84 98 Za 67
92310 Sèvres 92 51 Cb 56
86800 Sèvres-Anxaumont 86 100 Ac 69
71100 Sevrey 71 106 Ef 68
74320 Sévrier 74 132 Ga 73
18140 Sévry 18 103 Ce 66
89550 Sevry 89 90 Dd 61
68290 Sewen 68 94 Gf 62
19430 Sexcles 19 138 Ca 78
54550 Sexey-aux-Forges 54 56 Ga 57
54840 Sexey-les-Bois 54 56 Ga 56
52330 Sexfontaines 52 75 Fa 59
63190 Seychalles 63 128 Dc 74
47350 Seyches 47 136 Ab 81
04140 Seyne 04 157 Gc 82
30580 Seynes 30 154 Eb 84
83140 Seyne-sur-Mer, la 83 171 Ff 90
74600 Seynod 74 132 Ga 73
31560 Seyre 31 165 Be 88
40180 Seyresse 40 161 Yf 86
74910 Seyssel 74 119 Ff 73
31600 Seysses 31 164 Bb 88
32130 Seysses-savès 32 164 Ba 87
38170 Seyssinet 38 144 Fe 77
38180 Seyssins 38 131 Fe 78
38200 Seyssuel 38 130 Ef 75
74210 Seythenex, Faverges- 74 132 Gb 74
74430 Seytroux 74 120 Gd 71
51120 Sézanne 51 53 De 56
39270 Sézéria 39 119 Fd 69
26620 Sèzes, les 26 144 Fe 80
29180 Seznec 29 78 Vf 60
65120 Sia 65 175 Zf 91
07570 Sialles 07 142 Ec 79
87260 Siardeix 87 125 Bc 74
65500 Siarouy 65 162 Aa 89
26170 Sias, les 26 156 Fc 83
38740 Siauds, les 38 144 Ff 79
43300 Siaugues-Sainte-Marie 43 141 Dd 78
27250 Siaulles, le 27 49 Ae 56
19100 Siaurat 19 138 Bc 78
19230 Siauve, la 19 125 Bc 76
64470 Sibas 64 161 Za 90
64470 Sibas-Abense 64 161 Za 90
29250 Sibiril 29 62 Vf 56
62270 Sibiville 62 29 Cb 47
31190 Sicardou 31 164 Bc 88
63840 Sicaud 63 129 Df 76
44320 Sicaudais, la 44 96 Ya 65
36600 Sicaudières, les 36 101 Bc 65
38460 Siccieu-Saint-Julien-et-Carisieu 38 131 Fb 74
58700 Sichamps 58 103 Db 66
63660 Sichard 63 129 Df 75
68290 Sickert 68 94 Gf 62
50690 Sideville 50 33 Yb 51
18270 Sidiailles 18 114 Cb 69
20224 Sidossi CTC 180 Ka 95
17490 Siecq 17 123 Ze 74
67160 Siegen 67 59 Ia 55
34520 Sièges 34 153 Db 86
39360 Sièges 39 119 Fe 71
89190 Sièges, les 89 72 Dd 59
57480 Sierck-les-Bains 57 44 Gc 52
68510 Sierentz 68 95 Hc 63
57410 Siersthal 57 58 Hc 54
76690 Sierville 76 37 Ba 51
40180 Siest 40 161 Yf 87
81120 Sieurac 81 151 Ca 86
09130 Sieuras 09 164 Bc 89
38350 Siévoz 38 144 Ff 79
67320 Siewiller 67 57 Hb 55
04000 Sieyes, les 04 157 Gb 84
46150 Siffray 46 137 Bc 81
06910 Sigale 06 158 Gf 85
33690 Sigalens 33 148 Zf 82
11130 Sigean 11 179 Cf 90
45110 Sigloy 45 87 Cb 61
31440 Signac 31 176 Ad 91
37360 Signal, le 37 85 Ac 63
83870 Signes 83 171 Ff 89
52700 Signéville 52 75 Fb 59
86380 Signy 86 99 Ab 68
08460 Signy-L'Abbaye 08 41 Ec 50
08380 Signy-le-Petit 08 41 Eb 49
08370 Signy-Montlibert 08 42 Fb 51
77640 Signy-Signets 77 52 Da 55
16200 Sigogne 16 123 Zf 74
41370 Sigogne 41 86 Bc 62
68240 Sigolsheim 68 60 Hb 60
04300 Sigonce 04 157 Ff 85
05700 Sigottier 05 144 Fe 82
24240 Sigoulès 24 136 Ac 80
85110 Sigournais 85 97 Za 68
04200 Sigoyer 04 157 Ff 83
05130 Sigoyer 05 144 Ff 82
18250 Sigurès, les 18 88 Cd 65
05200 Siguret 05 145 Gd 81
77520 Sigy 77 72 Db 58
76780 Sigy-en-Bray 76 37 Bc 51
71250 Sigy-le-Châtel 71 118 Ed 69
43300 Silcusin 43 141 Dd 78
56480 Silfiac 56 79 Wf 60
20222 Silgaggia CTC 181 Kc 92
07240 Silhac 07 142 Ed 79
33770 Sillac 33 134 Za 82
81350 Sillac 81 151 Cb 84
38590 Sillans 38 131 Fc 76
83690 Sillans-la Cascade 83 171 Gb 87
86320 Sillars 86 112 Ae 70
33690 Sillas 33 148 Zf 82
57420 Sillegny 57 56 Ga 55
64120 Sillègue 64 161 Yf 88
72140 Sillé-le-Guillaume 72 67 Zf 59
72460 Sillé-le-Philippe 72 68 Ac 60
76740 Silleron 76 37 Ae 49
51500 Sillery 51 53 Ea 53
25330 Silley-Amancey 25 107 Ga 66
74330 Sillingy 74 120 Ga 73
86200 Silly 86 99 Aa 67
61310 Silly-en-Gouffern 61 48 Aa 56
57420 Silly-en-Saulnois 57 56 Gb 55
02460 Silly-la-Poterie 02 52 Da 53
60330 Silly-le-Long 60 52 Ce 54
57530 Silly-sur-Nied 57 56 Gc 54
60430 Silly-Tillard 60 38 Ca 53
55000 Silmont 55 55 Fb 56
67260 Siltzheim 67 57 Ha 54
57535 Silvange 57 56 Ga 53
20215 Silvareccio CTC 181 Kc 94
20215 Silvarecciu = Silvareccio CTC 181 Kc 94
52120 Silvarouvres 52 74 Ee 60
04200 Silve, la 04 157 Ff 83
64350 Simacourbe 64 162 Ze 88
01250 Simandre 01 119 Fc 71
71290 Simandre 71 106 Ef 69
69360 Simandres 69M 130 Ef 75
71330 Simard 71 106 Fb 68
16430 Simarde, la 16 124 Ab 74
62123 Simencourt 62 29 Cd 47
13109 Simiane-Collongue 13 170 Fc 88
04150 Simiane-la-Rotonde 04 156 Fd 85
85210 Simon-la-Vineuse 85 110 Yf 69
17270 Simonneau 17 135 Ze 77
58330 Simonots, les 58 104 Dc 66
32420 Simorre 32 163 Ae 88
53360 Simplé 53 83 Za 61
59780 Sin 59 30 Db 45
60390 Sinancourt 60 38 Bf 52
44522 Sinandière, la 44 82 Ye 64
38650 Sinard 38 144 Fd 79
02300 Sinceny 02 40 Db 51
74440 Sincerneret 74 121 Gd 72
21530 Sincey-lès-Rouvray 21 90 Ea 64
67440 Sindelsberg 67 58 Hc 56
40110 Sindères 40 146 Za 84
46230 Sindou 46 150 Bd 82
63690 Singles 63 127 Cd 75
24500 Singleyrac 24 136 Ac 80
57410 Singling 57 57 Hb 54
08430 Singly 08 42 Ee 51
67440 Singrist 67 58 Hc 56
12600 Sinhalac 12 139 Ce 79
48100 Sinières-Planes 48 140 Da 81
59450 Sin-le-Noble 59 30 Da 46
30420 Sinsans 30 154 Ea 86
09310 Sinsat 09 177 Bd 92
48300 Sinzelles 48 141 De 80
65190 Sinzos 65 163 Ab 89
32110 Sion 32 162 Aa 86
19120 Sioniac 19 138 Be 79
44590 Sion-les-Mines 44 82 Yc 62
88630 Sionne 88 75 Fd 58
85270 Sion-sur-L'Océan 85 96 Xf 68
54300 Sionviller 54 57 Gd 57
24430 Siorac 24 136 Ad 77
24600 Siorac-de-Ribérac 24 124 Ac 77
24170 Siorac-en-Périgord 24 137 Af 80
36160 Sioudray 36 114 Ca 69
50340 Siouville-Hague 50 33 Ya 51
33340 Sipian 33 122 Za 76
26400 Siquets, les 26 143 Ef 80
32430 Sirac 32 164 Af 86
62130 Siracourt 62 29 Cb 46
15150 Siran 15 138 Ca 79
34210 Siran 34 166 Cd 89
73230 Sire, le 73 132 Ff 75
65400 Sireix 65 174 Zf 91
46600 Siréjol 46 138 Bc 79
16440 Sireuil 16 123 Aa 75
24620 Sireuil 24 137 Ba 79
65370 Siridan 65 176 Ad 91
19220 Sirieix 19 126 Ca 77
19380 Sirieix, le 19 138 Be 78
39300 Sirod 39 107 Ff 68
05150 Sironne 05 156 Fd 82
64230 Siros 64 162 Zd 88
71250 Sirot 71 118 Ed 70
20233 Sisco CTC 181 Kc 92
20233 Siscu = Sisco CTC 181 Kc 92
AD400 Sispony ▫ AND 177 Bd 93
87300 Sissac 87 113 Af 72
02150 Sissonne 02 41 Df 51
02240 Sissy 02 40 Dc 50
82340 Sistels 82 149 Ae 84
04200 Sisteron 04 157 Ff 83
15100 Sistrières 15 140 Db 78
57870 Sitifort 57 57 Ha 56
33220 Sivadons, les 33 136 Aa 80
87130 Sivergnat 87 126 Bd 74
84400 Sivergues 84 156 Fc 86
56500 Siviac 56 80 Xa 61
71220 Sivignon 71 117 Ed 70
10130 Sivrey 10 73 Df 60
21230 Sivry 21 105 Ec 66
54610 Sivry 54 56 Gb 56
51800 Sivry-Ante 51 54 Ef 54
77115 Sivry-Courtry 77 71 Ce 57
55100 Sivry-la-Perche 55 55 Fb 54
08240 Sivry-lès-Buzancy 08 42 Ef 52
55110 Sivry-sur-Meuse 55 42 Fb 53
83140 Six-Fours-les-Plages 83 171 Fe 90
86260 Six-Maisons, les 86 100 Ae 68
86430 Six-Routes, les 86 112 Ae 71
74740 Sixt-Fer-à-Cheval 74 121 Ge 72
35550 Sixt-sur-Aff 35 81 Xf 62
29450 Sizun 29 62 Vf 58
29390 Skaer = Scaër 29 79 Wb 60
62164 Slack 62 26 Bd 44
86240 Smarves 86 112 Ac 69
76660 Smermesnil 76 37 Bc 49
20125 Soccia CTC 182 If 95
25600 Sochaux 25 94 Ge 63
64122 Socoa 64 160 Yb 88
88130 Socourt 88 76 Gb 58
59380 Socx 59 27 Cc 43
43350 Soddes 43 141 De 78
64400 Soeix 64 161 Zd 90
57330 Soetrich 57 44 Ga 52
49330 Sœurdres 49 83 Zc 62
89450 Sœuvres 89 90 De 64
58700 Soffin 58 89 Dc 65
27240 Sôgne, la 27 49 Ba 55
89260 Sognes 89 72 Dc 58
77520 Sognolles-en-Montois 77 72 Db 57
51520 Sogny-aux-Moulins 51 54 Ec 55
51340 Sogny-en-l'Angle 51 54 Ee 56
44310 Soherie, la 44 96 Yb 66
14190 Soignolles 14 48 Ze 54
28140 Soignolles 28 70 Be 59
77111 Soignolles-en-Brie 77 51 Ce 57
51210 Soigny 51 53 Dd 56
51700 Soilly 51 53 Dd 54
78200 Soindres 78 50 Be 55
70130 Soing-Cubry-Charentenay 70 93 Ff 63
41230 Soings-en-Sologne 41 86 Bd 64
18000 Soires 18 102 Cc 66
02200 Soissons 02 40 Dc 52
21270 Soissons-sur-Nacey 21 106 Fc 65
77650 Soisy-Bouy 77 72 Db 57
95600 Soisy-sous-Montmorency 95 51 Cb 55
91840 Soisy-sur-École 91 71 Cc 58
91450 Soisy-sur-Seine 91 51 Cc 57
02340 Soize 02 41 Ea 50
28330 Soizé 28 69 Af 60
51120 Soizy-aux-Bois 51 53 De 56
69360 Solaize 69M 130 Ef 75
74130 Solaizon 74 120 Gc 72
20240 Solaro CTC 183 Kb 97
12460 Solasols 12 139 Ce 80
26150 Solaure en Diois 26 143 Fc 80
67130 Solbach 67 77 Hb 58
49610 Solbre 49 83 Zc 64
46500 Sol-del-Pech 46 138 Bd 80
AD100 Soldeu ▫ AND 177 Be 93
04120 Soleilhas 04 158 Gd 85
89290 Soleines, les 89 90 Dd 62
25190 Solemont 25 94 Ge 64
60310 Solente 60 39 Cf 50
20145 Solenzara CTC 185 Kc 97
66270 Soler, le 66 179 Ce 92
18800 Solerieu 18 103 Ce 66
26130 Solérieux 26 155 Ee 82
77111 Solers 77 51 Ce 57
59730 Solesmes 59 30 Dc 47
72300 Solesmes 72 84 Ze 61
38460 Soleymieu 38 131 Fc 74
42560 Soleymieux 42 129 Ea 75
48220 Soleyrols 48 153 Df 83
40210 Solférino 40 146 Za 84
57420 Solgne 57 56 Gb 55
14540 Soliers 14 35 Ze 54
87110 Solignac 87 125 Bb 74
43130 Solignac-sous-Roche 43 129 Df 77
43370 Solignac-sur-Loire 43 141 Df 79
63500 Solignat 63 128 Db 75
61380 Soligny-la-Trappe 61 68 Ad 57
10400 Soligny-les-Étangs 10 72 Dd 58
20140 Sollacaro CTC 184 If 98
42940 Sollègue 42 129 Df 75
73500 Sollières-Envers 73 133 Ge 77
73500 Sollières-Sardières 73 133 Ge 77
83210 Solliès-Pont 83 171 Ga 89
83210 Solliès-Toucas 83 171 Ga 89
83210 Solliès-Ville 83 171 Ga 89
71960 Sologny 71 118 Ee 70
32120 Solomiac 32 149 Af 86
59740 Solre 59 31 Ea 47
59740 Solre-le-Château 59 31 Ea 47
59740 Solrinnes 59 31 Ea 47
12330 Solsac 12 139 Cc 82
45700 Solterre 45 88 Ce 61
47500 Solurac 47 137 Ba 82
71960 Solutré 71 118 Ee 71
11120 Somail, le 11 167 Cf 89
59490 Somain 59 30 Db 46
25520 Sombacour 25 108 Gb 67
21540 Sombernon 21 91 Ee 65
62179 Sombre 62 26 Be 43
62810 Sombrin 62 29 Cd 47
65700 Sombrun 65 162 Aa 88
49360 Somloire 49 98 Zc 66
59213 Sommaing 59 30 Dc 47
55250 Sommaisne 55 55 Fa 55
52130 Sommancourt 52 75 Fa 57
71540 Sommant 71 105 Eb 66
74440 Sommant 74 120 Gd 72
81170 Sommard le Fraisse 81 151 Bf 84
08240 Sommauthe 08 42 Ef 52
18500 Somme 18 102 Cb 66
51800 Somme-Bionne 51 54 Ee 54
89110 Sommecaise 89 89 Db 61
55320 Sommedieue 55 55 Fc 54
58140 Sommée 58 90 Df 65
55800 Sommeilles 55 54 Ef 55
02470 Sommelans 02 52 Db 54
55170 Sommelonne 55 55 Fa 56
51600 Sommepy-Tahure 51 54 Ed 53
08250 Sommerance 08 42 Ef 52
52150 Sommerécourt 52 75 Fd 59
60210 Sommereux 60 38 Bf 51
02260 Sommeron 02 41 Df 49
14400 Sommervieu 14 34 Zc 53
54110 Sommerviller 54 56 Gc 57
76440 Sommery 76 37 Bc 51
76560 Sommesnil 76 36 Ae 50
51320 Sommesous 51 53 Eb 56
51600 Somme-Suippe 51 54 Ed 54
51600 Somme-Tourbe 51 54 Ed 54
02480 Sommette 02 40 Da 50
25510 Sommette, la 25 108 Gd 65
10320 Sommeval 10 73 Df 60
51460 Somme-Vesle 51 54 Ed 55
52170 Sommeville 52 75 Fa 57
52220 Sommevoire 52 74 Ef 58
51330 Somme-Yèvre 51 54 Ee 55
30250 Sommières 30 154 Ea 86
86160 Sommières-du-Clain 86 112 Ac 71
82240 Somplessac 82 150 Bd 83
79110 Sompt 79 111 Zf 72
51320 Sompuis 51 54 Ec 56
51290 Somsois 51 74 Ed 57
08300 Son 08 41 Eb 51
33650 Son, le 33 135 Zc 81
46320 Sonac 46 138 Bf 80
63380 Sonazet 63 115 Cd 73
78120 Sonchamp 78 70 Bf 57
88170 Soncourt 88 76 Ff 58
52320 Soncourt-sur-Marne 52 75 Fa 59
68380 Sondernach 68 77 Ha 61
68480 Sondersdorf 68 95 Hc 64
38840 Sône, la 38 143 Fb 78
73400 Soney 73 132 Gc 74
60380 Songeons 60 38 Bf 51
39130 Songeson 39 107 Fe 69
01260 Songieu 01 119 Fe 73
51240 Songy 51 54 Ed 56
12700 Sonnac 12 138 Ca 81
17160 Sonnac 17 123 Ze 73
11230 Sonnac-sur-L'Hers 11 178 Bf 90
37500 Sonnay 37 99 Ab 66
38150 Sonnay 38 130 Ef 76
73000 Sonnaz 73 132 Ff 75
58140 Sonne 58 90 Df 65
16130 Sonneville 16 123 Ze 75
16170 Sonneville 16 123 Zf 74
02270 Sons-et-Ronchères 02 40 De 50
01580 Sonthonnax-la-Montagne 01 119 Fd 71
01560 Sonville 01 118 Fa 70
28160 Sonville 28 69 Bb 59
37360 Sonzay 37 85 Ac 63
40510 Soorts 40 160 Yd 86
40150 Soorts-Hossegor 40 160 Yd 87
06560 Sophia-Antipolis 06 173 Ha 87
68780 Soppe-le-Bas 68 94 Ha 62
68780 Soppe-le-Haut 68 94 Ha 62
09800 Sor 09 176 Af 91
70190 Sorans-lès-Breurey 70 93 Ga 64
02580 Sorbais 02 41 Df 49
32110 Sorbets 32 162 Zf 86
40320 Sorbets 40 162 Ze 87
55230 Sorbey 55 43 Fd 52
57580 Sorbey 57 56 Gb 54
03220 Sorbier 03 116 Dd 70
05150 Sorbiers 05 156 Fd 82
42290 Sorbiers 42 130 Ec 76
20152 Sorbollano CTC 185 Ka 98
08300 Sorbon 08 41 Ec 51
34520 Sorbs 34 153 Dc 85
20213 Sorbu Ocagnano CTC 181 Kc 94
20213 Sorbu Ocagnanu = Sorbo-Ocagnano CTC 181 Kc 94
08270 Sorcy-Bauthémont 08 41 Ed 51
55190 Sorcy-Saint-Martin 55 55 Fd 56
40300 Sorde-l'Abbaye 40 161 Yf 87
44650 Sorderie, la 44 97 Yc 67
40430 Sore 40 147 Zc 83
65350 Soréac 65 162 Aa 89
66690 Sorède 66 179 Cf 93
08090 Sorel 08 42 Ee 50
80240 Sorel 80 39 Da 48
80490 Sorel-en-Vimeu 80 38 Bf 48
28260 Sorel-Moussel 28 50 Bc 55
08800 Sorendal 08 42 Ef 49
81540 Sorèze 81 165 Ca 88
09110 Sorgeat 09 177 Bf 92
24420 Sorges et Ligueux en Périgord 24 125 Af 77
84700 Sorgues 84 155 Ef 84
64120 Sorhapuru 64 161 Za 89
64220 Sorhueta 64 160 Ye 89
50200 Sorière, la 50 33 Yc 54
17260 Sorignets, les 17 122 Zc 75
37250 Sorigny 37 100 Ae 65
04200 Sorin 04 157 Ga 83
85440 Sorin 85 109 Yc 70
79150 Sorinière, la 79 98 Zd 67
44840 Sorinières, les 44 97 Yc 66
20246 Sorio CTC 181 Kb 93
20246 Soriu = Sorio CTC 181 Kb 93
46400 Sorn 46 138 Bf 79
89570 Sormery 89 73 De 60
08150 Sormonne 08 41 Ed 50
19290 Sornac 19 126 Cb 74
AD300 Sornàs ▫ AND 177 Bd 93
70150 Sornay 70 92 Fe 65
71500 Sornay 71 106 Fb 69
54280 Sornéville 54 56 Gc 56
76540 Sorquainville 76 36 Ad 50
77690 Sorques 77 71 Ce 58
62170 Sorrus 62 28 Be 46
40180 Sort-en-Chalosse 40 161 Za 86
50310 Sortosville 50 33 Yd 52
50270 Sortosville-en-Beaumont 50 33 Yb 52
47170 Sos 47 148 Aa 84
06380 Sospel 06 159 Hc 85
86230 Sossais 86 99 Ac 67
65370 Sost 65 176 Ad 91
01260 Sothonod 01 119 Fe 73
20146 Sotta CTC 185 Kb 99
50260 Sottevast 50 33 Yc 51
50340 Sotteville 50 33 Yb 51
76300 Sotteville-lès-Rouen 76 37 Ba 52
76410 Sotteville-sous-le-Val 76 37 Ba 53
76740 Sotteville-sur-Mer 76 37 Ae 49
57170 Sotzeling 57 57 Gd 55
23230 Sou, le 23 114 Cb 71
81580 Soual 81 165 Ca 87
28400 Souancé-au-Perche 28 69 Af 59
62111 Souastre 62 29 Cd 48
32300 Soubaignan 32 163 Ac 87
24480 Soubartelle 24 137 Af 80

324 | Serres

32240 Soubère 32 147 Zf 85
34700 Soubès 34 153 Dc 86
30140 Soubeyran 30 154 Df 84
24700 Soubie 24 135 Aa 78
33840 Soubiran 33 147 Ze 82
47300 Soubirous 47 136 Ae 82
17780 Soubise 17 110 Yf 73
65700 Soublecause 65 162 Zf 87
17150 Soubran 17 123 Zc 76
23250 Soubrebost 23 114 Bf 73
26300 Soubredioux, les 26 143 Fa 79
49140 Soucelles 49 84 Zd 63
07380 Souche, la 07 141 Eb 81
83840 Souche, la 83 172 Gd 86
88650 Souche, le 88 77 Gf 59
43160 Souchère, la 43 129 De 77
18290 Souchet, le 18 102 Ca 66
62153 Souchez 62 29 Ce 46
57960 Soucht 57 58 Hc 55
39130 Soucia 39 119 Fe 69
69510 Soucieu-en-Jarrest 69M 130 Ee 74
46300 Soucirac 46 138 Bd 80
01150 Souclin 01 131 Fc 73
02600 Soucy 02 40 Da 53
89100 Soucy 89 72 Db 59
19370 Soudaine-Lavinadière 19 126 Be 75
44110 Soudan 44 82 Ye 62
79800 Soudan 79 111 Zf 70
24360 Soudat 24 124 Ad 75
41170 Souday 41 69 Af 60
51320 Soudé 51 54 Eb 56
19300 Soudeilles 19 126 Ca 76
51320 Soudé-le-Grand = Soudé-Sainte-Croix 51 54 Eb 56
51320 Soudé-le-Petit = Soudé-Notre-Dame 51 54 Eb 56
51320 Soudé-Notre-Dame = Soudé-le-Petit 51 54 Eb 56
51320 Soudé-Sainte-Croix = Soudé-le-Grand 51 54 Eb 56
27410 Soudière, la 27 49 Ae 54
30460 Soudorgues 30 154 De 84
51320 Soudron 51 53 Eb 55
31160 Soueich 31 176 Ae 90
09140 Soueix 09 177 Bb 91
81170 Souel 81 151 Bf 84
65430 Soues 65 162 Aa 89
80310 Soues 80 38 Ca 49
41300 Souesmes 41 87 Cb 64
67460 Souffelweyersheim 67 58 He 57
67620 Soufflenheim 67 59 Hf 56
05800 Souffles 05 144 Ga 79
87120 Souffrangeas 87 126 Be 75
16380 Souffrignac 16 124 Ad 75
36500 Sougé 36 101 Bc 67
41800 Sougé 41 85 Ae 62
35610 Sougéal 35 66 Yc 57
72130 Sougé-le-Ganelon 72 68 Zf 59
89520 Sougères-en-Puisaye 89 89 Db 63
89470 Sougères-sur-Sinotte 89 90 Dd 61
11190 Sougraigne 11 178 Cc 91
45410 Sougy 45 70 Be 60
58300 Sougy-sur-Loire 58 104 Dc 67
51600 Souhain-Perthes-lès-Hurlus 51 54 Ed 53
17600 Souhe 17 122 Za 74
55220 Souhesmes-Rampont, les 55 55 Fb 54
21140 Souhey 21 91 Ec 64
62810 Souich, le 62 29 Cc 47
85420 Souil 85 110 Zb 70
79800 Souil, le 79 111 Zf 71
11400 Souilhanels 11 165 Bf 88
11400 Souilhe 11 165 Bf 88
17270 Souillac 17 135 Ze 77
46200 Souillac 46 138 Bc 79
46300 Souillaguet 46 137 Bc 80
89420 Souillats, les 89 90 Ea 63
72380 Souillé 72 68 Ab 60
50300 Souillet 50 46 Yd 56
25270 Souillot, le 25 107 Gb 67
55220 Souilly 55 55 Fb 54
43340 Souils, les 43 141 De 79
33113 Souis 33 147 Zd 82
09000 Soula 09 177 Be 91
33780 Soulac-sur-Mer 33 122 Yf 75
43500 Soulage 43 129 Df 76
12800 Soulages 12 151 Cb 83
15100 Soulages 15 140 Db 78
12210 Soulages-Bonneval 12 139 Ce 80
34520 Soulagets 34 153 Dc 85
65100 Soulagnets 65 175 Aa 90
52230 Soulaincourt 52 75 Fb 58
10200 Soulaines-Dhuys 10 74 Ee 58
49610 Soulaines-sur-Aubance 49 84 Zc 64
49460 Soulaire-et-Bourg 49 83 Zc 63
28130 Soulaires 28 70 Bd 57
09320 Soulan 09 177 Bb 91
32810 Soulan 32 163 Ae 87
65170 Soulan 65 175 Ab 91
31230 Soulan, le 31 164 Af 89
27370 Soulanger, le 27 49 Af 53
51300 Soulanges 51 54 Ed 56
18220 Soulangis 18 102 Cd 65
18340 Soulangy 18 102 Cc 67
14700 Soulangy 14 48 Ze 55
16210 Soulard, le 16 124 Aa 77
11330 Soulatgé 11 178 Cd 91
52150 Soulaucourt-sur-Mouzon 52 75 Fe 59
10400 Soulaunoy 10 73 Dd 57
24540 Soulaures 24 137 Af 81
24560 Soulbarède 24 136 Ad 80
79100 Soulbrois 79 98 Ze 66
25190 Soulce-Cernay 25 94 Gf 65
81260 Soulègre 81 166 Cd 86
14260* Souleuvre en Bocage 14 47 Zb 55
40200 Souleyraou 40 146 Ye 83
12440 Souleysset 12 151 Cb 83
53210 Soulgé-sur-Ouette 53 67 Zc 60
34330 Soulié, le 34 166 Ce 87
05350 Soulier 05 145 Ge 80
23250 Soulier 23 114 Be 72
63820 Soulier 63 127 Ce 74
23340 Soulière 23 126 Ca 74
51130 Soulières 51 53 Df 55
47150 Souliès 47 137 Ae 81
79600 Soulièvres 79 99 Ze 68
33760 Soulignac 33 135 Ze 80
79270 Souligné 79 110 Zc 71
72210 Souligné-Flacé 72 68 Aa 61
72290 Souligné-sous-Ballon 72 68 Ab 60
17250 Soulignonne 17 122 Zb 74
10320 Souligny 10 73 Df 59
72370 Soulitré 72 68 Ac 60
85300 Soullans 85 96 Ya 68
50750 Soulles 50 46 Ye 54
47290 Soulodres 47 136 Ad 81
46240 Soulomès 46 138 Bd 81
88630 Soulosse-sous-Saint Elophe 88 75 Fe 58
81340 Souls 81 151 Cc 84
03370 Soult, le 03 115 Cc 70
15200 Soultz 15 127 Cb 77
68230 Soultzbach-les-Bains 68 77 Hb 60
68140 Soultzeren 68 77 Ha 60
68360 Soultz-Haut-Rhin 68 95 Hb 61
67120 Soultz-les-Bains 67 60 Hc 57
68570 Soultzmatt 68 60 Hb 61
67250 Soultz-sous-Forêts 67 58 Hf 55
44660 Soulvache 44 82 Yd 62
87130 Soumagnas 87 126 Bd 74
19320 Soumaille 19 126 Bf 77
89570 Soumaintrain 89 73 De 60
30125 Soumane 30 153 De 84
23600 Soumans 23 114 Cb 71
17450 Soumard 17 110 Yf 73
58150 Soumard 58 88 Cf 65
34600 Soumartre 34 167 Db 87
24640 Soumeil 24 125 Ba 77
23460 Soumeix 23 126 Bf 74
47120 Soumensac 47 136 Ab 80
17130 Souméras 17 123 Zd 77
09140 Soumère, la 09 176 Ba 91
34700 Soumont 34 167 Dc 86
14420 Soumont-Saint-Quentin 14 48 Ze 55
64420 Soumoulou 64 162 Ze 89
19290 Sounaleix 19 126 Ca 74
80290 Sounlicourt 80 38 Bf 50
03370 Souperons 03 115 Cc 69
11320 Soupex 11 165 Bf 88
77460 Souppes-sur-Loing 77 71 Ce 59
40250 Souprosse 40 147 Zb 86
81260 Souque, la 81 166 Cd 87
32170 Souques 32 163 Ac 88
40260 Souquet 40 146 Yf 85
64250 Souraïde 64 160 Yd 88
25250 Sourans 25 94 Gd 64
24460 Sourbarie 24 124 Ae 77
45590 Source 45 87 Bf 62
49440 Source 49 83 Yf 63
45100 Source, la 45 87 Bf 61
02110 Source de la Somme 02 40 Dc 49
69210 Sourcieux-les-Mines 69M 130 Ed 74
02140 Sourd, le 02 40 De 49
50150 Sourdeval 50 47 Za 56
50450 Sourdeval-les-Bois 50 46 Ye 55
19120 Sourdoire 19 138 Be 79
17170 Sourdon 17 110 Za 71
80250 Sourdon 80 39 Cc 50
77171 Sourdun 77 72 Dc 57
56300 Sourn, le 56 79 Xa 60
41800 Sournas, la 41 85 Ae 62
66730 Sournia 66 178 Cc 92
15200 Sourniac 15 127 Cb 77
04290 Sourribes 04 157 Ga 84
18240 Sours 18 88 Cf 64
28630 Sours 28 70 Bd 58
19550 Soursac 19 126 Cb 77
24400 Sourzac 24 136 Ac 78
46190 Sousceyrac-en-Quercy 46 138 Ca 79
74140 Sous-Etraz 74 120 Gb 71
49540 Sousigné 49 98 Zd 65
24380 Sous-le-Denis 24 136 Ae 78
08220 Sous-lès-Faux 08 41 Eb 50
23150 Sous-Parsat 23 114 Bf 72
26160 Souspierre 26 143 Ef 81
33790 Soussac 33 135 Aa 80
33460 Soussans 33 134 Zb 78
63210 Soussat 63 127 Ce 74
21350 Soussey-sur-Brionne 21 91 Ed 65
82150 Soussis 82 149 Ba 82
40140 Soustons 40 160 Ye 86
19160 Soustras 19 126 Cb 76
34190 Soutayrol 34 153 Dd 85
42260 Souternon 42 129 Df 73
23300 Souterraine, la 23 113 Bc 71
30600 Souteyranne, la 30 169 Ec 87
16150 Soutière, la 16 124 Ae 73
79310 Soutiers 79 111 Ze 69
60290 Soutraine 60 39 Cc 53
18520 Soutrin 18 103 Ce 66
39380 Souvans 39 107 Fd 67
71190 Souve 71 104 Ea 68
54115 Souveraincourt 54 76 Ga 58
30250 Souvignargues 30 154 Ea 86
16240 Souvigné 16 111 Aa 73
37330 Souvigné 37 85 Ac 63
79800 Souvigné 79 111 Ze 70
72400 Souvigné-sur-Même 72 68 Ad 59
72300 Souvigné-sur-Sarthe 72 84 Zd 62
03210 Souvigny 03 116 Db 69
37530 Souvigny-de-Touraine 37 86 Ba 64
41600 Souvigny-en-Sologne 41 87 Ca 63
72240 Souvré 72 68 Zf 60
65350 Souyeaux 65 163 Ab 89
12330 Souyri 12 151 Cd 82
49400 Souzay-Champigny 49 99 Zf 65
24590 Souzet 24 137 Bc 78
12200 Souzils 12 151 Bf 83
69610 Souzy 69M 130 Ec 74
91580 Souzy-la-Briche 91 71 Ca 57
20250 Soveria CTC 183 Ka 94
56270 Soy 56 79 Wd 62
26400 Soyans 26 143 Fa 81
16800 Soyaux 16 124 Ab 75
18200 Soye 18 102 Cc 68
25250 Soye 25 94 Gc 64
02490 Soyécourt 02 40 Da 49
80200 Soyécourt 80 39 Ce 49
18340 Soye-en-Septaine 18 102 Cc 66
52400 Soyers 52 92 Fe 61
07130 Soyons 07 142 Ef 79
55300 Spada 55 55 Fd 55
67340 Sparsbach 67 58 Hc 55
72700 Spay 72 84 Aa 61
44590 Spay, le 44 82 Yc 62
20270 Spazzola CTC 183 Kc 95
68720 Spechbach 68 95 Hb 62
68720 Spechbach-le-Bas 68 95 Hb 62
68720 Spechbach-le-Haut 68 95 Hb 62
31210 Spéhis, les 31 163 Ad 90
20226 Speloncato CTC 180 If 93
06530 Spéracèdes 06 172 Gf 87
67140 Sperberbaechtel 67 60 Hb 58
29540 Spézet 29 79 Wb 59
57350 Spicheren 57 57 Gf 53
55230 Spincourt 55 43 Fe 53
57490 Spittel = l'Hôpital 57 57 Ge 54
28630 Spoir 28 70 Bc 58
19550 Spontour 19 126 Cb 77
54800 Sponville 54 56 Fe 54
10200 Spoy 10 74 Ed 59
21120 Spoy 21 92 Fb 64
45480 Spuis 45 70 Ca 60
20226 Spuncatu = Speloncato CTC 180 If 93
59380 Spycker 59 27 Cb 43
22200 Squiffiec 22 63 Wf 57
29590 Squiriou 29 62 Vf 59
68850 Staffelfelden 68 95 Hb 62
93240 Stains 93 51 Cc 55
55500 Stainville 55 55 Fb 57
67420 Stampoumont 67 77 Hb 58
29250 Stang 29 62 Vf 57
29120 Stang, le 29 78 Vd 61
29720 Stang-ar-Bacol 29 78 Ve 61
29510 Stang-Kergoulay 29 78 Wa 60
29140 Stang-Tréblay 29 78 Wb 61
29500 Stang-Venn 29 78 Vf 60
13200 Stanislas 13 169 Ed 87
22680 Staol = Étables-sur-Mer 22 64 Xa 57
59190 Staple 59 27 Cc 44
58150 Station Géophysique du Nivernais 58 89 Da 65
67770 Stattmatten 67 59 Ia 56
20229 Stazzona CTC 183 Kc 94
59270 Steeht' je 59 29 Ce 44
59189 Steenbecque 59 29 Cc 44
59380 Steene 59 27 Cc 43
59114 Steenvoorde 59 30 Cd 44
59181 Steenwerck 59 30 Ce 44
67220 Steige 67 60 Hb 58
57430 Steinbach 57 57 Gf 55
68700 Steinbach 68 95 Ha 62
67790 Steinbourg 67 58 Hc 56
68440 Steinbrunn-le-Bas 68 95 Hc 62
68440 Steinbrunn-le-Haut 68 95 Hc 63
67160 Steinseltz 67 58 Hf 54
68640 Steinsoultz 68 95 Hc 63
62780 Stella-Plage 62 28 Bd 46
55700 Stenay 55 42 Fb 52
67170 Stephansfeld 67 58 He 56
68780 Sternenberg 68 94 Ha 62
68510 Stetten 68 95 Hc 63
89160 Stigny 89 90 Eb 62
67190 Still 67 60 Hc 57
57350 Stiring-Wendel 57 57 Gf 53
56300 Stival 56 79 Xa 60
67100 Stockfeld 67 60 He 57
08390 Stonne 08 42 Ef 51
68470 Storckensohn 68 94 Gf 61
68140 Stosswihr 68 77 Ha 60
67140 Stotzheim 67 60 Hc 58
67000 Strasbourg 67 60 He 57
67000 Straßburg = Strasbourg 67 60 He 57
59270 Strazeele 59 30 Cd 44
46600 Strenquels 46 138 Bd 79
46270 Struels, les 46 138 Ca 80
68580 Strueth 68 94 Ha 63
67290 Struth 67 58 Hb 55
57970 Stuckange 57 44 Gb 53
56300 Stumultan 56 79 Wf 60
67250 Stundwiller 67 59 Hf 55
57230 Sturzelbronn 57 58 Hd 54
67370 Stutzheim-Offenheim 67 58 Hd 57
90100 Suarce 90 94 Ha 63
20214 Suare CTC 180 Ie 94
20117 Suarella, Eccica- CTC 182 If 97
20620 Suariccia CTC 181 Kc 93
20137 Suartone CTC 185 Kb 100
70120 Suaucourt-et-Pisseloup 70 92 Fe 62
16260 Suaux 16 124 Ad 73
18570 Subdray, le 18 102 Cb 66
65670 Subergelle 65 163 Ac 89
87470 Subertange, la 87 126 Be 74
37310 Sublaines 37 86 Af 65
14400 Subles 14 34 Zb 53
18260 Subligny 18 88 Ce 64
89100 Subligny 89 72 Db 59
50870 Sublingy 50 46 Yd 56
36290 Subtray 36 101 Bb 68
38300 Succieu 38 131 Fc 75
64120 Succos 64 161 Yf 88
44240 Sucé-sur-Erdre 44 82 Yc 64
09220 Suc-et-Santenac 09 177 Bc 92
43400 Suchère, la 43 142 Eb 78
20140 Suddarò = Sollacaro CTC 184 If 98
12120 Suderie, la 12 152 Cc 83
48220 Sud Mont Lozère 48 153 De 82
81640 Suech 81 151 Ca 84
18130 Suée, la 18 102 Cd 67
34270 Sueilles 34 153 De 86
41500 Suèvres 41 86 Bc 62
63490 Sugères 63 128 Dc 75
63120 Sugier 63 129 De 74
08400 Sugny 08 42 Ed 52
64470 Suhare 64 161 Za 90
64780 Suhescun 64 160 Ye 89
58150 Suilly-la-Tour 58 89 Da 64
71220 Suin 71 117 Ec 70
51600 Suippes 51 54 Ed 54
77166 Suisnes 77 51 Ce 56
57340 Suisse 57 57 Gd 55
13800 Sulauze 13 170 Ef 87
29750 Suleur, le 29 78 Ve 61
01400 Sulignat 01 118 Ef 71
71500 Sulignat 71 118 Fa 69
20145 Sulinzara = Solenzara CTC 185 Kc 97
20143 Sullataia CTC 184 If 98
60380 Sully 60 38 Be 51
71240 Sully 71 106 Ee 69
71360 Sully 71 105 Ec 66
89630 Sully 89 90 Ea 64
45450 Sully-la-Chapelle 45 71 Cb 61
45600 Sully-sur-Loire 45 88 Cc 62
56250 Sulniac 56 80 Xc 62
30440 Sumène 30 153 De 85
68280 Sundhoffen 68 60 Hc 60
67920 Sundhouse 67 60 Hd 59
64470 Sunharette 64 161 Za 90
31110 Superbagnères 31 176 Ad 92
63610 Super-Besse 63 127 Cf 75
66210 Super-Bolquère 66 178 Ca 93
05250 Superdévoly 05 144 Ff 80
66480 Super-las-Illas 66 179 Ce 94
15300 Super-Lioran 15 139 Ce 78
74120 Super-Megève 74 133 Gd 73
04400 Super-Sauze 04 158 Ge 82
39300 Supt 39 107 Ff 67
06450 Suquet, le 06 159 Hb 85
38730 Surand, le 38 131 Fd 76
63720 Surat 63 116 Db 73
09400 Surba 09 177 Bd 91
38118 Surbaix 38 131 Fc 74
67250 Surbourg 67 58 Hf 55
20152 Surbuddà = Sorbollano CTC 185 Ka 98
80620 Surcamps 80 29 Ca 48
61500 Surdon 61 48 Ab 57
19400 sur-Dordogne 19 138 Bf 78
87130 Surdoux 87 126 Bd 75
61360 Suré 61 68 Ac 58
38134* Sure en Chartreuse, la 38 131 Fd 76
72370 Surfonds 72 68 Ac 61
02240 Surfontaine 02 40 Dc 50
17700 Surgères 17 110 Zb 72
12150 Surguières 12 152 Cf 82
58500 Surgy 58 89 Dd 63
88140 Suriauville 88 76 Ff 59
38150 Surieu 38 130 Ef 76
79220 Surin 79 110 Zd 70
86250 Surin 86 112 Ac 72
16270 Suris 16 124 Ad 73
24210 Surjac 24 125 Ba 77
01420 Surjoux 01 119 Fe 72
36300 Surjoux 36 100 Ba 68
74360 Sur-la-Fontaine 74 121 Ge 71
25380 Surmont 25 94 Gd 65
62850 Surques 62 27 Bf 44
14710 Surrain 14 47 Za 53
50270 Surtainville 50 33 Yb 52
27400 Surtauville 27 49 Ba 53
61310 Survie 61 48 Ab 55
04140 Surville 04 157 Gb 82
14130 Surville 14 35 Ab 53
27400 Surville 27 49 Ba 53
50250 Surville 50 46 Yb 53
95470 Survilliers 95 51 Cd 54
08090 Sury 08 42 Ed 50
58270 Sury 58 103 Dc 66
45530 Sury-aux-Bois 45 71 Cc 61
18300 Sury-en-Vaux 18 88 Ce 64
18260 Sury-ès-Bois 18 88 Ce 64
42450 Sury-le-Comtal 42 129 Eb 75
18240 Sury-près-Léré 18 88 Cf 64
56450 Surzur 56 80 Xc 63
64190 Sus 64 161 Zb 89
77390 Suscy-sous-Yèbles 77 71 Ce 57
64190 Susmiou 64 161 Zb 89
87130 Sussac 87 126 Bd 75
62810 Sus-Saint-Léger 62 29 Cc 47
34160 Sussargues 34 168 Ea 86
03450 Sussat 03 115 Da 72
64120 Sussaute 64 161 Yf 88
21430 Sussey 21 105 Ec 65
01260 Sutrieu 01 119 Fd 73
40110 Suzan 40 147 Zb 85
08130 Suzanne 08 42 Ed 51
80340 Suzanne 80 39 Ce 49
13130 Suzanne, la 13 170 Fa 88
52300 Suzannecourt 52 75 Fb 58
27420 Suzay 27 50 Bd 53
26400 Suze 26 143 Fa 80
26790 Suze-la-Rousse 26 155 Ef 83
72210 Suze-sur-Sarthe, la 72 84 Aa 61
84190 Suzette 84 155 Fa 84
60400 Suzoy 60 39 Cf 51
02320 Suzy 02 40 Dc 51
08390 Sy 08 42 Ef 51
39300 Syam 39 107 Ff 68
88410 Sybille, la 88 76 Ga 60
27240 Sylvains-les-Moulains 27 49 Ba 55
12360 Sylvanès 12 152 Cf 85
12360 Sylvanès-les-Bains 12 152 Cf 86
88120 Syndicat, le 88 77 Ge 60

T

64190 Tabaille-Usquain 64 161 Za 88
33550 Tabanac 33 135 Zd 80
73110 Table, la 73 132 Gb 76
85310 Tablier, le 85 109 Yd 69
09600 Tabre 09 177 Bf 91
16260 Tâche 16 124 Ac 73
79600 Tâche, la 79 99 Zf 68
58140 Tachely 58 104 De 65
17160 Tâcherie, la 17 123 Ze 74
32260 Tachoires 32 163 Ad 88
78910 Tacoignières 78 50 Be 55
44522 Tâcon 44 82 Ye 64
58420 Taconnay 58 89 Dc 65
54480 Taconville 54 77 Gf 57
22100 Taden 22 65 Xf 58
64330 Tadousse-Ussau 64 162 Ze 87
71480 Tageat 71 119 Fb 69
15260 Tagenac 15 140 Cf 79
20151 Taggia CTC 182 If 96
20230 Taglio-Isolaccio CTC 181 Kc 94
20144 Tagliu CTC 185 Kb 98
20230 Tagliu è Isolacciu = Taglio-Isolaccio CTC 181 Kc 94
71190 Tagnière, la 71 105 Eb 68
08300 Tagnon 08 41 Eb 52
68720 Tagolsheim 68 95 Hb 63
33380 Tagon 33 134 Za 81
68130 Tagsdorf 68 95 Hb 63
89560 Taigny 89 89 Dc 63
43300 Tailhac 43 140 Dc 78
84300 Taillades 84 155 Fa 86
34330 Taillades, les 34 167 Cf 87
55140 Taillancourt 55 75 Fe 57
33320 Taillan-Médoc, le 33 134 Zb 79
17350 Taillant 17 110 Zc 73
37140 Taille, la 37 84 Aa 65
61100 Taillebois 61 47 Zd 56
17350 Taillebourg 17 122 Zc 73
31210 Taillebourg 31 163 Ad 90
47200 Taillebourg 47 148 Ab 82
33580 Taillecavat 33 136 Aa 81
85220 Taillée, la 85 96 Yb 68
85450 Taillée, la 85 110 Za 70
41170 Taillefer 41 69 Ae 60
02600 Taillefontaine 02 39 Da 53
66400 Taillet 66 179 Ce 93
08230 Taillette 08 41 Ec 49
35500 Taillis 35 66 Ye 59
08240 Tailly 08 42 Fa 52
21190 Tailly 21 106 Ee 67
80270 Tailly 80 38 Bf 49
26600 Tain-l' Hermitage 26 142 Ef 78
50170 Tains 50 66 Yd 57
88100 Taintrux 88 77 Gf 59
71100 Taisey 71 106 Ee 68
59550 Taisnières-en-Thiérache 59 31 De 48
59570 Taisnières-sur-Hon 59 31 Df 47
80290 Taisnil 80 38 Ca 50
18370 Taissone 18 114 Cb 70
51500 Taissy 51 53 Ea 53
81130 Taïx 81 151 Ca 84
71250 Taizé 71 118 Ee 69
79100 Taizé 79 99 Zf 67
16700 Taizé-Aizie 16 111 Ab 72
79290 Taizon 79 99 Ze 66
08360 Taizy 08 41 Eb 51
65300 Tajan 65 163 Ac 89
20230 Talafredu CTC 183 Kc 95
11220 Talairan 11 179 Cd 90
43100 Talairat 43 128 Db 77
33590 Talais 33 122 Yf 76
19430 Talamet 19 138 Bf 79
57525 Talange 57 56 Gb 53
21240 Talant 21 91 Fa 64
29160 Tal-ar-Groas 29 62 Vd 59
33680 Talaris 33 134 Yf 78
20230 Talasani CTC 183 Kc 94
66360 Talau 66 178 Cb 93
42350 Talaudière, la 42 130 Ec 76
65500 Talazac 65 162 Aa 88
59310 Talbot, le 59 30 Db 46
41370 Talcy 41 86 Bc 62
89420 Talcy 89 90 Ea 63
33400 Talence 33 135 Zc 80
07340 Talencieux 07 130 Ee 77
35160 Talensac 35 65 Ya 60
12440 Talespues 12 151 Cc 82
24380 Talet, le 24 137 Ae 78
30570 Taleyrac 30 153 Dd 84
24330 Taleyrandies, les 24 137 Af 78
56650 Talhouet 56 80 We 62
15170 Talizat 15 140 Da 78
25680 Tallans 25 93 Gb 64
71240 Tallant 71 106 Ef 69
05130 Tallard 05 144 Ga 82
25870 Tallenay 25 93 Ga 65
63450 Tallende 63 128 Da 74
40260 Taller 40 146 Yf 85
43370 Tallobre 43 141 Df 79
74290 Talloires-Montim 74 132 Gb 73
20270 Tallone CTC 183 Kc 95
20270 Tallone CTC 183 Kc 96
79200 Tallud, le 79 98 Ze 69
85390 Tallud-Sainte-Gemme 85 98 Za 68
08250 Talma 08 42 Ef 52
80260 Talmas 80 39 Cb 48
21270 Talmay 21 92 Fc 64
17120 Talmont 17 122 Za 75
60590 Talmontiers 60 38 Be 52
85440 Talmont-Saint-Hilaire 85 109 Yc 70
58190 Talon 58 89 Dd 64
89500 Talouan 89 72 Dc 60
58240 Taloux 58 103 Da 68
51270 Talus-Saint-Prix 51 53 De 55
69440 Taluyers 69M 130 Ee 75
56930 Talvern-Nénez 56 64 Xa 61
34590 Tamariguières 34 168 Ea 87
13500 Tamaris 13 170 Fa 89
34450 Tamarissière, la 34 167 Dc 89
65330 Tamboury 65 163 Ac 89
50700 Tamerville 50 33 Yd 51
26510 Tamizat 26 156 Fc 82
58110 Tamnay-en-Bazois 58 104 De 66

Tamnay-en-Bazois | 325

24620 Tamniès 24 137 Ba 79
15100 Tanavelle 15 140 Da 78
21310 Tanay 21 92 Fb 64
76430 Tancarville 76 36 Ac 52
35133 Tanceraie, la 35 66 Ye 59
49310 Tancoigné 49 98 Zd 65
71740 Tancon 71 117 Eb 71
77440 Tancrou 77 52 Da 55
39400 Tancua 39 120 Ff 69
32700 Tane 32 149 Ae 85
62550 Tangry 62 29 Cc 46
09300 Tanière 09 177 Be 91
18330 Tanières, les 18 87 Ca 64
74440 Taninges 74 120 Gd 72
89430 Tanlay 89 90 Ea 61
68370 Tannach 68 77 Ha 60
08390 Tannay 08 42 Ee 51
58190 Tannay 58 89 Dd 64
59189 Tannay 59 29 Cc 45
83440 Tanneron 83 172 Gf 87
89350 Tannerre-en-Puisaye 89 89 Da 62
50580 Tannière, la 50 33 Yc 53
53220 Tannière, la 53 66 Za 58
02220 Tannières 02 53 Dd 53
55000 Tannois 55 55 Fb 56
61150 Tanques 61 48 Zf 56
54116 Tantonville 54 76 Ga 58
22150 Tantouille, la 22 64 Xc 59
50320 Tanu, le 50 46 Yd 56
81190 Tanus 81 151 Cb 84
61500 Tanville 61 68 Aa 57
17260 Tanzac 17 122 Zc 75
29670 Taole = Taulé 29 62 Wa 57
62215 Tap-Cul, le 62 27 Bf 43
12270 Tapie, la 12 151 Ca 83
09130 Tapioffoix 09 164 Bc 89
43380 Tapon 43 128 Dc 77
69220 Taponas 69D 118 Ee 72
16110 Taponnat-Fleurignac 16 124 Ac 74
31570 Tarabel 31 165 Be 87
83460 Taradeau 83 172 Gc 88
47380 Taradel 47 136 Ac 82
69170 Tarare 69D 117 Ec 73
13150 Tarascon 13 155 Ed 86
09400 Tarascon-sur-Ariège 09 177 Bd 91
65320 Tarasteix 65 162 Zf 89
82140 Taraut 82 150 Be 83
20214 Tarazone CTC 180 Ie 93
48310 Tarbes 48 140 Db 81
65000 Tarbes 65 162 Aa 89
25620 Tarcenay 25 107 Ga 66
39160 Tarcia 39 119 Fc 70
20135 Tarcu CTC 185 Kc 98
01510 Tard 01 131 Fd 73
28250 Tardais 28 69 Ba 57
23500 Tarderon, le 23 126 Ca 73
23170 Tardes 23 114 Cc 72
81630 Tardets, les 81 150 Bd 85
64470 Tardets-Sorholus 64 161 Za 90
85120 Tardière, la 85 98 Zb 69
62179 Tardinghen 62 26 Bd 43
42660 Tarentaise 42 130 Ec 76
66120 Targasonne 66 178 Ca 93
86100 Targé 86 100 Ad 68
03140 Target 03 115 Da 71
62580 Targette, la 62 29 Ce 46
63680 Targnat 63 128 Db 73
33760 Targon 33 135 Ze 80
33730 Targos 33 135 Zd 82
29860 Tariec 29 61 Vd 57
33730 Taris 33 147 Zd 82
03140 Tarjazet 03 115 Da 71
60400 Tarlefesse 60 39 Da 51
19170 Tarnac 19 126 Bf 74
64330 Taron-Sadirac-Viellenave 64 162 Ze 87
57260 Tarquimpol 57 57 Ge 56
20114 Tarrabucceta CTC 185 Ka 99
20234 Tarrano CTC 183 Kc 94
20234 Tarranu = Tarrano CTC 183 Kc 94
43370 Tarreyres 43 141 Df 79
32400 Tarsac 32 162 Zf 86
64360 Tarsacq 64 162 Zc 88
21120 Tarsul 21 91 Ef 63
46320 Tartabelle 46 138 Be 80
40400 Tartas 40 147 Zb 85
70500 Tartécourt 70 93 Ff 61
63190 Tarteire 63 128 Dc 74
02290 Tartiers 02 40 Db 52
47600 Tartifume 47 148 Ac 84
60120 Tartigny 60 39 Cc 51
21110 Tart-L'Abbaye 21 106 Fb 65
21110 Tart-le-Bas 21 106 Fb 65
21110 Tart-le-Haut 21 106 Fb 65
04330 Tartonne 04 157 Gc 84
44680 Tartouzerie, la 44 96 Ya 66
28190 Tartre 28 69 Bb 58
39140 Tartre, le 39 106 Fc 68
34130 Tartuguière 34 168 Ea 87
08380 Tarzy 08 41 Eb 49
32160 Tasque 32 162 Aa 87
24300 Tassat 24 124 Ad 75
72430 Tassé 72 84 Zf 61
39120 Tassenières 39 106 Fd 67
12310 Tassières, les 12 152 Cf 82
72540 Tassillé 72 67 Zf 61
20140 Tassinca CTC 184 Ie 98
69160 Tassin-la-Demi-Lune 69M 130 Ee 74
20134 Tasso CTC 183 Ka 97
20134 Tassu = Tasso CTC 183 Ka 97
07140 Tastavin 07 141 Ea 81
40140 Tastet 40 146 Ye 86
62500 Tatinghem 62 27 Cb 44
26410 Tatins, les 26 143 Fd 81
16360 Tâtre, le 16 123 Ze 76
20219 Tattone CTC 183 Ka 96
79370 Tauché 79 111 Ze 71
17170 Taugon 17 110 Za 71
40120 Tauladon 40 147 Zd 84
79220 Taulais 79 111 Ze 70
29670 Taulé = Taole 29 62 Wa 57
58350 Taules, les 58 89 Db 65
26770 Taulignan 26 155 Ef 82
66110 Taulis 66 179 Cd 93
13490 Taulisson, le 13 171 Fd 87
17920 Taupignac 17 122 Yf 74
56800 Taupont 56 81 Xd 61
81430 Taur 81 151 Cb 85
29630 Taureau 29 62 Wa 56
03700 Taureaux, les 03 116 Dc 72
33710 Tauriac 33 135 Zc 78
46130 Tauriac 46 138 Be 79
81630 Tauriac 81 150 Bd 85
12360 Tauriac-de-Camarès 12 152 Da 86
12800 Tauriac-de-Naucelle 12 151 Cb 84
07110 Tauriers 07 142 Eb 81
09160 Taurignan-Castet 09 176 Ba 90
12120 Taurines 12 152 Cc 84
66500 Taurinya 66 178 Cc 93
11220 Taurize 11 166 Cd 90
12600 Taussac 12 139 Cd 80
33480 Taussac 33 134 Za 79
34600 Taussac 34 167 Da 87
33138 Taussat 33 134 Yf 80
34330 Tautas, le 34 166 Ce 87
66720 Tautavel 66 179 Ce 92
63690 Tauvery, la 63 127 Cd 75
63690 Tauves 63 127 Cd 75
51150 Tauxières-Mutry 51 53 Ea 54
37310 Tauxigny-Saint-Bauld 37 100 Ae 65
47600 Tauziète 47 148 Ab 84
20167 Tavaco CTC 182 If 96
20167 Tavacu = Tavaco CTC 182 If 96
37220 Tavant 37 99 Ac 66
39500 Tavaux 39 106 Fc 66
02250 Tavaux-et-Pontséricourt 02 41 Df 50
30126 Tavel 30 155 Ee 84
20163 Tavera CTC 182 Ka 96
20218 Taverna CTC 181 Kb 94
71400 Tavernay 71 105 Eb 66
07580 Taverne 07 142 Ed 80
12390 Tavernes 12 151 Cc 82
83670 Tavernes 83 171 Ga 87
08270 Tavernes, les 08 41 Ed 51
30720 Tavernes, les 30 154 Ea 84
38320 Tavernolles 38 144 Fe 78
95150 Taverny 95 51 Cb 54
45190 Tavers 45 87 Bd 62
33840 Taves 33 147 Zf 82
70400 Tavey 70 94 Ge 63
03140 Taxat 03 116 Da 71
03140 Taxat 03 116 Db 71
03140 Taxat-Senat 03 116 Da 71
39350 Taxenne 39 107 Fe 65
66690 Taxo-d'Amont 66 179 Cf 93
53160 Tay, le 53 67 Zd 59
12120 Tayac 12 152 Cc 83
33460 Tayac 33 134 Zb 78
33570 Tayac 33 135 Zf 79
32120 Taybosc 32 149 Ae 86
09600 Taychel, le 09 177 Be 91
28190 Taye, la 28 69 Bc 58
69210 Taylan 69M 130 Ed 74
12440 Tayrac 12 151 Cb 83
47270 Tayrac 47 149 Af 83
12220 Tayral, le 12 139 Cb 82
12430 Taysses 12 152 Cd 84
58170 Tazilly 58 104 Df 68
65400 Tech, le 65 174 Ze 91
66230 Tech, le 66 179 Cd 94
38470 Têche 38 131 Fc 77
81600 Técou 81 151 Bf 85
33680 Tedey, le 33 134 Yf 79
20229 Teglia CTC 183 Kc 94
33470 Teich, le 33 134 Yf 81
23500 Teiffoux 23 126 Ca 74
58190 Teigny 58 89 De 64
19320 Teil 19 126 Ca 77
81260 Teil 81 166 Cd 86
07400 Teil, le 07 142 Ee 81
42240 Teil, le 42 129 Eb 76
56580 Teil, le 56 64 Xb 60
63460 Teilhède 63 115 Da 73
09500 Teilhet 09 165 Be 90
63560 Teilhet 63 115 Ce 72
44670 Teillais, la 44 82 Ye 62
35620 Teillay 35 82 Yc 62
45480 Teillay-le-Gaudin 45 70 Bf 59
45170 Teillay-Saint-Benoit 45 70 Ca 60
44440 Teillé 44 82 Ye 64
72290 Teillé 72 68 Ab 59
72540 Teillés, les 72 67 Ze 60
03410 Teillet 03 115 Cc 71
12240 Teillet 12 151 Cb 82
23110 Teillet 23 115 Cd 71
81120 Teillet 81 151 Cc 85
81190 Teillet 81 151 Cb 84
03410 Teillet-Argenty 03 115 Cd 71
50640 Teilleul, le 50 66 Za 57
24390 Teillots 24 125 Bb 77
81640 Teissarié, la 81 151 Ca 84
15250 Teissières-de-Cornet 15 139 Cc 79
15130 Teissières-lès-Bouliès 15 139 Cd 80
63470 Teissonnières 63 127 Cd 74
81190 Tel, le 81 151 Ca 83
29560 Telgruc-sur-Mer 29 62 Vd 59
56380 Telhaie, la 56 81 Xf 61
35380 Telhouët 35 65 Xe 60
54260 Tellancourt 54 43 Fd 51
49660 Tellandière, la 49 97 Yf 66
21270 Tellecey 21 92 Fb 65
61390 Tellières-le-Plessis 61 48 Ac 57
72220 Teloché 72 85 Ab 61
81340 Tels 81 151 Cc 84
16170 Temple, le 16 123 Zf 74
17160 Temple, le 17 111 Ze 73
19400 Temple, le 19 138 Bf 78
22130 Temple, le 22 64 Xe 58
33680 Temple, le 33 134 Za 79
36300 Temple, le 36 100 Bb 68
41100 Temple, le 41 86 Ba 62
41170 Temple, le 41 86 Af 61
56910 Temple, le 56 81 Xf 62
62180 Temple, le 62 28 Be 46
63600 Temple, le 63 129 De 76
79700 Temple, le 79 98 Zb 67
86300 Temple, le 86 112 Ad 70
19310 Temple-d'Ayen, le 19 125 Bb 77
44360 Temple-de-Bretagne, le 44 82 Yb 65
56220 Temple de Haut, le 56 81 Xd 63
35750 Temple-Helouin, le 35 65 Xf 60
24390 Temple-Laguyon 24 125 Ba 77
59175 Templemars 59 30 Da 45
53380 Templerie-d'Echerbé 53 66 Za 59
47110 Temple-sur-Lot, le 47 149 Ad 82
59242 Templeuve 59 30 Db 45
80240 Templeux-la-Fosse 80 39 Da 49
80240 Templeux-le-Guérard 80 40 Da 49
47500 Tempoure 47 137 Af 82
01230 Tenay 01 119 Fd 73
43190 Tence 43 142 Eb 78
38570 Tencin 38 132 Ff 77
06430 Tende 06 159 Hd 84
88460 Tendon 88 77 Ge 60
18350 Tendron 18 103 Cf 67
18160 Tendrons, les 18 102 Ca 68
36200 Tendu 36 101 Bd 69
62134 Teneur 62 29 Cb 46
23800 Tenèze 23 114 Be 70
37360 Ténières, les 37 85 Ad 63
72240 Tennie 72 68 Zf 60
03130 Tenons, les 03 117 Df 70
48500 Tenssonnieu, le 48 152 Da 83
57980 Tenteling 57 57 Gf 54
40700 Téoulé 40 161 Zc 86
65300 Tèpe 65 163 Ac 90
20270 Teppa CTC 183 Kc 96
01160 Teppes, les 01 119 Fb 72
86800 Tercé 86 112 Ad 69
61570 Tercey 61 48 Aa 56
04420 Tercier 04 158 Gc 83
23350 Tercillat 23 114 Ca 70
40180 Tercis-les-Bains 40 161 Yf 86
59114 Terdeghem 59 27 Cd 44
29630 Térénez 29 62 Wa 56
66130 Tererach 66 178 Cd 92
02700 Tergnier 02 40 Db 51
03420 Terjat 03 115 Cd 71
12560 Terménoux 12 152 Da 82
24410 Terme-Rouge, le 24 124 Ab 77
08250 Termes 08 42 Ee 53
11330 Termes 11 179 Cd 91
48310 Termes 48 140 Db 80
63640 Termes 63 115 Ce 73
13124 Termes, les 13 170 Fd 88
32400 Termes-d'Armagnac 32 162 Zf 86
73500 Termignon 73 133 Ge 77
74130 Termine 74 120 Gc 72
28140 Terminiers 28 70 Be 60
69620 Ternand 69D 117 Ed 73
21220 Ternant 21 106 Ef 65
49490 Ternant 49 84 Ab 63
58250 Ternant 58 104 Df 68
63870 Ternant 63 128 Da 74
79410 Ternanteuil 79 111 Zd 70
63340 Ternant-les-Eaux 63 128 Db 76
62127 Ternas 62 29 Cc 46
52210 Ternat 52 91 Fa 61
41800 Ternay 41 85 Ae 62
69360 Ternay 69M 130 Ee 75
86120 Ternay 86 99 Zf 66
15100 Ternes, les 15 140 Da 79
23140 Ternes, les 23 114 Ca 71
70270 Ternuay-Melay-et-Saint-Hilaire 70 94 Gd 62
02880 Terny-Sorny 02 40 Dc 52
16420 Terracher 16 112 Ae 73
19170 Terracot 19 126 Bf 75
87230 Terrade, la 87 125 Ba 74
12450 Terrail, le 12 152 Cd 83
46350 Terral, le 46 138 Bd 80
80600 Terramesnil 80 29 Cc 48
74470 Terramont 74 120 Gc 71
49540* Terranjou 49 83 Zd 65
71270 Terrans 71 106 Fb 67
01380 Terrasse, la 01 118 Fa 71
38660 Terrasse, la 38 132 Ff 77
42550 Terrasses 42 129 Df 76
42740 Terrasse-sur-Dorlay, la 42 130 Ed 76
24120 Terrasson-la-Villedieu 24 137 Bb 78
66300 Terrats 66 179 Ce 93
31580 Terrats, les 31 163 Ac 90
32700 Terraube 32 149 Ad 85
16230 Terrebourg 16 124 Ab 73
81120 Terre-Clapier 81 151 Cb 85
29890 Terre-du-Pont 29 62 Vd 56
50500 Terre-et-Marais 50 34 Ye 53
21290 Terrefondrée 21 91 Ef 62
46200 Terregaye 46 137 Bd 79
72110 Terrehault 72 68 Ac 59
40210 Terrenave 40 146 Yf 83
42100 Terrenoire 42 130 Ec 76
50560 Terrerie, la 50 33 Yc 54
20230 Terre Rosse CTC 181 Kc 94
72610 Terre-Rouge, la 72 85 Ab 61
27340* Terres de Bord 27 49 Ba 53
76640 Terres-de-Caux 76 36 Ad 50
25190 Terres-de-Chaux 25 94 Ge 65
14770 Terres de Druance 14 47 Zb 55
24420 Terrier 24 125 Ba 77
59266 Terriere, la 59 40 Db 48
85360 Terrière, la 85 109 Yd 70
36200 Terrier-Joli, le 36 113 Bc 69
17150 Terriers, les 17 122 Zc 76
12210 Terrisse 12 139 Ce 80
15160 Terrisse, la 15 128 Cf 77
11580 Terroles 11 178 Cb 91
08430 Terron 08 42 Ed 51
08400 Terron-sur-Aisne 08 42 Ee 52
46120 Terrou 46 138 Bf 80
46170 Terry 46 150 Bc 83
33410 Terry-de-Castel 33 135 Ze 81
26390 Tersanne 26 130 Fa 77
87360 Tersannes 87 113 Ba 71
74210 Tertenoz 74 132 Gb 74
41360 Tertre, le 41 85 Af 61
72240 Tertre, le 72 67 Zf 60
78980 Tertre-Saint-Denis, le 78 50 Bd 55
80200 Tertry 80 39 Da 49
79300 Terves 79 98 Zc 68
57180 Terville 57 56 Ga 52
12210 Tesq 12 139 Ce 81
47500 Tesquet 47 137 Af 81
78250 Tessancourt-sur-Aubette 78 50 Bf 54
16240 Tessé 16 111 Aa 72
61410 Tessé-Froulay 61 67 Zd 57
14250 Tessel 14 34 Zc 54
61140 Tessé-la-Madeleine 61 67 Zd 57
73210 Tessens 73 133 Gd 75
49160 Tesseul 49 84 Zf 64
17460 Tesson 17 122 Zc 75
24580 Tessonièras 24 137 Af 78
79600 Tessonnière 79 99 Ze 68
49280 Tessouale, la 49 98 Za 66
74370 Tessy 74 120 Ga 73
50420 Tessy-Bocage 50 46 Yf 55
50420 Tessy-sur-Vire 50 46 Yf 55
33380 Testarouch 33 134 Za 81
82160 Testas 82 150 Be 83
33260* Teste de Buch, la 33 134 Ye 81
12330 Testet 12 139 Cc 82
08110 Tétaigne 08 42 Fa 51
61310 Tête au Loup, la 61 48 Aa 56
59229 Téteghem 59 27 Cc 42
24230 Tête-Noire 24 135 Aa 79
57220 Téterchen 57 57 Gd 53
57385 Téting-sur-Nied 57 57 Gd 54
35630 Tetre, le 35 65 Yb 59
33710 Teuillac 33 135 Zc 78
81500 Teulat 81 165 Be 87
81430 Teulet 81 151 Cb 85
19430 Teulet, le 19 138 Ca 79
81600 Teulié 81 151 Ca 85
12200 Teulières 12 151 Ca 83
50630 Teurthéville-Bocage 50 33 Yd 51
50690 Teurthéville-Hague 50 33 Yb 51
33125 Teycheney 33 134 Zb 81
24300 Teyjat 24 124 Ad 75
34820 Teyran 34 168 Df 86
26220 Teyssières 26 156 Fa 82
46190 Teyssieu 46 138 Bf 79
19320 Teyssonnière 19 126 Ca 77
86250 Tezier 86 112 Ac 72
01120 Tfil 01 130 Fa 74
51230 Thaas 51 53 Df 57
17120 Thaims 17 122 Zb 75
17290 Thairé 17 110 Yf 72
17170 Thairé-le-Fagnoux 17 110 Za 71
58250 Thaix 58 104 De 67
19200 Thalamy 19 127 Cc 75
67320 Thal-Drulingen 67 57 Ha 55
67440 Thal-Marmoutier 67 58 Hc 56
68800 Thann 68 94 Ha 62
68590 Thannenkirch 68 60 Hb 59
67220 Thanvillé 67 60 Hc 59
14610 Thaon 14 35 Zd 53
88150 Thaon-les-Vosges 88 76 Gc 59
30430 Tharaux 30 154 Eb 83
89450 Tharoiseau 89 90 De 64
44730 Tharon-Plage 44 96 Xf 66
89200 Tharot 89 90 Df 63
72430 Thaulière, la 72 84 Ze 61
18210 Thaumiers 18 103 Cd 68
23250 Thauron 23 114 Be 72
18300 Thauvenay 18 88 Ce 65
65370 Thèbe 65 176 Ad 91
57450 Théding 57 57 Gf 54
46150 Thédirac 46 137 Bb 81
46500 Thégra 46 138 Be 80
56130 Théhillac 56 81 Xf 63
19160 Theil 19 127 Cb 76
19170 Theil 19 126 Be 75
50330 Theil, Gonneville-, le 50 33 Yd 51
03100 Theil, le 03 115 Cd 71
03240 Theil, le 03 116 Da 70
15140 Theil, le 15 127 Cc 78
23220 Theil, le 23 114 Bf 71
23700 Theil, le 23 115 Cc 73
41130 Theil, le 41 86 Bd 65
61250 Theil, le 61 68 Zf 58
61260 Theil, le 61 69 Ae 59
63520 Theil, le 63 128 Dc 75
87120 Theil, le 87 126 Be 74
87400 Theil, le 87 125 Bc 73
87510 Theil, le 87 113 Ba 73
14410 Theil-Bocage, le 14 47 Zb 55
35240 Theil-de-Bretagne, le 35 82 Yd 61
14130 Theil-en-Auge, le 14 48 Ab 52
19300 Theillac 19 126 Ca 76
41300 Theillay 41 87 Ca 65
27520 Theillement 27 49 Ae 53
87380 Theillornas 87 125 Bc 74
27230 Theil-Nolent, le 27 49 Ad 54
16240 Theil-Rabier 16 111 Aa 72
89320 Theil-sur-Vanne 89 72 Dc 60
63122 Theix 63 128 Da 74
23600 Theix, le 23 114 Ca 71
03170 Theix, les 03 115 Ce 70
56450 Theix-Noyalo 56 80 Xc 63
69620 Theizé 69D 118 Ed 73
69470 Thel 69D 117 Ec 72
69860 Thel, le 69D 118 Ed 71
28130 Théléville 28 70 Bd 57
72320 Théligny 72 69 Ae 59
35380 Thélin, le 35 81 Xf 61
42220 Thélis-la-Combe 42 130 Ed 77
54330 Thélod 54 76 Ga 57
08350 Thelonne 08 42 Ef 51
62580 Thélus 62 30 Ce 46
95450 Théméricourt 95 50 Bf 54
89410 Thèmes 89 72 Db 61
46120 Thémines 46 138 Be 80
46120 Théminettes 46 138 Bf 80
17460 Thénac 17 122 Zc 74
24240 Thénac 24 136 Ac 80
02140 Thenailles 02 41 Df 50
36800 Thenay 36 101 Bc 69
41400 Thenay 41 86 Bb 64
02390 Thenelles 02 40 Dc 50
73200 Thénésol 73 132 Gc 74
86310 Thenet 86 113 Af 69
37220 Theneuil 37 99 Ac 66
03350 Theneuille 03 103 Cf 69
79390 Thénezay 79 99 Zf 68
18100 Thénioux 18 102 Bf 65
21150 Thenissey 21 91 Ed 64
77520 Thénisy 77 72 Db 58
80110 Thennes 80 39 Cc 50
24210 Thenon 24 137 Ba 78
08240 Thénorgues 08 42 Ef 52
27520 Thénouville 27 49 Ae 53
33350 Theolat, le 33 135 Zf 79
06590 Théoule-sur-Mer 06 173 Gf 87
60510 Therdonne 60 38 Ca 52
50180 Thèreval 50 33 Ye 54
60380 Thérines 60 38 Bf 51
74210 Thermesay 74 132 Gb 74
65230 Thermes-Magnoac 65 163 Ad 89
12240 Théron, le 12 151 Cb 83
12600 Thérondels 12 139 Ce 79
12620 Thérondels 12 152 Cf 84
62129 Thérouanne 62 29 Cb 45
76540 Thérouldeville 76 36 Ad 50
39290 Thervay 39 107 Fd 65
36100 Théry 36 102 Ca 67
41140 Thesée 41 86 Bb 65
39110 Thésy 39 107 Ff 67
40990 Thétieu 40 146 Za 86
86320 Theuil, le 86 112 Ae 70
70120 Theuley 70 93 Fe 63
70600 Theuley-lès-Vars 70 92 Fd 63
36370 Theuret 36 113 Bb 69
05190 Théus 05 144 Gb 82
28360 Theuville 28 70 Bd 58
76540 Theuville 76 36 Ad 50
95810 Theuville 95 51 Ca 54
53000 Thévalles 53 67 Zb 60
29890 Théven 29 62 Vd 57
39150 Thévenins, les 39 107 Ff 69
29233 Theven-Kerbrat 29 62 Vf 56
47420 Thevet 47 148 Zf 83
36400 Thevet-Saint-Julien 36 102 Ca 69
50330 Théville 50 33 Yd 51
27330 Thevray 27 49 Ae 55
70190 They 70 93 Ga 64
38570 Theys 38 132 Ff 77
88800 They-sous-Montfort 88 76 Ff 59
54930 They-sous-Vaudémont 54 76 Ga 58
66200 Théza 66 179 Cf 93
17600 Thézac 17 122 Zb 74
47370 Thézac 47 149 Ba 82
34490 Thézan-lès-Béziers 34 167 Db 88
04200 Thèze 04 157 Ff 83
64450 Thèze 64 162 Zd 88
46250 Thèze, la 46 137 Ba 81
43210 Thézenac 43 129 Ea 77
54610 Thézey-Saint-Martin 54 56 Gb 55
30390 Théziers 30 155 Ed 85
01110 Thézillieu 01 119 Fd 73
80440 Thézy-Glimont 80 39 Cc 50
94320 Thiais 94 51 Cc 56
90100 Thiancourt 90 94 Gf 63
58260 Thianges 58 104 Dd 67
59224 Thiant 59 30 Dc 47
87170 Thias 87 125 Bb 74
87320 Thiat 87 113 Af 71
54470 Thiaucourt-Regniéville 54 56 Ff 55
54120 Thiaville-sur-Meurthe 54 77 Ge 58
18390 Thibauderie, la 18 102 Cd 66
01190 Thibauts, les 01 118 Fa 70
53350 Thibergères, les 53 83 Yf 61
27230 Thiberville 27 48 Ac 54
51510 Thibie 51 53 Eb 55
60240 Thibivillers 60 50 Bf 53
27800 Thibouville 27 49 Ae 54
57380 Thicourt 57 57 Gd 55
54300 Thiébauménil 54 77 Gd 57
25470 Thiébouhans 25 94 Gf 65
76890 Thiédeville 76 37 Af 50
10140 Thieffrain 10 74 Ec 59
70230 Thieffrans 70 93 Gb 64
88290 Thiéfosse 88 77 Ge 61
70320 Thiéloup 70 93 Gc 61
88220 Thiélouse 88 76 Gb 60
03230 Thiel-sur-Acolin 03 116 Dd 69
62560 Thiembronne 62 29 Ca 45
70230 Thiénans 70 93 Gb 64
59189 Thiennes 59 29 Cc 45
80300 Thiepval 80 29 Ce 48
77320 Thiercelieux 77 52 Dc 56
27140 Thierceville 27 50 Be 52
76540 Thiergeville 76 36 Ac 50
68600 Thierhurstkp 68 60 Hd 61
58160 Thiernay 58 103 Dc 67
02250 Thiernu 02 40 De 50
63300 Thiers 63 128 Dd 73
77570 Thiersanville 77 71 Ce 59
60520 Thiers-sur-Thève 60 51 Cd 54
27290 Thierville 27 49 Ae 53
55840 Thierville-sur-Meuse 55 55 Fc 53
06710 Thiéry 06 158 Ha 85
60310 Thiescourt 60 39 Cf 51
76540 Thiétreville 76 36 Ad 50
88260 Thiétry 88 76 Ga 60
28240 Thieulin, le 28 69 Ba 58
80640 Thieulloy-L'Abbaye 80 38 Bf 50
80290 Thieulloy-la-Ville 80 38 Bf 50
62130 Thieuloge, la 62 29 Cc 46
60210 Thieuloy-Saint-Antoine 60 38 Bf 51
07600 Thieuré 07 142 Ec 80
59270 Thieushouck, le 59 30 Cd 44
60480 Thieux 60 39 Cb 51
77230 Thieux 77 51 Ce 54
14170 Thiéville 14 48 Zf 54
62760 Thièvres 62 29 Cc 48

326 | Tamniès

27930 Tourneville 27 49 Ba 54
50660 Tourneville 50 46 Yc 55
19210 Tournevite 19 125 Bc 76
12700 Tournhac 12 138 Ca 81
15700 Tourniac 15 126 Cb 77
46150 Tourniac 46 137 Bb 81
14330 Tournières 14 34 Za 53
47350 Tournies 47 136 Ac 81
11220 Tournissan 11 166 Cd 90
45310 Tournoisis 45 70 Bd 60
07170 Tournon 07 142 Ec 81
73460 Tournon 73 132 Gb 75
47370 Tournon-d'Agenais 47 149 Af 82
36220 Tournon-Saint-Martin 36 100 Af 68
37290 Tournon-Saint-Pierre 37 100 Af 68
07300 Tournon-sur-Rhône 07 142 Ee 78
65220 Tournous-Darré 65 163 Ac 89
65330 Tournous-Devant 65 163 Ac 89
04530 Tournoux 04 145 Ge 82
71700 Tournus 71 118 Ef 69
03130 Tournus, les 03 117 Df 70
27510 Tourny 27 50 Bd 53
71120 Tourny 71 117 Eb 70
09200 Touron 09 177 Bb 91
82390 Touron 82 149 Ba 83
24140 Touron, le 24 136 Ad 79
19390 Tourondel 19 126 Bf 76
61190 Tourouvre au Perche 61 69 Ad 57
11200 Tourouzelle 11 166 Ce 89
11350 Tourreilles 11 178 Cb 90
32390 Tourrenquets 32 149 Ae 86
30170 Tourres 30 154 Df 85
06470 Tourres, les 06 158 Gf 83
83520 Tourres, les 83 172 Gd 88
47290 Tourrette 47 136 Ad 81
06690 Tourrette-Levens 06 159 Hb 86
31540 Tourrettes 31 165 Bf 88
83440 Tourrettes 83 172 Ge 87
26740 Tourrettes, les 26 142 Ee 81
16560 Tourriers 16 124 Ab 74
74500 Tourronde 74 121 Gd 70
05000 Tourronde, la 05 144 Ga 81
37000 Tours 37 85 Ae 64
42660 Tours, les 42 130 Ec 76
63380 Tours, les 63 115 Ce 73
37120 Tour-Saint-Gelin, la 37 99 Ac 66
73790 Tours-en-Savoie 73 132 Gc 75
80210 Tours-en-Vimeu 80 28 Be 48
51150 Tours-sur-Marne 51 53 Ea 54
63590 Tours-sur-Meymont 63 128 Dd 74
58240 Tour-sur-Jour 58 103 Db 68
34260 Tour-sur-Orb, la 34 167 Da 87
24420 Tourte 26 143 Fc 79
79100 Tourtenay 79 99 Zf 66
08130 Tourteron 08 42 Ed 51
79160 Tourteron 79 110 Zc 70
24390 Tourtoirac 24 125 Ba 77
63530 Tourtoule 63 128 Da 73
83690 Tourtour 83 172 Gb 87
09230 Tourtouse 09 164 Ba 90
47380 Tourtrès 47 136 Ac 81
09500 Tourtrol 09 165 Be 90
83170 Tourves 83 171 Ff 88
14130 Tourville-en-Auge 14 36 Ab 53
27370 Tourville-la-Campagne 27 49 Af 53
76630 Tourville-la-Chapelle 76 37 Bb 49
76410 Tourville-la-Rivière 76 37 Ba 53
76400 Tourville-les-Ifs 76 36 Ac 50
76550 Tourville-sur-Arques 76 37 Ba 49
14210 Tourville-sur-Odon 14 35 Zc 54
27500 Tourville-sur-Pont-Audemer 27 36 Ad 53
50200 Tourville-sur-Sienne 50 46 Yc 54
28310 Toury 28 70 Bf 59
77114 Toury 77 72 Dc 58
58300 Toury-Lurcy 58 104 Dc 68
63320 Tourzel-Ronzières 63 128 Da 75
76860 Tous-les-Mesnils 76 37 Af 49
76400 Toussaint 76 36 Ac 50
69780 Toussieu 69M 130 Ef 75
01600 Toussieux 01 118 Ee 73
77123 Tousson 77 71 Cc 58
73300 Toussuire, la 73 132 Gb 77
78117 Toussus-le-Noble 78 51 Ca 56
27500 Toutainville 27 36 Ac 52
71350 Toutenant 71 106 Fa 67
80560 Toutencourt 80 29 Cc 48
62650 Toutendal 62 28 Be 45
31460 Toutens 31 165 Be 88
49360 Toutlemonde 49 98 Zb 66
21460 Toutry 21 90 Ea 63
16360 Touvérac 16 123 Ze 76
19110 Touves 19 127 Cc 75
38660 Touvet, le 38 132 Ff 76
27290 Touville 27 49 Ae 53
37140 Touvois 37 84 Aa 65
44650 Touvois 44 96 Yb 67
27220 Touvoye 27 50 Bb 55
16600 Touvre 16 124 Ab 74
04240 Touyet, le 04 158 Ge 85
16120 Touzac 16 123 Zf 75
46700 Touzac 46 137 Ba 82
35500 Touzerie, la 35 66 Ye 60
43350 Touzet 43 129 De 77
17400 Touzetterie, la 17 110 Zc 73
20240 Tovisanu CTC 183 Kc 97
20270 Tox CTC 183 Kc 95
82600 Toyrats 82 150 Bb 86
19170 Toy-Viam 19 126 Bf 75
47290 Trabade 47 136 Ae 81
22350 Trabaillac 22 65 Xf 59
43230 Trabesson 43 128 Dd 77
43220 Tracol 43 130 Ec 77
13490 Traconnade 13 171 Fd 87
63740 Tracros 63 127 Ce 74
14310 Tracy-Bocage 14 47 Zb 54
60170 Tracy-le-Mont 60 39 Da 52
60170 Tracy-le-Val 60 39 Da 52
58150 Tracy-sur-Loire 58 88 Cf 65
14117 Tracy-sur-Mer 14 47 Zc 52
69860 Trades 69D 118 Ed 71
67310 Traenheim 67 60 Hc 57
20147 Traghino CTC 182 Ie 95
57580 Tragny 57 56 Gc 55
15320 Trailus 15 140 Db 78
86210 Trainebot 86 100 Ad 68
10400 Traînel 10 72 Dc 58
27480 Trainières, les 27 37 Bc 52
45470 Traînou 45 71 Ca 61
76580 Trait, le 76 37 Ae 52
70190 Traitiéfontaine 70 93 Ga 64
73170 Traize 73 131 Fe 74
63380 Tralaigues 63 115 Cd 73
33180 Trale, le 33 122 Zb 77
23260 Traleprat 23 127 Cb 74
20100 Tralicetu CTC 184 If 99
20250 Tralonca CTC 183 Kb 94
22640 Tramain 22 64 Xd 58
71520 Tramayes 71 118 Ed 71
71520 Trambly 71 117 Ed 71
62310 Tramecourt 62 29 Ca 46
51170 Tramery 51 53 De 53
65170 Tramezaïgues 65 175 Ab 92
65510 Tramezaygues 65 175 Ac 92
38300 Tramolé 38 131 Fb 75
54115 Tramont-Emy 54 76 Ff 58
54115 Tramont-Lassus 54 76 Ff 58
54115 Tramont-Saint-André 54 76 Ff 58
01390 Tramoyes 01 130 Ef 73
88350 Trampot 88 75 Fc 58
10290 Trancault 10 72 Dd 58
43120 Tranchard 43 129 Eb 77
24120 Tranche 24 137 Bb 78
85360 Tranche-sur-Mer, la 85 109 Yd 70
01160 Tranclière, la 01 119 Fb 72
28310 Trancrainville 28 70 Bf 59
72650 Trangé 72 68 Aa 60
36700 Tranger, le 36 101 Bb 67
58000 Trangy 58 103 Db 66
10140 Trannes 10 74 Ed 59
88300 Tranqueville-Graux 88 76 Ff 58
35610 Trans 35 65 Yc 58
53160 Trans 53 67 Ze 59
83720 Trans-en-Provence 83 172 Gc 87
80140 Translay, le 80 38 Be 49
62450 Transloy, le 62 30 Cf 48
44440 Trans-sur-Erdre 44 82 Yd 64
19260 Tranugie, la 19 126 Be 75
36230 Tranzault 36 101 Bf 69
40430 Traounquet 40 147 Zc 83
29590 Traourivin 29 62 Vf 59
12240 Trap, le 12 151 Cb 83
81450 Trap, le 81 151 Ca 85
03250 Trapière 03 116 De 72
24550 Trappe, la 24 137 Ba 80
53260 Trappe-du-Port-du-Salut 53 67 Zb 61
78190 Trappes 78 51 Bf 56
82100 Traques, les 82 149 Ba 85
12320 Tras-le-Bosc 12 139 Cc 81
11160 Trassanel 11 166 Cc 88
19370 Trassoudaine 19 126 Be 75
68210 Traubach-le-Bas 68 94 Ha 63
68210 Traubach-le-Haut 68 94 Ha 62
11160 Trausse 11 166 Cd 89
84850 Travaillan 84 155 Ef 83
81120 Travanet 81 151 Cb 86
19270 Travassac 19 125 Bd 77
02800 Travecy 02 40 Dc 50
22830 Traveneuc 22 65 Xf 59
55140 Traveron 55 75 Fe 57
30770 Travers, les 30 153 Dd 84
38860 Travers, les 38 144 Ga 78
73140 Traversaz, la 73 133 Gc 77
09200 Traverse, la 09 176 Ba 91
87250 Traverse, la 87 113 Bc 72
32450 Traversères 32 163 Ad 87
40120 Traverses 40 147 Ze 84
05600 Traverses, les 05 145 Gd 81
86190 Traversonne 86 99 Ab 69
32200 Travès 32 164 Af 86
70360 Traves 70 93 Ff 63
81120 Travet, le 81 151 Cc 86
88310 Travexin 88 77 Ge 61
20240 Travo CTC 183 Kc 97
56800 Travoléon 56 81 Xd 61
35190 Travoux 35 65 Yb 58
83530 Trayas, le 83 173 Gf 88
79240 Trayes 79 98 Zd 68
33430 Trazitz 33 148 Ze 82
56140 Tréal 56 81 Xe 61
29530 Tréambon 29 62 Wb 59
29370 Tréanna 29 78 Wa 60
29890 Tréas 29 62 Vd 57
56440 Tréauray 56 79 Wf 62
50340 Tréauville 50 33 Yb 51
29000 Tréauzon 29 78 Vf 60
56400 Tréavrec 56 80 Wf 62
29217 Trébabu 29 61 Vb 58
03240 Treban 03 116 Db 70
81190 Tréban 81 151 Cc 84
81340 Trébas 81 152 Cc 85
22980 Trébédan 22 65 Xe 58
22490 Trébéfour 22 65 Xf 57
11800 Trèbes 11 166 Cc 89
22560 Trébeurden 22 63 Wc 56
56440 Trébihan 56 80 We 61
65200 Trébons 65 162 Aa 90
31110 Trébons-de-Luchon 31 176 Ad 92
31290 Trébons-sur-la-Grasse 31 165 Be 88
29100 Tréboul 29 78 Vd 60
22340 Trébrivan 22 63 Wd 59
22510 Trébry 22 64 Xc 58
56780 Trec'h, le 56 80 Xa 63
21130 Tréclun 21 106 Fb 65
51130 Trécon 51 53 Ea 55
71520 Trécourt 71 117 Ec 71
22510 Trédaniel 22 64 Xc 58
22220 Trédarzec 22 63 We 56
35380 Trédeal 35 65 Xf 60
22250 Trédias 22 65 Xe 58
56250 Trédion 56 80 Xc 62
81320 Trédos 81 166 Ce 86
22300 Trédrez 22 63 Wc 56
22310 Tréduder 22 63 Wc 57
29690 Trédudon 29 62 Wa 58
29690 Trédudon-le-Moine 29 62 Wa 58
02490 Trefcon 02 40 Da 49
29550 Tréfeuntec 29 78 Ve 60
39300 Treffay 39 107 Ga 68
35380 Treffendel 35 65 Xf 60
29730 Treffiagat 29 78 Ve 62
44170 Treffieux 44 82 Yc 63
56250 Treffléan 56 80 Xc 62
38650 Treffort 38 144 Fd 79
01370 Treffort-Cuisiat 01 119 Fc 71
22340 Treffrin 22 63 Wc 59
56350 Trefin 56 81 Xf 63
29440 Tréflaouénan 29 62 Vf 57
29800 Tréflévénez 29 62 Ve 58
29430 Tréflez 29 62 Ve 57
51210 Tréfols 51 53 Dd 56
44290 Tréfoux 44 82 Ya 63
22630 Tréfumel 22 65 Xf 58
56800 Trégadoret 56 64 Xd 61
22950 Tregaeg = Trégueux 22 64 Xb 58
29260 Trégarantec 29 62 Ve 57
29560 Trégarvan 29 62 Ve 59
22730 Trégastel 22 63 Wd 56
22730 Trégastel-Plage 22 63 Wc 56
22400 Trégenestre 22 64 Xc 58
22540 Tréglamus 22 63 We 57
56490 Treglion 56 64 Xd 60
29870 Tréglonou 29 61 Vc 57
22400 Trégomar 22 64 Xd 58
22590 Trégomeur 22 64 Xa 57
22650 Trégon 22 65 Xe 57
35870 Trégondé 35 65 Xf 57
22200 Trégonneau 22 63 We 57
29250 Trégor 29 62 Vf 56
22110 Trégornan 22 79 Wd 59
44630 Trégouet 44 81 Ya 63
29970 Trégourez 29 78 Wa 60
46260 Trégoux 46 150 Be 82
56120 Trégranteur-la-Grillette 56 81 Xc 61
22420 Trégrom 22 63 Wd 57
29720 Tréguennec 29 78 Ve 61
29880 Tréguestan 29 61 Vc 57
22950 Trégueux = Tregaeg 22 64 Xb 58
22290 Tréguidel 22 64 Xa 57
22220 Tréguier 22 63 We 56
22130 Treguihé 22 65 Xe 57
29910 Trégunc 29 78 Wa 61
29190 Tréguron 29 78 Wa 59
44117 Trehé 44 81 Xe 64
41800 Trehet 41 85 Ad 62
35270 Tréheuc 35 65 Yb 58
56760 Tréhiguier 56 81 Xd 64
56890 Tréhonte 56 80 Xb 62
56430 Tréhorenteuc 56 64 Xe 60
29450 Tréhou, le 29 62 Vf 58
19170 Treich, le 19 126 Bf 74
19260 Treignac 19 126 Be 75
03380 Treignat 03 114 Cc 70
26390 Treignieux 26 130 Ef 77
58420 Treigny 58 89 Dc 65
89520 Treigny 89 89 Db 63
44119 Treillières 44 82 Yc 65
04510 Treille, la 04 157 Ga 84
13190 Treille, la 13 170 Fd 89
34360 Treille, la 34 167 Cf 88
11510 Treilles 11 179 Cf 91
45490 Treilles-en-Gâtinais 45 71 Cd 60
16130 Treillis 16 123 Zd 75
16560 Treillis 16 124 Ab 74
09140 Trein-d'Ustou, le 09 177 Bb 92
23480 Treix 23 114 Ca 73
52000 Treix 52 75 Fb 60
63710 Treizanches 63 128 Da 75
85600 Treize-Septiers 85 97 Ye 67
85590 Treize-Vents 85 98 Za 67
82110 Tréjouls 82 150 Bb 83
44630 Trélan 44 82 Yb 63
48340 Trélans 48 140 Da 82
35190 Trélat 35 65 Ya 58
49800 Trélazé 49 83 Zd 64
56330 Trélécan 56 80 Wf 62
22660 Trélévern 22 63 Wd 56
42130 Trelins 42 129 Ea 74
24750 Trélissac 24 124 Ae 77
22100 Trélivan 22 65 Xf 58
50660 Trelly 50 46 Yd 55
59132 Trélon 59 31 Ea 48
02850 Trélou-sur-Marne 02 53 Dd 54
35480 Trémac 35 82 Ya 61
29440 Trémagon 29 62 Vf 57
29800 Trémaouézan 29 62 Ve 57
22110 Trémargat 22 63 We 59
76640 Trémauville 76 36 Ad 51
29840 Trémazan 29 61 Vb 57
17390 Tremblade, la 17 122 Yf 74
35720 Tremblais, le 35 65 Ya 58
36290 Tremblais, le 36 100 Bb 67
10400 Tremblay 10 73 Dd 58
35460 Tremblay 35 66 Yd 58
27110 Tremblay, le 27 49 Af 54
28120 Tremblay, le 28 69 Bb 58
49520 Tremblay, le 49 83 Yf 62
89480 Tremblay, le 89 89 Dc 64
89520 Tremblay, le 89 89 Db 63
37360 Tremblaye, la 37 85 Ad 63
93290 Tremblay-en-France 93 51 Cd 55
28170 Tremblay-les-Villages 28 69 Bc 57
78490 Tremblay-sur-Mauldre, le 78 50 Bf 56
93290 Tremblay-Vieux-Pays 93 51 Cd 55
54385 Tremblecourt 54 56 Ff 56
03140 Trembles, les 03 115 Da 71
70100 Tremblois, le 70 92 Fd 64
08110 Tremblois-les-Carignan 08 42 Fb 51
08230 Tremblois-lès-Rocroi 08 41 Ec 49
09100 Tremège 09 165 Bd 90
35270 Trémeheuc 35 65 Yb 58
22310 Trémel 22 63 Wc 57
22590 Trémeloir 22 64 Xa 57
49340 Trémentines 49 98 Zb 66
29120 Tréméoc 29 78 Ve 61
22490 Tréméreuc 22 65 Xf 57
57300 Trémery 57 56 Gb 53
22250 Trémeur 22 64 Xe 58
88240 Trémeures, les 88 76 Gb 61
22290 Tréméven 22 64 Wf 56
29300 Tréméven 29 79 Wc 61
52110 Trémilly 52 74 Ee 58
38710 Tréminis 38 144 Fe 80
70400 Trémoins 70 94 Ge 63
24510 Trémolat 24 137 Ae 79
15100 Trémolière, la 15 140 Db 78
47140 Trémons 47 149 Af 82
49310 Trémont 49 98 Zd 66
61390 Trémont 61 68 Ab 57
55000 Trémont-sur-Saulx 55 55 Fa 56
88240 Trémonzey 88 76 Gb 61
22230 Trémorel 22 64 Xe 59
29190 Trémorgat 29 62 Wa 59
29920 Trémorvezen 29 78 Wb 62
56400 Trémouec 56 80 Xa 62
15270 Trémouille 15 127 Ce 76
24210 Trémouille, la 24 137 Af 77
12290 Trémouilles 12 152 Cd 83
15120 Trémouilles 15 139 Cd 80
63810 Trémouille-Saint-Loup 63 127 Cd 76
43340 Trémoul 43 141 De 79
09700 Trémoulet 09 165 Be 90
15500 Trémoulet 15 128 Da 77
19320 Trémoulet 19 126 Ca 77
63220 Tremoulet 63 128 Dd 76
56450 Trémoyec 56 80 Xc 63
41500 Tremplay 41 86 Bc 62
56110 Trémunut 56 78 Wb 60
22440 Tremuson 22 64 Xa 57
47700 Tren, le 47 148 Aa 83
15230 Trénac 15 139 Cf 79
39570 Trenal 39 106 Fc 69
18270 Trenay 18 114 Cb 69
40630 Trensacq 40 147 Zb 83
47140 Trentels 47 149 Af 82
56190 Trenue 56 81 Xd 63
22340 Tréogan 22 79 Wc 59
29720 Tréogat 29 78 Ve 61
29830 Tréompan 29 61 Vb 57
28500 Tréon 28 50 Bb 56
29290 Tréouergat 29 61 Vc 58
29390 Tréouzal 29 79 Wb 60
51380 Trépail 51 53 Eb 54
62780 Trépied 62 28 Bd 46
76470 Tréport, le 76 28 Bc 48
25620 Trépot 25 107 Ga 65
14690 Tréprel 14 47 Zd 55
38460 Trept 38 131 Fb 74
38930 Trésanne 38 143 Fd 79
55160 Tresauvaux 55 55 Fd 54
09000 Tresbens 09 177 Bd 91
35320 Tresbœuf 35 82 Yc 61
44420 Trescalan 44 81 Xd 64
62147 Trescault 62 30 Da 48
26410 Treschenu-Creyers 26 143 Fd 80
05700 Trescléoux 05 156 Fe 82
64300 Trescoint 64 161 Za 88
12170 Trescos 12 152 Cc 84
70190 Trésilley 70 93 Ga 64
51140 Treslon 51 53 De 53
77515 Tresmes 77 52 Cf 56
11420 Tresmezes 11 165 Be 89
58240 Tresnay 58 103 Db 68
33840 Trésot, le 33 148 Zf 83
46090 Trespoux-Rassiels 46 150 Bc 82
30330 Tresques 30 155 Ed 84
22100 Tressaint 22 65 Xf 58
34230 Tressan 34 167 Dc 87
57710 Tressange 57 43 Ff 52
79260 Tressauves 79 111 Ze 70
35720 Tressé 35 65 Ya 58
40170 Tresse 40 146 Ye 84
32700 Tressens 32 148 Ac 85
66300 Tresserre 66 179 Ce 93
33370 Tresses 33 135 Zd 79
22290 Tressignaux 22 63 Xa 57
59152 Tressin 59 30 Db 45
72440 Tresson 72 85 Ad 61
37310 Tressort 37 100 Af 65
22660 Trestel 22 63 Wd 56
03220 Treteau 03 116 Dd 70
77510 Trétoire, la 77 52 Db 55
13530 Trets 13 171 Fe 88
17160 Treuil, le 17 111 Zd 73
17610 Treuil, le 17 123 Zd 74
24380 Treuilh, le 24 137 Ae 78
36250 Treuilleau 36 101 Bd 67
22160 Treusvern 22 63 Wd 58
80300 Treux 80 39 Cd 49
29560 Treuzelom 29 62 Ve 59
77710 Treuzy-Levelay 77 72 Ce 59
71110 Tréval 71 117 Ea 71
56480 Trévannec 56 79 Wf 60
04270 Trévans 04 157 Gb 85
29570 Trevarguen 29 61 Vc 59
43600 Trevas 43 129 Eb 77
22600 Trévé 22 64 Xb 59
56130 Trévélo 56 81 Xd 63
56220 Trévelo 56 81 Xd 63
22410 Trévenais 22 64 Xa 57
90400 Trévenans 90 94 Gf 63
22160 Trévénec 22 63 Wc 58
22410 Tréveneuc 22 64 Xa 57
55130 Tréveray 55 75 Fc 57
22290 Trévérec 22 63 Wf 57
56450 Tréverel 56 80 Xc 63
35190 Trévérien 35 65 Ya 58
30750 Trèves 30 153 Dc 84
69420 Trèves 69M 130 Ee 75
49350 Trèves-Cunault 49 84 Ze 65
56700 Trévidel 56 80 We 62
81190 Trévien 81 151 Ca 84
14710 Trévières 14 47 Za 53
34270 Tréviers 34 153 Df 86
73100 Trévignin 73 132 Ff 74
29910 Trévignon 29 78 Wa 62
66130 Trévillach 66 179 Cd 92
11400 Tréville 11 165 Bf 88
25470 Trévillers 25 94 Gf 65
89420 Trévilly 89 90 Ea 63
22140 Trévoazan 22 63 We 56
03460 Trévol 03 103 Db 69
22660 Trévou-Treguignec 22 63 Wd 56
01600 Trévoux 01 118 Ee 73
29380 Trévoux, le 29 79 Wc 61
22100 Trévron 22 65 Xf 58
63930 Trévy, le 63 128 Dd 74
43290 Treyches 43 129 Eb 77
07310 Treynas 07 142 Eb 79
29890 Trez 29 62 Ve 57
29950 Trez, le 29 78 Vf 61
29560 Trez-Bellec-Plage 29 62 Vd 59
49260 Trézé 49 99 Zf 66
22140 Trézelan 22 63 We 57
03220 Trézelles 03 116 Dd 71
29810 Trézen 29 61 Vb 58
29100 Trézent 29 78 Ve 60
22450 Trézény 22 63 Wd 56
29217 Trez-Hir, le 29 61 Vb 58
11230 Tréziers 11 178 Bf 90
29440 Trézilidé 29 62 Vf 57
63520 Trézioux 63 128 Dc 74
35380 Trézon 35 65 Xf 61
16200 Triac-Lautrait 16 123 Zf 74
34270 Triadou, le 34 168 Df 86
85580 Triaize 85 110 Ye 70
50620 Tribehou 50 34 Ye 53
12390 Triboulan 12 139 Cc 82
12850 Tricherie, la 12 152 Cc 83
16220 Tricherie, la 16 124 Ad 75
86490 Tricherie, la 86 99 Ac 68
47470 Tricheries, les 47 149 Ae 83
89430 Trichey 89 90 Ea 61
19190 Tricolet 19 138 Be 78
47160 Tricot 47 148 Ab 83
60420 Tricot 60 39 Cd 51
60590 Trie-Château 60 50 Be 53
60590 Trie-la-Ville 60 50 Bf 53
78510 Triel-sur-Seine 78 51 Ca 55
67220 Triembach-au-Val 67 60 Hb 58
65220 Trie-sur-Baïse 65 163 Ac 89
38890 Trieux 38 131 Fc 75
54750 Trieux 54 43 Ff 53
59970 Trieux-de-Fresnes 59 31 Dd 46
21270 Triey 21 92 Fc 65
59250 Triez-Cailloux 59 30 Da 44
17150 Trigale, la 17 122 Zb 76
83840 Trigance 83 157 Gc 86
22490 Trigavou 22 65 Xf 57
17120 Trignac 17 122 Za 75
17130 Trignac 17 123 Zd 76
44570 Trignac 44 81 Xe 65
56910 Trignac 56 81 Xe 61
51140 Trigny 51 53 Df 53
44590 Triguel 44 82 Yc 63
45220 Triguères 45 72 Cf 61
77450 Trilbardou 77 52 Ce 55
66220 Trilla 66 178 Cd 92
77470 Trilport 77 52 Cf 55
67470 Trimbach 67 59 Ia 55
65120 Trimbareilles 65 175 Aa 92
35190 Trimer 35 65 Ya 58
86290 Trimouille, la 86 113 Ba 70
63230 Trimoulet 63 127 Cf 73
36190 Trimoulet, le 36 114 Bd 70
45410 Trinay 45 70 Bf 60
15110 Trinitat, la 15 140 Cf 80
05800 Trinité, la 05 144 Ff 80
06340 Trinité, la 06 173 Hb 86
22290 Trinité, la 22 63 Wf 56
22420 Trinité, la 22 63 Wd 57
22580 Trinité, la 22 64 Xa 56
27120 Trinité, la 27 50 Bb 55
29140 Trinité, la 29 78 Wa 61
29280 Trinité, la 29 61 Vc 58
29710 Trinité, la 29 78 Vd 61
50800 Trinité, la 50 46 Ye 56
73110 Trinité, la 73 132 Ga 76
27270 Trinité-de-Réville, la 27 49 Ad 55
61230 Trinité-des-Laitiers, la 61 48 Ac 56
76170 Trinité-du-Mont, la 76 36 Ad 51
56630 Trinité-Langonnet, la 56 79 Wd 60
56470 Trinité-sur-Mer, la 56 79 Wf 63
56190 Trinité-Surzur, la 56 80 Xc 63
89630 Trinquelin 89 90 Ea 64
58430 Trinquets, les 58 104 Ea 66
26750 Triors 26 143 Fa 78
79370 Triou 79 111 Ze 71
86330 Triou 86 99 Aa 67
12260 Trioulou 12 151 Bf 82
15600 Trioulou, le 15 139 Cb 81
41240 Tripleville 41 70 Bc 61
33230 Tripoteau 33 135 Zf 79
85290 Trique, la 85 98 Za 67
76170 Triquerville 76 36 Ad 51
27500 Triqueville 27 48 Ac 52
27330 Trisay 27 49 Ae 55
33730 Triscos 33 135 Zd 82
48200 Trisos 48 140 Db 80
59125 Trith-Saint-Léger 59 30 Dc 47
57385 Tritteling 57 57 Gd 54
12350 Trivale 12 151 Cb 82
81120 Trivale, la 81 151 Cb 85
81330 Trivale, la 81 151 Cc 86
12400 Trivalle 12 152 Ce 85
34520 Trivalle 34 153 Dc 86
81230 Trivalle, la 81 166 Ce 86
81120 Trivalou, le 81 151 Cb 86
19510 Trix 19 126 Bd 75
15400 Trizac 15 127 Cd 77
17250 Trizay 17 122 Za 73
28120 Trizay 28 69 Bc 58
28400 Trizay-Coutretot-Saint-Serge 28 69 Af 59
28800 Trizay-lès-Bonneval 28 69 Bc 59

328 | Tourneville

74470 Vailly 74 120 Gd 71
02370 Vailly-sur-Aisne 02 40 Dd 52
18260 Vailly-sur-Sauldre 18 88 Cd 64
36170 Vaines, les 36 113 Bc 69
50300 Vains 50 46 Yd 56
50360 Vains 50 33 Yd 52
25220 Vaire 25 93 Ga 65
85150 Vairé 85 96 Yb 69
25220 Vaire-Arcier 25 93 Ga 65
25220 Vaire-le-Petit 25 93 Ga 65
80800 Vaire-sous-Corbie 80 39 Cd 49
77360 Vaires-sur-Marne 77 51 Cd 55
44150 Vair-sur-Loire 44 83 Yf 64
84110 Vaison-la-Romaine 84 155 Fa 83
82800 Vaïssac 82 150 Bd 84
81640 Vaisse, la 81 151 Ca 84
48300 Vaissière, la 48 141 De 80
70180 Vaîte 70 92 Fe 63
70130 Vaivre, la 70 93 Fe 63
70220 Vaivre, la 70 93 Gc 61
70000 Vaivre-et-Montoille 70 93 Ga 63
25440 Val, le 25 107 Ff 66
27220 Val, le 27 50 Bb 55
56200 Val, le 56 81 Xe 62
56350 Val, le 56 81 Xf 63
83143 Val, le 83 171 Ga 88
24530 Valade 24 124 Ae 76
87500 Valade, la 87 125 Bb 76
87800 Valade, la 87 125 Bb 75
24220 Valades, les 24 137 Af 79
12330 Valady 12 139 Cc 82
27300 Valailles 27 49 Ad 54
28200 Valainville 28 70 Bc 60
41120 Valaire 41 86 Bb 64
07310 Valamas 07 142 Ec 79
14370 Valambray 14 48 Ze 54
03150 Valançon 03 116 Dc 71
22370 Val-André, le 22 64 Xc 57
49670 Valanjou 49 98 Zc 65
12210 Valat 12 139 Ce 81
85390 Valaudin 85 97 Za 68
61130* Val-au-Perche 61 69 Ad 59
26230 Valaurie 26 155 Ee 82
83120 Valaury 83 172 Gd 88
04250 Valavoire 04 157 Ga 83
70140 Valay 70 92 Fd 64
84210 Valayans, les 84 155 Ef 85
63610 Valbeleix 63 128 Cf 76
04200 Valbelle 04 157 Ff 84
48400 Valbelle 48 153 Dd 83
06470 Valberg 06 158 Gf 84
55300 Valbois 55 55 Fd 55
38740 Valbonnais 38 144 Ff 79
06560 Valbonne 06 173 Ha 87
05300 Val Buëch-Méouge 05 156 Fe 83
31510 Valcabrère 31 176 Ad 90
20243 Valcaccia CTC 183 Kc 96
50760 Valcanville 50 33 Ye 51
66340 Valcebollère 66 178 Ca 94
73500 Val-Cenis 73 133 Ge 77
04340 Valcivières 63 129 De 75
73320 Val-Claret 73 133 Gf 76
52100 Valcourt 52 74 Ef 57
26150 Valcroissant 26 143 Fc 80
83250 Valcros 83 172 Gb 89
83250 Valcros 83 171 Ga 89
62380 Val-d'Acquin, le 62 27 Ca 44
25800 Valdahon 25 108 Gc 66
88340 Val-d'Ajol, le 88 94 Gc 61
14350* Valdallière 14 47 Zb 55
60790 Valdampierre 60 51 Ca 53
35330 Val d'Anast 35 81 Xf 61
15320 Val d'Arcomie 15 140 Da 79
83200 Val d'Ardène 83 171 Ff 90
14210* Val d'Arry 14 35 Zc 54
10220 Val-d'Auzon 10 74 Ec 58
27930 Val-David, le 27 50 Bb 55
16230 Val-de-Bonnieure 16 124 Ab 73
57260 Val-de-Bride 57 57 Ge 56
54150 Val de Briey 54 56 Ff 53
74210 Val de Chaise 74 132 Gc 74
50260 Valdécie 50 33 Yc 52
14240 Val de Drôme 14 47 Za 54
74150 Val-de-Fier 74 119 Ff 73
83310 Valdegilly 83 172 Gc 89
57430 Val-de-Guéblange, le = Geblingen 57 57 Gf 55
76380 Val-de-la-Haye 76 37 Ba 52
11230 Val de Lambronne 11 165 Bf 90
52120 Valdelancourt 52 75 Fa 60
60430 Val-de-L'Eau, le 60 38 Ca 52
51150 Val de Livre 51 53 Ea 54
24510 Val de Louyre et Caudeau 24 136 Ae 79
06430 Val-del-Prat 06 159 Hd 84
89580 Val-de-Mercy 89 89 Dd 62
67350 Val de Moder 67 58 Hd 55
44650 Val-de-Morière, la 44 96 Yb 67
72140 Val-de-Pierre, le 72 68 Zf 59
39160 Val d'Epy 39 119 Fc 70
49370 Val d'Erdre-Auxence 49 83 Za 63
27100 Val-de-Reuil 27 49 Bb 53
81350 Valderiès 81 151 Cb 84
25640 Val-de-Roulans 25 93 Gb 64
06750 Valderoure 06 158 Ge 86
76890 Val-de-Saâne 76 37 Af 50
51130 Val-des-Marais 51 53 Df 55
05100 Val-des-Prés 05 145 Ge 79
83380 Val d'Esquières 83 172 Gd 88
51360 Val-de-Vesle 51 53 Eb 53
14140 Val-de-Vie 14 48 Ab 55
51340 Val-de-Vière 51 54 Ee 56
16250 Val de Vignes 16 123 Zf 75
67730 Val-de-Villé 67 60 Hc 59
33240 Val de Virvée 33 135 Zd 78
27940 Val d'Hazey, le 27 50 Bb 53
68210 Valdieu-Lutran 68 94 Ha 63
73150 Val-d'Isère 73 133 Gf 76
87330 Val d'Issoire 87 112 Af 72
86300 Valdivienne 86 112 Ad 69
35450 Val-d'Izé 35 66 Ye 59
89110 Val d'Ocre, le 89 89 Db 62
90300 Valdoie 90 94 Gf 62
69620 Val d'Oingt 69D 118 Ed 73
27190 Val-Doré, le 27 49 Af 55
27380* Val-d'Orger 27 50 Bc 52
55000 Val-d'Ornain 55 55 Fa 56
04530 Val d'Oronaye 04 145 Ge 82
50220 Valdoue, le 50 66 Ye 57
05150 Valdoule 05 143 Fc 82
56460* Val d'Oust 56 81 Xd 61
10190 Valdreux, le 10 73 Df 59
26310 Valdrôme 26 143 Fd 81
49190 Val-du-Layon 49 83 Zb 65
53340 Val-du-Maine 53 84 Zd 61
81090 Valdurenque 81 166 Cb 87
42110 Valeille 42 129 Eb 74
82150 Valeilles 82 149 Af 82
01140 Valeins 01 118 Ef 72
39300 Valempoulières 39 107 Ff 68
36600 Valençay 36 101 Bd 66
16460 Valence 16 112 Ab 73
26000 Valence 26 142 Ef 79
82400 Valence 82 149 Af 84
81340 Valence-d'Albigeois 81 151 Cc 84
77830 Valence-en-Brie 77 72 Cf 58
62170 Valencendre 62 28 Be 46
32310 Valence-sur-Baïse 32 148 Ac 85
59300 Valenciennes 59 30 Dd 46
38540 Valencin 38 130 Fa 75
41190 Valencisse 41 86 Bb 63
38730 Valencogne 38 131 Fd 76
72320 Valennes 72 69 Ae 61
04210 Valensole 04 157 Ff 85
32300 Valentées 32 163 Ac 87
25350 Valentigney 25 94 Ge 64
31800 Valentine 31 163 Ae 90
13011 Valentine, la 13 170 Fc 89
13119 Valentine, la 13 170 Fd 88
58800 Valentinges 58 90 De 65
94460 Valenton 94 51 Cc 56
33240 Valentons, les 33 135 Zd 79
79150* Val en Vignes 79 98 Zd 66
23500 Valeoux 23 126 Ca 74
34130 Valergues 34 168 Ea 87
04200 Valernes 04 157 Ff 83
18370 Valeron 18 114 Cb 70
60130 Valescourt 60 39 Cc 52
83610 Valescure 83 172 Gc 89
83700 Valescure 83 172 Ge 88
15270 Valessard 15 127 Cd 76
54480 Val-et-Châtillon 54 77 Gf 57
04170 Valette 04 158 Gd 84
07310 Valette 07 141 Eb 79
15400 Valette 15 127 Cd 77
30570 Valette 30 153 Dd 84
57510 Valette 57 57 Gf 54
12440 Valette, la 12 151 Cb 83
38350 Valette, la 38 144 Ff 79
57560 Valette, la 57 57 Ha 57
83200 Valette-du-Var, la 83 171 Ff 90
47290 Valettes 47 136 Ad 81
81630 Valettes, les 81 150 Be 85
84340 Valettes, les 84 155 Fb 83
24310 Valeuil 24 124 Ad 77
33340 Valeyrac 33 122 Za 76
46600 Valeyrac 46 138 Bd 78
73210 Valezan 73 133 Ge 75
67210 Valff 67 60 Hd 58
39240 Valfin, Vosbles- 39 119 Fd 70
39200 Valfin-lès-Saint-Claude 39 119 Fe 70
34270 Valflaunès 34 154 Df 86
42320 Valfleury 42 130 Ec 75
44110 Valfleury, le 44 82 Yd 62
36210 Val-Fouzon 36 101 Bd 65
61250 Valframbert 61 68 Aa 58
88270 Valfroicourt 88 76 Ga 59
05320 Valfroide 05 145 Gb 78
07110 Valgorge 07 141 Ea 81
14220 Valgoude, la 14 47 Zc 54
22690 Val-Hervelin 22 65 Ya 58
80750 Val-Heureux 80 29 Cb 48
54370 Valhey 54 57 Gc 56
62550 Valhuon 62 29 Cc 46
83170 Valiancelle 83 171 Ff 88
19200 Valiergues 19 127 Cb 76
03330 Valignat 03 115 Da 71
03360 Valigny 03 103 Ce 68
17270 Valin 17 135 Zf 78
80210 Valines 80 28 Bd 48
77154 Valjouan 77 72 Da 57
38740 Valjouffrey 38 144 Ff 79
15170 Valjouze 15 128 Da 78
42111 Valla, la 42 129 Df 74
30300 Vallabrègues 30 155 Ed 85
30700 Vallabrix 30 154 Ec 84
16730 Vallade, la 16 123 Aa 74
42131 Valla-en-Gier, la 42 130 Ed 76
23150 Vallaise 23 114 Ca 72
89580 Vallan 89 89 Dd 62
95810 Vallangoujard 95 51 Ca 54
79270 Vallans 79 110 Zc 71
23130 Vallansange 23 114 Cb 72
42600 Vallansange 42 129 Ea 75
10170 Vallant-Saint-Georges 10 73 Df 58
03380 Vallas, la 03 115 Cc 70
15270 Vallat 15 127 Cd 76
06220 Vallauris 06 173 Ha 87
86180 Valle 86 99 Ac 69
06420 Valle, la 06 158 Ha 84
20232 Vallecalle CTC 181 Kc 93
20234 Valle-d'Alesani CTC 181 Kc 95
20221 Valle-di-Campoloro CTC 183 Kc 94
20235 Valle-di-Rostino CTC 181 Kb 94
20229 Valle-d'Orezza CTC 183 Kc 94
02380 Vallée, la 02 40 Db 52
17250 Vallée, la 17 110 Za 73
18350 Vallée, la 18 103 Cf 66
22490 Vallée, la 22 65 Xf 57
27320 Vallée, la 27 50 Bb 56
27400 Vallée, la 27 49 Ba 53
37190 Vallée, la 37 99 Ac 65
44260 Vallée, la 44 82 Ya 65
50310 Vallée, la 50 33 Yd 52
56120 Vallée, la 56 64 Xb 60
58140 Vallée, la 58 90 De 65
72310 Vallée, la 72 85 Ad 62
72340 Vallée, la 72 85 Ad 62
76940 Vallée, la 76 36 Ae 52
85800 Vallée, la 85 96 Ya 68
02140 Vallée-au-Blé, la 02 40 De 49
61130 Vallée-Aubry 61 68 Ad 58
18240 Vallée-au-Paré, la 18 88 Ce 64
50270 Vallée-de-Beaubigny, la 50 33 Ya 52
37210 Vallée-de-Raye 37 85 Af 64
71640 Vallée de Vaux 71 105 Ee 68
66690 Vallée-Heureuse, la 66 179 Cf 93
02110 Vallée-Mulâtre, la 02 40 Dd 48
18140 Vallées 18 88 Cf 65
36600 Vallées 36 101 Bc 65
37150 Vallées 37 86 Af 65
45110 Vallées, les 45 87 Cb 61
89320 Vallées, les 89 72 Dc 60
89190* Vallées de la Vanne, les 89 72 Dc 59
02330 Vallées en Champagne 02 53 Dd 54
31290 Vallègue 31 165 Be 88
74520 Valleiry 74 120 Ff 72
63210 Valleix 63 127 Ce 74
20167 Valle-Mezzana CTC 182 Ie 96
18190 Vallenay 18 102 Cc 68
10500 Vallentigny 10 74 Ed 58
57340 Vallerange 57 57 Ge 55
30580 Vallérargues 30 154 Eb 84
30570 Valleraugue 30 153 Dd 84
37190 Vallères 37 85 Ac 65
52130 Valleret 52 75 Fa 58
24190 Vallereuil 24 136 Ad 78
70000 Vallerois-le-Bois 70 93 Gb 63
70000 Vallerois-Lorioz 70 93 Ga 63
20290 Valle Rose = Valroso CTC 181 Kc 93
25870 Valleroy 25 93 Ga 64
52500 Valleroy 52 92 Fe 62
54910 Valleroy 54 56 Ff 53
88270 Valleroy-aux-Saules 88 76 Ga 59
88800 Valleroy-le-Sec 88 76 Ga 59
89150 Vallery 89 72 Da 59
31570 Vallesvilles 31 165 Bd 87
17130 Vallet 17 123 Zd 77
44330 Vallet 44 97 Ye 66
27350 Valletot 27 36 Ad 52
87190 Vallette, la 87 113 Ba 71
27800 Valleville 27 49 Ae 53
20259 Vallica CTC 180 Ka 93
20114 Vallicello CTC 185 Ka 99
41240 Vallière 41 86 Bc 61
50200 Vallière 50 46 Yc 54
10210 Vallières 10 73 Ea 61
23120 Vallières 23 114 Ca 73
37230 Vallières 37 85 Ad 64
74150 Vallières 74 120 Ff 73
89260 Vallières 89 72 Dc 59
63700 Vallières, les 63 115 Ce 71
41400 Vallières-les-Grandes 41 86 Ba 64
30210 Valliguières 30 155 Ed 84
76190 Valliquerville 76 36 Ad 51
73450 Valloire 73 132 Gc 78
41150 Valloire-sur-Cisse 41 86 Ba 63
54830 Vallois 54 77 Gd 58
88260 Vallois, les 88 76 Ga 60
12600 Vallon 12 139 Cd 80
03190 Vallon-en-Sully 03 115 Cd 69
48210 Vallongue 48 153 Dc 83
05800 Vallonpierre 05 144 Gb 80
07150 Vallon-Pont-d'Arc 07 154 Ec 82
74340 Vallons, les 74 121 Ge 72
44450* Vallons-de-l'Erdre 44 82 Ye 63
72540 Vallon-sur-Gée 72 68 Zf 61
74660 Vallorcine 74 121 Gf 72
66600 Vall Oriole, la 66 179 Ce 91
71440 Vallots, les 71 106 Fa 68
10150 Vallotte, la 10 73 Ea 58
05290 Vallouise 05 145 Gc 79
05290* Vallouise-Pelvoux 05 145 Gc 79
65240 Val-Louron 65 175 Ac 92
89200 Valloux 89 90 Df 63
34570 Valmalle 34 168 De 87
13009 Valmante 13 170 Fc 89
66320 Valmanya 66 179 Cd 93
76690 Valmartin, le 76 37 Ba 51
34800 Valmascle 34 167 Db 87
73450 Valmeinier 73 133 Gc 77
76660 Val-Mesneret, le 76 37 Bc 50
57970 Valmestroff 57 44 Gb 52
11580 Valmigère 11 178 Cc 91
95760 Valmondais 95 51 Cb 54
21340 Val-Mont 21 105 Ed 66
76540 Valmont 76 36 Ad 50
73260 Valmorel 73 132 Gc 76
63440 Valmort 63 115 Da 72
57220 Valmunster 57 57 Gd 53
51800 Valmy 51 54 Ee 54
50700 Valognes 50 33 Yd 51
24290 Valojoulx 24 137 Ba 78
50330 Valonges 50 33 Yd 51
25190 Valonne 25 94 Gd 64
14290 Valorbiquet 14 48 Ab 54
25190 Valoreille 25 94 Ge 65
58230 Valottes, les 58 105 Ea 65
26110 Valouse 26 143 Fb 82
07110 Valousset 07 141 Eb 81
73110 Val-Pelouse 73 132 Gb 76
10200 Val-Perdu, le 10 74 Ee 59
05460 Valpreveyre 05 145 Gf 80
46800 Valprionde 46 149 Ba 82
43210 Valprivas 43 129 Ea 77
89500 Valprotonde 89 72 Dc 60
91720 Valpuiseaux 91 71 Cb 58
34650 Valquières 34 167 Db 87
34350 Valras-Plage 34 167 Db 89
89110 Valravillon 89 89 Dc 61
84600 Valréas 84 155 Ef 82
01370 Val-Revermont 01 119 Fc 71
41800 Valrond 41 86 Af 62
34290 Valros 34 167 Dc 88
83670 Val-Rose 83 171 Ff 87
20290 Valroso CTC 181 Kc 93
46090 Valroufié 46 138 Bc 81
70160 Val-Saint-Eloi, le 70 93 Gb 62
91530 Val-Saint-Germain, le 91 70 Ca 57
89270 Val-Saint-Martin, le 89 90 De 62
50300 Val-Saint-Père, le 50 46 Yd 57
14340 Valsemé 14 48 Aa 53
38740 Valsenestre 38 144 Ga 79
05130 Valserres 05 144 Ga 82
43230 Vals-le-Chastel 43 128 Dd 77
69170 Valsonne 69D 117 Ec 73
39190 Val-Sonnette 39 106 Fc 69
43750 Vals-près-le-Puy 43 141 Df 78
39320 Val Suran 39 119 Fc 70
73440 Val-Thorens 73 133 Gd 77
88230 Valtin, le 88 77 Ha 60
15300 Valuéjols 15 140 Cf 78
07400 Valvignères 07 142 Ed 82
12220 Valzergues 12 139 Cb 82
39240 Valzin en Petite Montagne 39 119 Fd 70
63580 Valz-sous-Châteauneuf 63 128 Dc 76
51330 Vanault-le-Châtel 51 54 Ee 55
51340 Vanault-les-Dames 51 54 Ee 55
79120 Vançais 79 111 Aa 71
72310 Vancé 72 85 Ad 62
67730 Vancelle, la 67 60 Hb 59
01200 Vanchy 01 119 Ff 72
69140 Vancia 69M 130 Ef 73
25580 Vanclans 25 108 Gc 66
01660 Vandeins 01 118 Fa 71
44850 Vandel 44 82 Ye 65
54890 Vandelainville 54 56 Ff 54
70190 Vandelans 70 93 Ga 64
79170 Vandeleigne 79 111 Ze 72
54115 Vandeléville 54 76 Ff 58
60490 Vandélicourt 60 39 Ce 51
62690 Vandelincourt 62 29 Cd 46
58290 Vandenesse 58 104 De 67
21320 Vandenesse-en-Auxois 21 105 Ed 65
51140 Vandeuil 51 53 De 53
51700 Vandières 51 53 De 54
54121 Vandières 54 56 Ga 55
54500 Vandœuvre-lès-Nancy 54 56 Gb 57
25230 Vandoncourt 25 94 Gf 64
17700 Vandré 17 110 Zb 72
27380 Vandrimare 27 37 Bc 52
08400 Vandy 08 42 Ee 52
48400 Vanels, les 48 153 Dd 83
88430 Vanémont 88 77 Gf 59
10210 Vanlay 10 73 Ea 60
70130 Vanne 70 93 Ff 63
89320 Vanne 89 72 Dc 59
79270 Vanneau, le 79 110 Zc 71
57340 Vannecourt 57 57 Gd 55
27210 Vannecrocq 27 48 Ac 53
56000 Vannes 56 80 Xb 63
58130 Vannes, les 58 103 Db 66
54112 Vannes-le-Châtel 54 76 Fe 57
45510 Vannes-sur-Cosson 45 87 Cb 62
39300 Vannoz 39 107 Ff 68
07140 Vans, les 07 154 Ea 82
07690 Vansoc 07 130 Ed 77
57070 Vantoux 57 56 Gb 54
70700 Vantoux-et-Longevelle 70 93 Ff 64
21400 Vanvey 21 91 Ee 61
77370 Vanvillé 77 72 Da 57
24600 Vanxains 24 124 Ab 77
57070 Vany 57 56 Gb 54
17500 Vanzac 17 123 Ze 76
79120 Vanzay 79 111 Aa 71
74270 Vanzy 74 119 Ff 72
86120 Vaon 86 99 Aa 66
81140 Vaour 81 150 Be 84
38470 Varacieux 38 131 Fc 77
44370 Varades 44 83 Yf 64
13920 Varage 13 170 Ef 88
83670 Varages 83 171 Ff 87
24270 Varagnac 24 125 Bb 76
46500 Varagne 46 138 Be 80
24360 Varaignes 24 124 Ad 75
46260 Varaire 46 150 Be 82
17400 Varaize 17 111 Zd 73
01160 Varambon 01 119 Fb 72
21110 Varanges 21 106 Fb 65
54110 Varangéville 54 56 Gb 57
36500 Varanne 36 101 Bc 67
79100 Varanne 79 99 Zf 66
37140 Varanterie, la 37 84 Ab 65
14390 Varaville 14 48 Zf 53
48000 Varazoux 48 140 Dd 82
38760 Varces-Allières-et-Risset 38 144 Fe 78
63740 Vareille 63 127 Ce 74
23340 Vareille, la 23 126 Bf 74
23300 Vareilles 23 113 Bc 71
48000 Vareilles 48 141 Dd 82
48190 Vareilles 48 141 De 82
63210 Vareilles 63 127 Cf 74
71800 Vareilles 71 117 Eb 71
89320 Vareilles 89 72 Dc 59
87260 Vareilles, les 87 125 Bc 74
24380 Varen 82 151 Bf 84
76119 Varengeville-sur-Mer 76 37 Af 49
50250 Varenguebec 50 46 Yd 52
28800 Varenne 28 70 Bc 59
86220 Varenne 86 100 Ad 67
43520 Varenne, la 43 141 Eb 78
49270 Varenne, la 49 82 Ye 65
49370 Varenne, la 49 83 Za 63
28200 Varenne-Ferron, la 28 69 Bb 60
71110 Varenne-L'Arconce 71 117 Ea 70
03170 Varennes 03 115 Cd 70
03410 Varennes 03 115 Cd 70
21210 Varennes 21 90 Eb 65
23170 Varennes 23 114 Cb 71
24150 Varennes 24 136 Ae 80
31450 Varennes 31 165 Be 88
36300 Varennes 36 100 Ba 69
36330 Varennes 36 101 Be 68
37600 Varennes 37 100 Af 66
43300 Varennes 43 140 Dc 78
43580 Varennes 43 141 De 78
63450 Varennes 63 128 Da 74
71430 Varennes 71 117 Ea 69
80560 Varennes 80 29 Cd 48
82370 Varennes 82 150 Bc 85
86110 Varennes 86 99 Ab 68
89144 Varennes 89 90 De 61
89240 Varennes 89 89 Dc 62
18500 Varennes, les 18 102 Cb 65
49330 Varennes, les 49 83 Zd 62
71600 Varenne-Saint-Germain 71 117 Ea 70
45290 Varennes-Changy 45 88 Cd 61
55270 Varennes-en-Argonne 55 55 Fa 53
91480 Varennes-Jarcy 91 51 Cd 56
71240 Varennes-le-Grand 71 106 Ef 68
71000 Varennes-lès-Mâcon 71 118 Ee 71
58400 Varennes-lès-Narcy 58 103 Da 65
43270 Varennes-Saint-Honorat 43 141 Dd 77
71480 Varennes-Saint-Sauveur 71 119 Fb 70
71800 Varennes-sous-Dun 71 117 Ec 71
03150 Varennes-sur-Allier 03 116 Dc 71
52400 Varennes-sur-Amance 52 92 Fd 61
36210 Varennes-sur-Fouzon 36 101 Bd 65
71270 Varennes-sur-le-Doubs 71 106 Fb 67
49730 Varennes-sur-Loire 49 99 Aa 65
63720 Varennes-sur-Morge 63 116 Db 73
77130 Varennes-sur-Seine 77 72 Cf 58
03220 Varennes-sur-Têche 03 116 Dd 71
63500 Varennes-sur-Ussan 63 128 Db 75
58640 Varennes-Vauzelles 58 103 Da 66
58640 Varennes-Vauzelles 58 103 Da 66
12150 Varès 12 152 Cf 82
47400 Varès 47 148 Ac 82
60400 Varesnes 60 39 Da 51
39270 Varessia 39 119 Fd 69
19240 Varetz 19 125 Bc 77
49490 Varie, la 49 84 Aa 63
70800 Varigney 70 93 Gb 61
09120 Varilhes 09 177 Bd 90
51330 Varimont 51 54 Ee 55
18190 Varines, les 18 102 Cc 68
60890 Varinfroy 60 52 Da 54
02190 Variscourt 02 41 Df 52
28140 Varize 28 70 Bd 60
57220 Varize 57 57 Gc 54
15240 Varleix 15 127 Cc 77
88450 Varmonzey 88 76 Gb 59
87290 Varnat 87 113 Bb 71
83840 Varneige 83 158 Gd 86
55300 Varnéville 55 55 Fd 55
76890 Varneville-Bretteville 76 37 Ba 51
55000 Varney 55 55 Fa 56
70240 Varogne 70 93 Gb 62
21490 Varois-et-Chaignot 21 92 Fa 64
50330 Varouville 50 33 Yd 50
77910 Varreddes 77 52 Cf 54
50580 Varreville 50 46 Yb 53
05560 Vars 05 145 Ge 81
16330 Vars 16 124 Aa 74
70600 Vars 70 92 Fd 63
57880 Varsberg 57 57 Gd 53
19130 Vars-sur-Roseix 19 125 Bc 77
76890 Varvannes 76 37 Af 50
17380 Varzay 17 110 Zb 72
17460 Varzay 17 122 Zb 74
58210 Varzy 58 89 Dc 64
20240 Vasalla CTC 183 Kb 97
27910 Vascœuil 27 37 Bc 52
85270 Vases, les 85 96 Xf 68
79340 Vasles 79 99 Zf 69
14600 Vasouy 14 35 Ab 52
57560 Vasperviller 57 57 Ha 57
73670 Vassaux, les 73 132 Ff 76
63910 Vassel 63 128 Db 74
18110 Vasselay 18 102 Cc 66
38890 Vasselin 38 131 Fc 75
02290 Vassens 02 40 Da 52
02220 Vasseny 02 40 Dc 52
26420 Vassieux-en-Vercors 26 143 Fc 79
51320 Vassimont-et-Chapelaine 51 53 Ea 56
55800 Vassincourt 55 55 Fa 56
02160 Vassogne 02 40 De 52
76890 Vassonville 76 37 Ba 50
14410 Vassy 14 47 Zb 55
51700 Vassy 51 53 De 54
58140 Vassy 58 90 De 64
58700 Vassy 58 103 Dc 65
89200 Vassy 89 90 Df 63
89420 Vassy 89 90 Eb 63
89560 Vassy 89 89 Dc 63
50630 Vast, le 50 33 Yd 51
76119 Vastérival 76 37 Af 49
50440 Vasteville 50 33 Yb 51
43430 Vastres, les 43 142 Eb 79
36150 Vatan 36 101 Be 66
54122 Vathiménil 54 77 Gd 57
76270 Vatierville 76 37 Bc 50
38470 Vatilieu 38 131 Fc 77
27150 Vatimesnil 27 50 Bd 53
57580 Vatimont 57 57 Gc 55
86330 Vâtre 86 99 Aa 67
51320 Vatry 51 54 Eb 56
45490 Vattereau 45 71 Cd 60
76110 Vattetot-sous-Beaumont 76 36 Ac 51
76111 Vattetot-sur-Mer 76 36 Ab 50
27430 Vatteville 27 50 Bb 53
76940 Vatteville-la-Rue 76 36 Ae 52
37150 Vau, le 37 86 Ba 65
37530 Vau, le 37 86 Ba 64
45340 Vau, le 45 71 Cc 60
14490 Vaubadon 14 34 Za 53
79360 Vaubalier 79 111 Zd 71
71800 Vauban 71 117 Eb 71
55250 Vaubecourt 55 55 Fa 55
02600 Vauberon 02 52 Da 52

330 | Vailly

88500 Vaubexy 88 76 Gb 59
22210 Vaublanc, le 22 64 Xc 59
35420 Vaubondon 35 66 Ye 58
53300 Vaucé 53 67 Zb 58
50240 Vaucel 50 66 Yd 57
14400 Vaucelles 14 47 Zb 53
25360 Vauchamps 25 93 Gb 65
51210 Vauchamps 51 53 Dd 55
10190 Vauchassis 10 73 Df 59
60400 Vauchelles 60 39 Cf 51
80132 Vauchelles 80 28 Bf 48
80560 Vauchelles-lès-Authie 80 29 Cc 48
80620 Vauchelles-lès-Domart 80 29 Ca 48
58220 Vauchery 58 89 Da 64
21340 Vauchignon, Cormot- 21 105 Ed 67
10140 Vauchonvilliers 10 74 Ed 59
70170 Vauchoux 70 93 Ga 63
49320 Vauchrétien 49 83 Zd 65
51480 Vauciennes 51 53 Df 54
60117 Vauciennes 60 52 Da 53
58140 Vauclaix 58 104 De 65
51300 Vauclerc 51 54 Ed 56
04170 Vaucluse 04 158 Gd 84
05150 Vaucluse 05 156 Fd 82
25380 Vauclusotte 25 94 Ge 65
10240 Vaucogne 10 74 Ec 57
70120 Vauconcourt-Nervezain 70 93 Fe 63
27680 Vaucorne, le 27 36 Ad 52
55140 Vaucouleurs 55 75 Fe 57
54370 Vaucourt 54 57 Ge 56
77580 Vaucourtois 77 52 Cf 55
57530 Vaucremont 57 56 Gc 54
19260 Vaud 19 126 Be 75
74310 Vaudagne 74 121 Ge 73
60240 Vaudancourt 60 50 Be 53
71120 Vaudebarrier 71 117 Eb 70
71760 Vaudelin 71 104 Df 68
49260 Vaudelnay 49 99 Ze 66
14170 Vaudeloges 14 48 Zf 55
51380 Vaudemanges 51 53 Eb 54
54330 Vaudémont 54 76 Ga 58
10260 Vaudes 10 73 Eb 59
51600 Vaudesincourt 51 54 Ec 53
02320 Vaudesson 02 40 Dc 52
89320 Vaudeurs 89 73 Dd 60
89970 Vaudevanne, le 89 73 De 60
07410 Vaudevant 07 142 Ed 78
54740 Vaudeville 54 76 Gb 58
88000 Vaudéville 88 77 Gd 59
55130 Vaudeville-le-Haut 55 75 Fd 58
70130 Vaudey 70 93 Fe 63
22590 Vaudic, le 22 64 Xa 57
54740 Vaudigny 54 76 Gb 58
39300 Vaudioux, le 39 107 Ff 68
58220 Vaudoizy, le 58 89 Db 64
55230 Vaudoncourt 55 43 Fd 53
57220 Vaudoncourt 57 56 Gc 54
88140 Vaudoncourt 88 76 Fe 59
36400 Vaudouan 36 114 Bf 69
77123 Vaudoué, le 77 71 Cd 58
77141 Vaudoy-en-Brie 77 52 Da 56
57320 Vaudreching 57 57 Gd 53
52150 Vaudrecourt 52 75 Fd 59
52330 Vaudrémont 52 74 Ef 60
27100 Vaudreuil, le 27 49 Bb 53
31250 Vaudreuille 31 165 Bf 88
50310 Vaudreville 50 33 Yd 51
39380 Vaudrey 39 107 Fd 67
62131 Vaudricourt 62 29 Cd 45
80230 Vaudricourt 80 28 Bd 48
50310 Vaudrimesnil 50 33 Yd 54
62380 Vaudringham 62 29 Ca 45
25360 Vaudrivillers 25 93 Gc 65
10210 Vaudron 10 73 Eb 61
14500 Vaudry 14 47 Za 55
72320 Vaufargis 72 69 Ae 60
13009 Vaufrèges 13 170 Fc 89
25190 Vaufrey 25 94 Gf 64
72300 Vaugaillard 72 84 Zd 62
37230 Vaugareau 37 85 Ad 64
11200 Vaugelas 11 166 Ce 90
26400 Vaugelas 26 143 Fa 80
10190 Vaugelé 10 73 De 59
89800 Vau-Germain 89 90 De 62
86600 Vaugeton 86 111 Aa 70
21450 Vaugimois 21 91 Ec 62
84160 Vaugines 84 156 Fc 86
69670 Vaugneray 69M 130 Ed 74
22150 Vau-Gouro, le 22 64 Xb 58
91640 Vaugrigneuse 91 71 Ca 57
86210 Vaugueil 86 100 Ae 68
91430 Vauhallan 91 51 Cb 56
38114 Vaujany 38 132 Ga 78
69860 Vaujon 69D 117 Ed 71
19220 Vaujour 19 126 Ca 77
10160 Vaujuronnes 10 73 De 59
59150 Vaulandry 49 84 Zf 63
41150 Vauliard 41 86 Ba 63
89700 Vaulichères 89 90 Df 61
15300 Vaulmier, le 15 127 Cd 77
38410 Vaulnaveys-le-Haut 38 144 Fe 78
86190 Vaulorin 86 99 Aa 69
87140 Vaulry 87 113 Ba 72
89200 Vault-de-Lugny 89 90 Df 64
62390 Vaulx 62 29 Ca 47
74150 Vaulx 74 120 Ff 73
69120 Vaulx-en-Velin 69M 130 Ef 74
38890 Vaulx-Milieu 38 131 Fb 75
62159 Vaulx-Vraucourt 62 30 Cf 48
60590 Vaumain, le 60 50 Bf 52
03220 Vaumas 03 116 Dd 70
04200 Vaumeilh 04 157 Ff 83
04000 Vaumet 04 157 Gb 84
60117 Vaumoise 60 52 Cf 53
60420 Vaumont 60 39 Cd 51
89320 Vaumort 89 72 Dc 60
24800 Vaunac 24 125 Af 76
43200 Vaunac 43 129 Ea 78
26400 Vaunaveys-la-Rochette 26 143 Fa 80
05140 Vaunières 05 144 Fd 81
61130 Vaunoise 61 68 Ac 58
28240 Vaupillon 28 69 Af 58
10700 Vaupoisson 10 73 Eb 57
55270 Vauquois 55 55 Fa 53
31250 Vauré 31 165 Bf 88
16190 Vaure, la 16 124 Ab 76
95490 Vauréal 95 51 Ca 54
77710 Vauredennes 77 72 Cf 59
12220 Vaureilles 12 151 Cb 82
23110 Vaureix 23 115 Cc 72
24390 Vaures 24 125 Ba 77
02200 Vaurezis 02 40 Db 52
63230 Vauriat, le 63 127 Cf 73
47150 Vauris 47 137 Af 81
60390 Vauroux, le 60 38 Bf 52
02860 Vaurseine 02 40 De 52
79190 Vaussais 79 111 Aa 72
86190 Vausseau, la 86 99 Zf 69
79420 Vausseroux 79 111 Zf 69
71540 Vaussery 71 105 Eb 66
81330 Vaute, la 81 151 Cc 85
79420 Vautebis 79 111 Zf 69
90150 Vauthiermont 90 94 Ha 62
79190 Vauthion 79 111 Aa 72
53500 Vautorte 53 66 Za 59
76560 Vautuit 76 36 Ae 50
76630 Vauvage, la 76 37 Bb 49
13126 Vauvenargues 13 171 Fd 87
30600 Vauvert 30 169 Eb 86
36400 Vauvet 36 102 Bf 69
14800 Vauville 14 36 Aa 53
50440 Vauville 50 33 Ya 51
70210 Vauvillers 70 93 Ga 61
80131 Vauvillers 80 39 Ce 49
74120 Vauvray 74 133 Gd 73
03190 Vaux 03 115 Cd 70
15170 Vaux 15 140 Da 78
16210 Vaux 16 123 Aa 77
19110 Vaux 19 127 Cc 76
31540 Vaux 31 165 Bf 88
36180 Vaux 36 101 Bc 67
37150 Vaux 37 86 Ba 64
57130 Vaux 57 56 Ga 54
58190 Vaux 58 89 De 64
58800 Vaux 58 104 Dd 65
60390 Vaux 60 38 Ca 52
60420 Vaux 60 39 Cd 51
71250 Vaux 71 118 Ed 70
80340 Vaux 80 39 Ce 49
86700 Vaux 86 111 Ab 71
89000 Vaux 89 89 Dd 62
49150 Vaux, le 49 84 Ze 63
50320 Vaux, le 50 46 Yd 55
41300 Vaux, les 41 87 Bf 64
79110 Vaux, les 79 111 Zf 72
02320 Vauxaillon 02 40 Dc 52
02110 Vaux-Andigny 02 40 Dd 48
52200 Vauxbons 52 92 Fa 61
35550 Vaux-Bourg 35 81 Xf 62
02200 Vauxbuin 02 40 Db 52
02160 Vauxcéré 02 53 Dd 52
08130 Vaux-Champagne 08 41 Ed 52
58130 Vaux d'Amognes 58 103 Db 66
55400 Vaux-devant-Damloup 55 55 Fc 53
80260 Vaux-en-Amiénois 80 38 Cb 49
69460 Vaux-en-Beaujolais 69D 118 Ed 72
01150 Vaux-en-Bugey 01 119 Fc 73
08240 Vaux-en-Dieulet 08 42 Ef 52
71460 Vaux-en-Pré 71 105 Ed 69
02590 Vaux-en-Vermandois 02 40 Da 50
25160 Vaux-et-Chantegrue 25 108 Gb 68
52400 Vaux-la-Douce 52 92 Fe 61
55500 Vaux-la-Grande 55 55 Fc 56
55500 Vaux-la-Petite 55 55 Fc 57
16320 Vaux-Lavalette 16 124 Ab 76
61150 Vaux-le-Bardoult 61 48 Zf 56
70700 Vaux-le-Moncelot 70 93 Ff 64
77000 Vaux-le-Pénil 77 71 Ce 57
08250 Vaux-lès-Mouron 08 54 Ee 53
08210 Vaux-lès-Mouzon 08 42 Fa 51
55300 Vaux-lès-Palameix 55 55 Fd 54
25770 Vaux-les-Prés 25 107 Ff 65
08220 Vaux-lès-Rubigny 08 41 Eb 50
39360 Vaux-lès-Saint-Claude 39 119 Fe 70
80140 Vaux-Marquenneville 80 38 Be 49
08270 Vaux-Montreuil 08 41 Ed 51
69820 Vauxrenard 69D 118 Ed 71
16170 Vaux-Rouillac 16 123 Zf 74
01110 Vaux-Saint-Sulpice 01 119 Fd 73
21440 Vaux-Saules 21 91 Ee 64
52190 Vaux-sous-Aubigny 52 92 Fb 63
14400 Vaux-sur-Aure 14 47 Zb 53
52130 Vaux-sur-Blaise 52 74 Ef 58
21560 Vaux-sur-Crône 21 92 Fb 65
27120 Vaux-sur-Eure 27 50 Bc 54
77710 Vaux-sur-Lunain 77 72 Cf 59
17640 Vaux-sur-Mer 17 122 Yf 75
39800 Vaux-sur-Poligny 39 107 Fe 68
52300 Vaux-sur-Saint-Urbain 52 75 Fb 58
78740 Vaux-sur-Seine 78 50 Bf 54
14400 Vaux-sur-Seulles 14 34 Zc 53
80800 Vaux-sur-Somme 80 39 Cd 49
86220 Vaux-sur-Vienne 86 100 Ad 67
02220 Vauxtin 02 40 Dd 52
08150 Vaux-Villaine 08 41 Ec 50
63610 Vauzelle 63 128 Cf 76
36330 Vauzelles 36 101 Bd 68
55000 Vavincourt 55 55 Fb 56
51300 Vavray-le-Grand 51 54 Ee 56
51300 Vavray-le-Petit 51 54 Ee 56
42120 Vavres, les 42 117 Ea 72
01250 Vavrette, la 01 119 Fb 72
54120 Vaxainville 54 77 Ge 57
88330 Vaxoncourt 88 76 Gc 59
57170 Vaxy 57 57 Gd 55
44170 Vay 44 82 Yb 63
09110 Vaychis 09 177 Be 92
46230 Vaylats 46 150 Bd 82
46110 Vayrac 46 138 Be 79
87600 Vayres 87 124 Ae 74
91820 Vayres-sur-Essonne 91 71 Cc 58
46090 Vayrol 46 150 Bc 82
12450 Vayssac 12 152 Cd 83
12780 Vaysse, la 12 152 Cf 83
46300 Vaysse, la 46 137 Bc 80
12780 Vaysse-Rodié 12 152 Cf 83
48300 Vaysset, le 48 141 De 80
46240 Vayssière 46 138 Bd 80
46300 Vayssière, la 46 137 Bc 80
48400 Vayssière, la 48 153 Dd 82
43580 Vazeilles, Esplantas 43 141 Dd 79
43320 Vazeilles-Limandre 43 141 De 78
82220 Vazerac 82 150 Bb 83
03450 Veauce 03 115 Da 72
42340 Veauche 42 129 Eb 75
18300 Veaugues 18 88 Ce 65
79230 Veaumoreau 79 111 Ze 71
26600 Veaunes, Mercurol- 26 142 Ef 78
22250 Veau-Ruset 22 64 Xe 58
76190 Veauville-lès-Baons 76 36 Ae 51
84340 Veaux 84 155 Fb 83
86450 Veaux 86 100 Ae 68
03210 Veaux, les 03 116 Db 70
09310 Vèbre 09 177 Be 92
15240 Vebret 15 127 Cd 76
48400 Vébron 48 153 Dd 83
57370 Veckersviller 57 57 Hb 55
57920 Veckring 57 56 Gc 52
88200 Vecoux 88 77 Gd 61
80800 Vecquemont 80 39 Cc 49
52300 Vecqueville 52 75 Fa 58
13129 Vedeau, le 13 169 Ee 88
36120 Vedeaux 36 102 Ca 68
87310 Vedeix 87 125 Af 74
84270 Vedène 84 155 Ef 85
20160 Vedolaccia CTC 182 Ie 96
19160 Vedrenne 19 127 Cb 76
19300 Vedrenne 19 126 Bf 76
87270 Vedrenne 87 113 Bb 73
19220 Vedrenne, la 19 126 Ca 77
48200 Védrine, la 48 140 Db 80
48310 Védrinel, le 48 140 Da 80
15100 Védrines-Saint-Loup 15 140 Db 78
55000 Véel 55 55 Fa 56
19120 Végennes 19 138 Be 79
54450 Vého 54 77 Ge 57
37250 Veigné 37 85 Ae 65
74140 Veigy-Foncenex 74 120 Gb 71
81500 Veilhes 81 165 Be 87
16200 Veillard 16 123 Ze 74
41230 Veilleins 41 87 Be 64
21360 Veilly 21 105 Ed 66
87440 Veimpeire 87 125 Af 75
66300 Veïnat-d'en-Llense 66 179 Cd 93
15310 Veissière, la 15 139 Cb 78
63610 Veissière, la 63 128 Cf 76
69650 Veissieux 69M 118 Ee 73
19260 Veix 19 126 Bf 75
19170 Véjoles 19 126 Bf 75
54840 Velaine-en-Haye 54 56 Ga 56
55500 Velaines 55 55 Fb 56
54280 Velaine-sous-Amance 54 56 Gb 56
38620 Velanne 38 131 Fd 76
21370 Velars-sur-Ouche 21 91 Ef 65
13880 Velaux 13 170 Fb 87
71550 Velée 71 105 Ea 66
60510 Velennes 60 38 Cb 52
80160 Velennes 80 38 Ca 50
70100 Velesmes-Echevanne 70 92 Fe 64
25410 Velesmes-Essarts 25 107 Ff 65
70100 Velet 70 92 Fd 64
71190 Velet 71 105 Ea 67
82000 Velhaguet 82 150 Bb 85
34220 Vélieux 34 166 Ce 88
24230 Vélines 24 136 Aa 79
78140 Vélizy-Villacoublay 78 51 Cb 56
86230 Vellèches 86 100 Ad 67
70110 Vellechevreux-et-Courbenans 70 94 Gd 63
70700 Velleclaire 70 93 Ff 64
70000 Vellefaux 70 93 Ga 63
70700 Vellefrey-et-Vellefrange 70 93 Fe 64
70240 Vellefrie 70 93 Gb 62
70600 Velleguibelle 70 92 Fd 63
70000 Velleguindry-et-Levrecey 70 93 Ga 63
70000 Velle-le-Châtel 70 93 Ga 63
70240 Velleminfroy 70 93 Gb 63
70700 Vellemoz 70 93 Fe 64
21230 Velleneuve 21 105 Ec 66
84740 Velleron 84 155 Fa 85
25430 Vellerot-lès-Belvoir 25 94 Gd 64
25530 Vellerot-lès-Vercel 25 108 Gc 65
36330 Velles 36 101 Bd 68
52500 Velles 52 92 Fe 61
90100 Vellescot 90 94 Ha 63
54290 Velle-sur-Moselle 54 76 Gb 57
25430 Vellevans 25 94 Gc 65
70130 Vellexon Quetrey-et-Vaudey 70 93 Fe 63
70700 Velloreille-lès-Choye 70 92 Fe 64
85770 Velluire 85 110 Za 70
21350 Velogny 21 91 Ec 64
20230 Velone-Orneto CTC 183 Kc 94
70300 Velorcrey 70 93 Gb 62
84800 Velorgues 84 155 Fa 85
55600 Velosnes 55 43 Fc 51
88270 Velotte-et-Tatignécourt 88 76 Gb 59
62124 Vélu 62 30 Cf 48
79600 Véluché 79 99 Zf 68
57220 Velving 57 57 Gd 53
51130 Vélye 51 53 Ea 55
15590 Velzic 15 139 Cd 79
95470 Vémars 95 51 Cd 54
39160 Vemay, le 39 119 Fb 70
27940 Venables 27 50 Bb 53
87140 Vénachat 87 113 Bb 72
20231 Venaco CTC 183 Kb 95
20231 Venacu = Venaco CTC 183 Kb 95
85190 Venansault 85 97 Yc 68
06450 Venanson 06 159 Hb 84
21150 Venarey-les-Laumes 21 91 Ec 63
19360 Venarsal 19 126 Bd 77
03190 Venas 03 115 Ce 70
84210 Venasque 84 156 Fa 85
06140 Vence 06 173 Ha 86
49150 Vendanger 49 84 Zf 64
34740 Vendargues 34 168 Df 87
03110 Vendat 03 116 Dc 72
33930 Vendays-Montalivet 33 122 Yf 76
49650 Vende, la 49 84 Aa 65
59218 Vendegies-au-Bois 59 31 Dd 47
59213 Vendegies-sur-Ecaillon 59 30 Dd 47
63350 Vendègre 63 116 Dc 73
35140 Vendel 35 66 Ye 59
63150 Vendel 63 127 Ce 75
50200 Vendelée, la 50 46 Yd 54
02490 Vendelles 02 40 Da 49
12400 Vendeloves 12 152 Cf 85
34230 Vendémian 34 168 Dd 87
71120 Vendenesse-lès-Charolles 71 117 Ec 70
71130 Vendenesse-sur-Arroux 71 104 Ea 69
67550 Vendenheim 67 58 He 56
14250 Vendes 14 34 Zc 54
15240 Vendes 15 127 Cc 77
43200 Vendets 43 129 Eb 77
02800 Vendeuil 02 40 Dc 50
60120 Vendeuil-Caply 60 38 Cb 51
14170 Vendeuvre 14 48 Zf 55
86380 Vendeuvre-du-Poitou 86 99 Ab 68
10140 Vendeuvre-sur-Barse 10 74 Ec 59
59175 Vendeville 59 30 Da 45
02420 Vendhuile 02 40 Db 48
02540 Vendières 02 52 Dc 55
62232 Vendin 62 29 Cd 45
31460 Vendine 31 165 Be 87
62880 Vendin-le-Vieil 62 30 Cf 46
36500 Vendœuvres 36 101 Bc 68
24320 Vendoire 24 124 Ab 76
41100 Vendôme 41 86 Ba 62
42590 Vendranges 42 117 Ea 73
85250 Vendrennes 85 97 Yf 68
34350 Vendres 34 167 Db 89
08160 Vendresse 08 42 Ee 51
02160 Vendresse-Beaulne 02 40 De 52
77440 Vendrest 77 52 Da 54
10800 Vendue-Mignot, la 10 73 Ea 60
35410 Venecelle 35 66 Yc 60
48000 Venède 48 140 Dd 82
35410 Veneffles 35 66 Yc 60
30200 Vénéjan 30 155 Ed 83
13770 Venelles 13 170 Fc 87
17100 Vénérand 17 123 Zc 74
70100 Venère 70 92 Fe 64
38460 Vénérieu 38 131 Fb 75
31810 Venerque 31 164 Bc 88
81440 Vénès 81 165 Cb 86
18190 Venesmes 18 102 Cb 67
76730 Vénestanville 76 37 Af 50
77250 Veneux-les-Sablons 77 72 Ce 58
54540 Veney 54 77 Ge 58
50150 Vengeons 50 47 Za 56
86200 Véniers 86 99 Aa 66
25870 Venise 25 93 Ga 64
70500 Venisey 70 93 Ff 62
69200 Vénissieux 69M 130 Ef 74
02200 Vénizel 02 40 Dc 52
89210 Venizy 89 73 De 60
11120 Venlenac-en-Minervois 11 167 Cf 89
45760 Vennecy 45 70 Ca 61
25390 Vennes 25 108 Gd 66
47350 Vennes, les 47 136 Ab 81
54830 Vennezey 54 77 Gc 58
18300 Venoize 18 88 Ce 65
27110 Venon 27 49 Ba 53
38610 Venon 38 144 Fe 77
38520 Vénosc 38 144 Gb 79
87130 Venouhant 87 126 Bd 74
86480 Venours 86 111 Aa 70
89230 Venouse 89 89 De 61
89290 Venoy 89 90 Dd 62
06660 Vens 06 158 Gf 83
33590 Vensac 33 122 Yf 76
63260 Vensat 63 116 Db 72
13122 Ventabren 13 170 Fb 87
46170 Ventaillac 46 150 Bc 82
48160* Ventalon en Cévennes 48 153 Df 83
05300 Ventavon 05 157 Ff 82
07470 Vente 07 141 Ea 80
50260 Vente aux-Saulniers, la 50 33 Yc 52
51140 Ventelay 51 53 De 52
09120 Ventenac 09 177 Be 90
11610 Ventenac-Cabardès 11 166 Cb 89
23230 Ventenat 23 114 Cb 71
05130 Venterol 05 157 Ga 82
26110 Venterol 26 155 Fa 82
27180 Ventes, les 27 49 Ba 55
61170 Ventes-de-Bourse, les 61 68 Ab 57
72600 Ventes-du-Four 72 68 Ab 58
76390 Ventes-Mésangères, les 76 37 Bd 50
76680 Ventes-Saint-Rémy 76 37 Bb 50
43170 Venteuges 43 140 Dd 79
51480 Venteuil 51 53 Df 54
73200 Venthon 73 132 Gc 74
82290 Ventillac 82 150 Bb 84
20240 Ventiseri CTC 183 Kc 97
46500 Ventoulou 46 138 Be 80
84390 Ventouret, le 84 156 Fc 84
16460 Ventouse 16 112 Ab 73
48130 Ventouzet, le 48 140 Db 81
63490 Ventre 63 128 Dc 75
88310 Ventron 88 94 Gf 61
13500 Ventrons, les 13 170 Fa 88
61190 Ventrouze, la 61 69 Ae 57
57430 Ventzviller 57 57 Gf 55
20215 Venzolasca CTC 181 Kc 94
50450 Ver 50 46 Yd 55
33240 Vérac 33 135 Zd 79
20113 Vera Martini CTC 184 If 98
42520 Véranne 42 130 Ed 76
34400 Vérargues 34 168 Ea 86
76190 Ver-à-Val, le 76 36 Ae 51
01170 Veraz 01 120 Ga 71
11580 Véraza 11 178 Cb 91
60410 Verberie 60 39 Ce 53
52000 Verbiesles 52 75 Fb 60
25530 Vercel-Villedieu-le-Camp 25 108 Gc 65
59227 Verchain-Maugré 59 30 Dc 47
74440 Verchaix 74 121 Ge 72
26340 Vercheny 26 143 Fb 80
74210 Verchères 74 132 Gb 74
49700 Verchers-sur-Layon, les 49 98 Ze 66
69510 Verchery 69M 130 Ee 74
62310 Verchin 62 29 Cb 46
71870 Verchizeuil 71 118 Ee 70
62560 Verchocq 62 29 Ca 45
42370 Verchu 42 117 Df 72
39190 Vercia 39 106 Fc 69
74340 Vercland 74 121 Ge 72
26510 Verclause 26 156 Fc 82
26170 Vercoiran 26 156 Fc 83
50240 Verconcey 50 66 Yd 57
80120 Vercourt 80 28 Be 47
01680 Vercraz 01 131 Fd 74
04140 Verdaches 04 157 Gc 83
81110 Verdalle 81 166 Ca 87
33340 Verdasse, la 33 122 Za 76
33490 Verdelais 33 135 Ze 81
77510 Verdelot 77 52 Dc 55
54450 Verdenal 54 77 Ge 57
60112 Verderel-lès-Sauqueuse 60 38 Ca 51
50190 Verderie, la 50 46 Yc 53
59710 Verderie, la 59 30 Da 45
60140 Verderonne 60 39 Cc 53
41240 Verdes 41 70 Bc 61
20229 Verdese CTC 183 Kc 94
64400 Verdets 64 161 Zc 89
74440 Verdevant 74 120 Gd 72
51120 Verdey 51 53 De 56
12170 Verdier 12 152 Cd 84
19140 Verdier 19 126 Bd 76
19240 Verdier 19 125 Bc 77
46160 Verdier 46 138 Be 81
81260 Verdier 81 166 Cd 87
19200 Verdier, le 19 127 Cc 76
38710 Verdier, le 38 144 Fe 80
63790 Verdier, le 63 127 Cf 75
81140 Verdier, le 81 151 Bf 85
83560 Verdière, la 83 171 Ff 87
18300 Verdigny 18 88 Ce 64
16140 Verdille 16 123 Zf 73
36800 Verdinguet, le 36 101 Bc 68
44810 Verdinière, la 44 82 Yc 64
12380 Verdolle, la 12 152 Cd 85
24520 Verdon 24 136 Ad 80
51210 Verdon 51 53 Dd 55
79300 Verdon, le 79 98 Zd 68
21330 Verdonnet 21 90 Eb 62
33123 Verdon-sur-Mer, le 33 122 Yf 75
33860 Verdot 33 123 Zd 77
09310 Verdun 09 177 Be 92
27400 Verdun 27 49 Ba 54
43580 Verdun 43 141 Dd 79
55100 Verdun 55 55 Fc 54
11400 Verdun-en-Lauragais 11 165 Ca 88
82600 Verdun-sur-Garonne 82 150 Bb 85
71350 Verdun-sur-le-Doubs 71 106 Fa 67
71340 Verdures, les 71 117 Df 71
18600 Vereaux 18 103 Cf 67
74140 Vereitre 74 120 Gb 71
74290 Vérel 74 132 Gb 73
73330 Verel-de-Montbel 73 131 Fe 75
73230 Verel-Pragondran 73 132 Ff 75
69420 Verenay 69M 130 Ee 75
34600 Vérénoux 34 167 Da 87
37270 Véretz 37 85 Ae 64
70180 Vereux 70 92 Fd 63
31590 Verfeil 31 165 Bd 87
82330 Verfeil-sur-Seye 82 151 Bf 83
30630 Verfeuil 30 154 Ec 83
70100 Verfontaine 70 92 Fc 64
57260 Vergaville 57 57 Ge 55
35680 Vergéal 35 66 Ye 60
83111 Vergelins, les 83 172 Gb 87
70200 Vergenne, la 70 94 Gc 63
89240 Vergeot 89 89 Dc 62
23140 Verger 23 114 Ca 71
35260 Verger 35 65 Ya 56
36170 Verger 36 113 Bc 70
44290 Verger 44 82 Yb 63
35160 Verger, le 35 65 Ya 60
86110 Verger-sur-Dive 86 99 Aa 68
39570 Verges 39 107 Fe 69
87400 Verges, les 87 125 Bc 74
76280 Vergetot 76 36 Ab 51
43320 Vergezac 43 141 De 78
30310 Vergèze 30 169 Eb 86
63330 Vergheas 63 115 Cd 72
20138 Verghia CTC 182 Ie 98
20224 Verghio CTC 182 If 95
20224 Verghju = Verghio CTC 182 If 95
13310 Vergière 13 169 Ee 87
84220 Vergiers, les 84 155 Fb 85
80270 Vergies 80 38 Bf 49
89600 Vergigny 89 73 De 61
71960 Vergisson 71 118 Ee 71
16220 Vergnas 16 124 Ad 74
19370 Vergnas 19 126 Be 75
23480 Vergnas 23 114 Ca 73
03600 Vergnaud 03 115 Ce 71
15190 Vergne 15 127 Ce 76
15310 Vergne 15 139 Cb 78
17330 Vergné 17 110 Zc 72
19320 Vergne 19 126 Ca 77
86400 Vergné 86 112 Ab 71
15140 Vergne, la 15 139 Cc 78
17360 Vergne, la 17 135 Zf 78
17400 Vergne, la 17 110 Zc 73
19800 Vergne, la 19 126 Be 77
23250 Vergne, la 23 114 Bf 72
63740 Vergne, la 63 127 Ce 74
16270 Vergne-Noire, la 16 112 Ad 73
85440 Vergne-Rocard, la 85 109 Yc 69

A B C D E F G H I J K L M N O P Q R S T U V W X Y Z

Vergne-Rocard, la I 331

07160 Vergnes 07 142 Ec 79
23700 Vergnes, les 23 115 Cd 73
18140 Vergniol, le 18 103 Cf 65
23320 Vergnioux, le 23 114 Bd 71
12470 Vergnoles 12 139 Cf 81
19400 Vergnolles 19 138 Bf 78
82230 Vergnous, les 82 150 Bc 84
32720 Vergoignan 32 162 Ze 86
71400 Vergoncey 71 105 Ec 67
43360 Vergongheon 43 128 Db 76
49420 Vergonnes 49 83 Yf 62
04170 Vergons 04 158 Gd 85
43300 Vergonzac 43 141 Dd 78
48400 Vergougnous, le 48 153 De 83
25110 Vergranne 25 93 Gc 64
24380 Vergt 24 136 Ae 78
02490 Verguier, le 02 40 Da 49
62131 Verguin 62 29 Cd 45
71580 Vériat 71 106 Fc 69
29590 Véridy 29 62 Vf 59
71700 Verière 71 106 Ef 69
49125 Verigne 49 83 Zd 63
83630 Vérignon 83 172 Gb 87
28190 Vérigny 28 70 Bb 57
87920 Vérinas 87 125 Bb 74
42440 Vérine 42 129 De 74
17540 Vérines 17 110 Za 71
43130 Vérines 43 129 Df 77
60320 Vérines 60 52 Ce 53
71440 Vérissey 71 106 Fa 68
71260 Vérizet 71 118 Ef 70
01270 Verjon 01 119 Fc 70
71590 Verjux 71 106 Ef 67
80400 Verlaines 80 39 Da 50
70400 Verlans 70 94 Ge 63
42620 Verlecoup 42 116 De 71
15200 Verlhac 15 127 Cc 77
82230 Verlhac-Tescou 82 150 Bd 85
42410 Verlieu 42 130 Ee 76
89330 Verlin 89 72 Db 60
62830 Verlincthun 62 28 Be 45
59237 Verlinghem 59 30 Cf 44
02490 Vermand 02 40 Da 49
80320 Vermandovillers 80 39 Ce 49
30380 Vermeil 30 154 Ea 84
09500 Vermeille 09 165 Be 90
81660 Vermeils 81 166 Cc 87
62980 Vermelles 62 29 Ce 46
89270 Vermenton 89 90 De 63
89200 Vermoiron 89 90 De 63
25150 Vermondans 25 94 Ge 64
88210 Vermont, le 88 77 Ha 58
58230 Vermot 58 90 Df 65
43810 Vermoyal 43 129 Df 77
29840 Vern 29 61 Vb 58
63700 Vernade, la 63 115 Cf 71
18210 Vernais 18 103 Ce 68
69390 Vernaison 69M 130 Ee 75
09120 Vernajoul 09 177 Bd 91
51330 Vernancourt 51 54 Ee 55
49390 Vernantes 49 84 Aa 64
39570 Vernantois 39 107 Fd 69
30530 Vernarède, la 30 154 Ea 83
38460 Vernas 38 131 Fb 74
43270 Vernassal 43 141 De 78
37600 Vernaterie, la 37 100 Af 66
09250 Vernaux 09 177 Be 92
01190 Vernay 01 118 Ef 70
37120 Vernay 37 99 Ac 66
42300 Vernay 42 117 Ea 72
69430 Vernay 69D 117 Ed 72
74200 Vernaz, la 74 120 Gd 71
49220 Vern-d'Anjou 49 83 Za 63
25110 Verne 25 93 Gc 64
42660 Verne 42 129 Ec 77
43200 Verne 43 142 Eb 77
71300 Verne, la 71 105 Ec 69
34520 Vernède, la 34 153 Dc 85
48400 Vernède, la 48 153 Dd 82
63390 Vernède, la 63 115 Ce 72
13116 Vernègues 13 170 Fb 86
23420 Verneide, la 23 115 Cc 73
23170 Verneiges 23 114 Cc 71
73110 Verneil, le 73 132 Gb 76
72360 Verneil-le-Chétif 72 85 Ab 62
03190 Verneix 03 115 Ce 70
19160 Vernejoux 19 127 Cb 76
19450 Vernejoux 19 126 Be 76
36600 Vernelle, la 36 101 Bd 65
58170 Vernes 58 104 Df 68
83560 Vernes, les 83 171 Fe 87
09700 Vernèses 09 165 Bd 89
71310 Vernes-Guyotte 71 106 Fb 67
31810 Vernet 31 164 Bc 88
03200 Vernet, le 03 116 Dc 72
04140 Vernet, le 04 157 Gc 83
09700 Vernet, le 09 165 Bd 89
43320 Vernet, le 43 141 De 78
63700 Vernet, le 63 115 Cf 71
63580 Vernet-la-Varenne 63 128 Dc 76
12260 Vernet-le-Bas 12 138 Bf 81
66820 Vernet-les-Bains 66 178 Cc 93
48400 Vernets, les 48 140 Dc 81
63710 Vernet-Sainte-Marguerite, le 63 128 Cf 75
63970 Verneuge 63 128 Cf 74
63470 Verneugheol 63 127 Cd 74
03360 Verneuil 03 102 Cd 68
16310 Verneuil 16 124 Ae 74
18210 Verneuil 18 102 Cd 68
51700 Verneuil 51 53 De 54
58300 Verneuil 58 104 Dd 67
03500 Verneuil-en-Bourbonnais 03 116 Db 70
60550 Verneuil-en-Halatte 60 51 Cd 53
55600 Verneuil-Grand 55 43 Fc 51
77390 Verneuil-l'Etang 77 52 Ce 57
37120 Verneuil-le-Château 37 100 Ac 66
87360 Verneuil-Moustiers 87 113 Ba 70
55600 Verneuil-Petit 55 43 Fc 51
02380 Verneuil-sous-Coucy 02 40 Db 51
27130* Verneuil-sur-Avre et d'Iton 27 49 Af 56
36400 Verneuil-sur-Igneraie 36 102 Ca 69
37600 Verneuil-sur-Indre 37 100 Ba 66
78480 Verneuil-sur-Seine 78 50 Bf 55
02000 Verneuil-sur-Serre 02 40 De 51
87430 Verneuil-sur-Vienne 87 125 Ba 73
29380 Verneur 29 79 Wb 61
27390 Verneusses 27 48 Ac 55
57130 Vernéville 57 56 Ga 54
05100 Verney 05 145 Gd 78
38114 Verney, le 38 144 Ga 78
38690 Verney, le 38 131 Fc 76
73500 Verney, le 73 133 Ge 77
73450 Verneys, les 73 145 Gc 78
12160 Vernhe 12 152 Cc 83
12410 Vernhes, les 12 152 Ce 83
72170 Vernie 72 68 Aa 59
49122 Vernière, la 49 98 Za 66
81530 Vernières 81 151 Cc 86
25580 Vernierfontaine 25 108 Gb 66
72240 Verniette 72 68 Zf 60
43380 Vernines 43 140 Db 77
63210 Vernines 63 127 Cf 75
09340 Verniolle 09 165 Bd 90
38150 Vernioz 38 130 Ef 76
50370 Vernix 50 46 Ye 56
89130 Vernoi, le 89 89 Db 62
49390 Vernoil 49 84 Aa 64
37330 Vernoille 37 85 Ab 63
21210 Vernois 21 90 Eb 65
39210 Vernois 39 107 Fd 68
39140 Vernois, le 39 106 Fc 68
25190 Vernois-le-Fol 25 94 Gf 64
25430 Vernois-lès-Belvoir 25 94 Gd 65
21260 Vernois-lès-Vesvres 21 92 Fa 63
70500 Vernois-sur-Mance 70 93 Fe 61
15160 Vernols 15 127 Cf 77
07260 Vernon 07 141 Eb 81
27200 Vernon 27 50 Bc 54
45190 Vernon 45 87 Bd 62
86340 Vernon 86 112 Ac 70
87400 Vernon 87 125 Bd 73
10200 Vernonvilliers 10 74 Ee 59
07430 Vernosc-lès-Annonay 07 130 Ee 77
21120 Vernot 21 91 Ef 64
71670 Vernotte 71 105 Ed 67
70130 Vernotte, la 70 93 Ff 63
41230 Vernou-en-Sologne 41 87 Be 63
28500 Vernouillet 28 50 Bb 56
78540 Vernouillet 78 50 Bf 55
77670 Vernou-la-Celle-sur-Seine 77 71 Cf 58
37210 Vernou-sur-Brenne 37 85 Af 64
01560 Vernoux 01 118 Fa 70
79240 Vernoux-en-Gâtine 79 98 Zc 69
07240 Vernoux-en-Vivarais 07 142 Ed 79
79170 Vernoux-sur-Boutonne 79 111 Ze 72
89150 Vernoy 89 72 Da 60
35770 Vern-sur-Seiche 35 65 Yc 60
58640 Vernuches 58 103 Da 66
15260 Vernuéjol 15 140 Cf 79
03390 Vernusse 03 115 Cf 71
57420 Verny 57 56 Gb 54
20172 Vero CTC 182 If 96
89510 Véron 89 72 Db 60
29380 Véronique, la 29 78 Wb 61
26340 Véronne 26 143 Fb 80
21260 Véronnes 21 92 Fb 63
21260 Véronnes-les-Petites 21 92 Fb 63
71220 Verosvres 71 117 Ec 70
08240 Verpel 08 42 Ef 52
88520 Verpellière 88 77 Ha 59
38290 Verpillière, la 38 131 Fa 75
80700 Verpillières 80 39 Ce 50
10360 Verpillières-sur-Durce 10 74 Ed 60
13670 Verquières 13 155 Ef 85
62113 Verquigneul 62 29 Cd 45
73460 Verrens-Arvey 73 132 Gb 75
08220 Verrerie, la 08 41 Eb 50
24310 Verrerie, la 24 124 Ad 76
36200 Verrerie, la 36 101 Bd 69
36330 Verrerie, la 36 101 Be 68
41170 Verrerie, la 41 69 Af 60
67510 Verrerie, la 67 58 He 55
70200 Verrerie, la 70 94 Gd 62
74570 Verrerie, la 74 120 Gb 73
85240 Verrerie, la 85 110 Zc 69
88330 Verrerie-de-Portieux, la- 88 76 Gc 58
34220 Verrerins-des-Moussans 34 166 Cd 88
43580 Verreyroles 43 141 Dd 79
21540 Verrey-sous-Drée 21 91 Ee 64
21690 Verrey-sous-Salmaise 21 91 Ed 64
10240 Verricourt 10 74 Ec 58
49400 Verrie 49 99 Ze 65
85130 Verrie, la 85 97 Yf 67
24130 Verrière 24 136 Ab 79
31380 Verrière, la 31 150 Bc 86
78990 Verrière, la 78 50 Bf 56
08390 Verrières 08 42 Ef 52
10390 Verrières 10 73 Ea 59
12520 Verrières 12 152 Da 83
14250 Verrières 14 34 Zc 53
16130 Verrières 16 123 Ze 75
18340 Verrières 18 102 Cc 67
48600 Verrières 48 141 Dd 79
51800 Verrières 51 54 Ef 54
63320 Verrières 63 128 Da 75
86410 Verrières 86 112 Ad 70
26260 Verrières, les 26 142 Ef 78
70700 Verrières, les 70 93 Fe 64
25300 Verrières-de-Joux 25 108 Gc 67
25580 Verrières-du-Grosbois 25 108 Gb 65
49112* Verrières-en-Anjou 49 83 Zd 63
42600 Verrières-en-Forez 42 129 Df 75
61110 Verrières 61 69 Ae 58
45300 Verrine 45 71 Cb 60
79200 Verrine 79 99 Ze 68
86110 Verrine 86 99 Aa 68
79120 Verrines 79 111 Aa 71
79370 Verrines-sous-Celles 79 111 Ze 71
72200 Verron 72 84 Zf 62
86420 Verrue 86 99 Ab 67
79310 Verruyes 79 111 Ze 69
71240 Vers 71 106 Ef 69
74160 Vers 74 120 Ga 72
46090 Vers, Saint-Géry- 46 138 Bd 82
92430 Versailles 92 51 Cb 56
14700 Versainville 14 48 Ze 55
42220 Versanne, la 42 130 Ed 77
24330 Versannes, les 24 137 Af 78
71110 Versaugues 71 117 Ea 70
52250 Verseilles-le-Bas 52 92 Fb 62
52250 Verseilles-le-Haut 52 92 Fb 62
39300 Vers-en-Montagne 39 107 Ff 68
02800 Versigny 02 40 Dc 51
60440 Versigny 60 52 Ce 54
43200 Versilhac 43 141 Eb 78
38890 Versin 38 131 Fc 75
28630 Vers-lès-Chartres 28 70 Bc 58
12400 Versols-et-Lapeyre 12 152 Cf 85
14790 Verson 14 35 Zd 54
01210 Versonnex 01 120 Ga 71
74150 Versonnex 74 120 Ff 73
73700 Versoye-les-Granges 73 133 Ge 75
30210 Vers-Pont-du-Gard 30 155 Ed 85
39230 Vers-sous-Sellières 39 107 Fd 68
80480 Vers-sur-Selle 80 38 Cb 49
60950 Ver-sur-Launette 60 51 Ce 54
14114 Ver-sur-Mer 14 47 Zc 52
40420 Vert 40 147 Zc 84
78930 Vert 78 50 Be 55
19140 Vert, le 19 125 Bc 76
19220 Vert, le 19 138 Ca 78
19250 Vert, le 19 126 Cb 75
38210 Vert, le 38 131 Fc 77
46140 Vert, le 46 150 Bb 82
79170 Vert, le 79 111 Zd 72
59730 Vertain 59 30 Dd 47
63910 Vertaizon 63 128 Db 74
39130 Vertamboz 39 107 Fe 69
21330 Vertault 21 90 Ec 61
17550 Vert-Bois 17 109 Ye 73
77760 Verteau 77 71 Cd 59
24320 Verteillac 24 124 Ac 76
28500 Vert-en-Drouais 28 50 Bb 56
47260 Verteuil-d'Agenais 47 137 Ac 82
16510 Verteuil-sur-Charente 16 111 Ab 73
02140 Verte-Vallee, la 02 41 Df 49
62830 Vertevoie, la 62 28 Be 45
73170 Verthemex 73 132 Fe 75
33180 Vertheuil 33 122 Za 77
74210 Verthier 74 132 Gb 74
89260 Vertilly 89 72 Dc 58
24330 Vertiol 24 137 Af 78
91810 Vert-le-Grand 91 71 Cc 57
91710 Vert-le-Petit 91 71 Cc 57
63480 Vertolaye 63 129 De 75
62180 Verton 62 28 Bd 46
44120 Vertou 44 97 Yd 66
38390 Vertrieu 38 131 Fc 73
63390 Verts, les 63 115 Ce 72
77240 Vert-Saint-Denis 77 71 Cd 57
51130 Vert-Toulon 51 53 Df 55
51130 Vertus 51 53 Ea 55
81800 Vertus 81 150 Be 85
55200 Vertuzey 55 55 Fd 56
62240 Verval, le 62 28 Bf 44
16330 Vervant 16 124 Aa 73
17400 Vervant 17 111 Zd 73
88600 Vervezelle 88 77 Ge 59
87120 Verviale 87 126 Bd 74
02140 Vervins 02 41 Df 49
24700 Very 24 136 Ab 79
55270 Véry 55 55 Fa 53
74330 Véry 74 120 Ga 73
71960 Verzé 71 118 Ee 70
72600 Verzé 72 68 Ab 58
11250 Verzeille 11 166 Cb 90
51360 Verzenay 51 53 Ea 54
57420 Verzon 57 56 Ga 54
03140 Verzun 03 115 Da 71
51380 Verzy 51 53 Ea 54
88160 Vés, les 88 94 Ge 61
52700 Vesaignes-sous-Lafauche 52 75 Fc 59
52800 Vesaignes-sur-Marne 52 75 Fb 60
01170 Vesancy 01 120 Ga 70
26220 Vesc 26 143 Fa 81
90200 Vescemont 90 94 Gf 62
57370 Vescheim 57 58 Hb 56
39240 Vescles 39 119 Fd 70
01560 Vescours 01 118 Fa 70
20215 Vescovato CTC 181 Kc 94
18360 Vesdun 18 115 Cc 69
01220 Vésenex-Crassy 01 120 Ga 70
51320 Vésigneul-sur-Coole 51 54 Ec 56
51240 Vésigneul-sur-Marne 51 54 Ec 55
58140 Vésigneux 58 90 Df 64
45200 Vésine 45 71 Ce 60
01570 Vésines 01 118 Ef 70
78420 Vesinet, le 78 51 Cb 55
02350 Vesles-et-Caumont 02 40 De 50
02840 Veslud 02 40 De 51
27870 Vesly 27 50 Bd 53
50430 Vesly 50 46 Yc 53
74210 Vésonne 74 132 Gb 74
70000 Vesoul 70 93 Ga 63
14290 Vespière-Friardel, la 14 48 Ac 54
35460 Vesquerie 35 66 Yd 58
22350 Vesquerie, la 22 65 Xf 59
12720 Vessac 12 153 Db 84
13740 Vesse, la 13 170 Fb 88
07200 Vesseaux 07 142 Ec 81
50170 Vessey 50 66 Yd 57
71880 Vessey 71 105 Ee 68
43170 Vesseyre 43 140 Dc 79
48140 Vessière, la 48 140 Db 79
30600 Vestric-et-Candiac 30 169 Eb 86
21350 Vesvres 21 91 Ed 64
52190 Vesvres-sous-Chalancey 52 92 Fb 62
21580 Vesvrotte 21 91 Ef 63
95510 Vétheuil 95 50 Be 54
74100 Vétraz-Monthoux 74 120 Gb 71
20147 Vetriccia CTC 182 Ie 95
20113 Vetricella CTC 184 If 98
36600 Veuil 36 101 Bd 66
02810 Veuilly-la-Poterie 02 52 Db 54
76980 Veules-les-Roses 76 36 Ae 49
76450 Veulettes-sur-Mer 76 36 Ad 49
03320 Veurdre, le 03 103 Da 68
38113 Veurey-Voiroize 38 131 Fd 77
51520 Veuve, la 51 54 Eb 54
41150 Veuves 41 86 Ba 64
21360 Veuvey-sur-Ouche 21 105 Ee 65
21520 Veuxhaulles-sur-Aube 21 74 Ee 61
12200 Veuzac 12 151 Ca 82
41150 Veuzain-sur-Loire 41 86 Ba 64
58150 Vèvres 58 89 Da 65
39570 Vevy 39 107 Fd 69
88110 Vexaincourt 88 77 Ha 58
27420* Vexin-sur-Epte 27 50 Bd 53
14570 Vey, le 14 47 Zd 55
14700 Vey, le 14 48 Zf 55
06530 Veyans, les 06 172 Gf 87
05350 Veyer, le 05 145 Ge 80
48400 Veygalier 48 153 Dd 83
48600 Veymen, le 48 141 De 80
57100 Veymerange 57 44 Ga 52
05400 Veynes 05 144 Fe 81
34510 Veyrac 34 167 Dc 88
34560 Veyrac 34 168 Dd 88
87520 Veyrac 87 113 Ba 73
34490 Veyran 34 167 Da 88
07000 Veyras 07 142 Ed 80
24210 Veyre 24 125 Ba 78
12720 Veyreau 12 153 Db 83
63960 Veyre-Monton 63 128 Da 74
33870 Veyres 33 135 Ze 79
01560 Veyriat 01 118 Fa 70
87130 Veyrieras 87 126 Bd 74
74290 Veyrier-du-Lac 74 132 Gb 73
81500 Veyrière, la 81 150 Be 86
15350 Veyrières 15 127 Cc 77
19200 Veyrières 19 127 Cc 76
19340 Veyrières 19 127 Cd 75
47250 Veyries 47 148 Aa 82
24370 Veyrignac 24 137 Bb 80
24470 Veyrinas 24 125 Af 75
17270 Veyrines 17 135 Ze 78
24250 Veyrines-de-Domme 24 137 Ba 80
24380 Veyrines-de-Vergt 24 136 Ae 78
38630 Veyrins-Thuellin, Les Avenières 38 131 Fd 75
50500 Veys 50 33 Yf 53
46230 Veysset 46 150 Bd 83
24410 Veyssière 24 123 Zf 77
63630 Veyssière, la 63 128 Dd 76
38460 Veyssilieu 38 131 Fb 74
87130 Veytizout, la 87 126 Be 74
01100 Veyziat 01 119 Fd 71
60117 Vez 60 52 Da 53
15130 Vézac 15 139 Cd 79
15200 Vézac 15 127 Cb 77
24220 Vézac 24 137 Bb 79
79170 Vezançais 79 111 Ze 72
89700 Vézannes 89 90 Df 61
02290 Vézaponin 02 40 Db 52
15160 Vèze 15 128 Cf 77
25660 Vèze, la 25 107 Ga 65
89450 Vézelay 89 90 De 64
54330 Vézelise 54 76 Ga 58
90400 Vézelois 90 94 Gf 63
15130 Vezels-Roussy 15 139 Cd 80
30360 Vézénobres 30 154 Ea 84
38510 Vézeronce-Curtin 38 131 Fc 75
12200 Vèzes 12 151 Ca 82
70130 Vezet 70 93 Ff 63
43390 Vézézoux 43 128 Dc 76
51210 Vézier, le 51 52 Dc 56
86120 Vézières 86 99 Aa 66
27700 Vézillon 27 50 Bc 53
02130 Vézilly 02 53 De 53
54260 Vezin 54 43 Fd 52
86410 Vézinière, la 86 112 Ad 70
35132 Vezin-le-Coquet 35 65 Yb 60
89700 Vézinnes 89 90 Df 61
49340 Vezins 49 98 Zb 66
50540 Vezins 50 66 Ye 57
12780 Vézins-de-Lévézou 12 152 Cf 83
12200 Vézis 12 151 Ca 83
72600 Vezot 72 68 Ab 58
12520 Vezouillac 12 152 Da 83
20242 Vezzani CTC 183 Kb 95
66120 Via 66 178 Ca 94
28150 Viabon 28 70 Be 59
12800 Viaduc du Viaur 12 151 Cc 84
44860 Viais 44 97 Yc 66
12230 Viala, le 12 153 Dc 84
12560 Viala, le 12 152 Da 82
34520 Viala, le 34 153 Dc 85
48220 Viala, le 48 153 De 82
48700 Viala, le 48 140 Dc 80
12470 Viala-Bas, le 12 140 Cf 81
48000 Viala-Bas, le 48 140 Dc 81
12250 Viala-du-Pas-de-Jaux 12 152 Da 85
34210 Vialanove 34 166 Ce 88
81240 Vialanove 81 166 Cd 87
15140 Vialard 15 139 Cc 78
19400 Vialard, le 19 138 Bf 78
46260 Vialars 46 151 Bf 82
48220 Vialas 48 154 Df 82
48220 Vialasse, la 48 153 Df 82
12260 Vialatelle 12 151 Bf 82
19200 Vialatte, la 19 127 Cc 76
81260 Vialavert 81 166 Cc 87
24630 Viale 24 125 Ba 75
12800 Viala, la 12 151 Cc 83
64330 Vialer 64 162 Ze 87
43350 Vialette 43 141 Df 78
43380 Vialette, la 43 128 Dc 77
48120 Vialette, la 48 140 Dc 79
12780 Vialettes, les 12 152 Cf 83
19390 Viallaneix 19 126 Bf 76
63350 Vialle 63 116 Dc 73
19150 Vialle, la 19 126 Be 77
19200 Vialle, la 19 127 Cc 75
19800 Vialle, la 19 126 Bf 76
63560 Vialle, la 63 115 Ce 72
43580 Vialle-Destours, la 43 141 Dd 78
43270 Vialles, les 43 129 De 77
63740 Vialles, les 63 127 Ce 74
24290 Vialot 24 137 Ba 78
40120 Vialote 40 147 Ze 84
38960 Vials, les 38 131 Fd 76
81530 Viane 81 166 Cd 86
21430 Vianges 21 105 Eb 66
47230 Vianne 47 148 Ab 83
10380 Viâpres-le-Grand 10 73 Ea 57
10380 Viâpres-le-Petit 10 73 Ea 57
95270 Viarmes 95 51 Cc 54
12290 Viarougé 12 152 Cf 83
34450 Vias 34 167 Dc 89
17130 Viauds, les 17 123 Zd 77
12130 Viaurals 12 140 Da 81
46100 Viazac 46 138 Ca 81
46320 Viazac 46 138 Be 80
12290 Vibal, le 12 152 Ce 83
57670 Vibersviller 57 57 Gf 55
76760 Vibeuf 76 37 Af 50
16120 Vibrac 16 123 Zf 75
17130 Vibrac 17 123 Zd 76
72320 Vibraye 72 69 Ae 60
30190 Vic 30 154 Ec 85
36400 Vic 36 102 Bf 69
21140 Vic-de-Chassenay 21 90 Eb 64
21360 Vic-des-Prés 21 105 Ed 66
09220 Vicdessos 09 177 Bc 92
50760 Vicel, le 50 33 Ye 51
65500 Vic-en-Bigorre 65 162 Aa 88
32190 Vic-Fezensac 32 148 Ab 86
63340 Vichel 63 128 Db 76
02210 Vichel-Nanteuil 02 52 Db 53
28480 Vichères 28 69 Af 59
23220 Vichez 23 114 Bf 70
03200 Vichy 03 116 Dc 72
34110 Vic-la-Gardiole 34 168 De 88
73700 Viclaire 73 133 Gf 75
63270 Vic-le-Comte 63 128 Db 75
30260 Vic-le-Fesq 30 154 Ea 85
32300 Vicnau 32 163 Ac 87
20160 Vico CTC 182 Ie 96
80260 Vicogne, la 80 29 Cb 48
59590 Vicoigne 59 30 Dc 46
35780 Vicomté, la 35 65 Xf 57
22690 Vicomté-sur-Rance, la 22 65 Ya 58
03450 Vicq 03 116 Da 72
52400 Vicq 52 92 Fd 61
59264 Vicq 59 31 Dd 46
78490 Vicq 78 50 Bf 56
87220 Vicq 87 125 Bc 74
40380 Vicq-d'Auribat 40 146 Za 86
36400 Vicq-Exemplet 36 102 Ca 69
87260 Vicq-sur-Breuilh 87 125 Bc 75
86260 Vicq-sur-Gartempe 86 100 Af 68
50330 Vicq-sur-Mer 50 33 Yd 50
36600 Vicq-sur-Nahon 36 101 Bd 66
76560 Vicquemare 76 37 Af 50
14170 Vicques 14 48 Zf 55
21390 Vic-sous-Thil 21 90 Eb 64
02290 Vic-sur-Aisne 02 40 Da 52
15800 Vic-sur-Cère 15 139 Cd 79
57630 Vic-sur-Seille 57 57 Gd 56
14430 Victot-Pontfol 14 35 Zf 54
20160 Vicu = Vico CTC 182 Ie 96
61360 Vidai 61 68 Ac 58
46260 Vidaillac 46 150 Be 82
23250 Vidaillat 23 114 Bf 73
15230 Vidalenche, la 15 139 Ce 78
48700 Vidalès, le 48 140 Dc 80
34330 Vidals, les 34 166 Cd 87
81230 Vidals, les 81 166 Ce 86
83550 Vidauban 83 172 Gc 88
84300 Vidauque 84 155 Fa 86
83390 Vidaux, les 83 171 Gb 89
47420 Videau 47 148 Zf 83
50630 Videcosville 50 33 Yd 51
87600 Videix 87 124 Ae 74
91890 Videlles 91 71 Cc 58
15170 Videt 15 140 Da 77
65220 Vidou 65 163 Ab 89
50810 Vidouville 50 34 Za 54
65700 Vidouze 65 162 Zf 88
63520 Vie, la 63 128 Dc 75
86160 Vieil-Airoux 86 112 Ac 71
49150 Vieil-Baugé, le 49 84 Zf 63
51330 Vieil-Dampierre, le 51 54 Ef 55
27930 Vieil-Evreux, le 27 50 Bb 54
62770 Vieil-Hesdin 62 29 Ca 46
65360 Vieille-Adour 65 162 Aa 90
43100 Vieille-Brioude 43 128 Dc 77
62136 Vieille-Chapelle 62 29 Ce 45
62162 Vieille-Église 62 27 Ca 43
78125 Vieille-Eglise-en-Yvelines 78 50 Bf 56
36110 Vieille-Epine, la 36 101 Be 67
89110 Vieille Ferté, la 89 89 Db 61
08500 Vieille-Forge 08 42 Ed 49
41360 Vieille-Haie, la 41 85 Af 61
39380 Vieille-Loye, la 39 107 Fd 66
27330 Vieille-Lyre, la 27 49 Ae 55
19150 Vieillemar 19 126 Bf 77
86250 Vieille-Métive 86 112 Ac 72
18170 Vieille-Morte, la 18 102 Cb 68
56130 Vieille Roche 56 81 Xd 64
86150 Vieilles-Forges, les 86 112 Ae 72
30500 Vieilles-Fumades, les 30 154 Eb 83
45260 Vieilles-Maisons-sur-Joudry 45 88 Cc 61
15500 Vieillespesse 15 140 Da 78
79130 Vieille-Touche, la 79 98 Zd 69
31320 Vieille-Toulouse 31 164 Bc 87
15120 Vieillevie 15 139 Cc 81
31290 Vieillevigne 31 165 Bd 88
44116 Vieillevigne 44 97 Yd 67

332 | Vergnes

23210 Vieilleville 23 113 Be 72
02540 Vieils-Maisons 02 52 Dc 55
02160 Viel-Arcy 02 40 Dd 52
65400 Vielettes 65 174 Ze 91
32400 Viella 32 162 Zf 87
65170 Vielle-Aure 65 175 Ab 92
64170 Viellenave-d'Arthez 64 162 Zd 88
64190 Viellenave-de-Navarrenx 64 161 Zb 88
64270 Viellenave-Sur-Bidouze 64 161 Yf 88
40560 Vielle-Saint-Girons 40 146 Ye 85
64150 Vielleségure 64 161 Zb 88
40240 Vielle-Soubiran 40 148 Ze 84
40320 Vielle-Tursan 40 162 Zd 86
58150 Vielmanay 58 89 Da 65
21540 Vielmoulin 21 91 Ee 65
81570 Vielmur-sur-Agout 81 165 Ca 87
43490 Vielprat 43 141 Df 79
08270 Viel-Saint-Remy 08 41 Ed 51
12450 Viel-Vayssac 12 152 Cd 83
21270 Vielverge 21 92 Fc 65
24170 Vielvic 24 137 Af 80
30450 Vielvic 30 154 Df 82
19220 Vielzot 19 126 Ca 77
79200 Viennay 79 99 Ze 68
38200 Vienne 38 130 Ef 75
95510 Vienne-en-Arthies 95 50 Be 54
14400 Vienne-en-Bessin 14 34 Zc 53
45510 Vienne-en-Val 45 87 Ca 62
51800 Vienne-la-Ville 51 54 Ef 53
51800 Vienne-le-Château 51 54 Ef 53
84750 Viens 84 156 Fd 85
88430 Vienville 88 77 Gf 59
04150 Vière 04 156 Fd 84
04420 Vière 04 157 Gc 83
05190 Vière 05 144 Gb 81
88240 Vierge, la 88 76 Gb 61
03300 Viermeux 03 116 Dd 72
23170 Viersat 23 115 Cc 71
28700 Vierville 28 70 Bf 58
50480 Vierville 50 46 Ye 52
14710 Vierville-sur-Mer 14 47 Za 52
18100 Vierzon 18 102 Ca 65
02210 Vierzy 02 52 Db 53
59271 Viesly 59 30 Dc 48
14410 Viessoix 14 47 Zb 55
50340 Viesville, la 50 33 Yb 51
83400 Viet, la 83 171 Ga 90
25340 Viéthorey 25 94 Gc 64
01260 Vieu 01 119 Fe 73
01430 Vieu-d'Izenave 01 119 Fd 72
03430 Vieure 03 115 Cf 70
34390 Vieussan 34 167 Cf 87
28120 Vieuvicq 28 69 Bb 59
53120 Vieuvy 53 66 Za 58
14930 Vieux 14 35 Zd 54
81140 Vieux 81 151 Bf 85
61160 Vieux Bailleul, le 61 48 Zf 56
59232 Vieux-Berquin 59 29 Cd 44
87220 Vieux Boisseuil 87 125 Bb 74
40480 Vieux-Boucau-les-Bains 40 146 Yd 86
03600 Vieux-Bourg 03 115 Ce 71
16100 Vieux-Bourg 16 123 Zd 74
35190 Vieux-Bourg 35 65 Ya 58
37230 Vieux-Bourg 37 85 Ad 64
40330 Vieux-Bourg 40 161 Zb 87
41800 Vieux-Bourg 41 85 Ae 62
61370 Vieux-Bourg 61 48 Ac 56
85540 Vieux-Bourg 85 109 Yd 69
14130 Vieux-Bourg, le 14 36 Ab 53
22150 Vieux-Bourg, le 22 64 Xb 59
22500 Vieux-Bourg, le 22 63 Xa 56
22800 Vieux-Bourg, le 22 64 Wf 58
44540 Vieux-Bourg, le 44 82 Ye 63
44590 Vieux-Bourg, le 44 82 Yc 62
29190 Vieux-Bourg-de-Lothey 29 62 Vf 59
22230 Vieux-Bourg-Saint-Nicolas, le 22 64 Xd 59
49125 Vieux-Briollay, le 49 83 Zd 63
16350 Vieux-Cérier, le 16 112 Ac 73
85160 Vieux-Cerne, le 85 96 Xf 67
77370 Vieux-Champagne 77 72 Da 57
89570 Vieux-Champs 89 73 De 60
25600 Vieux-Charmont 25 94 Gf 63
21460 Vieux-Château 21 90 Ea 64
69840 Vieux-Château 69D 118 Ed 71
59690 Vieux-Condé 59 31 Dd 46
58230 Vieux-Dun, le 58 90 Df 65
68480 Vieux-Ferrette 68 95 Hb 63
80120 Vieux-Fort-Mahon, le 80 28 Bd 46
14270 Vieux-Fumé 14 48 Zf 54
37530 Vieux-Joué, le 37 85 Af 64
08190 Vieux-lès-Asfeld 08 41 Ea 52
76630 Vieux Ifs, les 76 37 Bc 49
57635 Vieux-Lixheim 57 57 Ha 56
77320 Vieux-Maisons 77 52 Dc 56
76750 Vieux-Manoir 76 37 Bb 51
22420 Vieux-Marché, le 22 63 Wd 57
24340 Vieux-Mareuil 24 124 Ad 76
07330 Vieux-Mayres, le 07 141 Ea 80
59138 Vieux-Mesnil 59 31 Df 47
29600 Vieux-Moulin 29 62 Wb 57
60350 Vieux-Moulin 60 39 Cf 52
88210 Vieux-Moulin 88 77 Gf 58
52200 Vieux-Moulins 52 92 Fb 61
18330 Vieux-Nançay, le 18 87 Cb 64
22140 Vieux Poirier, le 22 63 We 57
61150 Vieux-Pont 61 48 Zf 57
14140 Vieux-Pont-en-Auge 14 48 Aa 54
27680 Vieux-Port 27 36 Ad 52
59600 Vieux-Reng 59 31 Ea 47
40410 Vieux-Richet 40 147 Zb 82
76390 Vieux-Rouen-sur-Bresle 76 38 Be 50
76160 Vieux-Rue, la 76 37 Bb 52
16350 Vieux-Ruffec 16 112 Ac 72
38490 Vieux-Saint-Ondras 38 131 Fd 75
29690 Vieux-Tronc, le 29 62 Wb 58
35610 Vieux-Vil 35 66 Yc 57
26160 Vieux-Village 26 143 Ef 81
27600 Vieux-Villez 27 50 Bb 53
49680 Vieux-Vivy, le 49 84 Zf 65
35490 Vieux-Vy-sur-Couesnon 35 66 Yd 58
65230 Vieuzos 65 163 Ac 89
21310 Viévigne 21 92 Fb 64
52310 Viéville 52 75 Fa 59
88500 Viéville 88 76 Gb 58
27500 Viéville, la 27 36 Ad 53
50260 Viéville, la 50 33 Yc 51
54470 Viéville-en-Haye 54 56 Ff 55
55210 Viéville-sous-les-Côtes 55 55 Fe 54
06430 Vievola 06 159 Hd 84
21230 Viévy 21 105 Ec 66
41290 Vievy-le-Rayé 41 86 Bb 61
65120 Viey 65 175 Aa 91
38450 Vif 38 144 Fe 78
02540 Viffort 02 52 Dc 55
30120 Vigan, le 30 153 Dd 85
46300 Vigan, le 46 137 Bc 80
15200 Vigean, le 15 127 Cc 77
86150 Vigeant, le 86 112 Ad 71
87110 Vigen, le 87 125 Bb 74
19410 Vigeois 19 125 Bd 76
65100 Viger 65 175 Zf 90
23140 Viges 23 114 Ca 71
23140 Vigeville 23 114 Ca 72
20110 Viggianello CTC 184 If 98
20110 Vighjaneddu = Viggianello CTC 184 If 98
45600 Viglain 45 88 Cb 62
12500 Vignac 12 140 Cf 81
40170 Vignacot 40 146 Ye 85
80650 Vignacourt 80 38 Cb 48
20121 Vignale CTC 182 If 96
20272 Vignale CTC 183 Kc 95
20290 Vignale CTC 181 Kc 93
20170 Vignalella CTC 185 Ka 99
46800 Vignals, les 46 150 Bb 83
81200 Vignals, les 81 166 Cb 88
19470 Vignane 19 126 Be 76
14700 Vignats 14 48 Zf 55
34600 Vignats, les 34 167 Db 87
40270 Vignau, le 40 147 Ze 86
23000 Vignaud 23 114 Be 71
33380 Vignaud 33 134 Za 81
85580 Vignaud, le 85 109 Ye 70
31480 Vignaux 31 164 Ba 86
33950 Vigne, la 33 134 Ye 80
56140 Vigne, la 56 81 Xe 61
59118 Vigne, la 59 30 Da 44
36120 Vigneau, le 36 101 Bf 68
85220 Vigneau, le 85 96 Ya 68
05120 Vigneaux, les 05 145 Gd 80
10400 Vigneaux, les 10 72 Dd 57
37340 Vigneaux, les 37 85 Ab 64
77450 Vignely 77 52 Ce 55
60162 Vignemont 60 39 Ce 51
84300 Vignères, les 84 155 Fa 85
71550 Vignerux 71 105 Eb 66
58190 Vignes 58 89 De 64
64410 Vignes 64 162 Zd 87
89420 Vignes 89 90 Ea 63
48210 Vignes, les 48 153 Db 83
52700 Vignes-la-Côte 52 75 Fb 59
54360 Vigneulles 54 76 Gb 57
55210 Vigneulles-lès-Hattonchâtel 55 55 Fe 55
55600 Vigneul-sous-Montmédy 55 42 Fc 51
44360 Vigneux-de-Bretagne 44 82 Yb 65
02340 Vigneux-Hocquet 02 41 Df 50
91270 Vigneux-sur-Seine 91 51 Cc 56
11330 Vignevieille 11 178 Cd 90
38890 Vignieu 38 131 Fc 75
35630 Vignoc 35 65 Yb 59
58190 Vignol 58 89 De 64
20119 Vignola CTC 182 If 97
72170 Vignole 72 68 Aa 59
21200 Vignoles 21 106 Ef 66
33770 Vignolle, la 33 134 Zb 81
16300 Vignolles 16 123 Zf 75
16370 Vignolles 16 123 Zd 74
86330 Vignolles 86 99 Aa 67
06420 Vignols 06 158 Ha 84
19130 Vignols 19 125 Bc 77
33330 Vignonet 33 135 Zf 79
52320 Vignory 52 75 Fa 59
55200 Vignot 55 55 Fd 56
36110 Vignots, les 36 101 Be 67
18110 Vignoux-sous-les-Aix 18 102 Cc 65
18500 Vignoux-sur-Barangeon 18 102 Cb 65
57420 Vigny 57 56 Gb 55
74520 Vigny 74 120 Ga 72
89210 Vigny 89 73 De 60
95450 Vigny 95 50 Bf 54
36160 Vigoulant 36 114 Ca 70
31320 Vigoulet-Auzil 31 164 Bc 87
15230 Vigouroux 15 139 Ce 79
36170 Vigoux 36 113 Bc 69
82500 Vigueron 82 149 Ba 85
57640 Vigy 57 56 Gb 53
49310 Vihiers 49 98 Zc 66
36160 Vijon 36 114 Ca 70
AD200 Vila ◘ AND 177 Bd 93
12490 Vila-du-Tarn 12 152 Cf 84
79170 Vilaine 79 111 Ze 71
87250 Vilarcoin 87 113 Bb 72
58400 Vilatte 58 103 Da 65
77540 Vilbert 77 52 Cf 56
54700 Vilcey-sur-Trey 54 56 Ff 55
86320 Vildard 86 112 Ae 70
22980 Vildé-Guingalan 22 65 Xf 58
35120 Vildé-la-Marine 35 65 Ya 57
01320 Vilette 01 119 Fb 73
78930 Vilette 78 50 Be 55
03350 Vilhain, le 03 115 Ce 69
16220 Vilhonneur 16 124 Ac 74
04200 Vilhosc 04 157 Ga 83
33950 Villa-Algérienne 33 134 Ye 80
91100 Villabé 91 71 Cc 57
18800 Villabon 18 103 Ce 66
24120 Villac 24 125 Bb 77
10600 Villacerf 10 73 Df 58
54290 Villacourt 54 76 Gc 58
10290 Villadin 10 73 De 59
70110 Villafans 70 94 Gc 63
18700 Village, le 18 87 Cb 64
14250 Village-de-Juaye, la 14 34 Zb 53
18100 Village-d'en-Haut 18 102 Ca 65
50190 Village-Fautrat 50 33 Yd 53
68128 Village-Neuf 68 95 Hd 63
73210 Villages 73 133 Ge 75
38850 Villages du Lac de Paladru 38 131 Fc 76
40550 Village-sous-les-Pins, le 40 146 Ye 85
28150 Villages Vovéens, les 28 70 Bd 59
77970 Villagnon, Bannost- 77 52 Db 57
33650 Villagrains 33 135 Zc 81
87190 Villagrand 87 113 Bb 71
27270 Villaie, la 27 48 Ac 54
18140 Villain 18 103 Ce 66
58460 Villaine 58 89 Dc 64
49540 Villaine, la 49 84 Zd 65
21450 Villaines-en-Duesmois 21 91 Ed 62
72600 Villaines-la-Carelle 72 68 Ab 58
72400 Villaines-la-Gonais 72 68 Ad 60
53700 Villaines-la-Juhel 53 67 Ze 58
21500 Villaines-les-Prévôtes 21 90 Eb 63
37190 Villaines-les-Rochers 37 100 Ac 65
95570 Villaines-sous-Bois 95 51 Cc 54
72150 Villaines-sous-Lucé 72 85 Ac 61
72270 Villaines-sous-Malicorne 72 84 Zf 62
76280 Villainville 76 36 Ab 51
35460 Villais 35 66 Yd 58
11000 Villalbe 11 166 Cb 89
27240 Villalet 27 49 Ba 55
11600 Villalier 11 166 Cc 89
45310 Villamblain 45 70 Bd 60
24140 Villamblard 24 136 Ad 78
35420 Villamée 35 66 Ye 58
41100 Villamoy 41 86 Bb 62
28200 Villampuy 28 70 Bd 60
54260 Villancy 54 43 Fd 52
33730 Villandraut 33 135 Zd 82
37510 Villandry 37 85 Ad 64
39120 Villangrette 39 106 Fb 67
11600 Villanière 11 166 Cc 88
20167 Villanova CTC 182 Ie 97
58370 Villapourçon 58 104 Df 67
73440 Villaranger 73 132 Gc 76
73730 Villarc, le 73 132 Gc 75
17470 Villarçay 17 111 Zd 73
41100 Villarceau 41 86 Bb 62
28150 Villarceaux 28 70 Bd 59
73420 Villarcher 73 132 Ff 75
01220 Villard 01 120 Ga 70
03220 Villard 03 116 Dd 71
04260 Villard 04 158 Gd 83
23150 Villard 23 114 Bf 72
23210 Villard 23 114 Be 72
23800 Villard 23 114 Be 71
63350 Villard 63 116 Dc 73
63980 Villard 63 128 Dd 76
69790 Villard 69D 117 Ec 71
71520 Villard 71 117 Ec 70
73700 Villard 73 133 Ge 75
74420 Villard 74 132 Ga 74
74420 Villard 74 120 Gc 71
87370 Villard 87 113 Bc 72
01270 Villard, le 01 119 Fb 70
04000 Villard, le 04 157 Gb 84
04850 Villard, le 04 158 Ge 82
05260 Villard, le 05 144 Ga 81
05290 Villard, le 05 145 Gc 79
05400 Villard, le 05 144 Ff 81
05460 Villard, le 05 145 Gf 80
05500 Villard, le 05 144 Ga 80
05600 Villard, le 05 145 Gd 80
05600 Villard, le 05 145 Ge 80
06470 Villard, le 06 158 Gf 84
23460 Villard, le 23 126 Bf 74
43190 Villard, le 43 141 Eb 78
43500 Villard, le 43 129 Df 76
43510 Villard, le 43 141 De 79
43700 Villard, le 43 141 Ea 78
48230 Villard, le 48 140 Db 82
71160 Villard, le 71 117 Df 69
71580 Villard, le 71 106 Fc 69
73290 Villard, le 73 132 Fe 75
73400 Villard, le 73 132 Gc 74
73440 Villard, le 73 132 Gc 76
73450 Villard, le 73 145 Gc 77
73460 Villard, le 73 132 Gb 75
73500 Villard, le 73 133 Gd 77
73550 Villard, le 73 133 Gd 76
73670 Villard, le 73 132 Fe 76
74230 Villard, le 74 132 Gc 74
83780 Villard, le 83 172 Gc 87
05480 Villar-d'Arène 05 145 Gc 78
73260 Villard-Benoît 73 132 Gc 75
38190 Villard-Bonnet 38 132 Ff 77
71480 Villard-Chapelle 71 119 Fb 70
04400 Villard-d'Abas, le 04 158 Gd 83
04400 Villard-de-Faucon, le 04 158 Ge 82
38250 Villard-de-Lans 38 143 Fd 78
05500 Villard de Laye, le 05 144 Ga 81
73800 Villard-d'Héry 73 132 Ga 75
58150 Villardeau 58 88 Cf 64
11250 Villardebelle 11 178 Cc 90
38710 Villard-Julien 38 144 Fe 79
73390 Villard-Léger 73 132 Gb 75
38530 Villard-Noir 38 132 Ga 76
38520 Villard-Notre-Dame 38 144 Ga 78
05500 Villardon, le 05 144 Ga 80
11600 Villardonnel 11 166 Cb 88
38114 Villard-Reculas 38 144 Ga 78
38520 Villard-Reymond 38 144 Ga 78
63440 Villards 63 115 Cf 72
23430 Villards, les 23 113 Bd 73
42380 Villards, les 42 129 Df 76
38119 Villard-Saint-Christophe 38 144 Fe 79
39200 Villard-Saint-Sauveur 39 119 Ff 70
73110 Villard-Sallet 73 132 Ga 76
39260 Villards-d'Héria 39 119 Fe 70
74230 Villards-sur-Thônes, les 74 120 Gc 73
39200 Villard-sur-Bienne 39 119 Ff 70
73270 Villard-sur-Doron 73 133 Gd 74
39130 Villard-sur-l'Ain 39 107 Fe 68
77730 Villaré 77 52 Db 55
73300 Villarembert 73 132 Gb 77
38710 Villarent 38 144 Fe 79
11220 Villar-en-Val 11 166 Cc 90
07590 Villaret 07 141 Df 80
30570 Villaret 30 153 Dc 84
43260 Villaret 43 141 Ea 78
48150 Villaret 48 153 Dc 84
48190 Villaret 48 141 De 81
12150 Villaret, le 12 152 Da 83
73440 Villaret, le 73 132 Gc 76
73460 Villaret, le 73 132 Gb 75
73550 Villaret, le 73 133 Gd 76
05350 Villargaudin 05 145 Ge 80
70110 Villargent 70 94 Gc 63
73260 Villargerel 73 133 Gd 75
21210 Villargoix 21 90 Eb 65
31380 Villariès 31 150 Bc 86
73700 Villarivon 73 133 Ge 75
05800 Villar-Loubière 05 144 Ga 80
73600 Villarlurin 73 133 Gd 76
04200 Villarnaud 04 157 Ff 83
58220 Villarnaud 58 89 Da 65
36200 Villarnoux 36 113 Bd 69
73500 Villarodin-Bourget 73 133 Ge 77
73640 Villaroger 73 133 Gf 75
73480 Villaron 73 133 Gf 76
05400 Villarons, les 05 144 Ff 81
73110 Villaroux 73 132 Ga 76
16200 Villars 16 123 Zf 74
16320 Villars 16 124 Ab 75
16420 Villars 16 112 Af 73
21430 Villars 21 105 Eb 65
24530 Villars 24 124 Ae 76
28150 Villars 28 70 Bd 59
42390 Villars 42 129 Ec 76
58360 Villars 58 104 Df 67
84400 Villars 84 156 Fc 85
71700 Villars, le 71 118 Ef 69
11250 Villar-Saint-Anselme 11 178 Cb 90
05100 Villar-Saint-Pancrace 05 145 Gd 79
04370 Villars-Colmars 04 158 Gd 84
52120 Villars-en-Azois 52 74 Ee 60
17260 Villars-en-Pons 17 122 Zc 75
21140 Villars-et-Villenotte 21 90 Ec 63
21700 Villars-Fontaine 21 106 Ef 66
04370 Villars-Heyssier 04 158 Gd 84
70500 Villars-le-Pautel 70 93 Ff 61
25310 Villars-lès-Blamont 25 94 Gf 64
17770 Villars-les-Bois 17 123 Zd 74
01330 Villars-les-Dombes 01 118 Fa 72
90100 Villars-le-Sec 90 94 Gf 64
25410 Villars-Saint-Georges 25 107 Fe 66
52400 Villars-Saint-Marcellin 52 93 Fe 61
52160 Villars-Santenoge 52 91 Ef 62
25150 Villars-sous-Ecot 25 94 Ge 64
06710 Villars-sur-Var 06 158 Ha 85
11600 Villarzel-Cabardès 11 166 Cc 89
11300 Villarzel-du-Razès 11 166 Cb 90
11150 Villasavary 11 165 Ca 89
23250 Villatange 23 114 Be 72
31860 Villate 31 164 Bc 88
23800 Villate, la 23 113 Bd 71
23110 Villatte, la 23 114 Cb 72
23140 Villatte, la 23 114 Cb 71
23270 Villatte, la 23 114 Ca 70
04140 Villaudemard 04 157 Gb 82
87190 Villaudrand 87 113 Bb 71
31620 Villaudric 31 150 Bc 86
41500 Villaugon 41 86 Bc 62
06750 Villaute 06 158 Gd 86
41800 Villavard 41 85 Af 62
41700 Villavrain 41 86 Bc 64
74370 Villaz 74 120 Gb 73
58400 Ville 58 103 Da 65
60138 Ville 60 39 Cf 51
67220 Villé 67 60 Hb 58
38650 Ville, la 38 143 Fd 79
40430 Ville, la 40 147 Zc 82
69470 Ville, la 69D 117 Ec 72
73730 Ville, la 73 133 Gc 75
88100 Villé, le 88 77 Gf 59
22190 Ville-Agan, la 22 64 Xb 57
66650 Ville-Amont, la 66 179 Da 94
56490 Villéan, la 56 64 Xd 60
22250 Ville-Apparillon, la 22 64 Xe 59
28150 Villeau 28 70 Bd 59
36140 Ville-au-Bertrand, la 36 114 Bf 70
22640 Ville-Aufray, la 22 64 Xd 58
54620 Ville-au-Montois 54 43 Fe 52
54380 Ville-au-Val 54 56 Ga 55
56800 Ville-au-Vy, la 56 81 Xd 61
10140 Ville-aux-Bois, la 10 74 Ed 59
10500 Ville-aux-Bois, la 10 74 Ee 58
02340 Ville-aux-Bois-lès-Dizy, la 02 41 Df 51
02160 Ville-aux-Bois-lès-Pontavert, la 02 41 Df 52
41160 Ville-aux-Clercs, la 41 86 Ba 61
28250 Ville-aux-Nonains, la 28 69 Ba 57
22150 Ville-aux-Péchoux, la 22 64 Xb 59
54800 Ville-aux-Prés 54 56 Ff 54
61310 Villebadin 61 48 Aa 56
41000 Villebarou 41 86 Bb 63
37460 Villebaslin 37 100 Bb 66
23350 Ville-Basse 23 114 Bf 70
50410 Villebaudon 50 46 Yf 55
11250 Villebazy 11 178 Cb 90
22250 Ville-Bedel, la 22 64 Xd 59
77710 Villebéon 77 72 Cf 59
41290 Villeberfol 41 86 Bb 62
49400 Villebernier 49 99 Zf 65
36500 Villebernin 36 101 Bb 67
21350 Villeberny 21 91 Ed 64
87140 Villebert 87 113 Bb 72
28220 Villebeton 28 69 Bc 60
21700 Villebichot 21 106 Fa 66
22300 Ville-Blanche, la 22 63 Wd 56
22330 Ville-Blanchet, la 22 64 Xd 59
89340 Villeblevin 89 72 Da 59
01150 Villebois 01 131 Fc 73
16320 Villebois-Lavalette 16 124 Ab 76
05700 Villebois-les-Pins 05 156 Fd 83
28190 Villebon 28 69 Bb 58
28800 Villebon 28 70 Bc 59
89150 Villebougis 89 72 Da 59
37370 Villebourg 37 85 Ad 63
41270 Villebout 41 69 Bb 61
41330 Villebouzon 41 86 Bb 62
47380 Villebramar 47 136 Ac 81
22940 Ville-Bresset, la 22 64 Xb 58
03310 Villebret 03 115 Cd 71
22130 Ville-Briend, les 22 64 Xe 57
07160 Villebrion 07 142 Ec 79
82370 Villebrumier 82 150 Bc 85
54890 Villecay-sur-Mad 54 56 Ff 54
18160 Villecelin 18 102 Cb 68
41160 Villecellier 41 86 Bc 61
77250 Villecerf 77 71 Cf 59
23430 Villechabrolle 23 113 Bd 72
36250 Villechaise 36 101 Bd 67
39320 Villechantria 39 119 Fc 70
36100 Villechaud 36 102 Bf 68
58200 Villechaud 58 88 Cf 64
41310 Villechauve 41 86 Af 63
63330 Villechelexi 63 115 Cd 72
69770 Villechenève 69M 130 Ec 74
36400 Villechère 36 102 Bf 68
10410 Villechétif 10 73 Ea 59
89320 Villechétive 89 72 Dd 60
50140 Villechien 50 66 Za 57
23360 Villechiron 23 114 Be 70
02490 Villecholles 02 40 Da 49
44520 Villechoux 44 82 Ye 63
89300 Villecien 89 72 Db 60
55600 Villécloye 55 43 Fc 51
22400 Ville-Cochard, la 22 64 Xd 57
35610 Villecolière 35 66 Yc 57
22510 Ville-Commeaux, la 22 64 Xc 58
12580 Villecomtal 12 139 Cd 81
32730 Villecomtal-sur-Arros 32 163 Ab 88
21120 Villecomte 21 91 Fa 63
91580 Villeconin 91 71 Ca 57
80190 Villecourt 80 39 Cf 50
94440 Villecresnes 94 51 Cd 56
83690 Villecroze 83 172 Gb 87
34700 Villecun 34 167 Db 86
11200 Villedaigne 11 167 Cf 89
35380 Ville-Danet, la 35 65 Xe 60
85750 Ville-d'Angles, la 85 109 Yd 70
79160 Ville-Dé 79 110 Zc 69
23500 Villedeau 23 126 Cb 73
79170 Ville-des-Eaux 79 111 Zd 72
55260 Ville-devant-Belrain 55 55 Fc 55
55150 Ville-devant-Chaumont 55 55 Fc 53
15100 Villedieu 15 140 Da 78
16210 Villedieu 16 124 Aa 77
21330 Villedieu 21 90 Ec 61
41130 Villedieu 41 87 Bd 65
42110 Villedieu 42 129 Ea 74
72430 Villedieu 72 67 Zf 61
84110 Villedieu 84 155 Fa 83
17470 Villedieu, la 17 111 Ze 72
23340 Villedieu, la 23 126 Bf 74
24120 Villedieu, la 24 137 Bb 78
48700 Villedieu, la 48 140 Dd 80
87380 Villedieu, la 87 125 Bc 75
25240 Villedieu, les 25 107 Gb 68
86340 Villedieu-du-Clain, la 86 112 Ac 70
79800 Villedieu-du-Perron, la 79 111 Zf 70
82290 Ville-Dieu-du-Temple, la 82 150 Bb 84
70160 Villedieu-en-Fontenette, la 70 93 Gb 62
49450 Villedieu-la-Blouère 49 97 Yf 66
41800 Villedieu-le-Château 41 85 Ad 62
61160 Villedieu-les-Bailleul 61 48 Aa 56
50800 Villedieu-les-Poêles-Rouffigny 50 46 Ye 55
36320 Villedieu-sur-Indre 36 101 Bd 67
20279 Ville-di-Paraso CTC 180 If 93
20200 Ville-di-Pietrabugno CTC 181 Kc 92
37460 Villedômain 37 101 Bb 66
37110 Villedômer 37 85 Af 63
51390 Ville-Dommage 51 53 Df 53
22600 Ville-Donnio, la 22 64 Xb 59
17230 Villedoux 17 110 Yf 71
11800 Villedubert 11 166 Cc 89
35460 Ville-du-Bois, la 35 66 Yd 58
91620 Ville-du-Bois, la 91 51 Cb 57
18210 Ville-du-Bout, la 18 102 Cd 68
74360 Ville-du-Nant 74 121 Ge 71
25650 Ville-du-Pont 25 108 Gc 66
41190 Villée 41 86 Ba 63
52130 Ville-en-Blaisois 52 74 Ef 58
44460 Ville-en-Pierre, la 44 81 Ya 63
74250 Ville-en-Sallaz 74 120 Gc 72
51500 Ville-en-Selve 51 53 Ea 54
51170 Ville-en Tardenois 51 53 De 53
54210 Ville-en-Vermois 54 76 Gb 57
55160 Ville-en-Woëvre 55 55 Fd 54
22330 Ville-Ermel 22 64 Xc 59
22130 Ville-es-Marchand, la 22 65 Xf 57
35430 Ville-ès-Nonais, la 35 65 Ya 57
53410 Ville-Etable, la 53 66 Yf 60
16240 Villefagnan 16 111 Aa 72
89240 Villefargeau 89 89 Dd 62
36100 Villefavant 36 101 Be 67
87190 Villefavard 87 113 Bb 71
21350 Villeferry 21 91 Ed 64
11570 Villefloure 11 166 Cc 90
22960 Ville-Folle, la 22 64 Xb 58
79170 Villefollet 79 111 Ze 72
38090 Villefontaine 38 131 Fa 75
87520 Villeforceix 87 113 Af 73
11230 Villefort 11 178 Ca 91

Villefort | 333

27950 Villez-sous-Bailleul 27 50 Bc 54
27110 Villez-sur-le-Neubourg 27 49 Af 54
69910 Villié-Morgon 69D 118 Ee 72
37260 Villière, la 37 100 Ad 65
18160 Villiers 18 102 Cb 68
36260 Villiers 36 102 Bf 67
36290 Villiers 36 100 Bb 67
36370 Villiers 36 100 Ba 69
41230 Villiers 41 87 Be 64
41330 Villiers 41 86 Bb 62
41500 Villiers 41 86 Bc 62
45150 Villiers 45 87 Ca 61
45360 Villiers 45 88 Ce 63
45480 Villiers 45 70 Ca 59
58150 Villiers 58 89 Da 64
62170 Villiers 62 28 Bd 46
86190 Villiers 86 99 Aa 68
86190 Villiers 86 99 Ab 68
86200 Villiers 86 99 Aa 66
95840 Villiers-Adam 95 51 Cb 54
37330 Villiers-au-Bouin 37 85 Ab 63
52130 Villiers-aux-Bois 52 74 Ef 57
52110 Villiers-aux-Chênes 52 74 Ef 58
51260 Villiers-aux-Corneilles 51 73 De 57
89260 Villiers-Bonneux 89 72 Dc 58
53170 Villiers-Charlemagne 53 83 Zb 61
17510 Villiers-Couture 17 111 Zf 73
77190 Villiers-en-Bière 77 71 Cd 58
79360 Villiers-en-Bois 79 111 Zd 72
27640 Villiers-en-Désœuvre 27 50 Bc 55
52100 Villiers-en-Lieu 52 54 Ef 56
79160 Villiers-en-Plaine 79 110 Zc 70
41100 Villiersfaux 41 86 Af 62
50680 Villiers-Fossard 50 34 Yf 54
10700 Villiers-Herbisse 10 53 Ea 57
91190 Villiers-le-Bâcle 91 51 Ca 56
95400 Villiers-le-Bel 95 51 Cc 54
10210 Villiers-le-Bois 10 73 Eb 61
28630 Villiers-le-Bois 28 70 Bd 58
10220 Villiers-le-Brûlé 10 74 Ec 58
21400 Villiers-le-Duc 21 91 Ee 62
45130 Villiers-le-Gast 45 70 Bd 61
78770 Villiers-le-Mahieu 78 50 Be 55
28130 Villiers-le-Mornier 28 50 Bd 57
16240 Villiers-le-Roux 16 111 Aa 72
52190 Villiers-lès-Aprey 52 92 Fb 62
14480 Villiers-le-Sec 14 47 Zc 53
52000 Villiers-le-Sec 52 75 Fa 60
95720 Villiers-le-Sec 95 51 Cc 54
89160 Villiers-les-Hauts 89 90 Ea 62
78660 Villiers-les-Oudets 78 70 Bf 58
89630 Villiers-lès-pos 89 90 Df 64
89320 Villiers-Louis 89 72 Dc 59
89630 Villiers-Nonains 89 90 Df 64
89130 Villiers-Saint-Benoît 89 89 Db 62
02310 Villiers-Saint-Denis 02 52 Db 55
78640 Villiers-Saint-Frédéric 78 50 Bf 56
77560 Villiers-Saint-Georges 77 52 Dc 57
28800 Villiers-Saint-Orien 28 70 Bc 60
08000 Villiers-Semeuse 08 42 Ee 50
77760 Villiers-sous-Grez 77 71 Cd 59
61400 Villiers-sous-Mortagne 61 68 Ad 57
10210 Villiers-sous-Praslin 10 73 Eb 60
58210 Villiers-sur-Beuvron 58 89 Dc 64
79170 Villiers-sur-Chizé 79 111 Ze 72
27940 Villiers-sur-le-Roule 27 50 Bb 53
41100 Villiers-sur-Loir 41 86 Ba 62
52320 Villiers-sur-Marne 52 75 Fa 59
94350 Villiers-sur-Marne 94 51 Cd 56
77580 Villiers-sur-Morin 77 52 Cf 55
91700 Villiers-sur-Orge 91 51 Cb 57
14520 Villiers-sur-Port 14 47 Zb 52
77114 Villiers-sur-Seine 77 72 Dc 58
52210 Villiers-sur-Suize 52 75 Fb 61
89110 Villiers-sur-Tholon 89 89 Dc 61
58500 Villiers-sur-Yonne 58 89 Dd 64
89360 Villiers-Vineux 89 73 Df 61
21430 Villiers-en-Morvan 21 105 Eb 66
01800 Villieu-Loyes 01 119 Fb 73
01800 Villieu-Loyes-Mollon 01 119 Fb 73
57550 Villing 57 57 Gd 53
14310 Villodon 14 47 Zc 54
16230 Villognon 16 123 Aa 73
89740 Villon 89 90 Eb 61
88150 Villoncourt 88 77 Gd 59
14610 Villons-les-Buissons 14 35 Zd 53
45190 Villorceau 45 86 Bd 62
58200 Villorget 58 88 Cf 64
63380 Villosanges 63 115 Cd 73
60390 Villotran 60 51 Ca 52
47400 Villotte 47 148 Ab 82
88320 Villotte 88 76 Fe 60
89130 Villotte 89 89 Db 62
89240 Villotte, la 89 89 Dd 62
55250 Villotte-devant-Louppy 55 55 Fa 55
21690 Villotte-Saint-Seine 21 91 Ee 64
55260 Villotte-sur-Aire 55 55 Fc 55
21400 Villotte-sur-Ource 21 91 Ee 61
36500 Villours 36 101 Bd 67
88350 Villouxel 88 75 Fd 58
77480 Villuis 77 72 Dc 58
58140 Villurbain 58 90 De 64
08370 Villy 08 42 Fb 51
89800 Villy 89 90 De 61
14310 Villy-Bocage 14 34 Zc 54
21350 Villy-en-Auxois 21 91 Ed 64
10140 Villy-en-Trodes 10 74 Ec 59
76260 Villy-le-Bas 76 37 Bc 49
10800 Villy-le-Bois 10 73 Ea 60
74350 Villy-le-Bouveret 74 120 Ga 72
76630 Villy-le-Haut 76 37 Bc 49
10800 Villy-le-Maréchal 10 73 Ea 59
21250 Villy-le-Moutier 21 106 Ef 66
74350 Villy-le-Pelloux 74 120 Ga 72
14700 Villy-lez-Falaise 14 48 Zf 55
20230 Vilone Orneto = Velone-Orneto CTC 183 Kc 94
70240 Vilory 70 93 Gb 62
55110 Vilosnes 55 42 Fb 53
55110 Vilosnes-Haraumont 55 42 Fb 53
57370 Vilsberg 57 58 Hb 56
53160 Vimarcé 53 67 Ze 59
19800 Vimbelle 19 126 Be 76
48240 Vimbouches 48 153 De 83
12310 Vimenet 12 152 Cf 82
48100 Vimenet 48 140 Dc 81
88600 Vioménil 88 77 Gd 59
73160 Vimines 73 132 Ff 75
82440 Viminies 82 150 Bc 84
14370 Vimont 14 35 Ze 54
45700 Vimory 45 71 Ce 61
61120 Vimoutiers 61 48 Ab 55
77520 Vimpelles 77 72 Da 58
62580 Vimy 62 30 Ce 46
77230 Vinantes 77 52 Ce 54
34260 Vinas 34 152 Da 86
11110 Vinassan 11 167 Da 89
17510 Vinax 17 111 Ze 72
38470 Vinay 38 131 Fc 77
51530 Vinay 51 53 Df 54
72240 Vinay 72 68 Aa 60
66320 Vinça 66 179 Cd 93
39190 Vincelles 39 106 Fc 69
51700 Vincelles 51 53 Dd 54
71500 Vincelles 71 106 Fb 69
89290 Vincelles 89 90 Dd 62
89290 Vincelottes 89 90 Dd 62
73480 Vincendières 73 133 Gf 77
94300 Vincennes 94 51 Cc 55
33126 Vincent 33 135 Ze 79
39230 Vincent-Froideville 39 106 Fc 68
03420 Vincents 03 115 Cd 72
38570 Vincents, les 38 132 Ga 77
36400 Vinceuil 36 102 Bf 68
88450 Vincey 88 76 Gb 58
20250 Vincinacce CTC 183 Kb 95
62310 Vincly 62 29 Cb 45
02340 Vincy 02 41 Ea 50
74330 Vincy 74 120 Ga 73
77139 Vincy-Manœuvre 77 52 Cf 54
02340 Vincy-Reuil-et-Magny 02 41 Ea 50
71110 Vindecy 71 117 Ea 70
50250 Vindefontaine 50 46 Yd 52
16430 Vindelle 16 124 Aa 74
50500 Vindelonde 50 34 Yd 53
51120 Vindey 51 53 De 56
81170 Vindrac-Alayrac 81 151 Bf 84
12420 Vines 12 139 Ce 79
10700 Vinets 10 73 Eb 57
36110 Vineuil 36 101 Bd 67
41350 Vineuil 41 86 Bc 63
41400 Vineuil 41 86 Bb 64
60500 Vineuil-Saint-Firmin 60 51 Cc 53
71250 Vineuse, la 71 118 Ed 70
71250 Vineuse sur Fregande, la 71 117 Ed 70
07110 Vinezac 07 142 Eb 81
66600 Vingrau 66 179 Ce 91
02290 Vingré 02 40 Db 52
61250 Vingt-Hanaps 61 68 Aa 57
76540 Vinnemerville 76 36 Ad 50
89140 Vinneuf 89 72 Da 58
44590 Vinois, la 44 82 Yc 63
18300 Vinon 18 88 Ce 65
83560 Vinon-sur-Verdon 83 171 Fe 86
48500 Vinous, les 48 153 Db 82
57940 Vinsberg 57 56 Gb 53
63420 Vins-Haut 63 128 Da 77
26110 Vinsobres 26 155 Fa 82
11230 Vinsou 11 178 Ca 91
83170 Vins-sur-Carami 83 171 Ga 88
57660 Vintrange 57 57 Ge 55
81240 Vintrou, le 81 166 Cc 87
19290 Vinzan 19 126 Ca 74
03130 Vinzelle 03 116 De 71
12320 Vinzelle, la 12 139 Cc 81
63350 Vinzelles 63 116 Dc 73
71680 Vinzelles 71 118 Ee 71
74500 Vinzier 74 120 Gd 70
07340 Vinzieux 07 130 Ee 77
64130 Viodos-Abense-de-Bas 64 161 Za 89
02220 Violaine 02 52 Dc 53
02600 Violaine 02 52 Db 53
62138 Violaines 62 30 Ce 45
35330 Violais, la 35 81 Xf 61
42780 Violay 42 129 Ec 73
84150 Violès 84 155 Ef 84
35420 Violette 35 66 Ye 58
25380 Violette, la 25 108 Gd 65
87800 Violezeix 87 125 Bb 75
05310 Violins, les 05 145 Gc 80
52600 Violot 52 92 Fc 62
34380 Viols-le-Fort 34 168 De 86
88260 Vioménil 88 76 Gb 60
07610 Vion 07 142 Ee 78
72300 Vion 72 84 Ze 62
73310 Vions 73 132 Fe 74
57130 Vionville 57 56 Ff 54
26150 Viopis 26 143 Fb 80
46600 Viors 46 138 Bd 79
88170 Vioucourt 88 76 Ff 59
32300 Viozan 32 163 Ac 88
03370 Viplaix 03 114 Cc 70
09120 Vira 09 177 Be 90
66220 Vira 66 178 Cc 92
81640 Virac 81 151 Ca 84
15600 Virade, la 15 139 Cb 80
50690 Virandeville 50 33 Yb 51
34460 Viranel 34 167 Da 88
15300 Virargues 15 140 Cf 78
14500 Vire 14 47 Za 55
71260 Viré 71 118 Ef 70
89160 Vireaux 89 90 Ea 62
49420 Virebouton 49 83 Yf 62
54290 Virecourt 54 76 Gb 58
72350 Viré-en-Champagne 72 67 Ze 61
33460 Vire-Fougasse 33 134 Zb 78
33720 Virelade 33 135 Zd 81
39240 Viremont 39 119 Fd 70
14500 Vire Normandie 14 47 Za 55
46700 Vire-sur-Lot 46 137 Ba 82
08320 Vireux-Molhain 08 42 Ee 48
08320 Vireux-Wallerand 08 42 Ee 48
50600 Virey 50 66 Yf 57
70150 Virey 70 92 Fe 64
71530 Virey 71 106 Ef 67
10260 Virey-sous-Bar 10 74 Eb 60
51800 Virginy 51 54 Ee 53
01440 Viriat 01 118 Fb 71
42140 Viricelles 42 129 Ec 75
38730 Virieu 38 131 Fc 76
01510 Virieu-le-Grand 01 131 Fd 73
01260 Virieu-le-Petit 01 119 Fe 73
42140 Virigneux 42 129 Ec 74
01300 Virignin 01 131 Fe 74
38980 Viriville 38 131 Fb 77
17800 Virlet 17 123 Zd 75
63330 Virlet 63 115 Ce 72
63700 Virlet 63 115 Cf 71
57340 Virming 57 57 Ge 55
78220 Viroflay 78 51 Ca 56
87130 Virolle 87 126 Bd 74
87220 Virolle 87 125 Bc 74
17260 Virollet 17 122 Zb 75
79360 Virollet 79 111 Zd 72
80150 Vironchaux 80 28 Be 47
17290 Virson 17 110 Za 72
76110 Virville 76 36 Ac 51
02300 Viry 02 40 Db 51
39360 Viry 39 119 Fe 71
71120 Viry 71 117 Ec 70
74580 Viry 74 120 Ga 72
91170 Viry-Châtillon 91 51 Cc 56
84820 Visan 84 155 Ef 83
63250 Viscomtat 63 129 De 74
65120 Viscos 65 175 Zf 91
62156 Vis-en-Artois 62 30 Cf 47
39800 Viseney, le 39 107 Fd 67
21500 Viserny 21 90 Eb 63
21230 Visignot 21 105 Ec 66
65200 Visker 65 162 Aa 90
80140 Vismes 80 38 Be 48
12400 Vispens 12 152 Ce 85
05700 Vissac, le 05 144 Fd 82
43300 Vissac-Auteyrat 43 141 Dd 78
30770 Vissec 30 153 Dc 85
35130 Visseiche 35 66 Ye 61
34350 Vistoule, la 34 167 Db 89
12210 Vitarelle, la 12 139 Ce 81
46210 Vitarelle, la 46 138 Ca 80
81090 Vitarelle, la 81 166 Cb 87
81490 Vitarelle, la 81 166 Cc 87
82700 Vitarelle, la 82 150 Bb 85
46300 Vitarelles, les 46 137 Bb 80
81220 Viterbe 81 165 Bf 86
54123 Viterne 54 76 Ga 57
15220 Vitrac 15 139 Cb 80
24200 Vitrac 24 137 Bb 80
63410 Vitrac 63 115 Cf 73
81120 Vitrac 81 151 Ca 86
12420 Vitrac-en-Viadène 12 139 Ce 80
16310 Vitrac-Saint-Vincent 16 124 Ac 74
19800 Vitrac-sur-Montane 19 126 Bf 76
61300 Vitrai-sous-Laigle 61 49 Ae 56
03360 Vitray, Meaulne- 03 103 Cd 69
28360 Vitray-en-Beauce 28 70 Bc 59
28270 Vitray-sous-Brezolles 28 49 Ba 56
79600 Vitré 79 99 Zf 68
86350 Vitré 86 112 Ac 71
79370 Vitré, Beaussais- 79 111 Ze 71
35500 Vitré = Gwitreg 35 66 Ye 60
39350 Vitreux 39 107 Fe 65
54330 Vitrey 54 76 Ga 58
70500 Vitrey-sur-Mance 70 93 Fe 62
54300 Vitrimont 54 76 Gc 57
05110 Vitrolles 05 157 Ff 82
13127 Vitrolles 13 170 Fb 88
84240 Vitrolles 84 156 Fd 86
94400 Vitry 94 51 Cc 56
45530 Vitry-aux-Loges 45 71 Cb 61
62490 Vitry-en-Artois 62 30 Cf 47
71600 Vitry-en-Charollais 71 117 Ea 70
52160 Vitry-en-Montagne 52 92 Fa 62
51300 Vitry-en-Perthois 51 54 Ed 56
58420 Vitry-Laché 58 104 Dd 65
51240 Vitry-la-Ville 51 54 Ec 55
10110 Vitry-le-Croisé 10 74 Ed 60
51300 Vitry-le-François 51 54 Ed 56
71250 Vitry-lès-Cluny 71 118 Ed 70
52800 Vitry-lès-Nogent 52 75 Fc 61
57185 Vitry-sous-Justemont 57 56 Ga 53
71140 Vitry-sur-Loire 71 104 De 68
55150 Vittarville 55 43 Fc 52
21350 Vitteaux 21 91 Ed 64
76450 Vittefleur 76 36 Ad 50
88800 Vittel 88 76 Ff 59
57670 Vittersbourg 57 57 Gf 55
57580 Vittoncourt 57 56 Gc 54
54700 Vittonville 54 56 Ga 55
80150 Vitz-sur-Authie 80 29 Ca 47
74250 Viuz-en-Sallaz 74 120 Gc 72
74540 Viuz-la-Chiésaz 74 132 Ga 74
02870 Vivaise 02 40 Dd 51
42310 Vivans 42 117 Df 71
20219 Vivario CTC 183 Kb 95
20219 Vivariu = Vivario CTC 183 Kb 95
82140 Vivens 82 150 Be 83
63840 Viverols 63 129 Df 76
66490 Vivès 66 179 Ce 93
52160 Vivey 52 91 Fa 62
17120 Vivier 17 122 Za 74
42380 Vivier 42 129 Ea 76
49220 Vivier 49 83 Za 63
16240 Vivier, le 16 111 Zf 73
36200 Vivier, le 36 113 Bd 69
41500 Vivier, le 41 86 Bc 63
66730 Vivier, le 66 178 Cc 92
08440 Vivier-au-Court 08 42 Ee 50
02600 Vivières 02 52 Da 53
17510 Vivier-Jusseau, le 17 111 Zf 73
07220 Viviers 07 142 Ee 82
23350 Viviers 23 114 Ca 70
24370 Viviers 24 137 Bc 79
34830 Viviers 34 168 Df 86
57590 Viviers 57 56 Gc 55
89700 Viviers 89 90 Df 62
17430 Viviers, les 17 110 Za 72
73420 Viviers-du-Lac 73 132 Ff 75
88260 Viviers-le-Gras 88 76 Ff 60
81500 Viviers-lès-Lavaur 81 165 Be 87
81290 Viviers-lès-Montagnes 81 165 Cb 87
88500 Viviers-lès-Offroicourt 88 76 Ga 59
10110 Viviers-sur-Artaut 10 74 Ec 60
54260 Viviers-sur-Chiers 54 43 Fd 52
35960 Vivier-sur-Mer, le 35 65 Yb 57
09500 Viviès 09 177 Be 90
12110 Viviez 12 139 Cb 81
16120 Viville 16 123 Zf 75
16430 Viville 16 124 Ab 74
72170 Vivoin 72 68 Aa 59
64450 Vivon 64 162 Zd 88
86370 Vivonne 86 112 Ab 70
27400 Vivonvay 27 49 Bb 53
49680 Vivy 49 84 Zf 65
21400 Vix 21 91 Ed 61
85770 Vix 85 110 Za 70
42110 Vizezy 42 129 Ea 74
38220 Vizille 38 144 Fe 78
65120 Vizos 65 175 Zf 91
18800 Vizy 18 103 Ce 66
20219 Vizzavona CTC 183 Ka 96
19390 Vlalle, la 19 126 Bf 76
07690 Vocance 07 130 Ed 77
63500 Vodable 63 128 Da 75
68420 Vœgtlinshofen 68 60 Hb 60
57320 Vœlfing-lès-Bouzonville 57 57 Gd 53
67430 Vœllerdingen 67 57 Ha 55
36260 Vœu 36 101 Bf 66
68600 Vogelgrun 68 60 Hd 60
73420 Voglans 73 132 Ff 75
07200 Vogüé 07 142 Ec 81
02140 Voharies 02 40 De 50
88220 Void-de-Girancourt 88 76 Gc 60
88220 Void-de-la-Bure, le 88 76 Gb 60
88260 Void-d'Escles, le 88 76 Gb 60
49310 Voide, le 49 98 Zc 66
55190 Void-Vacon 55 55 Fd 56
10200 Voigny 10 74 Ee 59
51800 Voilemont 51 54 Ee 54
25110 Voillans 25 93 Gc 64
52130 Voillecomte 52 74 Ef 57
57580 Voimhaut 57 56 Gc 54
54134 Voinémont 54 76 Ga 57
63620 Voingt 63 127 Cd 74
77540 Voinsles 77 52 Da 56
51130 Voipreux 51 53 Ea 55
25580 Voires 25 107 Gb 66
25580 Voires 25 108 Gb 66
02170 Voirie 02 40 De 49
85170 Voirie, la 85 97 Yd 68
38500 Voiron 38 131 Fd 76
27520 Voiscreville 27 49 Ae 53
28700 Voise 28 70 Be 58
77950 Voisenon 77 71 Cd 57
52400 Voisey 52 93 Fe 61
21400 Voisin 21 91 Ed 62
33380 Voisin, le 33 134 Za 81
39150 Voisinal, le 39 107 Ga 69
52200 Voisines 52 92 Fb 61
89260 Voisines 89 72 Dc 59
77860 Voisins 77 52 Cf 55
03230 Voisins, les 03 104 Dd 69
78960 Voisins-le-Bretonneux 78 51 Ca 56
19300 Voissange 19 126 Bf 76
38620 Voissant 38 131 Fe 76
17400 Voissay 17 110 Zc 73
63210 Voissieux 63 127 Cf 74
18300 Voisy 18 88 Ce 65
39210 Voiteur 39 107 Fd 68
70310 Voivre, la 70 94 Gd 62
88470 Voivre, la 88 77 Gf 58
88240 Voivres, les 88 76 Gb 60
72210 Voivres-lès-le-Mans 72 84 Aa 61
59470 Volckerinckhove 59 27 Cb 43
79170 Volée, la 79 111 Zd 71
71600 Volesvres 71 117 Ea 70
68600 Volgelsheim 68 60 Hd 60
89710 Volgré 89 89 Db 61
57100 Volkrange 57 44 Ga 52
67290 Volksberg 67 58 Hb 55
63120 Vollore-Montagne 63 129 De 74
63120 Vollore-Ville 63 128 Dd 74
57220 Volmerange-lès-Boulay 57 56 Gc 53
57330 Volmerange-les-Mines 57 43 Ga 52
57720 Volmunster 57 58 Hc 54
21190 Volnay 21 106 Ee 66
72440 Volnay 72 85 Ac 61
70180 Volon 70 92 Fe 63
04290 Volonne 04 157 Ga 84
20290 Volpajola CTC 181 Kc 93
15220 Volpiliac 15 139 Cc 79
48150 Volpilière, la 48 153 Db 83
71220 Volsin 71 105 Ec 69
57940 Volstroff 57 44 Gb 53
48190 Volte, la 48 141 De 82
26560 Voluy 26 156 Fd 83
26470 Volvent 26 143 Fc 81
89240 Volvent 89 89 Dc 62
09230 Volvestre 09 164 Ba 90
63530 Volvic 63 128 Da 73
04130 Volx 04 157 Ff 85
88700 Vomécourt 88 77 Gd 59
88500 Vomécourt-sur-Madon 88 76 Gb 58
07140 Vompdes 07 154 Ea 82
52500 Voncourt 52 92 Fe 62
08400 Voncq 08 42 Ed 52
21270 Vonges 21 92 Fc 65
01540 Vonnas 01 118 Ef 71
32100 Vopillon 32 148 Ab 85
01230 Vorages 01 119 Fc 73
70190 Voray-sur-l'Ognon 70 93 Ga 64
61160 Vorché 61 48 Zf 56
38340 Voreppe 38 131 Fd 77
43800 Vorey 43 129 Df 77
02860 Vorges 02 40 Dd 51
25320 Vorges-les-Pins 25 107 Ff 66
18340 Vorly 18 102 Cc 67
36150 Vornault 36 101 Be 66
18130 Vornay 18 102 Cd 67
12160 Vors 12 151 Cc 83
89400 Vorvigny 89 73 Dd 60
74700 Vorziers, les 74 120 Gd 73
39240 Vosbles- 39 119 Fd 70
21700 Vosne-Romanée 21 106 Ef 66
10130 Vosnon 10 73 Df 60
22230 Vot, le 22 64 Xd 60
37240 Vou 37 100 Af 66
01590 Vouais 01 119 Fd 71
51260 Vouarces 51 73 Df 57
21230 Voudenay 21 105 Ec 66
10150 Voué 10 73 Ea 58
52320 Vouécourt 52 75 Fa 59
70500 Vougécourt 70 76 Ff 61
21640 Vougeot 21 106 Ef 65
39260 Vouglans 39 119 Fd 70
10210 Vougrey 10 73 Eb 60
74500 Vougron 74 120 Gd 70
42720 Vougy 42 117 Ea 72
74130 Vougy 74 120 Gc 72
16330 Vouharte 16 123 Aa 74
17700 Vouhé 17 110 Zb 72
79310 Vouhé 79 111 Ze 69
70200 Vouhenans 70 94 Gc 63
36310 Vouhet 36 113 Bb 70
16400 Vouil-et-Giget 16 124 Aa 75
79230 Vouillé 79 111 Zd 71
86190 Vouillé 86 99 Ab 69
85450 Vouillé-les-Marais 85 110 Za 70
51340 Vouillers 51 54 Ee 56
36100 Vouillon 36 102 Bf 68
14230 Vouilly 14 47 Yf 53
25420 Voujeaucourt 25 94 Ge 64
21290 Voulaines-les-Templiers 21 91 Ee 62
77580 Voulangis 77 52 Cf 55
86400 Voulême 86 111 Ab 72
16250 Voulgézac 16 124 Aa 75
79150 Voulmentin 79 98 Zc 67
86700 Voulon 86 111 Ab 70
02140 Voulpaix 02 41 De 49
34390 Voulte, la 34 167 Cf 87
79150 Voultegon 79 98 Zc 67
07800 Voulte-sur-Rhône, la 07 142 Ee 80
77560 Voulton 77 52 Dc 57
77940 Voulx 77 72 Cf 59
86580 Vouneuil-sous-Biard 86 112 Ab 69
86210 Vouneuil-sur-Vienne 86 100 Ad 68
29870 Vourch 29 61 Vc 57
38210 Vourey 38 131 Fd 77
69390 Vourles 69M 130 Ee 75
90400 Vourvenans 90 94 Gf 63
03140 Voussac 03 115 Da 71
38520 Voûte, la 38 144 Ga 78
89270 Voutenay-sur-Cure 89 90 De 63
19130 Voutezac 19 125 Bc 77
16220 Vouthon 16 124 Ac 74
55130 Vouthon-Bas 55 75 Fd 58
55130 Vouthon-Haut 55 75 Fd 58
53600 Voutré 53 67 Ze 60
17340 Voutron 17 110 Yf 72
85120 Vouvant 85 110 Zb 69
01200 Vouvray 01 119 Fe 72
37210 Vouvray 37 85 Ae 64
72160 Vouvray-sur-Huisne 72 68 Ad 60
72500 Vouvray-sur-Loir 72 85 Ac 62
21430 Vouvres 21 105 Ec 65
88170 Vouxey 88 76 Fe 58
86170 Vouzailles 86 99 Aa 68
16410 Vouzan 16 124 Ac 75
86200 Vouzeray 86 99 Ab 66
18330 Vouzeron 18 87 Cb 65
08400 Vouziers 08 42 Ee 52
41600 Vouzon 41 87 Ca 63
51130 Vouzy 51 53 Ea 55
10260 Vove 10 73 Eb 59
28360 Vovelles 28 70 Bd 58
28150 Voves 28 70 Bd 59
28360 Vovette 28 70 Bd 58
01510 Vovray 01 119 Fe 73
74350 Vovray-en-Bornes 74 120 Ga 72
02250 Voyenne 02 40 De 50
80400 Voyennes 80 39 Cf 50
57560 Voyer 57 57 Ha 57
86200 Voyette, la 86 99 Ab 66
03110 Vozelle 03 116 Dc 72
76690 Vquebeuf 76 37 Bb 51
56250 Vraie-Croix, la 56 81 Xc 62
80240 Vraignes-en-Vermandois 80 39 Da 49
80640 Vraignes-lès-Hornoy 80 38 Bf 50
52310 Vraincourt 52 75 Fa 59
55120 Vraincourt 55 55 Fa 54
79290 Vraire 79 98 Ze 66
27370 Vraiville 27 49 Ba 53
86310 Vrassac 86 112 Af 69
50330 Vrasville 50 33 Yd 50
51150 Vraux 51 54 Eb 54
88140 Vrecourt 88 75 Fe 59
59870 Vred 59 30 Db 46
70150 Vregille 70 93 Ff 65
02880 Vregny 02 40 Dc 52
80170 Vrély 80 39 Ce 50
57640 Vrémy 57 56 Gb 54
50260 Vrétot, le 50 33 Yb 52
39700 Vriange 39 107 Fd 65
44270 Vrignais, le 44 96 Yb 67
08330 Vrigne-au-Bois 08 42 Ef 50
08350 Vrigne-Meuse 08 42 Ef 50
17210 Vrignon 17 123 Ze 77
45300 Vrigny 45 71 Cb 60
51390 Vrigny 51 53 Df 53
61570 Vrigny 61 48 Zf 56
79150 Vrillé 79 98 Zc 67
58220 Vrillon 58 89 Db 64
89520 Vrilly 89 89 Da 63
25300 Vrine, la 25 108 Gc 67
79100 Vrines 79 99 Ze 67

A B C D E F G H I J K L M N O P Q R S T U V W X Y Z

Vrines | 335

44540 Vritz 44 83 Yf 63
08400 Vrizy 08 42 Ee 52
60112 Vrocourt 60 38 Bf 51
51330 Vroil 51 54 Ef 55
03420 Vrolle 03 115 Cd 71
80120 Vron 80 28 Be 47
54330 Vroncourt 54 76 Ga 58
52240 Vroncourt-la-Côte 52 75 Fd 60
89700 Vrouerre 89 90 Df 62
88500 Vroville 88 76 Gb 59
57640 Vry 57 56 Gb 53
44640 Vue 44 96 Ya 65
25840 Vuillafans 25 107 Gb 66
25300 Vuillecin 25 108 Gb 67
10160 Vulaines 10 73 Dd 59
77160 Vulaines-lès-Provins 77 72 Db 57
77870 Vulaines-sur-Seine 77 71 Ce 58
74520 Vulbens 74 120 Ff 72
73700 Vulmis 73 133 Ge 75
57420 Vulmont 57 56 Gb 55
20153 Vuttera i Bagni = Guitera-les-Bains CTC 183 Ka 97
70400 Vyans-le-Val 70 94 Ge 63
70130 Vy-le-Ferroux 70 93 Ff 63
70230 Vy-lès-Filain 70 93 Gb 63
70200 Vy-lès-Lure 70 94 Gc 63
70120 Vy-lès-Rupt 70 93 Ff 63
25430 Vyt-lès-Belvoir 25 94 Gd 64

W

62180 Waben 62 28 Bd 46
59147 Wachemy 59 30 Cf 45
60420 Wacquemoulin 60 39 Cd 51
62250 Wacquinghen 62 26 Be 44
08200 Wadelincourt 08 42 Ef 50
80150 Wadicourt 80 28 Bf 47
08220 Wadimont 08 41 Eb 50
55160 Wadonville-en-Woëvre 55 55 Fe 54
67220 Wagenbach 67 77 Hb 58
08270 Wagnon 08 41 Ec 51
62161 Wagnonlieu 62 29 Ce 47
59261 Wahagnies 59 30 Da 46
68130 Wahlbach 68 95 Hc 63
67170 Wahlenheim 67 58 He 56
62770 Wail 62 29 Ca 46
62217 Wailly 62 29 Ce 47
62310 Wailly 62 29 Ca 45
80160 Wailly 80 38 Ca 50
62170 Wailly-Beaucamp 62 28 Be 46
68230 Walbach 68 60 Hb 60
67360 Walbourg 67 58 He 55
67350 Walck, la 67 58 Hd 55
67430 Waldhambach 67 57 Hb 55
57720 Waldhouse 57 58 Hc 54
68640 Waldighofen 68 95 Hb 63
67700 Waldolwisheim 67 58 Hc 56
57320 Waldweistroff 57 44 Gd 52
57480 Waldwisse 57 44 Gd 52
08220 Waleppe 08 41 Ea 51
68130 Walheim 68 95 Hb 63
59127 Walincourt-Selvigny 59 30 Db 48
02210 Wallée 02 52 Dc 53
59135 Wallers 59 30 Dc 46
59132 Wallers-Trélon 59 31 Eb 48
59190 Wallon-Cappel 59 27 Cc 44
57720 Walschbronn 57 58 Hc 54
57870 Walscheid 57 57 Ha 54
57370 Waltembourg 57 57 Hb 56
68510 Waltenheim 68 95 Hc 63
67670 Waltenheim-sur-Zorn 67 58 Hd 56
55250 Waly 55 55 Fa 54
59400 Wambaix 59 30 Db 48
62140 Wambercourt 62 29 Ca 46
60380 Wambez 60 38 Bf 51
59118 Wambrechies 59 30 Cf 44
62770 Wamin 62 29 Ca 46
76660 Wanchy-Capval 76 37 Bc 49
62128 Wancourt 62 30 Cf 47
59870 Wandignies-Hamage 59 30 Db 46
62560 Wandonne 59 29 Ca 45
67520 Wangen 67 60 Hc 57
67710 Wangenbourg-Engenthal 67 58 Hb 57
59830 Wannehain 59 30 Db 45
62123 Wanquetin 62 29 Cd 47
67610 Wantzenau, la 67 58 He 57
08460 Warby 08 41 Ed 50
08000 Warcq 08 42 Ee 50
55400 Warcq 55 55 Fd 53
62120 Wardrecques 62 29 Cc 44
51800 Wargemoulin-Hurlus 51 54 Ee 54
59144 Wargnies-le-Grand 59 31 Dd 47
80670 Wargnies 80 38 Cb 48
59144 Wargnies-le-Petit 59 31 De 47
59380 Warhem 59 27 Cc 43
59870 Warlaing 59 30 Db 46
62450 Warlencourt-Eaucourt 62 30 Ce 48
62760 Warlincourt-lès-Pass 62 29 Cd 47
80300 Warloy-Baillon 80 39 Cd 48
60430 Warluis 60 38 Ca 52
62123 Warlus 62 29 Ce 47
80270 Warlus 80 38 Bf 49
62810 Warluzel 62 29 Cc 47
51110 Warmeriville 51 41 Eb 52
62120 Warne 62 29 Cc 45
08090 Warnécourt 08 42 Ed 50
54400 Warnimont 54 43 Fe 51
59219 Warpont 59 31 Df 48
80500 Warsy 80 39 Cd 50
80170 Warvillers 80 39 Ce 50
02630 Wasigny 02 40 Dd 48
08270 Wasigny 08 41 Ec 51
59252 Wasnes-au-Bac 59 30 Db 47
59290 Wasquehal 59 30 Da 44
67310 Wasselheim = Wasselonne 67 58 Hc 57
67310 Wasselonne 67 58 Hc 57

68230 Wasserbourg 68 60 Ha 60
52130 Wassy 52 74 Ef 58
62142 Wast, le 62 26 Be 44
80230 Wathiehurt 80 28 Bd 47
02830 Watigny 02 41 Eb 49
55160 Watronville 55 55 Fd 54
80220 Wattebléry 80 38 Bd 49
59143 Watten 59 27 Cb 43
62380 Watterdal 62 28 Ca 44
59139 Wattignies 59 30 Da 45
59680 Wattignies-la-Victoire 59 31 Ea 47
62890 Wattine, le 62 27 Ca 44
59150 Wattrelos 59 30 Db 44
68700 Wattwiller 68 95 Hb 61
60130 Wavignies 60 39 Cc 51
54890 Waville 54 56 Ff 54
62380 Wavrans-sur-L'Aa 62 29 Ca 44
62130 Wavrans-sur-Ternoise 62 29 Cb 46
59220 Wavrechain-sous-Denain 59 30 Dc 47
59111 Wavrechain-sous-Faulx 59 30 Db 47
55150 Wavrille 55 43 Fc 53
59136 Wavrin 59 30 Cf 45
59119 Waziers 59 30 Da 46
68600 Weckolsheim 68 60 Hd 60
68290 Wegscheid 68 94 Gf 62
57412 Weidesheim 57 57 Ha 54
67160 Weiler 67 58 Hf 54
67340 Weinbourg 67 58 Hc 55
57720 Weiskirch 57 58 Hc 54
57290 Weislingen 57 58 Hb 55
67160 Weissenburg = Wissembourg 67 58 Hf 54
67500 Weitbruch 67 58 He 56
67340 Weiterswiller 67 58 Hc 55
57990 Welfer-Ippling 57 57 Ha 54
60420 Welles-Pérennes 60 39 Cc 51
59670 Wemaers-Cappel 59 27 Cc 44
67510 Wengelsbach 67 58 He 54
68220 Wentzwiller 68 95 Hc 63
68480 Werentzhouse 68 95 Hc 63
59117 Wervicq-Sud 59 30 Da 44
62380 Westbécourt 62 27 Ca 44
59380 West-Cappel 59 27 Cd 43
68250 Westhalten 68 60 Hb 61
67310 Westhoffen 67 60 Hc 57
67230 Westhouse 67 60 Hd 58
67440 Westhouse-Marmoutier 67 58 Hc 56
62575 Westhove 62 27 Cb 44
62129 Westrehem 62 29 Cb 45
62960 Westrehem 62 29 Cc 45
68920 Wettolsheim 68 60 Hb 60
67320 Weyer 67 57 Ha 55
67720 Weyersheim 67 58 He 56
51360 Wez 51 53 Eb 53
59320 Wez-Macquart 59 30 Cf 45
80140 Wiancourt 80 38 Bd 48
02420 Wiancourt 02 40 Db 49
67114 Wibolsheim 67 60 He 58
68820 Wickerschwihr 68 60 Hc 60
67270 Wickersheim-Wilshausen 67 58 Hd 56
59134 Wicres 59 30 Cf 45
62630 Widehem 62 28 Be 45
68320 Widensohlen 68 60 Hc 60
02120 Wiège-Faty 02 40 De 49
80170 Wiencourt-L'Équipée 80 39 Cd 49
62830 Wierre-au-Bois 62 28 Be 45
62720 Wierre-Effroy 62 26 Be 44
57200 Wiesviller 57 57 Ha 54
59212 Wignehies 59 41 Ea 48
08270 Wignicourt 08 41 Ed 51
68230 Wihr-au-Val 68 77 Hb 60
68180 Wihr-en-Plaine 68 60 Hc 60
67340 Wildenguth 67 58 Hc 55
68820 Wildenstein 68 77 Gf 61
67130 Wildersbach 67 60 Hb 58
62770 Willeman 62 29 Ca 46
59780 Willems 59 30 Db 45
68960 Willer 68 95 Hb 63
55500 Willeroncourt 55 55 Fc 56
68760 Willer-sur-Thur 68 94 Ha 61
62580 Willerval 62 30 Cf 46
57430 Willerwald 57 57 Ha 54
67370 Willgottheim 67 58 Hd 56
08110 Williers 08 42 Fb 50
59740 Willies 59 31 Ea 48
67270 Wilshausen 67 58 Hd 56
67270 Wilwisheim 67 58 Hd 56
62930 Wimereux 62 26 Bd 44
62126 Wimille 62 26 Bd 44
67290 Wimmenau 67 58 Hc 55
02500 Wimy 02 41 Ea 49
68130 Windenhof 68 95 Hc 63
57850 Windsbourg 57 77 Hb 57
67110 Windstein 67 58 Hd 55
67510 Wingen 67 58 He 54
67290 Wingen-sur-Moder 67 58 Hc 55
67170 Wingersheim les Quatre Bans 67 58 Hd 56
68570 Wintzfelden 68 77 Hb 61
62240 Wirwignes 62 28 Be 44
80270 Wiry-au-Mont 80 38 Bf 49
67130 Wisches 67 60 Hb 57
88520 Wisembach 88 77 Ha 59
55700 Wiseppe 55 42 Fb 52
62380 Wismes 62 29 Ca 45
62219 Wisques 62 29 Cb 44
62179 Wissant 62 26 Bd 43
67160 Wissembourg 67 58 Hf 54
02320 Wissignicourt 02 40 Dc 51
91320 Wissous 91 51 Cb 56

51420 Witry-lès-Reims 51 53 Ea 53
68310 Wittelsheim 68 95 Hb 62
68270 Wittenheim 68 95 Hc 62
62120 Witternesse 62 29 Cc 45
67230 Witternheim 67 60 Hd 59
68130 Wittersdorf 68 95 Hb 63
67670 Wittersheim 67 58 Hd 56
62120 Wittes 62 29 Cc 44
67820 Wittisheim 67 60 Hd 59
57905 Wittring 57 57 Ha 54
67370 Wiwersheim 67 58 Hd 57
62570 Wizernes 62 29 Cb 44
55210 Woël 55 56 Fe 54
57200 Woelfling-lès-Sarreguemines 57 57 Hb 54
67370 Woellenheim 67 58 Hd 57
80460 Woignarue 80 28 Bc 48
55300 Woimbey 55 55 Fc 55
80520 Woincourt 80 28 Bd 48
55300 Woinville 55 55 Fd 55
57140 Woippy 57 56 Ga 54
80140 Woirel 80 38 Be 49
68210 Wolfersdorf 68 94 Ha 63
68600 Wolfgantzen 68 60 Hd 60
67202 Wolfisheim 67 60 Hd 57
67260 Wolfskirchen 67 57 Ha 55
67700 Wolschheim 67 58 Hc 56
68480 Wolschwiller 68 95 Hc 64
67120 Wolxheim 67 60 Hd 57
59470 Wormhout 59 27 Cc 43
57915 Woustviller 57 57 Ha 54
68500 Wuenheim 68 95 Hb 61
88700 Wuillaume-Fontaine 88 77 Ge 59
57170 Wuisse 57 57 Gd 55
59143 Wulverdinghe 59 27 Cb 44
76940 Wuy, le 76 36 Ae 52
95420 Wy-dit-Joli-Village 95 50 Bf 54
59380 Wylder 59 27 Cc 43

X

88700 Xaffévillers 88 77 Gd 58
32200 Xaintrailles 32 163 Ae 87
47230 Xaintrailles 47 148 Ab 83
79220 Xaintray 79 110 Zd 70
16330 Xambes 16 123 Aa 74
54470 Xammes 54 56 Ff 55
88460 Xamontarupt 88 77 Gd 60
57630 Xanrey 57 57 Gd 56
85240 Xanton-Chassenon 85 110 Zb 70
88130 Xaronval 88 76 Gb 58
88220 Xatte, la 88 76 Gc 60
54300 Xermaménil 54 77 Gc 57
88220 Xertigny 88 76 Gc 60
54990 Xeuilley 54 76 Ga 57
54740 Xirocourt 54 76 Gb 58
55300 Xivray-et-Marvoisin 55 56 Fe 55
54490 Xivry-Circourt 54 43 Fe 52
57590 Xocourt 57 56 Gc 55
88400 Xonrupt-Longemer 88 77 Gf 60
54800 Xonville 54 56 Ff 54
57830 Xouaxange 57 57 Gf 56
88310 Xoulces 88 77 Gf 61
54370 Xousse 54 57 Ge 57
54370 Xures 54 57 Gd 56

Y

76480 Yainville 76 37 Ae 52
80135 Yaucourt-Bussus 80 28 Bf 48
22300 Yaudet, le 22 63 Wc 56
04300 Ybourgues 04 156 Fe 85
40160 Ychoux 40 146 Za 83
15210 Ydes 15 127 Cc 76
15210 Ydes Bourg 15 127 Cc 76
76640 Yébleron 76 36 Ad 51
77390 Yèbles 77 52 Ce 57
73170 Yenne 73 132 Fe 74
28130 Yermenonville 28 70 Bd 57
91560 Yerres 91 51 Cc 56
76760 Yerville 76 37 Af 50
81200 Yés, les 81 166 Cc 88
62610 Yeuse 62 27 Bf 44
45300 Yèvre-la-Ville 45 71 Cb 60
45300 Yèvre-le-Châtel 45 71 Cc 60
28160 Yèvres 28 69 Bb 59
10500 Yèvres-le-Petit 10 74 Ec 58
22120 Yffiniac 22 64 Xb 58
40110 Ygos-Saint-Saturnin 40 147 Zb 85
03160 Ygrande 03 115 Cf 69
76520 Ymare 76 37 Bb 52
28320 Ymeray 28 70 Be 57
19220 Ymons 19 126 Ca 77
28150 Ymonville 28 70 Be 59
28150 Ymorville 28 70 Bd 58
81430 Yole 81 151 Cc 85
15130 Yolet 15 139 Cd 79
08210 Yoncq 08 42 Fa 51
40170 Yons 40 146 Ye 84
50580 Yons, les 50 46 Yb 53
80132 Yonval 80 28 Be 48
63700 Youx 63 115 Ce 72
76111 Y Port 76 36 Ab 50
76540 Ypreville-Biville 76 36 Ad 50
50400 Yquelon 50 46 Yc 55
63270 Yronde-et-Buron 63 128 Db 75
63200 Yssac-la-Tourette 63 116 Da 73
19310 Yssandon 19 125 Bc 77
43200 Yssingeaux 43 141 Ea 78
15130 Ytrac 15 139 Cc 79
62124 Ytres 62 30 Cf 48
57970 Yutz 57 44 Gb 52
76560 Yvecrique 76 37 Ae 50
36200 Yvernaud 36 101 Bd 69
86170 Yversay 86 99 Ab 68
17340 Yves 17 110 Yf 72

84220 Yves, les 84 156 Fb 85
61210 Yveteaux, les 61 47 Ze 56
76190 Yvetot 76 36 Ae 51
50700 Yvetot-Bocage 50 33 Yc 52
22930 Yvias 22 63 Wf 56
16210 Yviers 16 123 Zf 77
22350 Yvignac 22 65 Xe 58
60410 Yvillers 60 51 Ce 53
76530 Yville-sur-Seine 76 37 Af 52
74140 Yvoire 74 120 Gb 70
41600 Yvoy-le-Marron 41 87 Bf 63
33370 Yvrac 33 135 Zd 79
16110 Yvrac-et-Malleyrand 16 124 Ac 74
61800 Yvrandes 61 47 Zb 56
72530 Yvré-Évêque 72 68 Ab 60
72330 Yvré-le-Pôlin 72 84 Aa 62
80150 Yvrench 80 28 Ca 47
80150 Yvrencheux 80 28 Bf 47
80520 Yvrench 80 28 Bd 48
49360 Yzernay 49 98 Zb 66
69510 Yzeron 69M 130 Ed 74
03400 Yzeure 03 103 Dc 69
37290 Yzeures-sur-Creuse 37 100 Af 68
80310 Yzeux 80 38 Ca 49
40180 Yzosse 40 161 Yf 86

Z

67700 Zabern = Saverne 67 58 Hc 56
68130 Zaessingue 68 95 Hc 63
88120 Zainvillers 88 77 Ge 61
20272 Zalana CTC 183 Kc 95
63420 Zanières 63 128 Da 76
63970 Zanières 63 127 Cf 75
57340 Zarbeling 57 57 Ge 55
57420 Zedrevaux 57 56 Gb 55
59470 Zegerscappel 59 27 Cc 43
67310 Zehnacker 67 58 Hc 56
67310 Zeinheim 67 58 Hc 56
64780 Zelhal 64 160 Ye 89
64240 Zelhay 64 160 Ye 88
57660 Zellen 57 57 Gf 55
68340 Zellenberg 68 60 Hb 60
67140 Zellwiller 67 60 Hd 58
67860 Zelsheim 67 60 Hd 59
59670 Zermazeele 59 27 Cc 44
23270 Zéros, les 23 114 Ca 70
20116 Zerubia CTC 185 Ka 98
47140 Zette 47 149 Ae 83
57905 Zetting 57 57 Ha 54
57320 Zeurange 57 44 Gd 52
20173 Zévaco CTC 182 Ka 97
20132 Zicavo CTC 183 Ka 97
20132 Zicavu = Zicavo CTC 183 Ka 97
20190 Zigliara CTC 184 If 97
20214 Zilia CTC 180 If 93
57370 Zilling 57 57 Hb 56
68720 Zillisheim 68 95 Hb 62
68230 Zimmerbach 68 60 Hb 60
68440 Zimmersheim 68 95 Hc 62
57690 Zimming 57 57 Gf 54
88330 Zincourt 88 76 Gc 59
67110 Zinswiller 67 58 Hd 55
57515 Zinzing 57 57 Ha 53
57290 Zittersheim 67 58 Hc 55
67270 Zœbersdorf 67 58 Hd 56
67260 Zollingen 67 57 Ha 55
57260 Zommange 57 57 Ge 56
20124 Zonza CTC 185 Kb 98
20140 Zoppu CTC 184 If 98
59440 Zorées 59 31 Df 48
67700 Zornhoff 57 58 Hc 56
62650 Zoteux 62 28 Bf 45
62890 Zouafques 62 27 Ca 44
57330 Zoufftgen 57 44 Ga 52
20112 Zoza CTC 184 Ka 98
20272 Zuani CTC 183 Kc 95
62500 Zudausques 62 27 Ca 44
62370 Zutkerque 62 27 Ca 43
67330 Zutzendorf 67 58 Hd 56
59123 Zuydcoote 59 27 Cc 42
59670 Zuytpeene 59 27 Cc 44